Dan Pfeffer
Will Redmond

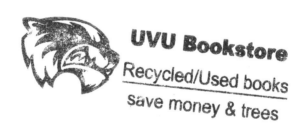

Personal Finance

10e

E. Thomas Garman

Virginia Tech University,
Professor Emeritus

Raymond E. Forgue

University of Kentucky

SOUTH-WESTERN
CENGAGE Learning

Australia • Brazil • Japan • Korea • Mexico • Singapore • Spain • United Kingdom • United States

SOUTH-WESTERN
CENGAGE Learning™

Personal Finance, Tenth Edition
E. Thomas Garman, Raymond E. Forgue

Vice President of Editorial, Business:
 Jack W. Calhoun

Publisher: Joe Sabatino

Acquisitions Editor: Mike Reynolds

Developmental Editor: Julia Chase

Marketing Manager: Nathan Anderson

Marketing Coordinator: Suellen Ruttkay

Sr. Marketing Communications
 Manager: Jim Overly

Content Project Manager: Holly Henjum

Media Editor: Scott Fidler

Frontlist Buyer, Manufacturing:
 Kevin Kluck

Permissions Account Manager/Images:
 John Hill

Permissions Account Manager/Text:
 Margaret Chamberlain-Gaston

Production Service/Compositor:
 S4 Carlisle Publishing Services

Sr. Art Director: Michelle Kunkler

Cover and Internal Designer:
 Lou Ann Thesing

Cover Image: © PhotoDisc/Alamy

For product information and technology assistance, contact us at
Cengage Learning Customer & Sales Support, 1-800-354-9706

For permission to use material from this text or product, submit all requests online at **www.cengage.com/permissions**
Further permissions questions can be emailed to
permissionrequest@cengage.com

Library of Congress Control Number: 2009927434

Student Edition ISBN 13: 978-1-4390-3902-1
Student Edition ISBN 10: 1-4390-3902-X

Instructor's Edition ISBN 13: 978-1-4390-4539-8
Instructor's Edition ISBN 10: 1-4390-4539-9

South-Western Cengage Learning
5191 Natorp Boulevard
Mason, OH 45040
USA

Cengage Learning products are represented in Canada by Nelson Education, Ltd.

For your course and learning solutions, visit **www.cengage.com**

Purchase any of our products at your local college store or at our preferred online store **www.ichapters.com**

Printed in Canada
1 2 3 4 5 6 7 13 12 11 10 09

Brief Contents

Contents

PART 3

Income and Asset Protection   281

10 Managing Property and Liability Risk   282

PART 4

Investments 373

13 Investment Fundamentals 374

14 Investing in Stocks and Bonds 408

Preface

A Note to the Student

The 10th edition offers reassurance to readers about what happened to the world's stock and credit markets, the American economy and its housing market. It carefully shows students how to be successful in these challenging times. This book reminds students of the values of their grandparents: "work hard, study, save, invest, and live within your means." The 10th edition creates a wide highway for students to travel on the path toward their personal financial success.

Hope alone is not enough. Armed with a solid understanding of the fundamental principles of personal finance, today's students can achieve great things, live productive lives, and do well financially even in these challenging economic times.

Our goal as authors is to give you the knowledge, tools, attitudes, and skills you need to be financially sound and strike your own personal balance. Along with the text, we have developed a full, rich companion website that you can use to learn as much as possible from your efforts and, perhaps more importantly, develop your own financial plans.

To the Instructor

This 10th edition of *Personal Finance* appropriately balances all the pieces of financial planning. It provides your students with the tools and knowledge they need for their short- and long-term financial success. In addition to updating and enhancing the quality of the content, this edition truly stimulates student interest in a half dozen new ways.

What is the greatest challenge in teaching personal finance? Instructors tell us "to connect all the pieces in a comprehensive manner," "to cover all the material in one course," "to accommodate different learning styles," "to show students the relevancy of the topics," "to visualize real-life examples," "to get students to do a reality check on their own finances," "to make topics interesting that are important later in life," "to teach the time value of money with lots of Excel spreadsheet exercises," "to deliver an effective e-package (including self-tests and decision-making worksheets)," and "to stimulate student interest such that the instructor receives verbal and nonverbal feedback in class." We have listened and responded. The 10th edition addresses those needs precisely. We have made many changes . . . for the better.

Topical Coverage of the 10th Edition

We have carefully constructed the 10th edition to address instructors' concerns about getting through all the necessary material for this course. The new, streamlined table of contents consists of 18 chapters total broken into 5 Parts: Financial Planning, Money Management, Income and Asset Protection, Investments, and Retirement and Estate Planning. In keeping with the difficult economic climate we again include a chapter entitled "Career Planning" that provides students with the steps they need for successful career planning. In addition, in every chapter where it is relevant we place the material in the context of today's challenging economic times.

Features

We have carefully designed pedagogical features to strengthen learning opportunities for students. Each feature is designed to communicate vital information meaningfully and to maintain student interest. The following features support student understanding and retention.

You Must Be Kidding, Right?   If you typically skip the opening case, now is the time to change your ways. This "instructor alert" feature opens every chapter with a short narrative about a financial topic and a question with four possible answers. The often surprising answers provide an excellent opportunity to engage students realistically in the chapter concepts.

What Do You Recommend?   These concise, realistic cases are pretests at the beginning of each chapter followed by leading questions tying the most important fundamental concepts in the chapter. The case acts as a pretest because students will be able to offer only simplistic, experience-based opinions and suggestions to respond to the questions. This will communicate to students how much they have to learn from reading the chapter. A corresponding posttest, "What Do You Recommend Now?," appears as part of the end-of-chapter pedagogy. At that point, student responses should be informed, practical, and action oriented. (See further discussion in the "End-of-Chapter Pedagogy" section.)

You Must Be Kidding, Right?

People with no prior credit history or one that shows poor repayment patterns in the past often wonder if they will ever be able to get credit, especially in an economy when credit is difficult to obtain. Simply put, why would any lender want to trust them? Which of the following is true about the availability of credit for people in such situations?

   A. No one will ever grant them credit.

   B. If they wait a few years, the situation could change.

   C. If they keep searching, they will find a lender that will treat them like everyone else.

   D. Credit is relatively easy to obtain even today.

The answer is B. When credit is tight it is difficult for people with a poor or no credit to obtain credit. When credit availability eases, certain lenders will accept such applicants although they will charge high interest rates. Building and maintaining a good credit history will always get you low interest rates!

Your Next Five Years   New to this edition, "Your Next Five Years" boxes in each chapter list actions students need to take to get a great start of being financially successful. These tips are sufficiently detailed to allow ready implementation. If students do all of these, they actually will become financially successful!

Your Next Five Years

In the next five years you can start achieving financial success by doing the following related to building and maintaining good credit:

1. Protect your credit reputation as carefully as you would safeguard your personal reputation.

2. Determine your own debt limit rather than rely on a lender before deciding to take on any debt

3. Obtain copies of your credit bureau reports regularly, and challenge all errors or omissions you find.

4. Never cosign a loan for anyone, including relatives.

5. Always repay your debts in a timely manner.

Do It NOW!   New to this edition, "Do It NOW!" boxes in each chapter list three key personal finance actions smart students should take immediately. They focus primarily on implementing some of the most pressing "Next Five Years" tips from the chapter.

Do It NOW!

Building and maintaining good credit is a must. Start today by:

1. Obtaining a free copy of your credit report (www .annualcreditreport.com) from one of the three national credit bureaus.

2. Confirming the accuracy of the report and if there are errors or omissions challenging them with all three bureaus.

3. Repeating steps two and three every four months staggering the bureaus to ensure that each request is free.

Instant Message   The "Instant Message" boxes provide quick, practical information on a variety of current financial issues and opportunities.

Instant Message

Are You Worried About Your Debts?

If you are worried about your debts then you should be. Your own gut feeling is often the best indicator.

Run the Numbers

Choosing Between Low-Interest-Rate Dealer Financing and a Rebate

Advertisements for new vehicles often offer low APRs for dealer-arranged loans. A cash rebate of $1000 to $3000 (or more) off the price of the car may be offered as an alternative to the low interest rate. If you intend to pay cash, then the cash rebate obviously represents the better deal. But which alternative is better when you can arrange your own financing?

To compare the two APRs accurately, you must add the opportunity cost of the forgone rebate to the finance charge of the dealer financing. The worksheet provides an example of this process. Suppose a dealer offers 2.9 percent financing for three years with a

$907 finance charge; alternatively, you can receive a $3000 rebate if you arrange your own financing. The price of the car before the rebate is $22,000. Assume you can make a $2000 down payment and that you can get a 6.5 percent loan on your own. This worksheet can be found on the *Garman/Forgue* companion website, or you can find similar worksheets at www.bankrate.com (search for "calculators") or www.kiplingers.com/tools.

The lower of the values obtained in steps 3 and 4 is the better deal. In this instance, the financing that you arranged on your own is more attractive. In fact, any loan you arrange that carries an APR lower than 12 percent compares favorably with the dealer-arranged financing in this case.

Step		Example	Your Figures
1.	Determine the dollar amount of the rebate.	$3000	
2.	Add the rebate amount to the finance charge for the dealer financing (dollar cost of credit).	+ $ 907	
3.	Use the n-ratio APR formula from Chapter 7 (Equation [7.2] on page xxx and replicated here as Equation [8.1]) to calculate an adjusted APR for the dealer financing.		

$$APR = \frac{Y(95P + 9)F}{12P(P + 1)(4D + F)} \qquad (8.1)$$

where

APR = **Annual percentage rate**
Y = Number of payment periods in one **year**
F = **Finance** charge in dollars
D = **Debt** (amount borrowed)
P = Total number of scheduled **payments**

$$APR = \frac{(12)[(95 \times 36) + 9][\$3000 + \$907]}{(12 \times 36)(36 + 1)[(4 \times \$20,000) + (\$3000 + \$907)]} \qquad = 12\%$$

4.	Write in the APR that you arranged on your own.	6.5%	

 Advice from a Pro...

Guard Your Privacy

Identity theft is the most common form of consumer fraud in the United States. It occurs whenever someone else uses your personal information, such as a credit card number, to steal from merchants, from credit card companies, or from you. Armed with a very little personal information, a clever thief can borrow someone's credit identity and run up thousands of dollars in debt. To protect your privacy, follow these guidelines:

- Offer no personal information (such as your address, telephone number, or Social Security number) to merchants when using a credit card. If the merchant requires identification beyond the credit card (for example, a driver's license), do not allow such information to be written down or photocopied.
- Save all purchase and ATM receipts, and regularly check them against statements from creditors and sellers.
- Do not give out your credit card or checking account number on the telephone to anyone you do not know or did not telephone directly yourself.
- Never give your **card verification value** over the phone or online to a merchant unless you initiated the contact with the merchant. This is the three- or four-digit code in the signature strip on the back of a credit card.
- Review your credit bureau report at least once each year through www.annualcreditreport.com.
- Report lost or stolen credit cards and suspicious billing information without delay, especially if you make Internet purchases.

- If your credit card is lost or stolen, or if you ever suspect fraudulent use of an account, contact one of the national credit bureaus because any one of them can put a "fraud alert" on your file at all three companies. Fraud alert messages notify potential credit grantors to verify your identification before extending credit in your name.
- Tell all of your financial services companies (banks, lenders, insurance companies) that you want to "opt out" of any information-sharing programs they maintain with affiliated or external companies.
- Never respond to e-mail messages from your bank stating that your account may have been compromised and you need to provide account information such as account numbers and passwords even if the e-mail message looks authentic. Your bank will never ask you for this type of information in an e-mail.
- Immediately change the marital status linked to your credit card account if you become married, separated, or divorced.
- Shred all credit card statements containing account numbers.
- Place a **security freeze** on your credit report, which is an effective way to prevent unauthorized credit accounts from being opened in your name. With a freeze you tell the credit bureaus not to release your financial records to anyone without your consent. You are issued a personal identification number (PIN) to give your authorization. In all but South Carolina there is a nominal charge for this service.

Karen Drage
Eastern Illinois University

What Do You Recommend NOW?

Now that you have read this chapter on building and maintaining good credit, what would you recommend to Carrie Savarin regarding:

1. Factors she should consider regarding her ability to take on additional debt?
2. The impact of her current debt on her ability to obtain a loan to buy a vehicle?
3. Where she might obtain financing for a vehicle loan?
4. The effect of taking on a loan on her overall financial planning?

Barry Austin Photography/Getty Images

Decision-Making Worksheets and Run the Numbers
These feature boxes guide students to their best personal finance decisions following a step-by-step process.

Did You Know? These boxes have interesting, catchy titles that encourage students to actually read the information, and classroom research demonstrates this technique works.

Concept Checks At the end of each major segment of each chapter, we provide one or more concept check questions tied to the major topics in that segment. These are aids to classroom discussion, serve as student assignments or simply provide students with a self-check to full understanding of the material.

Advice from a Pro . . . These feature boxes—written by some of the nation's best personal finance experts—offer authoritative, real-world advice on getting out of credit card debt, making purchases online, buying a used car, and paying for retirement on the layaway plan plus many other topics.

End-of-Chapter Pedagogy The end-of-chapter pedagogy carefully directs student learning of the concepts and principles key to success in personal finance.

What Do You Recommend Now? The same leading questions pertaining to the case at the beginning of the chapter are repeated in this section. At this point, however, instructors can anticipate higher-quality responses and a deeper level of understanding because students have read the chapter.

Big Picture Summary of Learning Objectives Three to four sentences review the chapter content following each of the chapter learning objectives.

Let's Talk About It Students are given an opportunity to converse about their personal experiences related to the chapter by addressing these questions.

Do the Math These questions apply the relevant quantitative mathematical calculations utilized in personal finance decision making. The companion website includes Excel calculators for these exercises.

Financial Planning Cases Students must apply key concepts when analyzing typical personal financial problems, dilemmas, and challenges that face individuals and couples. Because some cases are designed to be both continuous and independent of the other chapters' cases, each case can be analyzed by itself. The series of case questions requires data analysis and critical thinking, and this effort reinforces mastery of chapter concepts.

On the 'Net This end-of-chapter feature offers two or three Internet-based exercises, activities, and focused questions that expand the student's learning in a guided manner, allowing the student to research and apply chapter concepts while finding the answers.

Glossary A comprehensive end-of-text glossary that includes precise definitions of all key terms and concepts.

Complete Instructor Support

- **Instructor's Manual.** Written by main text author, Ray Forgue, this ancillary includes a variety of useful components: suggested course syllabi to emphasize a general, insurance, or investments approach to personal finance; learning objectives; a summary overview for use as a lecture outline; and teaching suggestions including student application exercises and tips for bringing the Web into the classroom. This item is found on the Instructor's Resource CD and instructor website.
- **Solutions Manual.** Written by main text author, Ray Forgue, and verified by Linda Bradley, University of Kentucky. Answers and solutions to all end-of-chapter questions and problems are included. This item is found on the Instructor's Resource CD and the instructor website.
- **PowerPoint slides.** The PowerPoint slides contain chapter outlines, figures, and tables from the main text, which were written by main text author Ray Forgue. eLecture material is available within the PowerPoint slides.
- **Instructor's Resource CD.** This instructor support CD offers electronic versions of the **Instructor's Manual, Solutions Manual,** and **PowerPoint slides.** In addition, the CD includes **ExamView,** a computerized Test Bank, which contains more than 3,100 questions. Approximately 30 percent of the questions are new or revised for this edition and all were carefully reviewed by main text author Ray Forgue. This program is very user friendly and permits editing of test questions and generation of class exams. In addition, an explanation is provided for all True-False questions for which the correct answer is "false," for all multiple-choice questions that require a mathematical computation and for all multiple-choice questions deemed as "difficult."
- **Instructor Website.** The instructor website that accompanies *Personal Finance* provides a wealth of supplemental materials to enhance learning and aid in course management. Features of the site include PowerPoint slides, downloadable Instructor Manual and Solution Manual files, Test Bank content, and a DVD guide.
- **Instructor DVD.** A DVD featuring personal finance tips from The Kiplinger Company. This Instructor DVD features video discussions with numerous personal finance professionals from The Kiplinger Company. These discussions contain personal finance tips illustrating and explaining pertinent topics such as job searching, income taxes, student loans, mortgage shopping, and more.

Kiplinger

Complete Student Support

- **My Personal Financial Planner** is a handbook for students to use in planning and organizing their personal finances. This booklet contains over 60 worksheets, schedules, and planners for financial planning. They are not "busywork" for students. Some of the worksheets mimic the calculations and planning exercises covered in the book, others are for your use in developing your own financial plans and activities.
- **Finance Central Premium Student Website** contains eLectures presentations, calculators, and worksheets to complete the end of chapter exercises, quizzes, online glossary, games, and flashcards. This content is accessible via an optional printed access card. Standalone instant access also available via iChapters.com.
- **Student Companion Website** is accessible without an access code. Students can find a short quiz there.

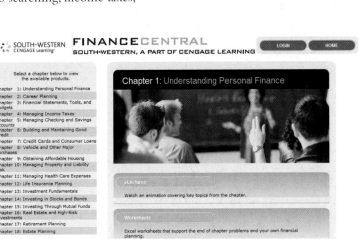

Acknowledgments

We would like to thank our reviewers and other experts, who offered helpful suggestions and criticisms to this and previous editions. This book is their book, too. We especially appreciate the assistance of the following individuals:

Tim Alzheimer, Montana State University

Gary Amundson, Montana State University–Billings

Dori Anderson, Mendocino College

Robert E. Arnold, Jr., Henry Ford Community College

Bala Arshanapalli, Indiana University Northwest

Hal Babson, Columbus State Community College

Anne Bailey, Miami University

Rosella Bannister, Bannister Financial Education Services

Richard Bartlett, Muskingum Area Technical College

Anne Baumgartner, Navy Family Service Center–Norfolk

John J. Beasley, Georgia Southern University

Kim Belden, Daytona Beach Community College

Pamela J. Bennett, University of Central Arkansas

Daniel A. Bequette, Hartwell College

Peggy S. Berger, Colorado State University

David Bible, Louisiana State University–Shreveport

George Biggs, Southern Nazarene University

Robert Blatchford, Tulsa Junior College

Susan Blizzard, San Antonio College

Karin B. Bonding, University of Virginia

Dean Brassington, Financial Educator Services

Anne Bunton, Cottey College

Paul L. Camp, Galecki Financial Management

Chris Canellos, Stanford University

Andrew Cao, American University

Diana D. Carroll, Carson–Newman College

Gerri Chaplin, Joliet Junior College

Steve Christian, Jackson Community College

Ron Christner, Loyola University

Charlotte Churaman, University of Maryland

Carol N. Cissel, Roanoke College

Thomas S. Coe, Xavier University of Louisiana

Edward R. Cook, University of Massachusetts–Boston

Patricia Cowley, Omni Travel

Kathy Crall, Des Moines Area Community College

Sheran Cramer, University of Nebraska–Lincoln

Ellen Daniel, Harding University

Joel J. Dauten, Arizona State University

Carl R. Denson, University of Delaware

Dale R. Detlefs, William M. Mercer, Inc.

A. Terrence Dickens, California State University

Charles E. Downing, Massasoit Community College

Alberto Duarte, InCharge Education Foundation

Sidney W. Eckert, Appalachian State University

Gregg Edwards, Monroe Community College

Jacolin P. Eichelberger, Hillsborough Community College

Gregory J. Eidleman, Alvernia College

Richard English, Augustana College

Evan Enowitz, Grossmont College

Don Etnier, University of Maryland–European Division

Judy Farris, South Dakota State University

Vicki Fitzsimmons, University of Illinois

Fred Floss, Buffalo State College

Paula G. Freston, Colby Community College

H. Swint Friday, University of South Alabama

Caroline Fulmer, University of Alabama

Wafica Ghoul, Davenport University

Joel Gold, University of South Maine

Elizabeth Goldsmith, Florida State University

Joseph D. Greene, Augusta State University

Paul Gregg, University of Central Florida

Jeri W. Griego, Laramie County Community College

Michael P. Griffin, University of Massachusetts–Dartmouth

Richard C. Grimm, Grove City College

David R. Guarino, Standard & Poor's

Hilda Hall, Surry Community College

Patty Hatfield, Bradley University

Andrew Hawkins, Lake Area Technical Institute

Janice Heckroth, Indiana University of Pennsylvania

Diane Henke, University of Wisconsin–Sheboygan

Roger P. Hill, University of North Carolina–Wilmington

Jeanne Hilton, University of Nevada

Laura Horvath, University of Detroit Mercy

David Houghton, Northwest Nazarene College

George Hruby, University of Akron

Samira Hussein, Johnson County Community College

Roger Ignatius, University of Maine-Augusta

James R. Isherwood, Community College of Rhode Island

Naheel Jeries, Iowa State University

Karen Jones, SWBC Mortgage Corporation

Marilyn S. Jones, Friends University

Ellen Joyner, Liberty National Bank–Lexington

Virginia W. Junk, University of Idaho

Peggy D. Keck, Western Kentucky University

Dennis Keefe, Michigan State University

Jim Keys, Florida International University

Haejeong Kim, Central Michigan University

Jinhee Kim, University of Maryland–College Park

Karen Eilers Lahey, University of Akron

Eloise J. Law, State University of New York–Plattsburgh

Andrew H. Lawrence, Delgado Community College

David W. Leapard, Eastern Michigan State University

Charles J. Lipinski, Marywood University

Janet K. Lukens, Mississippi State University

Ruth H. Lytton, Virginia Tech University

Kenneth Marin, Aquinas College

Kenneth Mark, Kansas Community College

Julia Marlowe, University of Georgia

Lee McClain, Western Washington University

Billy Moore, Delta State University

John R. Moore, Navy Family Services Center–Norfolk

Diane R. Morrison, University of Wisconsin–La Crosse

Steven J. Muck, El Camino College
Randolph J. Mullis, WEATrust
James Nelson, East Carolina State University
Donald Neuhart, Central Missouri State University
Oris L. Odom II, University of Texas–Tyler
William S. Phillips, Memphis State University
John Piccione, Rochester Institute of Technology
Carl H. Pollock, Jr., Portland State University
Angela J. Rabatin, Prince George's Community College
Gwen M. Reichbach, Dealers' Financial Services
Mary Ellen Rider, University of Nebraska
Eloise Lorch Rippie, Iowa State University
Edmund L. Robert, Front Range Community College
Clarence C. Rose, Radford University
David E. Rubin, Glendale Community College
Michael Rupured, University of Georgia
Peggy Schomaker, University of Maine
Barry B. Schweig, Creighton University
Elaine D. Scott, Bluefield State University
James Scott, Southwest Missouri State University
Wilmer E. Seago, Virginia Tech University
Kim Simons, Madisonville Community College
Marilyn K. Skinner, Macon Technical Institute
Rosalyn Smith, Morningside College

Horacio Soberon-Ferrer, University of Florida
Edward Stendard, St. John Fisher College
Mary Stephenson, University of Maryland-College Park
Eugene Swinnerton, University of Detroit Mercy
Lisa Tatlock, The Master's College
Francis C. Thomas, Port Republic, New Jersey
Stephen Trimby, Worcester State College
John W. Tway, Amber University
Shafi Ullah, Broward Community College
Dick Verrone, University of North Carolina–Wilmington
Jerry A. Viscione, Boston College
Stephen E. Wagner, Attorney at Law, Blacksburg, Virginia
Rosemary Walker, Michigan State University
Grant J. Wells, Michigan State University
Jon D. Wentworth, Southern Adventist University
Dorothy West, Michigan State University
Gloria Worthy, State Technical Institute-Memphis
Rui Yau, South Dakota State University
Alex R. Yguado, L.A. Mission College
Robert P. Yuyuenyongwatana, Cameron University
Martha Zenns, Jamestown Community College
Larry Zigler, Highland College
Virginia S. Zuiker, University of Minnesota

This 10th edition also has benefited from the contributions of some of the United States' best personal finance experts, who have shared some specialized expertise by contributing to a series of boxes titled "Advice from a Pro . . .":

Dennis R. Ackley, Ackley & Associates
Jan D. Andersen, California State University, Sacramento
Sophia Anong, Virginia Tech
Lorie Broberg, Oglala Lakota College
Bruce Brunson, Texas Tech University
Anthony J. Campolo, Columbus State Community College
Brenda J. Cude, University of Georgia
William Dean, Southern University
Lorraine R. Decker, Decker & Associates Inc.
Karen Drage, Eastern Illinois University
Patti Fisher, Virginia Tech
Jonathan Fox, The Ohio State University
Carol S. Fulmer, The University of Alabama
Jordan E. Goodman, MoneyAnswers.com
Holly Hunts, Montana State University
Alena C. Johnson, Utah State University
Hyungsoo Kim, University of Kentucky

Joan Koonce, University of Georgia
Frances C. Lawrence, Louisiana State University
Irene Leech, Virginia Tech
Lori Lothringer, Metropolitan Community College
Allen Martin, California State University-Northridge
Diann Moorman, University of Georgia
Aimee D. Prawitz, Northern Illinois University
Kathleen Prochaska-Cue, University of Nebraska–Lincoln
Ann Ranczuch, Monroe Community College
Jamie Richter, Northern Illinois University
Michael Ruff, Monroe Community College
Michelle Singletary, The Washington Post
Donald Stuhlman, Wilmington College, Delaware
Sherry Tshibangu, Monroe Community College
Robert O. Weagley, University of Missouri–Columbia
Jon Wentworth, Southern Adventist University
Dana Wolff, Southeast Technical Institute

We definitely wish to thank the many students who had the opportunity to read, critique, and provide input for various components of the *Personal Finance* project. Please keep sending us your e-mails. Jing-Jang Xiao (University of Rhode Island) prepared the financial calculator appendix found on the website.

This edition of *Personal Finance* benefited enormously from the editorial efforts of Julia Chase. In addition to being a fine manager and editor, she brought much insight, creativity, intelligence, and wisdom to the project. Linda Bradley's accuracy check efforts were incomparable. Holly Henjum and Lynn Steines did a superlative job supervising the production of this edition with its challenging format.

A project of this dimension could never have been completed without the patience, support, understanding, and sacrifices of our friends and families during the book's development, revision, and production. Tom Garman, professor emeritus and fellow at Virginia Tech University, lives in Summerfield, Florida, and stays in contact with his children and their spouses and significant others: Dana, Julia, Scott, David, Alieu, Isatou, Kumba, Alimatou, and Ousman. Thanks are owed to all. Tom also credits the mentors in his life—Ron West, Bill Boast, Bill McDivitt, and John Binnion—for guiding him along the way, particularly through their noble examples of compassion, commitment, and excellence. He also thanks Gerry Chambers for her love. Tom now serves as president of the nonprofit Personal Finance Employee Education Foundation (www.PersonalFinanceFoundation.org). Ray Forgue, recently retired from the University of Kentucky, lives near Greenville, South Carolina with his wife Snooky and her son, Stuart, and proudly watches over Ray's son Matthew and daughter Amy and Snooky's children Dru and Seth as they continue their working careers. Ray wishes to thank his mother, Mary, and brothers Bob, Gary, Joe, and Dave for their patience over the years as he spent time during vacation and holiday visits working on this book. Special thanks to Snooky, whose assistance on the first edition of *Personal Finance* continues to shine through to this current edition.

Finally, we wish to say "thank you" to the hundreds of personal finance instructors around the country who have generously shared their views, in person and by letter and e-mail, on what should be included in a high-quality textbook and ancillary materials. You demand the best for your students, and we've listened. *Personal Finance* is your book! The two of us and the superlative team of people at Cengage Learning have tried very hard to meet your needs in every possible way. We hope we have exceeded your expectations. Why? Because we share the belief that students need to study personal finance concepts thoroughly and learn them well so that they will be truly successful in their personal finances.

E. Thomas Garman
ethomasgarman@yahoo.com

Raymond E. Forgue
perfinypm@yahoo.com

P.S. Dear students: If you are going to save any of your college textbooks, be certain to keep this one because the basic principles of personal finance are everlasting. Also, you might want to present the book as a gift to a significant other, spouse, or parent.

Understanding Personal Finance

!You Must Be Kidding, Right?

Lauren Crawford invests $250 a month in her 401(k) retirement account, which earns an 8 percent annual return. After 35 years, how much money will she have in the account over and above the amounts she will contribute through the years?

A. $105,000

B. $210,000

C. $468,000

D. $573,000

The answer is C, $468,000 ($573,000 − $105,000). Lauren will contribute $105,000 ($3000 [$250 × 12] × 35). Lauren makes the big money ($468,000) off "the compounding money," not on the amount of money ($105,000) she put into her retirement plan. It's all about the magic of compound interest!

Learning Objectives

After reading this chapter, you should be able to:

1 Use the building blocks to achieving financial success.

2 Understand how the economy affects your personal financial success.

3 Apply economic principles when making financial decisions.

4 Perform time value of money calculations in personal financial decision making.

5 Make smart decisions about your employee benefits.

6 Identify the professional qualifications of providers of financial advice.

What Do You **Recommend?**

Se Ri Pak, age 23, recently graduated with her bachelor's degree in library and information sciences. She is about to take her first professional position as an archivist with a civil engineering firm in a rapidly expanding area in the U.S. Southwest. While in school, Se Ri worked part time, earning about $8000 per year. For the past two years, she has managed to put $1000 each year into an individual retirement account (IRA). Se Ri owes $15,000 in student loans on which she is obliged now to begin making payments. Her new job will pay $45,000. Se Ri may begin participating in her employer's 401(k) retirement plan immediately, and she can contribute up to 6 percent of her salary to the plan. Her employer will contribute 1/2 of 1 percent for every 1 percent that Se Ri contributes.

Susan Vogel/Photolibrary

What do you recommend to Se Ri on the importance of personal finance regarding:

1. Participating in her employer's 401(k) retirement plan?

2. Understanding the effects of her marginal tax rate on her financial decisions?

3. Factoring the current state of the economy into her personal financial planning?

4. Using time value of money considerations to project what her IRA might be worth at age 63?

5. Using time value of money considerations to project what her 401(k) plan might be worth when she is age 63 if she were to participate fully?

Your Next Five Years

In the next five years you can start achieving financial success by doing the following related to understanding personal finance:

1. Stay up-to-date with current economic conditions.

2. Use marginal and opportunity costs and time value of money calculations when making financial decisions.

3. Harness the power of compounding by saving a consistent amount each month for long-term goals.

4. Take responsibility for managing your own financial success.

5. Take advantage of tax sheltering through your employer's benefits program.

financial literacy
Knowledge of facts, concepts, principles, and technological tools that are fundamental to being smart about money.

personal finance
The study of personal and family resources considered important in achieving financial success; it involves how people spend, save, protect, and invest their financial resources.

financial responsibility
Means that you are accountable for your future financial well-being and that you strive to make wise personal financial decisions.

The 2008 housing/credit/stock market collapse and economic crisis was of historic proportions. Many people of your parents' ages saw the value of their homes shrink 20 percent while at the same time 40 percent of their retirement funds evaporated. Millions had their jobs disappear. Consumer confidence dropped to an all-time low. Today's ensuing slow recovery is fraught with fear about personal finances—the subject of this book that you are fortunate to be reading.

Can you successfully manage your personal finances in such an era of economic turbulence? Yes. And it will be challenging. Three-time *New York Times* Pulitzer Prize winner Thomas Friedman observes that, "We need to save more, invest more, consume less, and throw out most of our credit cards to bail ourselves out of this economic mess." That's good advice for your future. You can and will learn how to do these things because your long-term financial success depends upon it. The economy is going to be bumpy for the next few years. Yet many opportunities will arise for you to take smart actions to help assure your future financial success. This book provides prudent guidance for every step of the way.

Your **financial literacy** is your knowledge of facts, concepts, principles, and technological tools that are fundamental to being smart about money. Financial literacy empowers you. It improves your ability to handle day-to-day financial matters, helps you avoid the consequences of poor financial decisions that could take years to overcome, and helps you make informed and confident personal money decisions.

Personal finance is the study of personal and family resources considered important in achieving financial success; it involves how people spend, save, protect, and invest their financial resources. Topics in personal finance include financial and career planning, budgeting, tax management, cash management, credit cards, borrowing, major expenditures, risk management, investments, retirement planning, and estate planning. A solid understanding of personal finance topics offers you a better chance of success in facing the financial challenges, responsibilities, and opportunities of life. Such successes might include paying minimal credit costs, not paying too much in income taxes, purchasing automobiles at low prices, financing housing on excellent terms, buying appropriate and fairly priced insurance, selecting successful investments that match your needs, planning for a comfortable retirement, and passing on your estate with minimal transfer costs.

Financial responsibility means that you are accountable for your future financial well-being and that you strive to make good decisions in personal finance. Studying personal finance will help you avoid financial mistakes and show you how to take advantage of financial opportunities. The biggest barrier to achieving financial success is to live like you are rich before you are.

At the beginning of each chapter, we provide a short case vignette titled "What Do You Recommend?" Each case focuses on the financial challenges that can be experienced by someone who has not learned about the material in that chapter. You will be asked to think about what advice you might give the person as you study the chapter. Then at the end of each chapter, you will again be asked to provide more informed advice based on what you have learned. You will be smarter then!

The goal of this book is to provide you access to up-to-date information and rational suggestions to empower you to be able to make informed decisions about spending, managing money, maintaining creditworthiness, purchasing insurance, and saving and investing. Good decision making means you will control your personal financial destiny.

The Building Blocks to Achieving Personal Financial Success

1 Learning Objective
Use the building blocks to achieving financial success.

Today's marketplace provides a constant barrage of messages suggesting that you can spend and borrow your way to financial success, security, and wealth. These messages are very enticing for those starting out in their financial lives. In truth, overspending and overuse of consumer credit actually *impede* financial success!

Many people think that being wealthy is a function of how much you earn or inherit. In reality, it is much more closely related to your ability to understand the trade-offs and decisions that generate wealth for you. A **trade-off** is giving up one thing for another. For example, it is wise to give up some current spending in order to enjoy a financially comfortable retirement.

trade-off
Giving up one thing for another.

You have to do only a *few* things right in personal finance during your lifetime, as long as you don't do too many things wrong. Personal finance is not rocket science. You can succeed very well in your personal finances by making appropriate plans and taking sensible actions to implement those plans.

Spend Less So You Can Save and Invest More

First, recognize that financial objectives are rarely achieved without forgoing or sacrificing current **consumption** (spending on goods and services). This restraint is accomplished by putting money into **savings** (income not spent on current consumption) for use in achieving future goals. Some savings are actually **investments** (assets purchased with the goal of providing additional income from the asset itself). By saving and investing, people are much more likely to have funds available for future consumption. If you save for tomorrow, you will be happier today.

savings
Income not spent on current consumption.

investments
Assets purchased with the goal of providing additional income from the asset itself.

Effective financial management often separates the haves from the have-nots. The haves, observes Virginia Tech professor Celia Hayhoe, are those people who learn to live on less than they earn and are the savers and investors of society. The have-nots are the spenders who live paycheck to paycheck, usually with high consumer debt. To succeed in personal finance you should follow the adage to "Spend some and save some."

Saving for future consumption represents a good illustration of the human desire to achieve a certain **standard of living.** This standard is what an individual or group earnestly desires and seeks to attain, to maintain if attained, to preserve if threatened, and to regain if lost. At any particular time, individuals actually experience their **level of living.** In essence, your standard of living is where you would like to be, and your level of living is where you actually are.

standard of living
Material well-being and peace of mind that individuals or groups earnestly desire and seek to attain, to maintain if attained, to preserve if threatened, and to regain if lost.

Financial Success and Happiness

Financial success is the achievement of financial aspirations that are desired, planned, or attempted. Success is defined by the person that seeks it. Some define financial success as being able to actually live according to one's standard of living. Many seek **financial security,** which provides the comfortable feeling that your financial resources will be adequate to fulfill any needs you have as well as most of your wants. Others want to be **wealthy** and have an abundance of money, property, investments, and other resources. A fundamental truth of personal finance is that you cannot build financial security or wealth unless you spend less than you earn. As a result, you cannot reach your standard of living without somewhat restricting your level of living as you save and invest. That's the trade-off.

financial success
The achievement of financial aspirations that are desired, planned, or attempted, as defined by the person that seeks it.

financial security
The comfortable feeling that your financial resources will be adequate to fulfill any needs you have as well as most of your wants.

Buy Happiness with Money

Twenty-five percent of Americans believe that you can buy happiness with money.

Most Frequently Heard Advice

The most frequently heard advice from financial advisers is to reduce your debts so you can save more.

financial happiness
The experience you have when you are satisfied with your money matters, which is in part a result of practicing good financial behaviors.

Financial happiness encompasses a lot more than just making money. It is the experience you have when you are satisfied with your money matters. People who are happy about their finances are likely to be spending within a budget and taking steps to achieve their goals, and this happiness spills over in a positive way to feelings about their overall enjoyment of life. Financial happiness is in part a result of practicing good financial behaviors. Examples of such behaviors include paying bills on time, spending less than you earn, knowing where your money goes, and investing some money for the future. The more good financial behaviors you practice, the greater your financial happiness. In fact, simply setting financial goals contributes to financial happiness.

Using the Building Blocks

Bridging the gap between one's level of living and one's desired standard of living involves learning about how to achieve financial success. Figure 1.1 shows how the building blocks of a financially successful life fit together. Financial success and happiness come from using the building blocks of personal finance, such as having a foundation of regular income to provide basic lifestyle and savings, and establishing a financial base using employee benefits and checking and savings accounts. Other building blocks include setting financial goals, controlling expenditures, managing income taxes, handling credit cards, and investing in mutual funds and retirement plans. All of these factors are examined in the remaining chapters of the text.

 Concept Check 1.1

1. Describe financial success.
2. What is financial happiness?
3. What are the building blocks to achieving financial success?

Figure 1.1
Building Blocks to Achieving Financial Success

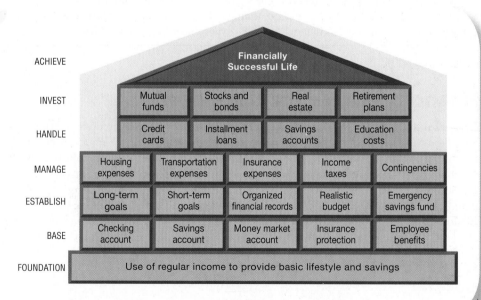

The Economy Affects Your Personal Financial Success

Your success in personal finance depends in part on how well you understand the economic environment; the current stage of the business cycle; and the future direction of the economy, inflation, and interest rates.

Where Are We in the Business Cycle?

An **economy** is a system of managing the productive and employment resources of a country, state, or community. The U.S. federal government attempts to regulate the country's overall economy to maintain stable prices (low inflation) and stable levels of employment (low unemployment). In this way, the government seeks to achieve sustained **economic growth,** which is a condition of increasing production (business activity) and consumption (consumer spending) in the economy—and hence increasing national income. Government policies also affect the economy. For example, tax cuts keeps money in consumers' pockets, which they are then likely to spend. Tax increases, in contrast, depress consumer demand.

Growth in the U.S. economy varies over time. The **business cycle** (also called the **economic cycle**) is a process by which the economy grows and contracts over time, and it can be depicted as a wavelike pattern of rising and falling economic activity in which the same pattern occurs again and again over time. As illustrated in Figure 1.2, the phases of the business cycle are expansion (when the economy is increasing), peak (the end of an expansion and the beginning of a contraction), contraction (when the economy is falling), and trough (the end of a contraction and beginning of an expansion).

The preferred stage of the economic cycle is the expansion phase, where production is at high capacity, unemployment is low, retail sales are high, and prices and interest rates are low or falling. Under these conditions, consumers find it easier to buy homes, cars, and expensive goods on credit, and businesses are encouraged to borrow to expand production to meet the increased consumer demand. The stock market also rises because investors expect higher profits.

Did You Know?

Top 3 Financial Missteps in Personal Finance

People slip up in personal finance when they do the following:

1. Only think about money matters when they have a financial problem
2. Spend more than they earn
3. Get financial advice from amateurs

economic growth
A condition of increasing production (business spending) and consumption (consumer spending) in the economy and hence increasing national income.

business cycle/ economic cycle
Business cycles can be depicted as a wavelike pattern of rising and falling economic activity; the phases of the business cycle include expansion, peak, contraction (which may turn into recession), and trough.

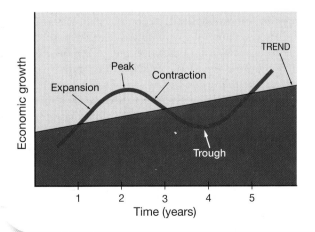

Figure 1.2
Business Cycle Phases

As the demand for credit increases, short-term interest rates rise because more borrowers want money. Consumers and businesses purchase more goods, exerting upward pressure on prices. Eventually, prices and interest rates climb high enough to stifle consumer and business borrowing, send stock prices down, and choke off the expansion. The result is a period of negligible economic growth or even a decline in economic activity.

In such situations, the economy often contracts and moves toward a **recession.** The federal government's Business Cycle Dating Committee officially defines a recession as "a recurring period of decline in total output, income, employment and trade, usually lasting from six months to a year and marked by widespread contractions in many sectors of the economy." During recessions, consumers become pessimistic about their future buying plans. The typical U.S. recession is marked by an average economic decline of 2 percent that lasts for ten months with an average unemployment rate exceeding 6 percent. Because of the severity of the recession that started in early 2008, characterized by extremely high unemployment, horrendous stock market declines, and falling housing prices, it is known as the Great Recession. There have been four recessions in the past 30 years.

Eventually the economic contraction ends, and consumers and businesses become more optimistic. The economy then moves beyond the trough toward expansion, where levels of production, employment, and retail sales begin to improve (usually rapidly), allowing the overall economy to experience some growth from its previously weakened state. The entire business cycle may take six to eight years.

What Is the Future Direction of the Economy?

recession
A recurring period of decline in total output, income, employment and trade, usually lasting from six months to a year and marked by widespread contractions in many sectors of the economy.

economic indicator
Any economic statistic, such as the unemployment rate, GDP, or the inflation rate, that suggests how well the economy is doing now and how well it might be doing in the future.

gross domestic product (GDP)
The nation's broadest measure of economic health; it reports how much economic activity (all goods and services) has occurred within the U.S. borders during a given period.

To make sound financial decisions, you need to know where we are in the business cycle, how well the economy is doing, and where the economy might be headed. You can do this by paying attention to some economic statistics that are regularly reported in the news as well as on cable TV business shows, such as "CNBC." Your knowledge will guide your long-term financial strategy. An **economic indicator** is any economic statistic, such as the unemployment rate, GDP, or the inflation rate (terms discussed in the next few paragraphs), that suggests how well the economy is doing and how well the economy might be doing in the future.

Procyclic Indicator A **procyclic** (or **procyclical**) economic indicator is one that moves in the same direction as the economy. Thus if the economy is doing well, this number typically is increasing, however if we are in a recession this indicator is decreasing. The gross domestic product is an example of a procyclic economic indicator. The **gross domestic product (GDP)** is the broadest measure of the economic health of the nation because it reports how much economic activity (all goods and services) has occurred within the U.S. borders. The government regularly announces the rate at which the GDP has grown during the previous three months (www.bea.gov/newsreleases/rels.htm). An annual rate of less than 2 percent is considered low growth; 4 percent or more is considered vigorous growth. Other examples of procyclic indicators are retail sales, industrial production, and number of employees on nonagricultural payrolls.

Countercyclic Indicator A **countercyclic** (or **countercyclical**) economic indicator is one that moves in the opposite direction as the economy. For example, the unemployment rate is countercyclic because it gets larger as the economy gets worse. Similarly, interest rates decline as the economy gets worse.

Leading Indicators **Leading economic indicators** are those that change before the economy changes, thus they help predict how the economy will do in the future. The stock market is a leading economic indicator because it usually begins to decline before the overall economy slows down. Then the stock market advances before the economy begins to pull out of a recession. Other examples of leading economic indicators are the number of new building permits, average number of weekly initial claims for unemployment insurance, and the consumer confidence index.

A widely watched leading economic indicator is the **consumer confidence index.** It indicates the degree of optimism that consumers are expressing about the state of the economy. It gives a sense of consumers' willingness to spend (www.conference-board.org). Growing confidence suggests increased consumer spending.

The **index of leading economic indicators (LEI)** is a composite index, reported monthly by the Conference Board, that suggests the future direction of the U.S. economy (www.conference-board.org). The LEI averages 10 components of growth from different segments of the economy, such as building permits, factory orders, and new private housing starts. Leading economic indicators are very important to investors as they help predict what the economy will be like in the future.

Use Economic Information in Your Financial Decision Making A point at which the economy is in the trough of a recession may be an excellent time to invest in stocks because the economy will soon expand and stock prices will rise. If economic indicators suggest that the economy is growing steadily, this may be a good time to invest in common stock and mutual funds as values are likely to continue to increase. If the economy begins to show clear signs of a slowdown, it may be a good time to invest in fixed-interest securities because interest rates are sure to fall as the government lowers its own interest rates to boost the economy. Also, this may be a good time to sell stocks as values are likely to decline as the economy slows.

What Is the Future Direction of Inflation, Prices, and Interest Rates?

Inflation and interest rates typically move in the same direction. **Inflation** is a steady rise in the general level of prices. Inflation is measured by the changing cost over time of a "market basket" of goods and services that a typical household might purchase. Inflation occurs when the supply of money (or credit) rises faster than the supply of goods and services available for purchases. It also may be attributed to excessive demand or sharply increasing costs of production.

Once expectations of inflation get too low, people anticipate falling prices. **Deflation** is a broad, sustained decline in prices of goods and services that is hard to stop once it takes hold. This causes less consumer spending, lower corporate profits, declining home values, rising unemployment, and lower incomes. The value of assets falls while debt payments become difficult. Deflationary pressures exist today in the United States and other countries. However, it is hoped that massive government spending will head off sustained price declines and stimulate economic growth. Inflation is the more typical condition in an economy and it can be self-perpetuating as well. Workers may ask for higher wages, thereby adding to the cost of production. In response to the increases in the costs of labor and raw materials, manufacturers will charge more for their products. Lenders, in turn, will require higher interest

leading economic indicators
Statistics that change before the economy changes, thus helping predict how the economy will do in the future, such as the stock market, the number of new building permits, and the consumer confident index.

index of leading economic indicators (LEI)
A composite index reported monthly by the Conference Board that suggests the future direction of the U.S. economy.

inflation
A steady and sustained rise in general price levels across economic sectors; measured by the changing cost over time of a "market basket" of goods and services that a typical household might purchase.

deflation
A broad, sustained decline in prices of goods and services that is hard to stop once it takes hold, causing less consumer spending, lower corporate profits, declining home values, rising unemployment, and lower incomes.

rates to offset the lost purchasing power of the loaned funds. Consumers will lessen their resistance to price increases because they fear even higher prices in the future. In times of moderate to high inflation, buying power declines rapidly, and people on fixed incomes suffer the most.

How Inflation Affects Income and Consumption   When prices are rising, an individual's income must rise at the same rate to maintain its **purchasing power,** which is a measure of the goods and services that one's income will buy. From an income point of view, inflation has significant effects. Consider the case of Scott Marshall of Chicago, a single man who took a job in retail management three years ago at a salary of $32,000 per year. Since that time, Scott has received annual raises of $800, $900, and $1000, but he still cannot make ends meet because of inflation. Although Scott received raises, his current income of $34,700 ($32,000 + $800 + $900 + $1000) did not keep pace with the annual inflation rate of 4.0 percent ($32,000 × 1.04 = $33,280; $33,280 × 1.04 = $34,611; $34,611 × 1.04 = $35,996). If Scott's cost of living rose at the same rate as the general price level, in the third year he would be $1296 ($35,996 − $34,700) short of keeping up with inflation. He would need $1296 more in the third year to maintain the same purchasing power that he enjoyed in the first year.

Personal incomes rarely keep up in times of high inflation. Your **real income** (income measured in constant prices relative to some base time period) is the more important number. It reflects the actual buying power of the **nominal income** (also called money income) that you have to spend as measured in current dollars. Rising nominal income during times of inflation creates the illusion that you are making more money, when in actuality that may not be true.

To compare your annual wage increase with the rate of inflation for the same time period, you first convert your dollar raise into a percentage, as follows:

$$\text{Percentage change} = \frac{\text{nominal income after raise} - \text{nominal income last year}}{\text{nominal income last year}} \times 100 \quad \textbf{(1.1)}$$

For example, imagine that John Bedoin, a single parent and assistant manager of a convenience store in Columbia, Missouri, received a $1600 raise to push his $37,000 annual salary to $38,600. Using Equation (1.1), John calculated his percentage change in personal income as follows:

$$\frac{(\$38,600 - \$37,000)}{\$37,000} \times 0.043 \times 100 = 4.3\% \star$$

After a year during which inflation was 4.0 percent, he did better than the inflation rate because his raise amounted to 4.3 percent. Measured in real terms, John's raise was 0.3 percent (4.3 − 4.0). In dollars, his real income after the raise can be calculated by dividing his new nominal income by 1.0 plus the previous year's inflation rate (expressed as a decimal):

$$\text{Real income} = \frac{\text{nominal income after raise}}{1.0 + \text{previous inflation rate}} \quad \textbf{(1.2)}$$

$$\frac{\$38,600}{1 + 0.040} = \$37,115$$

Clearly, a large part of the $1600 raise John received was eaten up by inflation. To John, only $115 ($37,115 − $37,000) represents real economic progress, while $1485 ($1600 − $115) was used to pay the inflated prices on goods and services. The $115 real raise is equivalent

---

★This equation shows how the percentage change is calculated for any difference between two measurements. Divide the difference between measurement 1 and measurement 2 by the value of measurement 1. For example, a stock selling for $65 per share on January 1 and for $76 on December 31 of the same year would have risen 16.92 percent during the year: ($76 − $65) ÷ $65 = 0.1692 or 16.92%.

---

purchasing power
Measure of the goods and services that one's income will buy.

real income
Income measured in constant prices relative to some base time period. It reflects the actual buying power of the money you have as measured in constant dollars.

nominal income
Also called money income; income that has not been adjusted for inflation and decreasing purchasing power.

to 0.31 percent ($115 ÷ $37,000) of his previous income, reflecting the difference between John's percentage raise in nominal dollars and the inflation rate.

How Inflation Is Measured

The U.S. Bureau of Labor Statistics measures inflation on a monthly basis using the **consumer price index (CPI).** The CPI is a broad measure of changes in the prices of all goods and services purchased for consumption by urban households. The prices of more than 400 goods and services (a "market basket") sold across the country are tracked, recorded, weighted for importance in a hypothetical budget, and totaled. In essence, the CPI is a cost of living index. The index has a base time period—or starting reference point—from which to make comparisons. The 1982 to 1984 time period represents the base period of 100. For example, if the CPI were 212 on January 1, 2010, the cost of living would have risen 112 percent since the base period $[(212 - 100) ÷ 100 = 1.12$ or 112%]. Similarly, if the index rises from 212 to 220 on January 1, 2011, then the cost of living will have increased by 3.8 percent over the year $[(220 - 212) ÷ 212 = 0.0377$ or 3.8%].

When prices rise, the purchasing power of the dollar declines, but not by the same percentage. Instead, it falls by the *reciprocal amount* of the price increase (the counterpart ratio quantity needed to produce unity). In the preceding illustration where prices increase between 2010 and 2011, prices rose 3.8 percent, whereas the purchasing power of the dollar declined 3.6 percent over the same period. [The previous year base of 212 divided by the index of 220 equals 0.9636; the reciprocal is 0.0364 $(1 - 0.9736)$, or 3.6%.]

Inflation pushes up the costs of the products and services we consume. If automobile prices rose 20 percent over the past five years, for example, then it will take $28,800 now to buy a car that once sold for $24,000. Conversely, the purchasing power of the car-buying dollar has fallen to 83.3 percent of its original power ($24,000 ÷ $28,800) five years ago. If your market basket of goods and services differs from that used to calculate the CPI, you might have a very different **personal inflation rate** (the rate of increase in prices of items purchased by a particular person). Inflation pushes up the cost of borrowing, so monthly car payments and home mortgage rates increase when inflation rises.

consumer price index (CPI)
A broad measure of changes in the prices of all goods and services purchased for consumption by urban households.

Track the Federal Funds Rate to Forecast Inflation

You can forecast interest rates by paying attention to changes in the **federal funds rate,** which is the rate that banks charge one another on overnight loans. Because it is set by the Federal Reserve Board (an agency of the federal government commonly referred to as the **Fed**) and regularly reported by the news media, the federal funds rate is a benchmark for business and consumer loans and an indication of future Fed policy. When the economy slows down too much the Fed reduces the federal funds rate and in turn lenders reduce their rates for short-term loans, thereby making it less costly to borrow and spend. In effect, the Fed pumps up the economy to spur business activity. When the Fed believes the economy is growing too fast, it raises the rate in an effort to reduce borrowing and slow down the economy.

federal funds rate
The rate that banks charge one another for overnight loans; set by the Federal Reserve Board.

fed
The Federal Reserve Board, which is an agency of the federal government.

How Inflation Affects Borrowing, Saving, and Investing

Interest is the price of money. During times of high inflation, interest rates on new loans for cars, homes, and credit cards rise. Even though nominal interest rates for savers rise as well, the increases do

interest
The price of borrowing money.

Advice from a Pro...

Seven Money Mantras for a Richer Life

1. It's not an asset if you are wearing it!
2. Is this a need or is it a want?
3. Sweat the small stuff.
4. Cash is better than credit.
5. Keep it simple.
6. Priorities lead to prosperity.
7. Enough is enough!

Michelle Singletary
Nationally syndicated *Washington Post* columnist ("The Color of Money") and author of *Spend Well, Live Rich: How to Get What You Want with the Money You Have.*

Reprinted with permission of the author.

The Fed meets regularly to discuss the economy and review federal interest rates.

Joe Pavel/ Federal Reserve Board /Landov

not provide "real" gains if the inflation rate is higher than the interest rate on savings accounts or certificates of deposit.

Smart investors recognize that the degree of inflation risk is higher for long-term lending (5 or 20 years, for example) than for short-term lending (such as a year) because the likelihood of error when estimating inflation increases when lots of time is involved. Therefore, long-term interest rates are generally higher than short-term interest rates. Similarly, stock market investors are negatively affected when inflation causes businesses to pay more when they borrow, thereby reducing their profits, and depressing stock prices. When inflation is at 5 percent annually, a dollar of profit that a company will earn a year from now will be worth only 95 cents in today's prices. If instead inflation was only 2 percent, that dollar would be worth 98 cents today. Such differences add up over many years. Throughout your financial life, you will want to factor the impact of inflation into your financial decisions in an effort to avoid its negative effects.

 Concept Check 1.2

1. Summarize the phases of the business cycle.
2. Describe two statistics that help predict the future direction of the economy.
3. Give an example of how inflation affects income and consumption.
4. Explain how the federal government measures inflation.

Think Like an Economist When Making Financial Decisions

3 Learning Objective

Apply economic principles when making financial decisions.

Understanding and applying basic economic principles will affect your financial success. The most important of these are opportunity costs, marginal utility and costs, and marginal income tax rate.

Opportunity Costs in Decision Making

The **opportunity cost** of a decision is the value of the next best alternative that must be forgone. Examples of personal opportunity costs are time, effort, and health, and examples of financial opportunity costs are interest, safety, and liquidity. Using the concept of opportunity costs allows you to address the personal consequences of choices because every decision inevitably involves trade-offs. For example, suppose that instead of reading this book you could have gone to a movie or watched television, but mainly you wanted to sleep. The lost benefit of that sleep—the next best alternative—is the opportunity cost when you choose to read. Knowing the opportunity cost of alternatives aids decision making because it indicates whether the decision made is truly the best option.

In personal finance, opportunity cost reflects the best alternative of what one could have done instead of choosing to spend, save, or invest money. For example, by deciding to put $2000 into a stock mutual fund for retirement rather than keeping the funds readily available in a savings account, you are giving up the option of using the money for a down payment on a new automobile. Keeping the money in a savings account has the opportunity cost of the higher return on investment that the stock mutual fund might pay. This opportunity to earn a higher rate of return is a primary consideration when making low-risk investment decisions.

Other challenging opportunity cost decisions are renting versus buying housing, buying a new or used car, buying or leasing a vehicle, working or borrowing to pay for college, purchasing life insurance or not, and starting early or late to save and invest for retirement. Another opportunity cost decision often is returning to college for a graduate degree.

If these costs are underestimated, then decisions will be based on faulty information, and judgments may prove wrong. Properly valuing the costs and benefits of alternatives represents a key step in rational decision making. The opportunity cost mathematics of the rent versus buy decision is illustrated later in Chapter 9.

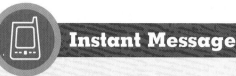

Instant Message

Save $4.66 for Every $1 Not Saved Earlier

If you want to retire at age 63, you will have to save about $4.66 beginning at age 40 to make up for every dollar you did not save at age 20.

opportunity cost
The opportunity cost of any decision is the value of the next best alternative that must be forgone.

Marginal Utility and Costs in Decision Making

Utility is the ability of a good or service to satisfy a human want. A key task in personal finance is to determine how much utility you will gain from a particular decision. For example, if you decide to spend $70 on a ticket to a concert, you might begin by thinking about what you might gain from the expenditure. Perhaps you'll enjoy a nice evening, good music, and so on.

Marginal utility is the extra satisfaction derived from having one more incremental unit of a product or service. **Marginal cost** is the additional (marginal) cost of one more incremental unit of some item. When known, this cost can be compared with the marginal utility received. Thinking about marginal utility and marginal cost can help in decision making because it reminds us to compare only the most important variables. It requires that we examine what we will really gain if we also experience a certain extra cost.

To illustrate this idea, assume that you consider spending $150 instead of $90 (an additional $60) for a front-row seat at the concert. What marginal utility will you gain from that decision? Perhaps an ability to see and hear more or the satisfaction of having one of the best seats in the facility. You would then ask yourself whether those extra benefits are worth 60 extra dollars. In practice, people are inclined to seek additional utility as long as the marginal utility exceeds the marginal cost.

In another example, imagine that two new automobiles are available on a dealership lot in Ferndale, Michigan, where chemical engineer Charlene Hicks is trying to make a purchase decision. Both vehicles are similar models, but from different manufacturers The first, with a sticker price of $29,100, has a moderate number of options; the second, with a sticker price of $30,800, has numerous options. Marginal analysis suggests that Charlene does not need

marginal utility
The extra satisfaction derived from gaining one more incremental unit of a product or service.

marginal cost
The additional (marginal) cost of one more incremental unit of some item.

to consider all of the options when comparing the vehicles. Instead, the concept of marginal cost says to compare the benefits of the additional options with the additional costs—$1700 in this instance ($30,800 − $29,100). Charlene need decide only whether the additional options are worth $1700.

Marginal Income Tax Rate in Decision Making

marginal tax rate
The tax rate at which your last dollar earned is taxed.

When making financial decisions, consider the economic effects of paying income taxes. Of particular importance is the **marginal tax rate**, which is the tax rate at which your last dollar earned is taxed. As income rises, taxpayers pay progressively higher marginal income tax rates. Financially successful people often pay U.S. federal income taxes at the 25 percent, or higher, marginal tax rate. For example, if Juanita Martinez, an unmarried office manager working in Atlanta, Georgia, has a taxable income of $66,000 and receives a $1000 bonus from her employer, she has to pay an extra $250 in taxes on the bonus income ($1000 × 0.25 = $250). Juanita also has to pay state income taxes of 6 percent, or $60 ($1000 × 0.06 = $60), and Social Security taxes of 7.65 percent, or $76.50 ($1000 × 0.0765 = $76.50). Therefore, Juanita pays an effective marginal tax rate of nearly 40 percent (25% + 6% + 7.65% = 38.65%), or $386.50, on the extra $1000 of earned income.

People who pay high marginal tax rates can do better by making tax-exempt investments, such as buying bonds issued by various agencies of states and municipalities. For example, Serena Miller, a married chiropractor with two children from Cleveland, Ohio, currently has $5000 in utility stocks earning 5 percent, or $250 ($5000 × 0.05), annually. She pays $62.50 in federal income tax on that income at her 25 percent marginal tax rate ($250 × 0.25), leaving her with $187.50 after taxes. Alternatively, a tax-exempt $5000 state bond paying 4 percent will provide Serena with a better after-tax return, $200.00 instead of $187.50. That is, she would receive $200.00 tax free from the state bond ($5000 × 0.04) compared with $187.50 ($250 − $62.50) after taxes on the income from the stocks.

tax-exempt income
Income that is totally and permanently free of taxes.

The Very Best Kind of Income Is Tax-Exempt Income   The very best kind of income, as this discussion implies, is **tax-exempt income**, which is income that is totally and permanently free of taxes. By legally avoiding paying one dollar in income taxes, you gain by not paying that dollar in taxes and, therefore, you receive the alternative use for that dollar. You also benefit by not having to earn another dollar to replace the one that might have been paid in taxes.

tax-sheltered income
Income exempt from income taxes in the current year but that will be subject to taxation in a later tax year.

The Second Best Kind of Income Is Tax-Sheltered Income   The second-best kind of income for individuals is **tax-sheltered** (or **tax-deferred**) **income**—that is, income that is exempt from income taxes in the current year but that will be subject to taxation in a later tax year. Figure 1.3 shows that tax-sheltered returns on savings and investments provide much greater returns than returns on which income taxes have to be paid because more money remains available to be invested. In addition, tax-sheltered funds grow more rapidly because compounding (the subject of the next section in this chapter) is enhanced when larger dollar amounts grow during the last years of an investment. Realize that eventually one must pay income taxes on the income deferred.

✔ Concept Check 1.3

1. Define *opportunity cost* and give an example of how opportunity costs might affect your financial decision making.
2. Explain and give an example of how marginal analysis makes some financial decisions easier.
3. Describe and give an example of how income taxes can affect financial decision making.

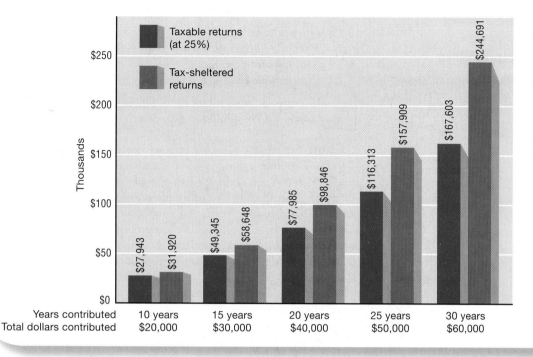

Figure 1.3
Tax-Sheltered Returns Are Greater Than Taxable Returns

In the illustration, the annual return is 8 percent and the annual contribution is $2000.

The Time Value of Money: Setting Dollar Values on Financial Goals

A dollar in your pocket today is worth more than a dollar received five years from now. Why? Time is money.

The **time value of money** (TVM) is perhaps the single most important concept in personal finance. It adjusts for the fact that dollars to be received or paid out in the future are not equivalent to those received or paid out today. It is easy to understand that a dollar received today is worth more than a dollar received five years from now because today's dollar can be saved or invested and in five years you expect it to be worth more than a dollar. The time value of money involves two components: future value and present value.

Two Common Questions in Personal Finance

To illustrate the time value of money, two questions in personal finance are commonly asked:

1. What will an investment (or a series of investments) be worth after a period of time? This question asks for a future value.

2. How much has to be put away today (or as a series of investments) to provide some dollar amount in the future? This question asks for a present value.

As you can see from these two questions, comparisons between time periods cannot be made without making adjustments to money values. Accordingly, time value of money calculations compare future and present values by taking into account the interest rate (or investment rate of return) and the time period involved.

The calculation of interest involves (1) the dollar amount, called the **principal,** (2) the rate of interest earned on the principal, and (3) the amount of time the principal is invested.

4 **Learning Objective**
Perform time value of money calculations in personal financial decision making.

time value of money
A method by which one can compare cash flows across time, either as what a future cash flow is worth today (present value) or what an investment made today will be worth in the future (future value).

principal
The original amount invested.

Instant Message

Reinvesting Means Compounding

If you earn 6 percent on a $1000 bond and spend your $60 annual interest every year for 20 years, you will have received $1200. But if you can reinvest your interest at 6 percent, you would net $2,262. Aha, the power of compounding.

compound interest
When interest on an investment itself earns interest.

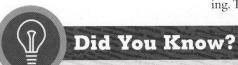

Did You Know?

State Lotteries Use Time Value of Money Calculations

How often have you heard or seen reports of lottery jackpots reaching extremely high amounts? Does the lottery actually pay out these amounts? Not really. Let's assume a lucky ticket holder wins a jackpot of $100 million. The announced jackpot is based on the assumption that the winner will receive the amount in a series of 20 annual payments of $5 million each, adding up to the $100 million advertised total. In fact, the lottery will invest a lump sum right away to fund the annual payments made over the 20 years. It needs to invest only $57,349,500 at 6 percent to fund the stream of $5 million payments ($5 million × 11.4699 from the 6 percent column and 20-year row of Appendix A.4). Alternatively, lottery winners may be permitted to take a "cash option" instead of the annual payments. In this case, a winner of a $100 million jackpot who chooses the cash option would receive only $57,349,500. The winner would also have to pay federal taxes, and perhaps state and city income taxes on this amount, resulting in an after-tax jackpot of closer to $35 million.

One way of calculating interest is called simple interest and is illustrated by the simple interest formula where

$$i = prt \text{ where} \tag{1.3}$$

p = the **principal** set aside
r = the **rate** of interest
t = the **time** in years that the funds are left on deposit

If someone saved or invested $1000 at 8 percent for four years, he would receive $320 in interest ($1000 × 0.08 × 4) over the four years.

Compounding   But something is missing here. The simple interest formula assumes that the interest is withdrawn each year and only the $1000 stays on deposit for the entire four years. Most people do *not* invest this way. Instead, they leave the interest earned in the account so that it will earn additional interest. This earning of interest on interest is referred to as compound interest. And compound interest is always assumed in time value of money calculations.

Earning **compound interest** (or **compounding**) is the best way to build investment values over time. Because of compound interest, money grows much faster when the income from an investment is left in the account. In fact, the deposit of $1000 in our example would grow to $4,661 after 20 years (the calculation is described in the following paragraph). Many of the techniques for building wealth that we describe in this book are based on compounding. The way to build wealth is to make money on your money, not simply to put money away. Yes, you need to put money away first. But compounding over time is what really builds wealth.

Compounding serves as the basis of all time value of money considerations. To see how this works, let us look again at our example in which $1000 is invested at 8 percent for four years. Here is how the amount invested (or principal) would grow using compounding:

At the end of year 1, the $1000 would have grown to $1080 [$1000 + ($1000 × 0.08)].

At the end of year 2, the $1080 would have grown to $1166.40 [$1080 + ($1080 × 0.08)].

At the end of year 3, the $1166.40 would have grown to $1259.71 [$1166.40 + ($1166.40 × 0.08)].

At the end of year 4, the $1259.71 would have grown to $1360.49 [$1259.71 + ($1259.71 × 0.08)].

Due to the effects of compounding, this investor would have earned an additional $40.49 ($360.49 − $320). While this amount might not seem like much, realize that a $1000 investment for a longer period—say, 40 years—earning 8 percent interest would grow to $21,724.52, providing $20,724.52 in interest over that time period. Simple interest would have resulted in only $3200 in interest ($1000 × 0.08 × 40). The benefit of compounding over that time period is an additional $17,524.52 in interest ($20,724.52 − $3200).

The results are even more dramatic if $1000 is invested at the end of each year for 40 years. The total at the end of 40 years would be $259,056, with $219,056 representing the interest on the invested funds. This illustration suggests one of the cardinal rules of personal financial planning: Getting rich is not a function of investing a lot of money. It is the result of investing regularly for long periods of time. The greatest investment strategy of all is compounding. Only through compounding will you attain the serious growth of your wealth over time.

Two Types of Time Value of Money Calculations   Essentially there are two types of time value of money calculations: (1) converting present values to future values (as illustrated in the preceding example) and (2) converting future values to present values. Within each type, the calculations differ slightly depending on whether a lump sum is involved or whether a series of payments (an annuity) is involved.

Calculating Future Values

Future value (FV) is the valuation of an asset projected to the end of a particular time period in the future. You can calculate the future value of a lump sum or the future value of a series of deposits.

future value
The valuation of an asset projected to the end of a particular time period in the future.

Future Value of a Lump Sum   Equation (1.4) can be used to calculate the future value of a lump sum:

$$FV = (\text{Present value of sum of money}) (i + 1.0)^n \qquad (1.4)$$

where i represents the interest rate and n represents the number of time periods. Applying this formula to our earlier example of investing $1000 at 8 percent for four years, we obtain

$$\$1360.49 = (\$1000)(1 + 0.08)^4$$

or

$$\$1360.49 = (\$1000)(1.08)(1.08)(1.08)(1.08)$$

While mathematically correct, these calculations can be cumbersome when using long time periods. Table 1.1 provides a quick and easy way to determine the future dollar value of an investment. For the preceding example, use the table in the following manner: Go across the top row to the 8 percent column. Read down the 8 percent column to the row for four years to locate the factor 1.3605 (at the intersection of the dark brown column and row). Multiply that factor by the present value of the cash asset ($1000) to arrive at the future value ($1360.50).

Appendix A.1 provides an even more complete table for calculating the future value of lump-sum amounts. Figure 1.4 demonstrates the importance of higher yields and longer time horizons by showing the effects of various compounded returns on a $10,000 investment. The $10,000 will grow to $57,435 in 30 years with an interest rate of 6 percent. Compounding $10,000 at 10 percent yields $174,494 over the same time period; at 14 percent, it yields a whopping $509,502! For practice you might want to confirm these results using Appendix A.1.

Table 1.1   Future Value of $1 After a Given Number of Periods

Periods	1%	2%	3%	4%	5%	6%	7%	8%	9%	10%
1	1.0100	1.0200	1.0300	1.0400	1.0500	1.0600	1.0700	1.0800	1.0900	1.1000
2	1.0201	1.0404	1.0609	1.0816	1.1025	1.1236	1.1449	1.1664	1.1881	1.2100
3	1.0303	1.0612	1.0927	1.1249	1.1576	1.1910	1.2250	1.2597	1.2950	1.3310
4	1.0406	1.0824	1.1255	1.1699	1.2155	1.2625	1.3108	1.3605	1.4116	1.4641
5	1.0510	1.1041	1.1593	1.2167	1.2763	1.3382	1.4026	1.4693	1.5386	1.6105
6	1.0615	1.1262	1.1941	1.2653	1.3401	1.4185	1.5007	1.5869	1.6771	1.7716
7	1.0721	1.1487	1.2299	1.3159	1.4071	1.5036	1.6058	1.7138	1.8280	1.9487
8	1.0829	1.1717	1.2668	1.3686	1.4775	1.5938	1.7182	1.8509	1.9926	2.1436
9	1.0937	1.1951	1.3048	1.4233	1.5513	1.6895	1.8385	1.9990	2.1719	2.3579
10	1.1046	1.2190	1.3439	1.4802	1.6289	1.7908	1.9672	2.1589	2.3674	2.5937

Figure 1.4
The Importance of Higher Yields and More Time (Future Value of a Single Investment of $10,000)

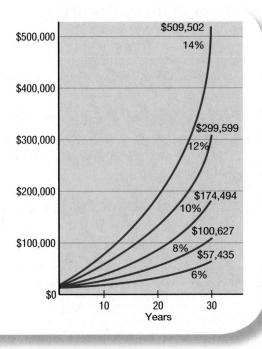

Figure 1.5
Rule of 72 Illustrated

Dividing the interest rate earned into 72 reveals how many years it takes for the principal to double.

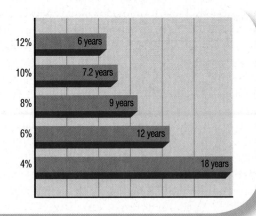

rule of 72
A formula for figuring the number of years it takes to double the principal using compound interest; simply divide the interest rate that the money will earn *into* the number 72.

Rule of 72 Reveals Number of Years for Principal to Double The **rule of 72** is a handy formula for figuring the number of years it takes to double the principal using compound interest. You simply divide the interest rate that the money will earn *into* the number 72. For example, if interest is compounded at a rate of 7 percent per year, your principal will double in 10.3 years (72 ÷ 7); if the rate is 6 percent, it will take 12 years (72 ÷ 6). The rule of 72 (see Figure 1.5) also works for determining how long it would take for the price of something to double given a rate of increase in the price. For example, if college tuition costs were rising 8 percent per year, the cost of a college education would double in just over nine years. In addition, the rule of 72 can be used to calculate the number of years before prices will double given a certain inflation rate. Just divide the inflation rate into 72.

Future Value of an Annuity People often save for long-term goals by putting away a series of payments. Appendix A.3 provides a complete table for calculating the future value of a stream of deposited amounts, referred to as an annuity. Figure 1.6 graphically

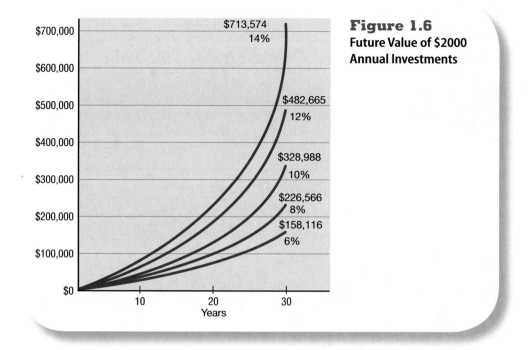

Figure 1.6
Future Value of $2000 Annual Investments

demonstrates the effects of various compounded returns on a $2000 annual investment made at the end of each year. The $2000 will grow to $91,524 in 20 years (read across the interest rate row in Appendix A.3 to 8 percent and then down the column to 20 years to obtain the factor of 45.762 to multiply by $2000) and to $226,566 in 30 years at an 8 percent rate. Compounding $2000 at 10 percent yields $114,550 in 20 years and $328,988 over 30 years; at 14 percent, it becomes $713,574 after 30 years! For practice you might want to confirm these results using Appendix A.3.

Calculating Present Values

Present value (or **discounted value**) is the current value of an asset (or stream of assets) that will be received in the future. You can calculate the present value of a lump sum to be received in the future or the present value of a series of payments to be received in the future.

present value
The current value of an asset (or stream of assets) that will be received in the future; also known as discounted value.

Present Value of a Lump Sum The present value of a lump sum is the current worth of an asset to be received in the future. Alternatively, it can be thought of as the amount you would need to set aside today at a given rate of interest for a given time period so as to have some desired amount in the future. Suppose you want to have $20,000 for the down payment on a new home in ten years. What would you need to set aside today to reach this goal if you could invest your money and receive a 7 percent return? Using Appendix A.2 you could look across the interest rate rows to 7 percent and then down to ten years to obtain the factor of 0.5083. Multiplying $20,000 by this factor reveals that $10,166 set aside today would allow you to reach your goal. (Note the connection here to the rule of 72: 7 percent divided into 72 is approximately 10.28, meaning that the investment would double in about 10.28 years. Indeed, $10,166 would approximately double to $20,000 in ten years.)

Present Value of an Annuity The present value of an **annuity** is the current worth of a stream of payments to be received in the future. Alternatively, it can be thought of as the amount you would need to set aside today at a given rate of interest for a given time period so as to receive that stream of payments. Suppose you want to have $30,000 per year

annuity
A stream of payments to be received in the future.

Instant Message

Web Calculators

Present and future value calculations can be readily performed on the Internet. Among the best calculators are those found at the following websites:

USA Today (www.usatoday.com/money/perfi/calculators/calculator.htm)

Financial Calculators (www.fincalc.com/)

KJE (www.dinkytown.net/)

Bankrate.com (www.bankrate.com)

CNNMoney (www.cgi.money.cnn.com/tools/)

Fool.com (www.fool.com/calcs/calculators.htm?source=LN)

Fidelity (www.moneychimp.com/calculator/compound_interest_calculator.htm)

for 20 years during your retirement. What amount would you need to have invested at retirement to reach this goal if you could invest your money and receive a 7 percent return? Using Appendix A.4 you could look across the interest rate rows to 7 percent and then down to 20 years to obtain the factor of 10.5940. Multiplying $30,000 by this factor reveals that $317,820 (10.5940 × $30,000) set aside at retirement would fund this stream of payments. Note the beauty of compound interest in this result. It takes only $317,820—not $600,000—to fund a $30,000 per year retirement for 20 years if you can earn 7 percent on your financial nest egg.★

✔ Concept Check 1.4

1. Explain the difference between simple interest and compound interest, and describe why that difference is critical.

2. What are the two components used when figuring the time value of money?

3. Use Table 1.1 to calculate the future value of (a) $2000 at 5 percent for four years, (b) $4500 at 9 percent for eight years, and (c) $10,000 at 6 percent for ten years.

Make Smart Money Decisions at Work

5 Learning Objective

Make smart decisions about your employee benefits.

Smart decisions about your employee benefits can increase your actual income by thousands of dollars each year. To do so wisely, select among employer-sponsored plans for health care, out-of-pocket spending for health and dependent care, life insurance, disability, long-term care, and retirement. These decisions often require you to calculate the tax-sheltered aspects of the employee benefits. Your benefits package might also include dental and vision care, child care, elder care, subsidized food services, and an educational assistance program.

employee benefit
Compensation for employment that does not take the form of wages, salaries, commissions, or other cash payments.

An **employee benefit** is compensation for employment that does not take the form of wages, salaries, commissions, or other cash payments. Examples include paid holidays, health insurance, and a retirement plan. The value of employee benefits often amounts to 30 percent or more of one's salary. Some employee benefits are tax sheltered, such as flexible spending accounts and retirement plans. Tax sheltered in this situation means that the employee avoids paying current income taxes on the value of the benefits received from the employer. The taxes may be postponed, or deferred, until a later date (usually a good idea)—perhaps until retirement, when the individual's income tax rate might be lower.

Flexible Benefit Plans Offer Tax-Free Money

flexible benefit plan
An employer-sponsored plan that gives the employee a choice of selecting either cash or one or more qualifying nontaxable benefits; also known as a cafeteria plan.

A **flexible benefit plan,** also known as a **cafeteria plan,** is an employer-sponsored plan that gives the employee a choice of selecting either cash or one or more qualifying nontaxable benefits. For example, an employer might offer $2500 annually to each employee to spend on one or more benefits, and you pay no income taxes on the value of the benefits. A flexible benefits plan might offer dependent care, adoption assistance, medical expense reimbursements,

★If you are using a financial calculator for time value of money calculations, see "How to Use a Financial Calculator" on the *Garman/Forgue* companion website, or you can use the present and future value calculators also found on the *Garman/Forgue* companion website, www.cengage.com/finance/garman.

insurance, or transportation benefits. Employees select the benefits they want. Employees working for employers that offer a cafeteria plan avoid having to pay out-of-pocket money for certain expenses.

Making Decisions About Employer-Sponsored Health Care Plans

Many employers offer employees a choice of **health care plans.** Employees usually can make a decision to change health plans once a year as well as when one's family situation changes, such as marriage. The premium for an unmarried employee could be $5000 or more annually depending upon the amount of coverage provided. Fortunately, the premiums for employees are either paid for entirely or subsidized by the employer. Some employers pay perhaps the first $3000 of annual premiums for employee health care coverage and require that employees pay the remainder.

Partly because of soaring costs of health care coverage, employers often offer multiple policies. These can range from an expensive plan, perhaps with a $6600 premium, that offers comprehensive coverage requiring little out-of-pocket spending by the employee to less expensive **high-deductible health care plan,** perhaps with a $3100 premium, requiring larger out-of-pocket health care spending by the employee. The *deductible* is the amount paid to cover expenses before benefits begin. Employees, especially healthy ones, hope to save money on premiums by choosing these policies.

Younger employers, particularly those who are typically healthy, often select high-deductible plans to save on the cost of premiums. For example, if an employer pays only the first $3000 in health care premiums for employees, an employee selecting the high-cost plan described previously has to pay $3600 ($6600 − $3000) annually, or $300 a month in premiums. This contrasts with a $100 annual premium for employees who select the high-deductible plan ($3100 − $3000). If the person experiences lots of health care expenses, he/she will have to pay additional costs.

Some employers also offer **health savings accounts (HSAs).** This special savings account is intended for people who have a high-deductible health care plan (with annual deductibles of at least $1000 for individuals and $2000 for families). Employees make tax-deductible contributions to a savings account to be used for eligible expenses. Employers may also contribute. The employee invests HSA funds and the money in the account grows tax free. Withdrawals are made to pay for medical expenses. The limits on contributions to an HSA savings account are $2900 per year for individuals and $5800 for families. The money in the account does not vanish if you don't spend it within a certain time period.

The tax-advantaged aspect of making a health care plan choice adds another dimension to making a good personal financial decision. Because many workers have an effective marginal tax rate (discussed earlier in the chapter) of nearly 40 percent, that same percentage can be *saved* or not spent by giving it to the government in taxes. The worker who contributes $3000, for example, to a health savings account saves approximately $1200 ($3000 × 0.40), further reducing his or her health care expenses.

Making Decisions About Employer's Flexible Spending Accounts

A **flexible spending account (FSA)** is an employer-sponsored account that allows employee-paid expenses for medical or dependent care to be paid with an employee's pretax dollars rather than after-tax income. Under a typical FSA, the employee agrees to have a certain amount deducted from each paycheck, and that amount is then deposited in a separate

---

health care plan
An employee benefit designed to pay all or part of the employee's medical expenses.

high-deductible health care plan
A plan that requires individuals pay a higher deductible to cover medical expenses before insurance plan payments begin; chosen to save money on premiums.

health savings accounts (HSAs)
Special savings account intended for people who have a high-deductible health care plan (with annual deductibles of at least $1000 for individuals and $2000 for families).

Instant Message

Don't Pay Extra Taxes
Contributing $1000 to a tax-advantaged employee benefit plan saves a worker as much as $400 that does not have to be paid to the government in taxes.

flexible spending account (FSA)
An employer-sponsored account that allows employee-paid expenses for medical or dependent care to be paid with an employee's pretax dollars rather than after-tax income.

pretax dollars
Money income that has not been taxed by the government.

tax-sheltered retirement plan
Employer-sponsored, defined-contribution retirement plans including 401(k) plans and similar 403(b) and 457 plans.

account called a flexible spending account. As eligible expenses are incurred, the employee requests and receives reimbursements from the account.

Funds in a dependent care FSA account may be used to pay for the care of a dependent younger than age 13 or the care of another dependent who is physically or mentally incapable of caring for himself or herself and who resides in the taxpayer's home. Funds in a health care FSA account may be used to pay for qualified, unreimbursed out-of-pocket expenses for health care.

The tax advantage of an FSA occurs because the amounts deducted from the employee's salary avoid federal income tax, Social Security taxes, and, in most states, state income taxes, thereby allowing selected personal expenses to be paid with pretax (rather than after-tax) income. Paying the expenses with **pretax dollars** (money income that has not been taxed by the government) lowers taxable income, decreases take-home pay, and increases effective take-home pay because of the reimbursements. The maximum annual contribution limits are usually $5000 for dependent care FSA and $3000 for medical care FSA.

Younger workers who anticipate few medical costs usually do not sign up for a medical FSA, although FSAs do pay for eyeglasses, contacts, copayments, and some over-the-counter medications. Workers with children or others to take care of financially, such as elderly or disabled parents, often sign up for dependent care FSA. Only about 20 percent of eligible employees participate in flexible spending accounts even though doing so saves money.

Before enrolling in an FSA, you need to estimate your expenses carefully so that the amount in the FSA does not exceed anticipated expenses. According to Internal Revenue Service (IRS) regulations, unused amounts are forfeited and are not returned to the employee—a condition called the "use it or lose it" rule. However, employers may offer a 2½-month grace period during which time you can continue to spend the previous year's FSA money. Many employers offer debit cards that withdraw money directly from an employee's FSA.

Examples of Good Financial Behaviors

Good financial behaviors to follow include these:

1. Develop a plan for financial future.
2. Start or increase savings.
3. Follow a budget or spending plan.
4. Reduce personal debts.
5. Pay credit card bills in full each month.
6. Control or reduce living expenses.
7. Comparison shops for purchases.
8. Use a credit/budget counselor if debt becomes unmanageable.
9. Use a financial planner when faced with complicated financial issues.
10. Set aside an emergency fund sufficient to live on for three to six months.
11. Contribute to a flexible spending account at work.
12. Calculate how much money you will need for retirement.
13. Sign up to participate in your employer's retirement plan.
14. Save and invest amounts sufficient to fund a financially successful retirement.

Making Decisions About Participating in Employer Insurance Plans

Life, disability, and long-term care insurance coverage is often available through employers. While the premiums charged for the group of employees for life insurance are not as low as those available in the general marketplace, some employers pay for part or all of employees' premiums. Coverage is typically one or two times the employee's salary. So, sign up for free or subsidized life insurance at work. The premiums for disability and long-term care insurance are often less expensive when purchased through one's employer. See Chapters 10, 11, and 12 to begin to purchase any needed insurance coverage.

Making Decisions About Participating in Your Employer's Retirement Plan

More than half of all workers are covered by an employer-sponsored, defined-contribution retirement plan, also called a **tax-sheltered retirement plan.** These include 401(k) plans and similar 403(b) and 457 plans. Employer-sponsored retirement plans provide four distinct advantages.

Prepare for a Long Retirement

You will likely work full time for 45 years, from ages 22 to 67. Saving for retirement during those years is critical since you are likely to live 20 or more years during retirement.

First Advantage: Tax-Deductible Contributions Tax-sheltered retirement plans provide tremendous tax benefits compared with ordinary savings and investment plans. Because pretax contributions to qualified plans reduce income, the current year's tax liability is lowered. The money saved in taxes can then be used to partially fund a larger contribution, which creates even greater returns. The 401(k) plan lets the IRS help employees finance their retirement plans because of the income taxes saved.

As Table 1.2 illustrates, you can save substantial sums for retirement with minimal effects on your monthly take-home pay. For example, a single person with a monthly taxable income of $4000 in the 25 percent marginal tax bracket who forgoes consumption and instead places $500 into a tax-sheltered retirement plan every month reduces monthly take-home pay from $3175 to $2800, or $375—that is certainly not an enormous amount. The net effect is that it costs that person only $375 to put away that $500 per month into a retirement plan. The immediate "return on investment" equals a fantastic 25 percent ($125 ÷ $500). In essence, the taxpayer puts $375 into his or her retirement plan and the government contributes $125. (Without the plan, the taxpayer would pay the $125 directly to the government.) A taxpayer paying a higher marginal tax rate realizes even greater gains. Because a substantial part of your contributions to a tax-sheltered retirement plan comes from money that you would have paid in income taxes, it costs you less to save more.

Instant Message

You Have a Promising Financial Future

The pessimism associated with recent stock market crashes and economic downturns is not your future. You are still in college. You have many years ahead in which to save, cautiously use credit, and invest wisely for your long-term future within an individual retirement account (IRA) or an employer-sponsored 401(k) retirement program.

Second Advantage: Employer's Matching Contributions To encourage saving for retirement, many employers "match" all or part of their employees' contributions, perhaps up to 6 percent of salary. An employee who saves $375 might receive an additional $375 a month from his/her employer. That's a 100 percent return on the employee's $375!

Third Advantage: Tax-Deferred Growth Because interest, dividends, and capital gains from qualified plans are taxed only after funds are withdrawn from the plan, investments in tax-sheltered retirement plans grow tax free. The benefits of tax deferral can be substantial.

For example, if a person in the 25 percent tax bracket invests $2000 at the end of every year for 30 years and the investment earns an 8 percent taxable return compounded annually, the fund will grow to $158,116 at the end of the 30-year period. If the same $2000 invested annually was instead compounded at 8 percent within a tax-sheltered program, it would grow to $226,566! The higher amount results from compounding at the full 8 percent and not paying any income taxes. (Figure 1.6 on page 19 illustrates these differences in returns.) Indeed, when the funds are finally taxed upon their withdrawal some years later, the taxpayer may be in a lower marginal tax bracket.

Table 1.2 **It Costs Only $375 a Month to Save $6000 a Year for Retirement**

Monthly Salary	$4,000	Monthly Salary	$4,000
Pretax retirement plan contribution	0	Pretax retirement plan contribution	500
Taxable income	4,000	Taxable income	3,500
Federal taxes*	825	Federal taxes*	700
Monthly take-home pay	3,175	Monthly take-home pay	2,800
You put away for retirement	0	Cost to put away $500 per month ($3175 − $2800)	375
		You put away for retirement	6,000

*From Chapter 4; 25 percent income tax rate, single.

Careful planning can result in a much more comfortable life when you retire.

Fourth Advantage: Starting Early Really Pays Off Big

Recall the rule of 72, which can be used to calculate the number of years it would take for a lump-sum investment to double. A 9 percent rate of return doubles an investment every eight years. Waiting eight years to begin saving results in the loss of one doubling. Unfortunately, it is the *last* doubling that is lost, as illustrated in Table 1.3. In that example, $48,000 ($96,000 − $48,000) is lost due to a hesitancy to invest $3000. This is a tremendous opportunity cost for waiting eight years to start.

The gains are awesome when you start early and make regular, continuing investments instead of delaying. For example, a worker who starts saving $25 per week in a qualified retirement plan at age 23 will have about $616,390 by age 65, assuming an annual rate of return of 9 percent. Waiting until age 33 to start saving, instead of beginning at age 23, results in a retirement fund of *only* about $242,230. The benefit of starting to invest early is $374,160 ($616,390 − $242,230). And

Instant Message

Income Does Not Create Wealth

People do not get wealthy by earning an income. Real wealth comes from increases in the value of assets over time such as the growth of investments within a 401(k) retirement program.

Table 1.3   Starting to Save Early Versus Starting Late

Starting Earlier		Starting Later	
Age	$ Value	Age	$ Value
23	$ 3,000	23	$ 0
31	6,000	31	3,000
39	12,000	39	6,000
47	24,000	47	12,000
55	48,000	55	24,000
63	$ 96,000	63	$ 48,000

Starting to save $3000 eight years earlier (age 23 instead of 31) earns the investor an extra $48,000 ($96,000 − $48,000) assuming a compound growth rate of 9 percent.

the total extra dollars invested over the ten years was a mere $13,000. Putting in $13,000 early results in an extra $374,160. This effect occurs because most of the power of compounding appears in the last years of growth.

Concept Check 1.5

1. Summarize the benefits of participating in a high-deductible health care plan at work.
2. Show a math example of why many employees participate in a tax-sheltered employee benefit plan, such as an HSA or 401(k) plan.
3. List two ways you can maximize the benefits from a tax-sheltered retirement program.

Did You Know?

Examples of Bad Financial Behaviors

Poor financial behaviors to avoid include the following:

1. Purchasing something expensive that was wanted but not needed
2. Reaching the maximum limit on credit card
3. Spending more money than available
4. Making credit purchase after running out of money
5. Obtaining cash advance on a credit card after running out of money
6. Using cash advance on a credit card to pay another
7. Receiving an overdue notice from a creditor
8. Paying credit card bill late
9. Paying service charge for paying a utility bill late
10. Making vehicle loan/lease payment late
11. Paying rent/mortgage late
12. Borrowing money from a coworker
13. Obtaining cash advance from employer
14. Borrowing from 401(k) retirement plan at work
15. Taking old employer's 401(k) money in cash when changing jobs
16. Using a debit card (or writing a check) with insufficient funds incurring hefty overdraft fees.

Where to Seek Expert Financial Advice

At various points in their lives, many people rely on the advice of a professional to make financial plans and decisions. Often this consultation is focused on a narrow area of their finances. Professional financial advisers, such as a family lawyer, tax preparer, insurance agent, credit counselor, or stockbroker, can be helpful. Too often these people are not impartial because they are salespeople for specific financial services. They typically want to sell you something rather than have your best interests at heart. People often find it helpful to obtain the services of more broadly qualified financial experts.

A **financial planner** is an investment professional who evaluates the personal finances of an individual or family and recommends strategies to set and achieve long-term financial goals. A good financial planner should be able to analyze a family's total needs in such areas as investments, taxes, insurance, education goals, and retirement and pull all of the information together into a cohesive plan. The planner may help a client select

 6 Learning Objective
Identify the professional qualifications of providers of financial advice.

financial planner
An investment professional who evaluates the personal finances of an individual or family and recommends strategies to set and achieve long-term financial goals.

Advice from a Pro...

Questions to Ask a Financial Planner

Your financial planner will influence your life and your future, so be sure to ask them these questions:

1. What experience do you have, such as work history and companies with which you have been associated?

2. Am I permitted a no-cost, initial consultation, and how much time is allowed?

3. What are your qualifications to practice financial planning, such as education, formal training, licenses, and credentials, and who can vouch for your professional reputation including some of your long-term clients?

4. What process do you follow to identify a client's financial goals?

5. Will you be the only person working with me or will an associate be involved in evaluating and updating the plan you suggest, and how often are formal reviews held with the client?

6. How do you evaluate investment performance, and how often?

7. May I see representative examples of financial plans, monitoring reports, and portfolios or actual case studies of your clients?

8. How much do you charge, what is your fee structure, how are you personally compensated, and if you earn commissions, how are they earned and from whom?

9. To whom do I take a complaint, if I had one?

10. Can I have a written agreement that details the points above and the services to be provided?

Joan Koonce
University of Georgia

Table 1.4 **Financial Planner Professional Certifications**

Many financial planners have voluntarily undergone training and satisfied various qualifications for particular professional certifications, as shown in Table 1.4. Certification examinations often require three years of work experience prior to sitting for the examination.

Certification	Description	Contact Information
Certified Financial Planner (CFP®)	Comprehensive financial planning; best-known certification	(800) 322-4237 www.cfp.net
Chartered Financial Consultant (ChFC)	Comprehensive financial planning in insurance industry	(888) 263-7265 www.theamericancollege.edu
Chartered Life Underwriter (CLU)	Life insurance	(888) 263-7265 www.theamericancollege.edu
Certified Public Accountant (CPA)	Income tax and estate planning	(888) 777-7077 www.aicpa.org
Personal Financial Specialist (PFS)	Personal finance credential for CPAs	(888) 777-7077 www.aicpa.org
Certified Trust and Financial Advisor (CTFA)	Trust, taxes, and personal finance credential for bankers	(202) 663-5092 www.aba.com
Accredited Financial Counselor (AFC)	Financial counseling and money management	(614) 485-9650 www.afcpe.org
Mutual Fund Chartered Counselor (MFCC)	Mutual funds	(800) 237-9990 www.cffp.edu
Registered Investment Adviser (RIA)	Investment adviser	(202) 551-6999 www.sec.gov

and prioritize goals and then rearrange assets and liabilities to fit the client's lifestyle, stage in the life cycle, and financial goals. When appropriate, planners should make referrals to outside advisers, such as attorneys, accountants, trust officers, real estate brokers, stockbrokers, and insurance agents. Effective financial advice helps you make better day-to-day financial decisions so you have more to spend, save, invest, and donate.

You can check the background of the planner you are considering. Self-regulatory organizations and government agencies are available to help.

- The Certified Financial Planner Board of Standards ([888] 237-6275; www.cfp.net) assists those searching for a CFP as well as accepts complaints.
- The National Association of Insurance Commissioners ([816] 842-3600; www.naic.org) directs inquiries to the appropriate state agency where you can check on planners who also sell insurance products.
- The Financial Industry Regulators Authority ([800] 289-9999; www.finra.com) oversees securities brokers.
- The Securities and Exchange Commission ([800] 732-0330; www.sec.gov) regulates investment advisers and all securities dealers.

Do It NOW!

Understanding the economy can help you manage your personal finances appropriately. Start today by:

1. Searching the Internet to identify the current stage in the business cycle,
2. Visiting www.bls.gov to determine the current inflation rate,
3. Going to www.conference-board.org to assess expectations for economic growth for the next 12 months.

How Financial Planners Are Compensated

One way or another, you will pay to get financial advice—commissions, fees, both—so assess the total costs up front as well as the opportunity costs. Financial planners earn their income in one of four ways:

1. **Commission-only financial planners and brokers** live solely on the commissions they receive on the financial products (such as investments or insurance) they sell to their clients. In this case, the plan will be "free," but a commission will be paid to the adviser by the source of the financial product, such as an insurance company or mutual fund. Advantage: Save money if you make only a few transactions.

2. **Fee-based financial planners** charge an up-front fee for providing services and charge a commission on any securities trades or insurance purchases that they conduct on your behalf. Advantage: Unlimited consultations with broker.

3. **Fee-offset financial planners** charge an annual or hourly fee. That fee will be reduced by any commissions earned off the purchase of financial products sold to the client. Advantage: Fee will be reduced as you trade investments.

4. **Fee-only financial planners** earn no commissions and work solely on a fee-for-service basis—that is, they charge a specified fee (typically $50 to $200 per hour or 1 percent of the client's assets annually) for the services provided. They usually need five or more one-hour appointments to analyze a client's financial situation and to present a thorough plan. Fee-only planners do not sell financial products, such as stocks or insurance. As a result and unlike other financial planners/brokers, they are not inclined to recommend products that earn them the highest commission. Finding a true fee-only financial planner is challenging. Advantage: Receive unbiased advice.

Remember, it's your money and your financial future. So when you use the services of a financial planner, don't be intimidated. Ask the hardest questions and don't leave the planner's office until you understand the answers.

Concept Check 1.6

1. What are the four ways financial planners may be compensated?
2. Describe two professional certification programs for financial planners.

What Do You Recommend NOW?

Now that you have read the chapter on the importance of personal finance, what do you recommend to Se Ri in the case at the beginning of the chapter regarding:

1. Participating in her employer's 401(k) retirement plan?

2. Understanding the effects of her marginal tax rate on her financial decisions?

3. Factoring the current state of the economy into her personal financial planning?

4. Using time value of money considerations to project what her IRA might be worth at age 63?

5. Using time value of money considerations to project what her 401(k) plan might be worth at age 63 if she were to participate fully?

Susan Vogel/Photolibrary

Big Picture Summary of Learning Objectives

1 Use the building blocks to achieving financial success.

Financial success and happiness comes from using the building blocks of personal finance, such as having a foundation of regular income to provide basic lifestyle and savings, and establishing a financial base using employee benefits and checking and savings accounts. Other building blocks include setting financial goals, controlling expenditures, managing income taxes, handling credit cards, and investing in mutual funds and retirement plans.

2 Understand how the economy affects your personal financial success.

Using your knowledge of where we are in the business cycle and tracking a few economic statistics will guide you to make modest adjustment in your long-term financial strategy.

3 Apply economic principles when making financial decisions.

Understanding and applying the basic economic principles of opportunity cost, marginal utility and cost, and marginal income tax rate will affect your financial success. The opportunity cost of a decision is the value of the next best alternative that must be forgone. Marginal cost is the additional (marginal) cost of one more incremental unit of some item. When known, this cost can be compared with the marginal utility received. One's marginal tax rate is the tax rate at which your last dollar is taxed.

4 Perform time value of money calculations in personal financial decision making.

Dollars to be received or paid out in the future are not equivalent to those received or paid out today. A dollar received today is worth more than a dollar received a year from now because today's dollar can be saved or invested; by next year, you expect it to be worth more than a dollar. The time value of money involves two components: future value and present value. The four basic time value of money calculations involve finding the future value of a lump sum, the future value of an annuity, the present value of a lump sum, and the present value of an annuity.

5 Make smart decisions about your employee benefits.

Smart decisions can increase your actual income by thousands of dollars each year. You need to wisely select among your employer-sponsored plans for health care, out-of-pocket spending for health and dependent care, life insurance, disability, and retirement. These decisions often require you to calculate the tax-sheltered aspects of the employee benefits.

6 Identify the professional qualifications of providers of financial advice.

When choosing a financial planner, know that many professional designations are meaningful in this field, such as CFP® and ChFC. Costs may be charged on a fee-only, commission-only, fee-based, or fee-offset basis.

Let's Talk About It

1. **Economic Growth.** How might some of the federal government's recent efforts to help foster economic growth impact your own financial situation?

2. **The Business Cycle.** Where is the United States in the economic cycle now, and where does it seem to be heading? List some indicators that suggest in which direction it may move.

3. **Personal Finance Mistakes.** What are some common mistakes that people make in personal finance? Which three are the worst, and why?

4. **Opportunity Costs.** People regularly make decisions in personal finance that have opportunity costs. List five financial decisions you have made recently and identify the opportunity cost for each.

Do the Math

1. **Future Value.** As a graduating senior, Gwen Kumora of Manhattan, Kansas, is eager to enter the job market at an anticipated annual salary of $34,000. Assuming an average inflation rate of 3 percent and an equal cost-of-living raise, what will Gwen's salary be in 10 years? In 20 years? (Hint: Use Appendix A.1 or calculations on the *Garman/Forgue* companion website.) To make real economic progress, how much of a raise (in dollars) does Gwen need to receive next year?

2. **Present and Future Values.** Rachael Berry, a freshman horticulture major at the University of Minnesota, has some financial questions for the next three years of school and beyond. Answers to these questions can be obtained by using Appendix A or the *Garman/Forgue* companion website.

   If Rachael's tuition, fees, and expenditures for books this year total $12,000, what will they be during her senior year (three years from now), assuming costs rise 6 percent annually? (Hint: Use Appendix A.1 or the *Garman/Forgue* companion website.)

   Rachael is applying for a scholarship currently valued at $5000. If she is awarded it at the end of next year, how much is the scholarship worth in today's dollars, assuming inflation of 3 percent? (Hint: Use Appendix A.2 or the *Garman/Forgue* companion website.)

   Rachael is already looking ahead to graduation and a job, and she wants to buy a new car not long after her graduation. If after graduation she begins a savings program of $2400 per year in an investment yielding 6 percent, what will be the value of the fund after three years? (Hint: Use Appendix A.3 or the *Garman/Forgue* companion website.)

   Rachael's Aunt Karroll told her that she would give Rachael $1000 at the end of each year for the next three years to help with her college expenses. Assuming an annual interest rate of 6 percent, what is the present value of that stream of payments? (Hint: Use Appendix A.4 or the *Garman/Forgue* companion website.)

3. **Present and Future Values.** Using the present and future value tables in Appendix A, the appropriate calculations on the *Garman/Forgue* companion website, or a financial calculator, calculate the following:

   (a) The future value of $400 in two years that earns 5 percent.

   (b) The future value of $1200 saved each year for ten years that earns 7 percent.

   (c) The amount a person would need to deposit today with a 5 percent interest rate to have $2000 in three years.

(d) The amount a person would need to deposit today to be able to withdraw $6000 each year for ten years from an account earning 6 percent.

(e) A person is offered a gift of $5000 now or $8000 five years from now. If such funds could be expected to earn 8 percent over the next five years, which is the better choice?

(f) A person wants to have $3000 available to spend on an overseas trip four years from now. If such funds could be expected to earn 7 percent, how much should be invested in a lump sum to realize the $3000 when needed?

(g) A person who invests $1200 each year finds one choice that is expected to pay 9 percent per year and another choice that may pay 10 percent. What is the difference in return if the investment is made for 15 years?

(h) A person invests $50,000 in an investment that earns 6 percent. If $6000 is withdrawn each year, how many years will it take for the fund to run out?

4. **Rule of 72.** Using the rule of 72, calculate how quickly $1000 will double to $2000 at interest rates of 2 percent, 4 percent, 6 percent, 8 percent, and 10 percent.

Financial Planning Cases

Case 1
Reasons to Study Personal Finance

Lindsey Beliveau Bailey of Redding, California, is a senior in college, majoring in sociology. She anticipates getting married a year or so after graduation. Lindsey has only one elective course remaining and is going to choose between another advanced class in sociology and one in personal finance. As Lindsey's friend, you want to persuade her to take personal finance. Give some examples of how Lindsey might benefit from the study of personal finance.

Case 2
A Closer Look at Financial Success

You have been asked to give a brief speech on how to achieve financial success. Define financial success and financial happiness, and summarize the building blocks to achieving financial success.

On the 'Net

Go to the Web pages indicated to complete these exercises.

1. Visit the Bureau of Labor Statistics Consumer Price Index homepage at www.bls.gov/cpi/ and link to information for various areas of the country and metropolitan areas of various sizes. Describe how prices have been changing for your area and city size during the past year.

2. Visit the Conference Board website, www.conference-board.org/economics/consumerConfidence.cfm/, for the latest information on the consumer confidence index and the index of leading economic indicators. What do the indexes say about the direction of the economy over the next six months to one year?

3. Visit the website of the Financial Planning Association at http://www.fpaforfinancialplanning.org/AboutFPA/CodeofEthics/. Read through the code of ethics for members of the organization. What does the code tell you about the members?

Visit the Garman/Forgue companion website . . .

www.cengage.com/finance/garman

Career Planning

!You Must Be Kidding, Right?

Jessica Springsteen is contemplating going to graduate school at night for a master's degree so she can advance her career and earn more than her current $44,000 salary income. She is a sales account manager for a health care organization, and she has a small online business selling gourmet foods. How much more income can Jessica expect over an anticipated 40-year career if she obtains the advanced degree?

A. $100,000

B. $300,000

C. $600,000

D. $900,000

The answer is C, $600,000. Over a 40-year working career, a person with a postgraduate degree can expect to earn more than $3 million, and this is about $600,000 more than a person with a bachelor's degree will earn. Getting an advanced degree is no guarantee of a bigger income, but the likelihood of such a reality is high!

Learning Objectives

After reading this chapter, you should be able to:

1 Identify the key steps in successful career planning.

2 Clarify your work-style personality.

3 Analyze the financial and legal aspects of employment.

4 Practice effective employment search strategies.

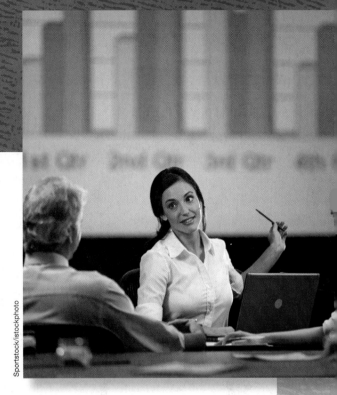

Sportstock/istockphoto

Ashley Linkletter, age 21, expects to graduate next spring with a bachelor's degree in business administration. Ashley's grades are mostly Bs and As, and she has worked part time throughout her college career. Ashley is vice president of the Student Marketing Association on her campus. She would like to work in management or marketing for a medium- to large-size employer. Because she loves the outdoors, Ashley thinks she would prefer a job in the Northwest, perhaps in northern California, Oregon, or Washington.

What would you recommend to Ashley on the importance of career planning regarding:

1. Clarifying her values and lifestyle trade-offs?
2. Enhancing her career-related experiences before graduation?
3. Creating career plans and goals?
4. Understanding her work-style personality?
5. Identifying job opportunities?

The level of unemployment in the United States is higher than normal because of the slow economy. As a result, many highly qualified people lost their jobs and are experiencing a career setback. To compete in this market career planning is an absolute necessity. Going from job to job may be okay while you are in college. And working for $12, $15, or $20 an hour and changing jobs for a $2-per-hour raise might be okay for a couple of years. But what you really should focus on is not a "job" but a career. A **career** is the lifework chosen by a person using their personal talent, education, and training. The general progression of one's career will include a number of related jobs.

You *can* control much of your financial future with effective career planning. Moving through the years in a career of your choice not only translates into jobs that are personally satisfying but also improves your level of living. A career translates into a base of income, employee benefits, additional educational experiences, advancement opportunities, and confidence in a secure financial future. Treat your career as a high priority, do-it-yourself project, and take control of where you are going and how you are going to get there.

career
The lifework chosen by a person to use personal talent, education, and training.

Key Steps in Successful Career Planning

1 Learning Objectives

Identify the key steps in successful career planning.

career planning
Finding employment that will use your interests and abilities and that will support you financially.

Career planning can help you identify an employment pathway that aligns your interests and abilities with the tasks expected and one that supports your preferred lifestyle. When you start looking for employment positions in your career plan, you will consider income, of course, but you also keep in mind opportunities for continued training, personal growth, and advancement. A career that suits you will give you opportunities to display your abilities in jobs you find satisfying while providing balance between work and your personal life.

During sluggish economic times you may need to adjust your expectations. Neither the pay nor the geographic location opportunities for employment may be quite what you expect. Realize, too, that the rest of your life will not be determined by your first professional job. No matter what job you choose, consider it a chance to do the required tasks effectively and learn about yourself. Use this information in planning your future. See Figure 2.1 for an illustration of the steps in career planning.

Career planning and financial planning go hand in hand. You can't advance very far in planning your financial life without also planning a career that will pay you adequately. Material on career planning has been included quite early in this book so that the principles and other information in the remaining chapters are relevant to you personally and to the way you want to make your living.

Figure 2.1
Steps in Career Planning

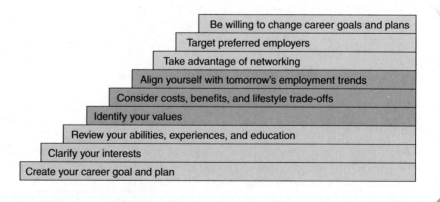

Career planning doesn't stop when you take your first career job. Rather, career planning is a continuous process that lasts throughout your life. Every time your life circumstances change, you will likely reconsider your career. But first you have to start. As you plan your career, you need to perform several steps, and you should take care to carry each step out to the best of your ability. The time and effort you put into your career planning effort will affect how much income you earn and how far you advance in your career. First, let's take a look at the key steps to successful career planning.

Create Your Career Goal and Plan

The workplace has changed dramatically. People used to take a single job and remain at the same company until they retired. Now, people change jobs five to ten times during their working years. You are not likely to remain with one employer a lifetime let alone ten years. You probably will completely change careers two or three times.

Thinking about a career goal helps you focus on what you want to do for a living. A **career goal** can be a specific job (e.g., cost accountant, teacher, human resources manager) or a particular field of work (e.g., health care, communications, construction). It helps guide you to do the kind of work you want in life rather than drift from job to job. Formulating a career goal requires thinking about your interests, skills, and experiences and learning about different careers and employment trends. The process of establishing a career goal motivates you to consider career possibilities that you may not have thought of otherwise.

To create a career goal, explore the jobs, careers, and trends in the employment marketplace that fit your interests and skills. Ask people you trust about their careers. Search websites such as those for the *Occupational Outlook Handbook* (www.bls.gov/oco/) and the *Occupational Outlook Quarterly* (www.bls.gov/opub/ooq/ooqhome.htm). Research the education requirements.

A **career plan** identifies employment that interests you; fits your abilities, skills, work style, and lifestyle; and provides strategic guidance to help you reach your career goal. It includes short-, medium-, longer-, and long-term goals as well as future education and work-related experiences that will serve to advance your career interests. Figure 2.2 provides an illustrative career plan.

Clarify Your Interests

Your **professional interests** are topics and activities about which you have feelings of curiosity or concern. Interests engage or arouse your attention. They reflect what you like to do. Interests, including occupational interests, are likely to vary over time.

You might consider making a list of your top ten interests. On that list will probably be some things you enjoy but have not done recently. Because of conflicting interests and alternative claims on your time, you cannot pursue all your interests. It is important in career planning to evaluate your interests; if you plan your career with your interests in mind, you will increase the likelihood of career satisfaction.

Interest inventories are measures that assist people in assessing and profiling the interests and activities that give them satisfaction. They compare how your interests are similar or dissimilar to the interests of people successfully employed in various occupations; the theory behind these interest inventories is that individuals with similar interests are often attracted to the same kind of work. These inventories can help you identify possible career goals that match your strongest personal interests.

The Strong Interest Inventory assessment is considered by many to be the gold standard of career exploration tools. The opportunity to take one or more interest inventory

Your Next Five Years

In the next five years you can start achieving financial success by doing the following related to career planning:

1. Map out a career plan by setting benchmarks as you move up the career ladder.
2. Identify your career planning values and live them in your selection of jobs and in your performance at work.
3. Continually enhance your education and professional training.
4. Seek out mentors on the job and in other professional settings.
5. Join and be active in the professional associations relevant to your career.

career goal
Identifying what you want to do for a living, whether a specific job or field of employment.

career plan
A plan that identifies employment that interests you; fits your abilities, skills, work style, and lifestyle; and provides strategic guidance to help you reach your career goal.

professional interests
Long-standing topics and activities that engage your attention.

interest inventories
Scaled surveys that assess career interests and activities.

Figure 2.2
Career Goals and Plans
for Harry Johnson

Harry Johnson began his working career following graduation from college by obtaining employment with a small commercial interior design firm. He has an undergraduate degree from a university accredited by the American Society of Interior Designers. He is happy that his first professional job is in his major field of interest.

Initial career goal: To become an interior designer. To design, plan, and supervise commercial/contract design projects.

Long-term career goal (20-plus years): Own or become a partner in a medium- to large-size commercial/contract interior design firm.

Short-term plans and goals in career establishment stage (3 to 6 years): Gain work experience in current job; receive employer compliments on quality of work; obtain continuing education credits for professional growth and development; secure higher-level design responsibilities, such as lead professional design team; volunteer for committee responsibilities in local and state professional associations; obtain substantial increases in income; receive promotions; learn operational aspects and marketing of the company.

Medium-term plans and goals in professional growth stage (7 to 12 years): Be promoted to the level of senior designer; consider going to work for another employer as a senior designer and, if necessary, move to another community; volunteer for higher-level service in professional associations; obtain a master of fine arts degree in interior design; become assistant to the firm's general manager.

Longer-term plans and goals in advancement stage (13 to 20 years): Become general manager of commercial design firm; seek out potential partners and sufficient financing to either buy out or start up a medium-size design firm.

assessments, usually for free or at a nominal cost, is available at most colleges and state-supported career counseling facilities. These assessments can also be completed online for a fee. (See, for example, www.discoveryourpersonality.com/Strong.html and www.careercc.com/career_assessment.shtml.)

Review Your Abilities, Experiences, and Education

Reviewing your abilities, aptitudes, experiences, and education is a key step in career planning. The purpose is to see how well they match up with your career-related interests.

professional abilities
Job-related activities that you can perform physically, mentally, artistically, mechanically, and financially.

Abilities Your **professional abilities** are the qualities that allow you to perform physically, mentally, artistically, mechanically, or financially job-related tasks. Most of us think of *ability* as a word describing how well we do something, a proficiency, dexterity, or technique, particularly one requiring use of the mind, hands, or body. Other examples of abilities include being skilled in working with people, being able to easily meet the public, and being good at persuading people.

Employer surveys indicate that the single most important ability needed for career success in the twenty-first century is computer skills. Also very highly ranked are communication skills and honesty/integrity. Consider making a list of your top ten abilities.

aptitudes
The natural abilities and talents that individuals possess.

Aptitudes are the natural abilities and talents that people possess. Aptitudes suggest that you have a tendency or inclination to learn and develop certain skills or abilities. Are you good with numbers? Do you find public speaking easy to do? Do you enjoy solving problems? What are your natural talents? Consider making a list of your top ten aptitudes.

Experiences College graduates have much more going for them than a degree and a string of part-time job experiences. Reviewing your experiences is a step in career planning. Evaluate what you have been doing in your life, including jobs and internships; participation in student organizations and community and church groups; leadership on school projects; and volunteer activities.

Those still in college can enhance their résumés by learning as much as possible in school, participating in clubs and other student organizations (including volunteering for committees and campus projects), getting involved in a faculty research project, and attending off-campus professional meetings in their major. Academic advisers can provide suggestions. Employers want workers with good writing and public speaking talents, strong computer skills, fluency in a second language, and an understanding of global commerce and industry. Experiences that use and develop these traits are a big plus for job seekers.

Education and Professional Training Going to college is excellent preparation for your career and your life. But college may not have provided you with all the skills and abilities to be successfully employed. A review of your abilities, experiences, and education may suggest you need to seek additional education and professional training.

Instant Message

Education and Earnings

Adults with a bachelor's degree earn an average of $56,000 compared with $34,000 for high school graduates and $82,000 for those with advanced degrees, reports the U.S. Census Bureau.

Identify Your Values

Thinking about and discovering what you want out of life gives you guidance for what to do to lead a satisfying life. Understanding yourself enables you to select a career path that best suits you. This is a key step in career planning.

Values are the principles, standards, or qualities considered worthwhile or desirable. Values provide a basis for decisions about how to live, serving as guides we can use to direct our actions. For something to be a value, it must be prized, publicly affirmed, chosen from alternatives, and acted upon repeatedly and consistently. Values are not right or wrong, or true or false; they are personal preferences.

People may place value on family, friends, helping others, religious commitment, honesty, pleasure, good health, material possessions, financial security, and a satisfying career. Examples of conflicting values are family versus satisfying career, religious beliefs versus pleasure, and material possessions versus financial security. When you make important decisions, you might be wise to think carefully to clarify your values before taking action. Consider making a list of your ten most important values.

values
The principles, standards, or qualities that you consider desirable.

Consider Costs, Benefits, and Lifestyle Trade-offs

Selecting a career involves making decisions about costs and benefits and **lifestyle trade-offs**.

lifestyle trade-offs
Weighing the demands of particular jobs with your social and cultural preferences.

Costs and Benefits When making career choices, you must weigh the benefits against the costs. The benefits could include a big salary, likelihood of personal growth and job advancements, and high job satisfaction. For some, the pluses might include the psychic benefit of a prestigious job with a high income. The costs might include living in a less desirable geographic area and climate, being too far from friends and family, sitting at a desk all day, working long hours, and doing too much travel.

Career planning should reflect your lifestyle preferences.

Masterfile

Lifestyle Trade-offs When considering any career, think about what lifestyle or social and cultural factors are important to you. For example, if access to big-name live entertainment, museums, and artistic activities is important, then working and living in a rural area may not be appropriate. If you like to visit new places, you may choose a career that involves frequent travel.

 Advice from a Pro...

Competencies of Successful People

People who are successful in their chosen careers, with their finances, and/or in life in general often possess and exhibit certain competencies.

1. Set goals in the various aspects of life and track progress toward attaining goals.
2. Use organizational tools such as lists as well as time management techniques.
3. Exhibit integrity.
4. Understand their motives and behave ethically.
5. Make a quality effort every time.
6. Accept accountability for their decisions and actions.
7. Exhibit good written and oral communication skills.
8. Demonstrate strong computer skills.
9. Open to new ideas.
10. Adapt easily to change.
11. Share knowledge to assist and mentor others.
12. Acquire advanced education and technical training and are life-long learners.
13. Take on new assignments and capitalize on the new skills learned.
14. Anticipate problems and work proactively to implement solutions.
15. Work well in teams and know when to lead and when to follow.
16. Project an image consistent with organizational values.
17. Understand operations, structure, and culture of organization.
18. Loyal to and supportive of company and boss.

Caroline S. Fulmer
The University of Alabama
Certified Leadership Trainer for the Achieve Global Corporation

Consider the following lifestyle options in your decision making:

- Urban/rural setting
- Close/far from work
- Own/rent housing
- City/suburban life
- Warm/cold climate
- Near/far from relatives
- Constant/variable climate

In addition, employers in certain careers provide more support for working parents. Employer-subsidized child care as well as flexible work hours might be available at a "family-friendly" workplace.

These are all quality-of-life issues, your quality of life. The challenges are greater for dual-career couples because they must communicate effectively when considering the impact of one person's career decisions on the other. (Chapter 5 offers some tips on communication skills.) Remember, you always have the freedom to change your life and career objectives as you learn more about yourself and the world of work.

Align Yourself with Tomorrow's Employment Trends

Right now, you may be focused on school—graduating and getting a good job. But you also need to find out where the jobs will be in the future. The job market today is rapidly changing—a result of economic downturns, corporate restructuring, downsizing, and globalization—and the career path you are considering now may not continue to be a good choice in the years ahead.

What, then, are the trends in employment? The aging U.S. population will create jobs in the service industries of finance, insurance, health care, recreation, and travel. Jobs are gravitating to existing population centers, particularly in warmer climates that have superior transportation systems. Jobs in manufacturing are largely going overseas to Mexico, Asia, Europe, and other countries, with the U.S. job market primarily demanding highly skilled workers in the service industries.

Strong job growth is projected for the twenty-first century in computer technology, business services, social services, child care, wholesale and retail sales, food services, hospitality, retirement facilities, travel, and human resources. All require good communication skills. High-demand occupations tend to pay high salaries and offer career advancement opportunities. They often require good computer skills. Table 2.1 shows the projected job growth in high-wage, high-growth occupations in the United States.

Take Advantage of Networking

Professional networking is the process of making and using contacts, such as individuals, groups, or institutions, to obtain and exchange information in career planning. Use social-networking sites, including MySpace, Facebook, and Linkedin. Every person you know or meet is a possible useful contact.

Networking requires that you make a conscious effort to use people you know and meet to maximize your job search process. Networking involves utilizing your social contacts, taking advantage of casual meetings, and asking for personal referrals. Most of your contacts will not be able to hire you, but they could refer you to the person who can, or they may be able to give you useful information about a potential employer.

Maintain a continually growing list of people who are family, neighbors, friends, college associates, coworkers, previous supervisors, teachers, professors, alumni, business contacts, and others

professional networking
Making and using contacts with individuals, groups, and other firms to exchange career information.

Table 2.1 Projected High-Wage, High-Growth Occupations

Job Title	Employment in 2014	Median Annual Income
General and operations managers	2,100,000	$115,000
Property association managers	454,000	$60,000
Business operations specialists	396,000	$79,000
Computer system analysts	640,000	$100,000
Sales managers	403,000	$122,000
Medical/health service managers	305,000	$102,000
Training and development specialists	261,000	$74,000
Marketing managers	228,000	$153,000
Industrial engineers	205,000	$98,000
Compensation benefits managers	70,000	$100,000
Technical writers	62,000	$81,000
Human resource managers	72,000	$122,000
Media and communications	46,000	$61,000
Air traffic controllers	28,000	$153,000
Accountants/auditors	1,440,000	$76,000
Child and social workers	324,000	$51,000
Public relations specialists	231,000	$66,000
Market research analysts	227,000	$81,000
Advertising promotions managers	77,000	$95,000

Source: Bureau of Labor Statistics, Table 15, High-wage, high-growth occupations, by educational attainment cluster and earnings; authors' income projections to 2014.

Instant Message

Get Staff Opinions on Employers

Find out what it is like to work at a specific company. When you do a background check on companies, you can seek out candid posts from current or former employees about salaries, company culture, and lousy bosses. But be wary about unsubstantiated information. See Jobster (www.jobster.com), LinkedIn (www.linkedin.com), and Vault (www.vault.com).

you know through civic and community organizations such as churches and business and social groups. Take note of where your contacts work and what types of jobs they have. Ask these people for 10 to 20 minutes of their time so you can seek information and suggestions from them. Perhaps meet at their workplaces (where you might meet other potential networking contacts), and afterward send them thank-you notes.

As many as three-quarters of all job openings may never be listed in want ads, so the people in your network become a vital source of information about employment opportunities. For this reason, expanding the number of people in your network is advantageous; some of the people you know will also likely share their networking contacts. Networking is the number one way people are successful in their job search.

Target Preferred Employers

Answering classified job advertisements probably is not the best way to start a career, unless you are lucky and the job listed is actually in your field of interest. A key step in the career search process is to think about both the industries in which you would prefer employment and which employers might be best for you.

If, for example, you want to work in the health care industry, you must research it. Get on the Internet. Go to the library. Visit the websites of health trade associations. Learn as much as you can about the health care industry. How broad is the industry? What types of companies are at the retail level? At the wholesale level? What kinds of firms provide services to the industry? Which companies are the largest? Which have the fastest growth rates? Which employers have employment facilities in geographic areas that are of interest to you? What are the leading companies? Which are the "employers of choice" that are family friendly or offer especially good benefits? What are the employee benefits at different companies? Knowing the industry and specific employers of interest to you tells you whom to target for employment in your career path.

Be Willing to Change Career Goals and Plans

Your career plan should be realistic and flexible. Your career interests and goals will change over time, especially as you continue your education, gain work experience, and see how your friends fare with their jobs and avocations. Teaching music education might be your first career, but you may eventually realize that the accompanying small income could keep you on a tight financial budget forever. This issue might encourage you to consider a total career change—perhaps to sales in the music industry or a related field, where incomes are higher.

Some people go the other way. For example, after some years in the field of accounting, you might change career goals and go to work in your longtime interest area of horticulture, which pays less. Your interests might evolve over time as well. For example, a person with a full-time job in retail store management might decide to turn a hobby of gun collecting into selling guns as an online business. Staying in a career path but changing jobs occurs, too. For example, some hospital nurses decide after a few years that they have made a wrong career choice. While the job pays well, it involves shift work and very long days. Those who want to remain in the nursing profession may decide to leave the hospital setting and go to work for a nursing home or college health facility.

Assessing yourself and your career plans every few years is important to achieving success in your working life. What do you find satisfying and not so satisfying? Honest answers will help you, particularly as your interests evolve. Your work experiences should hone your abilities and skills. Learning new skills on the job is common, and if that is not happening in a job, move on and change employers and perhaps careers.

Did You Know?

The Top 3 Financial Missteps in Career Planning

People slip up in career planning when they do the following:

1. Don't learn as much as possible about a company before going for an interview
2. Failing to match your interests and preferred work style with the requirements of the career
3. Failing to network by not getting involved in professional associations

 Concept Check 2.1

1. Distinguish between a job and a career.
2. How do your values affect your trade-offs in career planning?
3. What can be done to enhance your abilities and experiences without working in a job situation?
4. What are the components of career plans and goals?

Know Your Preferred Work-Style Personality

Every job requires the worker to function in relation to data, people, and things in differing work environments and corporate cultures. Your **work-style personality** is a unique set of ways of working with and responding to your job requirements, surroundings, and associates. When making a career selection, you must balance your work-style personality against the demands of the work environment.

2 Learning Objectives
Clarify your work-style personality.

work-style personality
Your own ways of working with and responding to job requirements, surroundings, and associates.

Decision-Making Worksheet

What Is Your Work-Style Personality?

It would be useful for you to consider a number of work values critical to the process of career selection, particularly in the areas of work conditions, work purposes, and work relationships. Rate how you value the following work values as either very important in my choice of career (VI), somewhat important in my choice of career (SI), or unimportant in my choice of career (UI).

Work-Style Factor	Your Rating of Importance		
	Very Important	Somewhat Important	Unimportant
1. Work Conditions			
Independence and autonomy			
Time flexibility			
Change and variety			
Change and risk			
Stability and security			
Physical challenge			
Physical demands			
Mental challenge			
Pressure and time deadlines			
Precise work			
Decision making			
2. Work Purposes			
Truth and knowledge			
Expertise and authority			
Esthetic appreciation			
Social conditions			
Material gain			
Achievement and recognition			
Ethical and moral			
Spiritual and transpersonal			
3. Work Relationships			
Working alone			
Public contact			
Close friendships			
Group membership			
Helping others			
Influencing others			
Supervising others			
Controlling others			

For additional values clarification, go back to the list and *circle the activities* that you want to do more often. The goal is to match your highest work-style values to career choices with similar work-style requirements.

Source: Adapted from D. C. Borchard, J. J. Kelly, and N. P. K. Weaver, *Your Career: Choices, Chances, Changes* (Dubuque, IA: Kendall/Hunt, 1990), Chapter 11.

You can begin by rating each work value as shown in the Decision-Making Worksheet "What Is Your Work-Style Personality?" Next, go back to the list and circle the activities that you prefer to do "most often." Armed with this information, you can now more clearly decide on careers that are most suitable for you.

Did You Know?

How to Work at Home Online

Technology has made it possible for many people to work at home online, as 1 in 15 workers has such an alternative work arrangement. Some people work off site for an employer, telecommuting (or teleworking) and perhaps spending one day every two weeks at the company office. Other people are self-employed entrepreneurs who run micro businesses. A good computer and software make it possible. Many excellent job opportunities exist.

Examples of online employment are Web hosting, desktop publishing, information processing, database administration, researcher, public relations, employee assistance counseling, telemarketing, personal care services, data entry, accounting, consulting, technical writing, editing, debt counseling, and project management. For ideas on working at home, see the Small Business Administration (www.sba.gov), National Association for the Self-Employed (www.nase.org), and Service Corps of Retired Executives (www.score.org).

 Concept Check 2.2

1. Summarize the three major parts of your work-style personality.

Financial and Legal Aspects of Employment

This section examines financial and legal aspects of employment to consider when analyzing your career plans, and it includes the Decision-Making Worksheet "Assessing the Value of a Second Income."

3 Learning Objectives
Analyze the financial and legal aspects of employment.

Compare Salary and Living Costs in Different Cities

Incomes range by geographic region, community, and size of employer. Median household income is lowest in the South, a little higher in the Midwest, higher still in the West, and highest in the Northeast. These regional differences reflect the industrial base, unemployment rates, general economic conditions, costs of living (especially for housing and transportation), and the supply and demand for skilled workers. Incomes in rural areas are usually much lower than in urban areas.

The highest incomes are paid in metropolitan areas exceeding 1 million in population. Higher salaries are paid in the largest communities for the reasons just mentioned but also because employers compete for the most skilled workers since so many people often live in these communities. Employers with fewer than 100 employees typically pay lower salaries for comparable positions than do larger employers.

Did You Know?

Value of Additional Education

Annual income

0 10 20 30 40 50 60 70 80

Years of age

College degree

High school diploma

Income over the Life Cycle According to Age and Education

Income varies over the life cycle. Higher incomes often go to those with more education or more specialized education. A recent high school graduate with a current income of $27,000 will earn a cumulative $2,036,000 over a 40-year working career. A person with an associate's degree earning $36,000 today will gross $2,700,000; one with a bachelor's degree earning $44,000 now will gross $3,300,000; and a person with a master's degree and a current income of $52,000 will receive a cumulative income of $3,900,000 over a 40-year working career. (The figures are based on 3 percent annual income increases in Appendix A.3.) Additional formal education normally leads to greater decision-making responsibilities in a career as well as a higher income.

Compare Using City Indexes   Comparing salary offers from employers located in different cities can be tricky without sufficient information on the approximate cost of living in each community. Sometimes those costs vary drastically. Information from the Internet reveals, for example, that life in a high-cost city such as Seattle is more expensive than life in a lower-cost city such as Portland, Oregon. The data are reported in index form, with the "average cost" community being given a rating of 100.

The following example demonstrates how to compare salary offers in two cities. Assume the Seattle (city 1) index is 138, and Portland's (city 2) is 114. You want to compare the buying power of a salary offer of $52,000 in Portland with a $65,000 offer in Seattle. The costs can be compared using Equations (2.1) and (2.2).

$$\text{Salary in city 1} \times \frac{\text{index city 2}}{\text{index city 1}} = \text{equivalent salary in city 2} \qquad \textbf{(2.1)}$$

$$\text{Seattle salary of } \$65,000 \times \frac{114}{138} = \$53,695 \text{ in buying power in Portland}$$

Thus, the $65,000 Seattle salary offer would buy $53,695 of goods and services in Portland, an amount more than the Portland offer of $52,000. All things being equal (and they are both nice cities), the Seattle offer is slightly better ($53,695 − $52,000 = $1,695).

To compare the buying power of salaries in the other direction, reverse the formula:

$$\text{Salary in city 2} \times \frac{\text{index city 2}}{\text{index city 1}} = \text{equivalent salary in city 1} \qquad \textbf{(2.2)}$$

$$\text{Portland salary of } \$52,000 \times \frac{138}{114} = \$62,947 \text{ in buying power in Seattle}$$

Seattle has a lot to offer, but it comes at a price.

Thus, the $52,000 Portland offer can buy only $62,947 of goods and services in Seattle—an amount less than the $65,000 Seattle salary offer. All things being equal, the Seattle offer is still better. For fairer comparisons, add the value of employee benefits and redo the calculations. Note that non-salary benefits are typically 25-30 percent of the salary for persons with a college degree.

Compare Salaries and Living Costs on the 'Net You may compare salary figures and the cost of living in different communities at the following websites (most use the ACCRA Cost of Living data [www.coli.org/]):

- CityRating.com (www.cityrating.com/costofliving.asp).
- CNNMoney.com (www.cgi.money.cnn.com/tools/costofliving/costofliving.html)
- Moving.com (www.moving.com/find_a_place/relosmart/rs.asp)
- Realtor.com (www.homefair.com/homefair/readart.html?art=bc_research)
- Salary.com (www.swz.salary.com/costoflivingwizard/layoutscripts/coll_start.asp)

Place Values on Employee Benefits

Employee benefits are tremendously important to employees, especially when comparing the benefits provided by one employer with another. **Employee benefits** (or **nonsalary benefits**) are forms of remuneration provided by employers to employees that result in the employee not having to pay out-of-pocket money for certain expenses. Examples include paid vacations, health care, paid sick leave, child care, tuition reimbursement, and financial planning services.

The topic of "making smart money decisions at work" was examined in Chapter 1, which provided details on selecting among employee benefits such as health care plans (including health savings accounts), flexible spending plans (such as dependent and health care FSA accounts), insurance (such as life, disability, and long-term care), and employer retirement plans.

employee benefits
Forms of remuneration provided by employers to employees that result in the employee not having to pay out-of-pocket money for certain expenses; also known as employee benefits.

Decision-Making Worksheet

Assessing the Benefits of a Second Income

A second income might add surprisingly little to your total earnings because of all the costs associated with earning it. In this example, a nonworking spouse is considering a job that pays $30,000 annually. The total accurate net amount of the extra $30,000 income is a mere $9205, thus adding only $767 a month to total earnings.

1. Second Income

Annual earnings	$30,000
Value of benefits (life insurance)	300
Total 1	$30,300

2. Expenses

Federal income taxes (25% rate × $30,000)	$ 7,500
State/local income taxes (6% rate × $30,000)	1,800
Social Security taxes (7.65% × $30,000)	2,295
Transportation and commuting (50 weeks @ $40)	2,000
Child care (8 months after-school only)	3,200
Lunches out (50 weeks, twice a week at $10)	1,000
Work wardrobe (including dry cleaning)	1,200
Other work-related expenses (magazines, dues, gifts)	300
Take-out food for supper (too tired to cook; $100 month)	1,200
Guilt complex purchases (to make up for time lost with others)	600
Total 2	$21,095

3. Net Value of Second Income

Total of 1 from above	$30,300
Subtract total of 2 from above	21,095
Total accurate net amount of second income	$ 9,205

You can place a monetary value on each employee benefit that is available. Some nonsalary benefits might not be applicable, such as child care if you are single. Others are supervaluable, such as a health plan, since a policy purchased in the private market for a single person might have a premium of $5000 a year. To put monetary values on employee benefits, you may (1) place a market value on the benefit or (2) calculate the future value of the benefit.

Place a Market Value on the Benefit If instead of enjoying a certain employee benefit, you had to pay out-of-pocket dollars for it, you can easily determine its market value. Private child care might cost $300 a week in your community; thus, when provided free from your employer, that is a whopping $15,000 ($300 × 50 weeks) saved annually. Actually, it is more because you would likely have to earn perhaps $22,000 to have $15,000 left over after paying $7000 in income and Social Security taxes. An employer-provided paid-for life insurance policy with a face value of $50,000 might cost $600 if you had to buy it yourself.

Advice from a Pro...

Career Advancement Tips

The essence of career advancement is to build your job-related knowledge and skills for the future by learning. You do not want to fall behind your coworkers and those who work for other employers, as they may be your future job market competitors. Change jobs when appropriate to obtain a different or better position that advances your career, or when deemed necessary to entirely alter your career. To advance in your career, consider the following:

- **Mentors.** Ask one or two people to serve as your mentors, people with whom you can regularly discuss your career progress. A mentor is an experienced person, often a senior coworker, who offers friendly career-related advice, guidance, and coaching to a less experienced person.
- **Traits.** Exhibit passion, self-discipline, confidence, and determination in your everyday responsibilities.
- **Volunteer.** Volunteer for new assignments.
- **Training.** Sign up for employer-sponsored seminars, training and certification opportunities.

- **Conferences.** Attend meetings and conferences in your field.
- **College Courses.** Take advanced college courses and complete a graduate degree.
- **Professional Reading.** Stay alert to what is happening in your career field by reading professional and trade publications.
- **Current Events.** Be up-to-date on current events and business and economic news by reviewing websites and reading newspapers, news magazines, and business periodicals.
- **Nonwork Activities.** Be actively involved in something besides work, such as coaching children's athletics, playing softball, singing in a choral group, or teaching reading to illiterate adults.

Dana Wolff
Southeast Technical Institute

Did You Know?

You May Give Up $200,000 If You Cash Out Your 401(k) Account

When changing jobs, nearly half of workers unwisely cash out all the money in their employer-sponsored retirement plan instead of leaving it with the old employer, transferring it to a new employer's 401(k) plan, or moving it to an IRA rollover account. If an individual has $50,000 in a 401(k) account and cashes it out, that person gives up $233,000 in future dollars over the following 20 years.

	If you cash out $50,000:	If you roll over $50,000:
20% federal income tax withholding	−$10,000	
5% additional tax (in 25% tax bracket)	−$2,500	
10% early-withdrawal penalty	−$5,000	
5% state/local income tax	−$2,500	
Total withdrawn	−$20,000	+$50,000
Money spent on new car, TV, home repair, vacation, etc.	−$30,000	Money invested in another tax-deferred retirement account that earns 8 percent annually
Total	−$50,000	+$50,000
Additional investment actions taken	None	None
Investment balance after 20 years	$0	$233,050

Instant Message

Focus on Take-Home Pay

An income of $37,000 shrinks to about $30,000 after subtracting federal income, Social Security and Medicare taxes. Additional deductions for contributions for medical care, retirement, and flexible benefits may drop the take-home pay to $27,000, or $2250 a month.

Calculate the Future Value of the Benefit The best income is income that is never taxed, called tax-exempt income. Chapter 1 examined this topic. Many employee benefits are of this type and that's great from your personal finance perspective. Future value calculations come into play when you are trying to place a value on an employee benefit that is tax sheltered. Such income is exempt from income taxes in the current year but is subject to taxation in a later tax year.

An employer that provides a 401(k) retirement plan offers a valuable benefit. If an employer provides a match of $1200 a year to the regular contributions of the employee, for example, those $1200 contributions will eventually be the worker's money. And it will grow free of income taxes until the funds are withdrawn. Over 20 years, the annual employer contributions of $1200 grow to more than $44,000 (using Appendix A.3). That's a good employee benefit!

Know Your Legal Employment Rights

You have legal rights both during the hiring process and after you are hired. When selecting employees, employers may not discriminate based on gender, race, color, national origin, age, marital status, pregnancy, or mental or physical disabilities (if the person can perform the essential job tasks). Laws in many states and cities also prohibit discrimination against gays and lesbians in the hiring process.

Once hired, you have many rights. Employers must do the following:

- Pay the minimum wage established by federal, state, or local laws
- Provide unemployment insurance
- Provide workers' compensation benefits to any employee on the job who is injured or becomes ill
- Pay Social Security taxes to the government, which are then credited to the employee's lifetime earnings account maintained by the Social Security Administration

Once hired, the law requires that hourly employees be paid overtime for extra work hours put in beyond the standard 40-hour workweek. (Salaried employees are not paid overtime, and the vast majority of college graduates have salaried jobs.) In addition, a woman cannot be forced to go on maternity leave before she wants to do so if she does choose to take leave. You have the rights not to be unfairly discriminated against or harassed and to be employed in a safe workplace.

You have the right to take leave for personal or family medical problems, pregnancy, or adoption. You also have the right to privacy in such personal matters. When you leave an employer, you have the right to continue your health insurance coverage, perhaps for as long as 18 months, by paying the premiums yourself. If you believe you have been wronged, you can assert your legal rights.

 Concept Check 2.3

1. Summarize how education level and age affect income.
2. Explain how to compare salary and living costs in different cities.
3. What two techniques can be used to place monetary values on employee benefits?
4. Choose three career advancement tips and explain how each one might apply in someone's personal situation.

Effective Employment Search Strategies

Once you have undertaken some career planning, you will want to get a job in your preferred career field. This is a process that takes much effort. A successful job search might require 25 to 30 hours per week of your time. Effective search strategies follow.

4 Learning Objectives

Practice effective employment search strategies.

Assemble a Résumé

The Internet is a valuable resource for you in all aspects of career planning, including preparing a résumé. A **résumé** is a summary record of your education, training, experience, and other qualifications. It is often submitted with a job application. Your résumé, usually one or two pages in length, should be carefully written and contain zero errors or inconsistencies in message, content, and appearance.

Its primary function is to provide a basis for screening people out of contention for jobs. When you supply a résumé, you are providing documentation for some kind of subjective evaluation against unknown criteria. Large employers, recruiters, and local and national websites screen résumés, and computer software is frequently used to scan them instead of humans. Use keywords from the job description such as "Microsoft Office" so the scanning process picks them up.

When it is necessary to technically fulfill a requirement in the employment process, tailor a special edition of your résumé to fit that special set of circumstances. Résumés are usually presented in a **chronological format** (information in reverse order with most recent first), **skills format** (aptitudes and qualities), or **functional format** (career-related experiences). See Figures 2.3, 2.4, and 2.5 for sample résumés. The most common mistake in a résumé is to fill it up with a long list of functions and responsibilities that you had in your previous jobs instead of evidencing the specific accomplishments that made a difference in the companies for which you worked.

Colleges have career centers with sample résumés and professional staff who can offer personal advice. You can also find examples of résumés on the Internet. Monster.com has 500,000 online résumés and ResumeMailman.com forwards résumés to recruiters. Simply posting your résumé on an Internet site or sending out résumés is not conducting a significant job search. Realize, of course, that your current employer can view your résumé if it is posted on the Internet.

Did You Know?

Prospective Employers Can Check Your Credit Report

Employers today sometimes obtain the credit reports of prospective job candidates. A lousy credit history can suggest a lot about a person's inability to manage important tasks. Federal law requires (1) that individuals are aware that consumer credit reports may be used for employment purposes and must agree to such use and (2) that individuals are to be notified promptly if information in a consumer report may result in a negative employment decision.

résumé
Summary record of your education, training, experience, and other qualifications.

chronological format
Résumé that provides your information in reverse order, with most recent first.

skills format
Résumé that emphasizes your aptitudes and qualities.

functional format
Résumé that emphasizes career-related experiences.

Identify Job Opportunities

The next step is to identify job opportunities that fit your skill set and provide opportunities for advancement in your career. Use the following resources, and keep track of your job search progress using the Decision-Making Worksheet "Keeping Track of Your Job Search Progress."

The Internet If you do not use the Internet in your job search, you are not likely to get the best job for your talents. You can use the Internet to obtain career advice, review job opportunities by industry and company, and conduct specialized job searches. You also can review résumés, create your résumé, create a cover letter, and post your résumé. The Internet allows you to review salary information, calculate living costs in different communities, and research career fairs. Just about all your search information on the Web can be saved for your future use.

Figure 2.3
Sample Chronological Résumé

CHRISTOPHER GORDON

SCHOOL ADDRESS: HOME ADDRESS:
2824 West Street   3055 Vallejo Street, Apt.12
Ames, IA 50211   Denver, CO 80303
(401) 555-1212   (303) 333-4141
E-mail: cgordon@yahoo.com

CAREER OBJECTIVE   Entry-level position as a metallurgical engineer.

EDUCATION   Bachelor of Science, Metallurgical Engineering, Iowa State
                        University, Ames, IA, June 2010.

                        Associate of Arts, Kishwaukee Community College, Malta,
                        IL, June 2006.

EXPERIENCE   August 2008–May 2010 (academic year, part time), Iowa
                        State University, Ames, IA, Research Assistant to Professor
                        John Binnion on metals and plastics, conducted research,
                        performed statistical analyses, wrote reports, led group
                        of interns.

                        Summer 2008 and Summer 2007 (full time), EMD Electro-
                        Motive Division, Metallurgical Engineering Department,
                        Chicago, IL, Internship (paid), tested materials, prepared
                        reports, participated in team efforts.

                        September 2004–April 2005, Volunteer, Village Nursing
                        Home, Denver, CO, updated some resident activities,
                        organized weekend volunteers.

CAMPUS ACTIVITIES   2008–2010, Associate Editor college newspaper, Iowa State
                        Progress; 2008, Vice President, ISU Metallurgical Society;
                        2006–2008, Hispanic Club, 2006–2008; Singer, University
                        Chorale; 2006, Tutor for College of Engineering computer
                        laboratory; 2007–2008, attended two national conferences
                        of American Society for Metals International.

HONORS   Etta Mae Johnson Scholarship (2008); College of Engineering
                        Academic Scholarship (2007); Most Valuable Member, ISU
                        Metallurgical Society (2007); Julie Lynn Marshall Scholarship
                        (2005).

REFERENCES   Available upon request.

Figure 2.4
Sample Functional Résumé

Jennifer Elizabeth Anklin
12144 Southwest 174th Loop
Tupelo, MS 38803
School: (662) 844-5698
Home: (662) 921-1213
Eanklin@hotmail.com

CAREER OBJECTIVE
Public relations or communications department with opportunities to learn.

EDUCATION
Bachelor of Science, University of Georgia, Consumer Economics and Housing with a minor
in communications, Athens, GA, May 2010; Associate of Arts, Mississippi Valley Community
College, Booneville, MS, August 2007.

CAREER-RELATED EXPERIENCES
Organized breakfast meetings, supervised new members, updated membership records,
organized annual auction, created administrative procedures, Chamber of Commerce,
Athens, GA, part time, 2008–10.
Maintained inventory records, monitored reordering systems, JC Penney Company, Athens,
GA, part time, 2007–08.
Updated merchandising records, redesigned sales floor layout, Johnson's Shoes, Booneville,
MS, part time, 2005–07.
Overseas experience building a school in Botswana.
Translated Spanish and French for Atlanta Translation Services.

CAMPUS CAREER-RELATED ACTIVITIES
Vice president, Sales and Merchandising Club; Treasurer, Aces Chorale Club; Secretary,
National Honor Society; Secretary, Alpha Kappa Alpha Sorority; Co-coordinator Speaker's
Committee, Consumer Club; Debate Club; attended SOCAP meetings in Atlanta; intramural
hockey; campus church choir.

COMPUTER SKILLS
Microsoft Office, Corel WordPerfect Office, Corel Paint Shop Pro X, Adobe Acrobat, Dazzle
Video Creator, QuickBooks Pro, Computer Assisted Design, Macromedia, FrontPage.

HONORS
Hanna Pallagrosi Academic Scholarship; Modu Samega-Janneh Service Award, College of
Family and Consumer Sciences, University of Georgia; Highest Monthly Sales Award,
JCPenney; Employee of the Month (twice), JCPenney.

REFERENCES
Furnished upon request.

Figure 2.5
Sample Skills Résumé

Joshua Fredrickson
2122 South 141th Street West, Apt. 340
San Antonio, TX 78204
School: (210) 207-5454
Home: (210) 419-1445
JFredrickson@hotmail.com

CAREER OBJECTIVE:
Professional position in human development with administrative responsibilities.

EDUCATION:
Master of Science, 2010, University of Texas at San Antonio, Human Development, San Antonio, TX; Bachelor of Science, 2007, University of Texas at San Antonio, Education and Human Development, San Antonio, TX; Associate of Arts, 2005, San Antonio College, San Antonio, TX.

CAREER-RELATED LEADERSHIP EXPERIENCES
- Organized and coordinated student session at national Family Relations Conference
- Hosted student session at Texas Family Relations Conference
- Led departmental graduate student study committee
- Treasurer of honor society Kappa Omicron Nu
- Organized speaker series for Kappa Omicron Nu
- Chaired Graduate Student Recruitment committee
- Vice President Study Body, San Antonio College
- Volunteer coordinator for neighborhood Meals-on-Wheels for adults

CAREER-RELATED WORK EXPERIENCE
- Administered intake procedures at Humanas Family Center
- Updated record-keeping systems for Humanas Family Center
- Planned learning activities for Gonzales Child Center
- Supervised parental security for Gonzales Child Center
- Presented research paper at Texas Family Relations Conference
- Attended two state Texas Family Relations Conferences
- Attended University of Utah summer seminar on human development
- Planned curriculum updates for Alamo Elder Center
- Trained and managed interns at campus family counseling center

CAREER-RELATED COMPUTER SKILLS
Word, Excel, Corel Graphics, Adobe Acrobat, SPSS, SAS.

HONORS
Henry B. Gonzales Public Service Scholarship, Lane Johnson Memorial Scholarship, Outstanding Member of Kappa Omicron Nu.

The Internet is robust with helpful resources for job seekers. Check out these websites:

www.ajb.dni.us
www.careerbuilder.com
www.careerjournal.com
www.flipdog.com
www.getthejob.com
www.hotjobs.yahoo.com
www.jobster.com

www.monster.com
www.nationjob.com
www.Plaxo.com
www.resumemachine.com
www.rileyguide.com
www.Twitter.com

Career Fairs **Career fairs** are university-, community-, and employer-sponsored opportunities for job seekers to meet with perhaps hundreds or even thousands of potential employers over one or more days. Here you can schedule brief screening interviews with a dozen or more employers in a single day. Career fairs are advertised in local newspapers, on television, and on the Internet. Search "career fairs" on the Internet as well as at Career-Builder.com and NationalCareerFairs.com.

career fairs
University-, community- and employer-sponsored events for job seekers to meet with many employers quickly to screen potential employers.

Classified Advertisements Advertisements in newspapers and professional and trade publications—as well as their Internet equivalents—are an excellent starting place in the job search process. Larger newspapers, such as the *Atlanta Constitution* and *Chicago Daily News* advertise jobs in large geographic areas. Others such as the *New York Times* and *Wall Street Journal* have jobs for the whole country. And others like the *Financial Times* (www.ft.com/jobs) describe overseas opportunities. Specialized trade publications and their Internet websites, in fields such as advertising (*Advertising Age*) and accounting (*Journal of Accountancy*), list numerous job openings. For other fields, see www.dir.yahoo.com/News_and_Media/Journals/.

Decision-Making Worksheet

Keeping Track of Your Job Search Progress

The job search process involves a tremendous number of details. Below is a list of task areas in worksheet format that you can use to help keep track of your job search progress. Create lots of columns to the right so you can input important information, such as dates when you completed each effort.

	Date Done	Date to Do More
1. Identify your values.	_____	_____
2. Decide on economic, psychic, and lifestyle trade-offs.	_____	_____
3. Clarify career-related interests.	_____	_____
4. Review abilities, experiences, and education.	_____	_____
5. Identify employment trends.	_____	_____
6. Create career goals and plans.	_____	_____
7. Target preferred employers.	_____	_____
8. Analyze your work-style personality.	_____	_____
9. Compare salary and living costs in different cities.	_____	_____
10. Place values on employee benefits.	_____	_____
11. Create an expanding list of networking contacts.	_____	_____
12. Obtain excellent letters of reference.	_____	_____
13. Compile revealing personal stories.	_____	_____
14. Assemble a résumé.	_____	_____
15. Assemble a cover letter.	_____	_____
16. Identify job opportunities:	_____	_____
a. Career fairs	_____	_____
b. Classified advertisements	_____	_____
c. Employment agencies	_____	_____
d. Internet	_____	_____
17. Interviewing	_____	_____
a. Research the company.	_____	_____
Create responses for anticipated interview questions.	_____	_____
b. Create positive responses to list of negative questions.	_____	_____
c. Evaluate your interview performance.	_____	_____
18. Send a thank-you note.	_____	_____
19. Accept the job.	_____	_____

Employment Agencies An **employment agency** is a firm specializing in locating employment positions for certain types of employees, such as secretaries, salespeople, engineers, managers, and computer personnel. Most employment agencies are paid fees by organizations that hire them to find new employees. Others charge the job hunter fees, sometimes very high amounts. Governments also have state or city employment offices that offer free services.

employment agency
Firm that locates employment for certain types of employees.

Write an Effective Cover Letter

A **cover letter** is a letter of introduction sent to a prospective employer designed to express your interest in obtaining an interview. The cover letter should be specifically written for each position for which you are applying. See Figure 2.6 for an example. Expand upon a couple of details from your résumé, explaining how your talents and experience can benefit the employer. Communicate your enthusiasm for the job. When appropriate, mention a networking contact.

cover letter
A letter of introduction sent to a prospective employer to get an interview.

Address your cover letter, written on high-quality paper, to a specific person and request a brief meeting. If the hiring manager's name is not in the job announcement, telephone the employer and speak with a receptionist in the correct department. Be candid about your reason for needing a specific person's name. Your letter should try to secure a face-to-face meeting to obtain more information and gather impressions. End the letter with a sentence stating that you will be telephoning or e-mailing within two weeks to reassert your interest in the position. Then, do so!

If you don't hear back, send another hard copy of your resume and cover letter and attach a hand-written note that says, "Second submission. I'm very interested."

Obtain Strong Reference Letters

College students too often simply ask a couple of professors they like to write them a letter of recommendation. Professors typically give their best judgments in these letters. This may include identifying some student weaknesses as well as strengths. Students who ask for a letter from an instructor who does not know them well also risk receiving a bland, boilerplate, or average kind of reference. Always provide a résumé to professors from whom you request letters as well as a copy of the job description for the position.

Ask only those professors who know you and your schoolwork well. Approach them with a request similar to "Are you willing to give me a positive letter of recommendation? I need one that points out my better qualities and performance here at college." If the instructor hesitates too long or gives you some negative feedback, it is time to consider asking a different professor for a recommendation. If your recommenders are willing to give you a separate copy of their letters, you will have them in your personal files for future use.

Did You Know?

Résumé Buzzwords for Skills, Traits, and Technical Expertise

When preparing your résumé, it is important to include buzzwords for skills, traits, and technical expertise that a potential employer will identify as desirable. This is especially important when computer software is used to scan résumés. See www.adwords.google.com. Following are examples of good buzzwords:

- **Attributes:** honesty, integrity
- **Skills:** oral, written, editing, mediating
- **Interests:** fun, avocations, volunteer efforts
- **Teamwork:** coordinated, designed, developed, led, researched
- **Computer literacy and expertise:** list programs and applications
- **Job responsibilities:** initiated, managed, monitored, planned, trained, supervised
- **Job accomplishments:** achieved, administered, built, created, designed, implemented, organized, produced

Apply

You can't get a job without applying for it. Personalize your cover letter and résumé to fit the specific job of interest. Send it to the prospective employer. Many large employers prefer to receive job inquiries via the Internet, often through their website. If so, follow the application instructions to the letter. Other employers prefer a written letter and résumé. It's often smart to do both.

Figure 2.6
Sample Cover Letter

June 23, 2010

Mrs. Juanita M. Pena, President
Pena Public Relations Agency, Inc.
4235 International Blvd NW
Atlanta, GA 30303

Dear Mrs. Pena:

We met briefly in Atlanta at last January's luncheon meeting of the Society of Consumer Affairs Professionals in Business. My professor at that time, Julia Marlowe, introduced us and stated that your company was "undoubtedly one of the most successful creative agencies" in the Atlanta community.

My work experience in public relations and sales, academic background in consumer economics and communications, and research about your firm has led me to the conclusion that I am very interested in seeking employment in your organization. Also, a former employee of yours, Amanda Allyson, now with Hewitt Advertising, told me that you were a fine boss and encouraged me to join your fast-growing company.

My abilities to research, organize, communicate, and lead can provide Pena Public Relations with a person with multiple skills who can adapt to fast-changing needs. My strengths include fluency in three languages, serious computer skills, technical writing, persuasion, and ease in meeting new people. Attending two colleges and living in three states has broadened my perspectives as has studying public relations from the consumer perspective. See my enclosed résumé for more details.

I look forward to the opportunity to meet with you to better communicate my qualifications and evaluate how they might fit the Pena Public Relations Agency. You may contact me at (662) 921-1213 or Eanklin@hotmail.com. Also, I will telephone you in two weeks.

Sincerely,

Jennifer Elizabeth Anklin
Jennifer Elizabeth Anklin
12144 Southwest 174th Loop
Tupelo, MS 38803

Enclosure

If you have not received a response to a job inquiry within two or three weeks, send a follow-up inquiry by adding a brief new opening sentence to your cover letter and send the revised letter with your résumé. When employers express interest in you as a prospective employee, they may request that you complete their official job application form. Be accurate in your responses.

Interview for Success

The interview is the single most important part of your search for employment. A **job interview** is a formal meeting to discuss an individual's job qualifications and suitability for an employment position. When you are invited for an interview, be prepared. Projecting a positive attitude will help.

job interview
Formal meeting between employer and potential employee to discuss job qualifications and suitability.

Do Some Research Before the Interview
Before the interview, research the company. Try to know more about it than the interviewer. Learn how the company makes money, its operations and history, profitability, expansion plans, and other recent developments. Also research the company's competitors and the industry. You can find details on the Internet as most companies have websites. Know what the company is good at and how this relates to your skills. Be familiar with the job description.

Compile Revealing Personal Stories
Assemble some personal stories about yourself that reveal some of your better characteristics. You could have five or more interviews for a single job, and during the interview process you are expected to talk about yourself. Therefore, prepare by writing down some concise stories or statements, perhaps about the time you took over care-giver duties for your siblings while your mother was hospitalized, or facilitated resolving some

internal conflicts among the officers in your student club, or assisted a high school teacher coordinate and supervise 20 students on a field trip, or worked 14 straight hours at Wal-Mart during a weather emergency. Preparing as many as a dozen stories will give you many ways to talk about your positive qualities without just saying, "I'm good." Everyone says that! Communicate that message about yourself in part by telling stories to illustrate your better qualities.

Prepare Questions to Ask the Interviewer A key to success in any interview is to show your enthusiasm and interest in the position and organization. Compliment the interviewer's company based on some facts learned in your preinterview research. Prepare some questions to ask, perhaps about future company plans, company policies, employee benefits, specific duties, and job expectations. You may want to inquire about the corporate culture, too. Write down your questions so you will have your thoughts clear in your mind.

Prepare Responses for Anticipated Interview Questions Your responsibilities during the interview are to remain calm, reveal your personality, be honest, convey your best characteristics, handle questions well, and communicate your enthusiasm about the job. Always answer in a controlled manner. During the interview, be confident that you are the best person for the job and project yourself accordingly.

Job interviewers seem to ask similar questions, so prepare some articulate responses to the following inquiries:

1. Tell me about yourself.
2. How would your instructors and previous employers describe you?
3. What did you like the most about college, and the least?
4. Tell me what you know about our company.
5. Why are you interested in working for this company?
6. What unique abilities and experiences qualify you for the job?
7. Describe some of your strengths and weaknesses.
8. What experiences have you had working with teams and coordinating such efforts?
9. Give an example of an ethical challenge you faced and tell how you handled it.
10. Relate a time when you were faced with a very difficult problem and how you handled it.
11. Describe the supervisors who motivated you to do your best work.
12. What were some of the best and worst aspects of your last job?
13. What do you do in your leisure time?
14. Describe your career plans for five and ten years from now.

Create Positive Responses to Negative Questions Be prepared to "turn any negative into a positive" when asked such questions. One popular negative question, of course, is, "What are your weaknesses?" Interviewers who ask these types of questions want to determine whether the applicant possesses certain qualities such as honesty, self-awareness,

Instant Message

How Truthful Do You Have To Be?

The short answer is to be as truthful as possible when interviewing. Don't volunteer information in an interview that might hurt you, but respond to questions accurately. Misrepresenting facts, making even small distortions, will cast doubt on everything in your résumé and on everything you said in the interview.

Instant Message

"Blink" Is Important in Interviewing

Malcolm Gladwell, author of Blink, argues that when you meet someone for the first time, "your mind takes about two seconds to jump to a series of conclusions." It is not intuition or a snap judgment; it is rapid rational thinking. Your appearance, smile, handshake, first few sentences, and tone of voice send critically important information to the interviewer. Practice and make your blink the best you can communicate. (See www.gladwell.com/blink/.)

Did You Know?

How to Interview over a Meal

More people lose a job interview over lunch than during the formal interview because they fail to realize that going to lunch is a continuation of the interview rather than a social situation. Employers want to hire people with some degree of refinement, people who will mix well with clients and executives. It is smart to engage in conversation over a meal, of course, but let the boss do most of the talking. Good etiquette tips include the following:

- Order a meal less expensive than the host.
- Keep your elbows off the table.
- Break (don't cut) your bread or roll before buttering.
- Use the bread knife (the small knife to the left of your plate).
- Use the small fork outermost from the plate for the first course.

- Don't salt and pepper your meal before tasting.
- Cut your meat one bite at a time.
- Don't talk with food in your mouth.
- Don't order beer, wine, or liquor.
- Avoid ordering soup or pastas because they can be too messy.
- Be extremely polite and respectful of the servers.
- Never complain about a meal.
- Leave it to your host to signal the server.
- If confused, be patient and follow the lead of the host.
- Leave your napkin on your chair when excusing yourself.
- When the meal is over, thank the host and state that you want the job.
- When appropriate, shake hands and say goodbye.

humility, sincerity, zest, and skill in managing shortcomings and mistakes. Denying weakness or being evasive means you don't get the job.

Practice your interview skills beforehand. Practice your responses, especially to negative questions. Perhaps make a videotape of a mock interview, and after evaluating your performance do it again.

Personality Tests One-third of employers give job candidates personality tests assessing team orientation, strengths important to a job, emotional intelligence, motivation, and true work-style inclinations. Don't try to game the employer by telling them what they want to hear—the "right" answer. Being honest confirms what the prospective employer already knows about you.

Be Ready for Telephone Interviews Present yourself in a professional manner when returning a telephone call or engaging in an interview. Have a pen or pencil and paper handy. Be aware of distractions in your surroundings, such as traffic noise. If needed, arrange to call the interviewer back when you find a quiet place. Speak clearly, and eliminate the "uhs" and "ums." The interviewer will notice if you take a sip of coffee or a bite out of a bagel. Try to eliminate as many annoyances as possible to improve your chances of getting the job. Professional recruiters estimate that perhaps only 20 percent of college seniors adequately prepare for their campus interviews.

After the Interview, Evaluate It and Send a Thank-You Note After a job interview, take a few minutes to objectively evaluate your performance. Write down any questions you were

Instant Message

Common Job Interview Mistakes

1. Displayed little knowledge of employer
2. Unprepared to discuss abilities, skills, and experience
3. Unable to discuss career plans and goals
4. Demonstrated little enthusiasm
5. Exhibited poor eye contact

asked that were different from what you expected and make some notes about ways to improve in your next interview. The more interviews you have, the better you will be able to present yourself. Also, immediately mail a thank-you note (don't e-mail it) expressing your appreciation for the opportunity to interview and restate your interest in the position.

Negotiate and Accept the Job

Wait until after the job has been firmly offered to discuss salary. Do not be the first to give a definitive dollar amount. Ask for the salary range for the position. Your objective in negotiating is to obtain a salary 20 percent above the highest figure because you are an exceptional candidate and you will perform at the highest level anticipated. Don't sell yourself short.

Be comfortable with silence, and wait for a response. If the offer is less than what you were expecting, explain that point. Be firm but amicable. This will enhance the employer's respect for you. Tell the employer that you are not willing to start at the bottom or middle of the salary ladder. Reiterate your two or three strongest selling points. Be certain to make a short list of these points beforehand. If the employer states that the offer is final, reply that you need a day or two to think it over. Never turn down an offer until you are absolutely positive you must do so.

If the terms are right, accept the job. Give your new employer your acceptance orally as well as in writing. Obtain a letter confirming your acceptance of the job at the agreed-upon salary with benefits such as moving expenses, flexible hours, and extra vacation days.

Did You Know?

How to Deal with Rejection

The job search process is filled with rejections. Before you land a job, you might have 5 or even 50 potential employers say "No!" Don't let employment rejections strip you of your self-esteem or you will begin to falsely think that there is something wrong with you. A rejection is simply an indicator that there is an inadequate match between your qualities and the employer's needs as perceived in the interview.

After a turndown, when possible ask the company for a review of the strengths and weaknesses of your interview. Make an effort to improve for the next interview. Then, forget the disappointment and move on with your job search.

Do It NOW!

Career planning is a must in today's job market. Start today by:

1. Preparing or updating your résumé.
2. Contacting your school's placement office to explore careers in your field.
3. Visiting one of your professors to seek a mentoring relationship.

Did You Know?

How to Get a Raise

Find out what people in your field earn by talking with others, reviewing trade publications, and checking online at sites such as Glassdoor.com, vault.com, payscale.com, salary.com, and HotJobs.com. Then talk with your boss and write down well-defined, achievable, and measurable goals that you can work toward. This may occur during a formal annual review. Document your accomplishments in writing and keep records. Throughout the year, perhaps on a quarterly basis, discuss these with your boss. Do so not in hallway conversations but in brief sit-down meetings.

Schedule a meeting with your boss before the scheduled time for the annual personnel review. Avoid mentioning how much you need a big raise (because bosses may not care and you might imply you are a poor money manager) and focus on your performance. If the boss cannot give you all the money you deserve, ask for a bigger bonus, enhanced health or retirement benefits, a more flexible work schedule, a change in work hours, permission to occasionally telecommute, or more vacation time.

Concept Check 2.4

1. Explain how networking can be used to one's advantage in career planning.
2. Offer suggestions on correctly assembling a résumé and cover letter, and explain how the two documents differ.
3. Summarize the best methods to identify job opportunities.
4. List five suggestions for interviewing with success.

What Do You Recommend NOW?

Now that you have read the chapter on the importance of career planning, what do you recommend to Ashley in the case at the beginning of the chapter regarding:

1. Clarifying her values and lifestyle trade-offs in career planning?
2. Enhancing her career-related experiences before graduation?
3. Creating career plans and goals?
4. Understanding her work-style personality?
5. Identifying job opportunities?

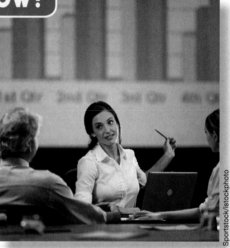

Sportstock/istockphoto

Big Picture Summary of Learning Objectives

1 Identify the key steps in successful career planning.

Career planning is identifying an employment pathway that aligns with your interests and abilities and that is expected to provide the lifestyle and work style you find enjoyable and satisfying. It includes defining your values, making lifestyle trade-offs, clarifying career-related interests, reviewing your talents, understanding employment trends, creating career goals, and targeting preferred employers.

2 Clarify your work-style personality.

Your work-style personality is a unique set of ways of working with and responding to one's job requirements, surroundings, and associates.

3 Analyze the financial and legal aspects of employment.

The financial side of career planning includes comparing salary and living costs in different cities and placing values on employee benefits.

4 Practice effective employment search strategies.

Smart job search strategies include networking, obtaining excellent reference letters, compiling revealing stories, assembling a résumé and cover letter, identifying job opportunities, and interviewing for success.

Let's Talk About It

1. **Interviewing Tips.** List three interviewing tips for new college graduates looking for employment during sluggish economic times.

2. **Interview Mistakes.** Thinking about some common mistakes that people make in job interviews, which five are the worst? Make a list of ten things people should do to improve success in an interview.

3. **Career Trade-offs.** People regularly make decisions in career planning that have trade-offs. List three career decisions that people are likely to face, and identify some economic, psychic, and lifestyle trade-offs for each.

4. **Keeping Track Topics.** Review the task areas in the Decision-Making Worksheet "Keeping Track of Your Job Search Progress," and identify what you think are the five that likely are the most difficult for people to accomplish. For each of the five, offer a suggestion that might help people accomplish the task.

Do the Math

1. **Economic Trade-off of Graduate School.** Delores Sotomajor hopes to earn an extra $600,000 over her remaining 40-year working career by going to night school to obtain a master's degree. If her income projection is correct, that's an average of $15,000 more income a year. Delores's employer is willing to pay $45,000 toward the $60,000 schooling costs, so she must pay out $15,000 of her own money.

   (a) What is the forgone lost future value of her $15,000 over the 40 years at 6 percent? (Hint: See Appendix A.1.)

   (b) What would be the forgone lost future value of $60,000 over 40 years if Delores had to pay all the costs for her master's degree? (Hint: See Appendix A.1.)

2. **Comparing Salary Offers.** Using Equation (2.1) or (2.2), if the cost-of-living index was 132 for Chicago and 114 for San Antonio, compare the buying power of a $50,000 salary in Chicago with a $47,000 offer in San Antonio.

3. **Future Value of Employer's Match.** Johann Winkle's employer makes a matching contribution of $1200 a year to his 401(k) retirement account at work. If the dollar amount of the employer's contribution increases 4 percent annually, how much will the employer contribute to the plan in the twentieth year from now? (Hint: See Appendix A.1.)

4. **Cashing Out 401(k) Plan.** Betty Amarrada has accepted a new job and is thinking about cashing out the $30,000 she has built up in her employer's 401(k) plan to use to buy a new car. If, instead, she left the funds in the plan and they earn 7 percent annually for the next 30 years, how much would Betty have in her plan? (Hint: See Appendix A.1.)

Financial Planning Cases

Case 1
Matching Yourself with a Job

After completing his associate of arts degree four months ago from a community college in Birmingham, Alabama, Jimmy Jackson has answered more than a dozen advertisements and interviewed several times in his effort to get a sales job, but he has had no success. Jimmy has never done sales work before, but he did take some business classes in college, including "Personal Selling." After some of the interviews, Jimmy telephoned some of those potential employers only to find that even though they liked him, they said they typically hired only those people with previous sales experience or who seemed to possess terrific potential.

   (a) If Jimmy actually was well suited for sales, which work values and work-style factors do you think he would rate as "very important"?

   (b) What would you recommend to Jimmy regarding how to find out about the depth of his interest in a sales career?

   (c) Assuming Jimmy has appropriate personal qualities and academic strengths to be successful in a sales career, what additional strategies should he consider to better market himself?

Case 2
Career Promotion Opportunity

Nina and Ting Guo of Des Plaines, Illinois, have been together for eight years, having married just after completing college. Nina has been working as an insurance salesperson ever since. Ting began working as a family counselor for the state of Illinois last year after completing his master's degree in counseling. Recently Nina's boss commented confidentially that he was going to recommend Nina to be the next person to be promoted, given a raise of about $15,000, and relocated to the home office in St. Louis, Missouri. Nina thinks that if offered the opportunity she would like to take it, even if it means that Ting will have to resign his new job.

   (a) What suggestions can you offer Nina when she gets home from work and wants to discuss with her husband her likely career promotion?

   (b) What lifestyle factors and costs and benefits issues should Nina and Ting probably discuss?

Case 3
Victor and Maria Hernandez Consider a Career Change

Throughout this book, we will present a continuing narrative about Victor and Maria Hernandez. Following is a brief description of the lives of this couple.

Victor and Maria, both in their late 30s, have two children: John, age 13, and Joseph, age 15. Victor has had a long sales career with a retail appliance store. Maria works part time as a dental hygienist. Victor is somewhat satisfied with his career but has always wondered about a career as a teacher in a public school. He would have to take a year off work to go to college to obtain his teaching certificate, and that would mean giving up his $43,000 salary for a year. Victor expects that he could earn about the same income as a teacher.

(a) What would his annual income be after 20 years as a teacher if he received an average 5 percent raise every year? (Hint: Use Appendix A.1.)

(b) Victor could earn $4000 each year teaching during the summers. What is the accumulated future value of earning those annual amounts over 20 years assuming a 5 percent raise every year? (Hint: Use Appendix A.3.)

Case 4
Harry and Belinda Johnson Consider Inflation and Children

Throughout this book, we will present a continuing narrative about Harry and Belinda Johnson. Following is a brief description of the lives of this couple.

Harry graduated with a bachelor's degree in interior design last spring from a large Midwestern university near his hometown. Belinda has a degree in business finance from a university on the West Coast. Harry and Belinda both worked on their school's student newspapers and met at a conference during their junior year in college. They were married last June and live in an apartment in Kansas City.

(a) Harry receives $3000 in interest income annually from a trust fund set up by his deceased father's estate. The amount will never change. What will be the buying power of $3000 in ten years if inflation rises at 3 percent a year? (Hint: Use Appendix A.2.)

(b) Belinda and Harry have discussed starting a family but decided to wait for perhaps five years in order to get their careers off to a good start and organize their personal finances. They also know that having children is expensive. They figure that the extra expense of a child would be about $5000 annually until high school graduation. How much money will they likely cumulatively spend on a child over 18 years assuming a 3 percent inflation rate? (Hint: Use Appendix A.3.)

On the 'Net

Go to the Web pages indicated to complete these exercises. You can also go to the *Garman/Forgue* companion website at www.cengage.com/finance/garman for an expanded list of exercises. Under General Business, select the title of this text. Click on the Internet Exercises link for this chapter.

1. Go to the website for the *Occupational Outlook Handbook* at www.bls.gov/oco/home.htm. Select two occupational areas that are of interest to you and for each determine the likely starting salary, career path, future salary expectations, and demand for people with the skills appropriate for the occupation.

2. Go to the website for the Bureau of Labor Statistics' assessment of the labor outlook in the United States at www.bls.gov/bls/employment.htm. Browse through the information provided to determine the current national unemployment rate for the nation as a whole and for a city or area of interest to you. Compare current statistics with those of one year ago and with projections for five and ten years in the future.

Visit the Garman/Forgue companion website . . .

www.cengage.com/finance/garman

Financial Statements, Tools, and Budgets

!You Must Be Kidding, Right?

The median net worth of American families is $95,000, and the mean amount is $453,000. (Those with high net worth pull the mean above the median.) What are the median and mean figures for families headed by a person less than 35 years of age?

A. $17,000 and $90,000

B. $31,000 and $130,000

C. $48,000 and $180,000

D. $61,000 and $199,000

The answer is A, $17,000 median and $90,000 mean. Median net worth goes up with age. It is $85,000 for families ages 35 to 44, $180,000 for ages 45 to 54, and $160,000 for ages 55 to 64. It's all about saving money and building wealth over time!

Learning Objectives

After reading this chapter, you should be able to:

1 Identify your financial values, goals, and strategies.

2 Use balance sheets and cash-flow statements to measure your financial health and progress.

3 Evaluate your financial strength and progress using financial ratios.

4 Maintain the financial records necessary for managing your personal finances.

5 Achieve your financial goals through budgeting.

What Do You Recommend?

Tara Moore/Getty Images

Robert and Nicole Patterson, both age 26, have been married for four years and have no children. Robert is a licensed electrician earning $46,000 per year, and Nicole earns $41,000 annually as a middle-school teacher. Robert would like to go to half time on his job and return to school on a parttime basis; he is one year short of finishing his bachelor's degree in engineering. His education expenses would be about $10,000 per year, which could be partially covered by student loans. He has not yet discussed his plans with Nicole.

Robert and Nicole have recently started saving for retirement through their employment and have set aside some savings for emergencies. They have substantial credit card debt and are still paying off their student loans. The couple rents a two-bedroom apartment. Robert always thought it smart to save all of their receipts, bank statements, and other financial documents. His system for organizing their records is very simple; each month he puts everything in a manila envelope and then puts the 12 envelopes into a box at the end of the year.

Robert knows that his educational plans will have financial implications for the couple. He wants to factor these financial issues into his discussion with Nicole about his plans. To this point, they have never developed financial statements or explicit financial goals.

What do you recommend to Robert for his talk with Nicole on the subject of financial planning regarding:

1. Determining what they own and owe?
2. Better understanding their patterns of family income and expenditure?
3. Using the information in Robert's newly prepared financial statements to summarize the family's financial situation?
4. Setting financial goals?
5. Evaluating their financial progress?
6. Setting up a record-keeping system to better serve their needs?
7. Starting a budgeting process to guide saving and spending?

What an economy! We have seen collapses in housing, credit and the stock market. While the economic recovery goes on, there is no doubt that the key lessons to be learned are to live below your means and build up your savings. Yet, *Kiplinger's Personal Finance Magazine* reports that 22 percent of U.S. consumers say they have no money left over after paying basic living expenses. How can these folks, and all of us, learn to manage our money more successfully and build savings over time?

This chapter provides the nitty-gritty details on how to go about becoming financially successful. You can attain your financial goals by setting goals and strategies that are consistent with your values. Along the way, you follow your spending plan, take appropriate actions to achieve results, and regularly measure your financial strength and progress. This anonymous quote sums up the theme of this chapter: "Living above your means can lead to financial ruin at a young age."

Financial Values, Goals, and Strategies

1 Learning Objectives

Identify your financial values, goals, and strategies.

Identifying your financial values and goals sets the stage for financial success. Values and goals keep a balance between spending and saving and help you stay committed to your financial plans. Once goals are set, you can develop the strategies necessary for their achievement. **Financial planning,** the process of developing and implementing a coordinated series of financial plans, can help you achieve financial success. By planning your finances, you seek to manage your income and wealth so that you reach your financial goals.

Figure 3.1 provides an overview of effective personal financial planning, and Table 3.1 illustrates one couple's overall financial plan. Your managerial efforts push you toward

Figure 3.1
How to Achieve Financial Goals

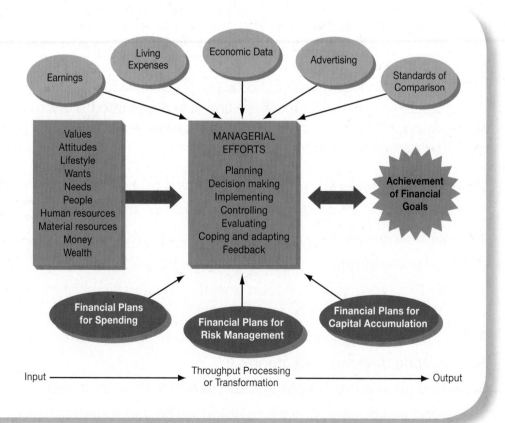

achieving financial success. The couple has made plans in 15 specific areas spread across three broad categories: (1) spending, (2) risk management, and (3) capital accumulation. Many people ignore certain areas (retirement planning is a common example) and act with only partial knowledge in other areas (relying on their employers' often inadequate disability income insurance, for example). Yet achieving success in financial matters requires effective financial planning in all 15 specific areas. The chapters in this book will provide enough detail so that you will feel confident and competent as you implement your financial plans that address all 15 areas.

Table 3.1 **Financial Plans, Goals, and Objectives for Harry (Age 23) and Belinda (Age 22) Johnson, Prepared in February 2010**

Financial Plan Areas	Long-Term Goals and Objectives	Short-Term Goals and Objectives
FOR SPENDING		
Evaluate and plan major purchases	Purchase a new car in two years.	Begin saving $200 a month for a down payment for a new car.
Manage debt	Keep installment debt under 10 percent of take-home pay.	Pay off charge cards at end of each month and do not finance any purchases of appliances or other similar products.
FOR RISK MANAGEMENT		
Medical costs	Avoid large medical costs.	Maintain employer-subsidized medical insurance policy by paying $135 monthly premium.
Property and casualty losses	Always have renter's or homeowner's insurance.	Make semiannual premium payment of $220 on renter's insurance policy.
	Always have maximum automobile insurance coverage.	Make premium payments of $440 on automobile insurance policy.
Liability losses	Eventually buy $1 million liability insurance.	Rely on $100,000 policy purchased from same source as automobile insurance policy.
Premature death	Have adequate life insurance coverage for both as well as lots of financial investments so the survivor would not have any financial worries.	Maintain employer-subsidized life insurance on Belinda. Buy some life insurance for Harry. Start some investments.
Income loss from disability	Buy sufficient disability insurance.	Rely on sick days and seek disability insurance through private insurers.
FOR CAPITAL ACCUMULATION		
Tax fund	Have enough money for taxes (but not too much) withheld from monthly salaries by both employers to cover eventual tax liabilities.	Confirm that employer withholding of taxes is sufficient. Have extra money withheld to cover additional tax liability because of income on trust from Harry's deceased father.
Revolving savings fund	Always have sufficient cash in local accounts to meet monthly and annual anticipated budget expense needs.	Develop cash-flow calendar to ascertain needs. Put money into revolving savings fund to build it up quickly to the proper balance. Keep all funds in interest-earning accounts.

Continued

Table 3.1 *(Continued)*

Financial Plan Areas	Long-Term Goals and Objectives	Short-Term Goals and Objectives
Emergency fund	Build up monetary assets equivalent to three months' take-home pay.	Put $150 per month into an emergency fund until it totals one month's take-home pay.
Education	Maintain educational skills and credentials to remain competitive.	Both take one graduate class per term.
	Have employer assist in paying for Belinda to earn a master of business administration (MBA).	
	Have Harry complete a master of fine arts (MFA), possibly a PhD in interior design.	
Savings	Always have a nice-size savings balance.	Save enough to pay cash for a good-quality DVD player.
	Regularly save to achieve goals.	
	Save a portion of any extra income or gifts.	Pay off Visa credit card balance of $390 soon.
	Save $26,000 for a down payment on a home to be bought within five years.	Begin saving $400 per month for a down payment on a new home.
Investments	Own substantial shares of a conservative mutual fund that will pay dividends equivalent to about 10 percent of family income at age 45.	Start investing in a mutual fund before next year.
	Own some real estate and common stocks.	
Retirement	Retire at age 60 or earlier on income that is the same as the take-home pay earned just before retirement.	Establish individual retirement accounts (IRAs) for Harry and Belinda before next year.
		Contribute the maximum possible amount to employer-sponsored retirement accounts.
Estate planning	Provide for surviving spouse.	Each spouse makes a will.

Your Next Five Years

In the next five years you can start achieving financial success by doing the following related to financial statements, tools, and budgets:

1. Develop financial goals and update and revise them annually.

2. Develop a cash-flow statement and spending plan every month to ensure that you spend significantly less than you make.

3. Track your net worth and financial ratios annually to assess your financial progress.

4. Use an uncomplicated but effective personal financial record-keeping system.

5. Openly and honestly communicate about money matters with loved ones on a regular basis.

Values Define Your Financial Success

Your **values** provide the underlying support and rationale for your financial and lifestyle goals. Your values are your fundamental beliefs about what is important, desirable, and worthwhile. They serve as the basis for your goals. All of us differ in the ways we value education, spiritual life, health, employment, credit use, family life, and many other factors. Personal financial goals grow out of these values because we inevitably consider some things more important or desirable than others. We express our values, in part, by the ways we spend, save, invest, and donate our money.

One major benefit of financial planning is using money wisely. People who are smart about personal finance typically value saving some of their income. They adhere to the personal finance philosophy of "Pay myself first." If you earn money, shouldn't you be "paid" first? Successful money managers do this instead of spending it all, or even worse spending even more than they earn by using lots of credit. They establish a current spending level based on the necessities of life. They set aside money for future spending, such as for a vehicle purchase, home, child's education, vacation home, and living expenses during the years of retirement.

values
Fundamental beliefs about what is important, desirable, and worthwhile.

Financial Goals Follow from Your Values

Successful financial planning evolves from your financial goals. **Financial goals** are the specific long-, intermediate-, and short-term objectives to be attained through financial planning and management efforts. Financial and lifestyle goals should be consistent with your values. To serve as a rational basis for financial actions, they must be stated explicitly in terms of purpose, dollar amounts, and the projected dates by which they are to be achieved.

financial goals
Specific objectives addressed by planning and managing finances.

Setting goals helps you visualize the gap between your current financial status and where you want to be in the future. Examples of general financial goals include finishing a college education, paying off debts (including education loans), meeting financial emergencies, taking a vacation, owning a home, accumulating funds to send children through college, owning your own business, creating a better peace of mind, ensuring family harmony, and having financial independence at retirement.

None of these goals, however, is specific enough to guide financial behavior. Specific goals should be measurable, attainable, relevant, and time related. Saving for retirement should begin with a calculation of how much money you will need in retirement (see Chapter 17), and saving for retirement should start soon after you begin a full-time job. Saving for a child's education should begin when your first child is born, if not earlier.

Consider the example of Heather Vogel, a dance instructor from Cincinnati, Ohio. Heather has just made the last $347 payment on her four-year car loan. She does not like being in debt, so she does not want to take out such a large loan again. Heather would like to put at least part of the money she has been paying monthly for the loan into a savings account, which would allow her to replace her current vehicle in five years. Heather figures that it would take about $22,500 to buy a similar inexpensive high-mileage vehicle in five years. She assumes she could earn a 3 percent return on her savings and, using Appendix Table A.3, has determined that she would need to save $4238 per year ($22,500 ÷ 5.3091 for five years at 3 percent interest from Appendix Table A.3), or roughly $353 per month.

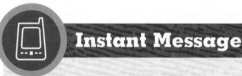

Instant Message

Turn Your Goals into Reality

The path toward turning a wish into reality begins with writing it down. If buying a condo is your goal, tape a photograph of a beautiful one on your refrigerator. Then tell others about your financial goal. The constant reminders will help you make it into a reality.

Heather's thinking offers a good example of how financial goal setting works. She recognized the value she put on staying out of debt and proceeded to the general goal of paying cash for her next car. After determining an overall dollar amount needed, she broke that amount down into first annual and then monthly amounts. For only $6 more per month than she has been paying on her loan ($353 − $347), Heather will be able to pay cash for her next car. This is the small sacrifice she is willing to make to avoid using credit to buy a vehicle in the future.

Financial Strategies Guide Your Financial Success

Financial strategies are pre-established plans of action to be implemented in specific situations. Heather Vogel implemented a very effective strategy in the preceding example. That is, when a loan has been repaid, start a savings program with the same monthly payment amount. Saving may be easier for Heather if she arranges for the amount she'd like to save to be automatically deposited from her paycheck into her savings account. Another effective savings strategy is to arrange for one-half of every raise to go into savings before you become accustomed to the additional income.

financial strategies
Preestablished action plans implemented in specific situations.

Heather's actions have nothing to do with her earning more money. Many people think that being wealthy is a function of how much you earn or inherit. Accumulating wealth is much more related to your ability to understand trade-offs among current and future wants and make the sacrifices that will save money and generate wealth for you. In Heather's case, all that remains for her to do is to put the strategy into action. She can then review her strategy annually and adjust it as necessary to keep pace with her shifting circumstances.

To sum up, successful financial planning includes the following elements that guide behavior: (1) specified values that underlie the plans, (2) explicitly stated financial goals, and (3) logical and consistent financial strategies. Smart financial strategies will be presented throughout this book, as they help you keep a balance between spending and saving. Only after this values-based process is complete do you take actions to achieve the goals. In other words, your financial planning comes before you take action.

Did You Know?

Money Topics to Discuss with Your Partner

Personal finances are complex enough for just one person, but when two people join their financial lives together, things can get very complicated. When you find the right partner, it is smart to do the following:

- **Change beneficiaries.** Life insurance policies, retirement accounts, and mutual fund accounts all have beneficiaries (the people who will receive the funds at your death) named when you set them up. (See Chapters 12, 15, 17, and 18.)
- **Coordinate employee benefits.** Couples often have two incomes today, so each has a menu of employee benefits from which to choose. As a result, one spouse may drop a benefit that is being received via the other's plan. For example, if one partner receives family coverage for health care for free or at a low monthly cost, perhaps the other can drop that aspect of his or her own plan. One spouse might then be able to add another benefit at no cost, such as paid education expenses. Your employee benefits officer can help you decide which options to select.
- **Update life insurance coverage.** Focus on term life insurance for the bulk of your needs. (See Chapter 12.)
- **Review auto and homeowner's insurance coverages.** Also inventory your personal property. (See Chapter 10.)
- **Get out of debt.** One or both of you may bring debts into the new family. Because a couple can live together a little more cheaply than two individuals who live apart, funds can be freed up to pay off credit card, student, and

other loans. This debt reduction has an added benefit: It sets the stage for getting a mortgage to buy your first home. (See Chapters 6, 7, and 9.)

- **Update names with government agencies.** If one or both partners' names are changed as a result of your new status, you need to notify the Social Security Administration and driver's licensing office of that change. You will need to show your marriage certificate as proof of the change.
- **Save for retirement separately.** Day-to-day living expenses will go down somewhat when you team up as a couple. Use some of that money to allocate additional amounts to your individual retirement plans. (See Chapter 17.)
- **Update estate transfer plans.** With a new number one in your life, you should change (or set up) your will, durable power of attorney, living will, and health care surrogate designations. (See Chapter 18 for more information on these documents.)
- **Close redundant bank accounts.** Reducing the number of accounts that each partner brings into the marriage can save money on account fees. Decide which accounts are yours, mine, or ours. (See Chapters 5 and 6 for more on managing accounts.)
- **Manage money together.** All of the topics in this chapter on financial planning should be undertaken as a team. (See Chapter 5 for how to effectively discuss money matters.)

 Concept Check 3.1

1. Summarize the financial planning process.
2. Explain the relationships among financial values, goals, and strategies.

Financial Statements Measure Your Financial Health and Progress

Financial statements are compilations of personal financial data that describe an individual's or family's current financial condition. They present a summary of assets and liabilities as well as income and spending of an individual or family. The two most useful statements are the balance sheet and the cash-flow statement.

A **balance sheet** (or **net worth statement**) describes an individual's or family's financial condition on a specified date (often January 1) by showing assets, liabilities, and net worth. It provides a current status report and includes information on what you own, what you owe, and what the net result would be if you paid off all of your debts. It answers the question "Where are you financially right now?"

A **cash-flow statement** (or **income and expense statement**) lists and summarizes income and expense transactions that have taken place over a specific period of time, such as a month or a year. It tells you where your money came from and where it went. It answers the question "Where did your money go?"

The Balance Sheet Is a Snapshot of Your Financial Status Right Now

To benchmark where you are on the wealth-building scale, determine your net worth. If you are indeed serious about your financial success, then you will sit down soon with pencil and paper or at your computer to see exactly where you stand. You do so by preparing your balance sheet, which summarizes the value of what you own minus what you owe. Your balance sheet should be updated at least once each year so that you can assess your progress. Net worth grows slowly. If you are successful in your career and follow the basic principles outlined in this book, there is no reason why you cannot have a net worth of $1 million, or $2 million or more, later in your life. Net worth typically peaks for people in their 60s and declines thereafter as they live off their financial nest egg in retirement.

Components of the Balance Sheet A balance sheet consists of three parts: assets, liabilities, and net worth. Your **assets** include everything you own that has monetary value. Your **liabilities** are your debts—amounts you owe to others. Your **net worth** is the dollar amount left when what is owed is subtracted from the dollar value of what is owned—that is, if all the assets were sold at the listed values and all debts were paid in full. Your net worth is the true measure of your financial wealth.

What Is Owned—Assets The assets section of the balance sheet lists items valued at their **fair market value**—what a willing buyer would pay a willing seller, not the amount originally paid or what it might be worth a year from now. It is useful to classify assets as monetary, tangible, or investment assets.

Monetary assets (also known as **liquid assets** or **cash equivalents**) include cash and low-risk near-cash items that can be readily converted to cash with little or no loss in value such as checking and savings accounts. They are primarily used for maintenance of living expenses, emergencies, savings, and payment of bills.

Tangible (or **use**) **assets** are personal property whose primary purpose is to provide maintenance of one's everyday lifestyle. Tangible assets, such as furniture and vehicles, generally depreciate in value over time.

Investment assets (also known as **capital assets**) include tangible and intangible items that have a relatively long life and high cost and that are acquired for the monetary benefits they provide, such as generating additional income and appreciation (or increasing

2 Learning Objectives

Use balance sheets and cash-flow statements to measure your financial health and progress.

financial statements
Snapshots that describe an individual's or family's current financial condition.

balance sheet (or net worth statement)
Snapshot of assets, liabilities, and net worth on a particular date.

cash-flow statement (or income and expense statement)
Summary of all income and expense transactions over a specific time period.

assets
Everything you own that has monetary value.

liabilities
What you owe.

net worth
What's left when you subtract liabilities from assets.

monetary assets/liquid assets/cash equivalents
Assets that can be used as cash.

tangible (use) assets
Personal property used to maintain your everyday lifestyle.

investment (capital) assets
Tangible and intangible items acquired for their monetary benefits.

in value). Examples include stocks and bonds. Investment assets generally appreciate and are dedicated to the maintenance of one's future level of living.

Following are some examples of each kind of asset.

Monetary Assets

- Cash (including cash on hand, checking accounts, savings accounts, savings bonds, certificates of deposit, and money market accounts)
- Tax refunds due
- Money owed to you by others

Tangible Assets

- Automobiles, motorcycles, boats, bicycles
- House, condominium, mobile home
- Household furnishings and appliances
- Personal property (jewelry, furs, tools, clothing)
- Other "big ticket" items

Investment Assets

- Stocks, bonds, mutual funds, gold, partnerships, art, IRAs
- Life insurance and annuities (cash values only)
- Real property (and anything fixed to it)
- Personal and employer-provided retirement accounts

short-term (current) liability
Obligation paid off within one year.

long-term liability
Debt that comes due in more than one year.

What Is Owed—Liabilities The liabilities section of the balance sheet summarizes debts owed, including both personal and business-related debts. The debt could be either a **short-term** (or **current**) **liability,** an obligation to be paid off within one year, or a **long-term liability,** debts that do not have to be paid in full until more than a year from now. To be accurate, record debt obligations at their current payoff amounts (excluding future interest payments). Following are some examples of items to include in the liabilities section of a balance sheet, with some suggested subheadings.

Short-Term (or Current) Liabilities

- Personal loans owed to other people
- Credit card and charge account balances
- Other open-end credit obligations
- Professional services unpaid (doctors, dentists, chiropractors, lawyers)
- Taxes unpaid
- Past-due rent, utility bills, and insurance premiums

Long-Term Liabilities

- Automobile loans
- Real estate mortgages
- Home equity (second mortgage) loan
- Consumer installment loans and leases (although a lease is technically not a debt)
- Education loans
- Margin loans on securities

Net Worth—What Is Left Net worth is determined by subtracting liabilities from assets, as indicated in Equation (3.1), the *net worth formula:*

$$\text{Assets} - \text{liabilities} = \text{net worth} \qquad (3.1)$$

or

$$\text{What is owned} - \text{what is owed} = \text{net worth}$$

This formula assumes that if you converted all assets to cash and paid off all liabilities, the remaining cash would be your net worth. For example, if your items of value had a fair market value of $8000 and the amount you owe to others is $4500, your net worth, or wealth, is $3500 ($8000 − $4500). Figure 3.2 shows household net worth figure by age group. Calculating your net worth will give you a reading on where you stand and point out any trouble spots on your balance sheet.

Sample Balance Sheets The total assets on a balance sheet must equal the total liabilities plus the net worth. Both sides must balance, which is the source of the name "balance sheet." You decide how much detail to include to show your financial condition accurately on a given date.

The balance sheets shown in Table 3.2 (page 72) and Table 3.3 (page 73) reflect the degree of detail that might be included for a traditional college student and a couple with two children, respectively. Notice that Table 3.2 includes very few items. This pattern is typical of single people who have not acquired many objects of value. Observe also the excess of liabilities over assets. This situation is not unusual for college students, for whom debts often seem

Did You Know?

The Financial Planning Process

The financial planning process includes the following steps:

1. Set realistic financial goals
2. Evaluate your present financial condition
3. Develop a plan to reach your goals
4. Put your plan into action
5. Monitor your efforts to stay on track

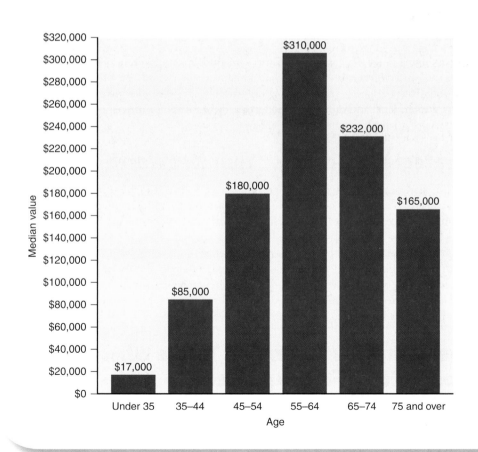

Figure 3.2
Net Worth by Age

Source: Base data from Survey of Consumer Finances. Authors' estimates for 2010.

Table 3.2 **Balance Sheet for a College Student—William Soshnik, January 1, 2010**

	Dollars	Percent
ASSETS		
Cash on hand	85	1.07
Checking account	335	4.21
Savings account	800	10.05
Personal property*	3,140	39.45
Automobile	3,600	45.23
Total Assets	$7,960	100.00
LIABILITIES		
Telephone bill past due	70	0.88
Bank loan—automobile	3,130	39.32
College loan	1,000	12.56
Government educational loan	4,500	56.53
Total Liabilities	$8,700	109.30
Net Worth	($740)	−9.30
Total Liabilities and Net Worth	$7,960	100.00

*At fair market value, list includes clothing, $400; dresser, $50; television, $150; chair, $30; table, $40; desk, $120; cooking/dining items, $50; and computer equipment, $2300.

insolvent
Carrying a negative net worth.

to grow much faster than assets do. In this case, the person is technically **insolvent** because he or she has a negative net worth. When students graduate and take on full-time jobs, typically their balance sheets change dramatically after a few years. The balance sheet in Table 3.3 shows greater detail and more items, reflecting the increasing financial complexity that typically occurs at later stages in a person's life.

Strategies to Increase Your Net Worth

You can increase your net worth by increasing assets, decreasing liabilities, or doing both. One way to increase assets and net worth is to cut back on spending. Perhaps consider forgoing the cup of coffee or soda you buy each day as you head to class, as any decrease in spending leaves money in the bank as an asset. Reducing expenses on high-cost items such as housing and transportation will have an even greater effect on assets. A second way to increase net worth is to increase income to build assets or pay down debts. For example, as you earn more money, perhaps consider saving most of the difference between your new income and your old income rather than using the added money for more spending. Paying off debt, especially high-interest credit card balances, increases net worth.

The Cash-Flow Statement Tracks Where Your Money Came From and Went

The cash-flow (or income and expense) statement summarizes the total amounts that have been received and spent over a period of time, usually one month or one year. It shows whether you were able to live within your income during that time period. It reflects the flow of funds in and out.

Table 3.3 **Balance Sheet for a Couple with Two Children—Victor and Maria Hernandez, January 1, 2010**

	Dollars	Percent
ASSETS		
Monetary Assets		
Cash on hand	260	0.08
Savings account	1,500	0.48
Victor's checking account	600	0.19
Maria's checking account	700	0.23
Tax refund due	700	0.23
Rent receivable	660	0.21
Total monetary assets	$ 4,420	1.43
Tangible Assets		
Home	176,000	56.79
Personal property	9,000	2.90
Automobiles	11,500	3.71
Total tangible assets	$196,500	63.40
Investment Assets		
Fidelity mutual funds	4,500	1.45
Scudder mutual fund	5,000	1.61
General Motors stock	2,800	0.90
New York 2016 bonds	1,000	0.32
Life insurance cash value	5,400	1.74
IRA	6,300	2.03
Real estate investment	84,000	27.10
Total investment assets	$109,000	35.17
Total Assets	$309,920	100.00
LIABILITIES		
Short-Term liabilities		
Dentist bill	120	0.04
Credit card debt	1,545	0.50
Total short-term liabilities	$ 1,665	0.54
Long-Term liabilities		
Sales finance company: automobile	7,700	2.48
Savings and loan: real estate	92,000	29.69
Total long-term liabilities	$ 99,700	32.17
Total Liabilities	$101,365	32.71
Net Worth	$208,555	67.29
Total Liabilities and Net Worth	$309,920	100.00

income
total income received such as reported on a cash flow statement.

expenses
total expenditures made in a specified time such as reported on a cash-flow statement.

surplus (or net gain or net income)
when total income exceeds total expenses such as reported on a cash flow statement.

deficit (or net loss)
when expenses exceed income such as reported on a cash flow statement.

cash basis
Only transactions involving actual cash received or cash spent are recorded.

A cash-flow statement includes three sections: **income** (total income received); **expenses** (total expenditures made); and **surplus** (or **net gain** or **net income**), when total income exceeds total expenses, or **deficit** (or **net loss**), when expenses exceed income. Such statements are usually prepared on a **cash basis,**[1] meaning the only transactions recorded are those involving actual cash received or cash that was spent.

Income/Cash Coming In

You may think of income as simply what is earned from salaries or wages, but there are other types of income that you should include on a cash-flow statement, such as the following:

- Bonuses and commissions
- Child support and alimony
- Public assistance
- Social Security benefits
- Pension and profit-sharing income
- Scholarships and grants
- Interest and dividends received (from savings accounts, investments, bonds, or loans to others)
- Income from the sale of assets
- Other income (gifts, tax refunds, rent, royalties, capital gains)

Expenses/Cash Going Out

All expenditures made during the period covered by the cash-flow statement should be included in the expenses section. The number and type of expenses shown will vary for each individual and family. Many people categorize expenses according to whether they are fixed or variable.

fixed expenses
Expenses that recur at fixed intervals.

Fixed expenses are usually paid in the same amount during each time period; they are typically inflexible and often contractual. Examples of such expenses include rent payments and automobile installment loans. It usually takes quite an effort to reduce a fixed expense.

variable expenses
Expenses over which you have substantial control.

Variable expenses are expenditures over which an individual has considerable control. Food, entertainment, and clothing are variable expenses, for example. Some categories, such as savings, can be listed twice, as both fixed and variable expenses. The following are examples of fixed and variable expenses that you might include in a cash-flow statement:

Fixed Expenses

- Savings and investments
- Retirement contributions (employer's plan, IRA)
- Housing (rent, mortgage, loan payment)
- Automobile (installment payment, lease)
- Insurance (life, health, liability, disability, renter's, homeowner's, automobile)
- Installment loan payments (appliances, furniture)
- Taxes (federal income, state income, local income, real estate, Social Security, personal property)

Variable Expenses

- Meals (at home and away)
- Utilities (electricity, water, gas, telephone)
- Transportation (gasoline and maintenance, licenses, registration, public transportation, tolls)

[1]An alternative method is accrual-basis budgeting that recognizes earnings and expenditures when money is earned and expenditures are incurred, regardless of when money is actually received or paid.

Jürg Carstensen/dpa/Corbis

When reducing variable expenses perhaps continue to enjoy cafe lattes and make bigger budget cuts elsewhere.

- Medical expenses
- Child care (nursery, baby-sitting)
- Clothing and accessories (jewelry, shoes, handbags, briefcases)
- Snacks (candy, soft drinks, other beverages)
- Education (tuition, fees, books, supplies)
- Household furnishings (furniture, appliances, curtains)
- Cable television (beyond basic services)
- Personal care (beauty shop, barbershop, cosmetics, dry cleaner)
- Entertainment and recreation (hobbies, socializing, health club, tapes/CDs, videotape/ DVD rentals, movies)
- Charitable contributions (gifts, church, school, charity)
- Magazine subscriptions
- Vacations and long weekends
- Credit card payments
- Savings and investments
- Miscellaneous (postage, books, magazines, newspapers, personal allowances, domestic help, membership fees)

There is no rigid list of categories to be used in the expenses section, but you do need to classify all of your expenditures in some way. Rather than just use fixed and variable expenses categories, you might also separate expenditures into savings/investments, debts, insurance, taxes, and household expenses. The more specific your categories, the deeper your understanding of your outlays.

Cash Surplus (or Cash Deficit) The surplus (deficit) section shows the amount of cash remaining after you have itemized income and subtracted expenditures from income, as illustrated by the following calculations using Equation (3.2), the *surplus/deficit formula*. (A business would call this amount its net profit or net loss.)

$$\text{Surplus (deficit)} = \text{total income} - \text{total expenses} \qquad (3.2)$$

or
$$\$1100 \text{ surplus} = \$12,500 - \$11,400$$
$$(\$800 \text{ deficit}) = \$14,900 - \$15,700$$

A surplus demonstrates that you are managing your financial resources successfully and do not have to use savings or borrow money to make financial ends meet. When the calculation shows a surplus, that amount is then available (in your checking and savings accounts) to spend, save, invest, or donate. A surplus is not really cash lying around on the kitchen table; it is the cash value reflected in the accounts on your balance sheet. Figure 3.3 shows the typical personal financial situation over the life cycle in present value dollars, from the wealth accumulation years through retirement.

Sample Cash-Flow Statements Table 3.4 and Table 3.5 show the cash-flow statements for a college student and a couple with two children, respectively. Table 3.5 vividly highlights the additional income needed to rear children and shows the increased variety of expenditures that characterize a family's (rather than an individual's) lifestyle. As a person earns more income, the cash-flow statement usually becomes more involved and detailed.

Did You Know?

Many People Are Poor Money Managers

Half of all adults say they do not budget. Four in ten say they are living beyond their means and rate themselves as fair or poor in managing money. To maintain a desired lifestyle, they spend every dollar they earn. They live paycheck to paycheck and they often turn to credit cards. These people are incompetent in money matters and their choices will forever make them the "have nots" in society rather than the "haves."

Figure 3.3
Personal Finance over the Life Cycle

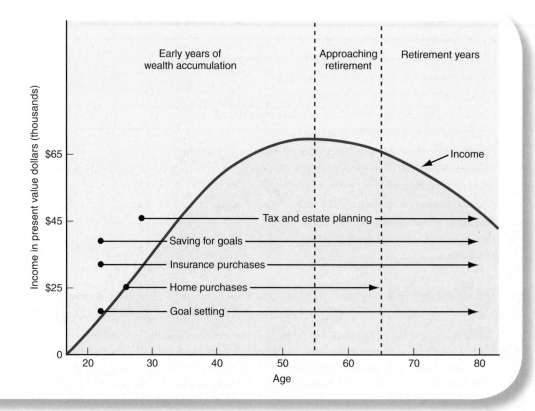

Table 3.4 **Cash-Flow Statement for a College Student—William Soshnik, January 1–December 31, 2010**

	Dollars	Percent
INCOME		
Wages (after withholding)	4,650	39.71
Scholarship	1,750	14.94
Government grant	2,500	21.35
Government loan*	2,600	22.20
Tax refund	210	1.79
Total Income	$11,710	100.00
EXPENSES		
Room rent (includes utilities)	1,500	12.81
Laundry	216	1.84
Food	1,346	11.49
Automobile loan payments	1,292	11.03
Automobile insurance	778	6.64
Books and supplies	932	7.96
Tuition	3,160	26.99
Telephone	282	2.41
Clothing	475	4.06
Gifts	300	2.56
Automobile expenses	600	5.12
Health insurance	102	0.87
Recreation and entertainment	360	3.07
Personal expenses	300	2.56
Total Expenses	$11,643	99.43
Surplus (deficit)	$ 67	0.57

*Technically, loans are not income. William plans to be a teacher, and his loan will be forgiven if he goes into teaching and remains in the profession for five years.

Table 3.5 **Cash-Flow Statement for a Couple with Two Children— Victor and Maria Hernandez, January 1, 2009–December 31, 2009**

	Dollars	Percent
INCOME		
Victor's gross salary	43,180	65.42
Maria's salary (parttime)	12,500	18.94
Interest and dividends	1,800	2.73
Bonus	600	0.91
Tax refunds	200	0.30
Net rental income	7,720	11.70
Total Income	$66,000	100.00

Continued

Table 3.5 *(Continued)*

	Dollars	Percent
EXPENSES		
Fixed Expenses		
Mortgage loan payments	12,000	18.18
Real estate taxes	2,400	3.64
Homeowner's insurance	760	1.15
Automobile loan payment	4,400	6.67
Automobile insurance and registration	1,191	1.80
Life insurance premiums	1,200	1.82
Medical insurance (employee portion)	2,980	4.52
Savings at credit union	1,260	1.91
Federal income taxes	6,800	10.30
State income taxes	3,100	4.70
City income taxes	720	1.09
Social Security taxes	4,260	6.45
Personal property taxes	950	1.44
Retirement IRAs	4,000	6.06
Total fixed expenses	$46,021	69.73
Variable Expenses		
Food	4,900	7.42
Utilities	2,100	3.18
Gasoline, oil, maintenance	3,100	4.70
Medical expenses	1,245	1.89
Medicines	750	1.14
Clothing and upkeep	1,950	2.95
Church	1,200	1.82
Gifts	900	1.36
Personal allowances	1,160	1.76
Children's allowances	960	1.45
Miscellaneous	500	0.76
Total variable expenses	$18,765	28.43
Total Expenses	$64,786	98.16
Surplus (deficit)	$ 1,214	1.84

 Concept Check 3.2

1. Distinguish between the balance sheet and cash-flow statement.
2. How should assets and liabilities be valued for the balance sheet?
3. Distinguish between fixed and variable expenses.

Financial Ratios Assess Your Financial Strength and Progress

Financial ratios are numerical calculations designed to simplify the process of evaluating your financial strength and the progress of your financial condition. Ratios serve as tools or yardsticks to develop saving, spending, and credit-use patterns consistent with your goals. Calculators for these ratios can be found on the *Garman/Forgue* companion website.

Basic Liquidity Ratio: Can I Pay for Emergencies?

Liquidity is the speed and ease with which an asset can be converted to cash. You can use the **basic liquidity ratio** to determine the number of months that you could continue to meet your expenses using only your monetary assets if all income ceases. A high ratio is desirable. For example, compare the monetary assets on the balance sheet for Victor and Maria Hernandez in Table 3.3 ($4420) with their monthly expenses in Table 3.5 ($64,786 ÷ 12 = $5399) using Equation (3.3):

$$\text{Basic liquidity ratio} = \frac{\text{monetary (liquid) assets}}{\text{monthly expenses}} \qquad \textbf{(3.3)}$$

$$= \frac{\$4420}{\$5399}$$

$$= 0.82$$

This financial ratio suggests that the Hernandezes may have insufficient monetary assets, unable to support them for even one month (0.82) if they are faced with a loss of income. According to researchers at the University of Texas, experts recommend that people have monetary assets equal to three months' expenses in emergency cash reserves. Surveys reveal that more than half of American families do not have that much savings. The exact amount of monetary assets necessary depends on your family situation and your job. A smaller amount may be sufficient for your needs if you have adequate income protection through an employee benefit program, are employed in a job that is definitely not subject to layoffs, or have a partner who works for money income. Households dependent on the income from a self-employed person with fluctuating income need a larger emergency cash reserve.

Asset-to-Debt Ratio: Do I Have Enough Assets Compared with Liabilities?

The **asset-to-debt ratio** compares total assets with total liabilities. It provides you with a broad measure of your financial liquidity. This ratio measures solvency and ability to pay debts, as shown in Equation (3.4). A high ratio is desirable. Calculations based on the figures in the Hernandezes' balance sheet (Table 3.3) show that the couple has ample assets compared with their debts because they own items worth more than three times what they owe. (Reversing the mathematics shows that they owe less than one-third of what they own.)

$$\text{Asset-to-debt ratio} = \frac{\text{total assets}}{\text{total debt}} \qquad \textbf{(3.4)}$$

$$= \frac{\$309,920}{\$101,365}$$

$$= 3.057$$

If you owe more than you own, then you are technically insolvent. While your current income may be sufficient to pay your current bills, you still do not have enough assets to cover

3 Learning Objectives
Evaluate your financial strength and progress using financial ratios.

financial ratios
Calculations designed to simplify evaluation of financial strength and progress.

liquidity
Speed and ease with which an asset can be converted to cash.

basic liquidity ratio
Number of months you could meet expenses using only monetary assets if all income ceases.

asset-to-debt ratio
Compares total assets with total liabilities.

all of your debts. Many people in such situations seek credit counseling, and some eventually declare bankruptcy. (These topics are discussed in Chapter 6, "Building and Maintaining Good Credit.") Many college students are temporarily insolvent, and that's okay because their earning capacity suggests that in only a few years their net worth will change for the better.

Debt Service-to-Income Ratio: Can I Meet My Total Debt Obligations?

debt service-to-income ratio
Compares dollars spent on gross annual debt.

The **debt service-to-income ratio** provides a view of your total debt burden by comparing the dollars spent on gross annual debt repayments (including rent or mortgage payments) with gross annual income. A ratio of 0.36 or less is desirable. Using data in Table 3.5, Equation (3.5) shows that the Hernandezes' $16,400 in annual loan repayments ($12,000 for the mortgage loan and $4400 for the automobile loan) amount to 24.85 percent of their $66,000 annual income. A ratio of 0.36 or less indicates that gross income is adequate to make debt repayments, including housing costs, and implies that you usually have some flexibility in budgeting for other expenses. This ratio should decrease as you grow older.

$$\text{Debt service-to-income ratio} = \frac{\text{annual debt repayments}}{\text{gross income}} \qquad (3.5)$$
$$= \frac{\$16,400}{\$66,000}$$
$$= 24.85\%$$

Debt Payments-to-Disposable Income Ratio: Can I Pay My Debts?

debt payments-to-disposable income ratio
Divides monthly disposable income into monthly debt repayments.

disposable income
Amount of income remaining after taxes and withholding; estimates funds available for debt repayment.

The **debt payments-to-disposable income ratio** divides monthly disposable personal income (not gross income) into monthly debt repayments (excluding mortgage debt). **Disposable income** is the amount of your income remaining after taxes and withholdings for such purposes as insurance and union dues. It estimates funds available for debt repayment. A ratio of 15 percent or less is desirable. A debt payments-to-disposable income ratio of 16 percent or more is considered problematic because the person is making high debt payments and quickly would be in serious financial trouble if a disruption in income occurred.

In the Hernandezes' case, their disposable monthly income from Table 3.5 is $3932.50 ([$66,000 − $2980 − $6800 − $3100 − $720 − $4260 − $950] ÷ 12). Their monthly debt repayments from Table 3.5 are $366.67 ($4400 ÷ 12). The result using Equation (3.6) is a debt payments-to-disposable income ratio of 9.32 percent.

$$\text{Debt payments-to-disposable income ratio} = \frac{\text{monthly nonmortgage debt repayments}}{\text{disposable income}} \qquad (3.6)$$
$$= \frac{\$366.67}{\$3932.50}$$
$$= 9.32\%$$

Investment Assets-to-Total Assets Ratio: Do I Need to Invest More?

investment assets-to-total assets ratio
Compares investment asset value with total assets.

The **investment assets-to-total assets ratio** compares the value of your investment assets with your total assets. This ratio reveals how well an individual or family is advancing toward their financial goals for capital accumulation, especially as related to retirement. A ratio of 50 percent or higher is desirable. A ratio of 10 percent might be appropriate for people in their 20s, 11 to 30 percent for those in their 30s, and above 30 percent for people in their 40s. Inserting the data from their balance sheet in Table 3.3 into Equation (3.7) shows that the Hernandezes have a ratio of 0.352 or 35.2 percent. As you can see, a little more than one-third of their total assets is made up of investment assets, a typical proportion for this stage in their lives.

$$\text{Investment assets-to-total assets ratio} = \frac{\text{investment assets}}{\text{total assets}} \qquad (3.7)$$

$$= \frac{\$109{,}000}{\$309{,}920}$$

$$= 0.352$$

Other Ways to Assess Financial Progress

You can use other data from your balance sheet and cash-flow statement to help analyze your finances. Consider the assets listed on the balance sheet for Victor and Maria Hernandez in Table 3.3. Do they have too few monetary assets compared with tangible and investment assets? Experts recommend that 15 to 20 percent of your assets be in monetary form and that this proportion increase as you near retirement. Do you have too much invested in one asset, or have you diversified, like the Hernandezes? Have your balance sheet figures changed in a favorable direction since last year? Is a growing proportion of your income coming from your investments? Are you making progress toward your financial goals? If not, ask: "Am I spending money where I really want to?," "In which categories can I reduce expenses?," and "Could I increase income?"

 Concept Check 3.3

1. Distinguish between the basic liquidity ratio and the asset-to-debt ratio.
2. Distinguish between the debt service-to-income ratio and the debt payments-to-disposable income ratio.
3. What can changes over time in your investment assets-to-total assets ratio tell you about your progress in reaching financial goals?

Financial Record Keeping Saves Time and Makes You Money

Financial records are documents that evidence financial transactions, such as bills, receipts, credit card receipts and statements, bank records, tax returns, brokerage statements, and paycheck stubs. Your financial records will help determine where you are, where you have been, and where you are going financially. They also help you save money as well as make money. Good records enable you to review the results of financial transactions as well as permit other family members to find them in an emergency. Organized records help you take advantage of all available tax deductions when filing income taxes and provide you with more dollars to spend, save, invest, or donate. Table 3.6 shows categories of financial records and the contents that might be included in each. Some records may be safely stored at home in a fire-resistant file cabinet or a safe. Other records should be kept in a **safe-deposit box.** Safe-deposit boxes are secured lock boxes available for rent ($50 to $250 per year) in banks. Two keys are used

4 Learning Objectives
Maintain the financial records necessary for managing your personal finances.

financial records
Documents that evidence financial transactions.

Table 3.6   Financial Records: What to Keep and Where

Category	Contents	
	In Home Files and Fireproof Home Safe	**In Safe-Deposit Box**
Financial plans/budgeting	Financial plans Balance sheets and cash-flow statements Current budget List of safe-deposit box contents Names and contact information for financial advisers	Names and contact information for financial advisers Copy of written financial plans, goals, and budgets
Career and employment	Current résumé College transcripts Letters of recommendation Employee benefits descriptions Written career plans	
Banking and financial services	Checkbook, unused checks, and canceled checks List of locations and account numbers for all bank accounts Checking and savings account statements Locations and access numbers for safe-deposit boxes Account transaction receipts	List of financial institutions and account numbers for all financial services accounts Certificates of deposit
Taxes	Copies of all income tax returns, both state and federal, for the past three years, including all supporting documentation Receipts for all donations of cash or property Log of volunteer expenses Receipts for property taxes paid	Copies of all income tax filings, both state and federal, for the past three years Records of securities purchased and sold
Credit	Utility and telephone bills Monthly credit card statements Receipts of credit payments List of credit accounts and telephone numbers to report lost/stolen cards Unused credit cards Credit reports and scores	List of credit accounts and telephone numbers to report lost/stolen cards
Housing, vehicles, and consumer purchases	Copies of legal documents (leases, mortgage, deeds, titles) Property appraisals and inspection reports Home repair/home improvement receipts Warranties Owners manuals for purchases Auto registration records Vehicle service and repair receipts Receipts for important purchases	Original legal documents (leases, mortgage, deeds, titles) Copies of property appraisals Vehicle purchase contracts (until vehicle is sold) Photographs or videos of valuable possessions

Table 3.6 *(Continued)*

	Contents	
Category	**In Home Files and Fireproof Home Safe**	**In Safe-Deposit Box**
Insurance	Original insurance policies List of insurance policies with premium amounts and due dates Premium payment receipts Calculation of life insurance needs Insurance claims forms and reports Medical records for family, including immunization records and list of prescription drugs	List of all insurance policies with company and agent names and addresses and policy numbers Listing with photographs or videotape of personal property
Investments	Records of stock, bond, and mutual fund transactions and certificate numbers Mutual fund statements Statements from brokers Reports from financial planner Company annual reports Retirement plan quarterly and annual reports Documents on business interests Written investment philosophy Written investment strategies	Contact information for all investment needs Stock and bond certificates Rare coins, stamps, and other collectibles
Retirement	Pension and retirement plan information Retirement statements Copies of all retirement plan transactions Copy of Social Security card Trust agreements Information on Social Security	Extra copy of all retirement plan transactions and statements
Estate planning	Copy of will Copies of advance directives (wills, living wills, medical powers of attorney, durable powers of attorney with originals with attorney) Copies of trust documents (originals with trustees/attorney)	Copy of will (original of all estate planning documents should be placed in attorney's office)
Personal information	Copy of birth certificate and marriage license Religious documents Copy of divorce decree, property settlement, and custody agreement Receipts for alimony and child support payments Custodial information for your children, relatives, and/or elderly parent	Passports while not being used Military and adoption papers Originals of birth, marriage, death certificates Originals of Social Security cards Originals of divorce decrees, property settlements, and custody agreements Master list of all important documents and their location Memory stick or CD containing soft copies of many financial records

to open such a box. The customer keeps one key, and the bank holds the other. Many people keep duplicates of important records at their workplace or with relatives because the likelihood of records at both locations being stolen or destroyed simultaneously is very small. You can purge or shred some of your records when you no longer need them, such as non-tax-related checks and credit card receipts more than a year old, expired insurance policies, and financial reports when supplanted with updated summary information.

 Concept Check 3.4

1. List some advantages of keeping good financial records.
2. Name three financial records that might best be kept in a safe-deposit box.

Reaching Your Goals Through Budgeting: Your Spending/ Savings Action Plan

5 Learning Objectives

Achieve your financial goals through budgeting.

Your financial success is largely a matter of choice, not a matter of chance. Your budget is where you make and implement those choices. Your budget is your plan for spending and saving. Budgeting forces you to consider what is important in your life, what things you want to own, how you want to live, what it will take to do that, and, more generally, what you want

 Advice from a Pro...

Get-Tough Ways to Cut Your Spending

If you always run out of money before the month is over, you may need to take some drastic steps to get your finances under control. Consider the following:

1. Stop paying bank fees by maintaining minimum balances and eliminating overdrafts.
2. Stop making ATM withdrawals.
3. Stop getting cash back from debit or credit card purchases to use for pocket money.
4. Spend only cash or money that you have, and leave debit and credit cards at home.
5. Stop using credit cards.
6. Refinance credit card debt at a credit union.
7. Do not eat out.
8. Cut back on excessive telephone use.
9. Don't pay for entertainment, rather do activities that are free.
10. Reduce or stop spending on luxuries such as clothing, movies, entertainment, memberships, hobbies, CDs, DVDs, and expanded cable channels.

11. Drop landline telephone service and use only a cell phone.
12. Find cheaper auto insurance.
13. Increase your 401(k) retirement contribution as it reduces income taxes.
14. Change income tax withholding to increase take-home pay.
15. Use a list when shopping, and stick to it.
16. Avoid shopping malls and discount stores.
17. Sell an asset, especially one that requires additional expenses, such as a boat or second car.
18. Build up an emergency fund of savings even if it means temporarily decreasing retirement-plan contributions.
19. Only buy used.
20. Make Christmas a nonspend holiday.
21. Move to lower-cost housing.
22. Increase income by working overtime or finding a second job.

Alena C. Johnson
Utah State University

to achieve in life. The budgeting process gives you control over your finances, and it empowers you to achieve your financial goals while simultaneously (and successfully) confronting any unforeseen events. In short, budgeting answers the question, "What is my spending/savings action plan?"

Some people do all their budgeting mentally—and do so successfully. Good for them! Many of us, however, need to see the actual numbers on paper or on a computer screen. A **budget** is a paper or electronic document used to record both planned and actual income and expenditures over a period of time. Your budget represents the major mechanism through which your financial plans are carried out and goals are achieved. The CNN/Money website provides an example (www.cgi.money.cnn.com/tools/budget101/budget_101.jsp) of online budgeting.

Figure 3.4 illustrates how to think about financial statements and budgeting. The cash-flow statement focuses on *where you have been* financially, the balance sheet shows *where you are* financially at the current time, and the budget indicates *where you want to go* in the future.

Action Before: Set Financial Goals

Creating and following a spending plan has three stages: before, during, and after. Before establishing your budget, take action to set financial goals. **Long-term goals** are financial targets or ends that an individual or family wants to achieve perhaps more than five years in the future. Such goals provide direction for overall financial planning as well as shorter-term budgeting. An example of a long-term goal is to create a $1 million retirement fund by age 60. Goals must be specific. They should contain dollar-amount targets and target dates for achievement.

If you have a small income or large debts, it may be unrealistic to think of long-term goals until any current financial difficulties are resolved. You may be unable to do much more than take care of immediate necessities, such as housing expenses, food, and utility bills. In such instances, you need to focus on short-term efforts to improve your financial situation. You may need to focus on paying down debt, not adding to it.

Instant Message

The Single Secret of Budgeting Success

With some money in emergency savings, perhaps $500 or $2000, to pay for vehicle repairs and unexpected travel, you never will have to pay with plastic for things that are not in your budget.

budget
Paper or electronic document used to record both planned and actual income and expenditures over a period of time.

Instant Message

Rules for Successful Budgeting

Keep it simple

Make it personal

Keep it flexible

Be positive

long-term goals
Financial targets to achieve more than five years in the future.

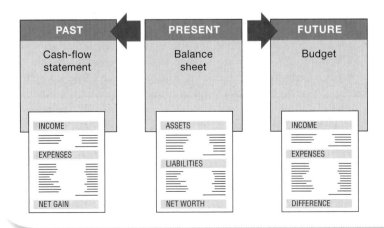

Figure 3.4
About Financial Statements and Budgets

Instant Message

Track Your Spending Online for Free

Instead of using a pad, pencil, and calculator to track your spending try a free website that offers budgeting functions. See Buxfer (www.buxfer.com), Geezeo (www.geezeo.com), Mint (www.mint.com), Wesabe (www.wesabe.com), and YodleeMoneyCenter (www.yodlee.com).

Instant Message

Compare Your Spending with Others

To compare your spending with that of people like you, describe your situation on the CNNMoney website at www.cgi.money.cnn.com/tools/instantbudget/instantbudget_101.jsp.

Instant Message

List the Benefits of Reaching Your Financial Goals

List the benefits to yourself that will occur when you reach a particular financial goal. You are likely to achieve a financial goal when you are convinced that it is "your goal," when you make an emotional commitment to the goal, when your short-term goals lead to your long-term goals, and when you can visualize receiving the benefits of your goals.

intermediate-term goals
Financial targets that can be achieved within one to five years.

budget estimates
Projected dollar amounts to receive or spend in a budgeting period.

Establishing unrealistic short-term goals sets up a high likelihood of failure. Instead, set financial targets that are almost too easy to meet. For example, you may want to save $350 per month to use as a down payment on a home in five years. That may seem like a lot. Start perhaps painlessly by saving $100 per month for a few months. Then put away $150 for two months, $200 for two months, then $250, then $300, and finally $350 so that by the end of the first year you are on target.

Intermediate-term goals are financial targets that can be achieved between one year and perhaps three to five years. Examples of intermediate-term goals are creating an emergency fund amounting to three months of income within four years, saving $22,500 within three years for a down payment on a home, taking a $4000 vacation to China in two years, paying off $8000 in credit card debt in one and a half years, and paying off a college loan in five years. Short-term goals are financial targets or ends that can be achieved in less than a year, such as finishing college, paying off an auto loan, increasing savings, purchasing assets (i.e., vehicle, furniture, television, stereo, clothes), reducing high-interest debt, taking an annual vacation, attending a wedding, buying life insurance, and making plans for retirement.

You need to be as clear as possible about what your financial goals are. The goals worksheet in Figure 3.5 provides examples of how much to save to reach long-, intermediate-, and short-term goals. People can view such savings as a fixed expenditure (such as withholding from a paycheck to contribute to an employer's retirement plan or to transfer to a savings account). Other savings may be a variable such as saving what is left over after all expenditures are made.

Prioritizing your goals makes sense. But what are your most important goals? One certain priority should be to pay off high-interest credit cards as soon as possible. Another is to contribute as much as you can afford to a retirement plan. Many college graduates buy a new car soon after getting their first job to celebrate having "made it." Before you're lured into following suit, give careful consideration to your priorities and remember that every action carries not only the dollar cost of the action taken but also the opportunity cost of the alternatives forgone. To achieve your long-term goals, you may have to sacrifice by deferring some of your short-term desires.

Action Before: Make and Reconcile Budget Estimates

Before the month begins, you make and reconcile budget estimates of income and expenditures. Here you resolve conflicting needs and wants by revising estimates as necessary. You can't have everything in life—especially this month—even though you might want it.

Make Budget Estimates **Budget estimates** are the projected dollar amounts in a budget that one plans to receive or spend during the period covered by the budget. Begin by estimating total gross income from all sources, and review take-home pay and then discretionary income. For example, Jonny Deppe's annual gross income is $60,000 and after employer withholdings for taxes, insurance, and union dues, his **take-home pay** (also called disposable income) is $48,000. This is the money available for spending, saving, investing, and donating. Focus also on your **discretionary income.** This is the money left over once the

Date worksheet prepared Feb. 20, 2010

1 LONG-TERM GOALS	2 AMOUNT NEEDED	3 MONTH & YEAR NEEDED*	4 MONTHS TO SAVE	5 DATE START SAVING	6 MONTHLY AMOUNT TO SAVE (2 ÷ 4)
European vacation	$3,000	Aug. 2012	30	Feb. '10	$100
Down payment on new auto	5,000	Oct. 2013	45	Jan. '10	111

Date worksheet prepared Feb. 20, 2010

1 INTERMEDIATE-TERM GOALS	2 AMOUNT NEEDED	3 MONTH & YEAR NEEDED*	4 MONTHS TO SAVE	5 DATE START SAVING	6 MONTHLY AMOUNT TO SAVE (2 ÷ 4)
Down payment on home	$26,078	Dec. 2014	60	Jan. '10	$435

Date worksheet prepared Feb. 20, 2010

1 SHORT-TERM GOALS	2 AMOUNT NEEDED	3 MONTH & YEAR NEEDED*	4 MONTHS TO SAVE	5 DATE START SAVING	6 MONTHLY AMOUNT TO SAVE (2 ÷ 4)
Partial down payment on new auto	$1,332	Dec. '10	12	Jan. '10	$111
House fund	4,815	Dec. '10	12	Jan. '10	401
Christmas vacation	700	Dec. '10	12	Jan. '10	58
Summer vacation	600	Aug. '10	6	Mar. '10	100
Anniversary party	250	June '10	5	Feb. '10	50

*Goals requiring five years or more to achieve require consideration of investment return and after-tax yield, which will be presented in Chapter 4.

Figure 3.5
Goals Worksheet for Harry and Belinda Johnson

necessities of living are covered, such as paying for housing, food, and other necessities. It is usually the money that is really "controllable" and often makes up the bulk of money available to pay for one's variable expenses. After Jonny pays his rent, food, utilities, and car payment, his discretionary income is $18,000.

Table 3.7 presents budget estimates for a college student, a single working person, a young married couple, a married couple with two young children, and a married couple with two college-age children. The college student's budget requires monthly withdrawals of previously deposited savings to make ends meet. The single working person's budget allows for an automobile loan, but not much else. The young married couple's budget permits one automobile loan, an investment program, contributions to individual retirement accounts, and significant spending on food and entertainment. The budget of the married couple with two young children allows for only an inexpensive automobile loan payment even though one spouse has a parttime job to help with the finances. The budget of the married couple with two college-age children permits a home mortgage payment, ownership of two paid-for automobiles, savings and investment programs, and a substantial contribution for college expenses.

take-home pay/disposable income
Pay received after employer withholdings for taxes, insurance, and union dues.

discretionary income
Money left over after necessities such as housing and food are paid for.

Table 3.7   Sample Monthly Budgets for Various Family Units

Classifications	College Student	Single Working Person	Young Married Couple	Married Couple with Two Young Children	Married Couple with Two College-Age Children
INCOME					
Salary	300	2,800	2,200	3,500	4,400
Salary	0	0	2,100	860	1,600
Interest and dividends	5	15	15	15	80
Loans/scholarships	300	0	0	0	0
Savings withdrawals	570	0	0	0	500
Total Income	$1,175	$2,815	$4,315	$4,375	$6,580
EXPENSES					
Fixed Expenses					
Retirement contributions	$ 0	$ 20	$ 360	$ 180	$ 340
IRA	0	20	160	180	200
Savings (withheld)	0	20	20	10	100
Housing	350	750	900	1,100	1,300
Health insurance	0	0	60	150	140
Life and disability insurance	0	0	20	60	40
Homeowner's or renter's insurance	0	0	40	60	80
Automobile insurance	0	80	90	60	140
Automobile payments	0	280	345	220	0
Loan 1 (TV and stereo)	0	80	80	40	0
Loan 2 (other)	0	40	40	0	50
Federal and state taxes	30	455	715	600	710
Social Security taxes	23	210	330	305	385
Real estate taxes	0	0	0	0	40
Investments	0	0	60	100	300
Total fixed expenses	$ 403	$1,955	$3,220	$3,065	$3,825
Variable Expenses					
Other savings	$ 0	$ 60	$ 150	$ 0	$ 0
Food	180	230	270	340	350
Utilities	40	80	90	140	145
Automobile gas, oil, maintenance	0	90	110	90	100
Medical	10	30	40	70	50
Child care	0	0	0	260	0
Clothing	20	50	60	50	40
Gifts and contributions	10	20	40	60	80
Allowances	20	75	60	100	180
Education	400	0	0	0	1,500
Furnishing and appliances	10	10	30	20	20
Personal care	10	45	25	30	30
Entertainment	40	120	100	60	120
Vacations	17	30	40	30	60
Miscellaneous	15	20	80	60	80
Total variable expenses	$ 772	$ 860	$1,095	$1,310	$2,755
Total Expenses	$1,175	$2,815	$4,315	$4,375	$6,580

It is essential to make reasonable budget estimates. If you have seven Christmas gifts to buy and expect to spend $50 for each, it's easy to make an estimate of $350. If you want to go out to dinner once each week at $50 per meal, estimate an expense of $200 per month. Avoid using unrealistically low figures by simply being fair and honest in your estimates. Then add up your totals.

Revise Budget Estimates When trying to make your spending conform with your budget goals sometimes you will find the math is alarming! When initial expense estimates exceed income estimates, three choices are available: (1) earn more income, (2) cut back on expenses, or (3) try a combination of more income and fewer expenses. The process of reconciling needs and wants is a healthy exercise. It helps identify your priorities by telling you what is important in your life at the current time, and it identifies areas of sacrifice that you might make. Revising your short-term financial goals may also be required.

You have no choice: You must reconcile conflicting wants to revise your budget until total expenses do not exceed income. Perhaps you can change some "must have" items to "maybe next year" purchases. Perhaps you can keep some quality items but reduce their quantity. For example, instead of $200 for four meals at restaurants each month, consider dining out twice each month at $60 per meal. You'll save $40 and still have two really nice meals. Your actions on money matters override your words, so act accordingly.

Table 3.8 presents the annual budget for Harry and Belinda Johnson and reflects their efforts to reconcile their budget estimates until the total planned expenses fall below the total planned income. Harry and Belinda are "paying themselves first," in the amount of $400 per month, to save to buy their own home. The Johnsons have a little way to go to fully reconcile their annual budget estimates.

Action Before: Plan Cash Flows

Before the month begins, you plan your cash flows. Income usually remains somewhat constant month after month, but expenses do rise and fall sharply. As a result, people occasionally complain that they are "broke, out of money, and sick of budgeting." This challenge can be anticipated by using a cash-flow calendar and eliminated with a revolving savings fund.

The budget estimates for monthly income and expenses in Table 3.8 have been recast in summary form in Table 3.9, providing a **cash-flow calendar** for the Johnsons. This is a very useful budgeting tool. Annual estimated income and expenses are recorded in this calendar for each budgeting time period in an effort to identify surplus or deficit situations. In the Johnsons' case, planned annual income exceeds expenses. The couple starts out the year with many expenses, resulting in deficits for the next six months. Later in the year, income usually exceeds expenses, but they are still faced with a deficit at year's end.

Effective management of cash flow can involve curtailing expenses during months with financial deficits, increasing income, using savings, or borrowing. If you borrow money and pay finance charges, the credit costs will further increase your monthly expenses.

For this reason alone, it is smart to "borrow from yourself" by using a **revolving savings fund.** This is a variable expense classification budgeting tool into which funds are allocated in an effort to create savings that can be used to balance the budget later so as to avoid running out of money. Establishing such a fund involves planning ahead—much like a college student does when saving money all summer (creating a revolving savings fund) to

Instant Message

Cut the Dollars Not the Pennies

Harvard law professor and bankruptcy expert Elizabeth Warren says that you should not cut out the café lattes to manage your money better. Instead of making penny cuts, enjoy the coffee and then make real dollar cuts elsewhere in your spending such as in housing, cars, preschool, child care, and health care. And cut back on the credit card charges.

Did You Know?

The Top 3 Financial Missteps in Budget Planning

People slip up in budget planning when they do the following:

1. Fail to plan for occasional, nonmonthly expenditures
2. Underestimate how much they spend each month
3. Use credit cards to "balance" their budget

cash-flow calendar
Budget estimates for monthly income and expenses.

revolving savings fund
Variable budgeting tool that places funds in savings to cover emergency or higher-than-usual expenses.

Table 3.8   Annual Budget Estimates for Harry and Belinda Johnson

	Jan.	Feb.	Mar.	Apr.	May	June	July	Aug.	Sept.	Oct.	Nov.	Dec.	Yearly Total	Monthly Average
INCOME														
Harry's salary	2,500	2,500	2,500	2,500	2,500	2,500	2,575	2,575	2,575	2,575	2,575	2,575	30,450	2,537.50
Belinda's salary	3,000	3,000	3,300	3,300	3,300	3,300	3,300	3,300	3,300	3,300	3,300	3,300	39,000	3,250.00
Interest	24	24	24	25	26	27	27	28	30	31	33	33	332	27.67
Trust	0	0	0	0	0	0	0	0	3,000	0	0	0	3,000	250.00
TOTAL INCOME	$5,524	$5,524	$5,824	$5,825	$5,826	$5,827	$5,902	$5,903	$8,905	$5,906	$5,908	$5,908	$72,782	$6,065.17
EXPENSES														
Fixed Expenses														
Rent	900	900	900	900	900	900	950	950	950	950	950	950	11,100	925.00
Health insurance	135	135	135	135	135	135	135	135	135	135	135	135	1,620	135.00
Life insurance	9	9	9	9	9	9	9	9	9	9	9	9	108	9.00
Home purchase fund	400	400	400	400	400	400	400	400	400	400	400	400	4,800	400.00
Renter's insurance	0	0	0	0	0	220	0	0	0	0	0	0	220	18.33
Automobile insurance	0	0	0	0	0	440	0	0	0	0	0	440	880	73.33
Auto loan payment	285	285	285	285	285	285	285	285	285	285	285	285	3,420	285.00
Student loan	145	145	145	145	145	145	145	145	145	145	145	145	1,740	145.00
Savings/emergencies	24	24	70	150	85	150	150	28	150	150	150	150	1,281	106.75
Harry's retirement plan	150	150	150	150	150	150	154	154	154	154	154	154	1,824	152.00
Belinda's retirement	120	120	132	132	132	132	132	132	132	132	132	132	1,560	130.00
Internet	50	50	50	50	50	50	50	50	50	50	50	50	600	50.00
Cable television	35	35	35	35	35	35	35	35	35	35	35	35	420	35.00
Federal income taxes	767	767	848	848	848	848	854	854	854	854	854	854	10,050	837.50
State income taxes	266	266	284	284	284	284	289	289	289	289	289	289	3,402	283.50
Social Security	421	421	444	444	444	444	450	450	450	450	450	450	5,318	443.17
Total fixed expenses	$3,707	$3,707	$3,887	$3,967	$3,902	$4,627	$4,038	$3,916	$4,038	$4,038	$4,038	$4,478	$48,343	$4,028.58
Variable Expenses														
Savings/investments	0	0	0	0	0	0	0	0	3,000	0	0	0	3,000	250.00
Revolving savings fund	140	140	140	140	140	0	250	0	215	190	0	0	1,355	112.92
Food	350	350	350	350	350	350	350	350	350	350	350	350	4,200	350.00
Utilities	150	150	150	150	100	100	100	100	100	125	125	150	1,500	125.00
Telephones	70	70	70	70	70	70	70	70	70	70	70	90	860	71.67
Auto expenses	115	115	115	115	115	115	115	115	115	115	115	115	1,380	115.00
Medical	100	100	100	100	100	100	100	100	100	100	100	100	1,200	100.00
Clothing	180	180	180	180	180	180	180	180	180	180	180	180	2,160	180.00
Church and charity	100	100	100	100	175	100	100	100	100	100	100	100	1,275	106.25
Gifts	80	80	160	75	120	20	20	60	60	60	60	20	815	67.92
Christmas gifts	0	0	0	0	0	0	0	0	0	0	400	300	700	58.33
Public transportation	60	60	60	60	60	60	60	60	60	60	60	60	720	60.00
Personal allowances	200	200	200	200	200	200	200	200	200	200	200	200	2,400	200.00
Entertainment/meals	240	240	240	240	240	240	240	240	240	240	240	240	2,880	240.00
Automobile license	0	0	0	0	0	40	0	0	0	0	0	0	40	3.33
Vacation (Christmas)	0	0	0	0	0	0	0	0	0	0	0	700	700	58.33
Vacation (summer)	0	0	0	0	0	0	0	600	0	0	0	0	600	50.00
Anniversary party	0	0	0	0	0	250	0	0	0	0	0	0	250	20.83
Miscellaneous	32	32	72	78	74	75	79	62	77	78	75	75	809	67.42
Total variable expenses	$1,817	$1,817	$1,937	$1,858	$1,924	$1,900	$1,864	$2,237	$4,867	$1,868	$2,075	$2,680	$26,844	$2,237
TOTAL EXPENSES	$5,524	$5,524	$5,824	$5,825	$5,826	$6,527	$5,902	$6,153	$8,905	$5,906	$6,113	$7,158	$75,187	$6,265.58
Difference (available for spending, saving, and investing)	$ 0	$ 0	$ 0	$ 0	$ 0	−700	$ 0	−250	0	0	−205	−1,250	−2,405	
Revolving savings withdrawals						700		250			205	200	1,355	
Uncovered shortfall	$ 0	$ 0	$ 0	0	$ 0	$ 0	$ 0	$ 0	$ 0	$ 0	$ 0	$ 0	−$1,050	−$1,050

Table 3.9 Cash-Flow Calendar for Harry and Belinda Johnson

Month	1 Estimated Income	2 Estimated Expenses	3 Surplus/Deficit (1 – 2)	4 Cumulative Surplus/Deficit
January	$ 5,524	$ 5,524	0	0
February	5,524	5,524	0	0
March	5,824	5,824	0	0
April	5,825	5,825	0	0
May	5,826	5,826	0	0
June	5,827	6,527	−700	−700
July	5,902	5,902	0	−700
August	5,903	6,153	−250	−950
September	8,905	8,905	0	−950
October	5,906	5,906	0	−950
November	5,908	6,113	−205	−1,155
December	5,908	7,158	−1,250	−2,405
Total	$72,782	$75,187	−$2,405	

draw on during the school months. You establish a revolving savings fund for two purposes: (1) to accumulate funds for large irregular expenses, such as automobile insurance premiums, medical costs, Christmas gifts, and vacations; and (2) to meet occasional deficits due to income fluctuations.

Table 3.10 shows the Johnsons' revolving savings fund. When preparing their budget, the Johnsons realized that in June, August, November, and December they were going to have significant deficits. They decided to begin setting aside $140 per month to cover the June deficit. To do so, they decided to wait to start building their emergency fund. By June they had $700 in their revolving savings fund to cover the June deficit. Continued use of the revolving savings fund helped them meet the August and November deficits as well.

The Johnsons will still be $1050 short in December. Lacking that much money, the couple has three alternatives: (1) use some of Harry's trust fund money to cover the deficit, (2) dip into their emergency savings in December, or (3) cut back on their expenses enough throughout the year to create sufficient surpluses. Ideally, the Johnsons want to have sufficient emergency funds by the end of the year to establish their revolving savings fund for the following year. Cutting back on expenses may be their best option.

Action During Budgeting Period: Control Spending

Budget controls are techniques to maintain control over personal spending so that planned amounts are not exceeded. They give feedback on whether spending is on target and provide information on overspending, errors, emergencies, and exceptions or omissions. Following are examples of budget controls:

Monitor Unexpended Balances to Control Overspending The number one method to control overspending is to monitor unexpended balances in each of your budget classifications. You can accomplish this task by using a budget design that keeps a declining balance, as illustrated by parts (a) and (b) of Figure 3.6. Other budget designs, such as those shown in parts (c) and (d) of Figure 3.6, need to be monitored differently. As illustrated

Table 3.10   **Revolving Savings Fund for Harry and Belinda Johnson**

Month	Large Expenses	Amount Needed	Deposit into Fund	Withdrawal from Fund	Fund Balance
January		0	140	0	140
February		0	140	0	280
March		0	140	0	420
April		0	140	0	560
May		0	140	0	700
June	Party and insurance premiums	700	0	700	0
July		0	250	0	250
August	Vacation	250	0	250	0
September		0	215	0	215
October		0	190	0	405
November	Holiday gifts	205	0	205	200
December	Holiday gifts and vacation	1,250	0	200	0
Total		$2,405	$1,355	$1,355	−$1,050

To help keep to a budget, use your check register to keep track of purchases.

in parts (c) and (d) of the figure, simply calculate subtotals every week or so, as needed, during a monthly budgeting period.

Budget for Shopping Trips
Set a budget for every shopping trip, and don't spend a penny more.

Use a Subordinate Budget
subordinate budget
Detailed listing of planned expenses within a single budgeting classification.

A **subordinate budget** is a detailed listing of planned expenses within a single budgeting classification. For example, an estimate of $1200 for a vacation could be supported by a subordinate budget as follows: motel, $700; restaurants, $300; and entertainment, $200.

(a)

Food Budget: $90			
DATE	ACTIVITY	AMOUNT	BALANCE
2-6	Groceries	$20	$70
2-9	Dinner out	18	52
2-14	Groceries	11	

(b)

DATE	ACTIVITY	AMOUNT BUDGETED	EXPENDITURES	BALANCE
2-1	Budget estimate	$90		$90
2-6	Groceries		$20	70
2-9	Dinner out		18	52
2-14	Groceries		11	41
2-20	Groceries		25	16
2-28	February Totals	$90	$74	$16

(c)

DATE	ACTIVITY	Food Budget: $90	Clothing Budget: $30	EXPENDITURES Auto Budget: $60	Rent Budget: $275	Savings Budget: $60	Utilities Budget: $40	TOTAL Budget: $680	REMARKS
2-1	Gasoline			10				10	
2-6	Groceries	20						20	Had friends over
2-8	Gasoline			17				17	Good price
2-9	Dinner out	18						18	
2-14	Groceries	11						11	Pepsi on sale
2-15	Subtotals	/49		/27				/76	

(d)

		INCOME Salary	Other	TOTAL	EXPENDITURES Food	Clothing	Auto	Rent	Savings	Utilities	TOTAL	REMARKS
Estimates		700	40	740	90	30	60	275	60	40	680	
Balance forwarded from January		—	—	—	6	—	14	—	—	2	28	
Sum		700	40	740	96	30	74	275	60	42	708	

DATE	ACTIVITY	CASH IN										
2-1	Paycheck	700	700									
2-1	Texaco-gasoline						10				10	
2-6	Safeway-groceries				20						20	Had friends over
2-8	7/11-gasoline						17				17	Good price
2-9	Dinner out-pizza				18						18	
2-14	Giant-groceries				11						11	Pepsi on sale
2-15	Subtotals	/700			/49		/27				/76	
2-16	Cell phone									41	41	
2-28	Totals	700		40	740	83	28	27	275	60	41	660	Good month

Figure 3.6
Record-Keeping Formats

Pay by Check to Record the Purpose of Expenditures

Each check contains a space to record the purpose. The check stub or register also provides a place to record explanations of expenditures. If you use automatic teller machines (ATMs) to withdraw cash or use debit cards to pay for day-to-day expenditures, record these withdrawals in the check register *immediately*. Retain the paperwork and write the purpose of each expense on the back of each. Deposit all checks received to your checking account without receiving a portion in cash; if you need cash, write a check or make an ATM withdrawal.

Keep Track of Credit Transactions

Some people do not record their credit transactions until they receive a statement. It is easy to continue buying on credit without recognizing the amount of indebtedness until the statement arrives. Record each credit transaction when it occurs; if you misplace a receipt, you still have a record available for verification.

budget exceptions
When budget estimates differ from actual expenditures.

Justify Exceptions to Avoid Lying to Yourself

Budget exceptions occur when budget estimates in various classifications differ from actual expenditures. Exceptions usually take the form of overexpenditures, but can also occur in the over- or underreceipt of earnings. Simply spending extra income instead of recording it is not being honest with yourself. Recording the truth—by writing a few words to explain the exception—gives you the information to control your finances. If the exception is an expenditure, then immediately determine how to make up for the overexpenditure by reducing other expenses in your spending plan.

envelope system
Placing exact amounts into envelopes for each budgetary purpose.

For the Strongest Control, Use the Envelope System

The **envelope system** of budgeting entails placing exact amounts of money into envelopes for purposes of strict budgetary control. Here you place money equal to the budget estimate for the various expenditure classifications in envelopes at the start of a budgeting period and write the classification name and the budget amount on the outside of each envelope. As expenditures are made, record them on the appropriate envelope and remove the proper amounts of cash. When an envelope is empty, funds are exhausted for that classification.

Action After: Evaluate Budgeting Progress

Evaluation occurs at the end of each budgeting cycle. The purpose is to determine whether the earlier steps in your budgeting efforts have worked, and it gives you feedback to use for the next budget cycle. You review by comparing actual amounts with budgeted amounts, evaluating whether your objectives were met, and assessing the success of the overall process as well as your progress toward your short- and long-term goals.

In some budget expenditure classifications, the budget estimates rarely agree with the actual expenditures—particularly in variable expenses. A **budget variance** is the difference between the amount budgeted and the actual amount spent or received. The remarks column, as illustrated in parts (c) and (d) of Figure 3.6 (page 93), can help clarify why variances occurred. Overages on a few expenditures may cause little concern. If excessive variances have prevented you from achieving your objectives or making the budget balance, then take some action. Serious budget controls might have to be instituted or current controls tightened.

Whatever your goals, it feels good when you make progress toward them, and it is thrilling to achieve them. If you did not achieve some of your objectives, you can determine why and then adjust your budget and objectives accordingly. It is okay to revise your plans. Suppose the Johnsons find that they are unable to set aside the planned $400 for their new home. By evaluating their budget, they find that unexpected

Instant Message

Before You Buy

If you want to *save $1,000* this year, ask yourself these questions before you buy!

1. Did I plan to buy this?
2. If I have to pay cash, do I still want it?
3. What will happen if I don't buy this?
4. Do I need this... or just want it?

Source: Created by the LFE Institute, a corporate skill-based financial literacy curriculum developer. Copyright © LFE Institute, www.lfeinstitute.com.

medical expenses and an out-of-state trip to visit a sick relative led them to dip into their savings. Because they understand why the objective was not achieved, they can set their sights on reaching the goal during the next budgeting time period.

Financial Software Tools to Manage Your Money

Financial software and planning tools, including many on the Internet, make managing your money—including record keeping—a snap. Financial software offers many benefits. Laborious calculations are sharply reduced, banking transactions can be performed with automatic updating of financial records, the balance sheet and cash-flow statements are automatically updated when transactions occur, and your financial plans can be developed.

Some comprehensive Web portals on personal finances are Yahoo! Finance (www .finance.yahoo.com), MSN Money Central (www.moneycentral.com), and Quicken .com (www.quicken.com). You will find all kinds of easy-to-use financial tools, including bill paying, banking, vehicle loan rate comparisons, mortgage shopping, online tax preparation, stock screening, stock quotes, online brokers, retirement calculators, and breaking news stories. (See also www.CNNmoney.com, www.Fool.com, www .Kiplinger.com, www.USAToday.com, www.Yahoo.com, http://www.yodlee.com, and www.Mint.com.

Record Keeping In the process of budgeting, **record keeping** is the process of recording the sources and amounts of dollars earned and spent. Recording the estimated and actual amounts for both income and expenditures helps you monitor your money flow. Keeping track of income and expenses is the only way to collect sufficient information to evaluate how close you are to achieving your financial objectives. For those who keep records on paper, Figure 3.6 shows four samples of self-prepared record-keeping formats that vary in complexity. Most people record earnings and expenditures when they occur. When writing in the "activity" and "remarks" columns in your record, be descriptive because you may need the information later.

Adding Up Actual Income and Expenditures After the budgeting period has ended—usually at the beginning of a new month—you need to add up the actual income received and expenditures made during that period. You can perform this calculation on a form for each budget classification, as shown in parts (a) and (b) of Figure 3.6 or on a form with all income and expenditure classifications, as in parts (c) and (d) of Figure 3.6. Such calculations indicate where you may have overspent within your budget categories. If you are new at budgeting, do not be too concerned about overspending; it occurs in some classifications almost always, only to be balanced by underspending in other categories. Use such information to refine your budget estimates in the future. In three or four months, you will be able to estimate your expenses much more accurately. The *Garman/Forgue* companion website provides budgeting software as well as numerous other templates, calculators, and worksheets that you can use in your own personal financial planning.

What to Do with Budgeted Money Left over at the End of the Month At the end of the budgeting time period, some budget classifications may still have a positive balance. For example, perhaps you estimated the electric bill at $100, but it was only $80. You may then ask, "What do I do with the $20 surplus?" You also may ask, "What happens to budget classifications that were overspent?"

People handle the **net surplus** (the amount remaining after all budget classification deficits are subtracted from those with surpluses) in any of the following ways:

- Carry the surpluses forward
- Put into a revolving savings fund

budget variance
Difference between amount budgeted and actual amount spent or received.

record keeping
Recording sources and amounts of dollars earned and spent.

net surplus
Amount remaining after all budget classification deficits are subtracted from those with surpluses.

Do It Now!

Financial success requires getting your spending under control. Start today by:

1. Putting a note pad in your pocket to record every single expense of $1 or more for one month.
2. Preparing a cash-flow statement at the end of the month.
3. Setting up a spending plan for the next month that provides for savings for at least one of your goals.

Instant Message

Become an Un-Consumer

The Compact is an online group that supports each other in their efforts to avoid unnecessary consumption. See www.groups.yahoo.com/group/thecompact.

- Build a cash reserve by depositing in a savings account
- Pay down credit card debt
- Put toward a mortgage or other loan
- Invest in a retirement account
- Spend like "made money"

The budgeting form in part (d) of Figure 3.6 (page 93) allows for carrying balances forward to the next period. Some people carry forward deficits, with the hope that having less available in a budgeted classification the following month will motivate them to keep expenditures low. Because variable expense estimates are usually averages, it is best not to change the estimate based on a variation that occurs over just one or two months. If estimates are too high or low for a longer period, you will want to make adjustments.

Using financial software for budgeting takes the drudgery out of making and using a spending plan. And it gets to be easy after a few months. Budgeting can help you succeed financially.

Did You Know?

Wealth-Building Principles

1. Set clear financial goals both in the short and long term.
2. Save by paying yourself first out of your paycheck.
3. Pay credit card balances in full each month.
4. Spend less than you earn.
5. Participate in the retirement plan at work and/or through an IRA.
6. Take full advantage of your employer's match on retirement savings.
7. Buy a home for the tax advantages.
8. Pay off your home before retirement.
9. Be patient when investing for the long term.
10. Live every day knowing that your financial future is under control.

Concept Check 3.5

1. Identify two actions that should be performed before establishing a budget.

2. What are budget estimates and offer some suggestions on how to go about making budget estimates for various types of expenses.

3. Distinguish between a cash-flow calendar and a revolving savings fund, and tell why each is important.

4. Offer three suggestions for effective budget controls.

What Do You Recommend NOW?

Now that you have read the chapter on financial planning, what do you recommend to Robert for his talk with Nicole on the subject of financial planning regarding:

Tara Moore/Getty Images

1. Determining what they own and owe?

2. Better understanding their patterns of family income and expenditure?

3. Using the information in Robert's newly prepared financial statements to summarize the family's financial situation?

4. Setting financial goals?

5. Evaluating their financial progress?

6. Setting up a record-keeping system to better serve their needs?

7. Starting a budgeting process to guide saving and spending?

Big Picture Summary of Learning Objectives

1 Identify your financial values, goals, and strategies.

By identifying your financial values, goals, and strategies, you can always keep a balance between spending and saving and stay committed to your financial success. You may create financial plans in three broad areas: plans for spending, plans for risk management, and plans for capital accumulation.

2 Use balance sheets and cash-flow statements to measure your financial health and progress.

Financial statements are compilations of personal financial data designed to furnish information on money matters. The balance sheet provides information on what you own, what you owe, and what the net result would be if you paid off all your debts. The cash-flow statement lists income and expenditures over a specific period of time, such as the previous month or year.

3 Evaluate your financial strength and progress using financial ratios.

Financial ratios are numerical calculations designed to simplify the process of evaluating your financial strength and the progress of your financial condition. Ratios serve as tools or yardsticks to develop saving, spending, and credit-use patterns consistent with your goals.

4 Maintain the financial records necessary for managing your personal finances.

Your financial records will help determine where you are, where you have been, and where you are going financially. They also help you make money.

5 Achieve your financial goals through budgeting.

Budgeting is all about logical thinking about your finances. Budgeting forces you to consider what is important in your life, what things you want to own, how you want to live, what it will take to do that, and, more generally, what you want to achieve in life. A budget is a process used to record both projected and actual income and expenditures over a period of time, and it represents the major mechanism through which your financial plans are carried out and goals are achieved.

Let's Talk About It

1. **Families.** During slugging economic times the federal government's budgeting priority is to spend much more money than it takes in. What happens to families that try that, and why?

2. **Your Values.** What are your three most important personal values? Give an example of how each of those values might influence your financial plans.

3. **Cash Flow.** College students often have little income and many expenses. Does this reduce or increase the importance of completing a cash-flow statement on a monthly basis? Why?

4. **Financial Ratios.** Of the financial ratios described in this chapter, which two might be most revealing for the typical college student? Which two are the most revealing for a retiree?

5. **Why Budget.** Do you have a budget? Why or why not? What do you think are the major reasons why people do not make formal budgets?

6. **Budgeting Mistake.** What is the biggest budget-related mistake that you have made? What would you do differently?

Do the Math

1. **Ratio Analyses.** Review the financial statements of Victor and Maria Hernandez (Table 3.3 and Table 3.5) and respond to the following questions:

   (a) Using the data in the Hernandezes' balance sheet, calculate an investment assets-to-net worth ratio. How would you interpret the ratio? The Hernandez family appears to have too few monetary assets compared with tangible and investment assets. How would you suggest that they remedy that situation over the next few years?

   (b) Comment on the couple's diversification of their investment assets.

   (c) Calculate the asset-to-debt ratio for Victor and Maria. How does this information help you understand their financial situation? How do their total assets compare with their total liabilities?

   (d) The Hernandezes seem to receive most of their income from labor rather than investments. What actions would you recommend for them to remedy that imbalance over the next few years?

   (e) The Hernandezes want to take a two-week vacation next summer, and they have only eight months to save the necessary $2400. What reasonable changes in expenses might they consider to increase net surplus and make the needed $300 per month?

2. **Construct Financial Statements.** John Green has been a retail salesclerk for six years. At age 35, he is divorced with one child, Amanda, age 7. John's salary is $36,000 per year. He regularly receives $250 per month for child support from Amanda's mother. John invests $100 each month ($50 in his mutual fund and $50 in U.S. savings bonds). Using the following information, construct a balance sheet and a cash-flow statement for John.

ASSETS	Amount
Vested retirement benefits (no employee contribution)	$3,000
Money market account (includes $150 of interest earned last year)	5,000
Mutual fund (includes $200 of reinvested dividend income from last year)	4,000
Checking account	1,000
Personal property	5,000
Automobile	3,000
U.S. savings bonds	3,000

LIABILITIES	Outstanding Balance
Dental bill (pays $25 per month and is included in uninsured medical/dental)	$ 450
Visa (pays $100 per month)	1,500
Student loan (pays $100 per month)	7,500

ANNUAL EXPENSES	Amount
Auto insurance	$ 780
Rent	9,100
Utilities	1,200
Phone	680
Cable	360
Food	3,000
Uninsured medical/dental	1,000
Dry cleaning	480
Personal care	420
Gas, maintenance, license	2,120
Clothes	500
Entertainment	1,700
Vacations/visitation travel	1,300
Child care	3,820
Gifts	400
Miscellaneous	300
Taxes	6,400
Health insurance	2,440

3. **Budgeting and Income Projections.** Sharon and Dick DeVaney of Monument, Colorado, have decided to start a family next year, so they are looking over their budget (illustrated in Table 3.7 as the "young married couple"). Sharon thinks that she can go on half-salary ($1050 instead of $2100 per month) in her job as a graduate assistant for about 18 months after the baby's birth; she will then return to full-time work.

(a) Looking at the DeVaneys' current monthly budget, identify categories and amounts in their $4315 budget where they realistically might cut back $1050. (Hint: Federal and state taxes should drop about $290 as their income drops.)

(b) Assume that Sharon and Dick could be persuaded not to begin a family for another two to three years until Sharon finishes graduate school. What specific budgeting recommendations would you give them for handling (i) their fixed expenses and (ii) their variable expenses to prepare financially for an anticipated $1050 loss of income for 18 months as well as the expenses for the new baby?

(c) If the DeVaneys' gross income of $4315 rises 6 percent per year in the future, what will their income be after five years? (Hint: See Appendix A.1 or the *Garman/Forgue* companion website.)

Financial Planning Cases

Case 1
Manipulation of a Cash-Flow Statement

Using the cash-flow statement developed by William Soshnik (see Table 3.4), enter the data from the *Garman/Forgue* companion website. The program will calculate the totals.

(a) Print the cash-flow statement, and compare the results with the text for accuracy.

(b) What original source records might William use to develop his cash-flow statement?

(c) Use the data in the cash-flow statements for William (Table 3.4) and for Victor and Maria Hernandez (Table 3.5) to advise William on how his financial life will change as he becomes older.

Case 2
Budget Control for a Recent Graduate

Mike Staten, a political scientist from Tucson, Arizona, graduated from college eight months ago and is having a terrible time with his budget. Mike has a regular monthly income from his job and no really large bills, but he likes to spend. He exceeds his budget every month, and his credit card balances are increasing. Choose three budget control methods that you could recommend to Mike, and explain how each one could help him gain control of his finances.

Case 3
A Couple Creates an Educational Savings Plan

Stanley Marsh and Wendy Testaburger of Gary, Indiana, have two young children and have been living on a tight budget. Their monthly budget is illustrated in Table 3.7 on page 88 as the "married couple with two young children." Wendy and Stanley are nervous about not having started an educational savings plan for their children. Wendy has just begun working on a parttime basis at a local accounting firm and earns about $860 per month; this income is reflected in the Marsh-Testaburgers' budget. They have decided that they want to save $200 per month for the children's education, but Wendy does not want to work more hours away from home.

(a) Review the family's budget and make suggestions about how to modify various budget estimates so that they could save $200 per month for the education fund.

(b) Briefly describe the effect of your recommended changes on the Marsh-Testaburgers' lifestyle.

Case 4
Victor and Maria Hernandez

Victor and Maria, both in their late 30s, have two children: John, age 13 and Joseph, age 15. Victor has had a long sales career with a major retail appliance store. Maria works parttime as a dental hygienist. The Hernandezes own two vehicles and their home, on which they have a mortgage. They will face many financial challenges over the next 20 years, as their children drive, go to college, and leave home and go out in the world on their own. Victor and Maria also recognize the need to further prepare for their retirement and the challenges of aging.

Victor and Maria Hernandez Think About Their Financial Statements and Budgets

Victor and Maria Hernandez spent some time making up their first balance sheet, which is shown in Table 3.3. Victor and Maria are a bit confused about how various financial activities can affect their net worth.

(a) Assume that their home is now appraised at $192,000 and the value of their automobile has dropped to $9500. Calculate and characterize the effects of these changes on their net worth on their asset-to-debt ratio.

(b) If Victor and Maria take out a bank loan for $1545 and pay off their credit card debts totaling $1545, what effects would these changes have on their net worth?

(c) If Victor and Maria sell their New York 2016 bond and put the cash into the savings account, what effects would this have on their net worth and basic liquidity ratio?

Case 5
Harry and Belinda Johnson

Harry graduated with a bachelor's degree in interior design last spring from a large Midwestern university near his hometown. Belinda has a degree in business finance from a university on the West Coast. Harry and Belinda both worked on their school's student newspapers and met at a conference during their junior year in college. They were married last June and live in an apartment in Kansas City. They currently own one car and Belinda uses public transportation to commute to work. Harry and Belinda look forward to advancing in their careers, buying their own home, and having children.

The Johnsons' Financial Statements Suggest Budgeting Problems

Harry and Belinda both found jobs in the same city. Harry works at a small interior design firm and earns a gross salary of $2500 per month. He also receives $3000 in interest income per year from a trust fund set up by his deceased father's estate; the trust fund will continue to pay that amount until 2020.

Belinda works as a salesperson for a regional stock brokerage firm. She earns $3000 per month, and when she finishes her training program in another two months, her gross salary will increase $300 per month. Belinda has many job-related benefits, including life insurance, health insurance, and a credit union. The Johnsons live in an apartment located approximately halfway between their places of employment. Harry drives about 10 minutes to his job, and Belinda travels about 15 minutes via public transportation to reach her downtown job. Harry and Belinda's apartment is very nice, but small, and it is furnished primarily with furniture given to them by their families. Soon after starting their first jobs, Harry and Belinda decided to begin their financial planning. Fortunately each had taken a college course in personal finance. After initial discussion, they worked together for two evenings to develop the two financial statements presented on page 101.

(a) Briefly describe how Harry and Belinda probably determined the fair market prices for each of their tangible and investment assets.

(b) Using the data from the cash-flow statement developed by Harry and Belinda, calculate a basic liquidity ratio, asset-to-debt ratio, debt service-to-income ratio, debt payments-to-disposable income ratio, and investment assets-to-total assets ratio. What do these ratios tell you about the Johnsons' financial situation? Should Harry and Belinda incur more debt?

(c) The Johnsons enjoy a high income because both work at well-paying jobs. They have spent parts of three evenings over the past several days discussing their financial values and goals together. As shown in the upper portion of Figure 3.5, they have established three long-term goals: $3000 for a European vacation to be taken in 2 ½ years, $5000 needed in October 2013 for a down payment on a new automobile, and $26,078 for a down payment on a home to be purchased in December 2014. As shown in the lower portion of the figure, the Johnsons did some calculations to determine how much they had to save for each goal—over the near term—to stay on schedule to reach their long-term goals as well as pay for two vacations and an anniversary party. After developing their balance sheet and cash-flow statement (shown on page 101), the Johnsons made a budget for the year (shown in Table 3.8). They then reconciled various conflicting needs and wants until they found that total annual income exceeded expenses. Next, they created a revolving savings fund (Table 3.10) in which they were careful to include enough money each month to meet all of their short-term goals. When developing their cash-flow calendar for the year (Table 3.9), they noticed a problem: substantial cash deficits during four months of the year. In fact, despite their projected high income, they anticipate a deficit for the year. To meet this problem, they do not anticipate increasing their income, using savings, or borrowing. Instead, they are considering modifying their needs and want to reduce their budget estimates to the point where they would have a positive balance for the year. Make specific recommendations to the Johnsons on how they could make reductions in their budget estimates. Do not offer suggestions that would alter their new lifestyle drastically, as the couple would reject these ideas.

Balance Sheet for Harry and Belinda Johnson— January 1, 2010

	Dollars	Percent
ASSETS		
Monetary Assets		
Cash on hand	1,178	5.48
Savings (First Federal Bank)	890	4.14
Savings (Far West Savings and Loan)	560	2.60
Savings (Smith Brokerage Credit Union)	160	0.74
Checking account (First Federal Bank)	752	3.50
Total monetary assets	$ 3,540	16.45
Tangible Assets		
Automobile (3-year-old Toyota)	11,000	51.13
Personal property	2,300	10.69
Furniture	1,700	7.90
Total tangible assets	$15,000	69.72
Investment Assets		
Harry's retirement account	1,425	6.62
Belinda's retirement account	1,550	7.20
Total investment assets	2,975	13.83
Total Assets	$21,515	100.00
LIABILITIES		
Short-Term Liabilities		
Visa credit card	390	1.81
Sears card	45	0.21
Dental bill	400	1.86
Total short-term liabilities	$ 835	$3.88
Long-Term Liabilities		
Student loan (Belinda)	3,800	17.66
Automobile loan (First Federal Bank)	8,200	38.11
Total long-term liabilities	$12,000	55.78
Total Liabilities	$12,835	59.66
Net Worth	$ 8,680	40.34
Total Liabilities and Net Worth	$21,515	100.00

Cash-Flow Statement for Harry and Belinda Johnson July 1–December 31, 2009 (First Six Months of Marriage)

	Dollars	Percent
INCOME		
Harry's gross income ($2500 × 6)	15,000	41.64
Belinda's gross income ($3000 × 6)	18,000	49.97
Interest on savings account	24	0.07
Harry's trust fund	3,000	8.33
Total Income	$36,024	100.00
EXPENSES		
Fixed Expenses		
Rent	5,400	14.99
Renter's insurance	220	0.61
Automobile loan payment	1,710	4.75
Automobile insurance	420	1.17
Medical insurance (withheld from salary)	750	2.08
Student loan payments	870	2.42
Life insurance (withheld from salary)	54	0.15
Cable television	540	1.50
Health club	300	0.83
Savings (withheld from salary)	900	2.50
Harry's retirement plan (6% of salary)	900	2.50
Belinda's retirement plan (4% of salary)	720	2.00
Federal income taxes (withheld from salary)	4,600	12.77
State income taxes (withheld from salary)	1,600	4.44
Social Security (withheld from salary)	2,520	7.00
Automobile registration	90	0.25
Total fixed expenses	$21,594	59.94
Variable Expenses		
Food	2,300	6.38
Utilities	750	2.08
Telephone	420	1.17
Gasoline, oil, maintenance	700	1.94
Doctor's and dentist's bills	710	1.97
Medicines	345	0.96
Clothing and upkeep	1,900	5.27
Church and charity	800	2.22
Gifts	720	2.00
Christmas gifts	350	0.97
Public transportation	720	2.00
Personal allowances	1,040	2.89
Entertainment	980	2.72
Vacation (holiday)	700	1.94
Vacation (summer)	600	1.67
Miscellaneous	545	1.51
Total variable expenses	$13,580	37.70
Total Expenses	$35,174	97.64
Surplus (deficit)	$ 850	2.36

On the 'Net

Go to the Web pages indicated to complete these exercises. You can also go to the *Garman/Forgue* companion website at www.cengage.com/finance/garman for an expanded list of exercises. Under General Business, select the title of this text. Click on the Internet Exercises link for this chapter.

1. Visit *Kiplinger's Personal Finance Magazine* website at www.kiplinger.com/tools/. There you will find a link to a long list of calculators that can be used in various present and future value calculations. Select four that you believe would be particularly useful in the aspects of personal financial planning that were discussed in this chapter.

2. Visit the website for SRI Consulting at www.sric-bi .com/VALS/presurvey.shtml where you will find the VALS questionnaire. This short questionnaire will help you identify your values in the context of the values of other members of American society.

3. Visit the website for the Economic Policy Institute at www.epi.org/content.cfm/datazone_fambud_budget where you can find an example of a family budget for many areas of the United States. Calculate the budget for an area of interest to you. How useful do you think such a calculator would be for a family interested in developing its own budget?

Visit the Garman/Forgue companion website . . .

www.cengage.com/finance/garman

PART 2

Managing Income Taxes

!You Must Be Kidding, Right?

Bharat Persaud's employer gave him a $2000 bonus last year, and when Bharat was filling out his federal income tax form, he discovered that $1000 of it moved him from the 15 percent marginal tax rate to 25 percent. How much tax will Bharat pay on the $1000?

   A. $150

   B. $180

   C. $250

   D. $380

The answer is C. The federal marginal tax rate is applied to your last dollar of earnings. The first $1000 of Bharat's bonus is taxed at the marginal tax rate of 15 percent ($150), but the second $1000 is taxed at 25 percent ($250). Be aware of your marginal tax rate!

Learning Objectives

After reading this chapter, you should be able to:

1 Explain the nature of progressive income taxes and the marginal tax rate.

2 Differentiate among the eight steps involved in calculating your federal income taxes.

3 Use appropriate strategies to avoid overpayment of income taxes.

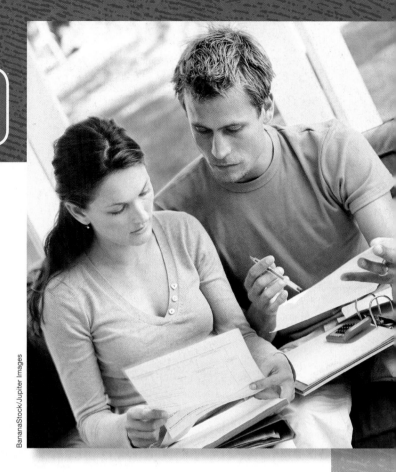

Tom Hutchinson and Gerry Martin plan to get married in two years. Tom earns $44,000 per year managing a fast-food restaurant. He also earns about $10,000 per year selling jewelry that he designs at craft shows held monthly in various nearby cities. Right after they get married, Tom plans to go back to college full time to finish the last year of his undergraduate degree. Gerry earns $58,000 annually working as an institutional sales representative for an insurance company. Both Tom and Gerry each contribute $100 per month to their employer-sponsored 401(k) retirement accounts. Tom has little additional savings, but Gerry has accumulated $18,000 that she wants to use for a down payment on a home. Gerry also owns 300 shares of stock in an oil company that she inherited four years ago when the price was $90 per share; now the stock is worth $130 per share. Tom and Gerry live in a state where the state income tax is 6 percent.

What would you recommend to Tom and Gerry on the subject of managing income taxes regarding:

1. Using tax credits to help pay for Tom's college expenses?

2. Determining how much money Gerry will realize if she sells the stocks, assuming she pays federal income taxes at the 25 percent rate?

3. Buying a home?

4. Increasing contributions to their employer-sponsored retirement plans?

5. Establishing a sideline business for Tom's jewelry operation?

Your Next Five Years

In the next five years you can start achieving financial success by doing the following related to managing income taxes:

1. Sign up for tax-advantaged employee benefits at your workplace.

2. Contribute to your employer-sponsored 401(k) retirement plan at least up to the amount of the employer's matching contribution.

3. Buy a home to reduce income taxes.

4. Do your own tax return so you can learn how to reduce your income tax liability.

5. Maintain good tax records.

tax planning
Seeking legal ways to reduce, eliminate, or defer income taxes.

taxable income
Income upon which income taxes are levied.

1 Learning Objective

Explain the nature of progressive income taxes and the marginal tax rate.

taxes
Compulsory government-imposed charges levied on citizens and their property.

progressive income tax
Tax rate increases as taxable income increases.

marginal tax bracket (MTB)/ marginal tax rate
One of six income-range segments at which income is taxed at increasing rates. Also known as **marginal tax rate.**

marginal tax rate
The tax rates that apply to income in each tax bracket range. Also known as **marginal tax bracket.**

Managing your money effectively includes efforts to avoid paying unnecessary sums to the government in taxes. These efforts will provide you with more money to do with what you want. "The avoidance of taxes is the only intellectual pursuit that carries any reward," wrote economist John Maynard Keynes.

You should pay your income tax liabilities in full, but that's all—there is no need to pay a dime extra. To achieve this goal, you need to adopt a **tax planning** perspective designed to reduce, defer, or eliminate some income taxes. To get started, you should recognize that you pay personal income taxes only on your **taxable income.** This amount is determined by subtracting various exclusions, adjustments, exemptions, and deductions from total income, with the result being the income upon which the tax is actually calculated. Details for these calculations are provided later. For now, simply remember that the main idea in managing income taxes is to reduce your taxable income as much as possible while maintaining a high level of total income. The result will reduce your actual tax liability. By carefully analyzing and managing the subject of income taxes to your advantage, you can avoid overpayment of income taxes. Then you will have more money available every year to manage, spend, save, invest, and donate—activities that are the focus of the remainder of this book.

Progressive Income Taxes and the Marginal Tax Rate

Taxes are compulsory charges imposed by a government on its citizens and their property. The U.S. Internal Revenue Service (IRS) is the agency charged with the responsibility for collecting federal income taxes based on the legal provisions in the *Internal Revenue Code.*

The Progressive Nature of the Federal Income Tax

Taxes can be classified as progressive or regressive. The federal personal income tax is a **progressive tax** because the tax rate progressively increases as a taxpayer's taxable income increases. A higher income implies a greater ability to pay. As Table 4.1 shows, the higher portions of a taxpayer's taxable income are taxed at increasingly higher rates under the federal income tax. A **regressive tax** operates in the opposite way. That is, as income rises, the tax demands a decreasing proportion of a person's income. An example is a state sales tax, since a rate of perhaps 5 percent might have to be paid by everyone regardless of income.

The Marginal Tax Rate Is Applied to the Last Dollar Earned

The **marginal tax bracket (MTB)** is one of the six income-range segments that are taxed at increasing rates as income goes up. This is also called the **marginal tax rate.** The tax rates apply only to the income in each tax bracket range. Recall from Chapter 1 that the marginal tax rate is applied to your last dollar of earnings. Depending on their income, taxpayers fit into one of the brackets (as shown in Table 4.1) and, accordingly, pay at one of those marginal tax rates: 10 percent, 15 percent, 25 percent, 28 percent, 33 percent, or 35 percent. Each year the taxable income levels for the tax brackets are adjusted to reduce the effects of inflation,

Table 4.1 The Progressive Nature of the Federal Income Tax

Segment of Taxable Income	Marginal Tax Rate*
First $8,350	10%
Over $8,350 but not over $33,950	15%
Over $33,950 but not over $82,250	25%
Over $82,250 but not over $171,550	28%
Over $171,550 but not over $372,950	33%
Over $372,950	35%

*Tax rates for single taxpayer.

a process called **indexing.** Indexing keeps taxpayers from being unfairly forced to pay more taxes as they receive raises simply to keep up with inflation.

Your marginal tax rate is perhaps the single most important concept in personal finance. It tells you the portion of any extra taxable earnings—from a raise, investment income, or money from a second job—you must pay in income taxes. Correspondingly, it measures the tax reduction benefits of a tax-deductible expense that allows you to reduce your taxable income. Consider this example of how the marginal tax rate might apply. Susan Bassett is from Syracuse, New York (see Figure 4.1). Part of her $60,000 gross income ($9350 [$3650 + $5700]) is not taxed, the next $8350 is taxed at 10 percent, the next $25,600 is taxed at 15 percent, and the remaining $16,700 of Susan's $60,000 taxable income is taxed at 25 percent. Thus, Susan is in the 25 percent marginal tax bracket because the *last* dollar that she earned is taxed at that level.

All tax rates cited in this chapter are for income tax returns filed in 2009. The mathematics shown in Figure 4.1 are based on the **IRS tax table** (used for tax returns with incomes up to $100,000) and **tax-rate schedules** (used for tax returns with incomes above $100,000).

indexing
Yearly adjustments to tax brackets that reduce inflation's effects on tax brackets.

IRS tax table
Used to figure income tax returns for incomes up to $100,000.

tax-rate schedules
Equations to figure taxes for returns with incomes above $100,000.

The Marginal Tax Rate Affects Your Financial Decisions

The marginal tax rate can affect many financial decisions that you make. Consider, for example, what happens if you are in the 25 percent marginal tax bracket and you make a $100 tax-deductible contribution to a charity. The charity receives the $100, and you deduct the $100 from your taxable income. This deduction results in a $25 reduction in your federal income tax ($100 × 0.25). In effect, you give $75 and the government "gives" $25 to the charity.

Figure 4.1
How Your Income Is Really Taxed (Example: Susan Bassett with a $60,000 Gross Income)

$3,650 personal exemption is not taxed
$5,700 standard deduction is not taxed
Next $8,350 of income is taxed at 10%

Income Segment			Next $25,600 of income is taxed at 15%	Remaining $16,700 of income is taxed at 25%		TOTALS

TOTALS = $60,000

Amount of Income Tax: 0 + 0 + $835.00 + $3,840.00 + $4,175.00 = $8,850

Susan's marginal tax rate is 25%.

Did You Know?

How to Determine Your Marginal Tax Rate

You can determine your marginal tax rate by following this example.

1. Robert Heatherton is single and has a taxable income of $27,825, and looking at the illustrated tax table (Table 4.3) he finds his tax on that amount of income ($3756).

2. Add $100 to that income for a total of $27,925, and find the tax on that amount ($3771).

3. Calculate the difference between the two tax amounts ($3771 – $3756). The extra $15 in taxes from a $100 increase in income reflects a federal marginal tax rate of 15 percent.

effective marginal tax rate
The total marginal rate reflects all taxes on a person's income, including federal, state, and local income taxes as well as Social Security and Medicare taxes.

average tax rate
Proportion of total income paid in income taxes.

Your Effective Marginal Tax Rate Is Probably 43 Percent

The **effective marginal tax rate** describes a person's total marginal tax rate on income after including federal, state, and local income taxes as well as Social Security and Medicare taxes. To determine your effective marginal tax rate on income, add all of these other taxes to your federal marginal tax rate. For example, a single taxpayer earning a taxable income between $33,950 and $82,250 will pay federal income taxes at a marginal rate of 25 percent, a combined Social Security and Medicare tax rate of 7.65 percent, a state income tax rate of 6 percent, and a city income tax rate of 4 percent. These taxes result in an effective marginal tax rate of 43 percent (25 + 7.65 + 6 + 4 = 42.65, rounded to 43). Many employed taxpayers pay an effective marginal tax rate of 43 percent or higher!★

Your Average Tax Rate Is Lower

Many people wonder what proportion of their total income they pay in income taxes.

Your **average tax rate** gives the answer to this question. For example, the average tax rate on Susan Bassett's total income (the illustration in Figure 4.1) is 14.75 percent ($8850 ÷ $60,000), somewhat more than the average of 9.1 percent for all U.S. taxpayers. Because total income is not fully taxed by the federal government, the average tax rate is always less than the marginal tax rate. But it is the marginal tax bracket that is most important because knowing what that rate is helps you make better financial decisions.

 Concept Check 4.1

1. Distinguish between a progressive and a regressive tax.
2. What is a marginal tax bracket, and how does it affect taxpayers?
3. Explain why many taxpayers have a marginal tax rate as high as 43 percent.

Eight Steps in Calculating Your Income Taxes

2 Learning Objectives
Differentiate among the eight steps involved in calculating your federal income taxes.

There are eight basic steps in calculating federal income taxes:

1. Determine your total income.
2. Determine and report your gross income after subtracting exclusions.
3. Subtract adjustments to income.
4. Subtract either the IRS's standard deduction amount for your tax status or your itemized deductions.
5. Subtract the value of your personal exemptions.

★About 60 million people have no federal income tax liability as their incomes are too low; however they do pay Social Security taxes.

Figure 4.2
The Process of Income Tax Calculation

6. Determine your preliminary tax liability.

7. Subtract tax credits for which you qualify.

8. Calculate the balance due the IRS or the amount of your refund.

Figure 4.2 graphically depicts these eight steps in the overall process of federal income tax calculation. The idea is to reduce your income so that you pay the smallest amount possible in income taxes. You do so by reducing total income by removing nontaxable income and then subtracting exclusions, deductions, exemptions, and tax credits, as indicated in the unshaded boxes in Figure 4.2.

1. Determine Your Total Income

Practically everything you receive in return for your work or services and any profit from the sale of assets is considered income, whether the compensation is paid in cash, property, or services. Listing these earnings will reveal your **total income**—compensation from all sources—and much of it, but not all, will be subject to income taxes.

Income to Include   For most people, earned income is reported to them annually on a Form W-2, Wage and Tax Statement. Employers must provide W-2 information (see Figure 4.3) by January 31 of the next year. If you also receive income from interest or dividends or other sources, those sources may send you a Form 1099. In addition to providing it to you, all this information is sent to the IRS.

The federal income tax is a "pay as you go" tax. Through **payroll withholding,** an employer takes a certain amount from an employee's income as a prepayment of an individual's

total income
Compensation from all sources.

payroll withholding
The IRS requirement that an employer withhold a certain amount from an employee's income as a prepayment of that individual's tax liability for the year, and it is sent to the government where it is credited to the taxpayer's account.

Figure 4.3
W-2 Form

a Control number		22222	OMB No. 1545-0008		

b Employer identification number (EIN) 37-12345678

c Employer's name, address, and ZIP code
Financial Knowledge Communications
1245 Oak Street
Oak Park, IL 60302

d Employee's social security number 123-45-6789

e Employee's first name and initial Yasuo Konami

1 Wages, tips, other compensation 65,000.00
2 Federal income tax withheld 10,400.00
3 Social security wages 65,000.00
4 Social security tax withheld 4,030.00
5 Medicare wages and tips 65,000.00
6 Medicare tax withheld 94.25
9 Advance EIC payment
10 Dependent care benefits
11 Nonqualified plans

15 State IL Employer's state ID number 37-1411 9877
17 State income tax 1,950.00

Form **W-2** Wage and Tax Statement
Copy 1—For State, City, or Local Tax Department
Department of the Treasury—Internal Revenue Service

tax liability for the year and sends that amount to the IRS, where it is credited to that particular taxpayer's account. People who are self-employed or receive substantial income from an employer that is not required to practice payroll withholding, such as lawyers, accountants, consultants, and owners of rental property, must pay estimated taxes. They are required to estimate their tax liability and pay their **estimated taxes** in advance in quarterly installments on April 15, June 15, September 15, and the following January 15.

The following types of income are included when you report your income to the IRS:

estimated taxes
People who are self-employed or receive substantial income from an employer that is not required to practice payroll withholding (such as lawyers and owners of rental property) are required by the IRS to estimate their tax liability and pay them in advance in quarterly installments.

- Wages and salaries
- Commissions
- Bonuses
- Professional fees earned
- Hobby income
- Tips earned
- Severance pay
- Fair value of anything received in a barter arrangement
- Debts forgiven
- Alimony received
- Scholarship and fellowship income spent on room, board, and other living expenses
- Grants and the value of tuition reductions that pay for teaching or other services
- Annuity and pension income received
- Withdrawals and disbursements from retirement accounts, such as an individual retirement account (IRA) or 401(k) retirement plan (discussed in Chapter 17, "Retirement Planning")
- Military retirement income
- Social Security income (a portion is taxed above certain income thresholds)
- Disability payments received if you did not pay the premiums

- Damage payments from personal injury lawsuits (punitive damages only)
- Value of personal use of employer-provided car
- State and local income tax refunds (only if the taxpayer itemized deductions during the previous year)
- Employee productivity awards
- Awards for artistic, scientific, and charitable achievements unless assigned to a charity
- Prizes, contest winnings, and rewards
- Gambling and lottery winnings
- All kinds of illegal income
- Fees for serving as a juror or election worker
- Unemployment benefits
- Net rental income
- Royalties
- Investment, business, and farm profits
- Interest income (this includes credit union dividends)
- Dividend income (including mutual fund capital gains distributions even though they are reinvested)

Include Capital Gains and Losses in Total Income An **asset** is property owned by a taxpayer for personal use or as an investment that has monetary value. Examples of assets include stocks, mutual funds, bonds, land, art, gems, stamps, coins, vehicles, and homes. The net income received from the sale of an asset above the costs incurred to purchase and sell it is a **capital gain.** A **capital loss** results when the sale of an asset brings less income than the costs of purchasing and selling the asset. Capital gains and losses on investments must be reported on your tax return. Capital gains from the sale or exchange of property held for *personal use,* such as on a vehicle or vacation home, must be reported as income, but losses on such property are not deductible. There is no tax liability on any capital gain until the stock, bond, mutual fund, real estate, or other investment is sold.

A **short-term gain** (or **loss**) occurs when you sell an asset that you have owned for one year or less; it is taxed at the same rates as ordinary income. A **long-term gain** (or **loss**) occurs when you sell an asset that you have owned for more than one year (at least a year and a day), and it is taxed at special low rates. Long-term capital gains are taxed at a maximum rate of 15 percent, and the rate is only 5 percent for taxpayers in the lower two brackets (15 and 10 percent) except for 2010 when the rate is zero.

Capital losses may be used first to offset capital gains. If there are no capital gains, or if the capital losses are larger than the capital gains, you can deduct the capital loss against your other income, but only up to a limit of $3000 in one year. If your net capital loss is more than $3000, the excess carries forward to the next tax year, up to an annual $3000 maximum.

asset
Property owned by a taxpayer for personal use or as an investment that has monetary value.

capital gain
The net income received from the sale of an asset above the costs incurred to purchase and sell it.

capital loss
The net loss of income that results when the sale of an asset brings less income than the costs of purchasing and selling an asset.

short-term gain/loss
A profit or loss on the sale of an asset that has been held for one year or less.

long-term gain/loss
A profit or loss on the sale of an asset that has been held for more than a year.

Instant Message

Mortgage Debt Forgiveness

A new law says if you sold your home for less than you owed, restructured your mortgage, or had your home foreclosed where part of the debt was canceled that amount generally will not be treated as income.

2. Determine and Report Your Gross Income After Subtracting Exclusions

Gross income consists of all income (both earned and unearned) received in the form of money, goods, services, and property that a taxpayer is required to report to the IRS. To determine gross income, you need to determine which kinds of income are not subject to federal taxation and, therefore, need not be reported as part of gross income. These amounts are called **exclusions.**

gross income
All income in the form of money, goods, services, and/or property.

exclusions
Income not subject to federal taxation.

Income to Exclude The more common exclusions (some are subject to limits) are as follows:

- Gifts
- Inherited money or property
- Income from a carpool
- Income from items sold at a garage sale for a sum less than what you paid
- Cash rebates on purchases of new cars and other products
- Tuition reduction, if not received as compensation for teaching or service
- Federal income tax refunds
- State and local income tax refunds for a year in which you claimed the standard deduction
- Scholarship and fellowship income spent on course-required tuition, fees, books, supplies, and equipment (degree candidates only)
- Withdrawals from state-sponsored Section 529 plans (prepaid tuition and savings) used for education
- Prizes and awards made primarily to recognize artistic, civic, charitable, educational, and similar achievements
- Return of money loaned
- Withdrawals from medical savings accounts used for qualified expenses
- Earnings accumulating within annuities, cash-value life insurance policies, Series EE bonds, and qualified retirement accounts
- Interest income received on tax-exempt government bonds issued by states, counties, cities, and districts
- Life insurance benefits received
- Combat zone pay for military personnel
- Welfare, black lung, workers' compensation, and veterans' benefits
- Value of food stamps
- First $500,000 ($250,000 if single) gain on the sale of a principal residence
- Disability insurance benefits if you paid the insurance premiums
- Social Security benefits (except for high-income taxpayers)
- Rental income from a vacation home if not rented for more than 14 days
- First $5000 of death benefits paid by an employer to a worker's beneficiary
- Travel and mileage expenses reimbursed by an employer (if not previously deducted by the taxpayer)
- Employer-provided per diem allowance covering only meals and incidentals
- Amounts paid by employers for premiums for medical insurance, workers' compensation, and health and long-term care insurance
- Moving expense reimbursements received from an employer (if not previously deducted by the taxpayer)
- Employer-provided commuter highway vehicle transportation and transit passes (up to $120 per month for both) and parking (up to $230 per month)
- Value of premiums for first $50,000 worth of group-term life insurance provided by an employer
- Employer payments (up to $5000) for dependent care assistance (for children and parents)
- Benefits from employers that are impractical to tax because they are so modest, such as occasional supper money and taxi fares for overtime work, company parties, holiday gifts (not cash), and occasional theater or sporting events

- Employer contributions for employee expenses for adoption, education (up to $5250 annually), long-term care, moving, pension, health care, life and disability insurance, and health and medical savings accounts
- Employee contributions to flexible spending accounts
- Reimbursements from flexible spending accounts
- Interest received on Series EE and Series I bonds used for college tuition and fees
- Child support payments received
- Property settlement in a divorce
- Compensatory damages in physical injury cases

3. Subtract Adjustments to Income

In the process of determining your taxable income, you make **adjustments to income** (or **adjustments**). These allowable subtractions from gross income include items such as moving expenses to a new job location (including college graduates who move to take their first job as long as it is at least 50 miles from their old residence); higher-education expenses for tuition and fees (up to $4000); student loan interest for higher education, including that paid by a parent ($2500 maximum); reservists' travel expenses (for more than 100 miles); contributions to qualified personal retirement accounts (IRA and 401[k] accounts) and health savings accounts; alimony payments; interest penalties for early withdrawal of savings certificates of deposit; business expenses; net operating losses; capital losses (up to $3000); and certain expenses of self-employed people (such as health insurance premiums). Adjustments are subtracted from gross income to determine **adjusted gross income (AGI).** Subtracting adjustments to income from gross income results in a subtotal.

To illustrate the value of adjustments to income, consider a person with a gross income of $50,000 who contributes $1000 to certain types of **qualified retirement accounts** (plans that the IRS has approved to encourage saving for retirement). The adjustment reduces gross income to $49,000 and, therefore, saves $250 in income taxes (calculated using Table 4.2). (Contributions to retirement plans are covered later in this chapter and in Chapter 17.)

adjustments to income
Allowable subtractions from gross income.

adjusted gross income (AGI)
Gross income less any exclusions and adjustments.

qualified retirement accounts
IRS-approved retirement savings programs.

Table 4.2 Tax-Rate Schedules

SINGLE

If taxable income is over—	But not over—	The tax is:
$ 0	$ 8,350	10% of the amount over $0
$ 8,350	$ 33,950	$835 plus 15% of the amount over $8350
$ 33,950	$ 82,250	$4675 plus 25% of the amount over $33,950
$ 82,250	$171,550	$16,750 plus 28% of the amount over $82,250
$171,550	$372,950	$41,754 plus 33% of the amount over $171,550
$372,950	No limit	$108,216 plus 35% of the amount over $372,950

MARRIED FILING JOINTLY

If taxable income is over—	But not over—	The tax is:
$ 0	$ 16,700	10% of the amount over $0
$ 16,700	$ 67,900	$1670 plus 15% of the amount over $16,700
$ 67,900	$137,050	$9350 plus 25% of the amount over $67,900
$137,050	$208,850	$26,637.50 plus 28% of the amount over $137,050
$208,850	$372,950	$46,741.50 plus 33% of the amount over $208,850
$372,950	No limit	$100,894.50 plus 35% of the amount over $372,950

Advice from a Pro...

A Sideline Business Can Reduce Your Income Taxes

A sideline business can open many doors to tax deductions. We would never recommend spending money for a tax deduction; however, if you're going to spend the money anyway, you should do everything you can to make it tax deductible.

By having your own business, every dollar you spend attempting to make a profit becomes tax deductible. You can deduct expenses for auto, travel, office, office equipment (e.g., desk, chair, computer), contributions to self-funded retirement accounts, health insurance premiums, educational expenses, entertainment, business gifts, and more. You can deduct salaries of employees, even if they are your children, other relatives, or friends.

The business does not have to be your primary employment. If you lose money in the business, you can deduct those losses from your other income. The IRS says that you must do what a "reasonable business person" would do to make a profit. If you do not meet that test, the IRS will classify the operation as a hobby business, require you to report the income, and disallow the deductions.

Anthony J. Campolo
Columbus State Community College

---

above-the-line deductions
Adjustments subtracted from gross income whether taxpayer itemizes deductions or not.

Adjustments are called **above-the-line deductions** because they may be subtracted from gross income even if itemized deductions are not claimed. Adjustments may be taken regardless of whether the taxpayer itemizes deductions or takes the standard deduction amount (discussed next).

4. Subtract Either the IRS's Standard Deduction for Your Tax Status or Your Itemized Deductions

standard deduction
Fixed amount that all taxpayers may subtract from their adjusted gross income if they do not itemize their deductions.

filing status
Description of a taxpayer's marital status on last day of tax year.

Taxpayers may reduce income further by the amount of the standard deduction. Or they can list, or itemize, their deductions. They can use either method, but not both. You want to use the larger of the two. The **standard deduction** is a fixed amount that all taxpayers (except some dependents) who do not choose to itemize deductions may subtract from their adjusted gross income. In effect, it consists of the government's permissible estimate of any likely tax-deductible expenses these taxpayers might have. Two out of three taxpayers take the standard deduction.

The standard deduction amount depends upon **filing status,** a description of your marital status on the last day of the year. A return can be filed with a status of a single person, a married person (filing separately or jointly), or a head of household. For example, the standard deduction amounts are $5700 for single individuals and twice as much, $11,400, for married people filing jointly. Those who are age 65 or older and/or blind may claim an extra amount for their standard deduction. Homeowners are allowed to increase their standard deduction by the additional amount of their state and local real estate taxes, up to $500 or $1000 for married couples.

itemized deductions
Tax-deductible expenses.

Taxpayers whose tax-deductible expenses, called **itemized deductions,** exceed the standard deduction amount may deduct the larger amount instead of taking the standard deduction. For example, single people might list all of their possible tax deductions and find that they total $6000, which is more than the standard deduction amount of $5700 permitted for single taxpayers. The tax form lists the following six classifications of itemized deductions:

1. Medical and Dental Expenses
2. Taxes You Paid
3. Interest You Paid

Lynn Goldsmith/Corbis

Charitable contributions are typically tax deductible.

4. Gifts to Charity

5. Casualty and Theft Losses

6. Job Expenses and Most Other Miscellaneous Deductions

Examples of deductions in each of these categories follow.

1. Medical and Dental Expenses (Not Paid by Insurance) in Excess of 7.5 Percent of Adjusted Gross Income

- Medicine and drugs
- Insurance premiums for medical, long-term, care and contact lenses
- Medical services (doctors, dentists, nurses, hospitals, long-term health care)
- Sterilizations and prescription contraceptives
- Costs of a physician-prescribed course of treatment for obesity
- Expenses for prescription drugs/programs to quit smoking
- Medical equipment and aids (contact lenses, eyeglasses, hearing devices, orthopedic shoes, false teeth, wheelchair lifts)
- Fees for childbirth preparation classes
- Costs of sending a mentally or physically challenged person to a special school
- Home improvements made for the physically disabled (ramps, railings, widening doors)
- Travel and conference registration fees for a parent to learn about a child's disease
- Transportation costs to and from locations where medical services are obtained, using a standard flat mileage allowance

2. Taxes You Paid

- Real estate property taxes (such as on a home or land)
- Personal property taxes (such as on an automobile or boat when any part of the tax is based on the value of the asset)
- State, local, and foreign income taxes

■ Sales taxes on new vehicle purchase (for 2010 but may be extended)

■ State and local sales taxes (instead of state and local income taxes but this cannot be taken if the new vehicle sales tax is deducted [see above])

3. Interest You Paid

■ Interest paid on home mortgage loans

■ "Points" treated as a type of prepaid interest on the purchase of a principal residence

■ Interest paid on home-equity loans

■ Interest paid on loans used for investments

■ Mortgage insurance premiums on new loans

4. Gifts to Charity

■ Cash contributions to qualified organizations such as churches, schools, and charities (receipt required for $250 or more)

■ Noncash contributions at **fair market value** (what a willing buyer would pay to a willing seller); IRS says that personal property must be in "good used condition or better" to qualify

■ Mileage allowance for travel and out-of-pocket expenses for volunteer charitable work

■ Charitable contributions made through payroll deduction

fair market value
Amount a willing buyer would pay to a willing seller for a charitable item.

5. Casualty and Theft Losses (Not Paid by Insurance) in Excess of 10 Percent of Adjusted Gross Income

■ Casualty losses (such as from storms, vandalism, and fires) in excess of $100

■ Theft of money or property in excess of $100

■ Mislaid or lost property if the loss results from an identifiable event that is unexpected or unusual (such as catching a diamond ring in a car door and losing the stone)

6. Job Expenses and Most Other Miscellaneous Deductions in Excess of 2 Percent of Adjusted Gross Income (Partial Listing)

■ Union or professional association dues and membership fees

■ Subscriptions to magazines, journals, and newspapers used for business or professional purposes

■ Books, software, tools, and supplies used in a business or profession

■ Tools and supplies for use in a profession

■ Cost of computers and cell phones required as a condition of your job

■ Clothing and uniforms not suitable for off-the-job usage as ordinary wearing apparel (protective shoes, hats, safety goggles, gloves, uniforms), laundering and cleaning

■ Unreimbursed employee business expenses (but only a portion of the cost of meals and entertainment), including long-distance telephone calls, cleaning and laundry, and car washes (of business vehicle)

■ Investment-related expenses (e.g., computer software, fees for online trading, adviser fees, investment club expenses, IRA fees, safe-deposit box rental, subscriptions to investment magazines and newsletters, tax preparation fees)

■ Legal fees that pertain to tax advice in a divorce or alimony payments

■ Travel costs between two jobs, using a flat mileage allowance

- Job-related car expenses (but not commuting to a regular job), using a flat mileage allowance or actual expenses
- Commuting costs to a temporary workplace
- Commuting costs that qualify as a business or education expense
- Medical examinations required (but not paid for) by an employer to obtain or keep a job
- Appraisal fees for charitable donations or casualty losses
- Education expenses if required to keep your job or improve your job or professional skills (but not if the training readies you for a new career)
- Job-hunting expenses for typing, printing, résumé advice, career counseling, want ads, telephone calls, employment agency fees, mailing costs, and travel for seeking a job in your current career field
- Transportation, food, and entertainment costs for job hunting (which does not have to be successful) in your current career

7. Other Miscellaneous Deductions Allowed at 100 Percent

- Gambling losses (but only to offset reported gambling income)
- Business expenses for workers with disabilities

Given the considerable number of deductions listed here and numerous others for which you might qualify, it makes sense to take time to estimate how much you can count up in possible itemized deductible expenses. If the amount exceeds the standard deduction amount or is even close, go back and carefully itemize deductions and deduct the larger amount.

5. Subtract the Value of Your Personal Exemptions

An **exemption** (or **personal exemption**) is a legally permitted amount deducted from adjusted gross income based on the number of people supported by the taxpayer's income. An exemption may be claimed for the taxpayer and qualifying dependents, such as a spouse (if filing jointly), children, parents, and other dependents earning less than a specific income and for whom the taxpayer provides more than half of their financial support. For example, a husband and wife with two young children would have four exemptions.

A person can serve as an exemption on only one tax return—his or her own or another person's (usually a parent). Each exemption reduces taxable income by $3650. The value of an exemption is phased out for those with higher incomes. If you are claimed as a dependent on a parent's return you may not claim a personal exemption for yourself, as only one person receives the exemption.

6. Determine Your Preliminary Tax Liability

The steps detailed to this point have explained how to determine your taxable income. Taxable income is calculated by taking the taxpayer's gross income, subtracting the adjustments to

Did You Know?

Keep Your Tax Records a Long Time

You should never discard records relating to home purchases, contributions to retirement accounts, and investments. Because you have the burden of proving that the numbers you provided to the IRS are accurate, when in doubt about keeping a tax record, do not throw it out. Record keeping is fundamental in tax matters, and being able to prove your deductions is crucial to keeping more of your money.

Did You Know?

Obtaining Income Tax Preparation Guidance

Your Federal Income Tax: For Individuals, Publication 17, is the IRS's 100-plus-page book for preparing your income taxes. In addition, all federal income tax forms, regulations, guides, and answers to frequently asked questions can be obtained from the IRS at (800) TAX-3676, or at www.irs.gov. The IRS help line is (800) TAX-1040. Half of taxpayers pay someone to prepare the return.

Tax guides that offer advice on how to reduce income taxes and computer software to assist in filling out your return are available at bookstores. The best and most readable tax guide is the annual *J. K. Lasser's Your Income Tax.* Popular computer software programs to help prepare income tax returns include Quicken TurboTax (www.turbotax.com), TaxACT (www.taxact.com), and H&R Block's TaxCut (www.taxcut.com).

exemption (or personal exemption)
Legally permitted amount deducted from AGI based on number of people that taxpayer's income supports.

Table 4.3 Tax Table*

If Taxable Income Is		Your Tax Is	
At Least	But Less Than	Single	Married Filing Jointly
20,200	20,250	2,616	2,199
20,250	20,300	2,624	2,206
23,550	23,600	3,119	2,701
23,600	23,650	3,126	2,709
26,050	26,100	3,494	3,076
26,100	26,150	3,501	3,084
26,300	26,350	3,531	3,114
26,350	26,400	3,539	3,121
27,750	27,800	3,749	3,331
27,800	27,850	3,756	3,339
27,850	27,900	3,764	3,346
27,900	27,950	3,771	3,354
33,950	34,000	4,681	4,261
34,000	34,050	4,694	4,269
39,900	39,950	6,169	5,154
39,950	40,000	6,181	5,161
41,300	41,350	6,519	5,364
41,350	41,400	6,531	5,371
49,100	49,150	8,469	6,534
49,150	49,200	8,481	6,541
49,450	49,500	8,556	6,586
49,500	49,550	8,569	6,594
53,000	53,050	9,444	7,119
53,050	53,100	9,456	7,126
53,100	53,150	9,469	7,134
60,000	60,050	11,194	8,169
60,050	60,100	11,206	8,176
74,100	74,150	14,719	10,906
74,150	74,200	14,731	10,919
90,200	90,250	18,983	14,931
90,250	90,300	18,997	14,944

*These segments of the tax table are derived from IRS tax-rate schedules.

alternative minimum tax (AMT)
A special higher tax rate of 26 or 28 percent that must be paid rather than the regular tax called for in the standard marginal tax brackets for certain high-income taxpayers that is triggered for people with excessive deductions.

income, subtracting the amount permitted for the number of exemptions allowed, and subtracting either the standard deduction or total itemized deductions.

The amount of taxable income is then used to determine taxpayers' preliminary tax liability via the tax tables or tax-rate schedules for their filing status (such as single or married filing jointly).★ The following examples illustrate how to determine tax liability. Table 4.3 shows segments of the tax table.

1. A married couple filing jointly has a gross income of $50,000, adjustments of $5000, two exemptions ($3650 each), and itemized deductions of $8285. They take the standard deduction of $11,400 because their itemized deductions do not exceed that amount.

Gross income	$50,000
Less adjustments to income	− 5,000
Adjusted gross income	45,000
Less standard deduction for married couple	− 11,400
Subtotal	33,600
Less value of two exemptions	− 7,300
Taxable income	26,300
Tax liability (from Table 4.3)	$ 3,114

2. A single person has a gross income of $56,000, adjustments of $4000, one exemption, and itemized deductions of $8400. She subtracts her itemized deductions because the amount exceeds the $5700 standard deduction value.

Gross income	$56,000
Less adjustments to income	− 4,000
Adjusted gross income	52,000
Less itemized deductions	− 8,400
Subtotal	43,600
Less value of one exemption	− 3,650
Taxable income	39,950
Tax liability (from Table 4.3)	$ 6,181

3. A married couple with a gross income of $137,000 has adjustments of $4000, two exemptions, and itemized deductions of $9800. The standard deduction value for a married couple is taken because it exceeds the itemized deductions.

Gross income	$137,000
Less adjustments to income	− 4,000
Adjusted gross income	133,000
Less standard deduction	− 11,400
Subtotal	121,600
Less value of two exemptions	− 7,300
Taxable income	114,300
Tax liability (from Table 4.2)†	$ 20,950

★The **alternative minimum tax (AMT)** was originally designed to ensure that the rich pay at least some income taxes. Today, however, instead of paying income taxes at the standard tax rates, several million high-income taxpayers must pay the higher AMT rate or 26 or 28 percent because it is triggered for people with excessive deductions. Examples include taxpayers who have several children and income from tax-exempt sources. When the value of those benefits is added back to your income, it results in an AMT amount that may exceed your regular tax.

†The tax liability is calculated from the tax-rate schedules in Table 4.2 because the taxable income exceeds $100,000. The tax liability is computed on taxable income as follows: $114,300 − $67,900 = $46,400 × 0.25 = $11,600 + $9350 = $20,950).

7. Subtract Tax Credits for Which You Qualify

You may be able to lower your preliminary tax liability through tax credits. **Tax credits** provide bigger tax breaks than do tax deductions because they represent a dollar-for-dollar subtraction from your tax liability. A credit directly reduces your tax liability, as opposed to tax deductions that reduce the income subject to tax. A $1000 tax deduction saves $250 in taxes if you are in the 25 percent bracket. A $1000 tax credit saves you $1000.

You may take tax credits regardless of whether you itemize deductions. A **nonrefundable tax credit** may reduce your tax liability only to zero; if the credit is more than your tax, the excess is not refunded to you. A **refundable tax credit** can reduce your taxes to below zero and the excess will be refunded to the taxpayer. Credits are often subject to income limits, meaning that high-income taxpayers may not be eligible for a particular credit.

American Opportunity Tax Credit The **American Opportunity Tax Credit** enhances the provisions of tax credit programs to help defray college expenses for the first four years of postsecondary education. (This replaces the Hope Scholarship credit.) The tax credit is for 100 percent of qualified tuition, fees and course materials paid by the taxpayer during the taxable year not to exceed $2000, plus 25 percent of the next $2000 in qualified tuition, fees and course materials. The total credit does not exceed $2500. The money must have been spent for qualified tuition and expenses for textbooks, supplies, equipment, and student activity fees if required as a condition of enrollment. The credit can be claimed in two taxable years for individuals enrolled on at least a half-time basis during any part of the year. Forty percent of the credit is refundable. The credit is for 2010, although it may be extended by Congress.

Lifetime Learning Credit The **lifetime learning credit** (nonrefundable) may be claimed every year for tuition and related expenses paid for all years of postsecondary education undertaken to acquire or improve job skills. The expenses for one or more courses may be for yourself, your spouse, or your dependents. The student need not be pursuing a degree or other recognized credential. This credit amounts to 20 percent of the first $10,000 paid, for a maximum of $2000 for all eligible students in a family. There is no limit on the number of years the credit may be taken for the student. The lifetime learning and Hope Scholarship credits may not be claimed for the same student expenses for the same tax year.

First-Time Home Buyer Credit The **first-time home buyer credit** is an $8000 refundable tax credit for those who purchased a home between April 2008 and July 2009, although this credit may be extended by Congress.

Earned Income Credit The **earned income credit (EIC)** is refundable, and it may be claimed not only by workers with a qualifying child but also, in certain cases, by childless workers. This credit (or a portion of it) is available for joint filers whose earned income and adjusted gross income are less than about $43,000. The maximum credit is about $5600 for a family with two children, about $3000 for a family with one child, and about $450 for a single person with no qualifying children. The greatest EIC credits go to those with the lowest taxable incomes.

 Instant Message

Income Tax Websites

Popular websites for information about income taxes include the following:

- Internal Revenue Service (www.irs.gov)
- H&R Block (www.hrblock.com/taxes/tax_tips/index.html)
- J. K. Lasser (www.wiley.com/WileyCDA/Section/id-301689.html)
- Kiplinger (www.kiplinger.com/money/taxes/)

tax credit
Dollar-for-dollar decrease in tax liability; also known as credit.

nonrefundable tax credit
A tax credit that can reduce one's tax liability only to zero; however, if the credit is more than the tax liability, the excess is not refunded.

refundable tax credit
A tax credit that can reduce one's income tax liability to below zero and the excess is refunded to taxpayer.

American Opportunity Tax Credit
A partially refundable tax credit of up to $2500 a year to help defray college expenses for the first four years of postsecondary education.

lifetime learning credit
A nonrefundable tax credit that may be claimed every year for tuition and related expenses paid for all years of postsecondary education undertaken to acquire or improve job skills.

first-time home buyer credit
An $8000 refundable tax credit for those who purchased a home between April 2008 and July 2009. (This credit may be extended by Congress.)

earned income credit (EIC)
A refundable tax credit that may be claimed by workers with a qualifying child and in certain cases by childless workers.

child tax credit
A refundable tax credit of $1000 or more that may be taken by low and moderate income families for each qualifying child younger than age 17 claimed as a dependent.

child and dependent care credit
A nonrefundable tax credit that may be claimed by workers who pay employment-related expenses for care of a child or other dependent if that care gives them the freedom to work, seek work, or attend school full time.

adoption tax credit
A nonrefundable tax credit of up to $12,150 available for the qualifying costs of an adoption.

mortgage interest tax credit
A nonrefundable tax credit of up to $2000 for mortgage interest paid may be claimed under special state and local government programs that provide a "mortgage credit certificate" for people who purchase a principal residence or borrow funds for certain home improvements.

Retirement savings contribution credit
A nonrefundable tax credit (also known as a **saver credit**) of up to $1000 available for some low and moderate income taxpayers.

tax refund
Amount the IRS sends back to taxpayer if withholding and estimated payments exceed tax liability.

tax balance due
Money you must pay to the IRS if withholding and quarterly payments are insufficient to cover tax liability.

Child Tax Credit   Low and moderate income families may claim a refundable **child tax credit** of $1000 or more for each qualifying child younger than age 17 claimed as a dependent.

Child and Dependent Care Credit   The **child and dependent care credit** (nonrefundable) may be claimed by workers who pay employment-related expenses for care of a child or other dependent if that care gives them the freedom to work, seek work, or attend school full time. Depending on your income, the maximum credit is 35 percent of qualifying care expenses up to a $1050 maximum credit ($3000 in expenses × 0.35) for one dependent and a maximum credit of $2100 for two or more dependents. Taxpayers may claim a dependent care tax credit and a child tax credit, if their expenses qualify.

Adoption Credit   An **adoption tax credit** (nonrefundable) of up to $12,150 is available for the qualifying costs of an adoption.

Mortgage Interest Credit   A **mortgage interest tax credit** (nonrefundable) of up to $2000 for mortgage interest paid may be claimed under special state and local government programs that provide a "mortgage credit certificate" for people who purchase a principal residence or borrow funds for certain home improvements. The home must not cost more than 90 to 110 percent of the average area purchase price.

Retirement Savings Contribution Credit   A nonrefundable **retirement savings contribution credit** (also known as a **saver credit**) of up to $1000 is available for singles with an AGI of less than $27,750 and married couples whose AGI is less than $55,500.

Elderly or Disabled Tax Credit   Individuals who are age 65 or older or who are permanently and totally disabled may claim a nonrefundable federal tax credit that can be as much as $1125.

Energy-Savings Tax Credits   If you placed an energy-savings vehicle (such as a hybrid car) in service during the year or upgraded heating and cooling equipment, windows, solar panels, skylights, solar water heaters, fuel cell equipment, and insulation, you may qualify for one or more refundable credits. There is also a plug-in electric drive vehicle credit that may be $2500 or more.

Making-Work-Pay Tax Credit   A refundable tax credit at a rate of 6.2 percent applies to earned income (after taxes are taken out). The credit can be up to $400 for individuals and up to $800 for couples for 2010, and this credit may be extended. To refund the money the government reduces the income taxes withheld from workers' paychecks.

Instant Message

File a Return to Get a Refundable Tax Credit

Claiming a credit may allow you to get money from the government even though you owed no income taxes for the year. To get a refundable tax credit you must file a return. You also may qualify for the earned income credit, child tax credit, or American Opportunity Tax Credit.

8. Calculate the Balance Due the IRS or the Amount of Your Refund

If the amount withheld (shown on your W-2 form) plus any estimated tax payments you made is greater than your final tax liability, then you are entitled to receive a **tax refund.** If the amount is less than your final tax liability, then you have a **tax balance due.** If you owe money, you pay by check, money order, or credit card. The IRS imposes a convenience fee of 2.5 percent of the amount charged on a credit card.

Taxpayers may file their returns by mail or online; visit www.irs .gov and click on "ElectronicIRS." You should file your return on time to avoid a penalty. If you owe the IRS and you are broke, you can borrow to pay the taxes or contact the IRS about setting up an installment plan that will repay the debt within three years. Taxpayers hear from the IRS within three weeks if they have failed to sign the return, neglected to attach a copy of the Form W-2, made an error in arithmetic, or figured the tax incorrectly. Figure 4.4 shows a completed 1040 Form for a taxpayer.

 Concept Check 4.2

1. Give five examples of income that must be included in income reported to the Internal Revenue Service.

2. How are long-term and short-term capital gains treated differently for income tax purposes?

3. Give five examples of income that is excluded from IRS reporting.

4. List three examples of adjustments to income.

5. Distinguish between a standard deduction and a personal exemption.

6. What advice on filing a Form 1040X can you offer someone who did not file a federal income tax return last year or in any one of the past three years?

7. List five examples of tax credits.

 Instant Message

File IRS Form 1040X to Obtain Refunds for Previous Years

Anyone who was eligible for a refundable tax credit may file to receive it retroactively for the previous three tax years using Form 1040X. Use this easy-to-complete form to obtain a refund when correcting any tax filing mistakes.

 Instant Message

Invest Your Tax Refund into an IRA

Taxpayers may direct the IRS to split their refund into various checking, saving, or investment accounts. Thus, you may earmark all or part of it into a new or existing individual retirement account (IRA) online with a financial institution or mutual fund. An IRA can be opened online in minutes without making an initial deposit.

Avoid Taxes Through Proper Planning

While the U.S. tax laws are strict and punitive about compliance (although the IRS audits less than 0.5 percent of all returns), they remain neutral about whether the taxpayer should take advantage of every "break" and opportunity possible. The strategies described here will enable you to reduce your tax liability.

3 Learning Objective

Use appropriate strategies to avoid overpayment of income taxes.

Practice Legal Tax Avoidance, Not Tax Evasion

Tax evasion involves deliberately and willfully hiding income, falsely claiming deductions, or otherwise cheating the government out of taxes owed. It is illegal. A waiter who does not report tips received and a babysitter who does not report income are both evading taxes, as is a person who deducts $150 in charitable contributions but who fails to actually make the donations.

Tax avoidance means reducing tax liability through legal techniques. It involves applying knowledge of the tax code and regulations to personal income tax planning. Tax evasion results in penalties, fines, interest charges, and a possible jail sentence. In contrast, tax avoidance boosts your income because you pay less in taxes; as a result, you will have more money available for spending, saving, investing, and donating.

tax evasion
Deliberately and willfully hiding income from the IRS, falsely claiming deductions, or otherwise cheating the government out of taxes owed; it is illegal.

tax avoidance
Reducing tax liability through legal techniques.

Form **1040**
Department of the Treasury—Internal Revenue Service
U.S. Individual Income Tax Return (99)   IRS Use Only—Do not write or staple in this space.

For the year Jan. 1–Dec. 31, or other tax year beginning _____ , ending _____ , 20 ___   OMB No. 1545-0074

Label
(See instructions on page 14.)
Use the IRS label. Otherwise, please print or type.

Your first name and initial   **Yasuo**   Last name   **Konami**

Your social security number   **123 45 6789**

If a joint return, spouse's first name and initial   Last name

Spouse's social security number

Home address (number and street). If you have a P.O. box, see page 14.   **3333 Third Avenue**   Apt. no. **12**

▲ You **must** enter your SSN(s) above. ▲

City, town or post office, state, and ZIP code. If you have a foreign address, see page 14.   **Oak Park, IL 60302**

Checking a box below will not change your tax or refund.

Presidential Election Campaign ▶ Check here if you, or your spouse if filing jointly, want $3 to go to this fund (see page 14) ▶   ☐ You ☐ Spouse

Filing Status
Check only one box.

1 ☒ Single
2 ☐ Married filing jointly (even if only one had income)
3 ☐ Married filing separately. Enter spouse's SSN above and full name here. ▶
4 ☐ Head of household (with qualifying person). (See page 15.) If the qualifying person is a child but not your dependent, enter this child's name here. ▶
5 ☐ Qualifying widow(er) with dependent child (see page 16)

Exemptions

6a ☒ **Yourself.** If someone can claim you as a dependent, **do not** check box 6a
b ☐ Spouse
c Dependents:

(1) First name Last name	(2) Dependent's social security number	(3) Dependent's relationship to you	(4) ✓ if qualifying child for child tax credit (see page 17)
			☐
			☐
			☐
			☐

If more than four dependents, see page 17.

d Total number of exemptions claimed

Boxes checked on 6a and 6b   **1**
No. of children on 6c who:
• lived with you
• did not live with you due to divorce or separation (see page 18)
Dependents on 6c not entered above
Add numbers on lines above ▶   **1**

◀ Report number of exemptions

Income

Attach Form(s) W-2 here. Also attach Forms W-2G and 1099-R if tax was withheld.

If you did not get a W-2, see page 21.

Enclose, but do not attach, any payment. Also, please use Form 1040-V.

7 Wages, salaries, tips, etc. Attach Form(s) W-2 | 7 | 65,000 —
8a **Taxable** interest. Attach Schedule B if required | 8a | 200 —
b **Tax-exempt** interest. **Do not** include on line 8a | 8b |
9a Ordinary dividends. Attach Schedule B if required | 9a |
b Qualified dividends (see page 21) | 9b |
10 Taxable refunds, credits, or offsets of state and local income taxes (see page 22) | 10 |
11 Alimony received | 11 |
12 Business income or (loss). Attach Schedule C or C-EZ | 12 |
13 Capital gain or (loss). Attach Schedule D if required. If not required, check here ▶ ☐ | 13 |
14 Other gains or (losses). Attach Form 4797 | 14 |
15a IRA distributions | 15a | b Taxable amount (see page 23) | 15b |
16a Pensions and annuities | 16a | b Taxable amount (see page 24) | 16b |
17 Rental real estate, royalties, partnerships, S corporations, trusts, etc. Attach Schedule E | 17 |
18 Farm income or (loss). Attach Schedule F | 18 |
19 Unemployment compensation | 19 |
20a Social security benefits | 20a | b Taxable amount (see page 26) | 20b |
21 Other income. List type and amount (see page 28) | 21 |
22 Add the amounts in the far right column for lines 7 through 21. This is your **total income** ▶ | 22 | 65,200 —

◀ Report income here

Adjusted Gross Income

23 Educator expenses (see page 28) | 23 |
24 Certain business expenses of reservists, performing artists, and fee-basis government officials. Attach Form 2106 or 2106-EZ | 24 |
25 Health savings account deduction. Attach Form 8889 | 25 |
26 Moving expenses. Attach Form 3903 | 26 |
27 One-half of self-employment tax. Attach Schedule SE | 27 |
28 Self-employed SEP, SIMPLE, and qualified plans | 28 |
29 Self-employed health insurance deduction (see page 29) | 29 |
30 Penalty on early withdrawal of savings | 30 |
31a Alimony paid b Recipient's SSN ▶ _____ | 31a |
32 IRA deduction (see page 30) | 32 | 4,000 —
33 Student loan interest deduction (see page 33) | 33 | 1,100 —
34 Tuition and fees deduction. Attach Form 8917 | 34 |
35 Domestic production activities deduction. Attach Form 8903 | 35 |
36 Add lines 23 through 31a and 32 through 35 | 36 | 5,100
37 Subtract line 36 from line 22. This is your **adjusted gross income** ▶ | 37 | 60,100

◀ Subtract adjustments to income

For Disclosure, Privacy Act, and Paperwork Reduction Act Notice, see page 88.   Cat. No. 11320B   Form **1040** (2008)

Figure 4.4
Federal Income Tax Form 1040 (Yasuo Konami)

Form 1040 (2008)
Page **2**

Tax and Credits	**38**	Amount from line 37 (adjusted gross income)	**38**	60,100 —

39a Check if: ☐ **You** were born before January 2, 1944, ☐ Blind. ☐ **Spouse** was born before January 2, 1944, ☐ Blind. } Total boxes checked ▶ 39a ☐

b If your spouse itemizes on a separate return or you were a dual-status alien, see page 34 and check here ▶ 39b ☐

c Check if standard deduction includes real estate taxes or disaster loss (see page 34) ▶ 39c ☐

40	Itemized deductions (from Schedule A) or your standard deduction (see left margin) .	**40**	7,000 —
41	Subtract line 40 from line 38	**41**	53,100 —

Standard Deduction for—
- People who checked any box on line 39a, 39b, or 39c **or** who can be claimed as a dependent, see page 34.
- All others:

Single or Married filing separately, $5,700

Married filing jointly or Qualifying widow(er), $11,400

Head of household, $8,350

Tax Credit (handwritten margin note)

42	If line 38 is over $119,975, or you provided housing to a Midwestern displaced individual, see page 36. Otherwise, multiply $3,500 by the total number of exemptions claimed on line 6d .	**42**	3,650 —
43	**Taxable income.** Subtract line 42 from line 41. If line 42 is more than line 41, enter -0-	**43**	49,450 —
44	**Tax** (see page 36). Check if any tax is from: **a** ☐ Form(s) 8814 **b** ☐ Form 4972	**44**	8,556
45	**Alternative minimum tax** (see page 39). Attach Form 6251	**45**	
46	Add lines 44 and 45 . . . . ▶	**46**	

47	Foreign tax credit. Attach Form 1116 if required . . .	47
48	Credit for child and dependent care expenses. Attach Form 2441	48
49	Credit for the elderly or the disabled. Attach Schedule R . .	49
50	Education credits. Attach Form 8863	50
51	Retirement savings contributions credit. Attach Form 8880 .	51
52	Child tax credit (see page 42). Attach Form 8901 if required .	52
53	Credits from Form: **a** ☐ 8396 **b** ☐ 8839 **c** ☐ 5695	53
54	Other credits from Form: **a** ☐ 3800 **b** ☐ 8801 **c** ☐ _____	54

55	Add lines 47 through 54. These are your **total credits**	**55**	
56	Subtract line 55 from line 46. If line 55 is more than line 46, enter -0- . . . . ▶	**56**	

Other Taxes	**57**	Self-employment tax. Attach Schedule SE	**57**	
	58	Unreported social security and Medicare tax from Form: **a** ☐ 4137 **b** ☐ 8919 . .	**58**	
	59	Additional tax on IRAs, other qualified retirement plans, etc. Attach Form 5329 if required . .	**59**	
	60	Additional taxes: **a** ☐ AEIC payments **b** ☐ Household employment taxes. Attach Schedule H	**60**	
	61	Add lines 56 through 60. This is your **total tax** . . . . ▶	**61**	

Payments	**62**	Federal income tax withheld from Forms W-2 and 1099 . .	62	
	63	2008 estimated tax payments and amount applied from 2007 return	63	10,400 —

If you have a qualifying child, attach Schedule EIC.

64a	**Earned income credit (EIC)**	64a
b	Nontaxable combat pay election	64b
65	Excess social security and tier 1 RRTA tax withheld (see page 61)	65
66	Additional child tax credit. Attach Form 8812 . . .	66
67	Amount paid with request for extension to file (see page 61)	67
68	Credits from Form: **a** ☐ 2439 **b** ☐ 4136 **c** ☐ 8801 **d** ☐ 8885	68
69	First-time homebuyer credit. Attach Form 5405	69
70	Recovery rebate credit (see worksheet on pages 62 and 63) . .	70

71	Add lines 62 through 70. These are your **total payments** . . . . . . ▶	**71**	10,400 —

Refund	**72**	If line 71 is more than line 61, subtract line 61 from line 71. This is the amount you **overpaid**	**72**	
Direct deposit? See page 63 and fill in 73b, 73c, and 73d, or Form 8888.	**73a**	Amount of line 72 you want **refunded to you.** If Form 8888 is attached, check here ▶ ☐	**73a**	1,844 —
	▶ **b**	Routing number _____ ▶ **c** Type: ☐ Checking ☐ Savings		
	▶ **d**	Account number _____		
	74	Amount of line 72 you want **applied to your 2009 estimated tax** ▶	74	

Amount You Owe	**75**	**Amount you owe.** Subtract line 71 from line 61. For details on how to pay, see page 65 ▶	**75**	
	76	Estimated tax penalty (see page 65)	76	

Third Party Designee
Do you want to allow another person to discuss this return with the IRS (see page 66)? ☐ **Yes.** Complete the following. ☐ **No**

Designee's name ▶ _____ Phone no. ▶ ( ) _____ Personal identification number (PIN) ▶ _____

Sign Here
Joint return? See page 15. Keep a copy for your records.

Under penalties of perjury, I declare that I have examined this return and accompanying schedules and statements, and to the best of my knowledge and belief, they are true, correct, and complete. Declaration of preparer (other than taxpayer) is based on all information of which preparer has any knowledge.

Your signature	Date	Your occupation	Daytime phone number
Yasuo Konami	3-1-10	Media Specialist	(630) 555-1234
Spouse's signature. If a joint return, **both** must sign.	Date	Spouse's occupation	

Paid Preparer's Use Only

Preparer's signature ▶		Date	Check if self-employed ☐	Preparer's SSN or PTIN
Firm's name (or yours if self-employed), address, and ZIP code ▶			EIN	
			Phone no. ( )	

Form **1040** (2008)

✪ **Printed on recycled paper**

(Margin annotation boxes, right side:)
- Take larger of itemized deductions or standard deduction
- Subtract value of exemptions
- Taxable income
- Subtract tax credits
- Calculate balance owed or refund
- Do not forget to sign your return

A Dollar Saved from Taxes Is Really Two Dollars—or More

These three reasons ought to motivate you to find legal ways to reduce your tax liability.

opportunity cost
Most valuable alternative that must be sacrificed to satisfy a want or need.

1. **The opportunity cost.** As noted in Chapter 1, the most valuable alternative that must be sacrificed to satisfy a want is called an **opportunity cost.** An opportunity cost is measured in terms of the value of this forgone option, and it is reflected by the cost of what one must do without or what one could have bought instead. By paying $1 in taxes, you lose the alternative use of that dollar.

2. **Earning another dollar to replace one given to the IRS.** If you pay a dollar too much in taxes, you may need to earn another dollar to replace it. A dollar saved in taxes, therefore, may be viewed as two dollars in your pocket.

3. **Earnings on a dollar not given to the IRS.** If the two dollars saved are invested, the earnings from that investment further expand your savings.

Strategy: Reduce Taxable Income via Your Employer

It may seem illogical to suggest that to lower your tax liability you should reduce your income. The objective is to reduce *taxable* income. Reducing your federal taxable income also will reduce the personal income taxes imposed by state and local governments. Three useful ways of reducing taxable income are premium-only plans, dependent care flexible spending accounts, and defined-contribution retirement plans. Employees often are already paying for these expenses out of their own pockets with after-tax dollars, thus these plans allow people to reduce taxes on money they are already spending.

Contributions to these employer-sponsored plans are entirely free of federal, state, and Social Security and Medicare taxes. The amount withheld to pay for the benefit is deducted from a worker's salary before taxes are calculated. In effect, the IRS subsidizes or helps pay for part of your planned expenses. If your effective marginal tax rate is 43 percent, that is how much savings you obtain by participating. So if you contribute $5000 in pretax income per year to one or more employer-sponsored plans, you immediately save $2150 because you do not have to pay that amount to the IRS.

premium-only plan (POP)
An IRS approved plan offered by some employers that allows employees to withhold a portion of their pretax salary to pay their premium contributions for employer-provided health benefits.

Premium-Only Plan   Many large employers offer a **premium-only plan (POP)** that allows employees to withhold a portion of their pretax salary to pay their premium contributions for employer-provided health benefits. Benefits could include health, dental, vision, and disability insurance. Amounts withheld are not reported to the IRS as taxable income. For example, if Nhon Ngo, a restaurant manager in Dallas, has $40 per month ($480 annually) withheld through his employer to pay for his share of the employer-sponsored health insurance premium, he saves $206 ($480 × 0.43 [effective marginal tax rate]) a year because he does not have to send that amount to the government in taxes.

transportation reimbursement plan
An IRS approved plan offered by some employers that allows employees the opportunity to withhold a portion of their pretax salary to pay for work-related transportation expenses because it reduces the individual's income tax liability.

Transportation Reimbursement Plan   A **transportation reimbursement plan** is a similar pretax program. This employer plan allows you the opportunity to save money by using payroll deduction with pretax salary dollars to pay for work-related transportation expenses, such as transit passes, van-pool commuting, and qualified parking. If Nhon contributes $600 in pretax income to his employer's transportation plan, he saves $258 ($600 × 0.43).

Dependent Care Flexible Spending Account   An attractive benefit for employees who pay for child care or provide care for a parent is a salary reduction plan known as a **flexible spending account (FSA)** (also called an **expense reimbursement account**). An FSA allows an employee to fund qualified medical expenses on a pretax basis through salary reduction to pay for out-of-pocket unreimbursed expenses for health care (usually a maximum of $3000 annually) and dependent care (maximum $5000 annually) that are not covered by insurance. Examples are annual deductibles, office copayments, over-the-counter drugs, prescriptions, and orthodontia. The salary reductions are not included in the individual's taxable earnings reported on Form W-2, and reimbursements from an FSA account are tax free.

Suppose Nhon in the preceding example has $1200 annually withheld through his employer to be used to pay out-of-pocket medical expenses (e.g., eyeglasses, chiropractors, physician copayments) plus another $3000 to pay out-of-pocket expenses for dependent care of his child. Nhon's $4200 ($1200 + $3000) in FSA withholdings reduces his costs by $1806 ($4200 × 0.43).

FSAs are subject to a **use-it-or-lose-it rule,** which means that any unspent dollars in the account at the end of the year are forfeited and not returned to the employee. The IRS allows a 2½-month additional "grace period" if your employer provides this extension. As a result, you should make conservative estimates of your expenses when you elect your choices. For example, if you had $1000 withheld for medical expenses but spent only $700 over the year, the balance of $300 goes back to your employer, not to you.

Defined-Contribution Retirement Plan

Contributing money to a qualified employer-sponsored retirement plan reduces income taxes. A **defined-contribution retirement plan** (described in Chapters 1 and 17) is an IRS-approved retirement plan sponsored by an employer to which employees may make pretax contributions that lower their tax liability. The most popular plan is known as a **401(k) retirement plan,** although other variations exist as well.

The amount of money that an employee contributes to his or her individual account via salary reduction does not show up as taxable income on the employee's W-2 form. For example, if you contribute $2000 to your employer's retirement plan, this immediately saves you money that you will not have to pay in taxes.

An extra benefit of a defined-contribution retirement plan is that employers often offer full or partial **matching contributions** to employees' accounts up to a certain proportion and/or limit of the contributions made by the employee participant. For example, if you invest $2000 into your 401(k) plan and your employer matches half of what you contribute, that is an immediate return of 50 percent ($1000 ÷ $2000) on your investment! The employer's "match" is essentially free money.

All of the dollars in a qualified retirement plan are likely to be invested in alternatives such as stocks and stock mutual funds, where they will grow free of income taxes. Income taxes must be paid when withdrawals are made, presumably during retirement.

Strategy: Make Tax-Sheltered Investments

Investments are often made with **after-tax dollars,** which means that the individual earned the money and paid income taxes on it. They take their after-tax money and invest it. (Investment alternatives are examined in Chapters 13 through 16.) The returns earned from these investments usually result in taxable income.

Tax laws encourage certain types of investments or other taxpayer behaviors by giving them special tax advantages over other activities. As a result, numerous **tax-sheltered investments** exist. The tax laws allow certain income to be exempt from income taxes in the current year or permit an adjustment, reduction, deferral, or elimination of income tax liability. When making investment decisions, investors should consider tax-sheltered investments.

Some of the best tax-sheltering opportunities are offered to people who wish to save and invest for their retirement. Retirement accounts are not investments themselves but rather

---

flexible spending account (FSA) (or expense reimbursement account)
An IRS approved plan for employers that allows an employee to fund qualified medical expenses on a pretax basis through salary reduction to pay for out-of-pocket unreimbursed expenses for health and dependent care that are not covered by insurance.

use-it-or-lose-it rule
An IRS regulation requiring that unspent dollars in a flexible spending account at the end of a calendar year be forfeited, unless the employer allows a 2 ½ month grace period for spending the funds.

defined-contribution retirement plan
IRS-approved retirement plan sponsored by employers that allows employees to make pretax contributions that lower their tax liability.

matching contributions
Employer programs that match employees' 401(k) contributions up to a particular percentage.

after-tax dollars
Money on which employee has already paid taxes.

tax-sheltered investments
Investments that yield returns that are tax advantaged.

the "housing" for tax-advantaged investments. Several additional tax-sheltered opportunities exist that can help reduce one's tax liability.

Investing with Pretax Income

pretax income
The amount of income withheld from a worker's salary before taxes are calculated.

Making an investment contribution with **pretax income** means that you do not have to pay taxes this year on the income. For example, Britney Speigel made a $1000 contribution into an IRA that qualified as an adjustment to income. Britney's $1000 will not count as taxable income this year. This will save her $250 ($1000 × 0.25), assuming she pays income taxes at the 25 percent rate. Instead of paying the $250 in taxes on the $1000 in income, she can invest the $1000 in a stock mutual fund (discussed in Chapter 15) within her IRA account. Britney's $1000 includes $250 that otherwise would have gone to the government in taxes. This tax shelter is available with most retirement accounts. In effect, investing with pretax income is an interest-free deferral of taxes, $250 in this case, to fund one's investment.

Tax-Deferred Investment Growth

tax deferred
Income, dividends, or capital gains that are allowed to grow without taxes until distributions are taken.

When income, dividends, or capital gains are **tax deferred,** the investor does not pay the current-year tax liability. For example, if Adam Reynolds received $2000 in interest from his investments, he would owe $500 in income taxes this year assuming he pays at the 25 percent marginal tax rate. If his investments were either in tax-deferred alternatives or made within tax-deferred accounts, the law allows the taxes to be paid sometime in the future (or perhaps never at all). This benefit is substantial. Investments can grow faster because the money that would have gone to the government in taxes every year can remain in the investment to accumulate. The tax-free growth of such investments is called **tax-deferred compounding.**

tax-deferred compounding
Tax-free growth of tax-deferred investments.

Assume that Kyle Broflosken, who pays combined federal and state income taxes at the 30 percent rate, opens two mutual fund accounts: a regular taxable investment account and a tax-sheltered IRA investment account. Kyle puts $1000 into each account. One year later, each account is worth $1090. The extra $90 in each case represents investment growth derived from interest, dividends, and capital gains. The $90 increase in the regular taxable account is considered taxable income. If Kyle took out $27 to pay the tax liability, that would leave a net amount of $1063 in the account. In contrast, the whole $90 increase in the tax-sheltered account can stay there and continue to grow at a pretax annual rate of return rather than an after-tax rate. This means that the extra $27 in the tax-sheltered account is an asset that Kyle can keep out of Uncle Sam's reach for years and years; it can be invested and reinvested again and again. By the time income taxes must finally be paid—probably during retirement—Kyle might be in a lower tax bracket. In effect, the government "loans" tax-free money to Kyle to help fund his retirement plan.

individual retirement account (IRA)
Investment accounts that reduce current year income and that are allowed to accumulate tax free.

IRA

The amount contributed (up to $5000 annually) to an **individual retirement account (IRA)** is considered an adjustment to income, which reduces your current-year income tax liability. Investments inside the IRA (such as stocks and stock mutual funds) accumulate tax free. Income taxes are owed on any eventual withdrawals, likely during retirement. This type of IRA is also known as a traditional individual retirement account.

Roth IRA
An individual retirement account of investments made with after-tax money; the interest on such accounts is allowed to grow tax free, and withdrawals are also tax free.

Roth IRA

Contributions (up to $4000 annually) to a **Roth IRA** accumulate tax free and withdrawals are tax free. There is no tax break on contributions, as they are made with after-tax money. This is an excellent investment vehicle for people with a long-term investment horizon. IRAs are examined in Chapter 17.

Coverdell education savings account (or education savings account)
An IRS approved way to pay the future education costs for a child younger than age 18 whereby the earnings accumulate tax free and withdrawals for qualified expenses are tax free.

Coverdell Education Savings Account

Contributions of up to $2000 per year of after-tax money may be made to a **Coverdell education savings account** (also known as an **education savings account** and formerly known as an "education IRA") to pay the future education costs for a child younger than age 18. Earnings accumulate tax free and withdrawals for qualified expenses are tax free. The money can be used to pay for public, private, or religious school expenses, from kindergarten through trade school or college, including tuition, fees, room and board, tutoring, uniforms, home computers, Internet access and related technology, transportation, and extended day care.

Qualified Tuition Programs

There are two types of **qualified tuition programs,** and these are known as **529 plans.** Under the **prepaid educational service plan** an individual purchases tuition credits today for use in the future. Also known as a state-sponsored **prepaid tuition plan,** this program allows parents, relatives, and friends to purchase a child's future college education at today's prices by guaranteeing that amounts prepaid will be used for the future tuition at an approved institution of higher education in a particular state. The funds may be used to pay for tuition only—not room, board, or supplies.

The second qualified (Section 529) tuition program, called a **college savings plan,** is set up for a designated beneficiary. You may contribute up to $12,000 per year per child of after-tax money to a 529 college savings plan. Withdrawals are tax free if made for qualified education expenses such as tuition, room, and board. If one child does not go to college, the funds may be transferred to another relative. One may contribute to both a Section 529 plan and an education IRA for the same beneficiary in the same year.

Government Savings Bonds

Series EE and Series I **government savings bonds** are promissory notes issued by the federal government. The income is exempt from state and local taxes. You may defer the income tax until final maturity (30 years) or report the interest annually. Reporting the interest in a child's name is advisable when it can be offset totally by the child's standard deduction. You may exclude accumulated interest from bonds from income tax in the year you redeem the bonds to pay qualified educational expenses. (See Chapter 14 for more information on these and similar bonds.)

Municipal Bonds

Municipal bonds (also called **munis**) are long-term debts issued by local governments and their agencies used to finance public improvement projects. Interest is free from federal and state taxes if the bond is purchased in one's state of residence. Taxpayers in higher-income brackets (28 percent or more) often take advantage of these kinds of investments. (See Chapter 14.) Smart investors choose the bonds that pay the better return after payment of income taxes. The formula to decide whether a taxable investment or nontaxable investment is better for you appears in the box "How to Compare Taxable and After-Tax Yields."

Here is an example to illustrate the benefits of municipal bonds. Assume that Lauren Rider, a retiree living in Lincoln, Nebraska, currently has $100,000 in a certificate of deposit earning 4.5 percent, or $4500 annually ($100,000 × 0.045). She pays $1125 in tax on this income at her 25 percent federal marginal tax rate ($4500 × 0.25), leaving her a net after-tax return of $3375. Investing in a tax-exempt $100,000 municipal bond paying 3.9 percent would provide Lauren with a better after-tax return. She would receive $3900 ($100,000 × 0.039) tax free from a municipal bond, compared with $3375 ($4500 − $1125) after taxes on the certificate of deposit. The increase in her after-tax income would be $525 ($3900 − $3375).

Capital Gains on Housing

A big tax shelter is available to homeowners when they sell their homes. Those with appreciated principal residences are allowed to avoid taxes on capital gains of up to $500,000 if married and filing jointly and on gains up to $250,000 if single. The home must have been owned and used as the taxpayer's private residence for two out of the past five years prior to the date of the sale.

---

qualified tuition program
IRS approved plans whereby individuals may save and invest after-tax money for college and the withdrawals are free if made for qualified education expenses.

prepaid educational service plan
Type of qualified tuition program that allows purchase of a child's future college education at today's prices, locking in tuition prices. Also known as **prepaid tuition plan.**

college savings plan
One of the two types of qualified tuition programs that is set up for a designated beneficiary.

municipal bonds (munis)
Long-term debt issued by state and local governments and their agencies to finance public improvement projects; usually tax-free interest to buyer.

Did You Know?

Consider the Tax Consequences of Managing Income Taxes

This is an example of how one couple—model taxpayers—took numerous tax deductions to reduce their income taxes. Ron and Marilyn West of Longmont, Colorado, have a complex income return because they have both made it a habit to learn about tax-saving strategies and to take advantage of them whenever possible. The Wests have a son in elementary school and a daughter in college; Ron's disabled mother, who requires in-home nursing care, lives in their home as well. Because Marilyn went to work immediately after high school, she only recently started taking college classes at night. Last year, she spent $1000 on night-school tuition.

Part of the Wests' income comes from tax-exempt sources. The table shows their total income and demonstrates how they arrived at a very low final tax liability. The couple has taken advantage of applicable exclusions, adjustments, deductions, exemptions, and credits. Their deductions and tax credits, typical for a couple with three dependents, result in a tax liability of only $2804. The marginal tax rate for the West family is 15 percent. Their average tax rate for all income is 2.8 percent ($2804 ÷ $100,550). For a family with such a substantial income, they have been extremely successful in lowering their tax liability.

Total Income		Dollars
Ron's salary (self-employed)	$ 54,200	
Marilyn's salary	35,570	
Marilyn's year-end bonus	1,000	
State income tax refund (itemized last year)	180	
Interest on savings account	350	
Interest on tax-exempt state bonds	2,000*	
Gift from Marilyn's mother	2,500*	
Carpool income (Ron's van pool)	250*	
Reimbursements from flexible spending accounts	4,500*	
Total all income		$100,550
*Minus Excludable Income		
($2000 + $2500 + $250 + $4500 from above)		− $ 9,250
Gross Income		$ 91,300
Adjustments to Income		
Contribution—Ron's retirement account	$ 4,000	
Contribution—Marilyn's IRA	2,500	
Flexible spending account for health care	500	
Flexible spending account for dependent care	4,000	
College tuition and fees (daughter)	3,000	
Minus Adjustments to Income		− 14,000
Adjusted Gross Income (AGI)		$ 77,300
Deductions		
Medical expenses (includes long-term care premiums)	6,900	
Exclusion (7.5% of AGI)	− 5,798	
Total net medical expenses	$ 1,102	

Did You Know?

Taxes

Real property	2,800
Personal property (vehicles)	210
Total deductible taxes	$ 3,010

Interest Expenses

Home mortgage interest	10,800
Home-equity loan interest	460
Total deductible interest expenses	$11,260

Contributions

Church	1,200
Other qualified charities	240
Charitable travel	90
Total deductible contributions	$ 1,530

Casualty or Theft

Lost diamond ring (uninsured)	8,100
Insurance reimbursement	− 0
Reduction	− 100
Exclusion (10% of AGI)	− 7,730
Total deductible casualty loss	$ 270

Miscellaneous

Union dues (Ron)	480
Safe-deposit box	30
Unreimbursed job expenses	460
Cost of Ron looking for a new job	900
Investment publications	60
Financial planning tax advice	150
Tax publications	40
Subtotal	2,120
Less 2% of AGI	− 1,546
Total net miscellaneous deductions	$ 574

Total Itemized Deductions	− 17,746
Minus Exemptions (5 @ $3650)	− 18,250
Taxable Income	$41,304
Tax Liability (from Table 4.3)	$ 5,364

Tax Credits

Hope Scholarship credit (Marilyn)	−1,000
Dependent care credit (Ron's mother)	− 960
Child tax credit (son)	− 600
Minus total tax credits	− 2,560
Final Tax Liability	$ 2,804

Did You Know?

How to Compare Taxable and After-Tax Yields

Investors may choose to put their money into vehicles that provide taxable income, such as stocks, corporate bonds, and stock mutual funds. Taxpayers also have the opportunity to lower their income tax liabilities by investing in tax-exempt municipal bonds, money market funds that invest in municipal bonds, and other tax-exempt ventures. (These investment alternatives are discussed in Chapter 14.)

Because of their tax-exempt status, these investments offer lower nominal returns than taxable alternatives. But after considering the effects of taxes, the actual return to an investor on a tax-exempt investment may be higher than the after-tax yield on a taxable corporate bond.

To find out whether a taxable investment pays a higher after-tax yield than a tax-exempt alternative, the investor must determine the after-tax yield of each alternative. The **after-tax yield** is the percentage yield on a taxable investment after subtracting the effect of federal income taxes that will need to be paid on the investment. The after-tax yield on a tax-exempt investment is the same as the nominal yield because you do not have to pay income taxes on income from this kind of investment. So the question is, "How does the investor calculate the after-tax yield on a taxable investment?"

When you know the taxable yield, use Equation (4.1) to determine the equivalent after-tax yield on a taxable investment. Only then can you decide which investment is better. For example, suppose Bobby Bigbucks pays income taxes at

the 35 percent combined federal and state marginal tax rate and is considering buying either a municipal bond that pays a 3.5 percent yield or a taxable corporate bond that pays a 5.7 percent yield. Equation (4.1) calculates the equivalent after-tax yield on the corporate bond:*

$$\begin{aligned}
\text{After-tax yield} &= \text{taxable yield} \\
&\quad \times (1 - \text{federal marginal tax rate}) \quad (4.1)\dagger \\
&= 5.7 \times (1.00 - 0.35) \\
&= 5.7 \times 0.65 \\
&= 3.71
\end{aligned}$$

The answer is 3.71 percent. Thus, a 5.7 percent taxable yield is equivalent to an after-tax yield of 3.71 percent. Eureka! Now Bobby knows that he should buy the corporate bond paying 5.7 percent because its after-tax yield of 3.71 percent is higher than the 3.5 percent paid by the municipal bond. These differences may look small, and they are, but over time they add up. For example, the extra 0.21 percent (3.71 − 3.50) yield on a $20,000 bond investment for 20 years amounts to $840 [$20,000 × 0.0021 × 20 (bond interest is not compounded)]. That's real money!†

The higher your federal tax rate, the more favorable tax-exempt municipal bonds become as an investment compared with taxable bonds. The tax-exempt status of municipal bonds does not apply to capital gains. When you sell an investment for more than what you paid for it, you will owe federal income taxes on the capital gain.

*This and similar equations can be found and used on the Garman/Forgue companion website.
†The formula can be reversed to solve for the equivalent taxable yield when one knows the tax-exempt yield. To continue the example, the return for Bobby on a 3.71 percent tax-exempt bond is equivalent to a taxable yield of 5.7 percent [3.71 ÷ (1.00 − 0.35)]. If Bobby finds a tax-exempt bond paying more than 3.71 percent, he should consider buying it.

after-tax yield
The percentage yield on a taxable investment after subtracting the effect of federal income taxes that will need to be paid on the investment.

Strategy: Postpone Income

Another way to reduce income tax liability is to postpone income. This goal is achieved by purposefully making arrangements to receive some of this year's income in the next year, when your marginal tax rate might be lower, perhaps only 25 percent rather than 28 percent. A 3 percent tax savings (paying at the 25 percent rate rather than 28 percent) on $2000 of income is $60 ($2000 × 0.03), enough to pay for a meal in a quality restaurant. For example, if you expect a year-end commission check of $2000, the extra income this year might be enough to push you into a higher marginal tax bracket. If your employer is willing to give the commission check a January date, the income need not be reported until the following year.

You might expect to be in a lower tax bracket in the following year because you anticipate less sales commissions or know that you will not work full time (for example, if you return to school, have a child, or decide to travel). Retired people may be able to postpone withdrawals of income from retirement plans, and entrepreneurs may delay billing customers for work.

Advice from a Pro...

Buy a Home to Reduce Income Taxes

Hanna Pallagrosi of Rome, New York, took a sales position at a retail chain store two years ago, where she earned a gross income of $46,736. Hanna wisely made a $1000 contribution to her IRA. Her itemized deductions came to only $3800, so she took the standard deduction and personal exemption amounts. The result was a tax liability of $6046. Hanna was not happy about paying what she thought was a large tax bill that year.

Gross income	$46,736
Less adjustment to income	− 1,000
Adjusted gross income	45,736
Less value of one exemption (old figure)	− 3,200
Subtotal	42,536
Less standard deduction (old figure)	− 5,000
Taxable income	37,536
Tax liability (from old tax table not shown)	$ 6,046

Last year Hanna did not receive a raise. Nonetheless, Hanna continued to contribute $1000 into her IRA. To reduce her federal income taxes, she also became a homeowner after using some inheritance money to make the down payment on a condominium. During the year, she paid out $9126 in mortgage interest expenses and $1995 in real estate taxes.

After studying various tax publications, Hanna determined that she had $3814 in other itemized deductions that, when combined with the interest and real estate taxes, totaled $14,935. These deductions reduced Hanna's tax liability dramatically.

Gross income	$46,736
Less adjustment to income	− 1,000
Adjusted gross income	45,736
Less itemized deductions	− 14,935
Subtotal	30,801
Less value of one exemption	− 3,650
Taxable income	27,401
Tax liability (from Table 4.3)	$ 3,723

Hanna correctly concluded that the IRS "paid" $2323 ($6046 − $3723) toward the purchase of her condominium and her living costs because she did not have to forward those dollars to the government. An additional benefit for Hanna is that she now owns a home whose value could appreciate in the future. The best advice is to buy a home to reduce income taxes.

Frances C. Lawrence
Louisiana State University

Strategy: Shift Income to a Child

A parent who runs their own business may pay a child up to $9350 ($3650 [value of exemption] + $5700 [value of standard deduction]) in earned income, assuming no other income to the child before any income tax liability occurs for the child. Thus, the parent can deduct the payments and the child owes no tax.

A parent also can shift income-generating investment assets to the name of a child who then may receive as much as $950 in tax-free investment income (known by the IRS as **unearned income**). The next $950 is taxed at the child's rate. If a child is under age 19 (or up to 24 for full-time students), the amount above $1900 is taxed as though it were the income of the parent. This is called the **kiddie tax.**

Strategy: Bunch Deductions

Many people find that they do not have enough itemized deductions to exceed the standard deduction amount. By shifting the payment dates of some deductible items, you can increase your deductions. For example, if a single person has about $5500 of deductible expenses this year, she could prepay some items in December to push the total over the $5700 threshold and benefit by taking the excess deductions now. The next year she can take the standard deduction amount instead of itemizing.

This process is known as **bunching deductions.** Items that may be prepaid include medical expenses, dental bills, real estate taxes, state and local income taxes, the January

unearned income
Investment returns in the form of rents, dividends, capital gains, interest, or royalties.

kiddie tax
A tax on a portion of the unearned income of those 24 and younger typically earned on money placed in a savings or investment account by a parent in an effort to avoid capital-gains taxes.

bunching deductions
A technique to save on income taxes by prepaying tax deductible expenses in a year in advance so as to increase one's itemizations higher than the standard deduction threshold and taking the standard deduction in the following year.

payment of estimated state income taxes, personal property taxes that have been billed (e.g., on autos and boats), dues in professional associations, and charitable contributions. You may mail the payments or charge them on credit cards by December 31.

Strategy: Take All of Your Legal Tax Deductions

Although you should not spend money just to create a tax deduction, you are encouraged to take all of the deductions to which you are entitled. One way to increase itemized deductions, for example, is to purchase a home with a mortgage loan. The large amounts of money homeowners expend for both interest and real estate taxes are deductible.

Here are some other approaches to increase your deductions and keep more tax dollars in your pocket. Assume you are in the 15 percent marginal tax bracket and itemize deductions. Cash contributions made to people collecting door to door or at a shopping center during holidays are deductible, even though receipts are not given. Fifty dollars in contributions deducted can save you $7.50 in taxes. Instead of throwing out an old television set, donate it. An $80 charitable contribution for a TV will save you $12 in taxes. These amounts may sound like "small change," but lots of little tax deductions can quickly add up to more than $100, and that's real money!

Expenses for business-related trips can be a fruitful area for tax deductions. If you are in the 15 percent tax bracket and take one business trip per year, perhaps incurring $400 in deductible expenses, you will save another $60 in taxes, assuming your miscellaneous deductions already exceed 2 percent of your AGI. The IRS also permits tax deductions for the costs expended on occasional job-hunting trips. In other words, depending on your tax bracket, the U.S. government pays the bill for 15 or 25 percent of such expenditures.

Strategy: Buy and Manage a Real Estate Investment

Tax losses are paper losses in the sense that they may not represent actual out-of-pocket dollar losses. They are created when deductions generated from an investment (such as depreciation and net investment losses) exceed the income from an investment.

Taxpayers are allowed to deduct certain real estate losses against ordinary taxable income, such as salary, interest, dividends, and self-employment earnings. Deductions are allowed for real estate investors who (1) have an adjusted gross income of $150,000 or less and (2) actively participate in the management of the property. Here the investor may deduct up to $25,000 of net losses from a "passive investment," such as real estate, against income from "active" sources, such as salary. For example, a residential real estate investment property might generate an annual cash income $1000 greater than the out-of-pocket operating costs associated with it. After depreciation expenses on the building are taken as a tax deduction, the resulting $1500 tax loss may then be used to offset other income. This tax break begins to phase out for those with higher incomes. (For more details see Chapter 16, "Real Estate and High-Risk Investments.")

Do It NOW!

Managing your income taxes should not wait until you file in the spring. Start today by:

1. projecting your taxable income and total withholding for this year.
2. estimating your federal tax liability based on your income projection using this year's tax tables or schedules.
3. revising your W-4 form with your employer as necessary to withhold more if you estimate owing more in taxes or to withhold less to get an immediate raise in take-home pay if you expect a refund.

Did You Know?

Top 3 Financial Missteps in Managing Income Taxes

People slip up in managing income taxes when they do the following:

1. Turn all their income tax planning over to someone else
2. Overwithhold income to receive a refund next year
3. Ignore the impact of income taxes in their personal financial planning

tax losses
Paper losses that may not represent actual losses created when deductions generated from an investment exceed income from the investment.

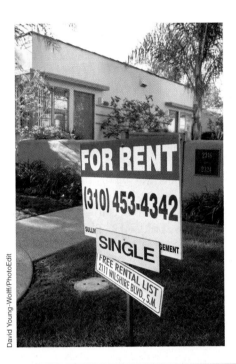

David Young-Wolff/PhotoEdit

Certain real estate losses are tax deductible.

Concept Check 4.3

1. Distinguish between two types of tax-sheltered investment returns.
2. Explain how to reduce income taxes via your employer, and name three employer-sponsored plans to do so.
3. Summarize the differences between an individual retirement account (IRA) and a Roth IRA.
4. Identify three strategies to avoid overpayment of income taxes (different from above), and summarize the essence of each.

What Do You Recommend NOW?

Now that you have read the chapter on managing income taxes, what advice can you offer Tom Hutchinson and Gerry Martin in the case at the beginning of the chapter regarding:

1. Using tax credits to help pay for Tom's college expenses?
2. Determining how much money Gerry will realize if she sells the stocks, assuming she pays federal income taxes at the 25 percent rate?
3. Buying a home?
4. Increasing contributions to their employer-sponsored retirement plans?
5. Establishing a sideline business for Tom's jewelry operation?

BananaStock/Jupiter Images

Big Picture Summary of Learning Objectives

1 Explain the nature of progressive income taxes and the marginal tax rate.

The federal personal income tax is a progressive tax because the tax rate increases as a taxpayer's taxable income increases. The marginal tax rate is applied to your last dollar of earnings. Your effective marginal tax rate is probably 43 percent.

2 Differentiate among the eight steps involved in calculating your federal income taxes.

There are eight steps in calculating your income taxes. Certain types of income may be excluded. Regulations permit you to subtract adjustments to income, exemptions, deductions, and tax credits before determining your final tax liability.

3 Use appropriate strategies to avoid overpayment of income taxes.

You can reduce your tax liability by following certain tax avoidance strategies, such as putting your money in tax-sheltered investments, reducing taxable income via your employer, and investing pretax money for tax-deferred compounding. Other strategies are to postpone income, bunch deductions, take all your legal deductions, and buy and manage a real estate investment.

Let's Talk About It

1. **During Slugging Economic Times.** Congress is likely to make the federal income tax more progressive by increasing the marginal tax rate for the highest earning taxpayers. Is this a good idea or bad, and why?

2. **Filing a Tax Return.** Many college students choose not to file a federal income tax return, assuming that the income taxes withheld by employers "probably" will cover their tax liability. Is such an assumption correct? What are the negatives of this practice if the employers withheld too much in income taxes? What are the negatives if the employers did not withhold enough in income taxes?

3. **Fairness of Capital Gains.** Long-term capital gains are taxed at a rate of 15 or 5 percent. What is your opinion on the fairness of these lower capital gains tax rates as compared with the marginal rates applied to income earned from employment that range as high as 35 percent?

4. **Reporting Cash Income.** Some college students earn money that is paid to them in cash and then do not include this as income when they file their tax returns. What are the pros and cons of this practice?

5. **Sideline Business.** Identify two possible sideline businesses that you might engage in to reduce your income tax liability.

6. **Tax Credits.** Name three tax credits that a college student might take advantage of while still in college or during the first few years after graduation.

7. **Reduce Tax Liability.** Identify five strategies to reduce income tax liability that you will likely take advantage of in the future.

Do the Math

1. **Find Tax Liability.** What would be the tax liability for a single taxpayer who has a gross income of $33,975? (Hint: Use Table 4.3, and don't forget to first subtract the value of a standard deduction and one exemption.)

2. **Marginal Tax Rate.** What would be the marginal tax rate for a single person who has a taxable income of (a) $20,210, (b) $27,800, (c) $26,055, and (d) $90,230? (Hint: Use Table 4.3.)

3. **Calculate Tax Liability.** Find the tax liabilities based on the taxable income of the following people: (a) married couple, $74,125; (b) married couple, $53,077; (c) single person, $27,880; (d) single person, $53,000. (Hint: Use Table 4.3.)

4. **Use Tax Table.** Joseph Addai determined the following tax information: gross salary, $59,400; interest earned, $90; IRA contribution, $1000; personal exemption, $3650; and itemized deductions, $3950. Calculate Joseph's taxable income and tax liability filing single. (Hint: Use Table 4.3.)

5. **Use Tax Rate Schedule.** Anthony Clark determined the following tax information: salary, $144,000; interest earned, $2000; personal exemption, $3650; itemized deductions, $9000; qualified retirement plan contribution, $7000. Calculate Anthony's taxable income and tax liability. (Hint: Use Table 4.2.)

Financial Planning Cases

Case 1

A New Family Calculates Income and Tax Liability

Stephanie Nichols and her two children, Austin and Alexandra, moved into the home of her new husband, Glenn Sandler, in Ames, Iowa. Stephanie is employed as a union organizer, and her husband manages a vegetarian food store. The Nichols-Sandler family income consists of the following: $40,000 from

Stephanie's salary; $42,000 from Glenn's salary; $10,000 in life insurance proceeds from a deceased aunt; $140 in interest from savings; $4380 in alimony from Stephanie's ex-husband; $14,200 in child support from her ex-husband; $500 cash as a Christmas gift from Glenn's parents; $90 from a friend who rides to work in Stephanie's vehicle; and a $1600 tuition-and-books scholarship Stephanie received to go to college part time last year.

(a) What is the total of the Nichols-Sandler reportable gross income?

(b) After putting $5600 into qualified retirement plan accounts last year, what is their adjusted gross income?

(c) How many exemptions can the family claim, and how much is the total value allowed the household?

(d) How much is the allowable standard deduction for the household?

(e) Their itemized deductions are $13,300, so should they itemize or take the standard deduction?

(f) What is their taxable income for a joint return, and what is their marginal tax rate?

(g) What is their final federal income tax liability? (Hint: Use Table 4.3.)

(h) If Stephanie's and Glenn's employers withheld $6300 for income taxes, does the couple owe money to the government or do they get a refund? How much?

Case 2
Taxable Versus Tax-Exempt Bonds

Art Williams, radio station manager in Franklin County, New Jersey, is in the 25 percent federal marginal tax bracket and pays an additional 5 percent in taxes to the state of New Jersey. Art currently has more than $20,000 invested in corporate bonds bought at various times that are earning differing amounts of taxable interest: $10,000 in ABC earning 5.9 percent; $5000 in DEF earning 5.5 percent; $3000 in GHI earning 5.8 percent; and $2000 in JKL earning 5.4 percent. What is the after-tax return of each investment? To calculate your answers, use the after-tax yield formula (or the reversed formula) on page 130, or the *Garman/Forgue* companion website.

Case 3
Taxable Versus Nontaxable Income

Identify each of the following items as either part of taxable income or an exclusion, adjustment or an allowable itemized deduction from taxable income for LaDainian Tomison and Megan Smithfield, a married couple from San Diego:

(a) LaDainian earns $45,000 per year.

(b) LaDainian receives a $1000 bonus from his employer.

(c) Megan receives $40,000 in commissions from her work.

(d) Megan receives $300 in monthly child support.

(e) LaDainian pays $200 each month in alimony.

(f) LaDainian contributes $2000 to his retirement account.

(g) Megan inherits a car from her aunt that has a fair market value of $3000.

(h) Megan sells the car and donates $1500 to her aunt's church.

(i) LaDainian receives a $5000 gift from his mother.

Case 4
Victor and Maria Reduce Their Income Tax Liability

The year before last, Victor earned $51,000 from his retail management position and Maria began working full-time and earned $45,000 as a dental hygienist. After they took the standard deduction and claimed four exemptions (themselves plus their two children), their federal income tax liability was about $12,000. After hearing from friends that they were paying too much in taxes, the couple vowed to try to never again pay that much. Therefore, the Hernandezes embarked on a yearlong effort to reduce their income tax liability. This year they tracked all of their possible itemized deductions, and both made contributions to qualified retirement plans at their places of employment.

(a) Calculate the Hernandezes' income tax liability for this year as a joint return (using Table 4.3) given the following information: gross salary income (Victor, $56,000; Maria $51,000); state income tax refund ($400); interest on checking and savings accounts ($250); holiday bonus from Maria's employer ($240); contributions to qualified retirement accounts ($5000); itemized deductions (state income taxes, $2700, real estate taxes, $2600; mortgage interest, $6300; charitable contributions, $2500); and exemptions ($3650 each) for themselves and their two children.

(b) List five additional strategies that Victor and Maria might consider for next year's tax planning to reduce their tax liability.

Case 5
The Johnsons Calculate Their Income Taxes

Several years have gone by since Harry and Belinda graduated from college and started their working careers. They both earn good salaries. They believe that they are paying too much in federal income taxes. The Johnsons' total income last year included Harry's salary of $63,000, Belinda's reportable income of $81,000 after subtracting her 401(k) deposits, $300 interest on savings and checking, and $3000 interest income from the trust that is taxed in the same way as interest income from checking and savings accounts. Harry deposits $3000 per year into a traditional IRA.

(a) What is the Johnsons' reportable gross income on their joint tax return?

(b) What is their adjusted gross income?

(c) What is the total value of their exemptions?

(d) How much is the standard deduction for the Johnsons?

(e) The Johnsons are buying a home that has monthly mortgage payments of $3000, or $36,000 a year. Of this amount, about $32,800 goes for interest and real estate property taxes. The couple has an additional $14,000 in itemized deductions. Using these numbers and Table 4.3, calculate their taxable income and tax liability.

(f) Assuming they had a combined $18,000 in federal income taxes withheld, how much of a refund will the Johnsons receive?

(g) What is their marginal tax rate?

(h) Based on gross income, what is their average tax rate?

(i) List three additional ways that the Johnsons might reduce their tax liability next year.

On the 'Net

Go to the Web pages indicated to complete these exercises. You can also go to the *Garman/Forgue* companion website at www.cengage.com/finance/garman for an expanded list of exercises. Under General Business, select the title of this text. Click on the Internet Exercises link for this chapter.

1. Visit the website for the Internal Revenue Service at www.irs.gov. Use the search function to find "Publication 501." Use this publication to determine (a) whether you must file a return, (b) who can claim you as an exemption, and (c) how much your standard deduction is.

2. Visit the website for the Internal Revenue Service's primary tax information document for taxpayers—Publication 17, *Your Federal Income Tax*—at www.irs.gov/publications/p17/index.html. Scroll down the menu to "Education Credits." There you will find information on the Hope Scholarship credit and the lifetime learning credit. How might these two credits help you lower your or your parents' overall federal income tax bill?

3. Visit the website for the Federation of Tax Administrators at www.taxadmin.org/fta/rate/. Click on "tax rates." There you will find a table with tax rates for all states that levy an income tax. Based on what you found, what is your combined federal and state marginal tax rate?

Visit the Garman/Forgue companion website . . .

www.cengage.com/finance/garman

Managing Checking and Savings Accounts

! You Must Be Kidding, Right ?

Patti Patterson realized about two weeks ago that she had misplaced her debit card. At first she was not worried because she reasoned that it had to be somewhere at home. Last week she received her savings account statement. She looked at her statement today and found that $200 had been withdrawn from her account on five different occasions ($1000 total). She immediately called her bank to report the fraudulent withdrawals. How much of this money will Patti lose because of the unauthorized withdrawals?

A. $0

B. $50

C. $500

D. $1000

The answer is C, $500. Because Patti waited more than two days after realizing the card was lost to report it to her financial institution, federal law states that she is liable for the first $500 in unauthorized uses. If she had notified the bank within two days, her loss would have been only $50. If Patti failed to notify her bank of the loss within 60 days, the law states that she would lose all of the money taken fraudulently. It's smart to immediately report a lost debit card!

Learning Objectives

After reading this chapter, you should be able to:

1 Identify the tools of monetary asset management and the types of companies that provide such financial services.

2 Earn interest and pay no or low fees on your checking accounts.

3 Make the best use of the benefits of savings accounts.

4 Explain the importance of placing excess funds in a money market account.

5 Describe electronic money management, including your legal protections.

6 Discuss your personal finances and money management more effectively with loved ones.

What Do You Recommend?

Photodisc/Alamy

Mark Rosenberg and Trina Adams are to be married in two months. Both are employed full time and currently have their own apartments. Once married, they will move into Trina's apartment because it is larger. They plan to use Mark's rent money to begin saving for a down payment on a home to be purchased in four or five years. Mark has a checking account at a branch of a large regional commercial bank near his workplace where he deposits his paychecks. He also has three savings accounts—one at his bank and two small accounts at a savings and loan association near where he went to college. Mark pays about $30 per month in fees on his various accounts. In addition, he has a $10,000 certificate of deposit (CD) from an inheritance; this CD will mature in five months. Trina has her paycheck directly deposited into her share draft account at the credit union where she works. She has a savings account at the credit union as well as a money market account at a stock brokerage firm that was set up years ago when her father gave her 300 shares of stock. She also has $4300 in an individual retirement account invested through a mutual fund.

What would you recommend to Trina and Mark on the subject of managing checking and savings accounts regarding:

1. Where they can obtain the services that they need for managing their monetary assets?

2. Their best use of checking accounts and savings accounts as they begin saving for a home?

3. The use of a money market account for managing their monetary assets?

4. Their use of electronic banking?

5. How they can best discuss the management of their money and finances?

Your Next Five Years

In the next five years you can start achieving financial success by doing the following related to checking and savings accounts:

1. Use a free, interest-earning checking account for your day-to-day spending needs.

2. Start now to build an emergency fund sufficient to cover three months of living expenses.

3. Use a pay-yourself-first approach as you begin to build other savings through high-interest accounts.

4. Use investment vehicles for wants that will not occur until five or more years in the future.

5. Use all your checking and savings accounts appropriately by never overdrawing the accounts and by reconciling them monthly.

monetary assets
Cash and low-risk, near-cash items that can quickly be converted into cash.

Your financial success will depend in part on how well you manage your **monetary assets.** These assets were defined in Chapter 3 as cash and low-risk, near-cash items that can be readily converted to cash with little or no loss in value. If you are a typical college student, your monetary assets are the largest component of your net worth and are the major focus of the activities you consider "personal finance."

People use monetary assets in one of three ways. First, they spend them. They buy food, clothing, entertainment, and a long list of products and services. Spending often requires cash or the use of a check or a debit card to access funds in a checking account. (Using credit is covered in Chapters 6 and 7.) Checking accounts are appropriate places to keep money that you will spend within the next three to six months or so. The second way that people use monetary assets is to set aside funds to meet needs that will occur six months to five years in the future. You could keep these funds in a checking account, but savings accounts pay more interest. With savings accounts, the focus is on holding money safely until needed in the future. Even though some banks go bankrupt every year, keep in mind that the money in most checking and savings accounts is fully insured by the federal government. The third way that people use monetary assets is to make investments. Here the goal is to earn a better return on your money for the long term. Investments are the best places to put money you will not need for 5, 10, or even 20 years in the future. The beauty of investments is that over long periods of time it is quite possible to earn three or four times more than the original amount deposited. Investments are examined in Chapters 13 through 17.

What Is Monetary Asset Management?

1   Learning Objective

Identify the tools of monetary asset management and the types of companies that provide such financial services.

monetary asset (cash) management
How you handle your monetary assets.

liquidity
Ease with which an asset can be converted to cash.

Monetary asset (cash) management encompasses how you handle all of your monetary assets, including cash on hand, checking accounts, savings accounts and certificates of deposit, and money market accounts. The goal is to maximize interest earnings and to minimize fees while keeping funds safe and readily available for living expenses, emergencies, and saving and investment opportunities. Successful monetary asset management allows you to earn interest on your money while maintaining reasonable liquidity and safety. **Liquidity** refers to the speed and ease with which an asset can be converted to cash. Your funds are safe when they are free from financial risk.

The Three Tools of Monetary Asset Management

As illustrated in Figure 5.1, monetary asset management relies on three major tools:

1. Low-cost, interest-earning checking accounts from which to pay ongoing, current living expenses.

2. Interest-earning savings accounts in local financial institutions in which you deposit funds for upcoming expenditures or to accumulate funds for future investments.

3. Money market accounts in local financial institutions or other financial services providers. These accounts pay higher interest rates than checking and savings accounts. They have limited check-writing privileges and, thus, are a cross between a checking and a savings account.

Instant Message

Lifeline Banking May Save You Money

College students who are financially independent of their parents may qualify for a very low-cost lifeline banking account.

Checking account	Savings account	Money market account
• NOW checking (pays interest)	• Statement savings ($+1/4\%$) • Certificate of deposit ($+1/3\%$ to $+2\%$)	• Money market deposit account ($+1/3\%$) • Super NOW ($+2/5\%$) • Money market mutual fund ($+1/2\%$ to $+3/4\%$) • Asset management account ($+1/2\%$ to $+3/4\%$)

Figure 5.1
Three Tools of Monetary Asset Management (with Illustrative Interest Rates Earned on Deposited Funds)

Who Provides Monetary Asset Management Services?

The **financial services industry** comprises companies that provide checking, savings, and money market accounts and possibly credit, insurance, investment, and financial planning services. These companies include depository institutions such as banks and credit unions, stock brokerage firms, mutual funds, financial services companies, and insurance companies. Table 5.1 matches these various types of firms with the financial products and services that they offer. As you can see, there is considerable overlap. For example, State Farm, which most people recognize as an insurance company, also owns a mutual fund and a bank.

financial services industry
Companies that provide monetary asset management and other services.

Depository Institutions **Depository institutions** are organizations licensed to take deposits and make loans. They all can offer some form of government account insurance

depository institutions
Organizations licensed to take deposits and make loans.

Table 5.1 Today's Providers of Monetary Asset Management Services

Providers	What They Sell	Examples of Well-Known Company Names
Depository institutions (banks, mutual savings banks, savings and loan associations, and credit unions)	Checking, savings, lending, credit cards, investments, and trust advice	CitiBank, Chase, Bank of America, Wells Fargo
Mutual funds	Money market mutual funds, tax-exempt funds, bond funds, and stock funds	Fidelity, T. Rowe Price, Vanguard
Stock brokerage firms	Securities investments (stocks and bonds), mutual funds, and real estate investment trusts	Schwab, Fidelity
Financial services companies	Checking, savings, lending, credit cards, securities investments, real estate, investments, insurance, accounting and legal advice, and financial planning	American Express, A. G. Edwards, Raymond James
Insurance companies	Property and liability, health and life insurance, credit services, financial planning services.	Allstate, Aetna, State Farm

Instant Message

Press "Credit" When Using Your Debit Card

Debit card fees are now much more common when you make purchases with the card. Press the "credit" key instead and sign your name on the receipt and no fee will be charged.

Did You Know?

The Top 3 Financial Missteps in Managing Checking and Savings

People slip up in managing checking and savings accounts when they do the following:

1. Pay high fees unnecessarily for bounce protection
2. Keep too much money in a checking account where it earns very little interest
3. Fail to reconcile their accounts on a regular basis

credit union (CU)
Member-owned, not-for-profit federally insured financial institutions that provide checking, savings, and loan services to members.

federal deposit insurance
Insures deposits, both principal amounts and accrued interest, up to $250,000 per account for most accounts.

on their customers' deposits and are government regulated. They offer a wide range of financial services. Examples of depository institutions are commercial banks, savings banks, and credit unions. Although each is a distinct type of institution, people often call them all simply *banks*.

Commercial banks are corporations chartered under federal and state regulations. They offer numerous consumer services, such as checking, savings, loans, safe-deposit boxes, investment services, financial counseling, and automatic payment of bills. Accounts in federally chartered banks are insured against loss by the **Bank Insurance Fund (BIF)** of the **Federal Deposit Insurance Corporation (FDIC),** which is an agency of the federal government. President Barack Obama has recommended that Congress create a National Bank Supervisor to monitor all federally chartered banks and federal branches of foreign banks.

Savings banks (or **savings and loan associations–S&Ls**) focus primarily on accepting savings and providing mortgage and consumer loans. They offer checking services through interest-earning NOW accounts (discussed later in this chapter). Savings banks generally pay depositors an interest rate about 0.10 to 0.20 percentage points higher than the rate found at commercial banks. The FDIC insures accounts in all federally chartered savings banks through the FDIC's **Savings Association Insurance Fund (SAIF).**

A **credit union (CU)** also accepts deposits and makes loans. Credit unions operate on a not-for-profit basis and are owned by their members. The members/owners of the credit union all share some common bond, such as the same employer, church, trade union, or fraternal association. People in the family of a member are also eligible to join. Federally chartered credit unions have their accounts insured through the **National Credit Union Share Insurance Fund (NCUSIF),** which is administered by the National Credit Union Administration (NCUA). State-chartered credit unions are often insured by NCUSIF, and most others participate in private insurance programs. Credit unions usually pay higher interest rates and charge lower fees than commercial banks or savings banks.

A **mutual savings bank (MSB)** is similar to a savings bank in that it also accepts deposits and makes housing and consumer loans. State laws permit these banks to operate in only 17 states, primarily those in the eastern United States. They are called "mutual" because the depositors own the institution and share in the earnings. Generally, MSBs have the FDIC's BIF coverage. Like savings banks, they offer interest-earning checking accounts.

Deposit Insurance Protects Your Money

Deposits in depository institutions are insured against loss of both the amount on deposit and the accrued interest by various insurance funds. This **federal deposit insurance**★ for your deposits at any one institution works as follows:

1. The maximum insurance on all of your single-ownership (individual) accounts (held in your name only) is $250,000.
2. The maximum insurance on all of your joint accounts (accounts held with other individuals) is $250,000.
3. The maximum insurance on all of your retirement accounts is $250,000.
4. A maximum of $250,000 in insurance per beneficiary is available on **payable at death accounts** (accounts set up so that the funds go to a designated person(s) upon the death of the account holder).

★ The amounts will drop to $100,000 unless the federal government extends the $250,000 coverage past December 31, 2013.

Thus, individuals might have several increments of insurance for their accounts at any one institution. Funds on deposit at other institutions will also have these same limits. So if you had $140,000 in individual accounts at each of two different institutions, you would have a total of $280,000 of deposit insurance.

Other Financial Services Providers   Depository institutions are not the only providers of monetary asset management services. Mutual funds, stock brokerage houses, and insurance companies provide some cash management services as well. The one service they do not provide are government insured checking and savings accounts. Note that many of these same companies also own banks and thus do provide insured deposits through their banking entities.

Mutual funds are investment companies that raise money by selling shares to the public and then invest that money in a diversified portfolio of investments. Most have created cash management accounts to provide a convenient and safe place to keep money while awaiting alternative investment opportunities. Note that money deposited in a mutual fund is not insured by the federal government, although some mutual fund companies purchase insurance privately for the noninvestment portions of customers' accounts. Mutual funds are the subject of Chapter 15.

Stock brokerage firms are licensed financial institutions that specialize in selling and buying stocks, bonds, and other investments and providing advice to investors. They earn commissions based on the buy and sell orders that they process. Stock brokerage firms typically offer cash or mutual fund accounts into which clients may place money while waiting to make investments. The noninvestment portion of an account (for example, cash held in the account prior to making an investment) is insured by the Securities Investor Insurance Corporation, a nongovernment entity.

Insurance companies provide property, liability, health, life, and other insurance products. Many offer monetary asset services, such as money market accounts. Some also offer vehicle loans and credit cards.

mutual funds
Investment companies that raise money by selling shares to the public and then invest that money in a diversified investment portfolio.

 Concept Check 5.1

1. Identify the primary goals of monetary asset management.
2. Explain the circumstances when it would be appropriate to have funds in a checking account, a savings account, or in investments.
3. Describe the primary differences between depository institutions and other financial services providers.
4. Describe your insurance protections when you have funds on deposit in a depository institution.

Tool #1—Interest-Earning Checking Accounts

2 Learning Objective
Earn interest and pay no or low fees on your checking accounts.

A **checking account** at a depository institution allows you to write checks against amounts you have on deposit. Checks transfer your deposited funds to other people and organizations. Checking accounts also can be accessed by using a **debit card** (or **check card**) in an automated teller machine (ATM) or a point-of-sale (POS) terminal at a retail store. When you use a debit card, funds are instantaneously removed from your account. You can also access your checking account via telephone or home computer. Whenever you deposit money into, withdraw funds from, or make any payment out of a checking account make sure you record the transaction with its date, amount, purpose, and your new balance in the

checking accounts
At depository institutions, allow depositors to write checks against their deposited funds, which transfer deposited funds to other people and organizations.

You should reconcile your bank accounts monthly.

Evok20 | Dreamstime.com

check register you received when you obtained your blank checks. This section examines the types of checking accounts available and checking account charges, fees, and penalties.

Types of Checking Accounts

interest-earning checking account
Any account on which you can write checks that pays interest.

tiered interest
Common type of NOW account that pays lower interest on smaller deposits and higher interest on larger balances.

Checking accounts may or may not pay interest. Interest-paying accounts with no or very low fees are available since all depository institutions offer some form of **interest-earning checking account** (also called a **negotiable order of withdrawal [NOW] account**). A **share draft account** is the credit-union version of a NOW account. Costs for a share draft account are typically lower than those for a checking account at a bank or savings bank. NOW accounts and share draft accounts may pay higher interest rates on larger balances (such as amounts above $1000). The combination of a base rate and a higher rate is called **tiered interest.** For example, an account might pay 1 percent on the first $2000 and 1.25 percent on any additional funds in the account.

A **lifeline banking account** offers access to certain minimal financial services that every consumer needs—regardless of income—to function in our society. An applicant's income and net worth determine acceptance into a lifeline program. The cost of lifeline banking accounts is extremely low, often about $5 per month although they do not pay interest.

Checking Account Minimum-Balance Requirements

Most interest-earning checking accounts have a minimum-balance requirement that, if not met, will result in the assessment of a monthly fee. In addition, interest earned is usually not paid for a month when the account falls below the minimum. An account with no minimum-balance requirement is preferable. Checking account users should always consider the amount of interest that will be lost and the fees that will be imposed.

Did You Know?

What Happens When You Write a Check?

When you write a check, you either simultaneously make a copy that serves as your record that the check was written or make a note of the transaction in your check register. When the check is paid by your bank it is said to have **cleared** the bank. The check itself is treated in one of two ways. First, in the traditional method, a **canceled check** is sent to your bank so that the funds can be paid to whomever you had written the check. Second, in the method now most commonly used, the check is scanned by the receiving bank (or even the business to which you gave it) and an electronic **substitute check** is created and transmitted immediately to your bank. As a result the check can clear your bank in a matter of minutes or hours. Your checking account statement will indicate which checks cleared via a substitute check. Substitute checks are an acceptable version of the original check written by you. Under the Check Clearing for the 21st Century

Act, your bank must quickly correct any errors in the processing of your check if the substitute check and the original check are both paid by your bank. Check your statement each month to ensure that this type of error has not occurred.

A **stop-payment order** tells your bank not to honor a check when it's presented for payment. To issue such an order, you can telephone your bank and stop payment on the check. In any event, a stop-payment order works only if the check has not yet cleared. And with electronic processing, check clearing can occur in a matter of minutes as can debit card transactions. Be aware that if the verbal stop-payment order is not followed up with a written instruction to the bank, the person or merchant to whom the check was written can *still* cash the check after 14 days. Even with a written request, the check can be cashed after six months unless the order has been renewed.

Did You Know?

About Payment Instruments for Special Needs

There are four types of payment instruments that you might find useful from time to time.

Traveler's Checks

Traveler's checks are issued by large financial institutions (such as American Express, Visa, and Carte Blanche) and sold through various outlets. They are accepted almost everywhere. Purchasers typically pay a fee of 1 percent of the amount of the traveler's checks written in specific U.S. denominations ($10, $20, $50, and $100) and in many foreign currencies. All traveler's check companies guarantee replacement of lost checks if their serial numbers are identified.

Money Orders

A **money order** is a checking instrument bought for a particular amount with a fee assessed based on the amount of the order. Many financial institutions including retailers such as Wal-Mart and the U.S. Postal Service sell money orders.

Certified Checks

A **certified check** is a personal check drawn on your account on which your financial institution imprints the word *certified*, signifying that the account has sufficient funds to cover its payment. The financial institution simultaneously places a hold on that amount in the account until the check clears. The fee for a certified check is $5 to $15.

Cashier's Checks

Some payees insist on receiving payment in the form of a **cashier's check** drawn on the account of the financial institution itself and, thus, backed by the institution's finances. To obtain such a check, you would pay the financial institution the amount of the cashier's check and pay a fee of $5 to $15.

Instant Message

Free Checking Is Not Really Free

Lots of banks offer "free" checking accounts. What this means is that there is no minimum-balance requirement or monthly maintenance fee on the account and no fee for writing too many checks. However, there will be fees for writing checks when there are insufficient funds in the account, using another bank's ATM, inactivity on the account, and other events.

Decision making becomes more difficult when the institution offers an interest-earning account in combination with either a minimum- or average-balance requirement. With a **minimum-balance account,** the customer must keep a certain amount (perhaps $500 or $700) in the account throughout a specified time period (usually a month or a quarter) to avoid a flat service charge (usually $5 to $15). A fee is assessed whenever the triggering event occurs—that is, when the balance drops below the specified minimum. With an **average-balance account,** a service fee is assessed only if the average daily balance of funds in the account drops below a certain level (perhaps $800 or $1000) during the specified time period (usually a month or a quarter).

In addition to monthly fees, institutions may assess many other fees. People interested in getting their money's worth in banking would be wise to avoid as many of the charges shown in Table 5.2 as possible.

Table 5.2   Costs and Penalties on Checking and Savings Accounts

Account Activity	Reasons for Assessing Costs or Penalties	Assessed on Checking or Savings
Automated teller machine (ATM) transactions	A customer's account is assessed a fee (often $1) for each transaction on an ATM; an additional fee may be charged for using an ATM not owned by the financial institution.	Checking, savings
Telephone, computer, or teller information	Fees are assessed for access or requests for account information by telephone, by computer, or in person (often $2 per transaction) after a number of free requests (perhaps three) have been made.	Checking, savings
Maintenance fees on a minimum-balance account (often waived if paychecks are directly deposited electronically)	The account balance falls below a set minimum amount, such as $300. A set fee of $5 to $15 per month is often charged.	Checking
Maintenance fees on an average-balance account (often waived if paychecks are directly deposited electronically)	The average daily account balance for the month falls below a set amount, such as $500. The cost is usually based on a set fee, a scaled amount (the more the account falls below the average, the greater the cost), or a percentage of the amount the account falls below the average.	Checking
Stop-payment order	A customer asks the financial institution to not honor a particular check; the fee is $15 to $30 per check.	Checking
Bad check "bounced" for insufficient funds	Costs of $20 to $40 or more are assessed for each check written or deposited to your account marked "insufficient funds."	Checking
Early account closing	Charges are assessed if a customer closes an account within a month or quarter of opening it. Charges range from $5 to $10.	Checking, savings
Delayed use of funds	Amounts deposited by check cannot be withdrawn until rules allow it.	Checking, savings
Inactive accounts	A monthly penalty may be assessed for inactive accounts (ones with no activity for six months to a year).	Checking, savings
Excessive withdrawals	Some savings institutions assess a penalty ($1 to $3) when withdrawals exceed a certain number per month.	Savings
Early withdrawal	Amounts withdrawn before the end of a quarter earn no interest for that quarter.	Savings
Deposit penalty	Deposits made during the current quarter earn no interest until the beginning of the next quarter.	Savings

Concept Check 5.2

1. Distinguish between an interest-paying checking account and a lifeline account.
2. What is meant by *free* checking?
3. List three checking account fees or penalties that you could easily avoid by using your account appropriately.

Instant Message

Using Checking Accounts in Budgeting

Copies of your written checks, your check register, and your debit card receipts are very useful in budgeting as they provide a record of money spent. Keep track of all checks written and retain all debit card receipts until you can verify their accuracy in your account statement.

Tool #2—Savings Accounts

The second tool of monetary asset management is a **savings account.** A savings account provides you with a readily accessible source of emergency cash and a temporary holding place for funds in excess of those needed for daily living expenses. Funds on deposit in a savings account are considered time deposits rather than **demand deposits** (another term for checking accounts). **Time deposits** are savings that are expected to remain on deposit in a financial institution for an extended period. Institutions have a rule requiring that savings account holders give 30 to 60 days' notice for withdrawals, although this restriction is seldom enforced. Some time deposits are **fixed-time deposits,** which specify a period that the savings *must* be left on deposit, such as six months or three years; certificates of deposit (CDs) fit this description.

Statement Savings Accounts

The typical savings account offered by depository institutions is the statement savings account (also called a passbook savings account). Statement savings accounts permit frequent deposits or withdrawals of funds. No fees are assessed as long as a low minimum balance ($25 to $100) is maintained. Statement savings account holders are provided with printed receipts to document their account transactions, and transactions usually can be accessed through ATMs. The process for opening a savings account is similar to that for a checking account.

Certificates of Deposit

A **certificate of deposit (CD)** is an interest-earning savings instrument purchased for a fixed period of time. The required deposit amounts range from $100 to $100,000, while the time periods range from seven days to eight years. The interest rate in force when the CD is purchased typically remains fixed for the entire term of the deposit. Depositors collect their principal and interest when the CD expires. Interest rates on longer-term CDs are usually higher than the comparable rates on shorter-term instruments. Certificates of deposit are insured through the FDIC or the NCUSIF if purchased through an insured depository institution.

Variable-rate certificates of deposit (or **adjustable-rate CDs**) are also available. These instruments pay an interest rate that is adjusted (up or down) periodically. Typically, savers are allowed to "lock in," or fix, the rate at any point before their CDs mature. This variability detracts from the main virtue of the fixed-rate CD—predictability. The best variable-rate CDs have a guaranteed minimum interest rate. **Bump-up CDs** allow savers to bump up the interest rate once to a higher market rate, if available, and to add up to 100 percent of the initial deposit whenever desired.

Money withdrawn from a CD before the end of the specified time period is subject to interest penalties. For certificates held less than one year, the depositor may lose a minimum of one month's interest; on certificates held more than a year, the depositor may lose a

3 Learning Objective

Make the best use of the benefits of savings accounts.

stop-payment order
Notifying your bank not to honor a check when it's presented for payment.

minimum-balance account
Checking account that requires customers to keep a certain minimum amount for a specified time period to avoid fees.

average-balance account
Checking account for which service fees are assessed if the account's average daily balance drops below a certain level during specified time.

savings account
Account that provides an accessible source of emergency cash and a temporary holding place for extra funds that will earn some interest.

certificate of deposit (CD)
An interest-earning savings instrument purchased for a fixed period of time.

Advice from a Pro...

Endorse Your Checks Properly

Endorsement is the process of writing on the back of a check to legally transfer its ownership, usually in return for the cash amount indicated on the face of the check. Choosing the proper type of endorsement can protect you from having the check cashed by someone else against your wishes.

A check with a **blank endorsement** contains only the payee's signature on the back. Such a check immediately becomes a bearer instrument, meaning that anyone who attempts to cash it very likely will be allowed to do so, even if the check has been lost or stolen. You would be wise to never make a blank endorsement prior to depositing or cashing a check.

A **special endorsement** can be used to limit who can cash a check; to make this kind of endorsement, you write the phrase *Pay to the order of [name]* on the back along with

your signature. A special endorsement can easily be put on a check that you want to sign over to another person. Such a "two-party check" is hard to cash other than by depositing it in an account at a financial institution.

A **restrictive endorsement** uses the phrase *For deposit only* written on the back along with the signature. It authorizes the financial institution to accept the check only as a deposit to an account. No one else can cash such a check. Checks deposited by mail should always be endorsed this way. In addition, you can include the name of the financial institution and the account number as part of the endorsement to make it even more restrictive.

Kathleen Prochaska-Cue
University of Nebraska–Lincoln

Did You Know?

How to Ladder Your CDs?

Most people who place money in CDs like them because the funds are insured and, thus, have no risk. But that is not exactly true. You see, when you put money in a CD, you have locked in an interest rate. What if rates in general go up while your money is in the CD? You are stuck at the lower rate. Or if rates come down, you will have to renew at the lower rate when the CD matures. Laddering is a technique that smoothes out the fluctuations in interest rates.

Here's how laddering works. Let's say you have $10,000 you would like to put into a CD. To start, simply go to www.bankrate.com and find the best rate you can get at the time. Then you purchase five CDs: CD #1 for $2000 for a one-year term, CD #2 for $2000 for a two-year term, CD #3 for $2000 for a three-year term, CD #4 for $2000 for a four-year

term, and CD #5 for $2000 for a five-year term. If you want to have fewer rungs on the ladder, simply divide your initial funds by three or four rather than five.

As the CDs mature, you renew each of them for five years. After five years, you continue to have one CD mature each year, and you renew at the highest current market rate you can find (you do not have to stay with the same financial institution). As interest rates fluctuate over time, you always have some CDs at lower rates and some at higher rates. As a result, you are always earning an average rate overall, thus avoiding the possibility of having all of your money accruing very low rates. And you always will be able to access at least some of your money within a relatively short time frame.

Advice from a Pro...

Protect Yourself from Overdraft Fees

An **overdraft** occurs any time you write a bad check or use a debit card when there are insufficient funds in the account. If funds to cover the usage are not available, the bank will charge you a fee of perhaps $25 or even $40, and the merchant to whom a **bad check** was written will charge you a similar fee. The fees could total $80 for one bad check or overdraft! It is easy to fall victim to these charges if you are not careful. One reason is that banks can choose the order in which they process checks/debits. Let's say you write a large check one day. The next day you use your debit card for three small purchases and the check shows up at your bank for payment. There might be enough money in your account to cover the three small items but not the check. The bank can choose to process the check first. You are now overdrawn and the three debit card items are overdrafts, as well. You now have four overdrafts. If the bank had cleared the debits first you would only have had one overdraft.

Almost all banks in the United States subscribe to Chex Systems, a company that lists several million people who have either written bad checks in the past or committed checking account fraud. It does not matter to Chex Systems whether the overdraft was later repaid—the person's name stays on the list anyway. Most banks and credit unions will not open a new account for five years for anyone on the list. (You can get a copy of your Chex Systems report at www.chexhelp.com.) Writing too many bad checks will also reflect poorly on a person's credit rating. (This topic is examined in Chapter 6.)

Your bank offers three ways to avoid overdraft fees:

1. **Automatic funds transfer agreement.** The amount necessary to cover an overdraft will be transmitted from your savings account to your checking account, as long as you keep sufficient funds in your savings account. An automatic funds transfer agreement is the least expensive of these three alternatives.

2. **Automatic overdraft loan agreement.** The needed funds will be automatically loaned to you by your bank if you have an overdraft line of credit or will be charged as a cash advance to your Visa or MasterCard credit account with the same bank. Note that the loan may be advanced in fixed increments of $100. If you need only $10, for example, you will consequently be responsible for paying interest on amounts not needed. A cash advance fee of $10 or more may also be assessed by the credit card company.

3. **Courtesy overdraft/bounce protection.** The bank will honor overdrafts up to a certain limit, such as $1000, by loaning the money to the account holder. In return, the customer must pay a $25 to $40 fee for each overdraft. Then, the customer must repay the funds usually within less than one month. Most large banks automatically sign you up for this protection unless you specifically decline it. Many new users of checking accounts rack up high levels of fees because they do not understand this protection. Why? Because the bank typically does not alert or stop you when you use your debit card or write a check when there are insufficient funds. Use of a debit card for $3.50 for a drink and some chips could trigger a fee 10 times as high. You must keep track of your own account balance and ensure that you have enough in your account each and every time you access the funds.

Almost $2 billion in overdraft fees were assessed by banks last year, most commonly to young and low-income customers. Will you be a victim? The choice is yours. Consider these ways to deal with overdrafts listed from best to worst:

Ways to cover your overdrafts	Examples of possible cost for EACH overdraft. You should know what YOUR bank charges
Practice good account management	$0; you have no overdrafts
Automatic funds transfer agreement	$0 to $5 transfer fee
Overdraft line of credit	$15 annual fee + 18% APR
Automatic overdraft loan from a credit card	$3 to $10 cash-advance fee + 18% APR
Courtesy overdraft/ bounce protection	$20 to $30
Bounced check	$40 to $60 ($25 to $40 bank fee + $20 to $30 merchant fee)

Patti Fisher, Sophia Anong, and Irene Leech
Virginia Tech

Instant Message

Uninsured CDs

Beware that some so-called CDs are actually "investment certificates." They are not insured and can be recalled by the financial institution and reissued at a lower interest rate prior to their maturity. Always ask "Is this a CD or an investment certificate?" If it's a CD, then verify that information.

minimum of three months' interest. If the penalty exceeds the interest amount, you will get back less than you deposited. Consequently, before putting money into a CD, make sure that it is appropriate to tie up your funds in this way.

You have no reason to restrict yourself to a nearby institution when searching for the highest CD yields. CD yields are updated weekly at www.bankrate.com. You might also check with a stock broker about a **brokered certificate of deposit** as these also pay higher yields. Most CDs enjoy the added protection of federal deposit insurance.

Did You Know?

How to Reconcile Your Bank Accounts

It is a very good idea to maintain records of the activities occurring in your various banking accounts. You should record all checks written, debit card transactions, and deposits in your check register as they take place. It is also a good idea to go online every few days to confirm deposit and withdrawal (or checking) transactions.

You also should conduct an **account reconciliation** in which you compare your records with your bank's records, checking the accuracy of both sets of records and identifying any errors. The best time to do so is when you receive your monthly account statement from your bank. Account reconciliation is a three-step process:

1. Bring your own records up-to-date.
2. Bring the bank's records up-to-date.
3. Reconcile the results from Steps 1 and 2.

If the revised balance in your records and the revised balance from the bank statement differ, you will need to find where the error occurred. First, check the additions and subtractions in your records. Next, make sure that all previous entries in your records are properly reported on the account statement.

Looking for errors when Steps 1 and 2 yield differing results is a necessary but tedious task. Fortunately, it is less likely to be necessary today because of electronic banking. Many people go online frequently to check their balances and review their account activity for accuracy. In this way, they can catch errors early and are always very confident that their balances are exactly as shown in their own records. Here is a table you can use to guide your reconciling efforts.

	Amount
STEP 1: Bring Your Own Records Up-to-Date	
1. Enter balance from your check register.	$
2. Add deposits not yet recorded.	$
3. Subtract checks and other withdrawals not yet recorded.	$
4. Subtract bank fees and charges included in the monthly statement and not yet recorded.	$
5. Add interest earned.	$
ADJUSTED CHECKBOOK REGISTER BALANCE	
STEP 2: Bring the Account Statement Up-to-Date	
1. Enter ending balance from bank statement.	$
2. Add deposits made since bank statement closing date.	$
3. Add outstanding checks written since bank statement closing date.	$
ADJUSTED BANK STATEMENT BALANCE	$

STEP 3: Compare adjusted checkbook register balance and adjusted bank statement balance. If the two balances do not match, identify where the error occurred.

How to Save

Americans have the lowest savings rates among the major countries of the world, even though they sharply increased their personal saving since the beginning of the Great Recession. When asked, they typically complain that there simply is no money left over at the end of the month. In a sense, they are correct, but they are thinking about savings in the wrong way. Wise individuals take a different approach. They follow the adage **"pay yourself first,"** which means to treat savings as the first expenditure after—or even before—getting paid. Build savings into your budget right from the beginning. In this way, you can effectively build funds to provide for large, irregular expenditures or unforeseen expenses; meet short-term goals; or save for retirement, a down payment on a home, or children's college education. Saving is not glamorous; slow and steady wins the race.

Your first savings goal is to accumulate enough money to cover living expenses (perhaps 70 percent of gross income) for three to six months. This money will serve as an **emergency fund** in case of job layoff, long illness, or other serious financial calamity. For a person with a $60,000 gross annual income, a three-month emergency fund would be $10,500 ($60,000 ÷ 12 = $5000; $5000 × 0.70 = $3500 for each month). People who should consider keeping more funds available—perhaps income to cover six months to a year of living expenses—include those who depend heavily on commissions or bonuses or who own their own businesses.

Most people do not have a sufficient emergency savings fund. Instead, they rely on credit cards when an emergency or unforeseen need arises. This is an unwise way to manage finances. Creating an emergency savings fund can be done by breaking it into monthly savings targets and then setting aside the money until you reach the goal. Other savings goals can be saved for using similar techniques discussed in Chapter 3. If you have more than one or two goals, you can set up savings, or investment, accounts for each goal. In this way, you can keep track of your progress and keep money separately identified.

pay yourself first
Treating savings as the first expenditure after—or even before—getting paid rather than simply the money left over at the end of the month.

annual percentage yield (APY)
Return on total interest received on $100 deposit for 365-day period, given institution's simple annual interest rate and compounding frequency.

Instant Message

Be a Regular Saver

Be smart! Start saving regularly when you are young. Divide long-term goals into short-term benchmarks. Then when sufficient amounts are accumulated, move the funds from savings into higher-yielding investments.

Savings Account Interest

The calculation of interest to be paid on deposits in financial institutions is primarily based on four variables:

1. Amount of money on deposit
2. Method of determining this balance
3. Interest rate applied to the balance
4. Frequency of compounding (such as annually, semiannually, quarterly, monthly, or daily)

The Truth in Savings Act requires depository institutions to disclose a uniform, standardized rate of interest so that depositors can easily compare various checking and savings options that pay interest. This rate, called the **annual percentage yield (APY),** is a percentage based on the total interest that would be received on a $100 deposit for a 365-day period given the institution's annual rate of simple interest and frequency of compounding. The more frequent the compounding, the greater the effective return for the saver. The institution must use the APY as its interest rate in advertising and in other disclosures to savers.

Wise money managers select the savings option that pays the highest APY and avoid institutions that assess excessive costs and penalties. Given the same APY, savers should choose an institution that compounds interest daily. Comparison shopping could easily earn you an extra $10 to $20 each year on a $1500 savings account balance.

Instant Message

Use a Savings Calculator

A very easy-to-use savings calculator can be found at http://partners.leadfusion.com/tools/kiplinger/savings03/tool.fcs. You can determine how much to save to reach your goal or find out what your savings will be worth at a future date.

Did You Know?

The Tax Consequences of Saving for Children's College?

A long-term goal of many families is saving for their children's college education. The best ways follow:

Put Money in a Section 529 College Savings Plan. Named after the related section of the Internal Revenue Service Code, many states have established a **Section 529 college savings plan.** Deposits into a 529 plan are not deductible, but withdrawals for qualified educational expenses are tax free. Section 529 plans offer two options: prepaid tuition or an investment plan. A state-sponsored prepaid tuition plan allows parents, relatives, and friends to purchase a child's future college education at today's prices by guaranteeing that today's payment will be used for the future tuition payments at an approved institution of higher education in a particular state. In a 529 investment plan, the state offers an investment program usually through a mutual fund from which the funds can be drawn when the child is in college.

Put Money in a Coverdell Education Savings Account (ESA). Nondeductible contributions up to a maximum of $2000 per year may be made to a **Coverdell education savings account** (formerly known as an education IRA) to pay the future education costs for a child younger than age 18. The money and earnings on the account can be withdrawn later tax free to pay for public, private, or religious school expenses, K–12 (expires in 2011), trade school, or college, including tuition, fees, tutoring, uniforms, home computers, educational computer software, and room and board.

Put Money for College in a Custodial Account. A **custodial account** is one opened in the name of a child younger than age 14 under the provisions of the Uniform Gifts to Minors Act (or Uniform Transfers to Minors Act). These funds can be used for college expenses. Taxpayers in the 10 percent and 15 percent tax brackets are able to sell assets, such as stocks or mutual funds, without paying any capital gains taxes. However, the so-called **kiddie tax** rule applies to unearned income (such as interest and dividends) of a minor child. This rule limits the ability of children to have their unearned income taxed at the child's low tax rate (presumably lower than the parent's tax rate). For children younger than age 18, the first $950 of unearned

income (the income earned from an investment) earned on custodial account assets is tax free to the child. The next $950 is taxed at the child's tax rate. Unearned income in excess of $1900 is taxed at the parent's (likely higher) rate. When children reach age 18, they will pay tax solely based on their own income tax bracket. Assets held in a custodial account for a long time should not be sold until the individual reaches age 18. At that point, the kiddie tax rules will no longer apply and, assuming the child falls into one of the two lowest tax brackets, he or she will qualify for the 0 percent tax rate on capital gains, making the profit free of federal taxes.

Discount bonds (also called **zeroes** or **zero coupon bonds**) are municipal, corporate, and government bonds that pay no annual interest. Discount bonds are sold to investors at sharp discounts from their face value and may be redeemed at full value upon maturity. For example, a $100 **Series EE savings bond** sold by the federal government can be purchased for $50, one-half its face amount. The interest, which is usually compounded semiannually, accumulates within the bond itself, and the return to the investor comes from redeeming the bond at its stated face value at the maturity date. Parents can invest in discount bonds through a custodial account to help pay for a child's college education. The phantom income "paid" to the child is generally so small that little, if any, income taxes are due each year as the interest accrues. An advantage of Series EE savings bonds is that taxes on the interest that accrues each year are deferred until redemption. The interest is tax free at redemption if the proceeds are used to fund the child's college education.

Put Money in a Roth IRA. Contributions to a Roth IRA account and the earnings within it accumulate tax free, and withdrawals are entirely free of tax after age 59½. Withdrawals before age 59½ are subject to the IRS's early distribution 10 percent withdrawal penalty. Before age 59½ the contributions to a Roth IRA account, but not the *earnings,* can be used for college expenses (or any purpose) without incurring the penalty. Withdrawals of deposits in a traditional IRA for college expenses also avoid the 10 percent penalty, but income taxes are due on the amounts withdrawn.

Smart savers also consider the fees and penalties outlined in Table 5.2 when deciding where to open a savings account.

An account with a grace period provides the depositor with a small financial benefit. A **grace period** is the period (in days) during which deposits or withdrawals can be made and still earn interest from a given day of the interest period. For example, if deposits are made by the tenth day of the month, interest might be earned from the first day of the month. For withdrawals, the grace period generally ranges from three to five days. Thus, if a saver withdrew money from an account within three to five days of the end of the interest period, the savings might still earn interest as if the money remained in the account for the entire period.

Instant Message

Interest Is Taxable

Any interest earned on your checking and savings accounts must be reported as income on your federal and state income tax returns. Your financial institutions should send you a **Form 1099** statement that reports your interest income for the previous year; that information also is sent to the IRS.

Concept Check 5.3

1. Describe reasons to keep money in a savings account rather than a checking account.
2. Distinguish between statement savings accounts and CDs.
3. Explain the benefits of a pay-yourself-first approach to saving.
4. Describe how can you use information about APY to your advantage.

grace period
Period (in days) for which deposits or withdrawals can be made without any penalty.

Tool #3—Money Market Accounts

Most people use checking and savings accounts as the cornerstones of their monetary asset management efforts. When income begins to exceed expenses on a regular basis, perhaps by $300 or $500 each month, a substantial amount of excess funds can quickly build up. Although this situation is a comfortable one, it is wise from a monetary asset management point of view to move some of the excess funds into an account that pays more interest.

A **money market account** is any of a variety of interest-earning accounts that pays relatively high interest rates (compared with regular savings accounts) and offers some limited check-writing privileges. A money market account provides both checking and savings tools at a higher interest rate than other accounts. Such accounts are offered by banks, savings banks, credit unions, stock brokerage firms, financial services companies, and mutual funds. The types of money market accounts are super NOW accounts, money market deposit accounts, money market mutual funds, and asset management accounts.

4 Learning Objective
Explain the importance of placing excess funds in a money market account.

money market account
Interest-earning accounts that pay relatively high interest rates and offer limited check-writing privileges.

Super NOW Accounts

A **super NOW account** is a government-insured money market account offered through depository institutions. It takes the form of a high-interest NOW account with limited checking privileges (usually a maximum of six checks per month). The initial minimum deposit typically ranges from $1000 to $2500. If the average balance falls below a specified amount (such as $1000), the account reverts to earning interest at the lower rate offered on a regular NOW checking account. Depositors can withdraw their funds (using checks or a debit card or electronically) at any time without penalty.

Money Market Deposit Accounts

A **money market deposit account (MMDA)** is also a government-insured money market account offered through a depository institution. It has minimum-balance requirements and

money market deposit account (MMDA)
Government-insured money market account with minimum-balance requirements and tiered interest rates.

Did You Know?

How Ownership of Accounts (and Other Assets) Is Established

When you open a new account, you will be asked to sign a signature card that can be used to verify the signatures of the owners of the account. Accounts can be owned either individually or jointly.

An **individual account** has one owner who is solely responsible for the account and its activity. At the death of the individual owner, the account becomes part of his or her estate and will go to heirs in accordance with the owner's will. If desired, individual accounts can be set up with a payable at death designation whereby a person is named in the account to receive the funds upon the death of the individual owner. This allows that person to gain quick access to the funds after the owner's death but does not give the person any rights to the account while the owner is still alive.

A **joint account** has two or more owners, each of whom has legal rights to the funds in the account. The forms of joint ownership discussed here apply to all types of property, including automobiles and homes, as well as checking and savings accounts. Three types of joint ownership exist:

1. **Joint tenancy with right of survivorship** (also called simply **joint tenancy**) is the most common form of joint ownership, especially for husbands and wives. In this case, each person owns the whole of the asset and can dispose of it without the approval of the other(s). With accounts at financial institutions, the financial institution will honor checks or withdrawal slips possessing any of the owners' signatures. An advantage of a joint account is that in case of death of one of the owners, the property continues to be owned by the surviving account holder(s).

2. **Tenancy in common** is a form of joint ownership in which two or more parties own the asset, but each retains control over a separate piece of the property rights. In most states, the ownership shares are presumed to be equal unless otherwise specified. When one owner dies, however, his or her share in the asset is distributed to his or her heirs according to the terms of a will (or if no will exists, according to state law) instead of automatically going to the other co-owners.

3. **Tenancy by the entirety,** which is recognized in about 30 states, is restricted to property held between a husband and a wife. Under this arrangement, no one coowner can sell or dispose of his or her portion of an asset without the permission of the other. This restriction prevents transfers by one owner without the knowledge of the other.

Dual-earner couples often prefer to own some property together and some property separately. If you own a business and default on a loan, for example, your creditors usually cannot attach your home if it is in your spouse's name. Nonworking spouses, however, should get their name on all deeds and investments; in the event of divorce, courts typically award property to the people who legally own it. In **community property states**—in which most of the money and property acquired during a marriage are legally considered the joint property of both spouses—the rights of both husbands and wives are equally protected. (These jurisdictions include Arizona, California, Idaho, Louisiana, Nebraska, Nevada, New Mexico, Puerto Rico, Texas, Washington, and Wisconsin.)

---

tiered interest rates that vary with the size of the account balance. Institutions are allowed to establish fees for transactions and account maintenance, and account holders typically are limited to three to six transactions each month. Often the customer must deposit $1000 to open an account. If the average monthly balance falls below a certain amount, such as $2500, the entire account earns interest at the lower rate of a regular NOW account. MMDAs generally pay higher interest rates than super NOW accounts.

Money Market Mutual Funds

money market mutual fund (MMMF)
Money market account in a mutual fund rather than at a depository institution.

A **money market mutual fund (MMMF)** is a money market account in a mutual fund investment company (rather than at a depository institution). It pools the cash of thousands of investors and earns a relatively safe and high return by buying debts with very short-term maturities (always less than one year). Interest is calculated daily, and an investor can withdraw funds at any time. Money market mutual funds typically pay the highest rate of return that can be earned on a daily basis by small investors.

MMMFs require a minimum deposit ranging from $500 to $1000. Dozens of mutual fund companies offer unlimited check writing with no minimums on check amounts. Electronic transfers are permitted, but ATMs cannot be used because MMMFs are not depository institutions. Although MMMFs are not insured by any federal agency, they are considered extremely safe. Some funds buy only debts of the U.S. government and therefore are virtually risk free. To open an MMMF account, you can contact a mutual fund company; more details are provided in Chapter 15.

Instant Message

It Is Easy to Find a Money Market Mutual Fund

You can find money market mutual funds easily online. Some of these MMMFs are managed by American Century (www.americancentury.com), Dreyfus (www.dreyfus.com), Fidelity (www.fidelity.com), Scudder (www.scudder.com), and www.T. Rowe Price (www.troweprice.com).

Asset Management Accounts

An **asset management account (AMA;** also known as an **all-in-one account)** is a multiple-purpose, coordinated package that gathers most of the customer's monetary asset management vehicles into a unified account and reports them on a single monthly statement. Included in this package might be transactions in a money market mutual fund and in checking, credit card, debit card, loan, and stock brokerage accounts. Also known as **central asset accounts,** AMAs are offered through depository institutions, stock brokerage firms, financial services companies, and mutual funds. Such an account enables you to conduct all of your financial business with one institution. Typically, $10,000, spread across all subaccounts, is required to open an AMA. Some AMAs assess an annual fee, usually $100. Notice that this would be a 1 percent fee on a $10,000 deposit ($100 ÷ $10,000) and reduce your return by 1 percentage point. AMAs usually have other features that attract investors as well—for example, free credit and debit cards, a rebate of 1 percent on credit card purchases, free traveler's checks, inexpensive term life insurance, and an investment advisory newsletter.

asset management account (AMA, all-in-one account, or central asset accounts)
Multiple-purpose, coordinated package that gathers most monetary asset management vehicles into a unified account and reports activity on a single monthly statement to the client.

 Concept Check 5.4

1. Explain the benefits of opening a money market account.
2. Distinguish between a super NOW account and a money market account.
3. Identify the feature of depository institution accounts not available with money market mutual funds.
4. List some benefits of an asset management account.

Electronic Money Management

Monetary asset management can be summed up today with the phrase "paper, plastic, or neither." "Paper" comprises the traditional cash- and check-based systems. "Plastic" is the use of a debit or other type of card to access your funds. "Neither" is the use of your computer to access and use your accounts.

Most major banks now provide access to their banking services via websites. "Internet banks" operate entirely online, and they often pay the highest interest rates. **Electronic money management** occurs whenever transactions are conducted without using paper documents. Most of these activities involve **electronic funds transfers (EFTs),** in which funds are shifted electronically (rather than by check or cash) among your various accounts and to and from other people and businesses.

5 Learning Objective
Describe electronic money management, including your legal protections.

electronic funds transfers (EFTs)
Funds shifted electronically (rather than by check or cash) among various accounts or to and from other people and businesses.

Did You Know?

Using "Plastic" in Monetary Asset Management

There are many types of plastic devices used to access your money.

1. ATM cards allow you to withdraw money from or transfer money among your checking and savings accounts at an automatic teller machine. You must use a personal identification number (PIN) to use the card.

2. Debit cards do ATM cards one better—you can use them to make purchases via a point-of-sale (POS) terminal at retail outlets. Using a debit card to make a purchase immediately transfers money from your account. You typically use a PIN or provide your signature when using a debit card.

3. Stored-value cards contain a magnetic strip or bar code that encrypts the amount of money stored via the card. Some stored-value cards can be "reloaded" with additional funds. Colleges often use this type of card for student meal plans and other spending both on and off campus. Stored-value cards are much like a mini-checking account you can use wherever the card is accepted. A gift card is an example of a stored-value card. There are risks associated with gift cards since many have an expiration date and should the retail company go bankrupt or close in your area, the cards may be impossible to redeem.

4. Electronic benefits transfer (EBT) cards are used by the government to pay military personnel and provide Social Security and other government benefits. They are much like a stored-value card, but the holder does not "load" the card—the payer does so.

5. Credit cards allow you to make purchases or obtain cash with credit from the bank or retailer that issued the cards. These are debts that must be paid back, often with interest.

Instant Message

Reduce and Avoid ATM Fees

Minimize your ATM fees by making fewer large withdrawals rather than more frequent small withdrawals. Avoid fees altogether by using your own bank's ATMs.

Instant Message

Use Direct Deposit to Save Money and Time

Many financial institutions offer no-fee checking accounts to customers who have their paychecks electronically sent from their employer via **direct deposit.** In addition, the institution may charge a lower interest rate on loans and credit card accounts for customers who use direct deposit.

ATM transaction fee
Payments levied each time an automated teller machine (ATM) is used.

Electronic Money Management Can Be Easy But Is Not Always Free

There are costs assessed for the use of some electronic banking.

An **ATM transaction fee** may be assessed for using an ATM. Fees may be levied by your financial institution as well as by the institution that provides the ATM if you are using an ATM linked to a national network. For example, you might pay your institution $1 to $3 and another $1 to $3 (or more) to the machine provider. Making frequent, small withdrawals can be expensive: a $2 ATM fee is just 1 percent of a $200 withdrawal but is 10 percent of a $20 withdrawal.

Transaction fees of $1 to $3 also may be assessed whenever you make a purchase via a POS terminal at a retail store. This is most likely to happen when you use a PIN number. Such a usage is called an "online" transaction and occurs when you hit the "debit" button on the terminal. You can usually avoid the fee if you hit "credit" instead and the transaction becomes an "off-line" transaction. Rather than use your PIN, you sign for the purchase. The transaction is still a debit transaction but is processed in a way that costs less for your bank. You also have additional legal protections for "off-line" transactions as discussed later.

Fees can be assessed for other uses of electronic money management. Some banks charge for online banking services such as bill paying and verification of your account balances. Often these fees for these services are a fixed monthly rate for all usage that may be cheaper than writing checks and mailing payments. These paper-based services are often free. You can avoid almost all such fees by shopping for an account and paying attention to your banking habits. Otherwise you will waste money on unnecessary banking fees.

Using Electronic Banking Safely

Federal and state regulations have been adopted to provide protections for the use of debit cards and other electronic banking. The Electronic Funds Transfer Act is the governing law, and the Federal Reserve Board's Regulation E provides specific guidelines on ATM and debit card liability. Cards can be issued only if the card cannot be used until validated and the user is informed of his or her liability for unauthorized use as well as other terms and conditions. When you sign up for electronic banking services, the depository institution must inform you of your rights and responsibilities in a written **disclosure statement.**

Users must be provided with written receipts when using an ATM or POS terminal. These receipts show the amount of the transaction, the date on which it took place, and other pertinent information. General protection of a customer's account takes the form of a **periodic statement** sent by the financial institution that shows all electronic transfers to and from the account, fees charged, and opening and closing balances. Smart users of electronic banking services and electronic funds transfers (EFTs) regularly compare the information on this periodic statement with their written receipts.

periodic statements
Consumer-protecting recaps that show all electronic transfers to and from accounts, fees charged, and opening and closing balances.

Fixing Errors If you find an error in your periodic statement, notify the issuing organization in writing as soon as possible. Use the notification procedures found in the disclosure statement accompanying your monthly statement. If the institution needs more than ten business days to investigate and correct a problem, generally it must return the amount in question to your account while it conducts the investigation. If an error did occur, the institution must permanently correct it promptly. If the institution decides that no error occurred, it must explain its decision in writing and let you know that it has deducted any amount temporarily credited during the investigation. In such a case, the institution must honor withdrawals against the credited amount for five days, allowing you time to deposit additional funds. You may ask for copies of the documents on which the institution relied in its investigation and again challenge the outcome if you believe that a mistake was made.

Instant Message

Guard Your PINs

Your personal identification numbers (PINs) "unlock" your accounts. You should write them down in case you forget them, but never keep the written record with the card. Do not use easily guessed PINs such as your birth date (112389) or repeated digits (444333). Use as complicated a PIN as your bank will allow.

Protections for Lost Cards The sooner you report the loss of an ATM or debit card, the more likely you will be to limit your liability if someone uses the card without your permission. Cardholders are liable for only the first $50 of unauthorized use if they notify the issuing company within two business days after the loss or theft of their card or PIN. Note that fraudulent "online" debit card transactions using a PIN are *not* afforded this protection. After two days, cardholder liability for unauthorized use rises to $500. Some issuers, including Visa and MasterCard, have voluntarily waived enforcement of this liability. However, you risk unlimited loss for the card's misuse if, within 60 days after the institution mails your financial statement to you, you do not report an unauthorized transfer or withdrawal. Thus, you could lose all of the money in your account. These regulations apply to debit cards and other cards used to make electronic funds transfers (EFTs). States may have laws that provide additional protection for consumers in EFT transactions.

Most homeowner's and renter's insurance policies (discussed in Chapter 10) already cover your liability for theft of both debit and credit cards. If you are not currently protected, such insurance coverage generally can be added. Many companies sell similar insurance as a separate policy for an annual premium of $30 to $60. In addition, some firms sell a **card registration service** that will notify all companies with which you have debit and credit cards in the event of loss. For $30 to $60 per year, you need make only one telephone call to report all card losses. Of course, you can also notify debit and credit card companies yourself at no cost.

card registration service
Firm that will notify all companies with which you have debit and credit cards if your cards are lost or stolen.

Did You Know?

How to Protect Against the Privacy Risks from Using Your Cell Phone to Manage Money

More and more people today are using their cell phones and PDAs for managing money and transferring personal financial data. Many fail to consider that the data stored in the device is ripe for identity theft. The data can fall into the wrong hands if the phone is lost, stolen, or simply replaced. Here are some things you can do to protect yourself.

1. **Do not store ID numbers and passwords** in your phone.

2. **Use complex passwords** of eight or more characters including symbols, numbers, and both upper and lower case letters. Change passwords every few months.

3. **Use the blocking mechanism** such as a password (and make it complex) provided with your device.

4. **Erase the flash-chip memory** using the "hard reset" function (or destroy the chip and/or SIM card) when discarding, trading-in, or recycling your phone.

Protect Your Privacy Yourself Having the law and insurance on your side when banking electronically or online is a good thing, but it is better to not have problems in the first place. Here are some tips for reducing the risk:

- Never bank via computer on a wireless system away from home. Use your wireless system at home only if it is thoroughly protected.

- Never provide account information if you get an unsolicited e-mail from your bank. It's likely from a scam artist.

- When finished banking via computer, always hit the log off button at the top of the page and then close the browser window.

- Avoid using someone else's computer to manage your account. If you do, shut down the computer completely when finished.

- Regularly change your passwords and keep them to yourself.

- Study your statements. Ask about anything that looks unusual or the least bit in error.

- Make and save paper copies of all your electronic transactions until you can verify their accuracy on your next account statement.

 Concept Check 5.5

1. Distinguish among credit cards, debit cards, and a stored-value card.
2. List the steps you should take if you find an error in your periodic statement regarding an electronic transaction.
3. Summarize the rules that apply if you lose your ATM or debit card and it is used without your authorization.

The Psychology of Money Management

6 Learning Objective

Discuss your personal finances and money management more effectively with loved ones.

A common cause of tension in personal relationships is conflict over money. Some people seem unable to work together to perform even the fundamental tasks of managing money, such as reconciling the checking account, creating a workable budget, and paying bills on time. Often one of the partners brings a great deal of debt to a relationship. Other couples get into financial trouble because they use credit too often. Mutual trust in money matters can be developed—and must be—to have happy interpersonal relationships and achieve financial success.

Managing Money and Making Financial Decisions Are Different

Managing money includes such tasks as handling the checkbook, overseeing the budget, and doing the household shopping. Couples should agree on who will carry out these day-to-day chores and then carry through on their responsibilities. Financial experts recommend that each person in a relationship keep some money of his or her own. For dual-earning couples, this can be accomplished by setting up three checking accounts: a discretionary account for each individual (two accounts) and a third joint account. Then clearly specify the budget categories related to each account. Each partner can then feel that he or she has access to money that the other partner does not control. These feelings of autonomy encourage independence and self-control in a relationship rather than dependency on the other person.

While managing family money is a significant task, decision making is where most disagreements arise. Shared decision making is the best model when setting goals; when contemplating any major expense, such as buying automobiles and housing; and when conferring on key topics such as insurance, estate planning and investments, and long-term financial plans.

People Ascribe Strong Emotions to Money

People often ascribe a number of emotions to money, including freedom, trust, self-esteem, guilt, indifference, envy, security, comfort, power, and control. They bring with them the patterns, beliefs, and attitudes that were prevalent in their family of origin. It is essential to recognize the importance of these emotions. Many people want to hold on to their fiscal autonomy as long as possible, and they may be embarrassed to inquire about how much others—even loved ones—spend, earn, or owe. For many people, money is an area of self-suspected incompetence. Judith Viorst, author of *Necessary Losses,* suggests that becoming responsible and adept at managing one's financial matters represents a true passage into adulthood. This evolution involves communicating effectively with others on money matters.

How to Talk About Financial Matters

Discussions about money matters are not always easy. Some people who are entirely rational about other issues are unpredictable or even careless in money matters. Adults need to accept that honest differences may exist among people and respect these values. The following ideas will help you discuss money with more confidence and candor.

Get to Know Yourself The first step in learning to talk with others about financial matters is to understand your own approach to money. Consider the emotions described earlier to help get you started. It is constructive to discuss any differences in how you view yourself as compared with how your partner views you.

Focus on Commonalities Successful communication about money requires that the effort be aimed toward agreeing on common goals and reaching a consensus of opinion without substantially compromising the views of others.

Learn to Manage Financial Disagreements Give all family members time to express their views when discussing financial matters. Each also needs to listen to what others are saying and feeling. If talking proves too difficult, have each person separately write down his or her concerns. By swapping notes, ideas and concerns can be shared. Schedule a time and place for financial talks, decide on agenda items, and leave other conflicts outside the door. When necessary, agree to disagree or postpone difficult decisions until a later time—but do so consciously and not simply out of procrastination.

Did You Know?

How to Develop Money Sense in Children

A major theme of this chapter is that checking, savings, and investments are an integral part of reaching your financial goals. By progressively building savings funds, you can achieve financial success. Parents can help children develop money sense by providing them with opportunities to manage their own money while still young and guiding this behavior toward appropriate patterns. Parents can do the following to increase their children's ease in handling money:

1. **Give an allowance.** Even children as young as five years old should have some money of their own. An allowance should be the source of these funds in the preteen years. The amounts of allowance should fit the family income level. Allowances are a means for teaching money management.

2. **Encourage work.** Once children reach their preteen years, there are many opportunities to earn their own money. When children see what it takes to make money, it is easier for them to know the real cost of spending.

3. **Set reasonable limits.** Children should be given age-appropriate limits for spending in various categories and should be required to save a portion, perhaps 50 percent, of their money. However, parents should not stop children from "wasting their money" or bail them out of every mistake. We learn best from experience, not from what someone else tells us is best.

4. **Teach them to make good choices through increasingly complex activities.** The dollar amounts and the areas of discretionary spending can increase as the child becomes older. A 7-year-old might be allowed to spend his or her own money on toys, snacks, and gifts to charity at church or school. A 14-year-old might be allowed to buy meals and clothing as well. More responsibility and autonomy should be given only as the child exhibits the ability to handle previous, less complicated tasks.

5. **Help them learn to wait.** Children should have autonomy over at least some of their own money. But the remainder, perhaps 50 percent, should be saved. Then when children desire some high-cost item, they can see that saving for a while can help them reach their goal.

6. **Talk about family finances with children.** In many families, money matters are a taboo subject. Children need to see that parents must work at managing the family finances. They should know what it costs to raise a family and to make ends meet. Otherwise, kids will grow up with unrealistic expectations and behaviors that will be passed on to their children.

7. **Be a role model.** Children learn more from what they see than what they are told. Avoid borrowing money from a child. They will learn that credit is easy. And, certainly, pay them back on time if you do borrow. Otherwise, they will think they can borrow without paying back. Save money yourself, and tell your children that saving means that you can't have something you, or they, want right away.

Use Positive "I" Statements   Messages focusing on "I" describe the behavior in question, the feelings you experienced because of the behavior, and any tangible effect on you. For example, a spouse might say, "I feel upset when we use credit cards because I do not know where we will find the money to pay the bills at the end of the month." "I" messages say three things: what (the behavior), I feel (feelings), and because (reason). Using "I" messages helps build stronger relationships because they tell the other person "I trust you to decide what change in behavior is necessary." Beware of "I" statements that begin with "I need you to. . . ." "You" statements are blaming statements, such as "You always . . . ," "You never . . . ," and "If you don't, I will. . . ." These statements have a high probability of being condescending to other people, of making them feel guilty, and of implying that their needs and wants are not as important as yours.

Be Honest and Talk Regularly   Achieving consensus requires that each person be honest when talking about money matters. It further demands that couples regularly talk about finances. Perhaps begin by deciding to talk about money matters for only 10 minutes at a time. Also be prepared to compromise. When you make decisions together act on them. Focus attention on current financial activities and issues as well as long-term financial planning. Use

Jupiterimages

Each member of the family should be aware of and involved with important financial decisions.

these discussions to forge overall long-term strategies for dealing with your family finances. Once the proper base has been established, short-term issues are more likely to fall into place.

Complications Brought by Remarriage

Remarriage merges financial histories, values, and habits as well as households. Some remarried couples—and those choosing to live together following a previous relationship—have substantial combined incomes bolstered by child-support payments from a former spouse. In many cases, at least one person may be paying (instead of receiving) alimony and child support. When "his," "her," and "our" children are included in the household, living expenses can be quite steep. Special concerns for blended families include determining who assumes financial responsibility for biological offspring and stepchildren; handling resentment over alimony and child-support payments; and managing unequal assets, incomes, responsibilities, and debts. Even gift giving can become a quandary. These challenges can be mitigated with effective communication.

Many remarried people use "his" and "hers" funds and require the legally responsible parent owing financial support to a previous spouse or to children to make such payments out of his or her own money. Professor Jean Lown of Utah State University suggests that, "What is best is what the couple can agree on."

Do It NOW!

Avoid Overdraft Fees

Avoiding overdraft fees is a must. Start today by:

1. Finding out what type of overdraft protection you have, if any, on your checking accounts.

2. Signing up for automatic funds transfer to be used first if you make an overdraft.

3. Making sure that your bank will block use of your debit card if there are insufficient funds in the account at the time of the usage.

✔ Concept Check 5.6

1. Explain why it is difficult for many people in relationships to talk about money matters.

2. Identify four ways you could more effectively communicate about money matters.

3. List four things that parents can do to help their children be better money managers.

What Do You Recommend NOW?

Now that you have read the chapter on managing checking and savings accounts, what would you recommend to Mark Rosenberg and Trina Adams in the case at the beginning of the chapter regarding:

1. Where they can obtain the monetary asset management services that they need?
2. Their best use of checking accounts and savings accounts as they begin saving for a home?
3. The use of a money market account for their monetary asset management?
4. Their use of electronic banking in the future?
5. How they can best discuss the management of their money and finances?

Big Picture Summary of Learning Objectives

1 Identify the tools of monetary asset management and the types of companies that provide such financial services.

Maximizing interest earnings and minimizing fees on savings and checking accounts is the goal of monetary asset management. The five primary providers of monetary asset management services include depository institutions (such as banks and credit unions), stock brokerage firms, mutual funds, financial services companies, and insurance companies.

2 Earn interest and pay no or low fees on your checking accounts.

The first tool of monetary asset management is an interest-earning checking account that is used to pay monthly living expenses. When setting set up an account, consider charges, fees, and penalties.

3 Make the best use of the benefits of savings accounts.

Your second tool of monetary asset management is a savings account in which you can place funds not needed for six months to five years into the future. Some longer-term savings instruments such as certificates of deposit (CDs) allow you to safely earn even higher returns if you are willing to forgo liquidity.

4 Explain the importance of placing excess funds in a money market account.

Your third tool of monetary asset management is a money market account. When your income begins to exceed expenses on a regular basis, it is wise to move excess funds into such an account, which typically pays a higher interest rate. The funds can be left in the account while you consider other investment options. Money market accounts include super NOW accounts, money market deposit accounts, money market mutual funds, and asset management accounts.

5 Describe electronic money management, including your legal protections.

Electronic money management occurs whenever banking transactions are conducted via computers without the customer using paper documents. Electronic banking includes the use of automatic teller machines (ATMs), point-of-sale (POS) terminals, debit cards, and stored-value cards. The Electronic Funds Transfer Act protects consumers who use electronic money management.

6 Discuss your personal finances and money management more effectively with loved ones.

Recognize the psychological and emotional aspects of money and identify your own approaches to money. Communicate openly and frequently about money matters by using "I" statements.

Let's Talk About It

1. **Bank Account Fees.** Describe some examples of checking and savings account transactions that result in assessment of fees or penalties. Which are the least and most avoidable?

2. **Avoiding Overdraft Fees.** You know someone who recently had $84 in overdraft fees for three small debit card transactions. Explain to him why such high fees resulted from such small transactions and the relative benefits of having an automatic funds transfer agreement versus an automatic overdraft loan agreement versus overdraft protection

3. **Forms of Account Ownership.** When would you recommend using an individual account, a joint tenancy with right of survivorship account, and a tenancy by the entirety account for your monetary assets?

4. **Earning Higher Interest on Your Savings.** When might it be appropriate for you save via a certificate of deposit versus a money market account?

5. **Lost/Stolen Debit Cards.** What should you do if your ATM or debit card is lost or stolen? Why?

6. **Talking About Money.** Have you ever had a disagreement with a friend or family member over a money issue? How might you communicate differently now than you did previously?

Do the Math

1. **Invest Now or Later?** Twins Barbara and Mary are both age 27. Beginning at age 27, Barbara invests $2000 per year for 10 years and then never sets aside another penny. Mary waits 10 years and then invests $2000 per year for the next 30 years. Assuming they both earn 7 percent, how much will each twin have at age 67? (Hint: Use Appendixes A.1 and A.3 or visit the *Garman/Forgue* companion website.)

2. **Reconciling a Checking Account.** Andrew Parker has a checking account at the credit union affiliated with his university. Illustrated below are his check register and monthly statement for the account. Reconcile the checking account and answer the following questions.

   (a) What is the total of the outstanding checks?
   (b) What is the total of the outstanding deposits?

   (c) Why is there a difference between the uncorrected balance in the check register and the balance on the statement?

   (d) What is the updated and correct balance in the check register below?

3. **Saving for College.** You want to create a college fund for a child who is now 3 years old. The fund should grow to $30,000 in 15 years. If an investment available to you will yield 6 percent per year, how much must you invest in a lump sum now to realize the $30,000 when needed? (Hint: Use Appendix A.2 or visit the *Garman/Forgue* companion website.)

4. **Saving for Retirement.** You plan to retire in 40 years. To provide for your retirement, you initiate a savings program of $4000 per year yielding 7 percent. What will be the value of the retirement fund at the beginning of the twenty-third year? (Hint: Use Appendix A.3 or visit the *Garman/Forgue* companion website.)

Account Name	Andrew Parker	Period of Activity	11/2/09–12/01/09
Account #	**123-45678**		

Summary of Your Activity This Month

Date	Activity	Amount	Balance
11/02			$412.66
11/04	Debit Card POS Transaction	$17.46	395.20
11/09	Check #237	$33.33	361.87
11/12	Direct Deposit	w	1238.86
11/13	Debit Card POS Transaction	$84.56	1154.30
11/13	EFT	$22.00	1132.20
11/15	Check #238	$645.00	487.30
11/23	Debit Card POS Transaction	$68.87	418.43
11/27	Debit Card POS Transaction	$43.00	375.43
11/28	Deposit	$200.00	575.43
11/30	Check #239	$125.00	450.43
11/30	Service Charge	$4.50	445.93
11/30	ATM Withdrawal	100.00	345.93
12/01	Check # 240	46.00	299.93

Continued

Date	Check #	Payee/ Payor	For	Amount	Balance
11/01					412.66
11/03	Debit Card	CVS	Cold Meds	17.46	395.20
11/05	237	Univ. Book-store	Of Mice and Men	33.33	361.87
11/12	Deposit	PNC Bank	Payday-Yeah!	876.99	1238.86
11/12	238	ABC Property Mgmt.	Rent	645.00	593.86
11/13	Debit Card	Kroger's	Groceries	84.56	509.30
11/13	Elec-tronic Payment	Maysville Water	Water Bill	22.00	487.30
11/23	Debit Card	Kroger's	Groceries	67.88	419.42
11/23	Debit Card	Applebee's	Dinner With Karen	43.00	376.42
11/27	Deposit	Mom	For Utilities	200.00	576.42
11/27	239	Duke Power	Electric/ Heat Bill	125.00	451.42
11/27	240	Conoco	Gas	46.00	405.42
11/30	Debit Card	ATM With-drawal	Carry Around Money	100.00	305.42
12/01	241	Comcast	Cable Bill	53.88	252.54

Financial Planning Cases

Case 1

A Lobbyist Considers Her Checking Account Options

Shudan Lee, a lobbyist for the textile industry living in Spring-field, Virginia, has had a no interest checking account at a com-mercial bank for three years. The bank requires a minimum balance of $500 to avoid an account charge, and Shudan has always maintained this balance. Recently, she heard that a nearby savings and loan association is offering NOW accounts paying 1.5 percent interest on the average daily balance of the account. This institution requires a minimum balance of $300, but a for-feiture of monthly interest occurs if the account falls below this

minimum. Given her past habits at the commercial bank, Shudan feels that the $500 minimum would be easy to maintain. She is seriously thinking about moving her money to the NOW account.

(a) What is the main reason Shudan should move her checking account?

(b) What should Shudan know about the differences among NOW accounts offered at various financial institutions?

(c) If Shudan maintained an average balance of $1000 in a NOW checking account earning 1.5 percent interest, how much interest would she have earned on her money after one year? (Hint: Use Appendix A.1 or visit the *Garman/Forgue* companion website. Do not forget to subtract Shudan's initial lump-sum deposit from the derived answer.)

(d) How much more would Shudan have earned in one year if she decided to invest in a money market mutual fund paying 2 percent interest instead of the NOW account? (Hint: Use Appendix A.1 or visit the *Garman/Forgue* companion website.)

Case 2

Deciding Among the Tools of Monetary Asset Management

Kwaku Addo earns $4200 per month take-home pay and has the funds directly deposited in his checking account. He spends only about $3500 per month, and the excess funds have been building up in his account for about one year.

(a) What other types of accounts are available to Kwaku?

(b) How might he manage his accounts to earn as much interest as possible and keep his money safe?

(c) How might he use electronic money management to accomplish these tasks?

Case 3

Use of a Computer Banking Service

Trent Searle, a service station owner from Roy, Utah, pays a $10 monthly fee for home banking so he can pay all his bills online though his bank. His friend Scott Simpson feels that Trent is wasting his money on the service. Trent has a net income of $3000 per month, plus other earnings from some investments. In addition, he is part owner of an apartment complex, which gives him approximately $1000 per month in income. He always tries to put his excess earnings into solid investments so that they might bring future income and security.

(a) What specific computer banking services would help a person such as Trent?

(b) Justify Trent's paying the $10 monthly fee for computer banking.

Case 4

Victor and Maria Hernandez Need to Save Money Fast

The Hernandez family is experiencing some financial pressures, even though the couple has a combined income of $66,000. Also, their eldest son, Joseph, will start college in only three years. Maria is contemplating going to work full time to add about $25,000 to the family's annual income.

(a) How will this change in income affect the family's emergency fund needs?

(b) How much should they save annually for the next three years if they want to build up Joseph's college fund to $20,000, assuming a 6 percent rate of return and ignoring taxes on the interest? (Hint: Use Appendix A.1 or visit the *Garman/Forgue* companion website.)

(c) Given their 25 percent marginal tax rate, what is the Hernandezes' after-tax return and how would that affect the amount they would need to save each year?

(d) What savings options are open to the Hernandezes that could reduce or eliminate the effects of taxes on their savings program?

Case 5

How Should the Johnsons Manage Their Cash?

In January, Harry and Belinda Johnson had $3540 in monetary assets (see page 101): $1178 in cash on hand; $890 in a statement savings account at First Federal Bank earning 1.0 percent interest compounded daily; $560 in a statement savings account at the Far West Savings and Loan earning 1.1 percent interest compounded semiannually; $160 in a share account at the Smith Brokerage Credit Union earning a dividend of 1.3 percent compounded quarterly; and $752 in their non–interest-earning regular checking account at First Interstate.

(a) What specific recommendations would you give the Johnsons for selecting checking and savings accounts that will enable them to effectively use the first and second tools of monetary asset management?

(b) Their annual budget, cash-flow calendar, and revolving savings fund (see Tables 3.8, 3.9, and 3.10 on pages 90–92) indicate that the Johnsons will have additional amounts to deposit in the coming year. What are your recommendations for the Johnsons regarding use of a money market account? Why?

(c) What savings instrument would you recommend for their savings, given their objective of saving enough to purchase a new home? Support your answer.

(d) If the Johnsons could put most of their cash on hand ($1000) into a money market account earning 1.4 percent, how much would they have in the account after one year?

On the 'Net

Go to the Web pages indicated to complete these exercises.

1. Visit the website for the Federal Reserve Bank of Kansas City, where you will find an article (http://federalreserveconsumerhelp.gov/index.cfm?nav=9498) on checking accounts. Browse through the articles to find five things you could do that will help you get the most out of your checking account.

2. Visit the website for Bankrate.com at http://www.bankrate.com/brm/rate/chk_sav_home.asp for information about checking accounts. Use the search box to find articles on "Check 21," which governs check clearing and processing. How might the rules of Check 21 affect your use of your checking account?

3. Visit the Bankrate.com website at http://www.bankrate.com/brm/rate/deposits_home.asp where you will find information about rates of return on certificates of deposit. What is the best rate for a one-year CD and a five-year CD in a large city near your home (look in the state, then the city)? How do these rates compare with the average rates nationally and the highest rates nationally?

4. Visit the website for FDIC at http://www.fdic.gov/. Use the search box to find articles on "internet bank." Read the article titled "Safe Internet Banking." After reading the information, make a list of important positive and negative aspects of Internet banking. Is Internet banking right for you?

Visit the Garman/Forgue companion website . . .

Building and Maintaining Good Credit

!You Must Be Kidding, Right?

People with no prior credit history or one that shows poor repayment patterns in the past often wonder if they will ever be able to get credit, especially in an economy when credit is difficult to obtain. Simply put, why would any lender want to trust them? Which of the following is true about the availability of credit for people in such situations?

A. No one will ever grant them credit.

B. If they wait a few years, the situation could change.

C. If they keep searching, they will find a lender that will treat them like everyone else.

D. Credit is relatively easy to obtain even today.

The answer is B. When credit is tight it is difficult for people with a poor or no credit to obtain credit. When credit availability eases, certain lenders will accept such applicants although they will charge high interest rates. Building and maintaining a good credit history will always get you low interest rates!

Learning Objectives

After reading this chapter, you should be able to:

1 Explain reasons for and against using credit.

2 Establish your own debt limit.

3 Achieve a good credit reputation.

4 Describe the common sources of consumer credit.

5 Identify signs of overindebtedness and describe the options that are available for debt relief.

What Do You Recommend?

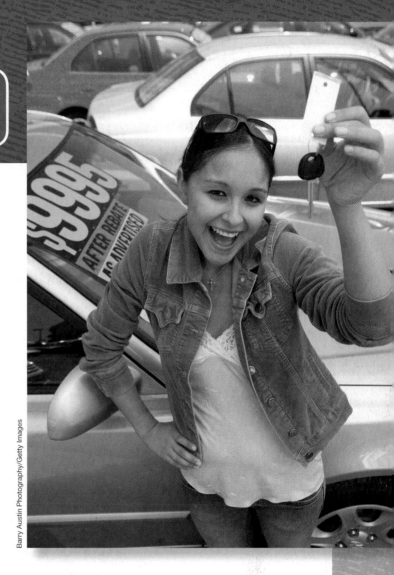

Carrie Savarin, age 25, is a nurse practitioner with the local health department. She earns $65,000 per year, with about $9000 of her income coming from overtime pay. Her disposable income is about $3300 per month. Her employer provides a qualified tax-sheltered retirement plan to which Carrie contributes 4 percent of her salary and for which she receives an additional 4 percent matching contribution from her employer. (She could contribute up to 6 percent with an equal employer match.) Carrie has $19,000 in outstanding student loans on which she will pay $354 per month over the next five years, and her total credit card debt is $3000 on which she has been paying $120 per month. Otherwise, she is debt free. Carrie would like to purchase a new or late-model used car to replace the car she has been driving since her senior year in high school. She has $2000 to use as a down payment.

What would you recommend to Carrie on the subject of building and maintaining good credit regarding:

1. Factors she should consider regarding her ability to take on additional debt?

2. The impact of her current debt on her ability to obtain a loan to buy a vehicle?

3. Where she might obtain financing for a vehicle loan?

4. The effect of taking on a loan on her overall financial planning?

Your Next Five Years

In the next five years you can start achieving financial success by doing the following related to building and maintaining good credit:

1. Protect your credit reputation as carefully as you would safeguard your personal reputation.

2. Determine your own debt limit rather than rely on a lender before deciding to take on any debt.

3. Obtain copies of your credit bureau reports regularly, and challenge all errors or omissions you find.

4. Never cosign a loan for anyone, including relatives.

5. Always repay your debts in a timely manner.

credit
A term used to describe an arrangement in which goods, services, or money is received in exchange for a promise to repay at a future date.

loan
Consumer credit that is repaid in equal amounts over a set period of time.

credit cards
Cards that allow repeated use of credit as long as the consumer makes regular monthly payments.

1 Learning Objective
Explain reasons for and against using credit.

Your financial success depends heavily on your ability to make the sacrifices necessary to spend less than you earn. This also suggests that you must use credit wisely. You must use credit only when necessary, pay low interest rates, make payments on time, and repay debts as quickly as possible. This can be challenging during sluggish economic times when credit is less available and employment opportunities are limited. But the advice is sound in good times and bad.

The term **credit** describes an arrangement in which goods, services, or money is received in exchange for a promise to repay at a future date. Most commonly, consumer credit takes the form of a **loan** that is repaid in equal payments over a set period of time or **credit cards,** which allow repeated use of credit as long as regular, monthly payments are maintained.

Many of us have conflicting feelings about the use of credit. On one hand, we may know people who have overused credit, got into financial trouble, perhaps because of unemployment, and wound up ruining their financial futures.

The failure to fully understand the nature of the credit can come back to haunt us when things do not go as planned. On the other hand, we may be attracted to the ease of using a credit card to pay for a vehicle or college expenses. There are good reasons for using credit but only when used wisely. Two keys are to set reasonable debt limits for yourself and know the best sources of credit. Follow this wise advice: "If you worry about your debts, you are already in trouble!" To succeed financially you need to establish and maintain a good credit reputation.

You also should be aware of your options for eliminating excessive debt should you ever get into financial difficulty. These topics are covered in this chapter. Chapters 7, 8, and 9 will help you understand the types of credit available and their costs.

Reasons For and Against Using Credit

Credit represents a form of trust established between a lender and a borrower. If the lender believes that a prospective borrower has both the ability and the willingness to repay money, then credit will be extended. The borrower is expected to live up to that trust by repaying the lender. For the privilege of borrowing, a lender requires that a borrower pay interest and sometimes other charges.

You can distinguish between good and bad uses of credit. Among the good uses are a mortgage loan to buy a home, a loan to open a business, and student loans. These purposes have benefits because the funds are invested in ways that can have a long-term payoff. Bad uses of credit include using a credit card to support a lifestyle that you can not otherwise afford and borrowing to buy groceries, overly expensive and otherwise unaffordable vehicles and homes.

Good Uses of Credit

Credit can be used in very positive ways to enhance personal financial planning. Following are some of the reasons people use credit:

1. **For convenience.** Using credit cards simplifies the process of making many purchases. It provides a record of purchases, and it can be used as leverage if disputes later arise. Convenience use of credit is growing. For example, many of us now use credit cards at the grocery store and the gas station. Convenience use is justified *only* if the card balance is paid in full each month, however. You do not want to be paying for today's restaurant meal for months or years in the future.

2. **For emergencies.** Consumers may use credit to pay for unexpected expenses such as emergency medical services or automobile repairs.

3. **To make reservations.** Most motels, hotels, and car rental agencies require some form of deposit to hold a reservation. A credit card number can serve as such a deposit, allowing guaranteed reservations to be made over the telephone. In many cases, the hotel will notify the credit card issuer to put a hold on your account for the anticipated total amount of the charge. This common practice is called **credit card blocking.**

4. **To own expensive products sooner.** Buying "big ticket" items such as a home or automobile on credit allows the consumer to enjoy immediate use of the product. Many expensive items would not be purchased (or would be bought only after several years of saving) without the opportunity to pay for them over time. The expected life of the product should be at least as long as the repayment period on the debt.

5. **To take advantage of free credit.** Merchants sometimes offer "free" credit for a period of time as an inducement to buy. Free credit, however, should not be used to buy a more expensive item than you can afford. Known as "same as cash" plans, these programs allow the buyer to pay later without incurring finance charges. The free credit lasts for a defined time period, but interest may be owed for the entire time period if the buyer pays even one day after the allotted free-credit period ends.

6. **For protection against rip-offs and frauds.** Internet and telephone purchases made on a credit card can be contested with the credit card issuer under the guidelines of the Fair Credit Billing Act (discussed later).

7. **To obtain an education.** The high cost of education has forced many students to use student loans. This may be one of the better uses of credit, as the borrower is investing in himself or herself to raise the quality of life and/or income in the future.

credit card blocking
Hotels or other service providers use a credit card number to secure reservations and charge the anticipated cost of services.

The Downside of Credit

Despite its benefits, the use of credit has a downside. Negative aspects include interest costs, the potential for overspending, credit's negative effect on your financial flexibility, and concerns about privacy.

Use of Credit Reduces Financial Flexibility The greatest disadvantage of credit use comes from the loss of financial flexibility in personal money management. As the old German proverb states, "He who borrows sells his freedom." The money that you pay each month on your debts is money you could have spent elsewhere on other opportunities. Credit use also reduces your future buying power, as the money you pay out on a loan includes a finance charge as well as the principal. In fact, credit can be seen as a promise for you to "work for the creditor" in the future to pay off your debt.

It Is Very Tempting to Spend More Money A major disadvantage of credit is that its use can lead to overspending. Using a credit card to buy $425 worth of new clothes and paying $25 per month for 20 months (a total of $500: $425 + $75 interest charge) may seem less painful than paying cash for a planned purchase of only $300 worth of clothes. The problem is this: Once you begin carrying credit card debt, it may seem easier to buy more on credit, especially if you have more than three or four cards—as is typical for U.S. credit card holders.

Instant Message

Debt Reduces Your Ability to Save and Invest

Saving and investing over long periods of time is the key to building wealth. Taking on excessive debts early in life will seriously compromise your goal of being financially successful.

Instant Message

"Chase"ing College Students on Facebook

As an indicator of how important the college market is to credit card companies, Chase Bank is Facebook's exclusive credit card sponsor, and ads for Chase credit cards appear on the popular social-networking website.

Becoming a Financially "Overstretched American"   Consumers with monthly nonmortgage debt repayments amounting to 15 percent of monthly take-home pay or more are considered to be precariously in debt. They teeter on the brink of disaster. They run a high risk by not paying bills on time, which results in a poor credit reputation, damage to employment prospects, an increase in rates paid for insurance, and sometimes the loss of items purchased. During the recent economic meltdown many people who were precariously in debt could not weather the loss of income as a result of layoffs and other financial setbacks. Some were victims of **predatory lending** when dishonest or deceptive lenders took advantage of their lack of understanding of credit matters. For example, many homebuyers ended up with mortgage payments they could not afford, due to confusing and misleading terms and conditions as well as outright fraud. Predatory mortgage lending resulted in many homes being sold to people who could not truly afford to make the monthly payments and the subsequent national crisis of mortgage foreclosures.

interest
In this context, interest is the "rent" you pay for using credit.

finance charge
Total dollar amount paid to use credit.

annual percentage rate (APR)
Expresses the cost of credit on a yearly basis as a percentage rate.

Interest Itself Is Costly   **Interest** represents the price of credit. It is the "rent" you pay while you use someone else's money. When stated in dollars, interest makes up part of the **finance charge**, which is the total dollar amount paid to use credit (including interest and any other required charges such as a loan application fee). The Truth in Lending Act requires lenders to state the finance charge both in dollars and as an **annual percentage rate (APR)**. The APR expresses the cost of credit on a yearly basis as a percentage rate. For example, a single-payment, one-year loan for $1000 with a finance charge of $140 has a 14 percent APR.

Knowing the APR simplifies making comparisons among credit arrangements. The lower the APR, the lower the true cost of the credit. The APR can be used to compare credit contracts with different time periods, finance charges, repayment schedules, and amounts borrowed. Many states have **usury laws** (sometimes called **small loan laws**) that establish the maximum loan amounts, interest rates, and credit-related fees for different types of loans from various sources. These maximum rates can vary from 18 percent to as much as 54 percent. The laws of the state in which the lending institution is located apply, rather than the laws of the state in which the borrower lives. These regulations apply to the annual fee, late payment fee, and other fees charged on a bank credit card.

 Concept Check 6.1

1. Which two good uses of credit seem most reasonable to you? Which do not?
2. Explain the two downsides of credit that would be most worrisome for you?
3. Distinguish between the APR and the finance charge on a debt.

You Should Set Your Own Debt Limit

2 Learning Objective
Establish your own debt limit.

debt limit
Overall maximum you believe you should owe based on your ability to meet repayment obligations.

You should set your **debt limit**, which is the overall maximum you believe you should owe based on your ability to meet the repayment obligations. Most people's debt limit is, and should be, lower than what lenders are willing to offer. Lenders are willing to take chances that some borrowers will not repay. In fact, this was one of the issues that led to the recent credit crisis. Lenders for several years were very willing to lend and many people assumed that if the lender thought they could repay that in fact they could. They were wrong. You should not take such a chance when making your own credit decisions.

When considering a new loan, many people simply look at the monthly payment required. This view is shortsighted and it is easy to get a low monthly payment simply by

Advice from a Pro...

Guard Your Privacy

Identity theft is the most common form of consumer fraud in the United States. It occurs whenever someone else uses your personal information, such as a credit card number, to steal from merchants, from credit card companies, or from you. Armed with a very little personal information, a clever thief can borrow someone's credit identity and run up thousands of dollars in debt. To protect your privacy, follow these guidelines:

■ Offer no personal information (such as your address, telephone number, or Social Security number) to merchants when using a credit card. If the merchant requires identification beyond the credit card (for example, a driver's license), do not allow such information to be written down or photocopied.

■ Save all purchase and ATM receipts, and regularly check them against statements from creditors and sellers.

■ Do not give out your credit card or checking account number on the telephone to anyone you do not know or did not telephone directly yourself.

■ Never give your **card verification value** over the phone or online to a merchant unless you initiated the contact with the merchant. This is the three- or four-digit code in the signature strip on the back of a credit card.

■ Review your credit bureau report at least once each year through www.annualcreditreport.com.

■ Report lost or stolen credit cards and suspicious billing information without delay, especially if you make Internet purchases.

■ If your credit card is lost or stolen, or if you ever suspect fraudulent use of an account, contact one of the national credit bureaus because any one of them can put a "fraud alert" on your file at all three companies. Fraud alert messages notify potential credit grantors to verify your identification before extending credit in your name.

■ Tell all of your financial services companies (banks, lenders, insurance companies) that you want to "opt out" of any information-sharing programs they maintain with affiliated or external companies.

■ Never respond to e-mail messages from your bank stating that your account may have been compromised and you need to provide account information such as account numbers and passwords even if the e-mail message looks authentic. Your bank will never ask you for this type of information in an e-mail.

■ Immediately change the marital status linked to your credit card account if you become married, separated, or divorced.

■ Shred all credit card statements containing account numbers.

■ Place a **security freeze** on your credit report, which is an effective way to prevent unauthorized credit accounts from being opened in your name. With a freeze you tell the credit bureaus not to release your financial records to anyone without your consent. You are issued a personal identification number (PIN) to give your authorization. In all but South Carolina there is a nominal charge for this service.

Karen Drage
Eastern Illinois University

lengthening the time period over which the loan will be repaid. You should assess your overall debt obligations. There are three ways to determine your debt limit:

1. Debt payments-to-disposable income method

2. Ratio of debt-to-equity method

3. Continuous-debt method

Debt Payments-to-Disposable Income Method

To use the **debt payments-to-disposable income method,** you first need to decide the percentage of your disposable personal income that can be spent for regular debt repayments, excluding the first mortgage loan on a home and credit card charges that are paid in full each month. **Disposable income** is the amount of your income remaining after taxes and withholding for such purposes as insurance and union dues. Table 6.1 shows some

debt payments-to-disposable income method
Percentage of disposable personal income available for regular debt repayments aside from set obligations.

disposable income
Amount of income remaining after taxes and withholding for such purposes as insurance and union dues.

Table 6.1   Debt-Payment Limits as a Percentage of Disposable Personal Income*

Percent	Current Debt Situation	Borrower's Feelings	Take on Additional Debt?
0	No debt at all	No stress about personal finances	Taking on some consumer debt is fine
10 or less	Little debt	Borrower feels no stress from debt repayment obligations	More debt could be undertaken cautiously
11 to 14	Safe debt limit but fully extended financially	Borrower is moderately stressed about pressure from debt repayment obligations	Should not acquire more debt, and a debt-consolidation loan from a credit union may be a good option
15 to 18	Precariously overindebted	Borrower starts to feel seriously stressed about debts and hopes no emergency arises	Absolutely should not take on more debt
19 to 28	Seriously overindebted	Borrower feels overwhelming stress and is desperate about debts	Contact a nonprofit credit counseling company
29+	Excessively overindebted	Borrower feels hopeless or knows his or her debts are so large that he or she is doomed to financial failure	Contact a bankruptcy attorney

*Excluding home mortgage loan repayments and convenience credit card purchases to be repaid in full when the bill arrives.

monthly debt-payment limits expressed as a percentage of disposable personal income. As the table indicates, with monthly payments representing 15 to 18 percent of monthly disposable personal income, a borrower is precariously overindebted and fully extended; taking on additional debt would be unwise. This means that someone with an average income and an expensive car loan might not be able to afford to carry any credit card balances that carry over from month to month.

Once you decide the percentage that is appropriate for you, you can compare it with your **debt payments-to-disposable income ratio** as discussed in Chapter 3. In that chapter, we calculated a debt payments-to-disposable income ratio for the Hernandez family of 9.32 percent. As indicated by Table 6.1, they could take on new debt—but only cautiously.

Table 6.2 shows the effects on a budget of increasing debts. In the table, after deductions, disposable personal income amounts to $2200 per month. Current budgeted expenses (totaling the full $2200) are allocated in a sample distribution throughout the various categories. As you can see, increasing debt payments from $0 to $550 per month (for example, to buy a new automobile or home entertainment system on credit) has dramatic effects on this budget. A responsible financial manager must decide where to cut back to meet monthly credit repayments. As the debt load grows, each 5 percentage point increase makes it much more difficult to "find the money" and make the cutbacks. In this case, the borrower reduced expenditures on savings and investments immediately and then finally reduced the amount in this category to $50. Food was cut back, but only slightly. Utilities, automobile insurance, and rent are relatively fixed expenses; as a consequence, it is difficult to reduce these amounts without moving or buying a less expensive car. Entertainment expenses were steadily reduced, and newspapers and magazines were eliminated altogether.

Where would you make reductions? Spending a few minutes changing the figures in Table 6.2 will give you an idea of your priorities and the size of the debt limit that you might establish. Note that the debt payments-to-disposable income method focuses on the amount of monthly debt repayment—not the total debt. As a result, it also would be wise to consider the length of time that the severe financial situation caused by high debt payments might last. You could get yourself into financial trouble for many years.

Table 6.2   **Effects of Increasing Debt Payments on a Budget***

Gross income	$ 34,000
Deductions for taxes, 401(k), insurance	$ 7,600
Disposable personal income	$ 26,400
Monthly disposable income	$ 2,200

	No Debt	10% Debt	15% Debt	20% Debt	25% Debt
Rent	$ 700	$ 700	$ 700	$ 700	$ 700
Savings and investments	250	180	120	80	50
Food	280	250	240	220	210
Utilities (telephone, electricity, heat)	130	130	130	120	120
Insurance (automobile, renter's, and life)	80	80	80	80	80
Transportation expenses	100	90	90	80	80
Charitable contributions	60	50	50	40	40
Entertainment	140	120	110	100	80
Clothing	50	40	30	20	20
Vacations and long weekends	60	50	40	40	30
Medical/dental expenses	60	50	50	50	50
Newspapers and magazines	40	30	30	30	0
Cable TV	50	50	40	40	30
Personal care	30	20	20	20	20
Gifts and holidays	40	30	30	30	30
Health club	60	60	60	60	60
Miscellaneous	70	50	50	50	50
Debt repayments	0	220	330	440	550
TOTAL	**$2,200**	**$2,200**	**$2,200**	**$2,200**	**$2,200**

*One person's decisions on where to cut back expenses to make increasing monthly debt payments.

Ratio of Debt-to-Equity Method

Another method for determining your debt limit involves calculating the ratio of your consumer debt to your assets. In Chapter 3, we performed such an analysis for the Hernandez family when we calculated their asset-to-debt ratio. The **debt-to-equity ratio** is similar except that it uses the **equity** in a person's assets (the amount by which the value of those assets exceeds debts), excluding the value of a primary residence and the first mortgage on that home. This ratio recognizes that mortgage debt does not get people into trouble. In fact, mortgage debt is backed up by excellent collateral—one's own home.

From Table 3.3 on page 73, we see that the Hernandez family has assets of $133,920 ($4420—monetary assets; $20,500—tangible assets less the value of their home; and $109,000—investment assets). Their debts (excluding their home mortgage) total $9365 ($120 + $1545 + $7700). With $9365 in debts and $133,920 in assets, the Hernandezes have equity of $124,555 ($133,920 – $9365), or a debt-to-equity ratio of 0.08 ($9365 ÷ $124,555).

debt-to-equity ratio
Ratio of your consumer debt to your assets.

Instant Message

Are You Worried About Your Debts?

If you are worried about your debts then you should be. Your own gut feeling is often the best indicator.

The ratio of debt-to-equity method provides a quick idea of one's financial solvency. The larger the ratio, the riskier the likelihood of repayment. A ratio in excess of 0.33 is considered high. The Hernandezes are well under that limit, unlike the result found by calculating their debt payments-to-disposable income ratio. This contrast occurs primarily because of their real estate investment asset, on which they have no debt.

Continuous-Debt Method

Another approach for determining your debt limit is the **continuous-debt method.** If you are unable to get completely out of debt every four years (except for a mortgage loan), you probably lean on debt too heavily. You could be developing a credit lifestyle in which you will never eliminate debt and will continuously pay out substantial amounts of income for finance charges—likely $1200 or more per year, and that is like throwing away $100 every month for absolutely nothing!

Dual-Earner Households Should Consider a Lower Debt Limit

Having two incomes in a household has its benefits. Two people, each of whom earns $36,000 per year, will gross $72,000, with a disposable personal income of around $54,000, or $4500 monthly. It may seem that the couple can afford a much higher level of debt than before the incomes were combined. While the guidelines given in Table 6.1 are realistic, they would allow a doubling of debt payments if the addition of a second earner doubled household earnings.

Many young couples adopt a lifestyle based on two incomes. Their spending grows in tandem with their rising incomes. After a while, they are spending and borrowing to the limit.

Did You Know?

How to Manage Student Loan Debt

You should minimize your student loan debt because large debts make it more challenging to meet other financial goals such as buying a home and saving for retirement. Here are some tips for managing student loan debt:

1. **Choose the most advantageous repayment pattern allowed.** The standard repayment plan for student loan debt calls for equal monthly installments paid over ten years, but to pay the debt off faster, you can establish a graduated repayment plan whereby the payments are lower in the early years but then increase in later years.

2. **Pay electronically.** Make arrangements to have the monthly payment transferred electronically out of a checking account and you can receive a reduction in the interest rate.

3. **Make your repayments on time, every time.** In some programs, if you make the first 48 payments on

time, the interest rate will be reduced by 2 percentage points. Failing to repay in a timely manner can have dire consequences, including forfeiture of federal and state income tax refunds, as well as Social Security and veterans' benefits.

4. **Consolidate your student loans.** Consolidating your education loans means that all your existing loans are paid off and one new loan is created. This strategy may allow for a much more convenient repayment schedule. The interest rate may be lower, the monthly payment is usually lower, and the amount of time for repayment may be longer under the new loan. Loans can be consolidated through a private bank or through one of three government programs: Sallie Mae (www.salliemae .com), or Federal Direct Consolidation Loans (www .loanconsolidation.ed.gov).

Jose Luis Pelaez/Getty Images

Two incomes should not mean double debt.

This situation cannot go on forever, of course. Eventually they may begin to feel financially stressed and wonder, "How can we be so broke when we make so much money?" When a child comes along or one partner loses a job or overtime pay, they may quickly get into deep financial trouble as debts that had been manageable with two incomes quickly become over-whelming. Bad economic times can have devastatingly negative financial impacts on families who have taken on too much debt. Couples would be wise to set a debt limit based on the higher of their two incomes and build savings accounts and make investments early in their lives together. That will truly protect their future financial security. This is one of the smartest financial actions a couple can make—save extra money early in a relationship.

✔ Concept Check 6.2

1. Distinguish among the debt payments-to-disposable income, ratio of debt-to-equity, and continuous-debt methods for setting your debt limit.

2. What are the threshold levels for both the debt payments-to-disposable income and ratio of debt-to-equity methods that would indicate that a person is carrying too much debt?

3. Discuss how dual-earner households should consider their ability to carry additional debt.

Obtaining Credit and Building a Good Credit Reputation

Credit is widely and readily available to most of us today. It is not unusual for a customer to walk into a retail store such as Target or Home Depot and be offered a credit card account that can be used immediately. However, if the applicant has not used credit previously (no credit), or has bounced a lot of checks, or has failed to honor credit agreements in the past (bad credit), an offer of credit is typically not extended. Your success in obtaining credit hinges on an understanding of the credit approval process and having a good credit reputation.

3 Learning Objective
Achieve a good credit reputation.

Did You Know?

The Top 3 Financial Missteps in Building and Maintaining Good Credit

People slip up in building and maintaining good credit when they do the following:

1. Fail to regularly check the accuracy of credit bureau files
2. Let a lender's willingness to grant credit be an indicator of its affordability
3. Pay more than 14 percent of disposable income toward nonmortgage debt payments

credit application
Form or interview that provides information about your ability and willingness to repay debts.

credit history
Continuing record of a person's credit usage and repayment of debts.

The Credit Approval Process

To obtain credit, you must first complete a credit application. Based on the information in this application, the lender will investigate your credit history. The information is then evaluated (sometimes instantly via computer), and the lender decides whether to extend credit. When an application is approved, the rules of the account are contained in the credit agreement.

You Apply for Credit A **credit application** is a form or interview that requests information that sheds light on your ability and willingness to repay debts. This information helps lenders make informed decisions about whether they will be repaid by borrowers. Answering questions completely and honestly both on an application form and during an interview (if any) is important. If inconsistencies arise during the lender's subsequent investigation of the applicant's credit history, the lender could refuse the request for credit or charge a higher interest rate. At the time of application, always ask for a copy of the rules governing the account, including the APR and various repayment terms. However, these terms are not final and can change when the actual decision to lend is made. That is why you should read all credit contracts before signing.

Approximately 15 percent of all people who apply for credit are denied. Half of the unsuccessful applicants have no established **credit history** (a continuing record of a person's credit usage and repayment of debts) or their credit history contains negative information. A bad credit history is like having high blood pressure—you may not know you have a problem until something bad happens, such as when your loan application is rejected.

The Lender Obtains Your Credit Report Upon receiving your completed credit application, the lender conducts a **credit investigation** and compares the findings with the information on your application. The goal of the investigation is to assess the applicant's

Did You Know?

Unfair Credit Discrimination Is Unlawful

The Equal Credit Opportunity Act (ECOA) prohibits certain types of **unfair discrimination** (making distinctions among individuals based on unfair criteria) when granting credit. Under this law, a lender must notify an applicant within 30 days about the lender's acceptance or rejection of a credit application. The ECOA also requires the creditor to provide the applicant with a written statement, if requested, detailing the reasons for refusing credit. Rejecting a credit application due to poor credit history is legal. Conversely, it is illegal to reject applicants on the basis of gender, race, age, national origin, religion, or receipt of Social Security income or public assistance. Credit applications cannot ask for information that could be used in a biased manner, such as marital status and childbearing plans. (Applicants may offer such information

voluntarily, however.) If discrimination is proved in court, the lender may be fined as much as $10,000.

A creditor cannot require an applicant to disclose income from alimony, separate maintenance payments, or child support payments. If the borrower wants this income to be counted during the lender's evaluation of the application, the creditor can consider whether that income stream is received consistently. Information about a spouse or former spouse may not be requested unless the spouse will use the account, it is a joint account, or repayment of debts will rely on the spouse's income or other financial support. The law requires that credit granted in both spouses' names be used to build a credit history for the parties as a couple as well as for each individual spouse.

creditworthiness. Lenders want to know the applicant's prior credit usage and repayment patterns, income, length of employment, and home ownership status.

To conduct its investigation, the lender obtains a **credit report** from a **credit bureau** that keeps records of many borrowers' credit histories. Lenders pay a fee for each credit report requested. Credit bureaus compile information from merchants, utility companies, banks, court records, and creditors. Most of the more than 2000 local credit bureaus in the United States belong to national groups that collectively have access to the credit histories of more than 170 million adults.

All three of the major credit-reporting bureaus calculate and report credit scores to lenders. Lenders use a **credit score** (also known as **risk scoring**) in which a statistical measure is used to rate applicants on the basis of various factors deemed relevant to creditworthiness

credit report
Information compiled by a credit bureau from merchants, utility companies, banks, court records, and creditors about your payment history.

credit bureau
Firm that collects and keeps records of many borrowers' credit histories.

Did You Know?

How to Make Sense of Credit Scores

Although the credit-scoring systems in use today go by a number of brand names, the most well known is the FICO score developed by Fair, Isaac and Company (www.myfico .com). Because your credit file and the method of calculating the score may differ at each of the three major credit bureaus, your credit score at each may differ as well. (See "Managing Your Credit Bureau File for Free" on page 179.) Your credit scores are vitally important because they dictate whether you will be granted credit and at what interest rates. Under the Fair and Accurate Credit Transactions Act of 2003, credit bureaus must provide consumers with their credit scores upon request. A nominal fee (about $12) is charged for a credit score report.

FICO scores are produced via complex statistical models that correlate certain borrower characteristics with the likelihood of repayment. The exact methodologies employed in the models are closely held secrets, but the factors that are used in them are shared openly by Fair, Isaac and Company on the company's website:

1. **Payment history.** Are you late with your payments? How late? How often? On how many of your accounts?

2. **Amounts owed.** What is the balance on each of your credit obligations? (Even if you pay in full each month, there might be a balance on a given date.) How do the amounts owed vary on various types of accounts, such as credit cards versus loans? How many accounts have balances? Are you "maxed out" or nearly so on your cards, regardless of the dollar amount of your balances? (Credit scores are negatively affected if you have a balance on any card in excess of 30 percent of the credit limit on that card.) On loans, how much of the original loan is still owed?

3. **Length of credit history.** How long have you had each account? How long has it been since you used the accounts?

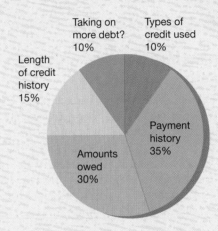

4. **Taking on more debt.** How many new accounts do you have? How long has it been since you opened a new account? How many recent inquiries have been made by lenders to which you have made application? If you had a period of poor credit usage in the past, for how long have you been in good standing?

5. **Types of credit used.** Do you have a good mix of credit usage, with reliance on multiple types depending on the purpose of the credit (for example, not using a credit card to buy a boat)? How many accounts in total do you have?

The FICO website provides suggestions on how to improve your FICO scores. For example, if you are "maxed out" on two cards and have low balances on others, you might shift some of the large balances to other cards. If you have many dormant accounts, you should close them. The chart above indicates the importance of each of the five factors in the development of FICO scores.

credit score (risk score)
Statistical measure used to rate applicants based on various factors deemed relevant to creditworthiness and the likelihood of repayment.

credit agreement
Contract that stipulates repayment terms for credit cards.

promissory note (note)
Contract that stipulates repayment terms for a loan.

Instant Message

Closing Accounts Does Not Help Your Credit Score

Many people think that closing credit card accounts will help a credit score. This is not the case. When accounts are closed it reduces the ratio between what you owe to the total amount of credit available on all credit cards, and that smaller window of credit available reduces your FICO score. Also, credit scores are higher when accounts have been open for longer periods of time. Therefore, if you feel you must close accounts, close your newest accounts, not the oldest.

and the likelihood of repayment. You also have the right to know your scores, although you usually must pay a fee to do so. The most well-known score is the FICO score developed by Fair, Isaac and Company.

The Lender Decides Whether to Accept the Application and Under What Terms

The approval or rejection of credit is based on the lender's judgment of the willingness and ability of the applicant to repay the debt. If the application is accepted, a contract is created that outlines the rules governing the account. For credit cards, this contract is called a **credit agreement.** For loans, the contract is called a **promissory note** (or simply, the **note**).

The actual lender always makes the decision about whether to grant credit. Credit scoring simply allows lenders to categorize credit users according to the perceived level of risk. Under the concept of **tiered pricing,** lenders may offer lower interest rates to applicants with the highest credit scores while charging steeper rates to more-risky applicants. Even people with low credit scores usually can find some lender that will say yes, however. The interest rates will be higher for those borrowers. Of course, some applicants represent such high risk that a lender will deny the application for credit. For this reason, you should always make sure that your credit bureau file is accurate before filling out a credit application.

Your Credit Reputation

The information about you that is contained in credit bureau files is one of the most important aspects of your financial life. It is used not only when lenders decide whether to approve your applications for credit but also when you apply for a job, insurance, and rental housing. Thus, it is important that you build a good credit reputation and confirm that the information in your file is as accurate and up-to-date as possible.

Building a Credit History

Some people who are new to the world of credit wonder whether they will ever get credit when they need it. They will if they establish a good credit history. This is what is meant when someone is said to have "good credit." The following steps can help you have "good credit":

1. **Establish both a checking account and a savings account.** Lenders see people who can handle these accounts as being more likely to manage credit usage properly.

2. **Have your telephone and other utilities billed in your name.** The fact that you can maintain a good payment pattern on your utility bills indicates that you can manage your money wisely and will do the same with your credit repayments.

3. **Request, acquire, and use an oil-company credit card.** These cards are easy to obtain. If one company refuses, simply apply to another company, as companies' scoring systems differ. Use the credit sparingly, and repay the debt promptly.

4. **Apply for a bank credit card.** Your own bank is the best place to start your search for a credit card. If not successful there, you usually can find some bank that will issue you a card (search at www.bankrate.com). The credit limit may be low (perhaps $500) and the APR high (perhaps 27 percent), but at least the opportunity exists to establish a credit history. Later, you can request an increase in the credit limit and a lower APR.

5. **Ask a bank for a small, short-term cash loan.** Putting these borrowed funds into a savings account at the bank will almost guarantee that you will make the required three or four monthly payments. In addition, the interest charges on the loan will be partially offset by the interest earned on the savings.

6. Pay off student loans. Some have their first exposure to credit through the student loans they use to attend college. Paying off these loans quickly through a series of regular monthly payments can show prospective lenders that you are a responsible borrower.

Managing Your Credit Bureau File for Free

Federal law requires credit bureaus to provide consumers with their credit reports upon request. You can obtain one report for free each year from each of the national credit bureaus. In addition, consumers must be notified if merchants report negative information to a credit bureau.

You should request a report periodically (certainly every year) or whenever you move, have a change in family status (marry, get divorced, or become widowed), or resolve any credit billing errors or disputes (to ensure that negative information is not in your file) or plan to sign up for new credit in the next few months. To obtain a free report, contact www.annualcreditreport.com. This is the **only** site that links you directly to the mechanism for obtaining a truly free report. If you contact one of the sites with similarly worded names or directly contact one of the three major credit-reporting bureaus you will be enticed to sign up for a **credit reporting service.** Such services allow you to access your report as often as daily and obtain your credit score, supposedly for free for a month or two. However, these offers are **negative option plans.** You are automatically signed up for a plan costing as much as $100 or more per year and your membership renews automatically unless you notify them that you want it to end at the end of the free period. A bad deal, especially when you can obtain all the information yourself for free.

The free annual credit report law allows you to check your credit for free every four months. How? By staggering your requests across the three national bureaus.* For example,

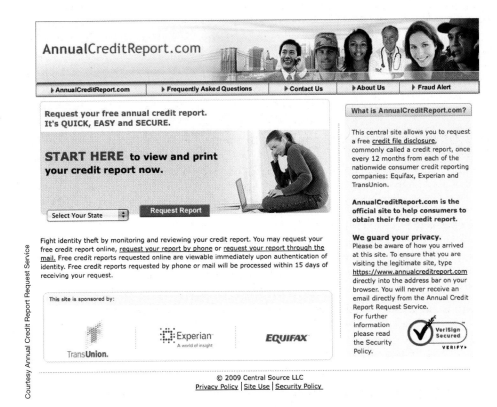

Courtesy Annual Credit Report Request Service

Review your credit report regularly to make sure it is accurate.

*The major credit bureaus often sell lists of consumer names in their files (albeit not the specific credit history information) for credit card marketing purposes. To have your name withheld for two years from this practice, call (888) 567-8688 or go online at www.optoutprescreen.com.

Instant Message

Your Credit Score Is Based on Your Credit Report

The importance of the accuracy of the information in your credit bureau file is emphasized by the fact that your credit score is determined solely by that information. Make sure your credit bureau files are accurate and be as concerned about your credit score as you are about your GPA.

Fair Credit Reporting Act (FCRA)
Requires that credit reports contain accurate, relevant, and recent information and that only bona fide users be permitted to review a file for approved purposes.

consumer statement
Your version of a credit issue that shows up on your credit report when the credit bureau refuses to drop a disputed claim.

in January you can request a report from Experian through www.annualcreditreport.com. Then, in May you can order a report from TransUnion. In September you can request a report from Equifax. Then in January, it's back to Experian. Because the bureaus all gather information from essentially the same sources, you can have some confidence that what appears on one file will be present in the others. If you find an error, contact all three to make the correction.

When you obtain your report, thoroughly inspect it for accuracy. The **Fair Credit Reporting Act (FCRA)** requires that reports contain accurate, relevant, and recent information and that only bona fide users be permitted to review a file for approved purposes. FCRA is partially enforced by consumers.

If you find an error or omission in a credit report from a particular credit bureau, you should immediately take steps to correct the information. Here's how:

1. Notify the original lender of the error and ask for confirmation.

2. Simultaneously notify the credit bureau that you wish to exercise your right to a reinvestigation under FCRA. Specifically, you should ask the bureau to "reaffirm" the item. If the credit bureau responds by stating that the information is accurate, you still have the right to challenge the item with the lender involved.

3. The bureau must reinvestigate the information within 45 days. If it cannot complete its investigation within 45 days, it must drop the information from your credit file.

4. If the information was erroneous, it must be corrected. If a report containing the error was sent to a creditor investigating your application within the past six months, a corrected report must be sent to that creditor.

5. If the credit bureau refuses to make a correction (perhaps because the information was "technically correct"), you may wish to provide your version of the disputed information (in 100 words or less) by adding a **consumer statement** to your credit bureau file. This statement will be included with any credit reports by that bureau.

Did You Know?

The Effects of Divorce on Your Credit

The breakup of a marriage affects the creditworthiness of both partners. The Federal Trade Commission makes the following suggestions for individuals seeking a divorce.

Pay careful attention to credit accounts held jointly, including mortgages, second mortgages, and credit cards. The behavior of one divorcing spouse will continue to affect the other individual as long as the accounts are held in both names. One party could make credit card charges, for example, and refuse to pay the debt, leaving the financial burden on the other party. When possible, ask creditors to close joint accounts and reopen them as individual accounts. Never accept a creditor's verbal assurance, either over the telephone or in person, that an account has been closed. Always insist

on written confirmation, including the effective date of the account closure.

When debts were accumulated in both names, a divorce decree has no legal effect on who technically owes which debts. Creditors can legally collect from *either* of the divorcing parties. If the person absolved of responsibility for the debt under the divorce decree is forced by a creditor to pay off the account, he must then go to court to seek enforcement of the divorce decree and collect reimbursement from the former spouse.

Both before and after a divorce, get a copy of your credit report from each of the three credit bureaus. Check them for accuracy and challenge any problem areas, such as accounts that continue to be shown in both names.

6. Also obtain a report from the other two bureaus to ensure that the error does not also appear in their files. If an error appears, correct it beginning at step #2.

7. Negative information in your file is generally not reportable after a period of seven years except for bankruptcy data, for which the time limit is ten years.

✔ Concept Check 6.3

1. Summarize the basic steps that occur when someone applies for credit.

2. What is a credit history, and what role do credit bureaus play in the development of your credit history?

3. What is a credit score, and what five major factors go into its calculation?

4. Identify five actions you can take to build a good credit reputation.

5. Summarize the protections provided under the Fair Credit Reporting Act.

Sources of Consumer Loans

Today's consumers have many sources of consumer loans from which to choose. Most consumer lending occurs through depository institutions and sales finance companies. Other sources include consumer finance companies, stockbrokers, and insurance companies. Table 6.3 shows the interest rates charged and example payment amounts and finance charges from these various sources of consumer loans.

4 Learning Objective
Describe the common sources of consumer credit.

Depository Institutions Loan Money to Their Banking Customers

Depository institutions include commercial banks, mutual savings banks, savings banks, and credit unions (see Chapter 5 for more-detailed descriptions of these institutions). They tend to make loans to their own customers and to noncustomers with good credit histories. Depository institutions offer highly competitive rates, partly because the funds loaned are obtained primarily from their depositors. The interest rate commonly ranges from 9 to 18 percent. Research indicates that many people who go elsewhere for loans actually meet the qualifications for depository institution lending and end up paying a higher interest rate than necessary.

Table 6.3 **What It Costs to Borrow Money**

Lender	Annual Percentage Rate	Two-Year Loan		Five-Year Loan	
		Monthly Payment	Finance Charge	Monthly Payment	Finance Charge
Life insurance company	6	$44.32	$ 63.68	$19.33	$159.80
Sales finance company	8	45.23	85.52	20.28	216.80
Credit union	10	46.14	107.36	21.25	275.00
Commercial bank	12	47.07	129.68	22.24	334.40
Mutual savings bank	12	47.07	129.68	22.24	334.40
Savings and loan association	12	47.07	129.68	22.24	334.40
Bank credit card	18	49.92	198.08	25.39	523.40
Consumer finance company	24	52.87	268.88	28.77	726.20

Credit costs money. Just how much can be seen by considering the cost of borrowing $1000 for two years and for five years from various sources at various interest rates.

Sales Finance Companies Loan Money to Buy Consumer Products

sales finance company
Seller-related lender whose primary business is financing sales for its parent company.

A **sales finance company** is a seller-related lender (such as GMAC Financial Services for General Motors Corporation and Ford Motor Credit) whose primary business is financing the sales of its parent company. Such firms specialize in making purchase loans, often with the item being bought serving as the collateral for the loan. Because the seller often works in close association with the sales finance company, credit can be approved on the spot.

Sales finance companies require collateral and deal only with customers who are considered medium to good risks. Thus, their interest rates are often competitive with those offered by depository institutions. Their interest rates may be even lower than those offered by other sources if the seller subsidizes the rate to encourage sales—as with the special low-APR financing often offered on new cars, for example. Most new-car loans today are made by sales finance companies.

Consumer Finance Companies Make Small Cash Loans

consumer finance company/ small loan company
Firm that specializes in making relatively small secured or unsecured loans that require monthly installment payments.

A **consumer finance company** specializes in making relatively small loans and is, therefore, also known as a **small-loan company.** These lenders range from the well-recognized CitiFinancial and Beneficial Finance Corporation to many local neighborhood lenders. Such companies make both secured and unsecured loans and require repayment on a monthly installment basis. They focus mainly on the **subprime lending** market. This market focuses

Did You Know?

About Alternative Lenders

A number of avenues through which to obtain credit are available that may not look like credit. Credit can come from unusual sources, including payday lenders, rent-to-own stores, and pawnshops.

Payday lenders (which are illegal in some states) are businesses that grant credit when they honor a personal check but agree not to deposit the check for a week or longer. The fees for check cashing are sometimes 20 percent or more of the amount of the check, pushing the APR (if the check is held for later deposit) to several hundred percent or higher.

A **rent-to-own program** provides a mechanism for buying an item with little or no down payment by renting it for a period of time, after which it is owned. Furniture, appliances, and electronic entertainment items are commonly sold via the rent-to-own approach. This form of credit is often used by people who believe they cannot qualify for credit purchases. These programs have two big drawbacks for consumers. First, the renter does not own the item until the final payment is made. Paying late or stopping payments will cause the

products to be seized with no allowance being made for the previous "rental" payments. Second, the actual cost for renting items is often exorbitantly high. For example, a TV worth $300 might be rented for $15 per week for one year, producing a finance charge of $480 (52 × $15 − $300).

A **pawnshop** is a lender that offers single-payment loans, often ranging from $100 to $500, for short time periods (typically one or two months), after the borrower turns over an item of personal property to the pawnshop. The dollar amount loaned is typically equal to one-third or less of the value of the item pawned. In most states, a borrower need merely turn over the item, present identification, and sign on the dotted line. The pawnshop owner can legally sell the item if the borrower fails to redeem the property by paying the amount due, plus interest, within the time period specified. The pawnshop typically charges an interest rate of about 5 percent per month plus a 2 percent monthly storage fee; thus, the annual combined "interest" amounts to 84 percent [(5 + 2) × 12]. Clearly, pawnshops represent the lender of last resort for borrowers.

on lending to people who normally would not qualify for credit with FICO scores of less than 620. The interest rates they charge are higher than those available from depository lenders because consumer finance companies focus on borrowers with low credit scores.

Approximately one-fifth of all loans granted by consumer finance companies are for the purpose of debt consolidation (described later). Other common uses of such loans are for travel, vacations, education, automobiles, and home furnishings. Some small-loan companies specialize in making loans by mail. They advertise in newspapers and magazines and on the Internet to attract borrowers, who complete a credit application and receive approval via mail.

Stockbrokers Loan Money to Their Clients

People build significant assets in investment accounts that may be earmarked for their children's college education, their own retirement, or other purposes. If you have a margin account (see Chapter 14), you can borrow from your stockbroker using your investments as collateral. Although many people prefer not to tap into these investment funds directly, it may be possible to borrow from or against these accounts. In addition, it may be possible to borrow from certain employer-sponsored, tax-sheltered retirement accounts (see Chapter 17), depending on the rules of the plan. Care must be taken to ensure that the loan plus interest is repaid so that the savings goal can still be met. Tax consequences may arise if retirement account loans are not repaid. (See Chapter 17 for details.)

Insurance Companies Loan Money to Their Policyholders

Insurance companies, such as State Farm or Allstate, offer car loans and credit cards to their policyholders. They may make these loans out of their own funds or have bank subsidiary companies set up to handle such loans. Insurance companies loan only to their customers with high credit scores. They can be a low-cost source from which to borrow money.

Policyholders who have cash-value life insurance policies can obtain loans based on the cash values built up in their policies. (This topic is examined in Chapter 12.) An advantage to borrowing on a cash-value life insurance policy is that the interest rates are low, ranging from 4 to 6 percent even though the policyholders actually are borrowing their own money. Many people fail to pay back such loans because no fixed schedule of repayment is established and insurance companies do not pressure borrowers to repay the debt. If the insured person dies before repaying the loan, the life insurance company will deduct the amount of the loan from the amount that would otherwise be paid on the policy.

Choose Your Source of Credit Wisely

As you have read above, you have many sources from which to borrow. Most borrowers want to hear a quick "yes" when they apply for credit and that goal can be made easier by applying to lenders who are willing to grant credit to almost anyone. But this is not the wisest approach for two reasons. First, lenders who make borrowing easy charge the highest interest rates. Second, such lenders grant credit to people with the low credit scores. When you borrow from such lenders the credit scoring system assumes you are doing so because you cannot get credit from lenders with high standards. The result is that your own credit score goes down when you borrow from consumer finance companies, debt consolidators, and payday lenders. Figure 6.1 provides a graphical representation of various lenders with those with the highest standards at the top of the pyramid and those with the lowest standards at the bottom. Always try to borrow from lenders as high on the pyramid as possible given your credit score.

Figure 6.1
The Credit Pyramid

Source: Michael Rupered,
© 2008 University of Georgia
Cooperative Extension. Used by
permission.

Concept Check 6.4

1. List the four types of depository institutions that are sources of credit for consumers.
2. Distinguish between a sales finance company and a consumer finance company.
3. Summarize how stockbrokers and insurance companies serve as sources of consumer credit.
4. Explain where you would go to obtain credit at the lowest cost.

Dealing with Overindebtedness

5 Learning Objective

Identify signs of overindebtedness and describe the options that are available for debt relief.

overindebted

When one's excessive personal debts make repayment difficult and cause financial distress.

People become **overindebted** when their excessive personal debts make repayment difficult and cause financial distress.

Ten Signs of Overindebtedness

1. **Exceeding debt limits and credit limits.** Are you spending more than 14 percent of your take–home pay on nonmortgage credit repayments? Do you sometimes reach the maximum approved credit limits on your credit cards?

2. **Not knowing how much you owe.** Have you lost track of how much you owe? Do you avoid reality by not adding up the total? Are you afraid to add up how much debt you have?

3. **Running out of money.** Are you using credit cards on occasions when you previously used cash? Are you borrowing to pay insurance premiums, taxes, or other large,

predictable bills? Are you borrowing to pay for regular expenses such as food or gasoline? Do you try to borrow from friends and relatives to carry you through the month?

4. **Paying only the minimum amount due.** Do you pay the minimum payment—or just a little more than the minimum—on your credit cards instead of making large payments to more quickly reduce the balance owed?

5. **Requesting new credit cards and increases in credit limits.** Have you applied for additional credit cards to increase your borrowing capacity? Have you asked for increases in credit limits on your current credit cards? Have you obtained a cash advance on one credit card to make the payment on another card?

6. **Paying late or skipping credit payments.** Are you late more than once a year in paying your mortgage, rent, car loan, or utility bills? Do you frequently pay late charges? Are you juggling bills to pay the utilities, rent, or mortgage? Are creditors sending overdue notices?

7. **Taking add-on loans.** Taking **add-on loans,** also called **flipping,** occurs when you refinance or rewrite a loan for an even larger amount before it has been completely repaid. Suppose that a loan of $1000 has been repaid down to $400. You decide to refinance the debt balance of $400 by borrowing $2000 and using the additional $1600 ($2000 − $400) for other purposes.

8. **Using debt-consolidation loans.** Are you borrowing, perhaps from a new source, to pay off old debts? Such action may temporarily reduce pressure on your budget, but it also indicates that you are overly indebted.

9. **Experiencing garnishment. Garnishment** is a court-sanctioned procedure by which a portion of the debtor's wages are set aside by the debtor's employer to pay debts. Wages and salary income, including that of military personnel, can be garnished. The Truth in Lending Act prohibits more than two garnishments of one person's paycheck. The total amount garnished cannot represent more than 25 percent of a person's disposable income for the pay period or more than the amount by which the weekly disposable income exceeds 30 times the federal minimum wage (whichever is less). In addition, the law prohibits garnishment from being used as grounds for employment discharge.

garnishment
Court-sanctioned procedure by which a portion of debtors' wages are set aside by their employers to pay debts.

10. **Experiencing repossession or foreclosure. Repossession** is a legal proceeding by which the lender seizes an asset (called **foreclosure,** if the property is a home) for nonpayment of a loan. When a lender repossesses property, the borrower may still owe on the debt because of a deficiency balance. A **deficiency balance** occurs when the sum of money raised by the sale of the repossessed collateral fails to cover the amount owed on the debt plus any repossession expenses (collection, attorney, and court costs) paid by the creditor.

repossession/foreclosure
Legal proceeding by which the lender seizes an asset.

deficiency balance
Occurs when money raised by sale of repossessed collateral doesn't cover the amount owed on the debt plus any repossession expenses.

Consider the tale of Betty Peterson, a staff sergeant in the army from San Diego, California, whose husband lost his civilian job. In an attempt to reduce expenditures, Betty voluntarily turned her Chevrolet HHR back to the finance company while still owing $11,000 on the debt. A month later, she was notified that the vehicle had been sold at auction for $7800; the proceeds were reduced to only $7100, however, due to collection and selling costs of $500 and attorney fees of $200. Betty was billed for a deficiency balance of $3900 ($11,000 − $7100). She would have been much better off had she sold the vehicle herself, as vehicles at auction usually sell for much less than their book values.

Federal Law Regulates Debt Collection Practices

The federal **Fair Debt Collection Practices Act (FDCPA)** prohibits third-party debt collection agencies from using abusive, deceptive, and unfair practices in the legitimate effort

Fair Debt Collection Practices Act (FDCPA)
Prohibits third-party debt collection agencies from using abusive, deceptive, or unfair practices to collect past-due debts.

debt collection agency
Firm that specializes in collecting debts that the original lender could not collect.

Get Out of Debt Before You Retire

People rarely go through life without taking on debt from time to time. But carrying debt into retirement is not a smart move. Even mortgage debt reduces significantly the flexibility you will need at that time in your life, so make paying off your home before retirement an important financial priority.

to collect past-due debts. **Debt (or credit) collection agencies** are firms that specialize in making collections that could not be obtained by the original lender. In some cases, they assist the original lender (for a fee); in other cases, they take over (purchase) the debt and become the creditor. When a debtor offers to make payment for several debts, the FDCPA requires that the amount paid must be applied to whichever debts the debtor desires. Banks, dentists, lawyers, and others who conduct their own collections (second-party collectors) are exempt from the provisions of the FDCPA. Nevertheless, many states have enacted similar laws that govern these second-party collectors.

Collection agencies are prohibited from telephoning the debtor at unusual hours, making numerous repeated telephone calls during the day, not applying payments to amounts under dispute, using deceptive practices (such as falsely claiming that their representatives are attorneys or government officials), making threats, or using abusive language. They also cannot telephone a debtor's employer. Even with these limitations, collection agencies can be irritatingly persistent when collecting past-due accounts. If the collection effort is not successful, as a last resort the creditor may take the debtor to court to seek a legal judgment against the debtor; this judgment may be collected by repossessing some of the debtor's property or garnishing wages.

Steps to Take to Get Out from Under Excessive Debt

Even the most well-meaning credit user can become overextended as a result of illness, unemployment, or divorce. What should you do if you realize that you are overly indebted?

1. **Determine your account balances and the payments required.** Find out exactly what it would take to pay off your balances today. This amount is not the same as the total of your remaining payments and probably includes penalties and late charges if you have been unable to keep up with your payments. Also ask your lenders to give you a monthly payment dollar amount needed to pay off the debts by the date previously agreed.

2. **Focus your budget on debt reduction.** Calculate the percentage of your budget necessary to make the payments on your debts, and then add 5 percent. Use this extra money to help pay your creditors by applying the extra money to the debt with the highest APR. The sacrifices required will pay off in the long run. Remember, paying off debts provides a higher "rate of return" than money in savings and investments, so "invest" your money in debt repayment first.

3. **Contact your creditors.** Try to work out a new payment plan with your creditors. Many lenders, including those that finance automobiles, may let you skip a payment. They want to see you solve your financial problems so you can avoid bankruptcy. Creditors are more likely to work with borrowers who come to them first rather than after collection efforts begin.

4. **Take on no new credit.** Return your credit cards to the issuer or lock them up so that you cannot use them. Disciplined action to reduce debt should show results in only a few months. If progress does not occur, seek professional help.

5. **Refinance.** Determine whether some loans can be refinanced to obtain a lower interest rate, especially mortgage loans. (See Chapter 9 for details.) Even if you refinance, keep making the same payment so you will pay the new loan off more quickly. Consumers who have difficulty making credit repayments may resort to a **debt-consolidation loan,** through which the debtor exchanges several smaller debts with varying due dates and interest rates for a single large loan. Obtaining a debt-consolidation

debt-consolidation loan
A loan taken out to pay off several smaller debts.

loan might be appropriate for someone who has acquired too much debt, but you should avoid the temptation to use this strategy simply to lower your total monthly payments. However, it is a smart move to use debt consolidation to lower APRs on existing debt.

6. **Avoid bad help.** Many companies claim that they want to help people in debt. A **credit repair company** (also known as a **credit clinic**) is a firm that offers to help improve or fix a person's credit history for a fee. Some are not so reputable, however. Avoid firms that charge a hefty advance payment ($250 to $2000). Also check aiccca.org and bbb.org for the reputation of any credit repair company you are considering.

   In reality, no company can remove or "fix" accurate but negative information in anyone's credit history. You can improve your future credit history by making on-time repayments. And you can correct errors in your credit bureau files on your own for free with little effort.

7. **Find good help.** You may be able to obtain free budget and credit advice from your employer, credit union, or labor union. Also, many banks and consumer finance companies offer advice to help financially distressed debtors, as do nonprofit **credit counseling agencies (CCAs).** Such an agency can make arrangements with unsecured creditors to collect payments from overly indebted consumers to repay debts, and it can provide individuals with credit counseling, assistance with financial problems, educational materials on credit and budgeting, and a **debt management plan (DMP).** A DMP is an arrangement whereby the consumer provides one monthly payment (usually somewhat smaller than the total of previous credit payments) that is distributed to all creditors. Creditor concessions, such as reduced interest rates, may also allow debtors to repay what they owe more quickly than would otherwise be possible. Credit counseling services are provided at a nominal cost on a face-to-face basis, online, or via the telephone. Seek an agency that is a not-for-profit agency that has 501(c)3 status from the IRS and that will do a full budget review for you. You can obtain consumer information and a referral by contacting the Association of Independent Consumer Credit Counseling Agencies ([800] 450-1794; www.aiccca.org) or the National Foundation for Credit Counseling ([800] 388-2227; www.nfcc.org). Call the Better Business Bureau for a reputation report as well.

credit repair company (credit clinic)
Firm that offers to help improve or fix a person's credit history for a (usually hefty) fee.

Instant Message

Debt Management Plans and Your Credit Score

Entering into a debt management plan will not lower your credit score. However, the credit score is not the only factor that lenders use when judging creditworthiness. Some lenders will look on a debt management plan unfavorably and deny credit or charge higher APRs for people who have been on a plan, compelling those people to search more extensively for good credit terms.

credit counseling agency (CCA)
Agency that can arrange payment schedules with unsecured creditors for overly indebted consumers and can provide individuals with credit counseling.

debt management plan (DMP)
Arrangement whereby consumer provides one monthly payment (usually somewhat smaller than the total of previous credit payments) that is distributed to all creditors.

bankruptcy
Constitutionally guaranteed right that permits people (and businesses) to ask a court to find them officially unable to meet their debts.

discharged debts
Debts (or portions thereof) that are excused as a result of a bankruptcy.

Bankruptcy as a Last Resort

When debts are so overbearing that life seems really bleak—a situation that may be aggravated by recent unemployment, illness, disability, death in the family, divorce, or small-business failure—many people consider filing a petition in federal court to declare bankruptcy. **Bankruptcy** is a constitutionally guaranteed right that permits people (and businesses) to ask a court to find them officially unable to meet their debts. Federal laws allow bankruptcy for consumers in two forms: Chapter 13 and Chapter 7. Some debts are never excused **("discharged debts")** through bankruptcy. These include education loans that have come due within the previous seven years, fines, alimony, child support, income taxes for the most recent three years, and debts for causing injury while driving under the influence of alcohol or drugs.

Before you can file for bankruptcy under either Chapter 7 or Chapter 13, you must complete credit counseling with an agency approved by the United States Bankruptcy Trustee's office. The purpose of this counseling is to give you an idea of whether you really need to file for bankruptcy or whether an informal repayment plan would get you back on

Did You Know?

How Long You Should Wait Before Declaring Bankruptcy

The thought of declaring bankruptcy is so onerous that many people wait too long to seek its protection. Both Chapter 7 and 13 bankruptcies allow debtors to keep a portion of their assets. For example, 401(k) retirement accounts are protected from creditors in bankruptcy. If a debtor begins taking money out of a retirement plan when faced with mounting debt and they ultimately must declare bankruptcy, they would have used up an asset that could have been 100% protected had they filed sooner. If the only way you can pay your debts is to tap your retirement plan you should consult a lawyer about whether the time already has come to seek bankruptcy protection.

Chapter 13 of the Bankruptcy Act (wage earner or regular income plan)
Designed for individuals with regular incomes who might be able to pay off some or all of their debts given certain court protections.

Chapter 7 of the Bankruptcy Act (straight bankruptcy)
Provides for the liquidation of assets with proceeds applied to paying off excusable debts to the degree possible.

Do It NOW!

Building and maintaining good credit is a must. Start today by:

1. Obtaining a free copy of your credit report (www.annualcreditreport.com) from one of the three national credit bureaus.

2. Confirming the accuracy of the report and if there are errors or omissions challenging them with all three bureaus.

3. Repeating steps two and three every four months staggering the bureaus to ensure that each request is free.

your economic feet. Once your bankruptcy case is over, you'll have to attend another counseling session, this time to learn personal financial management. Only after you submit proof to the court that you have fulfilled this requirement can you get a bankruptcy discharge wiping out your debts.

Chapter 13—Regular Income Plan

Chapter 13 of the Bankruptcy Act (also known as the **wage earner** or the **regular income plan**) is designed for individuals with regular incomes who might be able to pay off some or all of their debts given certain protections of the court. Under this plan, the debtor submits a debt repayment plan to the court that is designed to repay as much of the debt as possible, typically in three to five years. After the debtor files a petition for bankruptcy, the court issues an **automatic stay**—a court order that temporarily prevents all creditors from recovering claims arising from before the start of the bankruptcy proceeding. This action protects the debtor from collection efforts by creditors, including garnishments. Typically, no assets may be sold by the debtor or repossessed by the lender after a stay is granted.

After the court notifies all creditors of the petition for bankruptcy, a hearing is scheduled. With the help of a bankruptcy trustee (an agent of the bankruptcy court), who verifies the accuracy of a bankruptcy petition at a hearing and who distributes the assets according to a court-approved plan, the proposed repayment plan is reviewed (and modified, if necessary) and finally approved by the court. The debtor must then follow a strict budget while repaying the obligations. During this time, the bankrupt person cannot obtain any new credit without the permission of the trustee. If the debtor makes all scheduled payments, he or she is discharged of any remaining amounts due that could not be repaid within the repayment period.

Chapter 7—Immediate Liquidation Plan

Chapter 7 of the Bankruptcy Act, also called **straight bankruptcy**, provides for an immediate liquidation of assets. This option is permitted when it would be highly unlikely that substantial repayment could ever be made. Petitioners seeking to file Chapter 7 must pass a "means" test. Those who fail this test because their income is too high must file Chapter 13 instead.

When Chapter 7 is allowed, most of the bankrupt person's assets are given over to the bankruptcy trustee. Any assets that serve as collateral for loans are turned over to the appropriate secured creditors. Most of the remaining assets are sold, and the proceeds of the sales are distributed to the unsecured creditors of the bankrupt person. Any leftover debt is usually discharged by the court when the debtor emerges from bankruptcy. State and federal laws govern what assets the debtor can keep. In general, bankrupt people are allowed to keep a small amount of equity in their homes, an inexpensive automobile, and limited personal property.

Bankruptcy should be used as a last resort rather than as a quick fix or cure-all for overuse of credit. Bankruptcy remains on one's credit record for ten years. Because employers, landlords, and creditors check credit reports, people who have declared bankruptcy typically face years of trouble when renting housing, obtaining home loans, and getting credit cards. Discharged debtors usually emerge with little, if any, debt and a much improved net worth and a poor credit score. They also cannot use Chapter 7 bankruptcy again for at least six years. Therefore, some creditors will lend to such individuals, but at much higher interest rates than usual.

✓ Concept Check 6.5

1. Identify four signs of overindebtedness.
2. List the major provisions of the Fair Debt Collection Practices Act.
3. What services are provided by a credit counseling agency and how might a debt management plan work to provide relief for someone who is having debt problems?
4. Distinguish between Chapter 7 and Chapter 13 bankruptcy and explain who might be forced to use Chapter 13 rather than Chapter 7.

Did You Know?

Consumer Financial Protection Agency

The Obama Administration has proposed that Congress create a new agency, the Consumer Financial Protection Agency (CFPA). Its job would be to police the fine print on consumer products like credit cards and mortgages, as well as make rulings on what fees, penalties, and interest rates are fair.

What Do You Recommend NOW?

Now that you have read this chapter on building and maintaining good credit, what would you recommend to Carrie Savarin regarding:

1. Factors she should consider regarding her ability to take on additional debt?
2. The impact of her current debt on her ability to obtain a loan to buy a vehicle?
3. Where she might obtain financing for a vehicle loan?
4. The effect of taking on a loan on her overall financial planning?

Barry Austin Photography/Getty Images

Big Picture Summary of Learning Objectives

1 Explain reasons for and against using credit.

People borrow for a variety of reasons—for example, to deal with financial emergencies, to have goods immediately, and to obtain discounts in the future. Perhaps the greatest disadvantage of using credit is the ensuing loss of financial flexibility in personal money management. The annual percentage rate (APR) provides the best approximation of the true cost of credit.

2 Establish your own debt limit.

It is important to establish your own debt limit. Three methods can be used: the debt payments-to-disposable income method, the ratio of debt-to-equity method, and the continuous-debt method.

3 Achieve a good credit reputation.

In the process of opening a credit account, the lender investigates your credit history, obtains a credit score (such as a FICO score) from a credit bureau, and then determines whether to grant credit and under what conditions.

4 Describe the common sources of consumer credit.

Major sources of consumer loans include depository institutions (commercial banks, savings and loan associations, and credit unions), sales finance companies, and consumer finance companies. Loans are also available through insurance companies and stockbrokers. Depository institutions typically offer the best interest rates, although sales finance companies sometimes offer low rates to increase sales of the products being financed. In any case, only those people with high credit scores qualify for the best rates from any source.

5 Identify signs of overindebtedness and describe the options that are available for debt relief.

Among the signals of being overly indebted are exceeding credit-limit guidelines and running out of money too often. People experiencing serious financial difficulties can obtain professional assistance through nonprofit credit counseling agencies or by contacting an attorney about bankruptcy.

Let's Talk About It

1. **Good Versus Bad Debt.** If there is such a thing as good debt, what types of debt do you consider to be "good"? What types do you consider to be "bad"?

2. **Your Creditworthiness.** What aspects of your financial life make you creditworthy? What aspects would make it difficult for you to obtain credit?

3. **Assessing Your Debt Load.** How might students judge whether they are taking on too high a level of student loan debt?

4. **Where Could I Borrow for a Vehicle?** If you wanted to borrow money to buy a new or used car, where would you turn? Why?

5. **Your Privacy.** Are you concerned that the major national credit bureaus may have files containing information about you? What do you think about the process required to correct errors in those files?

6. **Easy Credit.** Is it too easy for college students to get credit cards? Do you know anyone who has gotten into financial difficulty because of overuse of credit cards?

7. **Feelings About Bankruptcy.** How do you feel about bankruptcy? When might bankruptcy be justified in your opinion? When might it not be justified?

Do the Math

1. **Taking Out a Motorcycle Loan.** Martin Jones is single and recently graduated from law school. He earns $9000 per month, an awesome salary for someone only 26 years old. However, he has $1,400 withheld for federal income tax, $540 for state income taxes, $686 for Social Security taxes, and $230 for health insurance every month. He has outstanding student loans of almost $80,000 on which he pays about $900 per month and a 0% auto loan payment of $300 on a new Pontiac G6 he purchased during law school. He is considering taking out a loan to buy a BMW motorcycle.

   (a) What is Martin's debt payments-to-disposable income ratio?

   (b) Based on your answer to "a" how would you advise Martin about his plan?

2. **Buying a Vacation Home.** Carmen and Juan Montoya have just finished putting their three daughters through college. As empty-nesters they are considering purchasing a vacation home on a nearby lake because prices have dropped in recent years. The house might also serve as a retirement home once they retire in 12 years. The Montoya's net worth is $283,000 including their home worth about $265,000 on which they currently owe $143,000 for their first mortgage. Their outstanding debts in addition to their mortgage include $12,500 on one car loan, $13,700 on a second car loan, and a $25,500 second mortgage on their home taken out to help pay for college expenses.

   (a) Calculate the Montoya's debt-to-equity ratio.

   (b) Advise them as to the wisdom of borrowing for a vacation home at this time.

Financial Planning Cases

Case 1
Reducing Expenses to Buy a New Car

Courtney Bennett recently graduated from college and accepted a position in Manhattan, Kansas, as an assistant librarian in the public library. Courtney has no debts, and her budget is shown in the first column of Table 6.2. She now faces the question of whether to trade in her old car for a new one requiring a monthly payment of $330. Taking the role of a good friend of Courtney, suggest how Courtney might cut back on her expenses so that she can afford the vehicle.

   (a) What areas might be cut back?

   (b) How much in each area might be cut back?

   (c) After finishing your analysis, what advice (and possibly alternatives) would you offer Courtney about buying the new car?

Case 2
Preparation of a Credit-Related Speech

Jacob Marchese of Auburn, Alabama, is the credit manager for a regional chain of department stores. He has been asked to join a panel of community members and make a ten-minute speech to graduating high-school seniors on the topic "Using Credit Wisely." In the following outline that Jacob has prepared, provide him with some suggested comments.

   (a) What is consumer credit?

   (b) Why might graduates use credit?

   (c) How can graduates use credit wisely?

Case 3

Debt Consolidation as a Debt Reduction Strategy

Justin Granovsky, an assistant manager at a small retail shop in Las Vegas, Nevada, had an unusual amount of debt. He owed $5400 to one bank, $1800 to a clothing store, $2700 to his credit union, and several hundred dollars to other stores and individuals. Justin was paying more than $460 per month on the three major obligations to pay them off when due in two years. He realized that his take-home pay of slightly more than $2100 per month did not leave him with much excess cash. Justin discussed an alternative way of handling his major payments with his bank's loan officer. The officer suggested that he pool all of his debts and take out an $11,000 debt-consolidation loan for seven years at 14 percent. As a result, he would pay only $206 per month for all his debts. Justin seemed ecstatic over the idea.

(a) Is Justin's enthusiasm over the idea of a debt-consolidation loan justified? Why or why not?

(b) Why can the bank offer such a "good deal" to Justin?

(c) What compromise would Justin make to remit payments of only $206 as compared with $460?

(d) If you assume that the debt-consolidation loan will cost more in total interest, what would be a justification for this added cost?

Case 4

Victor and Maria Advise Their Niece

Victor and Maria have always enjoyed a close relationship with Maria's niece Teresa, who graduated from college with a pharmacy degree. Teresa recently asked Maria for some assistance with her finances now that her education debts are coming due. She owes $19,000 in student loans and earns $44,000 per year in disposable income. Teresa would like to take on additional debt to furnish her apartment and buy a better car.

(a) What advice might Maria give Teresa about managing her student loan debt?

(b) If next year Teresa were to consolidate her loans into one loan at 8 percent interest, what advice might Maria give regarding Teresa's overall debt limit using both the debt payments-to-disposable income method and the continuous-debt method? (Hint: Use Table 6.3 on page 181 or visit the *Garman/Forgue* companion website to calculate monthly payments for various time periods.)

Case 5

The Johnsons Attempt to Resolve Their Credit and Cash-Flow Problems

Harry and Belinda have a substantial annual joint income—more than $70,000, in fact. Nevertheless, they expect to experience some cash-flow deficits during several months of the upcoming year (see Tables 3.8 and 3.9 on pages 90 and 91).

To resolve this difficulty, the couple is considering two options. One option is to open a credit card account and use it exclusively for those expenditures that will cause the deficits they face. Or they could talk to their bank about opening a line of credit that would allow them to borrow money by simply calling the bank and having money placed in their checking account.

(a) What are the advantages and disadvantages of the Johnsons opening these accounts?

(b) What financial calculations should Harry and Belinda undertake to see whether they could afford to borrow more money at this time?

(c) What might Harry and Belinda do before applying for credit to ensure that they will pay the lowest interest rate possible?

On the 'Net

Go to the Web pages indicated to complete these exercises.

1. Visit the website for obtaining a free credit report at www.annualcreditreport.com to order a copy of your credit report. Check the accuracy of the report and follow the directions provided to correct any errors. If no report is available on you, it should be because you have never used credit. If you have used credit and there is no report, you should notify the credit bureaus of this error.

2. Visit the website for the Federal Reserve Board at www.federalreserve.gov/consumers.htm. Locate its online copy of the *Consumer Handbook on Credit Protection Laws*. Identify one additional protection not discussed in this book that is provided by each of the following laws: the Fair Credit Billing Act, the Equal Credit Opportunity Act, and the Fair Credit Reporting Act.

3. Visit the website for Fair, Isaacs and Company at www.myfico.com/CreditEducation. Read up on how credit scoring works. Identify three actions you could take to improve your credit score.

Visit the Garman/Forgue companion website . . .

Credit Cards and Consumer Loans

!You Must Be Kidding, Right?

College students who have a credit card in their own name (and most do) have an average debt of $2700 at graduation. If they maintain that level of debt for ten years (because their payments only equal the charges they make plus interest), how much total interest will they pay?

A. $1200

B. $1800

C. $2700

D. $4860

The answer is D. A credit card with an 18 percent APR (typical for college students) translates to a 1.5 percent rate per month (18% ÷ 12). The $2700 debt multiplied by this rate equals $40.50 ($2700 × 0.015) per month in interest. And $40.50 multiplied by 120 months equals $4860. You must pay more than the required minimum monthly amount plus any new charges in order to reduce a credit card debt. Otherwise you will pay many thousands of dollars in interest and be in debt for years and years!

Learning Objectives

After reading this chapter, you should be able to:

1 Compare the common types of consumer credit, including credit cards and installment loans.

2 Describe the types and features of credit card accounts.

3 Manage your credit card accounts to avoid fees and finance charges.

4 Describe the important features of consumer installment loans.

5 Calculate the interest and annual percentage rate on consumer loans.

Michael Newman/PhotoEdit

Darrell Cochrane, a 31-year-old optician in Tampa, Florida, made $42,000 last year. Darrell avoided using credit and credit cards until he was 28 years old, when he missed three months of work due to a water-skiing accident. He made ends meet by obtaining two bank credit cards that, because of his lack of a credit history, carry 19.6 and 24 percent annual percentage rates (APRs). Darrell now has 11 credit card accounts open: five bank cards and six retail store cards. He uses them regularly, presenting whatever card a store will honor. He owes $13,000 on the 24 percent APR card and $4400 on the 19.6 percent APR card. His other three bank cards carry APRs of 11 percent, 12 percent, and 15 percent, and he owes $500 to $700 on each one. For the past year, Darrell has been making only the minimum payments on his bank cards. His retail cards all carry APRs in excess of 21 percent. Although he has managed to keep from running a balance on those cards during most months, occasionally these accounts have balances as well.

What would you recommend to Darrell on the subject of credit cards and consumer loans regarding:

1. His approach to using credit cards, including the number of cards he has?

2. Estimating the credit card interest charges he is paying each month?

3. How he might lower his interest expense each month?

4. Consolidating his credit card debts into one installment loan?

Your Next Five Years

In the next five years you can start achieving financial success by doing the following related to credit cards and consumer loans:

1. Pay all your credit card balances in full each month, or no longer than two or three months later.

2. Move credit card balances you do carry to lower-interest accounts and never make convenience purchases on the accounts on which you carry a balance.

3. Check your monthly billing statements against your receipts for accuracy every month and challenge all discrepancies.

4. Use student loans for direct education expenses only rather than to maintain a better lifestyle.

5. Choose installment loans based on the lowest annual percentage rate (APR) rather than monthly payment and years to repay.

1 Learning Objective

Compare the common types of consumer credit, including credit cards and installment loans.

installment credit (closed-end credit)
Credit arrangement in which the borrower must repay the amount owed plus interest in a specific number of equal payments.

open-ended (revolving) credit
Arrangement in which credit is extended in advance of any transaction so that borrowers do not need to reapply each time they need to use credit.

credit limit
Maximum outstanding debt that a lender will allow on an open-ended credit account.

cash advance
A cash advance is the use of a credit card to obtain cash rather than to make a purchase.

You cannot borrow your way to financial success. For proof ask some of the millions of Americans who because of the sluggish U.S. economy and job losses have been unable to pay their credit card bills or had their homes foreclosed. Using any kind of credit requires deliberate thinking and planning particularly when creditors are tightening lending standards. You need to first consider whether the reason you are borrowing is sound and then decide in advance how you will repay the debt. This is especially true for credit cards. Credit card usage can be managed so that you pay no interest at all. But this can occur only if you pay your balance in full every month. Planning how to repay an installment loan is also important because you commit to making a series of monthly payments for one to seven or more years. Smart borrowers understand the mathematics behind the calculation of the finance charges on these installment loans. Smart borrowers always focus on the **annual percentage rate (APR)** when comparing among various sources of credit. The APR is the cost of credit on a yearly basis as a percentage rate.

Types of Consumer Credit

Consumer credit is nonbusiness debt used by consumers for expenditures other than home mortgages. (Borrowing for housing has investment aspects that result in a separate classification; see Chapter 9.)

There are two types of consumer credit: installment credit and noninstallment credit.

■ With **installment credit** (also called **closed-end credit**), the borrower must repay the amount owed plus interest in a specific number of equal payments, usually monthly. For example, an $18,000 automobile loan might require monthly payments of $356 for 60 months at seven percent interest.

■ **Noninstallment credit** includes single-payment, open-ended credit, and service credit. **Single-payment loans** are the easiest of the three to understand. As an example, a borrower might take out a loan of $2000 at 12 percent interest for one year. If so, a single payment of $2240 ($2000 + $240 interest; $2000 × 0.12) would be due at the end of one year.

With **open-ended credit** (also called **revolving credit**), credit is extended in advance of any transaction so that the borrower does not need to reapply each time credit is desired. Credit cards are an example of open-ended credit. Any amounts owed will be repaid in full in a single payment or via a series of equal or unequal payments, usually made monthly. The borrower can use the account as long as the total owed does not exceed his or her **credit limit.** This credit limit is set by the lender and is the maximum outstanding debt allowed on the credit account. Credit limits vary with the perceived creditworthiness of the borrower.

Open-ended credit can be used to make purchases and, in some cases, to obtain cash advances. It is the most convenient type of credit, and it is also the most abused. Many open-ended accounts—but not all—use a credit card. A **credit** (or **charge**) **card** is a plastic card identifying the holder as a participant in the charge account plan of a lender, such as a retailer or financial institution.

Cash advances may be obtained at any financial institution that issues the type of card (Visa, MasterCard, and so on) being used. A cash advance is a cash loan from a credit card account. In most cases, the borrower receives cash, such as from an ATM. Alternatively, the funds may be transferred electronically into the cardholder's checking account.

A **personal line of credit** is a form of open-ended credit that allows the borrower access to a prearranged revolving line of credit provided by the lender (usually a commercial bank, savings bank, credit union, or brokerage firm). The essence of a line of credit is that borrowers can obtain a cash advance when needed and not reapply for a loan each time they need money. Like credit card accounts, a personal line of credit includes a credit limit and a flexible repayment schedule. Some people also use the equity in their home as collateral for a line of credit. This arrangement is referred to as a **home-equity line of credit.**

Service credit is granted to consumers by public utilities, physicians, dentists, and other service providers that do not require full payment when services are rendered. For example, your electric company allows you to use electricity all month and then sends you a bill that may not be due for 10 to 15 days. Service credit usually carries no interest, although penalty charges and interest may apply if payments are made late. Service may eventually be cut off for continued slow payment or nonpayment of the debt.

Concept Check 7.1

1. Distinguish between installment credit and open-ended credit.
2. Explain the basic features of revolving credit.
3. Describe how someone might use a personal line of credit.

Credit Card Accounts

Credit card accounts allow the borrower to pay the balance in full at any time or carry over a balance owed from month to month (travel and entertainment cards are an exception). If a balance is carried over, a **minimum payment** must be made each month to cover interest and a small payment on the amount owed (the **principal**). If at least the minimum payment amount is not received by the due date, the cardholder may be declared in **default** (the borrower has failed to make a payment of principal or interest when due or meet any other requirement of a credit agreement). Most cardholders maintain balances and can do so for years even as other charges are added to the same account. As long as the total debt remains below the credit limit, the user may continue to make charges against the account. When appropriate a borrower may ask a creditor to increase his or her credit limit.

Types of Credit Card Accounts

Credit card accounts include bank credit cards, retail credit cards, and travel and entertainment accounts (such as American Express's familiar "green card").

Bank Credit Cards A **bank credit card account** is an open-ended account at a financial institution allowing the holder to make purchases on credit almost anywhere. Visa, MasterCard, Discover, and Optima are the most commonly recognized bank card names. However, the actual lender is the bank, savings bank or credit union through which the card is offered. Visa, MasterCard, and the like are simply service providers that maintain the electronic network through which transactions are communicated. Participating merchants pay transaction fees (typically 1¼ to 5 percent) to these companies based on the dollar amounts

---

personal line of credit
Form of open-ended credit in which the lender allows the borrower access to a prearranged revolving line of credit.

Did You Know?

The Top 3 Financial Missteps in Credit Card and Consumer Loans

People slip up in credit cards and consumer loans when they do the following:

1. Fail to shop for the lowest APR on their credit cards and consumer loans
2. Regularly carry balances on credit card accounts
3. Use a credit card rather than lower-interest rate installment loans to make expensive purchases

Instant Message

Pay Close Attention to the APR

Always inquire about the APR if it is not readily apparent, and use it to compare rates from other lenders to obtain the best deal.

2 Learning Objective
Describe the types and features of credit card accounts.

minimum payment
Payment that must be made to a credit account each month to cover interest and a portion of the amount owed.

principal
Total amount owed on a credit account not including interest.

bank credit card account
Open-ended credit account with a financial institution that allows the holder to make purchases almost anywhere.

charged. Virtually all financial institutions offer bank credit cards, as do a number of consumer products companies, such as AT&T, Allstate Insurance, and Verizon. These companies contract with Visa, MasterCard, and a bank to offer **cobranded credit cards.**

Many bank credit card issuers periodically send **cash advance** (or **convenience**) **checks** to their cardholders. Of course, these instruments are not genuine checks but simply a check-equivalent way to take a cash advance. Customers can use these "checks" to make payments to others or themselves. If such a payment is used to make a payment on another credit card, it represents a **balance transfer.** If you receive convenience checks but do not want to use them, either put them in a safe place or destroy them immediately because they easily could be used fraudulently by someone else. As indicated in Figure 7.1 on page 198, a transaction fee is often charged for receiving cash advances, using convenience checks, or making balance transfers.

Some bank credit cards are a form of **prestige card,** often with a precious metal in the brand name such as "gold," "silver," or "platinum." These accounts require that the user possess higher credit qualifications and offer enhancements such as free traveler's checks and higher credit limits. Prestige cards may carry higher annual fees. Most holders of regular bank credit cards do not realize that they could obtain a higher credit limit on their standard card just by requesting one from the issuer.

Some Visa and MasterCard credit cards are identified as **affinity cards**—that is, standard bank cards with the logo of a sponsoring organization imprinted on the face of the card. The issuing financial institution often donates a portion of the annual fee and a small percentage of the amounts charged (perhaps 0.25, 0.5, or 1 percent) to the sponsoring organization. Sponsors may include charitable, political, sports, or other organized groups, such as the Sierra Club or Mothers Against Drunk Driving. Supporters of the sponsoring organization may be motivated to use an affinity card because the organization receives money from each transaction. Creditors rightly calculate that fewer delinquencies will occur among the particular group of people, so they can afford to transfer some dollars to the named organization.

cash advance (or convenience) checks
A check-equivalent way to take a cash advance on a credit card.

balance transfer
Full or partial payment on the balance of one credit card using a cash advance from another.

Instant Message

Cash Advances Are Very Expensive

Obtaining money via a credit card cash advance may seem easy. But it is very expensive. First, there is a transaction fee. It is usually a percentage of the amount taken (3 percent is common), but there is often a minimum amount that makes the percentage much higher on small advances. Then there is the interest that begins to accrue immediately even if you are not carrying a balance on the card. Plus, the interest rate on cash advances is often higher than for purchases.

retail credit cards
Allow customers to make purchases on credit at any of the outlets of a particular retailer.

Retail Credit Card Accounts   A **retail credit card** allows a customer to make purchases on credit at any of the outlets of a particular retailer or retail chain. Examples of credit card accounts at retail stores include those offered by JCPenney, Best Buy, and Shell Oil. Many retailers have alliances with a financial institution to offer a bank credit card that carries the retailer's logo and can also be used anywhere the bank credit card can be used.

Some smaller retail establishments offer open-ended accounts that do not use a credit card as the vehicle for using the account. With these retail charge accounts, customers simply ask to have the purchase put on their account for repayment at a later date.

travel and entertainment (T&E) cards
Bank credit cards that allow holders to make purchases at numerous businesses but that require the holder to repay the entire balance charged within 30 days.

Travel and Entertainment Cards   Travel and entertainment (T&E) cards are similar to bank credit cards in that they allow holders to make purchases at numerous businesses. The entire balance charged must be repaid within 30 days, however. The best-known T&E cards are those issued by American Express and Diners Club International. Such cards are often used by businesspeople for food and lodging expenses while traveling. They are somewhat more difficult to obtain than bank cards because applicants must have higher-than-average incomes to qualify for an account; in addition, applicants must pay an annual membership fee of $150 or more. T&E cards are not accepted at nearly as many outlets as are bank credit cards.

Did You Know?

How to Close a Credit Card Account Correctly

Credit card accounts are open-ended credit and, therefore, can remain open for decades even if you never use the card or stop using it at some point. Accounts are not closed if you cut up the cards. Instead, the lender must be formally notified of your request before the account will be officially closed. Here's what to do:

1. **Obtain the customer-service telephone number** for the lender from your most recent monthly statement. If you do not have a recent bill, obtain a copy of your credit report, which will list the contact information for the lender.

2. **Contact the lender** to request the address to which you should send your cancellation request. It will not be the same address to which you send your monthly payment.

3. **Send a written request** to close the account and request that the creditor send a confirmation that the account is, indeed, closed.

4. **Obtain a copy of your credit report.** After 90 days, from one of the three national credit bureaus (pay if necessary). If the account shows as closed, obtain free copies from the other two bureaus as confirmation at the next opportunity. If the account shows as still open at the first bureau, ask for a reinvestigation and also obtain copies from the other two bureaus to ensure the account shows closed appropriately.

Note that you cannot "close" an account on which you currently owe a balance. You can, however, ask the lender to no longer honor the card. Many people think that closing a credit card account will harm your credit score. Generally this is not true as it raises the ratio between the amount of credit card debt you can carry and the amount you do carry.

Common (But Not Always Beneficial) Aspects of Credit Card Accounts

Federal law requires credit card lenders to disclose all the rules governing the account to borrowers before they sign up for any card. Some of that information must be displayed in a uniform manner, as illustrated in the sample credit card disclosure box in Figure 7.1. The remainder of the information appears in the credit agreement (contract). Credit card issuers are free to change some of the rules on an account at any time as long as they notify the account holder of the change. This notification is usually included as an insert in the monthly bill for the account and often appears in very small print. You can avoid any penalties imposed by the new rules by paying off the account or by closing it. If you cannot pay the bill in full, you will be obligated to adhere to the new rules until you close the account. This section outlines some of the more important aspects of credit card accounts.

Teaser Rates Some cards carry a temporarily low **introductory rate (teaser rate)** to entice borrowers to apply for an account. Teaser APRs of 0 to 3.9 percent are common. In Figure 7.1, the teaser rate is 4.99 percent for purchases and 0.0 percent during the first six months the account is open. The APR typically reverts to a much higher fixed or variable interest rate after the introductory period ends. Some credit card borrowers take advantage of teaser rates by opening new accounts regularly and transferring the balances from other accounts to the new account to take advantage of the low introductory rate despite the high balance transfer fee that might exist. Customers with a good credit history can use this technique several times in succession.

introductory rate
A temporarily low initial interest rate to entice borrowers to apply for a credit card.

Figure 7.1
Sample Credit Card Disclosure Box

Federal law requires that key pieces of information be disclosed in direct-mail advertising and on applications for credit cards. An example of this required disclosure is provided here. To search for the best offers on credit cards, you can visit www.bankrate.com or www.cardtrack.com.

DETAILS OF RATE, FEE, AND OTHER COST INFORMATION	
As required by law, rates, fees, and other costs of this credit card offer are disclosed here. All account terms are governed by the Credit Card Agreement sent with the card. Account terms are not guaranteed for any period of time; all terms, including the APRs and fees, may change in accordance with the Agreement and applicable law.	
Annual Percentage Rate for purchases	The **introductory rate** (see notes below) is **4.99%** until the first billing after the sixth-month anniversary of the opening of the account. After that **9.99%** (variable rate).
Other APRs (all other APRs are variable)	**Balance Transfers:** The introductory rate is 0% until the first billing after the sixth-month anniversary of the opening of the account. After that **9.99%**. Cash Advances: **19.99%**. Default Rate: **27.99%** (see notes below).
Variable rate information	**Your APRs may vary** during each billing period. The rate for purchases and balance transfers is determined by adding 5.99% to the prime rate (see notes below). The rate for cash advances is determined by adding 15.99% to the prime rate but such rate will never be below 19.99%. The default is determined by adding no more than 23.99% to the prime rate.
Grace period for repayment of purchases	**Not less than 21 days** if you pay your total new balance in full each billing period by the due date. Payment must be received by 5 p.m. on the due date. There is **no grace period for balance transfers and cash advances.**
Method of computing the balance	**Average Daily Balance** (including new purchases).
Annual fee	$25
Minimum Finance Charge	$1.00
Miscellaneous fees	**Transaction fee for Cash Advances:** 3% of the amount of the transaction but not less than $20. **Transaction fee for Balance Transfers:** 3% of the amount of the transfer but not less than $50. There is no balance transfer fee during the six-month introductory period. **Late fee:** $15 on balances up to $500. $35 on balances over $500. **Over-the-limit fee:** $35. **Bounced check fee:** $35.
Notes	**Introductory rates:** Eligibility for introductory rate is subject to your maintaining good credit. Rates indicated in this offer are subject to change to reflect changes in the prime rate (see below) at the time of your application. **Default rate:** All of your APRs may increase if you default under any Card Agreement that you have with us because you fail to make a payment to us when due, you exceed your credit limit, or you make a payment to us that is not honored. Factors considered when determining your default rate may include the length of time your account with us has been open; the existence, seriousness, and timing of defaults under any Card Agreement you have with us; or other indications of account usage and performance on this or any other account you have with us. **Prime rate:** The prime rate (currently 4%) used to determine your APRs for each billing period is the U.S. prime rate published in the *Wall Street Journal* two business days prior to the billing date for that billing period.

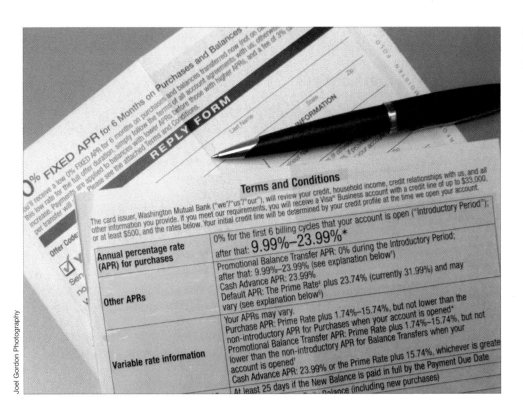

Extremely low APRs are usually temporary. Read the rules of your account carefully.

Default Rates Usually the introductory rate will be rescinded and the regular rate on the account will be applied if the borrower makes a late payment even once during the introductory period. A more serious downside to most credit card accounts is the assessment of a **default rate.** A default rate is a high APR that is assessed whenever a borrower fails to uphold certain rules of the account, such as being more than 60 days late or staying within the specified credit limit. The disclosure notice in Figure 7.1 indicates that if you are late making a payment even once during the introductory period, you will not only lose the teaser rate but also see a default rate of perhaps 27.99 percent APR (23.99 percent plus 4 percent [the current prime rate]).

default rate
A high APR that is assessed whenever a borrower fails to uphold certain rules of the account, such as making on-time payments or staying within the specified credit limit.

Variable Interest Rates Credit card accounts (and installment loans) carry either fixed or variable interest rates. **Variable interest rates** go up and down, usually monthly or annually, according to changes in interest rates in the economy as a whole. The example in Figure 7.1 has a variable interest rate with the prime rate used as a base rate. The **prime rate** is a key measure of interest rates in the economy and its fluctuations drive the changes in rates for all types of variable-rate credit. In recent years, the prime rate has ranged from 3.25 to 4 percent. As indicated in Figure 7.1, the card company lists the percentage rate that is added to the prime rate to determine the purchase (+5.99%), cash advance (+15.99%), and default rates (+23.99%) on the card.

variable interest rate cards
Have rates that change monthly or annually according to general changes in the economy as a whole.

 Instant Message

About 1 in 20 Credit Card Accounts Are in Default

Due to their ease of use, credit cards are the primary source of consumer debt other than home mortgages. About 5 percent of all credit card accounts typically are more than 30 days past due.

Preapproved Credit Card Offers Companies interested in expanding their base of credit customers sometimes pay credit bureaus to prescreen their files and identify people who pass certain tests of creditworthiness. A company may then send applications for credit to the prescreened people. Some consumers will have been preapproved as part of this process, so they merely need to sign the notice to open the account. Note that being preapproved means only that you will be

annual fees
Charges levied against cardholders for the privilege of having an open account but that are not included in the advertised APR.

transaction fee
Charge levied against cardholders per use of the card and are not included in the APR advertised.

Instant Message

There Is Really No Such Thing as a Fixed-Rate Credit Card

Many bank credit cards are variable-rate cards. But even for those that are not, the card issuer can change the rate with as little as 45 days' notice.

Instant Message

When in Doubt—Opt Out

Federal law states that consumers have the right to opt out of receiving unsolicited credit card offers, which are based on your credit report. To put a stop to the mailings using the official system, dial (888) 5-OPT-OUT or visit https://www.optoutprescreen.com.

granted credit. Both the credit card debt limit and APR will be determined after you apply for an account.

Annual and Transaction Fees   Some bank credit card lenders assess **annual fees** ranging from $25 to $50 (or more). In addition, lenders may charge a **transaction fee** (a small charge levied each time a card is used). The card illustrated in Figure 7.1 assesses transaction fees for cash advances and balance transfers. Some lenders even charge a fee for printing the monthly credit bill. Most fees are not required to be included in the APR calculation because they cannot be known in advance. As you can see, an apparently low-rate card may turn into a high-cost card when all fees are considered.

Liability for Lost or Stolen Cards   The Truth in Lending Act limits a cardholder's **credit card liability** for lost or stolen credit cards. Under the law, if you notify the card issuer within two days of a loss or theft, you are not legally responsible for any fraudulent usage of the card. After two days, your maximum liability for fraudulent usage of the card (including telephone calling cards) prior to your notification is $50. You are not responsible for any fraudulent usage after you notify the issuer of the loss. Although your financial liability is low, some companies nevertheless specialize in selling credit card insurance (for an annual premium ranging from $15 to $49) that will pay creditors for the first $50 of unauthorized use of an insured person's lost or stolen credit cards. Such insurance is profitable for insurance companies—but an unnecessary expense for you. If you are insistent and perhaps talk with a credit card company supervisor, most will waive the $50 fee for unauthorized use as a gesture of goodwill to keep you as a good customer.

Late-Payment, Bounced Check, and Over-the-Limit Fees   Late-payment fees of $30 or more are often applied when the borrower fails to make a payment by the due date. Most card issuers assess a similar charge if you write a bad check when making your monthly payment. Many credit card issuers charge a significant ($20 to $50) over-the-limit fee when the cardholder exceeds his or her credit limit. Each of these fees is much higher than necessary in terms of the

Did You Know?

About Secured Credit Cards

A **secured credit card** (also called a **collateralized credit card**) is backed by collateral in the form of a savings account opened at the financial institution that issues the card. Banks offering secured credit cards typically charge an application fee and require the applicant to make a deposit of $500 to $1000 into a savings account. The person then receives a credit limit in the same amount on a bank credit card. The savings balance cannot be withdrawn as long as the card is

available for use. The deposit is refunded (with a small amount of interest) when the credit card balance is paid off and the account closed. Most people do not need a secured credit card, but those who have no alternative should consider obtaining one from a reputable institution, as scams abound in this market. Fees to open these accounts can be as high as 50 percent of the credit limit.

actual cost to the lender for these rule violations. Indeed, they represent a significant source of profits for credit card issuers. The account illustrated in Figure 7.1 assesses a $35 fee for each of these offenses.

Credit Card Insurance Many lenders encourage borrowers to sign up for **credit life insurance** that pays the unpaid balance of a loan—to the lender—in the event of the borrower's death. Credit life insurance is grossly overpriced and is a cost that can be avoided. The same can be said for **credit disability insurance,** which repays the outstanding loan balance if the borrower becomes disabled (with "disability" usually being very narrowly defined), and credit unemployment insurance.

 Concept Check 7.2

1. Distinguish among bank credit cards, retail credit cards, and travel and entertainment cards.
2. What are the differences and similarities between a cash advance and a balance transfer using a bank credit card?
3. Describe the positive and negative aspects of having a variable interest rate on a credit card.
4. What is a default rate and how might a cardholder come to have to pay this interest rate?
5. Describe five common fees assessed on credit card accounts and how they can be avoided.

 Advice from a Pro...

Control and Reduce Your Credit Card Debt

If your credit card debt rises to a hard-to-manage level, consider the following suggestions:

1. **Immediately stop** using your credit cards, and do not open new credit accounts or accept any new credit offers.
2. **Evaluate** all of your budgeted expenditures and plan to devote the largest possible amounts toward paying off your credit card balances.
3. **Work overtime** or take another job. Devote any extra income, such as a tax refund, toward paying these debts.
4. **Gather your most recent credit card statements,** sit down with pencil and paper, and write down the balance of each debt and the interest rate. Then set a payoff date and calculate the monthly payment you will need to pay off the debt by that date using a calculator like the ones found at www.bankrate.com or www.money.cnn.com.

5. **Consider transferring existing balances** on high-interest rate accounts to an account with a lower interest rate. Use caution, however, because brief introductory periods, transaction fees, and penalties may eliminate any potential savings.
6. **Pay the minimum amount due** on your cards with low interest rates, and pay as much as possible on the cards with the highest interest rates. Continue to do so until all of your debts are paid off.
7. **Consider seeking assistance** from a nonprofit credit counseling agency if after three to six months you are not making good progress toward paying off your credit card balances. It can negotiate with your creditors to lower your payments and interest rates and to reduce or eliminate late fees and over-the-limit charges.

Lorie Broberg
Oglala Lakota College

Managing Credit Cards Wisely

Credit cards can be a positive tool in personal financial management—when used appropriately. It is important to manage their use wisely. To do so, you must understand and monitor your credit statements, correct errors when appropriate, and also recognize how finance charges are computed. Your goal should be to use the credit card in a manner that avoids all fees, including finance charges. This means paying your balance in full every month. After all, credit card debt is the most expensive form of debt used by most people. As Andrew Tobias has observed "You want 21 percent risk free? Pay off your credit cards"

Credit Statements

credit statement

The monthly bill on a credit card account showing the charges and payments made, minimum payment required, and due date among other information; also called a *periodic statement*.

Active charge account holders receive a monthly **credit statement** (also called a **periodic statement**) that summarizes the charges, payments, finance charges, and other activity on the account. The significant features of credit statements are the billing date, due date, transaction and posting dates, grace period, minimum payment, and credit for merchandise returns and billing errors obtained. You also need to know how to correct errors in your credit statements. Figure 7.2 shows a monthly statement for a credit card.

billing/closing/ statement date

The last day for which any transactions are reported on the credit statement.

Billing Date   The **billing date** (sometimes called the **statement date** or **closing date**) is the last day of the month for which any transactions are reported on the statement. In Figure 7.2, this date is 5/22/10. Any transactions or payments made after this date will be recorded on the following month's credit statement. The statement is mailed to the cardholder a day or so after the billing date. The billing date is generally the same day of each month, and the time period between billing dates is referred to as the **billing cycle.**

Due Date   The due date is the specific day by which the credit card company should receive payment from you. In Figure 7.2, this date is 6/17/10. The period between the billing date and the due date—no less than 21 days—represents the time allowed for statements and payments to be mailed and for the borrower to make arrangements to pay. Federal law states that bills must be mailed to cardholders at least 14 days before payments are due. The account illustrated in Figure 7.2 has a 25-day grace period. If payment is received later than the due date, a credit bureau may be notified of slow payment. If no payment is received, the company may begin collection efforts but commonly they will simply carry the balance over to the next month and add a late payment penalty of $40 or more. More vigorous collection efforts will occur if the next month's payment is also missed.

Transaction and Posting Dates   The date on which a credit cardholder makes a purchase (or receives a credit, as described later in this chapter) is known as the **transaction date.** In the past, several days would pass before the credit card company was informed of the transaction and the charge was posted to the account (on the posting date). With the increased use of magnetic strip readers at retailers, however, these dates may be concurrent, with both matching the date on which the clerk or the customer "swipes" the card through the reader. Interest is charged from the posting date unless a grace period is offered; some lenders charge interest from the transaction date.

grace period

Time period between the posting date of a transaction and the payment due date during which no interest accrues.

Grace Period   A **grace period** is the time period between the posting date of a transaction and the due date, within which any new credit card purchases made during the billing cycle will avoid finance charges (also see Figure 7.1). Most cards provide a grace period only if the previous month's total balance was paid in full and on time. About one-third of cardholders pay their bills in full by the due date and receive, in effect, an interest-free loan on their new purchases during the next billing cycle. It is a smart financial move to use one credit card for convenience items that are paid in full each month and another credit card for

Figure 7.2
Sample Statement for a Revolving Charge Account

Source: Courtesy of Pikeville National Bank, Pikeville, KY.

items for which paying off the balance each month is not possible. Use a no-annual-fee card for the convenience purchases and a low-APR card for purchases for which you carry a balance. Avoid cards that do not offer a grace period. In Figure 7.2, the cardholder has a previous unpaid balance, $600, and was charged interest on the unpaid balance as well as on the new charges made within the billing cycle, starting from the date they were posted to the account. Thus, this example lacks a grace period because of the unpaid balance on the card.

Minimum Payment Amount

To meet their obligations, borrowers must make a **minimum payment amount** monthly that is no smaller than the amount required by

minimum payment amount
Lowest allowable monthly payment required by the lender.

Instant Message

Special Rules for Credit Card Applicants Age 18 to 20

Under the 2009 Credit Card Accountability, Responsibility and Disclosure (CARD) Act, when a person age 18-20 applies for a credit card the card issuer must verify that the person has sufficient independent income or require a cosigner.

Did You Know?

How Your Credit Card Payment Is Applied

Your credit card statement might have several different balances resulting from purchases, cash advances and uses for which you received a special low rate. Each balance might have a different interest rate. How then is your payment applied to these balances when you make a payment? Under the 2009 Credit Card Accountability, Responsibility and Disclosure (CARD) Act, whenever you make more than a minimum payment on your credit card account the lender must apply any excess above the minimum payment to the portion of the card debt that carries the highest APR.

credit receipt
Written evidence of any items returned that notes the specific amount and date of the transaction.

periodic rate
The APR for a charge account divided by the number of billing cycles per year (usually 12).

average daily balance
Sum of the outstanding balances owed each day during the billing period divided by the number of days in the period.

the creditor. In Figure 7.2, the cardholder has two options: pay the total amount due ($696.04) or make at least the minimum payment of $21. If the borrower pays the full amount due, finance charges on new purchases in the next billing cycle generally can be avoided. If a partial payment, such as the "total minimum payment due" of $21, is made, additional finance charges will be assessed and will be payable the following month.

Credit for Merchandise Returns and Errors   If you return merchandise bought on credit, the merchant will issue you a **credit receipt**—written evidence of the items returned that notes the specific amount of the transaction. In essence, the amount of the merchandise credit is charged back to the credit card company and eventually to the merchant. A credit may also be granted by the credit card company when a billing error has been made (discussed in the next section) or when an unauthorized transaction appears. Credits obtained in the current month should appear on the next monthly statement as a reduction of the total amount owed. The credit statement in Figure 7.2 shows a $21 credit.

Computation of Finance Charges

Companies that issue credit cards must tell consumers the APR applied as well as the method used to compute the finance charges. In addition, they must disclose the **periodic rate,** which is the APR for a charge account divided by the number of billing cycles per year (usually 12). For example, a periodic rate of 1½ percent per month would result from an APR of approximately 18 percent (actually a bit higher because of compounding); both figures must be disclosed. Typically, the finance charge is calculated by first computing the **average daily balance**—the sum of the outstanding balances owed each day during the billing period divided by the number of days in the period. The periodic rate is then applied against that balance. For example, a card with an 18 percent APR and a 1½ percent periodic rate and an average daily balance of $1000 would have a finance charge for the month of $15 ($1,000 × 0.015).

How Credit Card Average Daily Balances Are Calculated

Three methods are commonly used to calculate the average daily balance on a credit card billing statement:

1. **Average daily balance excluding new purchases.** The cardholder pays interest only on any balance left over from the previous month.

2. **Average daily balance including new purchases with a grace period.** The balance calculation includes the balance from the previous month and any new charges made during the billing cycle. The grace period allows for the exclusion of new charges made during the billing cycle only if the balance from the previous billing cycle was zero.

3. **Average daily balance including new purchases with no grace period.** The balance from the previous month and any new charges made during the billing cycle are included in the balance calculation, even if the previous month's balance was paid in full.

Advice from a Pro...

Avoid the Minimum Payment Trap

Do you currently have balances outstanding on your credit cards? If so, how long have you carried those balances? If you open an account in college and already have an unpaid balance of $2500 upon your graduation at age 22, you may find that the balance will not drop below $2500 for many years. This situation occurs when you continue to make purchases with the card but continue to send in only the required minimum payment amount. If $2500 is still owed on the account years later , then you have "permanent debt." In essence, you have never repaid the college charges. With an 18 percent APR, the finance charges on a principal of $2500 for 15 years will total $6750 (0.18 × $2500 × 15), almost three times as much as the debt itself!

The outlook is similarly bleak if you discontinue using the card for new purchases but still remit only the required minimum repayment amount. Credit card issuers often require a minimum monthly payment as low as 3 or 3½ percent of the outstanding balance. This tiny payment requirement is mathematically guaranteed to keep the user in debt for many, many years. To illustrate, a minimum payment of $75 (3 percent) on an outstanding balance of $2500 with a 1½ percent monthly periodic rate results in only one-half of the payment ($37.50 = $2500 × 0.015) going to reduce the actual debt (the principal). The other $37.50 is used to pay the monthly interest. At this rate of repayment, it will take more than six years to repay the $2500.

A ploy that card issuers frequently use is to allow cardholders to "skip a payment"—in essence, to make "a zero-dollar minimum payment." Interest will continue to accrue for the month during which no payment is made. This practice increases the total amount owed because the unpaid interest simply adds to the unpaid balance.

Such offers for a "low" or "zero-dollar" minimum payment illustrate the minimum payment trap. To avoid paying credit card charges for six to ten years, or even longer, you must make much larger monthly payments that go toward retiring your credit card balances. Better still, ask yourself—no, ask yourself twice—"Do I really need to charge it?"

The 2009 Credit Card Accountability, Responsibility and Disclosure Act requires that your credit card statement include the number of months it will take to pay off your card balance if you make only the minimum payment. Pay close attention to this information when deciding what payment amount to make.

Donald Stuhlman
Wilmington College, Delaware

The following chart illustrates finance charges vary for a hypothetical situation in which a borrower charges $1000 per month and pays only the minimum payment, except for every third month when the balance is paid in full. Executing this scheme four times over the course of a year would result in the finance charges shown in the chart under the two most common ways of computing the average daily balance and for low-, average-, and high-interest cards.

	Annual Percentage Rate		
	12.0%	17.3%	19.8%
Average daily balance (excluding new purchases)	$40.00	$ 57.60	$ 66.00
Average daily balance (including new purchases)*	$80.00	$115.20	$132.00

*This is the most common method used by credit card issuers.

Correcting Errors on Your Credit Card Statement

The **Fair Credit Billing Act (FCBA)** helps people who wish to dispute billing errors on revolving credit accounts. In effect, the FCBA permits a **chargeback** that is, the amount of the transaction is charged back to the business where the transaction originated. Withholding

Fair Credit Billing Act (FCBA)
Helps people who wish to dispute billing errors on revolving credit accounts.

chargeback
The amount of the transaction is charged back to the business where the transaction originated in the case of a dispute or challenge by the cardholder.

Instant Message

Billing Errors Are Common

The University of Michigan's Survey of Consumers shows that nearly one in six households reported an error on their credit card accounts.

dunning letters
Notices that make insistent demands for repayment.

payment to a credit card company is permitted when the cardholder alleges that a mathematical error has been made in a billing statement, when fraudulent use of the card appears to have occurred, or when (within certain reasonable limitations) a **goods and services dispute** asserts that the charges were for faulty, damaged, shoddy, defective, or poor-quality goods and services and you made a good-faith effort to try to correct the problem with the merchant. For goods and services disputes, the FCBA applies only to charges of more than $50 made in your home state or within 100 miles of your current mailing address. Most lenders apply the spirit of the FCBA to any goods and services disputes, regardless of the geographic distances involved.

You must make your billing error complaint within 60 days after the date on which the first bill containing the error was mailed to you. The lender then has 30 days to acknowledge your notification and, within 90 days, must either correct the error permanently, return any overpayment (if requested), or provide evidence of why it believes the bill to be correct (such as a copy of a charge slip you supposedly signed).

While the dispute is being investigated, creditors cannot assess interest on or apply penalties for nonpayment of the disputed amount, send **dunning letters** (notices that make insistent demands for repayment), or send negative information about your account to a credit bureau without stating that "some items are in dispute." A lender that does not follow the procedures correctly cannot collect the first $50 of the questioned amount, even if the bill was correct. Back interest and penalties may be charged if the disputed item is proved to be legitimately owed.

Take several actions when disputing an item on a billing statement:

1. **Send a written notice** of the error to the credit card issuer. The notice must be in writing to qualify for the protections provided under the FCBA. Instead of sending the notice to the same address where repayments are normally remitted, examine the billing statement thoroughly, looking for an address under the heading "Send Inquiries to" or something similar. If the error is an "unauthorized use" make sure you indicate this as these disputes have added protections.

2. **Also notify the merchant** involved of the error. Although the FCBA does not apply to merchants, it is often the merchant that caused the error and who is in the best position to clear up the error. Also tell the merchant that you are asserting your rights under the FCBA with the card issuer.

Shoppers frequently rely on purchase loans when buying "big ticket" items such as furniture and TVs.

Juice Images/PhotoLibrary

3. **Provide photocopies** (not originals) of any necessary documentation. Keep the originals to challenge any finding by the company that no error occurred.

4. **Withhold payment for disputed items.** If possible, pay the remaining amount owed in full to isolate a disputed item. Under the provisions of the FCBA, the card company must immediately credit your account for the amount in dispute.

5. **Review your credit bureau file** after the dispute has been settled to ensure that it does not include information regarding your refusal to repay the disputed amount.

Instant Message

Homeowner's Insurance May Cover Lost Cards

Most homeowner's and renter's insurance policies will pay the $50 fee you might be charged for unauthorized use of a lost or stolen credit card. (See Chapter 10 for details.)

 ### Concept Check 7.3

1. Describe how the finance charge is calculated on a credit card account.
2. What is the major benefit of having a credit card with a grace period?
3. Explain the steps you should take if you find an error on your credit card account billing statement.

Understanding Consumer Installment Loans

Consumers obtain installment credit in two ways. With a **cash loan,** the borrower receives cash and then uses it to make purchases, pay off other loans, or make investments. With a **purchase loan** (also called **sales credit**), the consumer makes a purchase on credit with no cash transferring from the lender to the borrower. Instead, the funds go directly from the lender to the seller. For example, a car buyer might obtain a purchase loan from the Ford Motor Credit to buy a new Ford Edge. With some purchase loans, the lender *is* the seller. For all consumer loans, the borrower will sign a formal **promissory note** (a written installment loan contract) that spells out the terms of the loan.

Installment Loans Can Be Unsecured or Secured

Credit can either be unsecured or secured. An **unsecured loan** is granted solely based on the good credit character of the borrower. Sometimes unsecured loans are called **signature loans** because they are backed up by only the borrower's signature. Because unsecured loans carry higher risk than secured debts, the interest rate charged on them is substantially higher.

A **secured loan** requires a cosigner or collateral. A **cosigner** agrees to pay the debt if the original borrower fails to do so. Being a cosigner is a major responsibility because a cosigner has the same legal obligations for repayment as the original borrower does. In case of default, a lender will go after the party—either the borrower or the cosigner—from whom it is more likely to collect the funds.

A loan secured with collateral means that the lender has a security interest in the property that is pledged as collateral. For example, the vehicle itself is the collateral on an automobile loan. The item of collateral does not necessarily need to be the property purchased with the loan. Typically, the lender records a lien in the county courthouse to make the security interest known to the public. A **lien** is a legal right to seize and dispose of (usually sell) property to obtain payment of a claim. When the loan is repaid, the lien will be removed. (The borrower should double check to make sure this removal occurs.)

4 Learning Objective
Describe the important features of consumer installment loans.

promissory note
Written installment loan contract that spells out the terms of the loan.

unsecured loan/ signature loan
Loan granted based solely on borrower's good creditworthiness.

secured loan
Loan that is backed by collateral or a cosigner.

lien
A legal right to seize and dispose of (usually sell) property to obtain payment of a claim. Once loan is paid, lien is removed.

In the event that the borrower fails to repay a loan, the creditor can exercise the lien and seize the collateral through repossession, sometimes without notice. Almost all credit contracts contain an **acceleration clause** stating that after a specific number of payments are unpaid (often just one), the loan is considered in default and all remaining installments are due and payable upon demand of the creditor. These clauses protect the lender's interest but can prove very difficult for borrowers. Don't be fooled if you miss a payment and the lender does not exercise the acceleration clause immediately: It can do so at any time after default occurs. Do not ignore a warning letter from a creditor!

acceleration clause
Part of a credit contract stating that after a specific number of payments are unpaid (often just one), the loan is considered in default and all remaining installments are due and payable upon demand of the creditor.

Purchase Loan Installment Contracts

Two kinds of contracts are used when purchasing goods with an installment loan:

- **Installment purchase agreements** (also called **collateral installment loans** or **chattel mortgage loans**), in which the title of the property passes to the buyer when the contract is signed
- **Conditional sales contracts** (also known as **financing leases**), in which the title does not pass to the buyer until the last installment payment has been paid

An installment purchase agreement provides a measure of protection for the borrower, as the creditor must follow all legal procedures required by state law when repossessing the property. Some state laws permit the lender to take secured property back as soon as the buyer falls behind in payments, possibly by seizing a car right from a person's driveway.

 Concept Check 7.4

1. Describe how a cash loan and a purchase loan differ.
2. Distinguish between a secured and an unsecured loan.
3. When might a lender enforce an acceleration clause on a loan and explain the impact of such an action by the lender.
4. Differentiate between an installment purchase agreement and a conditional sales contract.

Calculating Interest on Consumer Loans

5 Learning Objective

Calculate the interest and annual percentage rate on consumer loans.

Truth in Lending Act (TIL)
Requires lenders to disclose to credit applicants both the interest rate expressed as an annual percentage rate (APR) and the finance charge.

variable-rate (adjustable-rate) loans
Loans for which the interest rate varies with the monthly payment going up or down, allowing the loan to be paid off by the original end date.

The federal **Truth in Lending Act (TIL)** requires lenders to disclose to credit applicants both the interest rate expressed as an APR and the finance charge. The finance charge is the cost of credit expressed in dollars. The finance charge plus the original amount borrowed must be paid. It has been said that the hardest thing to do is to "make twelve easy payments."

Calculating an Installment Loan Payment

Installment credit typically comes with a **fixed interest rate,** meaning that the rate will not change over the life of the loan. Lenders often offer **variable-rate loans** (also called **adjustable-rate loans**) to borrowers. When the loan rate varies, the monthly payment will go up or down, allowing the loan to be paid off by the same date as originally established in the contract.

To help you figure out the required monthly payment for different loan amounts, Table 7.1 shows various monthly installment payments used to repay a $1000 loan at commonly

Table 7.1 Monthly Installment Payment (Principal and Interest) Required to Repay $1000*

APR†	Number of Monthly Payments						
	12	24	36	48	60	72	84
5	$85.61	$43.87	$29.97	$23.03	$18.87	$16.10	$14.13
6	86.07	44.32	30.42	23.49	19.33	16.57	14.61
7	86.53	44.77	30.88	23.95	19.80	17.05	15.09
8	86.99	45.23	31.34	24.41	20.28	17.53	15.59
9	87.45	45.68	31.80	24.88	20.76	18.03	16.09
10	87.92	46.14	32.27	25.36	21.25	18.53	16.60
11	88.38	46.61	32.74	25.85	21.74	19.03	17.12
12	88.85	47.07	33.21	26.33	22.24	19.55	17.65
13	89.32	47.54	33.69	26.83	22.75	20.07	18.19
14	89.79	48.01	34.18	27.33	23.27	20.61	18.74
15	90.26	48.49	34.67	27.83	23.79	21.14	19.27
16	90.73	48.96	35.16	28.34	24.32	21.69	19.86
17	91.20	49.44	35.65	28.85	24.85	22.25	20.44
18	91.68	49.92	36.15	29.37	25.39	22.81	21.02
19	92.16	50.41	36.66	29.90	25.94	23.38	21.61
20	92.63	50.90	37.16	30.43	26.49	23.95	22.21

*To illustrate, assume an automobile loan of $14,000 at 8 percent for five years. To repay $1000, the monthly payment is $20.28; therefore, multiply $20.28 (8% row and 60-month column) by 14 to give a monthly payment of $283.92. For amounts other than exact $1000 increments, simply use decimals. For example, for a loan of $14,500, the multiplier would be 14.5.

†For fractional interest rates of 5.5, 6.5, 7.5, and so on, simply take a monthly payment halfway between the whole-number APR payments. For example, the payment for 48 months at 9.5 percent is $25.12 ($25.36 − $24.88 = $0.48; $0.48 ÷ 2 = $0.24; $0.24 + $24.88 = $25.12).

seen APR interest rates and time periods. For loans of other dollar amounts, divide the borrowed amount by 1000 and multiply the result by the appropriate figure from the table. For example, an automobile loan for $12,000, financed at 10 percent interest, might be repaid in 36 equal monthly payments of $387.24 ($32.27 × 12). A loan for $3550 at 16 percent for 24 months will require monthly payments of $173.81 ($48.96 × 3.550).

The finance charge must include all mandatory charges to be paid by the borrower. In addition to interest, lenders may charge fees for a credit investigation; a loan application; or credit life, credit disability, or credit unemployment insurance. When fees are required, the lender must include them in the finance charge in dollars as part of the APR calculations. When the borrower elects these options voluntarily, the fees are not included in the finance charge and APR calculations, even though they raise the actual cost of borrowing. It is easy to calculate the finance charge on a consumer loan. First, multiply the monthly payment by the number of months and subtract the original amount borrowed. In the 36-month automobile loan example given earlier, the finance charge would be $1940.64 [($387.24 × 36) − $12,000]. Second, add any other mandatory charges.

Do It NOW!

Taking out student loans may be necessary but you can minimize their impact. Start today by:

1. Making a list of all your loans currently outstanding, the amounts owed, to whom and at what interest rates.

2. Projecting any money you will borrow between now and graduation.

3. Using the calculator at http://www.bankrate.com/brm/popcalc2.asp to determine your monthly payments if you were to pay off your total debt owed at graduation in 3 years, 5 years and 10 years.

Finance Charge and APR Calculations for Installment Loans

Interest accounts for the greatest portion of the finance charge. Three methods are used to calculate interest on installment and noninstallment credit: the declining-balance (sometimes called the simple-interest) method, the add-on interest method, and the discount method. The add-on method predominates at banks, savings banks, and consumer finance companies for installment loans for automobiles, furniture, and other credit requiring collateral. The declining-balance method is widely used by credit unions to calculate interest on loans. The declining-balance method is always used for credit cards and for most home mortgages.

The following discussion illustrates the calculation of the APR for installment loans using each of the three methods.

declining-balance method
Interest calculation method in which interest is assessed during each billing period (usually each month) based on the outstanding balance of the installment loan that billing period.

The Declining-Balance Method   With the **declining-balance method,** the interest assessed during each payment period (usually each month) is based on the current outstanding balance of the installment loan. The lender initially calculates a schedule (such as that given in Table 7.2) to have the balance repaid in full after a certain number of months. The borrower may vary the rate of repayment by making payments larger than those scheduled or may repay the loan in full at any time.

Here is an illustration of the declining-balance method for an installment loan. As shown in Table 7.2, at the end of the first month, a periodic interest rate (the monthly rate applied to the outstanding balance of a loan) of 1½ percent (18 percent annually divided by 12 months) is applied to the beginning balance of $1000, giving an interest charge of $15. Of the first monthly installment of $91.68, $15 goes toward the payment of interest and $76.68 ($91.68 − $15.00) goes toward payment of the principal.

amortization
Loan repayment method in which part of the payment goes to pay interest and part goes to repay principal. Extra payments toward principal shorten the life of the loan and decrease total amount of interest paid.

For the second month, the outstanding balance is reduced to $923.32 ($1000 − $76.68). Since the balance is $78.68 lower, the interest portion of the payment drops to $13.85 (0.015 × $923.32). Because the declining-balance method applies the periodic interest rate to the outstanding loan balance, the APR and the simple interest rate will differ only if fees (such as an application fee) boost the finance charge. (This method of paying off a loan, called **amortization,** is also discussed in Chapter 9 when we examine home mortgage loans.) Note that declining-balance loans carry no prepayment penalties.

Table 7.2   **Sample Repayment Schedule for $1000 Principal Plus Interest Using the Declining Balance Method (1½ Percent per Month)**

Month	Outstanding Balance	Payment	Interest	Principal	Ending Balance
1	$1,000.00	$91.68	$15.00	$76.68	$923.32
2	923.32	91.68	13.85	77.83	845.49
3	845.49	91.68	12.68	79.00	766.49
4	766.49	91.68	11.50	80.18	686.31
5	686.31	91.68	10.29	81.39	604.92
6	604.92	91.68	9.07	82.61	522.31
7	522.31	91.68	7.83	83.85	438.46
8	438.46	91.68	6.58	85.10	353.36
9	353.36	91.68	5.30	86.38	266.98
10	266.98	91.68	4.00	87.68	179.30
11	179.30	91.68	2.69	88.99	90.31
12	90.31	91.66	1.35	90.31	0

The Add-On Method

The add-on method is a widely used technique for computing interest on installment loans. With this method, the interest is calculated and added to the amount borrowed to determine the total amount to be repaid. Equation (7.1) is used to calculate the dollar amount of interest. Note that the interest rate used in this equation for the add-on method is an add-on rate and should not be confused with the APR.

With the **add-on interest method,** interest is calculated by applying an interest rate to the amount borrowed times the number of years. The add-on interest formula given in Equation (7.1) is used as follows:

$$I = PRT \qquad \text{(7.1)}\star$$

add-on interest method
Interest is calculated by applying an interest rate to the amount borrowed times the number of years to arrive at the total interest to be charged.

where
I = Interest or finance charges
P = Principal amount borrowed
R = Rate of interest (simple, add-on, or discount rate)
T = Time of loan in years

For example, assume that Megan Broman of New York City borrows $2000 for two years at 9 percent add-on interest to be repaid in monthly installments. Using Equation (7.1), her finance charge in dollars is $360 ($2000 × 0.09 × 2). Adding the finance charge ($360) to the amount borrowed ($2000) gives a total amount of $2360 to be repaid. When this amount is divided by the total number of scheduled payments (24), we find that Megan must make 24 monthly payments of $98.33.

Calculating the APR When the Add-On Method Is Used

Add-on rates and APRs are not equivalent. This is because the add-on calculation assumes the original debt is owed for the entire period of the loan. But of course the debt does go down as the debt is repaid. In the example just given, Megan does not have use of the total amount borrowed for the full two years. Equation (7.2) shows the n-ratio method of estimating the APR on her add-on loan.

$$\begin{aligned}
\text{APR} &= \frac{Y\,(95P + 9)\,F}{12P(P + 1)\,(4D + F)} \qquad \text{(7.2)}\star \\[6pt]
&= \frac{(12)(95 \times 24 + 9)(360)}{12(24)(24 + 1)[(4 \times 2000) + 360]} \\[6pt]
&= \frac{12(2289)(360)}{(288)(25)(8360)} \\[6pt]
&= \frac{9{,}888{,}480}{60{,}192{,}000} \\[6pt]
&= 16.4\%
\end{aligned}$$

where
APR = Annual percentage rate
Y = Number of payments in one year
F = Finance charge in dollars (dollar cost of credit)
D = Debt (amount borrowed or proceeds)
P = Total number of scheduled payments

Using Equation (7.2), the APR is 16.4 percent. Note that the APR is approximately double the add-on rate because, on average, Megan has use of only half of the borrowed money during the entire loan period.

Applying the Rule of 78s to Determine Prepayment Penalties

Most installment loan contracts that use the add-on method include a **prepayment penalty**—a special charge assessed to the borrower for paying off a loan early. Prepayment penalties take

prepayment penalty
Special charge assessed to the borrower for paying off a loan early.

★Calculations involving Equations (7.1) and (7.2) can be performed on the *Garman/Forgue* companion website.

into consideration the reality that borrowers should pay more in interest early in the loan period when they have the use of more money and increasingly less interest as the debt shrinks over time. With an add-on method loan, however, the interest is spread evenly across all payments rather than declining as the loan balance falls. If an add-on method loan is paid off early, the lender will use some penalty method to compensate for the lower interest component applied in the early months.

rule of 78s method/sum of the digits method for calculating prepayment penalties
A common method of calculating the prepayment penalty on a loan which uses the add-on method for calculating the interest.

The **rule of 78s method** (also called the **sum of the digits method**) is the most widely used method of calculating a prepayment penalty. Its name derives from the fact that, for a one-year loan, the numbers between 1 and 12 for each month add up to 78 (12 + 11 + 10 + 9 + 8 + 7 + 6 + 5 + 4 + 3 + 2 + 1). For a two-year loan, the numbers between 1 and 24 would be added, and so on for loans with longer time periods.

To illustrate the use of the rule of 78s method, consider the case of Devin Grigsby from West Lafayette, Indiana. He borrowed $500 for 12 months plus an additional $80 finance charge, and is scheduled to pay equal monthly installments of $48.33 ($580 ÷ 12). Assume Devin wants to pay the loan off after only six months. He might assume—incorrectly—that he would owe only $250 more because after six months he had paid $250 (one-half) of the $500 borrowed and $40 (one-half) of the finance charge, for a total of $290 in payments ($48.33 × 6). Actually, Devin still owes $268.46, including a prepayment penalty of $18.46. To calculate this amount using the rule of 78s method, the lender adds together all of the numbers between 12 and 7 (12 for the first month, 11 for the second, and so on for six months): 12 + 11 + 10 + 9 + 8 + 7 = 57. The lender assumes that during the first six months $58.46 [(57 ÷ 78) × $80]—not $40—of the finance charges was received from the $290 in payments Devin had made on the loan.★ Consequently, only $231.54 ($290.00 − $58.46) was paid on the $500 borrowed, leaving $268.46 ($500.00 − $231.54) still owed, for a prepayment penalty of $18.46 ($268.46 − $250.00).

discount method of calculating interest
Interest is calculated based on discount rate multiplied by the amount borrowed and by number of years to repay. Interest is then subtracted from the amount of the loan and the difference is given to the borrower. In this method, interest is paid up front before any part of the payment is applied toward the principal.

The Discount Method   The discount method is sometimes used by creditors to compute the interest on an installment loan. With the **discount method,** the interest is calculated based on a discount rate that is multiplied times the amount borrowed and multiplied by the number of years to repay. The interest is then subtracted from the amount of the loan and only the difference is given to the borrower. Thus, the interest is paid up front. When this method is applied to our earlier example involving Megan Broman, she would receive only $1640 [$2000 − ($2000 × 2 × 9%)] at the beginning of the loan period. Her monthly payment would be $83.33 ($2000 ÷ 24). Using Equation (7.2), the APR would be 19.8 percent (the APR rises because only $1640 is obtained while $2000 is repaid).

 Concept Check 7.5

1. Explain how the interest is calculated on a consumer loan that uses the declining-balance method.
2. Summarize how interest is calculated on a consumer loan that uses the add-on method.
3. What is the effect of the rule of 78s when a borrower repays an add-on method loan early.
4. Explain how the interest is calculated on a consumer loan that uses the discount method.

★If the loan was paid off after one month, the amount of interest paid is assumed to be ¹²⁄₇₈ of the $80 finance charge, or $12.31. For a loan paid in full after two months, the amount of interest paid is assumed to be ²³⁄₇₈ of the total (¹²⁄₇₈ for month 1 plus ¹¹⁄₇₈ for month 2), or $23.59.

What Do You Recommend NOW?

Now that you have read this chapter on credit cards and consumer loans, what would you recommend to Darrell Cochrane regarding:

1. His approach to using credit cards, including the number of cards he has?

2. Estimating the credit card interest charges he is paying each month?

3. How he might lower his interest expense each month?

4. Consolidating his credit card debts into one installment loan?

Michael Newman/PhotoEdit

Big Picture Summary of Learning Objectives

1 Compare the common types of consumer credit, including credit cards and installment loans.

Borrowers can use both installment and noninstallment credit. Open-ended credit is an example of noninstallment credit. It permits the customer to gain repeated access to credit without having to fill out a new application each time money is borrowed. The consumer may choose either to repay the debt in a single payment or to make a series of payments of varying amounts. Bank credit cards and travel and entertainment credit cards are the most commonly used open-ended credit accounts.

2 Describe the types and features of credit card accounts.

Credit card borrowers must adhere to all the rules of the account or risk being charged a number of punitive fees such as late-payment and bounced check fees. Borrowers also need to be wary of default rates, which may raise the APR on the account for any violation of the account rules. Some lenders apply default rates if the borrower falls behind in payments on other accounts, even if the borrower is in good standing on the lender's own account.

3 Manage your credit card accounts to avoid fees and finance charges.

Credit card statements provide a monthly summary of credit transactions and the calculation of any finance charges. Credit card issuers compute finance charges by multiplying the average daily balance by the periodic interest rate.

4 Describe the important features of consumer installment loans.

Consumer loans, also called installment loans, have several features that distinguish them from credit card accounts. Loans usually have a fixed payment for a fixed number of months. Once the loan is paid off, the account is closed and a new account would need to be opened if the person wants to take out another loan.

5 Calculate the interest and annual percentage rate on consumer loans.

Both the declining-balance and add-on methods are used to calculate the interest on installment loans, although the annual percentage rate (APR) formula gives the correct rate in all cases. With declining-balance loans, the dollar amount of interest incorporated in each monthly payment declines as the loan balance declines.

Let's Talk About It

1. **Borrowing in Tough Economic Times.** The great recession of 2008-09 was made more difficult for many people because of their high debt loads. How has your perception of carrying credit card debt, student loans and other borrowing changed as a result of the economic downturn?

2. **What Type of Borrowing Might Be Best?** If you wanted to borrow money to study abroad for a semester and could pay it back within two years after returning, would you prefer a single-payment loan, an installment loan, or a cash advance on a credit card?

3. **Are Rebates a Good Idea?** Some credit cards offer a 1 percent or higher rebate for all purchases made on the card. How would you feel about using such a card to get those rebates with the intention of paying the balance off in full each month?

4. **Default Rates.** Do you feel that the much higher default interest rates are justified if you are not repaying a credit card on time? Does your opinion differ if the default rate was applied because you were in trouble on another account and not on the account charging the default rate?

5. **The Declining Balance Method.** How do you feel about the fact that interest costs are higher in the early months of a declining-balance loan than they are in the later months?

6. **The Rule of 78s.** Are prepayment penalties such as that applied with the rule of 78s justified? Why or why not?

Do the Math

1. **Monthly Payments and Finance Charges.** Kimberly Jensen and Rebecca Parker of Mankato, Minnesota are both single. The pair share an apartment on the limited resources provided through Kimberly's disability check from Social Security and Rebecca's parttime job at a grocery store. The two grew tired of their old furniture and went shopping. A local store offered credit at an APR of 16 percent, with a maximum term of four years. The furniture they wish to purchase costs $2800, with no down payment required. Using Table 7.1 or the *Garman/Forgue* companion website, make the following calculations:

   (a) What is the amount of their monthly payment if they borrow for four years?

   (b) What are the total finance charges over that four-year period?

   (c) How would the payment change if Kimberly and Rebecca reduced the loan term to three years?

   (d) What are the total finance charges over that three-year period?

   (e) How would the payment change if they could afford a down payment of $500 with four years of financing?

   (f) What are the total finance charges over that four-year period given the $500 down payment?

   (g) How would the payment change if they could afford a down payment of $500 with three years of financing?

   (h) What are the total finance charges over that three-year period given the $500 down payment?

2. **Average Daily Balance and Finance Charges.** Talika Sampson, an antiques dealer from Wilmington, North Carolina, received her monthly billing statement for April for her MasterCard account. The statement indicated that she had a beginning balance of $600, on day 5 she charged $150, on day 12 she charged $300, and on day 15 she made a $200 payment. Out of curiosity, Talika wanted to confirm that the finance charge for the billing cycle was correct.

   (a) What was Talika's average daily balance for April without new purchases?

   (b) What was her finance charge on the balance in part (a) if her APR is 19.2 percent?

   (c) What was her average daily balance for April with new purchases?

   (d) What was her finance charge on the balance in part (c) if her APR is 19.2 percent?

3. **Average Daily Balance.** Elizabeth Mountbatten, a biologist from Lexington, Kentucky, is curious about the accuracy of the average daily balance shown on her most recent credit card billing statement, which appears in Figure 7.2 on page 203. Use the posting dates for her account to calculate her average daily balance and compare the result with the amount shown on the statement.

4. **Comparing APRs.** Timothy Sprater of Reno, Nevada, has been shopping for a loan to buy a new car. He wants to borrow $18,000 for four or five years. Timothy's credit union offers a declining-balance loan at 9.1 percent for 48 months, resulting in a monthly payment of $448.78. The credit union does not offer five-year auto loans for amounts less than $20,000, however. If Timothy borrowed $18,000, this payment would strain his budget. A local bank offered current depositors a five-year loan at a 9.34 percent APR, with a monthly payment of $376.62. This credit would not be a declining-balance loan. Because Timothy is not a depositor in the bank, he would also be charged a $25 credit check fee and a $45 application fee. Timothy likes the lower payment but knows that the APR is the true cost of credit, so he decided to confirm the APRs for both loans before making his decision.

(a) What is the APR for the credit union loan?

(b) Use the n-ratio formula to confirm the APR on the bank loan as quoted for depositors.

(c) What is the add-on interest rate for the bank loan?

(d) What would be the true APR on the bank loan if Timothy did not open an account to avoid the credit check and application fees?

5. **Rule of 78s.** Aaron Carson of Bishop, California, obtained a two-year installment loan for $1500 to buy some furniture eight months ago. The loan had a 12.6 percent APR and a finance charge of $204.72. His monthly payment is $71.03. Aaron has made eight monthly payments and now wants to pay off the remainder of the loan. The lender will use the rule of 78s method to calculate a prepayment penalty.

(a) How much will Aaron need to give the lender to pay off the loan?

(b) What is the dollar amount of the prepayment penalty on this loan?

Financial Planning Cases

Case 1

A Delayed Report of a Stolen Credit Card

Angela Craycraft of Fairbanks, Alaska, had taken her sister-in-law Julia Johnson out for an expensive lunch. When it came time to pay the bill, Joan noticed that her Visa credit card was missing, so she paid the bill with her MasterCard. While driving home, Angela remembered that she had last used the Visa card about a week earlier. She became concerned that a sales clerk or someone else could have taken it and might be fraudulently charging purchases on her card.

(a) Summarize Angela's legal rights in this situation.

(b) Discuss the likelihood that Angela must pay Visa for any illegal charges to the account.

Case 2

Clauses in a Car Purchase Contract

Virginia Rowland is a dentist in Hattiesburg, Mississippi, who recently entered into a contract to buy a new automobile. After signing to finance $18,000, she hurriedly left the office of the sales finance company with her copy of the contract. Later that evening, Virginia read the contract and noticed several clauses—an acceleration clause, a repossession clause, and a rule of 78s clause. When she signed the contract, Virginia was told these standard clauses should not concern her.

(a) Should Virginia be concerned about these clauses? Why or why not?

(b) Considering the rule of 78s clause, what will happen if Virginia pays off the loan before the regular due date?

(c) If Virginia had financed the $18,000 for four years at 7 percent APR, what would her monthly payment be, using the information in Table 7.1 or on the *Garman/Forgue* companion website?

Case 3

Victor and Maria Have a Billing Dispute

Maria Hernandez was reviewing her recent bank credit card account statement when she found two charges that she and Victor could not have made. The charges were for rental of a hotel room and purchase of a meal on the same day in a distant city. These charges totaled $219.49 out of the couple's $367.89 balance for the month.

(a) What payment should Maria make on the account?

(b) How should she notify her credit card issuer about the unauthorized use?

(c) Once the matter is resolved, what should Maria do to ensure that her credit history is not negatively affected by this error?

Case 4

The Johnsons' Credit Questions

Harry and Belinda need some questions answered regarding credit. Their seven-year-old car has been experiencing mechanical problems lately. Instead of buying a new set of tires, as planned for in March, they are considering trading the car in for a newer used vehicle so that Harry can have dependable transportation for commuting to work. The couple still owes $3600 to the bank for their current car, or $285 per month for the remaining 18 months of the 48-month loan. The trade-in value of this car plus $1000 that Harry earned from a freelance interior design job should allow the couple to pay off the auto loan and leave $1250 for a down payment on the newer car. The Johnsons have agreed on a sales price for the newer car of $14,250. The money planned for tires will be spent for other incidental taxes and fees associated with the purchase.

(a) Make recommendations to Harry and Belinda regarding where to seek financing and what APR to expect.

(b) Using the *Garman/Forgue* companion website or the information in Table 7.1, calculate the monthly payment for a loan period of three, four, and five years at 8 percent APR. Describe the relationship between the loan period and the payment amount.

(c) Harry and Belinda have a cash-flow deficit projected for several months this year (see Tables 3.8 and 3.9 on pages 90 and 91). Suggest how, when, and where they might finance the shortages by borrowing.

On the 'Net

Go to the Web pages indicated to complete these exercises.

1. Visit the website for Bankrate.com at http://www .bankrate.com/brm/rate/cc_home.asp, where you will find information on bank credit card interest rates around the United States. View the information for the lenders in a large city nearest your home. How does the information compare with the interest rates charged on your own credit card account(s)? How do the rates in the city you selected compare with those found elsewhere in the United States?

2. Visit the website for Interest.com at http://auto-loan .interest.com/index.asp. There you will find an auto loan calculator that determines the monthly payment for any declining-balance loan given a specified time period, interest rate, and loan amount. Assume you wish to borrow $12,000 to buy a car. Vary the time period and interest rate of the loan to see how these variations affect your monthly payment.

3. Do you owe money on one or more credit cards? Visit the Bankrate.com website at www.bankrate.com and click on "More calculators" to find a calculator that will tell you how long it will take to pay off your balances.

Visit the Garman/Forgue companion website . . .

www.cengage.com/finance/garman

Vehicle and Other Major Purchases

!You Must Be Kidding, Right?

When Ryan Levelle graduated from college three years ago, he really wanted a fully equipped Honda Civic. His monthly payment would be about $350 per month, about $70 more than he could afford. So that Ryan could meet his budget, the dealer suggested that he lease the vehicle and offered a 42-month lease option at $270 per month with a driving maximum of 12,000 miles per year. The contract had a $0.30 per mile fee at the end of the lease for any excess mileage. Now, with six more months on his lease, Ryan is already 1500 miles over the 42,000 (3.5 × 12,000) mileage limit in his contract. What is Ryan's best option at this point?

A. Turn back the vehicle now and pay the $450 (1500 × $0.30) for excess mileage.

B. Try to cut back on his driving to minimize his excess mileage fee, which could be higher than $2500 if he keeps driving at the same rate as he has been.

C. Stop driving the car and pay $450 for excess mileage when he turns it back at the end of the lease.

D. Continue driving the vehicle and buy it at the end of the lease by paying the residual value agreed upon when he entered into the contract.

The answer is D. None of the other options is financially practical. Ryan learned a hard lesson. Leases require a lower monthly payment but have hidden costs that often are not known until the very end of the contract!

Learning Objectives

After reading this chapter, you should be able to:

1 Explain the three steps in the planned buying process that occur prior to interacting with sellers.

2 Describe the five aspects of major purchases that require comparison shopping.

3 Negotiate and decide effectively when making major purchases.

4 Evaluate your purchase decisions and, if necessary, effectively seek redress.

What Do You Recommend?

Photodisc/Alamy

David and Lisa Cosgrove of Tacoma, Washington, are in their early 40s and have three children. They own three vehicles. Lisa drives an almost-new Toyota Camry; David uses a five-year-old Ford pickup; and Amber, the couple's 17-year-old daughter, drives a ten-year-old Dodge. Recently, a fire in their garage destroyed both the Dodge and the Camry. The Cosgroves received an insurance settlement of $21,900 on Lisa's car, although the loan payoff amount was $22,800. Amber's Dodge was not insured for fire. The couple wants to obtain replacement cars that are similar to those destroyed.

What do you recommend to David and Lisa on automobiles and other major purchases regarding:

1. How to search for two vehicles to replace those destroyed?

2. Whether to replace Lisa's vehicle with a new or used vehicle?

3. Whether to lease or buy a vehicle?

4. How to decide between a rebate and a special low APR financing opportunity if they decide to purchase a new vehicle for Lisa?

5. How to negotiate with the sellers of the vehicles?

planned buying
Thinking through all the details of a purchase from the initial desire to buy to your satisfaction after the purchase.

Planned buying entails thinking about the details of a purchase from the initial desire to buy to your satisfaction after the purchase. You should use planned buying principles any time, but they are especially important when you are buying a car or making other "big ticket" purchases during difficult economic times. The seven distinct steps that lead you through the planned buying process are illustrated in Figure 8.1. Steps 1, 2, and 3 occur before you interact with sellers: determining your needs and wants, performing preshopping research, and fitting a purchase into your budget. Comparison shopping and other interactions with sellers comprise the fourth step in the buying process. Steps 5 and 6—negotiating and making the decision—follow. The seventh and final step—evaluation of the decision—is taken after making the purchase. After reading this chapter, you will understand enough about the planned buying process to save money when buying expensive goods while still meeting your needs and many of your wants.

Do Your Homework

1 Learning Objective

Explain the three steps in the planned buying process that occur prior to interacting with sellers.

Let's look now at the first three steps, all of which should occur before you actually interact with sellers. They are, in a sense, the homework you do when preparing to buy.

What Do You Really Want?

need
Item thought to be necessary.

want
Item not necessary but desired.

A **need** is something thought to be a necessity; a **want** is unnecessary but desired. In truth, very few needs exist, yet in everyday language people talk often of "needing" certain things. In the planned buying process, it is best to avoid such thinking because once something is called a need, it may no longer be open to careful consideration. Instead, you should consider all purchase options to be wants. Of course, some wants are very important. The most important can be determined by prioritizing your wants. This approach allows for careful consideration of the benefits and costs of the options available. Costs should include opportunity costs as measured by some other goal or want that will become less attainable if a given want is satisfied. For example, buying a car with a retractable sunroof might mean that you cannot afford to purchase one with a remote start feature.

Setting priorities becomes more difficult when a decision is complex such as when buying a car or home. Consider the case of Sharon Wilson, a respiratory therapist from St. Paul, Minnesota. Sharon has been late to work several times in the past few months because her 12-year-old car has been having mechanical problems. Sharon wants to avoid being late. But, how? Should she buy a new car, a used car, lease a new car, repair her current car, or

preshopping research
Gathering information before actually beginning to interact with sellers.

Figure 8.1
The Steps in Planned Buying

7 Evaluating the decision
6 Making the decision
5 Negotiating
4 Comparison shopping
3 Fitting your budget
2 Preshopping research
1 Prioritizing wants

Did You Know?

How to Buy Smart

Buying wisely can save you 10 or more percent of your income during the course of a year. That sure beats trying for a 10 percent raise that may or may not be received. Smart buyers should practice the following habits:

Do Not Buy on Impulse

Buying without fully considering priorities and alternatives is called **impulse buying.** For example, let's say you're looking for a laptop computer and you decide to buy one on sale at a discount store. While at the store, you pick up two video games that you had not planned to buy. The extra $150 spent on the unplanned purchase ruins most of the benefits of your careful shopping for the computer itself.

Pay Cash

Paying cash whenever possible can save money in two ways. First, it helps control impulse buying, which is a temptation when you're paying with a credit card. Second, using credit adds to the cost of items you buy.

Buy at the Right Time

You can save $5 or $10 a week on food simply by stocking up on advertised specials. New cars are least expensive at the end of the month and the model year. Many items, such as sporting goods and clothing, are marked down near certain holidays and at the end of each season. But be certain that what you buy on sale is something you will really use.

Do Not Pay Extra for a "Name"

Buying generic and store-brand products represents a good way to save money. **Generic products** are sold under a general commodity name such as "whole-kernel corn" rather than a brand name such as Del Monte. Store-brand products, such as those sold by Sears (Kenmore), Kroger, or Safeway, are actually made by the brand-name manufacturers. Gasoline, vitamins, medicines, laundry and other soaps, and many grocery items are all products with minor quality differences.

Recognize the High Price of Convenience

Buying a few items daily at a convenience store rather than using a shopping list during a weekly visit to a supermarket can raise food bills by perhaps 30 percent. Shopping for furniture and appliances in one's local community may be convenient, but better prices on the same items may be found in larger, more competitive shopping areas or online.

take the bus to work? After considering these options, Sharon decided to buy a new car. Now she must determine which features are of high or low priority. To do so, Sharon developed the worksheet shown in Figure 8.2. Such a worksheet makes it easier to formalize her wants and helps Sharon decide on the right car for her.

Become an Expert

Smart shoppers learn as much as they can about a product or service before buying. This process starts with **preshopping research**— gathering information before actually beginning to interact with sellers. Manufacturers, sellers, and service providers are all important sources of information about products and services during preshopping research. Two other sources are friends and consumer magazines. If you know someone who drives a car you're considering, ask that person's opinion of it. You can also research the car in *Consumer Reports*, a magazine that objectively tests and reports on numerous product categories. Monthly issues of *Consumer Reports* generally provide a two- to five-page narrative analyzing the products and summarizing the information in chart form. *Consumer Reports Buying Guide*, which is published every December, lists facts and figures for all kinds of products. And each year, the April issue of *Consumer Reports* is devoted entirely to the purchase of automobiles. All this and more can be seen at www.ConsumerReports.org.

Your Next Five Years

In the next five years you can start achieving financial success by doing the following related to vehicles and other major purchases:

1. Check repair ratings history in the April issue of *Consumer Reports* magazine when planning to buy vehicles.

2. Purchase late-model, high-quality used vehicles and check their ownership history at www.carfax .com and any recall history at www.nhtsa.gov.

3. Obtain price information from at least three sources and aggressively negotiate prices and financing terms for major purchases.

4. Never tell a seller what payment you can afford.

5. Promptly and firmly seek redress when dissatisfied with purchases or services.

Figure 8.2
Priority Worksheet
(for Sharon Wilson)

AUTOMOBILE FEATURE	PRIORITY LEVEL		
	1	2	3
Adjustable steering column			✔
Side-impact airbags		✔	
Air conditioning		✔	
AM-FM radio	✔		
Antilock brakes		✔	
Automatic transmission	✔		
Keyless locking system	✔		
CD player			✔
Cruise control		✔	
4-Wheel (all-wheel) drive			✔
Power windows	✔		
Rear-window defroster	✔		
Sun roof / moon roof			✔
Theft-deterrent system			✔

Time invested in preshopping research pays off in better purchase decisions.

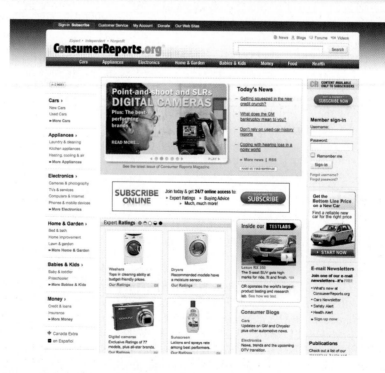

When shopping for any product, it may help to review publications dedicated to the topic, such as *Popular Photography, PC World, Car and Driver,* and *Sound & Vision.* Keep in mind, however, that these trade magazines accept advertising for the products on which they report and thus are not likely to be as unbiased as *Consumer Reports,* which does not accept any advertising. Another unbiased source of information on wise buying (and many other personal finance topics) is the federal government's Consumer Information Center (www.pueblo.gsa.gov).

What Price Should You Expect to Pay?

Advertising is often a key source of information about prices. You can also obtain price information through catalogs, on the telephone, and over the Internet. This situation differs for big-ticket items. While the prices of furniture, appliances, and vehicles may be advertised, that price is rarely the lowest price you can expect to pay. This is because sellers typically have the authority to negotiate an even lower price, if necessary, to make a sale; you can really bargain for a deal during sluggish economic times. Buyers should have a very good idea what price to expect to pay before going out to shop. Otherwise, they risk negotiating a price higher than necessary.

A key piece of price information for vehicles is the **manufacturer's suggested retail price (MSRP)**, which is aptly named because it is simply the suggested initial asking price. On new automobiles, the MSRP—called the **sticker price**—appears on a window sticker in the vehicle. There is often a **dealer sticker price** as well, which includes additional charges tacked on by the dealer; many of these are nothing more than attempts to generate additional revenue. The sticker prices should in no way be seen as the price that needs to be paid for a new vehicle or other big-ticket item. Instead, it should be viewed as a starting point for negotiations. Smart buyers can research the average retail and wholesale prices on new and used vehicles by visiting the websites for Edmunds (www.edmunds.com), Kelley Blue Book (www.kbb.com), or the National Automobile Dealers Association (www.nadaguides.com).

What Is a Fair Interest Rate?

Major purchases are often bought on credit. Interest rates for all types of loans, including vehicle loans, can be found at www.bankrate.com. Buyers should obtain multiple quotes from banks and credit unions. When shopping for a major purchase, ask your local bank or credit union for a **loan preapproval** before you visit sellers. This preshopping step will let you know how much you can borrow and at what interest rate.

A source of loans for new vehicles is sales financing arranged through the dealer or manufacturer. The interest rate on this credit is often low when manufacturers or dealers want to generate additional sales volume. The buyer must often choose between low-rate financing and a rebate (discussed later). See the Run the Numbers worksheet, "Choosing Between Low-Interest-Rate Dealer Financing and a Rebate," on page 224 for instructions on how to compare rebates, dealer/manufacturer financing, and other financing options.

Is a Rebate Available?

Many sellers offer rebates to encourage people to buy. With a **rebate**, the seller refunds a portion of the purchase price of the product either as a direct payment or a credit against future purchases (often through a gift card). Vehicle manufacturers offer rebates of $1000 to $5000 to purchasers of new vehicles as a way to generate more sales volume or to move slow-selling models. In most cases, the buyer must choose between the rebate and a low APR loan offer also being offered by the manufacturer. Many people choose to borrow the full price elsewhere and receive the rebate in cash. In effect, this option means that they are borrowing more money than the vehicle actually costs. Plus, the buyers also lose out on the opportunity for the low APR offer. The Run the Numbers Worksheet on the next page provides a way to calculate whether a rebate or the low APR financing is the better option. If you do decide to take the rebate on a new vehicle, you should apply the money to the down payment on the vehicle or pay extra on the first monthly payment on the loan. Rebates are common when purchasing products such as vehicles, cell phones, and computers. Why don't sellers simply lower the price of the item? First, rebate offers are temporary and thus do not affect the regular price of the item. Second, purchasers fail to redeem a high percentage

Instant Message

Buying Is Not Saving

Retailers love to say "buy now and save." When you buy something on sale, however, you aren't saving money—you are spending it.

Did You Know?

The Top 3 Financial Missteps in Big-Ticket Purchases

People slip up in purchasing vehicles and other big-ticket items when they do the following:

1. Rely upon the seller as their source of information for price, financing terms, and/or trade-in value

2. Tell a seller what they can afford to pay (because the seller can then avoid disclosing their lowest price)

3. Fail to complain when products fail to perform as expected

manufacturer's suggested retail price (MSRP)/ sticker price
Suggested initial asking price.

loan preapproval
Oral commitment from a bank or credit union agreeing to furnish credit for a purchase; lets buyers know how much they can borrow and at what interest rate.

rebate
A partial refund of a purchase price offered as an inducement to buy.

Run the Numbers

Choosing Between Low-Interest-Rate Dealer Financing and a Rebate

Advertisements for new vehicles often offer low APRs for dealer-arranged loans. A cash rebate of $1000 to $3000 (or more) off the price of the car may be offered as an alternative to the low interest rate. If you intend to pay cash, then the cash rebate obviously represents the better deal. But which alternative is better when you can arrange your own financing?

To compare the two APRs accurately, you must add the opportunity cost of the forgone rebate to the finance charge of the dealer financing. The worksheet provides an example of this process. Suppose a dealer offers 2.9 percent financing for three years with a $907 finance charge; alternatively, you can receive a $3000 rebate if you arrange your own financing. The price of the car before the rebate is $22,000. Assume you can make a $2000 down payment and that you can get a 6.5 percent loan on your own. This worksheet can be found on the *Garman/Forgue* companion website, or you can find similar worksheets at www.bankrate.com (search for "calculators") or www.kiplingers.com/tools.

The lower of the values obtained in steps 3 and 4 is the better deal. In this instance, the financing that you arranged on your own is more attractive. In fact, any loan you arrange that carries an APR lower than 12 percent compares favorably with the dealer-arranged financing in this case.

Step		Example	Your Figures
1.	Determine the dollar amount of the rebate.	$3000	_____
2.	Add the rebate amount to the finance charge for the dealer financing (dollar cost of credit).	+ $ 907	_____
3.	Use the n-ratio APR formula from Chapter 7 (Equation [7.2] on page 211 and replicated here as Equation [8.1]) to calculate an adjusted APR for the dealer financing.		

$$APR = \frac{Y(95P + 9)F}{12P(P + 1)(4D + F)} \qquad (8.1)$$

where

APR = **Annual percentage rate**

Y = Number of payment periods in one **year**

F = **Finance** charge in dollars

D = **Debt** (amount borrowed)

P = Total number of scheduled **payments**

$$APR = \frac{(12)[(95 \times 36) + 9]($3000 + $907)}{(12 \times 36)(36 + 1)[(4 \times $20,000) + ($3000 + $907)]} = 12\%$$

4.	Write in the APR that you arranged on your own.	6.5%	_____

(approaching 40 percent for some products) of rebates, which results in more profit for the seller. The most current details on manufacturers' rebates to both consumers and auto dealers can be found at Edmunds (www.Edmunds.com).

What Is My Trade-in Worth?   When buying vehicles, it is common, but not always advantageous, to trade in an old model when buying a new one. Vehicle buyers should know the true value of any vehicle they will trade in. Used-car trade-in values are available on the websites for Edmunds (www.edmunds.com), Kelley Blue Book (www.kbb.com), or the

Did You Know?

About "Gap" Insurance

New cars and low-mileage used cars depreciate (go down in value) very quickly after purchase, often as much as 25 percent after leaving the dealer's lot. If you take out a vehicle loan with a low down payment, it is possible that the value of the vehicle will go down faster than the amount owed. As a result, you can owe more on the vehicle than it is worth. This situation is referred to as being "upside down" and can last for up to two years after the initial purchase.

Being upside down can be a big problem when a newer vehicle is totaled in an accident. In such cases, the insurance company will reimburse for the value of the vehicle, not the amount owed on the loan. Many car dealers sell "gap" insurance that pays off the remainder of the loan if the insurance payment is insufficient to do so. While gap insurance is attractive, it is very profitable for the dealer and not such a good deal for the buyer. You should consider the possibility of being upside down as a sign that you are not making a large enough down payment or that you are buying a vehicle that is too expensive for you.

National Automobile Dealers Association (www.nadaguides.com). There you can find the likely trade-in value of the vehicle and the amount you could sell it for yourself. Armed with this information, you can more effectively negotiate a good trade-in allowance on your existing vehicle with a dealer.

Can I Afford It?

When considering a big-ticket item everyone wonders, "Can I afford it?" An unaffordable cash purchase can wreck your budget for one or two months; the negative effects of an ill-advised credit purchase, however, may last for years.

One way to view the cost of a major expenditure is to consider the cost per use of the product. For example, Paul Lenz, an autoworker

Instant Message

What Is an Informed Shopper?

Smart shoppers recognize that the seller is not an objective source of information. When making major purchases, you should go into the process with knowledge of what the item should cost, an appropriate interest rate if you will use credit, the availability of a rebate, and the value of any trade-in.

Did You Know?

The Truth About Rebates

You have seen the advertisements. Buy a new cell phone, computer printer, and many other products at a spectacularly low price. Then below the price are those dreaded words "after mail-in rebate." In order to boost sales, manufacturers of products could lower prices but why do that when they can offer a rebate that has only a 50 percent chance of being successfully redeemed? Yes, that is the average according to the Federal Trade Commission and the rate is even lower for products costing under $50. Why are so few rebates redeemed? Partly it is the consumer who messes up by waiting too long, making an error in the application or simply forgetting to redeem the rebate in the first place. But sellers are to blame as well. They often make the rules for redemption so difficult that the consumer is bound to make a mistake. How can you protect yourself?

1. **Comparison shop** to make sure you can't get the product somewhere else at a similar price without having to redeem a rebate.

2. **Read the rebate rules** carefully before buying. If the process seems too complicated, reconsider the purchase.

3. **Complete the form** as soon as you get home from making the purchase.

4. **Make photocopies** of all the paperwork that you send with the rebate.

5. **Follow your rebate** through the process using the Web tracking mechanism if one is provided.

6. **Complain** to your state's consumer protection office if your rebate does not arrive.

from Dothan, Alabama, is considering buying a high-quality video camera. He has researched several models in the $700 to $750 price range. Paul figures that he would use the camera about 20 times per year and knows that the average video camera lasts about seven years, giving him 140 uses. Dividing this figure into the price of a $700 model yields a cost per use of $5 ($700 ÷ 140), excluding the cost of videotapes and maintenance. It might be possible for Paul to save money by renting or borrowing a camera when he needs one. Or he could buy a less expensive camera.

To see how this process works with a more expensive purchase, consider how Sharon Wilson (see Table 8.1) might fit a new car into her budget. She estimates that the base sticker price of the car she wants will be about $16,000. This price includes her highest-priority wants. The lower-priority options will likely add a total of $2300 to the sticker price: side-impact airbags, $700; air conditioning, $700; antilock brakes, $600; and cruise control, $300. Buying a car with these features might cost Sharon $19,500 ($16,000 + $2300 for the options + $1200 for sales tax and title registration). She can use $2500 from her savings account as a down payment, receive $2000 for trading in her old car, and borrow the remaining $15,000. The actual price she will pay for the car will depend on her ability to negotiate the final price down from the sticker price. From her preshopping research, Sharon knows that the invoice price will be about 12 percent less than the sticker price, giving her some bargaining room. For example, Sharon might negotiate the price of the car down by 10 percent to $17,550 [$19,500 − ($19,500 × 0.10)].

The monthly payment that Sharon must fit into her budget will depend on five factors:

- Price she actually pays for the car
- Down payment she makes

Advice from a Pro...

Tips for Buying Online

People use the Internet to shop for appliances, vehicles, furniture, and other big-ticket items. Here's how you can become a better online shopper:

1. **Use only secure sites.** A secure site will feature a key or lock symbol on its screens or have a URL starting with "https" ("s" for secure). Sites displaying the VeriSign symbol must meet certain security standards.

2. **Only do business** with sellers for which you have complete contact information, including a "snail mail" (postal) address and telephone number.

3. **Review shipping policies** and costs as well as return policies before placing your order.

4. **Never use a debit card** for online purchasing. When the debit card transaction is executed, your cash is immediately transferred from your account to the seller's account. It may be difficult to persuade a seller to give you a refund when you pay by debit card. Purchases made via credit cards give you more protection because you may be able to ask that a purchase be charged back (see Chapter 6).

5. **Print and keep copies** of all purchase documents, warranties, credit card authorizations, and shipping notices.

6. **Use only one particular credit card** for online purchases. This practice will serve you well if your account number is stolen. In such a case, you can notify the one credit card issuer of the theft and block the card's future use without affecting your other accounts.

7. **Check the site's privacy policy.** Sites that display the TRUSTe symbol or Better Business Bureau Online seal have agreed to meet certain privacy standards.

8. **Opt out** of any list sharing that the seller might conduct with other merchants.

9. **Do not use your regular e-mail address.** Set up a free address at Yahoo!, Hotmail, or other provider and use it solely for online transactions. This will reduce the spam coming into your everyday e-mail account.

Brenda J. Cude
University of Georgia

Table 8.1 Fitting a Vehicle Payment into a Monthly Budget

	Prior Budget	Possible Cutbacks	New Budget
Food	$ 250	$ −30	$ 220
Clothing/laundry	120	−50	70
Vehicle maintenance and repairs	75	−50	25
Auto insurance	60	20	80
Gasoline	90	−20	70
Housing	450		450
Utilities	80		80
Telephone	50		50
Entertainment	150	−50	100
Gifts	50	−10	40
Church and charity	60		60
Personal care	60	−10	50
Savings	200	−50	150
Miscellaneous	70	−20	50
TOTAL	**$1,765**	**$−270**	**$1,495**
Car payment			318
TOTAL WITH CAR PAYMENT	**$1,765**	**$−270**	**$1,813**

- Time period for payback of the loan
- Amount she receives in trade for her old car
- Interest rate on the loan

For illustration, we will choose a down payment of $2500 and assume a 48-month time period (a common financing term). Sharon figures that she can get no more than $2000 for her old car. But what about the actual price and interest rate? Assuming that Sharon can reduce the price by 10 percent, she will need to borrow $13,050 ($17,550 − $2500 down − $2000 trade-in). If she obtains a loan with an 8 percent APR (based on her loan preapproval), Sharon estimates that her monthly payment would be about $318 (13.05 × 24.41, from Table 7.1 on page 209).

Table 8.1 shows Sharon's monthly budget. Her monthly take-home pay of $1765 is totally committed. To buy the automobile with options, she will need $318 per month and will have to change her budget drastically. For example, she could cut food expenditures ($30 per month); spend less on clothing ($50); cut entertainment, gifts, personal care, and miscellaneous items ($50, $10, $10, and $20, respectively); and put $50 less in savings (she was saving to buy a vehicle). In addition, her transportation-related expenses would change as follows: gasoline, −$20; maintenance and repairs, −$50; and insurance costs, +$20. (Always get an insurance quote before buying a vehicle.) In all, these efforts would raise only $270, still $48 short of the amount she needs for the car. Sharon's alternatives are to make more cutbacks in her budget, work overtime, or get a parttime job. She could also reduce her payments to about $264 per month by taking out a longer, 60-month loan (13.05 × $20.28, from Table 7.1 on page 209). She should be wary about having to operate on such a tight budget for five years, however. Sharon will pay much more in interest with a longer-term loan and might want to consider a less expensive new car or a used car.

Concept Check 8.1

1. What is planned buying?
2. Distinguish between *needs* and *wants,* and explain why it may be better to act as if no needs exist.
3. Describe the types of information you need to be your own expert when making big-ticket purchases.
4. Summarize the process to determine whether you can afford a particular purchase.

Use Comparison Shopping to Find the Best Buy

2 Learning Objective

Describe the five aspects of major purchases that require comparison shopping.

comparison shopping
Process of comparing products or services to find the best buy.

best buy
Product or service that, in the buyer's opinion, represents acceptable quality at a fair or low price for that quality level.

After completing the first three steps in planned buying, it is time to begin interacting with sellers. These interactions begin with comparison shopping. **Comparison shopping** is the process of comparing products or services to find the best buy. A **best buy** is a product or service that, in the buyer's opinion, represents acceptable quality at a fair or low price for that level of quality. Purchasing the product with the lowest price does not necessarily ensure a best buy; quality and features count, too. You can begin your comparison shopping online, but most likely you will need to visit different stores and talk to sellers directly.

Comparison shopping takes time and effort, but the payoff in both satisfaction and savings can be considerable. During the early steps in the comparison shopping process, shoppers should narrow their choices to specific makes and models and desired options. Then they should visit the appropriate sellers again. This time, shoppers will be much closer to the decision to buy and will be ready to discuss details, although they should not buy at this point. When comparison shopping, tell the salesperson exactly what interests you and ask about price and any dealer incentives and rebates that apply. You should inquire about financing options, leasing, warranties, and service contracts. Finally, test-drive the vehicle. The goal is to narrow the choice even further prior to negotiating for the very best deal, which is the next step in the buying process.

Compare Prices Using the "Rule of Three"

Prices on big-ticket items such as autos, furniture, appliances, and electronic equipment are rarely the same from seller to seller and vary from week to week. Hundreds or even thousands of dollars can be saved by searching for the best prices. Experts recommend use of the **"rule of three,"** which says to compare at least three alternatives before making any decision. When buying a car, compare the prices you find at dealers with the information from one of the websites devoted to vehicle prices listed on page 233.

Compare Financing Options

Sellers are not the only source of financing. Your bank or credit union loans money to make purchases. Also use websites such as bankrate .com or interest.com. Be on the lookout for "same as cash" offers on furniture, appliances, and electronics that allow you to delay interest or payment for, perhaps, 90 days to one year. If the product is paid off during this time period, you will not incur any finance charges. Be wary, however. Interest may be charged retroactively if a payment is late or if the purchase isn't fully paid off during the required time period.

Instant Message

Guard Your Privacy

Do not give out your Social Security number or allow the dealer to photocopy your driver's license before you go on a test drive. With that information the dealer can then access your credit report and estimate how much you can afford to pay and your ability to obtain financing elsewhere.

Did You Know?

The Keys to a Safe Car

The following pointers may help you buy a safer vehicle:

- **Check government safety test results.** The federal government crash-tests motor vehicles to analyze their safety. For results on various makes and models, call the National Highway Traffic Safety Administration (NHTSA) "auto hotline" at (800) 424-9393 or visit www.safercar .gov.
- **Check on recalls.** When buying a used car, visit www .nhtsa.gov to see whether the vehicle has been recalled. If so, confirm that the repairs have been made to the car you're considering; if not, buy elsewhere. Dealers are required to fix for free vehicles recalled for safety reasons.

- **Consider a model with additional airbags.** All new cars have driver and passenger front-seat airbags. For added protection, consider new and used models that also provide side-impact airbags.
- **Look for antilock brakes.** Antilock brakes are believed to reduce the possibility of skidding during sudden stops. They are especially helpful in rain and inclement winter conditions.
- **Think about theft.** Some makes and models of vehicles are much more attractive to thieves than others. These vehicles also require higher auto insurance premiums. Visit www.nhtsa.gov and search "vehicle theft ratings."

Consider Leasing Instead of Buying

Leasing a new vehicle is an increasingly attractive option to people who are in the market for a car. About 20 percent of the new cars "sold" each year are actually leased. It is even possible to lease used cars. Is leasing a better deal than financing? You cannot answer this question until you understand some basics of leasing.

When **leasing** a vehicle or any other product, you are, in effect, renting the product while the ownership title remains with the lease grantor. Regulation M issued by the Federal Reserve Board governs lease contracts. A requirement of this regulation is a mandatory disclosure of pertinent information about the lease that the consumer is considering. The disclosure form must summarize the offer of the **lessor** (leasing agency) to the **lessee** (consumer). The information in this form should be compared with the actual lease contract prior to signing to ensure that the lease signed is actually what was agreed upon verbally.

leasing
Renting a product while ownership title remains with lease grantor.

Leasing Terminology   Five terms are important in leasing:

1. **The gross capitalized cost (gross cap cost)** includes the price of the vehicle plus what the lessee paid to finance the purchase plus any other items the lessee agreed to pay for over the life of the lease, including insurance or a maintenance agreement.

2. **Capitalized cost reductions (cap cost reductions)** are monies paid on the lease at its inception, including any down payment, trade-in value, or rebate.

3. **The adjusted capitalized cost (adjusted cap cost)** is determined by subtracting the capitalized cost reductions from the gross capitalized cost.

4. **The residual value** is the projected value of a leased asset at the end of the lease time period.

5. **The money factor** (or **lease rate** or **lease factor**) measures the rent charge portion of your payment. Although the money factor is sometimes described by dealers as a figure for comparing leases, lease forms must carry the following disclosure about the money factor: "This percentage may not measure the overall cost of financing this lease."

gross capitalized cost (gross cap cost)
Includes vehicle price plus cost of any extra features such as insurance or maintenance agreements.

adjusted capitalized cost (adjusted cap cost)
Subtracting the capitalized cost reductions from the gross capitalized cost.

residual value
Projected value of leased asset at end of lease time period.

Rule number one when considering leasing: Always negotiate the purchase price before discussing a lease! Leasing requires an initial outlay of cash to pay for the first month's lease payment and a security deposit. Payments are based on the capitalized cost of the asset minus any capitalized cost reductions and the residual value. This difference represents the cost of

Instant Message

Buying Your Leased Vehicle

With either an open- or closed-end lease you may purchase the vehicle at the end of the lease period. With an open-end lease, you would pay the actual cash value. With a closed-end lease you would pay the residual value.

closed-end lease/ walkaway lease
Agreement in which the lessee pays no charge if the end-of-lease market value of the vehicle is lower than the originally projected residual value.

using the asset during the lease period; when divided by the number of months in the contract, it serves to establish the base for the monthly lease payment. (Some new vehicles are offered with single-payment leases in which the entire difference between the capitalized cost and residual value is paid up front.) With monthly payment leases, the payments are lower than monthly loan payments for equivalent time periods because you are paying for only the reduction in the asset's value—not its entire cost. To compare the costs of leasing versus buying, use the Decision-Making Worksheet, "Comparing Automobile Financing and Leasing."

Open- and Closed-End Leases   A lease may be either open end or closed end. In an **open-end lease,** you must pay any difference between the projected residual value of the vehicle and its actual market value at the end of the lease period. When a vehicle depreciates more rapidly than expected, the holder of an open-end lease has to pay extra money when the lease expires. For example, a vehicle with an $11,000 residual value but a $10,250 market value would require an end-of-lease payment of $750 ($11,000 − $10,250). The Consumer Leasing Act limits this end-of-lease payment to a maximum of three times the average monthly payment.

Most vehicle leases are closed-end leases. In a **closed-end lease** (also called a **walkaway lease**), the holder pays no charge if the end-of-lease market value of the vehicle is lower than the originally projected residual value. However, closed-end leases may carry some type of end-of-lease charge if the vehicle has greater than normal wear or excess mileage. For example, a four-year closed-end lease might require a $0.30 per mile

Run the Numbers

Comparing Automobile Financing and Leasing

This worksheet can be used to compare leasing and borrowing to buy a vehicle. Remember that the cost of credit is the finance charge—the extra that you pay because you borrowed. Leases also carry costs, but they are hidden in the contract. Indeed, some may remain unknown until the end of the lease period. These lease costs, which are indicated by an asterisk (*), are negotiable and are defined in the text. Ask the dealer for the price of each item, as these fees must be disclosed by dealers. Then complete the worksheet and compare the dollar cost of leasing with the finance charge on a loan for the same time period.

To make the comparison accurately, you must know the underlying price of the car as if you were purchasing it. Often you are not offered this value with a lease arrangement, so you should always negotiate a price for the vehicle before mentioning your interest in leasing.

Shop for a lease through dealers and independent leasing companies because costs vary widely. This worksheet can be found on the *Garman/Forgue* companion website, or you can find similar worksheets at www.bankrate.com (search for "calculators") or www.kiplingers.com/tools.

Step		Example	Your Figures
1.	Monthly lease payment (36 payments of $275, for example)	$ 9,900	_____
2.	Plus acquisition fee* (if any)	300	_____
	Plus disposition charge* (if any)	300	_____
	Plus estimate of excess mileage charges* (if any)	0	_____
	Plus projected residual value of the vehicle	4,500	_____
3.	Amount for which you are responsible under the lease	15,000	_____
4.	Less the adjusted capitalized cost (gross capitalized cost* less the capitalized cost reductions*)	12,600	_____
5.	Dollar cost of leasing to be compared with a finance charge if you purchased the vehicle	2,400	_____

excess mileage charge in excess of 55,000 miles. If you actually drove the vehicle 60,000 miles during the four years, you would be charged an extra $1500 [$0.30 × 5000 (60,000 − 55,000)].

Additional Leasing Fees   Other charges are possible with a lease. An **acquisition fee** is either paid in cash or included in the gross capitalization cost. It pays for a credit report, application fee, and other paperwork. A **disposition fee** is assessed when you turn in the vehicle at the end of the lease and the lessor must prepare it for resale. An **early termination charge** may also be levied if you decide to end the lease prematurely. Be wary of a lease with an early termination charge, even if you do not plan to end the lease early, because termination also occurs when a leased vehicle is traded in or is totally wrecked or stolen. Make sure you obtain a written disclosure of these charges well before you actually make your decision. The **early termination payoff** is the total amount you would need to repay if you end the lease agreement early; it includes both the early termination charge and the unpaid lease balance. In its early years, your lease may be financially upside down, which means that you owe more on the vehicle than it is worth.

Be Cautious About Leasing   Getting a good deal on any vehicle can be very complicated—leasing is even more so. First, be cautious if you talk about buying all through the negotiation process only to be offered a lease at the last minute. Because the monthly charge will be lower, you may be tempted to sign a deal that actually costs considerably more. Second, make sure all oral agreements related to trade-in value, mileage charges, and rebates are included in the lease contract. Third, watch out for additional fees being assessed, especially near the very end of the negotiations or in the final written lease.

One option for people considering a lease is a balloon automobile loan. You can arrange this type of financing through your bank or credit union. With a **balloon automobile loan,** you actually buy the vehicle with the last monthly payment equaling the projected residual value of the vehicle at the end of the loan period. This arrangement effectively lowers all the other earlier monthly payments to make them more competitive with lease payments. When the final balloon payment is due, perhaps $1000 to $7000, the borrower generally has three options:

1. **Sell the car** and pay the balloon payment with the proceeds (with luck, the vehicle will sell for a high enough amount).
2. **Pay the balloon payment** and keep the vehicle.
3. **Return the vehicle** to the lender to cover the balloon payment.

Compare Warranties

Warranties are an important consideration in comparison shopping. Almost all products have **warranties**—assurances by sellers that goods are as promised and that certain steps will be taken to rectify problems—even if only in the form of implied warranties. The longer the warranty and the more it covers, the better the warranty.

Under an **implied warranty,** the product sold is warranted to be suitable for sale (a **warranty of merchantability**) and to work effectively (a **warranty of fitness**) whether or not a written warranty exists. Implied warranties are required by state law. To avoid them, the seller can state in writing that the product is sold **as is.** If you buy any product "as is," you have no legal recourse if it fails to perform, even if the salesperson made verbal "promises" to take care of any problems. Used cars are often sold "as is."

Written and oral warranties are called **express warranties.** Companies that offer written express warranties must do so under the provisions of the federal Magnuson-Moss Warranty Act if the product is sold for more than $15. This law provides that any written warranty offered must be classified as either a full warranty or a limited warranty. A **full warranty** includes three stringent requirements:

1. A product must be fixed at no cost to the buyer within a reasonable time after the owner has complained.
2. The owner will not have to undertake an unreasonable task to return the product for repair (such as ship back a refrigerator).

---

excess mileage charge
Fees assessed at the end of a lease if the vehicle was driven more miles than originally specified in the lease contract.

balloon automobile loan
A loan that has a low monthly payment similar in amount to that required if the vehicle had been leased and with a large final payment similar in amount to the residual value under a lease.

warranty
Sellers' assurances that goods are as promised and that certain steps will be taken to rectify problems if they arise.

as is
Way for seller to get around legal requirements for warranties; buyer takes all risk of nonperformance or other problems despite any salesperson's verbal assurances.

full warranty
Warranty that meets three stringent promises: product must be fixed at no cost to buyer within reasonable time, owner will not have to undertake an unreasonable task to return product for repair, and defective product will be replaced with a new one or the buyer's money will be returned if product cannot be fixed.

3. A defective product will be replaced with a new one or the buyer's money will be returned if the product cannot be fixed after a reasonable number of attempts.

limited warranty
Any warranty that offers less than the three conditions for full warranty.

A **limited warranty** includes less than a full warranty. For example, it may offer only free parts, not labor. Note that one part of a product could be covered by a full warranty (perhaps the engine on a lawnmower) and the rest of the unit by a limited warranty. Read all warranties carefully, and note that both full and limited warranties are valid for only a specified time period.

Extended Warranties Are Overpriced

extended warranty/service contract/maintenance agreement/buyer protection plan
Agreement between the seller and buyer of product to repair or replace covered product components for some specified time period; purchased separately from product itself.

An **extended warranty** (or **service contract**) is an agreement between the contract seller (the dealer, manufacturer, or an independent company) and the buyer of a product to provide repair or replacement for covered components of the product for some specified time period. Extended warranties are sometimes given names such as **maintenance agreement** or **buyer protection plan.** These service contracts are purchased separately from the product itself (such as a vehicle, appliance, or electronics equipment). The cost is paid either in a lump sum or in monthly payments. Extended warranties are not insurance but act similarly. For example, a 40-inch LC HDTV could have an extended warranty that promises to fix anything that goes wrong during the third and fourth years of ownership; the manufacturer's warranty covers the first two years. This contract might cost $120 for one year, or $10 per month.

Although buying an extended warranty might provide peace of mind, it is unwise financially because it makes little economic sense to insure against risks that can, if necessary, be paid for out of current income or savings. Plus extended warranties are horribly overpriced. More than 80 percent of all service contracts are never used, and total payouts to consumers to make repairs amount to less than 10 percent of all money spent on the contracts. These contracts are prevalent in the vehicle, appliance, and electronics markets because of the high profits involved and the persuasiveness of salespeople, who typically earn a higher commission on the sale of an extended warranty than what they earn selling the product.

Think Twice About Extended Warranties

Extended warranties are generally not a good choice when buying electronics because the products rarely have problems beyond the warranty period. The exceptions are cell phones and laptops. Buy a service contract only from the actual manufacturer or dealer that sold the item.

Automobile manufacturers and dealers offer service contract plans; in addition, a number of independent companies offer service contracts for new vehicles. Often, a deductible of about $100 must be paid with each use of the contract. Repairs are usually covered and may include preventive maintenance for covered components. The cost for such a contract can exceed $700, and, if offered by the manufacturer or dealer, it can be added to the purchase price and financed with the purchase loan. If $700 is charged for the plan, $400 or more of this amount may be dealer profit, with $250 going to the salesperson. Sellers can afford to be more generous on a deal if they know that most of the money will be made back on the service contract.

 Concept Check 8.2

1. What is the goal of comparison shopping?

2. Explain why lease payments for a new vehicle are lower than loan payments for the same vehicle.

3. Describe the relationships among capital cost, capital cost reductions, and residual value in a lease.

4. Explain the difference between an implied warranty and an express warranty. How do they relate to the term *as is*?

5. What is an extended warranty? What is a disadvantage of such a contract?

Negotiate Effectively and Decide at Home

Negotiating and decision making follow comparison shopping in the buying process. If you move through these steps too quickly, you may pay too much even when you have done a great job with your preshopping research and comparison shopping. Sellers of such products sell every day, and they are highly skilled; in contrast, consumers are amateurs when it comes to buying big-ticket items. Smart shoppers learn to negotiate.

3 Learning Objective
Negotiate and decide effectively when making major purchases.

Successful Negotiators Are Armed with Information

Negotiating (or **haggling**) is the process of discussing the actual terms of an agreement with a seller. Consumers skip this step when making day-to-day purchases because prices in most stores are firm. With high-priced items—especially appliances, furniture, fine jewelry, and vehicles—there is an opportunity, and often an expectation, that offers and counteroffers will be made before arriving at the final price.

negotiating/haggling
Process of discussing actual terms of agreement with a seller, usually on higher-priced items.

Negotiating is challenging for consumers when buying vehicles because many variables must be considered, including the price of the vehicle, the trade-in value (if any), the possibility of a rebate, the prices of options, the interest rate, and possibly a service contract. The dealer can appear to be cooperative on one aspect and make up the difference elsewhere. The key to successful negotiation is to be armed with accurate information on all variables, especially the price, interest rate, and trade-in value.

Negotiate Your Price The complexity and uncertainty involved in negotiating the price of a new vehicle have inspired the development of special services intended to assist buyers. A **new-vehicle buying service** is a no-fee organization that arranges discount purchases for buyers of new cars who are referred to nearby participating automobile dealers that have agreed to charge specific discount prices. After you sign up, a local dealer will call you to offer a no-haggle price, which is often within 4 percent of the invoice price. The buying service earns its income by collecting a finder's fee from the dealer. **Professional shoppers,** in exchange for a fee (perhaps $150 to $450) based on the sticker price, will find the best available price from a nearby dealer and finalize the sale. Alternatively, for a lower fee (perhaps $100 to $200), they will obtain price quotes so you can finalize the deal yourself. The following websites offer more information about these services:

new-vehicle buying service
No-fee organization that arranges discount purchases for new-car buyers who are referred to nearby participating automobile dealers that have agreed to charge specific discount prices.

- www.autobytel.com
- www.autos.msn.com
- www.carsdirect.com
- www.autoweb.com
- www.autoadvisor.com
- www.carbargains.com

When negotiating a vehicle purchase, the key is to obtain a firm price from a dealer for the vehicle and optional equipment desired before discussing *any other* aspects of the deal. Rule number one in auto buying: Do not mention financing or a trade-in until you have pinned the salesperson down to a price! You will know from your preshopping research and comparison shopping what a good price for the vehicle in question would be.

Start your bargaining from this low price rather than the asking price or sticker price on the vehicle. Obtain prices from three or more dealers and then let each know that you have done so and whether or not their price is low compared with the others. The dealer will then have the chance to reduce the asking price to meet the competition. This smart strategy pressures the dealer to meet your needs rather than the other way around.

Always obtain a firm price for a vehicle before negotiating financing or a trade-in.

Stockbyte Stockbyte/PhotoLibrary

invoice price/seller's cost
Reflects the price the dealer has been billed from the manufacturer.

dealer holdback/dealer rebate
Dealer incentive in which the manufacturer allows dealers to hold back a percentage of invoice price, thereby providing the dealer with additional profit on the vehicle.

Consumers have caught on to the fiction of new-car sticker prices and now focus on the **invoice price** or **seller's cost,** which reflects the price the dealer has been billed from the manufacturer. But this may not be the price the dealer truly will have to pay when the vehicle is sold. This occurs because manufacturers often offer a **dealer holdback** (or **dealer rebate**) to dealers. A dealer holdback is a percentage of the invoice price that the dealer can hold back from (instead of paying to) the manufacturer, thereby providing the dealer with additional profit on the vehicle. Because of holdback incentives, dealers can sell a vehicle at or below invoice and still make a good profit. For example, a vehicle might have a sticker price of $27,890, an invoice price of $24,600, and a dealer holdback of 5 percent, or $1230. A negotiated price of $24,500 will still net the dealer a profit of $1130 [$1230 − ($24,600 − $24,500)]. Remember both the MSRP and invoice price are artificial numbers set by the manufacturer and dealer to allow room to negotiate a profitable price. For this reason, do not hesitate to negotiate for a price that is below the invoice price. Visit www .edmunds.com for a listing of current dealer holdback offers on various makes and models of vehicles.

Negotiate Your Interest Rate   Negotiating the interest rate, or APR, on a vehicle loan is not only possible but also essential to getting a good deal overall. Most vehicle borrowers accept that the dealer-arranged financing is the best the dealer can find. Buyers often do not know that the dealer benefits from having the borrower agree to a higher rate. Here is how the process works. The dealer asks the buyer to complete a loan application. The application is submitted to one or more lenders with whom the dealer has a preexisting affiliation. The lenders will assess the application and, if approved, suggest an APR. However, if the dealer suggests and gets an acceptance for a higher rate by the buyer (perhaps by saying that the buyer's credit score is low), the dealer (and salesperson) receives a higher fee for arranging the higher APR loan. In this way, the dealer can make money even if the profit off the sale of the vehicle itself is minimal. This is why it is so important to have a good credit history, know your credit score, and arrange the best financing you can on your own and accept the dealer financing only if it can beat your deal.

Negotiate Your Trade-in Getting a good deal on a vehicle purchase requires one more negotiation—your trade-in. You can pay a low price for the car you are buying, arrange a low-rate loan, and still not have a good deal if you do not receive what your trade-in is worth. Success here depends on knowing the value of your vehicle as a trade-in based on your preshopping research. The same online sources you used to get that information also have information on the average price at which similar vehicles are selling via private individuals. While it is true that trade-in values are usually lower than private sale values, you also have the costs of selling and the time involved if you decide not to accept the dealer's offer for your vehicle.

Trade-ins are another way for a seller to make more money on the transaction. In one common sales technique, called **high-balling,** a dealer offers a trade-in allowance that is much higher than the vehicle is worth. This apparent generosity may look very good to a buyer. But beware, the dealer is likely making up for this elsewhere, possibly in a higher-than-necessary price for the purchased vehicle. You will not know whether you are being high-balled unless you know the value of your trade-in.

Instant Message

Negotiating a Vehicle Purchase

When buying a car, you should negotiate the deal in this order:

1. Get a firm price for the vehicle.
2. Negotiate the lowest possible APR through the dealer, and borrow elsewhere if the rate is lower.
3. Obtain a firm commitment on a trade-in allowance, and sell the vehicle yourself if the allowance is too low.

high-balling
Sales tactic in which dealer offers a trade-in allowance that is much higher than the vehicle is worth.

Negotiating a Car Deal: An Illustration

Thousands of dollars are at stake when you buy a vehicle. Consider the case of Gary Joseph, a production manager from Northville, Michigan. Gary was in the market for a newer car. He had done his homework and narrowed his choice of vehicles and options down to one model and two dealerships. He also had arranged his own financing at 6.6 percent APR. Finally, he also knew the trade-in value of his current vehicle.

Gary presented his list of desired options to the first dealer and was shown a suitable car on the lot. When Gary inquired about price, the salesperson asked what monthly payment would fit affordably in his budget. Gary countered by saying that his budget was not important and that he wanted to know the price for the vehicle. When the salesperson responded that it was the dealership's policy to get the affordable payment amount before answering any questions, Gary insisted on a price from the salesperson. The salesperson then asked Gary whether he would be borrowing the money for the vehicle. Gary replied that he didn't know yet. The salesperson asked Gary if he had a trade-in vehicle. Gary replied, "Maybe, but let's get a price for the new car first." Finally, the salesperson gave him a price.

Gary said thank you and left the dealership, saying he would get back in touch with the salesperson. Later, he went to the other dealership and had a very similar discussion. He then went back and forth with the two dealers and obtained his best offer from the second dealer. Only then did Gary ask about the possibility of a loan. The salesperson arranged a loan with a 7.2 percent APR. Gary declined as he had a lower rate in hand. Then Gary asked about trading in his current car. The dealer offered him a trade-in allowance of $6200, $800 lower than what Gary knew the vehicle was worth ($7000) as a trade-in. Gary also knew he would likely be able to sell it himself for $7500. He countered the $7000 offer with that amount and ultimately

Instant Message

Play "Good Cop–Bad Cop" When Buying Vehicles

Many people are uncomfortable negotiating with sellers. Sellers understand this and are very good at putting people at ease with friendly talk and a supportive tone. But underneath, they are all business. How should you play the game? If you are a good negotiator, bring a friend along to be the friendly good cop while you focus on the deal and ask the hard questions. If you dislike negotiating, you can be the good cop, while your friend can ask the hard questions and focus on the business at hand.

Advice from a Pro...

How to Buy a Used Vehicle

Will Rogers once said, "We are the first nation in the history of the world to go to the poorhouse in an automobile." Don't let that be you. Most consumer-buying experts recommend purchasing late-model used cars to get the most from your car-buying dollar. You need to be careful when buying a used vehicle, however. Following are some basic steps that can help you avoid getting a lemon:

1. **Decide how much you can afford to spend.** Decide in advance how much you can afford.

2. **Decide which features and options you want.** Decide on features based on what is important to you. Are you concerned most about safety? comfort? ease of operation? Thinking about this will help you rank the features you want in a used car, such as power steering, air conditioning, or antilock brakes. Consider choosing an older model to obtain the features you value without spending too much more.

3. **Search for reliable makes and models in your price range.** The Internet is an excellent source of used-car pricing information. In addition, you should consult the most recent April issue of *Consumer Reports* for its lists of recommended used vehicles in various price ranges.

4. **Start your search.** Start with online sources and also use classified advertisements in your local newspaper and used-vehicle advertising publications. All of the online information sources included in this chapter list local dealership offerings for specific makes and models.

5. **Select source.** New-car dealerships tend to offer the nicer, more reliable, and more expensive used vehicles. Used-car dealerships, on the other hand, tend to have the widest range of quality. Private individuals deserve your attention because they usually own the vehicle and know its history. Used cars sold by rental agencies such as Hertz and Avis can be good choices because the cars have been regularly maintained.

6. **Avoid credit rebuilders.** Dealers who use terms such as "credit rebuilders" or "buy here/pay here" give the impression that they are willing to lend to all buyers quickly and easily. While their lending standards certainly are

lower, they also charge very high interest rates and offer contract terms that are quite unforgiving of late and/or missed payments.

7. **Quickly rule out the unworthy.** Regardless of the source, immediately rule out any vehicle that seems to have a problem or raises a question in your mind. Do the same for sellers who do not seem cooperative. Too many vehicles are available to waste your time considering poor-quality vehicles or wrestling with uncooperative sellers.

8. **Check your selections carefully.** By now you should have narrowed your choice to two or three specific vehicles. Inspect them inside and out. Take along a friend who is knowledgeable about cars if you are not car savvy. Ask for maintenance records if the seller is an individual or a rental company. Ask the dealer for the name, address, and phone number of the previous owner and give that person a telephone call. Before you agree to buy any vehicle, have your mechanic examine it. Although the examination may cost $50 to $75, it could help you avoid purchasing a vehicle with problems and save hundreds of dollars in repairs later. If the seller refuses to allow you to take the car to your own mechanic for an inspection, it is time to walk away from this sale.

9. **Check your vehicle's history.** You want to know whether your vehicle has ever been wrecked or salvaged. You also want to know its ownership history. Carfax.com is a good source for this information. Ask the seller to pay for this service. Vehicles coming off lease can be a good choice, and they are often still under original warranty.

10. **Negotiate and decide.** Never pay the asking price for a used vehicle. Get all verbal promises and guarantees in writing. If a seller will not put his or her words in writing, shop elsewhere. Finally, return to the quiet of your home to consider your alternatives and to make your final decision. If necessary, put down a small refundable deposit to hold the vehicle for a day or two while you make your decision.

Aimee D. Prawitz and Jamie A. Richter
Northern Illinois University

accepted a $7200 trade-in allowance, thereby saving himself the time and money needed to sell the vehicle himself.

Gary did everything right. He focused first on price, playing one dealership off against the other. He arranged his own financing and took the lowest APR. He negotiated his trade-in separately. Notice that he never once talked about monthly payments with the dealer. He knew that the dealer could manipulate other aspects of the deal to fit Gary's monthly payment goal and still make plenty of money off the deal. Gary was not finished, however. As a smart shopper, he knew he should take the information he had and go home to make the final decision.

Instant Message

Buy Used Cars and Use Them Up

The best way to buy vehicles with the lowest overall cost is to buy late-model used cars and drive them for ten or more years. New cars lose 25 percent of their value in the first year.

Make the Decision

It is unwise to make buying decisions for expensive purchases inside a retail store or showroom. By waiting until you get home to make the final decision, you are free of pressure from a salesperson and free of your own need to "get it over with." After taking some time to rationally consider all of the consequences of the purchase, you can return to the dealer's showroom and close the sale.

A **decision-making grid** allows you to visually and mathematically weigh the decision you are about to make. Table 8.2 depicts a grid for someone deciding among three different washing machines. The first task in developing such a grid is to determine the various criteria for making the decision. In Table 8.2, these factors include price, durability, and styling. Each criterion is assigned a weight that reflects the importance each has in the mind of the purchaser. Each brand and model under consideration is then given a score (from 1 to 10 in this case) that indicates how well it performs on that criterion. The score (S) is multiplied by the weight (W) to obtain a weighted score. The total of the weighted scores for each brand/model can then be compared with the totals for the other choices to determine which one "wins." In Table 8.2, Appliance C, which has a total score of 8.0, would be chosen. A grid of this type helps bring objectivity to your decision-making process and can be of benefit, especially when buying big-ticket items.

Finalizing a Car Deal

After negotiating a good deal and making your final decision, it would be nice if you could simply return to the dealer and sign the necessary papers. But even then there is opportunity for the dealer to push for a little more profit. One technique that is used at this point is called **low-balling.** This involves quoting and getting a verbal agreement from a buyer for an artificially low price. Then the salesperson attempts to raise the already negotiated price

low-balling
A sales tactic where the seller quotes an artificially low price to obtain a verbal agreement from a buyer and then attempts to raise the negotiated price when it comes time to finalize the written contract.

Table 8.2 **Decision-Making Grid (Illustrated for a Washing Machine)**

Criteria	Decision Weight (W)	Appliance A		Appliance B		Appliance C	
		Score (S)*	W × S	Score (S)*	W × S	Score (S)*	W × S
Price	30%	9	2.7	7	2.1	5	1.5
Durability	25%	6	1.5	8	2.0	10	2.5
Features	20%	6	1.2	8	1.6	10	2.0
Warranty	15%	6	0.9	10	1.5	8	1.2
Styling	10%	10	1.0	6	0.6	8	0.8
TOTAL	**100%**		**7.3**		**7.8**		**8.0**

*Using a 10-point scale where 10 is the highest score.

Instant Message

Do Not Lease Just to Have a Nicer Ride

Leases work best for people who wish to drive a new vehicle every two or three years and will, thus, always have a car payment. If you do choose a leasing option, your goal should be to lower your monthly cost rather than to "buy more car." Otherwise, in just a few years, you will find that you have spent big bucks for a vehicle you must turn back in or pay extra to buy as a used vehicle.

buyer's order
Written offer that names a specific vehicle and all charges; only sign such offers after the salesperson and sales manager have signed *first*.

when it comes time to finalize the written contract. For example, after agreeing on the price of a vehicle with a buyer, the salesperson states that, as a formality, the approval of a manager is necessary. While the buyer is dreaming of driving home in the new car, the salesperson and the manager are talking about how much more they can get for the vehicle. When the salesperson returns, he or she indicates that there is a problem. Perhaps the trade-in value is too high, or the sticker price can't be discounted by quite as much as planned, or the price of a certain option has increased. In reality, of course, low-balling is simply a ruse to allow the dealer to get more money. Smart buyers stand firm and insist on the deal that had been negotiated.

Finally, it is time to sign the papers. Commonly at this point the salesperson turns the buyer over to another member of the sales team whose specific job it is to have all the papers signed to finalize the sale, the loan, and the transfer of the title and registration of the vehicle. Sign only a **buyer's order** that names a specific vehicle and all charges. And do so only after the salesperson and sales manager have signed *first*. Then verify that all aspects of the deal are as originally agreed, sign your name, and drive away in your new vehicle.

Concept Check 8.3

1. List some of the complexities in vehicle buying and offer your advice on how to get a best buy.
2. What three aspects of a vehicle purchase should be negotiated? In what order?
3. Why should you make major purchase decisions at home?
4. Summarize how to use a decision-making grid.

Evaluate Your Decision

4 Learning Objective
Evaluate your purchase decisions and, if necessary, effectively seek redress.

redress
Process of righting a wrong.

The planned buying process comes full circle when you evaluate your decision. The purpose of this step is to determine where things went well and where they went less smoothly. The lessons learned will prove useful when you need to make a similar purchase in the future. Sometimes the process was so successful that you may want to compliment the seller.

In other cases, you may want to complain about the product or service so as to obtain **redress**—that is, to right the wrong. This process should start with the actual seller, as indicated in Table 8.3. Seeking redress through the first three channels in the complaint procedures as shown in the table can rectify almost all consumer complaints.

Table 8.3   Complaint Procedure (Levels and Channels of Complaining)

Levels to Bring Your Complaint	Channels for Complaint
1. Local business	Salesperson → supervisor → manager/owner
2. Manufacturer	Consumer affairs department → president/chief executive officer
3. Self-regulatory organizations	Better Business Bureau → trade associations → mediation/arbitration panels
4. Consumer action agencies	Private consumer action groups → media action lines → government agencies
5. Small-claims or civil court	Small-claims court → civil court

Alternative dispute resolution programs are industry- or government-sponsored programs that provide an avenue to resolve disputes outside the formal court system. Vehicle manufacturers utilize these programs as part of their warranty procedures. **Mediation** is a procedure in which a neutral third party works with the parties involved in the dispute to arrive at a mutually agreeable solution. In **arbitration,** a neutral third party hears (or reads) the claims made and the positions taken by the parties to the dispute and then issues a ruling that is binding on one or both parties.

All states have new-vehicle **lemon laws** that provide guidelines for arbitrators to use to order a dealer's buyback of a "lemon." A common definition of a lemon in these laws is a vehicle that was in the shop for repairs four times for the same problem in the first year after purchase. (For the specific definition in your state, visit www.carlemon.com.) To enforce a lemon law, the buyer must go through the warranty process specified in the owner's manual. Eventually, if the problem is not resolved, an arbitration hearing will be held through which the owner can request a buyback. Some states have also enacted used-vehicle lemon laws.

Sometimes your best efforts at redress may not prove successful. As a result, you might consider taking legal action in **small-claims court.** In this state court, civil matters are often resolved without the assistance of attorneys (in some states, attorneys are actually prohibited from representing clients in small-claims courts). Small-claims courts usually place restrictions on the maximum amount under dispute, typically ranging from $500 to $2500, for which a claim may be made in those courts. To file a small-claims court action, contact your local county courthouse and ask which court hears small claims.

alternative dispute resolution programs
Industry- or government-sponsored programs that provide an avenue to resolve disputes outside the formal court system.

lemon laws
State laws that provide guidelines for arbitrators to use to order a dealer's buyback of a "lemon" as defined under the law—commonly if a car that has been in the shop four or more times to fix the same problem.

small-claims court
State courts in which civil matters are often resolved without attorney assistance.

 Do It NOW!

Becoming a smart shopper does not have to wait until you make a major purchase such as a vehicle. Start today by:

1. Making a list before going to the grocery store and then buying only what is on the list unless the item is on sale and you know you will be using it soon.

2. Trying the generic version of food products you regularly buy to see if the name brand really is worth the extra cost.

3. Setting up a filing system for the warranty information and receipts for all products you buy that have a warranty.

Concept Check 8.4

1. Outline the steps to go through to seek redress.
2. Distinguish between mediation and arbitration.
3. How do lemon laws work?

What Do You Recommend NOW?

Now that you have read this chapter on vehicle and other major purchases, what do you recommend to David and Lisa Cosgrove regarding:

Photodisc/Alamy

1. How to search for two vehicles to replace those destroyed?
2. Whether to replace Lisa's vehicle with a new or used vehicle?
3. Whether to lease or buy a vehicle?
4. How to decide between a rebate and a special low APR financing opportunity? Should they decide to purchase a new vehicle for Lisa?
5. How to negotiate with the sellers of the vehicles?

Big Picture Summary of Learning Objectives

1 Explain the three steps in the planned buying process that occur prior to interacting with sellers.

The planned buying process includes three steps that occur prior to interacting with sellers: prioritizing wants, obtaining information during preshopping research, and fitting the planned purchase into the budget. These steps represent the homework needed when preparing to buy.

2 Describe the five aspects of major purchases that require comparison shopping.

To interact effectively with sellers, you should comparison shop to find the best buy. When purchasing vehicles and other big-ticket items, this shopping process includes comparing prices, financing arrangements, leasing options, warranties, and extended warranties.

3 Negotiate and decide effectively when making major purchases.

Negotiating with sellers involves obtaining a fair price, low-cost financing, and a high trade-in allowance. After negotiating, the final decision should be made at home.

4 Evaluate your purchase decisions and, if necessary, effectively seek redress.

The planned buying process comes full circle when you evaluate your decision. The purpose of this step is to determine where things went well, where they went less smoothly, and how you can make better purchase decisions in the future. When things have not gone well, you can use mediation, arbitration, lemon laws, or small-claims court to resolve matters.

Let's Talk About It

1. **Buying Name Brands.** Do you or a family member tend to buy name-brand versions of certain products? Which ones? Why or why not?

2. **Steps in the Planned Buying Process.** Do you think all of the steps in the planned buying process are used when buying simple everyday products (such as a loaf of bread or a half-gallon of milk) or are they used only when buying big-ticket items?

3. **Positives and Negatives of Leasing.** What benefits do you see in leasing a vehicle? What negatives exist when leasing?

4. **A Bad Purchase Decision.** What is the worst purchase decision you have ever made? What step(s) in the planned buying process could you have done better in that situation?

5. **Do You Complain?** When was the last time you were seriously dissatisfied with a purchase? Did you complain? Why or why not? If you complained, what was the outcome?

Do the Math

1. **Buy Versus Lease.** Amanda Forsythe of Tampa, Florida, must decide whether to buy or lease a car she has selected. She has negotiated a purchase price of $24,700 and could borrow the money to buy from her credit union by putting $3000 down and paying $515 per month for 48 months at 6.5 percent APR. Alternatively, she could lease the car for 48 months at $310 per month by paying a $3000 capital cost reduction and a $350 disposition fee on the car, which is projected to have a residual value of $8100 at the end of the lease. Use the Decision-Making Worksheet on page 230 to advise Amanda about whether she should buy or lease the car.

2. **Rebate Versus Low Interest Rate.** Kyle Parker of Fayetteville, Arkansas, has been shopping for a new car for several weeks. So far, he has negotiated a price of $27,000 on a model that carries a choice of a $2500 rebate or dealer financing at 2 percent APR. The dealer loan would require a $1000 down payment and a monthly payment of $564 for 48 months. Kyle has also arranged for a loan from his bank with a 7 percent APR. Use the Decision-Making Worksheet on page 224 to advise Kyle about whether he should use the dealer financing or take the rebate and use the financing from the bank.

Financial Planning Cases

Case 1
Purchase of a New Refrigerator

Tracy Sullivan, a financial consultant from Spokane, Washington, is remodeling her kitchen. Tracy, who lives alone, has decided to replace her refrigerator with a new model that offers more conveniences. She has narrowed her choices to two models. The first is a basic 16-cubic-foot model with a bottom freezer for $799. The second is a 25.4-cubic-foot model with side freezer for $999. Additional features for this model include icemaker, textured enamel surface, and ice and water dispenser. Tracy's credit union will loan her the necessary funds for one year at a 12 percent APR on the installment plan. Following is her budget, which includes $2140 in monthly take-home pay.

Food	$ 300
Entertainment	120
Clothing	60
Gifts	70
Charities	75
Car payment	330
Personal care	60
Automobile expenses	120
Savings	130
Housing	825
Miscellaneous	50
Total	**$2140**

(a) What preshopping research might Tracy do to select the best brand of refrigerator?

(b) Using the information in Table 7.1 on page 209 or the *Garman/Forgue* companion website, determine Tracy's monthly payment for the two models.

(c) Fit each of the two monthly payments into Tracy's budget.

(d) Advise Tracy to help her make her decision.

Case 2
A Dispute over New-Car Repairs

Christopher Hardison, a high school football coach from Oklahoma City, Oklahoma, purchased a new SUV for $28,000. He used the vehicle often; in fact, in less than nine months he had put 14,000 miles on it. A 24,000-mile, two-year warranty was still in effect for the power-train equipment, although Christopher had to pay the first $100 of each repair cost. After 16,500 miles and in month 11 of driving, the car experienced some severe problems with the transmission. Christopher took the vehicle to the dealer for repairs. A week later he picked the car up, but some transmission problems remained. When Christopher took the car back to the dealer, the dealer said that no further problems could be identified. Christopher was sure that the problem was still there, and he was amazed that the dealer would not correct it. The dealer told him he would take no other action.

(a) Was Christopher within his rights to take the car back for repairs? Explain why or why not.

(b) What logical steps might Christopher follow if he continues to be dissatisfied with the dealer's unwillingness or inability to repair the car?

(c) Should Christopher seek any help from the court system? If so, describe what he could do without spending money on attorney's fees.

Case 3
Victor and Maria Hernandez Buy a Third Car

The Hernandezes' older son, Hector, has reached the age at which it is time to consider purchasing a car for him. Victor and Maria have decided to give Maria's old car to Hector and buy a later-model used car for Maria.

(a) What sources can Victor and Maria use to access price and reliability information on various makes and models of used cars?

(b) What sources of used cars might be available to Victor and Maria, and what differences might exist among them?

(c) How might Victor and Maria check out the cars in which they are most interested?

(d) What strategies might Victor and Maria employ when they negotiate the price for the car they select?

Case 4
The Johnsons Decide to Buy a Car

The Johnsons have decided to move out of their apartment and into some form of owned housing. Although they have not decided what type of housing they will buy, they know that Belinda will no longer be able to ride the bus to work. Recognizing this fact, they are in the market for another car. They have decided not to buy a new car but think they have some room in their budget for a used car, given the raises each has received this year (see Table 3.3 on page 73). Harry and Belinda estimate that they could afford to spend about $3200 on an inexpensive used car by making a down payment of $600 and financing the remainder over 24 months at $120 per month.

(a) Make suggestions about how the $120 might be integrated into the Johnsons' budget (Table 3.3 on page 73) without changing the amount left over at the end of each month. Harry and Belinda want to retain that extra money to help defray some of the added expenses of home ownership.

(b) Which sources of used cars should they consider? Why?

(c) Assume that the Johnsons have narrowed their choices to two cars. Both have air conditioning, AM-FM radio, and automatic transmission. The first car is an eight-year-old Chevrolet with 102,000 miles; it is being sold for $3400 by a private individual. The car has a six-cylinder engine, and the seller has kept records of all repairs, tune-ups, and oil changes. It will need new tires in about six months. The second car is a nine-year-old, two-door Ford with 116,000 miles, being sold by a used-car dealership. It has a four-cylinder engine. Harry contacted the previous owner and found that the car was given in trade on a new car about three months ago. The previous owner cited no major mechanical problems but simply wanted a bigger car. The dealer is offering a written 30-day warranty on parts only. The asking price is $3200. Which car would you advise the Johnsons to buy? Why?

On the 'Net

Go to the Web pages indicated to complete these exercises. You can also go to the *Garman/Forgue* companion website at www.cengage.com/finance/garman for an expanded list of exercises. Under General Business, select the title of this text. Click on the Internet Exercises link for this chapter.

1. Visit the website for the Kelly Blue Book at www.kbb.com. For a used vehicle you currently own or one you would like to own, determine its "used car retail value," "trade-in value," and "private party value." Why do the three values differ?

2. Visit the website of *Consumer Reports* magazine at www.consumerreports.org and click on the "Cars" tab and then the "Car Buying Advice" tab. You will be sent to a page containing tips on buying new and used cars. In what ways are the strategies similar and in what ways do they differ from the tips offered in this book for buying a used car?

3. Visit the website of the Federal Reserve Board at http://www.federalreserve.gov/pubs/leasing where you will find a link titled "Keys to Vehicle Leasing" that expands upon the information in this book. Use this information to generate a list of pros and cons of leasing versus purchasing a vehicle. By clicking on "sample leasing form" on this Web page, you can view and print a copy of the required vehicle leasing disclosure form.

Visit the Garman/Forgue companion website . . .

www.cengage.com/finance/garman

Obtaining Affordable Housing

!You Must Be Kidding, Right?

Horst Brandt recently bought a new home and borrowed $140,000 at 6.25 percent interest for 30 years. His monthly payment for interest and principal will be $862. A friend suggested that Horst should have easily been able to find a loan at 6.0 percent with a monthly payment of $839. Horst dismissed his friend's comments, arguing that the difference in the monthly payments was no big deal. His friend replied, "Horst, it's not the monthly payment, it's the interest." How much more in interest will Horst pay over the life of the loan because he took a loan with the higher rate?

A. $350   **C.** $8280

B. $4200   **D.** $10,500

The answer is C. Horst will be making a higher payment for each and every month for 30 years. While the difference in the monthly payment seems small [$23 ($862 − $839) per month in this example], even a small difference in the interest rates on mortgage loans can add up to thousands of dollars in extra interest over the life of the loan. That is why searching for the lowest possible interest rate is so important when borrowing to buy a home!

Learning Objectives

After reading this chapter, you should be able to:

1 Decide whether renting or owning your home is better for you both financially and personally.

2 Explain the up-front and monthly costs of buying a home.

3 Describe the steps in the home-buying process.

4 Distinguish among the conventional and alternative ways of financing a home and list the advantages and disadvantages of each.

5 Identify the important aspects of selling a home.

What Do You Recommend?

AP Photo/Danny Johnston

Libby Clark has worked for a major consumer electronics retailer since graduating from college. The company has operations across the country with regional headquarters in Atlanta, Denver, Minneapolis, and Boston. She has been based in the Atlanta area for the past three years and given the recent declines in home prices there she has begun to think about buying a home rather than renting her townhouse apartment. Then, last month, Libby was promoted to deputy regional director for the Denver region. The promotion represents a key step for becoming a regional director in four or five years. Regional directors may or may not be promoted from within their current region.

What do you recommend to Libby on the subject of buying a home regarding:

1. Buying or renting housing in the Denver area?
2. Steps she should take prior to actively looking at homes?
3. Finding a home and negotiating the purchase?
4. The closing process in home buying?
5. Selecting a type of mortgage to fit her needs?
6. Things to consider regarding the sale of her home should she ultimately be promoted to a position in another of the four regions?

Your Next Five Years

In the next five years you can start achieving financial success by doing the following related to obtaining affordable housing:

1. Read your leases and other real estate contracts thoroughly before signing.

2. Save the money for a down payment within a tax-sheltered Roth IRA account.

3. Get your finances in order before shopping for a new home by reducing debt, budgeting better, and clearing up anything that keeps you from having a high credit score.

4. Buy a home as soon as it fits your budget and lifestyle so you can take advantage of special income tax deductions and price appreciation over time.

5. If you make a down payment of less than 20 percent on a home, cancel private mortgage insurance as soon as the equity in your home pushes the loan-to-value ratio down to 80 percent.

You probably are renting housing right now because about 90 percent of all younger people rent. In contrast, approximately 80 percent of people aged 55 to 64 are homeowners. Given these statistics it is likely that you eventually will decide between renting and buying housing and probably will buy. At that point, you will have to think about the financial benefits of renting versus buying and take a good hard look at what it really costs to buy a home.

Is a home an investment or just a place to live? Over the past 20 years housing values increased less than 4% annually or less than half what was earned on a diversified portfolio of stocks and bonds over the same time frame. If you decide to buy, you will obtain a **mortgage loan**—a loan to purchase real estate in which the property itself serves as collateral. There are many types of mortgage loans, and borrowers need to understand their options—now more than ever before.

The recent decline in housing prices occurred partly because millions of Americans took out complicated mortgages in previous years. For many, mortgages that, at first, seemed affordable turned out later to be unaffordable as the monthly repayment amounts increased due to rising interest rates. In addition, many people speculated in housing expecting values to continue to rise. But as Eli Broad, a housing development entrepreneur observed, "You can't have anything going up 10 percent to 20 percent to 30 percent indefinitely." Rising payments and declining values were a disaster for many homeowners. Further, those trying to sell their homes in such a market lost money in the process. You must understand the process of selling housing as well as how to buy at the right price.

mortgage loan
Loan to purchase real estate in which the property itself serves as collateral.

1 Learning Objective
Decide whether renting or owning your home is better for you both financially and personally.

Should You Rent or Buy Your Home?

Whether to rent or buy depends on your preferences and what you can afford. In the short run, renting is usually less expensive than buying. In the long run, the opposite is true.

Rented Housing

People may choose to rent their housing for several reasons. For some, the large down payment and high monthly loan payments are barriers to buying a home. Some people simply prefer the easy mobility of renting or want to avoid many of the responsibilities associated with buying. Prospective renters need to consider the monthly rental fees and related expenses, the lease agreement and restrictions, and tenant rights.

rent
Cost charged for using an apartment or other housing space.

Rent, Deposit, and Related Expenses   **Rent** is the cost charged for using an apartment or other housing space. It is usually due on a specific day each month, with a late penalty being assessed if the tenant is tardy in making the payment. Other fees could be assessed for features such as use of a clubhouse and pool, exercise facilities, cable television, and space for storage and parking.

A **damage deposit** is an amount given in advance to a landlord to pay for repairing the unit beyond the damage expected from normal wear and tear. It is often charged before the tenant moves in and is often equal to one month's rent. You may also be required to pay a **security deposit** to ensure that you do not move without paying your rent. Again, this amount is often equal to the last month's rent payment. Thus, an apartment with a monthly rent of $800 might require payment of $800 for the first month's rent, an $800 security deposit, and an $800 damage deposit for a total of $2400.

Lease Agreement and Restrictions

A **lease** is a contract specifying the legal responsibilities of both the tenant and the landlord. It identifies the amount of rent and security deposit, the length of the lease (typically one year), payment responsibility for utilities and repairs, penalties for late payment of rent, eviction procedures for nonpayment of rent, and procedures to follow when the lease ends. Leases often state whether the security deposit accumulates interest, how soon the unit must be inspected for cleanliness after the tenant vacates the premises, and when the security deposit (or the balance) will be forwarded to the tenant. Local laws may also address these issues.

Two types of leases generally govern tenant–landlord relationships. The first provides for **periodic tenancy** (for example, week-to-week or month-to-month residency), where the agreement can be terminated by either of the parties if they give proper notice in advance (for example, one week or one month). Without such notice, the agreement stays in effect. This arrangement also typically applies in situations in which no written lease is established. The second type of lease provides for **tenancy for a specific time,** usually for one year. When this period expires, the agreement terminates unless prior notice is given by both parties that the agreement will be renewed.

Lease agreements may contain a variety of restrictions that are legally binding on tenants. For example, pets may or may not be permitted; when they are permitted, landlords often require a larger security deposit. Excessive noise from home entertainment systems or parties may be prohibited as well. To protect other renters from overcrowding, a clause may limit the number of overnight guests. An important restriction applies to **subleasing** (wherein an original tenant leases the property to another tenant). Here a tenant who moves before the lease expires may need to obtain the landlord's permission before someone else can take over the rental unit. The new tenant may even have to be approved, and the original tenant will retain some financial liability until the term of the original lease expires.

Tenant Rights

Tenants have a number of legal rights under laws in most states and many local communities. Some important rights are as follows:

- Prohibitions against **harassment** (rent increases, eviction, or utility shutoff) for reporting building-code violations or otherwise exercising a tenant's legal rights.

- Assurances of some legally prescribed minimum standard of **habitability** for items such as running water, heat, and a working stove and the safety of access areas such as stairways.

- The right to make minor repairs and deduct the cost from the tenant's next rent payment. This right is subject to certain restrictions, such as giving sufficient prior written notification to the landlord.

- Prompt return of a security deposit, with limits placed on the kinds of deductions that can be made. Landlords must explain specific reasons for deductions. Some state laws require that interest be paid on security deposits.

- The right to file a lawsuit against a landlord for nonperformance. Such suits can be brought in a small-claims court.

Did You Know?

How to Make Sure Your Security Deposit Is Returned

If you leave a rental unit clean and undamaged, you have a legal right to a refund of your security deposit when you move out. Several steps will help ensure that you receive a full refund:

- Make a list of all damages and defects when you first move into the unit. Have the landlord sign this list.
- Maintain the unit and keep it clean.
- Notify the landlord promptly (in writing, if necessary) of any maintenance problems and malfunctions.
- Give proper written notice of your intention to move out at least 30 days in advance of the lease expiration.
- Make a written list of all damages and defects after moving out but prior to turning over the keys. Have the landlord sign this second list.
- Use certified mail (with a return receipt) to request the return of your security deposit and to inform the landlord of your new address.
- Use small-claims court (see Chapter 8), if necessary, to obtain a court-ordered refund.

lease
In this context, a contract specifying both tenant and landlord legal responsibilities.

subleasing
An arrangement in which the original tenant leases the property to another tenant.

Instant Message

Don't Rent Without a Lease

Renting housing without a formal, written lease may seem like an easy and congenial way to do business, but it is fraught with potential for disagreements later. Always get your rental agreements in writing. Illustrative leases can be found at nolo.com.

Owned Housing

Americans have historically chosen single-family dwellings to satisfy their owned-housing desires. Other alternatives are popular, too, such as condominiums, cooperatives, manufactured housing, and mobile homes.

single-family dwelling
Housing unit that is detached from other units.

Single-Family Dwellings
A **single-family dwelling** is a housing unit that is detached from other units. Buyers have many choices available for both new and existing homes with varying floor plans and home features. Some people prefer the modern kitchens and other features found in newer homes; others prefer the larger rooms, higher ceilings, and completed landscaping of older homes.

Condominiums and Cooperatives
The terms **condominium** and **cooperative** describe forms of ownership rather than types of buildings. These forms of ownership typically cost less than single-family dwellings, offer recreation facilities, and have little if any maintenance obligations.

condominium (condo)
Form of ownership with the owners holding legal title to their own housing unit among many with common grounds and facilities owned by the developer or homeowner's association.

With a **condominium** (or **condo**), the owner holds legal title to a specific housing unit within a multiunit building or project and owns a proportionate share in the common grounds and facilities. The entire complex is run by the owners through a **homeowner's association.** Besides making monthly mortgage payments, the condominium owner must pay a monthly **homeowner's fee** that is established by the homeowner's association. This fee covers expenses related to the management of the common grounds and facilities and insurance on the building. Some areas of concern for condominium owners include potential increases in homeowner's fees and limited resale appeal of the unit.

cooperative (co-op)
Form of ownership in which owner holds a share of the corporation that owns and manages a group of housing units as well as common grounds and facilities.

With a **cooperative** (or **co-op**), the owner holds a share of the corporation that owns and manages a group of housing units. The value of this share is equivalent to the value of the owner's particular unit. The owner also holds a proportional interest in all common areas. A monthly fee for the cooperative covers the same types of items as does a condominium fee and also includes an amount to cover the professional management of the complex as well as payments on the cooperative's mortgage debt. (The pro rata share for interest and property taxes is deductible on each shareholder's income tax return.)

Be sure to factor homeowner's association fees into the monthly income needed to purchase a condominium.

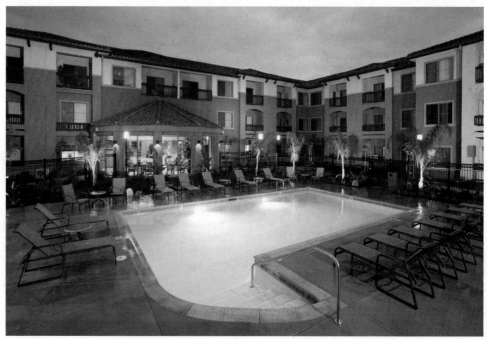

Chet Frohlich/PhotoLibrary

Manufactured Housing and Mobile Homes **Manufactured housing** consists of fully or partially factory-built housing units designed to be transported (often in portions) to the home site. Final assembly and readying of the housing for occupancy occurs at the home site. **Mobile homes,** in contrast, are fully factory-assembled housing units that are designed to be towed on a frame with a trailer hitch. Mobile homes depreciate in value every year just like automobiles.

Who Pays More—Renters or Owners?

According to conventional wisdom, homeowners enjoy a financial advantage over renters when total housing costs are calculated over many years. Renters generally pay out less money in terms of annual cash flow, but owners receive annual income tax advantages and they usually see increases in the value of their homes over time that can improve their financial situation. However, as evidenced by events of the past few years there is no guarantee that housing values will increase in a uniform fashion over the years; they might even decline. Your goal in buying a place to live should not be driven by dreams of possible financial gain. Buying is still a smart move and you must crunch the numbers to be absolutely certain the housing you choose is purchased at the right price and is affordable. Affordability must include not only the monthly payment but other additional homeownership expenses such as homeowner's association fees.

Based on Cash Flow, Renters Appear to Win The Run the Numbers worksheet "Should You Buy or Rent?" on page 251 illustrates a comparison between a small condominium and an apartment with similar space and amenities. For the apartment, rent would total $1000 per month. Assume you could buy the condominium for $180,000 by using $36,000 in savings as a down payment and borrowing the remaining $144,000 for 30 years at 7 percent interest. As the worksheet shows, renting would have a cash-flow cost of $11,010 after a reduction for the interest that could be earned on your savings (after-taxes). Buying requires several expenses beyond the monthly mortgage payment, including a monthly $150 homeowner's fee ($1800 annually) in our example. In this case, the cash-flow cost of buying is $17,621, or $6701 more than renting.

After Taxes and Appreciation, Owners Usually Win To make the comparison more accurate, you must also consider the tax and appreciation aspects of the two options. If you rent, you would pay $270 ($1080 × 0.25) in income taxes on the interest on the amount in your savings account ($36,000) not used for a down payment. If you buy the condominium, $1464 of the $11,496 in annual mortgage loan payments during the first year will go toward the principal of the debt, and the remainder—$10,032 ($11,496 − $1464)—will go toward interest. Both mortgage interest and real estate property taxes qualify as income tax deductions. If you are in the 25 percent marginal tax bracket, your taxes would be reduced by $2508 ($10,032 × 0.25) as a result of deducting the mortgage interest and by $750 ($3000 × 0.25) as a result of deducting the real estate tax. In effect, every time you make a payment you will get some of it back from the government.

Condominiums also have a likelihood of appreciation, or increase, in the home's value. A very conservative assumption would be that the condominium will increase in value by 1 percent per year. A home valued at $180,000 would, therefore, be worth $181,800 ($180,000 × 1.01) after one year, a gain of $1800. In this case, buying is financially better than renting by approximately $451 ($11,550 − $11,099).

Note that the calculations above compare somewhat equivalent housing types. The process is more complicated when you want to compare renting an apartment with buying a

Instant Message

Understand Your Deed Restrictions

Most existing communities, new housing developments, and cooperative and condominium associations have **deed restrictions** established by local zoning laws or by the developer. These rules govern such things as minimum lot size, the outside appearance and landscaping of the property, allowable secondary buildings, parking of vehicles, and other aspects of the use and appearance of the property. You should ask for and read the deed very carefully before buying.

house. You definitely should still do the math but recognize that you are comparing unlike properties. It is probable that you will find that buying a home is significantly more expensive than renting for the first few years. But if you stay in the home for 5 to 7 years or longer the financial situation improves for the homeowner especially for those with a fixed interest rate loan. This assumes you do not pay too much for it in the first place.

People who bought homes in recent years hoping to **flip** them for a quick profit sometimes found the opposite to be true. They lost money when they had to sell at a price lower than desired because the market was flooded with too many properties for sale, including foreclosed homes. The same thing happened to people who bought homes they could not afford while hoping that an increase in value would allow them to refinance for better terms after a couple of years. Worst off were people who bought homes with little or no down payment. When the value of their homes decreased they found themselves **upside down** (also known as **under water**) meaning that they owed more than the homes were worth. Declining home values were also noticed by lenders.

Any slip-up in making mortgage payments resulted in **foreclosure.** This is a process in which the lender sues the borrower to prove default and asks the court to order the sale of the property to pay the debt. Ironically, home buyers are finding home prices substantially lower today than a few years ago so these may be good times to do some careful shopping to buy a home.

foreclosure
Process in which the lender sues the borrower to prove default and asks the court to order the sale of the property to pay the debt.

Did You Know?

About Buying a Foreclosed Property

A major reason for the declines in home prices in recent years is the large number of foreclosed properties on the market. If there are four homes for sale in a neighborhood and one is a foreclosure residence, prices on the other three properties are typically lowered to the value of the one in foreclosure. Foreclosure properties can be found on such websites as www.Foreclosure.com, www.Foreclosures.com and www.RealtyTrac.com, which charge monthly subscription fees for access to their databases. If interested in buying such a property you must know how foreclosure works. Here are the three stages of foreclosure:

1. **Preforeclosure. Preforeclosure** is the time between when the homeowner has been notified by the lender that they are in default and when the lender has filed a notice of foreclosure with the local county clerk where the property is located. To purchase such a property you would negotiate a price directly with the owner who may or may not know that foreclosure is imminent. The owner may be willing to take a price lower than the market value especially if the offer is above the mortgage balance. Here the owner can get out of the loan and avoid foreclosure and perhaps still recoup some money. Time is of the essence at this stage as the actual foreclosure can take place in as little as 30 days.

2. **Foreclosure Action.** Once foreclosure occurs the bank will attempt to sell the home at a **foreclosure auction.** Most of the people bidding on these homes are professionals as the buyer must come up with the cash immediately. In many instances the bids are too low that the lender rejects them all.

3. **Short Sale.** If the auction produces no bids sufficiently high to pay off the outstanding debt the lender typically takes ownership of the property. The lender then will attempt to sell the property on its own or through a real estate agent. This is known as a **short sale** because the lender will accept less than the full mortgage amount. The process for purchasing a property in a short sale requires that offers are taken to the lender for approval. Lenders are tough negotiators as they want to get as much money as possible for the property but may be willing to wave closing costs and other fees making the overall cost more affordable. The lender agrees to absorb the loss although they might demand the homeowner make some kind of payment or share the loss.

There are some potential pitfalls when buying a foreclosed residence. The property is likely to need repairs, so insist upon a professional home inspection. Also, taxes and other assessments may be owed. You should hire a real estate attorney to help when making an offer and for the closing.

Run the Numbers

Should You Buy or Rent?

This worksheet can be used to estimate whether you would be better off renting housing or buying. If you are renting an apartment and planning to buy a house, qualitative differences will enter into your decision. This worksheet will put the financial picture into focus. A similar worksheet can be found on the Ginnie Mae website at http://www.ginniemae.gov/rent_vs_buy/rent_vs_buy_calc.asp?Section=YPTH.

	Example Amounts		Your Figures	
	Rent	**Buy**	**Rent**	**Buy**
Annual Cash-Flow Considerations				
Annual rent ($1000/month) or mortgage payments ($958.00/month)*	$12,000	$11,496	_____	_____
Property and liability insurance	360	725	_____	_____
Private mortgage insurance *if you pay less than 20% of down*	N/A	0	N/A	_____
Real estate taxes *payment*	0	3000	_____	_____
Maintenance	0	600	_____	_____
Other housing fees	0	1800	_____	_____
Less interest earned on funds not used for down payment (at 3%)	1080	N/A	_____	N/A
Cash-Flow Cost for the Year	**$11,280**	**$17,621**	_____	_____
Tax and Appreciation Considerations				
Less principal† repaid on the mortgage loan	N/A	1464	N/A	_____
Plus tax on interest earned on funds not used for down payment (25% marginal tax bracket)	270	N/A	_____	N/A
Less tax savings due to deductibility of mortgage interest‡ (25% marginal tax bracket)	N/A	2508	N/A	_____
Less tax savings due to deductibility of real estate property taxes (25% marginal tax bracket)	N/A	750	N/A	_____
Less appreciation on the dwelling (2.5% annual rate)	N/A	1800	N/A	_____
Net Cost for the Year	**$11,550**	**$11,099**	_____	_____

*Calculated from Table 9.4 on page 267.
†Calculated according to the method illustrated in Table 9.2 on page 265.
‡Mortgage interest tax savings equal total mortgage-payments minus principal repaid multiplied by the marginal tax rate.

Concept Check 9.1

1. Explain the purpose and value of a lease for both the renter and the landlord.
2. Distinguish between periodic tenancy and tenancy for a specific time when renting housing.
3. Identify three ways that home buyers can save on their income taxes.
4. Illustrate how housing buyers can pay less than renters when taxes and appreciation of housing values are considered.

What Does It Cost to Buy a Home?

2 Learning Objective

Explain the up-front and monthly costs of buying a home.

Buying housing represents the largest outlay of funds over most people's lifetime. Some of these costs occur up-front. The largest of these is usually the down payment. Others, such as the mortgage payment, occur monthly. A few items, such as real estate property taxes, require both an initial outlay and recurring monthly payments. Table 9.1 illustrates these outlays for the purchase of a $185,000 home with $25,000 down financed by a 30-year mortgage at 6.5 percent interest. This same example is used repeatedly throughout this chapter to illustrate the costs of home buying (it is near the median price for first-time buyers in metropolitan areas).

Table 9.1   Illustrated Up-Front and Monthly Costs When Buying a Home (Purchase Price of a Home, $185,000 with $25,000 Down; Closing on July 1)

Home-Buying Costs	At Closing	Monthly
Payments Required Up-Front		
Down payment	$25,000	
Points (2)	3,200	
Attorney's fee	500	
Title search	200	
Title insurance (to protect lender)	320	
Title insurance (to protect buyer)	320	
Loan origination fee	800	
Credit reports	75	
Home inspection	400	
Recording fees	250	
Appraisal fee	250	
Termite and radon inspection fee	130	
Survey fee	100	
Notary fee	150	
Payments Required Monthly		
Principal and interest (from Table 9.3 for a $160,000 loan for 30 years at 6.5%)		$1,011.31
Mortgage insurance		53.33
Warranty insurance		30.00
Payments Required Up-Front and Then Monthly		
Property taxes ($2160 for the entire year, $1080 for first half-year, then $180 monthly)	1,080*	180.00
Homeowner's insurance ($1200 for the entire year; $600 for first half-year, then $100 monthly)	600†	100.00
Subtotal	**$33,375**	**$1,374.64**
Less amount owed by seller	−1,080*	—
Total	**$32,295**	**$1,374.64**

*Would be received from seller, who legally owes these taxes, and then deposited in escrow account to be available when the tax bill comes due at the end of the year.
†Would be paid to escrow account to be available when the premium for the next year is due.

Did You Know?

The Tax Consequences of Buying a Home

Home ownership makes you eligible for three big tax breaks.

1. **Mortgage interest and real estate taxes are tax deductible on federal (and most state) income tax returns.** These amounts usually exceed the IRS's standard deduction (see Chapter 4). You can then take advantage of even more deduction opportunities that are available to taxpayers who itemize.

2. **You can save the funds to buy a home in a tax-sheltered account.** Individuals can use Roth IRAs (see Chapter 17) to save for retirement. Once the account is five years old as much as $10,000 may be withdrawn tax free and penalty free, provided that a qualifying, first-time home buyer uses the funds for home-buying costs. This mechanism even allows parents or grandparents to make withdrawals from their Roth IRAs to help young family members buy their first home.

3. **The profits made by selling a home can be tax free.** If you sell a home for more than you originally paid, you have a **capital gain.** Gains are ordinarily taxable, but homeowners can avoid paying taxes on gains by buying a home that is more expensive, thus rolling the gain into the new home. Capital gains of up to $500,000 if married and filing jointly and up to $250,000 if single may be avoided. To qualify, the home must have been owned and used as the principal residence for two of the last five years prior to the date of the sale. In the first few years of home ownership, any appreciation likely will be offset by the anticipated sales commission. This explains the advice that you should not buy a home unless you know you will live in it for three years.

Most Up-Front Costs Are Due at the Closing

First-time home buyers are faced with high initial costs when buying a home. These include the down payment and closing costs. **Closing costs** include fees and charges other than the down payment and may vary from 2 to 10 percent of the mortgage loan amount. The down payment and closing costs must be paid at a meeting called the **closing** at which ownership of the property is transferred. All the parties to the purchase, sale, and the mortgage loan are represented at the closing. Up-front costs are indicated in green in Table 9.1.

closing costs
Include fees and charges other than the down payment and may vary from 2 to 10 percent of the mortgage loan amount.

The Down Payment The **down payment** on a home is simply the portion of the purchase price that is not borrowed. The buyer actually writes a check to the seller for that amount. In this example, we assume that the prospective homeowner has $25,000 to use as a down payment on a $185,000 home and will, thus, need to borrow $160,000.

down payment
Portion of the purchase price that is not borrowed.

Points A **point** (or **interest point**) is a fee equal to 1 percent of the total loan amount. Any charges for points must be paid in full when the home is bought, although sometimes they can be added to the amount borrowed. Lenders use points to increase their returns on loans. For example, a lender might advertise a loan as having an interest rate 0.25 percentage point below prevailing rates but then charge 1 point. Any points are, in effect, prepaid interest and compensate the lender for having a low interest rate. In our example, the lender charged 2 points on the $160,000 loan, resulting in a charge of $3200. By law, interest points must be included when calculating the APR for the loan. Interest points are deductible on federal income tax returns.

Point/interest point
Fee equal to 1 percent of the total mortgage loan amount.

Attorney Fees Home buyers should hire an attorney to review documents and advise and represent them prior to and during closing. Attorney fees commonly amount to 0.5 percent of the purchase price of the home, although some attorneys do this work for a flat fee ($500 in our example).

title
Legal right of ownership interest to real property.

deed
Written document used to convey real estate ownership.

Title Search and Insurance

The **title** to real property is the legal right of ownership interest. In real estate transactions, the title is transferred to a new owner through a **deed,** which is a written document used to convey real estate ownership.

Four types of deeds are used:

1. A **warranty deed** is the safest, as it guarantees that the title is free of any previous mortgages.

2. A **special warranty deed** guarantees only that the current owner has not placed any mortgage encumbrances on the title.

3. A **quitclaim deed** transfers whatever title the current owner had in the property with no guarantee.

4. A **deed of bargain and sale** conveys title with or without a guarantee that the seller had an ownership interest.

Instant Message

Joint Ownership Is Best When Couples Buy a Home

Both married couples and unmarried persons buying a home together should generally put the ownership in both names using joint tenancy with right of survivorship. If one of the parties dies, the other will have clear title to the entire property.

A title search and the purchase of title insurance protect the buyer's title to the property. Your attorney or title company will conduct a **title search** by inspecting court records and prepare a detailed written history of property ownership called an **abstract.** The seller normally pays the fees for this process ($200 in our example). Lenders often require buyers to purchase **title insurance** because it protects the lender's interest if the title is later found faulty. Premiums for title policies vary among title companies. The one-time charge at closing may amount to 0.20 percent of the amount of the loan for each policy ($320 [$160,000 × 0.002] in our example). Homeowners who wish to insure their own interest must purchase a separate title insurance policy (another $320 in our example).

title insurance
Protects the lender's interest if the title search is later found faulty.

home inspection
Conducted to ensure that the home is physically sound and that all operating systems are in proper order.

appraisal fee
Fee charged for a professionally prepared estimate of the fair market value of the property by an objective party.

Miscellaneous Fees

When a prospective mortgage borrower applies for a loan, the lender may charge a **loan origination fee** at the closing to process the loan ($800 or half of a point in our example). In addition, credit reports ($75 in our example) are needed before a home buyer can obtain a loan—and the borrower pays the fee for this report as well. Another important up-front cost is the **home inspection** ($400 in our example) conducted to ensure that the home is physically sound and that all operating systems are in proper order. Title and deed recording fees ($250 in our example) are charged to transfer ownership documents in the county courthouse. An **appraisal fee** ($250 in our example) may be required to obtain a professionally prepared estimate of the fair market value of the property by an objective party. If you are charged an appraisal fee, you have the right to receive a copy of the appraisal. Occasionally, termite and radon inspections ($130 in our example) are required by local laws and these are a good idea even when not required. A **survey** ($100 in our example) is sometimes required to certify the specific boundaries of the lot. Finally, separate **notary fees** ($150 in our example) may be charged for the services of those legally qualified to certify (or notarize) signatures.

Monthly Costs Include Both Principal and Interest

Once a home is purchased, the monthly costs can consume as much as 30 or 40 percent of your disposable income. These costs include the portion of your monthly payment that goes to principal (the amount you owe) and interest. Additional monthly costs include mortgage insurance, home warranty insurance, property taxes, and/or homeowner's insurance. Monthly costs are indicated in blue in Table 9.1.

PITI
Elements of a monthly real estate payment consisting of principal, interest, real estate taxes, and homeowner's insurance.

Mortgage Principal and Interest

A mortgage loan requires repayment of both principal (P) and interest (I), which are the first two letters of the acronym **PITI,** which real estate agents and lenders often use to indicate a mortgage payment that includes principal, interest, real estate taxes, and homeowner's insurance. In the example in Table 9.1, the mortgage payment for principal and interest on a 30-year mortgage for $160,000 at 6.5 percent is $1011.31. (Later in this chapter, you will learn how the P and I components for any mortgage loan are calculated).

Mortgage Insurance   Lenders today expect a 70 to 80 percent **loan-to-value (LTV) ratio** when a home is purchased. The LTV ratio is simply the loan amount divided by the value of the home (the purchase price initially). An 80 percent LTV ratio translates into a 20 percent down payment, an amount that is difficult to come by for most first-time buyers. Fortunately, a number of special programs allow for lower down payments for first-time buyers. When a buyer makes a lower down payment that results in an LTV higher than that desired by the lender, the lender requires that the borrower purchase mortgage insurance.

loan-to-value (LTV) ratio
Original or current outstanding loan balance divided by the home value.

Mortgage insurance insures the difference between the amount of down payment required by the lenders desired LTV ratio and the actual, lower down payment. In this way, the lender is assured of payment of the loan balance if the home were later repossessed for default and sold for less than the amount owed. Mortgage insurance may be obtained from several sources and can be canceled when the LTV ratio reaches the desired percent as the loan is paid down. You can obtain mortgage insurance from the following sources.

mortgage insurance
Insures the difference between the amount of down payment required by an 80 percent LTV ratio and the actual, lower down payment.

- **Private Mortgage Insurance. Private mortgage insurance (PMI)** is obtained from a private company. The largest private mortgage insurer is the Mortgage Guaranty Insurance Corporation (MGIC, pronounced "magic"). The cost of PMI varies from 0.25 to 2.0 percent of the debt, depending on the degree to which the loan-to-value ratio exceeds the lender-desired percentage. In our example, the loan-to-value ratio is 86.5 percent ($160,000 ÷ $185,000) and the lender required 80 percent (20 percent down). As a result, the annual private mortgage insurance premium is 0.4 percent of the mortgage loan (0.004 × $160,000) and is $640, or $53.33 per month ($640 ÷ 12).

  private mortgage insurance (PMI)
  Mortgage insurance obtained from a private company.

  Instead of making monthly payments for PMI, it may be possible to obtain lender-paid mortgage insurance. In such a case, the lender pays the mortgage insurance premium and in return charges a higher interest rate on the loan of perhaps an additional ¼ to ¾ of a percentage point. In this way, the mortgage insurance premium is tax deductible because it represents part of the interest payments. But in this case, the insurance cannot be canceled when the LTV ratio hits the desired percentage without completely refinancing the loan.

- **FHA Mortgage Insurance.** To encourage lending, the **Federal Housing Administration (FHA)** of the U.S. Department of Housing and Urban Development (HUD) insures loans that meet its standards. To obtain such mortgage insurance, the borrower must be creditworthy and the home must meet the FHA's minimum-quality standards. (For information on HUD mortgage programs, visit http://www.hud.gov/buying/index.cfm.) FHA mortgage insurance premiums may be paid as a single up-front, lump-sum payment or may be financed and paid in monthly amounts in the same way as private mortgage insurance.

  federal housing administration (FHA)
  An arm of the U.S. Department of Housing and Urban Development (HUD) that insures loans that meet its standards to encourage home ownership.

- **VA Mortgage Insurance.** The federal **Department of Veterans Affairs (VA)** promotes home ownership among military veterans (active-duty, reserve, and National Guard veterans may qualify) by providing the lender with a guarantee against buyer default. In effect, the VA (www.homeloans.va.gov) guarantee operates much like FHA or private mortgage insurance—that is, the lender is guaranteed a portion of the loan's value in the event that the home must be repossessed and sold.

Home Warranty Insurance   All homes for sale carry some type of implied warranty (see Chapter 8). In most states, home sellers must complete and sign a form verifying the condition of home features and major mechanical equipment at the time of sale. A seller who knowingly hides serious defects might be liable, but the buyer will have to hire an attorney and sue to prove this point. Also, many new-home builders provide an express warranty good for one year on the new homes they sell.

Home warranty insurance, another option for the homeowner, operates much like a service contract (also discussed in Chapter 8). Insurance companies sell this type of insurance on existing homes through real estate agents and builders. The example in Table 9.1 has a $30-per-month home warranty insurance protection. Typically, the homeowner must pay the first $100 to $500 of any repair.

Some Fees Are Paid Both Up-Front and Monthly

Some home-buying costs do not fit neatly into an up-front or monthly pattern. This is because they are billed annually. Property taxes and homeowner's insurance are examples. **Taxes (T)** and **insurance (I)** represent the last two letters of PITI. To ensure that these are paid when due, the lender usually requires that monthly installments be paid into an escrow account. An **escrow account** is a special reserve account at a financial institution in which funds are held until they are paid to a third party. When the insurance and tax bills are due, the lender pays them out of the escrow account.

Real Estate Property Taxes
Real estate property taxes must be paid to local governments and may range from 1 to 4 percent of the value of the home. The total property tax ($2160 in our example) is due once each year when the government sends out its tax bill. However, if a buyer takes possession during the tax year, the buyer must pay the taxes accrued so far into the escrow account at the closing ($1080, or 6 × $180 here) to ensure that sufficient funds will be available when the bill comes due at the end of the year. Then the monthly amount ($180 in our example) is paid thereafter into the escrow account. (Because it is the seller who really owed the taxes for the six months prior to the sale, the seller will pay the buyer $1080 on the day of the closing.)

Homeowner's Insurance
Lenders always require homeowners to insure the home itself in case of fire or other calamity. Both the home and its contents can be covered in a typical homeowner's insurance policy. (Chapter 10 covers this information in detail.) The annual premium for such insurance must be paid each year in advance ($1200 in this example). Lenders require prepayment of the estimated insurance premium each month ($100 here) into the escrow account. In our example illustrated in Table 9.1, the purchaser must be prepared to pay one-half year's premium ($600 here) on the closing day so that there will be sufficient funds in the account to pay the next year's full premium in six months when it is due.

The Bottom Line?

The wise financial planner will carefully estimate all initial and monthly costs of housing. Focusing only on the down payment and the monthly payment for principal and interest does not tell the whole story. In our example, the borrower put only 13.5 percent of the purchase price ($25,000 ÷ $185,000) as a down payment but with points and other up-front costs actually had to come up with 17.46 percent ($32,295 ÷ $185,000) at the closing. Thus, the closing costs represented almost 4 percent (17.46% − 13.5%) of the purchase price. Similarly, the monthly payment for principal and interest was $1011.31, but the actual monthly outlay will be $1374.64, an increase of 36 percent [($1374.64 − $1011.31) ÷ $1011.31]. This is the real dollar amount that buyers must fit into their budget when trying to determine whether they can afford to buy a home.

escrow account
Special reserve account at a financial institution in which funds are held until they are paid to a third party—in this case, for home insurance and for property taxes.

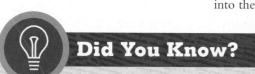

Did You Know?

About Real Estate Property Taxes

Real estate property taxes are based on the value of buildings and land. To calculate these taxes, local government officials first establish a **fair market value** for the owner's home and land. Next, the **assessed value** of the property is calculated. A home with a fair market value of $160,000, for example, might have an assessed value of $120,000. Although you can do little to influence the tax rate on real estate property, you can claim that assessed valuation of your home is too high. If your appeal is successful, your tax bill will be lowered accordingly. About one-half of all appeals succeed.

Concept Check 9.2

1. What is the standard down payment amount on a mortgage loan?
2. If you make a down payment that is lower than standard, identify the extra cost you will be required to pay.
3. Why do lenders use points in home loans, and who is responsible for paying points?
4. Explain why the down payment and mortgage principal and interest understate the actual up-front and monthly costs of home ownership.
5. When should you request that private mortgage insurance be canceled if such insurance was required at the time of purchase of a home?
6. Identify the components of PITI.

The Steps of Home Buying

The steps in the home-buying process closely resemble the planned buying steps outlined in Chapter 8. It may take several weeks or months to find a home that represents a good value and another four to five months to actually move into the home. Special attention will need to be paid to the seven steps outlined in Figure 9.1.

3 Learning Objective
Describe the steps in the home-buying process.

Get Your Finances in Order

You need to be financially ready to buy a home. Three tasks ease the process: doing a credit checkup, accurately estimating all monthly housing costs, and fitting projected housing costs into your budget.

Do a Credit Checkup Your credit history can make or break your chances of buying the home of your dreams. Obtain copies of your credit report and your credit scores from all three major credit reporting agencies (lenders use all three) about six months in advance of buying housing; you can then clear up any errors before the loan application process begins. See Chapter 6, pages 179 to 181 for the steps to take to correct errors in your credit report. Most people can improve their credit scores by correcting errors and rearranging credit accounts. See http://www.myfico.com/CreditEducation/ImproveYourScore.aspx for suggestions.

Use Internet Resources to Estimate Your Monthly Housing Costs It is vital to have an accurate estimate of what you will have to pay on a monthly basis for your new home. And it is not enough to just estimate the amount of the payment for principal and interest on your mortgage loan. Other costs must be considered, too. You should include all likely components of the monthly payment into your budget: the principal and interest, property taxes, homeowner's insurance, mortgage insurance, and perhaps a home warranty fee. You should also consider any additional costs you might pay for utilities. Heating, air conditioning, electric, and water are all areas for which homeowners generally pay more than renters. Including a 50 percent increase from what you are currently spending might be appropriate. Resources are available on the Internet to help estimate housing costs.

1. Start by choosing the type of home you would like to own and the neighborhood in which you would like to live.
2. Go to the www.realtor.com website to search for housing that matches your interests. You will be able to estimate the selling

Did You Know?

The Top 3 Financial Missteps When Buying Housing

People slip up in buying their home when they do the following:

1. Take out a mortgage loan inappropriate for their financial situation
2. Pay too much for a home and at too high an interest rate
3. Fail to request that private mortgage insurance be canceled when the loan-to-value ratio drops to 80 percent

Figure 9.1
Steps in the Process of Buying a Home

You should plan on it taking about 6 months to buy a home from the time you begin your efforts until you actually move in.

6 months before moving in	**1. Get your finances in order.** • Ensure that your credit bureau file is accurate and request any updates or corrections as necessary. • Estimate all your expected monthly housing costs. • Adjust your budget to fit the costs expected.
3 to 5 months before moving in	**2. Prequalify for a mortgage.** • Shop for best rates. • Estimate affordability using front- and back-end ratios. • Consult several lenders and mortgage brokers.
2 to 4 months before moving in	**3. Search for a home online and in person.**
2 months before moving in	**4. Agree to terms with a seller.** • Negotiate a price with the seller and give the seller earnest money. • Have your lawyer go over the purchase contract with you. • Sign the purchase contract with the seller. • Have the home inspected by someone you hire.
1 to 2 months before moving in	**5. Obtain a mortgage loan. Decide on the best type of mortgage loan for you.** • Formally apply for a mortgage from the desired lender. • Consider locking-in an interest rate if rates are likely to go up before the closing. • Arrange for a lawyer to help you go over the contract and the good-faith estimate of closing costs.
2 to 4 weeks before moving in	**6. Prepare for the closing.** • Make moving arrangements. • Activate all utilities. • Initiate the change of address process.
The Big Day	**7. Attend the closing.** • Correct any errors in the contract or uniform settlement statement. • Sign your name. Write the big checks. • Celebrate!!!!

price of similar housing and, by subtracting your available down payment amount, estimate the amount you will need to borrow.

3. Go to the www.bankrate.com website to estimate the current interest rates on mortgage loans in your market.

4. Use the calculator at www.bankrate.com to estimate the monthly payment for a loan of the amount you need at the prevailing interest rates.

5. Add an additional 30 to 40 percent (it was 36 percent in the Table 9.1 example) to the monthly payment on the loan itself for such things as homeowner's insurance, property taxes, maintenance, and upkeep.

Fit the Housing Costs into Your Budget   Once you have an estimate of the monthly costs associated with buying a home, you will need to see how these costs fit into your budget. You can follow a similar process as outlined in Chapter 8 on pages 226–227 to fit your payment into your budget. Some mortgages are set up for lower payments initially with possible (for adjustable-rate loans) and planned (for some loans tailored for first-time buyers) increases in the monthly payment. You will need to anticipate these and factor them into your budget to ensure that you will be able to afford any payment increases that could occur in the future. If your budget cannot accommodate your estimate of monthly costs, you may need to revise your goals by downsizing the type of home you desire or choosing housing in another neighborhood. Then readjust the estimate of your monthly housing costs and fit these revised numbers into your budget.

Prequalify for a Mortgage

It is really smart to begin looking into whether you will qualify for a mortgage loan given the price range of homes that you like and your intended down payment. You also need to make a preliminary decision about the time period of the loan and the choice between a fixed or variable interest rate (topics covered later in this chapter). A primary goal is to find the lowest APR for loans available. A good place to start is with the financial institutions in which you have your checking and savings accounts. In addition, you can search for low-rate loans at www.bankrate.com. Helpful information can be found at the websites for the U.S. Department of Housing and Urban Development (www.hud.gov/buying/) and the Federal National Mortgage Association (www.homepath.com).

Once you have an idea of the interest rate you might pay, you can consult lenders to determine whether you would actually qualify for a mortgage in the amount you would like. Lenders use two rules of thumb to estimate the maximum affordability of housing expenses: the front-end ratio and the back-end ratio.

 ## Did You Know?

The Income Needed to Qualify for a Mortgage

The table below gives you a quick idea of how much income you need to buy a home at a certain price using a front-end ratio of 28 percent. The illustration is for a 30-year loan with a 20 percent down payment. For each home price, the top figure in each row shows the monthly payment for principal, interest, real estate taxes, and homeowner's insurance for the interest rates; the bottom figure shows the required gross annual income to qualify for the loan. For example, a 7 percent loan on a $180,000 home requires a monthly payment of $1183 plus an income of $50,700 to qualify. Taxes and insurance are assumed to be 1.5 percent of the purchase price (divided by 12 months). Visit the *Garman/Forgue* companion website to perform these calculations for a variety of home prices and interest rates.

	Price of Home						
Interest Rate	$120,000	$150,000	$180,000	$210,000	$240,000	$270,000	$300,000
5.5	695	869	1,043	1,216	1,390	1,564	1,363
	29,800	37,200	44,700	52,100	59,600	67,000	74,500
6.0	725	907	1,088	1,269	1,451	1,634	1,814
	31,100	38,900	46,600	54,400	62,200	70,000	77,700
6.5	757	946	1,135	1,324	1,514	1,703	1,892
	32,400	40,600	48,700	56,800	64,900	73,000	81,100
7.0	789	986	1,183	1,380	1,577	1,775	1,971
	33,800	42,300	50,700	59,200	67,600	76,100	84,500
7.5	821	1,027	1,232	1,437	1,642	1,848	2,053
	35,200	44,000	52,800	61,600	70,400	79,200	88,000
8.0	854	1,068	1,282	1,495	1,709	1,922	2,136
	36,600	45,800	54,900	64,100	73,200	82,400	91,500

front-end ratio
Compares the total annual PITI expenditures for housing with the loan applicant's gross annual income to assess the borrower's ability to pay the mortgage.

back-end ratio
Compares the total of all monthly PITI expenditures plus auto loans and other debts with gross monthly income.

mortgage broker
Individual or company that acts as an intermediary between borrowers and lenders.

- The **front-end ratio** compares the total annual expenditures for housing (the principal and interest on the mortgage plus the real estate taxes and insurance) with the loan applicant's gross annual income. Generally, the total annual expenditures should not exceed 25 to 29 percent of gross annual income. Applying a 28 percent front-end ratio, a young couple with a combined gross annual income of $73,000 could qualify for a mortgage requiring total annual expenditures of less than $20,440 (0.28 × $73,000), or $1703 per month.

- The **back-end ratio** compares the total of all monthly debt payments (for the mortgage, real estate taxes, and insurance, plus auto loans and other debts) with gross monthly income. Generally, lenders require that monthly debt payments do not exceed 33 to 41 percent of gross monthly income. Applying a back-end ratio of 38 percent, the same couple could qualify for any loan that does not result in total monthly debt repayments exceeding $2311 (their monthly income of $6083 [$73,000 ÷ 12] × 0.38). During the housing boom of the mid-2000s some lenders allowed people to buy homes with back-end ratios as high as 50 percent. Such practices were ripe for disaster. You should never rely on what a lender says you can afford. If you think you will lose sleep at night because of a high mortgage payment you should instead buy a home that costs less.

Over one-half of all mortgage loans today are arranged through a mortgage broker. A **mortgage broker** is an individual or company that acts as an intermediary between borrowers and lenders. In other words, a broker helps lenders find borrowers and borrowers find lenders. Either the lender or the borrower may pay the fee charged by the broker. If the lender pays this fee, the broker legally represents the lender. If the borrower pays it, the broker legally represents the borrower. Thus, if you want the broker to work to find you the lowest possible rate, you should be prepared to pay for the service.

Moderate- and low-income families often find it difficult to save the 20 percent down payment required by lenders. FHA- and VA-insured loans (discussed earlier in this chapter) provide some opportunity for low down payments but are not available to all borrowers or on all homes. Other programs have been developed for low-income buyers and people buying homes for the first time. Lenders in your area can provide you with information about programs that target these special-needs groups. Through such programs, it may be possible to buy a home with a low (or no) down payment and at a low, government-subsidized interest rate.

Did You Know?

About Buying a Home on Two Incomes

Many young couples base their ability to afford housing on their combined incomes, and that is not a smart financial practice. Such a decision locks them into a required full-time, dual-income lifestyle once they have purchased a home. Family obligations or a job loss may later disrupt their ability or willingness to continue that lifestyle. Instead, they might be better off gauging housing affordability on just one income or on parttime work for the second income.

Instant Message

Keep Your Debts Low If You Want to Buy a Home

Student loan, car loan, and credit card payments can easily disqualify a potential home buyer based on the back-end ratio. If you plan on buying a home some day, you need to be very careful about how much debt you take on while in school and after graduation.

Search for a Home Online and in Person

Searching for a home requires a commitment of time. You do not want to be impulsive when you will be committing yourself to many thousands of dollars of expense. You can find housing in any number of ways, but the Internet is most helpful. You can narrow your choices to excellent prospects without ever leaving home. Simply go to www.realtor.com and search for homes in your community. You will be able to see floor plans, photos, descriptions of features and condition, and price-related information. Once you have found some homes you would like to see, you can contact the seller or the real estate agent handling the properties.

Agree to Terms with the Seller

Once you have your finances in order and have received assurances that you can qualify for a mortgage, you can start looking for a home

Did You Know?

How to Search for a Home

You can be a more effective home shopper if you do the following:

- **Make a list** in advance of special features or "must have" items that you are looking for in your new home.
- **Drive around the neighborhood** before you visit a property. Get out of the car and listen. Are there industrial noises or excessive highway noises? Any pet noises from the neighbors? Then ask the real estate agent and/or seller about any aspects that are of interest to you such as types of neighbors and availability of parks and schools.
- **Look at only two or three properties** in one day at most. Looking at too many homes at one time can be confusing and exhausting.

- **Bring a notepad and tape measure** with you. Make sketches of the floor plans that you like. Bring along a camera or video equipment.
- **Obtain written information** describing details about the home. Ask about special home features, utility costs (you can confirm these with the utility company), and any recent improvements and repairs.
- **Check for slope and sags** by rolling a small rubber ball along floors, countertops, and door frames.
- **Walk around the outside of the property** to assess the external condition of the home and yard. Look for signs of water damage to the home or drainage issues in the yard.

---

in earnest. Sellers generally put a price on the property that is 5 to 15 percent higher than the amount that they actually expect to receive. Therefore, you may want to make an offer to buy that is somewhat lower than the asking price. Perhaps $10,000 to $30,000 is at stake here. Some buyers today make a very low offer, perhaps 20 to 25 percent less than the asking price, and hope that a distressed seller will sell.

Make an Offer to Buy The written offer to purchase real estate is called a **purchase offer** (or an **offer to purchase**). Of course, you will specify a price, but other aspects of the sale may be included in your offer as well. Examples of conditions include successful termite and radon inspections; a home inspection of the plumbing, heating, cooling, and electrical systems; and inclusion of the living room drapes and kitchen and other appliances. When you make an offer, you need to give the seller some **earnest money** as a deposit; 1 or 2 percent of the purchase price should be sufficient to show your good faith when making an offer to purchase the seller's property. This money is returned if the seller rejects the offer.

purchase offer/offer to purchase
Written offer to purchase real estate.

earnest money
Funds given to seller as a deposit to hold the property until a purchase contract can be negotiated.

Respond to a Counteroffer Most home sellers do not accept the first offer from a prospective buyer. Instead, they usually make a **counteroffer,** which is a legal offer to sell (or buy) a home at a different price and perhaps with different conditions from those outlined in the original offer. You can assume that a seller who is willing to make a counteroffer may also be willing to sell at a slightly lower price. Thus, if you make a counteroffer falling between the two prices, a sale will usually result. Of course, if you push the seller too far, you risk having the seller back out of the negotiations altogether.

Negotiate and Sign a Purchase Contract A **purchase contract** (or **sales contract**) is the formal legal document that outlines the actual agreement that results from the real estate negotiations. It includes the final negotiated price and a list of conditions that the seller has agreed to accept. When the purchase contract is signed, the seller keeps the earnest money as a deposit.

You want to make sure that your earnest money is protected by including one or more **contingency clauses** in the purchase offer. These clauses specify that certain conditions must be satisfied before a contract is binding. One recommended clause would stipulate that the seller must refund the earnest money if the buyer cannot obtain satisfactory financing

purchase contract/sales contract
Formal legal document that outlines the actual agreement that results from the real estate negotiations.

contingency clauses
Specify that certain conditions must be satisfied before a contract is binding.

Did You Know?

The Role of Real Estate Agents

A **real estate broker (agent)** is a person licensed by a state to provide advice and assistance, for a fee, to buyers or sellers of real estate. Real estate brokers who are members of the National Association of Realtors often use the registered trademark of **Realtor®** to describe themselves. Brokers typically earn a commission of 5 to 7 percent on the sale price of a home. The seller—not the buyer—usually pays this commission. **Flat-fee brokers,** who charge a flat fee for their services rather than a percentage-based commission, are also available in most real estate markets.

Almost any agent can show you housing that is **listed** (under contract with the seller and the broker) by the realty firm. In addition, many communities have a **multiple-listing (or open-listing) service,** which is an information and referral network among real estate brokers allowing properties listed with a particular broker to be shown by all other brokers.

Buyers should understand that a real estate agent can play three possible roles. The **listing agent** is the party with whom the seller signs the listing agreement. Listing agents advertise the property, show it to prospective buyers, and assist the seller in negotiations. They receive a commission when the home is sold and owe the seller undivided loyalty. A **selling agent** is any real estate agent that seeks out buyers for a home. Listing agents also play this role, but any real estate agent can search for buyers to whom to sell a property.

Most home buyers use a real estate agent in their search for a home. They should understand that the agent's legal obligation is to the party who will pay his or her fee or commission—generally the seller! Buyers should be wary of this potential conflict of interest and hire their own broker if they need such services. That is, home buyers who want an agent to represent their interests should obtain the services of a **buyer's agent.** This person serves as the buyer's representative in the real estate negotiations and transaction.

Why is the distinction among the three types of agents important? Consider the example of a buyer who has asked a selling agent to help him find a home. During negotiations, the potential buyer decides to offer $175,000 for a property with an asking price of $189,000 but tells the selling agent that he would be willing to go as high as $180,000. The selling agent would then be legally obligated to tell the seller about this $180,000 figure.

---

real estate broker
Person licensed by a state to provide advice and assistance, for a fee, to buyer or sellers of real estate.

good-faith estimate
Lender's list of all the costs associated with the loan, including the annual percentage rate (APR), application and processing fees, closing costs, and any other charges that must be paid when the deal is legally consummated.

loan commitment/loan preapproval
Lender's promise to grant a loan.

within a specified time period, usually 30 days. Other important contingency clauses should allow the buyer to opt out of the deal if the home fails to pass certain aspects of the home inspection (for example, the inspection uncovers a major structural defect). Of course, if at this point you simply change your mind about buying, you will forfeit your earnest money and may be sued for damages.

Apply for a Mortgage Loan

Only after you sign a purchase contract do you formally apply for a mortgage loan on the specific home you have selected. The potential lender usually approves or turns down this request within a few days.

When you apply for a mortgage, the lender must give you a **good-faith estimate** of all the costs associated with the loan, including the annual percentage rate, application and processing fees, and any other charges that must be paid when the deal is legally consummated. Table 9.1 provides an example of the type of information in the good-faith estimate.

The exact interest rate on your mortgage may be the current rate at the time of application or the rate in force at the time of closing. If you expect rates to rise between the time you apply for the loan and the actual closing, you may wish to pay a small fee to obtain a **mortgage lock-in.** This agreement includes a lender's promise to hold a certain interest rate for a specified period of time, such as 60 days. It may be part of, but is not the same as, a **loan commitment** (or **loan preapproval),** which is a lender's promise to grant a loan.

Did You Know?

Your Credit Score Affects the Mortgage Rate You Pay

Mortgage lenders charge interest rates based on your credit score. Here are illustrative credit scores and the corresponding mortgage loan interest rates.

Credit Score	APR
760–850	5.1%
700–759	5.3%
680–699	5.6%
660–679	5.8%
640–659	6.0%
620–639	6.7%
600–619	7.0%
Below 600	It is unlikely that a loan could be obtained and, if so, only in the subprime market.

Loan applicants whose scores are lower than desired are turned down or, more commonly, referred to a lender in the **subprime market,** which serves higher-risk applicants with credit scores below 620. Borrowers who are placed in this market are often happy to have obtained a loan. However, such loans carry higher interest rates than normal and have terms and conditions that can lead to future repayment difficulties. Some subprime borrowers actually may qualify for loans at standard rates if they take steps to improve their credit scores and search more extensively.

Prepare for the Closing

After you have obtained a mortgage, you are not yet finished. Of course, you will want to do all the usual tasks associated with moving; giving notification of your change of address, hiring a moving company (or not), getting your utilities shut off at your old residence and on at your new are examples. But there are two very important additional steps to take that can save you thousands of dollars and many headaches.

Hire Your Own Inspector   Recall that you should always have a contingency clause included in your purchase contract so that you can back out of the deal if the house fails to pass the home inspection. The inspector should look for termite infestation, wood rot, and radon gas as well as examine the general condition of the home, including heating/cooling, plumbing, and electrical. You should pay the inspector yourself and should not choose one based on the recommendation of the seller's real estate agent. You want an independent person who is well qualified to look out for your interests. If the inspector finds problems, you can negotiate with the seller for an adjustment in the purchase price of the home or, in severe cases, use the contingency clause to back out of the deal. Be careful about allowing the seller to arrange the repair as they may choose the cheapest and quickest solution, not necessarily the one that adequately repairs the problem.

Hire an Attorney   The good-faith estimate that you receive is a legal document outlining your entire up-front and monthly home-buying costs. Hiring an attorney to go over the estimate and your

Instant Message

Buyers Have a Right to Full Disclosure

Federal law governs the information that must be disclosed to real estate purchasers. A list of these disclosures can be found by going to www.hud.gov and searching for the keyword "RESPA" to learn more about your rights under the Real Estate Settlement Procedures Act.

Instant Message

Protect Your Credit Score While Waiting for Your Mortgage to Close

In the weeks leading up to the closing for a home purchase, it may be tempting to begin buying furniture, appliances, outdoor equipment, and other costly items for the home. Think twice if doing so means racking up high balances on your credit cards. Your mortgage lender will raise your interest rate if you significantly change your credit score before closing.

purchase contract to ensure that everything is in order is money well spent. Many of the closing costs are negotiable, and your attorney can advise on how to keep these costs to a minimum.

Sign Your Name on Closing Day

uniform settlement statement
Lists all of the costs and fees to be paid at the closing.

To complete the sale, the buyer, the seller, and their chosen representatives generally gather in the lender's office for the closing. At the closing, all required documents are signed and payments are made. A key document is the **uniform settlement statement,** which lists all of the costs and fees to be paid at the closing. You have the right to see this statement one business day before the closing so that you can avoid surprises and can compare the fees with the good-faith estimate provided earlier. Challenge any discrepancy.

Concept Check 9.3

1. Distinguish between the two rules of thumb that lenders use to assess housing affordability.
2. What services does a mortgage broker offer?
3. What services do real estate agents provide for buyers?
4. Why should a buyer be cautious about working with a seller's agent?
5. Explain the benefits of having contingency clauses in a home purchase agreement.

Financing a Home

4 Learning Objective
Distinguish among conventional and alternative ways of financing a home and list the advantages and disadvantages of each.

People often rent housing for five years or more while they save enough to make a down payment to purchase a home. Some couples postpone having children, while other people cut back on entertainment and vacations and put off making major purchases. Before buying, you must become knowledgeable about mortgage loans and learn how they are used to purchase a home.

The Mathematics of Mortgage Loans

Mortgage loans are available from depository institutions (described in Chapters 5 and 7) and mortgage finance companies. In exchange for the loan, the lender (**mortgagee**) has a **lien** on the real estate—that is, the legal right to take and hold property or to sell it in the event the borrower (**mortgagor**) defaults on the loan.

The term *mortgage* receives its name from the concept of amortization, which is the process of gradually paying off a loan through a series of periodic payments to a lender. Each payment is allocated in two ways:

1. **A portion goes** to pay the simple interest on outstanding debt for that month multiplied by the periodic (monthly) interest rate.

2. **The remainder goes** to repay a portion of the principal, which is the debt remaining from the original amount borrowed.

As the principal is paid down, increasingly smaller portions of the payments will be required to pay interest while the portion of the payments devoted to the principal will grow larger. These changes in the allocation of each payment are illustrated in Figure 9.2.

Note the slow decline in the amount of each monthly payment going toward interest. A high proportion of each monthly payment during the early years of a mortgage loan is allocated to interest. This is because the outstanding debt remains very high. Table 9.2 shows the interest and principal payment amounts for the first three months of a $160,000,

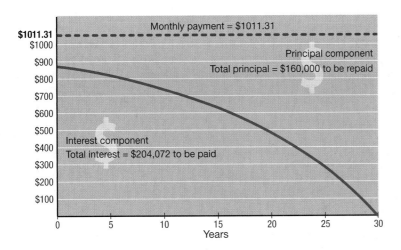

Figure 9.2
Change in Principal and Interest Components of the Monthly Payment on a $160,000 Mortgage Loan at 6.5 Percent Interest Rate for 30 Years

Table 9.2 Amortization Effects of Monthly Payment of $1011.31 on a $160,000, 30-Year Mortgage Loan at 6.5 Percent

First Month

$160,000 × 6.5% × 1/12	=	$ 866.67 Interest payment
$1,011.31 − 866.67	=	$144.64 Principal repayment
$160,000 − 144.64	=	$159,855.36 Balance due

Second Month

$159,855.36 × 6.5% × 1/12	=	$865.88 Interest payment
$1,011.31 − 865.88	=	$145.43 Principal repayment
$159,855.36 − 145.43	=	$159,709.93 Balance due

Third Month

$159,709.93 × 6.5% × 1/12	=	$865.10 Interest payment
$1,011.31 − 865.10	=	$146.21 Principal repayment
$159,709.93 − 146.21	=	$159,563.72 Balance due

30-year, 6.5 percent mortgage loan. For the first month, $866.67 goes for interest costs, and only $144.64 goes toward retirement of the principal of the loan. Table 9.3 provides a partial **amortization schedule** for the same loan. When you take out a mortgage loan, you will receive a full amortization schedule for each month of the loan listing all the monthly payments, the portions that will go toward interest and principal, and the debt remaining after each payment is made.

It takes many years of monthly payments to significantly reduce the outstanding balance of the loan. At any point, the amount that has been paid off (including the down payment) plus any appreciation in the value of the home represents the homeowner's **equity** (the dollar value of the home in excess of the amount owed on it). Figure 9.3 illustrates the buildup of equity in a home that results from reductions in the amount owed and the growth in the home's value. Note that the bulk of the increase in equity is a result of increases in the market value of the home. Additional payments can be directed toward the principal at any time to reduce the amount owed, increase equity, and reduce the eventual total amount of interest paid on the loan.

amortization schedule
List that shows all the monthly payments, the portions that will go toward interest and principal, and the debt remaining after each payment is made throughout the life of the loan.

equity
Dollar value of the home in excess of the amount owed on it.

Table 9.3 Partial Amortization Schedule for a $160,000, 30-Year (360-Payment) Mortgage Loan at 6.5 Percent

Payment Number (Month)	Monthly Payment Amount	Portion to Principal Repayment	Portion to Interest	Total of Payments to Date	Outstanding Loan Balance
1	$1,011.31	$144.64	$866.67	$1,011.31	$159,855.36
2	1,011.31	145.43	865.88	2,022.62	159,709.93
3	1,011.31	146.21	865.10	3,033.93	159,563.72
12	1,011.31	154.33	856.98	12,135.72	158,057.31
24	1,011.31	164.66	846.64	24,271.44	156,138.84
60	1,011.31	200.01	811.30	60,678.60	149,577.55
120	1,011.31	276.58	734.73	121,357.20	135,365.22
180	1,011.31	382.46	628.85	182,035.80	115,712.16
240	1,011.31	528.88	482.43	242,714.40	88,535.58
300	1,011.31	731.34	279.97	303,393.00	50,955.32
360	1,011.31	1,005.86	5.45	364,071.60	0

Figure 9.3
Change in Loan Balance and Owner's Equity for a $185,000 Home Purchased with $25,000 Down at a 6.5 Percent Interest Rate for 30 Years

(Assumes a 4% Annual Market Price Increase)

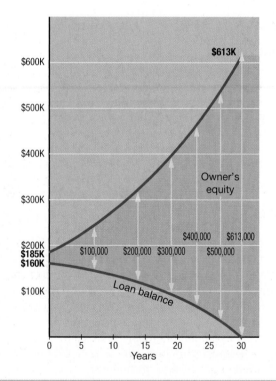

Factors Affecting the Monthly Payment on a Mortgage

Three factors affect the monthly payment on a mortgage loan: the amount borrowed, the interest rate charged, and the length of maturity of the loan.

The Amount Borrowed The payment schedule illustrated in Table 9.4 gives the monthly payment required for each $1000 of a mortgage loan at various interest rates. Using this table, you can calculate the monthly payment for mortgage loans of different amounts. For example, the $160,000 mortgage loan described earlier (6.5 percent for 30 years) costs $6.3207 per $1000 per month. Thus, 160 × $6.3207 equals $1011.31.

Making a down payment that is larger than required lowers the borrower's monthly payments. For example, a down payment of 30 percent, or $55,500, would lower the monthly payment on the loan to $818.53 [$6.3207 × ($185,000 − $55,500) ÷ 1000]. A smaller loan also carries lower total interest costs and may qualify for an interest rate that is perhaps 0.5 percentage points lower. In that case, the payment for the same loan would amount to only $776.42 [$5.9955 × ($185,000 − $55,500) ÷ 1000].

The Interest Rate The higher the interest rate, the higher the monthly payment on a mortgage loan (see Table 9.4). For example, a $1011.31 monthly payment is required for a $160,000 mortgage loan taken out for 30 years at 6.5 percent. If the interest rate were 7.5 percent, the monthly mortgage payment would be $1118.74 (160 × $6.9921), an increase of over $107. The effects are even greater when you consider the total of all the monthly payments and the total interest paid over the life of the loan. The 6.5 percent loan will have total payments of $364,072 (360 × $1011.31) with total interest of $204,072 ($364,072 − $160,000.00). For the 7.5 percent loan, total payments are $402,746 (360 × $1118.74) and

Table 9.4 **Estimating Mortgage Loan Payments for Principal and Interest (Monthly Payment per $1000 Borrowed)**

Interest Rate (%)	Payment Period (Years)			
	15	20	25	30
4.5	$7.6499	$6.3265	$5.5583	$5.0669
5.0	7.9079	6.5996	5.8459	5.3682
5.5	8.1708	6.8789	6.1409	5.6779
6.0	8.4386	7.1643	6.4430	5.9955
6.5	8.7111	7.4557	6.7521	6.3207
7.0	8.9883	7.7530	7.0678	6.6530
7.5	9.2701	8.0559	7.3899	6.9921
8.0	9.5565	8.3644	7.7182	7.3376
8.5	9.8474	8.6782	8.0523	7.6891
9.0	10.1427	8.9973	8.3920	8.0462
9.5	10.4422	9.3213	8.7370	8.4085
10.0	10.7461	9.6502	9.0870	8.7757

Note: To use this table to figure a monthly mortgage payment, divide the amount borrowed by 1000 and multiply by the appropriate figure in the table for the interest rate and time period of the loan. For example, a $160,000 loan for 30 years at 6.5 percent would require a payment of $1011.31 [($160,000 ÷ 1000) × 6.3207]; over 20 years, it would require a payment of $1192.91 [($160,000 ÷ 1000) × 7.4557]. For calculations for different interest rates, visit the *Garman/Forgue* companion website.

total interest is $242,746 ($402,764 − $160,000.00). Thus, the added cost for the 30-year loan at 7.5 percent is $38,674 over the life of the loan.

Length of Maturity of the Loan   Table 9.5 illustrates the relationships among maturity length, monthly payment, and interest cost for a $100,000 loan at various interest rates. A longer term of repayment results in a smaller payment (for loans with the same interest rate). More total interest is paid over the longer repayment time period despite the lower monthly payment. For example, the monthly payment on a 7 percent loan is $775 for 20 years but only $665 for 30 years. When the loan is paid back in 20 years, the total interest costs are much lower ($86,000 rather than $139,400, for a savings of $53,400).

Some borrowers choose a mortgage loan with a comparatively short 15-year maturity. The advantages include a faster buildup of equity, lower total interest, and a quicker payoff of the loan. These advantages can also be gained with a 20- or 30-year mortgage by simply paying additional amounts toward the principal during the time period of the loan. It is wise to take a longer repayment period even if you plan to pay off the loan in 15 (or fewer) years. With that strategy, the faster payoff is optional rather than mandatory.

The Conventional Mortgage Loan

conventional mortgage
A fixed-rate, fixed-term, fixed-payment mortgage loan.

A **conventional mortgage** is a fixed-rate, fixed-term, fixed-payment mortgage loan. Borrowers like conventional mortgages because they are so predictable. For example, a $160,000 loan could be granted at a 6.5 percent annual interest rate over a period of 30 years with a fixed monthly payment of $1011.31. The payment is the same for month after month and year after year. Most borrowers see a conventional fixed-rate loan as the best possible choice because the amount of all future payments is known in advance.

The Adjustable-Rate Mortgage Loan

adjustable-rate mortgage (ARM)/variable-rate mortgage
Mortgage in which the borrower's interest rate fluctuates according to some index of interest rates based on the rising or falling cost of credit in the economy—thus transferring interest rate risk to the borrower.

With an **adjustable-rate mortgage (ARM)**—sometimes called a **variable-rate mortgage**—the borrower's interest rate fluctuates according to some index of interest rates based on the rising or falling cost of credit in the economy. With an ARM, the risk of interest rate changes is assumed by the borrower, not the lender. As a consequence, the monthly payment could

Table 9.5   Monthly Payment and Total Interest to Repay a $100,000 Loan

Length of Loan	Interest Rate (%)				
	6	6.5	7	7.5	8
30 years	$600	$632	$665	$699	$734
	116,000	127,500	139,400	151,600	164,200
25 years	644	675	707	739	772
	93,200	102,500	112,100	121,700	131,600
20 years	716	745	775	806	836
	71,800	78,800	86,000	93,400	100,600
15 years	844	871	899	927	955
	51,900	56,800	61,800	66,900	71,900

Note: Figures are rounded. The top figure in each pair is the monthly payment, and the bottom figure is the total interest paid to the nearest $100.

You can use this table to calculate the monthly payment and total interest on any loan at these same interest rates. Simply divide the amount of the loan by $100,000 and multiply that figure by the amounts shown in the table. For example, the loan $160,000 at 6.5% for 30 years illustrated in this chapter has a monthly payment of $1011 (1.6 × $632) and total interest of $204,000 (1.6 × $127,500).

increase or decrease, usually on an annual basis, but sometimes monthly. Borrowers with ARMs should always determine the "worst case" scenario for interest rate increases under their loan contract and calculate the monthly payment that would result.

ARM rates are usually 1 to 3 percentage points below conventional mortgage rates. Lenders sometimes offer an even lower **teaser rate** to entice people to borrow using an ARM. Such a loan will carry an interest rate for the first year or so that may be 1 to 3 percentage points below the regular ARM loan rates, a substantial savings over a conventional mortgage. Borrowers using an ARM with a teaser rate must be prepared for the higher monthly payments that will occur when interest rates rise in the future. If you do not feel you can afford even a minimal increase in the rate you should not take out this type of loan.

Most ARMs have **interest-rate caps** that limit the amount by which the interest rate can increase (perhaps no more than 2 percent per year and no more than 5 percent over the life of the loan). **Payment caps,** in contrast, limit the amount by which the payment can vary on an ARM. Having a loan with a payment cap but without an equivalent interest-rate cap is an invitation to **negative amortization,** which occurs when monthly payments are actually smaller than necessary to pay the interest. This practice will result in a principal loan balance that rises rather than falls. Payment caps are an invitation to financial disaster. Many variations of ARMs exist.

teaser rate
Low interest rate that lenders sometimes use to lure buyers; these rates will be low for the first year or so and then will rise to more realistic rates.

negative amortization
Occurs when monthly payments are actually smaller than necessary to pay interest on the loan, which will result in a rising principal loan balance.

Alternative Mortgage Loans

Most alternative lending approaches aim to keep the monthly payment as low as possible, especially in the early years of the loan. This also permits borrowers to purchase larger, more expensive homes than they might be able to afford with a conventional loan. Do not take out an alternative loan to buy a home unless you are positive you can afford it. Remember that in recent years millions of Americans made the wrong decision by taking out these types of loans and then defaulted.

Interest-Only Mortgage With an **interest-only mortgage** loan, you pay only the interest on the mortgage in monthly payments for a fixed term. No monthly payment is made on the debt itself. After the end of that term, usually five to seven years, you can refinance, pay the balance in a lump sum, or start paying off the principal with a commensurate jump in the monthly payment. The obvious lure of an interest-only mortgage is its lower monthly payment. However, if the value of the home were to decrease, negative amortization would occur possibly leading to the borrower becoming upside down on the mortgage.

Instant Message

Be Very Wary of Option ARM Mortgages

One of the contributors to the housing foreclosure crises was the use of **option ARM** mortgages structured to have low monthly payments in the early years. Option ARMs give the borrower the option of paying the standard payment, an interest-only payment, and even worse, a less than interest payment resulting in negative amortization. Many people took out option ARMs that had artificially low teaser rates for the first years of the loan. Then, perhaps after 4 years the rate would "reset" to market rates with a new payment perhaps $200 or more higher than the earlier payments. Millions of mortgages became unaffordable and went into foreclosure after the rate reset.

interest-only mortgage
Mortgage in which the borrower pays only the interest on the mortgage in monthly payments for a fixed term, then either refinances the principal, pays off the principal, or starts paying the higher monthly payment with the principal payments added in.

graduated-payment mortgage
Mortgage in which borrower pays smaller-than-normal payments in the early years but payments gradually increase to larger-than-normal payments in later years.

Graduated-Payment Mortgage With a **graduated-payment mortgage,** smaller-than-normal payments are required in the early years, but payments gradually increase to larger-than-normal payments in later years. The interest rate is fixed, but payments early in the life of the mortgage may be lower than necessary to pay even the interest, resulting in possible negative amortization. Graduated-payment mortgages are attractive to buyers who expect substantial increases in their income in the future. You should be very certain of such increase before you think about using a graduated payment mortgage

Lender Buy-Down Mortgage With a **lender buy-down mortgage,** a base interest rate is set for the loan that is perhaps 0.5 percentage points higher than the interest rate for a conventional mortgage. For the first year, the borrower pays a rate 2 percentage points below the base rate. In the second year, the rate is 1 point below the base rate. In the third and future years, the base rate would be changed. These changes are known in advance and

Advice from a Pro...

Cancel Private Mortgage Insurance as Soon as Possible

Most first time home buyers cannot make the standard loan-to-value ratio of 80 percent (20 percent down) and must buy private mortgage insurance. PMI premiums must be paid until the unpaid balance drops to 80 percent of the home's value. As the borrower makes mortgage payments over time, the amount of principal remaining to be paid will decline until eventually the 80 percent threshold is reached. At that point, the lender must notify the borrower of the opportunity to drop the PMI.

As illustrated in Figure 9.3, a borrower might start out owing $160,000 or 86.5 percent of the value of the home. It takes about six years to reach the 80 percent threshold ($148,000 = 0.80 × $185,000) simply by making loan payments. The good news is that the value of the home may increase much faster than the loan principal declines.

In the example in Figure 9.3, the 80 percent threshold will be reached in about three years because of the rising value of the home.

When that threshold is attained, the borrower can ask the lender to cancel the PMI. Lenders usually require an appraisal of the property before doing so, but the cost of the appraisal (perhaps $300) represents money well spent. It is a smart move to make such a request, and it is even smarter to continue making the same monthly payment on the mortgage after the PMI is removed. The extra amount will be applied to the principal of the loan, thereby paying it off even sooner.

Michael Ruff and Sherry Tshibangu
Monroe Community College

---

are contractual. First-time home buyers often use buy-down mortgages to take advantage of lower monthly payments in early years of the loan. The borrower must be confident that these increases will fit into their planned budget before considering this type of mortgage.

Rollover (Renegotiable-Rate) Mortgage

A **rollover mortgage** consists of a series of short-term loans for 2- to 5-year time periods but with total amortization spread over the usual 25 to 30 years. The loan is renewed for each time period at the market interest rates that prevail at the time of the renewal. The beginning interest rate on rollover mortgages can be deceptively attractive for a first-time home buyer. Interest rates are low in today's market; thus there is only one way interest rates can go in the future—up.

Shared-Appreciation Mortgage

With a **shared-appreciation mortgage,** the lender offers an interest rate about one-third less than the market rate. In exchange, the lender gains the right to receive perhaps one-third of any appreciation in the home's value when the home is sold or ten years after the time of the loan.

Growing-Equity Mortgage

The **growing-equity mortgage (GEM)** is meant for people who design their loan in advance to reduce interest costs by paying off the mortgage loan early. One form of GEM is the **biweekly mortgage,** which calls for payments to be made every two weeks that represent half of the normal monthly payment. The borrower, therefore, makes 26 payments per year. For example, a $200,000, 7 percent, 30-year loan requires a $1330.60 monthly payment for a total of $15,967.20 (12 × $1330.60) paid in one year. On a biweekly basis with payments of $665.30 ($1330.60 ÷ 2), the total amount paid each year would be $17,297.80 ($665.30 × 26). The difference of $1330.60 ($17,297.80 − $15,967.20) is equivalent to one extra monthly payment per year and is applied to the principal of the loan. Under the biweekly repayment plan, a loan may be repaid in approximately 20 years, rather than the 30 years dictated by the monthly payment plan.

biweekly mortgage
A form of growing-equity mortgage (GEM) that calls for payments of half of the normal payment to be made every two weeks; the borrower thus makes 26 payments a year and reduces the principal amount by one full payment each year; this reduces the mortgage term to about 20 years on a 30-year mortgage.

Setting up a loan as a GEM from the beginning forces you to make the agreed-upon additional payments. However, almost all mortgages use the declining-balance method of calculating interest (See Chapter 7) thus permitting payment of additional amounts toward principal at any time. Thus, you can voluntarily pay additional amounts on the principal without being locked into it as you would with a growing equity mortgage. For example, even paying an additional $70 (or $1400.60) per month on the preceding loan would allow the loan to be paid off in just over 25 years and would save almost $50,000 in interest costs.

Assumable Mortgage

With an **assumable mortgage,** the buyer pays the seller a down payment generally equal to the seller's equity in the home and takes responsibility for the mortgage loan payments for the remaining term of the seller's existing mortgage loan. The buyer's goal is to obtain the loan at the original interest rate, which should be below current market rates. This approach will work only if the original mortgage loan agreement does not include a **due-on-sale clause.** Such a clause requires that the mortgage loan be fully paid off if the home is sold. It can impose a burden on the seller because it prohibits a buyer from assuming the mortgage loan.

Seller Financing

Seller financing occurs whenever the seller of a home agrees to accept all or a portion of the purchase price in installments rather than as a lump sum. Usually seller financing is a short-term arrangement, however, with payments based on amortization occurring over perhaps 20 years and a balloon payment due after perhaps five years. That is, all principal not paid after five years would be due at once.

In most seller financing, the buyer obtains the title to the property when the deal is closed and the contract is signed. In contrast, a **land contract** (or **contract for deed**) brings greater risk for the buyer because all terms in the contract (including payment of the debt) must be satisfied before transfer of title will occur. As a result, if you move before paying off

assumable mortgage
Buyer pays the seller a down payment generally equal to the seller's equity in the home and takes responsibility for the mortgage loan payments for the remaining term of the seller's existing mortgage loan.

due-on-sale clause
Requires that the mortgage loan be fully paid off if the home is sold. It can impose a burden on the seller because it prohibits a buyer from assuming the mortgage loan.

land contract/contract for deed
Brings greater risk for the buyer because all terms in the contract (including payment of the debt) must be satisfied before transfer of title will occur.

Did You Know?

About Second Mortgage Loans

Home values have increased significantly in recent years, allowing many people to see higher-than-expected increases in their home equity. You can use a second mortgage to borrow based on this home equity, with the property serving as collateral for both the first and second mortgage loans. A **second mortgage** is an additional loan on a residence besides the original mortgage. In case of default, the amount owed on the original mortgage must be paid first. Because of this additional risk, the interest rate on a second mortgage is often 2 to 5 percentage points higher than current market rates for first mortgages.

Historically, people have used second mortgages to pay for major remodeling projects, finance college costs for children, pay off medical bills, or start a business. Today, some people use these funds for everyday living expenses, an unwise practice dubbed "eating one's house."

Two types of second mortgages exist:

- The **home-equity installment loan,** where a specific amount of money is borrowed for a fixed time period with fixed monthly payments.
- The **home-equity line of credit,** where a maximum loan amount is established and the loan operates as open-ended credit, much like a credit card account. These line-of-credit loans often have variable interest rates and flexible repayment schedules.

The credit limit on a second mortgage loan is usually set at 80-90 percent of the home's appraised value minus the amount owed on the first mortgage. For example, a person with a home appraised at $200,000 with a balance owed of $100,000 on a first mortgage might be allowed to take out a $60,000 second mortgage [($200,000 × 0.80) − $100,000].

Run the Numbers

Should You Refinance Your Mortgage?

It is sometimes advantageous to refinance an existing mortgage when interest rates decline. In **mortgage refinancing,** a new mortgage is obtained to pay off and replace an existing mortgage. Most often it is undertaken to lower the monthly payment on the home by taking out a loan with a lower interest rate.

The example here illustrates how to determine whether refinancing your mortgage is a wise choice. The original mortgage for $130,000 was obtained seven years ago at an 8 percent interest rate for 30 years. The monthly payment is $953.89. After seven years, the principal owed has declined to $120,200. If interest rates for new mortgages have declined to 6.5 percent, the owner could take out a new mortgage at the lower rate for a monthly payment of 840.28. Borrowing $120,200 for 23 years at 6.5 percent saves approximately

$114 per month ($954 − $840). However, refinancing may have some up-front costs, including a possible prepayment penalty on the old mortgage and closing costs for the new mortgage. The question then becomes, will these costs exceed the monthly savings gained with a lower payment?

The following worksheet provides a means for estimating whether refinancing offers an advantage. It compares the future value of the reduced monthly payments (line 5) with the future value of the money used to pay the up-front costs (estimated here at 2%) of refinancing (line 8). The homeowner would need to estimate the number of months he or she expects to own the home after refinancing. Given an estimate of four years in this example, the net savings would be $1747 (subtracting line 8 from line 5), and refinancing would benefit the owner. A similar worksheet can be found at http://www.cgi.money.cnn.com/tools/cutmortgage/cutmortgage.html.

Decision Factor	Example	Your Figures
1. Current monthly payment	$ 954	_____
2. New monthly payment	840	_____
3. Monthly savings (line 1 – line 2)	114	_____
4. Additional years you expect to live in the house	4	_____
5. Future value of an account balance after 4 years if the monthly savings were invested at 3% after taxes (using the calculator on the *Garman/Forgue* companion website)	5,806	_____
6. Prepayment penalty on current loan (1%)	1,202	_____
7. Points and fees for new loan (2%)	2,404	_____
8. Future value of an account balance after 4 years if the prepayment penalty and closing costs ($3606) had been invested instead at 3% after taxes (using the calculator on the *Garman/Forgue* companion website)	4,059	_____
9. Net saving after 48 months (line 5 – line 8)	$ 1,747	_____

It may also be possible to borrow more than the current balance on the existing loan, thereby utilizing some of the equity built up in the home. Borrowers refinancing for more than the amount owed should understand that rebuilding the equity to its previous level may take many years.

the contract in full, you forfeit all money paid in installments to the seller and any appreciation in the home's value. You build no equity until the contract is completed.

reverse mortgage/home-equity conversion loan
Allows a homeowner older than age 61 to continue living in the home and to borrow against the equity in a home that is fully paid for and to receive the proceeds in a series of monthly payments, often over a period of 5 to 15 years or for life.

Reverse Mortgage A **reverse mortgage,** also known as a **home-equity conversion loan,** allows a homeowner older than age 61 to borrow against the equity in a home that is fully paid for and to receive the proceeds in a series of monthly payments for life. The contract allows the person to continue living in the home. Essentially, the borrower trades his or her equity in the home in return for a fixed monthly income and/or a line of credit that can be drawn upon at the option of the homeowner. The most likely prospects for such loans are elderly people who have paid off their mortgages but are strapped for income. The mortgage does not have to be paid back until the last surviving owner sells the house, moves out permanently, or dies.

Instant Message

Be Cautious About Tapping Your Equity to Pay Other Debts

Homeowners sometimes refinance a mortgage to pay off credit card debts and vehicle loans or buy large-screen TVs. This, of course, reduces the equity in their homes. Today, because of declines in home values, one in five homeowners has negative equity. Thus, if they move they will owe money to their lender. Spending one's home equity is financially dangerous.

Concept Check 9.4

1. Explain why the portions of a monthly mortgage payment that are allocated toward interest and toward principal will vary as the loan is repaid.

2. Distinguish between a conventional mortgage loan and an adjustable-rate loan.

3. Identify the two ways that home buyers build equity in their property.

4. Define negative amortization and describe one way that it might occur on a variable-rate loan.

5. Specify one advantage and one disadvantage of an interest-only mortgage loan.

Selling a Home

While most of this chapter deals with buying a home, important considerations also arise when you are selling a home. It is extremely important to do minor painting, cleaning, and repairing before listing your home for sale. Sellers also are required by law to disclose known defects in the home to the real estate agent and that information goes to potential buyers.

5 Learning Objective
Identify the important aspects of selling a home.

Should You List with a Broker or Sell a Home Yourself?

Knowing that the sales commission to a broker on a $200,000 home could be $12,000 provides motivation for some homeowners to consider selling their homes themselves. The key

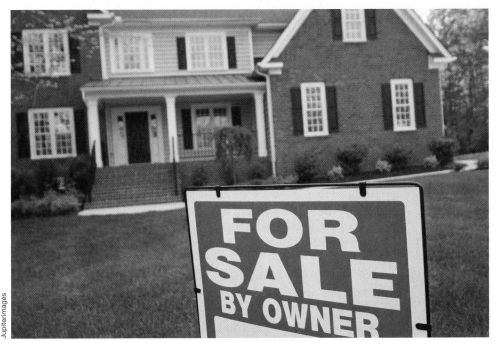

FSBOs can save a home seller money but usually take longer to sell.

Jupiterimages

FSBO
For sale by owner; commonly pronounced "fizbo"; home sold directly by the homeowner to save on sales commission paid to a real estate broker.

listing agreement
Agreement that brokers require homeowners to sign that permits the broker to list the property exclusively or with a multiple-listing service.

broker's commission
Largest selling cost in selling a home; these commissions often amount to 6 percent of the selling price of the home.

real estate transfer taxes
Community-assessed taxes paid by the seller and also sometimes by the buyer based on the purchase price of the home or the equity the seller has in the home.

to success in a **FSBO** (for sale by owner; commonly pronounced "fizbo") is to know what price to ask for your home. Asking too little could cost you much more than the commission paid to a broker. Setting the price too high keeps potential buyers away.

Many homeowners begin by contacting a few real estate agents to get their opinions on how much the home is worth. Agents are often quite willing to give their opinions because the homeowner might list the home with them if it does not sell quickly. Placing a for-sale sign on your lawn and spending about $500 on advertising the property should keep your telephone ringing for a few months with inquiries.★ If your home does not sell, you might want to list it with a broker.

Brokers require that homeowners sign a **listing agreement** permitting them to list the property exclusively or with a multiple-listing service. A multiple-listing service may work best because it allows every broker in the community to show and sell the home. Brokers "qualify" prospective buyers—distinguishing between serious buyers and people who are just looking or cannot afford the home. If your broker cannot find a buyer within 60 days, consider signing an agreement with another broker that might prove more aggressive in advertising and selling your property. If a sale occurs (or begins) during the time period of the listing agreement, you must pay a commission to the broker for any sale to a buyer not listed as an exception in the listing agreement.

Selling Carries Its Own Costs

The largest selling cost is the **broker's commission.** These commissions often amount to 6 percent of the selling price of the home. Some sellers are unaware that brokers may negotiate their commission. Smart sellers also pay for a title search, a professional appraisal, and their own home inspection as well.

Most mortgage loans are paid off before maturity because people move and sell their homes. Mortgage loan contracts often have a clause that specifies a **prepayment fee** or penalty, which can range from 1 to 3 percent of the original mortgage loan. On a $160,000 mortgage loan, for example, the charge might vary from $1200 to $4800. Usually, the penalty is only for an early payoff in the first few years of the loan.

Local communities may assess **real estate transfer taxes.** These taxes are paid by the seller and also possibly the buyer. The tax is based on the purchase price of the home or the equity the seller has in the home. These tax rates can be as high as 2 or 4 percent, that is, $4000 or $8000 on a $200,000 home. When paid by the seller, they may affect the offer that the seller is willing to accept for the home.

Do It NOW!

Planning to buy a home does not have to wait until you are established in your career. Start today by:

1. Talking to family members or friends who have bought a home to obtain their insights into the process including any not-so-pleasant surprises.

2. Exploring the housing market at www.realtor.com for the geographic area where you might live if you get a job offer in that location.

3. Setting a reasonable goal for a down payment amount and calculating how much you would have to save per month to reach it at http://partners.leadfusion.com/tools/kiplinger/savings03/tool.fcs.

Be Wary of Seller Financing

Some sellers who have experienced trouble when marketing their homes have successfully resorted to many variations of seller financing, although difficulties can arise with these options. Suppose you have a home worth $200,000 with a mortgage loan balance of $90,000 and equity of $110,000. The buyer assumes the existing mortgage loan, puts up $40,000 in cash, and takes out a second mortgage from *you* to repay the $70,000 over five years. At closing, the broker receives a commission of $12,000, and you come away with only $28,000 cash—a small sum to use in making a down payment on another home. Also, seller financing carries a risk that the buyer may not be able to make the second mortgage payments to you and could potentially default on the loan.

★For more information on selling your own home, visit www.sellyourhomeyourself.com or http://www.fizbolistings.com/sell.aspx.

Concept Check 9.5

1. List some disadvantages of trying to sell a home yourself.
2. List one advantage and one disadvantage of using a real estate broker to sell a home.
3. Describe two costs associated with selling a home in addition to the real estate commission.

What Do You Recommend NOW?

AP Photo/Danny Johnston

Now that you have read the chapter on buying housing, what do you recommend to Libby Clark regarding:

1. Buying or renting housing in the Denver area?
2. Steps she should take prior to actively looking at homes?
3. Finding a home and negotiating the purchase?
4. The closing process in home buying?
5. Selecting the type of mortgage to fit her needs?
6. Things to consider regarding the sale of her home should she ultimately be promoted to a position in another of the four regions?

Big Picture Summary of Learning Objectives

1 Decide whether renting or owning your home is better for you both financially and personally.

When choosing housing, renters must consider the costs of rent, a security deposit, and related items. Home buyers can choose among single-family dwellings, condominiums, cooperative housing, manufactured housing, and mobile homes. Renters generally pay out less money in terms of cash flow in the short run, whereas owners enjoy tax advantages and generally see an increase in the market value of their homes, making them better off financially in the long run.

2 Explain the up-front and monthly costs of buying a home.

Home buyers understand that they will make a down payment and then make monthly principal and interest payments on their mortgage. What many don't understand is that closing costs for interest points and other aspects of the purchase can add 5 percent or more to the amount needed up-front at the closing. Similarly, monthly charges for private mortgage insurance (PMI), homeowner's insurance, and real estate property taxes can add 25 percent or more to their monthly payment for principal and interest.

3 Describe the steps in the home-buying process.

The home-buying process includes (a) getting your finances in order, (b) prequalifying for a mortgage, (c) searching for a home online and in person, (d) agreeing to terms with a seller, (e) obtaining a mortgage loan, (f) preparing for the closing, and (g) signing your name on closing day.

4 Distinguish among conventional and alternative ways of financing a home and list the advantages and disadvantages of each.

Mortgage loans for homes are amortized. Amortization is the process of gradually paying off a mortgage through a series of periodic payments to a lender, with a portion of each payment going toward the principal and another portion going toward the interest owed. Conventional mortgages and adjustable-rate mortgages are the most common types of housing loans. Numerous alternative types of mortgages are available that have reduced the importance of the long-term, fixed-rate mortgage loan and that provide new ways to keep the monthly payment as low as possible.

The mathematics of buying a home shows how loan payments are calculated and how the portion of each monthly payment that goes toward interest declines, resulting in the portion that goes toward the principal increasing with each subsequent payment.

5 Identify the important aspects of selling a home.

When selling a home, it is wise to consider the pros and cons of listing with a real estate broker versus selling the home yourself, the transaction costs of selling, and the pitfalls of seller financing.

Let's Talk About It

1. **The Housing Collapse.** How has the recent foreclosure crises and collapse in home values affected your thinking about buying a home someday?

2. **Renting Versus Buying.** What do you see as the advantages and the disadvantages for you of renting or buying housing at the current time? How might your feelings change in the future, such as within five years?

3. **Feelings About Long-Term Debt.** In the early years of the standard 30-year mortgage loan, as little as 10 percent of the monthly payment actually goes toward repaying the debt. As a result, it takes many, many years for the loan balance to come down to any significant extent. Explain how that affects your feelings about taking on such a long-term obligation.

4. **Who Can Help You.** What experts could you turn to for assistance during the home-buying and loan application processes? What conflicts of interest most concern you?

5. **Alternative Mortgages.** Would you prefer a conventional mortgage to adjustable-rate mortgage or some of the other alternatives described in this chapter to finance a home purchase? Why?

6. **Negotiating the Purchase of a Home.** Some closing costs on a home purchase are negotiable. Would you feel comfortable entering into a discussion of these items? Why or why not?

Do the Math

1. **Deciding to Buy.** Walter and Marcie Jensen of Atlanta, Georgia, both of whom are in their late 20s, currently are renting an unfurnished two-bedroom apartment for $880 per month, plus $130 for utilities and $34 for insurance. They have found a condominium they can buy for $170,000 with a 20 percent down payment and a 30-year, 7 percent mortgage. Principal and interest payments are estimated at $905 per month, with property taxes amounting to $110 per month and a homeowner's insurance premium of $450 per year. Closing costs are estimated at $3200. The monthly homeowner's association fee is $275, and utility costs are estimated at $160 per month. The Jensens have a combined income of $57,000 per year, with take-home pay of $4100 per month. They are in the 15 percent tax bracket, pay $225 per month on an installment loan (ten payments left), and have $39,000 in savings and investments outside of their retirement accounts.

   (a) Can the Jensens afford to buy the condo? Use the results from the *Garman/Forgue* companion website or the information on pages 259–260 to support your answer. Also, consider the effect of the purchase on their savings and monthly budget.

   (b) Walter and Marcie think that their monthly housing costs would be lower the first year if they bought the condo. Do you agree? Support your answer.

   (c) If they buy, how much will Walter and Marcie have left in savings to pay for moving expenses?

   (d) Available financial information suggests that mortgage rates might drop over the next few months. If the Jensens wait until the rates drop to 6.0 percent, how much will they save on their monthly mortgage payment? Use the information in Table 9.4 or the *Garman/Forgue* companion website to calculate the payment.

2. **Mortgage Affordability.** Seth and Cassie Moore of Holyoke, Massachusetts, have an annual income of $120,000 and want to buy a home. Currently, mortgage rates are 7 percent. The Moores want to take out a mortgage for 30 years. Real estate taxes are estimated to be $4800 per year for homes similar to what they would like to buy, and homeowner's insurance would be about $720 per year.

   (a) Using a 28 percent front-end ratio, what are the total annual and monthly expenditures for which they would qualify?

   (b) Using a 36 percent back-end ratio, what monthly mortgage payment (including taxes and insurance) could they afford given that they have an automobile loan payment of $470, a student loan payment of $350, and credit card payments of $250? (Hint: Subtract these amounts from the total monthly affordable payments for their income to determine the amount left over to spend on a mortgage.)

   (c) If mortgage interest rates are around 7 percent and the Moores want a 30-year mortgage, use the information in the Did You Know box on page 259 to estimate how much they could borrow given your answer to part b. (Hint: Subtract the monthly real estate taxes and homeowner's insurance from your part b answer first.)

3. **Rent Versus Buy.** Phillip Guadet of Monroe, Louisiana, has been renting a small, two-bedroom house for several years. He pays $950 per month in rent for the home and $300 per year in property and liability insurance. The owner of the house wants to sell it, and Phillip is considering making an offer. The owner wants $130,000 for the property, but Phillip thinks he could get the house for $120,000 and use his $25,000 in 5 percent certificates of deposit that are ready to mature for the down payment. Phillip has talked to his banker and could get a 7 percent mortgage loan for 25 years to finance the remainder of the purchase price. The banker advised Phillip that he would reduce his debt principal by $1850 during the first year of the loan. Property taxes on the house are $1800 per year. Phillip estimates that he would need to upgrade his property and liability insurance to $500 per year and would incur about $1000 in costs the first year for maintenance. Property values are increasing at about 3.5 percent per year in the neighborhood. Phillip is in the 25 percent marginal tax bracket.

   (a) Use Table 9.4 to calculate the monthly mortgage payment for the mortgage loan that Phillip would need.

   (b) How much interest would Phillip pay during the first year of the loan?

   (c) Use the Run the Numbers worksheet, "Should You Buy or Rent?" on page 251 to determine whether Phillip would be better off buying or renting based on his cash flow.

4. **Refinancing a Mortgage.** Kevin Tutumbo of Rochester Hills, Michigan, has owned his home for 15 years and expects to live in it for five more years. He originally borrowed $105,000 at 8 percent interest for 30 years to buy the home. He still owes $85,750 on the loan. Interest rates have since fallen to 6.5 percent, and Kevin is considering refinancing the loan for 15 years. He would have to pay 2 points on the new loan with no prepayment penalty on the current loan.

   (a) What is Kevin's current monthly payment?

   (b) Calculate the monthly payment on the new loan.

   (c) Advise Kevin on whether he should refinance his mortgage using the Run the Numbers worksheet, "Should You Refinance Your Mortgage?" on page 272.

Financial Planning Cases

Case 1

Michael and Jonathan Weigh the Benefits and Costs of Buying Versus Renting

Michael Higginbottom and Jonathan Van Ness of Logan, Utah, are trying to decide whether to rent or purchase housing. Both men are single. Michael favors buying and Jonathan leans toward renting, and both seem able to justify their particular choice. Michael thinks that the tax advantages are a very good reason for buying. Jonathan, however, believes that cash flow is so much better when renting. See whether you can help them make their decision.

   (a) Does the home buyer enjoy tax advantages? Explain.

   (b) Discuss Jonathan's belief that cash flow is better with renting.

   (c) Suggest some reasons why Michael might consider renting rather than purchasing housing.

   (d) Suggest some reasons why Jonathan might consider buying rather than renting housing.

   (e) Is there a clear-cut basis for deciding either to rent or to buy housing? Explain why or why not.

Case 2

Emma Chooses Among Alternative Mortgage Options

Emma Rafferty of San Mateo, California, has examined several options for new home financing. She has been favoring alternative mortgage plans because of currently high mortgage rates. Emma hopes that the market rate will drop in a couple of years.

(a) What broad concerns are present with alternative mortgages?

(b) What financing option would you suggest for Emma, assuming she is able to use any type of mortgage available? Why?

(c) How would you advise Emma if she was considering using an option ARM mortgage to buy her home?

Case 3

Jeremy Decides to Sell His Home Himself

Jeremy Jorgensen of St. Paul, Minnesota, is concerned about the costs involved in selling his home, so he has decided to sell his home himself rather than pay a broker to do it.

(a) How would you advise Jeremy if he asked you whether he should sell the house himself or list with a broker? Explain your answer.

(b) Would Jeremy really save money by selling his home himself if he considers his time as part of his costs? Why or why not?

(c) Can you suggest any ways that Jeremy might reduce his selling costs without doing the selling himself? Explain.

Case 4

Victor and Maria Hernandez Learn About Real Estate Agents

Victor and Maria have been thinking about selling their home and buying a house with more yard space so that they can indulge their passion for gardening. Before they make such a decision, they want to explore the market to see what might be available and in what price ranges. They will then list their house with a real estate agent and begin searching in earnest for a new home.

(a) What services could a real estate agent provide for the couple, and what types of agents could represent them as they sell their current home?

(b) A friend has advised them that they really need a buyer's agent for the purchase of a new home. Explain to the Hernandezes the difference between buyer's and seller's agents.

Case 5

The Johnsons Decide to Buy a Condominium

Belinda Johnson's parents and maternal grandmother have combined their finances and presented Harry and Belinda with $25,000 with which to purchase a condominium. The Johnsons have shopped and found one that they like very much. They could either borrow from the condominium developer or obtain a loan from one of three other mortgage lenders. The financial alternatives are presented in the chart that follows, and data for the condo are summarized in the accompanying table on page 279.

(a) Which plan has the lowest total up-front costs? The highest?

(b) What would be the full monthly payment for PITI and PMI for each of the options?

(c) If the Johnsons had enough cash to make the 20 percent down payment, would you recommend lender 1 or lender 2? Why?

(d) Assuming that the Johnsons will need about $3000 for moving costs (in addition to closing costs), which financing option would you recommend? Why?

Financing Details on a Condominium Available to the Johnsons

Price: $140,000. Developer A will finance the purchase with a 10 percent down payment and a 30-year, 6.5 percent ARM loan with 2 interest points. The initial monthly payment for principal and interest is $796.41 ($126,000 loan after the down payment is made; 126 × $6.3207). After one year, the rate rises to 8 percent, with a principal plus interest payment of $921.91. At that point, the rate can go up or down as much as 2 percent per year, depending on the cost of an index of mortgage funds. There is an interest-rate cap of 5 percent over the life of the loan. Taxes are estimated to be about $1500, and the homeowner's insurance premium should be about $600 annually. A mortgage insurance premium of $78 per month must be paid monthly on the two 10 percent down options.

On the 'Net

To complete these exercises, go to the *Garman/Forgue* companion website at www.cengage.com/finance/garman. Under General Business, select the title of this text. Click on the Internet Exercises link for this chapter, and answer the questions that appear on the Web page.

1. Visit the website for Bankrate.com (http://www .bankrate.com/brm/rate/mtg_home.asp), where you will

Condo: Price, $140,000; Taxes, $1500; Insurance, $600

	Developer A	Lender 1	Lender 2	Lender 3
Loan term and type	30-year ARM★	30-year CON†	15-year CON	20-year REN‡
Interest rate	6.5%	7.5%	8%	7.5%
Down payment	$ 14,000	$ 28,000	$ 28,000	$ 14,000
Loan amount	126,000	112,000	112,000	126,000
Points	2,520	1,120	0	3,780
Principal and interest payment	796.41	783.12	1204.12	1015.04
PMI	78	0	0	78

★Adjustable-rate mortgage.
†Conventional.
‡Renegotiable every five years.

find information on mortgage interest rates around the United States. View the information for the lenders in a large city near your home. How does the information compare with the interest rates on your own credit card account(s)? How do the rates in the city you selected compare with other rates found in the United States?

2. Visit the website for the United States Department of Housing and Urban Development, where you will find a calculator (http://www.hud.gov/buying/index .cfm#afford) that helps you determine the amount you can afford for the purchase of a home given your income and funds available for a down payment, closing costs, and other home-buying expenses. Enter the data requested for your current situation. What does the calculator tell you about your housing affordability? Change the entered data for some point in the future when you project a better financial situation for yourself. How do the results change?

3. Visit the website for the National Association of Realtors (www.realtor.com), where you can search for owned housing in various locales around the United States. Look for housing in your community. Were you able to find housing that meets your criteria price range and other criteria? Also search for similar housing in the San Diego, California (high-cost) and Syracuse, New York (low-cost) metropolitan areas. Compare these cost results with the housing found in your area.

Visit the Garman/Forgue companion website . . .

www.cengage.com/finance/garman

Managing Property and Liability Risk

!You Must Be Kidding, Right?

Tiffany Blake recently caused an automobile accident when she had a blowout on the freeway. The cost of repairs to Tiffany's car will be $13,200, which exceeds the car's $12,500 fair market value. The damage to the other two vehicles was $17,800 and $6400, respectively. Fortunately, no one was injured in the accident. On the advice of her insurance agent, Tiffany had purchased an auto insurance policy with a $500 collision deductible and liability limits of $25,000/$50,000/$15,000. What dollar amount of her losses will be covered by her policy?

A. $12,700   **C.** $36,200

B. $27,000   **D.** $37,400

The answer is B. The company will pay her $12,000 after her $500 deductible for the loss of her vehicle. The company will also pay $15,000 for the damage to the other vehicles which is the limit for property damage liability under her policy. Tiffany will be personally responsible for the remainder since like most people, she did not carry sufficient liability protection.

Learning Objectives

After reading this chapter, you should be able to:

1 Apply the risk-management process to address the risks to your property and income.

2 Explain basic insurance terms and the relationship between risk and insurance.

3 Design a homeowner's or renter's insurance program to meet your needs.

4 Design an automobile insurance program to meet your needs.

5 Describe other types of property and liability insurance.

6 Summarize how to make an insurance claim.

What Do You Recommend?

Ted Foxx/Alamy

George and Emily Cosgrove of Athens, Georgia, recently had a fire in their garage that destroyed two of their cars and did considerable damage to the garage and to the outside of their home. After receiving their reimbursements from their homeowner's and automobile insurance policies, the Cosgroves realized that they were severely underinsured. One vehicle was not insured for fire, and the insurance on their dwelling amounted to only 60 percent of its current replacement value.

What do you recommend to George and Emily about managing property and liability risk regarding:

1. The risk-management steps they should take to update their insurance coverages?

2. The relationship between severity and frequency of loss when deciding whether to buy insurance?

3. Adequately insuring their home?

4. The use of deductibles and policy limits to keep their automobile insurance premiums at a manageable level while still maintaining vital coverage?

Your Next Five Years

In the next five years you can start achieving financial success by doing the following related to managing property and liability risk:

1. Maintain adequate auto insurance with appropriate limits and deductibles as well as under- and uninsured motorist protections.

2. Buy renters insurance with limits tied to the actual cash value of your property.

3. As soon as you begin your career (if not sooner) purchase an umbrella liability insurance policy with a minimum of a $1 million limit.

4. Once each year, reassess the types and amounts of insurance coverage you need and then comparison shop insurance prices and coverage.

5. Maintain a verifiable inventory of all your insured property so that in the event of a loss you can collect what is coming to you.

Up to this point, this book has focused on ways to manage your money and strategies for using financial resources to achieve your personal goals. But it is just as important to protect your resources and assets from the possibility of financial loss from accidents, acts of nature, illness or injury, and death. Uninsured and underinsured losses often result in people declaring personal bankruptcy. The uninsured loss leads to overuse of credit that then snowballs out of control. Many people are experiencing such difficulties during today's challenging economic times. You can manage the risk of such losses through the effective use of insurance. This chapter focuses on property and liability losses that occur from accidents and acts of nature. Chapter 11 focuses on losses related to illness or injury, and Chapter 12 looks at losses related to death.

The items you own and your day-to-day activities expose you to two types of losses. First, your property might be damaged. **Property insurance** protects you from financial losses resulting from the damage to or destruction of your property or possessions. Second, you might be held responsible, **(legally liable),** for losses suffered by others. **Liability insurance** protects you from financial losses suffered by others for which you are legally liable. The most commonly purchased forms of property and liability insurance are insurance for your home and its contents and insurance for your use and ownership of vehicles.

Risk and Risk Management

1 Learning Objective

Apply the risk-management process to address the risks to your property and income.

property insurance
Protection from financial losses resulting from the damage to or destruction of your property or possessions.

liability insurance
Protection from financial losses suffered when you are held liable for others' losses.

risk
Uncertainty about the outcome of a situation or event.

People Often Misunderstand the Concept of Risk

Risk is uncertainty about the outcome of a situation or event. It arises out of the possibility that the outcome will differ from what is expected. In the area of financial losses, risk consists of uncertainty about both whether the financial loss will occur and how large it might be. There are two types of risk. **Speculative risk** exists in situations where there is potential for gain as well as for loss. Investments such as those made in the stock market involve speculative risk. **Pure risk** exists when there is no potential for gain, only the possibility of loss. Fires, automobile accidents, illness, and theft are examples of events involving pure risk. Insurance only addresses pure risk.

Many people think of "odds" or games of chance when they hear the word risk. In fact, risk and chance are different concepts. The difference between the two is subtle but very important. An event with a 95 percent chance of occurring is highly likely to occur. Thus, both uncertainty and risk are low. An event with a 0.000001 percent chance of occurring is highly likely *not* to occur. Thus, both uncertainty and risk are low. When an event has a moderate chance of occurring—5 percent, for example—the uncertainty and risk are relatively high because it is difficult to predict the one person in 20 who will experience the event. In such cases, insurance often represents a wise choice for reducing risk.

The Risk-Management Process

risk management
Process of identifying and evaluating purely risky situations to determine and implement appropriate management.

Risk management is the process of identifying and evaluating situations involving pure risk to determine and implement the appropriate means for its management. The goal is to minimize any risk or potential for risk through advance planning. Risk management entails making the most efficient arrangements *before* a loss occurs. Risk management is an essential part

Table 10.1   The Risk-Management Process

	Possessions	**Activities**	**Accompanying Perils**
Step 1 *Identify sources of risk.*	Vehicle House Jewelry	Driving Smoking Traveling	Accident Fire Theft
Step 2 *Estimate risk and potential losses.*	(a) Determine the likely frequency of losses associated with each exposure. (b) Determine the potential severity and magnitude of losses associated with each exposure.		
Step 3 *Choose how to handle risk.*	(a) Avoid risk. (b) Retain risk. (c) Control losses. (d) Transfer risk. (e) Reduce risk.		
Step 4 *Implement the risk-management plan.*	(a) Refrain from certain activities. (b) Take extra precautions. (c) Buy insurance.		
Step 5 *Evaluate and adjust the program.*			

of personal financial management because it preserves the benefits of all your other financial planning efforts. Risk management usually requires the purchase of insurance although insurance is only one of the ways to handle risk, and it is not always the best choice.

The risk-management process involves five steps; Table 10.1 outlines these steps in the risk-management process.

Step 1: Identify Sources of Risk

Sources of risk, called **exposures,** are the items you own and the activities in which you engage that expose you to potential financial loss. Owning and/or driving an automobile are common exposures. To determine your exposures to risk, you should take an inventory of what you own and what you do.

Your exposures fall into five categories:

1. First, you may suffer a loss to your property, such as can happen during a house fire.
2. Second, you could be held legally responsible for losses suffered by others such as if you cause an automobile accident.
3. Third, you may become ill or be injured and have costs associated with health care.
4. Fourth, you may suffer a loss of income as a result of illness or accident.
5. Five, your family may incur expenses and suffer a loss of income as a result your death.

You also need to identify the perils that you face. A **peril** is any event that can cause a financial loss. Fire, wind, theft, vehicle collision, illness, and death are all examples of perils.

peril
Any event that can cause a financial loss.

Step 2: Estimate Risk and Potential Losses

Once you identify your exposures to risk, you estimate both loss frequency and loss severity. **Loss frequency** refers to the

Did You Know?

The Top 3 Financial Missteps in Managing Property and Liability Risk

People slip up in managing property and liability risk when they do the following:

1. Buy only the legal minimum coverage on the liability insurance on their vehicle

2. Fail to keep good records (e.g., lists, photos, receipts) that could serve to document insured property losses

3. Pay high premiums because they select low deductibles on property insurance for their home and car

likely number of times that a loss might occur over a period of time. **Loss severity** describes the potential magnitude of the loss(es).

Many people wonder whether they should buy insurance when loss frequency is low, for example, if they are young and healthy or if they live in a safe neighborhood. This is not a good way to think about potential losses because they still could occur and if loss frequency is low, the insurance premium would be small. Figure 10.1 illustrates the relationship between loss severity and loss frequency in risk management.

What is much more important is loss severity. "How much might I lose?" is the question you should ask. When considering possible property losses, you simply make an estimate of the value of the property. Liability losses are more complicated because the severity of the loss depends on the circumstances of the person you harm. For example, if you caused an accident that permanently disabled a young heart surgeon with three small children, you would be liable for the surgeon's care, lost earnings over his or her lifetime, and future care and education of the children. A loss of several million dollars is not out of the question in such a situation.

Step 3: Choose How to Handle Risk   The risk of loss may be handled in five ways: risk avoidance, risk retention, loss control, risk transfer, and risk reduction. Each strategy may be appropriate for certain circumstances, and the mix that you choose will depend on the source of the risk, the size of the potential loss, your personal feelings about risk, and the financial resources you have available to pay for losses.

■ **Risk avoidance.** The simplest way to handle risk is to avoid it. With this approach, you would refrain from owning items or engaging in activities that expose you to possible financial loss. For example, choosing not to own an airplane or not to skydive limits your exposure. Avoiding risk is not always practical, however.

risk retention
Consciously accepting that some risks simply arise in the course of one's life and consciously retaining that risk.

deductible clause
Requires that the policyholder pays an initial portion of any loss.

■ **Risk retention.** A second way to handle risk is to retain or accept it. The risk that the shrubbery around your house might die during a dry spell is such a retained risk. Conscious risk retention plays an important role in risk management. For example, you can use a **deductible clause** in an insurance policy to retain an initial portion of the risk. In this way you pay the first few dollars of a loss (perhaps $200 or $500) before the insurance company will reimburse for a loss. Risk retention due to

Figure 10.1
The Relationship Between Severity and Frequency of Loss

	HIGH SEVERITY	LOW SEVERITY
LOW FREQUENCY	Purchase insurance to cover the potentially large losses. Their infrequency will make premiums affordable.	Consider retaining risk because the frequency and severity of loss are both low.
HIGH FREQUENCY	Purchase insurance. Loss control efforts can be useful in reducing the necessarily high premiums.	Retain risk but also budget for losses that are likely to be frequent.

ignorance or inaction is unwise. For example, many people foolishly put off the purchase of life insurance after having children because they consider it to be a morbid, unpleasant task.

- **Loss control.** Loss control, the third method of handling risk, is designed to reduce loss frequency and loss severity. For example, installing heavy-duty locks and doors will reduce the *frequency* of theft losses. Installing fire alarms and smoke detectors cannot prevent fires but will reduce the *severity* of losses from them. Insurance companies often require loss-control efforts or give discounts to policyholders who implement them.

- **Risk transfer.** A fourth way to handle risk is to transfer it. In a risk transfer, an insurance company agrees to reimburse you for a financial loss. For example, a professional football team's star running back might take out an insurance policy on his legs. In this case, the uncertainty is simply transferred from the running back or his team to an insurance company. Insurance represents one method of transferring risk, although not all risk transfers can be classified as insurance because insurance goes beyond merely transferring risk to the actual reduction of risk.

- **Risk reduction.** The fifth way to handle risk is to reduce it to acceptable levels. Insurance is used by policyholders when they arrange for all or a portion of their risk to be covered by an insurance company, thereby reducing their personal level of risk.

Step 4: Implement the Risk-Management Program
The fourth step in risk management is to implement the risk-handling methods you have chosen. For most households, this means buying insurance to transfer and reduce risk. This involves selecting types of policies and coverage, dollar amounts of coverage, and sources of insurance protection.

People often wonder what types of insurance to buy and how many dollars of coverage to choose. You should use the maximum possible loss as a guide for the dollar amount of coverage to buy. This way of thinking makes use of the **large-loss principle** which states "insure the risks that you cannot afford and retain the risks that you can reasonably afford." In

loss control
Designing specific mechanisms to reduce loss frequency and loss severity.

risk reduction
Includes mechanisms, such as insurance, that reduce the overall uncertainty about the magnitude of loss.

large-loss principal
A basic rule of risk management that encourages us to insure the risks that we cannot afford and retain the risks that we can reasonably afford.

Renters need insurance too.

Instant Message

Buy—Don't Be Sold—Insurance

Always remember that your goal is to "buy" the insurance you need at a fair price. Do not let yourself be "sold" more or less insurance coverage than you need at excessive prices. Visit www.insquote.com and www.quotesmith.com once you have decided what insurance you need.

other words, pay for small losses out of your own pocket and purchase as much insurance as necessary to cover large, catastrophic losses that will ruin you financially. The example earlier of an auto accident that injures a heart surgeon would bring you such ruin because you would be held responsible for those losses. Consequently, you would want high dollar amounts of liability coverage on your auto insurance.

Step 5: Evaluate and Adjust the Program   The final step in risk management entails periodic review of your risk-management efforts. The risks people face in their lives change continually. Therefore, no risk-management plan should be put in place and then ignored for long periods of time. For certain exposures, such as ownership of an automobile, an annual review is appropriate. For areas involving life insurance, a review should occur about once every three to five years or whenever family structure and employment situations change. The necessary adjustments should be implemented promptly to reflect changes over your life cycle. Many people keep existing policies that no longer fit their needs (too little or too much coverage) simply because they buy once and ignore their insurance needs for years.

Concept Check 10.1

1. Distinguish between pure risk and speculative risk.
2. Explain the distinctions between risk and odds.
3. Distinguish among the five common risk exposures that most people face.
4. Describe the five steps of risk management.
5. Based on likelihood of loss and severity of loss, explain why one is more important when deciding whether to buy insurance.

Understanding How Insurance Works

2 Learning Objective

Explain basic insurance terms and the relationship between risk and insurance.

insurance

Mechanism for transferring and reducing pure risk through which a large number of individuals share in the financial losses suffered by members of the group as a whole.

premium

Comparatively small, predictable fee with which individuals or companies can replace an uncertain—and possibly large—financial loss.

insurance policy

Contract between the person buying insurance (the insured) and the insurance company (the insurer).

Insurance is a mechanism for transferring and reducing pure risk through which a large number of individuals share in the financial losses suffered by members of the group as a whole. Insurance protects each individual in the group by replacing an uncertain—and possibly large—financial loss with a certain but comparatively small fee. This fee, called the **premium,** has four components:

- The individual's share of the group's losses
- Insurance company reserves set aside to pay future losses
- A proportional share of the expenses of administering the insurance plan
- An allowance for profit (when the plan is administered by a profit-seeking company)

Insurance premiums are usually assessed on an annual or semiannual basis and the coverage is paid for in advance. You generally will be charged an extra amount if you choose to make the payments monthly.

The **insurance policy** is the contract between the person buying insurance (the **insured**) and the insurance company (the **insurer**). It contains language that describes the rights and responsibilities of both parties. Most people do not take the time to read and understand their insurance policies. As a result, insurance remains one of the least understood purchases people make. You can do a much better job of managing your risks if you understand the basic terms and concepts used in the field of insurance.

Basic Terms?

Hazards Make Losses More Likely to Occur

A **hazard** is any condition that increases the probability that a peril will occur. Driving under the influence of alcohol represents an especially dangerous hazard. Three types of hazards exist:

- A **physical hazard** is a particular characteristic of the insured person or property that increases the chance of loss. An example of a physical hazard is high blood pressure in a person covered by health insurance.

- A **morale hazard** exists when a person is indifferent to a peril. For example, a morale hazard exists if the insured party, knowing that theft insurance will pay for the loss, becomes careless about locking doors and windows.

- A **moral hazard** exists when an insured person wants a peril to occur so that he or she can collect on an insurance policy.

Insurance companies often limit or deny coverage if a loss occurs as a result of a morale or moral hazard.

hazard
Any condition that increases the probability that a peril will occur.

Only Certain Losses Are Insurable

Certain minimum requirements must be met for a loss to be considered insurable—in particular, the loss must be fortuitous, financial, and personal. **Fortuitous losses** are unexpected in terms of both their timing and their magnitude. A loss caused by a lightning strike and fire to your home is fortuitous; a loss caused by a decline in the market value of your home is not because it is reasonable to expect home values to rise and fall over time. A **financial loss** is any decline in the value of income or assets in the present or future. Financial losses can be measured objectively in dollars and cents. When you become sick, you suffer as a result of the discomfort, inconvenience, lost wages, and medical bills. Insurance will cover only the lost wages and medical bills, however, because these losses—but not the others—can be objectively measured. Finally, **personal losses** can be directly suffered by specific individuals or organizations rather than society as a whole.

The Principle of Indemnity Limits Insurance Payouts

The **principle of indemnity** states that insurance will pay *no more* than the actual financial loss suffered. For example, an automobile insurance policy will pay only the actual cash value of a stolen automobile. This principle prevents a person from gaining financially from a loss (certainly a moral hazard). The principle of indemnity does not guarantee that insured losses will be totally reimbursed. Every policy includes **policy limits,** which specify the maximum dollar amounts that will be paid under the policy. These limits explain why there is no such thing as "full coverage" insurance—there is always the potential that a loss will exceed the limits on a policy. As a result, insurance purchasers must carefully select policy limits sufficient to cover their potential losses.

principle of indemnity
Insurance will pay *no more* than the actual financial loss suffered.

policy limits
Specify the maximum dollar amounts that will be paid under the policy.

Factors That Reduce the Cost of Insurance

Some features of insurance policies can lower your premiums without significantly reducing the protection offered. These features include deductibles, coinsurance, hazard reduction, and loss reduction.

A **deductible** is an initial portion of any loss that must be paid before the insurance company will provide coverage. For example, automobile collision insurance often includes a $200 deductible and that means that the first $200 of loss to the car must be paid by the insured. The insurer then pays the remainder of the loss, up to the limits of the policy. You usually have a choice of deductible amounts and the higher the deductible the more you will save on your premium. This is because the insurance company will have fewer small losses to pay.

coinsurance
Method by which the insured and the insurer share proportionately in the payment for a loss.

Coinsurance is a method by which the insured and the insurer share proportionately in the payment for a loss. For example, health insurance policies commonly require that the insured pay 20 percent of a loss and the insurer pay the remaining 80 percent. Substantial premium reductions can be realized through coinsurance, but you must be prepared to pay your share of losses. The following **deductible and coinsurance reimbursement formula** can be used to determine the amount of a loss that will be reimbursed when the policy includes a deductible and a coinsurance clause:

$$R = (1 - CP)(L - D) \tag{10.1}$$

where

R = Reimbursement
CP = Coinsurance percentage required of the insured
L = Loss
D = Deductible

As an example, assume you have a health insurance policy with a $100 deductible per hospital stay and a 20 percent coinsurance requirement. If the hospital bill is $1350, the reimbursement will be $1000, calculated as follows:

$$
\begin{aligned}
R &= (1.00 - 0.20)(\$1{,}350 - \$100) \\
&= (0.80)(\$1{,}250) \\
&= \$1{,}000
\end{aligned}
$$

Hazard reduction is action taken by the insured to reduce the probability of a loss occurring. Insurance companies often offer reduced premiums to insureds who practice hazard reduction—for example, to nonsmokers.

Loss reduction is action taken by the insured to lessen the severity of loss if a peril occurs. Smoke alarms and fire extinguishers in the home are examples of loss reduction efforts. These items will not prevent fires, but their use may lead to less severe damage. Many insurers offer reduced premiums to policyholders who practice loss reduction.

The Essence of Insurance

Insurance consists of two basic elements: the reduction of risk and the sharing of losses. When you buy insurance, you exchange the uncertainty of a potentially large financial loss for the certainty of a fixed insurance premium, thereby reducing your risk. As Yogi Berra once said "It is tough to make predictions. Especially about the future." But predictions are much easier for an insurance company than for an individual. This is because risk is reduced for the insurer through the **law of large numbers:** As the number of members in a group increases, predictions about the group's behavior become increasingly more accurate. This greater accuracy decreases uncertainty and, therefore, risk.

law of large numbers
As the number of members in a group increases, predictions about the group's behavior become increasingly accurate.

To illustrate, consider a city of 100,000 households in which the probability of a fire striking a household is 1 in 1000, or 0.1 percent. Thus, 100 home fires are likely to occur each year in this community. If we focus on groups of 100 households at a time, we cannot predict very accurately whether a fire will strike a house in a given group. Some groups might have two or three fires, while others might experience none. If we combine all the households into one group, however, we can more accurately predict that 100 fires will occur (100,000 × 0.001). Even if 103 fires occurred, our prediction would be in error by only a

Did You Know?

How to Read an Insurance Policy

Insurance policies do not invite casual reading. Consequently, many people fail to thoroughly examine their policies until a loss occurs, only to find that they had misunderstood the terms of the agreement. You can avoid such problems by systematically reading a policy before you purchase it, focusing on eight points:

1. **Perils covered.** Some policies list only the perils that are covered; others cover all perils except those listed. The definition of certain perils may differ from that used in everyday language.

2. **Property covered.** Like perils, the property covered under a policy may be listed individually, or only the excluded property may be listed. When the property is listed individually, any new acquisitions must be added to the policy.

3. **Types of losses covered.** Three types of property losses can occur: (a) the loss of the property itself, (b) extra expenses that may arise because the property is rendered unusable for a period of time, and (c) loss of income if the property was used in the insured's work.

4. **People covered.** Insurance policies may cover only certain individuals. This information usually appears on the first page of the policy but may be changed subsequently in later sections.

5. **Locations covered.** Where the loss occurs may have a bearing on whether it will be covered. It is especially important to know which locations are not covered.

6. **Time period of coverage.** Policies are generally written to cover specific time periods. Restrictions may exclude coverage during specific times of the day or certain days of the week or year.

7. **Loss control requirements.** Insurance policies often stipulate that certain loss control efforts must be maintained by the insured. For example, coverage for a vehicle may be denied if the owner knowingly allows it to be driven by an unlicensed person.

8. **Amount of coverage.** All insurance policies specify the maximum amount the insurer will pay for various types of losses.

The information on these eight points may be spread throughout a policy. In fact, coverage that appears to be provided in one location actually may be denied elsewhere. Carefully review the entire policy to determine the protection it provides. If necessary, telephone the salesperson or company to obtain clarification.

---

small percentage. Insurance companies, which may have millions of customers, can be even more accurate in their group predictions.

Individual insurance purchasers benefit regardless of whether they actually suffer a loss because of the reduction of risk. This is the essence of insurance. Reduced risk gives one the freedom to drive a car, own a home, and plan financially for the future with the knowledge that some unforeseen event will not result in financial disaster.

Who Sells Insurance?

Sellers of insurance, called **insurance agents,** represent one or more insurance companies. They have the power to enter into, change, and cancel insurance policies on behalf of these companies. Two types of insurance agents exist: independent agents and exclusive agents.

Independent insurance agents are independent business people who act as third-party links between insurers and insureds. Such agents earn commissions from the companies they represent and will place each insurance customer with the company that they believe best meets that customer's particular needs.

Exclusive insurance agents represent only one insurance company for a specific type of insurance. They are employees of the insurance company they represent. Life insurance, for example, is often sold through exclusive insurance agents.

Instant Message

Check Up on Your Company and Agent

Insurance companies must have the financial strength to pay losses as promised. You can assess your company's financial strength at www.standardandpoors.com by clicking on "Ratings" and then "Insurance." Always seek out an agent who has the appropriate professional designations—chartered life underwriter (CLU) in life insurance and chartered property and casualty underwriter (CPCU) in automobile and homeowner's insurance.

insurance agent
Representative of an insurance company authorized to sell, modify, service, and terminate insurance contracts.

Did You Know?

How Companies Select Among Insurance Applicants

The purchase of insurance begins with an offer by the purchaser in the form of a written or oral policy application. The insurer typically issues a temporary insurance contract, called a **binder,** which is replaced at a later date with a written policy. The application then goes through a process of **underwriting**—that is, the insurer's procedure for deciding which insurance applicants to accept. To describe the process of underwriting, it is necessary to first understand how insurance rates are set.

An **insurance rate** is the price charged for each unit of insurance coverage. Rates represent the average cost of providing coverage to various **classes of insureds;** these classes consist of insureds who share similar characteristics. For example, automobile insurance policyholders may be classified by age, gender, marital status, and driving record, as well as by the make and model of vehicle that they drive.

When underwriters receive an application, they assign the applicant to the appropriate class. They then determine whether the rates established for that class are sufficient to provide coverage for that applicant. Underwriters divide insurance applicants into four groups:

- *Preferred* applicants have lower-than-average loss expectancies and may qualify for lower premiums.
- *Standard* applicants have average loss expectancies for their class and pay the standard rates.
- *Substandard* applicants have higher-than-average loss expectancies and may be charged higher premiums and have restrictions placed on the types or amounts of coverage they may purchase.
- *Unacceptable* applicants have loss expectancies that are much too high and are rejected.

You can save money by confirming with your agent that you have been placed in the proper class for premium-determination purposes. Verifying that you are in the proper class is also important because a claim may be denied if premiums were based on an inappropriate classification.

direct sellers
Companies that market insurance policies through salaried employees, mail-order promotions, newspapers, the Internet, and even vending machines.

Not all companies use agents to market their policies. Companies referred to as **direct sellers** market their policies through salaried employees, mail–order promotions, newspapers, the Internet, and even vending machines. Any type of insurance can be sold directly. For risk managers who know what coverage they need, the lowest insurance premiums can be found with direct sellers.

Each type of seller presents both advantages and disadvantages. Independent agents may provide more personalized service and can select among several companies to meet a customer's needs. Exclusive agents can provide personalized service as well but are limited to the policies offered by the one company they represent and their sales commissions tend to be low.

✔ Concept Check 10.2

1. Define *insurance.*
2. Distinguish among the three types of hazards.
3. Why is the principle of indemnity so important to insurance sellers?
4. Identify four key points to review when reading an insurance policy.
5. Summarize how to use deductibles, coinsurance, hazard reduction, and loss reduction to lower the cost of insurance.
6. Differentiate among independent agents, exclusive agents, and direct sellers.

Homeowner's Insurance

Whether you own or rent housing, you face the possibility of suffering property and liability losses. **Homeowner's insurance** combines the liability and property insurance coverages needed by homeowners and renters into a single-package policy. Four types of homeowner's insurance are available for people who own houses, another type for the owners of condominiums, and one other type for those who rent housing.

Coverages

The standard homeowner's insurance policy is divided into two sections.

Property Insurance   Section I provides protection for various types of property damage losses, including the following: (1) damage to the dwelling, (2) damage to other structures on the property, (3) damage to personal property and dwelling contents, and (4) expenses arising out of a loss of use of the dwelling (for example, food and lodging). Additional coverages are usually provided for such items as debris removal, trees and shrubs, and fire department service charges.

An important variable related to Section I of a policy involves the number of loss-causing perils that are covered. **Named-perils policies** cover only those losses caused by perils that are specifically mentioned in the policy. **All-risk (or open-perils) policies** cover losses caused by all perils other than those specifically *excluded* by the policy. All-risk policies provide broader coverage because hundreds of perils can cause property losses, but only a few would be excluded. Common exclusions are flood and earthquake but these can be purchased for an additional premium if desired.

Liability Insurance   Section II deals with liability insurance. Whenever homeowners are negligent or otherwise fail to exercise due caution in protecting visitors, they may potentially suffer a liability loss. **Homeowner's general liability protection** applies when you are legally liable for the losses of another person. Homeowners often wish to take responsibility for the losses of another person regardless of the legal liability. Consider, for example, a guest's child who suffers burns from touching a hot barbecue grill. **Homeowner's no-fault medical payments protection** will pay for bodily injury losses suffered by visitors regardless of who was at fault. In the preceding example, such coverage would help pay for the medical treatment of the visitor's burns. **Homeowner's no-fault property damage protection** will pay for property losses suffered by visitors to your home. An example of such a loss might be damage to a friend's leather coat that was chewed by your dog.

Types of Homeowner's Insurance Policies

Six distinct types of homeowner's insurance policies exist: HO-1 through HO-4, HO-6, and HO-8. They are described in detail in Table 10.2 and more generally in the sections that follow. The same terms and identifying numbers are generally used by most insurance companies.

Basic Form (HO-1)   The **basic form (HO-1)** is a named-perils policy that covers 11 property-damage–causing perils and provides three areas of liability-related protection: personal liability, property damage liability, and medical payments. The most common perils that can cause property damage—fire and lightning, windstorm, theft, and smoke—are covered in the basic homeowner's policy. People who have finished basements (perhaps a TV room or spare bedroom) should purchase additional sewer backup coverage, as this possibility is not one of the 11 named perils.

3 Learning Objective
Design a homeowner's or renter's insurance program to meet your needs.

homeowner's insurance
Combines liability and property insurance coverages that homeowners and renters typically need into single-package policies.

named-perils policies
Cover only losses caused by perils that the policy specifically mentions.

all-risk (open-perils) policies
Cover losses caused by all perils other than those that the policy specifically excludes.

homeowner's general liability protection
Applies when you are legally liable for another person's losses, other than those that arise out of use of vehicles or your professional duties.

basic (homeowner's insurance) form (HO-1)
Named-perils policy that covers 11 property-damage–causing perils and provides three areas of liability-related protection: personal liability, property damage liability, and medical payments.

Table 10.2   **Summary of Homeowner's Insurance Policies**

	HO-1 (Basic Form)	HO-2 (Broad Form)	HO-3 (Special Form)
Perils covered (descriptions are given below)	Perils 1–11	Perils 1–18	All perils except those specifically excluded for buildings; perils 1–18 on personal property (does not include glass breakage)
Property coverage/limits			
House and any other attached buildings	Amount based on replacement cost, minimum $15,000	Amount based on replacement cost, minimum $15,000	Amount based on replacement cost, minimum $20,000
Detached buildings	10 percent of insurance on the home (minimum)	10 percent of insurance on the home (minimum)	10 percent of insurance on the home (minimum)
Trees, shrubs, plants, etc.	5 percent of insurance on the home, $500 maximum per item	5 percent of insurance on the home, $500 maximum per item	5 percent of insurance on the home, $500 maximum per item
Personal property	50 percent of insurance on the home (minimum)	50 percent of insurance on the home (minimum)	50 percent of insurance on the home (minimum)
Loss of use and/or additional living expense	10 percent of insurance on the home	20 percent of insurance on the home	20 percent of insurance on the home
Credit card, forgery, counterfeit money	$1000	$1000	$1000

Liability coverage/limits (for all policies)

Comprehensive personal liability	$100,000
No-fault medical payments	$1000
No-fault property damage	$500

Special limits of liability

For the following classes of personal property, special limits apply on a per-occurrence basis (e.g., per fire or theft): money, coins, bank notes, precious metals (gold, silver, etc.), $200; computers, $5000; securities, deeds, stocks, bonds, tickets, stamps, $1000; watercraft and trailers, including furnishings, equipment, and outboard motors, $1000; trailers other than for watercraft, $1000; jewelry, watches, furs, $1000; silverware, goldware, etc., $2500; guns, $2000.

List of perils covered

1. Fire, lightning
2. Windstorm, hail
3. Explosion
4. Riots
5. Damage by aircraft
6. Damage by vehicles owned or operated by people not covered by the homeowner's policy
7. Damage from smoke
8. Vandalism, malicious mischief
9. Theft
10. Glass breakage
11. Volcanic eruption
12. Falling objects (external sources)
13. Weight of ice, snow, sleet
14. Collapse of building or any part of building (specified perils only)
15. Leakage or overflow of water or steam from a plumbing, heating, or air-conditioning system
16. Bursting, cracking, burning, or bulging of a steam or hot water heating system, or of appliances for heating water
17. Freezing of plumbing, heating, and air-conditioning systems and home appliances
18. Injury to electrical appliances and devices (excluding tubes, transistors, and similar electronic components) from short circuits or other accidentally generated currents

HO-4 (Renter's Contents Broad Form)	HO-6 (For Condominium Owners)	HO-8 (For Older Homes)
Perils 1–9,11–18	Perils 1–18	Perils 1–11
10 percent of personal property insurance on additions and alterations to the apartment	$1000 on owner's additions and alterations to the unit	Amount based on actual cash value of the home
Not covered	Not covered (unless owned solely by the insured)	10 percent of insurance on the home (minimum)
10 percent of personal property insurance, $500 maximum per item	10 percent of personal property insurance, $500 maximum per item	5 percent of insurance on the home, $500 maximum per item
Chosen by the tenant to reflect the value of the items, minimum $6000	Chosen by the homeowner to reflect the value of the items, minimum $6000	50 percent of insurance on the home (minimum)
20 percent of personal property insurance	40 percent of personal property insurance	20 percent of insurance on the home
$1000	$1000	$1000

Note: This table describes the standard policies. Specific items differ from company to company and from state to state. When you want a limit that exceeds the standard limit for your company, you usually can increase the limit by paying an additional premium.

Broad Form (HO-2)

The **broad form (HO-2)** is a named-perils policy that covers 18 property-damage–causing perils and provides protection from the three liability-related exposures.

Special Form (HO-3)

The **special form (HO-3)** provides open-perils protection for four types of property losses: losses to the dwelling, losses to other structures, landscaping losses, and losses generating additional living expenses. Contents and personal property are covered on a named-perils basis for 17 of the 18 common homeowner's perils (the exception is glass breakage). In terms of liability protection and in all other respects, the coverage under HO-3 is the same as under HO-2.

special (homeowner's insurance) form (HO-3)
Provides open-perils protection (except for the commonly excluded perils of war, earthquake, and flood) for four types of property losses.

Renter's Contents Broad Form (HO-4)

The **renter's contents broad form (HO-4)** is a named-perils policy that protects the insured from losses to the contents of a dwelling rather than the dwelling itself. It covers 17 perils and provides liability protection. HO-4 is ideal for renters because it provides protection from losses to dwelling contents and personal property and provides for additional living expenses if the dwelling is rendered uninhabitable by one of the covered perils. Although insurance is relatively inexpensive, only one-fourth of all renters carry HO-4 protection.

renter's contents broad form (HO-4)
Named-perils policy that protects the insured from losses to the contents of a rented dwelling rather than the dwelling itself.

Condominium Form (HO-6)

The **condominium form (HO-6)** is a named-perils policy protecting condominium owners from the three principal losses they face: losses to contents and personal property, losses due to the additional living expenses that may arise if one of the covered perils occurs, and liability losses. (The building itself is insured by the management of the condominium.) Two additional coverages are included in the HO-6 policy as necessary to meet the specific

 Instant Message

Renter's Insurance Is Not Expensive

Renter's insurance can cost as little as $20 per month, and discounts are available if you buy from the same company that provides your auto coverage.

needs of the condominium unit owner. The first is protection against losses to the structural alterations and additions that condominium owners sometimes make when they remodel their units. The second is supplemental coverage for the dwelling unit to protect the condominium owner if the building is not sufficiently insured.

Older Home Form (HO-8)   The replacement value of an older home may be much higher than its market or actual cash value. The **older home form (HO-8)** is a named-perils policy that provides actual-cash-value protection on the dwelling. It does not provide that the dwelling be rebuilt to the same standards of style and quality, as those standards may be prohibitively expensive today. Instead, the policy provides that the dwelling be rebuilt to make it serviceable.

Buying Homeowner's Insurance

Four questions must be answered when buying a homeowner's policy.

1. How much coverage will you need to replace the dwelling itself?
2. How much coverage will you need on the contents and personal property in general.
3. How much protection will you need for items such as jewelry, money, guns, or antiques that have specific limits?
4. How much coverage will you need for liability protection?

How Much Coverage Is Needed on Your Dwelling?   If you own your home, your first step is to determine the dwelling's replacement value. You could either use the services of a professional liability appraiser and/or consult with your insurance agent to determine replacement value.

replacement-cost requirement
Stipulates that a home *must* be insured for 80 percent of its replacement value (some companies require 100 percent) in order for any loss to be fully covered.

Homeowner's insurance policies usually contain a **replacement-cost requirement** that stipulates that a home *must* be insured for 80 percent of its replacement value (some companies require 100 percent). Thus, a home with a replacement value of $200,000 would need to be insured for $160,000 (or perhaps $200,000), and this amount would be the maximum that the insurance company would be obligated to pay for a total loss (after payment of the deductible by the policyholder). If you fail to meet your replacement-cost requirement, you will not be considered fully insured and must coinsure partial losses as well. The amount of reimbursement for partial losses will be calculated using the **replacement-cost-requirement formula:**

$$R = (L - D) \times [I \div (RV \times 0.80 \text{ or } 1.00)] \qquad (10.2)$$

where

R = Reimbursement payable
L = Amount of loss
D = Deductible, if any
I = Amount of insurance actually carried
RV = Replacement value of the dwelling

Consider the example of Chris Shearer from Las Cruces, New Mexico, who owns a home with a replacement value of $200,000 with a $500 deductible. Chris had insured his home for $144,000, even though the policy required coverage of 80 percent of the replacement cost. Last month a fire in his home caused damage amounting to $80,500. Applying Equation (10.2), Chris's calculations are as follows:

$$
\begin{aligned}
R &= (\$80,500 - \$500) \times [\$144,000 \div (\$200,000 \times 0.80)] \\
&= \$80,000 \times (\$144,000 \div \$160,000) \\
&= \$80,000 \times 0.90 \\
&= \$72,000
\end{aligned}
$$

As this calculation shows, Chris will be reimbursed for only $72,000 of his loss. His failure to insure his house for 80 percent of its replacement cost, or $160,000 ($200,000 × 0.80), means he will be covered for only 90 percent ($144,000 ÷ $160,000) of its value, and he must pay 10 percent of any partial loss—in this case, $8000. Three out of four homes in the United States are underinsured by an average of 35 percent.

Meeting an 80 percent replacement-cost requirement enables you to avoid coinsurance on small losses but might still result in inadequate coverage on large losses that, though rare, exceed the policy limit. Thus, it is wise to insure your dwelling for 100 percent of its replacement cost. However, you will also want to increase your limits each year to keep up with inflation in housing construction costs. To do so, you can sign up for **inflation guard protection** to have your insurance company increase your coverage automatically each year.

How Much Coverage Is Needed on Your Personal Property?   Making a **personal property inventory** of, and placing a value on, all the contents of your home are time-consuming but important tasks. Table 10.3 shows the inventory and valuation for the contents of and personal property in a typical living room. You should conduct such an inventory for each room, the basement, garage, shed, and yard possessions. When totaled, these values will enable you to select proper policy coverage limits. Most homeowner's policies are designed to automatically cover contents and personal property for up to 50 percent of the coverage on the home. For example, if your home is insured for $240,000, you would have $120,000 in personal property insurance. If you need more coverage, simply notify your agent.

Table 10.3   **Personal Property Checklist: Living Room**

Item	Date Purchased	Purchase Price	Actual Cash Value	Replacement Cost
Furniture				
Sofa	8/05	$ 750	$ 375	$ 950
Chair	11/03	250	100	375
Lounger	12/06	575	300	695
Ottoman	12/06	100	50	120
Bookcase	4/08	275	225	300
End table (2)	7/09	300	250	300
Appliances				
TV	1/09	550	500	600
DVD	6/08	400	300	400
Wall clock	7/03	60	10	100
Furnishings				
Carpet	6/02	375	50	600
Painting	12/06	125	225	225
Floor lamp	4/04	150	50	225
Art (three items)	10/08	600	600	800
Table lamp	4/04	75	40	100
Table lamp	5/08	125	100	135
Throw pillows	7/05	45	20	60
TOTAL		**$4,755**	**$3,195**	**$5,985**

Instant Message

Stay Out of the Doghouse

Over one-third of homeowner's insurance liability claims are associated with dog bites. Make sure your insurance company knows that you have a dog. And raise your liability limits for better protection.

actual cash value (of personal property)
Represents the purchase price of the property less depreciation.

How Much Coverage Is Needed on Personal Property That Has Specific Limits?

Some types of personal property may be subject to specific item limits. For example, the typical homeowner's insurance policy provides maximum coverages of $200 for cash, $5000 for personal computers, and $1000 for jewelry. This is because most people do not have such items above these values. If your inventory reveals a higher valuation on such items, you can simply ask your company for extra coverage and pay the higher premium required.

Notice that Table 10.3 lists three estimates for the value of the contents of a room: the purchase price, the actual cash value, and the replacement cost. Historically, property insurance policies paid only the **actual cash value** of an item of personal property, which represents the purchase price of the property less depreciation. The **actual-cash-value (ACV) formula** is

$$ACV = P - [CA \times (P \div LE)] \qquad (10.3)$$

where

$$P = \text{Purchase price of the property}$$
$$CA = \text{Current age of the property in years}$$
$$LE = \text{Life expectancy of the property in years}$$

Consider the case of Marianna Kinard, a music teacher from Orangeburg, South Carolina, whose 9-year-old heating/air-conditioning unit was struck by lightning. The unit cost $2400 when new and had a total life expectancy of 12 years. Its actual cash value when it was struck by lightning was

$$
\begin{aligned}
ACV &= \$2,400 - [9 \times (\$2,400 \div 12)] \\
&= \$2,400 - (9 \times \$200) \\
&= \$600
\end{aligned}
$$

contents replacement-cost protection
Option sometimes available in homeowner's insurance policies (including the renter's form) that pays the full replacement cost of any personal property.

Marianna could not replace the unit for $600. A more realistic replacement cost might be $3000. **Contents replacement-cost protection** is an option sometimes available in homeowner's insurance policies that pays the full replacement cost of any personal property. The standard limitation that applies to contents (50 percent of insured value of the dwelling) remains in effect if contents replacement-cost protection is purchased. The overall limit on contents may need to be raised, as it is easy to reach the 50 percent figure when replacement-cost valuation is used.

How Much Coverage Is Needed for Liability Losses?

Standard homeowner's policies provide $100,000 of personal liability coverage, $1000 of no-fault medical expense coverage, and $500 of no-fault property damage coverage. It is smart to apply the large-loss principle here and increase the policy limits for all three of these coverages (or consider an umbrella liability policy discussed later). The extra cost is small because the odds of these larger losses are low.

 Concept Check 10.3

1. Describe the types of losses covered under the property insurance portion of a homeowner's policy.
2. Give three examples of liability protection under homeowner's insurance policies.
3. List the six types of homeowner's insurance policies (HO-1 through HO-4, HO-6, and HO-8).
4. Identify four types of personal property for which the covered loss is limited to a specific dollar amount under standard homeowner's insurance policies (see Table 10.2).
5. List the three questions you should ask yourself when determining the policy limits for a homeowner's insurance policy.

Automobile Insurance

Driving a car is the largest single exposure to catastrophic losses for most Americans. A split-second error in driving judgment or simple bad luck can result in many tens of thousands of dollars of automobile-related property damage and personal injury losses. **Automobile insurance** combines the liability and property insurance coverages needed by automobile owners and drivers into a single-package policy. It is illegal to operate a motor vehicle without assuming financial responsibility for any losses you might cause. Most states require automobile owners to purchase automobile insurance to meet this responsibility (although there are many illegally uninsured drivers on the roads).

Losses Covered

Automobile insurance combines four distinct types of coverage: (1) liability insurance, (2) medical payments insurance, (3) protection against uninsured and underinsured motorists, and (4) insurance for physical damage to the insured automobile. Each coverage has its own policy limits, conditions, and exclusions. Table 10.4 summarizes the coverage provided by automobile insurance policies for people not specifically excluded in the policy.

Coverage A—Liability Insurance Liability insurance covers the insured when he or she is held responsible for losses suffered by others. Two types of liability can arise out of the ownership and operation of an automobile. **Automobile bodily injury liability** occurs when a driver or car owner is held legally responsible for bodily injury losses suffered by other people, including pedestrians. **Automobile property damage liability** occurs

4 Learning Objective
Design an automobile insurance program to meet your needs.

automobile insurance
Combines the liability and property insurance coverages that most car owners and drivers need into a single-package policy.

automobile bodily injury liability
Occurs when a driver or car owner is held legally responsible for bodily injury losses that other people, including pedestrians, suffer.

automobile property damage liability
Occurs when a driver or car owner is held legally responsible for damage to others' property.

Table 10.4 Summary of Automobile Insurance Coverages

Section	Type of Coverage	People Covered	Property Covered	Recommended Limits
A	LIABILITY INSURANCE			
	(1) Bodily injury liability	Relatives living in insured's household driving an owned or nonowned automobile	Not applicable	At least legally required minimums or $250,000/$500,000, whichever is greater
	(2) Property damage liability	Relatives living in insured's household driving an owned or nonowned automobile	Automobiles and other property damaged by insured driver while driving	At least legally required minimum or $100,000, whichever is greater
B	MEDICAL PAYMENTS	Passengers in insured automobile or nonowned automobile driven by insured family member	Not applicable	$50,000 or higher
C	UNINSURED AND UNDERINSURED	Anyone driving insured car with permission and insured family members driving nonowned automobiles with permission	Not applicable	$50,000/$100,000 or higher, if available
D	PHYSICAL DAMAGE			
	(1) Collision	Anyone driving insured car with permission	Insured automobile	Actual cash value less deductible
	(2) Comprehensive	Not applicable	Insured automobile and its contents	Actual cash value less deductible

Instant Message

Bodily Injury Losses Can Be Very High

A one-day stay in a hospital intensive care unit can cost upwards of $50,000. An accident with several severe injuries can result in losses in excess of $300,000. When buying a policy remember to select high liability limits as they are a must.

when a driver or car owner is held legally responsible for damage to the property of others. Such damage can include damage to another vehicle, a building, or roadside signs and poles.

The most common type of automobile insurance policy is the **family auto policy (FAP).** A FAP covers the vehicle owner, relatives living in the vehicle owner's household, and people who have the owner's permission to drive the vehicle. In addition, any other vehicle that the owner borrows with permission is similarly covered for all family members.

The policy limits for FAPs are quoted as **split liability limits,** usually three numbers such as 100/300/50, with each number representing a multiple of $1000 (Figure 10.2). The first number gives the maximum that will be paid for liability claims for *one* person's bodily injury losses resulting from an automobile accident ($100,000 in our example). The second number indicates the overall maximum that will be paid for bodily injury liability losses to *any number* of people resulting from an automobile accident ($300,000 in our example). The third number specifies the maximum that will be paid for property damage liability losses resulting from an accident ($50,000 in our example).

In some policies, the liability limits are stated as a **single liability limit,** such as $250,000. Under such policies, all property and bodily injury liability losses resulting from an accident would be paid until the limit is reached. These policies are referred to as **personal auto policies (PAPs).** Family members of the vehicle owner may or may not be covered under a PAP when driving the vehicle, depending on the policy provisions.

Liability insurance covers only the insured for losses suffered by others. It does not pay for bodily injury losses suffered by the insured or for property damage to the insured's car. Injured passengers of an at-fault driver may collect under the driver's liability coverage, but only

Figure 10.2
Automobile Liability Insurance Policy Limits

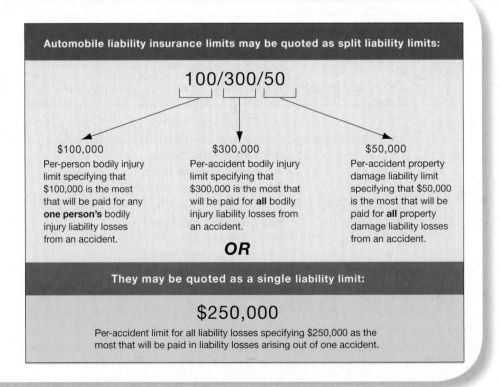

after exhausting the coverage provided under medical payments (discussed later) and only after reimbursement is made to people injured in other vehicles or as pedestrians. Driving a rental car exposes you to the same potential liabilities as driving your own vehicle. If you have automobile liability insurance, such liabilities will usually be covered while you drive a rented car. Check your coverage before you rent a car so you can avoid buying overpriced insurance from the rental agency.

Coverage B—Medical Payments Insurance

Automobile medical payments insurance covers bodily injury losses suffered by the driver of the insured vehicle and any passengers regardless of who is at fault. Medical losses occurring within one year and as a direct result of an accident will be reimbursed up to the limits of the policy. Automobile medical payments insurance also covers insured family members who are injured while passengers in any car or who are injured by a car when on foot or riding a bicycle. Medical payments coverage is subject to a single policy limit, which is applied per person, per accident.

In such states that have adopted some type of no-fault automobile insurance, insureds collect first (and possibly only) from their own insurance companies for bodily injury losses resulting from an automobile accident. In these states, the medical payments coverage, which is often referred to as **personal injury protection (PIP)**, covers the driver and any passengers for bodily injury losses as well as possibly lost wages and rehabilitation expenses. Under medical payments or PIP, drivers and their injured passengers collect directly from the driver's insurance. If the driver was not at fault, then the driver's insurer pays the claims and subsequently may choose to exercise subrogation rights against the at-fault party. **Subrogation rights** allow an insurer to take action against a negligent third party (and that party's insurance company) to obtain reimbursement for payments made to an insured. Subrogation rights are limited in no-fault states.

Coverage C—Uninsured and Underinsured Motorist Insurance

Sometimes the driver at fault in an automobile accident carries no insurance or has insufficient liability insurance coverage. To protect against such uncovered losses, an insured can purchase uninsured and underinsured motorist insurance as part of his or her own automobile insurance policy. When the medical payments coverage is exhausted, the uninsured and underinsured motorist coverage will provide protection. **Uninsured motorist insurance** protects the insured and the insured's passengers from bodily injury losses (and, in a few states, property damage losses) resulting from an automobile accident caused by an uninsured motorist. It provides protection above that extended under the automobile medical payments insurance. **Underinsured motorist insurance** protects the insured and his or her passengers from bodily injury losses (and, in some cases, property damage losses) when the at-fault driver has insurance but that coverage is insufficient to reimburse the losses.

The limits for uninsured motorist insurance are quoted in a manner similar to that for automobile liability insurance. For example, uninsured motorist protection with limits of 50/100 would provide a maximum of $50,000 for any one injured person and a maximum of $100,000 for multiple bodily injury losses in the same accident. Most states require insurers to offer uninsured and underinsured motorist insurance. Such insurance is a smart risk-management choice and carries a very low premium—often less than $50 per year.

Coverage D—Physical Damage Insurance

A number of perils can cause property losses to an insured automobile. **Automobile physical damage insurance** provides protection against losses caused by damage to your car from collision, theft, and other perils. The most common peril is, of course, a collision with another vehicle or an object. The next most common peril is theft.

Instant Message

Save Money the Right Way on Auto Insurance

The two ways to save money on auto insurance are to raise your deductible and lower your liability limits. Raising your deductible is the smarter move. Choosing lower limits is unwise, as you will be personally liable if an accident exceeds those limits.

automobile medical payments insurance
Insurance that covers bodily injury losses suffered by the driver of the insured vehicle and any passengers, regardless of who is at fault.

personal injury protection (PIP)
Medical payments coverage for the driver and any passengers for bodily injury losses as well as possibly lost wages and rehabilitation expenses common in no-fault accident states.

subrogation rights
Allow an insurer to take action against a negligent third party (and that party's insurance company) to obtain reimbursement for payments made to an insured.

Coverage C—uninsured and underinsured motorist insurance
Coverage that an insured can purchase as part of automobile insurance that covers the insured in an accident with an uninsured or underinsured driver at fault.

Did You Know?

How to Save Money on Insurance

There is no point in paying more for insurance than necessary. Here are some suggestions for achieving this goal.

Select Appropriate Coverages and Limits. Buy only needed coverages, and select policy limits appropriate for the largest potential losses.

Retain Risks That Are Affordable. Retain risks that you can afford—by raising a deductible, for example—and only insure against losses that would be financially unaffordable.

Take Advantage of Discounts. Most insurance companies offer discounted premiums for policyholders who buy multiple policies (for example, both automobile and home-owner's insurance) from them.

Engage in Loss Control. Many companies charge lower premiums to policyholders who take steps to reduce the probability or severity of loss. For example, discounts are available if you install dead-bolt door locks or a fire extinguisher in your home. Ask your agent what you need to do to qualify.

Shop Around for the Lowest-Cost Coverage. Insurance premiums from one company can be twice as much as that charged by another company and for essentially the same coverage, so considerable savings can be realized by seeking quotes from multiple agents and direct sellers. To obtain a quote, simply telephone an agent or direct seller and provide some basic descriptive information. You can also use a Web-based quote service such as www.quotesmith.com or www.insquote.com.

The insurance regulatory agency in your state (to find yours, visit www.naic.org/state_web_map.htm) may publish helpful insurance buyer's guides that discuss how to buy specific types of insurance, compare premiums, and rate the companies providing such insurance. In addition, *Consumer Reports* magazine periodically publishes feature articles that discuss insurance.

---

collision insurance
Reimburses insureds for losses to their vehicles resulting from a collision with another car or object or from a rollover.

comprehensive automobile insurance
Protects against property damage losses to an insured vehicle caused by perils other than collision and rollover.

Collision insurance reimburses an insured for losses resulting from a collision with another car or object or from a rollover. The insurer pays the cost of repairing or replacing the insured's car, regardless of who is at fault. When the other driver is at fault, subrogation rights may allow the insurer to obtain reimbursement through that driver's property damage liability protection. Collision insurance is written with a deductible that usually ranges from $100 to $1000. If you carry collision insurance coverage on your own car, you are generally covered when you drive someone else's car with that person's permission. Most automobile insurance policies provide for collision coverage on rental cars if such coverage applies to your owned vehicle. Again, check with your agent before you rent a car.

Comprehensive automobile insurance protects against property damage losses caused by perils other than collision and rollover. Covered perils include fire, theft, vandalism, hail, and wind, among many others. Comprehensive insurance is written on an open-perils basis, and it often includes a deductible ranging from $100 to $500.

When you have a loss that qualifies under collision and comprehensive insurance, an estimate of the repair cost will be made. If this estimate exceeds the value that the insurance company puts on the vehicle, the lower of the two figures is paid, less any deductible. Insurance companies set vehicle values based on the average current selling price of vehicles of the same make, model, and age and the vehicle's mileage and condition prior to the occurrence of the damage.

Other Protections

Two other inexpensive but helpful coverages are available to automobile insurance buyers. **Towing coverage** pays the cost of having a disabled vehicle transported for repairs. It usually pays only the first $25 or $50 per occurrence but will cover any towing need—not just assistance needed due to an accident. **Rental reimbursement coverage** provides a rental car when the insured's vehicle is being repaired after an accident or has been stolen. It often has a daily payout limit of $20 to $30 and, therefore, may provide only part of the funds needed to obtain replacement transportation.

Frances Twitty/istockphoto.com

Drivers need to make sure they have sufficient liability coverage in the event of an accident— the person at fault is typically responsible for all damages.

Buying Automobile Insurance

The smart risk manager will shop carefully for automobile insurance because of its high cost. The task is to select the proper automobile insurance program while keeping premiums as low as possible. Because coverages are fairly standardized and premiums vary widely, comparison shopping for premium prices often saves hundreds of dollars.

The first step toward designing an adequate automobile insurance program involves identifying the types of losses that might occur. This task is easy because the standard policies cover most of the losses that you can reasonably expect to face as a result of owning and driving a vehicle.

Next, you must determine the amount of coverage you need. At a minimum, you must conform to the financial responsibility requirements mandated by your state. Because medical expenses and automobile repair costs can be enormous, it is wise to buy high liability limits. Limits of at least $250,000/$500,000/$100,000 are commonly recommended. Similarly high limits for uninsured and underinsured motorist coverage are advisable. Limits recommended for automobile medical expense coverage are a minimum of $100,000 per person. It may be tempting to decline some of the coverages provided in a policy to reduce the overall premium. For example, lower premiums may be obtained by eliminating collision coverage, as the charge for such coverage typically represents 30 to 40 percent of the total automobile insurance premium. This cost-saving strategy is

Did You Know?

The Best Way to Title Vehicles

Couples may be tempted to put major assets in both names, and sometimes that is the best way to go. For automobiles, however, the decision is complicated. The owner of a vehicle is legally liable for accidents caused by the driver. If both partners own an automobile, both could be sued. Thus, it is smart to title an automobile in only one name. For couples with two vehicles, each should be owned separately.

Did You Know?

How Automobile Insurance Would Apply to an Accident

Just how the myriad provisions in an automobile insurance policy apply to a specific accident mystifies many people. As a result, the claims process may generate considerable dissatisfaction after an accident. The example given here and outlined in the following chart is intended to clarify the application of the multiple coverages and limits.

In September of last year, Donna Redman, a college student from Austin, Texas, caused a serious accident when she failed to yield to an approaching vehicle while attempting to make a left turn. Donna suffered a broken arm and facial cuts, resulting in medical costs of $1254. Her passenger, Philip Windsor, was seriously injured with head and neck wounds requiring surgery, a two-week hospital stay, and rehabilitation. Philip's injuries generated medical costs of $17,650. The driver of the other car, John Monk, suffered serious back and internal injuries and facial burns that resulted in some disfigurement. His medical care costs totaled $22,948. His passenger, Annette Monk, suffered cuts and bruises requiring minor medical care at a cost of $423.

Both cars were completely destroyed in the accident. Donna's 10-year-old Buick was valued at $2150. John's Mazda Miata was valued at $19,350. The force of the impact spun John's car around, causing it to destroy a traffic-signal control box (valued at $3650).

Both Donna and John were covered by family automobile policies with liability limits of $20,000/$50,000/$15,000 and medical payment limits of $5000 per person and $100 collision coverage deductibles. In total, Donna had to pay $11,048 out of her own pocket, as the policy limits were exceeded by John's medical costs and the property damage. If she had taken out a single-limit personal automobile policy for $65,000 (the total of her $50,000 per-accident bodily injury liability and $15,000 per-accident property damage liability), then she would have incurred no out-of-pocket liability losses.

An additional point needs to be raised concerning situations in which an accident victim suffers serious, permanent injuries that are not fully reimbursed by the insurance policy protecting the driver at fault. In our example, John suffered very painful injuries resulting in permanent disfigurement. He may wish to sue Donna for his pain and suffering and for his unpaid medical expenses. If he were to file such a suit, Donna would be provided with legal assistance by her insurance company. Any judgment that exceeds the policy limits (remember that Donna's per-person policy limit has already been reached) will be Donna's responsibility, however. Both Donna and John were terribly underinsured.

Donna Redman's Accident: Who Pays What?

Coverage	Donna's Policy	John's Policy
Liability (limits) (multiples of $1000):	(20/50/15)	(20/50/15)
Bodily injury:		
John Monk	$20,000	
Annette Monk	423	
Philip Windsor	12,650	
Property damage:		
John Monk's car	15,000	
Medical payments (limits):	($5,000)	($5,000)
John Monk	5,000*	
Annette Monk	5,000*	
Donna Redman	1,254	
Philip Windsor	5,000	
Collision coverage (limits):	(ACV, $100 deductible)	(ACV, $100 deductible)
Donna's car	2,050	
John's car	19,250*	
Donna's out-of-pocket expenses:		
John Monk's bodily injury	2,948	
John Monk's car	4,350	
Traffic-signal control box	3,650	
Collision insurance deductible	100	
TOTAL	**$11,048**	

*Included in Donna's column because John's company filed a claim against Donna by exercising its subrogation rights.

Decision Making Worksheet

Buying Automobile Insurance

Even though automobile insurance premiums can vary by hundreds of dollars annually among companies, only four in ten consumers shop around when they buy or renew coverage.

You can use the following worksheet to record automobile insurance premium quotations obtained from insurers.

Remember to add surcharges for previous claims and other factors as well as to subtract discounts for which you might qualify. If you must join an organization (for example, the American Automobile Association) to obtain coverage from an insurer, add the membership fees to the final premium.

Coverage Type	Coverage†/Amount of Deductible	Premium* Company A (example)	Company B (your figures)	Company C (your figures)
A. Liability insurance				
Bodily injury	250/500	$132	_____	_____
Property damage	100	58	_____	_____
B. Medical payments/personal injury protection				
Medical payments	100	$51	_____	_____
PIP (no-fault states)	N/A	N/A	N/A	N/A
C. Uninsured/underinsured motorist protection				
Uninsured motorist	50/100	$28	_____	_____
Underinsured motorist	50/100	$17	_____	_____
D. Physical damage protection				
Collision coverage	$100 deductible	$126	_____	_____
	$200 deductible	111	_____	_____
	$500 deductible	88	_____	_____
	$1,000 deductible	62	_____	_____
Comprehensive	no deductible	59	_____	_____
	$100 deductible	41	_____	_____
	$200 deductible	34	_____	_____
	$500 deductible	24	_____	_____
Total premium		438	_____	_____
Plus surcharges		N/A	_____	_____
Less discounts		33	_____	_____
Final premium*		**$405**	_____	_____

*Premium for six months for a midsize car in a medium-size city based on a $200 collision deductible and a $100 comprehensive deductible.
†Multiples of $1000.

recommended only for cars having a book value of less than $2000. Elimination of other nonessential coverages (for example, comprehensive or uninsured/underinsured motorist insurance) would yield little savings while sharply reducing protection.

 Concept Check 10.4

1. Identify the four types of automobile insurance coverage.
2. Explain the meaning of the numbers 100/200/75.
3. Identify who is protected by medical payments coverage.
4. Distinguish between collision and comprehensive insurance.
5. Explain why selecting a policy with a high deductible and high liability limits is better than one with a low deductible and low liability limits.

Protection for Other Property and Liability Loss Exposures

5 Learning Objective

Describe other types of property and liability insurance.

Some people need protection against property and liability losses that are not covered by homeowner's or automobile insurance policies.

Comprehensive Personal Liability Insurance

Owning a home and driving a car are not the only sources of potential liability you may face. Consider the case of Will Crain, a pharmacist from Missoula, Montana. While climbing in a restricted area, he accidentally loosened some rocks, which fell down the slope and seriously injured hikers below. Because Will was in a restricted area and had failed to warn the hikers of his presence, he was held liable for their injuries and ordered to pay a court judgment of $178,000. Recall that the standard homeowner's insurance policy provides comprehensive personal liability insurance up to a specified limit, usually $100,000. Individuals who lack such coverage can purchase a separate **comprehensive personal liability policy.** Those with homeowner's (including renter's) insurance who desire higher limits should ask their insurance agent to raise the limits on their existing policy.

Flood and Earthquake Insurance

Standard homeowner's insurance policies exclude losses caused by flood and earthquakes. This is because these types of losses are subject to **adverse selection.** This means that people who are most likely to suffer such losses know that they are and those that are least likely know that, too. As a result, only those people with high probabilities of loss will want to buy the coverage thereby violating the law of large numbers. But if you live in a flood prone area or earthquake zone your risk of loss should be addressed. The **National Flood Insurance Program** is a Federal government program that makes flood insurance available in counties where flood is common. **Earthquake insurance** can be purchased only from a private insurance company either as a separate policy or as an endorsement to an existing homeowner's or renter's insurance policy.

Professional Liability Insurance

Professionals such as physicians, lawyers, and accountants can be held legally liable for losses suffered by their patients or clients. **Professional liability insurance** (sometimes called **malpractice insurance**) protects individuals and organizations that provide professional services when they are held liable for the losses of their clients. Policy limits, deductibles, premiums, and other characteristics of such policies vary widely depending on the profession involved. Professional liability policies are written with policy limits of $250,000 or more. A $1 million professional liability policy written for a family therapist may cost as little as $300 per year; in contrast, some surgeons pay $60,000 or more per year for professional liability insurance.

professional liability insurance/malpractice insurance
Protects individuals and organizations that provide professional services when they are held liable for their clients' losses.

Umbrella Liability Insurance

It is possible to lose one's entire life savings as a result of a single liability loss. **Umbrella** (or **excess**) **liability insurance** is a catastrophic liability policy that covers liability losses in excess of those covered by any underlying homeowner's, automobile, or professional liability policy. Such policies provide two benefits. First, the types of losses covered are broader than those recognized by more narrowly defined policies. Second, these policies provide for high dollar amounts of coverage over and above the basic policies. To be covered for these higher limits, you must carry the basic coverages as well.

Figure 10.3 shows how umbrella policies work. In this example, the insured has an automobile insurance policy with total liability limits of $130,000 (the total liability coverage for one accident is $100,000 per bodily injury plus $30,000 for property damage), a homeowner's insurance policy with liability protection of $100,000, and a $150,000 professional liability insurance policy. If the insured bought an umbrella policy with a $1 million limit and then experienced a $750,000 professional liability loss, the umbrella policy would provide protection of $600,000 after the professional liability policy limits were exceeded. Umbrella policies are relatively low in cost when purchased to supplement basic policies (perhaps $150 to $200 per year for an additional $1 million of protection) and protect against virtually all liability exposures that a person might face.

umbrella (excess) liability insurance
Catastrophic liability policy that covers liability losses in excess of those covered by any underlying homeowner's, automobile, or professional liability policy.

floater policies
Provide all-risk protection for accident and theft losses to movable property regardless of where the loss occurs.

Floater Policies

Floater policies provide all-risk protection for accident and theft losses to movable property (such as cameras, sporting equipment, MP3 players, and clothing) regardless of where the loss occurs. Floater protection for personal property is part of the standard homeowner's insurance policy. Property owned for business purposes is excluded. This means that a mechanic's tools, a lawyer's books, and a Karaoke DJ's equipment, for example, would not be covered. A separate floater policy would be required.

Many items of personal property are transported in automobiles and kept at temporary residences such as motel rooms. Automobile insurance policies do not cover portable personal property. If it is covered under a homeowner's policy at home, however, personal property will be covered elsewhere under the floater protection provided by the homeowner's policy. For example, a compact disc player permanently installed in a car would not be considered portable and thus would be covered by the automobile policy. If it can be removed for use indoors, the CD player would be covered under the homeowner's (or renter's) policy.

Did You Know?

About Wedding Insurance

The cost of an average wedding is about $30,000. Much of that amount must be paid up-front. If either party backs out, there is not much you can do. But, what if something happens and the wedding must be postponed? There is insurance for such situations. Wedding insurance generally covers situations such as these: (1) a member of the immediate families dies or becomes ill (preexisting illness is excluded); (2) a guest is injured; (3) caterers fail to provide a service; (4) clothing providers and photographers do not deliver their services; and (5) gifts are stolen or damaged. It is a good idea to use a credit card for many of the expenses. That is because of the dispute protections provided for credit card purchases (see Chapter 7) that are not available for debit, check, or cash purchases.

Did You Know?

What's Covered While You Are Away at College

College students often wonder about what kind of insurance coverage they have while they are attending school away from home. Students who have moved into their own residence to live year-round need to buy their own renter's and automobile insurance policies. This is because the family's homeowner's and auto coverages will only apply if the student (1) lives in a dorm or fraternity/sorority house or (2) lives off campus in what is clearly a temporary arrangement (that is, the student returns home during semester breaks and over the summer).

If you are covered by your family's policies, here are some guidelines to remember:

1. Property stored away from home is often covered for up to 10 percent of the coverage on the home. If the family home is insured for $150,000, for example, then $15,000 of coverage applies—and this is probably adequate for most students. Remember, however, this is a family total.

If three siblings are away at school simultaneously, it may be inadequate. Additional coverage can be purchased through your homeowner's insurance agent.

2. Expensive items such as jewelry or computers may be subject to specific limits in the homeowner's insurance policy. Purchase additional protection for these items if necessary.

3. Auto insurance rates are based on where the vehicle is garaged (or parked) at night. The insurance agent should be notified if a covered vehicle is used while away at school. It is better to pay a slightly higher rate than to face denial of payment for a loss because of misinformation. A discount is common for a college student listed on a parent's policy if the student does not have a car at school and the school is at least 100 miles from the parent's home.

Figure 10.3
How Umbrella Liability Policies Work

Advice from a Pro...

Applying the Large-Loss Principle to Property and Liability Insurance

You should always buy adequate insurance for the highest possible loss. Although rare, such losses can destroy your financial future. That thinking underlies the large-loss principle discussed earlier. Here is how to apply the principle to property and liability insurance.

For your property insurance, you should select limits that equal the value of the property involved. A $240,000 home should be insured for $240,000. Select all-risk policies rather than named-peril policies. Yes, the cost may be high but the loss of your property would be much worse.

The purchase of an umbrella liability policy is the best way to apply the large-loss principle to liability insurance. Never buy the legal minimums for auto insurance. Causing an accident that destroys one newer-model vehicle can exceed most state minimum limits.

You can afford to apply the large-loss principle through the use of higher deductibles. Ask yourself: "What is the largest loss I can afford to cover myself?" Then choose the highest deductible that does not exceed what you can afford to cover. The money saved by selecting a higher deductible can be used to pay for higher policy limits. For example, on a 100/300/50 auto policy with a $100 deductible, you can save as much as $300 per year by simply raising the deductibles to $1000! Then you can apply some of those savings to buy a $1,000,000 umbrella policy to protect yourself from a catastrophe.

Jan D. Andersen, PhD
Emeritus Associate Professor
California State University, Sacramento

 Concept Check 10.5

1. Explain how purchasing an umbrella liability insurance policy applies the large-loss principle.
2. Are you preparing for a professional career that might expose you to liability losses? How might you protect yourself from such losses?
3. Give two examples of someone who might want to purchase a floater insurance policy.

How to Collect on Your Property and Liability Losses

The direct benefit of owning insurance becomes evident when a loss occurs and it is time to file a claim. Even when you have a legitimate claim, however, you may want to consider whether you should do so. A small claim might be best ignored.

Recall that insurance is for the losses you cannot afford. Filing frequent claims (or even notifying the agent of a loss) can result in an increase in your rates. One claim probably will not cause a problem. Having a second claim within a two-year period may be looked at negatively. Of course, if you have a large claim, you would want to file for its recovery. Here's what you should do when you have a loss.

6 Learning Objective
Summarize how to make an insurance claim.

Contact Your Insurance Agent

The first step—contacting your agent—should be taken as soon as possible, but only after you have decided that you will ultimately file a claim. Follow the agent's instructions regarding who to contact next (including filing a written police report) and what to do to minimize the magnitude of the loss. Then keep the company informed of everything relevant to the loss, even if it requires daily or weekly contact until the claim is settled. The tenacious claimant is likely to collect fully on a loss.

Instant Message

Getting Started on Your Personal Property Inventory

Your balance sheet can serve as a starting point when developing your personal property inventory. Provide any additional details needed for the items listed for insurance purposes.

Do It NOW!

Managing property and liability risks protects you from losses that could severely damage your financial future. Start today by:

1. Completing steps one and two of the risk management process.
2. Assessing your automobile insurance coverage and making changes as necessary.
3. Buying renters insurance if you rent your housing.

Document Your Loss

You carry the burden of proof whenever a property or liability loss occurs. Adequate documentation of the circumstances and the amount of the loss is essential. In the absence of such documentation, the insurance company will generally interpret the situation in the manner most favorable to its interests, not yours.

The best way to document a theft, fire, or other personal property loss is with pictures. Photograph or videotape all valuable property in your home when you purchase it or when you obtain insurance coverage. Write the date of purchase, price paid, description, model name and number, and serial number (if any) of the property on the back of the photograph or verbally record it on the videotape. Prepare a list describing any items not photographed or videotaped. Keep such records in a safe-deposit box, in a file cabinet at work, or with a relative. If a loss occurs, present a *copy* of your documentation to the agent or insurance company.

You should always file a police report if you become involved in an automobile accident. Insureds also should prepare a narrative giving the time and place of the accident, the direction of travel and estimated speed of the cars involved, the road and weather conditions, and the behavior of all parties involved. Include a diagram of the accident scene showing the location of the vehicles before, during, and after the time of impact, plus the locations of traffic lights and signs and any landmarks (for example, road construction or repairs). If possible, obtain the names and contact information for witnesses. Police reports are also advisable (and often required) when filing a theft claim of any type.

File Your Claim

insurance claim
Formal request to the insurance company for reimbursement for a covered loss.

claims adjuster
Person designated by the insurance company to assess whether the loss is covered and to determine the dollar amount that the company will pay.

release
Insurance document affirming that the dollar amount of the loss settlement is accepted as full and complete reimbursement.

An **insurance claim** is a formal request to the insurance company for reimbursement for a covered loss. All of the documentation and information will be requested by the insurance agent or a **claims adjuster** (the person designated by the insurance company to assess whether the loss is covered and to determine the dollar amount that the company will pay). Insurance companies require that claims be made in writing, although the adjuster may assist you in completing the necessary forms.

Sign a Release

Part of the final step in the claims-settlement process is to sign the **release,** which is an insurance document affirming that the dollar amount of the loss settlement is accepted as full and complete reimbursement and that the insured will make no additional claims for the loss against the insurance company. Signing the release absolves the insurance company of any further responsibility for the loss. Resist the temptation to sign a release until you are sure that the full magnitude of the loss has become evident.

 Concept Check 10.6

1. What is the best way to establish documentation for potential losses to your personal property?
2. Describe what you should do to file a claim most effectively when involved in an automobile accident.
3. Describe the term *release* and explain why signing a release too soon might work to your disadvantage.

What Do You Recommend NOW?

Now that you have read the chapter on risk management and property liability insurance, what would you recommend to George and Emily in the case at the beginning of the chapter regarding:

Ted Foxx/Alamy

1. The risk-management steps they should take to update their insurance coverages?

2. The relationship between severity and frequency of loss when deciding whether to buy insurance?

3. Adequately insuring their home?

4. The use of deductibles and policy limits to keep their automobile insurance premiums at a manageable level while still maintaining vital coverage?

Big Picture Summary of Learning Objectives

1 Apply the risk-management process to address the risks to your property and income.

Personal financial managers practice risk management to protect their present and future assets and income. Risk management entails identifying the sources of risk, evaluating risk and potential losses, selecting the appropriate risk-handling mechanism, implementing and administering the risk-management plan, and evaluating and adjusting the plan periodically.

2 Explain basic insurance terms and the relationship between risk and insurance.

Insurance is a mechanism for reducing pure risk by having a larger number of individuals share in the financial losses suffered by all members of the group. It is used to protect against pure risk but cannot be used to protect against speculative risk, which carries the potential for gain as well as loss. Likewise, insurance cannot be used to provide payment in excess of the actual financial loss suffered. Insurance consists of two elements: the reduction of pure risk through application of the law of large numbers, and the sharing of losses.

3 Design a homeowner's or renter's insurance program to meet your needs.

Homeowner's insurance is designed to protect homeowners and renters from property and liability losses. Six types of homeowner's insurance are available, including one geared toward renters. Homeowner's policies can be purchased on a named-perils or an open-perils basis.

4 Design an automobile insurance program to meet your needs.

Automobile insurance is designed to protect the insured against property and liability losses arising from use of a motor vehicle. These policies typically provide liability insurance (both bodily injury and property damage liability), medical payments or personal injury protection insurance, property insurance on your car, and underinsured and uninsured motorist insurance. The most commonly purchased type of automobile insurance is the family automobile policy. The premium for automobile insurance is based on the characteristics of the insured driver, including age, gender, marital status, and driving record.

5 Describe other types of property and liability insurance.

Other important types of property and liability insurance include floater policies (to protect personal property regardless of its location), professional liability insurance, and umbrella liability insurance.

6 Summarize how to make an insurance claim.

The insured is responsible for documenting and verifying a loss. Photographs or videotapes of the insured property are ideal for documenting claims made under a homeowner's insurance policy. A police report provides the best documentation for claims made under an automobile insurance policy.

Let's Talk About It

1. **Auto Insurance Claims.** What experiences have you or a family member had with the automobile insurance claims process? What might you have done differently or better?

2. **Actual Cash Value.** Many people complain that property insurance policies should pay more than what the insurance companies say is the actual cash value of the property, such as for a motor vehicle that is in beautiful condition. How do you feel about this issue, and what would happen if insurance companies were more generous in their reimbursements?

3. **Auto Liability Limits.** Do you know the liability limits on the automobile insurance policy under which you are covered? Are the limits appropriate?

4. **Personal Property Protection.** Is your personal property, such as furniture and computer, covered under a homeowner's or renter's insurance policy? If not, why not? If so, what are the policy limits?

5. **Insurance Underwriting.** How do you feel about being grouped into classes in the insurance underwriting process? Do you feel that insurance companies should treat all people alike?

Do the Math

1. **How Much of Fire Loss Will Be Covered?** Toula and Ian Miller of St. Clairsville, Ohio, recently suffered a fire in their home. The fire, which began in a crawl space at the back of the house, caused $24,000 of damage to the dwelling. The garage, valued at $8400, was totally destroyed but did not contain a car at the time of the fire. Replacement of the Millers' personal property damaged in the home and garage amounted to $18,500. In addition, $350 in cash and a stamp collection valued at $3215 were destroyed. While the damage was being repaired, the Millers stayed in a motel for one week and spent $1350 on food and lodging. The

house had a value of $95,000 and was insured for $68,400 under an HO-3 policy with a $250 deductible. Use Table 10.2 to answer the following questions. (Hint: You must first determine whether the Millers have adequate dwelling replacement coverage and, if not, what percentage of the necessary 80 percent coverage they do have. The resulting answer will determine the percentage of the loss to the dwelling covered, and consequently the amount to be reimbursed by the insurance company.)

(a) Assuming that the deductible was applied to the damage to the dwelling, calculate the amount covered by insurance and the amount that the Millers must pay for each loss listed: the dwelling, the garage, the cash and stamp collection, and the extra living expenses.

(b) How much of the amount of the personal property loss would be covered by the insurance policy? Paid for by the Millers?

(c) Assuming that they have contents replacement-cost protection on the personal property, what amount and percentage of the total loss must be paid by the Millers?

2. **Sufficient Dwelling Coverage?** Adam Barrow of Columbia, Missouri, has owned his home for ten years. When he purchased it for $178,000, Adam bought a $160,000 homeowner's insurance policy. He still owns that policy, even though the replacement cost of the home is now $300,000.

(a) If Adam suffered a $20,000 fire loss to the home, what percentage and dollar amount of the loss would be covered by his policy?

(b) How much insurance on the home should Adam carry to be fully reimbursed for a fire loss?

3. **How Much of an Auto Accident Loss Will Be Covered?** Ashley Diamond of Laramie, Wyoming, drives an eight-year-old Toyota valued at $9600. She has a $75,000 personal automobile policy with $10,000 per person medical payments coverage and both collision ($200 deductible) and comprehensive coverage. David Smith of Fort Collins, Colorado, drives a four-year-old Chevrolet Malibu valued at $9500. He has a 25/50/15 family automobile policy with $20,000 in medical payments coverage and both collision ($100 deductible) and comprehensive insurance. Late one evening, while he was driving back from Rocky Mountain National Park, David's car crossed the centerline of the road, striking Ashley's car and forcing it into a ditch. David's car also left the road and did extensive damage to the front of a roadside store. The following table indicates the damages and their dollar amounts.

Item	Amount
Bodily injuries suffered by Ashley	$ 6,800
Bodily injuries suffered by Fran, a passenger in Ashley's car	28,634
Ashley's car	9,600
Bodily injuries suffered by David	2,700

Bodily injuries suffered by Cecilia, a passenger in David's car	12,845
David's car	9,500
Damage to the roadside store	14,123

Complete the following chart and use the information to answer these questions:

(a) How much will Ashley's policy pay Ashley and Fran?

(b) Will subrogation rights come into play? In what way?

(c) How much will David's bodily injury liability protection pay?

(d) To whom and how much will David's property damage liability protection pay?

(e) To whom and how much will David's medical protection pay?

(f) How much reimbursement will David receive for his car?

(g) How much will David be required to pay out of his own pocket?

David Smith's Accident: Who Pays What?

Coverage	David's Policy	Ashley's Policy
Liability (limits)	____	____
Bodily injury	____	____
Ashley	____	____
Fran	____	____
Cecilia	____	____
Medical payments (limits)	____	____
David	____	____
Ashley	____	____
Fran	____	____
Cecilia	____	____
Collision coverage (limits)	____	____
David's car	____	____
Ashley's car	____	____
David's out-of-pocket expenses	____	____
Fran's bodily injury	____	____
Excess property damage losses	____	____
Collision insurance deductible	____	____
TOTAL	____	____

Financial Planning Cases

Case 1

The Princes' Auto Insurance Is Not Renewed

Mark and Kelly Prince of Jacksonville, Florida, face a crisis. Their automobile insurance company has notified them that their current coverage expires in 30 days and will not be renewed. Both Mark and the Princes' younger son had two minor, at-fault accidents during the past year. Their children are otherwise good drivers, as are both parents. The Princes are confused because they know families whose members have much worse driving records but still have insurance.

(a) Explain to Mark and Kelly why their policy might have been canceled.

(b) Use the box on page 302 to give Mark and Kelly some pointers on how to save money on their new policy.

Case 2

Abigail Contemplates a New Homeowner's Insurance Policy

Abigail Elizabeth Proctor of Bedford, Oregon, recently bought a home for $200,000. The previous owner had a $160,000 HO-1 policy on the property, and Abigail can simply pay the premiums to keep the same coverage in effect. Her insurance agent called her and cautioned that she would be better off to upgrade the policy to an HO-2 or HO-3 policy. Abigail has turned to you for advice. Use the information in Table 10.2 to advise her.

(a) What additional property protection would Abigail have if she purchased an HO-2 policy?

(b) What additional property protection would Abigail have if she purchased an HO-3 policy?

(c) What property protection would remain largely the same whether Abigail had an HO-1, HO-2, or HO-3 policy?

(d) Advise Abigail on what differences in liability protection, if any, exist among the three policies.

Case 3

A Student Buys Insurance for a Used Car

Makiko Iwanami, a student from Osaka, Japan, is in one of your classes. She is considering the purchase of a used car and has been told that she must buy automobile insurance to register the car and obtain license plates. Makiko has come to you for advice, and you have decided to focus on three aspects of automobile insurance.

(a) Explain how liability insurance works in the United States. Advise Makiko about which liability insurance limits she should select.

(b) Makiko is especially impressed that automobile insurance includes medical payments coverage because she has no health insurance. Explain why the medical payments coverage does not actually solve her health insurance problem, and describe the type of coverage it provides.

(c)   Makiko plans to pay cash for the car and doesn't want to spend more than $3000. Outline the coverage provided by collision insurance and factors that might make such coverage optional for Makiko.

Case 4

An Argument About the Value of Insurance

You have been talking at a party to some friends about insurance. One young married couple in the group believes that insurance is really a waste of money in most cases. They argue, "The odds of most bad events occurring are so low that you need not worry." Furthermore, they say, "Buying insurance is like pouring money down a hole; you rarely have anything to show for it in the end." Based on what you have learned from this chapter, how might you argue against this couple's point of view?

Case 5

The Hernandezes Consider Additional Liability Insurance

Victor and Maria's next-door neighbor, Jasmine Saunders, was recently sued over an automobile accident and eventually was held liable for $437,000 in damages. Jasmine's automobile policy limits were 100/300/50. Because of the shortfall, she had to sell her house and move into an apartment. Victor and Maria are now concerned that a similar tragedy might potentially befall them. They have a homeowner's policy with $100,000 in comprehensive personal liability coverage, an automobile policy with 50/100/25 limits, Maria has a small ($100,000) professional liability policy for her dental hygiene practice.

(a)   How might Victor and Maria more fully protect themselves through their homeowner's and automobile insurance policies?

(b)   What additional benefits would they receive in buying an umbrella liability policy?

Case 6

The Johnsons Decide How to Manage Their Risks

The financial affairs of the Johnsons have become much more complicated since we began following them in Chapter 2. Both Harry ($275 per month) and Belinda ($300 per month) have been given raises at work. They have purchased a $140,000 condominium that has added about $400 per month to their housing expense. They have purchased a used car for $3200, adding about $120 per month to their expenses. As a result of these changes, Harry and Belinda realize that they now face greater risks in their financial affairs. They have decided to review their situation with an eye toward managing their risks more effectively. Use Table 10.1, their net worth and income and expense statements at the end of Chapter 2, and other information in this chapter to answer the following questions:

(a)   What are Harry and Belinda's major sources of risk from home and automobile ownership, and what is the potential magnitude of loss from each?

(b)   Given the choices listed in step 2 of Table 10.1, how should the Johnsons handle the sources of risk listed in part a?

On the 'Net

Go to the Web pages indicated to complete these exercises. You can also go to the *Garman/Forgue* companion website at www.cengage.com/finance/garman for an expanded list of exercises. Under General Business, select the title of this text. Click on the Internet Exercises link for this chapter.

1. Visit the website for the National Association of Insurance Commissioners at http://www.insurance.naic.org/state_web_map.htm/, where you will find a map where you can link to the Insurance Commission in your state. Determine the minimum automobile insurance liability limits in your state. How well insured do you feel someone would be if they carried only these minimums?

2. Visit the website for the National Association of Insurance Commissioners, where you will find a map at http://www.naic.org/state_web_map.htm through which you can link to your state insurance regulator's website. If available in your state, obtain an insurance buyer's guide for automobile and homeowner's insurance that describes policy provisions and compares insurance rates. Use these rate comparisons to select two automobile insurance companies that would be appropriate for your needs. Write or telephone the companies to obtain specific premium quotations for the desired insurance protection. Do the same for single-family dwelling, condominium, or renter's insurance, depending on your circumstances.

3. Visit the website for the Insurance Institute for Highway Safety at http://www.iihs.org/ratings/default.aspx. For your own vehicle and one or two you would like to own, check how the vehicles stack up against the competition in terms of injury protection.

Visit the Garman/Forgue companion website . . .

www.cengage.com/finance/garman

Managing Health Expenses

!You Must Be Kidding, Right?

Amber Parker is a 32-year-old married mother with two children, ages 3 and 4. She used to work out of her home as a medical transcriptionist for a local hospital that offered a health care plan. Last year Amber suffered severe head injuries in a bicycling accident. Amber's wounds have healed and she has regained her ability to speak but is not yet able to walk on her own or use her hands and arms very well. Amber is recuperating at home but requires a daily paid caregiver to assist with her personal needs. Her children now go to daycare and it may be 5 years before she can work again. Which of the following aspects of her injury were covered by Amber's health care plan?

A. Her hospital stay and surgery

B. Her at-home custodial care

C. The cost of daycare for her children

D. Her lost income

The answer is A. Having a health care plan is a must. But your protection is incomplete until you have addressed the need for rehabilitation and custodial care as well as for the potential lost income from a period of disability!

Learning Objectives

After reading this chapter, you should be able to:

1 Identify ways that people can manage the financial burdens resulting from illness or injury.

2 Distinguish among the types of protection for direct health expenses.

3 Describe the general benefits and limitations of health care plans.

4 Develop a plan for protecting your income when you cannot work due to disability.

5 Explain how to protect yourself from the expenses for long-term care.

Jupiterimages

Danielle DiMartino is a 36-year-old single mother with two children, ages 10 and 14. Her 10-year-old daughter has a history of ear infections that require doctor's office visits four or five times per year. Danielle's 71-year-old mother lives with the family for financial reasons; she has hereditary high blood pressure and high cholesterol as well as diabetes. Danielle's mother has enrolled in Medicare Parts A and B.

Danielle's employer pays all or a portion of the cost for a health care plan to cover the company's workers, their spouses, and their dependents. Danielle has four options: (1) the basic HMO managed by a local university medical school/hospital with no additional cost for Danielle, but with additional cost of $122 per month to cover her children, (2) a health insurance plan with a PPO at that same medical center for an additional cost of $245 per month, (3) a traditional health insurance plan that provides access to virtually all health care providers in her community for $455 per month, and (4) a high-deductible plan with a $5000 deductible at no additional cost. Danielle's employer offers no disability income or long-term care group plan. She does receive 10 sick days per year, which can accumulate to 60 days if not taken. Danielle has accumulated 30 days.

What do you recommend to Danielle DiMartino on the subject of managing health expenses regarding:

1. Choosing among the four alternatives available to her?

2. Danielle's concerns about providing for her mother's health care needs?

3. How Danielle can cover her long-term care risk?

4. Danielle's need for disability income insurance?

Your Next Five Years

In the next five years you can start achieving financial success by doing the following related to managing health expenses:

1. Sign up for an employer-sponsored premium conversion plan and a flexible spending arrangement for health care, whenever they are available, to save money on taxes.

2. Consider using a high-deductible health care plan and health savings account if you are unable to afford the high costs of an HMO or traditional health insurance plan.

3. Always maintain coverage for direct health care expenses when changing employers using the COBRA law or a short-term health plan for protection.

4. Take advantage of employer-sponsored long-term disability income insurance if available or consider purchasing protection individually.

5. Regularly reevaluate your need for long-term care insurance against your resources for providing such care on your own.

1 Learning Objective

Identify ways that people can manage the financial burdens resulting from illness or injury.

group health plan
Sold collectively to an entire group of people rather than to individuals, such as the group health care policies offered by employers.

Instant Message

Group Health Plans Are Best

Participating in a group plan is desirable for three reasons: First, group health coverage costs less than an individual plan. Second, employers often pay all or the major portion of the cost. Third, people who have existing health problems are less likely to be rejected because of their condition.

Few things in life are more important than your good health. When illness or injuries do strike, three possible issues may affect your finances.

1. **The direct costs of the required health care,** such as the cost of hospital stays, surgeries, and visits to the doctor's office.

2. **The cost of your rehabilitation and custodial care** such as care in a nursing home.

3. **The income lost** when you cannot work due to illness or injury.

This chapter looks at the ways you can address these three financial concerns. You should not take them lightly. Medical debts are the number one cause of bankruptcy.

Addressing the Financial Burdens of Illness or Injury

On average, more than $7500 is spent on health care for each American every year. About 85 percent of Americans are covered by a health care plan that will pay a portion of these costs. You can obtain protection as an individual or as a member of a group. A **group health plan** is sold collectively to an entire group of people rather than to individuals. The health care plan offered by an employer or to students enrolled in a particular college is an example of a group plan. Years ago most workers could rely on their employer to provide them with a health care plan. But as prominent businessman, Herb Kohl, has observed "Businesses want to offer solid, affordable health insurance to their employees, but it is getting harder to find every year." As a result, Americans today are more responsible for paying for their health care than previous generations.

Each of the three types of losses resulting from illness or injury can be addressed in multiple ways. Of course, you can pay all of your own expenses. That is not always practical or smart. We provide a summary of your options here and in Table 11.1.

1. Covering Your Direct Health Care Costs

Direct health care can be paid for by a health maintenance organization (HMO), traditional health insurance, or a high-deductible health care plan (each is defined later). These three types of plans may cover as much as 90 to 100 percent of one's costs and comprise the plans typically offered by employers. Purchased as an individual, these plans can cost $600 or more per month for an individual and $1200 or more for family coverage.

People age 65 or over can enroll in the **Medicare** program, which is the federal government's health care program for the elderly. Medicare is divided into two parts. **Medicare Part A** is the hospitalization portion of the program; it requires no premium. **Medicare Part B** is the supplementary health expense insurance portion for outpatient care, doctor office visits, or certain other services of the Medicare program; it requires payment of a monthly premium (approximately $112). Both components require the patient to pay a portion of their costs.

Low-income individuals and families may qualify for **Medicaid,** a government health care program funded jointly by the federal and state governments. Eligibility for Medicaid is based on household income and net worth. The **S-CHIP program,** which is a government program similar to Medicaid, covers children whose parents are middle income but do not have access to a private health care plan.

Medicare
The federal government's health care program for the elderly.

Medicaid
A government health care program for low-income people funded jointly by the federal and state governments.

long-term care insurance
Provides reimbursement for costs associated with custodial care in a nursing facility or at home.

2. Covering Your Rehabilitative and Custodial Care Costs

Accident victims, people with chronic disease, and the elderly often have needs that go beyond direct health care. At one extreme is the need for a stay in a nursing home and at the other might be a short period of time during which a patient receives rehabilitation. Health care plans tend to cover only "medically necessary" care, not for rehabilitation and custodial needs. **Long-term care insurance** provides reimbursement for costs associated with custodial care in a nursing facility or at home. A key feature of Medicaid is its coverage of long-term custodial care. Elderly who have "spent down" their assets on long-term care expenses may be eligible to receive Medicaid reimbursement for a portion of these costs. Those in the greatest need for long-term care insurance tend to be those in the middle-income range. They lack the financial resources to pay for nursing home care (perhaps $5000 per month) and have too high of an income to qualify for Medicaid.

Instant Message

Three Ways to Obtain Health Care Benefits

Health benefits can come from three sources. First, your employer might provide them as an employee benefit. Second, you might qualify for a government program. Three, you can buy protection as an individual.

3. Covering Your Lost Income

Anyone with a job can lose income when they become sick or are injured. Many employers offer sick days and other time off that can be used as necessary. Some employers may offer **disability income insurance** that replaces a portion of the income lost when you cannot work because of illness or injury. These plans come in two forms. A **short-term disability income insurance plan** replaces a portion of one's income for a short period of time; perhaps up to two years. Short-term plans are sometimes partially paid for by the employer. Employers may also offer a group **long-term disability income insurance plan** for coverage periods of five or more years. The employee is usually required to pay the full premium for such coverage. If your employer does not offer either of these plans, you may buy them on your own.

Workers who are eligible can collect **Social Security Disability Income Insurance** benefits from the federal government if their disability is total (meaning they cannot work at any job) and is expected to last one year (or until death if that is anticipated within one year). The amount of these benefits is based on the worker's average lifetime earnings subject to Social Security tax and, thus, might not be sufficient to adequately support young workers and their families.

Older workers who become disabled may have another option available. Many have built up considerable funds in a tax-sheltered retirement account. These funds can be utilized to replace lost income when disabled.

disability income insurance
Insurance that covers a portion of the income lost when you cannot work because of illness or injury.

Social Security Disability Income Insurance
Under this government program, eligible workers can collect some income for up to one year if their disabilities are total, meaning that they cannot work at any job.

Did You Know?

The Top 3 Financial Missteps in Managing Health Expenses

People slip up in managing health expenses when they do the following:

1. Go unprotected for health care when changing jobs
2. Duplicate employer-provided health care protection with their employed spouse
3. Ignore the need for disability income insurance

Table 11.1   Types of Protection from Health-Related Expenses

	Direct Health Care			**Rehabilitative and Custodial Care**	**Lost Income**
Provider of Coverage?	• Health maintenance organizations (HMOs) • Medicare for those age 65 and over • Medicaid for low-income/low-wealth individuals	• Traditional health insurance • Medicare for those age 65 and over • Medicaid for low-income/low-wealth individuals	• Consumer-driven health insurance plans	• Long-term care insurance • Medicaid for low-income/low-wealth individuals	• Disability income insurance • Social Security for eligible workers and their families
Services Covered?	Provide hospital, surgical, and medical services directly through their own hospital and physicians or under contract with such providers	Reimburses or pays for hospital, surgical, medical, and other health care costs	Reimburse or pay for hospital, surgical, medical, and other health care costs that exceed a high deductible of $5000 or more	Reimburses for costs associated with custodial care (not direct medical care)	Provides a monthly income to replace that lost when the insured is unable to work due to accident or injury
Payment Mode?	Charge a monthly fee on a prepaid basis	Charges monthly premiums for the insurance coverage	Charge monthly premiums for the insurance coverage	Charges monthly or annual premiums	Charges a monthly premium
Purchased By?	Individuals or by employers as an employee benefit	Individuals or by employers as an employee benefit	Individuals or by employers as an employee benefit	Individuals	Individuals or by employers as an employee benefit

Type of Expense

 Concept Check 11.1

1. List three ways that group health plans are better than individually purchased plans.
2. Identify the five mechanisms available to help people pay for direct health care costs.
3. Explain why someone might want to purchase long-term care insurance.
4. Explain how someone might replace the income lost due to illness or injury.

---

2 Learning Objective

Distinguish among the types of protection for direct health expenses.

health care plan
Generic name for any program that pays or provides reimbursement for direct health care expenditures.

Sources of Protection from Direct Health Care Costs

A **health care plan** is a generic name for any program that pays or provides reimbursement for direct health care expenditures. When a health plan is available as an employee benefit, the employer typically pays the cost for the worker (and possibly other members of the worker's immediate family) for the lowest-cost plan the employer offers. Employees can choose a higher-priced option or add family members to the coverage by paying an additional charge.

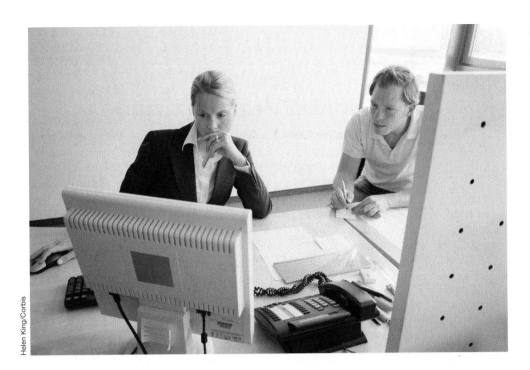

Helen King/Corbis

New employees often must choose from among a menu of health care plans soon after being hired.

New employees generally must make a choice among the available plans within the first few days of being hired.

Health Maintenance Organizations

Health maintenance organizations (HMOs) provide a wide array of health care services, including hospital, surgical, and preventive health care. Some HMO plans require a small copayment of $5 to $25 for each office visit or prescription. A goal of HMOs is to catch any medical problem early which helps keep overall costs low by reducing the probability of subsequent high-cost medical treatment. HMO plans are available to groups and individuals.

HMOs Provide Prepaid Health Care   The monthly fee charged by an HMO is actually a prepayment for your health care. The fee is based on the health services that the average plan member would tend to use. HMOs do not put dollar limits on how much health care can be used. Instead, they list the types of health care they will provide under the contract.

How HMOs Work   HMO subscribers are assigned a **primary-care physician** by the HMO or choose one from a list of physicians employed by the HMO. The primary-care physician usually must order all procedures and approve referrals to specialized health care providers (for example, a cardiologist) within the HMO. HMOs are one of several types of **managed care plans.** Such plans seek to control the conditions under which health care can be obtained. Examples of controls include preapproval of hospital admissions, restrictions on which hospital or doctor can be used, and mandates regarding the type of procedures that will be employed to treat a specific health problem. If the HMO itself does not provide a particular type of care, the primary care physician refers the patient to a local hospital or clinic for those services. One HMO variation is the **individual practice organization (IPO),** a structure in which the HMO contracts with—rather than hires—groups of physicians. These

Instant Message

Making Changes in Your Group Plan

When you work for an employer that offers a group health plan, you must wait until the next **open-enrollment period** to make changes in coverage or switch among alternative plans. Open-enrollment periods occur once each year and last for about one month. Open-enrollment period requirements are generally waived for such family changes as births, adoptions, divorce, and marriage.

health maintenance organizations (HMOs)
Health insurance plans that provide a broad range of health care services for a set monthly fee on a prepaid basis.

managed care plans
Any health care plan that controls the conditions under which health care can be obtained.

The Difference Between Health Insurance and HMOs

Health insurance pays for or reimburses you for your care. HMOs actually provide your health care.

comprehensive health insurance
Insurance that provides protection against financial losses resulting from hospital, surgical, and medical expenditures with policy limits as high as $1 million or more.

preferred provider organization (PPO)
Group of health care providers (doctors, hospitals, and other health care providers) who contract with a health insurance company to provide services at a discount.

Check the Quality of Your Health Care Providers

The National Committee for Quality Assurance maintains a website that provides its ratings of HMOs, hospitals, clinics, and physicians (www.ncqa.org).

consumer-driven health care
An approach to health care protection where the consumer elects a health care plan with a high deductible and high overall policy limits.

high-deductible health care plan
Can either be traditional health insurance or an HMO that follows the consumer-driven health care philosophy by charging relatively high deductibles.

physicians maintain their own offices in various locations around a community and serve as the primary-care physicians and specialists for the HMO.

Traditional Health Insurance

Health insurance provides protection against direct medical expenses resulting from illness and injury. It may cover hospital, surgical, and other medical expenditures. These coverages can be purchased separately, but most consumers and employers prefer **comprehensive health insurance** because it combines these protections into a single policy with policy limits of $1 million or more. Unlike with HMOs, where you are prepaying for health care in advance, health insurance is based on the concept of reimbursement for losses, with the patient choosing the type of care based on the advice of his or her physician. For this reason, health insurance plans are often referred to as **indemnity plans** or **fee-for-service plans** because they compensate the insured for the cost of care received.

Health insurance plans often identify a **preferred provider organization (PPO)**. A PPO is a group of health care providers (doctors, hospitals, and other health care providers) who contract with a health insurance company to provide services at a discount. This discount is then passed along to the policyholders in the form of reductions or elimination of deductibles and coinsurance requirements if they choose the PPO providers for their health care.

Consider the case of Dru Cameron, who works in the field of international marketing. Her firm's health insurance plan has contracted with a PPO representing a local university's teaching hospital and its affiliated physicians. Because Dru chose the university hospital for treatment of a broken ankle, she saved $150 on the $250 deductible and did not have to pay the usual 20 percent coinsurance share of office visit charges. She gave up the right to go to her family doctor, who is not a PPO member, although she could still see that physician for other health care needs in the future.

A **provider-sponsored network (PSN)**, also called a **provider-sponsored association,** is a group of cooperating physicians and hospitals who have banded together to offer a health insurance contract. Such networks operate primarily in rural areas, where access to HMOs may be limited. As a group, the members of the PSN coordinate and deliver health care services and manage the insurance plan financially. They contract with outside providers for health services that are not available through members of the group.

Consumer-Driven Health Care

Consumer-driven health care is an approach to health care protection where the consumer elects a health care plan with a high deductible and high overall policy limits. A **high-deductible health care plan** can either be traditional health insurance or an HMO. Deductibles for these plans can start at $1100 ($2200 for a family) but can be as high as $5000 per year. The plans will have an out-of-pocket limit of $5500 for an individual or $11,000 for a family per year. High-deductible plans have much lower premiums than other plans because workers pay a much larger portion of health care bills. When offered by an employer the plan is less costly for the employer, as well. People who must buy their own

Did You Know?

How Medicare Differs from Medicaid

Medicare is funded by means of the Medicare payroll tax. This tax is paid by both workers and employers, much like the Social Security tax. Its beneficiaries include people age 65 and older who are eligible for Social Security retirement benefits, federal civilian employees age 65 and older who retired after 1982, people who are eligible for Social Security disability benefits, and individuals with kidney disorders that require kidney dialysis treatments.

Medicare is divided into two parts. Medicare Part A is the hospitalization portion of the program; it requires no premium. Medicare Part B is the supplementary health expense insurance portion for outpatient care, doctor office visits, or certain other services of the Medicare program; it requires payment of a monthly premium.

Eligibility for Medicaid is based on household income and net worth. The health services provided through this program generally include hospital, surgical, and medical care. In some states, dental care for children may be covered as well. A key feature of Medicaid is its coverage of custodial long-term and nursing home care. Elderly who have "spent down" their assets on long-term care expenses may be eligible to receive Medicaid reimbursement for a portion of their nursing home costs.

---

health care plan, especially younger workers, often find the lower premiums for a high-deductible plan attractive.

The question, then, is how to afford the high out-of-pocket cost when health care is needed. The answer is with a **health savings account (HSA).** An HSA is a tax-deductible savings account into which individuals and/or their employers can deposit tax-sheltered funds for use to pay medical bills including the deductibles and other out-of-pocket costs required by a high-deductible plan. The maximum annual deposit is either the annual deductible under their high-deductible plan or $3000 for an individual or $5950 for a family plan, whichever is lower. Another common feature of consumer driven health care is a **health reimbursement account (HRA).** An HRA consists of funds set aside by employers to reimburse employees for qualified medical expenses. Thus, the employer helps employees pay their medical bills. An HRA is funded solely by an employer. There is no limit on the employer's contributions, which are excluded from an employee's taxable income.

The principle behind consumer driven health care is that when consumers are spending more of their own health care dollars initially they will become knowledgeable and informed patients/employees and will spend their own money more carefully than they would spend an employer's or health plan's funds. The higher out-of-pocket spending by consumers will encourage them to shop around, compare prices, pick and choose among options, and all the other things consumers normally do when making expensive purchases. Plus, they are more apt to try to stay healthy in the first place. In return the consumer receives a high level of protection from a catastrophic, high-cost disease or injury.

Here is how these three plans might fit together for an employee working for an employer that offers a choice of health care plans. The worker might choose the high-deductible plan from the options provided. The employee could then set up an HSA to set aside funds to pay the high deductible required by the HSA with the employer possibly providing funds for the HSA, as well. As an incentive for choosing the high-deductible plan the employer could also fund an HRA for the employee. (Note that some employers fund HRAs even if the employee does not want to choose the high-deductible plan.)

What if you have no access to an employer-provided health care plan? Here you could buy a high-deductible plan on your own and set up an HSA to set aside funds to pay the high deductible and other costs associated with the HSA. Should you work for an employer that provided an HRA, you would be provided additional assistance.

health savings account (HSA)
Tax-deductible savings accounts into which individuals or employers can deposit tax-sheltered funds to pay medical bills.

health reimbursement account (HRA)
Funds that employers set aside to reimburse employees for qualified health expenses.

Advice from a Pro...

Be Smart When Shopping for an Individual Health Plan

Shopping for an individual health care plan (a plan that is not provided through a group) requires a comparison of the many options available. You should focus your attention on three areas: (1) the cost, (2) the company, and (3) the plan itself.

The Cost

A sound health insurance plan, when purchased outside of a group, can easily cost more than $600 per month for a typical family of four. Obviously, comparison shopping is essential. When you apply for an individual health care plan, the company's decision whether to accept you is based on a number of underwriting factors, including your age, gender, occupation, family and personal health history, and physical condition. Each of these factors has a bearing on the likelihood of health-related expenditures and, therefore, the cost.

    Medical information bureaus (similar to credit bureaus) maintain files on insurance applicants.* Both medical and nonmedical information is maintained in these files. If you are charged more or turned down for credit or insurance because of information in such a file, you should know your consumer rights. If you were denied coverage or charged extra, you have the right to be told that the information came from a medical information bureau. You can then request a copy of the report to verify the accuracy of the information.

The Company

It is important to choose a financially sound health care company. Wise financial planners always ask about the percentage of premiums collected by an insurance company that is subsequently paid out to reimburse the losses of the participants. The **claims ratio (payout ratio)** formula is

$$\text{Claims ratio} = \frac{\text{losses paid}}{\text{premiums collected}} \qquad (11.1)$$

    Top companies typically have claims ratios that exceed 90 percent. At the other extreme are companies (especially those that sell hospital indemnity and dread disease insurance by mail, over the telephone, or through newspaper inserts) that have claims ratios of less than 25 percent. The lower the claims ratio, the lower the return (the actual benefits) to the policyholder on the premium dollar paid.

The Plan

The smart way to compare health care plans is to set some criteria for judging whether a policy provides the needed coverage. The plans that do provide the needed coverage (and have high claims ratios) can then be compared on a price basis. No plan should be purchased "sight unseen." If an agent or company will not allow you to study a plan for a few days, buy your policy elsewhere.

Holly Hunts
Montana State University

*To obtain a copy of your report ($8 or free within 30 days of an adverse report), write the Medical Information Bureau at P.O. Box 105, Essex Station, Boston, MA 02112; call (617) 426-3660 for an application; or visit http://www.mib.com/html/request_your_record.html.

Instant Message

What If Your Employer Does Not Offer a Health Care Plan?

A high-deductible health care plan in conjunction with an HSA can be a low-cost option for people who do not have access to a health care plan through their employment. The monthly premium might be about $200.

 ## Concept Check 11.2

1. Distinguish between health maintenance organizations (HMOs) and traditional health insurance.
2. Identify two benefits of selecting a preferred provider organization (PPO) when seeking health care.
3. Explain the linkage between high-deductible health care plans and health savings accounts (HSAs) and health reimbursement accounts (HRAs).

---

3 Learning Objective
Describe the general benefits and limitations of health care plans.

Making Sense of Your Health Plan Benefits

You can save yourself considerable confusion, delay, and money if you understand your health plan benefits before illness or injury strikes. If you have a group plan, you will receive a

certificate of insurance that outlines your benefits. If you have purchased a plan on your own, you should become familiar with your health insurance policy or your HMO contract. Here are some questions to ask yourself and background information to understand what you find in these documents.

certificate of insurance
Paper or booklet that outlines group health insurance benefits.

What Types of Care Are Covered?

The typical health care plan covers hospital room and board expenses, surgical procedures both as an inpatient and outpatient, prescription drugs, diagnostic tests, visits to the doctor's office, and many other aspects of health care. Dental and vision care are generally not covered. You can buy separate **dental expense insurance** (possibly as a group plan through your employer) to provide reimbursement for dental care expenses. Orthodontic treatment is typically excluded. High deductibles and coinsurance requirements and low policy limits can make dental plans less beneficial than they might appear. **Vision care insurance** provides reimbursement for eye examinations and purchase of glasses and contact lenses. Vision care insurance is typically written on a group basis as an employee benefit. For an individual, vision care insurance is probably not a good buy because the highest expenses for eye care arise out of diseases and injuries to the eyes, which would be covered under basic health care plans.

dental expense insurance
Insurance that provides reimbursement for dental care expenses.

Health plans contain provisions that exclude coverage for certain **preexisting conditions.** These are health conditions or symptoms that were known to the participant or diagnosed within a certain time period, usually one or two years, before the effective date of the plan. Preexisting conditions can be excluded for a period of time after a plan goes into effect or, possibly, permanently. Group plans exclude fewer preexisting conditions than individual plans. Plans may also dictate waiting periods for specific types of expenses. For example, maternity benefits often have a one-year waiting period.

preexisting conditions
Medical conditions or symptoms that the plan participant knew about or had been diagnosed within a certain time period before the plan effective date.

Did You Know?

What Can Happen to Your Health Plan When You Graduate

Many college students lose their health care coverage when they graduate because they are no longer eligible as a family member under a parent's plan. You might be tempted to go without coverage for a time because of its high cost, you expect to have a job soon that will provide coverage, or simply because you are healthy and expect to stay that way. This latter reason is shortsighted because young people do get sick or are injured. For example, young adults are at higher risk for automobile injuries and your car insurance will cover only a small portion of your medical bills if you are seriously injured in an accident. So what should you do?

1. **Try to stay on a parent's plan.** Some states require companies to allow you to do this for a few months. Also check to see if it is an option via a plan's COBRA provisions. You would need to pay the premium but as a group member you will pay lower rates and the coverage is broader than with other options.

2. **Buy short-term health insurance.** These plans can be paid for monthly for a term of six months or a year and may be renewable. Coverage for a premium of perhaps $200 per month may be available. These plans are not as comprehensive, of course, but they cover the basics. Select a plan with a high limit and a high deductible to be covered for a serious illness. You can pay for routine doctor's office visits out-of-pocket.

Going without health insurance has an added risk. If you develop a serious medical condition while uninsured, it will be considered a preexisting condition and make coverage difficult or impossible to obtain in the future. Bottom line . . . stay insured.

About Accident and Dread Disease Health Insurance

Accident and dread disease health insurance is often purchased by people who have no other health care plan or fear that their health care plan will fall short of their needs. **Accident insurance** pays a specific amount per day—for example, $100 for a hospital stay arising out of an accident—or a specific amount for the loss of certain limbs or body parts—for example, $2000 for the loss of a finger or an arm. **Dread disease insurance** provides reimbursement for medical expenses arising out of the occurrence of a specific disease, such as cancer. These plans are typically highly overpriced and provide benefits much less generous than implied in sales promotions. Since the average daily cost for a hospital stay is more than $1200, these policies cover very little.

guaranteed renewable policies
Policies that must be continued in force as long as the policyholder pays the required premium.

Who Is Covered?

Health care plans can be written to cover an individual, a family, or a group. Few misunderstandings arise when an individual is the focus of the coverage, but family policies can be more complex. Generally, a family consists of a parent or parents and dependent children. Are children who are born while the plan is in effect automatically covered from the moment of birth? What about stepchildren? At what age are children no longer covered? These questions must be answered to ensure that all family members receive adequate protection.

When Does Coverage Begin and End?

Individual and group health care plans are usually written on an annual basis. An annual plan beginning on January 1 will start at 12:00 A.M. that day and end at 11:59 P.M. on December 31. Any illness that begins during the year will be covered. But will coverage continue if the plan expires while you are in the hospital? The answer is usually yes. Similarly, a surgical procedure performed after a plan expires but for an illness or injury for which treatment was originally begun during the plan period may be covered.

Health care plans must be renewed each year. If you are in a group plan, you can renew your participation during the plan's open-enrollment period. Renewal of individual plans is handled in one of three ways. **Optionally renewable policies** may be canceled or changed by the plan provider but only at the time of expiration and renewal, often with 30 days' notice. **Guaranteed renewable policies** must be continued in force as long as the policyholder pays the required premium. Premiums may change but only if the change applies to an entire class of participants rather than to an individual participant. Guaranteed renewability is recommended for health care plans and

How to Avoid Duplication of Employee Health Care Benefits

Dual-income households often have overlapping health care benefits. For example, both Harry and Belinda Johnson's employers provide partially subsidized family health insurance plans as employee benefits. The Johnsons chose to be covered under Belinda's policy because it provides more protection and is less expensive. Belinda's coverage is fully paid for and she can add Harry to the plan for $125 per month.

Harry's employer offers a flexible approach toward providing employee benefits. Employees are provided with $800 per month to be used for any of the employee benefits available from a menu of benefits offered by the employer. If Harry chose his employer's health care plan, he would need to pay $375 of the $800 for this benefit. He could use the remaining $425 for life insurance, dental insurance, disability income

insurance, or an additional contribution into his 401(k) plan. Harry has decided to forgo his health insurance and will pay the extra $125 to be covered under Belinda's plan. As a result, he has $675 ($800 − $125) available for other options. Harry decided to sign up for disability and dental expense insurance and have the remainder go into his 401(k) plan.

With a group all employees are usually covered, but new members may have to endure a waiting period before receiving protection. If the group includes the employees of a business, different protection may be offered for full-time and part-time employees. The family of the group member may be covered, but, once again, the definition of "family" must be understood.

long-term care insurance. **Noncancelable policies** must be continued in force without premium changes up to age 65 as long as the participant pays the required premium. Noncancelable policies are recommended when buying disability income insurance.

How Much Must You Pay Out of Your Own Pocket?

Health care plans contain provisions that specify the level of payments for covered expenses.

Deductibles   **Deductibles** are clauses in health care plans that require you to pay an initial portion of medical expenses annually before receiving reimbursement. A deductible of $200 per year, for example, would mean that the patient must pay the first $200 of the medical costs for the year. Family plans generally include a deductible for each family member (again, perhaps $200 per year) with a maximum family deductible (perhaps $500 per year). Once the deductible payments for individual family members reach the maximum family deductible ($500 in this example), further individual deductibles will be waived.

Copayments   A **copayment,** which is a variation of a deductible, requires you to pay a specific dollar amount each time you have a specific covered expense item. A copayment is often required for visits to the doctor's office and prescription drugs. For example, you might have to pay $25 for each prescription, with the insurer paying the remainder. A copayment differs from a deductible in that it might require that you pay $35 for each office visit even after the deductible is met.

Coinsurance   A **coinsurance clause** requires you to pay a proportion of any loss suffered. The typical share is 80/20, with the insurer paying the larger percentage. Usually, a coinsurance cap limits the annual out-of-pocket payments required of the patient when meeting the coinsurance. The following example illustrates how a deductible of $250 and an 80/20 coinsurance provision with a $1000 coinsurance cap work together to determine the coverage for an $8760 health care bill. Because the deductible is the responsibility of the insured party, the patient pays the first $250. The coinsurance ratio is applied to the remaining $8510 ($8760 − $250) until the portion paid by the patient reaches the coinsurance cap. Thus, $1000 is covered by the insured and $4000 by the insurer. The additional expenses of $3510 ($8510 − $1000 − $4000) are covered 100 percent by the insurance company up to the overall limits of coverage (perhaps $100,000). In this example, the insured party will pay $1250 ($250 deductible + $1000 coinsurance) and the insurer will pay $7510 ($4000 coinsurance + $3510 remaining charges).

Policy Limits   Policy limits specify the maximum dollar amounts that a health insurance plan will pay to reimburse a covered loss. To illustrate policy limits for a health insurance plan, we will consider the case of Karl Gruenfeld, an unmarried electrician from Council Bluffs, Iowa.

■ **Item limits** specify the maximum reimbursement for a particular health care expense. Karl's policy contains a $75 maximum per X ray. Karl suffered a heart attack and had X-ray expenses of $840 (seven sets of X rays at $120 each). The policy will pay

deductibles
Clauses in health care plans that require you to pay an additional portion of health expenses annually before receiving reimbursement.

Instant Message

Health Care Plans Have a Grace Period

Health plans contain provisions for a grace period (typically 30 days), which prevents the lapse of a policy if a payment is late. The policy remains fully in force during the grace period but only if the insured pays the premium before the end of the grace period.

copayment
A variation of a deductible requires you to pay a specific dollar amount each time you use your benefits for a specific covered expense item.

coinsurance clause
Requires insured to pay a proportion of any loss suffered.

item limits
Specify the maximum reimbursement for a particular health care expense.

Did You Know?

Practicing a Healthy Lifestyle Can Save You Money

Health care plans have always charged more (or even denied coverage) for people with preexisting health conditions. Nowadays, healthy care plans are also giving discounts to people who maintain a healthy lifestyle.

   Most common are discounts for non-smokers and those who quit. Discounts are also offered those who drink alcohol in moderation, exercise regularly and meet good health-risk assessment targets for weight, blood pressure and cholesterol levels. Maintaining good health also pays off financially due to reduced chronic disease in later years resulting in a longer and more productive career and a healthier retirement.

Instant Message

HMOs Do Not Have Dollar Limits

HMO plans generally do not have maximum policy limits specified in dollars. Instead, they limit the health care services they will provide for a specified diagnosis.

Instant Message

Know Your Limits

Aggregate dollar limits are always higher than time period limits, which are in turn higher than episode limits. A policy with high aggregate limits may seem attractive, but it may not be a good buy if the episode limits are too low. Analyze each limit separately to determine whether it provides sufficient protection.

$525 (7 × $75) of this expense, and Karl must pay the remaining $315.

■ **Episode limits** specify the maximum payment for health care expenses arising from a single episode of illness or injury, with each episode being considered separately. Karl's policy contains an episode limit of $75,000 for all covered expenses. After his heart attack, Karl was hospitalized for two weeks and incurred $78,000 in medical charges (including the covered portion of the X rays). His policy will pay $75,000 of these charges. One month later, Karl suffered burns in a cooking accident at his home and was hospitalized for two days, incurring hospital care costs of $4310. His policy will pay these expenses in full because the second hospitalization is considered a separate episode rather than a continuation of the first which would have put him over the $75,000 limit.

Disputes may arise over whether a recurrence of an illness represents a separate episode. A **recurring clause** clarifies conditions under which a recurrence of an illness is considered a continuation of the first episode or a separate episode. If the recurrence is considered a separate episode, the deductible may need to be paid, but reimbursement will be available up to the full episode limit. If the recurrence is considered a continuation of the original episode, the second deductible will not apply, but the loss may exceed the episode limit.

■ **Annual limits** specify the maximum payment for covered expenses occurring within one year. Consider Karl's heart attack and burn hospitalizations. If his policy had contained a $100,000 annual limit, Karl would have used $82,310 ($78,000 + $4310) of this amount and would have only $17,690 ($100,000 − $82,310) remaining for the year.

■ A **lifetime** or **aggregate limit** places an overall maximum on the total amount of reimbursement available under a policy. If Karl's policy has an aggregate limit of $500,000, no more than $500,000 will be reimbursed for all medical expenses that Karl incurs during the life of the policy.

lifetime/aggregate limit
Places an overall maximum on the total amount of reimbursement available under a policy.

coordination-of-benefits clause
Prevents an individual from collecting insurance benefits that exceed the loss suffered by noting the order in which plans will pay if the insured individual is covered by multiple plans.

premium conversion plans
With premium conversion, the employee's share of the premiums is paid with pretax dollars; those amounts are not included when the employer reports the employee's income to the IRS.

Coordination of Benefits

A **coordination-of-benefits clause** prevents you from collecting insurance benefits that exceed the loss suffered. Such a clause designates the order in which plans will pay benefits if multiple plans apply to a loss. The primary plan is the first applied to any loss when more than one plan provides coverage. If it fails to reimburse 100 percent of the loss, then any secondary (or excess) plans will be applied in order until the loss is fully paid or until benefits are exhausted, whichever occurs first.

 Concept Check 11.3

1. What are preexisting conditions and how do they affect coverage under health plans?
2. Distinguish among a deductible, a copayment, and coinsurance.
3. Explain COBRA rights and portability rights that apply when you leave a job that has a group health care plan.
4. Distinguish among item limits, episode limits, time period limits, and aggregate limits as used in health care plans.
5. Distinguish among optionally renewable, guaranteed renewable, and noncancelable health care plans.
6. List three ways you can save on taxes when paying for health care or insurance.

Did You Know?

The Tax Consequences of Managing Health Expenses

The Internal Revenue Code allows several avenues for reducing income taxes when you spend your own money on health care plan premiums and health care expenses:

1. Many employees may save on taxes when they use **premium conversion plans** to pay their health care insurance premiums (discussed in Chapter 1). With premium conversion, the employee's share of the premiums is paid with pretax dollars; those amounts are not included when the employer reports the employee's taxable income to the IRS.

2. Many employers offer **flexible spending arrangements,** allowing employees to place a portion of their salary into an account that is used to pay some of their

health care expenditures, including employee-paid health plan premiums (discussed in Chapter 1). Flexible spending accounts are a "use it or lose it" proposition. Thus, you should set aside only an amount that you are sure you will use.

Health care expenditures (including a portion of certain long-term care insurance premiums) can be used as itemized deductions on one's income tax return. Only the amount that exceeds 7.5 percent of the adjusted gross income is deductible. Self-employed people may deduct (as a business expense, not an itemized deduction) the cost of health care plan premiums for themselves and their dependents.

Advice from a Pro...

Maintain Your Health Care Plan Between Jobs

What happens when you no longer work for an employer that offers a group health care plan and you want to continue the coverage? You can assert your **COBRA rights** (Consolidated Omnibus Budget Reconciliation Act of 1985). These rules allow you to remain a member of a group health plan for as long as 18 months if you worked for an employer with more than 20 workers. COBRA applies to you and to any of your dependents who had been covered under the employer's plan. COBRA rights apply to your dependents for 36 months. These rights must be exercised within 60 days after the termination of employment, and you must pay the full premiums

(including both the employee's and the employer's portions) plus a 2 percent administrative fee.

Eligibility to remain under the group plan eventually will run out. Federal law also mandates **guaranteed portability** that allows you to convert your group coverage to individual coverage within 180 days before COBRA ends, if that is part of the employer's plan originally or as amended. Your individual policy premiums will be higher but the waiting period and preexisting condition provisions will not apply.

William Dean
Southern University

Protecting Your Income During Disability

A number of resources are available for income protection during a period of disability. Many U.S. workers have sick-pay benefits that can help ease the burden of a short period of disability, such as four weeks. Disability income insurance is probably the most overlooked type of insurance though it is vitally important for all workers. For example, a 22-year-old without dependents would probably need no life insurance but would likely need disability

4 Learning Objective

Develop a plan for protecting your income when you cannot work due to disability.

flexible spending arrangements
Employer arrangements that allow employees to place a portion of their salary into an account that is used to pay some of their health care expenditures, including employee-paid health plan premiums.

COBRA rights
The Consolidated Omnibus Budget Reconciliation Act of 1985 that allows a former employee to remain a member of a group health plan for as long as 18 months if the employee worked for an employer with more than 20 workers.

guaranteed portability
Provision that allows an individual to convert group coverage to individual coverage within 180 days before COBRA ends.

insurance for support during a period of disability. While employer-based retirement plans provide benefits to workers who become disabled while still employed, such benefits plans fall far short of fully meeting the needs of workers who have accumulated little or no retirement savings.

Level of Need

The first question to ask when contemplating disability income insurance is, "How much protection do I need?" The dollar limits on disability income policies are written either in increments of $100 per month or as a percentage of monthly income. Policy coverage is limited to 60 to 80 percent of the insured's after-tax earnings. Note that the government's Social Security disability income program may provide more than $20,000 annually in tax-free income to the family of a fully insured disabled worker. See Appendix B at the end of the book or the *Garman/Forgue* companion website for an illustration of how to estimate these benefits, or visit www.ssa.gov/top10.html.

Determining the amount of additional protection needed is challenging because some sources of help may not actually be available for all disabilities. It is smart to complete the calculations in the Run the Numbers feature, "Determining Disability Income Insurance Needs." You can use the figure obtained in the worksheet as a starting point when shopping for disability income insurance protection.

A young person with no dependents might have a greater need for disability insurance than life insurance.

Important Disability Income Insurance Policy Provisions

Once you have estimated your level of need, you can begin your search for a disability income insurance policy. Look first for the major policy provisions, discussed in the following paragraphs, that meet your needs. Disability income insurance policies are complicated so avoid relying on the verbal assurances of the agent selling the policy and do your own analysis and seek the advice of a financial planner.

Waiting Period The **waiting period (elimination period)** in a disability income policy is the time period between the onset of the disability and the date that disability benefits begin. Because disability income benefits are paid monthly, the first check will not arrive until 30 days after the end of the waiting period.

Benefit Period The **benefit period** in a disability income policy is the maximum period of time for which benefits will be paid. It begins when the elimination period ends. The benefit period is usually stated in years but may instead state a specific age when benefits will cease. Most disability income policies will not pay past age 65.

Degree of Disability Policies can be written on an "own-occupation" or "any-occupation" basis. An **own-occupation policy** will provide benefits if you can no longer perform the occupation you had at the time you became disabled. An **any-occupation policy** will provide full benefits only if you cannot perform any occupation. In effect, an

Instant Message

Disability Income or Life Insurance?

At age 22, a person's chances of becoming disabled for at least three months are seven times greater than his or her chances of dying. Disability income insurance is more important for young, single adults than life insurance.

waiting period
Long-term care policies can pay benefits from the first day of nursing home care or they can include a waiting period. Premiums drop with longer waiting periods.

benefit period
Length of time that the individual for whom a policy is written would likely need the care.

any-occupation policy
Provides full benefits only if you cannot perform any occupation.

Run the Numbers

Determining Disability Income Insurance Needs

The determination of disability insurance needs begins with your current monthly after-tax income.

From this figure, subtract the amounts you would receive from Social Security disability and other sources of disability income. The resulting figure will provide an estimate of extra coverage needed.

Decision Factor	Example	Your Figures
1. Current monthly after-tax income	$2,100	_____
2. Minus previous established disability income protections	+ $ 907	_____
(a) Monthly Social Security disability benefits	_____	_____
(b) Monthly benefit from employer-provided disability insurance	600	_____
(c) Monthly benefit from private disability insurance	_____	_____
(d) Monthly benefit from other government disability insurance	_____	_____
Total Subtraction	−1,350	_____
3. Estimated monthly disability income insurance needs	$ 750	_____

Did You Know?

Workers' Comp Pays If You Are Hurt on the Job

If you are injured on the job or become ill as a direct result of your employment, state law requires your employer to pay any resulting medical costs. **Workers' compensation insurance** covers employers for liability losses for injury or disease suffered by employees that result from employment-related causes. The benefits to the employee include health care, recuperative care, replacement of lost income, and, if necessary, rehabilitation. Thus, workers' compensation insurance covers the full range of health-related losses. Because only those losses resulting from work-related accidents are covered and benefits are limited, workers' compensation can only supplement your total health insurance plan.

residual clause
Feature of own-occupation policies that allows for some reduced level of disability income benefits when a partial—rather than full—disability strikes.

Social Security rider
Provides an extra dollar amount of protection if a person fails to qualify for Social Security disability benefits (70 percent of all applicants are rejected).

any-occupation policy is an income replacement policy, as it makes up a portion of the difference between what you were earning prior to becoming disabled and what you can earn while disabled. Own-occupation policies are more generous and, therefore, cost more. Some policies provide own-occupation coverage during the first two years of a disability, and then switch to an any-occupation basis with income replacement for the remaining years of the benefits. Such **split-definition policies** are likely to provide benefits for rehabilitation and retraining at insurance company expense.

A **residual clause** is a feature of own-occupation policies that allows for some reduced level of disability income benefits when a partial—rather than full—disability occurs. Consider the case of Françoise LaDeux, a criminal lawyer in Providence, Rhode Island, who purchased a disability policy offering a benefit of $3000 per month. Françoise later developed multiple sclerosis and was forced to cut back her workload by 50 percent, thereby taking a 50 percent pay cut. Her disability policy had a residual clause, so she received $1500 (0.50 × $3000) per month during her disability.

Social Security Rider   If you have figured your disability income insurance needs assuming that you would receive Social Security benefits, you will find yourself with inadequate protection if your Social Security application is denied (70 percent of all applicants are rejected). To provide an extra dollar amount of protection if you fail to qualify for Social Security disability benefits, a **Social Security rider** may be added to your policy. Consider the case of Karen Gifford, a florist from Urbana, Illinois. Karen determined that her disability insurance needs would be $1400 per month after assuming that she would receive $1000 from Social Security if she were to become disabled. She could have purchased a $2400-per-month policy and removed all uncertainty, but the premium would have been more than she could afford. Instead, she bought a $1400 policy with a $1000 Social Security rider for a premium savings of 30 percent.

Cost-of-Living Adjustments   You are wise to seek out a policy with a **cost-of-living clause**, which will increase your benefit amount to keep up with inflation. You might also consider buying a policy that limits benefits to a percentage of income rather than a specific dollar amount per month. With such a policy, your potential monthly benefit would increase automatically as your income increases.

✔ Concept Check 11.4

1. Explain how you determine your level of need for disability income insurance.
2. Identify the major policy provisions to consider when purchasing disability income insurance.
3. Distinguish between any-occupation and own-occupation disability income insurance plans.
4. Describe how you might adjust the waiting period on a disability income insurance policy in order to affordably obtain a longer benefit period.

Did You Know?

How to Afford an Expensive Health-Related Risk

Recall from Chapter 10 that it is smart to insure against the losses you cannot afford and handle more affordable losses on your own. This large-loss principle should be your guide for health-related risks as well. Here is how to apply it:

1. If you do not have access to a health care plan at work and have limited resources to buy a health care plan on your own, you can use a high-deductible health care plan in conjunction with a health savings account (HSA) (see page 323). This will affordably protect you against catastrophic direct medical costs.

2. Select a long benefit period for both your disability income and long-term care insurance needs. For an

equivalent dollar amount, you can buy many more years of protection by extending the waiting period only slightly as illustrated graphically here.

For $X you might buy a plan with a short waiting period (WP) and a short benefit period (BP):

WP	BP	Coverage Has Run Out

Even better, for the same $X you might buy a plan with a slightly longer waiting period (WP) and a much longer benefit period (BP):

WP	BP	Coverage Has Run Out

Planning for Long-Term Care

Many health care episodes include a period of time when the patient no longer needs skilled medical care but does need assistance to a degree that requires confinement in a nursing home or special help at home. This need is especially prevalent with the extremely elderly and patients with certain conditions such as Alzheimer's disease. Such costs are not covered by HMOs, health insurance, or Medicare because the care is usually considered "not medically necessary" by these providers.

Factors to assess when considering a long-term care policy include the following:

1. **The degree of impairment required for benefits to begin.** Insurance companies use the inability to perform a certain number of **activities of daily living (ADLs)** as a criterion for deciding when the insured becomes eligible for long-term care benefits. Typically, a policy pays benefits when a person cannot perform two or three ADLs without assistance. The ADLs commonly used in this type of decision making are bathing, bladder control, dressing oneself, eating without assistance, toileting (moving on and off the toilet), and transferring (getting in and out of bed). Because bathing is often one of the first ADLs that is lost, a policy that does not list bathing as a criterion makes it more difficult to reach the threshold at which benefits become available.

2. **The level of care covered.** The levels of nursing home care are usually categorized three ways. **Skilled nursing care** is intended for people who need intensive care, meaning 24-hour-a-day supervision and treatment by a registered nurse, under the direction of a doctor. **Intermediate care** is appropriate for people who do not require around-the-clock nursing but who are not able to live alone. **Custodial care** is suitable for many people who do not need skilled nursing care but who nevertheless require supervision (for example, help with eating or personal hygiene). Insurance companies' definitions of these levels of care may differ and must be considered when

5 Learning Objective

Explain how to protect yourself from the expenses for long-term care.

activities of daily living (ADLs)
Insurance companies use the inability to perform a certain number of such activities as a criterion for deciding when the insured becomes eligible for long-term care benefits.

skilled nursing care
Intended for people who need intensive care, that is, 24-hour-a-day supervision and treatment by a registered nurse under the direction of a doctor.

Do It NOW!

Maintaining coverage in a health care plan is essential to protect your future financial success. Start today by:

1. Learning exactly what group health care coverage you actually do have through your job, your school, and/or your parents.

2. Investigating the possibility of saving on income taxes via a premium conversion plan, flexible spending arrangement, or health savings account (HSA).

3. Identifying one behavior that you engage in that could lead to health problems later in life and taking steps to reduce their impact.

benefit amount
Long-term care plans are generally written to provide a specific dollar benefit per day of care.

policies are evaluated. Although the largest expenses related to long-term care result from a stay in a nursing home, many people are able to remain in their homes with the assistance of visiting nurses, therapists, and even housekeepers. Long-term care policies can be written to cover such in-home care.

3. **The person's age.** The younger the person when the policy is purchased, the lower the premium as the odds of needing care increase with age. The trade-off lies between buying young and paying premiums for many years versus waiting to purchase a policy, at which time it may be difficult to afford coverage because of preexisting conditions and consequently high policy costs.

4. **The benefit amount.** Long-term care plans are generally written to provide a specific dollar benefit per day of care. If the cost per day for nursing homes in your geographic area is typically $140, you might buy a policy for $110 per day, thereby coinsuring for a portion of the expenses.

5. **The benefit period.** Although it is possible to buy a policy with lifetime benefits, this option can be very expensive. The average nursing home stay is about two and one-half years. A policy with a three-year limit might cost one-third less than a policy with a lifetime benefit period.

6. **The waiting period.** Policies can pay benefits from the first day of nursing home care or they can include a waiting period. Selecting a 30-day or 90-day waiting period can significantly reduce premiums.

7. **Inflation protection.** If a policy is purchased prior to age 60, the buyer faces a significant risk in that inflation may render the daily benefit woefully inadequate when care is ultimately needed. Some policies increase the daily benefit by 4 or 5 percent per year to adjust for inflation, but this protection adds considerably to the premium. The younger your age when a policy is purchased, the more you need inflation protection.

 Concept Check 11.5

1. Describe the protections provided by long-term care insurance.

2. Distinguish between the benefit period and the waiting period for a long-term care policy.

3. List three aspects of long-term care insurance that affect the cost of a policy.

What Do You Recommend NOW?

Now that you have read the chapter on health care planning, what do you recommend to Danielle DiMartino in the case at the beginning of the chapter regarding:

1. Choosing among the four alternatives available to her?

2. Danielle's concerns about providing for her mother's health care needs?

3. Danielle's need for her own disability income insurance?

4. How Danielle can cover her long-term care risk?

Jupiterimages

Big Picture Summary of Learning Objectives

1 Identify ways that people can manage the financial burdens resulting from illness or injury.

Health-related losses include the cost of direct health care, the cost of rehabilitation and custodial care, and the lost income when one is ill or injured. Protection from the costs of direct health care is provided by a health care plan. Long-term care insurance can protect you from rehabilitation and custodial care costs. Disability income insurance can replace income lost while disabled.

2 Distinguish among the types of protection for direct health expenses.

HMOs, traditional health insurance, and consumer-driven health plans address the need for direct health care. HMOs provide health care on a prepaid basis. Health insurance will reimburse you or pay your medical bills directly. Consumer-driven health care plans require that consumers pay a higher portion of the costs out of pocket. Health savings accounts provide a tax-sheltered way to save up the funds to pay these costs. Health reimbursement accounts allow an employer to help pay these costs for an employee.

3 Describe the general benefits and limitations of health care plans.

Health care policies contain language that outlines coverage in general and, more important, describes the limitations and conditions that determine the level of protection afforded under the plan. Some of the more important plan provisions include what types of care are covered, who is covered under the plan, and the time period for the coverage. Important limitations on coverage include deductibles and copayments, coinsurance requirements, and policy limits.

4 Develop a plan for protecting your income when you cannot work due to disability.

Disability income insurance replaces a portion of the income lost when you cannot work as a result of illness or injury. The amount you need is equal to your monthly after-tax income less any benefits to which you are entitled (for example, Social Security). By selecting among various policy provisions, you can tailor a policy that fills any gaps in your existing disability protection.

5 Explain how to protect yourself from the expenses for long-term care.

Long-term care insurance provides a per-day dollar reimbursement when the insured person must stay in a nursing home or other long-term care facility. It is not designed to provide health care protection, as that coverage is available through other plans such as an HMO, private insurance, or Medicare/Medicaid. Medicaid does provide long-term care benefits, but Medicare does not.

Let's Talk About It

1. **Your Health Care Plan.** Are you covered by a health care plan? If so, what do you see as the largest potential for losses if you become ill or injured? How well do you understand the plan?

2. **HMOs Versus Health Insurance.** HMO plans and health insurance plans take different approaches to health care. What are the major differences between the two types of plans? Which plan would you prefer for your own health care protection?

3. **Long–Term Care Insurance.** Are you covered by a long-term care insurance plan? What would happen if you became so incapacitated that such care was necessary? What could you do?

4. **Disability Income Insurance.** Are you covered by disability income insurance? What would happen if you were unable to work for two or three years because of illness or injury?

Do the Math

1. **Health Care Coverage Amounts.** Christina Haley of Clyde, North Carolina, age 61, recently suffered a severe stroke. She was in intensive care for 12 days and was hospitalized for 18 more days. After being discharged from the hospital, she spent 45 days in a nursing home for medically necessary nursing and rehabilitative care. Christina had a comprehensive health insurance plan through her employer. The policy had a $1000 deductible, a $50,000 episode limit, and a $250,000 aggregate limit with an 80/20 coinsurance clause with a $2000 coinsurance cap. Christina's policy covered the medically necessary services performed in a nursing home setting. Her total bill was $125,765.

   (a) How much of Christina's expenses were paid by her insurance policy?

   (b) How much did Christina pay?

2. **Health Care Coverage Amounts.** Michael Howitt of Berkley, Michigan, recently had his gallbladder removed. His total bill for this event, which was his only health care expense for the year, came to $13,890. His health insurance plan has a $500 annual deductible and an 80/20 coinsurance provision. The cap on Michael's coinsurance share is $2000.

   (a) How much of the bill will Michael pay?

   (b) How much of the bill will be paid by Michael's insurance?

Financial Planning Cases

Case 1
A New Employee Ponders Disability Insurance

Jim Napier of Indiana, Pennsylvania, recently took a new job as a manufacturer's representative for an aluminum castings company. While looking over his employee benefits materials, he discovered that his employer would provide 10 sick days per year, and he can accumulate these to a maximum of 60 sick days if any go unused in a given year. In addition, his employer provides a $1000-per-month, short-term, one-year total disability policy. When he called the employee benefits office, Jim found that he might qualify for $500 per month in Social Security disability benefits if he became unable to work. Jim earns a base salary of $2000 per month and expects to earn about that same amount in commissions, for an average after-tax income of $3100 per month. After considering this information, Jim became understandably concerned that a disability might destroy his financial future.

(a) What is the level of Jim's short-term, one-year disability insurance needs?

(b) What is the level of Jim's long-term disability insurance needs?

(c) Help Jim select from among the important disability insurance policy provisions to design a disability insurance program tailored to his needs.

Case 2
A CPA Selects a Health Care Plan

Your friend Taliesha Jackson of Stillwater, Oklahoma, recently changed to a new job as a CPA in a moderate-size accounting firm. Knowing that you were taking a personal finance course, she asked your advice about selecting the best health insurance plan. Her employer offered five options. In addition, she could open a flexible spending arrangement and pay any premiums she must pay through a premium conversion plan:

- **Option A:** A comprehensive health insurance plan with a $500 annual deductible and an 80 percent/20 percent coinsurance clause with a $2000 out-of-pocket limit. The policy has a $500,000 lifetime limit. Taliesha must pay $60 per month toward this plan.

- **Option B:** Same as option A except that a PPO is associated with the plan. If Taliesha agrees to have services provided by the PPO, her annual deductible drops to $100 and the coinsurance clause is waived. As an incentive to get employees to select option B, Taliesha's employer will provide dental expense insurance worth about $40 per month.

- **Option C:** A comprehensive health insurance plan with a $200 annual deductible and a 90 percent/10 percent coinsurance clause with a $1000 out-of-pocket limit. This has a $1 million lifetime limit. Taliesha must pay $150 per month toward the cost of this plan.

- **Option D:** Membership in an HMO. Taliesha will have to contribute $40 extra each month if she chooses this option.

- **Option E:** A high-deductible health plan at no monthly cost to Taliesha. The annual deductible is $3000. There is a 90 percent/10 percent coinsurance provision. The annual out-of-pocket maximum is $5000. Her employer offers a $1000 health reimbursement account, and if she chooses, Taliesha can set up an HSA to help her pay her expenses during the year.

(a) To help her make a decision, Taliesha has asked you to list two positive points and two negative points about each plan. Prepare such a list.

(b) Why might Taliesha's employer provide an incentive of dental insurance if she chooses option B?

(c) Which plan would you recommend to Taliesha? Why?

Case 3
The Hernandezes Face the Possibility of Long-Term Care

Victor Hernandez recently learned that his uncle has Alzheimer's disease. While discussing this tragedy with Maria, he realized that two of his grandparents probably had the disease, although no formal diagnosis was ever made. As a result, Victor and Maria have become interested in how they might protect themselves from the financial effects of long-term health care.

(a) What factors should the Hernandezes consider as they shop for long-term care protection?

(b) Victor is still in his 40s. How does his age affect their decisions related to long-term care protection?

Case 4
The Johnsons Consider Buying Disability Insurance

Although Belinda's employer offers a generous employee benefit program, it does not provide disability income protection other than 8 sick days per year, which may accumulate to 20 days if Belinda does not use them. Harry also has no disability income insurance. Although both have worked long enough to qualify for Social Security disability benefits, Belinda has estimated that Harry would receive about $640 and she would receive about $800 per month from Social Security. Harry and Belinda realize that they could not maintain their current living standards on only one salary. Thus, the need for disability income insurance has become evident even though they probably cannot afford such protection at this time. In fact, they chose not to purchase the disability waiver of premium option when they purchased their life insurance. Advise them on the following points:

(a) Use the Run the Numbers Worksheet on page 331 to determine how much disability insurance Harry and Belinda each need. Use the December salary figures from Table 3.8 on page 90. To determine the amount of taxes and Social Security paid by each, assume that Harry, whose salary represents approximately 42 percent of their total income, paid a comparable percentage of the taxes.

(b) Use the information on pages 331–332 to advise the Johnsons about their selections related to the following major policy provisions:

1. Elimination period
2. Benefit period
3. Residual clause
4. Social Security rider
5. Cost-of-living adjustments

On the 'Net

Go to the Web pages indicated to complete these exercises. You can also go to the *Garman/Forgue* companion website at www .cengage.com/finance/garman for an expanded list of exercises. Under General Business, select the title of this text. Click on the Internet Exercises link for this chapter.

1. Visit the website for the National Committee for Quality Assurance at www.ncqa.org, where you will find "report cards" on quality and accreditation status of health plans. If you are covered by a health plan, search for information on your plan. If you are not covered or if data are not available on your plan, select a major city and obtain the report on a plan in that city. What information, criteria, and other data in the report might assist you in assessing the quality of any plan?

2. Visit the website for the Social Security Administration and use its online calculator at http://www.ssa.gov/ retire2/AnypiaApplet.html to determine whether you are currently eligible to receive Social Security disability insurance benefits if you become disabled and the projected level of those benefits.

3. Visit the website for Yahoo! Finance at http:// finance.yahoo.com/how-to-guide/insurance/18447 and read its discussion of understanding long-term care insurance. How might such protection fit into your risk-management program or that of your family?

Visit the Garman/Forgue companion website . . .

www.cengage.com/finance/garman

Life Insurance Planning

!You Must Be Kidding, Right?

Michelle and Jason Bailey are in their early 30s and expecting their first child next month. Each earns about $40,000 per year. Currently, they have $20,000 life insurance policies on each of their lives with the other named as the beneficiary. They bought these policies a few years ago to pay for death-related expenses if tragedy struck. They are thinking about adding another $300,000 each to their protection to replace the income lost if one of them passed away. How much will Michelle and Jason each pay for this additional protection?

A. About $25 per month

B. About $50 per month

C. About $100 per month

D. About $200 per month

The answer is A. Term life insurance for people in their 30s costs about $1 per $1000 of coverage per year. Thus, Michelle and Jason could each buy this insurance for $300 each or about $25 per month. If they chose instead to buy cash-value life insurance, they would likely pay $200 or more each per month. Always buy inexpensive term life insurance so that you replace the lost income needed by your dependents if you were to pass away!

Learning Objectives

After reading this chapter, you should be able to:

1 Understand the reasons why you might need life insurance and calculate the appropriate amount of coverage.

2 Distinguish among types of life insurance.

3 Explain the major provisions of life insurance policies.

4 Apply a step-by-step strategy for implementing a life insurance plan.

What Do You Recommend?

Junial/Dreamstime LLC

Karen Bridgeman, age 28, and her husband Will, age 30, are planning to start a family in the next year. Both have small cash-value life insurance policies ($25,000 and $50,000, respectively) that their parents purchased when they were children. Karen is a real estate attorney and earns $90,000 per year. She plans to continue working after having a child. Karen's employer offers a 401(k) plan into which she contributes a maximum of 6 percent of her salary each year matched by her employer one-half of 1 percent for each 1 percent that Karen contributes. Her employer does not offer employer-paid life insurance. Will is a high-school teacher and track coach and makes $49,000 per year. His employer pays the full cost of his retirement pension plan. An optional supplemental retirement plan is available into which Will can contribute 5 percent of his salary, but he has not done so as yet. Will has an employer-provided life insurance policy equal to twice his annual salary. Will and Karen have no other life insurance on their lives.

What do you recommend to Karen and Will on the subject of life insurance planning regarding:

1. Their changing need for life insurance once they have a child?

2. What types of life insurance they should consider and whether they should purchase multiple policies?

3. Coordinating their retirement savings and other investments with their life insurance program?

4. Shopping for life insurance?

In the next five years you can start achieving financial success by doing the following related to life insurance planning:

1. Calculate your life insurance needs every three years or when major life events occur, such as the birth of a child.

2. Comparison shop for term life insurance on the Internet to obtain the lowest possible rates.

3. Employ the principle of "buy term life insurance and invest the rest" with guaranteed renewable term life insurance.

4. Fund your tax-sheltered retirement plan with the money saved by purchasing term rather than cash-value insurance.

5. Protect against failing health by selecting guaranteed renewable term policies and cash-value policies that have a guaranteed insurability option.

life insurance
An insurance contract that promises to pay a dollar benefit to a beneficiary upon the death of the insured person.

1 Learning Objective
Understand the reasons why you might need life insurance and calculate the appropriate amount of coverage.

final expenses
One-time expenses occurring just prior to or after a death.

Instant Message

Buying Life Insurance Versus Investing

Most college students will live into their 80s, although about 20 percent will die before retirement. Use life insurance to protect against an early death and make investments to prepare for a long life.

George Burns once observed "if you live to be one hundred, you've got it made. Very few people die past that age." But for most of us death will come earlier even if we do not know when. With the uncertainty of when death will occur comes financial risk. Two financial problems arise because you cannot know how long you will live. The first problem is the *risk of living too long*. This is the possibility that you will outlive your savings during retirement. Life insurance is *not* the best way to address the living-too-long problem. Instead, you should invest through tax-sheltered retirement savings plans (discussed in Chapter 17). The second is the *risk of dying too soon*. This is the possibility that you might die before adequately providing for the financial well-being of loved ones, especially your spouse and children. **Life insurance** protects your loved ones against the possibility that you may die too soon. As you will see, term life insurance does this best.

Most Americans buy insufficient life insurance coverage. The need for life insurance is greatest in the child-rearing years because the income of one or more adults is needed to support a child financially. As children grow up, they need fewer years of financial support and the necessity of life insurance on the income earner levels off and then declines. Eventually, growth in assets, primarily through a retirement plan, replaces the need for life insurance. Americans also tend to buy the wrong type of life insurance—cash-value—when term insurance costs 85 to 90 percent less. A smart financial strategy is to use the money saved by buying term insurance to invest in a tax-sheltered retirement plan. This approach is referred to as "buy term and invest the rest."

How Much Additional Life Insurance Do You Need?

The primary reason for buying life insurance is to allow your family members to continue with their lives free from the financial burdens that your death would bring. Income can be made available for spouse and children. Insurance proceeds can safeguard home ownership. Future college or other educational plans can remain intact. The bottom line? Your purchase of life insurance is to benefit your loved ones, not yourself.

What Needs Must Be Met?

Financial losses that arise from dying too soon include expenditures for final expenses; the lost income of the deceased; and funds for a readjustment period, debt repayment, and possibly education expenses for a surviving spouse and children.

Final-Expense Needs **Final expenses** are one-time expenses occurring just prior to or after a death. The largest of these expenses is for the funeral and burial of the deceased, which could cost more than $10,000. Travel expenses for family members to provide emotional support and to attend a funeral can be quite high as can food and lodging expenses for mourners. Severe and costly disruptions of family life can last for months. Finally, there are costs associated with settling the estate of the deceased. These can also be paid for with life insurance proceeds. These expenses are one area of financial loss that is common to people of all ages.

Income-Replacement Needs Once someone else becomes financially dependent on you, your lost income will be the major financial loss resulting from your premature death. Included in this lost income is the value of any essential employee benefits, such as health care plan for your dependents. Dual-earner families who depend on both incomes to maintain the desired level of living should plan on protecting both sources of income.

Readjustment-Period Needs Families often need a period of readjustment after the death of a loved one. This period may last for several months to two or three years and may have financial consequences that require substantial life insurance proceeds. For example, the death of a parent with young children may require the surviving spouse to forgo employment for a while. Similarly, a surviving employed spouse may need to take time off from a job to obtain further education.

Debt-Repayment Needs Some people want to buy enough additional life insurance to pay off all installment loans, credit cards, and the outstanding balance on the home mortgage. This is understandable but a family that has provided adequately for the replacement of lost income probably will not need to make specific insurance provisions for the repayment of most debts. It is sometimes helpful however, to buy enough additional life insurance to pay off all debts other than the mortgage in order to simplify the finances of the survivors. Then, the life insurance purchased to replace lost income will also cover the mortgage payments just as they were before death.

College-Expense Needs Many families with small children already have a college savings plan in place. Adequate replacement of lost income should allow for continuation of the plan. But most families also use current income to handle expenses when the children are in college and the death of a family income provider may, therefore, impede the ability to meet this need. The solution: Earmark a dollar amount of life insurance proceeds for future college expenses. A suggested amount would be the current cost of tuition and room and board and expenses for four years at a desired institution.

Other Special Needs Many families have special needs that must be considered in the life insurance planning process. A family with a disabled child might have special needs if that child is likely to require medical or custodial care as an adult. Wealthier families might need extra life insurance to pay federal estate taxes and state inheritance taxes (covered in Chapter 18).

How Can You Meet the Need?

There are three ways you can meet your need for protection from losses described above; government benefits, existing assets and life insurance.

Government Benefits Can Reduce the Level of Need Widows, widowers, and their dependents may qualify for various government benefits—most notably **Social Security survivor's benefits,** which are paid to a surviving spouse with children or to the children directly if there is no surviving spouse. The level of benefits depends on income earned during the lifetime of the deceased. (Details on estimating Social Security benefits are provided in Appendix B and on the *Garman/Forgue* companion website.) If eligible, a family can receive as much as $25,000 per year, but these benefits generally cease when the youngest child reaches age 18.

Instant Message

Husbands and Wives Need Their Own Life Insurance Plans

Husbands and wives should integrate their life insurance plans, but both need individual policies. This is true even if one partner makes the bulk of the family income. The cost of replacing the household labor of a stay-at-home spouse should be included in life insurance planning.

Social Security survivor's benefits
Government program benefits paid to a surviving spouse and children.

Adequate life insurance can ensure that important goals, such as paying for a child's education, are met should a parent die.

Joelle Gould/istockphoto.com

Existing Assets Can Help Meet the Needs

As time passes, individuals and families usually acquire at least a minimal amount of savings and investments. The funds held in savings accounts, certificates of deposit, stocks, bonds, and mutual funds often are specifically earmarked for some special goal, such as retirement, travel, or college for children. In the event of a premature death, they could be used to pay final and readjustment expenses as well as to replace lost income, even though it might be wiser to retain these funds for their originally intended purpose. Pension funds and retirement plans of the deceased, such as 401(k) plans and IRAs (discussed in Chapter 17), may be viewed as resources. Younger families should be wary of using retirement money for living expenses after the death of an income provider, however, as this strategy may jeopardize the surviving spouse's retirement.

Life Insurance Can Close Any Remaining Gap in Needs

Life insurance is the simplest form of insurance. It protects against only one peril—death. The benefit the policy will pay in cash is known in advance. If the policy is for $100,000, then the policy will pay the **beneficiary** (the person named in the policy to receive the funds) an amount very close to $100,000. This payment will occur within a few days once a death certificate is presented to the insurance company. Beneficiaries may use the funds in any way

beneficiary
Person who receives life insurance proceeds, as per the policy.

they wish without paying income taxes on the proceeds. However, if the funds are put in the bank or invested in some way, any interest or dividends earned will be subject to income taxation.

Employers often provide life insurance to their employees as an employee benefit. In addition, many people have existing life insurance that was purchased for them as children or that they purchased previously. These coverages can reduce the need for additional life insurance purchases.

What Dollar Amount of Life Insurance Do You Need?

Determining the magnitude of the losses resulting from a premature death can be complicated. Two methods are commonly used: a multiple-of-earnings approach and a needs-based approach. The needs-based approach is more accurate and reflects the changes in family status, income, assets, and age that will occur over your life cycle.

The Multiple-of-Earnings Approach: Easy but Flawed
The **multiple-of-earnings approach** estimates the amount of life insurance needed by multiplying your income by some number, such as 5, 7, or 10. Thus, someone with an annual income of $40,000 would need $200,000 to $400,000 in life insurance. Life insurance agents suggest this approach.

Another multiple-of-earnings approach is to use the interest factors from Appendix A.4 for an expected investment rate of return and a given number of years of need. The logic here is that at death, the survivor could invest the funds received from the life insurance policy on the person who has died to provide a flow of income for the number of years desired. For example, a father who wishes to provide his family with income of $40,000 for 20 years at a real rate of return of 4 percent (after inflation and taxes) would need to have about $550,000 ($40,000 × 13.59) of life insurance protection on his life.

The shortcoming of the multiple-of-earnings approach can be seen in the wide range of dollar amounts that result. This approach addresses only one of the factors affecting life insurance needs—income-replacement needs and does not take into consideration such factors as age, family situation, and other assets that could cover the lost income.

The Needs-Based Approach: A Better Method
The **needs-based approach** for estimating life insurance needs considers all of the factors that might potentially affect the level of need. It improves upon the calculations of the multiple-of-earnings approach by including a more accurate assessment of income-replacement needs and incorporates factors that add to and reduce the level of need. The Run the Numbers worksheet, "The Needs-Based Approach to Life Insurance" (page 346), illustrates calculations made via the needs-based approach. You would be wise to calculate your current needs for life insurance and then to revisit those calculations every three years and when changes occur in your employment or family situation or your health status.

Instant Message

Retirees Need Little or No Life Insurance

Life insurance needs typically decrease while assets increase over the course of one's life. At some point, savings and investments should exceed potential losses and eliminate the need for life insurance—especially after age 60.

Did You Know?

The Top 3 Financial Missteps When Protecting Loved Ones Through Life Insurance

People slip up in managing life insurance when they do the following:

1. Let their life insurance agent persuade them on how much and what type of life insurance to buy

2. Buy cash-value life insurance during their 20s and 30s rather than term policies

3. Ignore their changing need for life insurance as their life progresses from young adulthood through retirement

needs-based approach
A superior method of calculating the amount of insurance needed that considers all of the factors that might potentially affect the level of need.

Run the Numbers

The Needs-Based Approach to Life Insurance

This worksheet provides a mechanism for estimating life insurance needs using the needs-based approach. The amounts needed for final expenses, income replacement, readjustment needs, debt repayment, college expenses, and other special needs are calculated and then reduced by funds available from government benefits and any current insurance or assets that could cover the need. This worksheet is also available on the *Garman/Forgue* companion website.

Factors Affecting Need	Example	Your Figures
1. Final-expense needs		
Includes funeral, burial, travel, and other items of expense just prior to and after death	$ 12,000	$_____
2. Income-replacement needs		
Multiply 75 percent of annual income* by the interest factor from Appendix A.4 that corresponds to the number of years that the income is to be replaced and the assumed after-tax, after-inflation rate of return. ($36,000 × 19.6004 for 30 years at a 3% rate of return)	+ 705,614	+_____
3. Readjustment-period needs		
To cover employment interruptions and possible education expenses for surviving spouse and dependents	+ 19,000	+_____
4. Debt-repayment needs		
Provides repayment of short-term and installment debt, including credit cards and personal loans	+ 10,000	+_____
5. College-expense needs		
To provide a fund to help meet college expenses of dependents	+ 75,000	+_____
6. Other special needs	+ 0	+_____
7. Subtotal (combined effects of items 1–6)	+ $821,614	+_____
8. Government benefits		
Present value of Social Security survivor's benefits and other benefits		
Multiply monthly benefit estimate by 12 and use Appendix A.4 for the number of years that benefits will be received and the same interest rate that was used in item 1.		
($2725 × 12 × 11.118 for 15 years of benefits and a 4% rate of return)	– 363,558	–_____
9. Current insurance assets	– 98,000	–_____
10. Life insurance needed	$ 360,056	$_____

*Seventy-five percent is used because about 25 percent of income is used for personal needs.

Calculating Life Insurance Needs for a Couple with Small Children

Consider the example of Zoel Raymond, a 35-year-old factory foreman from Holyoke, Massachusetts, who has a spouse (age 30) and three sons (ages 8, 7, and 3 years). Zoel earns $48,000 annually and desires to replace his income for 30 years, at which time his spouse would be approaching retirement. The "Example" column of the Run the Numbers worksheet above expands on the situation faced by Zoel.

1. **Final-expense needs.** Zoel estimates his final expenses for funeral, burial, and other expenses at $12,000.

2. **Income-replacement needs.** Zoel's income of $48,000 is multiplied by 0.75 and the interest factor of 19.604. This factor was used because Zoel decided that it would be best to replace his lost income for 30 years or until Mary, his wife, reached age 60 and passed through the Social Security blackout period. Zoel and Mary are moderate-risk investors and believe that she could earn a 3 percent after-tax, after-inflation rate of return on life insurance proceeds. Income-replacement needs based on these conditions amount to $705,614.

Instant Message

Life Insurance Can Provide a Flow of Future Income

Having the right amount of life insurance will allow your family to invest the proceeds received and then make withdrawals to replace the income you could have provided for them had you lived.

3. **Readjustment-period needs.** Mary is a columnist for a local newspaper, earning an annual income of $38,000. Allocating $19,000 for readjustment-period needs would allow her to take a six-month leave of absence from her job or meet other readjustment needs.

4. **Debt-repayment needs.** Zoel and Mary owe $10,000 on various credit cards and an auto loan. They also owe about $128,000 on their home mortgage. Mary would like to pay off all debts except the mortgage debt if Zoel dies. The mortgage debt would be affordable if Zoel's income was adequately replaced.

5. **College-expense needs.** Zoel estimates that it would currently cost $25,000 for each of his sons to attend the local campus of a public university. If he dies, $25,000 of the life insurance proceeds could be invested for each son. If invested appropriately, the funds would grow at a rate sufficient to keep up with increasing costs of a college education.

6. **Other special needs.** Zoel and Mary do not have any unusual needs related to life insurance planning, so they entered zero for this factor.

7. **Subtotal.** The Raymonds total items 1 through 6 on the worksheet and determine that the family's financial needs arising out of Zoel's death would amount to $821,614. Although this sum seems large to them, they have access to two resources that can reduce this figure, as indicated in items 8 and 9.

8. **Government benefits.** Zoel estimates that his family would qualify for monthly Social Security survivor's benefits of $2725.* These benefits would be paid for 15 years, until his youngest son turns 18. The present value of this stream of benefits is $363,558 (from Appendix A.4), assuming a 4 percent return for 15 years.

9. **Current insurance and assets.** Zoel has a $50,000 life insurance policy purchased five years ago. His employer also pays for a group policy equal to his $48,000 gross annual income. Zoel's major assets include his home and his retirement plan. Because he does not want Mary to have to liquidate these assets if he dies, he includes only the $98,000 insurance coverage in item 9.

10. **Life insurance needed.** After subtracting worksheet items 8 and 9 from the subtotal, Zoel estimates that he needs an additional $360,056 in life insurance. This amount may seem like a large sum of insurance, but Zoel can meet this need through term life insurance for as little as $30 per month.

Because Mary earns an income that is about 80 percent of Zoel's, her life insurance needs may be about 20 percent lower. To determine the specific amount, the couple must complete a worksheet for her as well. Next, the Raymonds will need to decide what type of life insurance is best and from whom to buy the additional life insurance needed. These topics are covered later in this chapter.

*Your personal Social Security benefits can be estimated by requesting a Social Security Statement from the Social Security Administration (www.ssa.gov). Appendix B also provides estimates.

Instant Message

Social Security Survivor Benefits Have a Blackout Period

Once the youngest child reaches age 18, a surviving spouse enters the **Social Security blackout period** and is ineligible for Social Security survivor benefits. The blackout period ends when the surviving spouse reaches age 60. The surviving spouse may then collect survivor's benefits until age 62, and then may begin collecting Social Security retirement benefits based on his or her own or the deceased spouse's retirement account, whichever provides the higher payment.

Calculating Life Insurance Needs for a Young Professional

Irene Leech of Rancho Cucamonga, California, recently graduated with a degree in tourism management and has accepted a position paying $43,000 per year. Irene is single and lives with her sister. She owes $14,500 on a car loan and $21,800 in education loans. She has about $7000 in the bank. Among her employee benefits is an employer-paid term insurance policy equal to her annual salary.

Irene has been approached by a life insurance agent who used the multiple-of-earnings approach to suggest that she needs $215,000 in life insurance, or about five times her income. Does she? If you apply the needs-based approach to Irene's situation, you will see the following:

- Irene estimates her final expenses at $10,000, which she entered for item 1. Because Irene has no dependents, she needs no insurance for income-replacement needs, readjustment-period needs, college-expense needs, or other special needs.

- Items 2, 3, 5, and 6 in the needs-based approach worksheet on page 346 are zero because Irene has no dependents.

- Irene's survivors will not qualify for any government benefits, so item 8 will also be zero.

- Irene would like to see her $14,500 automobile loan and $21,800 education loans repaid in the event of her death. She feels better knowing that her younger sister could inherit her car free and clear. She entered $36,300 for item 4.

- Irene has combined life insurance and assets of $50,000, so she entered that amount for item 8.

The resulting calculations show that Irene needs *no* additional life insurance ($10,000 + $36,300 − $50,000 = −$3700). The agent suggested that Irene buy now while she is young and rates are low. This, too, is not a smart approach. The lesson here is that you should not buy life insurance simply to lock in low rates. That would be like buying car insurance before you own a car. Unless you have a personal or family-based medical history that might interfere with the purchase of life insurance when needed later, you, like Irene, can wait until you actually need life insurance before buying a policy.

Concept Check 12.1

1. Distinguish between the dying-too-soon problem and the living-too-long problem and the best ways to address each.
2. List five types of needs that can be addressed through life insurance.
3. Explain why the multiple-of-earnings approach is less accurate than a needs-based approach to life insurance planning.
4. Identify two periods in a typical person's life cycle when the need for life insurance is low and one when it is high.

---

2 Learning Objective

Distinguish among types of life insurance.

term life insurance
"Pure protection" against early death; pays benefits only if the insured dies within the time period (term) that the policy covers.

There Are Only Two Basic Types of Life Insurance

Many people are confused by the wide variety of life insurance plans available. But, in reality, there are only two types of life insurance: term life insurance and cash-value life insurance. **Term life insurance** is often described as "pure protection" because it pays benefits only if the insured person dies within the time period (term) covered by the policy. The policy must be renewed if coverage is desired for another time period. In this way it acts much like car or homeowner's insurance. **Cash-value life insurance** pays benefits at death and includes a savings/investment element that can provide benefits to the policyholder prior to the death of the insured person. Thus, it includes a **cash value** representing the value of the investment element in the life insurance policy. Because of its investment aspect, many people automatically believe it is the better option. Cash-value life insurance costs much more than term insurance, however, and there are much better investment options as you will learn in upcoming chapters.

cash-value life insurance
Pays benefits at death and includes a savings/investment element that can provide a reduced level of benefits to the policyholder prior to the death of the insured person.

Term Life Insurance

Term life insurance contracts are most often written for time periods (or terms) of 1, 5, 10, or even 20 years. If the insured survives the specified time period, the beneficiary receives no monetary benefits. Term insurance can be purchased in contracts with face amounts in multiples of $1000, usually with a minimum face amount of $50,000. The **face amount** is the dollar value of life insurance protection as listed in the policy and used to calculate the premium. Variations on term life insurance include decreasing term insurance, guaranteed renewable term insurance, convertible term insurance, and credit (term) life insurance.

face amount
Dollar value of protection as listed in the policy and used to calculate the premium.

Unless otherwise stipulated by the original contract, you must apply for a new contract and may be required to undergo a medical examination to renew the policy. The premium will increase with each renewal, reflecting your increasing age and greater likelihood of dying while the new policy remains in force. If you have a health problem, you may be denied a new policy or be asked to pay even higher premiums. For example, a $100,000 five-year renewable term policy for a man age 25 might have an annual premium of $100; at age 35, the policy might cost $135; and at age 45, it might cost $220. Term policies are much less expensive than a new cash-value policy at any given age because they do not include a savings/investment element.

Guaranteed Renewable Term Insurance
Proving insurability at renewal may be difficult if you develop a health problem during the time period of a term policy. Term life insurance policies, however, are usually written as **guaranteed renewable term insurance.** The guarantee protects you against the possibility of becoming uninsurable. The number of renewals you can make without proving insurability may be limited, and a maximum age may be specified for these renewals (usually 65 or 70 years). Unless you are positive that you will not need a renewal, guaranteed renewable term insurance is recommended.

guaranteed renewable term insurance
Protects you against the possibility of becoming uninsurable.

Level-Premium Term Insurance
You can partially avoid term insurance premium increases as you grow older by buying **level-premium** (or **guaranteed level-premium**) **term insurance,** which is a term policy with a long time period (perhaps 5, 10, or 20 years). Under such a policy, the premiums remain constant throughout the entire life of the policy. Premiums charged in early years are higher than necessary to balance out the lower-than-necessary premiums in later years covered by the policy. Premiums on policies written for ten or more years usually remain constant for a five-year interval, then might increase to a new constant rate for another five- or ten-year interval. Such level-premium policies may include a **reenter provision,** requiring proof of good health at the beginning of each five-year interval. If health status changes, the insured must reenter the policy at a higher rate than originally anticipated. Be extremely wary of policies with such a provision, especially if you anticipate needing coverage beyond the initial level-premium interval.

level-premium term insurance
Term policy with long term under which premiums remain constant. Also called guaranteed level-premium term insurance.

Decreasing Term Insurance
With **decreasing term insurance,** the face amount of coverage declines annually, while the premiums remain constant. The owner chooses an initial face amount and a contract period, after which the face amount of the policy gradually declines (usually each year) to some minimum (such as $50,000) in the last year of the

contract. For example, a woman age 35 might buy a 30-year $200,000 decreasing term policy that declines by $5000 each year. The major benefit of decreasing term policies is that they more closely fit changing insurance needs, which typically decline as a person ages.

Convertible Term Insurance

convertible term insurance
Offers policyholders option of exchanging a term policy for a cash-value policy without evidence of insurability.

Convertible Term Insurance   Convertible **term insurance** offers the policyholder the option of exchanging a term policy for a cash-value policy without evidence of insurability. Usually, this conversion is available only in the early years of the term policy. Some policies provide for an automatic conversion from term to cash-value insurance after a specific number of years.

There are two ways to convert a term policy to a cash-value policy. First, you can simply request the conversion and begin paying the higher premiums required for the cash-value policy. The savings/investment element of the cash-value policy will begin accumulating as of the date of the conversion. Second, you can pay the company the cash value that would have built up had the policy originally been written on a cash-value basis. Although this lump sum may be a considerable amount, it does represent an asset for the policyholder. Furthermore, the new premiums will be based on your age at the time that you bought the original term policy, which may result in lower premiums.

Instant Message

Buying Life Insurance Through a Group Plan at Work

Unlike with health insurance, group life insurance rates are not lower than individual rates for people in good health. Alternatively, if you have a health condition, your group rates are likely to be much lower than what you might pay on your own.

Group Term Life Insurance   Group **term life insurance** is issued to people as members of a group rather than as individuals. Most such policies are written for a large number of employees, with premiums being paid in full or in part by the employer. Group life insurance premiums are average rates based on the characteristics of the group as a whole. If you are insured under a group plan, you need not prove your insurability, and you can usually convert the policy to an individual basis without proof of insurability if you leave the group. Such convertibility represents a major benefit for people whose health status makes individual life insurance unaffordable or unattainable.

Credit Term Life Insurance   Credit **term life insurance** will pay the remaining balance of a loan if the insured dies before repaying the debt. **Mortgage life insurance** specifically focuses on the repayment of mortgage debt. In essence, both these types of term insurance are decreasing term insurance with the creditor named as beneficiary. These products are grossly overpriced, and the only people who should consider their purchase are those who are uninsurable because of a serious health condition. Most people are insurable and can obtain term life coverage for a minimal cost, so they do not need credit or mortgage term life insurance.

Some Forms of Cash-Value Life Insurance Earn a Fixed Return

Cash-value life insurance pays benefits upon the death of the insured and also incorporates a savings/investment element. This cash value belongs to the owner of the policy rather than to the beneficiary (although they can be the same person). While the insured is alive, the owner may obtain the cash value by borrowing from the insurance company or by surrendering and canceling the policy. Cash-value insurance is referred to as **permanent insurance** because it does not need to be renewed and because coverage is maintained for the entire life of the insured as long as premiums are paid. The annual premiums for cash-value policies usually remain constant.

The premiums for newly written cash-value policies are always higher than those for term policies providing the same amount of coverage. This difference arises because only a portion of the premium is used to provide the death benefit; the remainder is used to keep the premium level and to build the cash value. Figure 12.1 illustrates the premium differences between cash-value and term life insurance policies.

Cash-value life insurance represents a combination of decreasing term insurance and an investment account that adds up to the face amount of the policy. Figure 12.2 illustrates this concept. Initially, for example, you might have $100,000 of insurance and no savings. Several years later, you might have built up $2000 in savings within the policy. In the event of your death, your beneficiary would collect $100,000, of which $2000 would be your own money. If you lived long enough, the cash value could equal—and might surpass—the $100,000 figure. In effect, your beneficiary would then collect your "savings account" rather than an insurance payment.

Even though the cash value of a life insurance policy accumulates throughout your life, only the face amount of the policy will be paid upon your death. In many ways, cash values represent a kind of forced saving that allows funds to build up while you buy life insurance. Several types of cash-value life insurance are available that pay a fixed rate of investment return.

Whole Life Insurance
Whole, or straight, life insurance is a form of cash-value life insurance that provides lifetime life insurance protection and expects you to pay premiums for life. The policy remains in effect and does not need to be renewed as long as the premiums are paid on time.

Limited-Pay Whole Life Insurance
Limited-pay whole life insurance is whole life insurance that allows premium payments to cease before you reach the age of 100. Two common examples are **20-pay life policies,** which allow premium payments to cease after 20 years, and **paid-at-65 policies,** which require payment of premiums only until the insured turns 65. Although premiums need be paid only for the specified time period, the insurance protection lasts for your entire life. As you might expect, the annual premiums for limited-pay insurance policies are higher than those for whole life insurance policies because the insurance company has fewer years to collect premiums. Limited-pay policies are said to

whole life insurance
Form of cash-value life insurance that provides lifetime life insurance protection and expects the insured to pay premiums for life. Also called straight life insurance.

limited-pay whole life insurance
Whole life insurance that allows premium payments to cease before the insured reaches the age of 100.

Figure 12.1
Comparison of Premium Dollars for Life Insurance

Cash-Value Policy

| Premium to pay for insurance protection, sales commissions, and company expenses | $ | Premium to provide for the building of cash value plus related company expenses |

Term Policy

| Premium to pay for insurance protection, sales commissions, and company expenses | $ | Dollars not spent on life insurance and available to invest |

Figure 12.2

The Fundamental Nature of Cash-Value Life Insurance

The $100,000 death benefit (face value) paid to the beneficiaries comprises a decreasing amount of life insurance and the policyholder's returned built-up cash values.

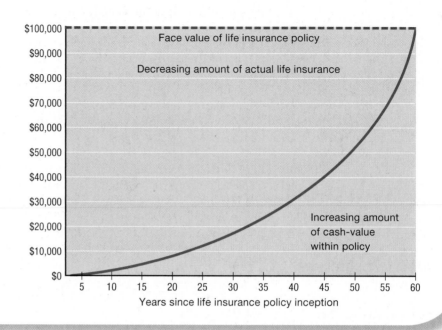

paid-up
Point at which the owner of a whole life policy can stop paying premiums.

be **paid-up** when the owner can stop paying premiums. An extreme version of limited-pay life insurance is **single-premium life insurance,** in which the premium is paid once in the form of a lump sum.

Adjustable Life Insurance   The three cornerstones of cash-value life insurance are the premium, the face amount of the policy, and the rate of cash-value accumulation. **Adjustable life insurance** allows you to modify any one of these three components, with corresponding changes occurring in the other two. These changes may be made without providing new proof of insurability. For example, you might feel that inflation has increased your need for life insurance. Adjustable life insurance would allow you to increase the face amount. In return, your premiums could increase, the cash-value accumulation could slow, or some combination of the two could apply.

Modified Life Insurance   **Modified life insurance** is whole life insurance for which the insurance company charges reduced premiums in the early years and higher premiums thereafter. The premiums are lower in early years because some of the protection during the early years is provided by term insurance. The period of reduced premiums can vary from one to five years. Modified life insurance is primarily designed for people whose life insurance needs are high (young parents, for example) but who cannot immediately afford the premiums required for a cash-value policy. Because modified life insurance uses term insurance in the early years, it accumulates cash value extremely slowly.

Endowment Life Insurance   **Endowment life insurance** pays the face amount of the policy either upon the death of the insured or at some previously agreed-upon date, whichever occurs first. The date of payment, called the endowment date, is commonly some specified number of years after issuance of the policy (for example, 20 or 30 years) or some specified age (such as 65). New endowment policies are no longer being written, however, and this type of policy will be phased out as existing policies "endow" and are converted to cash.

Some Forms of Cash-Value Life Insurance Earn a Variable Return

The rate at which the cash value accumulates in a cash-value policy depends on the rate of return earned. Some forms of cash-value insurance have a guaranteed minimum rate of return, often 4 percent, but pay a higher current rate depending on the success of the investments made by the insurance company with your premiums. Table 12.1 illustrates these rates. An understanding of these policies requires an examination of the premium, the cost of the insurance protection portion, the rate of return on the invested funds, and the company's expense charges.

Universal Life Insurance   **Universal life insurance** provides both the pure protection of term insurance and the cash-value buildup of whole life insurance, along with variability in the face amount, rate of cash-value accumulation, premiums, and rate of return. Initially, the purchaser selects a face amount, and the company quotes an annual premium. The annual premium goes into the cash-value fund, from which the company deducts the cost of providing the insurance protection and charges for company expenses. As time goes by, the owner of the policy may reduce or increase the premium, with corresponding changes occurring in the insurance protection or amount added to cash value. If premiums drop below the amount necessary to cover the insurance protection and expenses, funds are removed from the cash-value account to cover the shortfall.

Essentially, universal life insurance combines annual term insurance with an investment program. Universal life policies are usually available in initial face amounts of $100,000 or more. The rate of return is tied to some interest rate prevailing in the financial markets or is dictated by the insurance company. The rate of return often exceeds those available under fixed-rate cash-value policies.

universal life insurance
Provides the pure protection of term insurance and the cash-value buildup of whole life insurance, along with face amount variability, rate of cash-value accumulation, premiums, and rate of return.

Table 12.1   **Cash-Value Buildup—Guaranteed Versus Current Rates***

Policy Year	"Guaranteed" Cash-Surrender Value (4.0% rate)	"Current Rate" Cash-Surrender Value (7.6% rate)
1	$ 0	$ 0
2	0	236
3	585	886
4	1,280	1,577
5	1,993	2,377
6	2,723	3,187
7	3,470	4,212
8	4,234	5,258
9	5,016	6,302
10	5,816	7,419
15	10,089	14,748
20	14,738	25,812
25	19,888	39,419

*Figures are illustrative for a $50,000 universal life policy; the annual premium is $684.

Advice from a Pro...

Don't Be Fooled by "Vanishing-Premium" or "Return-of-Premium" Policies

Life insurance agents often pitch **vanishing-premium life insurance**, which is designed to allow policyholders to cease making premium payments after just a few years. In these plans, cash-value accumulations are used to pay premiums that no longer must be paid. While attractive at first glance, these policies contain a significant hazard. If the growth in cash-value accumulations proves insufficient to pay the premium, the owner of the policy will be billed for the premium shortfall—possibly after many years of having not paid premiums. Always assume any life insurance charge that can be imposed will be imposed.

A similar type of plan is called a **return-of-premium policy.** Here the policy promises to return all the premiums

paid if the insured person maintains the policy and lives past a certain number of years—usually 30. These policies cost more so that the extra funds can be invested to provide for the return of premiums. Insurance companies promote these policies as a way to avoid "wasting" your money. In reality, what they are trying to do is entice you to keep the policy in effect for a long time even if you do not need the coverage anymore. Instead buy term insurance and decide for yourself when it is best to drop a policy.

Hyungsoo Kim
University of Kentucky, Lexington, Kentucky

Variable Life Insurance   **Variable life insurance** allows you to choose the investments made with your cash-value accumulations and to share in any gains or losses. The face amount of your policy and the policy's cash value may rise or fall based on changes in the rates of return on the invested funds. The face amount of the policy usually will not drop below the originally agreed-upon amount, however. Instead, the cash value will fluctuate. If you are unfamiliar with markets for corporate stocks and bonds and mutual funds, however, you should probably avoid variable life insurance. Many variable life insurance policies contain provisions calling for the payment of fees and sales charges before the policyholder can share in any investment returns. Variable life insurance policies are complicated and should be read and analyzed very carefully before purchase.

variable-universal life insurance

Form of universal life insurance that gives the policyholder some choice in the investments made with the cash value accumulated by the policy. Also called flexible-premium variable life insurance.

Variable-Universal Life Insurance   **Variable-universal life insurance** is a form of universal life insurance that gives the policyholder some choice in the investments made with the cash value accumulated by the policy. It is sometimes called **flexible-premium variable life insurance.** The most popular form of cash-value life insurance, it most closely embodies the philosophy of "buy term and invest the difference." (Actually buying a term policy and putting your premium savings into investments is the wiser approach as transaction costs are much lower.) Because you select the investment vehicles (a combination of stocks, bonds, or money market mutual funds), you can potentially realize a higher rate of return than is possible under other cash-value policy types. With this flexibility comes the risk of a lower rate of return, of course. As a result, variable-universal life policies usually provide no minimum guaranteed rate of return. Table 12.2 summarizes the features of term life insurance, cash-value insurance with a fixed return, and cash-value insurance with a variable return.

Variable-universal life insurance also carries higher commissions and is more likely to require annual fees than other forms of life insurance. A 2 percent annual fee would change a policy with an annual return of 5 percent on its investments to one with a net 3 percent return. You should also compare the policy's investment component with alternative investments. (Investments are covered in Chapters 13 to 16.)

Table 12.2   Comparisons of Three Popular Life Insurance Policies

Feature	Term Insurance	Cash-Value Life Insurance	
		Whole Life Insurance	**Variable Life Insurance**
Cash-value accumulation	None	Fixed rate of accumulation	Variable accumulation as premium and interest rates vary
Rate of return paid on cash accumulations	Not applicable	Fixed	Variable with interest rates in the economy or as specified by company
Face amount	Fixed or declining during term of the policy; changeable at renewal	Fixed	Variable
Premiums	Low with increases at renewal	High and fixed	High but variable within limits
Cost of the death benefit portion	Low, with interest at renewal	Unknown	Known but can vary and may hide some expense charges
Company expense charges	Low but unknown; hidden in premium	Unknown; hidden in premium	Known; may be high

 Concept Check 12.2

1. Distinguish between term life insurance and cash-value life insurance.
2. Explain why the premiums for term insurance are so much lower than those of cash-value life insurance.
3. Describe the benefit of buying guaranteed renewable term insurance.
4. Explain why the amount of "insurance" declines over time under a cash-value life insurance policy.
5. Distinguish between cash-value life insurance with a fixed return and with a variable return.

Understanding Your Life Insurance Policy

A **life insurance policy** is the written contract between the insurer and the policyholder. It contains all of the information relevant to the agreement. Several parties will be named in the life insurance contract (policy). The **owner, or policyholder,** retains all rights and privileges granted by the policy, including the right to amend the policy and the right to designate who receives the proceeds. The **insured** is the person whose life is insured. In addition to the beneficiary, the owner will name a **contingent beneficiary** who will become the beneficiary if the original beneficiary dies before the insured. Although the owner and the insured are often the same person, it is possible for four different people to play all these roles.

3 Learning Objective

Explain the major provisions of life insurance policies.

owner/policyholder
Retains all rights and privileges granted by the policy, including the right to amend the policy and the right to designate who receives the proceeds.

insured
Individual whose life is insured.

Did You Know?

How Insurance Policies Are Organized

All insurance policies have five basic components including declarations, insuring agreements, exclusions, conditions, and endorsements. In order of their usual location in the policy, these five elements, contain information as follows:

1. **Declarations** provide the basic descriptive information about the insured person or property, the premium to be paid, the time period of the coverage, and the policy limits. Also included may be promises by the insured to take steps to control the losses associated with a specific peril. For example, a life insurance purchaser may promise not to smoke in exchange for paying a discounted premium. The information in the declarations is used to help determine the premium and for identification purposes.

2. **Insuring agreements** are the broadly defined coverages provided under the policy. The insurer makes these promises in return for the premium paid by the insured. For example, in life insurance, the insurer promises to pay the death benefit amount to the beneficiary in the event of the insured's death. In automobile insurance, the insuring agreements will often include definitions of a motor vehicle or insured premises to clarify the promises made.

3. **Exclusions** narrow the focus and eliminate specific coverages broadly stated in the insuring agreements. The insurer makes no promise to pay for these exceptions and special circumstances. For example, suicide is commonly excluded during the first two years of a life insurance policy. A common automobile insurance exclusion denies coverage under a family policy if the car is used primarily for business purposes. People who do not understand the exclusions in their policies may believe they are covered for a loss when, in fact, they are not.

4. **Conditions** impose obligations on both the insured and the insurer by establishing the ground rules of the agreement. For example, they might include procedures for making a claim after a loss, rules for cancellation of the policy by either party, and procedures for changing the terms of the policy. The insured who fails to adhere to the procedures or obligations described in the conditions may be denied coverage when a loss occurs.

5. **Endorsements** (or **riders** as they are sometimes called in life insurance) are amendments and additions to the basic insurance policy that can both expand and limit coverage to accommodate specific needs. When the terms of an endorsement or rider differ from the terms of the basic policy, the endorsement will be considered valid. Endorsements may be requested at any time during the life of the policy to expand coverage, raise the policy limits, and make other changes.

Policy Terms and Provisions Unique to Life Insurance

Life insurance policies define the terminology used in the policy and outline the basic provisions of such insurance. This information serves to clarify the meaning of the policy and the protection afforded the insurer and the policyholder.

The Application   The **life insurance application** is the policyholder's offer to purchase a policy. It provides information and becomes part of the life insurance policy (the contract). Any errors or omissions in the application may allow the insurance company to deny a request for payment of the death benefit.

Lives Covered   Most life insurance policies cover the life of a single person—the insured. It is also possible to cover two or more people with one policy, however. **First-to-die policies** cover more than one person but pay only when the first insured dies. These policies are less costly than separate policies written on each person, but the survivor then has no coverage after the first person dies. An alternative is the **survivorship joint life policy,** which pays when the last person covered dies.

The Incontestability Clause Life insurance policies generally include an **incontestability clause** that places a time limit—usually two years after issuance of the policy—on the right of the insurance company to deny a claim. This clause addresses the problems arising out of erroneous statements in the application.

incontestability clause
Places a time limit on the right of the insurance company to deny a claim.

The Suicide Clause Life insurance policies generally include a **suicide clause** that allows the life insurance company to deny coverage if the insured commits suicide within the first few years after the policy is issued. If the specified number of years (usually two) has elapsed, the full death benefit will be paid. If not, only the premiums paid up to that point will be refunded.

Cash Dividends **Insurance dividends** are defined by the Internal Revenue Service as a return of a portion of the premium paid for a life insurance policy; they are not considered taxable income. They represent the surplus earnings of the company when the difference between the total premium charged exceeds the cost to the company of providing insurance. Policies that pay dividends are called **participating policies,** and policies that do not pay dividends are called **nonparticipating policies.** Both term and cash-value policies may pay dividends. Owners of participating policies may receive dividends as a cash payment, leave them with the insurance company to earn interest, or use the dividends to purchase small amounts of additional paid-up life insurance.

insurance dividends
Surplus earnings of insurance company when the difference between the total premium charged exceeds the cost to the company of providing insurance.

participating policies
Life insurance policies that pay dividends.

Death Benefit The **death benefit** of a life insurance policy is the amount that will be paid upon the death of the insured person.

The amount of the death benefit may be either higher or lower than the face amount. It can be higher due to such items as earned dividends not yet paid or premiums paid in advance. Or it could be lower due to outstanding policy loans or unpaid premiums. Consider a $100,000 participating whole life policy with annual premiums of $1380. If the insured died halfway through the policy year, with an outstanding cash-value loan of $5000 and earned but unpaid dividends of $4000, the death benefit would be $99,690, calculated as follows:

death benefit
Amount that will be paid to beneficiary when the insured dies.

$100,000	Face amount
4,000	Unpaid dividends
+ 690	Premiums paid in advance (one-half year)
$104,690	Subtotal
− 5,000	Outstanding cash-value loan
$ 99,690	Death benefit

Grace Period Prompt payment of the premium is crucial to the continuation of coverage provided by any insurance policy. A **lapsed policy** is one that has been terminated because of nonpayment of premiums. More than one-half of all whole life policies lapse within ten years of being issued. If your life insurance policy lapses, you must prove insurability and pay any missed premiums, plus interest, to be reinstated. Alternatively, you might pay a higher premium for a new policy, reflecting your current age.

To help prevent a lapse, state laws generally require that cash-value and multiyear term policies include a **grace period,** that is, a period of time (usually 30 days following each premium due date) during which an overdue premium may be paid without a lapse of the policy. During the grace period, all provisions of the policy remain intact, but only if payment is made before the grace period ends. Assume, for example, that payment was due but not paid on January 1. If the insured were to die on January 15, the policy could be reinstated as long as payment was made by January 30, given a 30-day grace period. It also may be possible to "buy back" a lapsed cash-value policy by paying any missed premiums and the cash value that would have accumulated while the policy was lapsed.

grace period
Period of time during which an overdue premium may be paid without a lapse of the policy.

Multiple Indemnity   A **multiple indemnity clause** provides for a doubling or tripling of the face amount if death results from certain specified causes. It is most often used to double the face amount if death results from an accident. Such a clause is often included automatically as part of the policy at no extra cost, but sometimes a charge is assessed. If you are adequately insured, a multiple indemnity clause is unnecessary.

Settlement Options Allow the Beneficiary to Decide How to Receive the Death Benefit

settlement options
Choices from which the policyholder can choose in how the death benefit payment will be structured.

Settlement options are the choices that the life insurance beneficiary or policyholder has in determining how the death benefit payment will be structured. The owner may choose the option before death, or the beneficiary may select the option after the insured's death. Each option's appropriateness depends on the beneficiary's financial situation. The five settlement options are as follows:

1. **Lump sum.** The death benefit may be received as a lump-sum cash settlement immediately after death.

2. **Interest income.** The beneficiary can receive the annual interest earned from the death benefit. For example, the beneficiary would receive $4000 each year from a $100,000 death benefit earning 4 percent interest. The $100,000 principal would remain intact and would continue to earn interest until the death of the beneficiary, when it becomes part of his or her estate.

3. **Income of a specific amount.** The beneficiary may receive a specific amount of income per year from the death benefit. Under this option, payments cease when the death benefit and interest are exhausted. For example, a $100,000 death benefit earning 4 percent interest would provide a $15,000 annual income for approximately eight years.★

4. **Income for a specific period.** The beneficiary may receive an income from the death benefit for a specific number of years. For example, a widow with small children may choose to receive an income for 18 years. The insurance company would calculate a level of income that would allow for equal proceeds each year, with all funds, including interest, being exhausted at the end of the 18th year.

5. **Income for life.** The beneficiary may elect to receive an income for life. In such a case, the insurance company would use the life expectancy of the beneficiary to calculate the level of income that would allow for equal annual payments so that funds would be exhausted by the expected date of the beneficiary's death. If the beneficiary lives longer than expected, the income payments would continue.

Policy Features Unique to Cash-Value Life Insurance

Cash-value life insurance policies carry special features that all relate to the cash values built up in the policies.

The Policy Illustration   Prior to death, you may cash in the policy for the accumulated cash value, which cancels your insurance coverage, or you may borrow all or part of the cash value. You must repay the amount borrowed with interest, and any amount owed will be subtracted from the face amount of the policy if you die while the debt remains outstanding.

Cash-value life insurance policies generally provide a **policy illustration** that charts the projected growth in the cash value for given rates of return. Two rates are usually quoted:

★This option and options 4 and 5 are variations of an annuity and are covered further in Chapter 17.

the **guaranteed minimum rate of return** (the minimum rate that, by contract, the company is legally obligated to pay) and the **current rate** (the rate of return recently paid by the company to policyholders). Agents typically emphasize the current rate, perhaps by presenting a table that illustrates the rate of cash-value accumulation resulting from the two rates. Table 12.1 provides an example of such a table. Note the differences in the two cash-value columns in Table 12.1—you can readily understand why the agent would emphasize the current rate. Policy illustrations can easily be made to look much more optimistic than it is reasonable to expect. Only after the policy is in force for perhaps 10 to 20 years can an accurate picture be drawn. For this reason, it is smart to periodically ask your agent for an **in-force illustration** that shows the cash-value status of the policy and projections for the future given the current rate of return at the time of the illustration (rather than the rate used at the inception of the policy).

Policy illustrations can be helpful in many cases, but they can also be written in such a way as to make the policy look better than it really is. Asking a few pertinent questions can help cut through some of the misconceptions:

1. Is the "current rate" illustrated actually the rate paid recently? What was the current rate in each of the past five years?

2. What assumptions have been made regarding company expenses, dividend rates, and policy lapse rates?

3. Does all of my cash value earn a return at the current rate? (If not, the current rate is misleading.)

4. Is the illustration based on the "cash surrender value" or the "cash value"? (The cash surrender value is usually the lower value and reflects what will actually be paid if the policy is cashed in.)

Nonforfeiture Values
Nonforfeiture values are amounts stipulated in a life insurance policy that protect the cash value, if any, in the event that the policyholder chooses not to pay or fails to pay the required premiums. The policy owner can receive the accumulated cash-value funds in one of three ways. First, he or she may simply surrender the policy and receive the **cash surrender value,** which represents the cash value minus any surrender charges. In reality, the true measure of the cash value of a policy is its cash surrender value (the amount received when the policy is canceled). Second, the policy owner may continue the policy with the original face amount but for a time period shorter than the original policy. Third, the policy may be continued on a paid-up basis, with a new and lower face amount being established based on the amount that can be purchased with the accumulated funds. Table 12.3 illustrates the nonforfeiture values for a paid-at-65 cash-value policy. Note that a cash-value policy has very little cash surrender value unless you have held it for ten years or more.

Policy Loans
The owner of a cash-value policy may borrow all or a portion of the accumulated cash value. Interest rates charged for the loan will range from 2 to 8 percent, depending on the terms of the policy. In addition, the interest rate earned on the remaining cash value typically reverts to the guaranteed minimum rate while the loan remains outstanding. As a result, the cash value ultimately accumulated may be significantly reduced.

An **automatic premium loan** provision allows any premium not paid by the end of the grace period to be paid automatically with a policy loan if sufficient cash value or dividends have accumulated. In the first few years of a policy, this provision may not offer much benefit because cash value and dividends accumulate slowly. Eventually these funds may grow enough to pay premiums for a considerable length of time, thereby effectively preventing the lapse of the policy.

Many life insurance companies make a policy's death benefit available to a terminally ill insured through a **living benefit clause** that allows the payment of all or a portion of the

Table 12.3   **Cash-Value Life Insurance Nonforfeiture Values**

		A	B		C
			(Policyholder can choose A, B, or C.)		
Policy Year	Cash or Surrender Value*		**Period of $10,000 Term Insurance**		Face Value of Term Insurance Paid-up for Life†
			Years	Days	
0	$0		0	0	$0
2	0		0	0	0
3	60		2	81	240
4	190		7	35	720
5	310		10	282	1,140
10	1,000		19	351	3,160
15	1,790		22	346	4,900
20	2,690		23	122	6,410
30	4,350		21	228	8,260
35	5,390		20	286	9,140
40	6,520		For life	—	10,000
45	7,110		For life	—	10,000

For a $10,000, paid-at-65, limited-payment, cash-value life insurance policy for a male aged 25; the annual premium is $180.

*The policy has a back-end load that reduces the buildup of cash value in early years.

†Much lower commissions tend to be charged on term insurance policies.

death benefit prior to death if the insured contracts a terminal illness. This allows the policy to offer, in effect, long-term health care protection. These early payments are not cash-value loans, so it is possible to obtain more than the cash value accumulated in the policy. In addition, **viatical companies** specialize in buying life insurance policies from insureds for $0.50 to $0.80 per $1 of death benefit in return for being named beneficiary on the policy.

waiver of premium

Sets certain conditions under which an insurance policy would be kept in full force by the company without the payment of premiums.

Waiver of Premium   A **waiver of premium** sets certain conditions under which an insurance policy would be kept in full force by the company without the payment of premiums. It usually applies when a policyholder becomes totally and permanently disabled, but it may also apply under other conditions, depending on the policy provisions. In effect, the waiver-of-premium option (for an extra cost) protects against the risk of becoming disabled and being unable to pay premiums. This option can be expensive and may account for as much as 10 percent of the policy premium. If you are adequately covered by disability income insurance (see Chapter 11), then you might want to avoid this option.

guaranteed insurability (guaranteed purchase option)

Permits the cash-value policyholder to buy additional stated amounts of cash-value life insurance at stated times in the future without evidence of insurability.

Guaranteed Insurability   The **guaranteed insurability** (or **guaranteed purchase**) **option** permits the cash-value policyholder to buy additional stated amounts of cash-value life insurance at stated times in the future without evidence of insurability. This option differs from the guaranteed renewability option for term insurance in that it enables the owner to increase the face amount of the policy or to buy an additional policy. The policy might allow the exercise of these options when the insured turns 30, 35, or 40, or when he or she marries or has children. The added cost of this option is nominal and worthwhile.

Concept Check 12.3

1. Distinguish among the owner, the insured, the beneficiary, and the contingent beneficiary of a life insurance policy.

2. Briefly describe each of the five components of all insurance policies.

3. Identify the five settlement options for the payment of the proceeds of a life insurance policy to its beneficiary.

4. Besides taking the cash value as a lump sum, what are four more ways a cash-value policyholder may take the proceeds of the policy at cancellation?

5. Distinguish between an automatic premium loan and a waiver of premium option in a life insurance policy.

6. Explain how guaranteed renewability for term life insurance and guaranteed insurability for cash-value insurance protect insured people who develop serious health conditions.

Step-by-Step Strategies for Buying Life Insurance

Every year more than $150 billion of new life insurance is purchased in the United States. Does each individual really need life insurance? Was the policy purchased the right one, and was it purchased from a reputable company and agent? Did the buyer pay the right price?

4 Learning Objective

Apply a step-by-step strategy for implementing a life insurance plan.

First Ask Whether or Not, and For How Much, Your Life Should Be Insured

Anyone whose death will result in financial losses to others should be covered by life insurance unless other resources are sufficient to cover the losses. At a minimum, there will be final expenses such as for funeral and burial. Beyond that, the need depends on the person's family situation. Parents with minor children almost always need life insurance.

People who generally do not need life insurance include children and people with no dependents who have no desire to leave an estate. People who are sometimes unnecessarily insured include retirees who may have already built up assets sufficient to provide for income for survivors and to cover final expenses. The only way to really know how much additional life insurance you need is through the needs-based calculations covered earlier in this chapter. You should do this yourself and not rely on an insurance agent who has a vested interest in selling you some life insurance.

Properly Integrate Your Life Insurance into Your Overall Financial Planning

Advertising and sales promotion literature for cash-value life insurance often pushes the idea that this type of insurance is a good investment and is appropriate as a retirement savings vehicle. Most independent personal finance experts would disagree strongly. Instead, they typically advise people to take a broader perspective and think of life insurance

Did You Know?

About Life Insurance After Divorce

If you receive income from a former spouse through either alimony or child support, life insurance on that person is strongly advised. If a policy that was purchased while a couple was married remains in effect, it is wise to keep it. To be certain that the correct beneficiary is named, have that requirement stated in a court order and/or made part of the divorce decree and require written confirmation from the insurance company that the beneficiary is appropriately noted. The custodial parent should then be named as owner of the policy, thereby preventing the noncustodial parent from making any changes in the policy. Noncustodial parents will also need life insurance on their former spouses because they will probably receive custody of the children if the former spouse dies and may need additional income to support them.

Did You Know?

The Tax Consequences of Life Insurance

The proceeds of life insurance policies are not taxable income. Thus a survivor who receives a $100,000 check from an insurance company keeps all the money. He or she can spend, save, invest, or donate the funds. Some people might be persuaded by an insurance agent to consider cash-value life insurance to be a smart tax-advantaged way to invest for retirement. While life insurance does have some tax-sheltering aspects because the cash value built up in the policy is not subject to income taxes, cash-value life insurance does not compare favorably with 401(k) retirement plans available through your employer or with an IRA (discussed in Chapter 17):

1. The premiums paid on life insurance policies cannot be used to reduce taxable income; however, contributions to IRAs and 401(k) plans do offer this significant advantage.

2. The rate of return earned within cash-value life insurance policies has historically lagged well behind what can be achieved by a diversified portfolio of stock and bond mutual funds. (discussed in Chapters 13–15, and 17).

3. The commissions and expense charges on cash-value life insurance are substantially higher than those associated with investing in no-load mutual funds. Hence the net cost of investing in mutual funds is far lower than buying cash-value life insurance. (See Chapter 15.)

Conclusion: You should be contributing the maximum amount possible into available tax-sheltered retirement plans before you even begin to consider the purchase of cash-value life insurance as an appropriate way to save for retirement

as just one facet of their plans. Specifically, you should always think in terms of the two longevity risks: the risk of living too long and the risk of dying too soon. Investing through tax-sheltered retirement plans (not in expensive insurance policies) most effectively solves the living-too-long problem. Inexpensive term life insurance most effectively solves the dying-too-soon problem.

Your need for life insurance will change significantly over the course of your life. So should your life insurance plan. You should reassess your plan every two or three years and any time your family or employment situation changes. Keep these facts in mind:

- During childhood and while single, your need for life insurance is either nonexistent or very small because few, if any, other people rely on you for financial support.

- With marriage comes the increased responsibility for another person, although life insurance needs probably remain low because spouses usually have the potential to support themselves if the other partner were to die.

- The arrival of children, however, triggers a sharp increase in life insurance needs. Children often require as many as 25 years of parental support, during which time they usually have little ability to provide for themselves.

- As children grow older, the number of years of their remaining dependency declines, reducing the need for life insurance.

- Parents with grown children see a reduced need for life insurance because their retirement investment program will have grown large enough to cover the losses that death might bring.

- Retirement and widowhood reduce the need for life insurance or may even eliminate it altogether.

Figure 12.3 depicts a life insurance and investment plan recommended over an individual's life cycle. This plan is built on two cornerstones: (1) the purchase of term insurance for the bulk of life insurance needs (because term insurance is more flexible than cash-value insurance and provides more protection for each premium dollar) and (2) a systematic, regular

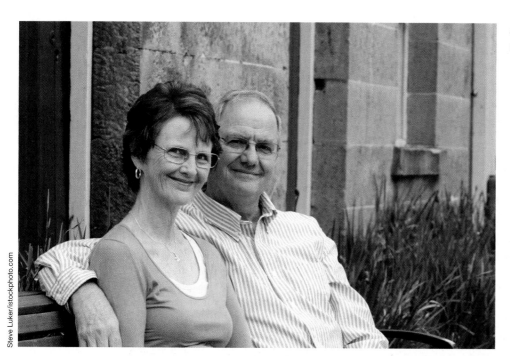

As a family ages, life insurance needs typically decrease.

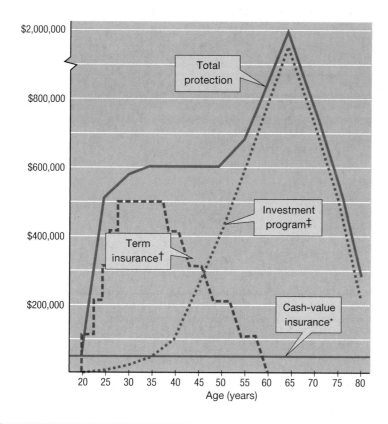

Figure 12.3
Wisely Using Life Insurance Investments over the Life Cycle

* With a guaranteed insurability option and paid-up at 65.

† Term insurance policies.

‡ Includes vested employer-sponsored retirement (e.g., 401[k]) plans. (See Chapter 17.)

Advice from a Pro...

Buy Term and Invest the Rest

The principle behind the strategy "buy term and invest the rest" is simple: If you invest the money difference between the cost of premiums for a term life insurance policy and the cost of premiums for a far more expensive cash-value policy, you will always come out ahead financially. To see why, consider the buildup of protection shown in the accompanying table for Seth Cameron, a 30-year-old art gallery administrator from New York who is considering life insurance policies. Seth could pay an $870 annual premium to buy a $100,000 whole life policy. Alternatively, he could spend $130 for the first-year premium of a $100,000 five-year renewable term policy and invest the $740 difference ($870 − $130) in a mutual fund account and earn a 5 percent after-tax rate of return.

If Seth dies tomorrow, the policy's beneficiary would receive both the $100,000 in insurance proceeds and the $740 in savings. After five years (age 35), Seth's annual $710 in savings would have grown to $4293; if he dies at that time, the total death benefit would be $104,293. If Seth dies years into the future, the estate is even further ahead because of the growing principal in the account. By age 60, Seth's mutual fund investment would have grown to $58,052. If the fund earned higher than 5 percent annually, the amount would be much greater. By the time Seth reached age 60, the term insurance premiums would exceed the premiums for the cash-value policy. However, his need for life insurance would presumably be eliminated or greatly reduced at that point. If Seth's children were self-supporting by then, he could probably drop the term insurance policy altogether. Nevertheless, his mutual fund account would remain to provide a financial nest egg of $58,052 or more to his heirs.

With the "buy term and invest the rest" strategy, Seth would have been insured more than 30 years at total premium cost of just $7350. By contrast, the cash-value policy would have required total premiums of $26,100 ($870 × 30) and the policy's cash value at year 30 would be about $44,000.

For "buy term and invest the rest" to work, however, the difference between the term and cash-value policy premiums must, in fact, be invested on a regular basis. Many people say that they will invest this money but then fail to follow through on that promise. You can succeed with a little discipline. The easiest way to ensure that your money is actually invested is to set up an automatic investment program (AIP) in which a mutual fund is authorized to withdraw money from your checking account, perhaps monthly, to buy mutual fund shares. When you agree to invest the "difference" automatically, the strategy will work well for you. (See Chapters 13 and 15.)

Estate Buildup If a Term Life Insurance Buyer Invests the Difference

Age	Premium for Five-Year Renewable Term	Difference (Not Spent on Whole Life)	Total Investment and Earnings* at 5%	Total Estate
30	$130	$740	$ 740	$100,740
35	150	720	4,293	104,293
40	180	690	9,657	109,657
45	210	660	16,328	116,328
50	240	630	24,668	124,668
55	590	290	35,139	135,139
60			58,052	58,052

*This illustration makes the following assumptions: The whole life policy premium for the same $100,000 in coverage is fixed at $870 every year; the buyer pays the five-year renewable term premium at the beginning of each year; and the difference is invested. Those amounts stay in the investments account all year, as does the previous year's ending balance. Investments earn a compounded 5 percent after-tax annual rate of return. Upon the insured's death, the beneficiary would receive the $100,000 face amount of the term life insurance policy plus the amount built up in the investments account earning 5 percent.

Source: Jordan E. Goodman, "America's Money Answers Man" (www.MoneyAnswers.com), author of *Everyone's Money Book* and *Everyone's Money Book* series.

investment program. The first type of life insurance to buy is a permanent cash-value policy with a guaranteed insurability option. A $20,000 to $50,000 policy is sufficient to cover final expenses, the only permanent need that is present throughout life. The remainder of your life insurance should consist of multiple term insurance policies that you start buying when you begin to have dependents. These should be five- or ten-year, level-premium, guaranteed renewable policies in increments of $100,000 or more. The policies should be layered so that you can drop policies as your need declines. By the time you reach retirement, you will have dropped all your term policies and the cash-value policy can remain to pay final expenses or be cashed in to provide a little retirement income. Of course, this scenario requires that you implement an investment program to save for retirement. Chapters 13 through 17 cover investments in sufficient detail to provide you with the necessary tools to construct this program.

layering term insurance policies
Purchasing level-premium term policies so that coverage grows when you need it most and then can be decreased as your needs change.

Did You Know?

How to Layer Your Term Insurance Policies for Only $60 per Month

Trying to meet one's life insurance needs with just one or two life insurance policies is not the best way to obtain protection over the life cycle. Life insurance needs fluctuate over one's lifetime, and you will need flexibility. Your life insurance needs are low (burial, debt repayment) until the moment when your first child is born or adopted. Then the need can easily spike up to $200,000 or $500,000 (or more). This need will remain high until the youngest child is approximately ten years old and then will decrease until your retirement age. You can meet the bulk of this need by **layering term insurance policies** so that coverage grows and then can be decreased as your needs change.

An example is provided in the following chart. It assumes that the person is age 25 when a first child is born and age 30 when a last child is born. In this example, the parents buy several level-premium term policies near the birth of the first child, with the policies having differing time periods. They buy another policy when their last child is born and another as the first child gets close to college age. As the children go out on their own, some of the earliest policies expire, thereby reducing the overall amount of insurance as the parents' needs decline.

One benefit of layering is affordability. Based on premium rates for healthy nonsmokers, the cost for the plan illustrated here would never be more than $60 per month.

Age	Buy	Policies in Force at Each Age	Total Coverage at Each Age
25	Policy 1, $100,000, 30 years	#1, #2, #3	$450,000
	Policy 2, $150,000, 25 years		
	Policy 3, $200,000, 20 years		
30	Policy 4, $150,000, 25 years	#1, #2, #3, #4	600,000
35		#1, #2, #3, #4	600,000
40	Policy 5, $50,000, 20 years	#1, #2, #3, #4, #5	650,000
45		#1, #2, #4, #5	450,000
50		#1, #4, #5	300,000
55		#5	50,000
60			0

State Insurance Departments Are a Good Consumer Resource

You can find information about life insurance companies through your state's insurance regulatory agency (www.naic.org/state_web_map.htm).

premium quote service
Offers computer-generated comparisons among 20 to 80 different companies.

insurance agent
Representative of an insurance company authorized to sell, modify, service, and terminate insurance contracts.

Where and How to Buy Your Life Insurance

The most important feature of any life insurance company is its ability to pay its obligations. The company you choose must have the stability and financial strength to survive for the many years your policy will remain in force. Ratings of the financial strengths of insurance companies are available from A.M. Best Company (www.ambest.com) and Standard & Poor's (www.standardandpoors.com).

You Can Get a Great Price Buying Life Insurance Online

Smart personal financial managers take a do-it-yourself approach to life insurance. They regularly calculate their needs and decide what types of insurance to buy and cancel in what increments. This allows them to use a **premium quote service** that offers computer-generated comparisons among 20 to 80 different companies. Premium quote services can be found at www.insure.com, www.quotescout.com, and www.accuquote.com. These websites also offer online life insurance needs calculators and a wealth of information on life insurance from an unbiased perspective. In addition, all the major life insurance companies have an online purchase system. Term insurance is easiest to buy this way, but even cash-value insurance can be purchased online.

Or You Can Use a Local Insurance Agent

An **insurance agent** is a representative of an insurance company authorized to sell, modify, service, and terminate insurance contracts. In the United States, life insurance is typically sold through exclusive agents who represent only one company, although some independent agents represent more than one company.

The life insurance agent must be qualified to design a program tailored to your specific needs and should understand the dynamics of family relationships, which influence all life insurance needs. The agent should have earned a professional designation, such as chartered life underwriter (CLU). To earn the CLU, an agent must have three years of experience and pass a ten-course program in life insurance counseling. Some agents also may have earned the certified financial planner (CFP) or chartered financial consultant (ChFC) designation (see Chapter 1, Table 1.4, page 26).

About Life Insurance Sales Commissions

Sales commissions are paid to the selling insurance agent every year that a life insurance policy remains in force. Very low sales commissions tend to be charged on term insurance policies—perhaps 10 percent or less of the premium if the policy is purchased directly rather than through an agent.

Sales commissions typically represent as much as 90 percent of the first-year premium paid for a cash-value life insurance policy. Over the next several years, commissions drop considerably (perhaps declining annually to 50, 40, 30, 20, and eventually 10 percent) so that more of the premium each year builds cash value.

You can buy all types of life insurance policies with low commissions on the Internet and through fee-only financial planners and fee-for-service insurance agents. Even policies sold with a low commission rate may have a surrender charge, which is a fee assessed if the policyholder withdraws some or all of the cash value accumulated. This charge is often highest in the early years of the policy but may be reduced or eliminated in later years. The policy illustrated in Table 12.1 has a surrender charge, for example. Ask about commissions and surrender charges whenever you shop for life insurance. Be wary of policies that have both high commissions and surrender charges.

Your agent should be willing to take the time to provide personal service and to answer all of your questions about the policy both before and after you purchase it. Always ask an agent about the first-year commission on any policies you are considering. In addition, you should check your agent's reputation with your state's insurance and securities investment regulatory agencies.

Compare Costs Among Policies   The price people pay for life insurance depends on their age, health, and lifestyle. Age is important, of course, because the probability of dying increases with age. A person who has a health problem such as heart disease or diabetes may pay considerably higher rates for life insurance or may not be able to obtain coverage at any price. People with hazardous occupations (police officers) or dangerous hobbies (skydivers) are often required to pay higher life insurance premiums as well. Life insurance companies typically offer their lowest prices to "preferred" applicants whose health status and lifestyle (for example, nonsmokers) suggest longevity. "Standard" and "impaired" applicants would pay more. Because companies differ in how they assign these labels to applicants, you should shop around for the best treatment.

Term life insurance premiums are usually quoted in dollars per $1000 of coverage. Generally, the higher the face amount of the policy, the lower the rate per $1000. For example, a company might sell term life insurance for $1 per $1000 per year when purchased in face amounts of $100,000 or more and for $1.25 per $1000 per year for policies of less than $100,000. Policies with face amounts of $1 million can cost less than $0.50 per $1000 per year for people younger than age 35.

It is easy to pay too much for term life insurance, especially if you do not comparison shop. The rates shown in Table 12.4 represent good values for term insurance. Note that smokers pay much higher premiums than nonsmokers because as a group smokers die ten years earlier than nonsmokers. Men pay more than women because they typically die three years earlier. Table 12.5 lists annual premiums that are near the average required for various types of insurance policies.

The cost of insurance measured in dollars per $1000 is not an appropriate way to compare term with cash-value insurance or when examining different types of cash-value insurance. Three methods are used to compare similar policies:

1. **Net cost method.** The **net cost** of a life insurance policy equals the total of all premiums to be paid minus any accumulated cash value and accrued dividends. It is calculated for a specific point in time during the life of the policy—for example, at the end of the 10th or 20th year. The net cost is often a negative figure, giving a false impression that the policy will pay for itself. You should ignore net cost calculations provided by a life insurance agent.

Table 12.4   Fair Prices for Term Life Insurance*

(Authors' estimates based on Internet shopping on the major quote services.)

Age	Nonsmokers		Smokers	
	Male	**Female**	**Male**	**Female**
18–30	$0.70	$0.67	$1.00	$0.95
35	$0.83	$0.74	$1.25	$1.15
40	$1.08	$1.00	$1.95	$1.60
45	$1.67	$1.60	$2.80	$2.40
50	$2.30	$2.20	$4.00	$3.25

*Multiply the rate by each $1000 of coverage and add $60 for estimated administrative fees. For example, a fair annual premium for a $50,000 policy for a 36-year-old male nonsmoker might be $101.50 ($0.83 × 50 = $41.50; $41.50 + $60 = $101.50).

Table 12.5   Typical Premiums* for Various Types of Life Insurance (Face Amount $100,000)

Policy Type	Policy Year							
	1	2	3	5	10	11	20	Age 65
Annual renewable term (guaranteed renewability to age 70)	$80	$81	$82	$83	$ 90	$ 92	$110	$2,400
Decreasing term (over 20 years)	160	160	160	160	160	160	160	0
Convertible term (within 5 years)	170	170	170	170	940	940	940	940
Whole life	870	870	870	870	870	870	870	870
Universal life	590	590	590	590	680	730	760	790
Limited-pay life (paid at age 65)	920	920	920	920	920	920	920	0

*Premiums quoted are for a 21-year-old male nonsmoker.

Do It NOW!

Having the proper amount and types of life insurance is essential to protect your loved ones' financial future. Start today by:

1. Finding out if and what type of life insurance you currently have.

2. Using the needs approach (a calculator can be found on this book's website) to determine your present need for additional life insurance.

3. Discussing the results of the above with your closest family members.

interest-adjusted net payment index (IANPI)
If a policy will remain in force until death, this method allows you to effectively measure the cost of cash-value insurance. The lower the IANPI, the lower the cost of the policy.

2. **Interest-adjusted cost index method.** A **cost index** is a numerical method used to compare the costs of similar plans of life insurance. The **interest-adjusted cost index (IACI)** measures the cost of life insurance, taking into account the interest that would have been earned had the premiums been invested rather than used to buy insurance. The lower the IACI, the lower the cost of the policy. Ask for 5-, 10-, 20-, and 30-year IACI values as well because companies have been known to manipulate their dividend and cash-value accumulations to look especially good at the 20-year point. You should insist on being told the index before you agree to buy a policy, and you should shop elsewhere if the agent refuses, resists, or implies that the index has little value.

3. **Interest-adjusted net payment index method.** The IACI assumes that the policy will be cashed in and surrendered at the end of a certain period (usually 20 years) rather than remaining in force until the death of the insured. If the policy will remain in force until death, you can use the **interest-adjusted net payment index (IANPI)** to effectively measure the cost of cash-value insurance. The lower the IANPI, the lower the cost of the policy.

Concept Check 12.4

1. List the benefits of buying term and investing the rest.
2. Identify the weaknesses of cash-value life insurance as a mechanism for saving for retirement.
3. Explain how the pattern of one's life insurance program should vary from young adulthood through retirement years.
4. Explain how you can benefit by layering your term insurance policies.

What Do You Recommend NOW?

Now that you have read the chapter on protecting loved ones through life insurance, what would you recommend to Karen and Will Bridgeman in the case at the beginning of the chapter regarding:

1. Their changing need for life insurance once they have a child?

2. What types of life insurance they should consider and whether they should purchase multiple policies?

3. Coordinating their retirement savings and other investments with their life insurance program?

4. Shopping for life insurance?

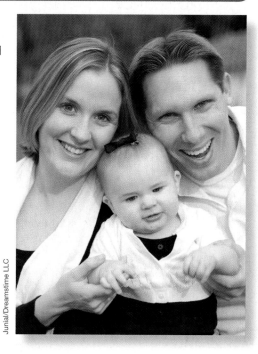

Junial/Dreamstime LLC

Big Picture Summary of Learning Objectives

1 Understand the reasons why you might need life insurance and calculate the appropriate amount of coverage.

Life insurance is designed to provide protection from the financial losses that result from death. The reasons to purchase life insurance change over the life cycle. The need for this type of protection is nonexistent or very small for children and single adults. Factors affecting life insurance needs include the need to replace income, final-expense needs, readjustment-period needs, debt-repayment needs, college-expense needs, availability of government programs, and ownership of other life insurance and assets. Two methods to calculate life insurance needs are the multiple-of-earnings approach and the needs-based approach. The needs-based approach is the more accurate of the two and should be conducted every three years or whenever your family situation changes.

2 Distinguish among types of life insurance.

Two basic types of life insurance exist: term life insurance and cash-value life insurance. Variations on term life insurance include decreasing term insurance, guaranteed renewable term insurance, convertible term insurance, and credit life insurance. Variations on cash-value insurance include whole life insurance, limited-pay life insurance, and universal and variable life insurance.

3 Explain the major provisions of life insurance policies.

A life insurance policy is a written contract between the insurance purchaser and the insurance company, spelling out in detail the terms of the agreement. When buying life insurance, you should pay attention to the policy's general terms and conditions, the special features of cash-value life insurance, and settlement options.

4 Apply a step-by-step strategy for implementing a life insurance plan.

Life insurance should be purchased to address the dying-too-soon problem. Your investments should manage the living-too-long problem. Addressing these two problems appropriately requires a small amount of cash-value life insurance, high amounts of term insurance while you are raising children, and a sound investment program to prepare for your retirement years. You should not purchase life insurance until you have determined the actual dollar amount and type of policy you need and compared premiums using various life insurance cost indices.

Let's Talk About It

1. **Thinking About Life Insurance.** What were your feelings about the need for life insurance before you read this chapter? What are they now? Have they been influenced by the recent poor economy?

2. **Are You Insured?** Are you covered by life insurance? If so, how much? Do you feel that you are over- or under-insured?

3. **Term Versus Cash-Value Insurance.** Why do you think people persist in buying cash-value life insurance when, in most cases, they would be better off buying term insurance and investing the money saved into a tax-sheltered retirement account?

4. **Life Insurance for Married Couples.** In many married-couple families, one of the spouses is the primary breadwinner and the other focuses more on homemaking duties. In your view, how does such an arrangement affect the approach that should be taken for each spouse in terms of life insurance?

5. **Life Insurance for Unmarried Couples.** Many young people today choose to cohabitate rather than marry (at least for some time period). Should this affect their thinking about life insurance?

Do the Math

1. **Life Insurance Needs for a Young Single.** Andrew Blake of Tuscaloosa, Alabama, is single and has been working as an admissions counselor at a university for three years. Andrew owns a home valued at $156,000 on which he owes $135,000. He has a two-year-old vehicle valued at $12,500 on which he owes $8000. He has about $3800 remaining on his student loans. His retirement account has grown to $7800, and he owns some stock valued at $4400. He has no life insurance and is considering buying some. How much should he buy?

2. **Life Insurance Needs for a Young Married Couple.** Kyle and Laura Parker from Ypsilanti, Michigan have been married for three years. They recently bought a home costing $212,000 using a $190,000 mortgage. They have no other debts. Kyle earns $42,000 per year and Laura $41,000. Each has a retirement plan valued at approximately $10,000. They recently received a mail offer from their mortgage lender for a mortgage life insurance policy of $190,000. Their only life insurance currently is a $20,000 cash-value survivorship joint life policy. They each would like to provide the other with support for five years if one of them should die.

    a. Assuming $10,000 in final expenses and $20,000 allocated to help make mortgage payments, calculate the amount of life insurance they need using the needs-based approach.

    b. How would their needs change if Laura became pregnant?

3. **Borrowing from a Cash-Value Life Insurance Policy.** Lauren Crow of Riverside, California, has a $100,000 participating cash-value policy written on her life. The policy has accumulated $4700 in cash value; Lauren has borrowed $3000 of this value. The policy also has accumulated unpaid dividends of $1666. Yesterday Lauren paid her premium of $1200 for the coming year. What is the current death benefit from this policy?

Financial Planning Cases

Case 1
Life Insurance for a Newly Married Couple

Just-married couples sometimes overindulge in the type and amount of life insurance that they buy. John and Nicole Greenwood of Murfreesboro, Tennessee, took a different approach. Both were working and had a small amount of life insurance provided through their respective employee benefit programs: John, $40,000, and Nicole, $50,000. During their discussion of life insurance needs and related costs, they decided that if Nicole completed her master's degree in industrial psychology, she would have better employment opportunities. Consequently, they decided to use money they had available for additional life insurance to pay for Nicole's education. They both feel, however, that they do not want to have inadequate life insurance.

(a) In what way does Nicole's return to school alter the Greenwoods' life insurance needs?

(b) Would you agree that the amount of life insurance provided by the Greenwoods' respective employers is adequate while Nicole is in school? Explain your response.

(c) Summarize how the Greenwoods' life insurance needs might change over their life cycle.

Case 2

Fraternity Members Contemplate Permanent Life Insurance

Zachary Chen is a college student from Prescott, Arizona. Soon to graduate, Zachary was approached recently by a life insurance agent, who set up a group meeting for several members of his fraternity. During the meeting, the agent presented six life insurance plans and was very persuasive about the benefits of a universal life insurance plan that his company calls Affordable Life II. Under the plan, the prospective graduate can buy $100,000 of permanent life insurance for a very low premium during the first five years and then pay a higher premium later when income presumably will have increased. Zachary was confused after the meeting, as were his friends. Armed with your knowledge from this personal finance book, you have been asked to respond to some of their questions.

(a) Do you think universal life insurance is a good deal for these people? Why or why not?

(b) How can the individual fraternity members decide how much life insurance they need?

(c) Life insurance cannot be as confusing as the agent made it seem. What clearer explanation would you give to the fraternity members?

(d) What type of life insurance, if any, would you advise for the fraternity brothers?

(e) How would they know if a life insurance policy is offered at a fair price?

Case 3

A Married Couple with Children Address Their Life Insurance Needs

Joseph and Samantha Hensley of Savannah, Georgia, are a married couple in their mid-30s. They have two children, ages five and three, and Samantha is pregnant with their third child. Samantha is a parttime book indexer who earned $15,000 after taxes last year. Because she performs much of her work at home, it is unlikely that she will need to curtail her work after the baby is born. Joseph is a family therapist; he earned $48,000 last year after taxes. Because both are self-employed, Samantha and Joseph do not have access to group life insurance. They are each covered by $50,000 universal life policies they purchased three years ago. In addition, Joseph is covered by a $50,000, five-year guaranteed renewable term policy, which will expire next year. The Hensleys are currently reassessing their life insurance program. As a preliminary step in their analysis, they have determined that Samantha's account with Social Security would yield the family about $1094 per month, or an annual benefit of $13,128, if she were to die. For Joseph, the figure would be $2072 per month, or an annual benefit of $24,864.

Both agree that they would like to support each of their children to age 22, but to date they have been unable to start a college savings fund. The couple estimates that it would cost $40,000 to put each child through a regional university in their state as measured in today's dollars. They expect that burial expenses for each spouse would total about $12,000, and they would like to have a lump sum of $50,000 to help the surviving spouse make payments on their home mortgage. They also feel that each spouse would want to take a six-month leave from work if the other were to die.

(a) Calculate the amount of life insurance that Samantha needs based on the information given. Use the Run the Numbers worksheet on page 346 or the *Garman/Forgue* companion website. Assume a 3 percent rate of return after taxes and inflation and an income need for 22 years because the unborn child will need financial support for that many years.

(b) Calculate the amount of life insurance that Joseph needs based on the information given. Use the Run the Numbers worksheet on page 346 or the *Garman/Forgue* companion website. Assume a 3 percent rate of return after taxes and inflation and an income need for 22 years because the unborn child will need financial support for that many years.

(c) If Samantha and Joseph purchased term insurance to cover their additional needs, how much more would each need to spend on life insurance based on the information in Table 12.4?

Case 4

Victor and Maria Hernandez Contemplate Switching Life Insurance Policies

Victor and Maria Hernandez have a total of $200,000 in life insurance. Victor has a $50,000 cash-value policy purchased more than 20 years ago when the couple was first married and a $100,000 group term policy through his employer. Maria has a $50,000 group term insurance policy through her employer. The couple has been approached by a life insurance agent who thinks that they need to change their policy mix because, he says, they are inadequately insured. Specifically, the agent has suggested that Victor cash in his cash-value policy and buy a new variable-universal life insurance policy.

(a) If Victor cashes in his policy, what options would he have when receiving the cash value?

(b) Determine what the $16,000 in cash value in Victor's life insurance policy would be worth in 20 years if that sum were invested somewhere else and earned an 8 percent annual return. (Hint: Use the *Garman/Forgue* companion website.)

(c) Would cashing in the policy be a wise decision? Why or why not?

(d) As the Hernandezes' children are now grown and out on their own, and both Victor and Maria are employed full time, give general reasons why Victor may need more or less insurance.

(e) Explain why it would be a bad idea for Victor to buy a variable-universal life insurance policy.

Case 5
The Johnsons Change Their Life Insurance Coverage

Harry and Belinda Johnson spend $9 per month on life insurance in the form of a premium on a $10,000, paid-at-65 cash-value policy on Harry. Belinda has a group term insurance policy from her employer with a face amount of $59,400 (1.5 times her annual salary). By choosing a group life insurance plan from his menu of employee benefits, Harry now has $30,900 (his annual salary) of group term life insurance. Harry and Belinda have decided that, because they have no children, they could reduce their life insurance needs by protecting one another's income for only four years, assuming the survivor would be able to fend for himself or herself after that time. They also realize that their savings fund is so low that it would have no bearing on their life insurance needs. Harry and Belinda are basing their calculations on a projected 4 percent rate of return after taxes and inflation. They also estimate the following expenses: $10,000 for final expenses, $6000 for readjustment expenses, and $5000 for repayment of short-term debts.

(a) Should the $3000 interest earnings from Harry's trust fund be included in his annual income for the purposes of calculating the likely dollar loss if he were to die? (See the discussions about the Johnsons at the end of Chapter 2.) Explain your response.

(b) Based on your response to the previous question, how much more life insurance does Harry need? Use the Run the Numbers worksheet on page 346 to arrive at your answer.

(c) Repeat the calculations to arrive at the additional life insurance needed on Belinda's life.

(d) How might the Johnsons most economically meet any additional life insurance needs you have determined they may have?

(e) In addition to their life insurance planning, how might the Johnsons begin to prepare for their retirement years?

On the 'Net

Go to the Web pages indicated to complete these exercises. You can also go to the *Garman/Forgue* companion website at www.cengage.com/finance/garman/ for an expanded list of exercises. Under Economics and Business select "Finance" and then "Personal Finance" and select the title of this text. Click on the Internet Exercises link for this chapter.

1. Visit the website for AccuQuote at www.accuquote.com to obtain a quote for the annual premium on a $200,000 guaranteed renewable, ten-year term policy for you. Then call a life insurance agent in your community to obtain a quote on the same term insurance coverage. How do the term rates quoted by your local agent compare with the rates found over the Internet? Also, ask for the quote on a $100,000 universal life policy with guaranteed insurability and waiver-of-premium options. Ask the agent to explain why the quotes for the two types of policies differ. Analyze his or her response based on what you learned in this chapter.

2. Visit the website for A.M. Best Company at www.am .best.com/ratings and check the ratings for the insurance company recommended by the agent in Exercise 1 as well as the company with the lowest cost for term insurance that you found on the Web. What do the ratings tell you about the relative strengths of those companies?

3. Visit the Life and Health Insurance Foundation for Education www.lifehappens.org website. Click on "Life Insurance" then "How much do I need" and then "Insurance needs calculator." Calculate your current need for life insurance. Then recalculate your need for five years from now given your estimates of your income and family situation.

Visit the Garman/Forgue companion website . . .

PART 4

Spencer Grant / PhotoEdit

Investment Fundamentals

!You Must Be Kidding, Right?

Twins Laura and Lauren Jackson have worked for the same employer for many years. They have always differed in their investment philosophies toward saving for retirement. Laura invested $5000 for 10 years starting at age 25 and never added any more money to the account. Lauren invested $5000 per year for 20 years starting at age 35 and never contributed more to her account. Assuming that they both earn an 8 percent annual return, how much more money will Laura have accumulated for retirement than Lauren by the time they reach age 65?

- **A.** $144,000
- **B.** $234,000
- **C.** $494,000
- **D.** $778,000

The answer is B, $234,000. Laura's account balance at age 65 is projected at $778,000 and Lauren's is $494,000. Even though Laura saved for only 10 years compared with Lauren's 20 years of saving, Laura's long-term investment approach had her starting to save for retirement early in her working career. Thus, she accumulated 47 percent more money than her sister ($234,000 ÷ $494,000). Starting early on long-term investment goals is a money-winning idea!

Learning Objectives

After reading this chapter, you should be able to:

1 Explain how to get started as an investor.

2 Discover your own investment philosophy.

3 Identify the kinds of investments that match your interests.

4 Describe the major factors that affect the rate of return on investments.

5 Decide which of the five long-term investment strategies you will utilize.

6 Create your own investment plan.

Pali Rao/istockphoto.com

Jennifer and Julia are sisters, both in their 20s. Jennifer drives a leased BMW convertible, and she makes about $42,000, including tips, as a part-time bartender at two different restaurants. Although she has no employee benefits, she enjoys having flexible work hours so that she can go to the beach and the local nightspots. Currently, Jennifer has $10,000 in credit card debt. She has $1500 in a bank savings account, and two years ago she opened an individual retirement account (IRA) with a $1000 investment in a mutual fund. Her sister Julia drives a paid-for Honda Civic, pays her credit card purchases in full each month, and sacrifices some of her salary by putting $100 per month into her employer's company stock through her 401(k) retirement account. Over the past seven years, the stock price, which was once about $40, has risen to almost $70, and Julia's 401(k) plan is now worth about $16,000. Julia also has invested about $14,000 in aggressive-growth mutual funds, and she plans to use that money for a down payment on a home purchase. She earns $58,000 as a manager of a restaurant, plus she receives an annual bonus ranging from $2000 to $4000 every January that she uses for a spring vacation in Mexico. Julia's employer provides many employee benefits.

What do you recommend to Jennifer and Julia on the subject of investment fundamentals regarding:

1. Getting more money to save and invest?

2. Prerequisites to investing for Jennifer?

3. Portfolio diversification for Julia?

4. Dollar-cost averaging for Jennifer?

5. Investment alternatives for Julia?

At many points in this book, we have encouraged you to set aside funds for the future, especially by accumulating funds through regular savings. This approach is a wise course of action, but building real wealth requires an additional consideration—earning a good rate of return on your money. The difference in the return is a major distinction between mere savings and investing.

For most of the past 25 years one of the best ways to make money over the long term was to invest in stocks, bonds, and mutual funds that invest in those vehicles. Despite the recent economic meltdown this remains the best advice. The earning power of the U.S. and world economies, even with serious fluctuations, endures. This chapter (and the following four) explains both why this is true and how to succeed during times of economic recession or in a rapidly growing economy. Being clueless about investing is not an option for those who want to achieve financial success.

This chapter begins by examining how to get started in investments. It then helps you identify your personal investment philosophy. The next section gives an overview of investment possibilities—whether you as an investor want to lend or own and whether you prefer to be a short- or long-term investor. We also examine the major factors that affect an investment's rate of return, such as market risk, inflation, time horizon, and taxes. Rather than trying to time the market, the wise investor uses the investment strategies of buy and hold, portfolio diversification, asset allocation, modern portfolio theory, and dollar-cost averaging. The chapter closes with step-by-step details on how to create your own investment plan.

Starting Your Investment Program

1 Learning Objective
Explain how to get started as an investor.

To help secure a desirable future lifestyle, you cannot spend every dollar that you earn today. Instead, you must sacrifice by setting aside some of your current income and investing it. You postpone the pleasure of using money for here-and-now consumption so you can have more in the future. To be financially successful, it is wise to start investing early in life, invest regularly, and stay invested. Why? Because, for every five years you delay investing, you will have to double your monthly investment amount to achieve the same goals. Remember: You—and no one else—are responsible for your own financial success.

Starting an investment program requires understanding how investing differs from savings, getting ready to invest, and deciding why you want to invest. Then after you find the money to invest, you can contemplate the types of returns you might anticipate from your investments.

Investing Is More Than Saving

investing
Putting saved money to work so that it makes you even more money.

Savings is the accumulation of excess funds by intentionally spending less than you earn. Investing is more. **Investing** is taking some of the money you are saving and putting it to work so that it makes you even more money. Your goals and the time it will take to reach those goals dictate the investment strategies you follow and the investment alternatives you choose.

securities
Assets suitable for investment, including stocks, bonds, and mutual funds.

The most common ways that people invest are by putting money into assets called **securities**, such as stocks, bonds, and mutual funds (often through their employer-sponsored retirement accounts), and by buying real estate. **Stocks** are shares of ownership in a corporation, and bonds represent loans to companies and governments. All of your investment assets make up your **portfolio**, the collection of multiple investments in different assets chosen to meet your investment goals.

stocks
Shares of ownership in a corporation.

portfolio
Collection of investments assembled to meet your investment goals.

Are You Ready to Invest?

Here are signs you are ready to begin an investment program:

- **You live within your income.** If you find yourself constantly running short of cash toward the end of the month or if you make only minimum payments on your credit card balances, you need to institute budget controls so you can live within your means.

- **You are able to save regularly.** A good financial manager forgoes some spending to save regularly to build an emergency fund, acquire goods and services, and achieve other goals. You can't invest unless you have some savings with which to begin.

- **You use credit wisely.** Pay off any high-interest debt. Pay credit card bills in full each month. Have a maximum credit limit sufficient to meet personal financial emergencies.

- **You carry adequate insurance.** Liability insurance protects your assets and lifestyle in the event you experience a loss and/or are sued. Health insurance is a must. Term life insurance protects the lifestyle of dependents.

Decide Why You Want to Invest

When you have reasons to invest, such as to buy a home or plan for a financially satisfying retirement, you will be more likely to consider "investments" as a high-priority category in your budget. Your investments can increase your income and help maximize your enjoyment of life. People invest for four reasons:

- To achieve financial goals, such as taking a vacation, purchasing a new car, making a down payment on a home, financing a child's education, or starting a business

- To gain wealth and a feeling of financial security

- To increase current income

- To meet retirement income needs

Where Can You Get the Money to Invest?

You must save money to have it for investing. See Figure 13.1 and the following suggestions:

- **Pay yourself first.** Live within your means every time you receive income by earmarking in your budget money for saving.

- **Save—don't spend—extra funds.** When unexpected money arrives, save part or all of it. Examples of extra money are a year-end employer bonus, a commission check, a salary raise, a gift of money, an inheritance, and an income tax refund. Also, when you have a surplus in a monthly budget category, save it.

- **Participate in your employer's retirement plan.** When your employer offers to match your contribution to a 401(k) retirement plan, invest at least enough to get the full match because it's free money.

- **Make saving automatic.** Have funds automatically transferred from your bank to a savings account as well as from your paycheck to your retirement plan.

- **Continue to make installment payments to yourself.** If you make installment repayments on a debt or lease, continue to make the "payments" to your savings account after the debt has been repaid.

- **Break a habit.** Put aside the money you would have spent on a former habit, such as buying lottery tickets, lattes at Starbucks, and enjoying restaurant lunches.

- **Get a part-time job.** Save the after-tax money earned from an extra job.

- **Scrimp for one month.** To succeed, cut back and question every possible expense. Knowing that this level of frugality will end after 30 days will help motivate you.

Your Next Five Years

In the next five years you can start achieving financial success by doing the following related to investment fundamentals:

1. Sacrifice some income and put some cash into a diversified investment portfolio for the future.

2. Accept more risk when investing for the long term.

3. Invest regularly through your employer's retirement plan.

4. Invest no more than 5 or 10 percent of your portfolio in any single company stock including that of your employer.

5. Rebalance your portfolio at least once a year based on your chosen asset allocation strategy.

Figure 13.1
"If You Want to Save $1000...."

Source: Created by the LFE Institute, a corporate skill-based financial literacy curriculum developer. Copyright © LFE Institute.

If you want to *save $1,000* this year, ask yourself these questions...before you buy!

1. Did I plan to buy this?

2. If I have to pay cash, do I still want it?

3. What will happen if I don't buy this?

4. Do I need this... or just want it?

financial risk
Possibility that an investment will fail to pay a return to the investor.

total return
Income an investment generates from current income and capital gains.

current income
Money received while you own an investment; usually received regularly as interest, rent, or dividends.

interest
Charge for borrowing money; investors in bonds earn interest.

capital gain
Increase in the value of an initial investment (less costs) realized upon the sale of the investment.

capital loss
Decrease in paper value of an initial investment; only realized if sold.

Instant Message

Creating Wealth

For most people it is difficult to accumulate wealth by saving out of earnings. Most wealth comes from capital gains. To create wealth, use your savings to invest in stocks, bonds, mutual funds, or real estate and/or start a business.

What Investment Returns Are Possible?

Figure 13.2 shows the long-term rates of return on some popular investments. When people invest their money, they take a **financial risk** (also called **business risk**)—namely, the possibility that the investment will fail to pay them any return to the investor. At the extremes, a company could have a very good year earning a considerable profit, or it could go bankrupt, causing investors to lose all of their money. Later in the chapter, we examine how investing poses a number of other kinds of risk.

Investors hope that their investments will earn them a positive **total return,** which is the income an investment generates from a combination of current income and capital gains. **Current income** is money received while you own an investment. It is usually received on a regular basis as interest, rent, or dividends. As we have noted elsewhere in the text, **interest** is the charge for borrowing money. Investors in bonds earn interest. **Rent** is payment received in return for allowing someone to use your real estate property, such as land or a building. A **dividend** is a portion of a company's earnings that the firm pays out to its shareholders. For example, Nina Hernandez from Oneonta, New York, purchased 100 shares of H&M stock at $45 per share ($4500) last year. The company paid dividends of $3 per share during the year, so Nina received $300 in cash dividends as current income.

A **capital gain** occurs only when you actually sell the investment; it results from an increase in the value of the initial investment. It is calculated by subtracting the total amount paid for the investment (including purchase transaction costs) from the higher price at which it is sold (minus any sales transaction costs). For example, if the price of H&M company stock rose to $52 during the year, Nina could sell it for a capital gain. If Nina paid a transaction cost of $1 per share at both purchase and time of sale, her capital gain would be $500 [($5200 − $100) − ($4500 + $100)].

Capital losses can occur as well. For most investments, a trade-off arises between capital gains and current income. Investments with potential for high capital gains often pay little current income, and investments that pay substantial current income generally have little or no potential for capital gains. Long-term investors are usually willing to forgo current income in favor of possibly earning substantial future capital gains.

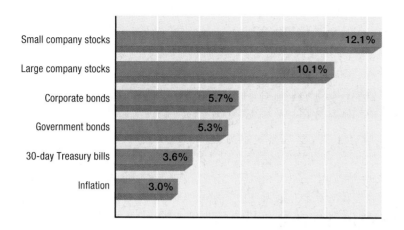

Figure 13.2
The Long-Term Rates of Return on Investments
(Annualized returns from 1926 through 2000)

The **rate of return,** or **yield,** is the total return on an investment expressed as a percentage of its price. It is usually stated on an annualized basis. For example, if Nina sells the H&M stock for $52 per share after one year, she will have a total return of $800 ($300 in dividends plus $500 in capital gains). Her yield would be 17.78 percent ($800 ÷ $4500).

rate of return/yield
Total return on an investment expressed as a percentage of its price.

 Concept Check 13.1

1. What should you do before you are ready to invest?
2. Identify three ways that you personally could find some money to invest in the next five years.
3. What are the two parts of an investor's total return?

Discover Your Investment Philosophy

Achieving financial success requires that you understand your investment philosophy and adhere to it when investing. Thus, you also need to know about investment risk and what to do about it. Keep in mind the advice offered by investment guru Warren Buffett, "The first rule of investing is don't lose money; the second rule is don't forget Rule No. 1."

2 Learning Objective
Discover your own investment philosophy.

How to Handle Investment Risk

Pure risk, which exists when there is no potential for gain, only the possibility of loss, was discussed in Chapter 10. Investments, in contrast, are subject to **speculative risk,** which exists in situations that offer potential for gain as well as for loss. **Investment risk** represents the uncertainty that the yield on an investment will deviate from what is expected. For most investments, the greater the risk the higher the potential return. This potential for gain is what motivates people to accept increasingly greater levels of risk, as illustrated in Figure 13.3. Nevertheless, many people remain seriously averse to risk.

This figure also provides insight about possible investment choices. Don't be overwhelmed because all of these investments are explained in the following chapters. You *will* learn how to make informed investment decisions for yourself.

speculative risk
Involves the potential for either gain or loss; equity investments might do either.

investment risk
The possibility that the yield on an investment will deviate from its expected return.

Figure 13.3
The Risk Pyramid Reveals the Trade-offs Between Risk and Return

Did You Know?

What Happened to All the Money?

Many trillions of dollars in stock market value, money in 401(k) retirement accounts, college savings funds, and equity in homes disappeared! The stock market crash and declining home prices means a lot of money no longer exists. Well, to be honest, it never existed because it was not money in the first place. Money is cash, and an investment or equity in a home is not cash until the asset is converted into cash. Potential money is not the same as cash.

risk premium
Amount that risk-averse investors require for taking on a riskier investment rather than a risk-free investment like U.S. government securities. The riskier the investment, the greater the premium demanded.

Instant Message

Accept More Risk

Most investors are too risk averse. You can accept more risk when investing for long-term goals.

Investors need the promise of a high return to warrant placing their money at risk in an investment. If you want a completely safe investment, you can invest in U.S. Treasury securities (discussed in Chapter 14), which are backed by the full faith and credit of the U.S. government. With this sort of investment, you loan your money to the federal government and it is later returned with interest. One form of Treasury securities is the short-term Treasury bill, or **T-bill,** which is a government IOU of one year of less. Because T-bills are risk-free investments, they pay too low a return for most people unless they are simply safeguarding their money to invest at a later time.

If you invest only in T-bills, you will miss out on the significantly higher returns that other investments, such as stocks and stock mutual funds, can provide. When making investments, people demand a **risk premium** for their willingness to make investments for which there is no guarantee of future success. This risk premium constitutes the difference between a riskier investment's return and the totally safe return on the T-bill. Industry experts figure that the amount of the risk premium for most investors is 3 percent or higher, although it varies depending upon the investment alternative. A top-quality corporate bond pays about 2 percentage points more than T-bills, so if the latter rate is 1.5 percent, the potential return to the bond investor should be about 6.5 percent (0.02 + 0.03 + 0.015). Because stocks historically earn at least 4 percentage points more than T-bills, the anticipated return to the stock investor should be 8.5 percent (0.045 + 0.04) or more. Higher-risk investments carry higher risk premiums. A variety of investment alternatives are available to fit each investor's requirements.

Ultraconservative Investors Are Really Just Savers

The world of investments offers many ways to save that present little or no risk of losing your principal and still earn respectable—albeit limited—returns. These financial vehicles include federally insured savings accounts, certificates of deposit, and EE bonds, as well as money market accounts. Ultraconservative investors, especially those who cannot sleep at night if they think their money is at risk, do not consider putting money into investments, choosing instead to stick with the safest options. Over the course of a year, an ultraconservative investor who places $1000 in one of these options will not lose a penny and will likely gain $15 to $20. In actuality, ultraconservative investors are not really investors. They are savers. As a result, they do not get ahead financially over the long term because taxes and inflation offset most, if not all, of their interest earnings. On the other hand, when asset values sharply decline ultraconservative investors still have their money!

Take a Risk-Tolerance Quiz

Find out how much risk you can comfortably tolerate by taking a risk-tolerance quiz at one of the following websites:

- Bankrate.com: www.bankrate.com/brm/news/investing/20011127a.asp
- MSN: www.moneycentral.msn.com/investor/calcs/n_riskq/main.asp
- WalletPop: http://www.walletpop.com/

What Is Your Investment Philosophy?

Investors have to take risks that are appropriate to reach their financial goals. The task is to find the right balance and make choices accordingly. You must weigh the risks of an investment with the likelihood of not reaching your goal. Your **risk tolerance** is your ability to weather changes in the values of your investments. To be successful in investing, your tolerance for risk must be factored into your investment philosophy. If you lose sleep over your investments, you know it is time to reduce your risk and adjust your investment philosophy.

An **investment philosophy** is one's general approach to tolerance for risk in investments, whether it is conservative, moderate, or aggressive, given the financial goals to be achieved. The more risk you take, within reason, the more you can expect to earn and accumulate over the long term. Smart investors follow their investment philosophy without wavering; they do not change course unless their basic objectives change.

Are You a Conservative Investor?
If you have a **conservative investment philosophy,** you accept very little risk and are generally rewarded with relatively low rates of return for seeking the twin goals of a moderate amount of current income and preservation of capital. **Preservation of capital** means that you do not want to lose any of the money you have invested. In short, you could be characterized as risk averse.

Conservative investors focus on protecting themselves. They do so by carefully avoiding losses and trying to stay with investments that demonstrate gains, often for long time periods (perhaps for five or ten years). Tactically, they rarely sell their investments. Investors who are approaching retirement or who are planning to withdraw money from their investments in the near future often adhere to a conservative investment philosophy.

Conservative investors typically consider investing in obligations issued by the government. Examples include Treasury bills, notes, and bonds (insured as to timely payment of principal and interest by the U.S. government), municipal bonds, high-quality (blue-chip) corporate bonds and stocks, balanced mutual funds (which own both stocks and bonds), certificates of deposit, and annuities. A **bond** is essentially a loan that the investor makes to a government or a corporation. Thus, a bond is a debt of the issuer. Over the course of a year, a conservative investor with $1000 could possibly lose $20 and is likely to gain $20 to $40.

Are You a Moderate Investor?
People with a **moderate investment philosophy** seek capital gains through slow and steady growth in the value of their investments along with some current income. They invite only a fair amount of risk of capital loss. Most have no immediate need for the funds but instead focus on laying the investment foundation for later years or building on such a base. Moderate investors are fairly comfortable during rising and falling market conditions. They remain secure in the knowledge

risk tolerance
An investor's ability and willingness to weather changes in security prices, that is, to weather market risk.

investment philosophy
Investor's general tolerance for risk in investments, whether it is conservative, moderate, or aggressive, given the investor's financial goals.

conservative investment philosophy (risk aversion)
Investors with this philosophy accept very little risk and are generally rewarded with relatively low rates of return for seeking the twin goals of a moderate amount of current income and preservation of capital.

bond
A debt instrument issued by an organization that promises repayment at a specific time and the right to receive regular interest payments during the life of the bond; from investor's standpoint, a loan that the investor makes to a government or a corporation.

moderate investment philosophy (risk indifference)
Investors with this philosophy accept some risk as they seek capital gains through slow and steady growth in investment value along with current income.

aggressive investment philosophy (risk seeker)
Investors with this philosophy primarily seek capital gains, often with a short time horizon.

that they are investing for the long term. Their tactics might include spreading investment funds among several choices and trading some assets perhaps once a year.

People seeking moderate returns consider investing in dividend-paying common stocks, growth and income mutual funds, high-quality corporate bonds, government bonds, and real estate. Over the course of a year, a moderate investor with $1000 could possibly lose $150 and is likely to gain $50 to $80.

Are You an Aggressive Investor?

If you choose to strive for a very high return by accepting a high level of risk, you have an **aggressive investment philosophy.** As such, you could be characterized as a risk seeker. Aggressive investors primarily seek capital gains. Many such investors take a short-term approach, remaining confident that they can profit substantially during major upswings in market prices.

People seeking exceptionally high returns consider investing in common stocks of new or fast-growing companies, high-yielding junk bonds, and aggressive-growth mutual funds. Such investors may put their money into limited real estate partnerships, undeveloped land, precious metals, gems, commodity futures, stock-index futures, and collectibles. Devotees of this investment philosophy sometimes do not spread their funds among many alternatives. Also, they may adopt short-term tactics to increase capital gains. For example, aggressive investors might place most of their investment funds in a single stock in the hope that it will rise 10 percent over 90 days, giving an annual yield of more than 40 percent. Those shares could then be sold and the money invested elsewhere.

Investment tactics for aggressive investors are discussed in Chapter 16. Aggressive investors must be emotionally and financially able to weather substantial short-term losses—such as a downward swing in a stock's price of 30 or 40 percent even though they might expect that an upswing in price will occur in the future. Over the course of a year, an aggressive investor with $1000 could possibly lose $300 and could gain $100, $150, or even more.

Should You Take an Active or Passive Investing Approach?

Another aspect of your personal investment philosophy is your level of involvement in investing. That is, do you want to be an active or passive investor?

active investor
An investor who wishes to manage her own account by carefully studying the economy, market trends, and investment alternatives; regularly monitoring these factors; and buying and selling three to four times a year to rebalance her or his portfolio.

Active Investing

An **active investor** carefully studies the economy, market trends, and investment alternatives; regularly monitors these factors; and makes decisions to buy and sell, perhaps three or four or more times a year, with or without the advice of a professional. In addition, because the prices of many investments vary with certain news events, world happenings, and economic and political variables, active investors stay alert. Knowing what is going on in the larger world helps active investors understand when to buy or to sell investments quickly so as to reap profits and/or reduce losses.

market efficiency
The speed at which new information is reflected in investment prices suggesting that security prices are reflective of their true value at all times because publicly available information has driven market prices to the correct level.

Active Investing in an Efficient Market

Market efficiency has to do with the speed at which new information is reflected in investment prices. The theory is that security prices are reflective of their true value at all times because publicly available information has driven market prices to the correct level. Stock analysts and investment managers believe they can make better choices than the average in part because they can act on information more quickly than other investors. But on average most do not.

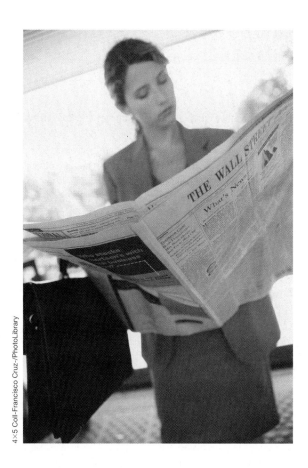

4×5 Coll-Francisco Cruz-/PhotoLibrary

An active investor keeps a close watch on the economy and financial markets.

The typical investor is even more challenged. When information is reported in the financial press, it is already too late for the typical investor to act and make a profit. And investors don't always even know which information is relevant. Therefore, individual investors cannot beat the market as they are just as likely to invest in an overpriced security rather than one which is undervalued. Thus, the typical investor will not consistently beat the market.

Passive Investing A **passive investor** does not actively engage in trading of securities or spend large amounts of time monitoring his or her investments. Such an individual may make regular investments in securities, such as mutual funds (described in Chapter 15), and his or her assets are rarely sold for short-term profits. Instead, passive investors simply aim to match the returns of the entire market. They ignore "hot" tips and the investment of the day touted in the financial press. They keep their emotions in check, and they earn higher returns than active investors over the long term. Most long-term investors utilize a passive approach.

Once you have clarified your investment philosophy and how involved you want to be as an investor, you will be able to make future investing decisions with confidence and conviction. You will be able to show patience by following your long-term views rather than make emotional and wrong decisions—in other words, mistakes—about your money. The investments you choose and the returns earned are likely to match your investment philosophy.

passive investor
An investor who does not actively engage in trading securities or monitoring his or her investments; seeks to match the market return via mutual funds or other managed investments in the longer term.

Did You Know?

Why Americans Are Lousy at Investing Their Money

Over the past decade, the typical investor in America—the average person who puts money into stock mutual funds—earned 5.0 percent a year, according to the consulting firm Dalbar. That is about half of what the S&P 500 stock market index delivered during that time. Over the past 20 years, the figures are worse, investors producing gains of 3.5 percent compared with stock market averages of 10 percent annually.

Why? American investors are inept. Investor behavior often turns into "herd behavior" with alternating times of euphoria and panic. Many people feel compelled to look at prices in the newspaper every day and watch or tune in the financial media, such as on CNBC and CNN, which sensationalize every blip of change in the stock markets.

Such negative information creates anxiety and this can lead to bad decision making.

Inexperienced investors make emotional errors when they fail to stay within the bounds of their personal investment philosophy. Greed leads to bad decisions, such as chasing the latest investment fad. Impatience leads to jumping in and out of investments. Investors who buy what they do not understand often wind up with a mishmash of investments. They buy high and sell low. This unhappy result arises when people forget to match their financial decisions with their disposition toward risk and their broad long-term goals. Your job as an investor is to be a steward of your financial security and not get caught up in the passions of the moment.

So What Should You Do?

Smart investors understand their personal investment philosophy. Some people are very conservative by nature. Others take a moderate approach to risk while others tend to be very aggressive and enjoy risk. Actually, none of these philosophies is correct all the time. Much more important is the time horizon of the goal for which you are investing. When investing for a short-term goal you would want to be very conservative to ensure that a sudden drop in the market would not jeopardize your reaching the goal before the market has time to recover. When investing for long-term goals you can afford to be more aggressive. That is why the stock market is a good place to save for retirement. Even at retirement age you can leave a portion of your portfolio in stocks since you still have 20 to 25 years before needing the last dollars out of your nest egg.

 Concept Check 13.2

1. Summarize your investment philosophy and general approach to tolerance for risk.
2. Indicate whether you view yourself as an active or passive investor, and explain why.
3. Summarize why so many people are lousy investors and not very successful.

Identify the Kinds of Investments You Want to Make

3 Learning Objective

Identify the kinds of investments that match your interests.

The investments you choose should match your interests. Before investing, think about lending versus owning, short term versus long term, and how to select investments that are likely to provide your desired potential total return.

Do You Want to Lend or Own?

You can invest money in two ways, by lending or by owning. When you lend your money, you receive some form of IOU and the promise of repayment plus interest. The interest is a form of current income while you hold the investment. Lending investments rarely result in capital gains.

You can lend by depositing money in banks, credit unions, and savings and loan associations (via savings accounts and certificates of deposit) or by lending money to governments (via Treasury notes and bonds as well as state and local bonds), businesses (corporate bonds), mortgage-backed bonds (such as Ginnie Maes), and life insurance companies (annuities). These lending investments, or **debts,** generally offer both a fixed maturity and a fixed income. With a **fixed maturity,** the borrower agrees to repay the principal to the investor on a specific date. With a **fixed income,** the borrower agrees to pay the investor a specific rate of return for use of the principal. Such investments allow lenders to be fairly confident that they will receive a certain amount of interest income for a specified period of time and that the borrowed funds will eventually be returned. Thus, the return is somewhat assured. No matter how much profit the borrower makes with your funds, the investing lender receives only the fixed return promised at the time of the initial investment.

Alternatively, you may invest money through ownership of an asset. Ownership investments are often called **equities.** You can buy common or preferred corporate stock (to obtain part ownership in a corporation) in publicly owned companies, purchase shares in a mutual fund company (which invests your funds in corporate stocks and bonds), put money into your own business, purchase real estate, buy commodity futures (pork bellies or oranges), or buy investment-quality collectibles (such as rare antiques or stamps). Ownership investments have the potential for providing current income; however, the emphasis is usually upon achieving substantial capital gains.

debts
Lending investments that typically offer both a fixed maturity and a fixed income.

fixed maturity
Specific date on which borrower agrees to repay the principal to the investor.

fixed income
Specific rate of return that borrower agrees to pay the investor for use of the principal (initial investment).

equities
Ownership equities such as common or preferred stocks, equity mutual funds, real estate, and so on that focus on capital gains more than on income.

Making Short-, Intermediate-, and Long-Term Investments

If you are investing for a short-term time horizon of less than a year or an intermediate-term of perhaps up to five years, you want to be confident that you preserve the value of what you have. After all, you don't want to lose money in an investment when you need to use that money for a near-term goal, such as college tuition, or be forced to sell an investment because you need cash in a hurry. People with a short or intermediate time horizon require investments that offer some predictability and stability. As a result, these investors are usually more interested in current income than capital gains. If you are investing to achieve long-term goals, by contrast, you want your money to grow, and, therefore, you are likely to keep your money in the same investments for 10 or 15 years. Long-term investors usually invite more risk by seeking capital gains as well as current income. Table 13.1 provides an overview of investments for various time horizons, and Table 13.2 on page 387 gives an overview of investment alternatives that might best fit your needs.

Choose Investments for Their Components of Total Return

When investing, you want to build a portfolio of investments that will provide the necessary potential total return through current income and capital gains in the proportions that you desire. One stock might provide an anticipated cash dividend of 1.5 percent and an expected annual price appreciation of 6 percent, for a total anticipated return of 7.5 percent. Another choice offering the same projected total return might be a stock with expected annual cash dividends of 2.5 percent and capital gains of 5 percent.

Table 13.1   Investments for Various Time Horizons

Time Periods	Possible Investments
Less than 2 years	NOW checking account
	Savings account
	Money market account
	Certificates of deposit
	Treasury issues/corporate bonds maturing within 2 years
2 to 5 years	Corporate bonds maturing within 5 years
	Ginnie Mae bonds
	Stocks paying high dividends
	Balanced mutual funds
6 to 10 years	Stocks paying high dividends
	Ginnie Mae bonds
	Short-term bonds
	Long-term bonds
	Long-term certificates of deposit (CDs)
	Growth and income mutual funds
	Real estate
More than 10 years	Growth stocks
	Long-term bonds
	Precious metals
	Aggressive-growth mutual funds
	Real estate

✔ Concept Check 13.3

1. Summarize your personal views on lending or owning investments.
2. Which type of investment return—current income or capital gains—seems more attractive to you? Why?

Risks and Other Factors Affect the Investor's Return

4 Learning Objective

Describe the major factors that affect the rate of return on investments.

Because of the uncertainty that surrounds investments, people often follow a conservative course in an effort to keep their risk low. Being too conservative when investing means that they also risk not reaching their financial goals. To be a successful investor, you must understand the major factors that affect the rate of return on investments. Being informed, you can then take the appropriate risks when making investment decisions.

Table 13.2 Overview of Investment Alternatives

This chapter provides background information to help you to initially assess which types of investments might best suit your needs. The next four chapters examine details of investment alternatives. After reading those chapters, you will have learned enough about investments to make informed decisions.

- **Stocks.** Shares of ownership in the assets and earnings of a business corporation. Examples: Blue-chip stocks (like Dow Chemical, Exxon Mobil, and General Electric), well-known growth stocks (like Microsoft and McDonald's), lesser-known growth stocks (like American Greeting and Healthdyne), and income stocks (like water and electricity companies).

- **Bonds.** Interest-bearing negotiable certificates of long-term debt issued by a corporation, a municipality (such as a city or state), or the federal government. Examples: U.S. savings bonds, Series EE bonds, corporate bonds, high-yield corporate bonds, municipal bonds, and zero-coupon bonds.

- **Mutual funds.** An investment company that combines the funds of investors who have purchased shares of ownership in it and then invests that money in a diversified portfolio of stocks and bonds issued by other corporations or governments. Examples: Fidelity Growth Fund, Calvert Social Investment, and Vanguard Growth Index.

- **Real estate.** Property consisting of land; all structures permanently attached to that land; and accompanying rights and privileges, such as crop and mineral rights. Examples: residential housing units, commercial properties, residential lots, raw land.

- **High-risk investments.** Alternatives that have the potential for significant fluctuations in return over short time periods, perhaps only days or weeks. Examples: collectibles (baseball cards, posters, sports jerseys, comic books, stamps, rare coins, antiques), precious metals and stones, and options and futures contracts.

Random Risk Is Reduced by Diversification, Eventually

Random risk (also called **unsystematic risk**) is the risk associated with owning only one investment of a particular type (such as stock in one company) that, by chance, may do very poorly in the future because of uncontrollable or random factors, such as labor unrest, lawsuits, and product recalls. If you invest in only one stock, its value might rise or fall. If you invest in two or three stocks, the odds are lessened that all of their prices will fall. Such **diversification**—the process of reducing risk by spreading investment money among several investment opportunities—provides one effective method of managing random risk. The principle holds that when you own different types of investment assets in a portfolio, some assets should be rising when others are falling. It results in a potential rate of return on all of the investments that is lower than the potential return on a single alternative, but the return is more predictable and the risk of loss is lower. Diversification averages out the high and low returns.

Research suggests that you can cut random risk in half by diversifying into as few as five stocks or bonds; you can eliminate random risk by holding 15 or more stocks or bonds. Rational investors diversify so as to reduce random risk, and over the long term—as little as a decade—it works.

random/unsystematic risk
Risk associated with owning only one investment of a particular type (such as stock in one company) that, by chance, may do very poorly in the future due to uncontrollable or random factors that do not affect the rest of the market.

diversification
Process of reducing risk by spreading investment money among several investment opportunities.

Market Risk and the Economic Meltdown

Diversification among stocks or bonds cannot eliminate all risks. Some risk would exist even if you owned all of the stocks in a market because stock (and bond) prices in general move up

market risk/systematic risk/ undiversifiable risk
Risk that the value of an investment may drop due to influences and events that affect all similar investments.

and down over time. This movement results in **market risk** (also known as **systematic** or **nondiversifiable risk**). In this case, the value of an investment may drop due to influences and events that affect all similar investments. Examples include a change in economic, social, political, or general market conditions; fluctuations in investor preferences; or other broad market-moving factors, such as a recession or a terrorist attack. Market risk can be reduced, though only partially, by dividing your portfolio among several different markets. Normally, not all markets will decline at the same time, but it can happen.

Economists generally believe that all uncertainty can be reduced to measurable risk and that unregulated markets should be stable. However, the recent economic meltdown demonstrates the ever-present possibility of a systemic mistake in the logic of efficient markets as all types of investments fell in unison. The crisis was brought about by the financial system itself because, almost unbelievably, both liquidity and confidence in the credit, investment and real estate markets disappeared simultaneously. This proves that once-in-a-lifetime financial disasters not only can occur but are always possible, and the financial markets definitely need robust government regulation.

U.S. and world markets are continuing to recover. Over the short term, diversification cannot protect your investments against market declines but at least some of your investments will hold their value or most of it. Market risk is the risk that remains after an investor's portfolio has been fully diversified within a particular market, such as stocks. Over the years, market risk has averaged about 8 percent. As a consequence of this risk, the return on any single securities investment (such as a stock), through no fault of its own, might vary up and down about 8 percent annually. The total risk in an investment consists of the sum of the random risk and the market risk.

Instant Message

Time Reduces the Risk of Owning Stock

Since 1927 the worst 20-year performance for stocks was a gain of 3 percent. Until 2008 the worst over 10 years was only −1 percent. Over 1 year it was −43 percent. In the past 80 years, the chance of making money during any one year in the stock market is 66 percent. Over 5 years, the probability increases to 81 percent; over 10 years it rises to 89 percent.

Other Types of Investment Risks

A number of other investment risks affect investor returns:

- **Business failure risk.** **Business failure risk,** also called **financial risk,** is the possibility that the investment will fail, perhaps go bankrupt, and result in a massive or total loss of one's invested funds. Investigate thoroughly before investing. See Chapters 14, 15, and 16.

- **Inflation risk.** Inflation risk may be the most important concern for the long-term investor. **Inflation risk,** also called **purchasing power risk,** is the danger that your money will not grow as fast as inflation and therefore not be worth as much in the future as it is today. Over the long term, inflation in the United States has averaged 3.1 percent annually. Thus, the cumulative effects of inflation diminish your investment return. Historically, common stocks and real estate have reduced inflation risk, as values tend to rise with inflation over several years. However, houses, real estate, and other ownership investments are also subject to **deflation risk.** This is the chance that the value of an investment will decline when overall prices decline.

- **Time risk.** The role of time affects all investments. The sooner your invested money is supposed to be returned to you—the **time horizon** of an investment—the less the likelihood that something could go wrong. The more time your money is invested, the more it is at risk. For taking longer-term risks, investors expect and normally receive higher returns.

- **Business-cycle risk.** As we discussed in Chapter 1, economic growth usually does not occur in a smooth and steady manner. Instead, periods of expansion lasting three or four years are often followed by contractions in the economy, called recessions, that may last a year or longer. The profits of most industries follow the business cycle. Some businesses do not experience business-cycle risk because they continue to earn profits during economic downturns. Examples are gasoline retailers, supermarkets, and utility companies.

- **Market-volatility risk.** All investments are subject to occasional sharp changes in price as a result of events affecting a particular company or the overall market for similar investments. For example, the value of a single stock, such as that of a technology company like Microsoft, might change 10 or even 30 percent in a single day. Also, all technology stocks could decline 2 or perhaps 5 percent if two or three competitors announce poor earnings. In an average year, the price of a typical stock fluctuates up and down by about 50 percent; thus, the price of a stock selling for $30 per share in January might range from $15 to $45 before the end of the following December. In difficult economic times it is not unusual for overall stock market prices to fall (or rise) 3, 4, or 5 percent in a single day. Terrifying daily swings are likely to remain a constant during turbulent economic times. Such swings may be today's new normal. Yet, long-term investors need not be overly concerned with such short-term fluctuations.

- **Liquidity risk.** Liquidity is the speed and ease with which an asset can be converted to cash. You can convert your savings into cash instantly. You can sell your stocks and bonds in one day, although it may take four days to have the proceeds available in cash. Real estate is **illiquid** because it may take weeks, months, or years to sell.

- **Reinvestment risk.** Reinvestment risk is the risk that the return on a future investment will not be the same as the return earned by the original investment.

- **Marketability risk.** When you have to sell a certain asset quickly, it may not sell at or near the market price. This possibility is referred to as **marketability risk.** Selling real estate in a hurry, for example, may require the seller to substantially reduce the price in order to sell to a willing buyer.

Transaction Costs Reduce Returns

Buying and selling investments may result in a number of transaction costs. Examples include "fix-up costs" when preparing a home for sale, appraisals for collectibles, and storage costs for precious metals. **Commissions** are usually the largest transaction cost in investments. These are fees or percentages of the units or selling price paid to salespeople, agents, and companies for their services—that is, to buy or sell an investment. The commission charged to buy an investment (one commission) and then later sell it (a second commission) is partially based on the value of the transaction. Typical ranges for commissions are as follows: stocks, 1.5 to 2.5 percent (although trades can be made on the Internet for less than $20); bonds, 0 to 2.0 percent; mutual funds, 0 to 8.5 percent; real estate, 4.5 to 7.5 percent; options and futures contracts, 4.0 to 6.0 percent; limited partnerships, 10.0 to 15.0 percent; and collectibles, 15.0 to 30.0 percent. You can increase your investment returns by holding down transaction costs.

commissions
Fees or percentages of the selling price paid to salespeople, agents, and companies for their services in buying or selling an investment.

Leverage May Increase Returns

Another factor that can affect return on investment is **leverage.** In the leveraging process, borrowed funds are used to make an investment with the goal of earning a rate of return in excess of the after-tax costs of borrowing. Investing in real estate for its rental income provides an illustration of leverage, as shown in Table 13.3. Assume that a person can buy a small office building either by making a $30,000 down payment and borrowing $270,000 or by paying $300,000 cash. If the rental income is $30,000 annually ($2500 per month) and the person pays income taxes at a 25 percent rate, a higher return can be obtained using credit to buy the building because the yield would be 31.38 percent versus a 7.5 percent yield when paying cash.

leverage
Using borrowed funds to invest with the goal of earning a rate of return in excess of the after-tax costs of borrowing.

Table 13.3 Leverage Illustration: Buying Real Estate

	Pay Cash	Use Credit
Purchase price of office building	$300,000	$300,000
Amount borrowed	0	− 270,000
Amount invested	300,000	30,000
Rental income ($2500 per month)	30,000	30,000
Minus tax-deductible interest (6.5%, 30-year loan on $270,000)	− 0	− 17,450
Net earnings before taxes	30,000	12,550
Minus income tax liability (25% bracket)	− 7,500	− 3,137
Rental earnings after taxes	$22,500	$9,413
	÷ 300,000	÷ 30,000
Percentage return on amount invested	7.5%	31.38%

Did You Know?

Leverage Was a Cause of the U.S. Credit Meltdown

The credit meltdown in the United States occurred largely because many financial institutions were leveraged 30:1 in unregulated securities. This means that for every $30 of assets on their books, they put up a mere $1 of equity and borrowed the other $29. Thus, they had to lose only about 3% of their $30 in assets and their $1 was wiped out. The failure of one leveraged transaction immediately created 10 more similar crises. The overly leveraged financial institutions could not make loans or new investments because they lacked the equity to do so. Unable to raise new equity they faced bankruptcy. Faced with the failure of the entire U.S. financial system the American government began its rescue efforts.

Leverage can prove particularly beneficial when substantial capital gains occur, as this strategy sharply boosts the return on the investment. Assume that at the end of one year, the value of the building described in the previous example has appreciated 7 percent and you could sell it for $321,000 (excluding commission costs). If you had purchased the property for $300,000 cash and then sold it for $321,000, the capital gain on the sale would be 7 percent (the $21,000 return divided by the $300,000 originally invested). If you had bought it using credit, the capital gain would be 70 percent (the $21,000 return divided by the $30,000 originally invested, ignoring transaction costs, taxes, and inflation).

Leverage has a potential negative side for individual investors as well. In the preceding example, if you used credit to purchase the property, you would need a minimum rental income of $20,479 (from Table 9.3 on page 266, 6½ percent interest on a 30-year loan) to make the mortgage loan payments. A few months of vacancy or expensive repairs to the building could result in a losing situation. Furthermore, any decline in value would be magnified when you use leverage. You can become financially overextended by using leverage for investments, a factor that you should not ignore.

Concept Check 13.4

1. Distinguish between random risk and market risk.
2. Summarize three other risks that may affect investment returns.
3. Explain how transactions costs, leverage, and income taxes increase or decrease investment returns.

Establishing Your Long-Term Investment Strategy

Investing is not rocket science! Anyone reading this book and following its recommendations for making long-term investments can become a successful investor. To succeed, you must establish your own long-term investment strategies. Fortunately, this is easy because there are only five strategies to follow, and they all "hang together." And once learned, as the Nike slogan goes, you "Just do it!" And start investing as early in life as possible, as illustrated in Figure 13.4 and Table 13.4.

5 Learning Objective

Decide which of the five long-term investment strategies you will utilize.

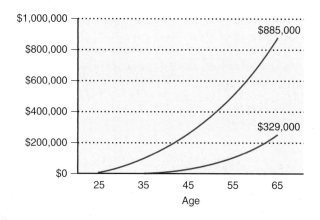

Figure 13.4
A 10-Year Delay in Investing Can Cost You $500,000

Delaying ten years before starting to save $2000 a year in a tax-deferred account that earns a 10 percent return can cost you $500,000. Saving $2000 a year between age 25 and 65 accumulates to $885,000, but if you don't start to save until age 35, you accumulate only $329,000. Thus, the $20,000 that you did not invest between ages 25 and 35 will cost you $556,000 by the time you reach age 65.

Table 13.4   The Wisdom of Starting to Invest Early in Life

Age	Early Investor*		Late Investor†	
	Cumulative Investment	Account Value	Cumulative Investment	Account Value
30	$ 2000	$ 2,180	$ 0	$ 0
35	10,000	13,047	0	0
40	20,000	33,121	2,000	2,180
45	0	50,960	10,000	13,047
50	0	78,408	20,000	33,121
55	0	120,641	30,000	64,007
60	0	185,621	40,000	111,529
65	0	285,601	50,000	184,648

Conclusion: $20,000 gets the early investor $285,601; $50,000 gets the late investor only $184,648.

*The early investor invested $2000 at the beginning of every year from ages 30 to 39 (ten years of cumulative investing totaling $20,000), and the funds compounded at 9 percent annually.

†The late investor invested $2000 at the beginning of every year from ages 40 to 64 (25 years of cumulative investing totaling $50,000), and the funds compounded at 9 percent annually.

real rate of return

Return on an investment after subtracting the effects of inflation and income taxes.

Long-term investors seek growth in the value of their investments that exceeds the rate of inflation. In other words, they want their investments to provide a positive **real rate of return.** This is the return after subtracting the effects of both inflation and income taxes. A long-term investor generally wants to hold an investment as long as it provides a return commensurate with its risk, often for 10 or 15 years or more.

Did You Know?

Calculate the Real Rate of Return (After Taxes and Inflation) on Investments

1. **Identify the rate of return before income taxes.** Perhaps you think that a stock will offer a return of 10 percent in one year, including current income and capital gains.

2. **Subtract the effects of your marginal tax rate on the rate of return to obtain the after-tax return.** If you are in the 25 percent federal income tax bracket, the calculation is $(1 - 0.25) \times 0.10 = 0.075 = 7.5$ percent.

3. **Subtract the effects of inflation from the after-tax return to obtain the real rate of return on the investment after taxes and inflation.** If you estimate an annual inflation of 4 percent, the calculation gives 3.5 percent (7.5 percent − 4.0 percent). Thus, your before-tax rate of return of 10 percent provides a real rate of return of 3.5 percent after taxes and inflation.

securities markets

Places where stocks and bonds are traded (or in the case of electronic trading, the way in which securities are traded).

bear market

Market in which securities prices have declined in value by 20 percent or more from previous highs, often over the course of several weeks or months.

bull market

Market in which securities prices have risen 20 percent or more over time.

In addition to understanding the overall economic picture (see Chapter 1), long-term investors understand how the **securities markets** (places where stocks and bonds are traded) are performing as a whole. That is, are the markets moving up, moving down, or remaining stagnant? A securities market in which prices have declined in value by 20 percent or more from previous highs, often over the course of several weeks or months, is called a **bear market.** Since 1926, several bear markets have occurred, and the bear market that started in 2007 saw stock prices decline more than 50 percent. A **bull market** results when securities prices have risen 20 percent or more over time. Historically, the more than 20 bull markets have seen an average gain of 110 percent. The bull market of the 1990s saw stock prices increase more than 300 percent!

A *bull* in the market is a person who expects securities prices to go up; a *bear* expects the general market to decline. The origin of these terms is unknown, but some suggest that they refer to the ways that the animals attack: Bears thrust their claws downward, and bulls move their horns upward. Historically, bear markets last, on average, about 9 months; bull markets average 29 months in length.

Long-Term Investors Understand Market Timing

market volatility

The likelihood of large price swings in securities due to a company's success (or lack of it) and various market conditions.

Long-term investors must be able to withstand some **market volatility,** the likelihood of large price swings in their chosen securities. The price of a typical stock fluctuates up and down by about 50 percent every year due to the company's success (or lack of it) and various market conditions.

Benjamin Graham, investment sage and author of *The Intelligent Investor*, argues that the investor should be interested in the possibility of profiting from wide fluctuations in prices. The opportunity of volatility is to buy stocks wisely when they are underpriced and sell them wisely when they rise above that value, and this is known as **value investing** (examined in Chapter 14). Staying focused on the value of an individual investment is more important than its price, particularly in times of market turmoil.

This contrasts with the speculative approach of buying or selling on the anticipated direction of the overall market as this is **market timing.** These investors try to "time" their investments, hoping to capture most of the upside of rising stock prices while avoiding most of the downside. **Market timers** pull out of stocks or bonds in anticipation of a market decline or hold back from investing until the market "settles down."

To succeed in timing the market, you need to know just the right time to buy and just the right time to sell, know what signals suggest you take action, and exhibit the discipline to do it. Research shows that most of the market's gains are realized in a few trading days that occur every now and then. If market timers are out of the market on those days, they lose. In times of rising markets, it is very easy for market timers to sell too early and as a result miss out on much larger profits as the bull market continues to push up prices even more. Those who sell after a sudden drop in investment value, a "down market," actually lock in their losses. And what do these investors do if the stock market drops even further? What contributes the most to successful investing is not timing, but time.

Instant Message

Out of the Market? You Missed a 45% Gain

If you had been out of stocks during the market's ten best days in the past decade, according to Charles Schwab, you would have missed out on 45 percent of the gains.

market timing
Investing, perhaps speculatively, in an effort to "time" the markets by buying or selling on the anticipated direction of the overall market, hope to capture most of the upside of rising stock prices while avoiding most of the downside.

market timers
Long-term investors who pull out of stocks or bonds in anticipation of a market decline or hold back from investing until the market "settles down"—that is, when they expect prices to climb.

Short-term buying and selling is more like gambling than investing.

Jupiter Images

buy and hold/buy to hold
Investment strategy in which investors buy a widely diversified mix of stocks and/or mutual funds, reinvest the dividends by buying more stocks and mutual funds, and hold on to those investments almost indefinitely.

Strategy 1: Buy and Hold Anticipates Long-Term Economic Growth

The secret to investment success is benign neglect. Long-term investors need to relax with the confidence and knowledge that investing regularly and not trading frequently will create a substantial portfolio over time. Long-term investors do not follow or react emotionally to the day-to-day changes that occur in the market. Ignore them is the best advice. Because most people are sensitive to short-term losses, daily monitoring could motivate one to make shortsighted buying and selling decisions. Selling high-quality assets in a bear market is a poor strategy because bear markets are typically short in duration. It is tough to do, but it is smart to buy more shares when prices are lower during market downturns because rising prices in a bull market always follow a bear market. Investors who remain invested in the stock market are rewarded with the opportunity to earn the historic average return of the equities markets, which is over 10 percent annually.

Most long-term investors use the investment strategy **buy and hold** (also called **buy to hold**). That is, they buy a widely diversified mix of stocks and/or mutual funds, reinvest the dividends by buying more stocks and mutual funds, and hold on to those investments almost indefinitely. With this approach, the investor expects that the values of the assets will increase over the long run in tandem with the growth of the U.S. and world economies. The investments may pay some current income as well. The investor's emphasis is on holding the assets through both good and bad economic times with the confidence that their values will go up over the long term. This is a wise strategy. Critics argue that "buy and hold" is a discredited concept, but they are wrong because this is still the best approach for investing over 20 years or longer.

Buy and hold does not mean buy and ignore. Investors are unwise to blindly hold on to an investment for years. Instead, review all holdings at least once a year to make sure that each remains a good investment. Questions to ask: "Is the valuation too high?"; "Has the fundamental outlook of the company changed?"; "Does this asset still fit my investment plan?"; "Would I buy it today?" If necessary, sell the asset.

Strategy 2: Dollar-Cost Averaging Buys at "Below-Average" Costs

dollar-cost averaging/cost averaging
Systematic program of investing equal sums of money at regular intervals regardless of the price of the investment.

below-average costs
Average costs of an investment if more shares are purchased when the price is down and fewer shares when the price is high.

Dollar-cost averaging (or **cost averaging**) is a systematic program of investing equal sums of money at regular intervals regardless of the price of the investment. In this approach, the same fixed dollar amount is invested in the same stock or mutual fund at regular intervals over a long time. Since investments generally rise more than they fall, the "averaging" means that you purchase more shares when the price is down and fewer shares when the price is high. Most of the shares are, therefore, purchased at **below-average costs.**

This strategy avoids the risks and responsibilities of investment timing because the stock purchases are made regularly (usually every month) regardless of the price. It also ignores all outside events and short-term gyrations of the market, providing the investor with a disciplined buying strategy. A well-diversified stock mutual fund would be an excellent choice for dollar-cost averaging.

Table 13.5 shows the results of dollar-cost averaging for a stock under varying market conditions (commissions are excluded). As an example, assume that you invest $300 into a stock every three months. Notice that dollar-cost averaging is successful in all three scenarios illustrated.

Table 13.5 Dollar-Cost Averaging for a Stock or Mutual Fund Investment

	Fluctuating Market			Declining Market			Rising Market		
	Regular Investment	Share Price	Shares Acquired	Regular Investment	Share Price	Shares Acquired	Regular Investment	Share Price	Shares Acquired
	$ 300	$15	20	$ 300	$15	20	$ 300	$ 6	50
	300	10	30	300	10	30	300	10	30
	300	15	20	300	10	30	300	12	25
	300	10	30	300	6	50	300	15	20
	300	15	20	300	5	60	300	20	15
Totals	$1,500	$65	120	$1,500	$46	190	$1,500	$63	140
	Average share price: $13.00 ($65 ÷ 5)*			Average share price: $9.20 ($46 ÷ 5)*			Average share price: $12.60 ($63 ÷ 5)*		
	Average share cost: $12.50 ($1500 ÷ 120)†			Average share cost: $7.89 ($1500 ÷ 190)†			Average share cost: $10.71 ($1500 ÷ 140)†		

*Sum of share price total ÷ number of investment periods.

†Total amount invested ÷ total shares purchased.

Dollar-Cost Averaging in a Fluctuating Market

To illustrate the effects of dollar-cost averaging, assume that you first invested funds during the "fluctuating market" shown in Table 13.5. Because the initial price is $15 per share, you receive 20 shares for your investment of $300. Then the market drops—an extreme but easy-to-follow example—and the price falls to $10 per share. When you buy $300 worth of the stock now, you receive 30 shares. Three months later, the market price rebounds to $15 and you invest another $300, receiving 20 shares. The price then drops and rises again.

 Advice from a Pro...

Use a Dividend-Reinvestment Plan to Dollar-Cost Average

More than 1000 well-known companies allow investors to purchase shares of stock directly from them without the assistance of a stockbroker and then to continue to invest on a regular basis without paying brokerage commissions. Such a program is known as a **dividend-reinvestment plan (DRIP).** You simply sign up with the company, agreeing to buy a certain number of shares and to reinvest cash dividends into more shares of stock for little or no transaction fee. Investors' accounts are credited with fractional shares, too.

Wal-Mart is illustrative. It requires a minimum investment of $250, and continuing investments of $50 thereafter. The enrollment fee is $20 plus $0.10 per share. Most companies will buy back shares for a transaction fee of only $10.

Companies offering DRIPs include Ameritech, ExxonMobil, Home Depot, Tenneco, Wal-Mart, McDonalds, and Sears, Roebuck and Company. For a list of companies offering direct purchases, see the Securities Transfer Association at www.sharebuilder.com or the Direct Stock Purchase Plan Clearinghouse at www.dripinvestor.com/clearinghouse/home.asp.

Buying shares regularly through a DRIP is a great example of dollar-cost averaging. It allows you to take advantage of fluctuating stock prices by purchasing on a regular basis at below-average costs.

Jon Wentworth
Southern Adventist University

average share price
Calculated by dividing the share price total by the number of investment periods.

average share cost
Actual cost basis of the investment used for income tax purposes, calculated by dividing the total amount invested by the total shares purchased.

You now own 120 shares, thanks to your total investment of $1500. The **average share price** is calculated by averaging the amounts paid for the investment: Simply divide the share price total by the number of investment periods. In this example, the average share price is $13 ($65 ÷ 5). The **average share cost,** a more meaningful amount, is the actual cost basis of the investment used for income tax purposes. It is calculated by dividing the total amount invested by the total shares purchased. In this example, it is $12.50 ($1500 ÷ 120). Based on the recent price of $15 per share, each of your 120 shares is worth on average $2.50 ($15 − $12.50) more than you paid for it. Thus, your gain is $300 (120 × $2.50; or $15 × 120 = $1800, $1800 − $1500 = $300).

Dollar-Cost Averaging in a Declining Market   Markets may also decline over a time period. The "declining market" columns in Table 13.5 (representing a prolonged bear market of 15 months) show purchases of 190 shares for increasingly lower prices that eventually reach $5 per share at the bottom of the business cycle. In a declining market, if you keep investing using dollar-cost averaging, you will purchase a large volume of shares. If you sell when the market is down substantially, you will not profit. In this example, you have purchased 190 shares at an average cost of $7.89, and they now have a depressed price of $5. Selling at this point would result in a substantial loss of $550 [$1500 − (190 × $5)]. Dollar-cost averaging requires that you continue to invest if the longer-term prospects suggest an eventual increase in price.

Dollar-Cost Averaging in a Rising Market   During the "rising market" in Table 13.5, you continue to invest but buy fewer shares. The $1500 investment during the bull market bought only 140 shares for an average cost of $10.71. In this rising market, you profit because your 140 shares have a recent market price of $20 per share, for a total value of $2800 (140 × $20).

Almost anyone can profit in a rising market. If you use dollar-cost averaging over the long term, you will continue to buy in rising, falling, and fluctuating markets. The overall result will be that you buy more shares when the cost is down, thereby lowering the average share cost to below-average prices. The totals in Table 13.5, for example, reveal an overall investment of $4500 ($1500 + $1500 + $1500) used to purchase 450 shares (120 + 190 + 140) for an average cost of $10 per share ($4500 ÷ 450). With the recent market price at $20, you will realize a long-term gain of $4500 ($20 current market price × 450 shares = $9000; $9000 − $4500 invested = $4500 gain). Note that the dollar-cost averaging method would remain valid if the time interval for investing were monthly, quarterly, or even semiannually; benefits are derived from the regularity of investing.

Dollar-Cost Averaging Offers Two Advantages   First, it reduces the average cost of shares of stock purchased over a relatively long period. Profits occur when prices for an investment fluctuate and eventually go up. Although this approach does not eliminate the possibility of loss, it does limit losses during times of declining prices. Profits accelerate during rising prices. Second, dollar-cost averaging dictates investor discipline. This strategy of investing is not particularly glamorous, but it is the only approach that is almost guaranteed to make a profit for the investor. It takes neither brilliance nor luck, just discipline. People who invest through individual retirement accounts (IRAs), employee stock ownership programs, and 401(k) retirement plans (discussed in Chapter 17) enjoy the benefits of dollar-cost averaging when they invest regularly.

Strategy 3: Portfolio Diversification Reduces Portfolio Volatility

Owning too much of any one investment creates too great a financial risk. Experts advise that you never keep more than 5 or 10 percent of your assets in one investment, including your employer's stock. Many workers who did not diversify properly have seen their

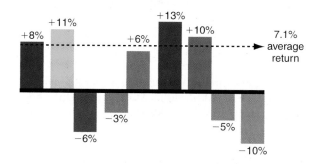

Figure 13.5

Diversification Averages Out an Investor's Return

The chart at the left represents a hypothetical mix of winning and losing investments after one year. The investment on the far left, for instance, increased in value 8 percent; another declined 10 percent. While some investments lost value, over the year those losses were offset with the gains of others, and the overall portfolio earned a 7.1 percent average return.

retirement funds disappear or be drastically reduced in value when their employers' stocks plunged in price.

Diversification is the single most important rule in investing. **Portfolio diversification** is the practice of selecting a collection of different asset classes of investments (such as stocks, bonds, mutual funds, real estate, and cash) that are chosen not only for their potential returns but also for their dissimilar risk–return characteristics.

The goal of portfolio diversification is to create a collection of investments that will provide an acceptable level of return and an acceptable exposure to risk. This outcome can be achieved because asset classes typically react differently to economic and marketplace changes. The major benefit of having a diversified portfolio is that when one asset class performs poorly, there is a good chance that another will perform well, and vice versa.

For example, you might buy a number of mutual funds, perhaps including a balanced fund, an asset-allocation fund, a life-cycle fund, and an aggressive-growth fund. Similarly, you could invest in three or four stocks within an industry group, instead of just one, and then invest in several industry groups, plus invest in a bond mutual fund and a certificate of deposit.

Diversification reduces portfolio volatility while averaging out an investor's return. (See Figure 13.5.) Diversification lowers the odds that you will lose money investing and increases the odds that you will make money. Table 13.6 illustrates that the gains in the equity portion of a diversified portfolio are modest in a rising market (up 10%) and while losses in a declining market (down 50%) are substantial they are not devastatingly horrible as is the case in a portfolio that is too heavy in equities. Diversification protects against such dire losses.

portfolio diversification
Practice of selecting a collection of different asset classes of investments (such as stocks, bonds, mutual funds, real estate, and cash) that are chosen not only for their potential returns but also for their dissimilar risk–return characteristics.

Table 13.6 Stock Market Turmoil Proves the Case for Diversification

Beginning Portfolio Values			Ending Portfolio Values	
Portfolio A—Balanced			**Stocks Jump 10%**	**Stocks Crash 50%***
Cash	Bonds	Equities†		
10%	45%	45%		
$20,000	$90,000	$90,000	+$9,000	$45,000
Portfolio B—Heavy on Equities				
Cash	Bonds	Equities†		
5%	10%	85%		
$10,000	$20,000	$170,000	$170,000	$85,000

*Decline from previous high in stock market prices during severe economic recession.

†Equity portion of portfolio rises or falls with changes in stock market prices.

Strategy 4: Asset Allocation Keeps You in the Right Investment Categories for Your Time Horizon

Research shows that more than 90 percent of returns earned by long-term investors result from having one's assets allocated in a diversified portfolio. Most of the return comes not from specific investments but rather is derived from owning the right asset categories at the right time.

asset allocation
Form of diversification in which investor decides on proportions of an investment portfolio that will be devoted to various categories of assets.

Asset allocation, a form of diversification, is deciding on the proportions of your investment portfolio that will be devoted to various categories of assets. Asset allocation helps preserve capital by selecting assets so as to protect the entire portfolio from negative events while remaining in a position to gain from positive events. This strategy helps control your exposure to risk. Economist Gary Brinson says "Asset allocation is the overwhelmingly dominant contributor to total return."

To achieve an appropriate mix of growth, income, and stability in your portfolio, you need a combination of three investments: (1) stocks and/or stock mutual funds (equities), (2) bonds (debt), and (3) cash (or cash equivalents like Treasury securities). Asset allocation requires that you keep your equities, debt, and cash at a fixed ratio for long time periods, occasionally rebalance the allocations, perhaps quarterly or annually, so as to continue to meet your investment objectives.

Your allocation proportions and investment choices need to reflect your age, income, family responsibilities, financial resources, risk tolerance, goals, retirement plans, and investment time horizon. You need not change the proportions of your asset allocation until your broad investment goals change—possibly not for another five or ten years. When your investment objectives change, perhaps because of marriage, birth of a child, child graduating from college, loss of employment, divorce, or death of a spouse, you will need to change your asset allocation as well.

Figure 13.6 illustrates model portfolios that reflect varying degrees of risk tolerance and time horizons. A young, risk-tolerant, long-term investor with an aggressive investment philosophy might have a portfolio that is 100 percent in equities because equities offer the highest return over the long term and the remainder in cash (within a money market fund). Younger investors also have ample time to ride out market fluctuations and make up any major losses. A moderate approach with a time horizon of six to ten years might have an equities-bond-cash portfolio of 60/30/10 percent.

Portfolio rebalancing is the process of bringing the different asset classes back into proper relationship following a significant change in one or more of them. You must reset your asset allocation at least once a year to return your portfolio to the proper mix of stocks, bonds, and cash when they no longer conform to your plan. Here is why. Assume you have a moderate investment philosophy and started out with a 40/40/10 bond-equities-cash portfolio, and a year later stock values increased 37 percent and bonds lost 5 percent. The result: Your portfolio is now 40 percent toward stocks and less than 40 in bonds. It is too risky. As shown in Figure 13.7, this means selling some of your equities and using the proceeds to buy more bonds, thus rebalancing it according to your previously determined asset allocations. When rebalancing, you will be selling high and buying low—the goal of all investors. It is temperamentally difficult for investors to rebalance. They don't like to sell assets that have increased in value because they hope those values will continue to increase.

Instant Message

Asset Allocation Rules of Thumb

Consider these two rules of thumb to guide the stock and bond allocation of your portfolio:

1. The percent to invest in equities is 110 minus your age, multiplied by 1.25. For example, if you are 40 years old, calculate as follows: 110 − 40 = 70; 70 × 1.25 = 87.5. Therefore, a 40-year-old investor is advised to maintain a portfolio where 87.5 percent of the assets are in equities and 12.5 percent in bonds (or cash equivalents).

2. The percent to invest in equities is found by subtracting your age from 120. Put the resulting number in the form of the percentage of your portfolio to invest in stocks. Put the remainder in bonds. So if you are age 30, put 90 percent (120 − 30) in stocks and 10 percent in bonds. Every year, subtract your age from 120 again and rebalance your portfolio as needed.

0–5 Years	6–10 Years	11+ Years	Risk Tolerance/ Investment Philosophy
10% Cash 30% Bonds 60% Equities	20% Bonds 80% Equities	100% Equities	High Risk/Aggressive
20% Cash 40% Bonds 40% Equities	10% Cash 30% Bonds 60% Equities	20% Bonds 80% Equities	Moderate Risk/Moderate
35% Cash 40% Bonds 25% Equities	20% Cash 40% Bonds 40% Equities	10% Cash 30% Bonds 60% Equities	Low Risk/Conservative

Figure 13.6
Model Portfolios
and Time Horizons

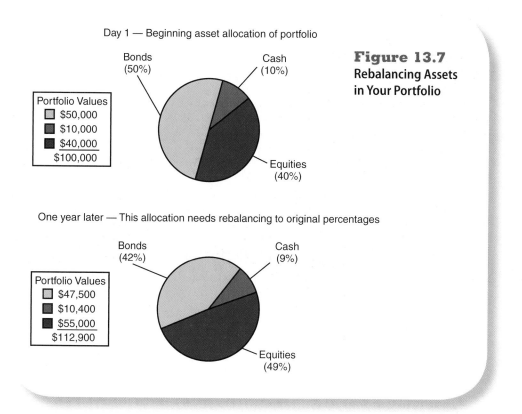

Day 1 — Beginning asset allocation of portfolio

Bonds (50%)   Cash (10%)

Portfolio Values
☐ $50,000
▨ $10,000
■ $40,000
$100,000

Equities (40%)

Figure 13.7
Rebalancing Assets
in Your Portfolio

One year later — This allocation needs rebalancing to original percentages

Bonds (42%)   Cash (9%)

Portfolio Values
☐ $47,500
▨ $10,400
■ $55,000
$112,900

Equities (49%)

Rebalancing is an appropriate form of market timing as it provides some of the benefits of timing without the risk.

Employees who participate in their employer-sponsored retirement plan may have access to services to automatically rebalance their retirement assets. Instead of being a do-it-yourself investor, a worker can sign up for the services of a **limited managed account.** Once you have decided on your preferred asset allocation and signed a contract with a vender approved by your employer, the company sells and buys your mutual fund assets, usually quarterly, on your behalf to adjust your portfolio back to your specific standards. The service is free or a nominal fee is charged.

modern portfolio theory (MPT)
Goal is to identify the investor's acceptable level of risk tolerance and then find an optimal portfolio of assets that will have the highest expected returns for that level of risk.

Monte Carlo analysis
Technique that performs a large number of trial runs of a particular portfolio mix of investments, called simulations, to find an optimal allocation for a particular investor's goals and risk tolerance.

Strategy 5: Modern Portfolio Theory Evolves from Asset Allocation

A sophisticated application of asset allocation can be accomplished using **modern portfolio theory (MPT).** Here, the goal is to identify the investor's acceptable level of risk tolerance and then find an optimal portfolio of assets that will have the highest expected returns for that level of risk. A popular form of MPT is **Monte Carlo analysis.** This technique performs a large number of trial runs of a particular portfolio mix of investments, called simulations. It calculates hundreds or even thousands of possible investment combinations to determine the probability that a particular selection of investments will reach an investor's goal, such as a specific retirement income at a certain point in the future. See the green and yellow portions in Figure 13.8. (See Chapter 17 for more information.)

Figure 13.8
Monte Carlo Analysis from Financial Engines

The analysis and recommendations pictured are hypothetical and are provided for illustrative purposes only. This illustration should not be relied on for investment advice.

Source: Copyright © Financial Engines. Used with permission.

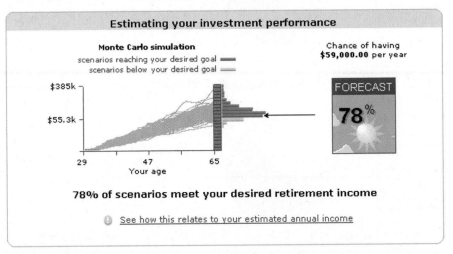

How we create your Forecast

Overview

How much you'll have in the future depends on how your investments perform over time. To give you our best estimate, we explore thousands of possible economic scenarios using a technique known as "Monte Carlo" simulation. The animation below is a visual representation of this process.

Estimating your investment performance

Monte Carlo simulation
scenarios reaching your desired goal ▬
scenarios below your desired goal ▬

Chance of having
$59,000.00 per year

FORECAST
78%

$385k
$55.3k

29   47   65
Your age

78% of scenarios meet your desired retirement income

ⓘ See how this relates to your estimated annual income

Each economic scenario we explore makes different, realistic assumptions about inflation, interest rates, and returns on asset classes (stocks, bonds, and so forth) for each year of possible growth.
To make sense out of the thousands of estimated portfolio values, we carefully sort and count them. Then we show you three very important numbers. Your median estimate is the most likely of the three, but you should be prepared for the downside just in case:

- **Upside:** if your investments perform well, you may end up with a portfolio in the best 5% of the scenarios.
- **Median:** if your investments perform average, you may end up with a portfolio near the middle of the scenarios.
- **Downside:** if your investments perform poorly, you may end up with a portfolio in the worst 5% of the scenarios.

Advice from a Pro...

When to Sell an Investment

It is time to sell an investment when one of the following conditions has been met:

- Something significant about the company's business or its earnings has changed dramatically for the worse since you bought the company's stock.
- The stock is doing so well that it is overvalued, and the share price is much higher than what you believe the company is worth.

- The investment is performing poorly and causing you undue anxiety. The great financier Bernard Baruch advised, "Sell down to the level where you are sleeping well."
- You need cash for a worthwhile purpose, and this investment appears the most fully priced.
- The investment no longer fits your situation or goals, and you have a more promising place to invest your money.

Diann Moorman
University of Georgia

 Concept Check 13.5

1. Summarize why smart people conclude that it is impossible to beat the average stock market returns, and then note why some marker timers try anyway.
2. Summarize what the buy-and-hold strategy is all about.
3. Explain the concept of dollar-cost averaging including why one invests at below-average costs.
4. What is asset allocation and why does it work?
5. What is the goal of portfolio diversification and how is this accomplished?

 Did You Know?

The Top 3 Financial Missteps in Investing

People slip up in investing fundamentals when they do the following:

1. Buy and sell more than they should
2. Diversify less than they should
3. Hold on to a bad investment long after evidence shows it was a bad decision

Creating Your Own Investment Plan

To create an **investment plan,** which is a reflection of your investment philosophy and your logic on investing to reach specific goals, see the illustrated plan for Jamie Richter in Figure 13.9. You can begin creating your own investment plan, using Figure 13.8 as a model, by identifying your financial goals and explaining your investment philosophy as called for in Steps 1 and 2.

To help in your thinking review for Step 3 in Figure 13.9, review Table 13.1 for the time horizons of various investments. (Terms new to you are explained in the chapters that follow.) What are the time horizons for your investment goals? Are you building up an amount for a down payment on a home, creating a college fund for a child, or putting away money for retirement? Or are all three time horizons relevant? Keep in mind why you are investing and proceed accordingly. Now calculate the numbers. How much money do you need to achieve each goal, and by when? What is the total of your current investment assets? Do the math.

Step 4 in Figure 13.9 asks about investment alternatives. Review Figure 13.2 on the long-term rates of return on various investments and Table 13.2 for alternatives. Then

 6 Learning Objective

Create your own investment plan.

investment plan
An explanation of your investment philosophy and your logic on investing to reach specific goals.

Figure 13.9

Jamie Richter's Investment Plan

After some thinking and reading, Jamie, age 24, jotted down some investment plan notes.

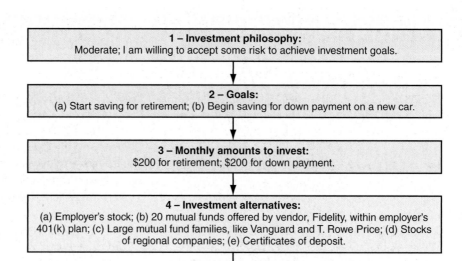

1 – Investment philosophy:
Moderate; I am willing to accept some risk to achieve investment goals.

2 – Goals:
(a) Start saving for retirement; (b) Begin saving for down payment on a new car.

3 – Monthly amounts to invest:
$200 for retirement; $200 for down payment.

4 – Investment alternatives:
(a) Employer's stock; (b) 20 mutual funds offered by vendor, Fidelity, within employer's 401(k) plan; (c) Large mutual fund families, like Vanguard and T. Rowe Price; (d) Stocks of regional companies; (e) Certificates of deposit.

5 – Rationale for decisions:
For every dollar invested I will receive an immediate 50 percent return because my employer's policy is to match 401(k) contributions 50 cents on the dollar for the first 6 percent of earnings. Starting next month, begin investing in my employer's 401(k) plan to earn $100 monthly matching contribution as this gives me a 50 percent immediate return ($200 of my money plus $100 of my employer's money).

Rationale: (a) Employer's stock may be risky; (b) Really do not know much about local stocks; (c) Down payment funds go into money market account to accumulate and then earn higher rate on certificates of deposit.

6 – Key risk factors:
(a) Do not need retirement funds for 30 or more years, so I can invite more risk for a higher return; (b) I expect to need the down payment funds within 3 to 4 years, so the investment cannot be risky.

7 – Anticipated return:
(a) Hopefully 7 to 8 percent on the retirement investments; (b) For the down payment funds, hopefully 3 to 4 percent in a money market account, and perhaps 4 to 5 percent in a certificate of deposit.

8 – Actions to take:
(a) Fill out 401(k) forms in Human Resources Department to withhold $200 monthly and invest it in a mutual fund with an investment objective of moderate- to high-growth; (b) Open an account at large mutual fund company and automatically send $200 monthly from my banking account to a money market account until sufficient funds accumulate to buy a certificate of deposit.

Did You Know?

The Tax Consequences in Investment Fundamentals

There are some favorable aspects to income taxes to think about when making investments.

1. **After-tax return.** When comparing similar investments, your objective is to earn the best after-tax return. This return is the net amount earned on an investment after payment of income taxes. (See Equation [4.1] on page 130.)

2. **Income versus capital gain.** Current investment income, such as dividends and interest, is taxed at one's marginal tax bracket, likely 25 percent. Capital gains are taxed at special lower rates, likely at 10 or 15 percent.

3. **Tax-deferred investments.** The income and capital gains from investments within employer-sponsored retirement accounts are not subject to income taxes until the funds are withdrawn.

4. **Tax-exempt income.** Income earned from municipal bonds is exempt from income taxes.

5. **Tax-exempt investments.** The income and capital gains from investments within Roth IRA accounts are not subject to income taxes, unless the funds are removed from the account within 5 years.

examine Figure 13.3 because it shows the trade-offs between risk and return on investment alternatives. Next take a pencil and delete some investment choices that do not appeal to you or match your investment philosophy. You will be left with alternatives that better fit your investment goals, philosophy, and time horizon. Now you have an investment plan, so record your responses to Steps 5, 6 and 7. All that remains is to put your plan into action. That means filling out forms to open an investment account, writing checks for your first investing dollars, and overseeing your investments. These topics are examined in the chapters that follow.

Do It NOW!

Investing is the key to financial success. Start today by:

1. Saving even a small amount through a pay-yourself-first philosophy perhaps by using payroll withholding.

2. Identifying the percentages you would allocate to stocks, bonds and cash equivalents using an asset allocation strategy to save for retirement.

3. Visiting www.finance.yahoo.com every weekday for one month to become familiar with how and why the stock market moves from day to day.

Concept Check 13.6

1. Review Tables 13.1 and 13.2 and Figures 13.1 and 13.2, and record in writing an investment plan to fund your retirement, presumably one of your own long-term goals.

What Do You Recommend NOW?

Now that you have read the chapter on investment fundamentals, what do you r|ecommend to Jennifer and Julia on the subject regarding:

1. Getting more money to save and invest?

2. Prerequisites to investing for Jennifer?

3. Portfolio diversification for Julia?

4. Dollar-cost averaging for Jennifer?

5. Investment alternatives for Julia?

Big Picture Summary of Learning Objectives

1 Explain how to get started as an investor.

Before investing, think about your goals, why you want to invest, and whether you are ready to invest. After you find the money to invest, contemplate the types of returns you might anticipate. Investors hope that their investments will earn them a positive total return, which is the income an investment generates from current income and capital gains.

2 Discover your own investment philosophy.

Achieving financial success requires that you understand your investment philosophy and adhere to it when investing. An investment philosophy is one's general approach to tolerance for risk in investments, whether it is conservative, moderate, or aggressive, given the financial goals to be achieved. You also need to know about investment risk and what to do about it.

3 Identify the kinds of investments that match your interests.

Before investing your money, you need to think about lending versus owning, short term versus long term, and how to select investments that are likely to provide your desired potential total return.

4 Describe the major factors that affect the rate of return on investments.

Because of the uncertainty that surrounds investments, people often follow a conservative course in an effort to keep their risk low. Being too conservative when investing means that they risk not reaching their financial goals. To be a successful investor, you must understand the major factors that affect the rate of return on investments so you can then take the appropriate risks when making investment decisions. Key concepts include random and market risk and time horizon.

5 Decide which of the five long-term investment strategies you will utilize.

To succeed as an investor, you must establish your own long-term investment strategy. Most investors accept the fact that they cannot time the market with any consistency. Long-term investors are passive investors. They wisely ignore the ups and downs of the stock market and the business cycle and simply use the five investment strategies of buy and hold, diversification, asset allocation, modern portfolio theory, and dollar-cost averaging.

6 Create your own investment plan.

An investment plan is an explanation of your investment philosophy and your logic on investing to reach specific goals. Steps include identifying your goals, contemplating which types of investments might best fit your investment goals, clarifying your investment philosophy, reviewing possible investments that match specific investment time horizons, calculating the numbers using appropriate time horizons, learning about investment alternatives, and narrowing down your choices.

Let's Talk About It

1. **Your Investing Success.** Describe your thoughts about the likelihood of your long-term investing success given the recent severe downturn in the economy and stock markets?

2. **Why Invest.** Why should people invest? Give three reasons each for college students, young college graduates in their 20s, couples with young children, and people in their 50s.

3. **When to Invest.** The text outlines certain prerequisites to investing. Make a list of likely dates when you think you will have accomplished each prerequisite (perhaps in one, two, or three years). Give one or more reasons for selecting those dates.

4. **What Is Your Tolerance for Risk in Investing?** Is it the same as for other members of your class? Why or why not?

5. **Your Investment Philosophy.** Is your investment philosophy conservative, moderate, or aggressive? Give two reasons to support the adoption of your philosophy. How does your view compare with the philosophies of other members of your class?

6. **Your Investment Strategy.** The text discusses five strategies for long-term investors. Which one appeals to you most? Give two reasons why you find this strategy attractive.

7. **Invest How Much?** Assume you have graduated from college and have a good-paying job. If you had to commit to investing regularly right now, how much money would you put away every month? Explain why. How does your view compare with the views of other members of your class?

Do the Math

1. **Annual Investments.** Michael and Jessica Mackewich, who live in Fresno, California, have as a new investment goal to create a college fund for their newborn daughter. They estimate that they will need $200,000 in 18 years. Assuming that the Mackewiches could obtain a return of 6 percent, how much would they need to invest annually to reach their goal? Use Appendix A.3 or the *Garman/Forgue* companion website.

2. **Number of Years.** Michael's mother, who lives in New Port Richey, Florida, wants to help pay for her grandchild's education. How many years will it take her to reach her goal of $30,000 if she invests $1000 per year, earning 6 percent? Use Table A.3 or the *Garman/Forgue* companion website.

3. **Future Cost.** If one year of college currently costs $15,000, how much will it cost Joshua's new daughter, Serena, in 18 years, assuming a 5 percent annual rate of inflation? Use Appendix A.1 or the *Garman/Forgue* companion website.

4. **Returns and Actions.** Samantha Rennakker from Collegedale, Tennessee, has $50,000 in investments at the beginning of the year that consisted of a diversified portfolio of stocks (40 percent), bonds (40 percent), and cash equivalents (20 percent). Her returns over the past 12 months were 13 percent on stocks, 6 percent on bonds, and 4 percent on cash equivalents.

   (a) What is Samantha's average return for the year?

   (b) If Samantha wanted to rebalance her portfolio to its original position, what specific actions should she take?

5. **Early Investor Wins.** Eric and Adam, who are twins living in Rexburg, Idaho, took different approaches to investing. Eric saved $2000 per year for 10 years starting at age 23 and never added any more money to the account. Adam saved $2000 per year for 20 years starting at age 35. Assuming that the brothers earned an 8 percent return, who had accumulated the most by the time they reached age 63? Use Appendixes A.1 and A.3 or the *Garman/Forgue* companion website.

6. **Taxable or Tax-Free.** Ashley Rivera of Milford, Nebraska, has a choice of two investments: a $1000 tax-free municipal bond that pays 4.3 percent interest or a $1000 taxable corporate bond that pays 6.3 percent interest. Both bonds will mature in five years. If Ashley is in the 25 percent tax bracket, which bond should she choose? Use the information on page 130 or the *Garman/Forgue* website.

Financial Planning Cases

Case 1

A Veteran's Short-Term Goal Is to Buy a Condominium

Christopher Witherspoon, a paraplegic disabled veteran of the U.S. Marines and self-employed "computer nerd" from Minneapolis, Minnesota, hopes to continue his savings and investment program for five more years before making a down payment on a condominium. The home that he wants to purchase is currently priced at $250,000.

(a) Should Christopher invest his money during the next three years by lending or owning? Why?

(b) What investment choices should Christopher consider for this condominium goal? (Hint: See Tables 13.1 and 13.2 and Figure 13.3.)

(c) If housing inflation is 4 percent for each of the next five years, about how much will the condominium cost then?

Case 2
A First-Time Investor Gets a Head Start

Jennifer Marsh, a recent dental school graduate from Indiana, Pennsylvania, is thinking about jump-starting a retirement savings plan by investing the $50,000 gift that her elderly uncle gave her. She also wants to invest $1000 a month for the next 25 years for retirement. Jennifer knows little about investments and does not seem to have a big desire to learn.

(a) What can you suggest to Jennifer about figuring out her investment philosophy? (Hint: Mention the information in Figure 13.3 in your response.)

(b) Would you recommend active or passive investing for her, and why?

(c) Should Jennifer be a lender or owner?

(d) Identify three risks to her retirement investments that Jennifer should try to avoid, and explain how she can avoid them.

(e) Select two of the five recommended investment strategies to recommend to Jennifer, and explain why she should follow them.

(f) If Jennifer's $50,000 is invested in a standard investment account and her $1000 monthly is invested in a tax–sheltered account, with each account growing at 8 percent annually for 25 years, how much money will she have accumulated? (Hint: Adjust the lump-sum investment for taxes.)

Case 3
Victor and Maria Hernandez Try to Catch Up on Their Investments

The expenses associated with sending two children through college prevented Victor and Maria Hernandez from adding substantially to their investment program. Now that their younger son, Brian, has completed school and is working full time, they would like to build up their investments quickly. Victor is 47 years old and wants to retire early, perhaps by age 60. In addition to the retirement program at his place of employment, Victor believes that their investment portfolio, currently valued at $70,000, will need to triple to $210,000 by retirement time. He and Maria realize that they will have to sacrifice a lot of current spending to save and invest for retirement.

(a) What rate of return is needed on the $70,000 portfolio to reach their goal of $210,000 (assuming no additional contributions)? Use Appendix A.3 or visit the *Garman/Forgue* companion website.

(b) Victor and Maria think they will need a total of $400,000 for a retirement financial nest egg. Therefore, they will need to create an additional sum of $190,000 through new investments. Assuming an annual return of 8 percent, how much do the Hernandezes need to invest each year to reach their goal of $190,000? Use Appendix A.3 or visit the *Garman/Forgue* companion website.

(c) If they assume a 6 percent annual return, how much do the Hernandezes need to invest each year to reach their goal of $190,000? Use Appendix A.3 or visit the *Garman/Forgue* companion website.

Case 4
The Johnsons Start an Investment Program

Harry and Belinda's finances have improved in recent months, even though they have incurred new debts for an automobile loan and a condominium. The improvement has occurred because they cut back their spending on discretionary items (clothing, food, and entertainment) and because Harry also received a sizable increase in salary after changing employers. His new job as an assistant designer at Medical Facilities Inc. pays $6000 more than his other job. The new job is also closer to home, reducing Harry's commuting time. The Johnsons have decided to forgo some current spending to concentrate on getting a solid investment program under way while they have two incomes available. They are willing to accept a moderate amount of risk and expect to invest between $200 and $400 per month over the next five years. Assuming that they have an adequate savings program, respond to the following questions:

(a) In what types of investments (choose only two) might the Johnsons place the first $2000? (Review Tables 13.1, 13.2, and 13.6 for ideas and available options, and consider the types of investment risks inherent in each choice.) Give reasons for your selections.

(b) In what types of investments might they place the next $4000? Why?

(c) What types of investments should they choose for the next $10,000? Why?

On the 'Net

Go to the Web pages indicated to complete these exercises.

1. Visit the website for the Motley Fool at http://www
.fool.com/school/13steps/13steps.htm. Read the article
discussing its 13 steps to "foolish" investing. Which of the
13 steps were you aware of before reading this chapter?
Which did you become aware of after reading this
chapter and the article?

2. Visit the website for investment beginners at
About.com at http://beginnersinvest.about.com/od/

assetallocation1/a/aa102404.htm to read its article on
asset allocation. Identify the asset allocation percentages
with which you would feel most comfortable now. How
might your views change in five years? Twenty years?

3. Visit the website for Investopedia and read its article on
the risk pyramid at http://www.investopedia.com/
articles/basics/03/050203.asp. Contrast your risk
tolerance for short-term and long-term investing after
reading the article. Did your views change after reading
the article? If so, in what ways?

Visit the Garman/Forgue companion website . . .

www.cengage.com/finance/garman

Investing in Stocks and Bonds

!You Must Be Kidding, Right?

Brothers Ricky and Marvin Morton differ in investment philosophies—Ricky is conservative and Marvin holds a moderate investing outlook. Their father left each of them $100,000 when he died ten years ago, and Ricky invested in common stocks while Marvin invested in corporate bonds. After ten years, how much more money is Ricky likely to have in his account than Marvin?

A. $35,000

B. $53,000

C. $163,000

D. $216,000

The answer is B, $53,000. One could typically expect to obtain a long-term average annual return of 8 percent on U. S. common stocks compared with 5 percent on corporate bonds. A $100,000 common stock portfolio that returned 8 percent annually would accumulate to $216,000 in ten years while a bond portfolio earning 5 percent annually over the same time period would grow to $163,000. Ricky's willingness to accept more risk by investing in common stocks may provide him with a balance bigger than his brother's by a whopping 32.5 percent!

Learning Objectives

After reading this chapter, you should be able to:

1 Explain how stocks and bonds are used as investments.

2 Classify common stocks according to their major characteristics.

3 Describe fundamental and numerical ways to evaluate stock values.

4 Determine whether an investment's potential rate of return is sufficient.

5 Use the Internet to evaluate common stocks in which to invest.

6 Summarize how stocks are bought and sold.

7 Describe how to invest in bonds.

What Do You Recommend?

Monkey Business Images/2009, used under license Shutterstock.com

Caitlin Diaz, age 42, is a senior Web designer for a communications company in Lansing, Michigan. She earns $92,000 annually. From her salary, Caitlin contributes $200 per month to her 401(k) retirement account, through which she invests in the company's stock. Caitlin is divorced and has custody of her three children, 10-year-old twins and a 12-year-old. Her ex-husband pays $1500 per month in child support. Caitlin and her former spouse contribute $3000 each annually to a college fund for their children. Over the past 15 years, Caitlin has built a $300,000 stock portfolio after starting by investing the proceeds of a $50,000 life insurance policy following the death of her first husband. Currently, her portfolio is allocated 40 percent into preferred stocks (paying 4.5 percent); 30 percent into cyclical, blue-chip common stocks (P/E ratio of 14); 10 percent into Treasury bonds (paying 3.2 percent); 10 percent into municipal bonds (paying 2.2 percent); and 10 percent into AAA corporate bonds (paying 4.6 percent). Today's comparable corporate bonds pay 5 percent. Caitlin's total return in recent years has been about 6 percent annually. Her investment goals are to have sufficient cash to pay for her children's education and to retire in about 18 years.

What do you recommend to Caitlin on the subject of stocks and bonds regarding:

1. Investing for retirement in 18 years?

2. Owning blue-chip common stocks and preferred stocks rather than other common stocks given Caitlin's investment time horizon?

3. The wisdom of owning municipal bonds rather than corporate bonds?

4. The likely selling price of her corporate bonds, if sold today?

5. Investments that might be appropriate to fund her children's education?

Your Next Five Years

In the next five years you can start achieving financial success by doing the following related investing in stocks and bonds:

1. Include stocks and bond or mutual funds that own stocks and bonds in your investment portfolio.

2. Use fundamental analysis to determine a company's basic value before investing in any individual stock.

3. Resist putting money into so-called hot stocks.

4. Invest part of the conservative portion of your portfolio in TIPS (Treasury Inflation-Protected Securities) to beat inflation.

5. When you have children use zero-coupon bonds to help save for their education.

To earn a larger return than offered by conservative investments, you must accept more risk. Historically, common stocks, for example, have earned substantially more than cash savings, often twice as much. When you invest in stocks and bonds, you can increase returns significantly while increasing risk only slightly. These investments belong in everyone's investment portfolio because they provide opportunities for conservative, moderate, and aggressive investors alike.

This is true despite the recent meltdown of U.S. and global stocks. During distressed economic times the price of an individual stock might fall 5 or 10% or more in one day! Investors lock in losses *only* if they sell what they own. And keep in mind that prices might rebound the next day or week or month. The principles of long-term investing—the essence of this chapter—are valid because over time turbulent stock and bond markets calm down and provide investors fairly predictable returns. In fact, a good time to invest is when the share prices of high-quality firms have been beaten down to affordable levels. When the stock markets are down that means they are "on sale" as prices are lower than usual. You should realize that economic slumps eventually always spark a powerful market recovery. The typical post-recession rally in prices on the stock market is a 50 percent increase over the following 18 months. Investing is an act of faith and confidence in the future of the U.S. and global economies. History argues that by the time students in college are ready to retire stock market prices will have tripled or quadrupled.

Buying individual stocks and bonds feels risky to investors because the rate of return and value of these securities fluctuate up and down over time. Investment expert Peter Lynch says "The real key to making money in stocks is not to get scared out of them." Accordingly, investors often choose to invest in stocks and bonds indirectly through mutual funds, the subject of Chapter 15. Because stocks and bonds are the basic securities used in the world of investing, you need to understand how they are used. When wisely selected, they are excellent choices for long-term investors. Keep in mind when investing in securities that the price—the value today—is not the same thing as money. Such assets are not money until you sell and convert them to cash. Owning an investment portfolio worth $1 million, for example, is not real money. The price of a stock, bond, or mutual fund is simply the market's "best guess" on what it is worth today.

The Role of Stocks and Bonds in Investments

1 Learning Objective

Explain how stocks and bonds are used as investments.

privately-held corporation
One that issues stock purchased by a relatively small number of people and is not traded on a public stock exchange.

start-up capital
Funds initially invested in a business enterprise.

securities
Negotiable instruments of ownership or debt, including common stock, preferred stock, and bonds.

Individual investors provide the money corporations use to create sales and earn profits. The investor shares in those profits. A **corporation** is a state-chartered legal entity that can conduct business operations in its own name. A **public corporation** is one that issues stock purchased by the general public and traded on stock markets such as the New York Stock Exchange. In contrast, the stock of a **privately-held corporation** is held by a relatively small number of people and is not traded on a public stock exchange. The ability to sell shares of ownership to investors offers a corporation the opportunity to develop into a firm of considerable size. It can continue to exist even as ownership of its shares changes hands. AT&T, for example, has issued more than 4 million shares of stock.

A corporation's financial needs will vary over time. To begin its operations, a new corporation needs **start-up capital** (funds initially invested in a business enterprise). During its life, a corporation may need additional money to grow. To raise capital and finance its goals, it may issue three types of **securities** (negotiable instruments of ownership or debt): common stock, preferred stock, and bonds, which we mentioned in Chapter 13.

Common Stock

Stocks are shares of ownership in the assets and earnings of a business corporation. Each stock investor is a part owner in a corporation. **Common stock** is the most basic form of ownership of a corporation. For the investor, stocks represent potential income because the investor owns a piece of the future profits of the company. Investors have two expectations: (1) the corporation will be profitable enough that income will exceed expenses, thereby allowing the firm to pay **cash dividends** (a share of profits distributed in cash) and (2) the **market price** of a share of stock, which is the current price that a buyer is willing to pay a willing seller, will increase over time. Stocks usually require a low minimum investment. Common stocks pay annual returns about twice as high as preferred stocks and bonds. Investors expect to earn annual returns of 8 percent or higher on average over time from the combination of dividends and capital gains.

Each person who owns a share of stock—called a **shareholder** or **stockholder**—has a proportionate interest in the ownership (usually a very small slice) and, therefore, in the assets and income of the corporation. This **residual claim** means that common stockholders have a right to share in the income and assets of a corporation only after higher-priority claims are satisfied. These higher-priority claims include interest payments to those who own company bonds and preferred stocks.

Stockholders have a **limited liability,** as their responsibility for business losses is limited to the amount invested in the shares of stock owned. These amounts may be small or large, but the most the shareholder can lose is the original amount invested. If the corporation becomes bankrupt, the common stockholder's ownership value consists of the amount left per share after the claims of all creditors are satisfied first. Each common stockholder has **voting rights:** the proportionate authority to express an opinion or choice in matters affecting the company. Stockholders vote to elect the company's **board of directors.** This group of individuals sets policy and names the principal officers of the company, **management,** who run the firm's day-to-day operations. The number of votes cast by each shareholder depends on the number of shares he or she owns. Stockholders attend an annual meeting or vote by *proxy*—shareholders' written authorization to someone else to represent them and to vote their shares at a stockholder's meeting.

Preferred Stock

Preferred stock is a type of fixed-income ownership security in a corporation. Owners of a preferred stock receive a fixed dividend per share that corporations are required to distribute before any dividends are paid out to common stockholders. They receive no extra income from the stock other than their fixed dividend, even when the firm is highly profitable. The regular dividend payments appeal to retired investors and others who desire a reliable stream of income. While the income stream may be consistent, the market price of preferred stock is sensitive to interest rates. Preferred stockholders rarely have voting privileges.

Sometimes a corporation decides not to pay dividends to preferred stockholders because it lacks profits or simply because it wants to retain and reinvest all of its earnings. When the board of directors votes to skip *(pass)* making a cash dividend to preferred stockholders, holders of **cumulative preferred stock** must be paid that dividend before any future dividends are distributed to the common stockholders. For example, assume that a company passes on the first two quarterly dividends of $2.25 each to preferred stockholders, who expect to receive $9 each year ($2.25 × 4 quarters). If the company prospers and wants to give a cash dividend to its common stockholders in the third quarter, it must first pay the passed $4.50 to the cumulative preferred stockholders. Furthermore, the usual third-quarter cash dividend of $2.25 has to be made to the preferred

stocks
Shares of ownership in a business corporation's assets and earnings.

common stock
Most basic form of ownership of a corporation.

cash dividend
Cash profits that a firm distributes to stockholders.

market price
The current price of a share of stock that a buyer is willing to pay a willing seller.

stockholder/shareholder
Each person who owns a share of a company's stock holds a proportionate interest in firm ownership (a very small slice) and, therefore, in the assets and income of the corporation.

residual claim
Common stockholders have a right to share in the income and assets of a corporation after higher-priority claims are satisfied.

voting rights
Proportionate authority to express an opinion or choice in matters affecting the company.

preferred stock
Type of fixed-income ownership security in a corporation that pays fixed dividends.

cumulative preferred stock
Preferred stock for which dividends must be paid, including any skipped dividends, before dividends go to common stockholders.

convertible preferred stock
Can be exchanged at the option of the stockholder for a specified number of shares of common stock.

stockholders before the common stockholders can receive any dividends. In the case of **non-cumulative preferred stock,** the preferred stockholders would have no claim to previously skipped dividends. **Convertible preferred stock,** a unique security occasionally sold by companies, can be exchanged at the option of the stockholder for a specified number of shares of common stock.

Bonds

Individuals who want to invest by loaning their money can do so by buying bonds and becoming a creditor (again very small) of the business. As we noted in Chapter 13, a **bond** is an interest-bearing negotiable certificate of long-term debt issued by a corporation, the U.S. government, or a municipality (such as a city or state). Bonds are basically IOUs. Corporations and governments often use the proceeds from bonds to finance expensive construction projects and to purchase costly equipment.

principal
Face amount of a bond, or price originally paid for a bond.

maturity date
Date upon which the principal is returned to the bondholder.

With bonds, investors lend the issuer a certain amount of money—the **principal**—with two expectations: (1) they will receive regular interest payments at a fixed rate of return for many years, and (2) they will get their principal returned at some point in the future, called the **maturity date.** The regular pattern of dividends appeals to those who desire a reliable stream of income. The market price of bonds is sensitive to interest rates.

An Illustration of Stocks and Bonds: Running Paws Cat Food Company

To better understand how a corporation finances its goals by issuing common and preferred stock while also paying returns for stockholders, consider the example of Running Paws Cat Food Company. When reading through the example, imagine that the numbers have many more zeros to better visualize a company the size of Google or Microsoft.

Running Paws Is Born   Running Paws began as a small family business in Lincoln, Nebraska, started by Linda Webtek. She developed a wonderful recipe for cat food and sold the product through a local grocery store. As sales increased, Linda decided to incorporate the business, expand its operations, and share ownership of the company with the public by asking people to invest in the company's future. Running Paws issued 10,000 shares of common stock at $10 per share. Three friends each bought 2500 shares, and Linda signed over the cat food recipe and equipment to the corporation itself in exchange for the remaining 2500 shares. At that point, Running Paws had $75,000 in working capital (7500 shares sold at $10 each), equipment, a great recipe, and a four-person board of directors. Each of the directors worked for the firm, although they paid themselves very low salaries.

profit
Money left over after a firm pays all expenses and interest to bondholders.

after-tax profit
Money left over after a firm has paid expenses, bondholder interest, and taxes.

retained earnings
Money left over after firm has paid expenses, bondholder interest, taxes, preferred stockholder dividends, and common stockholder dividends.

Running Paws Begins to Grow   The sales revenues of a corporation like Running Paws are used to pay (1) expenses, (2) interest to bondholders, (3) taxes, (4) cash dividends to preferred stockholders, and (5) cash dividends to common stockholders, in that order. If money is left over after items 1 and 2 are paid, the corporation has earned a **profit.** If funds are available after item 3 is paid, the company has an **after-tax profit.** The average corporation pays out 40 to 60 percent of its after-tax profit in cash dividends to stockholders. The remainder, called **retained earnings,** is left to accumulate and finance the company's goals—often expansion and growth. In its early years, Running Paws retained all of its profits and distributed no dividends.

Common stockholders, such as the stockholders of Running Paws Cat Food Company, are not guaranteed dividends. However, most profitable companies do pay common stockholders a small dividend

Instant Message

Assume Your Investments Earn 5% to 6%

When planning for long-term financial goals, assume your investments will conservatively earn 3 percent after inflation or at least 5 percent to 6 percent a year. Your investment returns could be higher.

on a quarterly basis until increased earnings justify paying out a higher amount. Given that Running Paws retained all its earnings, you might wonder why people would invest in such a company. Two reasons explain the attraction. First, as a company becomes more efficient and profitable, cash dividends to common stockholders may not only begin but also become significant. Second, the market price of the stock may increase sharply as more investors become interested in the future profitability of a growing company. Common stock constitutes a share of ownership, thus as the company grows, the price of its common stock follows suit.

Increasing sales meant more production for Running Paws. Soon more orders were coming in from Chicago than the firm could handle. After three years, the owners of Running Paws decided to expand once again. They wanted to borrow an additional $100,000, but their business was so new and its future so uncertain that lenders demanded an extremely high interest rate. To raise the needed funds, the owners decided to issue 5000 shares of preferred stock at $20 per share, promising to pay a cash dividend of $1.80 per share annually, providing a 9 percent yield to investors. The preferred stock was sold to outside investors, but the original investors retained control of the company through their common stock.

Running Paws Becomes a National Company

Following its pattern of expanding into new markets, Running Paws soon developed additional lines of cat food that sold well. With the proceeds from the sale of preferred stock, and after a new plant in Brooklyn, New York, opened, the income of the four-year-old business finally exceeded expenses, and it had a profit of $13,000. The board of directors declared the promised preferred stock dividend of $9000 (5000 preferred shares × $1.80) but no dividend for common stockholders. In the following year, net profits after taxes amounted to $28,000. Once again the board paid the $9000 dividend to preferred stockholders but retained the remainder of the profits to finance continued expansion and improved efficiency.

Then one of the original partners wanted to exit the business and needed to sell her 2500 shares of stock, for which she had originally paid $25,000. Because Running Paws was beginning to show some profits, two other private investors recommended by a local stockbroker made offers to purchase her shares. The shares were sold at $16 per share, with 1500 shares going to one investor and 1000 shares to another investor. Thus, this original investor gained $15,000 in price appreciation ($16 × 2500 = $40,000; $40,000 − $25,000 = $15,000) when she sold out. (The corporation did not profit from this transaction.) Now five owners of the common stock, including the two new ones, voted for the board of directors, with each share representing one vote.

During the sixth year, the company's sales again increased and its earnings totaled $39,000. This time the board voted $9000 for the preferred stockholders and $5000 ($0.50 per share) for the common stockholders but retained the remaining $25,000. With the $5000 distribution, the common stockholders finally began to receive cash dividends.

Even with its success, Running Paws faced another decision. To distribute its products nationally would require another $400,000 to $500,000 for expansion costs. After much discussion, the board voted to sell additional shares of stock and issue some bonds.

The company planned to sell 10,000 shares of common stock at $25 per share. This would dilute the owners' proportion of ownership by half. Common stockholders, however, have a **preemptive right** to purchase additional shares before new shares are offered to the public. Thus, each current stockholder retained the legal right to maintain proportionate ownership by being allowed to purchase more shares.

Instant Message

Be Greedy When Others Are Fearful

Billionaire Warren Buffett, known as the "Oracle of Omaha" for running the tremendously successful investment conglomerate Berkshire Hathaway, observes that investors should be "fearful when others are greedy and greedy when others are fearful."

Instant Message

Investment Blogs

There is a vast array of investment blogs. Many are rubbish; some seem useful. Some favorites include www.RandomRoger.blogspot.com, www.Inventing Money.blogspot.com, www.AllFinancialMatters.com, www.GetRichSlowly.com, and www.MyMoneyBlog. See also the Stock Market Blogs Resource Page (http://seekingalpha.com/article/3033) and GetRichSlowly.org.

preemptive right
Right of common stockholders to purchase additional shares before a firm offers new shares to the public.

Bonds were sold, too.★ Running Paws issued two hundred $1000 bonds with a coupon rate of 8 percent. After several months, all of the new stock and bond shares were sold. After brokerage expenses, the company netted more than $190,000 from the bonds to help finance the expansion. On the stock sales, various local stockbrokers took selling commissions totaling $16,000, leaving $234,000 available for the company to use for expansion. These and other investors will follow the progress of Running Paws and buy and sell shares accordingly. The company will not benefit from this trading. Running Paws and its shareholders will benefit from a rising stock price because ownership in a growing company becomes increasingly valuable. If Running Paws continues to prosper, its board of directors might work toward having its stock listed on a regional stock exchange (discussed later in this chapter) to facilitate trading of shares and to further enhance the company's image.

 Concept Check 14.1

1. Distinguish between common stocks and bonds.
2. How do public corporations use stocks and bonds?
3. Why do individuals invest in stocks and bonds?

The Major Characteristics of Common Stocks

2 Learning Objective

Classify common stocks according to their major characteristics.

A first and easy step in evaluating stock issues is to examine the major characteristics of stock classifications. Here you determine which ones match your investment goals.

Price/Earnings Ratio and Beta

Price/earnings (P/E) ratio (or multiple)

The current market price of a stock divided by earnings per share (EPS) over the past four quarters; used as the primary means of valuing a stock.

Price/Earnings Ratio   The **price/earnings ratio (P/E ratio)** (or **multiple**) is the current market price of a stock divided by earnings per share (EPS) over the past four quarters. This ratio is the primary means of valuing a stock. It demonstrates how expensive the stock is versus the company's recently reported earnings, by revealing how much you are paying for each $1 of earnings. For example, if the market price of a share of Running Paws stock is currently $25 and the company's EPS is $1.60, the P/E ratio will be 16 ($25 ÷ $1.60 = 15.6, which rounds to 16). This value can also be called a 16-to-1 ratio or multiple, or a P/E ratio of 16. The P/E ratios of many corporations are widely reported on the Internet and in the financial section of newspapers. Stocks with low P/E ratios tend to have higher dividend yields, less risk, lower prices, and slower earnings growth.

To assess a company's financial status, you could compare that firm's P/E ratio with the P/E ratios for other similar stocks. The P/E ratios for corporations typically range from 5 to 25. The typical market average P/E is about 12, although it varies for different industries. Financially successful companies that have been paying good dividends through the years might have a P/E ratio ranging from 7 to 10. Rapidly growing companies would likely have a much higher P/E ratio—11 to 20. Speculative companies might have P/E ratios of 25 or 50 or even higher because they have low earnings now but anticipate much higher earnings in the future. Firms that are expected to have strong earnings growth generally have a high stock price and a correspondingly high P/E ratio.

trailing P/E ratio

Calculated using recently reported earnings, usually from the previous four quarters.

The standard P/E ratio is, in fact, called a **trailing P/E ratio** measure because it is calculated using recently reported earnings, usually from the previous four quarters. Investors

---

★Companies that need capital to begin or expand their operations sell new issues of stocks, bonds, or both to the investing public. New issues of stock are referred to as **initial public offerings (IPOs). Investment banking firms** serve as intermediaries between companies issuing new stocks and bonds and the investing public.

need to focus on future prospects when analyzing the value of a stock. A **projected P/E** or **forward price/earnings ratio** divides price by projected earnings over the coming four quarters, an estimate available via online stock quote providers. The **earnings yield,** which is the inverse of the P/E ratio (Running Paws' earnings yield is 6.4 percent [$1.60 ÷ $25]), helps investors think more clearly about expectations for investments.

Use Beta to Compare a Stock to Similar Investments

Beta is a number widely used by investors to predict future stock prices. The **beta value** (or **beta coefficient**) is a measure of an investment's volatility compared with a broad market index for similar investments over time. For large-company stocks, the S&P 500 Stock Index often serves as a benchmark. The average for all stocks in the market is a beta of +1.0, and a beta greater than 1.0 indicates higher-than-market volatility. Recall that market risk is assumed to be 8 percent, thus when the overall stock market increases 8 percent a stock with a 1.0 beta is likely to rise the same. Beta reports the relative history of an investment's up-and-down price changes.

Most stocks have positive betas between 0.5 and 2.0. A beta of less than 1.0 (0.0 to 0.9) indicates that the stock price is less sensitive to the market. This is because the price moves in the same direction as the general market, but not to the same degree. A beta of more than +1.0 to +2.0 (or higher) indicates that the price of the security is more sensitive to the market because its price moves in the same direction as the market but by a greater percentage. Higher betas mean greater risk relative to the market. A beta of zero suggests that the price of the stock is independent of the market, much like that of a risk-free U.S. Treasury security. You may look up betas for stocks at Quote.com (http://www.quote .com/beta/chart.action) and at Yahoo! Finance at http://screen.yahoo.com/stocks.html.

Cyclical and Countercyclical Stocks

The term **cyclical stock** describes the stock of a company whose profits are greatly influenced by changes in the economic business cycle. Such companies operate in consumer-dependent industries, such as automobiles, housing, airlines, retailing, and heavy machinery. The market prices of cyclical stocks mirror the general state of the economy and reflect the various phases of the business cycle. During times of prosperity and economic expansion, corporate earnings rise, profits grow, and stock prices climb; during a recession, these measures decline sharply. The stock of many firms characterized as blue-chip, income, growth, value, or speculative stocks can be described as cyclical stocks. Cyclical stocks have a beta of about 1.0.

A stock with a beta that is less than 1.0 or even a negative beta is called a **countercyclical (or defensive) stock** because it exhibits price changes contrary to movements in the business cycle. These stocks perform well even in an environment characterized by weak economic activity and sliding interest rates. Cigarette smokers, for example, do not quit during a recession, and people usually continue to go to movies, consume soft drinks, purchase cat and dog food, buy electric utility service, and grocery shop. The prices of countercyclical stocks remain steady during an economic recession.

✳ Income Stocks

A company whose stock is classified as an **income stock** characteristically may not grow too quickly, but year after year it pays a cash dividend higher than that offered by most companies. It does so because the firm has fairly high earnings and chooses to retain only a small portion of the earnings. To declare high cash dividends regularly, a company has to have a steady stream of profits. Stocks issued by telephone, electric, and gas utility companies fit this profile and are labeled income stocks. Investors in these companies usually are not very concerned with the P/E ratio or the growth potential of the price of the stock. The betas of such stocks are often less than 1.0. Individuals who desire some income from their portfolio are often attracted to income stocks.

---

projected P/E ratio
Because investors need to look to the future rather than the past, this measure divides price by projected earnings over the coming four quarters. Also known as forward price/earnings ratio.

earnings yield
Inverse of the P/E ratio; helps investors more clearly see investment expectations.

beta value/beta coefficient
A measure of stock volatility; that is, how much the stock price varies relative to the rest of the market.

cyclical stock
The stock of a company whose profits are greatly influenced by changes in the economic business cycle.

countercyclical (or defensive) stock
A stock that exhibits price changes contrary to movements in the business cycle.

income stock
A stock that may not grow too quickly, but year after year it pays a cash dividend higher than that offered by most companies.

✳ Growth Stocks

The term **growth stock** describes the stock of a company that offers the promise of much higher profits tomorrow and has a consistent record of relatively rapid growth in earnings in all economic conditions. The return to investors from growth stocks comes primarily from increases in share prices. Such stocks typically pay low or no dividends because most of their earnings are retained to maintain company growth.

Well-Known Growth Stocks   Stocks of companies that are leaders in their fields, that dominate their markets, and that have several consecutive years of above-industry-average earnings are considered **well-known growth stocks.** Investor awareness of such corporations is widespread, and expectations for continued growth are high. The P/E ratio is high, too. Many growth stocks have a glamorous reputation that improves or declines sharply in conjunction with the overall market and, therefore, have betas of 1.5 or more. Investors like well-known growth stocks because they typically pay some dividends and offer a good opportunity for price appreciation. In the past, well-known growth stocks have included those offered by Bristol-Myers Squibb (BMY), Genentech (DNA), Google (GOOG), Monsanto (MON), Panera Bread (PRNA), and Urban Outfitters (URBN).

Lesser-Known Growth Stocks   Because some **lesser-known growth stocks** are not as popular with investors, the P/E ratios for such firms are generally lower (although still high) than those of the more glamorous growth stocks. Often such firms represent regional businesses with strong earnings or companies that may be the third or fourth leading firm in an industry. In recent years, lesser-known growth stocks have included (with their stock symbols in parentheses): Berry Petroleum (BRY), Biogen Idec (BIIB), Knight Transportation (KNX), Momenta Pharmaceuticals (MNTA), and USANA Health Sciences (USNA). Their betas are usually 1.5 to 2.0 or higher.

Value Stocks

A **value stock** is one that tends to trade at a low price relative to its company fundamentals (dividends, earnings, sales, and so on) and thus is considered undervalued by a value investor. A **value investor** believes that the market isn't always efficient and that it is possible to find companies trading for less than they are worth. Value investors try to buy stocks when they are quoted below their fair value and sell them when they rise above that level.

Value stocks often operate within industries that benefit from a growing economy. Stocks that have a relatively high dividend yield, low price/sales ratio, and/or low P/E ratio are classified as value stocks. The low valuations that value stocks enjoy are often a result of some type of bad news (poor earnings report, bad press, legal issues, and so on). Although their stock prices may have changed, some past examples of value stocks have included Kraft Foods (KFT), Northrup Grumman (NOC), Toyota Motors (TM), and ValueClick (VCLK).

Speculative Stocks

The term **speculative stock** describes the stock of a company that has a potential for substantial earnings at some time in the future. These stocks are considered speculative because those earnings may never be realized. A speculative stock may have a spotty earnings record or is so new that no earnings pattern has emerged. Investors in these companies accept some risk because they expect the companies to be highly profitable in the future. They hope that the company will make a new discovery, invent a new product, or generate valuable information that later may push up the price of the stock, creating substantial capital gains.

Examples of speculative companies include computer graphics firms, Internet applications firms, small oil exploration businesses, genetic engineering firms, and some pharmaceutical manufacturers. For these firms, the P/E ratio fluctuates widely in tandem with the company's fortunes, and beta values exceeding 2.0 are common. For every speculative company that succeeds, many others do poorly or fail altogether. Although their stock prices may have changed, some past examples of speculative stocks have included Dean Foods Company (DF), Dynegy (DYN), Level 3 Communications (LVLT), and Rite Aid (RAD),

A **penny stock** is one that sells for less than $1 per share, and there are about 5000. They are typically issued by new companies with erratic sales, few profits, and only some hope of success. Penny stocks are sometimes sold over the telephone by high-pressure salespeople to unsophisticated investors. Legitimate stocks or not, these are very speculative investments.

Tech Stocks

Tech stocks are those in the technology sector. Technology firms are dominant in the stock market and include firms that offer technology-based products and services, biotechnology, Internet services, network services, wireless communications, and more. Some are large blue-chip firms, such as Microsoft (MSFT) and Cisco Systems (CSCO), while most are speculative ventures, such as Advanced Micro Devices (AMD), Hewlett-Packard (HPQ), and Intel (INTC).

Tech stocks
Stocks in the technology sector that offer technology-based products and services, biotechnology, Internet services, network services, wireless communications, and more.

*Blue-Chip Stocks — Dow Jones stocks

The term **blue-chip stocks** suggests a company that has been around for a long time, has a well-regarded reputation, dominates its industry (often with annual revenues of $1 billion or more), and is known for being a solid, relatively safe investment. Typically, blue-chip companies have a history of both good earnings and consistent cash dividends, and they grow at approximately the same rate as the overall economy. The term comes from poker, in which the highest chip denomination is colored blue.

Blue-chip stock shares are widely held by individual investors, mutual funds, and pension plans. The earnings of blue-chip companies (whose stocks are usually considered income stocks or well-known growth stocks) are expected to increase at a consistent but unspectacular rate because these highly stable firms are the leaders in their industries. Examples of such stocks are PepsiCo (PEP), Schlumberger (SLB), 3M (MMM), Wal-Mart (WMT), and Wells Fargo (WFC). Investing in such companies is considered much less risky than investing in other types of firms.

blue-chip stocks
A public corporation that has been around for a long time, has a well-regarded reputation, dominates its industry, and is known for being a solid, relatively safe investment.

*Large-Cap, Small-Cap, and Midcap Stocks

A company's size classification in the stock market is based on its **market capitalization**. This is the total value of a company's common stock shares determined at its current market price. **Large-cap stocks** are those of firms that have issued $3 billion to $4 billion (or more) of stocks. Most are considered blue-chip companies, too. Examples include Electronic Arts (ERTS), First Solar (FSLR), Norfolk Southern (NSC), Proctor & Gamble (PG), and Visa (V). Stocks of midsize and smaller firms often outperform large-cap stocks.

Midcap stocks are the stocks of those remaining companies that are quite substantial in terms of capitalization—perhaps $2 billion to $3 billion in size—but not among the very largest firms. Examples include Dolby Laboratories (DLB), Micros Systems (MCRS), and Priceline.com (PCLN). A **small-cap stock** is stock of a company that has a capitalization of $300 million to $2 billion. Examples include Cheesecake Factory (CAKE), Cubist Pharmaceuticals (CBST), and Sequenom (SQNM). **Microcaps** are firms with $300 million or less in capitalization. When the smaller firms achieve substantial increases in sales and earnings, their stock prices typically jump quite sharply. Examples are Frontier Oil (FTO), Gulfmark Offshore (GLF), and Meridian Bioscience (VIVO).

large-cap stocks
Those public corporations that are capitalized by issuing $3 billion to $4 billion (or more) of stocks; most are considered blue-chip companies.

How to Evaluate Stock Values

3 Learning Objective

Describe fundamental and numerical ways to evaluate stock values.

How do you know whether buying a particular stock is a good idea? Or when you should sell shares that you hold? To get answers, first use fundamental research analysis. Second, understand that evaluating stocks is largely about earnings. Third, use numerical measures to evaluate stock values. And fourth, use beta values to compare a stock to similar investments.

Use Fundamental Analysis to Evaluate Stocks

fundamental analysis
School of thought in market analysis that assumes each stock has an intrinsic (or true) value based on its expected stream of future earnings.

The premise underlying **fundamental analysis** is that each stock has an intrinsic (or true) value based on its expected stream of future earnings. Most professional stock analysts and investors take this approach to investing as they research corporate and industry financial reports. Fundamental analysis suggests that you can identify some stocks that will outperform others given the state of the economy. The fundamental approach presumes that a stock's basic value is largely determined by its current and future earnings trends, assets and debts, products, competition, and management's expertise to assess its growth potential. The aim is to seek out sound stocks—perhaps even unfashionable ones—that are priced below what they ought to be.

technical analysis
Method of evaluating securities that uses statistics generated by market activity, such as past prices and volume, over time to determine when to buy or sell a stock.

An opposing and minority view on valuing common stocks is advocated by proponents of **technical analysis,** often newsletter authors. This method of evaluating securities analyzes statistics generated by market activity, such as past prices and volume. Technical analysts do not attempt to measure a security's intrinsic value but instead use charts, graphs, mathematics, and software programs to identify and predict future price movements. Technical analysis has proved to be of little value, although some novice investors may find technical analysts' logic appealing.

Fundamental analysis suggests that you should consider investing only in companies that will likely be industry leaders—not necessarily the largest firms and fastest-growing industries, but the pacesetters in terms of profitability. You should invest in a stock because you have good reasons related to earnings and profitability, such as a new division that is turning around, competitors that are losing ground, product research that looks promising, or an industry that will be a future driver of profits in the economy.

Measuring Expected Stock Returns

corporate earnings
The profits a company makes during a specific time period indicate to many analysts whether to buy or sell a stock.

Corporate earnings are the profits a company makes during a specific time period. If a company cannot generate earnings now or in the future, stock market analysts and investors are not going to be impressed. As people reach this conclusion, there quickly will be more sellers than buyers of the company's common stock, and that will depress the stock's market price. Here are some numerical indicators of earnings.

earnings per share (EPS)
A firm's profit divided by the number of outstanding shares.

Earnings per Share   A company's **earnings per share (EPS)** is annual profit divided by the number of outstanding shares. It indicates the income that a company has available, on a per-share basis, to pay dividends and reinvest as retained earnings. The EPS is a measure of the firm's profitability on a common-stock-per-share basis, and it is helpful because investors can use it to compare financial conditions of many companies. The EPS is reported in the business section of many newspapers.

There are numerous websites that offer fundamental and technical analysis of stocks. The Motley Fool does so with humor.

In our example, assume that, next year after payment of $9000 in dividends to preferred stockholders, Running Paws had a net profit of $32,000. With 20,000 shares of stock, the company's EPS would be $1.60 ($32,000 ÷ 20,000).

Price/Sales Ratio

The **price/sales ratio (P/S ratio)** indicates the number of dollars it takes to buy a dollar's worth of a company's annual revenues. The P/S is obtained by dividing a company's total market capitalization by its sales for the past four quarters. For example, if Running Paws Cat Food Company's common stock currently sells for $25 per share and 20,000 shares of the company's stock are outstanding, its total capitalization is $500,000. If company revenues (sales of cat food) were $750,000 over the past year, the stock's P/S would be 0.67 ($500,000 ÷ $750,000). Stock analysts suggest investors avoid companies with a P/S greater than 1.5 and favor those having a P/S of less than 0.75. Many investors ignore the P/S, but it works better than the highly acclaimed P/E ratio in predicting which companies provide the best return, as explained in James P. O'Shaughnessy's *What Works on Wall Street.*

price/sales ratio (P/S ratio)
Tells the number of dollars it takes to buy a dollar's worth of a company's annual revenues; calculated by dividing company's total market capitalization by its sales for the past four quarters.

Numerical Measures to Evaluate Stock Prices

Several other numerical measures are used to evaluate stock performance. These numbers are readily available to investors on the Internet. Here are some numerical indicators that will help you assess future stock prices.

Cash Dividends

Stocks usually pay dividends. **Cash dividends** are distributions made in cash to holders of stock. They are the current income that you receive while you own shares in the company. The firm's board of directors usually declares a dividend on a quarterly basis (four times per corporate year), typically at the end of March, June, September, and December. Dividends are ordinarily paid out of current earnings, but, in the event of unprofitable times (low earnings or none), the money might come from cash reserves held by the company. Occasionally, a company will borrow to pay the dividend so as to maintain its reputation of consistently paying dividends. Later profits can be used to repay any funds borrowed for this purpose.

cash dividends
Distributions made in cash to holders of common and preferred stock typically paid four times a year.

Dividends per Share

dividends per share
Translates the total cash dividends paid out by a company to common stockholders into a per-share figure.

The **dividends per share** measure translates the total cash dividends paid out by a company to common stockholders into a per-share figure. For example, Running Paws might elect to declare a total cash dividend of $8000 for the year to common stockholders. In that case, cash dividends per share would amount to $0.40 ($8000 ÷ 20,000 shares).

Dividend Payout Ratio

dividend payout ratio
Dividends per share divided by earnings per share (EPS); helps judge likelihood of future dividends.

The **dividend payout ratio** is the dividends per share divided by EPS. It helps you judge the likelihood of future dividends. For example, imagine that Running Paws Cat Food Company earned $32,000 (after paying preferred stockholders), paid out a cash dividend of $8000 to company stockholders, and retained the remaining $24,000 to facilitate growth of the company. In this case, the dividend payout ratio equals 0.25 ($8000 ÷ $32,000). For that year, Running Paws paid a dividend equal to 25 percent of earnings. Newer companies usually retain most, if not all, of their profits to facilitate growth. An investor interested in growth would, therefore, seek a company with a low payout ratio. The lower the payout ratio, the greater the likelihood that the company will grow, resulting in capital gains for investors.

Dividend Yield

dividend yield
Cash dividend to an investor expressed as a percentage of the current market price of a security.

The **dividend yield** is the cash dividend paid to an investor expressed as a percentage of the current market price of a security. For example, the $0.40 cash dividend of Running Paws divided by the current $25 market price for its stock reveals a dividend yield of 1.6 percent ($0.40 ÷ $25). Growth and speculative companies typically pay little or no cash dividends, so they have limited dividend yields. Such companies are attractive to investors who are interested in capital gains.

Book Value

book value/shareholder's equity
Net worth of a company, determined by subtracting total liabilities from assets.

Book value (also known as **shareholder's equity**) is the net worth of a company, which is determined by subtracting the company's total liabilities from its assets. It theoretically indicates a company's worth if its assets were sold, its debts were paid off, and the net proceeds were distributed to the investors who own the outstanding shares of common stock.

Book Value per Share

book value per share
Reflects the book value of a company divided by the number of shares of common stock outstanding.

The **book value per share** reflects the book value of a company divided by the number of shares of common stock outstanding. Running Paws has a net worth of $230,000, which, when divided by 20,000 shares, gives a book value per share of $11.50.

Often little relationship exists between the book value of a company and its earnings or the market price of its stock. A stock's price usually exceeds its book value per share. The reason is that stockholders bid up the stock price because they anticipate earnings and dividends in the future and expect the market price to rise even more. When the book value per share exceeds the price per share, the stock may truly be underpriced.

Price-to-Book Ratio

price-to-book ratio (P/B ratio)
Current stock price divided by the per-share net value of a firm's plant, equipment, and other assets (book value).

The **price-to-book ratio (P/B ratio),** also called the **market-to-book ratio,** identifies firms that are asset rich, such as many banks, brokerage firms, and insurance companies. The P/B ratio is the current stock price divided by the per-share net value of the company's plant, equipment, and other assets (book value). It tells you the premium that you are paying for the net assets of the company.

In the Running Paws example, the book value per share of $11.50 would be divided into the recent price at which the stock was sold ($25 in this case); thus, the P/B ratio for Running Paws is 2.17. The current P/B ratio for most stocks lies between 2.1 and 1.0. The lower the ratio, the less highly a company's assets have been valued, indicating that the stock may be currently underpriced. If the ratio is less than 1, the assets may be utilized ineffectively. In such cases, an underperforming and undervalued company may become a target of a corporate takeover.

Concept Check 14.3

1. What is the focus of fundamental analysis?
2. Distinguish between EPS and the P/E ratio.
3. Summarize the differences among dividend payout ratio, dividends per share, and dividend yield.

About Employee Stock Options

Many employers give stock options to attract and retain employees. An **employee stock option (ESO)** is a gift, like a bonus, from an employer to an employee that allows employees to benefit from the appreciation of their employer's stock without putting any money down. The company gives the employee the right and opportunity to "exercise" the option by buying the stock sometime in the future at an "exercise" or "striking" price established when the option was given. If the company prospers, when the employee eventually decides to exercise the options, the current share price may be much higher than the exercise price, thus allowing the employee to buy the shares at a considerable discount.

Calculating a Stock's Potential Rate of Return

There is but a single reason to make an investment: to obtain a positive return. One indicator of return is an investment's **alpha statistic,** which quantifies the difference between an investment's expected return and its actual recent performance (outperforming or underperforming) given its risk. A stock or mutual fund with a positive alpha means the company did better than expected for its level of risk; a negative alpha indicates poor performance. Alphas for individual stocks, mutual funds, and other investments are available online through brokerage firms and advisory services. Alphas are an important statistic, but they are based on past performance and, thus, provide only a guide for future performance.

While you cannot know the exact performance of any investment in advance, you certainly will want to pay no more than the "right price" for the investment given its potential rate of return. Calculating returns on a potential investment involves five steps. Armed with these data, you will be better positioned to make informed decisions:

1. Use beta to estimate the level of risk of the investment.
2. Estimate the market risk.
3. Calculate the required rate of return.
4. Calculate the potential rate of return on the investment.
5. Compare the required rate of return with the potential rate of return on the investment.

4 Learning Objective

Determine whether an investment's potential rate of return is sufficient.

alpha statistic
Quantifies the difference between an investment's expected return and its actual recent performance (outperforming or underperforming) given its risk; positive values indicate better-than-market performance.

Use Beta to Estimate the Risk of the Investment

Beta is a useful piece of information when you want to estimate the rate of return you require on an investment in a stock, bond, or mutual fund before putting your money at risk. Betas for individual stocks, mutual funds, and other investments are available online from brokerage firms, advisory services, and investment magazines.

The following example illustrates how to use beta to estimate the amount of risk in an investment portfolio. Assume you are willing to accept more risk than the general investor and that you buy a stock with a beta of 1.5. If the average price of all stocks rises by 20 percent over time, the price of the stock you chose might rise by 30 percent, which is the beta of 1.5 multiplied by the increase in the market (1.5 × 20%). If the average price of all stocks drops in value by 10 percent, the price of the stock you chose might drop by 15 percent (1.5 × 10%).

Estimate the Market Risk

To estimate the required rate of return on an investment, you need to quantify the market risk. **Market risk,** also known as **systematic risk,** which we discussed in Chapter 13, is the risk associated with the effects of the overall economy on securities markets. It often causes the market price of a particular stock or bond to change, even though nothing has changed in the fundamental values underlying that security. Historical records indicate that 8 percent represents a realistic estimate of market risk for U.S. stocks. Market risk was substantially higher during the recent turbulence in stock markets and in the near term it remains elevated.

Calculate Your Required Rate of Return

The return on short-term U.S. Treasury bills has historically exceeded the rate of inflation by a slight degree. Thus, when T-bills pay 5 percent interest, the inflation rate might hover around 4 percent. This circumstance provides almost no gain for the investor. For this reason, investors often use the yield on Treasury bills as a base number that provides a zero **real rate of return**—that is, a zero return on investment after inflation and income taxes.

To calculate your required rate of return on an investment, multiply the beta value of an investment by the estimated market risk and then add the risk-free T-bill rate, as shown in Equation (14.1). For current T-bill rates, see http://www.treasurydirect.gov/indiv/products/prod_tbills_glance.htm, and http://www.treasurydirect.gov/RI/OFBills. Use Equation (14.1) to determine an **estimate of the required rate of return on an investment.**

estimate of the required rate of return on an investment
A calculation that multiplies the beta value of an investment by the estimated market risk and adds the risk-free T-bill rate that suggests to investors the return required to put their money at risk.

$$\text{Estimate of the required rate of return on an investment} = \text{T-bill rate} + (\text{beta} \times \text{market risk}) \qquad \textbf{(14.1)}$$

For example, assume you are considering investing in Running Paws Cat Food Company, which has a beta of 1.5. If you assume a market risk of 8 percent and the current T-bill rate is 2.0 percent, the total rate of return you will require on this investment is 14.0 percent [2.0 + (1.5 × 8.0)]. Investors need the promise of a return higher than 14 percent to put their money at risk in this investment.

Calculate the Stock's Potential Rate of Return

potential return
Determined by adding anticipated income (from dividends, interest, rents, or other sources) to future value of investment and then subtracting investment's original cost.

The **potential return** for any investment over a period of years can be determined by adding anticipated income (from dividends, interest, rents, or other sources) to the future value of the investment and then subtracting the investment's original cost. The investor using fundamental analysis can obtain the figures needed to construct the expected stream of future earnings for a company from a variety of sources. For example, you can use estimates for earnings and dividends gathered from large investment data firms such as Value Line or Standard & Poor's, an individual stock analyst's projections, or figures from the company itself, or you can create your own numbers.

Add Up Projected Income and Price Appreciation Table 14.1 illustrates how to sum up the projected income and price appreciation. You can convert these

Table 14.1 **One Investor's Projections of the Earnings and Dividends for Running Paws Cat Food Company**

End of Year	Earnings	Dividend Income
1	$2.76	$0.76
2	3.17	0.87
3	3.65	1.00
4	4.20	1.15
5	4.83	1.33
Total dividends		$5.11
Average annual dividend ($5.11 ÷ 5)		$1.02

Source: Reprinted with permission of Mark Eiger.

figures into a **potential rate of return** by calculating the approximate compound yield, as shown in Equation (14.2). This figure can then be compared with returns on other investments.

Example: Running Paws Cat Food Company

Based on a recommendation from his stockbroker, Martin Crane, who live in Seattle, is considering Running Paws Cat Food Company as a potential investment. Martin figures that the company's stock might provide a better return than inflation and income taxes for about five years. He has determined the following information about this stock investment: It is currently priced at $30 per share, its most recent 12-month earnings amounted to $2.40 per share, and the cash dividend for the same period was $0.66 per share.

Martin began the task of projecting the future value of one share of the stock by using the EPS information. He first calculated the P/E ratio to be 12.5 ($30 ÷ $2.40). Next, as illustrated in Table 14.1, Martin applied a 15 percent rate of growth estimate (the same rate that occurred in previous years, according to Running Paws' annual report) for the EPS for each year ($2.40 × 1.15 = $2.76; $2.76 × 1.15 = $3.17; and so forth). Using a P/E ratio of 12.5 (the same as the current ratio), Martin estimated the market price at the end of the fifth year to be $60.38 (12.5 × $4.83). This calculation gives a projected net appreciation in stock price over five years of $30.38 ($60.38 minus the current price of $30).

$$
\text{ACY} = \frac{\substack{\text{average} \\ \text{annual} \\ \text{dividend}} + \dfrac{\substack{\text{projected price} \\ \text{of stock}} - \substack{\text{current price} \\ \text{of stock}}}{\text{number of years projected}}}{\dfrac{\substack{\text{projected price} \\ \text{of stock}} + \substack{\text{current price} \\ \text{of stock}}}{2}}
\qquad \textbf{(14.2)}
$$

$$
= \frac{\$1.02 + \dfrac{\$60.38 - \$30.00}{5}}{\dfrac{\$60.38 + \$30.00}{2}}
$$

$$
= \frac{\$1.02 + \$6.08}{\$45.19}
$$

$$
= 15.7\%
$$

To project the future income of the investment in Running Paws—the anticipated cash dividends—Table 14.1 shows that Martin estimated a 15 percent growth rate in the cash dividend ($0.66 × 1.15 = $0.76; $0.76 × 1.15 = $0.87; and so forth). Adding the projected cash dividends over five years gives a total of $5.11. Martin obtained the potential return for one share of Running Paws over five years by adding anticipated dividend income ($5.11) to the future value of the investment ($60.38) less its original cost ($30.00), for a result of $35.49 ($5.11 + $30.38). Thus, Martin has projected that $30 invested in one share of Running Paws will earn a potential total return of $35.49 in five years.

The question now becomes, what is the percentage yield for this dollar return? The **approximate compound yield (ACY)** provides a measure of the annualized compound growth of any long-term investment. You can determine this value by using Equation (14.2). The calculation requires use of an *annual average* dividend rather than the specific projected dividends. In this example, the annual average dividend of $1.02 is computed by dividing the $5.11 in dividend income by five years. Substituting the data from Table 14.1 into Equation (14.2) and using the average annual dividend figure results in an approximate compound yield of 15.7 percent on the potential investment in one share of Running Paws stock for five years. (This formula can be found on the *Garman/Forgue* companion website.)

Compare the Required Rate of Return with the Potential Rate of Return on the Investment

Now the moment of decision making is at hand. You compare the estimated required rate of return on an investment (given its risk) with the investment's potential projected rate of return. In our example involving Running Paws Cat Food Company, the risk suggested a required rate of return of 14.0 percent. The investment's potential rate of return was projected to be 15.7 percent, which suggests that Running Paws is a good buy for Martin at the current selling price of $30—that is, the stock is underpriced. Once armed with projected rate of return information for an investment, you can compare it with other investments.

 Concept Check 14.4

1. Explain why individuals considering investing in stocks begin by thinking about the return on U.S. Treasury bills.
2. Explain how a stock with a beta of 1.0 differs from ones with a beta of 1.2 and 2.5.
3. Summarize the steps in calculating the potential rate of return on a stock investment.

Use the Internet to Evaluate and Select Stocks

5 Learning Objective

Use the Internet to evaluate common stocks in which to invest.

An overwhelming amount of information is available on stock investments. With more than 8000 U.S. public companies to choose from and another 50,000 stocks in other countries, stock selection takes time. Hundreds of investment resources exist, including television and radio shows, books, websites, blogs, and newsletters. What approach should you take? Use the Internet because everything you need is online. The Internet is a source of up-to-the minute, high-quality information on investments.

Begin by Setting Criteria for Your Stock Investments

The process of setting criteria for a stock investment starts with a review of your investment plan, as discussed in Chapter 13 and illustrated in Figure 13.9 on page 402. To make informed selections of the specific stock investments that match your investment goals, philosophy, and time horizon, begin by making decisions on criteria for your stock investments:

- What classifications of stocks are best suited for your goals?
- What market capitalization meets your desires?
- What specific numeric measures do you require on beta, sales, profitability, P/E ratio, dividends, payout ratio, and market price?
- What projected EPS growth do you require?
- Do you want to invest in an industry leader?

Basic Investment Information

Comprehensive investment websites provide updated news headlines; market overviews; market statistics; industry statistics; industry trends; corporate stock symbols; current stock market prices; specific company profiles, history, financials, prices, and outlook for the future; tips on how to build a portfolio; and stock-screening tools with search capabilities. Following are some popular websites for investing:

- The Motley Fool (www.fool.com)
- *Kiplinger's Personal Finance* (www.kiplinger.com/personalfinance/)
- CNNMoney.com (www.money.cnn.com/pf/index.html)
- Yahoo! Finance (www.finance.yahoo.com/marketupdate?u)
- BusinessWeek.com (www.businessweek.com/investor/)
- SmartMoney.com (http://www.smartmoney.com/)
- AOL Money Basics (http://money.aol.com/basics/index)

Set Up Your Portfolio Online

You can set up a portfolio through an online brokerage account or by using any of several websites. For example, see Kiplinger at www.Kiplinger.com and Yahoo! Finance (http://finance.yahoo.com). Both let you insert the number of shares you own and at what price. The site then tracks stock quotes to update the value of your holdings. Also see MSN MoneyCentral's Portfolio Manager at www.moneycentral.msn.com.

Stock Screening

You can research stocks, bonds, and mutual funds by using **stock-screening tools** available on the Internet. Screening enables you to quickly sift through vast databases of hundreds of companies to find those that best suit your investment objectives. For example, you can use the Kiplinger screening tool to filter thousands of stocks using 27 search criteria, and you can use Kiplinger's or another company's tools to identify dividend-paying stocks, small companies, and growth companies. You simply set the standard for screening, such as high P/E ratios, and the program sorts out the investment choices, including five-year EPS growth projections by professional stock analysts. You may be surprised to find how easy it is to screen stocks. The following websites offer stock-screening tools:

- Yahoo! Finance (http://screener.finance.yahoo.com/newscreener.html)
- Morningstar (http://screen.morningstar.com/stockselector.html?hsection=toolcenterstsel)
- MSN Money (http://moneycentral.msn.com/investor/finder/customstocksdl.asp)
- MarketWatch (http://www.marketwatch.com/tools/stockresearch/screener//)

stock-screening tools
Enable you to quickly sift through vast databases of hundreds of companies to find those that best suit your investment objectives.

Did You Know?

How to Use Online Stock Calculators

You can perform almost any kind of mathematical calculation necessary in investing by using one of the online investment websites. For example, by using AOL Money Basics (http://money.aol.com/calculators/stocks), you can get answers to these questions:

- Which is better: income or growth stock?
- What is my current yield from dividends?
- How much do commissions and fees affect my stock's rate of return?
- What stock price will achieve my target rate of return?
- What is the return on my stock if I sell now?
- Should I wait a year to sell my stock?
- Should I sell my stock now and invest the money elsewhere?

Get a Sense of the History of a Stock

You can study the price of stock movements over different time frames, including bull and bear markets, as well as make comparisons to various benchmarks such as the S&P 500 Index. See MarketWatch http://bigcharts.marketwatch.com/historical// and MoneyCentral at http://moneycentral.msn.com/investor/research/welcome.asp.

Go to the Source for Company Information

The investor's section of a company's website contains a wealth of information, including historical data, current happenings, upcoming actions, and latest earnings results. Public companies must regularly report their financial status to the government and the public, and this type of information is available at the company website and through other links.

Corporate filings required by the Securities and Exchange Commission are available on the Internet from the Electronic Data Gathering and Retrieval (EDGAR) project (www.edgar-online.com). Top online sources for stock, bond, and mutual fund information include Morningstar (www.morningstar.com) and Bloomberg (www.bloomberg.com). Each public company has its own website that offers insights from management about the future of the firm, and it is easy to request a company's annual report.

Every company registered with the SEC is required to file once each year to ensure public availability of accurate current information about the firm. It summarizes the firm's financial activities for the year. Its **10-K report** includes company provided information on sales, earnings, profit, and legal problems, and a forecast of the company's future. You can obtain 10-K reports from the SEC online (www.sec.gov).

The company's **annual report** is mostly a numbers-free publication that looks like a slick marketing magazine. While annual reports do contain some summarized financial information, they serve more as promotional corporate brochures.

When a company issues any new security, it files a **prospectus** with the Securities and Exchange Commission. This disclosure describes the experience of the corporation's management, the company's financial status, any anticipated legal matters that could affect the company, and potential risks of investing in the firm. The language is legalistic and full of technical jargon, but the interested investor may find it useful to sift through the details.

10-K report
A firm's financial statements and activity details for any publicly traded company appear in this mandatory report sent to the SEC annually.

annual report
Legally required yearly report about financial performance, activities, and prospects sent to major stockholders and made available to the general public.

prospectus
Highly legalistic information presented by a firm to the SEC and to the public with any new issue of stock.

Though annual reports contain some important information, many are mainly marketing tools for the corporation.

Security Analysts' Research Reports

Stock analysts working for independent stock advisory firms or stock brokerages write research reports on companies and industries, as illustrated in Figure 14.1 with a report from Standard & Poor's. Reports based on fundamental analysis are quite informative. The quality of advice is uneven, ranging from brilliant to pedestrian as analysts have a tendency to run with the herd and make similar recommendations. They often recommend buying certain stocks and rarely suggest selling. The prudent investor interprets "hold" recommendations as a signal to sell.

Stock Research Firms

The two most popular firms that offer stock advisory research services on a subscription basis to individual investors are Morningstar (www.morningstar.com) and Value Line (www.valueline.com). The cost for these services is in the hundreds of dollars per year. A Google search for "stock advisory newsletters" will reveal several dozen firms that offer guidance on stock selections, market updates, and investment advice. You may wish to avoid those that offer suggestions based on a "technical" or "chartist" approach to analyzing stocks rather than a mainstream approach that emphasizes fundamental research.

Amateur investors actually do have some advantages over the big stock research firms. Three to five years before analysts really start to follow such developments, local people can be among the first to see the industry in which they work start to turn around. They also may see nearby businesses with bright futures.

Economic Data

Investors need to stay aware of trends in the general economy. You need to know the stage of the business cycle (recession or prosperity) and the current interest and inflation rates, and you need to understand how economic conditions are likely to change over the next 12 to 18 months. (This topic was examined in Chapter 1.) Economic information is available through almost all media:

- Search engines: Yahoo!, Google, and Momma
- Big newspapers: *USA Today, Los Angeles Times, The Wall Street Journal*
- Business news: *BusinessWeek, Fortune, Forbes, Financial World*
- Personal finance: *Money* magazine and *Kiplinger's Personal Finance Magazine*
- Investment sources: *The Wall Street Journal, Barron's, Investor's Business Daily, MarketWatch*
- News magazines: *U.S. News & World Report, Time*

Stock Market Data

Reports on securities market indexes are provided around the clock in almost every media. "The Dow went up 300 points today." "The S&P 500 rose 168 points." When it is reported that "the Dow rose 110 points today in heavy trading," realize that these "points" are changes in the index, not actual dollar changes in the value of the stocks. A **securities market index** is an indicator of market performance. It measures the average value of a number of securities chosen as a sample to reflect the behavior of a more general market. Indexes aim to provide a comprehensive, unbiased, and stable barometer of a broad market. Investors use the indexes to determine trends to help in their decision making. Popular indexes include the following:

Dow Jones Industrial Average The **Dow Jones Industrial Average (DJIA)** is the most widely reported of all indexes. The DJIA follows prices of only 30 actively traded blue-chip stocks, including well-known companies such as American Express, AT&T, Caterpillar, Chevron, Coca-Cola, Merck, 3M, Wal-Mart, and Walt Disney. The average is

securities market index
Measures the average value of a number of securities chosen as a sample to reflect the behavior of a more general market.

Dow Jones Industrial Average (DJIA)
The most widely reported of all stock market indexes that tracks prices of only 30 actively traded blue-chip stocks, including well-known companies such as American Express and AT&T.

Figure 14.1
Illustrative Stock Analyst's Report

Reprinted by permission of Standard & Poor's, a division of the McGraw-Hill Companies, Copyright © 2009.

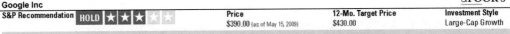

STANDARD &POOR'S

Google Inc

| S&P Recommendation | HOLD ★★★☆☆ | Price $390.00 (as of May 15, 2009) | 12-Mo. Target Price $430.00 | Investment Style Large-Cap Growth |

UPDATE: PLEASE SEE THE ANALYST'S LATEST RESEARCH NOTE IN THE COMPANY NEWS SECTION

GICS Sector Information Technology
Sub-Industry Internet Software & Services

Summary GOOG, which completed its initial public offering in August 2004, is the world's largest Internet company. It specializes in online search and advertising.

Key Stock Statistics (Source S&P, Vickers, company reports)

52-Wk Range	$589.92–247.30	S&P Oper. EPS 2009E	18.95	Market Capitalization(B)	$93.713	Beta	1.22
Trailing 12-Month EPS	$13.68	S&P Oper. EPS 2010E	21.46	Yield (%)	Nil	S&P 3-Yr. Proj. EPS CAGR(%)	14
Trailing 12-Month P/E	28.5	P/E on S&P Oper. EPS 2009E	20.6	Dividend Rate/Share	Nil	S&P Credit Rating	NA
$10K Invested 5 Yrs Ago	NA	Common Shares Outstg. (M)	315.9	Institutional Ownership (%)	80		

Price Performance

30-Week Mov. Avg. ···· 10-Week Mov. Avg. — — GAAP Earnings vs. Previous Year   Volume Above Avg. STARS
12-Mo. Target Price — Relative Strength ▲ Up ▼ Down ► No Change   Below Avg. ★

Options: ASE, CBOE, P, Ph

Analysis prepared by **Scott H. Kessler** on April 20, 2009, when the stock traded at **$ 386.61.**

Qualitative Risk Assessment

| LOW | MEDIUM | HIGH |

Our risk assessment reflects what we see as the Internet segment's emerging nature and relatively low barriers to entry, significant and mounting competition, substantial and increasing investment and related new offerings, our view of somewhat lacking corporate governance practices, and notable share-price volatility.

Quantitative Evaluations

S&P Quality Ranking   **NR**

| D | C | B- | B | B+ | A- | A | A+ |

Relative Strength Rank   **MODERATE**

55

LOWEST = 1   HIGHEST = 99

Revenue/Earnings Data

Revenue (Million $)

	1Q	2Q	3Q	4Q	Year
2009	5,509	--	--	--	--
2008	5,186	5,367	5,541	5,701	21,796
2007	3,664	3,872	4,231	4,827	16,594
2006	2,254	2,456	2,690	3,206	10,605
2005	1,257	1,385	1,578	1,919	6,139
2004	651.6	700.2	805.9	1,032	3,189

Earnings Per Share ($)

	1Q	2Q	3Q	4Q	Year
2009	4.49	E4.58	E4.79	E5.09	E18.95
2008	4.12	3.92	4.06	1.21	13.31
2007	3.18	2.93	2.93	3.79	13.29
2006	1.95	2.33	2.36	3.29	9.94
2005	1.29	1.19	1.32	1.22	5.02
2004	0.24	0.30	0.19	0.71	1.46

Fiscal year ended Dec. 31. Next earnings report expected: Late July. EPS Estimates based on S&P Operating Earnings; historical GAAP earnings are as reported.

Dividend Data

No cash dividends have been paid.

Highlights

➤ We believe that gross revenues will rise 10% in 2009 and 15% in 2010, benefiting from greater spending on Internet advertising, the appeal of search advertising, some market share gains, and international expansion. Revenue increases should continue to be paced, in our view, by GOOG's websites. We think GOOG continues to face challenges in many of its businesses not centered on its more traditional Internet search offerings. We believe the tough economic climate poses difficulties, but that GOOG is relatively well positioned.

➤ We think operating margins will improve in 2009 and 2010, reflecting less reliance on large content partners and a relatively new and aggressive focus on cost containment and cutting, offset by continuing investment in product and service innovation. Although revenues have been adversely affected by currency fluctuations, we believe a new hedging program has aided profits.

➤ Our EPS estimates include notable expenses related to stock-based compensation. We foresee only moderate growth in diluted outstanding shares through 2010.

Investment Rationale/Risk

➤ We believe the global recession, competitive pressures, and concerns about GOOG's size/power could detract from revenue growth. Nonetheless, its business model has been resilient. We are constructive on efforts to broaden its offerings, especially with Web applications (Apps) and mobile services, but believe it has in some cases paid excessive prices to do so. In November 2006, GOOG acquired YouTube for $1.8 billion in stock, and in March 2008 it purchased DoubleClick for $3.2 billion.

➤ Risks to our opinion and target price include possible market share losses, possible industry consolidation intended to better compete with GOOG, new offerings or partnerships that do not succeed as some expect, and challenges related to legal/regulatory issues.

➤ Our DCF model includes assumptions of a WACC of 10.5%, five-year average annual growth of 14%, and a perpetuity growth rate of 3%, and yields an intrinsic value of roughly $430, which is our 12-month target price. GOOG generates billions of dollars in annual free cash flow and recently had $15.8 billion in cash and marketable securities and no debt.

Please read the Required Disclosures and Analyst Certification on the last page of this report.

The McGraw-Hill Companies

calculated by adding the closing prices of the 30 stocks and dividing by a number adjusted for splits, spin-offs, and dividends.★

Standard & Poor's 500 Index

The popular **Standard & Poor's (S&P) 500 Index** reports price movements of 500 stocks of large, established, publicly traded firms. It includes stocks of 400 industrial firms, 40 financial institutions, 40 public utilities, and 20 transportation companies. Companies with the highest market values influence the index the greatest.

NASDAQ Composite Index

The **NASDAQ Composite Index** takes into account virtually all U.S. stocks (about 3000) traded in the over-the-counter market in the automated quotations system operated by the National Association of Securities Dealers. It provides a measure of companies not as popular or as large as those traded on the NYSE, including price behavior of many smaller, more speculative companies, although some big companies (such as Cisco Systems, Intel, and Microsoft) are listed as well.

Russell 3000 Index

The **Russell 3000 Index** measures the performance of the 3000 largest U.S. companies based on total market capitalization.

Wilshire 5000 Index

The **Wilshire 5000 Index** represents the total market value of practically all the 6000-plus U.S.-headquartered stocks that trade on major exchanges.

Foreign Stock Exchanges

Stock exchanges are located in major cities throughout the world, including London, Sydney, Tokyo, Toronto, and Kuala Lumpur. U.S. investors often check the stock exchanges throughout the night to gain a hint of what might happen that day in the U.S. stock market.

Securities Exchanges (Stock Markets)

As we first noted in Chapter 13, a **securities exchange** (also called a **stock market**) is a market where agents of buyers and sellers can find each other easily by providing an orderly, open plan to trade securities. Each exchange has its own rules, is subject to government regulation, and provides constant supervision and self-regulation. The transactions are performed in an organized physical location, such as the New York Stock Exchange (also known as the *"Big Board"*) and the American Stock Exchange, both in New York City. NYSE Euronet is the first trans-Atlantic stock exchange, and it is the world's biggest. For the convenience of traders, regional stock exchanges are located in Boston, Chicago, Philadelphia, and San Francisco. They all are called **organized exchanges.**

Electronic Communications Network and OTC Marketplace

The New York Stock Exchange along with other exchanges continues to move trading to an **electronic communications network (ECN).** This is a type of computer system that facilitates trading of financial products, such as stocks and currencies, outside of stock exchanges. ECNs have lower transaction costs and offering order matching outside of traditional exchange hours.

securities exchange/stock market
Market where agents of buyers and sellers can find each other easily by providing an orderly, open plan to trade securities.

organized exchanges
Actual physical location for a market, at which some securities prices are set by open outcry.

electronic communications network (ECN)
A type of computer system that facilitates trading of financial products, such as stocks and currencies, outside of traditional exchange hours.

★A **stock split** occurs when the shares of a stock owned by existing shareholders are divided into a larger number of shares. This may be an indicator that management expects better profits in the years ahead. Many companies provide a cash dividend to stockholders and sometimes companies declare a noncash dividend in the form of a **stock dividend.** Here the shareholder receives additional shares of the company's stock.

Did You Know?

Why Stock Prices Fluctuate in Value

Stocks fluctuate in price for lots of reasons, such as changes in interest rates, earnings, dividends, and profit forecasts. Investors notice or anticipate these changes and buy and sell accordingly. The prices on most stocks rise and fall about 50 percent during a year.

over-the-counter (OTC) marketplace
Electronic marketplace for securities transactions.

NASDAQ
National Association of Securities Dealers Automated Quotations system, which provides instantaneous information on securities offered by more than 3200 domestic and foreign companies.

Another electronic marketplace for securities transactions is called the **over-the-counter (OTC) marketplace.** In the OTC market, buyers and sellers negotiate transaction prices through a sophisticated telecommunications network connecting brokerage firms. The **NASDAQ** automated quotations system provides prices on securities offered by more than 3200 domestic and foreign companies.

Looking Up a Stock Price

What affects the price of a stock the most is supply and demand. When more people want to buy, the price goes up. When more people want to sell, the price goes down. If you know the company's stock symbol (search Google for "stock symbols"), the current price of any stock may be obtained by inputting the company symbol into Google or any of the other popular investment websites, such as Yahoo! Finance, MSN Money, and MarketWatch.

The millions of daily buying and selling transactions involving stocks, bonds, and mutual funds are summarized in the *Wall Street Journal,* the most widely read financial newspaper in the United States. Many daily newspapers publish abbreviated information, and security prices are quoted and traded to two decimal points. Stock quotations that might appear in the *Wall Street Journal* for Wal-Mart, a retailer, are illustrated in Figure 14.2.

Column 1: YTD % Change. The numbers in this column report the "year to date (YTD) as a percentage" change in the price (+8.6%) of Wal-Mart stock since January 1 of the current calendar year.

Columns 2 and 3: 52 Weeks, High and Low. This column shows that Wal-Mart stock traded at a high price of $63.08 and a low price of $41.50 during the previous 52 weeks, not including the previous trading day.

Column 4: Stock and Sym. This column gives the name of the stock (Wal-Mart in this example) and its abbreviated trading symbol (WMT).

Column 5: Div. The dividend amount is based on the last quarterly declaration by the company. For example, Wal-Mart last paid a quarterly dividend that, when converted to an annual basis, amounts to an estimated $0.28 annual dividend.

Figure 14.2
How Stocks Are Quoted

1	2	3	4		5	6	7	8	9	10
YTD	52 WEEKS					YLD		VOL		NET
%CHG	HI	LO	STOCK (SYM)		DIV	%	PE	100S	LAST	CNG
+17.2	45.29	28.70	Walgreen	WAG	.14	.4	44	27540	39.45	+0.59
+ 3.7	20.56	14.00	WallaceCS	WCS	.66	3.4	17	714	19.70	+0.06
+ 0.1	34.50	23.00	WaddReed A	WDR	.35	1.1	25	2228	32.24	+0.04
+ 8.6	63.08	41.50	Wal-Mart	WMT	.28	.4	42	104572	62.52	+0.82

+18.7	17.50	8.55▲	WacknhutCorr	WHC			18	448	16.45	−0.40
+ 0.1	34.50	23	WaddlReed A	WDR	.35	1.1	25	2228	32.24	+0.04
+17.2	45.29	28.70	Walgreen	WAG	.14	.4	44	27540	39.45	+0.59
+ 3.7	20.56	14	WallaceCS	WCS	.66	3.4	17	714	19.70	+0.06
+ 8.6	63.08	41.50	WalMart	WMT	.28	.4	42	104572	62.52	+0.82
+ 9.6	14.65	7.60	WalterInd	WLT	.12	1.0	12	1625	12.40	−0.10
+ 3.1	42.99	26.52	WashMut	WM s	1.00f	3.0	11	45891	33.71	−0.45
			WashMut	PIES	4.00	5.4	...	14	74.10	−0.40
			WashPost B	WPO	5.60	.9	25	51	596.90	−0.60
			WashREIT	WRE	1.33	4.9	20	590	26.99	−0.11
			WasteMgt	WMI	.01	...	34	15675	27.46	−0.52
			WtrPikTch	PIK			11	51	9.48	+0.38
			WatersCp	WAT			26	17787	32.76	+1.31
			Watsco	WSO	.12f	.7	19	3016	17.05	+1.46
			WatsnPharm	WPI			28	10379	30.22	+0.06
			WatsonWyatt A	WW			18	3106	26.45	+0.95
			WattsInd A	WTS	.24	1.5	16	3198	16.20	+0.45
			WausaMosin	WMO	.34	2.9	62	1503	11.87	...
			Weatherford	WFT			26	165427	46.09	−0.40
			WeiderNutrtn A	WNI	.15	8.6	dd	251	1.75	+0.01
			WeightWatchers	WTW n			1128	35.82	+0.62
			WeingtnRlty	WRI	3.33f	6.5	18	943	50.87	−0.04
			WeisMkts	WMK	1.08	3.8	18	121	28.09	−0.01
			Wellman	WLM	.36	2.3	61	1194	15.90	−0.11
+ 3.2	131.25	81.65▲	WelptHlth	WLP			19	4837	120.59	+3.09
+12.8	51.71	38.25	WellsFargo	WFC	1.04	2.1	25	45366	49.05	+0.16
+ 1.0	25.75	24.75	WellsFargo QUIPS	WPF n			410	25.38	−0.27
+ 9.6	32.78	20	Wendys	WEN	.24	.8	19	5596	31.97	−0.44
+ 6.9	63.25	45.10	Wendys TECONS		2.50	4.0	...	15	62.25	−0.55
+44.0	9.50	3.95	WescolInt	WCC			17	240	7.13	+0.37

Column 6: Yld %. The figure in this column represents the yield as a percentage of dividend income, calculated by dividing the current price of the stock into the recent estimated dividend. The yield of the Wal-Mart stock is 0.4 percent.

Column 7: PE. This figure provides the P/E ratio based on the current price. The earnings figure used to calculate the price is not published in the newspaper but is the latest available. When Wal-Mart's "last" or closing price of $62.52 is divided by earnings, it gives a P/E ratio of 42.

Column 8: Vol 100s. This figure indicates the total volume of trading activity for the stock measured in hundreds of shares. Thus, 10,457,200 shares of Wal-Mart were traded on that day.

Column 9: Last. The price of the last trade of the day before the market closed for Wal-Mart was $62.52.

Column 10: Net Cng. The net change, +$0.82, represents the difference between the closing price (last) on this day and the closing price of the previous trading day. Today's Wal-Mart closing (last) price of $62.52 was up $0.82 from the previous closing price, which must have been $61.70.

Using Portfolio Tracking to Monitor Your Investments

Keeping track of investments requires record keeping, particularly for income tax purposes. These tasks can be performed easily using a computer software program. **Portfolio tracking** automatically updates the value of your portfolio after you enter the symbols of the stocks you own and the number of shares held. Online portfolio tracking services also alert you to events that may affect your stocks. Tracking helps you stay on top of your holdings so you know which stocks are performing well, which are underperforming, and which might need to be sold. See MSN Money (http://moneycentral.msn.com), E★Trade (https://us.etrade.com/e/t/home), Morningstar (www.morningstar.com), and InvestorGuide.com.

portfolio tracking
Automatically updates the value of your portfolio after you enter the symbols of the stocks you own and the number of shares held.

Concept Check 14.5

1. Give three examples of the types of website resources available to investors on the Internet.
2. List five places where you can obtain investment information on a specific stock.
3. Distinguish between the Dow Jones Industrial Average and the S&P 500.
4. Where can you go to look up stock symbols and prices?

Buying and Selling Stocks

Securities transactions require the use of a licensed broker serving as a middleman between the seller and the buyer and collecting a fee on each purchase or sale of securities. A **stockbroker** (also known as an **account executive**) is licensed to buy and sell securities on behalf of the brokerage firm's clients. You can buy or sell securities through an online or human stockbroker who works for a brokerage firm that has access to the securities markets. Brokerage firms often provide investors with investment advice.

As a matter of convenience and to facilitate resale, investors prefer to leave securities certificates in the name of their brokerage firm rather than take physical possession themselves. Securities certificates kept in the brokerage firm's name instead of the name of the individual investor are known as the **security's street name.**

6 Learning Objective
Summarize how stocks are bought and sold.

stockbroker/account executive
Professional who is licensed to buy and sell securities on behalf of the brokerage firm's clients.

security's street name
Securities certificates kept in the brokerage firm's name instead of the name of the individual investor.

Figure 14.3
Securities Transactions

Brokers have a duty to assess each client's suitability for particular investments. Regulations also require that they disclose when they are selling securities owned by the firm for which they work. Figure 14.3 shows the flow of securities transactions.

Discount, Online, and Full-Service Brokers

cash account
A brokerage account that requires an initial deposit (perhaps as little as $100) and specifies that full settlement is due to the brokerage firm within three business days after a buy or sell order has been given.

discount brokers
Charge commissions to execute trades that are often 30 to 80 percent less than the fees charged by full-service brokers, but also offer fewer services.

online brokers
Such brokers, also called Internet or electronic brokers, have reduced the cost of executing a trade to perhaps $20 or even $10 because their primary business is online trading.

day trading
Occurs when an investor buys and sells stocks quickly throughout a day with the hope that prices will move enough to cover transaction costs and earn some profits.

To trade securities, you will need a brokerage firm to act as your agent. You can open an account at a full-service general brokerage firm or a discount brokerage firm. Each charges a commission for any trading it conducts on your behalf. You should make clear to the brokerage firm, in writing, your investment objectives and your desired level of risk. You can open an account rather easily at any brokerage firm. A **cash account** requires an initial deposit (perhaps as little as $100) and specifies that full settlement is due to the brokerage firm within three business days after a buy or sell order has been given. After each transaction, your account is debited or credited and written confirmation is immediately forwarded.

Discount Brokers   Many investors use **discount brokers** because they charge commissions to execute trades that are often 30 to 80 percent less than the fees charged by full-service brokers. These brokers feature low commissions because they have lower overhead. Most offer excellent research and investment tools. Transactions can be completed online as well as via a toll-free telephone number; investors can also obtain price quotes, check the status of their accounts, and transfer funds online or by phone. Popular discounters include Ameritrade, BUYandHOLD, E★Trade, Fidelity, Charles Schwab, Scottrade, ShareBuilder, Muriel Siebert, TradeKing.

Buying and Selling Stocks Online   Online brokers (also called **Internet** or **electronic brokers**) have reduced the cost of executing a trade to perhaps $20 or even $10 because their primary business is online trading. All the discount brokers noted also are online brokers. Online **day trading** occurs when an investor buys and sells stocks quickly throughout the day with the hope that the price will move enough to cover transaction costs and earn some profits. Day traders do not own stocks overnight. Transactions are executed

Did You Know?

Regulations Protect Against Investment Fraud

Public trust is vital to the success of the securities industry; without it, consumers will not invest. Regulation of securities markets aims to provide investors with accurate and reliable information about securities, maintain ethical standards, and prevent fraud against investors. This regulation occurs at four levels:

1. **Securities and Exchange Commission (SEC).** The SEC is a federal government agency that focuses on ensuring disclosure of information about securities to the investing public and on approving the rules and regulations employed by the organized securities exchanges. The SEC requires registration of listed securities with appropriate and updated information. It also prohibits manipulative practices, such as using insider information for illegal personal gain or causing the price of a security to rise or fall for false reasons. All states require registration of securities sold within their states, and they, too, regulate the securities industry.

2. **Self-Regulatory Agencies.** Financial Industry Regulatory Authority (FINRA), and other self-regulatory organizations enforce standards of conduct for their members and their member organizations. They dictate rules for listing and for trading securities.

3. **Brokerage Firms.** Individual brokerage firms have established standards of conduct for brokers that govern how they deal with investors.

4. **Security Investors Protection Corporation (SIPC).** A limited insurance program to protect the investing public when an SEC-registered brokerage firm goes bankrupt. Although investment losses are not covered, the SIPC protects each of an investor's accounts at a brokerage firm against financial loss as a result of unreturned securities and cash up to a total of $500,000, but no more than $100,000 in cash.

5. **Financial Services Oversight Council (FSOC).** President Barack Obama has recommended that Congress create the FSOC to monitor risk across the financial system.

---

online because they can be done quickly with low commissions. Day trading is a risky practice. One of billionaire Warren Buffett's commandments for getting ahead in personal finance states, "You will lose money if you trade stocks actively."

Full-Service General Brokerage Firms

A traditional **general brokerage firm** offers a full range of services to customers, including investment information and advice; research reports on companies, industries, general economic trends, and world events; an investment newsletter; recommendations to buy, sell, or hold stocks; execution of securities transactions by humans and online; and margin loans. Investors receive monthly statements summarizing all of the transactions in their account and commissions, dividends, and interest. Commissions and fees are higher than those of discount and online brokers; however, investors can discuss their investments with a qualified professional.

general (full-service) brokerage firms
Offer a full range of services to customers, including investment advice and research.

Broker Commissions and Fees

Brokerage firms receive a commission on each securities transaction to cover the direct expenses of executing the transaction and other overhead expenses. They have established fee schedules that they use when dealing with any except the largest investors. The fees reflect a commission rate that declines as the total value of the transaction increases. For example, in lieu of a minimum commission charge of $25, a brokerage firm might charge 2.8 percent on a transaction amounting to less than $800, 1.8 percent on transactions between

Advice from a Pro...

Check Your Stockbroker's Background

You can check the background of a stockbroker or a brokerage firm via the Financial Industry Regulatory Authority (FINRA) (http://www.finra.org/Investors/ToolsCalculators/BrokerCheck/index.htm).

Some investors neglect to investigate a stockbroker or firm and lose money as a result. The broker may abscond with the investor's funds; at other times, the investor receives poor advice. Don't let it happen to you!

Allen Martin
California State University–Northridge

$800 and $2500, 1.6 percent on amounts between $2500 and $5000, and 1.2 percent on amounts exceeding $5000.

round lots
Standard units of trading of 100 shares of stock and $1000 or $5000 par value for bonds.

Transaction costs are based on sales of **round lots,** which are standard units of trading of 100 shares of stock and $1000 or $5000 par value for bonds. An **odd lot** is an amount of a security that is less than the normal unit of trading for that particular security; for stocks, any transaction less than 100 shares is usually considered to be an odd lot. When brokerage firms buy or sell shares in odd lots, they may charge a fee of 12.5 cents (called an *eighth*) per share on the odd-lot portion of the transaction, which is called the *differential*.

odd lot
An amount of a security that is less than the normal unit of trading for that particular security; for stocks, any transaction less than 100 shares is usually considered to be an odd lot.

The payment of commissions can quickly reduce the return on any investment. A purchase commission of 2 percent added to a sales commission of another 2 percent, for example, means that the investor has to earn a 4 percent yield just to pay the transaction costs. Brokerage commissions typically range from $25 to 3 percent of the value of the transaction. The easiest way to hold down investing costs is to find a brokerage firm that charges low commissions.

How to Order Stock Transactions

Hundreds of millions of shares of securities are traded daily on the stock markets in the United States. Every trade brings together a buyer and a seller to complete the transaction at a given price.

floor broker
Brokerage firm's contact person at an exchange.

specialist
Person on floor of an exchange who handles trades of a particular stock in an effort to maintain a fair and orderly market.

The Process of Trading Stocks

Assume you instruct brokerage firm A to purchase a certain number of shares at a specific price. The firm relays the buy order to its representative, who coordinates trading. Because the brokerage firm has a seat on the exchange, the buy order is then given to the brokerage firm's contact person at the exchange—a **floor broker.** This broker contacts a **specialist,** a person on the floor of the exchange who handles trades of that particular stock in an effort to maintain a fair and orderly market. The buy order is then filled, either by taking shares from the specialist's own inventory or by matching it with another investor's sell order.

Matched or Negotiated Stock Price

Securities prices are either matched or negotiated.

MATCHED PRICE   On the organized stock exchanges, a match must occur between the buyer's price and the seller's price for a sale to take place. Therefore, a specialist could hold a specific order for a few minutes, a few hours, or even a week before making a match. With actively traded issues, a transaction is completed in just a few minutes. A slower-selling security can be traded more quickly if an investor is willing to accept the current market price (as discussed later).

bid price
Declared highest price anyone wants to pay for a security.

ask price
Declared lowest price that anyone is willing to accept to sell a security.

spread
Represents difference between bid price at which a broker/dealer will buy shares and higher ask price at which the broker/dealer will sell shares.

NEGOTIATED PRICE   In the over-the-counter market, the final transaction price is negotiated because two prices are involved. The **bid price** is the highest price anyone has declared that he or she wants to pay for a security. Thus, it represents the amount a brokerage firm is willing to pay for a particular security. The **ask price** is the lowest price anyone will accept at that time for a particular security. Thus, it represents the amount for which another brokerage firm is willing to sell a particular security.

The **spread** represents the difference between the bid price at which a broker/dealer will buy shares and the higher ask price at which the broker/dealer will sell shares. The spread can be as little as 5 cents per share, but it can range from 10 to 20 cents for OTC stocks. In addition to paying the ask price, investors typically pay a nominal sales commission to their stockbroker for executing the transaction.

If a buyer does not want to pay the asking price, he or she instructs the stockbroker to offer a lower bid price, which may or may not be accepted. If it is refused, the buyer might cancel the first order and raise the bid slightly in a second order in the hope that the owner will sell the shares at that price. Otherwise, the buyer may have to pay the full ask price to complete the deal. OTC trades usually occur at prices somewhere between the bid and ask figures.

Types of Stock Orders

Basically, there are only two types of orders—buy and sell. The stockbroker will buy or sell securities according to prescribed instructions in a process called *executing an order*. Those instructions can place constraints on the prices at which those orders are carried out. Following are examples of instructions that may accompany stock orders:

MARKET ORDER A **market order** instructs the stockbroker to execute an order at the prevailing market price—that is, the current selling price of the stock. A stockbroker can generally conduct the desired transaction within a few minutes. The floor broker tries to match the instructions from many investors with the narrow range of prices available from the specialist. Traders on the floor of the stock market typically shout and signal back and forth as part of this effort to match buyers and sellers. Most trades are market orders.

LIMIT ORDER A **limit order** instructs the stockbroker to buy or sell a stock at a specific price. It may include instructions to buy at the best possible price but not above a specified limit, or to sell at the best possible price but not below a specified limit. A limit order provides some protection against buying a security at a price higher than desired or selling at a price deemed too low. The stockbroker transmits the limit order to the specialist. The order is executed if and when the specified price (or better) is reached and all other previously received orders on the specialist's book have been considered.

A disadvantage for buyers who place a limit order is that they might miss an excellent opportunity. For example, assume you place a limit order with your stockbroker to buy 100 shares of Running Paws common stock at $60.50 or lower. You have read in the newspaper that the stock has recently been selling at $61 and $61.25, and you hope to save $0.50 to $1.00 on each share. On that same day, the company announces publicly that it plans to expand into the dog food area for the first time. Investor confidence in the new sales effort pushes the price up to $70. If you had given your stockbroker a market order instead, you would have purchased 100 shares of Running Paws at perhaps $61.50, which would have given you an immediate profit of $850 ($70 − $61.50 = $8.50; $8.50 × 100 shares = $850) on an initial investment of $6150 ($61.50 × 100).

A disadvantage for sellers placing a limit order is that it could result in no sale if the price drops because of negative news. Assume that you bought stock at $50 that is currently selling at $58 and that you have placed a limit order to sell at a price of no less than $60 so as to take your profit. The price could creep up to $59 and then fall back to $48, however. In this event, you did not sell the securities because the limit order was priced too high, and they are now worth less than what you originally paid for them. A limit order is best used when you expect great fluctuations in the price of a stock and when you buy or sell infrequently traded securities on the over-the-counter market. Limit orders account for about one-third of all trades.

STOP ORDER (STOP-LOSS ORDER) A **stop order** instructs a stockbroker to sell your shares of stock at the market price if a stock declines to or goes below a specified price. It is often called a **stop-loss order** because the investor uses it to protect against a sharp drop in price and thus to stop a loss. The specialist executes the order as soon as the stop-order price is reached and a buyer is matched at the next market price.

As an example of how to stop a loss, assume you bought 100 shares of Running Paws stock at $70. You are nervous about the

Did You Know?

How Over-the-Counter Securities Transactions Are Executed

In an OTC sale, a stockbroker at a brokerage firm representing a buyer communicates with another brokerage firm that has the desired securities. The second brokerage firm is more accurately known as a **broker/dealer** because, in addition to offering the usual brokerage services, it can "make a market" for one or more securities. That is, broker/dealers both buy and sell securities. **Market making** occurs when a broker/dealer attempts to provide a continuous market by maintaining an inventory of specific securities to sell to other brokerage firms and stands ready to buy reasonable quantities of the same securities at market prices. To avoid potential conflicts of interest with a client, when a stockbroker sells securities in which the brokerage firm has made a market, the buying investor must be informed of that fact.

company's entry into the competitive dog food business, however, and you fear that it might lose money. As a consequence, you place a stop order to sell your shares if the price drops to $56, thereby limiting your potential loss to 20 percent ($70 − $56 = $14; $14 ÷ $70 = 0.20). Some months later, you read in the financial section of your newspaper that even after six months Running Paws still has less than 1 percent of the dog food market. You call your stockbroker, who informs you that the price of Running Paws stock dropped drastically in response to the article, which was published in the previous day's *Wall Street Journal*. The broker reports that all of your shares were sold at $55, that the current price is $49, and that the sales transaction notice is already in the mail to your home. The stop order cut your losses to slightly more than 20 percent ($70 − $55 = $15; $15 ÷ $70 = 21.4 percent) and saved an additional loss of $6 ($55 − $49) per share. Thus, the stop order limited your loss to $1500 [(100 × $70 = $7000) − (100 × $55 = $5500)] instead of $2100 [(100 × $70 = $7000) − (100 × $49 = $4900)].

You can use a stop order to protect your profits, too. Assume you bought 100 shares of Alpo Dog Food Company at $60 per share, which now has a current selling price of $75. Your paper profit is $1500 ($75 − $60 = $15; $15 × 100 shares = $1500), less commissions. To protect part of that profit, you place a stop order with your stockbroker to sell at $65 if the price drops that low. If your stock is sold, you will have a real profit of $500 ($65 − $60 = $5; $5 × 100 shares = $500). If Alpo Dog Food stock climbs in price instead, perhaps in response to the bad news about Running Paws, the stop order would have cost you nothing. If the price does climb, you might replace the stop order with one having a higher price to lock in an even greater amount of profit.

TIME LIMITS   Investors have several ways to place time limits on their orders to buy or sell stocks. A **fill-or-kill order** instructs the stockbroker to buy or sell the stock at the market price immediately or else cancel the order. A **day order** is valid only for the remainder of the trading day during which it was given to the brokerage firm. Unless otherwise indicated, any order received by a stockbroker is assumed to be a day order. A **week order** remains valid until the close of trading on Friday of the current week. A **month order** is effective until the close of trading on the last business day of the current month. An **open order,** also

Did You Know?

The Tax Consequences of Investing in Stocks and Bonds

The government encourages investing through tax policies that favor investors.

Dividends and Interest
Taxes are low on dividend income. Funds put into regular investment accounts represent "after-tax money" (you earn an income, you pay taxes on that income, and then you invest some of the remaining money). Taxes are due on any interest, dividends, and capital gains in the year in which the income is received. Interest is taxable at the investor's marginal tax rate. Dividend income is taxed at a maximum rate of 15 percent for most people; a 5 percent rate applies to lower-income taxpayers.

Capital Gains and Losses
Capital gains taxes are low. No tax liability is incurred for any capital gains until the stock, bond, mutual fund, real estate,

or other investment is sold. When you sell an investment, such as a stock, the gain or loss is calculated by analyzing what you paid for the investment plus broker commissions and loads minus the selling price minus commissions or redemption fees. Short-term gains (for investments held less than one year) are taxed at the same rates as ordinary income. Long-term gains (for investments held at least a year and a day) are taxed at special rates: The maximum federal rate is 15 percent, and taxpayers in the 10 to 15 percent tax brackets pay a long-term capital gains tax of 5 percent. Long-term capital gain rates for collectibles such as stamps and coins are 28 percent. Capital losses can be used to offset capital gains or even your regular income. See Chapter 4.

called a **good-til-canceled (GTC) order,** remains valid until executed by the stockbroker or canceled by the investor. If you give an order longer than a week in duration, you should carefully monitor events and then alter the order if the situation changes substantially.

Margin Buying and Selling Short Are Risky Trading Techniques

For investors interested in taking on additional risk, there are two advanced trading techniques, and both involve using credit: buying stocks on margin and selling short. Buying stocks on margin involves using a line of credit from a stockbroker, thereby enabling the investor to effectively control many more shares with a small amount of cash. Investors who sell shares of stock short are actually selling shares they do not own.

Margin Trading Is Buying Stocks on Credit
Some investors open a margin account with a brokerage firm in addition to their cash account so they can buy securities using credit. Opening a **margin account** requires making a substantial deposit of cash or securities ($2000 or more) and permits the purchase of other securities using credit granted by the brokerage firm. Using a margin account to purchase securities, or **margin buying,** allows the investor to apply leverage that magnifies returns. In essence, the investor borrows money from the brokerage firm to buy more stocks and bonds than would be possible with his or her available cash. Both brokerage firms and the Federal Reserve Board regulate the use of credit to buy securities.

The **margin rate** is the percentage of the value (or equity) in an investment that is not borrowed. In recent years, it has ranged from 25 to 40 percent. Thus, if the margin rate is 40 percent, you can buy securities by putting up only 40 percent of the total price and borrowing the remainder from the brokerage firm. The securities purchased, as well as other securities in the margin account, are used as collateral. Margin lending is financed at competitive interest rates.

BUYING ON MARGIN CAN INCREASE RETURNS   Buying on margin is commonly used to increase the individual's return on investment. For example, assume that Greenfield Computer Company common stock is selling for $80 per share. You want to buy 100 shares, requiring a total expenditure of $8000. Using your margin account, you will make a cash payment of $3200 (0.40 × $8000), with the brokerage firm lending you the difference of $4800 ($8000 − $3200).

For the sake of simplicity, we will omit commissions from this example and assume that the brokerage firm lends the funds at 10 percent interest. Thus, your equity (market value minus amount borrowed) in the investment is $3200. If, as illustrated in Table 14.2, the price of Greenfield stock increases from $80 to $92 at the end of a year, you can sell your investment for proceeds of $9200, minus the amount invested ($3200), the amount borrowed ($4800), and the cost of borrowing ($4800 × 0.10 = $480), for a return of $720. Because you invested equity of only $3200 to obtain a profit of $720, you have earned a return of 22.5 percent ($720 ÷ $3200). If you had put up the entire $8000 and not bought on margin, your return on investment would have been only 15 percent ($9200 − $8000 = $1200; $1200 ÷ $8000 = 0.15). In this way, you can use credit to increase the rate of return on your own investment. Those with an aggressive investment philosophy might buy on margin because it gives them the opportunity to obtain a higher rate of return.

BUYING ON MARGIN CAN INCREASE LOSSES   If the price of a security bought on margin declines, however, leverage can work against you, as Table 14.2 also illustrates. For example, if the price of the Greenfield stock bought at $80 dropped to $70 after a year, you would lose $10 per share on the 100 shares, for a total loss of $1000. Your proceeds from selling the stock would be only $7000. If you bought the stock on 40 percent margin, these proceeds are offset by the cost of the investment ($3200), the margin loan from the broker

margin account
Account at a brokerage firm that requires a substantial deposit of cash or securities and permits the purchase of other securities using credit granted by the brokerage firm.

margin buying
Using a margin account to buy securities; allows the investor to apply leverage that magnifies returns—or losses.

margin rate
Set by the Fed, percentage of the value (or equity) in an investment that is not borrowed—recently 25 to 40 percent.

Table 14.2   How Buying on Margin Affects Investment Returns

	Cash Transaction	Margin Transaction
Price of stock rises (from $80 to $92 per share)		
Buy 100 shares at $80 (amount invested)	−$8,000	−$3,200
Sell 100 shares at $92 (proceeds)	9,200	9,200
Net proceeds	$1,200	$6,000
Minus amount borrowed	—	−4,800
Net	$1,200	$1,200
Minus cost of borrowing	—	−480
Return	$1,200	$720
Yield (return ÷ amount invested)	+15.0%	+22.5%
Price of stock declines (from $80 to $70 per share)		
Buy 100 shares at $80 (amount invested)	−$8,000	−$3,200
Sell 100 shares at $70 (proceeds)	7,000	7,000
Net proceeds	−$1,000	$3,800
Minus amount borrowed	—	−4,800
Net	−$1,000	$1,000
Minus cost of borrowing	—	−480
Return	−$1,000	−$1,480
Yield (return ÷ amount invested)	−12.5%	−46.25%
Price of stock declines (from $80 to $60 per share)		
Buy 100 shares at $80 (amount invested)	−$8,000	−$3,200
Buy 100 shares at $60 (proceeds)	6,000	6,000
Net proceeds	−$2,000	$2,800
Minus amount borrowed	—	−4,800
Net	−$2,000	−$2,000
Minus cost of borrowing	—	−480
Return	−$2,000	−$2,480
Yield (return ÷ amount invested)	−25.0%	−77.5%

($4800), and interest on the loan ($480), for a total deduction of $8480 and a net loss of $1480 ($7000 − $8480). Thus, a loss of $1480 on an investment of $3200 is a negative return of 46.25 percent (−$1480 ÷ $3200). The same $10 loss per share (from a price of $80 to $70 per share) would have been a negative loss of only 12.5 percent if the stocks were not bought on margin ($7000 − $8000 = −$1000; −$1000 ÷ $8000 = −0.125). Similarly, the example cited in Table 14.2 shows the magnitude of the loss due to a $20 decline in value as a negative return of 77.5 percent, compared with a loss of only 25 percent if the investor had not bought on margin.

A MARGIN CALL MAKES MATTERS EVEN WORSE   When the price of a stock declines to the point where the investor's equity is less than the required percentage, the brokerage firm will make a telephone call to the investor. A representative of the firm will tell the investor to immediately either put up more collateral (money or other stocks) or face having the investment liquidated. This procedure is known as a **margin call.** If the investor fails to put up the additional cash or securities to maintain a required level of equity in the margin account, the broker will sell the securities at the market price, resulting in a sharp financial loss to the investor. The investor is required to repay the broker for any losses. The margin call concept protects the broker that has loaned money on securities.

For example, in Table 14.2, the 100 shares of Greenfield priced at $80 were originally valued at $8000, consisting of investor's equity of $3200, or 40 percent ($3200 ÷ $8000), and $4800 borrowed from the brokerage firm. Assume that the stock price drops to $60 per share, resulting in a current market value of $6000 for the investment. Because the investor still owes $4800, his or her equity has dropped to $1200 ($6000 − $4800), which is now only 20 percent of the value of the securities ($1200 ÷ $6000), rather than the required 40 percent. The broker, operating with a 25 percent margin requirement, will immediately make a margin call and demand that funds or collateral be added to the account to bring the equity up to a minimum of 25 percent. In this example, to maintain a 25 percent margin, an additional $300 ($6000 × 0.25 = $1500; $1500 − $1200 = $300) would be required.

Did You Know?

How to Determine a Margin Call Stock Price

To determine the price at which a margin call for a stock will occur, use the formula given in Equation (14.3). This formula also appears on the *Garman/Forgue* companion website.

$$\text{Margin call stock price} = \frac{\text{amount owed broker} \div (1 - \text{margin call requirement})}{\text{number of shares bought}} \quad (14.3)$$

$$\$64 = \frac{\$4800 \div (1 - 0.25)}{100}$$

Substituting the figures from the Running Paws text example, the investor will receive a margin call if the stock price dropped below $64, as equity at this point is 25 percent.

Selling Short Is Selling Stocks Borrowed from Your Broker

Buying a security with the hope that it will go up in value—the goal of most investors—is called **buying long.** You might suspect, however, that the price of a security will drop. You can earn profits when the price of a security declines by **selling short.** In this trading technique, investors sell securities they do not own (borrowing them from a broker) and later buy the same number of shares of the security at a lower price (returning them to the broker). Thus, the investor earns a profit on the transaction. Brokerage firms require an investor to maintain a margin account when selling short because it provides some assurance that the investor can repay the firm for the borrowed stock, if necessary. As a result, some or all of an investor's funds deposited in a margin account are effectively tied up during a short sale. Many brokers hold the proceeds of a short sale, without paying interest, until the customer **covers the position** by buying it back for delivery to the broker.

AN EXAMPLE OF SHORT SELLING As an example, suppose you believe that the price of Greenfield stock will drop substantially over the next several months. You have heard that some top managers of the company may resign and that competitors are expected to introduce newer products. Accordingly, you instruct your broker to sell 100 shares of Greenfield at $80 per share ($80 × 100 = $8000). In this illustration, assume that you have a 40 percent margin requirement, which means you have committed $3200 (0.40 × $8000). The shares are actually borrowed by the broker from another investor or another broker. Several months later, Greenfield announces lower profits because of strong competition, and the share price drops to $70. Now you instruct your broker to buy 100 shares at the new price and use the purchased shares to repay the borrowed shares. You gain a profit of $1000 ($8000 − $7000), ignoring commissions, providing a return of 31.3 percent ($1000 ÷ $3200).

USING MARGIN TO SELL SHORT A very small price drop can provide big profits for the short-term investor who sells short *and* uses margin-buying techniques. As an example, imagine that you sell 100 shares of a $10 stock with a 40 percent margin requirement. The committed funds amount to $400 (0.40 × $1000). Even if the price of the stock declines by only $1, you still earn a significant profit: 100 shares sold at $10 equals $1000, minus 100 shares bought at $9 equals $900, for a profit of $100 and a return of 25 percent ($100 ÷ $400).

margin call
If a stock price declines to the point that the investor's equity is less than the required percentage, a representative of the brokerage firm makes a phone call and tells the investor to either put up more money or securities or face having the position bought on margin (liquidated).

buying long
Buying a security (especially on margin) with the hope that the stock price will rise.

selling short
Investors selling securities they do not own (borrowing them from a broker) and later buying the same number of shares of the security at a lower price (returning them to the broker).

covering a position
When an investor using a margin account buys back securities sold short or sells securities bought long.

The price could decline in just a day or two. This possibility of a fast, high return explains the allure of such investments.

Almost unlimited losses can occur with the use of margin to sell short if the price rises rather than falls. If the $10 stock soars to $22, for example, the loss will exceed the original investment: 100 shares sold at $10 equals $1000, minus 100 shares bought at $22 equals $2200, for a loss of $1200 and a negative return of 550 percent ($2200 ÷ $400). When the price of a security rises, short sellers are subject to margin calls.

Only a small proportion of investors sell stocks short because this approach is so risky. Selling short and buying on margin are techniques to be used only by sophisticated investors. Rydex Investments and ProFunds sell short index mutual funds, allowing market timers to profit during bear markets.

Concept Check 14.6

1. Summarize the differences among discount, online, and full-service brokers.
2. Distinguish between round lot and odd lot broker's commissions.
3. Summarize the differences among types of stock orders: market, limit, and stop order.
4. Explain what buying on margin is and how it can go wrong for an investor.
5. Explain what selling short is and how it can go wrong for an investor.

Investing in Bonds

7 Learning Objective

Describe how to invest in bonds.

While bonds usually offer a lower return to investors than stocks there are good reasons to include bonds in one's portfolio. The primary one is to reduce market risk. Others include obtaining a regular source of predictable although lower income, likelihood of profiting from possible future increases in the value of bonds, and matching some of one's assets to one's investment time horizon. A variety of bonds are available to the investor.

investment-grade bonds
Offer investors a reasonable certainty of regularly receiving periodic income (interest) and retrieving the amount originally invested (principal).

par value/face value
Some multiple of $1000 that is printed on a bond when issued and repaid at maturity.

speculative-grade bonds
Long-term, high-risk, high-interest-rate corporate (or municipal) IOUs issued by companies (or municipalities) with poor or no credit ratings. Also called junk bonds or high-yield bonds.

default rate
Percentage of bonds that do not repay principal at maturity and sometimes cease interest payments in the interim.

Investment-grade bonds offer investors a reasonable certainty of regularly receiving the periodic income (interest) and retrieving the amount originally invested (principal). Bonds are usually issued at a **par value** (also known as **face value**) of $1000. An investor typically earns a low to moderate return on bond investments, an appropriate yield when compared with the higher total returns earned on riskier stocks and stock mutual funds. Fewer than 800 of the 23,000 largest U.S. companies that issue bonds meet the highest investment-grade rating standards. Owning some bonds (or bond mutual funds) along with stocks and cash diversifies an investment portfolio. The Bond Market Association (http://www.investinginbonds.com/) sponsors a bond website.

Speculative-grade bonds pay a high interest rate. These are often called **junk bonds,** and they are long-term, high-risk, high-interest-rate corporate (or municipal) IOUs issued by companies (or municipalities) with poor or no credit ratings. The interest rates paid investors on junk bonds are 3.5 to 8 percent higher than those of Treasury bonds. Also called **high-yield bonds,** they carry investment ratings that are below traditional investment grade and carry a higher risk of default (not repay the bond investors). The **default rate** on high-quality bonds is less than 1 percent. The default rate on junk bonds typically is between 8 and 24 percent. For more information, see Bond Pickers (www.bondpickers.com) or www.defaultrisk.com or search Google using "high-yield bond offerings."

Individual investors often avoid buying individual junk bonds because of the substantial financial risk involved with owning too few investments. Instead, they reduce risk by diversifying their investments through a "high-yield income" bond mutual fund (see Chapter 15) that has junk bonds in its portfolio.

Corporate, U.S. Government, and Municipal Bonds

Three types of bonds are available: corporate bonds, U.S. government securities, and municipal government bonds.

Corporate Bonds   **Corporate bonds** are interest-bearing certificates of long-term debt issued by a corporation. They represent a needed source of funds for corporations. The dollar value of newly issued bonds is three times the dollar value of newly issued stocks. Because of tax regulations, corporations often finance major projects by issuing long-term bonds instead of selling stocks. One reason they do so is that payments of dividends to common and preferred stockholders are not tax deductible for corporations, unlike interest paid to bondholders. State laws require corporations to make bond interest payments on time. Therefore, companies in financial difficulty are required to pay bondholders before paying any short-term creditors.

Compared with other bonds, corporate bonds pay the highest interest rates. The default risk varies with the issuer. To help you in appraising the risks and potential rewards of bond investments, independent advisory services, such as Moody's Investors Service, Standard & Poor's, and Fitch, grade bonds for credit risk. These firms publish unbiased ratings of the financial conditions of corporations and municipalities that issue bonds. A **bond rating** represents the opinion of an outsider on the quality—or creditworthiness—of the issuing organization. It reflects the likelihood that the issuing organization will be able to repay its debt. Ratings for each bond issue are continually reevaluated, and they often change after the original security has been sold to the public. Investors have access to measures of the **default risk** (or **credit risk**), which is the uncertainty associated with not receiving the promised periodic interest payments as well as the principal amount when it becomes due at maturity. Bond rating directories are available in large libraries and online.

Table 14.3 shows the bond ratings used by Moody's and Standard & Poor's. The higher the rating, the greater the probable safety of the bond and the lower the default risk. The lower the rating of the bond, the higher the stated interest rate or the effective interest rate.

corporate bonds
Interest-bearing certificates of long-term debt issued by a corporation.

bond rating
An impartial outsider's opinion of the quality—or creditworthiness—of the issuing organization.

default risk/credit risk
Uncertainty associated with not receiving the promised periodic interest payments and the principal amount when it becomes due at maturity.

Table 14.3   **Summary of Bond Ratings**

Ratings		
Moody's	**Standard & Poor's**	**Interpretation of Ratings**
Aaa	AAA	High investment quality suggests ability to repay principal and interest on time. Aaa and AAA bonds are generally referred to as "gilt-edged" because issuers have demonstrated profitability over the years and have paid their bondholders their interest without interruption; thus, they carry the smallest risk.
Aa	AA	
A	A	
Baa	BBB	Medium-quality investments that adequately provide security to principal and interest. They are neither highly protected nor poorly secured; thus, they may have some speculative characteristics.
Ba	BB	
	B	
B	CCC	Lack characteristics of a desirable investment and investors have decreasing assurance of repayment as the rating declines. Elements of danger may be present regarding repayment of principal and interest.
Caa	CC	
Ca	C	
C	DDD	In default with little prospect of regaining any investment standing.
	DD	
	D	

Note: Bonds rated Baa and higher by Moody's and BBB and higher by S&P are investment-grade quality; Ba, BB, and lower-rated bonds are junk bonds.

When bonds are reduced in price from their face amount, more risk is involved. Higher ratings denote confidence that the issuer will not default and, if necessary, that the bond can readily be sold before its maturity date. Investment-grade corporate bonds may provide returns as much as 1.5 percentage points higher than the returns available on comparable U.S. Treasury securities.

U.S. Government Bills, Notes, and Bonds

U.S. Treasury securities are the world's safest investment because the government has never defaulted on its debt. U.S. Treasury securities are backed by the "full faith, credit, and taxing power of the U.S. government," and this all but guarantees the timely payment of principal and interest.

U.S. government securities are classified into two groups: (1) Treasury bills, notes, and bonds and (2) federal agency issue notes, bonds, and certificates. Treasury bills, notes, and bonds are collectively known as **Treasury securities,** or **Treasuries.** The federal government uses these debt instruments to finance the public national debt. Treasury securities have excellent liquidity and are simple to acquire and sell. Previously issued marketable Treasury securities are bought and sold in securities markets through brokers. New issues can be purchased online using the Treasury Direct Plan (www.publicdebt.treas.gov). Individuals may buy Treasury securities in amounts as small as $100. The interest rates on federal government securities are lower than those on corporate bonds because they are virtually risk free. The possibility of default is near zero. Individuals with a conservative investment philosophy are often attracted to the certainty offered by U.S. government securities. Investors can purchase Treasury securities through their bank or broker or directly from the Treasury. Investors often buy Treasury issues to protect a portion of their assets and to diversify their portfolios. Although interest income is subject to federal income taxes, interest earned on Treasury securities is exempt from state and local income taxes.

Treasury Bills, Notes, and Bonds

Treasury bills, or **T-bills,** are short-term government securities with maturities ranging from a few days to 52 weeks. Bills are sold at a discount from their face value (par). The difference between the original purchase price and what the Treasury pays you at maturity, the gain or "par," is interest. This interest is exempt from state and local income taxes but is reported as interest income on your federal tax return in the year the Treasury bill matures. Stated as an interest rate, the return on such investments is called a **discount yield.** For example, if you buy a $10,000 26-week Treasury bill for $9750 and hold it until maturity, your interest will be $250. An investor can hold a bill until maturity or sell it before it is due. When a bill matures, the proceeds can be reinvested into another bill or redeemed and the principal will be deposited into the investor's checking or savings account.

A **Treasury note** or **bond** is a fixed-principal, fixed-interest-rate government security issued for an intermediate or long term. Notes are issued for two, three, five, or ten years, and pay interest every six months. Treasury bonds have a maturity of 10 to 30 years. Notes and bonds exist only as electronic entries in accounts. The interest rate on notes and bonds is typically higher than the rates for T-bills because the lending period is longer. Interest payments is to be reported as interest income on one's federal tax return in the year received. When the security matures, the investor is repaid the principal. Investors can hold a note or bond until maturity or sell it.

I bonds are nonmarketable savings bonds backed by the U.S. government that pay an earnings rate that is a combination of two rates: a fixed interest rate that is set when the investor buys the bond and a semiannual variable interest rate tied to inflation that protects the investor's purchasing power. They are sold at face value, such as $50 for a $50 bond. Interest stops accruing 30 years after issue, and I bonds pay off only when redeemed. If you redeem an I bond within the first

---

Treasury securities
Known as Treasuries, securities issued by the U.S. government, including bills, notes, and bonds.

Treasury bills
Known as T-bills, U.S. government securities with maturities of one year or less.

discount yield
Difference between the original purchase price of a T-bill and what the Treasury pays you at maturity—the gain, or "par," is interest.

Treasury note/Treasury bond
Fixed-principal, fixed-interest-rate government security issued for an intermediate term or long term. Notes mature in ten years or less; bonds mature in more than ten years.

I bonds
Nonmarketable savings bonds backed by the U.S. government that pay an earnings rate that combines two rates: a fixed interest rate set when the investor buys the bond and a semiannual variable interest rate tied to inflation that protects the investor's purchasing power.

Instant Message

Reinvestment Risk

As we noted in Chapter 13, **reinvestment risk** (or **duration risk**) is the risk that the return on a future investment will not be the same as the return earned by the original investment in part because of falling interest rates. Also, because of inflation the promised rate of interest will turn out to be worth less over time.

five years, you will forfeit the three most recent months' interest; after five years, you will not be penalized. All earnings on savings bonds are exempt from both state and local income taxes, while federal taxes can be deferred until the bonds are either redeemed or reach final maturity. I bonds cashed in to pay education expenses are tax exempt.

Treasury Inflation-Protected Securities (TIPS) are marketable Treasury securities whose principal increases with changes in the Consumer Price Index. These inflation-indexed bonds are the only investment that guarantees that the investor's return will outpace inflation. TIPS bonds are sold in terms from 5 to 30 years, and interest is paid to TIPS owners every six months until they mature. The interest rate is set when the security is purchased, and the rate never changes. The principal is adjusted every six months according to the rise and fall of the consumer price index (CPI); if inflation occurs and the CPI rises, the principal increases. The government sends the interest payment on the new principal to the investor's account. The fixed interest rate on TIPS is applied to the inflation-adjusted principal; so if inflation occurs throughout the life of a TIPS security, every interest payment will be greater than the one before it. The amount of each interest payment is determined by multiplying the inflation-adjusted principal by one-half the interest rate. The inflation-adjusted amount added to the principal on a TIPS bond every six months is taxable, even though the investor does not receive the money until the bond matures. Thus, TIPS bonds pay "phantom taxable interest income," like **zero-coupon bonds** (described in the Advice from a Pro...box on page 445), so the investor pays federal income taxes on the interest earned each year. The investor uses other funds to pay the taxes on that income.

When TIPS mature, the federal government pays the inflation-adjusted principal (or the original principal if it is greater). Investors can hold a TIPS bond until it matures or sell it before it matures. The interest on TIPS bonds can be excluded from federal income tax when the bond owner pays tuition and fees for higher education in the year the bonds are redeemed.

U.S. government savings bonds are nonmarketable, interest-bearing bonds issued by the federal government and sold at face value. They are considered a low-risk savings product that earns interest while protecting one from inflation.

Series EE/E savings bonds are a secure savings product issued by the federal government that pays a fixed rate of interest for up to 30 years. Electronic **EE Savings Bonds** are sold at face value in TreasuryDirect. Paper EE Savings Bonds are sold at one-half of the face value and pay no annual interest, and they may be redeemed at full value upon maturity. For example, a $100 EE savings bond might be purchased for half of its face amount, $50. The interest, compounded semiannually, accumulates within the bond itself, and the return to the investor comes from redeeming the bond at its stated face value at the maturity date. Interest on Series EE bonds is exempt from state and local taxes. There is no federal income tax liability on the interest at redemption if the proceeds are used to fund the child's college education. (**Series HH savings bonds** (no longer sold) are issued at par and acquired only by exchanging Series EE bonds. Interest on Series HH bonds is exempt from state and local taxes.)

Federal Agency Debt Issues
More than 100 different bonds, notes, and certificates of debt are issued by various federal agencies that are government sponsored but stockholder owned. Examples of these agencies include Federal National Mortgage Association (Fannie Mae), Government National Mortgage Association (Ginnie Mae), and Student Loan Marketing Association (Sallie Mae). Ginnie Mae and Fannie Mae buy mortgage loans from lenders, thereby supplying them with more cash to make loans. Each security represents interest in a pool of mortgages that are sold to institutions and investors in units of $25,000 (they can also be purchased in smaller units through a mutual fund). When homeowners make their monthly mortgage payments to Ginnie Mae, part of the principal and interest is passed to investors.

The assets and resources of the issuing agency back these agency issues. Although the federal government does not guarantee the debt issued by such agencies, it did provide billions of dollars when Fannie Mae and Ginnie Mae faced default. Agency issues are not as widely

---

Treasury Inflation-Protected Securities (TIPS)
Marketable Treasury bonds whose value increases with inflation. These inflation-indexed $1000 bonds are the only investment that guarantees that the investor's return will outpace inflation.

zero-coupon bonds (zeros or deep discount bonds)
Municipal, corporate, and Treasury bonds that are issued at a sharp discount from face value and pay no annual interest but are redeemed at full face value upon maturity.

U.S. government savings bonds
Nonmarketable, interest-bearing bonds issued by the U.S. Treasury.

series EE savings bonds
Nonmarketable, interest-bearing bonds issued by the federal government that are issued at a sharp discount from face value and pay no annual interest, and they may be redeemed at full value upon maturity.

publicized as Treasury securities, yet they often pay a yield that is higher than the yield for comparable-term Treasury securities because of their somewhat higher degree of risk.

Municipal Government Bonds

municipal government bonds (munis)
Long-term debts (bonds) issued by local governments (cities, states, and various districts and political subdivisions) and their agencies.

Municipal Government Bonds   As we discussed in Chapter 4, **municipal government bonds** (also called **munis**) are long-term debts issued by local governments (cities, states, and various districts and political subdivisions) and their agencies. Their proceeds are used to finance public improvement projects, such as roads, bridges, and parks, or to pay ongoing expenses. Moody's Bond Record rates some 20,000 munis, and twice as many unrated securities exist. Bonds range in quality from AAA-rated state highway bonds to unrated securities issued by local governmental parking authorities.

The investor's interest income on municipal bonds is not subject to federal income taxes. This is because the U.S. Constitution requires that municipal bond interest be exempt from federal income tax. Because the interest income is tax free, municipal bonds are also known as **tax-free bonds** or **tax-exempt bonds.** Interest income on munis also is exempt from state and local income taxes when the investor lives in the state that issued the bond.

Municipal bonds offer a lower stated return than other bonds. However, if your marginal tax rate is higher than 25 percent, it generally makes economic sense to invest in municipal bonds because the after-tax return on a muni might be higher than that of a corporate bond. To compare the after-tax returns of investments, see page 130.

Capital gains on the sale of munis are taxable. Such gains may be realized when bonds are bought at a discount and then sold at a higher price or redeemed for full value at maturity. Bonds bought at a premium also may appreciate to produce a gain.

Unique Characteristics of Bond Investing

Bonds have certain characteristics that distinguish them from other investment alternatives.

coupon rate/coupon/coupon yield/stated interest rate
Interest rate printed on the certificate when the bond is issued.

Coupon Rate   The bond's **coupon rate** (also known as the **coupon, coupon yield,** or **stated interest rate**) is the interest rate printed on the certificate when the bond is issued. It reflects the total annual fixed rate of interest that will be paid. For example, Leslie Geradine Sherman, a retired teacher from Laramie, Wyoming, bought a 20-year, $1000 Running Paws Cat Food Company bond last week with a coupon rate of 7 percent that promises to pay her $70 in interest annually (bonds pay interest in two semiannual installments—$35 in this instance). A disadvantage of bonds is that the investment does not provide the automatic benefit of compounding of interest; therefore, investors have no choice but to find other places to invest interest payments.

serial bonds
Bonds that are retired serially; that is, each bond is numbered consecutively and matures according to a prenumbered schedule at stated intervals.

sinking fund
Bond feature through which money is set aside with a trustee each year for repayment of the principal portion of the debt at maturity.

indenture
Written, legal agreement between bondholders and debtor that describes terms of the debt by setting forth the maturity date, interest rate, and other details.

Serial or Sinking Fund   The coupon rate of a bond remains the same until the maturity date, when the face amount is due and the debt is required to be paid off (or **retired**). Corporate bonds often mature in 20 to 30 years. Occasionally, bonds are retired serially; that is, each bond is numbered consecutively and matures according to a prenumbered schedule at stated intervals. These investments are known as **serial bonds.** Many bonds include a **sinking fund** through which money is set aside with a trustee each year for repayment of the principal portion of the debt. The details about each bond issue are contained in its **indenture.** This written, legal agreement between a group of bondholders (representing each bondholder) and the debtor describes the terms of the debt by setting forth the maturity date, interest rate, and other factors.

secured bond
Pledges specific assets as collateral in indenture or has the principal and interest guaranteed by another corporation or government agency.

Secured or Unsecured   Bonds are issued as either secured or unsecured. A corporation issuing a **secured bond** pledges specific assets

Did You Know?

The Top 3 Financial Missteps of Investing in Stocks and Bonds

People slip up in investing in stocks and bonds when they do the following:

1. Buy and sell more often than they should
2. Diversify less than they should
3. Hold on to a poor performing investment too long

as collateral in the indenture or has the principal and interest guaranteed by another corporation or a government agency. In the event of default, the trustee could take legal action to seize and sell such assets. In the event of bankruptcy, the claims of secured creditors are paid first.

An **unsecured bond** (or **debenture**) does not name collateral as security for the debt and is backed only by the good faith and reputation of the issuing agency. Although secured bonds might appear safer than unsecured bonds, this assumption may not be true. The strong financial reputations of many large corporations enable them to offer unsecured bonds that are safer than the secured bonds of many other companies. All federal government bonds are unsecured and are backed by the U.S. government.

unsecured bond/debenture
Does not name collateral as security for debt; backed only by the good faith and reputation of the issuing agency.

Registered and Issued
By law, all bonds issued now are **registered bonds.** This provides for the recording of the bondholder's name so that checks or electronic funds transfers for payment of interest and principal can be safely forwarded when due. The Internal Revenue Service is notified of the payments as well. A registered bond can be transferred only when the registered owner endorses the transaction.

registered bond
Bondholder's name is recorded so that checks or electronic funds transfers for payment of interest and principal can be safely forwarded when due.

Book Entry
All bonds today are issued in **book-entry form,** which means that certificates are not issued. Instead, an account is set up in the name of the issuing organization or the brokerage firm that sold the bond, and interest is paid into this account when due. In the past, all corporations issued **bearer bonds** (also called **coupon bonds** because owners redeemed the coupons for interest). Some of these older bonds are still traded today.

book-entry form
Bond certificates aren't issued; rather, account is set up in name of the issuing organization or the brokerage firm that sold the bond, and interest is paid into this account when due.

Callable
An issuer might desire to exercise a **call option** when interest rates drop substantially. For example, assume a company issues bonds paying a $90 annual dividend (9 percent coupon rate). When interest rates drop perhaps to 7 percent, the 9 percent bonds may represent too high a cost for borrowing to the corporation. If the bonds have a **callable** feature, according to dates and terms detailed in the indenture, the issuer can redeem the bonds before the maturity date. In such a case, the issuer repurchases the bond at par value or by paying a premium, often one year's worth of interest. Approximately 80 percent of long-term bonds are classified as callable.

call option
Stipulation in an indenture that allows issuer to repurchase the bond at par value or by paying a premium, often one year's worth of interest. Bonds are thus callable.

 ## Advice from a Pro...

Zero-Coupon Bonds Pay Phantom Interest

Zero-coupon bonds (also called **zeros** or **deep discount bonds**) are municipal, corporate, and Treasury bonds that pay no annual interest. They are sold to investors at sharp discounts from their face value and may be redeemed at full value upon maturity. For example, a 7 percent, $1000 zero-coupon bond to be redeemed in the year 2025 might sell today for $258. Zeros pay no current income to investors, so investors do not have to be concerned about where to reinvest interest payments. The semiannual interest accumulates within the bond itself, and the return to the investor comes from redeeming the bond at its stated face value at the maturity date. In this manner, zeros operate much like Series EE savings bonds and T-bills. The maturity date for a zero could range from a few months to as long as 30 years.

Parents often invest in zero-coupon bonds to help pay for their children's college education, and they wisely establish ownership of the zeros in the child's name. The phantom income "paid" to the child is generally so small that little, if any, income taxes are due. Treasury zeros, unlike other zeros, are not callable.

People planning for retirement often buy zeros because they know exactly how much will be received at maturity. Even though the investor receives no interest money until maturity, the investor still pays income taxes every year on the interest that accumulates within the bond. Investors can avoid income taxes altogether by buying zeros in a qualified tax-sheltered retirement plan account.

Anne Ranczuch
Monroe Community College

Evaluating Bond Prices and Returns

Much of the economic turmoil in the U.S. and world investment markets emanated from the U.S. credit markets. Billions of dollars of credit securities were characterized as **toxic debt** as they were found to be backed by assets of dubious value and quickly became impossible to value or to sell without incurring tremendous losses. The bond rating companies of S&P, Moody's, and Fitch Ratings completely failed to properly evaluate and grade those securities in a reasonable and prudent manner. The resulting illiquidity in credit markets caused some institutions to go bankrupt and confidence in the ratings companies deservedly declined. In addition, the prices of other bonds quickly soared or declined 25 percent or more. As markets continue to return to normal, investors can again utilize the standard factors to evaluate bond prices and potential returns: interest rates, premiums and discounts, current yield, and yield to maturity.

Interest Rate Risk Results in Variable Value
A bond's price, or its value on any given day, is affected by a host of factors. These include its type, coupon rate, availability in the marketplace, demand for the bond, prices for similar bonds, the underlying credit quality of the issuer, and the number of years before it matures. Most important, the price also varies because of fluctuations in current **market interest rates** in the general economy. The state of the economy and the supply and demand for credit affect market interest rates. These are the current long- and short-term interest rates paid on various types of corporate and government debts that carry similar levels of risk.

Long-Term Interest Rates Set by Investors
Long-term rates are largely set by bond investors' buying and selling decisions, primarily based on their expectations of future inflation. Short-term interest rates are manipulated by the Federal Reserve Board, which is popularly known as the Fed. When inflation rises, the Fed often raises interest rates to discourage borrowing, which reduces consumer and business spending. When the economy slows, the Fed often lowers the interest rates on short-term Treasury issues in an attempt to stimulate economic activity by making borrowing cheaper for companies to borrow and expand.

Pricing a Bond in Today's Market

As we noted in Chapter 13, **interest rate risk** is the risk that interest rates will increase and bond prices will fall, thereby lowering the prices on older bond issues. This decline in value ensures that an older bond and a newly issued bond will offer potential investors approximately the same yield. Bonds generally have a **fixed yield** (the interest income payment remains the same) but a **variable value.**

For example, assume you own a 30-year bond with a face value of $1000 paying a semiannual coupon interest rate of 6 percent that has 20 years remaining until maturity. If interest rates in the general economy jump to 8 percent after one year, no one will want to buy your 6 percent bond for $1000 because it pays only $60 per year. If you want to sell it, the price of the bond will have to be lowered, perhaps to $802.80. The **value of bond** (or **bond selling price**) **formula**, Equation (14.4), shows the calculation involved. If rates on similar bonds are now paying 8 percent then the discount rate is 8 percent (or 4% twice a year for 40 payments). The task is to calculate the present value of the interest payments and the repayment lump sum. To do so use Appendixes A.2 and A.4 and look across the interest rows to 4% and down to 40 "n" periods.

Value of Bond = Present value of interest payments + present value of lump sum   **(14.4)**
$$= (\text{Annual interest payment}/2 \times \text{PVIFA}^{i,n}) + (\text{Lump sum} \times \text{PVIF}^{i,n})$$
where

i = new annual **interest** rate divided by 2
n = years to maturity times 2
$$= (\$60/2 \times \text{PVIFA}^{4\%,40}) + (\$1{,}000 \times \text{PVIF}^{4\%,40})$$
$$= (\$30 \times 19.7928) + \$1{,}000 \times 0.2083)$$
$$= \$593.78 + \$208.30 = \$802.08$$

---

market interest rates
Current long- and short-term interest rates paid on various types of corporate and government debts that carry similar levels of risk.

interest rate risk
Risk that interest rates will rise and bond prices will fall, thereby lowering the prices on older bond issues.

fixed yield
Interest income payment remains the same regardless of bond's price.

variable value
Because interest rates change, bonds may trade at a premium (more than face value) or at a discount (less than par) so that the yield equals the current yield for bonds with similar maturities and risk levels.

Conversely, if interest rates on newly issued bonds slip to 4 percent, the price of your 6-percent bond will increase sharply, perhaps to $1,273.55. Thus, investors might be willing to pay a **premium** of $273.55 ($1,273.55 − $1,000), which is a sum of money paid in addition to a regular price, to buy your $1000 bond paying 6 percent when other rates are only 4 percent. Remember that bond yields and prices move in opposite directions—as one goes up, the other goes down.

The price of a bond is most volatile in the following circumstances: (1) when it was sold at less than face value when first issued, (2) when the stated rate is low, and (3) when the bond maturity time is long. The investor who holds a bond to maturity might ignore such information.

premium
A sum of money paid in addition to a regular price.

Premiums and Discounts

When a bond is first issued, it is sold in one of three ways: (1) at its face value (the value of the bond stated on the certificate and the amount the investor will receive when the bond matures), (2) at a discount below its face value, or (3) at a premium above its face value. After a bond is issued, its market price changes in order to provide a competitive effective rate of return for anyone interested in purchasing it from the original bondholder.

As an example, assume that Running Paws Cat Food Company decided to issue 20-year bonds at 8.8 percent. While the bonds were being printed and prepared for sale, the market interest rate on comparable bonds rose to 9 percent. In this instance, Running Paws will sell the bonds at a slight discount to provide a competitive return. Discounts and premiums on bonds reflect changing interest rates in the economy and the number of years to maturity.

Current Yield

The **current yield** equals the bond's fixed annual interest payment divided by its bond price. It is a measure of the current annual income (the total of both semi-annual interest payments in dollars) expressed as a percentage when divided by the bond's current market price. When you buy a bond at par, its current yield equals its coupon yield. For example, a bond with a 5.5 percent coupon yield purchased at par for $1000 has a current yield of 5.5 percent. As bond prices fluctuate because of interest rate changes and other factors, the current yield also changes. For example, if Leslie paid $940 for a $1000 bond paying $55 per year, the bond's current yield is 5.85 percent, as shown by the **current yield formula,** Equation (14.5).

current yield
Equals the bond's fixed annual interest payment divided by its bond price.

$$\text{Current yield} = \frac{\text{current annual income}}{\text{current market price}} \qquad (14.5)$$

$$= \frac{\$55}{\$940}$$

$$= 5.85\%$$

A bond's current yield is based on the purchase price, not on the prices at which it later trades. The current yields for many bonds based on that day's market prices are available online and are published in the financial section of many newspapers.

The total return on a bond investment consists of the same components as the return on any investment: current income and capital gains. In Leslie's case, she will receive $1000 at the maturity date (20 years from now), even though she paid only $940 for the bond; therefore, her anticipated total return (or effective yield) will be higher than the 5.85 percent current yield. How much higher is accurately revealed by the yield to maturity (discussed next).

Yield to Maturity

Yield to maturity (YTM) is the total annual effective rate of return earned by a bondholder on a bond if the security is held to maturity. The YTM is the internal rate of return on cash flows of a fixed-income security. The YTM reflects both the current income and any difference if the bond was purchased at a price other than its face value

yield to maturity (YTM)
Total annual effective rate of return earned by a bondholder on a bond if the security is held to maturity—takes into consideration both the price at which the bond sold and the coupon interest rate to arrive at effective rate of return.

spread over the life of the bond. The market price of a bond equals the present value of its future interest payments and the present value of its face value when the bond matures.

Three generalizations can be made about the yield to maturity:

1. If a bond is purchased for exactly its face value, the YTM is the same as the coupon rate printed on the certificate.

2. If a bond is purchased at a premium, the YTM will be lower than the coupon rate.

3. If a bond is purchased at a discount, the YTM will be higher than the coupon rate.

For example, because Leslie bought her 20-year bond with a coupon rate of 5.5 percent at a discount for $940, her yield to maturity must be greater than the coupon rate because she will receive $60 more than she paid for the bond when she receives the $1000 at maturity. Exactly how much greater can be determined by calculating an approximate yield to maturity when contemplating a bond purchase because bonds that seem comparable may have different YTMs.

The **yield to maturity (YTM) formula,** Equation (14.6), which is duplicated on the *Garman/Forgue* companion website, factors in the approximate appreciation when a bond is bought at a discount or at a premium:

$$\text{YTM} = \frac{I + [(FV - CV)/N]}{(FV + CV)/2} \tag{14.6}$$

where

$$
\begin{aligned}
I &= \textbf{Interest} \text{ paid annually in dollars} \\
FV &= \textbf{Face value} \\
CV &= \textbf{Current value} \text{ (price)} \\
N &= \textbf{Number} \text{ of years until maturity}
\end{aligned}
$$

If Leslie paid $940 for a 20-year bond with a 5.5 percent coupon rate, the YTM is calculated as follows:

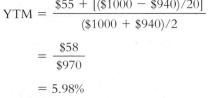

$$
\begin{aligned}
\text{YTM} &= \frac{\$55 + [(\$1000 - \$940)/20]}{(\$1000 + \$940)/2} \\
&= \frac{\$58}{\$970} \\
&= 5.98\%
\end{aligned}
$$

If you plan to buy and hold a bond until its maturity, you should compare YTMs instead of current yields when considering a purchase because YTMs fairly represent all factors. The current yield on a bond is not an effective measure of the total annual return to the investor; in fact, the fewer years until maturity, the worse an indicator it becomes. As just calculated, Leslie's 20-year bond with a coupon rate of 5.5 percent and a current yield of 5.85 percent has a YTM of 5.98 percent. If the same bond had been purchased with only 10 years until maturity, the YTM would be 6.29 percent; with 5 years until maturity, the YTM would be 6.90 percent; and with 2 years until maturity, the YTM would be 8.76 percent. Exact YTMs are online and listed in detailed bond tables available at large libraries and at brokers' offices.

Six Decisions for Bond Investors

Individuals interested in investing in bonds can review resources on the website of the Securities Industry and Financial Markets Association (http://www.investinginbonds.com/). It offers a free, searchable database of the latest corporate, government, municipal, and mortgage-backed bond issues and prices. Bond investors must make six decisions:

Do It NOW!

The smart investor in stocks and bonds studies particular securities thoroughly before investing. Start today by:

1. Identifying three types of individual stocks (see pages 415–417) that are appropriate for your investment goals.

2. Following the price fluctuations of those stocks for one or two months.

3. Assessing after one or two months whether the changes in price you saw were due primarily to movements in the stock market as a whole (market risk) or aspects of the companies' own success (random risk).

1. **Decide on credit quality.** Consider Treasury/agency, investment-grade corporate and municipal, and below investment-grade corporate and municipal.

2. **Decide on maturity.** Consider the time schedule of your financial needs: short, medium, or long term. Bonds with a short maturity have the lowest current yield but excellent price stability. Medium maturity bonds pay close to the higher rates earned on long-term bonds and enjoy much greater price stability.

3. **Determine the after-tax return.** Assuming equivalent risk, choose the bond that provides the better after-tax return because tax-exempt securities may offer a higher after-tax return than taxable alternatives. To compare the after-tax return of investments, see page 130.

4. **Select the highest yield to maturity.** Given similar bond securities with comparable risk, maturity, and tax equivalency, investors are wise to choose the one that offers the highest yield to maturity, as calculated by Equation (14.6).

5. **Consider selling.** When interest rates have dropped, consider selling because you can profit when rate decreases push up the value of your bond. Consider selling also if the bond rating has seriously slipped because it could mean greater risk and possible default.

6. **Think about investing in bond mutual funds.** Consider whether it is smarter to invest in bond mutual funds rather than individual bonds. This topic is examined in Chapter 15.

Instant Message

Check Bond Performance Online

BondInfo (http://www.nasdbondinfo.com/asp/bond_search.asp) is where you will find bond indexes and tools to gauge overall market direction and to measure the performance of corporate bond holdings against the broader market of more than 30,000 corporate bonds.

 Concept Check 14.7

1. Distinguish between investment- and speculative-grade bonds.

2. Give some reasons why individuals often invest in corporate bonds rather than Treasuries.

3. Summarize the differences among Treasury bonds, I bonds, and TIPS bonds.

4. Explain what interest rate risk is and tell what calculation individuals considering bond investments should use to avoid that problem when buying an existing bond.

What Do You Recommend NOW?

Now that you have read the chapter on stocks and bonds, what do you recommend to Caitlin Diaz in the case at the beginning of the chapter regarding:

1. Investing for retirement in 18 years?

2. Owning blue-chip common stocks and preferred stocks rather than other common stocks given Caitlin's investment time horizon?

3. The wisdom of owning municipal bonds rather than corporate bonds?

4. The likely selling price of her corporate bonds, if sold today?

5. Investments that might be appropriate to fund her children's education?

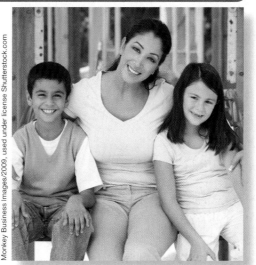

Monkey Business Images/2009, used under license Shutterstock.com

Big Picture Summary of Learning Objectives

1 Explain how stocks and bonds are used as investments.

Individual investors provide the money corporations use to create sales and earn profits. The investor shares in those profits.

2 Classify common stocks according to their major characteristics.

Common stocks may be broadly classified as either income or growth stocks. Other terms used to describe stocks are *blue chip, value, speculative,* and *tech.* Market capitalization is used to classify large-cap, midcap, and small-cap stocks.

3 Describe fundamental and numerical ways to evaluate stock values.

The investor studies certain fundamental factors, such as the company's sales, assets, earnings, products or services, markets, and management, to determine a company's basic value. To do so, investors examine several revealing ratios such as price/earnings (P/E), price/sales (P/S), and dividend payout, as well as revealing numbers such as book value per share. Individuals also estimate the value of a company by using beta to compare its history and expected future profitability with those of competing stocks.

4 Determine whether an investment's potential rate of return is sufficient.

Estimating and calculating returns on a potential investment involve using beta to estimate the level of risk of the investment, estimating the market risk, calculating the required rate of return, calculating the potential rate of return on the investment, and comparing the required rate of return with the potential rate of return on the investment.

5 Use the Internet to evaluate common stocks in which to invest.

Individuals begin evaluating stocks by setting criteria for a stock investment. This may involve using stock-screening software; obtaining security analysts' research reports, annual reports, 10-K reports, and prospectuses; acquiring economic and stock market data; and using portfolio-tracking services.

6 Summarize how stocks are bought and sold.

Securities transactions require the use of a licensed broker serving as a middleman between the seller and the buyer. You can buy or sell securities through an online or human stockbroker who works for a brokerage firm that has access to the securities markets. Many individuals use discount and online brokers rather than full-service brokers. Types of stock orders include market, limit, and stop orders. Buying on margin and selling short are risky trading techniques.

7 Describe how to invest in bonds.

Investment-grade bonds offer a reasonable certainty of regularly receiving the periodic income (interest) and retrieving the amount originally invested (principal). Junk bonds are available, too. Corporate bonds usually pay higher returns than government bonds. Interest rate risk results in variable value in bond investments.

Let's Talk About It

1. **Investing Today.** What counsel can you offer long-term investors who are hesitant to invest in stocks and bonds in today's economy?

2. **Three Good Companies.** Make a list of three products and services that you buy on a weekly or monthly basis and the companies that sell them. Offer your initial views on whether each company would be a good place to invest money.

3. **Two Useful Measures.** The text introduced a variety of ways to measure stock performance. Name two of those measures that you might use in your own decision making. Offer reasons for selecting those measures.

4. **Would You Buy?** You have just heard that Microsoft's stock price dropped $5. If you had the money, would you buy 100 shares? Give three reasons why or why not.

5. **Interesting Stock.** Review the three basic classifications of common stock and the other descriptive terms. Based on your personal comfort level for risk, which type of stock would be of interest to you? Give three reasons why.

6. **Sources of Information.** If you had an investment portfolio of stocks worth $20,000, identify three sources for information that you would likely use to keep abreast of current information affecting your investments.

7. **Potential Rate of Return.** Do you think anyone really calculates the potential rate of return on a particular investment? Should they? If so, offer a reason why.

8. **Invest Using Credit.** Buying on margin and selling short both involve using credit. Would you invest this way? Give two reasons why or why not.

9. **Interest in Bonds.** Do bonds interest you as an investment? Why or why not?

Do the Math

1. **Numerical Measures.** A stock sells at $15 per share.

   (a) What is the EPS for the company if it has a P/E ratio of 20?

   (b) If the company's dividend yield is 5 percent, what is its dividend per share?

   (c) What is the book value of the company if the price-to-book ratio is 1.5 and it has 100,000 shares of stock outstanding?

2. **Bond Selling Price.** What is the market price of a $1000, 8 percent bond if comparable market interest rates drop to 6.0 percent and the bond matures in 15 years?

3. **Market Price.** What is the market price of a $1000, 8 percent bond if comparable market interest rates rise to 10 percent and the bond matures in 14 years?

4. **Equivalent Taxable Yield.** For a municipal bond paying 5.4 percent for a taxpayer in the 25 percent tax bracket, what is the equivalent taxable yield? (Hint: See the footnote on page 130.)

5. **Equivalent Taxable Yield.** For a municipal bond paying 5.7 percent for a taxpayer in the 33 percent tax bracket, what is the equivalent taxable yield? (Hint: See the footnote on page 130.)

6. **Yield, Price, and YTM.** A corporate bond maturing in 15 years with a coupon rate of 9.9 percent was purchased for $980.

   (a) What is its current yield?

   (b) What will be its selling price in two years if comparable market interest rates drop 1.9 percentage points?

   (c) Calculate the bond's YTM using Equation (14.6) or the *Garman/Forgue* companion website.

7. **Yield, Price, and TYM.** A corporate bond maturing in 22 years with a coupon rate of 8.2 percent was purchased for $1100.

   (a) What is its current yield?

   (b) What will the bond's selling price be if comparable market interest rates rise 1.8 percentage points in two years?

   (c) Calculate the bond's YTM using Equation (14.6) or the *Garman/Forgue* companion website.

8. **Beta Calculations.** Michael Margolis is a single parent and a motivational training consultant from Rancho Cucamonga, California. He is wondering about potential returns on investments given certain amounts of risk. Michael invested a total of $6000 in three stocks ($2000 in each) with different betas: stock A with a beta of 0.8, stock B with a beta of 1.7, and stock C with a beta of 2.5.

   (a) If the stock market rises 12 percent over the next year, what will be the likely value of each investment?

   (b) If the stock market declines 8 percent over the next year, what will be the likely value of each investment?

9. **Investment Calculations.** Xiao and Shiao Jing-jian, newlyweds from New Castle, Delaware, have decided to begin investing for the future. Xiao is a 7-Eleven store manager, and Shiao is a high-school math teacher. The couple intends to take $3000 out of their savings for investment purposes and then continue to invest an additional $200 to $400 per month. Both have a moderate investment philosophy and seek some cash dividends as well as price appreciation.

   Calculate the five-year return on the investment choices in the table on page 452. Put your calculations in tabular form like that shown in Table 14.1. (Hint: At the end of the first year, the EPS for Running Paws will be $2.40 with a dividend of $0.66, and the EPS for Eagle Packaging will be $2.76 with a projected dividend of $0.86.)

   (a) Using the appropriate P/E ratios, what are the estimated market prices of the Running Paws and Eagle Packaging stocks after five years?

   (b) Show your calculations in determining the projected price appreciations for the two stocks over the five years.

   (c) Add the projected price appreciation of each stock to its projected cash dividends, and show the total five-year percentage returns for the two stocks.

   (d) Determine the average annual dividend for each stock, and use these figures in calculating the approximate compound yields for each.

   (e) Assume that the beta is 2.5 for Running Paws and 2.8 for Eagle Packaging. If the market went up 20 percent during the year, what would be the likely stock prices for Running Paws and Eagle Packaging?

   (f) Assume that inflation is approximately 4 percent and the return on high-quality, long-term corporate bonds is 8 percent. Given the Jing-jians' investment philosophy, explain why you would recommend (1) Running Paws, (2) Eagle Packaging, or (3) a high-quality, long-term corporate bond as a growth investment. Support your answer by calculating the potential rate of return using the information on page 422 or by using the *Garman/Forgue* companion website. The Jing-jians are in the 25 percent marginal tax bracket.

	Running Paws	Eagle Packaging
Current price	$30.00	$48.00
Current earnings per share (EPS)	$2.00	$2.30
Current quarterly cash dividend	$0.15	$0.18
Current P/E ratio	15	21
Projected earnings annual growth rate	20%	20%
Projected cash dividend growth rate	10%	10%

Financial Planning Cases

Case 1

Two Brothers' Attitudes Toward Investments

Kyle Broffoski, a guidance counselor in Freeport, Illinois, has purchased several corporate and government bonds over the years, and his total bond investment now exceeds $40,000. He prefers a variable-value investment with some inflation protection. His brother Ike, a highly paid physician, has more than $150,000 invested in various blue-chip income stocks in a variety of industries.

(a) Justify Kyle's attitude toward bond investments.

(b) Justify Ike's attitude toward stock investments.

(c) Explain why both brothers might be happy investing some of their money in TIPS bonds.

Case 2

A College Student Ponders Investing in the Stock Market

Richard Ford of Jefferson City, Tennessee, has $5000 that he wants to invest in the stock market. Richard is in college on a scholarship and does not plan to use the $5000 or any dividend income for another five years, when he plans to buy a home. He is currently considering a stock selling for $25 per share with an EPS of $1.25. Last year, the company earned $900,000, of which $250,000 was paid out in dividends.

(a) What classification of common stock would you recommend to Richard? Why?

(b) Calculate the P/E ratio and the dividend payout ratio for this stock. Given this information and your recommendation, would this stock be an appropriate purchase for Richard? Why or why not?

(c) Identify the components of the total return Richard might expect, and estimate how much he might expect annually from each component.

Case 3

An Aggressive Investor Seeks Rewards in the Bond Market

Karry Varcoe works as a drug manufacturer's representative based in Newton, Iowa. She has an aggressive investment philosophy and believes that interest rates will drop over the next year or two because of an expected economic slowdown. Karry, who is in the 25 percent marginal tax rate, wants to profit in the bond market by buying and selling during the next several months. She has asked your advice on how to invest her $15,000.

(a) If Karry buys corporate or municipal bonds, what rating should her selections have? Why?

(b) Karry has a choice between two $1000 bonds: a corporate bond with a coupon rate of 5.1 percent and a municipal bond with a coupon rate of 3.2 percent. Which bond provides the better after-tax return? (Hint: See Equation [4.1] on page 130.)

(c) If Karry buys fifteen 30-year, $1000 corporate bonds with a 5.1 percent coupon rate for $960 each, what is her current yield? (Hint: Use Equation [4.5].)

(d) If market interest rates for comparable corporate bonds drop 1 percent over the next 12 months (from 5.1 percent to 4.1 percent), what will be the approximate selling price of Karry's corporate bonds in (c)? (Hint: Use the *Garman/Forgue* companion website.)

(e) Assuming market interest rates drop 1 percent in 12 months, how much is Karry's capital gain on the $15,000 investment if she sells? How much was her current return for the two semiannual interest payments? How much was her total return, both in dollars and as an annual yield? (Ignore transaction costs.)

(f) If Karry is wrong in her projections and interest rates go up 1 percent over the year, what would be the probable selling price of her corporate bonds? (Hint: Use the *Garman/Forgue* companion website.) Explain why you would advise her to sell or not to sell.

Case 4

Victor and Maria Hernandez Wonder About Investing

Victor and Maria are considering making investments in stocks and bonds. They plan to invest between $8000 and $9000 every year for the next 13 years.

(a) Why should Victor and Maria consider buying common stock as an investment?

(b) If Victor and Maria bought a stock with a market price of $50 and a beta value of 1.8, what would be the likely price of an $8000 investment after one year if the general market for stocks rose 10 percent?

(c) What would the same investment be worth if the general market for stocks dropped 10 percent?

Case 5
The Johnsons Want Greater Yields on Investments

Harry and Belinda Johnson have saved $6000 toward a down payment on a luxury automobile they hope to purchase in the next three to five years. Because they are not receiving a very high rate of return on their money market account, they are seeking greater yields with bond investments. Examine the following table, which identifies eight investment alternatives, and then respond to the questions that follow. The coupon rates vary because the issue dates range widely, and market prices are above par because older bonds paid higher interest than today's issues.

(a) What is the current yield of each investment alternative? Use Equation (14.5) or visit the *Garman/Forgue*

companion website. (Write your responses in the proper column in the table.)

(b) What is the yield to maturity for each investment alternative? (Write your responses in the proper column in the table.) You may calculate the YTMs by using Equation (14.6) or by visiting the *Garman/Forgue* companion website.

(c) Knowing that the Johnsons follow a moderate investment philosophy, which one of the six corporate bonds would you recommend? Why?

(d) Given that the Johnsons are in the 25 percent federal marginal tax rate, what is the equivalent taxable yield for the municipal bond choice? Should they invest in your recommendation in part (c) or in the municipal bond? Why? You may calculate the equivalent taxable yield using the footnote on page 130.

(e) Which three of the eight alternatives would you recommend as a group so that the Johnsons would have some diversification protection for their $6000? Why do you suggest that combination?

Name of Issue	Bond Denomination	Coupon Rate Percent	Years Until Maturity	Moody's Rating	Market Price	Current Yield	YTM
Corporate ABC	$1000	7.0	4	Aa	$1400		
Corporate DEF	1000	7.5	20	Aa	1550		
Corporate GHI	1000	5.9	12	Baa	1250		
Corporate JKL	1000	7.8	5	Aaa	1500		
Corporate MNO	1000	6.1	15	B	1260		
Corporate PQR	1000	5.8	11	B	1200		
Treasury note	1000	7.9	3	—	1600		
Municipal bond	1000	4.1	20	Aa	1200		

On the 'Net

Go to the Web pages indicated to complete these exercises.

1. Visit the website for the U.S. Treasury Department at http://www.treasurydirect.gov/ and enter its Institutional section, where you will find the results of recent auctions for Treasury notes and bonds. What do the results of the auctions over the past year tell you about market expectations for movement of interest rates in the future? (Hint: Compare auction rates for bonds and notes with similar maturity periods.)

2. Visit the website for Kiplinger.com at http://www.kiplinger.com where you can find stock quotes for

most publicly traded companies. Type in the symbols for the following companies: Coca-Cola (KO), Google (GOOG), Microsoft (MSFT), and Disney (DIS). Evaluate these four firms on the basis of EPS, dividend yield, and P/E ratio. What do these data suggest to you about the relative attractiveness of these companies for investors?

3. Visit the website for Yahoo! Finance, where you can find a stock-screener utility at http://screen.yahoo.com/stocks.html. Search among the S&P 500 stocks for companies with a $50 minimum share price. How many companies meet this criterion? Select again using a P/E ratio from 0 to 20. How many companies meet this new criterion? Why is this list longer? Do you recognize any of the companies on either list?

Visit the Garman/Forgue companion website . . .

Investing Through Mutual Funds

!You Must Be Kidding, Right?

Twins Amanda and Daniel invest in mutual funds. Amanda majored in finance. For more than 20 years she invested in managed funds, counting on intelligent professional financial advisers to select the winning companies more often than not. Daniel majored in English; he invested in unmanaged index funds that achieve the same return as a particular market index by buying and holding all or a representative selection of securities in the index. After 20 years of investing, what is the likelihood that Amanda's investment portfolio balance will be better than Daniel's?

A. 10%

B. 20%

C. 30%

D. 40%

The answer is B or A but never C or D. Managed mutual funds generally do not earn returns for investors that exceed the overall market indexes. The fact is the average mutual fund manager earns a lower return at least 80 percent of the time. In most years, only 10 percent beat the market averages. Finding a mutual fund investment manager who can consistently beat the market is very challenging!

Learning Objectives

After reading this chapter, you should be able to:

1 Describe the features, services, and advantages of investing in mutual funds.

2 Differentiate mutual funds by investment objectives, types, and characteristics.

3 Summarize the fees and charges involved in buying and selling mutual funds.

4 Establish strategies to evaluate and select mutual funds that meet your investment goals.

What Do You Recommend?

David and Sarah Gent, a couple in their early 30s, have a 2-year-old child and enjoy living in a moderately priced downtown apartment. David, a librarian section manager, earns $50,000 annually. Sarah earns $59,000 as a merchandise buyer for a specialty store. They are big savers: Together they have been putting $1000 to $2000 per month into CDs, and the couple now has a portfolio balance worth $120,000 paying about 4 percent annually. The Gents are conservative investors and want to retire in about 20 years.

What do you recommend to David and Sarah on the subject of investing through mutual funds regarding:

1. Redeeming their CDs and investing their retirement money in mutual funds?

2. Investing in growth and income mutual funds instead of income funds?

3. Buying no-load rather than load funds?

4. Buying life-cycle mutual funds instead of balanced mutual funds?

5. Buying mutual funds through their employers' 401(k) retirement accounts?

Your Next Five Years

In the next five years you can start achieving financial success by doing the following related to investing through mutual funds:

1. Match your investment philosophy and financial goals to a mutual fund's objectives.

2. Invest only in no-load mutual funds that have low expenses and have no or a low 12b-1 fee.

3. Get the right mix of asset classes in your long-term fund investments through a sound asset allocation plan.

4. Sign up for automatic reinvestment of your mutual fund dividends.

5. Invest regularly in mutual funds through your employer's retirement plan.

1 Learning Objective

Describe the features, services, and advantages of investing in mutual funds.

mutual fund
Investment company that pools funds by selling shares to investors and makes diversified investments to achieve financial goals of income or growth, or both.

Most investors prefer to avoid buying individual stocks and bonds because of the high financial risk associated with owning too few investments. The average investor usually cannot accumulate a portfolio diversified enough to minimize the risk linked to the failure of a single holding. Investors often also lack both the ability and time required to research individual securities and manage such a portfolio. In an effort to avoid these problems, many people invest *in* the stock and bond markets *through* mutual funds, which typically buy hundreds of different stocks and bonds. Mutual funds make it easy and convenient for investors to open an account and continue investing. Half of all households invest through mutual funds.

Why Invest in Mutual Funds?

A **mutual fund** is an investment company that pools funds obtained by selling shares to investors and makes investments to achieve the financial goal of income or growth, or both. Mutual funds invest in a diversified portfolio of stocks, bonds, short-term money market instruments, and other securities or assets.

The fund might own common stock and bonds in such companies as AT&T, IBM, Sears, or Running Paws Cat Food Company (our example from Chapter 14). The combined holdings are known as a **portfolio,** as we noted in Chapter 13 and as shown graphically in Figure 15.1. The mutual fund company owns the investments it makes and the mutual fund investors own the mutual fund company. Unlike corporate shareholders, holders of mutual funds have no say in running the company, although they have equity interest in the pool of assets and a residual claim on the profits.

The economic recession and stock market meltdown—the worst decline in 80 years—severely impacted mutual fund returns because they, too, invest in stocks and bonds. The

Figure 15.1
How a Mutual Fund Works

mutual funds that invested in a widely diversified manner did not suffer losses nearly as great as many other narrowly focused funds. As the economy improves with rising retail sales, growing employment, and increasing business investment, the values of stocks and bonds and, thus, mutual funds will provide ample returns to millions of investors.

Net Asset Value

One measure of the investor's claim on assets is the net asset value. The **net asset value (NAV)** is the price one pays (excluding any transaction costs) to buy a share of a mutual fund; it is the per-share value of the mutual fund. It is calculated by summing the values of all the securities in the fund's portfolio, subtracting liabilities, and then dividing by the total number of shares outstanding.

net asset value (NAV)
Per-share value of a mutual fund.

$$\text{Net asset value} = \frac{\text{market value of assets} - \text{market value of liabilities}}{\text{number of shares}} \qquad (15.1)$$

For example, a mutual fund has 10 million shares outstanding, a portfolio worth $100 million, and its liabilities are $5 million. The net asset value of a single share is

$$\text{Net asset value} = \frac{\$100,000,000 - \$5,000,000}{10,000,000} = \frac{\$95,000,000}{10,000,000} = \$9.50 \text{ per share}$$

The NAV rises or falls to reflect changes in the market value of the investments held by the mutual fund company. This value is calculated daily after the major U.S. stock exchanges close, and a new NAV is posted in the financial media. If the assets held in a mutual fund increase in value the NAV will rise. For example, if a mutual fund owns IBM and General Electric common stocks and the prices of those stocks increase, the increased value of the underlying securities is reflected in the NAV of fund shares. The increase in NAV due to rising portfolio values is price appreciation. When investors sell shares at a net asset value higher than that paid when they purchased the shares (after transaction costs), they will have a capital gain.

Dividend Income and Capital Gains

A **mutual fund dividend** is income paid to investors out of profits that the mutual fund has earned from its investments. The dividend represents both ordinary income dividend distributions and capital gains distributions. **Ordinary income dividend distributions** occur when the fund pays out dividend income and interest (monthly, quarterly, or annually) it has received from securities it owns. **Capital gains distributions** represent the net gains (capital gains minus capital losses) that a fund realizes when it sells securities that were held in the fund's portfolio. Mutual funds distribute capital gains once a year, even though the gains occur throughout the year whenever securities are sold at a profit. When a fund pays out these distributions, the NAV drops by the amount paid. Figure 15.2 illustrates theses sources of mutual fund returns.

mutual fund dividend
Income paid to investors out of profits earned by the mutual fund from its investments.

ordinary income dividend distributions
Distributions that occur when the fund pays out dividend income and interest (monthly, quarterly, or annually) it has received from securities held in the fund.

capital gains distributions
Distributions representing the net gains (capital gains minus capital losses) that a fund realizes when it sells securities that were held in the fund's portfolio.

Advantages of Investing Through Mutual Funds

The type of mutual fund that is the focus in this chapter is an **open-end mutual fund.** Accounting for more than 90 percent of all funds, open-end mutual funds issue redeemable shares that investors purchase directly from the fund (or through a broker for the fund) instead of purchasing from investors on a stock market. They are always ready to sell new shares of ownership and to buy back previously sold shares at the fund's current NAV. Open-end mutual funds, numbering more than 8000, outnumber companies listed on the New York Stock Exchange (approximately 2800). Mutual funds offer a number of advantages to investors.

open-end mutual fund
Investment that issues redeemable shares that investors purchase directly from the fund (or through a broker for the fund).

Figure 15.2
Sources of Investor Returns from Owning Mutual Fund Shares

Sources of Investor Returns from Owning a Share in a Mutual Fund		
Current Income (returns received while you own a share)		Capital Gains (returns received when you sell your share)
Ordinary Dividend Income Distributions	Capital Gains Distributions	
The mutual fund receives dividends from the stocks and interest from the bonds it holds in its portfolio. These are passed on to you every three months (quarterly).	The mutual fund occasionally sells stocks and bonds in its portfolio. When it receives more from the sale than it paid for the securities, it achieves a capital gain. The gains are passed along to you each year (annually).	When you sell your share in the mutual fund, you receive the NAV of the share at its current market price. If that price is higher than the price you paid at purchase, you have a capital gain due to the increase in NAV. Your capital gain will be reduced by transaction costs.

fund investment advisers
Money managers, securities analysts, and traders of a mutual fund that have access to the best research; they select, buy, sell, and monitor the performance of the securities purchased; thus, they oversee the portfolio.

redeems
When an investor sells shares.

Instant Message

Financial Planning on the Web

To obtain an overall assessment of your financial progress and advice on how to achieve your goals, you may want to consult an online financial advisor to construct a financial plan. Prices vary from $250 to $500 or more. Check out Fidelity.com, Schwab.com, TrowePrice.com, and Vanguard.com. Answers to specific questions for $50 to $100 may be obtained on the Web and over the telephone from companies such as Myfinancialadvice.com.

Diversification   Mutual funds are broadly diversified in financial markets. They might own several hundred different securities, and all are represented in a single mutual fund share. The individual with $500 or $5000 to invest could never obtain such diversification. A diversified portfolio reduces the risk if a company or sector fails. **Random risk,** or **nonsystematic risk,** as we discussed in Chapter 13, is reduced. Recall that random risk arises when one owns only one investment of a particular type (such as stock in one company) that, by chance, may do very poorly in the future due to uncontrollable or random factors. Many investors find it easier to achieve diversification through ownership of mutual funds that own stocks and bonds rather than picking and then owning individual stocks and bonds.

Affordability   Individuals can invest in mutual funds with relatively low dollar amounts for initial purchases, such as $250 or $1000. Subsequent purchases can be as little as $50.

Professional Management   Many investors lack the knowledge, time, and commitment to worry about which of their stocks and bonds to buy and sell. Mutual fund investors like the fact that professional investment advisers registered with the Securities and Exchange Commission (SEC) manage their investment portfolio. The fund management company may control many millions or billions of dollars of assets. The **fund investment advisers** have access to the best research, and they select, buy, sell, and monitor the performance of the securities purchased; they oversee the portfolio. Investment advisers use the most current information, analytical tools, and investment techniques available. Fund investment advisers (money managers, securities analysts, and traders) share the same investment objective as the individual investor: to make money by increasing the net asset value of the mutual fund.

Liquidity   Mutual funds have good **liquidity,** a term we discussed in Chapters 5 and 13. You can very easily convert mutual fund shares into cash without loss of value because the investor sells (**redeems**) the shares back to the investment company. To do so, individuals simply pick up the telephone or go online. The price the investor gets depends upon the value of the portfolio and the resulting NAV.

Low Transaction Costs Because mutual funds trade in large quantities of shares, they pay far less in brokerage commissions than individual investors. Lower transaction costs result in higher returns for investors. Individuals purchase mutual fund shares from the fund itself (or through a broker for the fund) instead of from other investors on a secondary market, such as the New York Stock Exchange or NASDAQ stock market. Shares bought and sold are at the NAV plus any fees and charges that the fund imposes, and these are often low. While some funds charge significant fees on purchases and redemptions, individuals need not invest in them.

Uncomplicated Investment Choices Selecting a mutual fund is easier than selecting specific stocks or bonds. Mutual funds state their investment objectives, allowing investors to select funds that almost perfectly match their own objectives. Identifying mutual funds that meet certain investment criteria can be done easily using mutual fund screening software. This topic is examined later in this chapter.

Unique Mutual Fund Services

Mutual funds offer a number of valuable services that are unique to this type of investment and that are helpful and appealing to investors.

Convenience Mutual funds are extremely convenient for investors. Funds make it easy to open an account and invest in and sell shares. Fund prices are widely quoted. Services include toll-free telephone numbers, detailed records of transactions, and various checking and savings alternatives. Funds handle all the paperwork and record keeping, including accounting for fractional shares, so it is simple for investors to calculate taxable gains and losses when shares are sold.

Ease of Buying and Selling Shares Opening an account with a mutual fund company is just as simple as opening a checking account. After sending the fund your initial investment, you can easily buy more shares. Any number of shares can be sold at any time, or you can simply ask that a specific dollar amount be taken out by selling the appropriate number of shares. Each share is redeemed at the closing price—that is, the NAV—at the end of the trading day. Shares can be bought and sold by communicating with the company via telephone, wire, fax, mail, or online.

Check Writing and Electronic Transfers Mutual funds often offer interest-earning money market mutual funds in which investors can accumulate cash, accept dividends, or hold their money while making decisions about investing. They can write checks from money market funds. A money market fund invests exclusively in cash and cash equivalents. Investors can electronically transfer funds to and from mutual funds and banks.

Distribution of or Automatic Reinvestment of Income and Capital Gains Unlike most other investments, mutual funds allow investors to choose to receive interest, dividends, and capital gains payments or have them automatically reinvested to purchase additional fund shares (often without paying any commissions). This is **automatic reinvestment,** and it produces the same effects as the compounding of interest because the investor earns money on past earnings. Fractional shares are acquired as needed. Automatic reinvestment is one of the most appealing aspects of mutual funds for investors. Most shareholders wisely reinvest their mutual fund income to keep all of their capital fully invested, as illustrated in Figure 15.3.

According to Standard & Poor's Dave Guarino, "Automatic reinvestment of dividends is one of the most overlooked ways of accumulating wealth. In addition to the benefits of compounding, it also provides a mechanism to dollar-cost average investments."

automatic reinvestment
Investor's option to choose to automatically reinvest any interest, dividends, and capital gains payments to purchase additional fund shares.

Figure 15.3
The Wisdom of Automatic Dividend Reinvestment

Reinvesting income greatly compounds share ownership. Figure 15.3 illustrates the positive results obtained by reinvesting dividends. The initial $10,000 investment in S&P 500 Index Fund grew to $73,700 over 22 years instead of $42,623, because of the reinvestment of dividends.

Source: Data copyright ©2007 Standard & Poor's, a division of The McGraw-Hill Companies, Inc. Reprinted by permission of David Guarino.

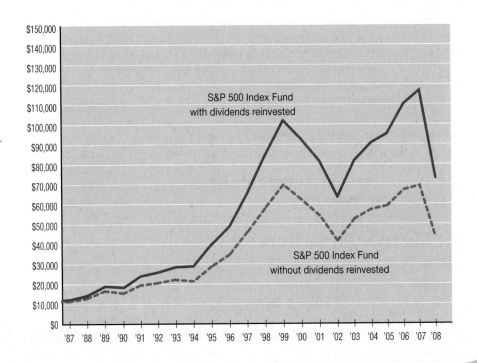

exchange privilege
Allowance for mutual fund shareholders to easily swap shares on a dollar-for-dollar basis for shares in another mutual fund within a mutual fund family. Also called switching, conversion, or transfer privilege.

exchange fee
Small amount charged to move money among funds within a mutual fund family.

mutual fund family
Investment management company that offers a number of different funds to the investing public, each with its own investment objectives or philosophies of investing.

Telephone and Internet Exchange Privileges
An **exchange privilege** (also called a **switching, conversion,** or **transfer privilege**) permits mutual fund shareholders to easily swap shares on a dollar-for-dollar basis for shares in another mutual fund managed by the same mutual fund family. Telephone and online transfers from one fund to another, such as moving money from a domestic stock fund to a Taiwan international fund, can be accomplished at no cost or for only a small charge, typically $5 or $10 per transaction, called an **exchange fee.** A **mutual fund family** is an investment management company that offers a number of different mutual funds to the investing public, each with its own investment objectives. There are more than 400 mutual fund families (see http://biz.yahoo.com/p/fam/a-b.html).

Automatic Investment
Funds often allow investors to make periodic monthly or quarterly payments using money automatically transferred from their bank accounts or paychecks to the mutual fund company. You can invest as little as $25 monthly or quarterly. You can change your investment selections without penalty by contacting the fund. This is an example of dollar-cost averaging. By regularly investing in mutual funds, you can build a substantial portfolio of assets over time.

Effortless Establishment of Retirement Plans
Mutual funds are perhaps the best option available to people saving for retirement through 401(k) plans and IRAs (topics examined in Chapter 17). An employee can direct his employer to transfer a specified dollar amount from every paycheck to a mutual fund to buy shares for a 401(k) plan; individuals can buy shares for their IRA accounts, too.

beneficiary designation
Allowance of fund holder to name one or more beneficiaries so that the proceeds bypass probate proceedings if the original shareholder dies.

Beneficiary Designation
When opening a mutual fund account, the investor must complete a form to designate a beneficiary in case of the investor's death. A **beneficiary designation** enables the shareholder to name one or more beneficiaries so that the proceeds go to them without going through probate. The delays and expenses of probate are discussed in Chapter 18.

Multiple Mechanisms for Withdrawing Income Mutual funds offer **withdrawal options** (also called **systematic withdrawal plans**) to shareholders who want to receive income on a regular basis from their mutual fund investments. Once enrolled in a withdrawal plan, the minimum withdrawal amount is $50. The fund forwards the amounts to you (or to anyone you designate) at regular intervals (monthly or quarterly). You can make regular withdrawals by (1) taking a set dollar amount each month, (2) cashing in a set number of shares each month, (3) taking the current income as cash, or (4) taking a portion of the asset growth.

withdrawal options/ systematic withdrawal plans Arrangements with a mutual fund company for shareholders who want to receive income on a regular basis from their mutual fund investments.

Concept Check 15.1

1. Explain how net asset value is calculated and how it is used by mutual funds.
2. List five advantages of investing in mutual funds.
3. Name five services that are unique to mutual funds.

Did You Know?

Types of Investment Companies

The Investment Company Act of 1940 distinguishes among investment companies. Open-end mutual funds are by far the most widely owned investment companies. Four other types exist:

1. **Closed-end mutual funds. Closed-end mutual funds** issue a limited and fixed number of shares at inception and do not buy them back. These companies operate with a fixed amount of capital. Closed-end shares are bought and sold on a stock exchange or in the over-the-counter market. After the original issue is sold, the price of a share depends primarily on the supply and demand in the market rather than the performance of the investment company assets. Closed-end shares are actively traded like common stocks and bonds, primarily on the New York Stock Exchange.

2. **Real estate investment trusts.** A special kind of closed-end investment company is a **real estate investment trust (REIT).** REITs invest in a portfolio of assets as defined in the trust agreement, such as properties, like office buildings and shopping centers (called an equity REIT), or mortgages (a mortgage REIT). Hybrid REITs invest in both. REITs have no predetermined life span. REIT shares are traded on stock exchanges, although many are illiquid investments.

3. **Unit investment trusts.** A **unit investment trust (UIT)** is a closed-end investment company that makes a

one-time public offering of only a specific, fixed number of units. A UIT buys and holds an unmanaged fixed portfolio of fixed-maturity securities, such as municipal bonds, for a period of time. This could be a few months or perhaps 50 years. Each unit represents a proportionate ownership interest in the specific portfolio of perhaps 10 to 50 securities. Sold by brokers for perhaps $250 to $1000 a unit, there is no trading of these securities, although brokers may repurchase and resell them.

4. **Exchange-traded funds.** An **exchange-traded fund (ETF)** is a basket of passively managed securities structured like an index fund (described later in this chapter) as it owns all or a representative set of securities that duplicate the performance of a market segment or index. There are ETFs for the S&P 500, called Spiders; the Dow Jones Industrial Average, called Diamonds; and Qubes based on the NASDAQ 100. There are over 800 ETFs, and their prices are set by market forces since they are listed on securities markets (primarily on the American Stock Exchange [AMEX]) and traded throughout the day by brokers. One in four investors has ETFs in their portfolios in part because of the extremely low costs, which are lower than mutual funds. The lowest fee of all (0.07%) is Vanguard Total Stock Market ETF (symbol VTI). "Enhanced ETFs" are available that track an index but overweigh companies with the greatest potential; that's a "managed ETF."

Fund Objectives, Types, and Characteristics

Most mutual funds are **managed funds,** meaning that professional managers are constantly evaluating and choosing securities using a specific investment approach. On a daily basis, active managers select the stocks and bonds in which to invest and sell them when they deem appropriate. The managers earn a fee for their services, and ultimately their choices are responsible for the performance of the fund. Often, however, investing in a managed mutual fund is not the best choice for investors. Index funds are unmanaged, and they are often the best choice for investors.

Before investing in any specific mutual fund, decide whether the fund's investment objectives are a good fit for you. The SEC requires funds to disclose their investment objective. Mutual funds may be classified in one of three categories: income, growth, and growth and income. Each type has different features, risks, and reward characteristics. The name of a fund gives a clue to its objectives.

Income Objective

A mutual fund with an **income objective** invests in securities that pay regular income in dividends or interest. One key to earning a good return is to buy a fund that has low expenses.

Money Market Funds Mutual fund companies and brokerage firms offer **money market funds.** They invest in highly liquid, relatively safe securities with very short maturities (always less than one year), such as CDs, government securities, and commercial paper (i.e., short-term obligations issued by corporations). You can write checks or use an ATM card to access a money market fund account. Issuers keep the NAV (the price of each share of the fund) at $1.

As we discussed in Chapter 5, money market funds (and there are more than 1000 of them) pay a higher rate of return than accounts offered through banks and credit unions. They are considered extremely safe. At the beginning of the recession the federal government temporarily provided insurance against losses for money market funds to increase investor confidence. **Tax-exempt money market funds** limit their investments to tax-exempt municipal securities with maturities of less than 90 days. The earnings are tax free to investors. **Government securities money market funds** appeal to investors' concerns about safety by investing solely in Treasury bills and other short-term securities backed by the U.S. government.

Bond Funds Bond funds (also called **fixed-income funds**) aim to earn current income higher than a money market fund without incurring undue risk by investing in a portfolio of bonds and other investments, such as preferred stocks and common stocks that pay high dividends. However, they do not ignore capital gains because bond fund prices fluctuate with changing interest rates. Bond funds are categorized by what they own and the maturities of their portfolio holdings.

- **Short-term corporate bond funds** invest in securities maturing in 1 to 5 years.
- **Short-term U.S. government bond funds** invest in Treasury issues maturing in 1 to 5 years.
- **Intermediate corporate bond funds** invest in investment-grade corporate securities with 5- to 10-year maturities.
- **Intermediate government bond funds** invest in Treasuries with 5- to 10-year maturities.

- **Long-term corporate bond funds** specialize in investment-grade securities maturing in 10 to 30 years.

- **Long-term U.S. government bond funds** invest in Treasury and zero-coupon bonds with maturities of 10 years or longer.

- **Mortgage-backed funds** invest in mortgage-backed securities issued by agencies of the U.S. government, such as Ginnie Mae (GNMA).

- **Junk bond funds** invest in high-yield, high-risk corporate bonds.

- **Municipal bond (tax-exempt) funds** invest in municipal bonds that provide tax-free income. Both investment-grade and high-yield municipal bond funds exist.

- **Single-state municipal bond funds** invest in debt issues of only one state.

- **World bond funds** invest in debt securities offered by foreign corporations and governments.

Growth Objective

A mutual fund that has a growth objective seeks capital appreciation. It invests in the common stock of companies that have above average growth potential, firms that may not pay a regular dividend but have the potential for large capital gains. Growth funds carry a fair amount of risk exposure, and this is reflected in substantial price volatility.

Aggressive growth funds (also known as **maximum capital gains funds**) seek the greatest long-term capital appreciation. Also known as **capital appreciation funds,** they make investments in speculative stocks with volatile price swings. They may employ high-risk investment techniques, such as borrowing money for leverage, short selling, hedging, and options. Lots of buying and selling occurs to enhance returns.

Growth funds seek long-term capital appreciation by investing in the common stocks of companies with higher-than-average revenue and earnings growth, often the larger and well-established firms. Such companies (like Wal-Mart, Microsoft, and Coca-Cola) tend to reinvest most of their earnings to facilitate future growth.

Growth and income funds invest in companies that have a high likelihood of both dividend income and price appreciation.

Value funds specialize in stocks that are fundamentally sound and whose prices appear to be low (low P/E ratios), based on the logic that such stocks are currently out of favor and undervalued by the market.

Midcap funds invest in the stocks of midsize companies with a market capitalization of $2 to $3 billion in size that are expected to grow rapidly.

Small-cap funds (or **small company growth funds**) invest in lesser-known companies with a market capitalization of $300 million to $2 billion in size that offer strong potential for growth.

Microcap funds invest in high-risk companies with a market capitalization of less than $300 million.

Sector funds concentrate their investment holdings in one or more industries that make up a targeted part of the economy that is expected to grow, perhaps very rapidly, such as energy, biotechnology, health care, and financial services.

Did You Know?

Stable-Value Funds Are Available Only Through Employer-Sponsored Retirement Plans

Stable-value funds are available through employer-sponsored retirement plans. This is a different breed of fund. Stable-value funds get their name in part because they buy an insurance policy designed to allow the fund to redeem shares at a stable price regardless of overall market prices. This gives investors some assurance that the fund will be able to maintain the net asset value of the portfolio. Stable-value funds invest in high-quality, intermediate-term investments, including **guaranteed investment contracts (GICs)** offered by insurance companies. A GIC guarantees the owner a fixed or floating interest rate for a predetermined period of time, and the return of principal is guaranteed. GIC funds increased in value during the worst of the economic recession while virtually all others declined.

aggressive growth funds
Funds that invest in speculative stocks with volatile price swings, seeking the greatest long-term capital appreciation possible. Also known as maximum capital gains funds and capital appreciation funds.

growth funds
Funds that seek long-term capital appreciation by investing in common stocks of companies with higher-than-average revenue and earnings growth, often the larger and well-established firms.

growth and income funds
Funds that invest in companies that have a high likelihood of both dividend income and price appreciation; less risk-oriented than aggressive growth funds or growth funds.

value funds
Funds specializing in stocks that are fundamentally sound whose prices appear to be low (low P/E ratios) based on the logic that such stocks are currently out of favor and undervalued by the market.

Advice from a Pro...

Invest Only "Fun Money" Aggressively

Once the investor has his or her financial plan in place, taking on more risk is acceptable—but *only* within the limits of the individual's "fun money." **Fun money** is a sum of investment money that you can afford to lose without doing serious damage to your total portfolio. You might, for example, resolve to trade with a specific sum, such as $5000, or perhaps no more than 2 or 3 percent of your portfolio. Keep such fun money in a separate account from your long-term investments. Decide mentally that if and when the money is gone, it has been spent on an activity that you enjoyed trying, but accept that the money lost is lost forever. In particular, avoid the temptation to "throw good money after bad" in trying to recover your losses.

Speculative investing is not much different from gambling. The biggest danger of fun-money investing is that you might be successful. Success can give you the confidence—

albeit perhaps false confidence—that you are a great investor. While you might be the next billionaire investor like Warren Buffett, such success is likely to tempt you to aggressively invest even more of the assets in your total portfolio. That approach can result in disaster.

Investing in aggressive growth mutual funds for some might be a lot of fun, particularly when the amount of money at stake is small. Over time, you will be best served by pursuing a disciplined investing plan with a focus on diversification. As financial columnist Jane Bryant Quinn observes, "The money you really need for life is better off in broadly diversified mutual funds, where a mistake is not forever."

Robert O. Weagley
University of Missouri–Columbia

Regional funds invest in securities listed on stock exchanges in a specific region of the world, such as the Pacific Rim, Australia, or Europe.

Precious metals and gold funds invest in securities associated with gold, silver, and other precious metals.

Global funds invest in growth stocks of companies listed on foreign exchanges as well as in the United States, usually multinational firms.

International funds invest only in foreign stocks throughout the world.

Emerging market funds seek out stocks in countries whose economies are small but growing. Fund prices are volatile because these countries tend to be less stable politically.

Growth and Income Objective

A mutual fund that has a combined growth and income objective seeks a balanced return made up of current income and capital gains. Such funds heavily invest in common stocks. They seek a return not as low as offered by funds with an income objective but not as high as that offered by funds with a growth objective. They invite less risk than growth funds.

Growth and income funds invest in companies expected to show average or better growth and pay steady or rising dividends.

Equity-income funds invest in well-known companies with a long history of paying high dividends as they emphasize income and capital preservation.

socially conscious funds
Funds that invest in companies that meet some predefined standard of moral and ethical behavior.

Socially conscious funds invest in companies that meet some predefined standard of moral and ethical behavior. Criteria could be progressive employee relations, strong records of community involvement, an excellent record on environmental issues, respect for human rights, and safe products (as well as no "sinful" products such as tobacco, guns, alcohol, gambling). See www.socialinvest.org for examples.

Balanced funds (or **hybrid funds**) keep a set mix of stocks and bonds, often 60 percent stocks and 40 percent bonds, in order to earn a well-balanced return of income and long-term capital gains.

Blend funds invest in a combination of stocks and money market securities, but no fixed-income securities, such as bonds.

Asset allocation funds invest in a mix of assets (usually stocks, bonds, and cash equivalents and sometimes international assets, gold, and real estate), and they buy and sell regularly to reduce risk while trying to outperform the market. The asset mix may be based on risk tolerance (aggressive, moderate, and conservative).

Target-date retirement funds (life-cycle funds) are asset allocation funds that offer investors premixed portfolios of stocks, bonds, and cash that investors of a certain age and risk tolerance might prefer. These are targeted to people in their 30s, 40s, 50s, 60s, and 70s. Target-date funds shift assets from aggressive to moderate to conservative securities as the retirement target date approaches. They seek to first grow and then preserve the portfolio assets. This is a no-hassle, "autopilot solution" way to invest.

Mutual fund funds earn a return by investing in other mutual funds. This provides extensive diversification, but expenses and fees are higher than average.

Index funds are called **unmanaged funds** because their managers do not evaluate or select individual securities. Being unmanaged, annual management fees are extremely low, perhaps only 0.20 to 0.30 percent. Both index funds and ETFs follow market benchmarks, and ETF management fees often are lower. The returns achieved by actively managed stock funds typically trail the stock market averages by about 1.5 percentage points per year. Burton Malkiel, professor of economics at Princeton University, says that very few individual investors or fund managers will do better than the indexes. "It's like looking for a needle in a haystack." He recommends that investors buy the haystack.

Instant Message

Index Funds Are Unmanaged

An **index fund** is a mutual fund whose investment objective is to achieve the same return as a particular market index by buying and holding all or a representative selection of securities in it. An S&P 500 index fund would effectively mirror the companies in the index, which are primarily large-cap U.S. stocks. A Russell 2000 Index Fund invests in the 2000 small-cap stocks in the index. Index funds offer a guarantee that the investor will get the same return that the market obtains. Billionaire Warren Buffett says "The best way to own common stocks is through an index fund."

balanced funds
Funds that keep a set mix of stocks and bonds, often 60 percent stocks and 40 percent bonds, in order to earn a well-balanced return of income and long-term capital gains.

asset allocation funds
Investments in a mix of assets (usually stocks, bonds, and cash equivalents and sometimes international assets, gold, and real estate); they buy and sell regularly to reduce risk while trying to outperform the market.

target-date retirement funds/life-cycle funds
Asset allocation funds that offer investors premixed portfolios of stocks, bonds, and cash that investors of a certain age and risk tolerance might prefer.

unmanaged fund
Fund with very low management fees since managers do not evaluate or select individual securities; ETFs and index funds are examples.

 Concept Check 15.2

1. How can investors use a money market fund?
2. Distinguish among mutual funds with an income objective, growth objective, and growth and income objective, and give two examples of each.
3. Distinguish between asset allocation and life-cycle funds.
4. Explain why investors like index mutual funds.

Mutual Fund Investing Fees and Charges

Individuals who invest through mutual funds pay transaction costs that often are less than those associated with buying individual stocks, bonds, and cash equivalent securities. Mutual fund investors do pay certain fees and charges for the benefits of diversification, professional management, liquidity, check writing, and record keeping. Funds also pay their operating expenses out of fund assets, and this means that investors indirectly pay these costs.

3 Learning Objective

Summarize the fees and charges involved in buying and selling mutual funds.

shareholder fees
Fees charged directly to investors for specific transactions, such as purchases, redemptions, or exchanges.

annual fund operating expenses
Normal operating costs of the business that are deducted from fund assets before shareholders receive earnings.

Did You Know?

The Top 3 Financial Missteps in Mutual Fund Investing

People slip up in mutual fund investing when they do the following:

1. Buy funds with high fees and expenses
2. Withdraw dividends rather than reinvesting
3. Chase performance by investing in "hot" funds

load funds
Mutual funds that always charge a "load" or sales charge upon purchase; the load is the commission used to compensate brokers.

front-end load
A sales charge paid when an individual buys an investment, reducing the amount available to purchase fund shares.

stated commission
The sales charge as a percentage of the amount invested.

low-load funds
Funds carrying sales charges of perhaps 1 to 3 percent; sold by brokers, via mail, and sometimes through mutual fund retailers located in shopping centers.

no-load funds
Funds that allow investors to purchase shares directly at the net asset value (NAV) without the addition of sales charges.

Shareholder fees are charged directly to investors for specific transactions, such as purchases, redemptions, or exchanges. **Annual fund operating expenses** are the normal operating costs of the business that are deducted from fund assets before earnings are distributed to shareholders. The fees and charges associated with investing in mutual funds are many, and they can be confusing; some can be avoided.

Load and No-Load Funds

All mutual funds are classified as either load or no-load funds. This refers to whether or not they assess a sales charge, or load, when shares are purchased.

Load Funds Always Charge Transaction Fees Funds that levy a sales charge for purchases are called **load funds.** Load funds are generally *sold* by stock brokerage firms, banks, and financial planners rather than marketed directly to investors by a mutual fund company. The load is the commission used to compensate brokers.

This commission, also called a **front-end load,** typically amounts to 3 to 8.5 percent of the amount invested; this reduces the amount available to purchase fund shares. For example, assume that you and your stockbroker have discussed the investment potential of the Conglomerate Cat and Dog Food Mutual Fund and you decide to invest $10,000. Because this load fund charges a commission of 8.5 percent (the maximum permitted by the SEC), the stockbroker receives $850 ($10,000 × 0.085). As a result, only $9150 of your money is actually available to purchase shares. Such a commission is much higher than stock transaction costs, which are usually 0.25 percent to 2 percent of the security's purchase price.

The sales charge may be shown either as the stated commission or as a percentage of the amount invested. The **stated commission** (8.5 percent in our example), is always somewhat misleading. In contrast, the percentage of the amount invested is a more accurate figure because it is based on the actual money invested and working. A stated commission of 8.5 percent actually amounts to 9.3 percent of the amount invested: $10,000 − $9150 = $850; $850 ÷ $9150 = 9.3%. If you want to invest a full $10,000 in this load fund, you will need to pay out $10,930 [$10,930 − ($10,930 × 8.5%) = $10,000]. Investments of $10,000 or more often receive a discount on the load.

So-called **low-load funds** may carry a sales charge of perhaps 1 to 3 percent. These funds may also be sold by brokers and are sold via mail and sometimes through mutual fund retailers located in shopping centers. About half of all mutual funds levy a load.

No-Load Funds A **no-load fund** sells shares at the net asset value without the addition of sales charges. These mutual fund companies let people purchase shares directly from the mutual fund company without the services of a broker, banker, or financial planner. Interested investors simply seek out advertisements for these funds in financial newspapers, magazines, and the Internet and make contact through toll-free telephone numbers, online, or mail. The SEC does allow funds to be called "no-load" even though they assess a "service fee" of 0.25 percent or less when shares are purchased.

Some No-Load Funds Assess 12b-1 Fees A **12b-1 fee** (named for the SEC rule that permits the charge) is an annual charge deducted by the fund company from a fund's assets to compensate underwriters and brokers for fund sales as well as to pay for advertising, marketing, distribution, and promotional costs. A 12b-1 fee is also known as a **distribution fee.** For no-load funds, these charges also pay for **trailing commissions,**

which is compensation paid to salespeople for months or years in the future. Although the funds do not call 12b-1 fees "loads" because they are not charged up front, they have the same effect as loads—that is, they reduce the investor's return.

These **hidden fees** decrease a shareholder's earning power each year without being described as a sales commission. A 12b-1 fee is actually a "perpetual sales load" because it is assessed on the initial investment as well as on reinvested dividends, every year, forever. The SEC caps 12b-1 fees at 0.75 percent, although it permits a 0.25 percent "service fee," which brings the total cap to 1 percent. Some funds stop assessing 12b-1 fees after four to eight years.

Some No-Load Funds Assess Deferred Load and Redemption Fees

Approximately 60 percent of no-load mutual funds (and many load funds) assess additional fees for transactions, such as deferred load and redemption charges. A **contingent deferred sales charge,** also known as a **back-end load,** is a sales commission that is imposed only when shares are sold. Deferred loads are often on a sliding scale. The fee may decline 1 percentage point for each year the investor owns the fund. For example, a fund might charge a 6 percent fee if an investor redeems the shares within one year of purchase, and then the fee declines on an annual basis, until it reaches zero after six years.

A **redemption charge** (or **exit fee**) is similar to a contingent deferred sales charge, although often it is much lower. A fund uses such a charge to reduce excessive trading of fund shares. The fee is usually 1 percent of the value of the shares redeemed. It disappears after the investment has been held for six months or a year. Long-term investors should not shy away from funds with redemption fees that disappear after a year.

Mutual Fund Share Classes

A single mutual fund may be available to investors in more than one class of shares: Class A, B, or C. The Classes A, B, and C all invest in the same portfolio of securities and have the same investment objectives but have different fee and expense patterns. As a result the performance results for each class will differ depending on how long you hold the shares. Class A shares charge a front-end load. Class B shares are sold on a no-load basis but with a 12b-1 fee and a contingent deferred sales charge. Class C shares also are sold on a no-load basis with a 12b-1 fee but have a redemption charge. Which class is best for you will depend highly on your expected holding time for the investment. To compare the costs of various funds and share classes for your expected holding period and estimated returns see FINRA's Mutual Fund Expense Analyzer (http://apps.finra.org/investor_Information/ea/1/mfetf.aspx

Disclosure of Fees in Standardized Expense Table

The SEC requires that mutual funds provide investors with a concise summary—in plain English—of the key information they need to make informed investment decisions. This summary prospectus will appear at the front of a fund's full prospectus. The full prospectus also must include a **standardized expense table** within its first three pages that describes and illustrates in an identical manner the effects of all of its fees and other expenses. (See Table 15.1.) This description must estimate the hypothetical total costs that a mutual fund investor would pay on a $1000 investment that earns 5 percent annually and is withdrawn after ten years. All figures must be adjusted to reflect the effects of loads and fees. Also look for the fund's **expense ratio,** the expense per dollar of assets under management. Some mutual funds are much more efficient than others, and the expense ratio could range from 0.2 percent to more than 4 percent. Expense ratios average 1.45 percent for diversified stock funds and 0.40 percent for index funds.

12b-1 fees/distribution fees
Annual fees that some "no-load" fund companies deduct from a fund's assets to compensate salespeople and pay other expenses.

trailing commission
Compensation paid to salespeople for months or years in the future.

contingent deferred sales charge/back-end load
A sales commission that is imposed only when shares are sold; often charges are on a sliding scale, with the fee dropping 1 percentage point per year that the investor stays in the fund.

redemption charge/exit fee
Similar to a deferred load but often much lower; used to reduce excessive trading of fund shares.

standardized expense table
SEC-required information that describes and illustrates mutual fund charges in an identical manner so that investors can accurately compare the effects of all of a fund's fees and other expenses relative to other funds.

expense ratio
Expense per dollar of assets under management.

Table 15.1 Mutual Fund Fee Table Required by Federal Law

This illustrative mutual fund fee table is hypothetical, and the estimated expenses are based on the U.S. Securities and Exchange Commission's Mutual Fund Cost Calculator (www.sec.gov/investor/tools/mfcc/get-started.htm).

Shareholder Fees		Annual Fund Operating Expenses	
A Maximum Sales Charge (Load) Imposed on Purchases (as a percentage of offering price)	4.5%	G Management Fee	0.52%
B Maximum Deferred Sales Charge (Load)	None	H Distribution (12b-1) Fee	0.25%
C Maximum Sales Charge (Load) on Reinvested Dividends	None	I Other Expenses	0.20%
		J Total Annual Fund Operating Expenses (Expense Ratio)	0.97%
		K Example	
		This example is intended to help an investor compare the cost of investing in different funds. The example assumes a $10,000 investment in the fund for one, three, five, and ten years and then a redemption of all fund shares at the end of those periods. The example also assumes that an investment returns 5 percent each year and that the fund's operating expenses remain the same. Although actual costs may be higher or lower, based on these assumptions an investor's estimated expenses would be:	
D Redemption Fee	None	1 year	$547
E Exchange Fee	None	3 years	$754
F Annual Account Maintenance Fee	None	5 years	$977
		10 years	$1,617

Source: Investment Company Institute (http://www.ici.org/funds/inv/bro_understanding_mfs.html#P502_43411). Reprinted by permission of Mike McNamee.

What's Best: Load or No Load?
Low Fee or High Fee?

Keep Your Investing Costs Low

Over time, the negative costs of fees and expenses greatly reduce investment returns. The expense ratios and investment balances 20 years later if a stock fund earns a 7% annual return on a $10,000 investment are as follows:

- actively managed mutual fund (1.9%; $29,190),
- index mutual fund (0.70%; $33,936),
- index ETF (0.07%; $38,193).

The sales commissions charged by load funds indisputably reduce total returns. When investment results are adjusted to account for the effects of sales charges, no-load mutual funds have an initial advantage because the investor has more money at work. In general, the shorter the time period you own the shares, the greater the negative impact of loads on the total return for the mutual fund investor. Up-front load charges are costly to the investor in the short run (less than five years), whereas annual 12b-1 charges are very costly over the long run.

If you pay 1 percent per year in 12b-1 fees for a mutual fund in which you invest for ten years, you will be giving up nearly 10 percent of your investment amount in trailing commissions. Yikes! You would be well advised to invest in a load fund rather than pay 12b-1 assessments if you plan to own the fund for more than five years.

Independent research has found that over five-year periods, lower-cost funds always deliver returns better than those offered by higher-cost funds. Even a small difference in fees can seriously affect long-term returns. For example, a $50,000 portfolio earning an 8 percent annual return would grow to $176,182 in 20 years with a

1.5 percent management fee. By comparison, over the same time span it would grow to $193,484 with a 1.0 percent fee and to $212,393 with a 0.5 percent fee. Over 30 years, the returns with these fee rates would be $330,718, $380,613, and $437,748, respectively. The negative effects of high fees on long-term returns are enormous.

The investor would be wise to invest in no-load fee mutual funds that have low management fees. "If you pick your own funds, sales charges [and loads] are a total waste of money," observes Fred W. Frailey, editor of *Kiplinger's Personal Finance Magazine*.

 ## Concept Check 15.3

1. Give three examples of fees and charges associated with load funds.
2. Which is better for most investors, load or no-load fund?
3. Summarize the effects of loads on investment returns.

 ## Did You Know?

Long-Term Returns for All Types of Stock Mutual Funds Are Roughly the Same

Data from the Investment Company Institute reveal that the type of stock mutual fund in which you invest over the long term makes very little difference. Over 10 or 20 years, the average annual returns for different types of diversified stock funds (growth, domestic equity, growth and income, equity income, and balanced) converge around 10 percent. The only secret to obtaining such a good return is to remain patient and keep investing. Returns over one, three, and five years vary widely, but over the long term, the returns of major categories of diversified stock mutual funds are roughly the same.

Selecting Funds in Which to Invest

Selecting mutual funds in which to invest is usually a do-it-yourself effort. A tremendous amount of objective information is available to help potential investors evaluate and select funds. To explain the process of selecting funds, let's follow Jessica Shipp's decision making. She is in sales and earns $51,000 annually; she lives in Sacramento, California. Figure 15.4 illustrates the process of selecting mutual fund investments, and Table 15.2 contains performance data for a number of large-cap mutual funds from *Kiplinger's Personal Finance* magazine.

The returns of mutual funds for the "previous 12 months" shown in Table 15.2 were very negative and illustrate the depth of the meltdown of stock values during the 2008 market decline. Note further that both the 5- and 10-year annualized returns were positive and more typical for large-cap mutual funds. Investors should never choose a mutual fund based on the most recent 12-month return, but instead should consider the selection suggestions that follow.

4 Learning Objective

Establish strategies to evaluate and select mutual funds that meet your investment goals.

Socially conscious funds such as Green Century appeal to those who want to choose investments in keeping with their social values.

Figure 15.4
The Process of Selecting a
Mutual Fund Investment

1. Review investment policy	Conservative
	Moderate
	Aggressive
2. Review investment goals	Goal
	Time horizon
	Return
	Taxes
3. Eliminate funds inappropriate for your investment goals	Income
	Growth
	Growth and income
	Specific fund types
4. Low load or no load?	
5. Investment advice needed?	For immediate investments
	For later portfolio review
6. Screen and compare funds that meet your investment criteria	Fund-screening tools
	Fees and charges
	Performance
	Services
7. Monitor your mutual fund portfolio	Portfolio monitoring on the 'Net
	Fund quotations in newspapers

Review Your Investment Philosophy and Investment Goals

Jessica began by reviewing her investment philosophy and financial goals. These topics were examined in Chapter 13. Jessica has a moderate investment philosophy, and she has a written investment plan (Figure 13.9 on page 402). The investment goal she is interested in investing in for now is retirement, and her investment time horizon is the next 30 years or more. She anticipates an annual return of at least 7 to 8 percent. She does not care about income taxes because these investments will be made within Jessica's tax-deferred 401(k) retirement plan at work.

Jessica does not have any lump sums available in a savings or money market account to use for investing. To help fund her retirement plans, she decided to have $200 a month withheld from her paycheck to invest in a mutual fund with a growth investment objective. Jessica's employer's 401(k) plan offers about 20 funds as well as company stock.

Eliminate Funds Inappropriate for Your Investment Goals

Jessica began by reviewing all fund classifications (pages 462–465) and balancing the risks and returns of various funds as illustrated in Figure 15.5. She wants to eliminate mutual funds inappropriate for her retirement investment goal.

Instant Message

Morningstar "Star" Ratings

Many investors review Morningstar mutual fund ratings for guidance in selecting funds in which to invest. Five stars for the best and one star for the worst. (See www .Morningstar.com or www.cnnmoney.com.) The star ratings are backward-looking, quantitative measures of past returns that are adjusted for risk, costs, and sales charges. Other fund analysts (*Kiplinger's Personal Finance Magazine, Money* magazine, *Consumer Reports,* and other investment publications) offer forward-looking, subjective recommendations of funds that they think have the best chance at success.

Table 15.2 Mutual Fund Performance

Fund	Symbol	Total return* 1 yr.	3 yrs.	5 yrs.	10 yrs.	Exp. ratio	Toll-free number
Large-Company Stock Funds							
Dodge & Cox Stock	DODGX	−53.8%	−22.2%	−9.9%	1.3%	0.52%	800-621-3979
Fidelity Contrafund	FCNTX	−40.8	−11.9	−2.1	0.6	0.89	800-544-9797
Longleaf Partners	LLPFX	−53.9	−21.9	−11.8	−1.3	0.89	800-445-9469
T. Rowe Price Equity Income	PRFDX	−49.9	−18.8	−8.7	−1.3	0.67	800-225-5132
Selected American Shares S	SLASX	−50.9	−19.2	−9.2	−2.3	0.88	800-243-1575
Vanguard Primecap Core	VPCCX	−38.9	−13.3	—	—	0.50	800-635-1511
Small- and Midsize-Company Stock Funds							
Baron Small Cap	BSCFX	−44.1%	−17.8%	−6.0%	3.1%	1.32%	800-442-3814
FBR Focus	FBRVX	−40.2	−13.9	−3.3	6.8	1.42	888-888-0025
Fidelity Low-Priced Stock	FLPSX	−45.7	−16.9	−5.5	6.0	0.98	800-544-9797
T. Rowe Price Mid-Cap Growth	RPMGX	−42.3	−15.1	−3.7	2.5	0.77	800-225-5132
T. Rowe Price Small-Cap Value	PRSVX	−45.0	−18.9	−5.6	5.6	0.81	800-225-5132
Vanguard Selected Value	VASVX	−43.3	−16.1	−5.7	3.1	0.38	800-635-1511
International/Global Funds							
Artio International Equity II A	JETAX	−50.2%	−14.7%	—	—	1.21%	800-387-6977
Dodge & Cox International Stock	DODFX	−55.8	−19.0	−4.3%	—	0.64	800-621-3979
Marsico Global	MGLBX	−50.6	—	—	—	0.75	888-860-8686
T. Rowe Price Emrg Mkts Stock	PRMSX	−63.4	−17.2	0.1	7.6%	1.24	800-225-5132
Go-Anywhere Funds							
CGM Focus	CGMFX	−59.9%	−9.2%	1.4%	15.1%	0.97%	800-598-0778
Fairholme Fund	FAIRX	−46.8	−13.2	−2.3	—	1.01	866-202-2263
FPA Crescent	FPACX	−25.5	−4.9	0.5	6.5	1.34	800-982-4372
Commodity Fund							
Pimco CommodityRealRet Strat D	PCRDX	−59.1%	−13.8%	−5.8%	—	1.24%	800-426-0107
Bond Funds							
Dodge & Cox Income	DODIX	−1.6%	2.8%	2.4%	5.1%	0.43%	800-621-3979
Fidelity Intermed Muni Income	FLTMX	2.8	3.6	2.9	4.5	0.37	877-208-0098
Harbor Bond Institutional	HABDX	−0.7	4.4	3.7	5.7	0.55	800-422-1050
Loomis Sayles Bond	LSBRX	−23.5	−4.2	0.5	5.4	0.94	800-633-3330
Vanguard Infltn-Prot Securities	VIPSX	−8.3	3.1	2.9	—	0.20	800-635-1511
Indexes							
S&P 500-STOCK INDEX		**−46.2%**	**−17.1%**	**−8.2%**	**−4.4%**		
RUSSELL 2000 INDEX		**−46.2**	**−20.6**	**−9.0**	**0.0**		
MSCI EAFE INDEX		**−52.8**	**−17.0**	**−4.6**	**−1.4**		
MERRILL LYNCH US BROAD MARKET INDEX		**3.0**	**5.1**	**3.8**	**5.6**		
DOW JONES—AIG COMMODITY INDEX		**−50.6**	**−10.3**	**−3.3**	**6.7**		

Source: Kiplinger's Personal Finance, Investing Section, 5/1/2009. Reproduced by permission.

Jessica recognizes that increasing the potential for higher returns also increases the risk to the investor's capital. Therefore, she eliminated the following types of funds: aggressive income funds, commodity funds, sector funds, and aggressive growth funds, as well as stock in the company where she works. She also realizes that investing too conservatively invites the risk of failure to achieve her goal of a financially successful retirement. Therefore, Jessica eliminated money market funds and balanced funds.

Figure 15.5
Balancing Risk and Returns
on Mutual Funds

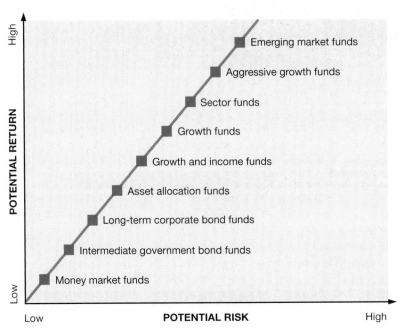

Note that increasing the potential for higher returns also increases the risk to the investor's capital.

Did You Know?

How to Learn About Mutual Funds

Information on mutual fund investing is vast, and current information about mutual funds is available from numerous sources.

Websites Focusing on Mutual Funds

- Yahoo! Finance (http://finance.yahoo.com/funds)
- The Motley Fool (http://www.fool.com/mutualfunds/mutualfunds.htm?source=LN)
- *Kiplinger's Personal Finance* (http://www.kiplinger.com/personalfinance/investing/funds/index.html)
- CNNMoney.com (http://money.cnn.com/pf/funds/index.html)
- BusinessWeek Online (http://www.businessweek.com/investor/funds.html)
- SmartMoney.com (http://www.smartmoney.com/funds/?nav=dropTab)
- AOL Money & Finance (http://money.aol.com/investing/funds?icid=investing:mutualfunds)

Personal Finance Magazines

Kiplinger's Personal Finance Magazine, Money, Business-Week, Consumer Reports, Forbes, Fortune, and *Worth.* Comprehensive examinations of the performance of numerous mutual funds are featured every year in the late August issue

of *Forbes,* the October issue of *Money,* a late February issue of *BusinessWeek,* and the September issue of *Kiplinger's Personal Finance Magazine.*

Financial Press

The Wall Street Journal, Barron's, Investor's Business Daily, and the business sections of newspapers such as *The New York Times* and *USA Today.*

Online News and Quote Services

CompuServe, Dow Jones News/Retrieval-Private Investor Edition, Farcast, Personal Journal, Quote.com, and Reuters Money Network.

Mutual Fund Investment Publications and Websites

Morningstar Mutual Funds, Morningstar No-Load Funds, Mutual Funds Update, Investment Companies Yearbook, IBC/Donoghue's Mutual Funds Almanac, Standard & Poor's, Lipper Mutual Fund Profiles, Moody's, and *The Value Line Mutual Fund Survey.* Dozens of newsletters that specialize in mutual funds are available, too. Morningstar (www.morningstar.com) and the Investment Company Institute (www.ici.org) provide information on thousands of funds. Some charge fees, and others are free.

Load or No-Load Funds?

The sales commissions charged by load funds indisputably reduce total returns. Jessica reasoned that since no-load mutual funds have an initial advantage—the investor has more money at work—she preferred no-load funds. Because her $200 a month was going into investment for retirement, she also thought that 12b-1 fees would be very costly over the long term. For the same reason, she wanted to avoid high management fees. She did not care about back-end loads and exit fees, as these largely disappear over time. Jessica decided to invest in one or more no-load mutual funds with no or low 12b-1 fees and very low expense ratios.

Investment Advice Needed?

Because Jessica is going to invest in no-load funds, she figured she did not need the services of a broker or financial adviser. Instead, she plans to use the tremendous resources that are available via the Vanguard website (http://www.vanguard.com/)—information, education, and professional advice. Jessica's employer offers investing and retirement planning seminars and workshops provided by Ernst & Young, Vanguard, T. Rowe Price, and other companies. Significant others are welcome to attend. Employer-sponsored financial advice may cover an employee's entire financial situation, including debt reduction, college planning, spousal assets, real estate, and other investments. Once Jessica's retirement assets build up to a substantial amount, perhaps $20,000 or more, she might be wise to seek additional professional investment advice.

Screen and Compare Funds That Meet Your Investment Criteria

When comparing the track records of mutual funds, there are a number of criteria to consider. These may include expenses; net asset value; minimum initial purchase; size of fund; ratings; past performance (perhaps one, three, five, and ten years); best and worst performance in up and down markets (volatility); fund manager tenure; and services. Jessica is interested in stock funds, international funds, and bond funds, low management fees, and no or low 12b-1 fees.

Jessica started searching for mutual fund investments at Vanguard (https://flagship.vanguard.com/VGApp/hnw/FundsMFSIntro?FROM=VAN), considered among the best mutual fund selection websites, and she began by typing in the fund symbols in "search." A **fund screener** or **fund-screening tool** permits an individual to screen all of the mutual funds in the market. Other mutual fund screening tools are available at the following websites:

- Yahoo! Finance (http://finance.yahoo.com/funds)
- Kiplinger.com (www.Kiplinger.com/investing/funds/)
- CNNMoney.com (http://money.cnn.com/pf/funds/)
- Fidelity (http://personal.fidelity.com/products/funds/?refhp=pr&ut=B10)

Jessica focused on large-cap funds, including those shown in Table 15.2. She researched funds using the Vanguard fund screener. She obtained online a profile prospectus from Vanguard on each of the funds she liked. A **profile prospectus** (or **fund profile**) describes the mutual fund, its investment objectives, and how it tries to achieve its objectives. Written in lay language, it offers a two- to four-page summary presentation of information contained in an SEC-required

fund screener/fund-screening tool
Permits investors to screen all of the mutual funds in the market to gauge performance.

profile prospectus/fund profile
Publication that describes the mutual fund, its investment objectives, and how it tries to achieve its objectives in lay terms rather than the legal language used in a regular prospectus.

 Did You Know?

About Mutual Fund Volatility

Volatility characterizes a mutual fund's (or any security's) tendency to rise or fall in price over a period of time. A measure of volatility is the **standard deviation,** which gauges the degree to which a security's historical return rises above or falls below its own long-term average return—and therefore may be likely to do so again in the future. A standard deviation is a probability indicator, not an economic forecast. The bigger an investment's standard deviation, the more volatile its price may be in the future. High volatility suggests greater long-term rewards but a greater-than-normal risk of short-term losses during economic downturns. Other common measures of risk are beta, the Sharpe Ratio, and R-squared. Publications like *Kiplinger's Personal Finance Magazine, Money, Morningstar,* and *U.S. News & World Report* provide volatility ratings for mutual funds.

Did You Know?

The Tax Consequences of Mutual Fund Investing

Ordinary income dividend distributions, capital gains distributions, and realized gains from the sale of mutual funds are generally subject to taxation.

- In regular investment accounts:
  - When you buy and hold mutual fund shares, you owe income taxes on any ordinary income dividends and on the fund's capital gains in the year you receive or reinvest them.
  - When you sell shares, you owe taxes on the capital gains earned on the difference between what you paid for the shares and the selling price (less transaction costs).
  - When purchasing a mutual fund in December, determine whether the fund has already made its end-of-year capital gains distribution. If you buy the fund before the **record date** (the date established by an issuer to determine who is eligible to receive a dividend or distribution), you will receive the income but you also will owe capital gains taxes for the whole year. Buying after the record date avoids that situation because you will not receive the distribution.

- Interest from a tax-exempt municipal bond fund is exempt from federal income taxes.

- In retirement accounts (such as a 401[k] or traditional IRA account), taxes are deferred until withdrawn.

legal prospectus that answers 11 key investor questions, including risks, fees, and details about the fund's ten-year performance record.

After reading fund details, looking at the numbers, and comparing performance, Jessica decided to split her monthly $200 investment between Vanguard Primecap Core (VPCCX) and Vanguard Selected Value (VASVX), partly because of their low expense ratios. (Any minimum initial investment fees are waived for investments via her employer's retirement plan.) Jessica thinks the fund managers will beat the average market returns, such as the S&P 500 index. Jessica might be right, or she might be wrong.

The next step is for Jessica to contact the human resources department at her employer and sign the documents to withhold $200 a month from her paycheck and invest $100 into each of the two funds. Jessica also knows that for every dollar invested she gets an immediate 50 percent return because her employer's policy is to match 401(k) contributions 50 cents on the dollar for the first 6 percent of earnings. Jessica's 401(k) balance in 12 months, therefore, will show $2400 in contributions and $1200 in employer matching contributions (that's an immediate 50 percent return on her $2400!), plus whatever gain occurs (hopefully not a loss) in NAV. Jessica's 401(k) balance next year is likely to be more than $3600. Chapter 17 examines retirement planning.

Monitor Your Mutual Fund Portfolio

Tracking your portfolio is imperative because investors do not want to keep an underperforming mutual fund in their portfolio for very long, assuming other similar funds are doing better. Detailed records are also useful when preparing income tax returns. If Jessica wants to invest outside of her 401(k) plan in the same or other no-load funds, she can purchase funds directly from mutual fund investment companies, such as family fund companies like Fidelity, T. Rowe Price, or any other mutual fund, like Gabelli, Neuberger, or Calvert.

The internet provides a broad variety of investment information and advice.

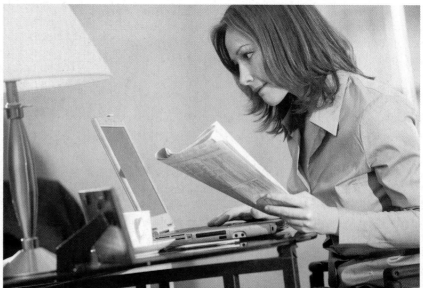

Use Portfolio Monitoring on the Internet

Monitoring a mutual fund portfolio is easy using any of the top-rated mutual fund websites cited earlier. For example, see Yahoo!'s portfolio manager capabilities at http://finance.yahoo.com/funds/monitoring_funds.

Check Fund Quotations in Newspapers

You can check closing prices online any time on any of the financial websites cited earlier or read quotes in newspapers. See Figure 15.6 for an illustration. Newspapers' quotations for no-load mutual funds list the name of the fund followed by columns for its net asset value, net change from the previous day, and year-to-date percentage return. For example, within the group listing for Fidelity Investments mutual funds, the Balanced Fund (abbreviated as Balanc) has a net asset value (NAV) of $15.14, a change in the net asset value (NET CHG) of −$0.20 from the closing price of the previous trading day, and a year-to-date percentage return (YTD %RET) of 1.1 percent. In mutual funds, the NAV is also known as the **mutual fund bid price.** Shareholders receive this amount per share when they redeem their shares—that is, the company is willing to pay this amount to buy the shares back. Also, the NAV is the amount per share an investor will pay to purchase a fund, assuming it is a no-load fund. A no-load fund is indicated as such by the alphabetic letter n at the end of the fund's name.

The **mutual fund ask price** (or **offer price**) is the price at which a mutual fund's share can be purchased by investors. It equals the current NAV per share plus sales charges, if any. If you wanted to buy or sell shares of Fidelity Balanced Fund, a no-load (note the superscript n in Figure 15.6) mutual fund, the price would be $15.14 per share. The funds listed without an n are load funds. The SEC requires that appropriate footnotes appear in newspaper listings of mutual funds to indicate other expenses and charges.

Do It NOW!

Investing in mutual funds may not be something you can do today but can start getting ready now. Start by:

1. Identifying five services provided by mutual funds (see pages 459–461) that appeal to you.

2. Identifying three of your long-term financial goals and determine whether you would seek a fund with a growth objective or growth and income objective for each goal.

3. Selecting one mutual fund from those listed in Table 15.2 on page 471 to follow for one or two months; then reassess your selection if warranted.

mutual fund bid price
Shareholders receive this amount per share when they redeem their shares, which is the same dollar amount as the NAV.

mutual fund ask (or offer) price
Price at which an investor can purchase a mutual fund's shares; current NAV per share plus sales charges.

Figure 15.6
How Mutual Funds Are Quoted

Fidelity Invest			
A Mgr	15.83	−0.24	− 4.3
AggrGr r	22.68	−0.76	− 37.1
AggrInt	11.60	−0.15	− 12.8
AMgrAggr	11.73	−0.35	− 10.0
AMgrGr	14.83	−0.29	− 6.8
AMgrIn	11.38x	−0.11	− 0.4
Balanc	15.14	−0.20	+ 1.1
BluCh	44.52	−1.34	− 13.6
Canad r	19.30	−0.21	− 8.2
CapAp	21.53	−0.57	− 3.1
ChinaReg	13.61	−0.08	− 7.4
Colns r	7.35	−0.04	− 1.3
		−5.55	− 7.6
		−0.45	− 11.2
		−0.28	− 5.2
		−0.29	− 0.5
		−0.35	− 12.1
		−0.29	− 5.2
		−0.39	− 11.2
		−0.68	− 3.9
		−0.15	− 11.7
		−0.09	− 4.5
		−0.86	− 2.8
		−0.47	− 4.9
		−0.21	− 18.8
		−0.13	− 15.0
		−4.03	− 8.2
		−0.33	− 1.2
		−1.02	− 7.6
		−0.06	− 10.3
		−0.40	− 8.4
GNMA	10.79	+0.01	+ 3.7
GloBal	15.90	−0.16	− 8.8

GovtInc	9.82	+0.02	+ 2.5
GroCo	55.13	−1.97	− 22.6
GroInc	38.56	−0.69	− 7.9
GroIncIl	9.33	−0.18	− 8.7
HighInc r	8.81	−0.01	− 2.5
Independnc	16.46	−0.60	− 25.0
IntBd	10.16	+0.02	+ 4.4
IntGov	9.66	+0.02	+ 3.6
IntGr	19.31	−0.26	− 15.0
IntlBnd	7.83	+0.04	− 4.2
InvGB	7.20	+0.01	+ 3.7
Japan r	11.86	−0.21	− 13.7
JpnSmCo r	7.64	−0.09	− 4.3
LargeCap	15.56	−0.41	− 12.3
LatinAm r	12.62	−0.13	− 3.4
LevCoSt	10.56	−0.15	+ 4.9
LowP r	26.61	−0.29	+ 15.1
MagIn	107.84	−2.46	− 8.9
MidCap	23.86	−0.49	− 8.1
MtgSec	10.78	+0.02	+ 3.5
NewMkt r	11.38	−0.04	+ 4.9
NewMill	27.27	−1.25	− 19.2
Nordic	19.60	−0.12	− 25.0
OTC	32.41	−1.42	− 21.0
Ovrse	29.16	−0.57	− 15.2
PcBas r	15.37	−0.27	− 11.1
Puritn	18.38	−0.19	− 0.9
RealE	19.49	−0.05	+ 8.3
STBF	8.74	+0.02	+ 4.4
SmallCap	13.54	−0.20	+ 0.2
SmCapSlc	15.06	−0.25	− 7.2
SE Asia r	10.68	−0.10	− 6.6
StratInc	9.13	+0.01	+ 3.2

NAME	NAV	NET CHG	YTD %RET
Fidelity Invest			
Balanc^n	15.14	− 0.20	+ 1.1
Contra	43.67	− 0.45	− 11.2
MidCap^n	23.86	− 0.49	− 8.1
MagIn	107.84	− 2.46	− 8.9

Concept Check 15.4

1. Tell why it is important to review your investment philosophy and goals when selecting mutual fund investments.
2. Explain how you would eliminate funds inappropriate for your investment goals, given your situation and assuming you were working full time.

What Do You Recommend NOW?

Now that you have read the chapter on mutual funds, what do you recommend to David and Sarah Gent in the case at the beginning of the chapter regarding:

1. Redeeming their CDs and investing their retirement money in mutual funds?
2. Investing in growth and income mutual funds instead of income funds?
3. Buying no-load rather than load funds?
4. Buying life-cycle mutual funds instead of balanced mutual funds?
5. Buying mutual funds through their employers' 401(k) retirement accounts?

Big Picture Summary of Learning Objectives

1 Describe the features, services, and advantages of investing in mutual funds.

A mutual fund is an investment company that pools funds obtained by selling shares to investors and makes investments to achieve the financial goal of income or growth, or both. The net asset value (NAV) is the per-share value of the fund. Advantages of mutual funds include diversification, affordability, and professional management. Unique services include ease of buying and selling, check writing, and effortless establishment of retirement plans.

2 Differentiate mutual funds by investment objectives, types, and characteristics.

A mutual fund with an income objective invests in securities that pay regular income in dividends or interest. A fund that has a growth objective seeks capital appreciation. A fund that has a combined growth and income objective seeks a balanced return made up of current income and capital gains. The name of a fund, such as aggressive growth fund, gives a clue to its objectives. Index funds and ETFs are popular because they earn the same return as a particular market index.

3 Summarize the fees and charges involved in buying and selling mutual funds.

Individuals who invest through mutual funds pay shareholder fees for specific transactions, such as purchases, redemptions, or exchanges. They also pay annual fund operating expenses that are deducted from fund assets before earnings are distributed to shareholders. Investors may be faced with load and no-load funds, 12b-1 fees, and deferred load and redemption fees.

4 Establish strategies to evaluate and select mutual funds that meet your investment goals.

The process of selecting mutual funds in which to invest is usually a do-it-yourself effort. The steps are (1) review investment philosophy, (2) review investment goals, (3) eliminate funds inappropriate for your investment goals, (4) choose low- or no-load funds, (5) decide whether investment advice is needed, (6) screen and compare funds that meet your investment criteria, and (7) monitor your mutual fund portfolio.

Let's Talk About It

1. **Investing in Tough Economic Times.** Comment on this statement: "A great time to invest is during times of economic turmoil when assets are undervalued."

2. **One Fund of Interest.** Review the objectives of mutual funds and the characteristics of various funds. Based on your investment philosophy and risk tolerance, which one type of fund would be of most interest to you if you are saving to buy a home several years from now? Give reasons why.

3. **Two Funds.** Assume you graduated from college a few years ago, had a good job paying $55,000 annually, and wanted to invest $300 per month in mutual funds for retirement. Which combination of two or more mutual funds would you think appropriate? Give reasons for each of your selections.

4. **Spread Your Money into Funds.** Assume that your uncle gave you $50,000 to invest solely in mutual funds. Based on your point in the life cycle and your investment philosophy, identify your investment goals and explain how you would spread your money into different funds.

5. **Good Choices.** Identify the types of mutual funds that would be good choices to meet the following investment objectives: emergency fund, house down payment, college fund for 2-year-old child, and retirement fund

for a 25-year-old. Give two reasons why each of your recommendations would be appropriate.

6. **Load or No-Load.** Which is a better choice for you, load or no-load mutual funds? Give some reasons.

Do the Math

1. **Profits and Taxes.** Ten months ago George Jetson, from Orbit City, Illinois, invested $1000 by buying 100 shares of the Can't Lose Mutual Fund, an aggressive growth no-load mutual fund. George reinvested his dividends all year so now has 112 shares. So far, the NAV for George's investment has risen from $10 per share to $13.25.

   (a) What is the percentage increase in the NAV of George's mutual fund?

   (b) If George redeemed the first 100 shares of his mutual fund investment for $13.25 per share, what would be his capital gain over the amount invested?

   (c) Assuming George pays income taxes at the 25 percent rate, how much income tax will he have to pay if he sells those first 100 shares?

2. **Mutual Fund Sales.** Two years ago, Stephanie, from Manhattan, Kansas, invested $1000 by buying 125 shares ($8 per share NAV) in the Can't Lose Mutual Fund, an aggressive growth no-load mutual fund. Last year she made two additional investments of $500 each (50 shares at $10 and 40 shares at $12.50). Stephanie reinvested all of her dividends. So far, the NAV for her investment has risen from $8 per share to $13.25. Late in the year, she sold 60 shares at $13.25.

   (a) What were the proceeds from Stephanie's sale of the 60 shares?

   (b) To use the Internal Revenue Service's average-cost basis method of determining the average price paid for one share, begin by calculating the average price paid for the shares. In this instance, the $2000 is divided by 215 shares (125 shares + 50 shares + 40 shares). What was the average price paid by Stephanie?

   (c) To finally determine the average-cost basis of shares sold, you multiply the average price per share times the number of shares sold—in this case, 60. What is the total cost basis for Stephanie's 60 shares?

   (d) Assuming that Stephanie has to pay income taxes on the difference between the sales price for the 60 shares and their cost, how much is this difference?

Financial Planning Cases

Case 1

Matching Mutual Fund Investments to Economic Projections

Glenn Sandler, a realtor for the past ten years in Ames, Iowa, is married and has two children. He is interested in investing in mutual funds. Glenn wants to put half of his $20,000 of accumulated savings into a stock mutual fund and then continue to invest $200 monthly for the foreseeable future, perhaps using the money for retirement starting in about 25 years. Glenn has limited his choices to the mutual funds listed in Table 15.2.

(a)   Glenn wants to invest the full $10,000 now and diversify his holdings into two mutual funds, an international fund and a stock fund. Which two funds listed in Table 15.2 do you recommend as investments for his $10,000? Why?

(b)   Glenn also wants to invest $200 per month into one mutual fund over the next 25 years. Which of the other funds listed in Table 15.2 would you recommend? Why?

Case 2

Selection of a Mutual Fund as Part of a Retirement Plan

Etta Mae Westbrook, a single mother of a six-year-old child, works in a marketing firm in Chestertown, Maryland, and is willing to invest $2000 to $3000 per year in a mutual fund. She wants the investment income to supplement her retirement pension starting in approximately 20 years and she has a moderate investment philosophy. Advise Etta Mae by responding to the following questions:

(a)   Should Etta Mae invest in a mutual fund with a growth objective, such as one of the stock funds listed in Table 15.2, or one with an income objective, such as a bond fund? Why?

(b)   Etta Mae wants to invest in a mutual fund that focuses on common stocks. Which two stock funds in Table 15.2 would you recommend that she avoid? Why?

(c)   Explain your reasons for suggesting Etta Mae invest in a load fund or a no-load fund.

Case 3

Victor and Maria Invest for Retirement

Victor and Maria Hernandez plan to retire in less than 15 years. Their current investment portfolio is distributed as follows:

40 percent in growth mutual funds, 40 percent in corporate bonds and bond mutual funds, and 20 percent in cash equivalents. They have decided to increase the amount of risk in their portfolio by taking 10 percent from their cash equivalent investments and investing in some mutual funds with strong growth possibilities.

(a)   Of the mutual stock and international funds listed in Table 15.2, which two would you recommend to meet the Hernandezes' goals? Why?

(b)   Would you recommend that the Hernandezes remain invested in those two funds during their retirement years? Why or why not?

Case 4

The Johnsons Decide to Invest Through Mutual Funds

After learning about mutual funds, the Johnsons are confident that they are a great way to invest, especially because of the diversification and professional management that funds offer. The couple has a financial nest egg of $9500 to invest through mutual funds. They also want to invest another $300 per month on a regular basis.

Although not yet completely firm, Harry and Belinda's goals at this point are as follows:

• They want to continue to build their retirement income to retire in about 36 years.

• They will need about $10,000 in six to eight years to use as supplemental income if Belinda has a baby and does not work for six months.

• They might buy a luxury automobile requiring a $10,000 down payment if they decide not to have a child.

Knowing that the Johnsons have a moderate investment philosophy, that they live on a reasonable budget, and that they have a well-established cash-management plan, advise them on their mutual fund investments by responding to the following questions:

(a)   After looking at Table 15.2, would you recommend they invest in a stock fund, a bond fund or both? Why?

(b)   How would you divide the $9500 between a stock fund and a bond fund? Why?

(c)   How much of the $300 monthly investment amount would you allocate to a stock fund and/or a bond fund? Why?

(d)   Some comparable mutual fund performance data on stock funds are shown in Table 15.2. Using only that information and assuming that you are recommending some funds for the Johnsons' retirement needs, which two funds would you recommend? Why?

(e) Assume that all three funds have above-average performance over the next ten years. Another bear market then occurs, causing the NAVs to drop 25 percent from the previous year. Would you recommend that the Johnsons sell their accumulated shares in the funds? Why or why not?

(f) Determine the value of the shares purchased with their $9500 original investment in ten years, assuming that the three funds' NAVs increase 8 percent annually for the next ten years. (Use the *Garman/Forgue* companion website.)

On the 'Net

Go to the Web pages indicated to complete these exercises.

1. Visit the website for Vanguard Investments and visit its education section at https://flagship.vanguard.com/VGApp/hnw/planningeducation/education. Compare the information provided in the "Mutual fund basics" section with the information in this text chapter. Develop a list of ten key points that every beginning investor in mutual funds should know. Also list four advantages that investing in stock mutual funds provides as opposed to direct purchase of stock.

2. Visit the website for CNNMoney. On its "Mutual Fund" page at http://money.cnn.com/pf/funds/index.html, access its "Fund winners and fund losers" section to review the best- and worst-performing funds over the past three months, past one year, and past five years. What differences do you detect in the lists? What might this information tell you about the approach that might be taken by investors with longer time horizons?

3. Visit the website for the Financial Industry Regulatory Authority (FINRA) at http://www.finra.org/Investors/index.htm, where you will find an "expense analyzer" for comparing the expenses of mutual funds. Compare the expenses for three of the funds identified as examples in this chapter.

Visit the Garman/Forgue companion website . . .

www.cengage.com/finance/garman

Real Estate and High-Risk Investments

!You Must Be Kidding, Right?

Friends Richard Belisle and Dave Sanders both have aggressive investment philosophies. Richard invests primarily in residential real estate, and Dave invests in commodities futures contracts. As longtime investors, they consider themselves experts, but occasionally each has experienced financial losses. What are the odds that the typical investor will make money investing in commodities futures contracts?

A. 50%

B. 30%

C. 20%

D. 10%

The answer is D. Ninety percent of individual investors in futures contracts lose money. Funds used for these investments should be only those that one can afford to lose!

Learning Objectives

After reading this chapter, you should be able to:

1 Demonstrate how you can make money investing in real estate.

2 Calculate the right price to pay for real estate and how to finance your purchase.

3 Assess the disadvantages of investing in real estate.

4 Summarize the risks and challenges of investing in collectibles, precious metals, and gems.

5 Explain why options and futures are high-risk investments.

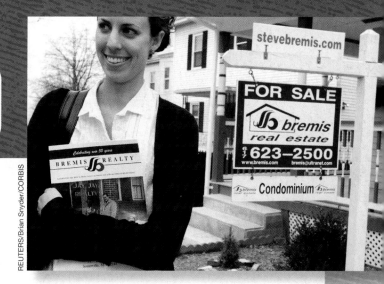

REUTERS/Brian Snyder/CORBIS

Jamie Day, a 37-year-old marketing manager for a large corporation in Long Beach, California, earns $110,000 per year. She saves about $1800 each month beyond her contributions to her employer's 401(k) retirement plan. To date, Jamie has been investing her 401(k) plan money primarily in aggressive stock mutual funds and the remainder in her employer's company stock. She has found excellent success investing in the mutual funds within the plan, and her investments have grown at a healthy pace through the years. Her total 401(k) holdings are worth $260,000.

Ever since her grandfather gave her some stocks as a child, Jamie has loved investing—and she has enjoyed a good track record with her efforts. Jamie is an active trader, often trading every three or four weeks, primarily in the oil, technology, and prescription drug industries. Every year she has some losses as well as gains. Her private portfolio is currently worth $160,000. Jamie has never bought or sold options or futures contracts, but her stockbroker suggested that she consider them. Jamie also has a friend who owns several residential rental properties who has asked her to consider investing as her partner in her next real estate venture.

What do you recommend to Jamie on the subject of real estate and high-risk investments regarding:

1. Investing in real estate?

2. Putting some of her money in a high-risk investment, like collectibles?

3. Investing in options and futures contracts?

**real estate
(or housing) bubble**
Rapid and unsustainable increases in home prices followed by sharp declines in values.

A home tends to accomplish more than just putting a roof over your head. It is also an investment because historically housing values have increased over the long term. A **real estate** (or **housing**) **bubble** for residential markets occurred in the United States between 2001 and 2006. The bubble saw rapid increases in home valuations until they were unsustainable. Then the real estate market crashed! Not since the 1930s has the United States seen home values plummet 20%, 40%, 50% or even more in some communities. The "for sale" prices on millions of foreclosed homes simultaneously pulled down the values of other homes. The results: (1) many people own homes that have declined in value, and (2) buying opportunities exist for new homeowners as prices are lower. Real estate today remains an investment option that is somewhat riskier than yesteryear but nevertheless is one that can pay ample returns.

**high-risk/speculative
investments**
Present potential for significant fluctuations in return, sometimes over short time periods.

Investors who seek high returns and are willing to accept greater risks might consider owning tangible assets such as collectibles, precious metals, and gems for their investment potential. Yet another higher risk alternative is options and futures contracts. All these are referred to as **high-risk (speculative) investments** because they have the potential for significant fluctuations in return, sometimes over short time periods. They are suitable only for investors with a moderate-to-aggressive investment philosophy.

Making Money Investing in Real Estate

1 Learning Objective

Demonstrate how you can make money investing in real estate.

Real estate investing is not the same as buying a home in which to live. Investing in real estate can provide you extra income now and give a boost to your future retirement plans. But to do so you have to do a lot of things right. Real estate is not rocket science, but investors must be smart about taxes, financing, insurance, and community economics. Dealing with tenants requires a business attitude not a willingness to give renters a good deal. Real estate investments are complex, and they are much riskier than investing in mutual funds and stocks.

real estate
Property consisting of land, all structures permanently attached to that land, and accompanying rights and privileges, such as crops and mineral rights.

direct ownership
Results when investor holds actual legal title to property.

Real estate is property consisting of land, all structures permanently attached to that land, and accompanying rights and privileges, such as crops and mineral rights. A real estate investment is termed **direct ownership** when an investor holds actual legal title to the property. For example, you can invest directly as an individual or jointly with other investors to buy properties designed for residential living, such as houses, duplexes, apartments, mobile homes, and condominiums. You also could invest in commercial properties designed for business uses, such as office buildings, medical centers, gasoline stations, and motels. You might buy raw land or residential lots, although they are extremely risky and often lose money for the investor.

Current Income and Capital Gains

Following are two key questions for real estate investors:

- Can you make current income while you own?
- Can you profit with capital gains when you sell the property?

The most important consideration for real estate investors is not whether the price will rise enough in a few years to make a profit. The boom days of the housing bubble are gone! The key question for real estate investors now is whether the rental income will be sufficient to make a profit. If you invest in a property and you are paying out more than the rental income coming in, you face three risks: (1) whether you can afford to continue paying out that money every month, (2) whether the price on the property will increase, and (3) whether the property actually will sell for more than what you paid for it. Get one or more of these wrong and you lose your invested money and maybe more.

To measure the current income in a real estate market, investors can begin by using the **price-to-rent ratio,** which averages 18 in the U.S. This numerical relationship might range from 11 to 26 depending upon local market conditions—meaning how high housing prices are. The larger the number, the less likely the investor can make money. In Seattle, Washington, a condominium renting for $1500 a month might sell for the high price of $390,000 for a ratio of 21.7 (12 × $1500 = $18,000; $390,000 ÷ $18,000 = 21.7), while a similar one in Dallas, Texas, might cost only $165,000 for a ratio of 9.17 (12 × $1500 = $18,000; $165,000 ÷ $18,000 = 9.17). Buying property with a high ratio will provide a profit only with a future increase in the value of the property.

Investors also calculate the **rental yield** on properties. This is a computation of how much income the investor might pocket from rent each year before mortgage payments as a percentage of the purchase price. Most properties yield about 4 percent of income annually, although the rental yield may be as little as 1 or 2 percent and as high as 8 or 9 percent. Less expensive properties often offer higher yields. The formula assumes half of rental income goes for expenses other than debt repayment.

$$\text{Rental yield} = \frac{(\text{rent} \div 2)}{\text{purchase price}} \qquad (16.1)$$

	Example A	Example B
Purchase price	$500,000	$150,000
Annual rent	36,000	26,000
Yield	3.6%	8.67%

Current Income Results from Positive Cash Flow

In real estate investing, current income takes the form of positive cash flow. For an income-producing real estate investment, you pay operating expenses out of rental income. If the property has a mortgage (a common occurrence), payments toward the mortgage principal and interest also must be made out of rental income. Operating expenses such as vacancies, taxes, mortgage payments, and repairs may eat up half of rental income.

The amount of rental income you have left after paying all operating expenses is called **cash flow.** The amount of cash flow—obtained by subtracting any cash outlays from the cash income—depends on the amount of rent received, the amount of expenses paid, and the amount necessary to repay the mortgage debt. Investors usually prefer a positive cash flow to a negative cash flow because any shortages represent out-of-pocket expenses for the investor.

Many real estate investments will not generate a positive cash flow, even though they may offer the likelihood of potential returns through price appreciation. Investors might consider managing a negative cash flow for a few years while waiting for capital gains to later materialize and then sell the property. Profits in real estate due to subsequent price appreciation can occur in geographic areas where prices are rising as well as in any one specific local market. Profits may occur because of special circumstances, such as more demand for housing due to construction of a new shopping mall or school, a new major employer coming to town or when the asking price of a particular property is sharply reduced and underpriced perhaps because of a divorce or foreclosure.

Your Next Five Years

In the next five years you can start achieving financial success by doing the following related to real estate and high-risk investments:

1. Focus heavily on the disadvantages before deciding to invest in real estate.

2. Invest only in real estate properties that have a positive cash flow.

3. Finance real estate investments with conventional mortgages, not mortgages with adjustable interest terms.

4. Use the discounted cash-flow method to help determine the right price to pay for any real estate investment.

5. If you put money into high-risk assets, limit your investment to no more than 10 percent of your portfolio.

price-to-rent ratio
Measures the current income in a real estate market; multiply the monthly rent by 12 and then divide the property price by this figure. The higher the number, the less likely you are to make money.

rental yield
A computation of how much income the investor might pocket from rent each year (before mortgage payments) as a percentage of the purchase price; divide the annual rent by 2 and then divide by the purchase price.

cash flow
Amount of rental income you have left after paying all operating expenses.

Price Appreciation Leads to Capital Gains

The **capital gain** earned in a real estate investment comes from price appreciation. It is the amount above ownership costs for which an investment is sold. In real estate, ownership costs include the original purchase price as well as expenditures for any capital improvements made to a property prior to sale. **Capital improvements** are costs incurred in making changes in real property—beyond maintenance and repairs—that add to its value. Paneling a living room, adding a new roof, and putting up a fence represent capital improvements.

Repairs are expenses (usually tax deductible against an investor's cash-flow income) necessary to maintain the value of the property. Repainting, mending roof leaks, and fixing plumbing are examples of repairs.

As an example, assume that Andrew Webb, an unmarried schoolteacher from Fort Wayne, Indiana, bought a small rental house as an investment five years ago for $120,000 in cash that he received as an inheritance. He fixed some roof leaks (repairs) for $1000 and then added a new shed and some kitchen cabinets (capital improvements) at a cost of $10,000 before selling the property this year for $160,000. As a result, Andrew happily realized a capital gain of $30,000 ($160,000 minus the $120,000 purchase price minus $10,000 in capital improvements).

Historically, residential real estate values could generally be expected to increase 3 percent annually, about the rate of inflation, or a little above. In some markets, prices do rise that much or more; however, prices can and have declined even in formerly hot real estate markets. In markets in which real estate is difficult to sell (too many properties on the market and too few buyers), perhaps because of continuing job losses in a slow regional economy, residential housing prices might decline 2 or 3 percent annually for a long time.

If you cannot comfortably forecast the future of what you invest in, such as price appreciation on a property in a local housing market, you are speculating. Using a mortgage loan to invest in real estate invites more risk. While price appreciation is where the big profits are in real estate, you can reduce risk by investing in property for which the expected rental income exceeds projected mortgage payments, property taxes, and maintenance costs.

Leverage Can Increase an Investor's Return

As we noted in Chapter 13, **leverage** involves using borrowed funds to make an investment with the goal of earning a rate of return in excess of the after-tax costs of borrowing. Lenders often allow investors to borrow from 75 to 90 percent of the price of a property.

capital improvements
Costs incurred in making value-enhancing changes (beyond maintenance and repair) in real property.

repairs
Usually tax-deductible expenses necessary to maintain property value.

Did You Know?

Foreclosure and Short Sales

Foreclosure is the legal and professional procedure in which a mortgagee, or other lienholder, usually a lender, repossesses a home and sells it because the borrower has fallen behind in making payments on the loan. Prior to foreclosure the home-owner has three options: (1) depart the property and try to repay the lender the deficiency, (2) declare bankruptcy, or (3) try to arrange a short sale. Sometimes the remaining balance owed on the home is more than the property is worth. The lender then pursues the homeowner for the deficiency.

In a **short sale** the lender accepts less than the full mortgage amount and often forgives whatever debt is left

unpaid. The **deficiency amount** is the difference between the amount owed and what the bank collects at the short sale. When a bank agrees to a short sale, the homeowner hires an agent to find a buyer. Offers are taken to the bank to seek approval. The lender agrees to absorb the loss although they might demand the homeowner make some kind of payment or share the loss. A debt that is forgiven may be subject to income taxes. A short sale may be a buying opportunity for investors although negotiating with banks is a cumbersome and lengthy process.

Did You Know?

What to Do Before Investing in Real Estate

1. Set up a limited liability corporation to own your real estate investments as it protects your personal assets in case someone injured on your rental property sues you.

2. Hire an accountant experienced in real estate investing.

3. Line up financing options before searching for properties.

4. Hire an inspector to inspect the physical condition of the property.

5. Hire a licensed contractor for plumbing, electrical, and expensive repair jobs rather than doing them yourself.

6. Consider hiring a management company to tend to your property; the cost is 5 to 10 percent of rental income.

7. Set aside $5000 as a contingency fund for unanticipated property problems.

8. Consider investing in properties only in locales where there are thriving businesses located near good schools, supermarkets, and public transportation.

A slumping economy can lead to unfinished units and losses for real estate investors.

Jack Smith/Bloomberg News/Landov

Suppose that Andrew, instead of paying cash for the house, had made a down payment of $25,000 and borrowed the remainder. What effect would this borrowing have on his return? In the first instance, Andrew paid $120,000 cash for the property and earned a 25 percent return on his investment ($30,000 ÷ $120,000) over the five-year period, or roughly 5 percent per year. In the second situation, using leverage, he would have an apparent return of 120 percent ($30,000 ÷ $25,000), or roughly 24 percent per year. The true return would be lower because of mortgage payments, interest expenses, property taxes, and repairs but would still be a double-digit return.

The **loan-to-value ratio** measures the amount of leverage in a real estate investment project. It is calculated by dividing the amount of debt by the value of the total original investment. For example, because his down payment was $25,000 on the $120,000 property, Andrew had a loan-to-value ratio of 79 percent ($95,000 ÷ $120,000), or 79 percent leverage.

loan-to-value ratio
Measures the amount of leverage in a real estate investment project by dividing the total amount of debt by the market price of the investment.

Do you like turtles?

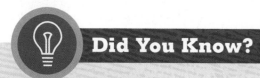

Did You Know?

The Top 3 Financial Missteps in Real Estate and High-Risk Investing

People slip up in real estate and high-risk investments when they do the following:

1. Assuming that real estate prices will go up and interest rates will not increase

2. Failing to factor in income lost due to vacancies and collection costs for tenants who do not pay

3. Not setting enough money aside for maintenance, repairs, unanticipated capital improvements, and rising real estate taxes

depreciation
Decline in value of an asset over time due to normal wear and tear and obsolescence.

Beneficial Tax Treatments

The U.S. Congress, through provisions in the Internal Revenue Code, encourages real estate investments by giving investors five special tax treatments. The first three may increase the real estate investor's income while the last two may enhance capital gains.

1. Depreciation Is Tax Deductible

Investors in real estate become successful by understanding the "numbers" of real estate investing. For example, assume that Jisue Han, a lawyer from Pewaukee, Wisconsin, invested $200,000 in a residential building ($170,000) and land ($30,000). She rents the property to a tenant for $24,000 per year. You might initially think that Jisue has to pay income taxes on the entire $24,000 in rental income. Wrong. IRS regulations allow taxpayers to deduct depreciation from rental income. **Depreciation** represents the decline in value of an asset over time due to normal wear and tear and obsolescence. A proportionate amount of a capital asset representing depreciation may be deducted against income each year over the asset's estimated life. Land cannot be depreciated.

Jisue can deduct an equal part of the building's cost over the estimated life of the property. IRS guidelines provide that residential properties may be depreciated over 27.5 years while nonresidential properties are allowed 39 years. Jisue calculates (from Table 16.1) the amount she can annually deduct from income to be $6182 ($170,000 ÷ 27.5). Table 16.1 shows the effects of depreciation on her income taxes, assuming Jisue pays income taxes at a combined federal and state rate of 36 percent. In this example, the depreciation deduction lowers taxable income on the property from $24,000 to $17,818 ($24,000 − $6182) and increases the return on the investment to 9.29 percent.

2. Interest Is Tax Deductible

Real estate investors incur many business expenses in attempting to earn a profit: interest on a mortgage, real estate taxes, insurance, utilities, accounting and legal costs, management bills, capital improvements, and repairs. The largest of these costs often is the interest expense, as properties are often purchased with a mortgage loan. Table 16.2 illustrates the effect of interest expenses on income taxes. Assume Jisue borrowed $175,000 to purchase her $200,000 property. After deducting annual depreciation of $6182 and interest expenses of $13,050, her taxable income is reduced to $4768. Because her income tax liability is only $1716, Jisue's after-tax return of $9234 yields 36.94 percent on her leveraged investment.

Table 16.1   Effect of Depreciation on Income Taxes and Return

			Without Depreciation	With Depreciation
Total amount invested	$200,000	Gross rental income	$24,000	$24,000
Cost of land	− 30,000	Less annual depreciation expense	0	6,182
Cost of rental building	$170,000	Taxable income	24,000	17,818
Depreciation for 27.5 years	$ 6,182	Income taxes (36 percent combined federal and state tax rate)	8,640	6,414
		After-tax return	$15,360	$17,586
		After-tax yield (divide return by $200,000)	7.68%	8.79%

Table 16.2 Additional Effect of Interest Paid on Income Taxes on Return

Gross rental income	$ 24,000
Less annual depreciation deduction	− 6,182
Subtotal	$17,818
Less interest expense for the year (7.5 percent mortgage loan)	− 13,050
Taxable income	$ 4,768
Cash flow after paying interest ($24,000 − $13,050)	10,950
Less income tax liability (0.36 × $4768)	− 1,716
After-tax return ($10,950 − $1716)	$ 9,234
After-tax yield [$9234 ÷ ($200,000 − $175,000)]	36.94%

Tax laws permit investors to deduct interest expenses (with the amount of the deduction allowed depending on the investor's marginal tax bracket). The interest deduction gives Jisue a cash flow after paying mortgage interest of $10,950 ($24,000 − $13,050). In essence, the $13,050 in interest is paid with $4698 ($13,050 × 36 percent combined federal and state income tax rate) of the money that was not sent to the federal and state governments and $8352 ($13,050 − $4698) of Jisue's money.

3. Rental Income Tax Regulations on Vacation Homes
If you rent out your vacation property for 14 or fewer days during the year, you can pocket the income tax-free as the IRS does not want to hear about this gain. The home is considered a personal residence, so you can deduct mortgage interest and property taxes just as you would for your principal residence. (That same tax break is available for those who rent their primary home for 14 days or less, say for people attending a major sporting event in your city.)

If you limit your use to fewer than 15 days or 10 percent of the time it is rented, whichever is greater, you are a landlord and you have turned the endeavor into a business. Spending lots of days in excess of the 14-day limit "maintaining" the property and fixing it up do not count as personal days. You also can deduct rental expenses up to the level of rental income you report prorated for the number of days it was rented out. When your adjusted gross income (AGI) is less than $100,000, a maximum of $25,000 of rental-related losses may be deducted each year to offset income from any source, including your salary. The $25,000 limit is gradually phased out as your AGI moves between $100,000 and $150,000. This ability to shelter income from taxes represents a terrific benefit for people who invest in real estate on a small scale.

4. Capital Gains Are Taxed at Reduced Rates
Capital gains on real estate are realized through price appreciation. For most taxpayers, long-term capital gains are taxed at a rate of 15 percent, and taxpayers in the 10 to 15 percent tax brackets pay a long-term capital gains tax of 5 percent. (See Chapter 4.)

5. Tax-Free Exchanges
Another special tax treatment results when a real estate investor trades equity in one property for equity in a similar property. If none of the people involved in the trade receives any other form of property or money, the transaction is considered a **tax-free exchange.** If one person receives some money or other property, only that person has to report the extra proceeds as a taxable gain. For example, assume you bought a residential rental property five years ago for $220,000 and today it is worth much more money. You trade it with your friend by giving $10,000 in cash for your friend's $280,000 single-family rental home. Your friend needs to report only the $10,000 as income

tax-free exchange
Arises when a real estate investor trades equity in one property for equity in a similar property and no other forms of property or money change hands.

this year. In contrast, you do not need to report your long-term gain, $50,000 ($280,000 − $10,000 − $220,000), until you actually sell the new property.

✔ Concept Check 16.1

1. What are the two key questions to consider before investing in real estate?
2. Distinguish between the price-to-rent ratio and the rental yield as measures of current income.
3. Give an example of how leverage can increase an investor's return in real estate.
4. Explain how two beneficial tax treatments are helpful to real estate investors.

Pricing and Financing Real Estate Investments

2 Learning Objective
Calculate the right price to pay for real estate and how to finance your purchase.

discounted cash-flow method
Effective way to estimate the value or asking price of a real estate investment based on after-tax cash flow and the return on the invested dollars discounted over time to reflect a discounted yield.

Sure ways to go wrong in a real estate investment are to pay too much for the property and finance it incorrectly.

Pay the Right Price

The **discounted cash-flow method** is an effective way to estimate the value or asking price of a real estate investment. It emphasizes after-tax cash flow and the return on the invested dollars discounted over time to reflect a discounted yield. Software programs are available to calculate the discounted cash flows. You also can use Appendix A.2, as illustrated in Table 16.3.

To see how this method works, assume that you require an after-tax rate of return of 10 percent on a condominium advertised for sale at $200,000. You estimate that rents can be increased each year for five years. After all expenses are paid, you expect to have after-tax cash flows of $4000, $4200, $4400, $4600, and $4800 for the five years. Assuming some price appreciation, you anticipate selling the property for $265,000 after all expenses are incurred. How much should you pay now to buy the property?

Table 16.3 explains how to answer this question. Multiply the estimated after-tax cash flows and the expected proceeds of $265,000 to be realized on the sale of the property by the present value of a dollar at 10 percent (the required rate of return). Add the present values together to obtain the total present value of the property—in this case, $181,097. The asking price of $200,000 is too high for you to earn an after-tax return of 10 percent. Your choices are to negotiate the price down, accept a return of less than 10 percent, hope that the sale price of the property will be higher than $265,000 five years from now, or consider another investment. The discounted cash-flow method provides an effective way to estimate real estate values because it takes into account the selling price of the property, the effect of income taxes, and the time value of money.

Instant Message

Find Information on Home Prices

To find prices on homes where you live, check out www.realtor.org and http://www.huduser.org/.

Financing a Real Estate Investment

Borrowing to finance a real estate investment is more expensive than borrowing to buy one's own home, often 0.5 to 1.5 percent percentage points above the rate for customary home-buyers. There is more risk because the investor does not live in the property. The minimum down payment for investors is often 20 or 25 percent. Most investors finance real estate investments with conventional fixed-rate, fixed-term mortgage loans.

Table 16.3 **Discounted Cash-Flow to Estimate Price**

	After-Tax Cash Flow	Present Value of $1 at 10 Percent*	Present Value of After-Tax Cash Flow
1 year	$ 4,000	0.909	$ 3,636
2 years	4,200	0.826	3,469
3 years	4,400	0.751	3,304
4 years	4,600	0.683	3,142
5 years	4,800	0.621	2,981
Sell property	$265,000	0.621	164,565
Present value of property			$181,097

*From Appendix A.2.

Advice from a Pro...

Timesharing Is Not an Investment

Timesharing is the joint ownership or lease of vacation property through which the principals occupy the property individually for set periods of time. Timesharing is not an investment, although it is promoted as a way to simultaneously invest and obtain vacation housing. For $5000 to $20,000, buyers can purchase one or more weeks' use of luxury vacation housing furnished right down to the salt-and-pepper shakers. Timeshare owners pay an annual maintenance fee of perhaps $100 to $300 for each week of ownership.

With **deeded timesharing,** the buyer obtains a legal title or deed to limited time periods of use of real estate. Purchasers become secured creditors who are guaranteed continued use of the property throughout any bankruptcy proceedings. They also really own their week (or two) of the property.

Most timeshares are sold without a deed. **Nondeeded timesharing** is a legal right-to-use purchase of a limited, preplanned timesharing period of use of a property. It is a long-term lease, license, or club membership permitting use of a hotel suite, condominium, or other accommodation, and the right to use expires in 20 to 25 years. It does not grant legal real estate ownership interest to the purchaser. If the true owner of the property—the developer—goes bankrupt, problems abound. Creditors can lock out the timeshare purchasers (technically they are tenants) from the premises.

It is very hard to sell a timeshare and sales commissions are 25 percent of the price. A survey from the Resort Property Owners Association says that the average timeshare unit languishes on the market for 4.4 years before being sold. At any point in time, 60 percent of all timeshares are up for sale. Timeshare sellers rarely receive more than 50 percent of their original investment in the sale.

Lori Lothringer
Metropolitan Community College

To make a smaller down payment and get a lower mortgage rate, some real estate investors buy a home, live in it for a year, and then rent it out as an investment. Another way to finance a real estate investment is through **seller financing** (or **owner financing**). This occurs when a seller is willing to self-finance a loan by accepting a promissory note from the buyer who makes monthly mortgage payments. No lending agency is involved. Investing buyers pay higher interest rates for seller financing. The seller may accept little or no down payment in exchange for an even higher interest rate, perhaps 1½ to 2½ percent above conventional mortgage rates. Owner-financed deals can be transacted very quickly.

seller financing/owner financing
When seller self-finances a buyer's loan by accepting a promissory note from buyer, who makes monthly mortgage payments.

Instant Message

Adjustable-Rate Mortgage Loans Are Risky

It is risky to buy real estate by financing it with an adjustable-rate mortgage (ARM) loan (see Chapter 9). When rates begin to rise—and they eventually will—the higher rates mean the investor is forced to write bigger and bigger monthly checks to the lender.

sweat equity property
Property that needs repairs but that has good underlying value; an investor buys the property at a favorable price and fixes it up to rent or sell at a profit.

3 Learning Objective

Assess the disadvantages of investing in real estate.

A popular way to start in real estate investing is to purchase **sweat equity property.** With this approach, you seek a property that needs repairs but has good underlying value. You buy this fixer-upper at a favorable price and "sweat" by spending many hours cleaning, painting, and repairing it to rent or sell at a profit.

 Concept Check 16.2

1. Summarize how the discounted cash-flow method helps determine the right price to pay for a real estate investment.

2. List three ways to finance a real estate investment, and tell why a conventional mortgage might be safer than another financing method.

Disadvantages of Real Estate Investing

Real estate investing can be very profitable. But it does have some significant disadvantages.

- **Business risk.** It is quite possible to lose money in real estate investments. Housing foreclosures, for example, depress the prices of many other homes in the same community. A local recession, perhaps because a large employer went bankrupt, can do the same. Zoning changes can slash housing values. Rents can not keep up with costs in communities in which industries and jobs are moving elsewhere or in deteriorating neighborhoods.

- **Complexity.** Real estate investments require much more investigation than do most other investments. Numerous assumptions about financial details in the future also must be made.

- **Large initial investment.** Direct investment in real estate generally requires many thousands of dollars, often with an initial outlay of $15,000, $30,000, $50,000 or more.

- **Lack of diversification.** So much capital is required in real estate investing that spreading risk is almost impossible.

- **Dealing with tenants.** Someone has to screen rental applicants for their credit histories, criminal records, work references, and experience with previous landlords. State laws may make it impossible to evict a deadbeat tenant for several months. Picking the wrong tenants can quickly turn a real estate property into a financial loss.

- **Time-consuming management demands.** Managing a real estate investment requires time for conducting regular inspections of the property, dealing with insurance companies, making repairs, and collecting overdue rents.

- **Low current income.** Expenses may reduce the cash-flow return to less than 2 percent or even generate a net loss in a given year.

- **Unpredictable costs.** Estimating costs is problematic. Investors cannot control increasing real estate tax assessments or when a central air-conditioning unit might break down.

- **Interest rate risk.** When interest rates rise, fewer people can afford to buy homes, and this puts downward pressure on prices and rents.

- **Legal fees.** The services of a real estate attorney will be needed to help handle the real estate purchase, sale, building inspections, zoning issues, tenant problems, insurance disputes, accounting, and any liability issues.

- **Illiquidity.** Real estate is expensive, and the market for investment property is much smaller than the securities market. As a result, it is common to experience trouble in selling. It may take months or even a year or more to find a buyer, arrange the financing, and close the sale of a real estate investment.

- **High transfer costs.** Substantial transfer costs, often representing 6 to 7 percent of the property's sale price, plus money for fix-up costs, may be incurred when real estate is bought or sold.

 Concept Check 16.3

1. Summarize why illiquidity, transfer costs, and unpredictable costs are disadvantages in real estate investing.

2. Identify the four tax deductions that can be taken by an income producing real estate investor.

Investing in Collectibles, Precious Metals, and Gems

Investors often think of assets as something they would like to own for the long term. When investing in collectibles, precious metals, and gems, the investor owns illiquid real assets, not intangible items represented by pieces of paper. While an asset may be bought for its long-term investment potential, profits might be earned in the short term. A **speculator** buys in the hope that someone else will pay more for an asset in the not-too-distant future. Speculators often buy or sell in expectation of profiting from market fluctuations. If you put money into these illiquid assets, limit your speculative investing to no more than 10 percent of your portfolio.

Collectibles

Collectibles are cultural artifacts that have value because of their beauty, age, scarcity, or popularity. They include baseball cards, posters, sports memorabilia, guns, photographs, paintings, ceramics, comic books, watches, lunchboxes, matchbooks, glassware, spoons, stamps, rare coins, art, rugs, cars, and antiques. The collectible markets are fueled by nostalgia, limited availability, and "what is hot to own today."

Making a Profit on Collectibles Is Not Easy
One key to success in collectibles is to invest in quality—the higher the better. Although buying collectibles can be fun and easy, turning a profit may not. The *only* return on collectibles occurs through price appreciation, and you *must sell* to realize a profit. That could be hard for you to do if the collectibles give you pleasure.

Items that are almost certain to lose value include those that are mass-produced and marketed as collectibles or limited editions. You often see these kinds of "collectibles" advertised on television and in newspapers and magazines. Another risk is the wholesale-to-retail price spread, which could be 50 or 100 percent. Prices on collectibles vary greatly from item to item and year to year. Markets are fickle. If the investor needs to convert the asset to cash, a sale may take days, weeks, or months, and the seller may be forced to accept a lower price. The collectibles industry is rife with forgeries, scams, and frauds, particularly in sports memorabilia.

Buying and Selling Collectibles on the Internet
You can buy collectibles on the Internet, using eBay for example, purchasing in minutes what you might never have

4 Learning Objective
Summarize the risks and challenges of investing in collectibles, precious metals, and gems.

speculator
An investor who buys in the hope that someone else will pay more for an asset in the not-too-distant future.

collectibles
Cultural artifacts that have value because of their beauty, age, scarcity, or popularity, such as antiques, stamps, rare coins, art, baseball cards, and so on.

Did You Know?

The Tax Consequences of an Income-Producing Real Estate Investment

When you are considering a real estate investment, you use the investment amount (purchase price or down payment) to begin the process of estimating the likely rate of return. This calculation may then be compared with other investment alternatives. Because some of the many assumptions in real estate calculations could be incorrect, caution is warranted in real estate analyses.

The following table shows five-year estimates for a hypothetical residential property in Rapid City, South Dakota, with a purchase price of $200,000. The building will be purchased with a $150,000 mortgage loan, so the buyer has to make a $50,000 down payment plus pay $8000 in closing costs. The gross rental income of $18,000 annually is projected to rise at an annual rate of 5 percent, vacancies and unpaid rent at 10 percent, real estate taxes at 7 percent, insurance at 8 percent, and maintenance at 10 percent. Virtually the entire payment for the 30-year, $150,000, 8 percent, fixed-rate mortgage loan is assumed to be interest during these early years. For income tax purposes, the land is valued at $20,000,

and the building is depreciated over 27.5 years. The amount of annual straight-line depreciation is calculated to be $6546 ($200,000 − $20,000 = $180,000; $180,000 ÷ 27.5 = $6546).

Note (in line D) how challenging it is to earn current income from rental properties. During the first year, the total cash-flow loss is projected to be $2808. However, because the income tax laws permit depreciation (line E, $6546) to be recorded as a real estate investment expense, even though it is not an out-of-pocket cost, the total taxable loss (line F) is projected to be $9354. This loss can be deducted on the investor's income tax returns. Because the investor pays a 30 percent combined federal and state income tax rate, the loss results in a first-year annual tax savings of $2806. Therefore, instead of sending the $2806 to the government in taxes, the investor can use that amount to help pay the operating expenses of the investment. Consequently, the net cash-flow income (line D) of $2808 is reduced by tax savings (line G) of $2806 to result in a net cash-flow gain after taxes of $2 ($2808 − $2806).

Estimates for a Successful Real Estate Investment

		Year				
		1	2	3	4	5
A.	Gross rental income	$ 18,000	$ 18,900	$ 19,845	$ 20,837	$ 21,879
	Less vacancies and unpaid rent	1,800	1,890	1,985	2,084	2,188
B.	Projected gross income	$ 16,200	$ 17,010	$ 17,860	$ 18,753	$ 19,691
C.	Less operating expenses					
	Principal and Interest $(P + I)$	$ 13,208	$ 13,208	$ 13,208	$ 13,208	$ 13,208
	Real estate taxes (T)	2,600	2,782	2,977	3,185	3,408
	Insurance (I)	800	864	933	1,008	1,089
	Maintenance	2,400	2,640	2,904	3,194	3,513
	Total operating expenses	$ 19,008	$ 19,494	$ 20,022	$ 20,595	$ 21,218
D.	Total cash flow (negative)	$ (2,808)	$ (2,484)	$ (2,162)	$ (1,842)	$ (1,527)
E.	Less depreciation expense	6,546	6,546	6,546	6,546	6,546
F.	Taxable income (or loss) $(D − E)$	$ (9,354)	$ (9,030)	$ (8,708)	$ (8,388)	$ (8,073)
G.	Annual tax savings (30 percent marginal rate)	2,806	2,709	2,612	2,516	2,422
H.	Net cash-flow gain (or loss) after taxes $(G − D)$	$ (2)	$ 225	$ 450	$ 674	$ 895

Assume that the property appreciates in value at an annual rate of 6 percent and will be worth $267,645 (line K) in five years ($200,000 × 1.06 × 1.06 × 1.06 × 1.06 × 1.06).

If it is sold at this price, a 6 percent real estate sales commission of $16,059 ($267,645 × 0.06) would reduce the net proceeds to $251,586 ($267,645 − $16,059).

Now we can calculate the **crude annual rate of return** on the property, as shown in the second table. A crude rate of return is a rough measure of the yield on amounts invested that assumes that equal portions of the gain are earned each year. The total return in this example was substantial. The investor made out-of-pocket cash investments of $50,000 for the down payment and $8000 in closing costs, and we subtract the accumulated net cash flow (line N) of $2242 (adding all the numbers across line H because the investor already has received that money) for a total investment (line O) of $55,758. The investor has a capital gain (line M) of $76,316. After dividing to determine the before-tax total return (line R) to obtain 137 percent, the crude annual rate of return (line S) is 27.4 percent annually over the five years (137 percent ÷ 5 years).

Crude Rate of Return on a Successful Real Estate Investment

Taxable cost

I.	Purchase price ($50,000 down payment; $150,000 loan)	$200,000
	Closing costs	8,000
	Subtotal	208,000
J.	Less accumulated depreciation	32,730
	Taxable cost (adjusted basis)	$175,270

Proceeds (after paying off mortgage)

K.	Sale price	$267,645
	Less sales commission	16,059
	Net proceeds	$251,586
L.	Less taxable cost (J)	175,270
M.	Taxable proceeds (capital gain)	$ 76,316

Amount invested

	Down payment	$ 50,000
	Closing costs	8,000
N.	Less accumulated net cash-flow gains	(2,242)
O.	Total invested	$ 55,758

Crude annual rate of return

P.	Total invested	$ 55,758
Q.	Taxable proceeds (capital gain from M)	$ 76,316
R.	Before-tax total return ($ 76,316 ÷ $55,758)	137%
S.	Crude before-tax annual rate of return (137 percent ÷ 5 years)	27.4%

found after searching for years in magazines, junk shops, flea markets, and auctions. Buying collectibles on the Internet is efficient and convenient, and it is easy to compare products and prices. It's hard to inspect them before purchase, however. Search Google for "collectibles." Note, however, that this is a very risky way to invest!

Gold and Other Metals

There is an allure to owning gold. It is beautiful to look at, hold, and own. Gold is a uniquely private, personal, and portable way to hold some genuine wealth. People around the world occasionally invest some of their assets in gold to preserve capital, reasoning that if their national economies crash they will be able to trade gold even if their country's paper currency is devalued. The prices of gold tend to increase in times of economic and political turmoil, war, and high inflation because investors fear a future that may be worse than today, perhaps a lot worse. Some other metals have a similar appeal to investors.

Gold Bullion   **Gold bullion** is often thought of as the large gold "bricks" that weigh about 28 pounds that people imagine are stored in Fort Knox. Each is worth more than $100,000. The term simply means a refined and stamped weight of precious metal. Gold bullion is traditionally purchased and traded in 1- and 10-ounce gold bars. Gold is expensive

gold bullion
A refined and stamped weight of precious metal.

Gold and other precious metals are highly volatile investments.

to own. There are fees for refining, fabricating, and shipping bullion. A sales charge of 5 to 8 percent is common. There are storage costs. When gold is sold, the bank or dealer buying it from an investor may insist on reassaying its quality, yet another cost for the investor. The investor may also choose to purchase insurance against fire and theft.

gold bullion coins
Various world mints issue these coins, which contain 1 troy ounce (31.15 grams) of pure gold.

Gold Bullion Coins   Some costs of investing in gold can be avoided by those wanting to take physical possession of gold bullion itself by owning modern **gold bullion coins,** each containing 1 troy ounce (31.15 grams) of pure gold issued by the various world mints. The most popular coins are the South African Krugerrand, Canadian Maple Leaf, and U.S. American Eagle. Other gold bullion coins are available, including the Great Britain Sovereign, Australian Kangaroo Nugget, and Chinese Panda. Minimum orders are 10 coins, and commissions are 2 to 4 percent when buying and selling. These gold bullion coins have total liquidity worldwide.

Gold Stocks, ETFs and Mutual Funds   When gold price rose to over $900 an ounce in 2008 at the beginning of the worldwide economic slowdown, it seemed to some like a good investment. Most people do not invest in gold because the asset does not pay interest or dividends and gold has been in a bear market for most of the past 25 years. In addition, government central banks have tons of stored bullion that they could sell (which would depress prices). As a result, almost no one recommends gold as an investment. Well, the gold promoters on television still do!

Promoters (and that is the correct term because traders only make money when something sells) always tell investors that they are crazy not to participate in the "ongoing gold boom." They are confident that economic conditions today are similar to 1980 when gold prices moved from $38 to more than $800. Such confidence is foolhardy. Gold was selling for $250 an ounce in 1998 and a decade later it sold for over $900. While this sounds like an appealing investment, consider further that if you bought $10,000 in gold in 1980 it would be worth $10,600 today and if you invested $10,000 that same year in a mutual fund that tracks the S&P 500 you would have over $200,000 today. Seriously!

Investors wanting to capitalize on world crises and rising gold prices may choose to invest in the stocks of gold mining companies and in mutual funds that own gold companies.

You may have heard of the Homestake Gold Mine, one of the early enterprises associated with the Gold Rush of 1876 in the northern Black Hills of what was then Dakota Territory. There are a handful of gold mining companies in the United States and dozens around the world. When there is turmoil in the world and people are fearful about the future, the prices of gold stocks rise, including gold mutual funds and gold exchange-traded funds (ETFs). For examples, see Eagle Wing Research (http://www.eaglewing.com) or SPDR Gold Shares (http://www.spdrgoldshares.com/sites/us/value/). Scams abound.

Silver, Platinum, Palladium, Rhodium   Some less popular metals also appeal to certain investors. Silver, platinum, palladium, and rhodium are metals used industrially and occasionally in jewelry. The values of these metals rise and fall with changes in demand. An investor might reason that since palladium is used in auto production that when demand in China and India for vehicles increases substantially the price of the metal will soar.

Precious Stones and Gems

Precious stones and gems, such as diamonds, sapphires, rubies, and emeralds, are also examples of high-risk investments. Investors purchase investment-grade gems as "loose gems" rather than as pieces of jewelry. Wholesale firms, not jewelers, sell the best-quality precious gems. The gem certification process may be touted as a science; it is not, rather it is educated guesswork. Obtaining two assessments of a stone's quality, particularly on stones of less than 1 carat, is likely to result in a variation of 10 to 20 percent.

Novice investors often buy at retail and then wind up trying to sell at retail. This approach is the opposite of smart investing—that is, buying low and selling high. Sales commissions on precious stones are high, and reselling is very difficult. Losing 20 to 50 percent of one's investment upon selling is common.

Did You Know?

Scams Abound in Collectibles, Precious Metals, and Gems

The average investor can't tell a diamond from cubic zirconium or a Monet from a Manet. The values of collectibles, gold, other precious metals, and precious gems rely in part upon the authority of "experts" who purport to determine their worth, and such blind trust invites risk for potential investors. When an asset does not generate a readily quantifiable return (such as rent, interest, or dividends), its value is determined by supply and demand—and rumors. Scams and frauds abound with these investments, as promoters and telemarketers tell tales about skyrocketing prices and high profit potentials to encourage their purchase. Collectibles, precious metals, and gems are not wise choices for the casual investor.

Concept Check 16.4

1.   Identify one collectible that might be an interesting investment, and explain why it might be difficult to make a profit.
2.   Explain why some investors buy gold and other precious metals, and tell why that type of investment might be appealing or unappealing to you.
3.   Identify some risks of investing in precious stones and gems.

Did You Know?

Trading in Currencies?

Investors deeply worried about the future, instead of owning gold, may find it more convenient to put some of their assets in the cash of the world's two safest currencies, the U.S. dollar and the Euro. Individuals may speculate on the changing daily values of the dollar, Euro, yen, pound, Swiss franc, and other currencies in the **forex** (foreign exchange trading). A "mini" account can be opened for only $300 at Forex Capital Markets (www.FXCM.com.) where you try out a practice account and then bet up to 200 times that amount by using margin. Currency trading is a high-risk investment!

Investing in Options and Futures Contracts

5 Learning Objectives

Explain why options and futures are high-risk investments.

Derivative securities are available for commodities, equities, bonds, interest rates, exchange rates, and indexes (such as a stock market index, consumer price index, and weather conditions). A **derivative** (or **derivative security**) is an instrument used by people to trade or manage more easily the asset upon which these instruments are based. Investors choose derivatives to either reduce risk by hedging against losses or taking on additional risk by speculating. The investor's returns are derived solely from changes in the underlying asset's price behavior. Two of the most common derivative instruments are options and futures contracts.

Options Allow You to Buy or Sell an Asset at a Predetermined Price

option

Contract to buy or sell a financial asset at a specified point in the future at a specified price.

An **option** is a contract to buy or sell an asset at some point in the future at a specified price. The most common type of option is a **stock option.**★ This security gives the holder (purchaser) the right, but not the obligation, to buy or sell a specific number of shares (normally 100) of a certain stock at a specified price (the **striking price**) before a specified date (the **expiration date,** typically three, six, or nine months).

stock option

Security that gives the holder the right to buy or sell a specific number of shares (normally 100) of a certain stock at a specified (striking) price before a specified expiration date.

Options Are Created by an Option Writer

An **option writer** signs an option contract through a brokerage firm and promises either to buy or to sell a specified asset for a fixed striking price. In return, the option writer receives an **option premium** (the price of the option itself) for standing ready to buy or sell the asset at the wishes of the option purchaser. Once written and sold, an option may change hands many times before its expiration. The **option holder** is the person who actually owns the option contract. The original option writer always remains responsible for buying or selling the asset if requested by the holder of the option contract.

option writer

Agrees to sell an option contract that promises either to buy or to sell a specified asset for a fixed striking price.

Two types of option contracts exist: calls and puts. A **call option** gives the option holder (buyer) the right, but not the obligation, to *buy* the optioned asset from the option writer at the striking price. A **put option** gives the option holder (buyer) the right, but not the obligation, to *sell* the optioned asset to the option writer at the striking price. The Did You Know? box "How to Make Sense of Option Contracts" explains the relationships between option writers and option holders for both puts and calls.

option holder

Person who buys and then owns an option contract.

Most option contracts expire without being exercised by the option holder, and the option writer is the only person to earn a profit. The profit results from the option premium charged when the option was originally sold. Buying and selling options are techniques used by both conservative and aggressive investors.

call option

Gives option holder the right to buy the optioned asset from the option writer at the striking price at any time before the expiration date.

Conservative Writers Profit by Selling Covered Calls

Selling calls can be a fairly safe way to generate income by conservative option writers who own the underlying asset (the stock). When they sell a call, it is described as a **covered option** because the writer owns the underlying stock. (If the writer does not own the asset, it is a **naked option,** a speculative position.) When used effectively by conservative option writers, calls can potentially pick up an extra return of perhaps 1 to 2 percent every three months and minimize risk at the same time. In effect, this conservative investor protects himself financially by hedging his investment against loss due to price fluctuation.

put option

Gives option holder the right to sell the optioned asset to the option writer at the striking price at any time before the option expires.

★Recall from Chapter 14 that some employers give stock options as a way to attract and retain employees. If the price of the underlying stock increases sufficiently, the employee can profit by exercising the option to buy the shares at the predetermined price and then quickly selling the shares at the higher current price.

Did You Know?

How to Make Sense of Option Contracts

An option is a contract that gives its holder the right, but not the obligation, to buy or sell an asset at a specified price. The two principal players in the options game are the option writer and the option holder. Their relationships are summarized below.

Calls

	Call option Has option to buy stock at a specific price	Call obligation Is obligated to sell stock at a specific price	
Option holder has the right to buy or sell.	Put option Has option to sell stock at a specific price	Put obligation Is obligated to purchase stock at a specific price	**Option writer** has possible obligation to sell or buy.

Puts

You can profit by selling a call on stock already owned, giving the buyer the right to purchase your shares at any time during a relatively short period at a fixed strike price. Here is an example.

Assume you have 1000 shares of ABC stock originally bought for $56 (total investment of $56,000) and you write a call to sell the shares at a strike price of $60. The option price is $2, so you gain an instant premium of $2000 (omitting commissions). Three scenarios are possible:

1. If the stock price does not change in three months, the call expires. As the covered call writer, you profit from the $2000 premium.

2. If the stock price rises to $65, the holder exercises the call and buys the stock at $60. Your profit is $6000 ($4000 from appreciation in the stock price from $56 to $60, plus the $2000 premium). You missed out on potentially greater profits, however, because you sold the stocks at the striking price of $60. Without the option, you could have sold the stock at $65 per share.

3. If the stock price drops to $50, the buyer of the call will not exercise it because the market price is less than the striking price. You keep the $2000 premium, which cuts your loss from $6000 to $4000 ($56 − $50 = $6; $6 × 1000 = $6000).

Conservative Investors Reduce Risks by Purchasing Covered Puts

Buying puts is a way to immunize a conservative investor's portfolio against severe price declines because they set up a "collar" to safeguard profits. Puts allow the holder of the contract to sell an asset at a specific striking price for a certain time period, commonly three months. For example, if you own 1000 shares of ABC stock originally purchased at $56 per share (total investment of $56,000), you hope that the market price of the stock will go up. If it goes down instead, you may suffer a loss. To reduce this risk, you could buy a put for 1000 shares at a striking price close to the purchase price of the stock—for example, $52. The total price of the option contract might be $2000 ($2 per share). Three scenarios are possible:

1. If the stock price does not change in three months, the put expires, and you are out only the $2000.

2. If the stock price rises to $65, you allow the put to expire because it is greater than the striking price, and again you are out only the $2000. Alternatively, you could sell your shares at $65 and realize a profit of $7000 ($65 × 1000 = $65,000; $65,000 − $56,000 − $2000 = $7000).

3. If the stock price drops to $50, you would exercise the put and sell your stock at the striking price of $52, thereby hedging your loss from $6000 ($56 − $50 = $6; $6 × 1000 = $6000) to $4000 ($56 − $52 = $4; $4 × 1000 = $4000).

Options Industry Websites

Websites for learning about the options industry include www.optionscentral.com, www.tradeking.com, www.cboe.com, and www.optionsxpress.com.

LEAPs

A **LEAP** is a Long-term Equity AnticiPation Security. It is an option with a much longer term than traditional stock or index options. Like options, a stock-related LEAP may be a call or a put, meaning that the owner has the right to purchase or sell shares of the stock at a given price on or before some set, future date. Unlike options, the given date may be up to two and a half years away.

Speculative Investors Try to Profit with Options

Aggressive investors in the options market attempt to profit in two ways. First, because a market typically exists for each security for a period of three months, the investor can hope for an increase in the value of the option. For example, if the price of a stock is rising, the holder of a call option might sell it to another investor for a higher price than that originally paid. Second, the investor can exercise the option at the striking price, take ownership of the underlying securities, and sell them at a profit.

Investors take a particularly speculative position when they do not own the underlying asset, as when they sell naked calls or sell naked puts. Option traders can suffer considerable losses. For example, the writer of a put may incur a loss when the market price of an optioned asset drops below the striking price. The writer would be forced to buy the asset from the option holder at a price higher than the market price. Writing naked options is high-risk investing!

Speculative Investors Buy Calls to Create Tremendous Leverage

The lure of a call is that the option holder can control a relatively large asset with a small amount of capital for a specified period of time. If the market price of the asset rises to exceed the striking price plus the premium, the holder could make a substantial profit. For example, Jeremy Dietrich, a technology expert from Aurora, Colorado, bought a stock option call on Xerox in March when the stock was selling for $55 per share. The striking price is $60, the expiration date is the third Friday in March, and the price (premium) of the call is $2 per share. The option contract cost is $200 ($2 × 100 shares under his control). Jeremy hopes that the per-share price for Xerox will rise. He prefers not to buy the stock outright because 100 shares of Xerox would cost him a great deal more—$5500 ($55 × 100).

For Jeremy to break even on the call option deal, the price of Xerox shares must rise to $62 before the call expires, as shown in Equation (16.2). If Jeremy exercises the call option, he can buy the stock at $60 from the option writer and sell it on the market for the current market price of $62 (ignoring commissions). In this instance, he earns $2 per share ($62 − $60), which offsets the $2 per share purchase price of the option. If the price of Xerox stock rises to $65, Jeremy would make a $3 profit per share, for a total profit of $300. Based on his $200 investment, this gain amounts to a 150 percent return ($300 ÷ $200) earned over a short period. If the Xerox stock price fails to reach $60 by late March, Jeremy's $200 in calls will expire with no value at all, and he will lose the amount he paid (invested) for the options.

Advice from a Pro...

How to Calculate Breakeven Prices for Option Contracts

Investors need to know the **breakeven price** for option contracts. At this price, the cost of a contract is negated by a profit (or the cost is reduced by hedging a loss). The breakeven prices for two types of option contracts—puts and calls— are calculated using Equations (16.2) and (16.3), respectively. If the striking price on a put option contract was $52 and the option contract cost $2000 and provided for the control of 1000 shares of stock, then the breakeven price of a share of the stock would be $50, as the calculation shows. If the striking price on a call was $60 and the option contract cost $200 and provided for the control of 100 shares of stock, then the breakeven price of a share of the stock would be $62.

$$\text{Puts breakeven price} = \text{striking price} - \frac{\text{contract cost}}{\text{number of shares under control}} \qquad (16.2)$$

$$\$50 = \$52 - \frac{2000}{1000}$$

$$\text{Calls breakeven price} = \text{striking price} + \frac{\text{contract cost}}{\text{number of shares under control}} \qquad (16.3)$$

$$\$62 = \$60 + \frac{\$200}{100}$$

When calculating the breakeven prices for both puts and calls, it is critical to include all transaction costs in the contract cost. These costs include the option premium and perhaps sizable commissions paid to brokers. Commissions will be paid on the option contract itself, and subsequent commissions may be paid related to execution or sale of the option contract. In the preceding put example, a price below $50 triggers the sale of 1000 shares that will come at an additional, and perhaps unanticipated, commission cost. This possibility leads to some sage advice: When planning, always consider the full and subsequent costs of the deal.

Jonathan Fox
The Ohio State University

Did You Know?

About Hedge Funds

Hedge funds are freewheeling risky investment pools for the extremely wealthy. They are global companies, beyond the regulations of the U.S. Securities and Exchange Commission (SEC), that use unconventional investment strategies. Hedge funds trade options and commodities, sell short, use leverage, risk arbitrage, buy and sell currencies, and invest in undervalued securities (poorly performing companies, those in bankruptcy, companies that may be merged).

Hedge funds can profit in times of market volatility as well as in a falling market. The investors are partners. Fees charged by the hedge fund manager are 2 to 5 percent of assets under management and 20 to 40 percent of the profits of the fund. None of the 8000 hedge funds can be offered or advertised to the general investing public in the United States. They are limited to "accredited investors and purchasers" who have incomes over $200,000 and a net worth over $1 million and who own more than $5 million in investments. Some hedge funds have had catastrophic losses and have gone bankrupt.

Selling Options You would want to sell a put or a call when the option's market price has risen sufficiently due to changes in the market price of the underlying asset to ensure a profit. Alternatively, you might sell an option to prevent further losses if its market price is dropping.

Commodities Futures Contracts

futures contract
Type of exchange-traded standardized forward contract that specifies the size of the contract, quality of product to be delivered, and delivery date.

A **futures contract** is similar to an option in that it is a type of forward contract that is standardized (usually in terms of size of contract, quality of product to be delivered, and delivery date) and traded on an organized exchange. The difference is that futures contracts require the holder to buy the asset on the date specified. If the holder does not want to buy the asset, he or she must sell the contract to some other investor or to someone who wants to actually use the asset.

Futures contracts usually focus on agricultural, commercial, and mining products. Organized commodities markets include the New York Coffee and Sugar Exchange; New York Cocoa Exchange; CME Group (pigs, pork bellies, eggs, potatoes, and cattle); Chicago Board of Trade (corn, wheat, soybeans, soybean oil, oats, silver, and plywood); International Monetary Market (foreign currencies and U.S. Treasury bills); New York Commodity Exchange (gold and silver); and New York Mercantile Exchange (platinum).

Economic Need Creates Futures Markets

Farmer Dave planting a 10,000-bushel soybean crop in Chana, Illinois, might want to sell part of it now to ensure the receipt of a certain price when the crop is actually harvested. Similarly, a food-processing company might want to purchase soybeans now to protect itself against sharp price increases in the future. Similarly, an orange juice manufacturer might want to lock in a supply of oranges at a definite price now rather than run the risk that a winter freeze might push up prices. These economic needs create futures markets.

Speculators May Trade in Futures Markets

The speculative investor who buys or sells a commodity contract is hoping that the market price of the commodity will rise (or fall) before the contract matures, usually 3 to 18 months after it is written. Futures offer the potential for extremely high profits because all futures contracts by definition are highly leveraged. Depending on the commodity, the volatility of the market, and the brokerage house requirements, an investor can put up as little as 5 to 15 percent of the total value of the contract. Some contracts require a deposit of only $300. Commissions average about $20 for each purchase and sale.

To illustrate the use of leverage in buying futures contracts, assume that Danielle Anthony, a scuba-diving instructor from Largo, Florida, purchases a wheat contract for 5000 bushels at $3.80 per bushel in July. The contract value is $19,000 ($3.80 × 5000), but Danielle puts up only $2500. Each $0.01 increase in the price of wheat represents a total of $50 profit to her ($0.01 × 5000). If the price rises $0.50 to reach $4.30 by late July, Danielle is "in the money" and will make $2500 ($0.50 × 5000 bushels) and double her investment by directing the futures exchange to close out her position. The theory is that she could buy the wheat for $3.80 per bushel (as stipulated in the contract) rather than the market price of $4.30 in late July. As an investor, Danielle does not actually want the wheat; she wants her profit by selling her contract. Another investor, perhaps a bread company, is likely to purchase that futures contract to obtain wheat at a below-market price.

The potential for loss exists, too. If the price drops $0.50 to reach $3.30, Danielle would lose $2500. If the price declines, the broker will make a margin call and ask Danielle

Do It NOW!

Investing in real estate or high-risk investments may not appeal to you. But if you are considering it you can start today by:

1. Imagining what you would do if you came into $50,000 that you could invest without any concern about losing the money. Would you invest all or some of it in high-risk investments? Explain why or why not?

2. Assuming that real estate is an option for this investment. Search your local newspaper for opportunities to

buy a house as a rental property and estimate the asking price for the property, the rate of interest you could expect for the mortgage, the likely rent you could charge and other factors.

3. Then calculating the net present value of the property to determine the price you should offer for the property.

to provide more money to back up the contract. If Danielle does not have these additional funds, the broker can legally sell her contract and "close out" the position, which results in a true cash loss for Danielle. Because of the risks involved, brokerage houses require their futures customers to have a minimum net worth of $50,000 to $75,000, exclusive of home and life insurance.

In each commodity transaction, a winner and a loser will emerge. A buyer of a futures contract benefits if the price of the commodity increases, but the seller suffers. When prices decline, the reverse is true. An estimated 90 percent of investors in the futures market lose money; 5 percent (mostly the professionals) make good profits from the losers; and the remaining 5 percent break even.

Futures Are a Zero-Sum Game Investors need to be aware that they are dealing in very sophisticated markets when they trade in options or futures. Trading in futures is a **zero-sum game** in which the wealth of all investors remains the same; the trading simply redistributes the wealth among those traders. Each profit must be offset by an equivalent loss; therefore, the average rate of return for all investors in futures is zero. The return actually becomes negative if transaction costs are included. In the world of options and futures, losers outnumber winners. Investors who get hooked on trading options and futures are courting disaster.

Did You Know?

Sure Ways to Lose Money in Investing

If you don't know a lot about the specific investments you are considering, you are sure to lose money. You may lose a lot. If you are a long-term investor, avoid these risky investments.

- Margin trading
- Short selling
- Options (puts and calls)
- Commodity futures (pork bellies, oranges)
- Limited real estate partnerships
- Gold, precious metals and gems
- Infomercial investment schemes

zero-sum game
Situation in which the wealth of all investors remains the same; the trading simply redistributes the wealth among those traders. Each profit must be offset by an equivalent loss; therefore, the average rate of return for all investors in futures is zero.

Concept Check 16.5

1. Distinguish between a call and a put for the options investor.
2. Summarize two ways a person with a conservative investment philosophy can profit in options.
3. Explain how a speculative options investor can lose a lot of money.
4. Offer reasons why futures contracts are not appropriate for the average investor.

What Do You Recommend NOW?

Now that you have read the chapter on real estate and high-risk investments, what do you recommend to Jamie on:

1. Investing in real estate?
2. Putting some of her money in a high-risk investment, like collectibles?
3. Investing in options and futures contracts?

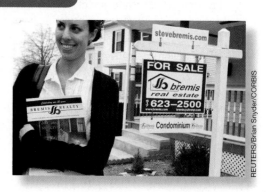

REUTERS/Brian Snyder/CORBIS

Big Picture Summary of Learning Objectives

1 Demonstrate how you can make money investing in real estate.

The key questions for real estate investors are: "Can you make current income while you own the property?" and "Can you profit with capital gains when you sell the property?" To help find answers, investors calculate the price-to-rent ratio and rental yield. Leverage enhances real estate returns, and the IRS offers investors five beneficial tax treatments, including depreciation and tax-deductible interest.

2 Calculate the right price to pay for real estate and how to finance your purchase.

The discounted cash-flow method is an effective way to estimate the value or asking price of a real estate investment. It takes into account the selling price of the property, the effect of income taxes, and the time value of money. There are many ways to finance a real estate investment, although a conventional mortgage loan is the most popular.

3 Assess the disadvantages of investing in real estate.

There are many disadvantages in real estate investing: large initial investment, lack of diversification, dealing with tenants, low current income, unpredictable costs, illiquidity, and high transfer costs.

4 Summarize the risks and challenges of investing in collectibles, precious metals, and gems.

When investing in collectibles, precious metals, and gems, the investor owns illiquid real assets, not intangible items represented by pieces of paper. The investor's only return comes from price appreciation, as they do not pay interest or dividends. While prices are set by supply and demand, promoters hype these high-risk investments. Changing investor tastes and rumors also influence prices.

5 Explain why options and futures are high-risk investments.

Derivatives, such as options and futures, are instruments used by market participants to trade or manage more easily the asset upon which these instruments are based. While all types of investors can profit in options, only "speculators" with an aggressive investment philosophy should consider trading in futures. Most investors in derivatives lose money, and losses can accumulate quickly.

Let's Talk About It

1. **Invest in Real Estate.** Describe what would encourage you to invest in real estate given that in many communities prices have declined severely.

2. **Reasons to Invest.** Assume you have $30,000 in cash. Give reasons why you might want to invest that money

in a real estate investment. Offer two reasons why others might not be willing to invest in real estate.

3. **Manage Tenants.** Do you think you could successfully deal with tenants and the management demands required in real estate investing?

4. **Disadvantages of Real Estate.** The text describes several disadvantages of real estate investments. Identify two that might stop you from investing in real estate. Identify ways to circumvent those two obstacles.

5. **Timeshare as an Investment.** Explain why timeshares should never be considered an investment. What are some reasons why people buy timeshares?

6. **Invest in High-Risk.** What percentage of your portfolio do you think should be invested in high-risk investments? Explain.

7. **Options and Futures.** Both options and futures are high-risk investments. Identify one that seems like an unwise idea, and explain why it is unappealing.

Do the Math

1. **Real Estate Investment Returns.** Justin Nicholas, an electrician from Great Bend, Kansas, is interested in the numbers of real estate investments. He has reviewed the figures in Table 16.2 and is impressed with the potential 36.9 percent return after taxes. Justin is in the 25 percent marginal tax bracket. Answer the following questions to help guide his investment decisions:

   (a) Substitute Justin's 25 percent marginal tax bracket (his state has no state income tax) in Table 16.2, and calculate the taxable income and return after taxes.

   (b) Why does real estate appear to be a favorable investment for Justin?

   (c) What one factor might be changed in Table 16.2 to increase Justin's return?

   (d) Calculate the after-tax return for Justin, assuming that he bought the property and financed it with a 7 percent, $170,000 mortgage with annual interest costs of $11,175.

2. **Vacation Condo Investment.** Elizabeth Bennett, a caterer from Columbus, Mississippi, is considering buying a vacation condominium apartment for $265,000 in Park City, Utah. Elizabeth hopes to rent the condo to others to keep her costs down. Answer the following questions to help Elizabeth with her decisions:

   (a) Elizabeth's $210,000, 30-year mortgage loan has a seven percent interest rate and costs $16,766 annually (from Table 9.4 on page 267). She figures that $14,900 of her mortgage payments will go for interest during the first year. On top of that are monthly

expenses for property taxes ($140), homeowner's insurance ($80), and homeowner's association fee ($100). Which of these costs will be tax deductible?

   (b) If Elizabeth is in the 30 percent combined federal and state marginal tax bracket, how much less in taxes will she pay if she buys this condo?

   (c) Given that she would like to personally use the condo for vacations totaling 10 to 12 days per year, how many days will Elizabeth have to rent it out before she would become eligible to deduct rental losses from her taxes?

   (d) Because Park City is primarily a winter ski resort, few condo renters can be found in the off season; therefore, Elizabeth is concerned about qualifying to deduct rental losses. Assuming she could rent the condo for $400 per day, summarize the IRS-approved rental alternative she could use to generate some tax-free income. Calculate the maximum amount of money Elizabeth could obtain using that plan.

   (e) Figure Elizabeth's annual net out-of-pocket cost to buy the condominium and rent it out minimally for tax-free income. List the costs and total on an annualized basis. Next, deduct the savings on income taxes as well as the presumed rental for the number of IRS-allowed days.

   (f) Using the figure derived in part (e), what would Elizabeth's out-of-pocket cost per day be to use the condo herself if she stayed there ten days each year? Fifteen days each year?

Financial Planning Cases

Case 1
Real Estate or Stocks?

Junhee Chang, a senior research analyst in Laramie, Wyoming, has bought and sold high-technology stocks profitably for years. Lately some of her stock investments have done poorly, including one company that went bankrupt. Emily, a longtime friend at work, has suggested that the two of them invest in real estate together because property values in some neighborhoods have been rising. Emily has looked at three small office buildings and some residential duplexes as possible investments.

   (a) Contrast the wisdom of investing in commercial office buildings versus the attraction of investing in residential properties.

   (b) List three of the advantages associated with real estate investments.

   (c) List three things that can go wrong for real estate investors.

Case 2
From Real Estate to Options and Futures

Brandon Williams and Jason Richardson, longtime partners in Storm Lake, Iowa, have bought and sold real estate properties for ten years. They have profited on many transactions although they had some substantial losses last year. Their portfolio of real estate is worth about $4.7 million, on which they owe $2.9 million. Jason has read about investing in options and futures contracts, and last week he talked with a stockbroker about the possibilities.

(a) Offer some reasons why Jason might gain by investing $100,000 or $200,000 in options and futures contracts.

(b) List some of the risks of options trading for Brandon and Jason.

(c) From an investor's point of view, contrast trading in futures contracts with buying highly leveraged real estate.

Case 3
Victor and Maria Consider Hedging an Investment with Puts

Victor and Maria Hernandez invested in 200 shares of Pharmacia Corporation common stock at $93 per share. They purchased the stock because the company is testing a new drug that may represent a significant medical breakthrough. The stock's value has already risen $8 in three months, in anticipation of the U.S. Food and Drug Administration's approval of the new drug. Many observers believe that the price of the stock could reach $120 if the drug is successful. If it does not prove to be the breakthrough anticipated, the price of the stock could drop back to the $85 range, or even lower. The Hernandezes are optimistic but feel that they should hedge their position a bit. As a result, they have decided to purchase two nine-month Pharmacia 100-share puts for $3 per share at a striking price of $93 per share. Ignore commissions when answering the following questions.

(a) What price would the Pharmacia stock need to reach for the Hernandezes to break even on their investment?

(b) How much would the Hernandezes gain if they sold the stock for $102 six months from now?

(c) How much would the return be as a percentage on an annualized basis?

(d) If the price of the stock dropped to $85 in six months, how much would the Hernandezes lose?

Case 4
The Johnsons Consider a Real Estate Investment

Harry and Melissa Johnson are considering purchasing a residential income property as an investment. The Johnsons want to achieve an after-tax total return of 10 percent. They are considering a property with an asking price of $190,000 that should produce $27,000 in gross rental income and $15,000 in net operating income.

(a) Calculate the present value of after-tax cash flow for the property, assuming that the after-tax cash-flow numbers are $8000 for the first year, $8400 for the second year, $8800 for the third year, $9200 for the fourth year, and $9600 for the fifth year, and that the selling price of the property will be $220,000 in five years. Prepare your information in a format similar to Table 16.3, using Appendix A.2 or the *Garman/Forgue* companion website to discount the future after-tax cash flows to their present values.

(b) Give the Johnsons your advice on whether they should invest in the property at its current price of $190,000.

On the 'Net

Go to the Web pages indicated to complete these exercises.

1. Visit the website for the Chicago Board of Trade (www.cbot.com). In its Education section, use the tutorials and glossary to answer the following questions:

   (a) What is a futures contract?

   (b) What is the difference between a stock market and a futures exchange?

   (c) Browse the site further to learn about the commodities that are traded on the CBOT.

2. Visit the website for Investopedia.com at www.investopedia.com. Search for "reducing risk with options." There you will see an article on how option investing can serve to reduce risk. When might investors want to use options in their investment portfolios?

Visit the Garman/Forgue companion website . . .

PART 5

PETER M. FISHER/CORBIS

Retirement Planning

!You Must Be Kidding, Right?

Lindsey Jones is 27 years old, and she recently took a new job. Lindsey had accumulated $6000 in her previous employer's 401(k) retirement plan, and she withdrew it to help pay for her wedding. How much less money will Lindsey have at retirement at age 67 if she could have earned 9 percent on the $6000?

- **A.** $6000
- **B.** $24,000
- **C.** $48,000
- **D.** $203,000

The answer is D. Spending retirement money for discretionary purposes, instead of keeping it in a tax-deferred account where it can compound for many years, is unwise. The lesson is to keep your retirement money where it belongs!

Learning Objectives

After reading this chapter, you should be able to:

1 Recognize that you are solely responsible for funding your retirement and must sacrifice some current spending and invest for your future lifestyle.

2 Estimate your Social Security retirement income benefit.

3 Calculate your estimated retirement savings needs in today's dollars.

4 Understand why you should save for retirement within tax-sheltered retirement accounts.

5 Distinguish among the types of employer-sponsored and personally established tax-sheltered retirement plans.

6 Make use of professional investment advisors and Monte Carlo simulations when deciding on how to invest for retirement.

7 Describe techniques for living in retirement without running out of money.

What Do You Recommend?

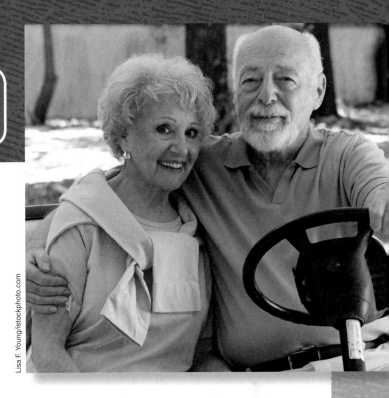

Lisa F. Young/istockphoto.com

Maryanne Johnson, age 32, worked for a previous employer for eight years. When she left that job, Maryanne left her retirement money in that employer's defined-contribution plan. It is now worth $120,000. After getting divorced and remarried four years ago, she has been working as an assistant food services manager for a large convention center in Indianapolis, Indiana, earning $80,000 per year. Maryanne contributes $267 each month (4 percent of her salary) to her account in her employer's 401(k) retirement plan. Her current employer provides a 100 percent match for the first 4 percent of Maryanne's salary contributions. Rules allow her to contribute another 7 percent on her own. Today, Maryanne's 401(k) account balance is $21,000. Her investments are equally divided among three mutual funds: a growth fund, a value fund, and an S&P index fund.

Maryanne's husband, Bob, is permanently disabled, and most of his medical expenses are paid for through Maryanne's health benefits at work. Bob receives $1000 per month in disability insurance benefits, and he earns about $5000 per year as a freelance cartoonist. Maryanne is hoping that she and Bob can retire when she is age 55.

What do you recommend to Maryanne and Bob on the subject of retirement and estate planning regarding:

1. The major steps in the process to determine the amount of Maryanne and Bob's retirement savings goal?

2. How Bob's net income could be invested in a personal tax-sheltered retirement account?

3. The kinds of investment accounts into which they might put additional money over the next 23 years if they determined they needed $1 million to meet their retirement savings goal?

4. The investment strategies that Maryanne and Bob might follow for accumulating their retirement funds?

Your Next Five Years

In the next five years you can start achieving financial success by doing the following related retirement planning:

1. Save continuously within a tax-sheltered employer-sponsored retirement plan at least the amount required to obtain the full matching contribution from your employer.

2. Start saving early in life by diversifying through mutual funds and limit company stock to no more than 10 percent of your portfolio.

3. Accept enough risk to increase the likelihood that you will have enough money in retirement.

4. Contribute to Roth IRA and traditional IRA accounts to supplement your employer-sponsored plans.

5. Keep your hands off your retirement money. Do not borrow it. Do not withdraw it. When changing employers, roll over the funds into the new employer's plan or a rollover IRA account.

Today's Americans are healthier, are better educated, will live longer, and have higher expectations than their counterparts from earlier generations. Your view may include retiring to a comfortable and happy life with little stress and lots of leisure. Enjoying financial security during your retirement years is not a matter of luck, as it takes planning and action. You must invest money you save during your retirement years, and do so wisely.

The first rule of wise retirement investing is diversification. As you get close to retirement, perhaps beginning around age 50 or 55, you must rebalance your portfolio toward safer, more conservative investment alternatives to protect against big losses. Millions of American retirees and near retirees were shocked when the stock market crashed in 2008 and 2009 and the value of their investments lost 40% to 50%. Such enormous declines occurred in portfolios that were not diversified. As a result, some individuals postponed their retirement dates while others went back to work. Those who had a diversified portfolio that year lost only about 20% and were in much better shape when the market started its rebound in 2009.

You cannot progress through life and achieve a financially successful retirement without investing. You simply sacrifice some current spending and start early. By contributing regularly, you can turn small monthly investments into hundreds, then thousands, and eventually millions of dollars over the years. Saving and investing 10% of your pay can provide a lump sum of $1,540,000 at age 65, while saving just 6% will provide only $924,000. Calculations are based on a 25-year old with a salary of $40,000 who receives 3 percent annual pay increases and the invested sums earn an 8 percent annual return. You can have a lot of fun investing, but please realize that building assets for retirement is serious business. While compiling such a seemingly enormous sum may seem like an impossible proposition today, you can and need to do it.

Retirement Planning Is Your Responsibility

1 Learning Objective

Recognize that you are solely responsible for funding your retirement and must sacrifice some current spending and invest for your future lifestyle.

retirement
The time in life when the major sources of income change from earned income (such as salary or wages) to employer-based retirement benefits, private savings and investments, income from Social Security, and perhaps part-time employment.

Retirement is the time in life when the major sources of income change from earned income (such as salary or wages) to employer-based retirement benefits, private savings and investments, income from Social Security, and perhaps part-time employment. (See Figure 17.1.) Planning for retirement has changed dramatically in recent years. Yesterday's employer-provided pensions were commonly a reward for 30-plus years of working for one employer, but they are no longer widely available. Instead, most employers today offer "voluntary" retirement plans to which employees may or may not choose to contribute.

As a result, both the responsibility of investing funds for retirement and the risk of making poor investments with these funds has been shifted from the employer to the employee. Thus the fact is that you—and only you—are solely responsible for meeting your retirement needs.

On the day when your regular full-time paycheck stops, you are retired. If you have not saved enough money to enjoy the lifestyle you prefer, you will have to lower your level of living, continue working part-time, or do both. Many of today's retirees continue to work part-time because they need to supplement their retirement income, enjoy working, and want an employer's subsidized health care benefits. Others continue working simply because they must do so to survive. You may choose to save and invest for your retirement, or you can work forever.

Financial planners say that people need 80 to 100 percent of their pre-retirement gross income (including Social Security benefits) to meet their expenses in retirement and maintain their lifestyle. This amount includes what you have to pay in income taxes. Achieving this goal will be a big challenge, but it is one you may choose to meet successfully. Alternatively,

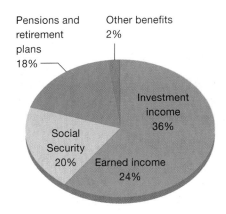

Pensions and retirement plans 18%

Other benefits 2%

Investment income 36%

Social Security 20%

Earned income 24%

Figure 17.1
Sources of Retirement Income

you may want to retire on 60 to 70 percent of your pre-retirement income and be satisfied living with less. As the American Savings Education Council says, "You have the power to choose today how you will spend your retirement tomorrow."

To prepare for a financially successful retirement, you must build a sufficient amount of savings and investments to supplement other sources of income in retirement, such as monthly checks from the **Social Security Administration (SSA).** To succeed in this endeavor, during your 30 or 40 years in the workforce you must select among the various retirement plans and accounts that are available to you and adequately fund them through regular and consistent savings. You must make sound investment decisions regarding your retirement assets. You are advised to start early to save and invest for retirement and to continue this effort throughout your working years. You can then let the magical powers of compounding fully fund your needs and wants during the latter third of your life.

 Instant Message

Cost of Delaying Saving for Retirement

Making steady contributions of $3000 every year to a tax-sheltered retirement account earning 8 percent annually for 30 years will accumulate to $340,000. Delaying 10 years before beginning to save accumulates only $137,000.

Concept Check 17.1

1. Summarize how retirement planning has changed in recent years and has now become each individual's responsibility.
2. List the financial planning actions that individuals must take during their working life to prepare for retirement.
3. Comment on the cost of delaying saving for retirement.

2 Learning Objective

Estimate your Social Security retirement income benefit.

Federal Insurance Contributions Act (FICA)
Act that authorizes Social Security and Medicare tax withdrawals from employee paychecks; amounts withheld go into Social Security trust fund accounts, which pay benefits to current retirees.

Understanding Your Social Security Retirement Income Benefits

The Social Security program has become the most successful and popular domestic government program in U.S. history. Funding for Social Security benefits comes from a compulsory payroll tax split equally between employee and employer. Social Security taxes withheld from wages are called **FICA taxes** (named for the **Federal Insurance Contributions Act**). The amounts withheld are put into the Social Security trust fund accounts from which benefits are paid to current program recipients.

Did You Know?

About Women and Retirement Planning

Women are less likely to get retirement benefits from their employers. This occurs, in part, because women are more likely to work for employers who do not offer a retirement plan. Because of their lower average incomes, women also receive less income than men from Social Security (about $900 per month compared with over $1100). Women live longer than men, so women should consider saving more money for retirement than men.

maximum taxable yearly earnings (MTYE)
The maximum amount to which the FICA tax is applied.

Social Security credits
Accumulated quarterly credits to qualify for Social Security benefits obtained by paying FICA taxes.

fully insured Social Security status
Requires 40 credits and provides workers and their families with benefits under the retirement, survivors, and disability programs; once status is earned, it cannot be taken away even if the eligible worker never works again.

Instant Message

Financing Social Security

Based on the Social Security Administration Trustees' best estimate, program costs will exceed tax revenues starting in 2016. Social Security's combined trust funds are projected to allow full payment of scheduled benefits until they become exhausted in 2037. While many young people doubt that Social Security will provide them benefits, there are solutions. Simple fixes that actually will work and are favored by people of both parties and all age groups are to increase the wage cap, increase the payroll tax, and change the benefit formula.

Your Contributions to Social Security and Medicare

Wage earners pay both FICA and Medicare taxes to the SSA. The FICA tax is paid on wage income up to the **maximum taxable yearly earnings (MTYE),** which comprises the maximum amount to which the FICA tax is applied. The MTYE figure—$106,800 for last year—is adjusted annually for inflation. The FICA tax rate has been 12.4 percent, consisting of 6.2 percent paid by employees and 6.2 percent paid by employers. Self-employed workers pay a FICA tax rate of 12.4 percent, twice that of wage earners, because they are their own employers. Thus, a self-employed person earning $106,800 per year would pay $6622 ($106,800 $\times$ 0.062 $\times$ 2) in FICA taxes on that income.

Wage earners and their employers also pay a 1.45 percent Medicare tax on all earnings. The MTYE limit does not apply to the Medicare tax. Thus, the typical worker sends 7.65 (6.2 + 1.45) percent of his or her earnings to the SSA. For example, a person earning $35,000 pays a combined FICA and Medicare tax of $2678 ($35,000 $\times$ 0.0765) and a person earning $110,000 pays $6622 ($106,800 $\times$ 0.062) plus $1595 ($110,000 $\times$ 0.0145), or a total of $8217.

How You Become Qualified for Social Security Benefits

You must be insured under the Social Security program before retirement, survivors, or disability insurance benefits can be paid to you or your family. The Social Security program covers nine out of every ten U.S. employees. Some federal, state, and local government employees are exempt because their employers have instituted other plans.

To qualify for benefits, a worker accumulates credits for employment in any work subject to the FICA taxes, including part-time and temporary employment. The periods of employment in which you earn credits need not be consecutive. Military service also provides credits. You earn **Social Security credits** for a certain amount of work covered under Social Security during a calendar year. For example, workers receive one credit if they earned $1090 during any one of the four 90-day periods during the year and the annual maximum of four credits if they earned $4360 (4 $\times$ $1090). The dollar figure required for each credit earned is raised annually to keep pace with inflation.

The number of credits you have earned determines your eligibility for retirement benefits and for disability or survivors benefits if you become disabled or die. Table 17.1 shows the length-of-work requirements to receive Social Security benefits. The SSA recognizes four statuses of eligibility.

Fully Insured   **Fully insured** status requires 40 credits and provides the worker and his or her family with eligibility for benefits under the retirement, survivors, and disability programs. Once obtained, this status cannot be lost even if the person never works again. Although it is required to receive retirement benefits, "fully insured" status does not imply that the worker will receive the maximum benefits allowable.

Currently Insured   To achieve **currently insured status,** six credits must be earned in the most recent three years. This status

Table 17.1 Length-of-Work Requirements for Social Security Benefits

Types of Benefits	Payable to	Minimum Years of Work Under Social Security
Retirement Survivors*	You, your spouse, child, dependent spouse 62 or older	10 years (fully insured status).
Full	Widow(er) 60 or older, disabled widow(er) 50–59, widow(er) if caring for child 18 years or younger, dependent children, dependent widow(er) 62 or older, disabled dependent widow(er) 50–61, dependent parent at 62	10 years (fully insured status).
Current	Widow(er) caring for child 18 years or younger, dependent children	1½ years of last 3 years before death (currently insured status).
Disability	You and your dependents	If younger than age 24, you need 1½ years of work in the 3 years prior to disablement; if between ages 24 and 31, you need to work half the time between when you turned 21 and your date of disablement; if age 31 or older, you must have 5 years of credit during the 10 years prior to disablement.
Medicare		
Hospitalization (Part A: automatic benefits)	Anyone 65 or older plus some others, such as the disabled	Anyone qualified for the Social Security retirement program is qualified for Medicare Part A at age 65; others may qualify by paying a monthly premium for Part A.
Medical expense (Part B: voluntary benefits)	Anyone eligible for Part A and anyone else 65 or older (payment of monthly premiums required)	No prior work under Social Security is required.

*A lump-sum death benefit no greater than $255 is also granted to dependents of those either fully or currently insured.
Source: U.S. Department of Health and Human Services.

provides for some survivors or disability benefits but no retirement benefits. To remain eligible for these benefits, a worker must continue to earn at least six credits every three years or meet a minimum number of covered years of work established by the SSA.

Transitionally Insured **Transitionally insured** status applies only to retired workers who reach the age of 72 without accumulating 40 credits (ten years). These people are eligible for limited retirement benefits.

Not Insured Workers younger than age 72 who have fewer than six credits of work experience are **not insured.**

How to Estimate Your Social Security Retirement Benefits

The actual dollar amount of Social Security benefits is based on the average of the highest 35 years of earnings during the working years. Your actual earnings are first adjusted, or **indexed** to account for changes in average wages since the year the earnings were received. The SSA then calculates your average monthly indexed earnings during the 35 years in which you earned the most. The agency applies a formula to these earnings to arrive at your **basic retirement benefit** (or **primary insurance amount**). This is the amount you would receive at your **full-benefit retirement age**—67 for those born in 1960 or later.

basic retirement benefit/ primary insurance amount
Amount of Social Security benefits a worker would receive at his or her full-benefit retirement age, which is 67 for those born after 1960.

full-benefit retirement age
Age at which a retiree is entitled to full Social Security benefits; 67 for those born in 1960 or later.

You can compute your own retirement benefit estimate using a program that you can download to your computer from http://www.ssa.gov/OACT/ANYPIA/. You will have three choices concerning when you want to begin receiving Social Security retirement benefits.

1. Begin Receiving Benefits at Your Full-Benefit Age

Once you have reached your full-benefit retirement age, you are eligible to receive your basic monthly retirement benefit. You can begin collecting these benefits even if you continue working full- or part-time. Your level of employment income will not affect your level of benefits, though it may affect the income taxes that you pay on your Social Security benefits (as discussed later in this chapter).

2. Begin Receiving Reduced Benefits at a Younger Age

You can choose to start receiving retirement benefits as early as age 62, regardless of your full-benefit retirement age. If you do so, however, your basic retirement benefit will be permanently reduced. The check will be permanently reduced 30 percent for people born after 1960. If you choose to take the earliest Social Security retirement benefits, you will be ahead financially if you do not survive to about age 80. Sixty percent of retirees elect to take their Social Security benefits early.

People considering early Social Security retirement benefits need to be aware that their checks will be reduced if they have earned income above the annual limit ($14,160 this year). Those who earn more than the annual limit have their Social Security benefits reduced $1 for every $2 in earnings. A person entitled to $1000 per month ($12,000 per year) in early retirement benefits who has an earned income of more than $37,000 should not apply for early Social Security benefits because he or she makes too much money to be eligible for any benefit.

3. Begin Receiving Larger Benefits at a Later Age

You can delay taking benefits beyond your full-benefit retirement age. In such a case, your benefit would be permanently increased by as much as 8 percent per year. You can continue to work even after you begin taking these delayed benefits. Again, your level of employment income will not affect your level of benefits, but it may affect the income taxes that you pay on your Social Security benefits.

Instant Message

Use Calculator to Decide on Collecting Social Security Benefits at 62 or Later

Go to Met Life's calculator to use their Social Security Decision Tool (http://www.metlife.com/fileassets/sscalc), which takes into account your current age, how close you are from retirement, gender, and life expectancy.

Check the Accuracy of Your Social Security Statement

Social Security Statement
A document that the Social Security Administration periodically sends to all workers, which includes earnings history, Social Security taxes paid, and an estimated benefit amount.

The **Social Security Statement** is a document that the SSA periodically sends to all workers. It includes a record of your earnings history, a record of how much you and your various employers paid in Social Security taxes, and an estimate of the benefits that you and your family might be eligible for now and in the future. You can also request a Social Security Statement at any time at www.ssa.gov/statement/ or by telephone at (800) 772-1213. When reviewing this statement, make sure that the SSA's records are up-to-date and accurate. Workers have three years to correct any errors.

✔ Concept Check 17.2

1. Summarize how workers become qualified for Social Security benefits.
2. Distinguish between the benefits provided under Social Security for a worker who is fully insured and a worker who is currently insured.
3. How is the dollar amount of one's Social Security benefit determined?
4. Explain what happens if you choose to retire earlier than your full retirement age, which is probably 67.

How to Calculate Your Estimated Retirement Needs in Today's Dollars

To plan for a financially successful retirement, you first need to set a goal. Otherwise, as one of the most quoted figures in sports, baseball legend Yogi Berra, says, "If you don't know where you are going, you will end up somewhere else." Your **retirement savings goal,** or **retirement nest egg,** is the total amount of accumulated savings and investments needed to support your desired retirement lifestyle. If you want to spend less than 15 minutes to get a basic idea of the savings you will need when you retire, see the American Savings Education Council's *Ballpark Estimate* (www.choosetosave.org/ballpark/) for a one-page worksheet.

Setting a personally meaningful retirement goal helps motivate people to take the necessary saving and investing actions. If you begin to save and invest for retirement early in life, the compounding effect on money over time will make it fairly easy for you to reach your retirement savings goal.

Projecting Your Annual Retirement Expenses and Income

Projecting your annual retirement expenses in current dollars and being knowledgeable about the sources of income that might support these expenditures lead logically to a key question that may be asked in several ways: "How much money must be set aside to provide that support?" or "What is my retirement savings goal?" or "How large a retirement nest egg do I need?" You can use the Run the Numbers worksheet, "Estimating Your Retirement Savings Goal in Today's Dollars" (page 515), to calculate this amount. In the following example, you will see how to use this worksheet to arrive at the amount that you would need to save each year to realize your desired, financially comfortable retirement lifestyle. Couples can use the same worksheet, but each person should prepare a worksheet. You do not have to remain clueless about how much money you will need when you retire. Simply do the math.

3 Learning Objective

Calculate your estimated retirement savings needs in today's dollars.

retirement savings goal/ retirement nest egg
Total amount of accumulated savings and investments needed to support desired retirement lifestyle.

Paul Simcock/ Iconica/Getty Images

Understanding your Social Security and employer-based retirement benefits is a first step in retirement planning.

An Illustration of Retirement Needs

Consider the case of Erik McKartmann, aged 35 and single, the manager of a weight-loss business in South Park, Colorado. Erik currently earns $50,000 per year. He has been contributing $160 per month ($1920 annually) into his account established through his employer's 401(k) plan. Erik plans to retire at age 62.

1. Erik has chosen not to develop a retirement budget at this time. Instead, he multiplied his current salary by 70 percent to arrive at an annual income (in current dollars) needed in retirement of $35,000 ($50,000 × 0.70). This amount was entered on line 1 of the worksheet. If Erik wants to increase the amount of dollars to support a higher retirement lifestyle, he can simply increase the percentage in the calculation.

2. Erik checked the SSA website to estimate his benefits. At age 62, he could expect a monthly benefit of $1100 (in current dollars). Multiplying by 12 gave an expected annual Social Security benefit of $13,200 (in current dollars), which Erik entered on line 2 of the worksheet.

3. Line 3 of the worksheet, which calls for Erik's expected pension benefit, is appropriate for defined-benefit plans. After discussing his expected employer pension with the benefits counselor at work, Erik found that his anticipated benefit under the plan would amount to approximately $5800 annually, assuming that he remained with the company until his retirement, so he entered that figure on line 3.

4. Erik adds lines 2 and 3 to determine his total estimated retirement income from Social Security and his employer pension. The amount on line 4 would be $19,000 ($13,200 + $5800).

5. Subtracting line 4 from line 1 reveals that Erik would need an additional income of $16,000 ($35,000 − $19,000) in today's dollars from savings and investments to meet his annual retirement income needs.

6. At this point, Erik has considered only his annual needs and benefits. Because he plans to retire at age 62, Erik will need income for 20 years based on his life expectancy. (Of course, Erik could live well into his 80s, which would mean that he would need the inflation-adjusted equivalent of his annual retirement expenditures for more than 20 years.) Using Appendix A.4 and assuming a return that is 3 percent above the inflation rate, Erik finds the multiplier 14.8775 where 3 percent and 20 years intersect. He then calculates that he needs an additional amount of $238,040 (14.8775 × $16,000) at retirement. That's a big number! And it is in current dollars. The number does not dissuade Erik from saving because he knows he has time and the magic of compounding on his side.

7. Erik's current savings and investments can be used to offset the $238,040 he will need for retirement. Erik has zero savings in his employer's 401(k) account; however, he does have some money invested in an IRA ($24,000), plus some other investments ($13,000). These amounts are totaled ($37,000) and recorded on line 7E.

8. If left untouched, the $37,000 that Erik has built up will continue to earn interest and dividends until he retires. Because he has 27 more years until retirement, Erik can use Appendix A.1 and, assuming a growth rate of 3 percent over 27 years, find the factor 2.2213 and multiply it by the total amount in line 7. Erik's $37,000 should have a future value of $82,188 at his retirement, so he puts this amount on line 8.

9. Subtracting line 8 from line 6 reveals that Erik's retirement nest egg will need an additional $155,852 at the time of retirement.

10. Using Appendix A.3 and a growth rate of 3 percent over 27 years, Erik finds a factor of 40.7096. When divided into $155,852, it reveals that he needs savings and investments of $3828 per year until retirement.

11. Erik records his current savings and investments of $2000 per year on line 11.

Run the Numbers

Estimating Your Retirement Savings Goal in Today's Dollars

This worksheet will help you calculate the amount you need to set aside each year in today's dollars so that you will have adequate funds for your retirement. The example here assumes that a single person is now 35 years old, will retire at age 62, has a current income of $50,000, currently saves and invests about $2000 per year, contributes zero to an employer-sponsored retirement plan, anticipates needing a retirement income of $35,000 per year assuming a spending lifestyle at 70 percent of current income ($50,000 × 0.70), and will live an additional 20 years beyond retirement. Investment returns are assumed to be 3 percent after inflation—a fair estimate for a typical portfolio. The financial needs would differ if the growth rate of the investments was less than 3 percent. This approach simplifies the calculations and puts the numbers to estimate retirement needs into today's dollars. The amount saved must be higher if substantial inflation occurs.

	Example	Your Numbers
1. Annual income needed at retirement in today's dollars (Use carefully estimated numbers or a certain percentage, such as 70% or 80%.)	$ 35,000	50,000
2. Estimated Social Security retirement benefit in today's dollars	$ 13,200	24,000
3. Estimated employer pension benefit in today's dollars (Ask your retirement benefit adviser to make an estimate of your future pension, assuming that you remain in the same job at the same salary, or make your own conservative estimate.)	$ 5,800	0
4. Total estimated retirement income from Social Security and employer pension in today's dollars (line 2 + line 3)	$ 19,000	24,000
5. Additional income needed at retirement in today's dollars (line 1 − line 4)	$ 16,000	26,000
6. Amount you must have at retirement in today's dollars to receive additional annual income in retirement (line 5) for 20 years (from Appendix A.4, assuming a 3% return over 20 years, or 14.8775 × $16,000)	$ 238,040	
7. Amount already available as savings and investments in today's dollars (add lines 7A through 7D, and record the total on line 7E)		
A. Employer savings plans, such as a 401(k), SEP-IRA, or profit-sharing plan	0	2,500
B. IRAs and Keoghs	$ 24,000	5,000
C. Other investments, such as mutual funds, stocks, bonds, real estate, and other assets available for retirement	$ 13,000	8,400
D. If you wish to include a portion of the equity in your home as savings, enter its present value minus the cost of another home in retirement	0	0
E. Total retirement savings (add lines A through D)	$ 37,000	
8. Future value of current savings/investments at time of retirement (using Appendix A.1 and a growth rate of 3% over 27 years, the factor is 2.2213; thus, 2.2213 × $37,000)	$ 82,188	
9. Additional retirement savings and investments needed at time of retirement (line 6 − line 8)	$ 155,852	
10. Annual savings needed (to reach amount in line 9) before retirement (using Appendix A.3 and a growth rate of 3% over 27 years, the factor is 40.7096; thus, $155,852 ÷ 40.7096)	$ 3,828	
11. Current annual contribution to savings and investment plans	$ 2,000	5,000
12. Additional amount of annual savings that you need to set aside in today's dollars to achieve retirement goal (in line 1) (line 10 − line 11)	$ 1,828	

Advice from a Pro...

Buy Your Retirement on the Layaway Plan

The large retirement savings goal dollar amount scares some people. To allay such concerns, the following novel approach to thinking about retirement saving has been suggested. You can look at your retirement as something you "buy." The "retail price" is the retirement nest egg goal itself. From that amount, you can subtract "discounts" for anticipated income from Social Security, employer-sponsored retirement accounts, personal retirement accounts, and any other funds you expect to have accumulated. Then you identify the difference—the shortfall indicated on line 9 of the Run the Numbers worksheet—and buy it on a "layaway plan." The additional amounts you periodically save and invest are, therefore, the "layaway payments" with which you "buy" your retirement. This is smart thinking!

Dennis R. Ackley
Ackley & Associates, Kansas City, Missouri

Did You Know?

Online Retirement Calculators

There are dozens of online retirement calculators, mostly free, that take only minutes to complete. These are educational tools that help get you thinking and perhaps acting about saving and investing for retirement. A simple calculator, such as Fidelity's interactive website (http://personal.fidelity.com/planning/retirement/content/myPlan/index.shtml), can get you started.

A more comprehensive calculator, such as T. Rowe Price's (http://www.troweprice.com/ric), uses Monte Carlo simulations. It calculates a projected monthly income stream throughout retirement taking into account current and future savings in employer-sponsored retirement plans, as well as other retirement accounts and regular taxable accounts, Social Security, other sources of income, expected number of years in retirement, and investment strategy before and after retirement.

Research suggests that those who calculate how much they need to save often end up having a more financially successful retirement. In your assumptions perhaps use a 5 percent long-term rate of return minus a 3 percent annual inflation rate, and try more than one calculator.

12. Erik subtracts line 11 from line 10 to determine the additional amount of annual savings that he should set aside in today's dollars to achieve his retirement goal. His shortfall totals $1828 per year. By saving an extra $153 each month ($1828 ÷ 12), he can reach his retirement goal established in step 1.

Suggestions to Fund Erik's Retirement Goal

Erik needs to continue what he is doing—saving and investing—plus save a little more so he can enjoy his lifestyle when his full-time career ends. Erik should discuss with his benefits counselor how much he can save and invest via the company's new 401(k) program.

Erik needs to save more for retirement by contributing an additional $1828 per year into his account within his employer's 401(k) plan—that is, about 3.7 percent of his salary. To create an extra margin of safety, and if the rules of his employer's retirement plan permit it, he could save even more of his salary. His employer might also make a matching contribution (discussed later) of some of Erik's 401(k) contributions.

The additional $1828 in current dollars assumes that the growth of his investments will be 3 percent higher than the inflation rate, a reasonable assumption. If his income goes up sharply, Erik should increase his savings because he will have a much larger amount of income to replace at retirement. Redoing the calculations every few years will help keep Erik informed and on track for a financially successful retirement.

 Concept Check 17.3 ·

1. List the steps in the process of estimating your retirement savings goal in today's dollars.
2. In the text example, what can Erik do to save more for his retirement?
3. Give your impression of the idea of buying retirement on the "layaway plan."

Why Invest in Tax-Sheltered Retirement Accounts?

The funds you put into regular investment accounts represent **after-tax money.** Assume, for example, that a person in the 25 percent tax bracket earns an extra $1000 and is considering investing those funds. She will pay $250 in income taxes on the extra income, which leaves only $750 in after-tax money available to invest. Furthermore, all earnings from the invested funds are also subject to income taxes each year as they are accrued. Matters are much different when you invest in **tax-sheltered retirement accounts.**

Your Contributions May Be Tax Deductible

Contributions may be "deductible" from your taxable income in the year the contributions are made. In this situation, you pay zero taxes on the contributed amount of income in the current year. This means that you are investing with **pretax money,** and the salary amount you defer, or contribute, to a tax-sheltered retirement account comes out of your earnings before income taxes are calculated. Thus, you gain an immediate elimination of part of your income tax liability for the current year. The advantage of using tax-deductible contributions is illustrated in Table 17.2. The maximum contribution varies (discussed later) depending upon the type of tax-sheltered account you are using.

4 Learning Objective
Understand why you should save for retirement within tax-sheltered retirement accounts.

after-tax money
Funds put into regular investment accounts; subject to income taxes.

tax-sheltered retirement accounts
Retirement account for which all earnings from the invested funds are not subject to income taxes.

pretax money
Investing with pretax money to a tax-sheltered retirement account comes out of your earnings before income taxes are calculated, thus gaining an immediate elimination of part of your income tax liability for the current year.

Table 17.2 The Financial Benefits of 401(k) Participation

Samantha Smarty participates in her employer's 401(k) retirement plan, and contributes $3600 of her $60,000 income. Her contributions are tax deductible, so this reduces her federal income taxes by $1900 ($9600 − $7700), and it takes another $500 off her state income tax liability ($3100 − $2600). Samantha's net take-home pay is reduced by only $800 ($47,300 − $46,100). Moreover, for a net outflow of only $800 Samantha gets to invest $3600. That's a 300 percent return ($3600 – $800 = $2400/$800) on her "investment." Whao! What a good deal!

	Not Participating in 401(k) Plan	Participating in 401(k) Plan
Income	$60,000	$60,000
Contribution to plan	– 0 –	3,600
Taxable income	60,000	56,400
Federal income tax	9,600	7,700
State income tax	3,100	2,600
Tax-home pay	$47,300	$46,100

tax-deferred
The individual does not have to pay current income taxes on the earnings (interest, dividends, and capital gains) reinvested in a retirement account.

Your Earnings Are Tax Deferred

Income earned on funds in tax-sheltered retirement accounts accumulates **tax deferred.** In other words, the individual does not have to pay income taxes on the earnings (interest, dividends, and capital gains) reinvested within the retirement account. A **withdrawal** is a removal of assets from an account.

You Can Accumulate More Money

You will have much more money when it is time to retire if you use tax-sheltered accounts for your investing instead of personal taxable accounts. The following examples assume that a person who pays combined federal and state income taxes at a 25 percent rate invests $3000 per year for 20 years in a diversified portfolio of stock, bonds, and mutual funds that earns 8 percent annually. Calculations are from Appendix A.4.

Example 1—$110,357: Make Annual After-Tax Investments That Are Not Tax Sheltered

The sum of $3000 in after-tax money is invested in a personal taxable account every year for 20 years. Because the 8 percent return is subject to annual income taxes, the return rate is effectively reduced to 6 percent [8 percent × (1 − 0.25)]. A $3000 annual investment for 20 years that earns 6 percent annually will grow to $110,357. The person has invested $60,000.

Example 2—$137,286: Make Annual After-Tax Investments That Are Tax Sheltered

The sum of $3000 in after-tax money is invested in a tax-sheltered account every year for 20 years. Because no income taxes are assessed on the interest, dividends, and capital gains while they accumulate, the return rate is 8 percent. A $3000 annual investment for 20 years that earns 8 percent annually will grow to $137,286. The person has invested $60,000.

Example 3—$137,286: Make Annual Pretax Investments That Are Tax Sheltered

The $3000 in pretax money is invested in a tax-sheltered account every year for 20 years. Pretax contributions to retirement accounts reduce the current year's income tax liability, so the investor saves $750 ($3000 × 0.25) in income taxes. Instead of the $750 going to the government, those dollars are used to reduce the amount the person had to invest. A $3000 annual investment for 20 years that earns 8 percent annually will grow to $137,286. Of the $60,000 invested, the person put in only $45,000 because $15,000 was money that would have otherwise gone to the IRS.

Example 4—$171,608: Make Annual Investments That Tax-Shelter Growth Plus Invest the Money That Would Have Gone to the IRS in Taxes

The $3000 in pretax money is invested in a tax-sheltered account every year for 20 years. Pretax contributions to qualified accounts reduce the current year's income tax liability, so the investor saves $750 ($3000 × 0.25) in income taxes. This time, however, the investor uses that $750 to help fund a larger contribution—$3750 instead of $3000. A $3750 annual investment for 20 years ($75,000 invested, although only $60,000 was the investor's money and $15,000 was money that would have otherwise gone to the IRS) that earns 8 percent annually will grow to $171,608.

You Have Ownership and Portability

portability
Upon termination of employment, employees with portable benefits can keep their savings in tax-sheltered accounts, transferring retirement funds from employer's account directly to another account without penalty.

Portability means that upon termination of employment, an employee can keep his or her savings in a tax-sheltered account by transferring the retirement funds from the employer's account to another account without penalty. Assets held in tax-sheltered retirement accounts are always owned by the person who opened the account (once the person is vested, as discussed later).

Your Withdrawals Might Be Tax Free

Taxes may or may not be due in the future when withdrawals occur. IRS regulations permit tax-free withdrawals from only one type of retirement account, the Roth IRA, which is discussed later. **Tax free** means that withdrawals are never taxed.

Instant Message

Beneficiary Designation Form

When you open a retirement account, you must sign a **beneficiary designation form.** This document contractually determines who will inherit the funds in that retirement account in case you die before the funds are distributed. This designation generally overrides any provisions in a will, and it keeps those assets out of one's estate, as discussed in Chapter 18.

Concept Check 17.4

1. Distinguish between after-tax money put into investments and pretax money.
2. Give your impression of the logic of the "net pay" numbers of participating in a 401(k) plan.
3. Explain what is meant by tax-sheltered investment growth on money contributed to qualified retirement accounts.

Employer-Sponsored and Personally Established Retirement Plans

Employers usually offer retirement plans to their employees because the promise of a secure retirement represents an effective way to recruit and retain valuable workers. An **employer-sponsored retirement plan** is an IRS-approved plan offered by an employer. These are called **qualified** plans. Approximately one-third of all workers at small firms voluntarily participate in an employer-sponsored retirement plan, compared with three-quarters of workers in medium-size to large firms. Participating in such a plan can serve as the cornerstone of your retirement planning. If you do not have access to an employer plan, you should make alternative preparations for retirement (discussed later in this chapter).

IRS regulations allow you to take advantage of other personally established, self-directed tax-sheltered retirement accounts. These are especially important if your employer offers no retirement plan. But even if you do have a plan at work, you can benefit from contributing to one or more personally established plans.

The **Employee Retirement Income Security Act (ERISA)** does not require companies to offer retirement plans, but it does regulate those plans that are provided. ERISA calls for proper plan reporting and disclosure to participants. Three types of employer-sponsored retirement plans are available: defined-contribution, defined-benefit, and cash-balance.

Today's Employer-Sponsored Defined-Contribution Retirement Plan

A **defined-contribution retirement plan** voluntarily offered by an employer is designed to provide a retiring employee a lump sum at retirement. It is distinguished by its "contributions"—that is, the total amount of money put into each participating employee's individual account. The eventual retirement benefit in such an employer-sponsored plan consists solely of assets (including investment earnings) that have accumulated in the various individual accounts. In a **noncontributory plan,** money to fund the retirement plan is contributed only by the employer.

5 Learning Objective

Distinguish among the types of employer-sponsored and personally established tax-sheltered retirement plans.

employer-sponsored retirement plan
An IRS-approved retirement plan offered by an employer (also called qualified plans).

Employee Retirement Income Security Act (ERISA)
Regulates employer-sponsored plans by calling for proper plan reporting and disclosure to participants in defined-contribution, defined-benefit, and cash-balance plans.

defined-contribution retirement plan
A retirement plan designed to provide a lump-sum at retirement; it is distinguished by its "contributions"—the total amount of money put into each participating employee's individual account.

contributory plan
The most common type of employee-sponsored defined-contribution retirement plan; accepts employee as well as employer contributions.

automatic enrollment plan
Plan in which the employer withholds up to 6 percent of an employee's salary and places it into a defined-contribution retirement plan.

self-directed
In defined-contribution plans, employees control the assets in their account—how often to make contributions to the account, how much to contribute, how much risk to take, and how to invest.

401(k) plan
Defined-contribution plan designed for employees of private corporations.

403(b) plan
Defined-contribution plan designed for eligible employees of not-for-profit institutions, such as colleges, hospitals, and religious organizations.

matching contribution
Employer benefit that offers a full or partial matching contribution to a participating employee's account in proportion to each dollar of contributions made by the participant.

In a **contributory plan,** money to fund the plan is provided by both the employer and the participant or solely by the employee. Most plans are contributory. This is the most popular retirement plan offered by employers today.

When you elect to participate and contribute to such a retirement plan, you take a portion of your salary and postpone receiving it. That money goes into your account. Because it goes there before you receive it, those funds are not subject to income taxes. Defined-contribution retirement plans are also known as **salary-reduction plans** because the contributed income is not included in an employee's salary. The tax-free contributions are designated as such on the employee's W-2 form. Financial expert Steve Lansing says a defined-contribution plan can be viewed as an interest-free loan from the government, via the income taxes saved, to help finance one's retirement.

Each employee's contributions are deposited with a **trustee** (usually a financial institution, bank, or trust company that has fiduciary responsibility for holding certain assets), which invests the money in various securities, including mutual funds, and sometimes the stock of the employer. Each employee's funds are managed in a separate account.

Employers who offer a defined-contribution account may choose to establish an **automatic enrollment plan** for employees. Employees are registered and the employer withholds up to 3 percent of the employee's salary and puts that amount into each worker's account in an automatically diversified portfolio. Over time, the employer may choose to automatically increase the withholding to 6 percent, or the company maximum. Employees have the right to "opt out" of this kind of "automatic" plan, although taking such action defeats a valuable way to save for retirement.

Defined-contribution retirement plans are described as **self-directed** because the employee controls where the assets in his or her account are invested. The individual selects where to invest, how much risk to take, how much to invest, and how often contributions are made to the account.

Over time, the balance amassed in such an account consists of the contributions plus any investment income and gains, minus expenses and losses. The contributions devoted to the account are specified ("defined"). The future amount in the account at retirement will not be known until the individual decides to begin making withdrawals. This uncertainty occurs because the sum available to the retiree depends on the success of the investments made. At retirement the retiree thus has a lump sum to manage during the rest of his or her lifetime.

Names of Defined-Contribution Plans
Several types of employer-sponsored defined-contribution plans exist. The most common are the 401(k), 403(b), and 457 plans (named after sections of the IRS tax code) and the SIMPLE IRA and SIMPLE 401(k). Each plan is restricted to a specific group of workers. You may contribute to these plans only if your employer offers them.

The **401(k) plan** is the best-known defined-contribution plan. It is designed for employees of private corporations. Eligible employees of non-profit organizations (colleges, hospitals, religious organizations, and some other not-for-profit institutions) may contribute to a **403(b) plan** that has the same contribution limits. Employees of state and local governments and non–church controlled tax-exempt organizations may contribute to **457 plans.** Only employees (not employers) make contributions into the plan. When the employing organization has 100 or fewer employees, it may set up a **Savings Incentive Match Plan for Employees IRA (SIMPLE IRA).** Regulations vary somewhat for each type of plan.

Matching Contributions
Many employers offer a full or partial **matching contribution** (up to a certain limit) to the employee's account in proportion to each dollar of contributions made by the participant. The match might be $1.00 per $1.00 up to the first 3 percent of pay. More common is $0.50 per $1.00 up to the first 6 percent of

Instant Message

How Much Should You Save?

Only about half of twenty-somethings say they have a retirement plan, such as an IRA or 401(k). People who start saving and investing for retirement during their 20s should aim to reserve 12 to 15 percent of their pretax income every year, *including* employer contributions, for this purpose. Those who have delayed planning for retirement until their late 30s or 40s should begin investing 20 to 25 percent annually in an effort to catch up, and they also may have to be more risk aggressive in their investment choices.

Table 17.3 How Much You Give Up Without Matching Contributions

You might consider working only for employers who offer matching contributions to your retirement account. For example, the matching 100 percent employer contributions shown below increase the retirement account balance after 30 years from $317,193 to $475,578 with a 2 percent match and to $634,386 with a 4 percent match. By increasing the employee's contribution from 4 percent ($70,000 × 0.04 = $2800) to 6 percent ($70,000 × 0.06 = $4200) to obtain the full 100 percent employer match on the first 6 percent of salary, the sum rises to almost $1 million after 30 years earning an 8 percent annual return. You should make contributions to your account at least up to the amount where you obtain the largest matching contribution from your employer. After all, the matching contributions are "free money."

Salary $70,000	Employee Contribution	100% Match of 2% of Salary	100% Match of 4% of Salary	100% Match of 6% of Salary
Employee contribution	$ 2,800	$ 2,800	$ 2,800	$ 4,200
Employer contributions	$ 0	$ 1,400	$ 2,800	$ 4,200
Total annual contributions	$ 2,800	$ 4,200	$ 5,600	$ 8,400
Account balance after 30 years earning 8%	$317,193	$475,578	$634,386	$951,579

pay. Because your employer makes a contribution to your account every time you do, in effect you obtain an "instant return" on your retirement savings. Saving $4000 a year with a $0.50 employer match immediately puts $2000 more into your retirement account. This concept is illustrated in Table 17.3. During difficult economic times employers sometimes reduce or eliminate their matching contributions to retirement plans.

Limits on Contributions There are limits on the maximum amount of income per year that an employee may contribute to an employer-sponsored plan. The maximum contribution limit to 401(k), 403(b), and 457 plans is $16,500; the maximum is $11,500 for SIMPLE IRA plans. These figures rise yearly with inflation.

Catch-Up Provision A **catch-up provision** permits workers age 50 or older to contribute an additional $5500 to most employer-sponsored plans. Millions of people who are getting a late start on saving—including women who have gone back to work after raising children—can put more money away for retirement.

catch-up provision
Permits workers age 50 or older to contribute an additional $5500 to most employer-sponsored plans ($1000 limit on IRA accounts).

Vesting Gives You Rights to Your Benefits Employers require a waiting period of one year before allowing new employees to participate in the company's retirement plan. To be eligible for any retirement benefits, an employee must first participate in the employer-sponsored retirement plan.

Vesting ensures that a retirement plan participant has the right to take full possession of all employer contributions and earnings if the employee is dismissed, resigns, or retires. If an employee has not worked long enough for the employer to be vested before leaving his or her job, the employer's contributions are forfeited back to the employer's plan. The employee has no rights to any of those funds. Once vested, the worker has a legal right to the entire amount of money in his or her account in a defined-contribution plan. No matter when you leave an employer, you always have a vested right to the money that you personally contributed to that retirement account. Some employers permit immediate vesting, whereby the employee owns the money just as soon as the employer deposits funds into the retirement account.

Employees, by law, must be vested no later than specified by one of the following options:

- **Cliff vesting.** The employee is fully vested within three years of employment.
- **Graduated vesting.** Employees must be at least 20 percent vested after two years of service and gain an additional 20 percent of vesting for each subsequent year until, at the end of year six, the account is fully vested.

vesting
Ensures that a retirement plan participant has the right to take full possession of all employer contributions and earnings if employee is dismissed, resigns, or retires.

graduated vesting
Schedule under which employees must be at least 20 percent vested after two years of service and gain an additional 20 percent of vesting for each subsequent year until, at the end of year six, the account is fully vested.

How to Manage Your Retirement Money After Leaving Your Employer

When changing employers or retiring, you may have four choices:

1. **Leave it.** You may be able to leave the money invested in your account at your former employer until you wish to begin taking withdrawals.

2. **Transfer it.** You may be able to transfer the money to a retirement account at a new employer.

3. **Transfer it.** You can transfer the money to an IRA.

4. **Take it.** You can take the money in cash and pay income taxes and penalties.

Options 2, 3, and 4 result in a **lump-sum distribution** because all the funds are removed from a retirement account at one time. Such a transfer must be executed correctly according to the IRS's "rollover regulations" or the taxpayer will be subject to a substantial tax bill, a **rollover penalty,** and perhaps a need to borrow money to pay the IRS. A **rollover** is the action of moving assets from one tax-sheltered account to another tax-sheltered account or to an IRA within 60 days of a distribution. This procedure preserves the benefits of having funds in a tax-sheltered account.

retirement plan contribution credit/saver's tax credit
Program to encourage low-income individuals to save for retirement, this tax credit ranges from 10 to 50 percent of every dollar they contribute to an IRA or employer-sponsored retirement plan up to $2000.

defined-benefit retirement plan
Employer-sponsored retirement plan that pays lifetime monthly annuity payments to retirees based on a predetermined formula.

pension
Sum of money paid regularly as a retirement benefit.

The IRS's **20 percent withholding rule,** the rollover penalty, applies if the participant takes direct possession of the funds (choice 4 in the previous list). This rule requires that an employer collect a 20 percent tax from any lump-sum distribution that is paid directly to a former employee. This amount is forwarded to the IRS to prepay some of the income taxes that will be owed on the withdrawn funds. To avoid the 20 percent withholding rule, a **trustee-to-trustee rollover** must occur. In this procedure (choices 2 and 3 in the list), the funds go directly from the previous employer's trustee to the trustee of the new account, with no payment to the employee occurring.

For example, a $300,000 lump-sum distribution made directly to an employee would result in that person receiving $240,000 and the employer withholding $60,000 for the IRS. Government regulations further require that the employee put the entire $300,000 into an account at another employer or a **rollover IRA** (an IRA opened to accept rollover funds) within 60 days—even though only $240,000 was actually received by the employee. The investor must supply the difference ($60,000 in this instance) on his or her own. Substantial penalties are assessed for noncompliance. The 20 percent amount that was withheld may be retrieved the following tax year by filing an income tax return to claim a refund. Because of such penalties most people avoid taking such distributions. The IRS wants taxpayers to transfer retirement funds in such a way that the previously untaxed money remains accountable and, eventually, taxable.

Retirement Plan Contribution Tax Credit for Low-Income and Moderate-Income Savers

Singles with adjusted gross incomes of less than $25,000 and joint filers earning less than $50,000 can claim a nonrefundable **retirement plan contribution credit** (also known as a **saver's tax credit**). This credit ranges from 10 to 50 percent of every dollar they contribute to an IRA or employer-sponsored retirement plan up to $2000.

Yesterday's Defined-Benefit Retirement Plan

The second type of employer-sponsored retirement plan, a **defined-benefit retirement plan,** pays lifetime monthly annuity payments to retirees based on a predetermined formula, usually in the form of annuity payments to retirees. It is commonly called a "pension" or a "final-average plan." A **pension** is a sum of money paid regularly as a retirement benefit. Pensions are paid to retirees, and sometimes their survivors, by the Social Security Administration, various government agencies, and some employers. Defined-benefit plans were the "standard" a generation ago, but today they are offered by less than one-fifth of employers, primarily because 401(k) retirement plans are less costly to provide employees.

Benefits in defined-benefit plans are based on the years of service at the employer, average pay in the last few working years, and a percentage. For example, an employee might have a defined annual retirement benefit of 2 percent multiplied by the number of years of service and multiplied by the average annual income during the last five years of employment. In this example, a worker with 20 years' service and an average income of $48,000 over the last five years of work would have an annual benefit of $19,200 (20 × 0.02 × $48,000), or $1600 per month. In another example, an employee with 30 years of service might qualify for 60 percent of the average income over the last five years of work. With a $48,000 average salary over those five years, this worker might receive $28,800 annually, or $2400 per month.

Since the employer contributes all the money, it assumes all the investment risks associated with creating sufficient funds to pay future benefits. Some employers offer both defined-benefit and defined-contribution plans to their employees. Vesting requirements and participant rights are the same for all retirement plans offered by an employer.

Normal or Early Retirement?

The earlier you retire, the smaller your monthly retirement pension from a defined-benefit plan will be because you will likely receive income for more years as a retired person. To illustrate, assume you are eligible for a full retirement pension of $28,800 per year at age 65. Your benefit may be reduced 5 percent per year if you retire at age 58 or reduced 3 percent per year if you retire at age 62. Smaller monthly pension payments are paid to the early retiree in a defined-benefit plan so that he or she will receive, in theory, the same present value amount of benefits as the person who retires later.

The financial advantage of taking early retirement depends in part on the person's life expectancy and the rate at which benefits are reduced. People who expect to live for a shorter period than the average expectancy may achieve a better financial position by retiring early. Most employees are allowed to work for as long as they choose, but companies generally do not increase benefits for employees who postpone retirement beyond age 65.

Disability and Survivors Benefits

Survivors and disability benefits also represent concerns for workers who have spouses or children or are financially responsible for caring for others. A person's full retirement pension forms the basis for any benefits paid to survivors and, when part of a retirement plan, for disability benefits as well. **Disability benefits** can be paid to employees who become disabled prior to retirement. People receiving either survivors or disability benefits are entitled to an amount that is substantially less than the full retirement amount. For example, if you were entitled to a retirement benefit of $2000 per month, your disability benefit might be only $1100 per month.

If a survivor is entitled to benefits that pension amount must be paid over two people's lives instead of a single person's life; consequently, the monthly payment is different. Using the benefit described in the preceding example, if your surviving spouse is five years older than you, he or she might be entitled to $1300 per month. In contrast, if your spouse is five years younger, he or she might be entitled to only $900 per month.

A qualified **joint and survivor benefit** (or **survivor's benefit**) is an annuity whose payments continue to the surviving spouse after the participant's death, often equal to at least 50 percent of the participant's benefit. This requirement can be waived if desired, but only after marriage—not in a prenuptial agreement. Federal law dictates that a spouse or ex-spouse who qualifies for benefits under the plan of a spouse or former spouse must agree in writing to a waiver of the spousal benefit. This **spousal consent requirement** protects the interests of surviving spouses. If the spouse does waive his or her survivor benefits, the worker's retirement benefit will increase. Upon the worker's death, the spouse will not receive any survivor benefits when a waiver has been signed. Unless a spouse has his or her own retirement benefits, it is usually wise to keep the spousal benefit.

disability benefits
Substantially reduced benefits paid to employees who become disabled prior to retirement.

joint and survivor benefit/survivor's benefit
Annuity whose payments continue to a surviving spouse after the participant's death; often equals at least 50 percent of participant's benefit.

spousal consent requirement
Federal law that protects surviving rights of spouse or ex-spouse to retirement or pension benefits unless the person signs a waiver of those rights.

Cash-Balance Plan—A Hybrid Employer-Sponsored Retirement Deal

cash-balance plan
Defined-benefit plan funded solely by an employer that gives each participant an interest-earning account credited with a percentage of pay on a monthly basis.

Some employers have established or amended their existing retirement plans to create a third type of employer-sponsored retirement plan, a hybrid of the defined-contribution and defined-benefit plans. A **cash-balance plan** is a defined-benefit plan that gives each participant an interest-earning account credited with a percentage of pay on a monthly basis. It is distinguished by the "balance of money" in an employee's account at any point in time. The employer contributes 100 percent of the funds and the employees contribute nothing. The employer contributes a straight percentage of perhaps 5 percent of the employee's salary every payday to his or her specific cash-balance account. Interest on cash-balance accounts is credited at a rate (perhaps 5 percent) guaranteed by the employer, and the employer assumes all the investment risk. As a result, the amount in the account grows at a regular rate. Employees can look ahead 5 or 25 years and calculate how much money will be in their account.

Vesting requirements for cash-balance plans are the same as those for other employer-sponsored retirement plans. At separation from employment or retirement, the vested employee has the right to all money in the account.

Many large employers are shifting to cash-balance retirement plans in part because they are often much less costly to administer. Cash-balance plans are controversial because when substituted for a defined-benefit plan, they typically give older workers smaller benefits. Recognizing this concern, many cash-balance plans now provide a higher contribution, sometimes as large as 10 percent, for those employees age 55 and older. Younger workers who are more inclined to move from job to job may appreciate a benefit that can move with them, rather than one that offers a substantial payout only after decades of job loyalty.

Only the defined-benefit retirement pension program brings a guaranteed monthly pension benefit, early retirement supplements, survivor annuities, and disability benefits. Cash-balance and 401(k) plans do not. Participants in the latter plans will need to tap into their retirement accounts to pay for disability and survivor needs, if necessary.

Did You Know?

Retirement Plan Insurance

ERISA established the Pension Benefit Guaranty Corporation (PBGC; www.pbgc.gov). Defined-benefit pension plans pay insurance premiums to the PBGC, which guarantees a certain minimum amount of benefits to eligible workers whose employers' plans are not financially sound enough to pay their obligations. The PBGC has taken over about 3500 plans. PBGC insurance never insures defined-contribution plans, but it does insure some cash-balance plans.

Additional Employer-Sponsored Retirement Plans

Some employers offer supplemental savings plans to employees.

employee stock-ownership plan (ESOP)
Benefit plan in which employers make tax-deductible gifts of company stock into trusts, which are then allocated into employee accounts.

ESOP   An **employee stock-ownership plan (ESOP)** is a benefit plan through which the employer makes tax-deductible gifts of company stock into a trust, which are then allocated into accounts for individual employees. When employees leave the company, they get their shares of stock and can sell them. In effect, the retirement fund consists of stock in the company. If the company prospers over time, the employees will own some valuable stock; if the company does poorly or goes bankrupt, the stock may be worthless. (Note that an ESOP is not an employee stock option, examined in Chapter 14, page 421, as an ESO is a gift, like a bonus, from an employer to an employee that allows employees to benefit from the appreciation of their employer's stock without putting any money down.)

To be properly diversified, experts recommend that employees have no more than 10 percent of their retirement assets invested in their employer's company stock. The *Pension Protection Act* provides that companies cannot require that you buy company stock to qualify for a match. If your contributions continue to be matched with stock, you are able to trade out of those shares after three years. If you already own company shares, you can sell a third at a time, over three years.

Profit-Sharing Plan A **profit-sharing plan** is an employer-sponsored plan that shares some of the profits with employees in the form of end-of-year cash or common stock contributions to employees' 401(k) accounts. The level of contributions made to the plan may reflect each person's performance as well as the level of profits achieved by the employer. Contributions might be fixed (perhaps at 10 percent of profits) or be discretionary. They can vary from year to year. Some companies offer a voluntary profit-sharing plan through which employees can regularly purchase shares of stock in the company at discounted prices.

profit-sharing plan
Employer-sponsored plan that allocates some of the employer profits to employees in the form of end-of-year cash or common stock contributions to employees' 401(k) accounts.

Withdrawing Retirement Money Early

For many people, the money accumulated in a 401(k) retirement account represents most—if not all—of their retirement savings.

Penalty-Free Withdrawals Although your employer may have rules for its retirement plan that restrict withdrawals, the IRS imposes no penalty for early withdrawals in three situations:

1. **Early retirement.** You may avoid a penalty if you are disabled or retire early and you are willing to receive annual distributions according to an IRS-approved annuity method for a time period of no less than five years. You must pay taxes on the withdrawn amount.

2. **Expenses for medical, college, and home buying.** You can make penalty-free withdrawals from an IRA account (but not an employer-sponsored plan) if you pay for medical expenses in excess of 7.5 percent of your adjusted gross income, you pay medical insurance premiums after being on unemployment for at least 12 weeks, you are disabled, you pay for qualified higher-education expenses, or the distribution of less than $10,000 is used for qualifying first-time home-buyer expenses. You may have to pay income taxes on the amount withdrawn.

3. **Account loan.** You may borrow up to half of your accumulated assets in an employer-sponsored account, not to exceed 50 percent of the balance, or $50,000, whichever is less. The borrower pays interest on the loan, which is then credited to the person's account. Loans must be repaid with after-tax money. If the employee changes employers, he or she must repay the unpaid balance of the loan within 30 days. Otherwise, the loan is reclassified as a withdrawal, which results in additional taxes and penalties. Borrowing diverts the money from its intended purpose, and the funds are no longer there to benefit from tax-deferred compounding. You may not borrow from IRA accounts.

Negative Impacts of Early Withdrawals When money is withdrawn from a tax-sheltered retirement account before the rules permit—perhaps to buy a car, take a vacation, remodel a home, or pay off a credit card debt—three bad things happen:

1. **More taxes are due to the government.** Early withdrawals—typically defined as a premature distribution before age 59½—are taxed as ordinary income. Assume William Wacky, a 35-year-old with $25,000 in a tax-sheltered retirement account, withdraws $8000 out of the account. If he pays combined federal and state income taxes at the 30 percent rate, his $8000 withdrawal must be included as part of his taxable income. That will cost him an extra $2400 ($8000 × 0.30) in income taxes.

2. **Penalties are assessed.** The IRS assesses a 10 percent penalty on early withdrawals. Because William withdrew $8000, he must also pay a penalty tax of $800 ($8000 × 0.10).

3. **The investment does not grow.** Withdrawing money means that the investment can no longer accumulate. The lost time for compounding will substantially shrink your retirement nest egg. William's withdrawal of $8000 out of the account that could have grown at 8 percent over the next 30 years costs him the forgone return of a whopping $80,502 (from Appendix A.1).

Summing up this example, William's early withdrawal of $8000 nets him only $4800 after taxes and penalties ($8000 − $2400 − $800), and he gave up a future value of more than $80,000 in his retirement account. More than 60 percent of workers age 18 to 34 take all the money out of their employer's tax-sheltered retirement account when they change jobs. Early withdrawals are unwise!

Personally Established Retirement Accounts

individual retirement account (IRA)
Personal retirement account to which a person can make annual contributions that provide tax-deferred growth and then decide how to invest the funds within the IRA.

An **individual retirement account (IRA)** is a personal retirement account to which a person can make one or more annual contributions. These accounts are created and funded at the discretion of the individual who sets them up. An IRA is much like any other account opened at a bank, credit union, brokerage firm, or mutual fund company. An IRA is not an investment but rather an account in which to hold investments, like stocks and mutual funds. You can invest IRA money almost any way you desire, including collectibles like art, gems, stamps, antiques, rugs, metals, guns, and certain coins and metals. You may change investments whenever you please.

You should consider investing in an IRA to augment your retirement savings. IRAs are similar to 401(k) plans in that you do not pay taxes each year on capital gains, dividends, and other distributions from securities held within the account. The maximum annual contribution you may make to an IRA is $5000 (which is indexed to inflation starting in 2010). An additional catch-up contribution of $1000 to an IRA may be made by people age 50 and older. You may not borrow from an IRA.

To fund the account, you may make a new contribution or transfer a lump-sum distribution received from another employer plan or another IRA account to your IRA account. Taxpayers can even opt on their tax return to allocate part or all of their refund for direct deposit into an IRA account.

traditional (regular) IRA
Account that offers tax-deferred growth; the initial contribution may be tax deductible for the year that the IRA was funded.

Traditional IRAs Shelter Investment Growth   A **traditional** (or **regular**) **IRA** offers tax-deferred growth. Your contributions may be tax deductible, which means that you can use all or part of your contributions to reduce your taxable income. Qualifying depends on how much your earnings are (restrictions exist to prevent some high-income earners from getting the deduction) and whether you and your spouse are eligible to participate in an employer-sponsored retirement plan. To see whether you qualify for a tax-deductible IRA, use the following guidelines:

1. If you have no retirement plan at work, you can invest in a traditional IRA and deduct the entire amount from your taxes.

2. If you are married and you are not an active participant in an employer retirement plan but your spouse is an active participant, you may deduct all of your contribution to a traditional IRA.

3. If you have a retirement plan at work, you may fully or partially deduct your IRA contribution only if your adjusted gross income qualifies. Also, if either spouse participates in an employer-sponsored retirement plan, the allowable contribution depends on the couple's income. The amount begins to be reduced for single taxpayers earning about $105,000 and $166,000 for joint returns.

spousal IRA
Account set up for spouse who does not work for wages; offers tax-deferred growth and tax deductibility.

4. If you have a nonworking spouse, that person may contribute to a **spousal IRA.** Each partner may invest up to the limit and deduct the full amount if the combined compensation of both spouses is at least equal to the contributed amount.

Distributions from traditional IRAs may be fully or partially taxable. If the account is funded solely by tax-deductible contributions, any distributions are fully taxable when received. If you also made nondeductible contributions, logically some amount should not be taxed at withdrawal as it has already been taxed earlier. You should maintain adequate records of all IRA contributions—even for 40 years or more—to avoid paying too much in taxes. That means saving all annual reports of account activities. The IRS requires that withdrawals from traditional IRAs begin no later than age 70½.

Roth IRAs Provide Tax-Free Income

A **Roth IRA** is a non-deductible, after-tax IRA that offers significant tax and retirement planning advantages. (Similar Roth 401(k)s and 403(b)s exist.) Contributions of up to $5000 annually to Roth IRAs are not tax deductible and funds in the account grow tax free. The maximum is indexed to inflation starting in 2010. Withdrawals are tax-free if taken at age 59½ or later (or if you are disabled) from an account held at least 5 years. Tax-free withdrawals may be made for qualifying first-time home-buyer expenses or to pay for educational expenses. Once you remove money from a Roth IRA, it is a withdrawal (not a loan), and you cannot put it back. There is no mandatory withdrawal schedule for Roth IRAs, and money in the account can pass to an heir free of estate taxes. A traditional IRA may be converted to a Roth IRA. If you are not eligible for a 401(k), consider starting a Roth or traditional IRA.

Keoghs and SEP-IRAs for Self-Employed Individuals

A **Keogh** (pronounced "Key-oh") is a tax-deferred retirement account designed for self-employed and small-business owners. Depending on the type of Keogh established (profit-sharing or money-purchase), an individual can save as much as 25 percent of self-employment earned income, with most plan contributions capped at $45,000 per participant. If the income comes from self-employment, contributions can still be made after age 70½. Money in Keoghs may be invested in real estate, and a Keogh can be converted to a SEP-IRA.

A **simplified employee pension–individual retirement account (SEP-IRA)** is a retirement savings account for sole proprietor's self-employment income and owners of small businesses looking to save only in profitable years. A SEP-IRA is easier to set up and maintain than a Keogh. The maximum contribution limit to a SEP-IRA is the same as for a Keogh. People with income from a sideline business can contribute substantial amounts to a SEP-IRA account. There also is a one-person 401(k) plan, which allows larger contributions than a Keogh or SEP-IRA plan.

Concept Check 17.5

1. Summarize the main differences between defined-contribution and defined-benefit pension plans.
2. Explain why defined-contribution retirement plans are called self-directed.
3. Offer your impressions of working for an employer that offers a sizable matching contribution compared with one that does not.
4. List three differences between a traditional IRA and a Roth IRA.
5. List three negative impacts of withdrawing money early from a tax-sheltered retirement account.

Did You Know?

You Can Open a Personally Established Retirement Account Almost Anywhere

Individual retirement accounts (IRAs) offer flexibility on where you can invest. Options may include trust accounts at financial institutions, such as a bank, credit union, savings and loan association, or mutual fund. Individuals often invest in mutual funds and stocks, particularly index funds. You can change investments whenever desired. You may choose to contribute once to a tax-sheltered retirement account and then never do so again, or you can contribute regularly for many years.

Instant Message

Roth IRA or Regular IRA?

Mutual fund websites provide worksheets to help you decide (in five minutes) whether a traditional IRA or a Roth IRA is best for you. See www.troweprice.com, www.kiplinger.com, or www.fidelity.com. These calculations will be based on your current age, current marginal tax rate, expected annual yield, years to retirement, years in retirement, and marginal income tax rate during the distribution years.

Instant Message

Where to Invest Extra Retirement Money

The best place to invest for retirement is in a 401(k) plan. Once you have earned the full company match, put extra money into a Roth IRA.

Roth IRA
IRA funded with after-tax money (and thus it is not tax deductible) that grows on a tax-deferred basis; withdrawals are not subject to taxation.

Keogh
Tax-deferred retirement account designed for self-employed and small-business owners.

Use Financial Advice and Monte Carlo Simulations

6 Learning Objective

Make use of professional investment advisors and Monte Carlo simulations when deciding on how to invest for retirement.

Two strategies are available when investing for retirement. Active investors can choose to manage their retirement portfolio, following a "do-it-yourself" approach. Passive investors, or "hands-off" investors, can put their retirement assets in an index fund or target-date retirement fund (both discussed in Chapter 15) or hire a professional to make the decisions. Professional advice for retirement assets is available, and advisers often use Monte Carlo simulations to help guide their recommendations.

Investment Advice for Retirement Assets

If you are just starting out in a 401(k) or have no other retirement assets, you might invest in a low-fee **target-date retirement fund** at a lower cost. (See Chapter 15.) These funds are the ultimate in disciplined, hands-off investing as you pick a date that matches the year you plan to retire. You get a diversified portfolio that automatically shifts the asset mix away from equities and toward more conservative fixed-income investments as you approach the year of your retirement.

A lot of people do not want to manage their own retirement assets. Employers who offer 401(k) accounts often make available to employees direct one-on-one financial investment advice to plan participants. For a fee, an outside professional investment manager can design a portfolio of mutual funds for you based upon those available within your 401(k) plan. An adviser also can rebalance your investments to keep the desired asset mix on track. Recommendations consider all one's retirement assets, including those of a spouse or significant other, not just money in a 401(k) account. Annual fees should be no more than one-third of 1 percent of your assets.

It is critical when accumulating funds for retirement to be well diversified and to rebalance your portfolio at least once a year. During the stock market crash of 2008–2009 the S&P 500 dropped 52 percent. In contrast, a portfolio that remained well-diversified had a positive return of over 5 percent annually from 1999 through 2008.

Did You Know?

The Top 3 Financial Missteps in Retirement Planning

People slip up in retirement planning when they do the following:

1. Starting to save for retirement in their thirties, or worse, their forties
2. Putting away too little money
3. Using mutual funds with high expense ratios for their 401(k) or IRA accounts

Did You Know?

Why You Should Avoid "High-Cost" Mutual Funds

Investing for retirement in low-cost or ultra-low-cost funds, such as an index fund or exchange-traded fund, is the single most effective strategy to fatten your retirement nest egg. The following calculations are based on research from T. Rowe Price and *Money*. Assume you are 30 years old, earn $40,000, and invest 6 percent of your salary with a $0.50 match on $1.00. Your salary increases 3 percent annually and your investments earn 8 percent a year. Low mutual fund expenses dramatically increase your retirement nest egg.

Cost of Mutual Fund Expenses	Retirement Nest Egg at Age 65
High expenses (1.5%)	$664,000
Moderate expenses (1.0%)	$732,000
Low expenses (0.5%)	$819,000
Ultra-low expenses (0.25%)	$852,000

Monte Carlo Simulations to Help Guide Retirement Investment Decisions

Employer-based financial advice must follow the requirements of the Pension Protection Act, including keeping employees informed about any possible conflicts of interest. The advice must be based on computer simulations of projected investment performance. Monte Carlo simulations are an evolution of the long-term investment strategy of asset allocation, as discussed in Chapter 13 (see pages 398–399).

Monte Carlo simulations, named for the famous casino site, can be used to model the performance of hundreds or even thousands of individual mutual funds and stocks through thousands of fluctuating securities markets. The simulations allow you to estimate the probability of reaching your financial goals. This sophisticated application of asset allocation identifies the investor's acceptable level of risk tolerance and then finds an optimal portfolio of assets that will have the highest expected returns for that level of risk.

The mathematical simulations are based on long-term historical risk and return characteristics for various mixes of stock, bond, and short-term investment asset classes. Each simulation estimates how much you need to save if your investments performed better or worse than expected, and it gives the odds that your assets will last throughout the retirement time period after you choose a given set of investments and establish a withdrawal amount. Note that these calculations are probabilities, not certainties.

By using Monte Carlo simulations, investors can get a more realistic view of how much their current investments may yield in retirement. Investors may learn that they are playing it too safe by investing too conservatively, and this may prevent them from reaching their goals. By evaluating the trade-offs among various combinations of retirement plan contribution levels, diverse investment mixes, overall portfolio risk, projected retirement age, and retirement income goals, Monte Carlo simulations let you understand how certain changes in these factors will affect the chance that you will have enough money in retirement. Some investors may have to learn to be comfortable with increased risk while others may have to save more or work longer. See Figure 17.2 for illustrative Monte Carlo calculations.

Monte Carlo simulations
Mathematical calculations that can be used to find an optimal portfolio of mutual funds and stocks that will have the highest expected returns for a certain level of risk.

Did You Know?

How to Invest Your 401(k) Money

When you sign up for your 401(k) plan at work, your employer will have established a number of investment vehicles from which you must choose. These are usually arranged through one or two mutual fund companies. You will likely have a stock fund, a growth stock fund, an index fund, a bond fund, and a money market fund at a minimum. In addition, you will likely be able to invest in your own company's stock and in an annuity. What should you choose for your contributions?

You should allocate no more than 10 percent to your company's stock because of the need to diversify. Similarly, you should not have more than 10 percent going into a money market fund because its returns are too low to build the financial nest egg you will need. Annuities, if desired, may be purchased with your money when you retire, so you should wait until then to make that decision. So that leaves various stock and bond funds.

A young, risk-tolerant, long-term 401(k) investor with an aggressive investment philosophy might have a portfolio with 100 percent in a growth stock fund. A more moderate approach might have a stock fund/bond fund/money market fund portfolio allocated 60/30/10 percent, respectively. As a young investor, you do not need to be conservative with your retirement money because you will have the time to ride out the ups and downs of the stock market. You can keep the same proportions of your asset allocation until your broad investment goals change—possibly not for another 25 or 30 years as you approach retirement.

Figure 17.2
Monte Carlo Simulation from Financial Engines

(The analysis and recommendations pictured are hypothetical and are provided for illustrative purposes only. This illustration should not be relied on for investment advice.)

Source: Copyright © Financial Engines. Used with permission.

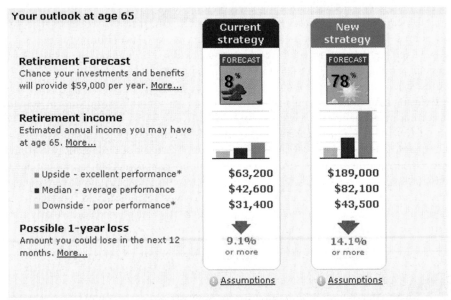

You're on track!

The Forecast for your new strategy looks good! Click the **Next** button to receive your Advice Action Kit.

Your decisions		
	Current	New
Your contribution	$3,400/year	$6,100/year
Employer contribution	$1,300/year	$1,300/year
Your investments	Current	Advice
Your risk level	Mod. conserv.(0.82)	Mod. aggr.(1.25)
Retirement age	65	67
Desired income	$59,000	$59,000
Minimum income	$42,000	$42,000

Your outlook at age 65

	Current strategy	New strategy
Retirement Forecast Chance your investments and benefits will provide $59,000 per year. More...	FORECAST 8%	FORECAST 78%
Retirement income Estimated annual income you may have at age 65. More...		
■ Upside - excellent performance*	$63,200	$189,000
■ Median - average performance	$42,600	$82,100
▪ Downside - poor performance*	$31,400	$43,500
Possible 1-year loss Amount you could lose in the next 12 months. More...	9.1% or more	14.1% or more
	Assumptions	Assumptions

*Note: There is a 5% chance you'll have less than the downside amount and a 5% chance you'll have more than the upside amount. Amounts shown are in pre-tax dollars and have been adjusted for inflation.

Your personalized investment advice is based on your decisions. How we created your investment advice.

Investment advice	Current strategy	New strategy
401(k) Account		
Redwood Money Market	5%	0%
Platinum Growth	17%	10%
Cypress Balanced Fund	11%	0%
Maple Bond Market	13%	13%
Sequoia Small Cap	25%	0%
Granite S&P 500 Index	29%	30%
Silver Growth and Income	0%	23%
Chestnut Idx:500 Idx	0%	24%

Software programs can be used to assist investors in creating an efficient portfolio using Monte Carlo simulations. Products are available from Financial Engines, Morningstar, Vanguard, and Financial Soundings. Many employers offer free or low-cost access to MPT software as an employee benefit (such as less than $15 annually through Financial Soundings [http://www.financialsoundings.com/]). Services might include retirement forecasts, annual report on progress toward retirement, portfolio monitoring, e-newsletters, and information on finances and investing. To try out interactive Monte Carlo simulations, see www.moneychimp.com/articles/risk/riskintro.htm.

When you take the appropriate retirement planning action steps, including a moderate amount of risk when investing, you will be able to relax with the confidence that you are making wise decisions about your investment assets and the knowledge that your money will grow and will be there to fund your lifestyle during the last third of your life.

Did You Know?

How to Recover from a Stock Market Crash

If you had $10,000 or $20,000 and lost half of it in a stock market crash, that amount can be saved again in a few years. However, if you lost $80,000 or more, the only way to recover is to start contributing more to your portfolio.

 Concept Check 17.6

1. Do you visualize yourself as a "do-it-yourself" or as a "hands-off" type of investor of retirement funds? Tell why.
2. Summarize the importance of low-cost mutual fund fees to long-term investing success.
3. Offer some impressions of Monte Carlo simulations as a tool to use in retirement planning.

Living in Retirement Without Running Out of Money

Once you have accumulated a substantial retirement nest egg, congratulate yourself. For many years you sacrificed spending and invested instead. Now your task is to plan your finances so you—and perhaps a significant other—can live during retirement without the

7 Learning Objective

Describe techniques for living in retirement without running out of money.

Planning an active retirement can include working part-time at something you enjoy.

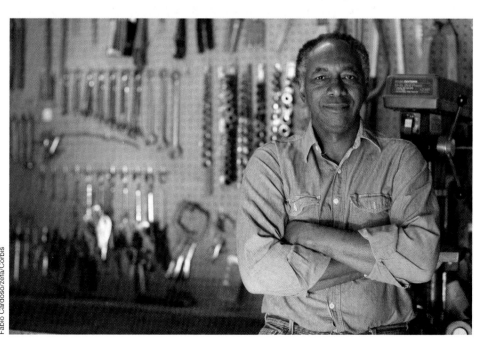

Fabio Cardoso/zefa/Corbis

worry of running out of money. To do so, you carefully manage your retirement account withdrawals, consider purchasing an annuity with a portion of your retirement funds, and/or work part-time during your early retirement years.

Figure Out How Many Years Your Money Will Last in Retirement

"How long will my retirement nest egg last?" The answer to this question depends on three factors: (1) the amount of money in the retirement nest egg, (2) the rate of return earned on the funds, and (3) the amount of money withdrawn from the account each year.

Appendix A.4 provides factors that can be divided into the money in a retirement fund to determine the amount available for spending each year. Consider the example of Kevin and Kelly Neu, 58-year-old retirees from Albuquerque, New Mexico, who want their $250,000 retirement nest egg to last 20 years, assuming that it will earn a 6 percent annual return in the future. The present value factor in the table in the "20 years" column and the "6 percent" row in Appendix A.4 is 11.4699. Dividing $250,000 by 11.4699 reveals that Kevin and Kelly could withdraw $21,796, or $1816 per month ($21,796 ÷ 12 months), for 20 years before the fund was depleted. But what if they live for 30 more years? The factor for 30 years is 13.7648, and the answer is $18,162, or $1513 per month. Table 17.4 indicates how long retirement money will last given certain withdrawal rates.

A slightly higher rate of withdrawal can significantly decrease your years of retirement income. For example, a portfolio of $1 million with a 4 percent annual withdrawal rate could provide 20-plus more years of retirement income than the same portfolio with a 5 percent annual withdrawal rate. People planning for retirement should be cautious and withdraw at a rate, perhaps 3½ to 4 percent, that is not likely to deplete their funds too rapidly. Then they can be more confident that their money will last the desired number of years.

Buy an Annuity and Receive Monthly Checks

annuity
Contract made with an insurance company that provides for a series of payments to be received at stated intervals (usually monthly) for a fixed or variable time period.

Rather than continuing to manage their own investments during retirement and make planned withdrawals over the years, some people take a portion of their retirement nest egg (such as one-third or one-half) to buy an annuity. An **annuity** is a contract made with an insurance company that provides for a series of payments to be received at stated intervals (usually monthly) for a fixed or variable time period. For retirees who buy an annuity, this

Table 17.4   How Long Will the Retirement Money Last?

The higher your withdrawal rate, the more likely it is that your portfolio will not last until you die. The basis for the following calculations is research by T. Rowe Price, Vanguard, and other online retirement planning websites. Here are the rates of withdrawals and the likelihood that a diversified portfolio earning a long-term historical rate of return will last through retirement, assuming 3 percent annual increases in withdrawals for inflation.

Withdrawal Rate Amount	Years in Retirement		
	20	30	40
3%	99%	99%	93%
4%	99%	86%	68%
5%	93%	61%	41%
6%	74%	35%	18%

means that an insurance company will manage a lump sum of their retirement nest egg and promise to send monthly distribution payments according to an agreed-upon schedule, usually for the life of the person covered by the annuity (the **annuitant**).

Immediate Annuity

This is best accomplished by purchasing an **immediate annuity** with a single payment during retirement. The income payments will then begin at the end of the first month after purchase. People who buy an immediate annuity typically do so with a lump sum of money rolled over from an IRA, from an employer's defined-contribution retirement account, from the cash-value or death benefit of a life insurance policy, or from other savings and investments.

Income Options

Annuities offer several options for drawing down the funds used to purchase the annuity. In the following examples of hypothetical income payments, assume that a 70-year-old retiree has purchased an annuity for $100,000. A **straight annuity** might provide a lifetime income of perhaps $790 monthly for the rest of the life of the annuitant only. An **installment-certain annuity** might provide a payment of $680 monthly for the rest of the life of the annuitant with a guarantee that if the person dies before receiving a specific number of payments his or her beneficiary will receive a certain number of payments for a particular time period (such as ten years in this example). A **joint-and-survivor annuity** might provide $640 monthly for as long as one of the two people—usually a husband and wife—is alive.

The purchase of an annuity can involve a variety of high sales commissions and fees, and, as such, they can substantially reduce the amount of income paid out. Annual expense ratios can range as low as 0.34 percent to 0.65 percent or higher. The trade-off is between the guaranteed payouts from an annuity that often carry high costs and the high risks of managing one's retirement investments. Those considering buying an annuity perhaps might begin with the AAA-rated, low-fee industry leader TIAA-CREF.

Variable and Deferred Annuities

A common type of annuity sold by insurance salespeople is called a **variable annuity.** This is an annuity whose value rises and falls like mutual funds, and it pays a limited death benefit via an insurance contract. Variable annuities are sold very aggressively because sellers earn commissions of 5 percent or more, and they charge annual fees that often average 3 percent or more. An investor will have to wait 15 to 20 years before an annuity becomes as efficient an investment as a mutual fund. Variable annuities are not a practical investment for 99 percent of investors. Another type of annuity is a **deferred annuity.** Here the person pays premiums during his or her life and income payments start at some future date, such as at retirement.

Employers Offer Annuities

Some employers who offer employees a 401(k) plan rather than a pension are giving them another way to collect a guaranteed paycheck. A **fixed-deferred annuity** provides that part of your 401(k) contribution buys a dollar amount of annuitized retirement income. Converting 20% or so of your retirement savings into a predictable source of income can keep you from outliving your money.

People should absolutely, positively not consider investing in an annuity until *all* other tax-sheltered vehicles to save and invest for retirement have been maximized. This means that people saving for retirement first contribute the legally permitted maximum amounts to 401(k), traditional IRA, and Roth IRA accounts, perhaps totaling $20,000 each year. The tax-sheltered benefits of these retirement accounts are far better than those offered by

Did You Know?

Tax Consequences in Retirement Planning

Tax-deferred retirement plans, like 401(k) plans and traditional IRAs, provide these benefits:

- Your contributions are tax deductible and are not subject to federal, state, and local income taxes.
- No income taxes are due on any earnings on the assets until withdrawn.
- Withdrawals are subject to income taxes at your marginal tax rate, which in retirement may be lower than your tax rate today.
- Other retirement income, such as from Social Security, pensions, employment, interest, dividends, and capital gains, is subject to income taxes.
- When you die, any beneficiary may choose to roll your 401(k) assets into his or her IRA tax free.

immediate annuity
Annuity, often funded by a lump sum from the death benefit of a life insurance policy or lump sum from a defined-contribution plan, that begins payments one month after purchase.

straight annuity
Provides lifetime payments for the life of the annuitant only.

joint-and-survivor annuity
Provides monthly payments for as long as one of the two people—usually a husband and wife—is alive.

variable annuity
Annuity whose value rises and falls like mutual funds and pays a limited death benefit via an insurance contract. Not as efficient as a mutual fund; costs are high for little return.

deferred annuity
Annuity plan in which annuitants pay premiums during their working lives, then take income payments at some future date, such as retirement.

Do It NOW!

Wise financial planners begin saving for retirement right away after beginning their careers. Start today by:

1. Calculating your retirement savings amount at both age 60 and 67 based on your projected income following graduation.

2. Deciding tentatively whether you would invest retirement saving in an employer-sponsored plan or a personally established tax-sheltered retirement account.

3. Thinking about the types of mutual funds you will use to invest for retirement as mutual funds will be the primary sources available to you.

a salesperson promoting a deferred annuity. Annuities are replete with numerous restrictions, administrative charges, commissions, purchase fees, withdrawal charges, and penalties. If you need life insurance, buy term life insurance, not an annuity; if you need to save for retirement, invest in mutual funds through tax-sheltered retirement accounts.

Consider Working Part-Time

For a variety of reasons, including reducing the worry of outliving one's retirement income, instead of retiring completely, some people choose to work part-time for a while during their early retirement years. They either continue working for their last employer or go to work part-time for a new employer. Reasons include wanting the extra income, enjoying being with coworkers, and obtaining employer-provided health care benefits. Predictions are that many retirees will work part-time if for no other reason than to continue to feel active and be a contributing member of society.

Concept Check 17.7

1. Use Appendix A.4 to calculate how much could be withdrawn each year from a $900,000 retirement nest egg earning 5 percent if you wanted the nest egg to last 20 years? How much less could be withdrawn so that the nest egg lasts 25 years?

2. Offer some positive and negative observations on the wisdom of buying an annuity with all or some of your retirement nest egg money when you retire.

What Do You Recommend NOW?

Now that you have read the chapter on retirement and estate planning, what do you recommend to Maryanne and Bob Johnson in the case at the beginning of the chapter regarding:

1. The major steps in the process to determine the amount of Maryanne and Bob's retirement savings goal?

2. How Bob's net income could be invested in a personal tax-sheltered retirement account?

3. The kinds of investment accounts into which they might put additional money over the next 23 years if they determined they needed $1 million to meet their retirement savings goal?

4. The investment strategies that Maryanne and Bob might follow for accumulating their retirement funds?

Big Picture Summary of Learning Objectives

1 Recognize that you are solely responsible for funding your retirement and must sacrifice some current spending and invest for your future lifestyle.

The responsibility of investing for retirement and the risk of making poor investments have been shifted from the employer to the employee. You are solely responsible for meeting your retirement needs, which may include health care costs.

2 Estimate your Social Security retirement income benefit.

The Social Security program is funded through FICA taxes on employees and employers, and the amounts withheld are put into trust fund accounts from which benefits are paid to current program recipients. Congress is expected to take action to maintain the solvency of the Social Security program. You must be fully insured under the Social Security program before retirement benefits can be paid.

3 Calculate your estimated retirement savings needs in today's dollars.

Your retirement nest egg is the total amount of accumulated savings and investments needed to support your desired retirement. This is calculated by projecting your annual retirement expenses and income and determining the amount of annual savings you need to set aside in today's dollars to achieve your retirement goal.

4 Understand why you should save for retirement within tax-sheltered retirement accounts.

Saving in tax-sheltered retirement accounts has tax advantages. Your contributions may be tax deductible and earnings may be tax deferred; thus, you can accumulate more money for retirement.

5 Distinguish among the types of employer-sponsored and personally established tax-sheltered retirement plans.

The three major types of employer-sponsored retirement plans are defined-contribution, defined-benefit, and cash-balance. Some employers make matching contributions to their employees' accounts. To receive benefits, an employee must be vested in an employer-sponsored retirement plan. You also may be able to contribute to personally established tax-sheltered retirement plans, such as an IRA or Roth IRA.

6 Make use of professional investment advisors and Monte Carlo simulations when deciding on how to invest for retirement.

Employers often provide financial advice for retirement assets, and the advice must be based in part on Monte Carlo simulations. These calculations allow you to estimate the probability of reaching your financial goals.

7 Describe techniques for living in retirement without running out of money.

Your choices at retirement are to carefully manage your retirement account withdrawals, consider purchasing an annuity with a portion of your retirement funds, and/or work part-time during your early retirement years. There are tables and techniques to calculate how long your money will last.

Let's Talk About It

1. **Retirement Investing Today.** What are your thoughts on this comment? "Younger workers today face some serious challenges in deciding where to invest their retirement funds."

2. **Why Calculate.** Do you know anyone who has estimated his or her retirement savings goal in today's dollars? Offer two reasons why many people do not perform those calculations. Offer two reasons why it would be smart for people to determine a financial target.

3. **Roth or Traditional IRA.** If you go to work for an employer that does not sponsor a retirement plan, which kind of personal retirement account would you establish? A traditional IRA or a Roth IRA? Give two reasons to support your response. How much money do you think could accumulate in the account before retirement?

4. **Help People Plan.** What kinds of people do you think are likely to not plan ahead and save for retirement in a tax-sheltered account? What might be done to help those people prepare for retirement?

5. **Retirement Planning Mistakes.** Of all the mistakes that people make when planning for retirement, which one might be likely to negatively affect your retirement planning? Give two reasons why.

6. **How to Invest.** If you had $10,000 in your employer's 401(k) plan retirement account, explain how you would invest these funds. Tell why.

Do the Math

1. **Tax-Sheltered Returns.** Timothy Clum, of Brookline, Massachusetts, is in the 25 percent tax bracket and is considering the tax consequences of

investing $2000 at the end of each year for 30 years, assuming that the investment earns 8 percent annually.

(a) How much will the account total if the growth in the investment remains sheltered from taxes?

(b) How much will the account total if the investments are not sheltered from taxes? (Hint: Use Appendix A.3 or the *Garman/Forgue* companion website.)

2. **Withdrawal Amount.** Over the years, Kyle and Erica Paget, of Clyde, North Carolina, have accumulated $200,000 and $220,000, respectively, in their employer-sponsored retirement plans. If the amounts in their two accounts earn a 6 percent rate of return over Kyle and Erica's anticipated 20 years of retirement, how large an amount could be withdrawn from the two accounts each month? Use the *Garman/Forgue* companion website or Appendix A.4 to make your calculations.

3. **Withdrawal Amount.** Kyle Paget from Question 2 is an aggressive investor *and* lucky. Assume that his $200,000 retirement nest egg will earn 8 percent while his wife Erica's investments earn 6 percent. How large an amount could be withdrawn from the two funds each month over the next 20 years? Use the *Garman/Forgue* companion website or Appendix A.4 to make your calculations.

4. **Savings Amount Needed.** Christine and Nathan Riley, of Coon Rapids, Minnesota, desire an annual retirement income of $40,000. They expect to live for 30 years past retirement. Assuming that the couple could earn a 3 percent after-tax and after-inflation rate of return on their investments, what amount of accumulated savings and investments would they need? Use Appendix A.4 or the *Garman/Forgue* companion website to solve for the answer.

5. **Annual Earnings.** Alicia and Juan Selenas, of Youngwood, Pennsylvania, hope to sell their large home for $280,000 and retire to a smaller residence valued at $150,000. After they sell the property, they plan to invest the $130,000 in equity ($280,000 − $150,000, omitting selling expenses) and earn a 4 percent after-tax return. Approximately how much annual income will be earned? Use Appendix A.4 or the *Garman/Forgue* companion website to solve for the answer.

6. **Twins Invest.** Kathryn Ake, of Fulton, New York, plans to invest $3000 in a mutual fund for the next 25 years to accumulate savings for retirement. Her twin sister, Kristin, plans to invest the same amount for the same length of time in the same mutual fund. Instead of investing with after-tax money, Kristin will invest through an employer-sponsored retirement plan. If both mutual fund accounts provide an 8 percent rate of return, how much more will Kristin have in her retirement account after 40 years? How much will Kristin have if she also invests the amount saved in income taxes?

Assume both women pay income taxes at a 25 percent rate. Use Appendix A.3 or the *Garman/Forgue* companion website to solve for the answer.

7. **Total Sum Accumulated.** Jenna Cowley, of Seguin, Texas, is currently putting 9 percent per year into her tax-sheltered employer-sponsored retirement plan at work. Jenna's employer matches $0.50 for each $1 that each employee contributes to his or her retirement account on amounts Jenna deposits up to 6 percent of her salary. Jenna's annual salary is $70,000. How much will Jenna accumulate after 28 years if her annual investments plus the employer's contributions grow at a 7 percent rate of return? How can Jenna protect herself from inflation in this plan? Use Appendix A.3 or the *Garman/Forgue* companion website to solve for the answer.

8. **More Aggressive Investing.** Cliff Wong, of Livonia, Michigan, wants to invest $4000 annually for his retirement 30 years from now. He has a conservative investment philosophy and expects to earn a return of 3 percent in a tax-sheltered account. If he took a more aggressive investment approach and earned a return of 5 percent, how much more would Cliff accumulate? Use Appendix A.3 or the *Garman/Forgue* companion website to solve for the answer.

Financial Planning Cases

Case 1
Estimating Early and Normal Retirement Benefits

Patrick Dietrick of Murfreesboro, Tennessee, age 37, is single and is making belated plans for his retirement from employment in state government. Based on his family's medical history he thinks he should base his plan on assuming he will live to age 85. He wants to maintain his current lifestyle without "scrimping" but still wants to actively save more for his retirement to take advantage of compounding. Currently, Patrick earns $44,000 per year, with an adjusted gross income of $43,000 and an after-tax income of $33,000. He anticipates receiving $10,000 from Social Security annually and $14,000 per year in a defined-benefit pension upon his retirement at age 67. If he retires at age 62, his pension benefits will be lowered to approximately $11,000. To date, Ben has about $10,000 in investments.

(a) Using the Run the Numbers worksheet on page 515, calculate the additional amount of annual savings that Patrick needs to set aside to reach his goal of retiring at age 62 with 80 percent of his current income.

(b) What amount is needed if he waits until his full benefit retirement age of 67? Use the same worksheet to solve for the answer.

(c) Why do you think the dollar amounts that Patrick will need to save are so drastically different for retiring at age 62 and at age 67?

(d) Would you recommend that Patrick invest in a traditional IRA or a Roth IRA? Why or why not?

Case 2
Calculation of Annual Savings Needed to Meet a Retirement Goal

Jessica Amberlin, age 40, single, and from Sacramento, California, is trying to estimate the amount she needs to save annually to meet her retirement needs. Jessica currently earns $30,000 per year. She expects to need 80 percent of her current salary to live on at retirement. Jessica anticipates that she will receive $800 per month in Social Security benefits. Using the Run the Numbers worksheet on page 515, answer the following questions.

(a) What annual income would Jessica need for retirement?

(b) What would her annual expected Social Security benefit be?

(c) Jessica expects to receive $500 per month from her defined-benefit pension at work. What is her annual benefit?

(d) How much annual retirement income will she need from savings?

(e) How much will Jessica need to save by retirement in today's dollars if she plans to retire at age 65 and live to age 90?

(f) Jessica currently has $5000 in a traditional IRA. Assuming a growth rate of 8 percent, what will be the value of her IRA when she retires?

(g) How much will she still need to save?

(h) What is the amount she needs to save each year to reach this goal?

Case 3
Deciding How to Invest Retirement Money

Emily Borden, from Georgetown, Delaware, recently graduated from college and started her first full-time job with a midsize company. Emily's employer offers a 401(k) defined-contribution, tax-sheltered retirement account in which she and her employer can place funds. She must select one or more options from among these seven investment choices: (1) her company's stock, (2) a low-risk bond mutual fund, (3) a growth stock fund, (4) an aggressive growth stock fund, (5) a stock index fund, (6) a money market fund, or (7) an annuity.

Into which option(s) would you suggest she invest, and indicate what percentage of the overall 100 percent of deposited funds she should put into that option. Explain the reasons for your choices.

Case 4
Victor and Maria's Retirement Plans

Victor, now age 61, and Maria, age 59, are retiring at the end of the year. Since his retail management employer changed from a defined-benefit retirement plan to a defined-contribution plan ten years ago, Victor has been contributing the maximum amount of his salary to several different mutual funds offered through the plan, although his employer never matched any of his contributions. Victor's tax-sheltered account, which now has a balance of $144,000, has been growing at a rate of 9 percent through the years. Under the previous defined-benefit plan, Victor is entitled to a single-life pension of $360 per month or a joint and survivor option paying $240 per month. The value of Victor's investment of $20,000 in Pharmacia stock eight years ago has now grown to $56,000.

Maria's earlier career as a dental hygienist provided no retirement program, although she did save $10,000 through her credit union, which was later used to purchase zero-coupon bonds now worth $28,000. Maria's second career as a pharmaceutical representative for Pharmacia allowed her to contribute about $37,000 to her retirement account over the past nine years. Pharmacia matched a portion of her contributions, and that account is now worth $130,000; its growth rate has ranged from 6 to 10 percent annually. When Maria's mother died last year, Maria inherited her home, which is rented for $900 per month; the house has a market value of $170,000. The Hernandezes' personal residence is worth $180,000. They pay combined federal and state income taxes at a 30 percent rate.

(a) Sum up the present values of the Hernandezes' assets, excluding their personal residence, and identify which assets derive from tax-sheltered accounts.

(b) Assume that the Hernandezes sold their stocks, bonds, and rental property, realizing a gain of $238,000 after income taxes and commissions. If that sum earned a 7 percent rate of return over the Hernandezes' anticipated 20 years of retirement, how large an amount could be withdrawn each month? How large an amount could be withdrawn each month if they needed the money over 30 years? How large an amount could be withdrawn each month if the proceeds earned 6 percent for 20 years? For 30 years?

(c) Victor's $144,000 and Maria's $130,000 in retirement funds have been sheltered from income taxes for many years. Summarize the advantages the couple realized by leaving the money in the tax-sheltered accounts. Offer them a rationale to keep the money in the accounts as long as possible before making withdrawals.

Case 5
The Johnsons Consider Retirement Planning

Harry Johnson's father, William, was recently forced into early retirement at age 63 because of poor health. In addition to the psychological drawbacks of the unanticipated retirement, William's financial situation is poor because he had not planned adequately for retirement. His situation has inspired Harry and Belinda to take a look at their own retirement planning. Together they now make about $72,000 per year and would like to have a similar level of living when they retire. Harry and Belinda are both 27 years old and recently received their annual Social Security Benefits Statements indicating that they could expect about $18,000 per year in today's dollars as retirement benefits at age 67. Although their retirement is a long way off, they know that the sooner they put a plan in place, the larger their retirement nest egg will be.

(a) Belinda believes that the couple could maintain their current level of living if their retirement income represented 75 percent of their current annual income after adjusting for inflation. Assuming a 4 percent inflation rate, what would Harry and Belinda's annual income need to be over and above their Social Security benefits when they retire at age 67? (Hint: Use Appendix A.1 or visit the *Garman/Forgue* companion website.)

(b) Both Harry and Belinda are covered by defined-contribution retirement plans at work. Harry's employer will contribute $1000 per year, and Belinda's employer $2000 per year in addition to the $3,240 total that Harry and Belinda can contribute. Assuming a 7 percent rate of return, what would their retirement nest egg total 40 years from now? (Hint: Use Appendix A.3 or visit the *Garman/Forgue* companion website.)

(c) For how many years would the retirement nest egg provide the amount of income indicated in Question a? Assume a 4 percent return after taxes and inflation.

(Hint: Use Appendix A.4 or visit the *Garman/Forgue* companion website.)

(d) One of Harry's dreams is to retire at age 55. What would the answers to Questions a, b, and c be if he and Belinda were to retire at that age?

(e) How would early retirement at age 55 affect the couple's Social Security benefits?

(f) What would you advise Harry and Belinda to do to meet their income needs for retirement?

On the 'Net

Go to the Web pages indicated to complete these exercises.

1. Visit the website for the Social Security Administration. There you will find a quick benefits calculator at http://www.ssa.gov/planners/calculators.htm that can be used to estimate your Social Security benefit in today's dollars. Use an income figure that approximates what you expect to earn in the first full year after graduating from college. When the calculator provides your answer, click on "break-even age" to see when you would be better off if you had waited until age 67 to begin taking benefits rather than age 62.

2. Visit the website for the U.S. Department of Labor. There you will find an article on 401(k) fees and the effects they can have on retirement savings at http://www.dol.gov/ebsa/publications/undrstndgrtrmnt.html. Develop a list of six questions that employees with a 401(k) plan might ask their employers about the fees charged under their plans.

3. Visit the website of the American Association of Retired Persons (AARP), where you will find AARP's views on how to fix the Social Security system at http://www.aarp.org/bulletin/socialsec/ss_ideas.html. How would the suggestions affect your retirement planning? Which of the suggestions would you support? Which would you oppose?

Visit the Garman/Forgue companion website . . .

www.cengage.com/finance/garman

Estate Planning

!You Must Be Kidding, Right?

Michael and Jessica have two children. In addition, Michael has a child from his previous marriage to Ashley. Unfortunately, one day a big bus hit and killed Michael. The assets in his IRA and 401(k) accounts amount to $700,000. Who is likely to get the $700,000 now that Michael has died?

A. First wife, Ashley

B. Second wife, Jessica

C. Children of first or second wife

D. Michael's mother

The answer is D, Michael's mother. Why? If Michael was like many unmarried guys starting a career who designate their mothers as the beneficiary, his mom will get all the money if he neglected to change the beneficiary and designate either of his wives or his children on his retirement accounts. Alternately, his first wife, Ashley, would get all the money if, when Michael married Jessica, he failed to fill out the form to change the beneficiary designation to his second wife. As you can see, estate tasks, such as designating beneficiaries, is not just for old people!

Learning Objectives

After reading this chapter, you should be able to:

1 Identify the ways that your estate can be transferred through contracts and a will.

2 Determine how trusts can be used to transfer assets and reduce estate taxes.

3 Summarize the benefits of preparing advance directive documents.

4 List the questions and documents needed to simplify the settlement and transfer of your estate.

5 Explain the potential impact of estate and inheritance taxes.

What Do You Recommend?

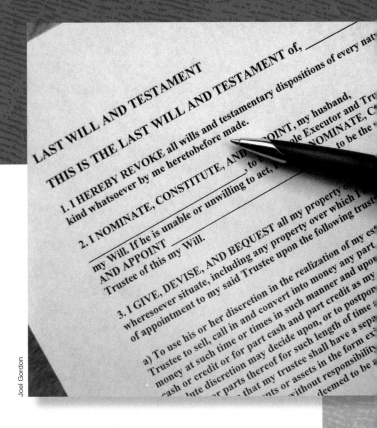

Orlando Molina, age 34, the ballet master at a professional ballet company, recently remarried after being single for several years. He shares custody of his son with his first wife. Orlando married into a ready-made family: Giselle, his new wife, who was divorced from her husband two years ago, has two children, Jamie and Jon. Like many married couples, Orlando and Giselle, who is a modern dance choreographer, have a variety of financial assets. These include bank accounts, money market accounts, mutual fund accounts, 401(k) plans, Roth IRAs, and whole life insurance policies. They also plan to buy a larger home in the near future. Soon after they returned from their honeymoon, Orlando's father, who is only 56 years of age, had a serious stroke. Despite undergoing physical therapy, he is now in a nursing home and likely will reside there for the remainder of his life. The financial and emotional impacts of the elder Mr. Molina's illness have forced Orlando and Giselle to talk about some delicate financial circumstances in their own family.

What do you recommend to Orlando and Giselle on the subject of estate planning regarding:

1. Beneficiary designations for their financial assets?
2. Joint ownership of their home, vehicles, and other property?
3. Making a will?
4. Establishing guardianship for the children?
5. Using advance directive documents to avoid a situation like that confronting Orlando's father?
6. Establishing trusts for their children?

Your Next Five Years

In the next five years you can start achieving financial success by doing the following related to estate planning:

1. Review the beneficiary and ownership designations in your life insurance policies, retirement plans, bank accounts, vehicles and other assets every three years or whenever your family situation changes, to make certain they will transfer the property according to your wishes.

2. Write your will and a letter of last instructions and revise them as major life events occur.

3. Prepare and regularly update advance directive documents so others can make the right decisions for you if you become incapacitated.

4. Discuss with your spouse or significant other your family's financial and estate plans once each year.

5. Inform one or two close family members and friends of the location of your financial records, advance directives, and will.

1 Learning Objective

Identify the ways that your estate can be transferred through contracts and a will.

estate
Your worldly possessions and financial assets less any debts you owe.

estate planning
The definite arrangements you make during your lifetime that are consistent with your wishes for the administration and distribution of your estate when you die.

probate
Court-supervised process that allows creditors to present claims against an estate and ensures the transfer of a decedent's assets to the rightful beneficiaries according to a properly executed and valid will or, when no will exists, to the people, agencies, or organizations required by state law.

Your **estate** consists of your worldly possessions and financial assets less any debts you owe. When you die all of your creditors must be notified of your death and can collect what they are owed from your estate. The remainder will be distributed to your heirs. Creditors have absolutely no legal right to collect from your surviving relatives unless the relative was also a party to the debt or a cosigner.

If you follow the guidance in this book you will spend wisely, save and invest, protect your assets and income with insurance, donate, and build and spend down a retirement nest egg. Now—not 10 or 20 years from today—is the time to think about the final financial planning task of transferring your estate to others. **Estate planning** comprises the specific arrangements you make during your lifetime for the administration and distribution of your estate when you die. Estate planning takes into consideration the needs of your survivors, making sure the greatest amount of the estate passes to the intended beneficiaries. It involves both financial and legal considerations, and a common goal is to minimize both taxes and legal expenses. Protecting and transferring your estate can be an emotional process. It is both smart and practical to take the fundamental steps while you are young and then update them as your life progresses.

How Your Estate Is Transferred

You probably will work hard over the course of your life to build a substantial estate. But, in fact, you have an estate now; however modest it might be. Pablo Picasso once said, "Only put off until tomorrow what you are willing to die having left undone." He may or may not have been thinking about estate planning but you should.

Your surviving family members do not conduct the distribution of your assets after death. The distributions are either set up by you before your death or through **probate** by which a special **probate court** allows creditors to present claims against an estate and ensures the transfer of a decedent's assets to the rightful beneficiaries. The probate court will make the distributions according to a properly executed and valid will or, when no will exists, to the people or organizations as required by state law. As you will see, there are steps you can and should take to minimize how much of your property has to be distributed by the probate court.

Most of Your Assets Can Be Set Up as Nonprobate Property

Figure 18.1 illustrates the different ways that your property can be distributed after your death. **Nonprobate property** is not transferred by the probate court. Nonprobate property includes assets transferred to survivors by contract such as by naming a beneficiary for your retirement plan or by owning assets with another person through joint tenancy with right of survivorship. Trusts (discussed in the next section) can also be used to transfer assets outside of probate court. One of the primary benefits of setting up assets as nonprobate property is time. Nonprobate property transfers immediately upon your death whereas probate can take between 4 and 18 months, or longer if there is no will. Avoiding probate court may also save money since your estate pays the cost of the probate process based on the value of the assets it must distribute. It also maintains your privacy because a public record is maintained of the probate process.★

★Visit http://www.geocities.com/athens/acropolis/6537/wills.htm to see some wills of famous people.

YOUR ENTIRE ESTATE	
Your nonprobate property is transferred at your death before your estate goes through probate court. These transfers can be implemented:	Your probate property is transferred by the probate court in accordance with:
By contracts you set up before death, such as: Beneficiary designations in life insurance and retirement plans Assets owned by joint ownership with rights of survivorship Payable-at-death clauses in bank accounts **By setting up trusts that designate who will receive the property at your death** Living trusts established while you are still alive Testamentary trusts designed to take effect at your death	**Your wishes as outlined in your will** **OR** **If you have no will, the intestate succession laws in your state**

Figure 18.1
How Your Estate
Is Distributed

Transfer Your Estate by Contracts

Described next are three ways to transfer by contract most or all of one's estate outside of probate. Transferring your estate by contract is an easy, do-it-yourself project. You just have to take a few minutes of time to fill out the appropriate forms.

1. Transfers by Beneficiary Contract Designation
The forms one fills out to open investment accounts or title certain assets often require that you name a beneficiary. Examples are IRAs, 401(k) plans, Keogh plans, bank and credit union accounts, stock brokerage accounts, mutual funds, and life and disability income insurance policies. A **beneficiary** is a person or organization designated to receive a benefit. A **beneficiary designation** is a legal form signed by the owner of an asset providing that the property goes to a certain person or organization in the event of the owner's death. The form also contains a place to designate a **contingent** (or **secondary**) **beneficiary** in case the first-named beneficiary has died. If no one has been named as beneficiary for a particular asset or if that person and a named contingent beneficiary have died, the property will go to one's estate and to probate court for distribution.

Retirement plan administrators are required by the Employee Retirement Income Security Act (ERISA) to pay benefits in the plan to the beneficiaries identified in the plan documents. Some people leave retirement savings to parents or siblings and never update the forms. Keeping your beneficiary designations current is extremely important, particularly if you become a parent or get married, divorced or remarried. If the employee dies without changing the beneficiary, an ex-spouse might inherit all of the retirement plan assets, even if state law generally views his children as the proper heirs. Divorce does not terminate an ex-spouse's status as the named beneficiary of a retirement plan or a life insurance policy even if the divorce decree says something to the contrary. The beneficiary designation itself must be changed.

2. Transfers by Property Ownership Contract Designation
Joint **tenancy with right of survivorship** (also called **joint tenancy;** see page 154) is the most common form of joint ownership, especially for husbands and wives. In this case, each person owns the whole of the asset, such as a bank account or home, and can dispose of it without the approval of the other owners. Assets owned in this way can include bank accounts,

nonprobate property
Does not go through probate; includes assets transferred to survivors by contract (such as beneficiaries listed on retirement accounts and bank accounts held with another person).

beneficiary
A person or organization designated to receive a benefit.

contingent (or secondary) beneficiary
The beneficiary in case the first-named beneficiary has died; also called the secondary beneficiary.

joint tenancy with right of survivorship/joint tenancy
Most common form of joint ownership, especially for husbands and wives, in which each person owns the whole of the asset, such as a bank account or home, and can dispose of it without the approval of the other owner(s).

Preparing a will ensures appropriate distribution of your assets upon your death.

Jim Arbogast/Getty Images

stocks, bonds, real estate, mutual funds, government bonds, and virtually any other type of asset. Upon the death of one owner, the surviving owners receive the property by operation of law rather than through the provisions of a will. Simply stated, the surviving owners owned the entire asset before the death and own all of it after death.

3. Transfers by Payable-on-Death Contract Designation

It is often impractical, undesirable, or inappropriate to own certain types of property using joint tenancy. For example, two elderly unmarried siblings might want each other to have access to funds in individual savings accounts earmarked to pay for their funerals but not have those accounts be available to the other sibling during life. They could, of course, designate each other as heirs in their wills. However, the funds would then remain tied up until the probate process is complete. To solve this dilemma, each could name the other to receive the funds upon their death using a **payable-on-death designation** for the account. With a payable-on-death bank account, the beneficiary has no rights to the funds until you pass on. Until that time, you are free to use the money kept in the bank account, to change the beneficiary, or to close the account. To access the funds, the named party would simply need to present the death certificate to the bank and show proper identification, and access to the account would be granted. The only real drawback to a payable-on-death designation is that you cannot name contingent beneficiaries on an account. An alternative could be to set up multiple accounts with payable-on-death designations for different loved ones.

Transfer the Rest of Your Estate via Your Will

Your **probate property** is simply all assets other than nonprobate property. Your probate property consists of what you owned individually and totally in your name, as well as the value of assets jointly owned through tenancy in common. In the latter case, your heirs will

payable-on-death designation
Status granted to individuals who are not joint tenants and who might need to access accounts without going through probate—the deceased signs the designation before death and the designee simply presents a death certificate to access the accounts.

probate property
All assets other than nonprobate property.

Did You Know?

How to Transfer Retirement Assets

As a condition of opening a retirement account, such as an IRA or 401(k), you are required to complete the form identifying your named beneficiary(ies) and contingent beneficiary(ies), the latter in case a primary beneficiary dies before you do. You may designate as a beneficiary a spouse, child, parent, sibling, or anyone else. Upon your death, a recipient (or his or her heirs) can choose to take the money directly or have the funds transferred into an existing or new IRA account. An IRA's tax shelter can last as long as its beneficiaries do. Transferring assets to a young child may keep the tax collector away for many years. Be certain to change your beneficiary when major life events occur, such as divorce, remarriage, or the birth of a child. Otherwise, the originally named beneficiaries (e.g., ex-spouse, ex-spouse's sister) may get the funds. Employer-based retirement plans operate in a similar manner, although typically the only beneficiary eligible to receive money is a surviving spouse.

receive your share, but not the coowner's share. A will is the smartest way to transfer your nonprobate assets upon your death. You definitely need a will unless all of your property is nonprobate property or will be transferred by contract. A will is not estate planning. It is written after all the other aspects of estate planning are completed.

Transfers with a Will Go to Your Desired Heirs

A **will** is a written document in which a person, the **testator,** tells how his or her remaining assets should be given away after death. In your will you name an **executor** (or **personal representative**). The executor identifies assets, collects any money due, pays off debts, liquidates assets, files final income tax and estate tax returns, and with the court's permission distributes the balance of any remaining money and property to the beneficiaries. Some people select a friend or relative to perform the executor's duties, whereas others name an accountant or attorney to play this role. The executor's fee for carrying out these complicated tasks ranges from 1 to 5 percent of the estate.

A simple will that is prepared by an attorney can cost $125 to $400. Minor changes in a will may be made with a **codicil** instead of revoking the existing will and writing a completely new one, as you would when making major changes. People usually know exactly what they want to do with their property, so they can use software and online programs to prepare an uncomplicated will. Examples include BuildaWill.com, Kiplinger's WILLPower, LegalZoom, and Quicken WillMaker.

If you die with a valid will, the probate court will transfer or distribute your property according to your wishes. A person who inherits or is entitled by law or by the terms of a will to inherit some asset is called an **heir.** A will that is properly drafted, signed, and witnessed is unlikely to be successfully challenged by someone who is dissatisfied with the intended distribution of assets. If you have a complicated estate, you should seek the assistance of an attorney who specializes in estate planning.

If you have minor children, you should appoint a legal **guardian** for each child in your will. This person is responsible for caring for and raising any child under the age of 18 and for managing the child's estate. The guardian should be someone who shares your values and views on child rearing. Financial columnist Michelle Singletary suggests that you might avoid as potential guardians those who are too old, too ill, or too tired from raising their own children, and those who don't really know the children. Consider naming an alternate candidate in case your first choice cannot take on this responsibility. If you have not taken steps to name a legal guardian, the court will appoint one.

will
Written document in which a person tells how his or her remaining assets should be given away after death; without a will, the property will be distributed according to state probate law.

executor/personal representative
Person responsible for carrying out the provisions of a will and managing the assets until the estate is passed on to heirs.

codicil
Legal instrument with which one can make minor changes to a will.

heir
Person who inherits or is entitled by law or by the terms of a will to inherit some asset.

guardian
Person responsible for caring for and raising any child under the age of 18 and for managing the child's estate.

Instant Message

Choose Your Executor Wisely

Your executor must be someone willing and able to do the job. The choice should not be based on emotional ties or any sense of personal obligation. The person should ideally live in the state where the will is to be probated. A legal background is not necessary but honesty and maturity are key attributes of a good executor.

letter of last instructions
Nonlegal instrument that may contain preferences regarding funeral and burial, material to be included in the obituary, and other information useful to the survivors, such as the location of important documents.

Many people prepare a **letter of last instructions** along with their will that may contain preferences regarding funeral and burial instructions, organ donation wishes, material to be included in the obituary, contact information for relatives and friends, and other information useful to the survivors, such as the location of important documents. Family members and others are not legally bound by details in a letter of last instructions but such a letter relieves them of the stress of making sometimes emotional decisions. A letter of last instructions may specify that certain pieces of jewelry or art not specified in your will that have more sentimental than monetary value are to go to specific people. If the will contains different instructions on these matters, the will prevails.

Your original will and letter of last instructions should be kept in a safe place, such as a lockable filing cabinet or home safe or at an attorney's office. Copies may be given to certain family members or friends.

Without a Will, Your Property May Not Go to Your Desired Heirs

When a person dies without a valid will, the deceased is assumed to have died **intestate.** Dying intestate can cost much more in taxes and cause legal, bureaucratic, and emotional struggles for survivors. In such a case, the probate court first ensures that the debts, income taxes, and expenses of the deceased are paid. Then, the probate court will divide all property

Did You Know?

Last Will and Testament of Harry Johnson

1 Introduction
Being of sound mind and memory, I Harry Johnson, do hereby publish this as my Last Will and Testament. I am married to Belinda Johnson, and my mother is Melinda Johnson.

2 Payment of Debts and Expenses
I hereby direct my Executor to pay my medical expenses, funeral expenses, debts, and the costs of settling my estate.

3 Distribution of Assets
I give my wife one-half of my possessions and all my personal effects. I give my mother one-quarter of my possessions. I give to Common Cause, a nonprofit organization, one-quarter of my possessions. If my wife, Belinda Johnson, predisposes me, I give her share to my mother, Melinda Johnson.

4 Simultaneous Death of Beneficiary
If any beneficiary of this Will, including any beneficiary of any trust established by this Will, other than my wife, shall die within 60 days of my death or prior to the distribution of my estate, I hereby declare that I shall be deemed to have survived such person.

5 Appointment of Executor and Guardian
I appoint my father-in-law, Martin Anderson, to be the Executor of this will and my estate, and provide if this executor is unable or unwilling to serve then I appoint the Trust Department of the Bank of America as alternate Executor. My Executor shall be authorized to carry out all provisions of this Will and pay my just debts, obligations, and funeral expenses.

6 Power of the Executor
The executor of this will has the power to receive payments, buy or sell assets, and pay debts and taxes owed on behalf of my estate.

7 Payment of Taxes
I direct my executor to pay all taxes imposed by governments.

8 Execution
In witness therefore, I hereby set my hand to this last Will and Testament, which consists of one page, this 31st day of January 2010.

9 Witness Clause
The above-named person signed in our presence and in our opinion is mentally competent.

_____	_____	_____
Witness 1	Address	Date
_____	_____	_____
Witness 2	Address	Date

and transfer assets to the legal heirs according to state law. If no surviving relatives exist (a rare situation), the estate will go to the state by **right of escheat.** Your friends and charities will get nothing.

If you die intestate, the laws in the state in which you lived prior to death determine how your property will be divided. The manner in which the assets are divided varies enormously from state to state. For example, one state might make the following distributions of a $120,000 estate: If a person with no surviving kin except a spouse dies without a will, the spouse receives the entire estate of $120,000. If the deceased had children with that spouse, the spouse takes $60,000 and the balance is divided equally between the spouse and their children. If the couple was not married, the children would get 100 percent. If the deceased also had children from another marriage, one-half of the estate goes to the spouse and the balance is divided among all his or her children. If a spouse and a parent survive the decedent, the spouse receives $60,000 and one-half of the balance, with the remainder passing to the parent.

As you can see, state laws contain a number of complex provisions that govern what constitutes a legal heir and how much (if any) of an estate an heir may be entitled to receive. What may appear least fair in the intestate distributions just described is that, if the decedent has no children, his or her spouse may be required to share the assets with a distant relative. Sadly, more than half of all adults and two-thirds of all parents with dependent children do not have wills.

intestate
When a person dies without a legal will.

Did You Know?

About Estate Planning for Unmarried Couples

It is becoming increasingly common for a couple to live together for a while before marriage. Estate planning is a must in these situations as the intestate laws in most states make no recognition of the rights of a partner whether a man and woman or of the same gender. The emphasis should be setting assets up as nonprobate property. Even with a will there are likely to be disputes between the surviving partner and the family of the deceased. Without careful estate planning the surviving partner is likely to get nothing.

Concept Check 18.1

1. What is probate, and why should people try to avoid probate court?
2. Distinguish between probate and nonprobate property.
3. Give three examples of how people transfer some estates by contract.
4. Give an example of what could happen to one's estate when one dies without a will.

Use of Trusts to Transfer Assets and Reduce Estate Taxes

Properly drawn trusts can save you and your family time, trouble, and money. These laudable objectives can be achieved only with the assistance of an experienced attorney who specializes in carefully drafting, planning, and executing strategies and techniques in estate planning.

By creating one or more trusts, portions of an estate can be transferred in a contractual manner to others in a way that avoids probate and may reduce or eliminate the federal estate tax. A **trust** is a legal arrangement between you as the **grantor** or creator of the trust and the **trustee,** the person designated to control and manage any assets in the trust. The agreement requires the trustee to faithfully and wisely manage and administer the assets to the benefit of the grantor and others. Trusts can be established to take effect during the grantor's life as well as upon his or her death.

People who should consider setting up a trust include those who have complex estates, hold relatively few liquid assets, desire privacy for their heirs, fear a battle over the provisions of a will, or live in a state with high probate costs or cumbersome probate procedures. Trusts may be created to safeguard the inheritances of survivors, reduce estate taxes, fund a child's education, provide the down payment on someone's home, provide financial assistance for minor children, manage property for young children or disabled elders, and provide income for future generations.

2 Learning Objective
Determine how trusts can be used to transfer assets and reduce estate taxes.

trust
Legal arrangement between you as the creator of the trust and the trustee, the person designated to faithfully and wisely manage any assets in the trust to your benefit and to the benefit of your heirs.

grantor
Creator of a trust—the person who makes a grant of assets to establish a trust. Also called the *settler, donor,* or *trustor.*

trustee
Person charged with carrying out the trust for the benefit of the grantor(s) and heirs.

Some of the terms associated with trusts are as follows:

- **Grantor:** The person who makes a grant of assets to establish a trust. Also called the **settler, donor,** or **trustor.**
- **Trustee:** The person or corporation to whom the property is entrusted to manage for the use and benefit of the beneficiary or beneficiaries.
- **Corpus:** The assets put into a trust. Also called the **trust estate** or **fund.**
- **Beneficiary:** The person for whose benefit a trust is created. Also called the **donee.**
- **Remainder beneficiaries:** The parties named in the trust who are to receive the corpus upon termination of the trust agreement.

Living Trusts

living trust
A trust that takes effect while the grantor is still alive.

There are two types of trusts: (1) **living trusts** that take effect while the grantor is alive and (2) testamentary trusts (see next section) that go into effect upon death.

Revocable Living Trusts

revocable living trust
Grantor maintains the right to change the trust's terms or cancel it at any time, for any reason, during his or her lifetime.

Revocable Living Trusts A **revocable living trust** is used to protect and manage a person's assets. The person creating the trust maintains the right to change its terms or cancel the trust at any time, for any reason, during his or her lifetime. Thus, living trusts often establish the grantor as the trustee. A revocable living trust can prove for the orderly management and distribution of assets if the grantor becomes incapacitated or incompetent. A new trustee can easily be named. A revocable living trust operates much like a will and proves difficult to contest. Its assets stay in the estate of the grantor at his or her death.

irrevocable living trust
Arrangement in which the grantor permanently gives up ownership and the right to control of the property, to change the beneficiaries, and to change the trustees.

Irrevocable Living Trusts An **irrevocable living trust** is an arrangement in which the grantor relinquishes ownership and control of property. Usually this involves a gift of the property to the trust. It cannot be changed or undone by the grantor during his or her lifetime. The grantor gives up three key rights under an irrevocable living trust: (1) control of the property, (2) change of the beneficiaries, and (3) change of the trustees. Because irrevocable trusts are generally considered separate tax entities, the trust pays any income taxes due. The assets in the trust bypass probate; however, transfers to a trust made within three years of death may be brought back into the decedent's estate.

 Did You Know?

Spouses Have Legal Rights to Each Other's Estates

The **partnership theory of marriage rights** is an assumption in the law that presumes that wedded couples share their fortunes equally. Thus, property acquired during the marriage and titled in the name of only one partner (other than property acquired by gift or inheritance) becomes the property of both spouses. A decedent who disinherits a surviving spouse or who leaves that person with less than a fair share of the estate is judged to have reneged on the partnership. A surviving spouse disinherited in this manner has some claim in probate court to a portion of the decedent's estate if he or she chooses to elect that option. All states give a surviving spouse the right to claim one-fourth to one-half of the other spouse's estate, no matter what a will provides. The remaining portion may pass to other heirs.

Furthermore, in states with **community property laws,*** the law assumes that the surviving spouse owns half of everything that both partners earned during the marriage, no matter how much was actually contributed by either partner and even if only one spouse held legal title to the property. States with community property laws provide the same spousal rights for marriages that end in divorce.

*Arizona, California, Idaho, Louisiana, Nevada, New Mexico, Puerto Rico, Texas, Washington, and Wisconsin.

Did You Know?

Use of a Charitable Remainder Trust to Boost Current Income

Effective use of an **irrevocable charitable remainder trust (CRT)** is popular for people who want to leave a portion of their estate to charity because it can boost one's income during the grantor's lifetime. You set up the trust and irrevocably give it assets. The trust then pays you income from the assets in the trust for a set period, usually for life, and possibly your spouse's life as well. The charity eventually receives the corpus of the CRT when you (and your spouse, if so arranged) die. For example, Amy Louisanta, a widow from Hyattsville, Maryland, increased the after-tax income on her $60,000 investment portfolio from $1000 to $4800 per year by earmarking the assets for the National Wildlife Federation.

According to her attorney, Matthew Paul, the CRT that Amy created quickly sold the assets without incurring any capital gains taxes and then reinvested the proceeds.

A CRT works well for people who show wealth on paper because of appreciated assets. The projected future value of the gift can be discounted to a present value. This amount can then be written off as a charitable contribution on Amy's current income tax return, saving her even more money. It is wise to give to a CRT because the donor can avoid capital gains taxes while still realizing the full benefit of the asset's current value.

Testamentary Trusts

The second broad category of trusts used in connection with estate planning comprises **testamentary trusts.** A testamentary trust becomes effective upon the death of the grantor according to the terms of the grantor's will or a revocable living trust. Such trusts can be designed to provide money or asset management after the grantor's death, to provide income for a surviving spouse and children, and to give assets to grandchildren or great-grandchildren while providing income from the assets to the surviving spouse and children, among other things.

Instant Message

Special Needs Trust

Some states have passed laws that allow parents to set aside money in a trust specifically for the benefit of a disabled child or adult while letting him or her retain all public benefits, like Medicaid or welfare. This kind of trust is called a **special needs trust.** This type of trust is used in situations where the grantee likely will never be able to handle their own affairs. It provides lifelong access to supplemental and emergency funds to cover expenses that public assistance does not. The trustee makes all the decisions to pay for access to assure suitable health, safety, and welfare. Without special arrangements, income from a trust will count against a special needs child who is receiving public aid.

 Concept Check 18.2

1. List some reasons why people establish trusts.
2. Distinguish between a grantor and a trustee.
3. Summarize the difference between living and testamentary trusts.
4. Explain what is so important about the difference between revocable and irrevocable trusts.

testamentary trust
Becomes effective upon death of the grantor according to the terms of the grantor's will or a revocable living trust. Such trusts can provide money or asset management after the grantor's death for the heirs' benefit.

Prepare Advance Directive Documents in Case You Become Incapacitated

3 Learning Objective
Summarize the benefits of preparing advance directive documents.

You can retain your dignity and save your loved ones the burden of making some very challenging decisions by writing down what you want to happen if you become incapacitated. Many illnesses, such as Alzheimer's disease, strokes, and cancer, can result in a period of mental incompetence and physical disability before death. Give copies of these documents to

Instant Message

Advanced Directives for Unmarried Couples

While state laws are evolving on the rights of unmarried couples, a loved one can be protected and have some legal power. To do so, name each other in your durable or springing power of attorney for finances and health care durable power of attorney.

durable power of attorney for finances
Document that appoints someone, called an attorney-in-fact, to handle your legal or business matters and sign your name to documents if illness prevents you from doing so yourself.

springing power of attorney
"Springs" into effect when a specified event occurs, usually mental incapacitation or disability.

advance medical directive
Statement of medical preferences, including designation of surrogate decision maker if patients become unable to make medical decisions for themselves in case of coma, dementia, or brain death.

Advance directives can help family members make appropriate decisions when a loved one is incapacitated.

members of your family and other responsible people in your life, and your wishes in these matters may be controlled as you desire.

Creating Advanced Directives for Finances

People over age 50 or 60 often create a **durable power of attorney for finances** well in advance of the onset of any medical problems. This is a document in which you appoint someone, called an attorney-in-fact, to handle your legal or business matters and sign his or her name to documents. It stays in effect as long as you live, unless you explicitly revoke it. This document should detail the specific aspects of your affairs that it covers and should even mention specific institutions (banks or brokerage firms, for example) and account numbers. A durable power of attorney gives the designated person virtually absolute power to manage your financial affairs, so choose a trusted individual who knows your wishes.

A **limited** (or **special**) **power of attorney** is narrower in scope and could be restricted to one specified act or a certain time period, such as signing your name at the closing of the sale of a home or managing your investment accounts. A **springing power of attorney** "springs" into effect when a specified event occurs, usually mental incapacitation or disability. This is often used to allow a spouse or family member to manage the grantor's affairs in case illness or injury makes him or her unable to act, while allowing him or her to retain power before the incapacity occurs.

Creating Advance Directives for Medical Care

An **advance medical directive** is a medical guideline that pertains to treatment preferences, including the designation of a surrogate decision maker in the event that a patient becomes unable to make medical decisions on his or her own behalf as a result of coma, dementia, brain death, or other serious medical condition. A **living will** specifies what types

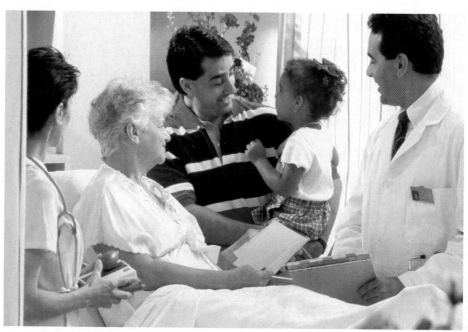

Gabe Palmer/Palmer/Kane Studio

of medical treatment are desired. It commonly states that "If I suffer an incurable, irreversible illness, disease, or condition and my attending physician determines that my condition is terminal, I direct that life-sustaining measures that would serve only to prolong my dying be withheld or discontinued."

This document may relieve family members of making a painful decision to allow a person's life to end. To be effective and to avoid varying interpretations, a living will must speak to specific circumstances. For example, a living will could dictate a "do not resuscitate order" designed to prohibit health care providers from attempting cardiopulmonary resuscitation (CPR) in case of cardiac or respiratory arrest. Federal law requires hospitals to inform patients of their rights to make such decisions about medical care. Living wills need to conform precisely to the statutes in the state in which the person lives.

A **health care proxy (or durable power of attorney for health care)** is a legal document in which individuals designate another person to make health care decisions if they are rendered incapable of making their wishes known. The person designated in the health care proxy has, in essence, the same rights to request or refuse treatment that the individual would have if capable of making and communicating decisions.

Instant Message

Estate Planning on the Web

Some routine legal estate planning matters can be handled without a lawyer. Nolo (www.nolo.com) is a publisher of self-help, lawyer-prepared legal books on such topics as writing a will or living trust and other ways to minimize estate taxes. Additional resources include:

- American Bar Association (http://www.abanet.org/ rppt/public/home.html)
- Nolo (http://www.nolo.com/resource.cfm/catID/ FD1795A9-8049-422C-9087838F86A2BC2B/309/)
- Cornell Law School (http://topics.law.cornell.edu/ wex/Estate_Planning)
- National Association of Estate Planners & Councils (http://www.naepc.org/)

health care proxy/durable power of attorney for health care
Legal document that appoints another person to make health care decisions if the writer of the proxy is rendered incapable of making his or her wishes known.

Concept Check 18.3

1. What does a durable power of attorney accomplish, and who should consider having one?
2. Distinguish between a limited power of attorney and a springing power of attorney.
3. Summarize the difference between a living will and a medical power of attorney.

4 Learning Objective

List the questions and documents needed to simplify the settlement and transfer of your estate.

Checklist to Settle and Transfer Your Estate

Creating a master checklist to your financial world by providing answers to estate planning questions and detailing the locations of related documents will simplify the settlement and transfer of your estate.

1. *Current will.* Location? Contact information for attorney? For financial adviser? For insurance agent?
2. *Powers of attorney.* Durable power of attorney? Advance medical directive? Medical power of attorney?
3. *Letter of last instructions.* Document locations? Who has copies?
4. *Funeral and burial arrangements.* Written instructions? Who has copies?
5. *Trusts.* Location? Attorney contact information?
6. *Official documents.* Birth? Prenuptial agreements? Marriage? Divorce? Guardianship? Military?
7. *Social Security numbers.* Yours? Spouse? Children?

Instant Message

Steps in Estate Planning

1. Inventory everything you own and owe.
2. Record reasonable estimates of each item's current value.
3. Prepare advance directives.
4. Create a comprehensive estate planning checklist describing all essential assets, documents, and financial information and where they are located.
5. Sit down with your spouse or significant other and discuss your wishes about who should get what and under what circumstances.
6. Decide which estate planning tools are the most appropriate choices for your situation.

Did You Know?

The Top 3 Financial Missteps in Estate Planning

People slip up in estate planning when they do the following:

1. Not having a will
2. Not having signed advance directive documents
3. Forgetting to update forms you have signed that contractually award assets, like life insurance and retirement and checking accounts, to ex-spouses, parents, siblings, and others because those instructions override your will

8. *Computer passwords.* Passwords for computer?

9. *Safe-deposit box.* Location? Key? Written record of contents?

10. *Employer.* Employee benefits? Contact information for supervisors and human resources department?

11. *Life insurance.* Policies? Employer group policy? Beneficiaries? Contingent beneficiaries? Agent(s)? Details on collecting benefits?

12. *Pension.* Potential benefits? Veteran's benefits?

13. *Retirement accounts.* IRA? 401(k)? Keogh? Annuities? Employer pension plans? Passwords?

14. *Social Security and Veterans Administration.* Current or potential benefits? Discharge papers? Records?

15. *Health insurance.* Coverage details? Employer policy?

16. *Disability income and long-term care insurance.* Policies?

17. *Financial statements.* Balance sheet, including artwork and family heirlooms? Cash-flow statement? Value of estate?

18. *Budget.* Details? Old records?

19. *Liabilities.* Credit cards? Vehicle loans/leases? Personal loans? Mortgages? Passwords?

20. *Cash management.* Bank information? Checking? Savings? Money market? Passwords? Certificates of deposit?

21. *Housing.* Deeds? Titles? Rental properties? Title insurance? Timeshares? Homeowner's policies?

22. *Automobiles/recreational vehicles.* Titles? Insurance policies?

23. *Investment assets.* Brokerage accounts? Mutual fund statements? Stocks? Bonds? Other assets? Written investment objectives? Passwords?

24. *Business interests.* Agreements? Ownership interest in a family-owned business? Legal counsel?

25. *Tax returns.* Last year's return? Previous returns? Current year's information? Gift and estate tax?

---

5 Learning Objective

Explain the potential impact of estate and inheritance taxes.

federal estate tax
Assessed against a deceased person's estate before property (real estate, stocks and bonds, business interests, and so on) is transferred to heirs or assigned according to terms of a will or state intestacy laws.

exclusion amount
The value of assets that may be transferred to heirs without incurring an estate tax—currently $3.5 million.

marital deduction
Allows an estate to pass on an unlimited amount of assets to a surviving spouse free of estate taxes.

 Concept Check 18.4

1. List five estate planning documents that should be easily found by your survivors.
2. List five different types of assets about which your survivors will need detailed information in order to claim them after your death.

Estate and Inheritance Taxes

The **federal estate tax** is assessed against the estate of a deceased person before property (real estate, stocks and bonds, business interests, and so on) is transferred to heirs or assigned according to terms of a will or state intestacy laws. It is a tax on the deceased's estate, not on the beneficiary who is to receive the property.

The first $3.5 million of a taxable estate is exempt from the federal estate tax in 2009. Referred to as the **exclusion amount,** it is the value of assets that may be transferred to heirs without incurring an estate tax. The **marital deduction** allows an estate to pass on

Did You Know?

About Life Insurance and Estate Planning

Life insurance proceeds are payable directly to the named beneficiary(ies) in the policy. If the proceeds of life insurance are payable to the estate of the deceased—which is exactly the wrong thing to do—they are included in the estate for federal estate tax purposes. Further, if the deceased, while alive, retained any ownership interest, such as the right to change beneficiaries or to borrow against any cash value of the policy, the proceeds are also included in the estate for estate tax purposes. Assigning ownership of the policy to someone else, such as the beneficiary, prior to death solves this estate transfer problem.

an unlimited amount of assets to a surviving spouse free of estate taxes. When the surviving spouse who inherited assets dies, the estate would be subject to any federal estate taxes in effect at that time.

You are not likely to be subject to federal estate taxes because less than 1 percent of all estates must pay estate taxes. Most estate taxes are paid by the extremely wealthy and the highest marginal tax rate is 45 percent for estates over the exclusion amount. Current law has the federal estate tax being repealed and going to zero in 2010. The law expires on January 1, 2011, meaning that the older estate tax exclusion amount ($1 million) and higher marginal tax rate (49%) from the early 2000's will become law again in 2011 unless Congress takes action. Many observers expect Congress to make the 2009, $3.5 million exclusion amount and 45 percent maximum marginal rate permanent. Seventeen states and the District of Columbia also have an estate tax, and since most are coupled with the federal estate tax, those taxes are zero when the federal tax is zero.

Eight states★ impose an **inheritance tax** assessed by the decedent's state of residence on *beneficiaries* who receive inherited property. This tax is based on how much the beneficiaries get and their right to receive it. In those states, transfers to spouses, children, and other close relatives may be either exempt or subject to a lower state inheritance tax rate. The beneficiaries are responsible for paying inheritance taxes, although typically the estate pays the taxes before distributing any remaining assets to the heirs.

inheritance tax
A tax imposed by eight states (i.e., Connecticut, Indiana, Iowa, Kentucky, Maryland, Nebraska, New Jersey, and Pennsylvania) that is assessed on the decedent's beneficiaries who receive inherited property.

Do It NOW!

Estate planning is not just for older persons or those with high levels of wealth. Start today by:

1. Taking an inventory of your inheritable assets and deciding to whom you would like them to go in the event of your death.

2. Determining how all of your bank and investment accounts are owned and changing the ownership form as appropriate to individual or joint with someone else of your choosing.

3. Preparing a will.

✔ Concept Check 18.5

1. What is the exclusion amount on the federal estate tax?
2. Tell how the marital deduction works in estate planning.
3. Comment on the likely impact of estate taxes and inheritance taxes at the state level on most people.

★Connecticut, Indiana, Iowa, Kentucky, Maryland, Nebraska, New Jersey, and Pennsylvania.

Advice from a Pro...

Ten Things Every Spouse Must Know

The following checklist contains items spouses should know about financial, estate, tax, and investment planning. After all, it is never what we know that will get us in trouble, but rather what we don't know.

1. Understand your current financial situation—assets and liabilities, net worth, and family income and expenses.

2. Have a plan for all emergencies. Know exactly what financial resources would be needed if your spouse were to become disabled or unemployed. Make certain your auto, homeowner's, and medical insurance coverage are adequate for your situation. Have sufficient cash on hand to pay your deductibles.

3. Carry sufficient life insurance on yourself and your spouse. Determine whether sufficient resources are available to raise your family and provide for your children's education if you or your spouse were to die. Know what benefits your spouse's employer offers and what benefits have been selected. Know who is the beneficiary at your spouse's death and if both you and your spouse were to die. Consider naming a trust as beneficiary instead of naming minor-age children as beneficiaries.

4. Verify that your estate documents (wills, trusts, guardianships, durable powers of attorney, and so on) reflect your current wishes for your family.

5. Understand your income taxes and pursue aggressive, but legal, strategies for reducing your tax liabilities. Don't sign a return you don't understand.

6. Create a written investment plan and follow it. Understand the rate of return that you must realize on your investments to achieve your goal. Monitor your results quarterly.

7. Know how to invest—when to buy and sell—so that you can consistently obtain a rate of return that will allow your family to achieve and maintain financial independence. Do not expect someone else to care more about your money than you do.

8. Have a plan for funding your children's education, home ownership, and your retirement. Complete sample FAFSA (Free Application for Federal Student Aid) forms when your child enters high school so you will understand what the government believes your family should be able to contribute for your child's college education.

9. Thoroughly understand your employer- and government-provided benefits. If they are not sufficient to achieve your goals, make a career change. There is no sense in riding a dead horse.

10. Communicate with your children and other members of your family to teach them about financial, estate, tax, and investment planning. Remember, the most expensive form of education is to learn through your own bad experiences.

Lorraine R. Decker
Decker & Associates Inc., www.DeckerUSA.com

Source: Decker, Lorraine R., CLU, ChFC, MSFS, President, Decker & Associates Inc., "Ten Things Every Spouse Must Know About Finance, Estate Tax, and Investment Planning." Copyright © 2009 by Decker & Associates Inc. Reprinted with permission.

What Do You Recommend NOW?

Now that you have read the chapter on estate planning, what do you recommend to Orlando and Giselle Molina in the case at the beginning of the chapter regarding:

1. Beneficiary designations for their financial assets?

2. Joint ownership of their home, vehicles, and other property?

3. Making a will?

4. Establishing guardianship for the children?

5. Using advance directive documents to avoid a situation like that confronting Orlando's father?

6. Establishing trusts for their children?

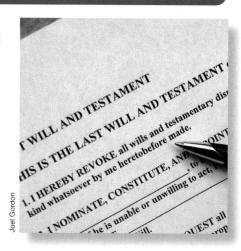

Joel Gordon

Big Picture Summary of Learning Objectives

1 Identify the ways that your estate can be transferred through contracts and a will.

After inventorying everything you own and owe, you may find that you can readily transfer most or all of your estate with a will and via contracts. Nonprobate property, which does not go through the court process of probate, includes assets transferred to survivors by contract (such as naming a beneficiary for your retirement plan or with bank accounts owned with another person through joint tenancy with right of survivorship).

2 Determine how trusts can be used to transfer assets and reduce estate taxes.

By creating one or more trusts, portions of an estate can be transferred in a contractual manner to others in a way that avoids probate and may reduce or eliminate the federal estate tax. A trust is a legal arrangement between you as the grantor or creator of the trust and the trustee, the person designated to control and manage any assets in the trust. Revocable and irrevocable trusts are used in estate planning as well as testamentary trusts.

3 Summarize the benefits of preparing advance directive documents.

Making advance directives can save your loved ones the burden of making some challenging decisions in case you become incapacitated. These documents include durable power of attorney, limited power of attorney, living will, and health care directive.

4 List the questions and documents needed to simplify the settlement and transfer of your estate.

Creating a master list of "CliffsNotes" to your financial world by providing answers to estate planning questions and listing the locations of related documents will simplify the settlement and transfer of your estate.

5 Explain the potential impact of estate and inheritance taxes.

The federal estate tax affects less than 1 percent of estates, and a surviving spouse may use the marital deduction to completely avoid the tax during his or her lifetime. Some states have state estate and inheritance taxes.

Let's Talk About It

1. **Wills for College Students.** Do college students really need a will at this point in their lives? Why or why not? What probably would happen to the typical college student's assets if he or she died without a will?

2. **Choosing an Executor.** What are some criteria that you would use to select the executor for your estate or the guardian for your children if you and your spouse or significant other died at the same time?

3. **Writing a Living Will.** If you were thinking about signing a living will, what are some provisions that you might put into the document?

4. **Writing a Letter of Last Instructions.** Identify topics that you would cover in your letter of last instructions.

5. **Creating Trusts for Grandchildren.** Do you think it is appropriate for parents and grandparents to put conditions in a trust set up for their children or grandchildren that relate to the behavior of those assets?

Do the Math

1. **Estimating the Size of an Estate.** Christopher Marcos, of Santa Clarita, California, died recently without a valid will. His probate estate for federal estate tax purposes was $3.2 million. Christopher's wife, Amanda, and three children were his only survivors. Answer the following questions, assuming that Christopher's state of residence followed the typical guidelines of division (one-half for the spouse with the children equally splitting the remainder):

    (a) What will be the dollar amount of the division of assets for the wife and children?

    (b) If Amanda has personal assets (beyond her inheritance from Christopher) that have a fair market value of $400,000, when she dies, how much will her estate total?

    (c) If Amanda now died without a will in 2011, what will be the dollar amount of the division of assets, assuming that she has no other children?

    (d) Assuming Amanda's estate paid $15,000 for her funeral expenses, $14,000 for probate costs, and $180,000 to pay off the remaining debts and mortgages, what was Amanda's taxable estate before subtracting the exclusion amount?

2. **Estimating Estate Taxes.** Laura Kim of Georgetown, Delaware, lives with her elderly grandmother, Haejeong. Her grandmother owns two profitable auto parts stores that are worth millions. Because current law has the federal estate tax going to zero in 2010 and then back to previous rules in 2011, the pair is wondering how these taxes might affect Haejeong's estate.

Laura hopes that her grandmother, who is in excellent health, lives at least another 20 years. If she doesn't, the federal estate tax will apply in all years except 2010. If Haejeong's probate estate is valued at $7.5 million, calculate the following:

(a) The amount of the estate subject to the federal estate tax if she dies in 2011 and Congress makes no change in the law.

(b) The amount of the federal estate tax if she dies in 2011 and Congress extends the 2009 exclusion amount and tax rate.

Financial Planning Cases

Case 1

A Couple Considers the Ramifications of Dying Intestate

Melissa Merryweather of Savannah, Georgia, is a 34-year-old police detective earning $58,000 per year. She and her husband, Joshua, have two children in elementary school. They own a modestly furnished home and two late-model cars. Melissa also owns a snowmobile. Both spouses have 401(k) retirement accounts through their employers, and their employers also provide them with $50,000 group term life policies. Melissa also has a $50,000 term life policy of her own. The couple has about $5000 in their joint checking account. Neither has a will.

(a) List four negative things that could happen if either Melissa or Joshua were to die without a will.

(b) What would be the most important negative consequence of not having a will if both Melissa and Joshua were to die together in an accident?

(c) Which assets could be jointly owned so that they will automatically transfer to the other spouse if either Melissa or Joshua dies?

(d) What qualities should Melissa and Joshua look for when naming the executors of their wills?

(e) Once they have completed and signed their wills, where should the Merryweathers keep the original documents and any copies?

Case 2

A Lottery Winner Practices Estate Planning

Your good friend, Brandon, has just announced that he has the sole winning ticket in the $7 million lottery drawing of last week. Brandon is 60 years old, divorced and lives in Orangeburg, South Carolina. He has two adult children

(Nicole and Heather) and four grandchildren. Recognizing that you are not an attorney, and knowing that your friend needs personal finance advice, offer some estate planning suggestions regarding the following points:

(a) Assume that Brandon's taxable estate now amounts to $7,200,000 and after the $3,500,000 exclusion, his remaining estate could be taxed at 45 percent. If he died tomorrow, how much would he owe? Give him that figure while offering him one single piece of advice.

(b) Name two types of trusts that Brandon might consider to reduce his eventual estate taxes and summarize what those trusts might help him accomplish.

(c) Offer Brandon some suggestions for things he might want to put into his letter of last instructions.

Case 3

Victor and Maria Update Their Estate Plans

Since retiring earlier this year, Victor and Maria have found that their assets amount to approximately $800,000, made up of the following: Victor's half-interest in their home ($90,000), his tax-sheltered pension plan ($144,000), his stock ($56,000), his personal property ($50,000), Maria's half-interest in their home ($90,000), the inherited home from her mother ($120,000), her tax-sheltered pension plan ($112,000), the present value (obtained from Victor's employer) of the survivors benefits under her husband's defined-benefit pension plan ($60,000), personal property ($50,000), and her zero-coupon bonds ($28,000).

(a) Offer the Hernandezes advice about how each might establish a durable power of attorney for finances.

(b) Should both Victor and Maria have living wills and a health care proxy? Why or why not?

(c) Victor purchased his $100,000 term life insurance policy through his employer, and he has been paying on his privately purchased $50,000 whole life insurance policy for many years (which now has a cash value of $30,000). Maria is listed as the beneficiary on both policies. Assuming that Victor owns both policies, what advice can you offer regarding ownership of the two policies?

(d) After adding up the value of the estate, what is the likelihood of having to pay federal estate taxes if Victor dies?

(e) Offer Victor and Maria some suggestions on how to ease the transfer of assets to their adult children and grandchildren.

Case 4

Belinda Johnson Helps Her Uncle Plan His Estate

Belinda Johnson has been approached by her uncle, Ryan Lawrence, who seeks advice about planning his estate. She has been handling some of Ryan's investments, and he trusts her judgment on financial matters. Ryan has a net worth of $2,340,000. At age 54, he is concerned about preparing his finances so that as much as possible of his estate will go to his heirs according to his wishes. Ryan has no will but has written down some of his ideas. He has no wife or children but wants to be able to provide for his mother, four nephews, Belinda, and a disabled sister.

(a) What is the first action Ryan should take in planning his estate?

(b) Why might an irrevocable living trust be a good idea for Ryan in providing for his mother and sister?

(c) What other types of trusts might Ryan use in his estate planning?

On the 'Net

Go to the Web pages indicated to complete these exercises.

1. Visit the website for Legacy Writer at www.legacywriter.com. Click on "Living Wills," where you can begin the process of developing a living will and other advance directives. Finishing the process will require payment of a fee, but for this exercise simply answer the questions asked. After doing so, is an advance directive something you would consider? Why or why not?

2. Upon death, a person's will can become a public document through the probate process. Visit the Court TV website at http://www.courttv.com/archive/legaldocs/newsmakers/wills/, where the wills of some famous people have been posted. Select a person whose will interests you. Identify one of the estate planning techniques outlined in this chapter that were used by that person.

3. Visit the website for the Internal Revenue Service at http://www.irs.gov/publications/p950/index.html, where you can find information on the federal gift and estate tax. Is this a tax you ever expect to pay? What are your views on this tax as an appropriate way to provide revenue to support government operations?

Visit the Garman/Forgue companion website . . .

Appendixes

Present and Future Value Tables

Many problems in personal finance involve decisions about money values at varying points in time. These values can be directly and fairly compared only when they are adjusted to a common point in time. Chapter 1 introduced the basic time value concepts. This appendix offers more details about the time value of money. In addition, it provides tables listing the future and present value of $1 with which to make calculations.

Four assumptions must be made to eliminate unnecessary complications:

1. Each planning period is one year long.

2. Only annual interest rates are considered.

3. Interest rates are the same during each of the annual periods.

4. Interest is compounded and continues earning a return in subsequent periods.

Tables of present and future values can be constructed to make these adjustments. **Future values** are derived from the principles of compounding the dollar values ahead in time. **Present values** are derived by discounting (which is the inverse of compounding) the dollar values and transferring them to an earlier point in time.

It is usually unnecessary to precisely identify whether the interest is paid/received at the *beginning* of a period or at the end of a period, or to know whether interest compounds daily or quarterly instead of annually. (These calculations require even more tables.) The following present and future value tables assume that money is accumulated, received, paid, compounded, or whatever at the *end* of a period. The tables can be used to compute the mathematics of personal finance with high certainty and to confirm (or reject as inaccurate) what people tell you about financial matters.

The most significant task is to find the correct table. Accordingly, each table is clearly described here, and illustrations of its use appear on the facing page where possible. In addition, the appropriate mathematical equation is shown and can be easily solved using a calculator.

Illustrations Using Appendix A.1: Future Value of a Single Amount ($1)

To use Appendix A.1 on page A-4, locate the future value factor for the time period and the interest rate.

1. You invest $500 at a 15 percent rate of return for 12 years. How much will you have at the end of that 12-year period?

The future value factor is 5.350; hence, the solution is $500 × 5.350, or $2675.

2. Property values in your neighborhood are increasing at a rate of 5 percent per year. If your home is presently worth $90,000, what will its worth be in 7 years?

The future value factor is 1.407; hence, the solution is $90,000 × 1.407, or $126,630.

3. You need to amass $40,000 in the next 10 years to make a balloon payment on your home mortgage. You have $17,000 available to invest. What annual interest rate must be earned to realize the $40,000?

$40,000 ÷ $17,000 = 2.353. Read down the periods (*n*) column to 10 years and across to 2.367 (close enough), which is found under the 9 percent column. Hence, the $17,000 invested at 9 percent for 10 years will grow to a future value of slightly more than $40,000.

4. An apartment building is currently valued at $160,000, and it has been appreciating at 8 percent per year. If this rate continues, in how many years will it be worth $300,000?

$300,000 ÷ $160,000 = 1.875. Read down the 8 percent column until you reach 1.851 (close enough to 1.875). This number corresponds to a period of 8 years. Hence, the $160,000 property appreciating at 8 percent annually will grow to a future value of $300,000 in slightly more than 8 years.

5. You have the choice of receiving a down payment from someone who wants to purchase your rental property as $15,000 today or as a personal note for $25,000 payable in 6 years. If you could expect to earn 8 percent on such funds, which is the better choice?

The future value factor is 1.587; hence, the future value of $15,000 at 8 percent is $15,000 × 1.587, or $23,805. Thus, it would be better to take the note for $25,000.

6. How much will an automobile now priced at $20,000 cost in 4 years, assuming an annual inflation rate of 5 percent?

Read down the 5 percent column and across the row for 4 years to locate the future value factor of 1.216. Hence, the solution is $20,000 × 1.216, or $24,320.

7. How large a lump-sum investment do you need now to have $20,000 available in 5 years, assuming a 10 percent annual rate of return?

The $20,000 future value is divided by 1.611 (10 percent at 5 years), resulting in a current lump-sum investment of $12,415.

8. You have $5000 now and need $10,000 in 9 years. What rate of return is needed to reach that goal?

Divide the future value of $10,000 by the present value of the lump sum of $5000 to obtain a future value factor of 2.0. In the row for 9 years, locate the future value factor of 1.999 (very close to 2.0). Read up the column to find that an 8 percent return on investment is needed.

9. How many years will it take your lump-sum investment of $10,000 to grow to $16,000, given an annual rate of return of 7 percent?

Divide the future value of $16,000 by the present value of the $10,000 lump sum to compute a future value factor of 1.6; look down the 7 percent column to find 1.606 (close enough). Read across the row to find that an investment period of 7 years is needed.

An alternative approach is to use a calculator to determine the future value, FV, of a sum of money invested today, assuming that the amount remains in the investment for a specified number of time periods (usually years) and that it earns a certain rate of return each period. The equation is

$$FV = PV \, (1.0 + i)^n \tag{A.1}$$

where

$FV = $ *Future Value*
$PV = $ *Present Value* of the investment
$i = $ *Interest* rate per period
$n = $ *Number* of periods the PV is invested

Appendix A.1 Future Value of a Single Amount ($1 at the End of n Periods)
(Used to Compute the Compounded Future Value of a Known Lump Sum)

n	1%	2%	3%	4%	5%	6%	7%	8%	9%	10%	11%	12%	13%	14%	15%	16%	17%	18%	19%	20%
1	1.0100	1.0200	1.0300	1.0400	1.0500	1.0600	1.0700	1.0800	1.0900	1.1000	1.1100	1.1200	1.1300	1.1400	1.1500	1.1600	1.1700	1.1800	1.1900	1.2000
2	1.0201	1.0404	1.0609	1.0816	1.1025	1.1236	1.1449	1.1664	1.1881	1.2100	1.2321	1.2544	1.2769	1.2996	1.3225	1.3456	1.3689	1.3924	1.4161	1.4400
3	1.0303	1.0612	1.0927	1.1249	1.1576	1.1910	1.2250	1.2597	1.2950	1.3310	1.3676	1.4049	1.4429	1.4815	1.5209	1.5609	1.6016	1.6430	1.6852	1.7280
4	1.0406	1.0824	1.1255	1.1699	1.2155	1.2625	1.3108	1.3605	1.4116	1.4641	1.5181	1.5735	1.6305	1.6890	1.7490	1.8106	1.8739	1.9388	2.0053	2.0736
5	1.0510	1.1041	1.1593	1.2167	1.2763	1.3382	1.4026	1.4693	1.5386	1.6105	1.6851	1.7623	1.8424	1.9254	2.0114	2.1003	2.1924	2.2878	2.3864	2.4883
6	1.0615	1.1262	1.1941	1.2653	1.3401	1.4185	1.5007	1.5869	1.6771	1.7716	1.8704	1.9738	2.0820	2.1950	2.3131	2.4364	2.5652	2.6996	2.8398	2.9860
7	1.0721	1.1487	1.2299	1.3159	1.4071	1.5036	1.6058	1.7138	1.8280	1.9487	2.0762	2.2107	2.3526	2.5023	2.6600	2.8262	3.0012	3.1855	3.3793	3.5832
8	1.0829	1.1717	1.2668	1.3686	1.4775	1.5938	1.7182	1.8509	1.9926	2.1436	2.3045	2.4760	2.6584	2.8526	3.0590	3.2784	3.5115	3.7589	4.0214	4.2998
9	1.0937	1.1951	1.3048	1.4233	1.5513	1.6895	1.8385	1.9990	2.1719	2.3579	2.5580	2.7731	3.0040	3.2519	3.5179	3.8030	4.1084	4.4355	4.7854	5.1598
10	1.1046	1.2190	1.3439	1.4802	1.6289	1.7908	1.9672	2.1589	2.3674	2.5937	2.8394	3.1058	3.3946	3.7072	4.0456	4.4114	4.8068	5.2338	5.6947	6.1917
11	1.1157	1.2434	1.3842	1.5395	1.7103	1.8983	2.1049	2.3316	2.5804	2.8531	3.1518	3.4785	3.8359	4.2262	4.6524	5.1173	5.6240	6.1759	6.7767	7.4301
12	1.1268	1.2682	1.4258	1.6010	1.7959	2.0122	2.2522	2.5182	2.8127	3.1384	3.4985	3.8960	4.3345	4.8179	5.3503	5.9360	6.5801	7.2876	8.0642	8.9161
13	1.1381	1.2936	1.4685	1.6651	1.8856	2.1329	2.4098	2.7196	3.0658	3.4523	3.8833	4.3635	4.8980	5.4924	6.1528	6.8858	7.6987	8.5994	9.5964	10.6993
14	1.1495	1.3195	1.5126	1.7317	1.9799	2.2609	2.5785	2.9372	3.3417	3.7975	4.3104	4.8871	5.5348	6.2613	7.0757	7.9875	9.0075	10.1472	11.4198	12.8392
15	1.1610	1.3459	1.5580	1.8009	2.0789	2.3966	2.7590	3.1722	3.6425	4.1772	4.7846	5.4736	6.2543	7.1379	8.1371	9.2655	10.5387	11.9737	13.5895	15.4070
16	1.1726	1.3728	1.6047	1.8730	2.1829	2.5404	2.9522	3.4259	3.9703	4.5950	5.3109	6.1304	7.0673	8.1372	9.3576	10.7480	12.3303	14.1290	16.1715	18.4884
17	1.1843	1.4002	1.6528	1.9479	2.2920	2.6928	3.1588	3.7000	4.3276	5.0545	5.8951	6.8660	7.9861	9.2765	10.7613	12.4677	14.4265	16.6722	19.2441	22.1861
18	1.1961	1.4282	1.7024	2.0258	2.4066	2.8543	3.3799	3.9960	4.7171	5.5599	6.5436	7.6900	9.0243	10.5752	12.3755	14.4625	16.8790	19.6733	22.9005	26.6233
19	1.2081	1.4568	1.7535	2.1068	2.5270	3.0256	3.6165	4.3157	5.1417	6.1159	7.2633	8.6128	10.1974	12.0557	14.2318	16.7765	19.7484	23.2144	27.2516	31.9480
20	1.2202	1.4859	1.8061	2.1911	2.6533	3.2071	3.8697	4.6610	5.6044	6.7275	8.0623	9.6463	11.5231	13.7435	16.3665	19.4608	23.1056	27.3930	32.4294	38.3376
21	1.2324	1.5157	1.8603	2.2788	2.7860	3.3996	4.1406	5.0338	6.1088	7.4002	8.9492	10.8038	13.0211	15.6676	18.8215	22.5745	27.0336	32.3238	38.5910	46.0051
22	1.2447	1.5460	1.9161	2.3699	2.9253	3.6035	4.4304	5.4365	6.6586	8.1403	9.9336	12.1003	14.7138	17.8610	21.6447	26.1864	31.6293	38.1421	45.9233	55.2061
23	1.2572	1.5769	1.9736	2.4647	3.0715	3.8197	4.7405	5.8715	7.2579	8.9543	11.0263	13.5523	16.6266	20.3616	24.8915	30.3762	37.0062	45.0076	54.6487	66.2474
24	1.2697	1.6084	2.0328	2.5633	3.2251	4.0489	5.0724	6.3412	7.9111	9.8497	12.2392	15.1786	18.7881	23.2122	28.6252	35.2364	43.2973	53.1090	65.0320	79.4968
25	1.2824	1.6406	2.0938	2.6658	3.3864	4.2919	5.4274	6.8485	8.6231	10.8347	13.5855	17.0001	21.2305	26.4619	32.9190	40.8742	50.6578	62.6686	77.3881	95.3962
26	1.2953	1.6734	2.1566	2.7725	3.5557	4.5494	5.8074	7.3964	9.3992	11.9182	15.0799	19.0401	23.9905	30.1666	37.8568	47.4141	59.2697	73.9490	92.0918	114.4755
27	1.3082	1.7069	2.2213	2.8834	3.7335	4.8223	6.2139	7.9881	10.2451	13.1100	16.7386	21.3249	27.1093	34.3899	43.5353	55.0004	69.3455	87.2598	109.5893	137.3706
28	1.3213	1.7410	2.2879	2.9987	3.9201	5.1117	6.6488	8.6271	11.1671	14.4210	18.5799	23.8839	30.6335	39.2045	50.0656	63.8004	81.1342	102.9666	130.4112	164.8447
29	1.3345	1.7758	2.3566	3.1187	4.1161	5.4184	7.1143	9.3173	12.1722	15.8631	20.6237	26.7499	34.6158	44.6931	57.5755	74.0085	94.9271	121.5005	155.1893	197.8136
30	1.3478	1.8114	2.4273	3.2434	4.3219	5.7435	7.6123	10.0627	13.2677	17.4494	22.8923	29.9599	39.1159	50.9502	66.2118	85.8499	111.0647	143.3706	184.6753	237.3763
40	1.4889	2.2080	3.2620	4.8010	7.0400	10.2857	14.9745	21.7245	31.4094	45.2593	65.0009	93.0510	132.7816	188.8835	267.8635	378.7212	533.8687	750.3783	1051.668	1469.772
50	1.6446	2.6916	4.3839	7.1067	11.4674	18.4202	29.4570	46.9016	74.3575	117.3909	184.5648	289.0022	450.7359	700.2330	1083.657	1670.704	2566.215	3927.357	5988.914	9100.438

Illustrations Using Appendix A.2: Present Value of a Single Amount ($1)

To use this table, locate the present value factor for the time period and the interest rate.

1. You want to begin a college fund for your newborn child; you hope to accumulate $30,000 by 18 years from now. If a current investment opportunity yields 7 percent, how much must you invest in a lump sum to realize the $30,000 when needed?

   The present value factor is 0.296; hence, the solution is $30,000 × 0.296, or $8880.

2. You hope to retire in 25 years and want to deposit a single lump sum that will grow to $250,000 at that time. If you can now invest at 8 percent, how much must you invest to realize the $250,000 when needed?

   The present value factor is 0.146; hence, the solution is $250,000 × 0.146, or $36,500. The present value of $250,000 received 25 years from now is $36,500 if the interest rate is 8 percent.

3. You have the choice of receiving a down payment from someone who wants to purchase your rental property as $15,000 today or as a personal note for $25,000 payable in 6 years. If you could expect to earn 8 percent on such funds, which is the better choice?

   The present value factor is 0.630; hence, the solution is $25,000 × 0.630, or $15,750. Thus, the present value of $25,000 received in 6 years is greater than $15,000 received now, and the personal note is the better choice.

4. You own a $1000 bond paying 8 percent annually until its maturity in 5 years. You need to sell the bond now, even though the market rate of interest on similar bonds has increased to 10 percent. What discounted market price for the bond will allow the new buyer to earn a yield of 10 percent?

   First, compute the present value of the future interest payments of $80 per year for 5 years at 10 percent (using Appendix A.4): $80 × 3.791, or $303.28. Second, compute the present value of the future principal repayment of $1000 after 5 years at 10 percent: $1000 × 0.621, or $621.00. Hence, the market price is the sum of the two present values ($303.28 + $621.00), or $924.28.

An alternative approach is to use a calculator to determine the present value, PV, of a single payment received some time in the future. The equation, which is a rearrangement of the future value Equation (A.1), is

$$PV = \frac{FV}{(10 + i)^n} \qquad \text{(A.2)}$$

where

$$PV = \textit{Present Value} \text{ of the investment}$$
$$FV = \textit{Future Value}$$
$$i = \textit{Interest} \text{ rate per period}$$
$$n = \textit{Number} \text{ of periods the PV is invested}$$

Appendix A.2 Present Value of a Single Amount ($1)
(Used to Compute the Discounted Present Value of Some Known Future Single Lump Sum)

n	1%	2%	3%	4%	5%	6%	7%	8%	9%	10%	11%	12%	13%	14%	15%	16%	17%	18%	19%	20%
1	0.9901	0.9804	0.9709	0.9615	0.9524	0.9434	0.9346	0.9259	0.9174	0.9091	0.9009	0.8929	0.8850	0.8772	0.8696	0.8621	0.8547	0.8475	0.8403	0.8333
2	0.9803	0.9612	0.9426	0.9246	0.9070	0.8900	0.8734	0.8573	0.8417	0.8264	0.8116	0.7972	0.7831	0.7695	0.7561	0.7432	0.7305	0.7182	0.7062	0.6944
3	0.9706	0.9423	0.9151	0.8890	0.8638	0.8396	0.8163	0.7938	0.7722	0.7513	0.7312	0.7118	0.6931	0.6750	0.6575	0.6407	0.6244	0.6086	0.5934	0.5787
4	0.9610	0.9238	0.8885	0.8548	0.8227	0.7921	0.7629	0.7350	0.7084	0.6830	0.6587	0.6355	0.6133	0.5921	0.5718	0.5523	0.5337	0.5158	0.4987	0.4823
5	0.9515	0.9057	0.8626	0.8219	0.7835	0.7473	0.7130	0.6806	0.6499	0.6209	0.5935	0.5674	0.5428	0.5194	0.4972	0.4761	0.4561	0.4371	0.4190	0.4019
6	0.9420	0.8880	0.8375	0.7903	0.7462	0.7050	0.6663	0.6302	0.5963	0.5645	0.5346	0.5066	0.4803	0.4556	0.4323	0.4104	0.3898	0.3704	0.3521	0.3349
7	0.9327	0.8706	0.8131	0.7599	0.7107	0.6651	0.6227	0.5835	0.5470	0.5132	0.4817	0.4523	0.4251	0.3996	0.3759	0.3538	0.3332	0.3139	0.2959	0.2791
8	0.9235	0.8535	0.7894	0.7307	0.6768	0.6274	0.5820	0.5403	0.5019	0.4665	0.4339	0.4039	0.3762	0.3506	0.3269	0.3050	0.2848	0.2660	0.2487	0.2326
9	0.9143	0.8368	0.7664	0.7026	0.6446	0.5919	0.5439	0.5002	0.4604	0.4241	0.3909	0.3606	0.3329	0.3075	0.2843	0.2630	0.2434	0.2255	0.2090	0.1938
10	0.9053	0.8203	0.7441	0.6756	0.6139	0.5584	0.5083	0.4632	0.4224	0.3855	0.3522	0.3220	0.2946	0.2697	0.2472	0.2267	0.2080	0.1911	0.1756	0.1615
11	0.8963	0.8043	0.7224	0.6496	0.5847	0.5268	0.4751	0.4289	0.3875	0.3505	0.3173	0.2875	0.2607	0.2366	0.2149	0.1954	0.1778	0.1619	0.1476	0.1346
12	0.8874	0.7885	0.7014	0.6246	0.5568	0.4970	0.4440	0.3971	0.3555	0.3186	0.2858	0.2567	0.2307	0.2076	0.1869	0.1685	0.1520	0.1372	0.1240	0.1122
13	0.8787	0.7730	0.6810	0.6006	0.5303	0.4688	0.4150	0.3677	0.3262	0.2897	0.2575	0.2292	0.2042	0.1821	0.1625	0.1452	0.1299	0.1163	0.1042	0.0935
14	0.8700	0.7579	0.6611	0.5775	0.5051	0.4423	0.3878	0.3405	0.2992	0.2633	0.2320	0.2046	0.1807	0.1597	0.1413	0.1252	0.1110	0.0985	0.0876	0.0779
15	0.8613	0.7430	0.6419	0.5553	0.4810	0.4173	0.3624	0.3152	0.2745	0.2394	0.2090	0.1827	0.1599	0.1401	0.1229	0.1079	0.0949	0.0835	0.0736	0.0649
16	0.8528	0.7284	0.6232	0.5339	0.4581	0.3936	0.3387	0.2919	0.2519	0.2176	0.1883	0.1631	0.1415	0.1229	0.1069	0.0930	0.0811	0.0708	0.0618	0.0541
17	0.8444	0.7142	0.6050	0.5134	0.4363	0.3714	0.3166	0.2703	0.2311	0.1978	0.1696	0.1456	0.1252	0.1078	0.0929	0.0802	0.0693	0.0600	0.0520	0.0451
18	0.8360	0.7002	0.5874	0.4936	0.4155	0.3503	0.2959	0.2502	0.2120	0.1799	0.1528	0.1300	0.1108	0.0946	0.0808	0.0691	0.0592	0.0508	0.0437	0.0376
19	0.8277	0.6864	0.5703	0.4746	0.3957	0.3305	0.2765	0.2317	0.1945	0.1635	0.1377	0.1161	0.0981	0.0829	0.0703	0.0596	0.0506	0.0431	0.0367	0.0313
20	0.8195	0.6730	0.5537	0.4564	0.3769	0.3118	0.2584	0.2145	0.1784	0.1486	0.1240	0.1037	0.0868	0.0728	0.0611	0.0514	0.0433	0.0365	0.0308	0.0261
21	0.8114	0.6598	0.5375	0.4388	0.3589	0.2942	0.2415	0.1987	0.1637	0.1351	0.1117	0.0926	0.0768	0.0638	0.0531	0.0443	0.0370	0.0309	0.0259	0.0217
22	0.8034	0.6468	0.5219	0.4220	0.3418	0.2775	0.2257	0.1839	0.1502	0.1228	0.1007	0.0826	0.0680	0.0560	0.0462	0.0382	0.0316	0.0262	0.0218	0.0181
23	0.7954	0.6342	0.5067	0.4057	0.3256	0.2618	0.2109	0.1703	0.1378	0.1117	0.0907	0.0738	0.0601	0.0491	0.0402	0.0329	0.0270	0.0222	0.0183	0.0151
24	0.7876	0.6217	0.4919	0.3901	0.3101	0.2470	0.1971	0.1577	0.1264	0.1015	0.0817	0.0659	0.0532	0.0431	0.0349	0.0284	0.0231	0.0188	0.0154	0.0126
25	0.7798	0.6095	0.4776	0.3751	0.2953	0.2330	0.1842	0.1460	0.1160	0.0923	0.0736	0.0588	0.0471	0.0378	0.0304	0.0245	0.0197	0.0160	0.0129	0.0105
26	0.7720	0.5976	0.4637	0.3607	0.2812	0.2198	0.1722	0.1352	0.1064	0.0839	0.0663	0.0525	0.0417	0.0331	0.0264	0.0211	0.0169	0.0135	0.0109	0.0087
27	0.7644	0.5859	0.4502	0.3468	0.2678	0.2074	0.1609	0.1252	0.0976	0.0763	0.0597	0.0469	0.0369	0.0291	0.0230	0.0182	0.0144	0.0115	0.0091	0.0073
28	0.7568	0.5744	0.4371	0.3335	0.2551	0.1956	0.1504	0.1159	0.0895	0.0693	0.0538	0.0419	0.0326	0.0255	0.0200	0.0157	0.0123	0.0097	0.0077	0.0061
29	0.7493	0.5631	0.4243	0.3207	0.2429	0.1846	0.1406	0.1073	0.0822	0.0630	0.0485	0.0374	0.0289	0.0224	0.0174	0.0135	0.0105	0.0082	0.0064	0.0051
30	0.7419	0.5521	0.4120	0.3083	0.2314	0.1741	0.1314	0.0994	0.0754	0.0573	0.0437	0.0334	0.0256	0.0196	0.0151	0.0116	0.0090	0.0070	0.0054	0.0042
40	0.6717	0.4529	0.3066	0.2083	0.1420	0.0972	0.0668	0.0460	0.0318	0.0221	0.0154	0.0107	0.0075	0.0053	0.0037	0.0026	0.0019	0.0013	0.0010	0.0007
50	0.6080	0.3715	0.2281	0.1407	0.0872	0.0543	0.0339	0.0213	0.0134	0.0085	0.0054	0.0035	0.0022	0.0014	0.0009	0.0006	0.0004	0.0003	0.0002	0.0001

Illustrations Using Appendix A.3: Future Value of a Series of Equal Amounts (an Annuity of $1 per Period)

To use this table, locate the future value factor for the time period and the interest rate.

1. You plan to retire after 16 years. To provide for that retirement, you initiate a savings program of $7000 per year in an investment yielding 8 percent. What will the value of the retirement fund be at the beginning of the seventeenth year?

   Your last payment into the fund will occur at the end of the sixteenth year, so scan down the periods (*n*) column for period 16, and then move across until you reach the column for 8 percent. The future value factor is 30.32. Hence, the solution is $7000 × 30.32, or $212,240.

2. What will be the value of an investment if you put $2000 into a retirement plan yielding 7 percent annually for 25 years?

   The future value factor is 63.250. Hence, the solution is $2000 × 63.250, or $126,500.

3. You are trying to decide between putting $3000 or $4000 annually for the next 20 years into an investment yielding 7 percent for retirement purposes. What is the difference in the value of investing the extra $1000 for 20 years?

   The future value factor is 41.0. Hence, the solution is $1000 × 41.0, or $41,000.

4. You will receive an annuity payment of $1200 at the end of each year for 6 years. What will be the total value of this stream of income invested at 7 percent by the time you receive the last payment?

   The appropriate future value factor for 6 years at 7 percent is 7.153. Hence, the solution is $1200 × 7.153, or $8584.

5. How many years of investing $1200 annually at 9 percent will it take to reach a goal of $11,000?

   Divide the future value of $11,000 by the lump sum of $1200 to find a future value factor of 9.17. Look down the 9 percent column to find 9.200 (close enough). Read across the row to find that an investment period of 7 years is needed.

6. If you plan to invest $1200 annually for 9 years, what rate of return is needed to reach a goal of $15,000?

   Divide the future value goal of $15,000 by $1200 to derive the future value factor 12.5. Look across the row for 9 years to locate the future value factor of 12.49 (close enough). Read up the column to find that you need an 8 percent return.

An alternative approach is to use a calculator to determine the total future value, *FV*, of a stream of equal payments (an annuity). The equation is

$$FV = \frac{[(1.0 + i)^n - 1.0] \times A}{i} \tag{A.3}$$

where

$FV = $ *Future Value* of the investment
$i = $ *Interest* rate per period
$n = $ *Number* of periods the *PV* is invested
$A = $ *Amount* of the annuity

Appendix A.3 Future Value of a Series of Equal Amounts (an Annuity of $1 Paid at the End of Each Period)
(Used to Compute the Compounded Future Value of a Stream of Income Payments)

n	1%	2%	3%	4%	5%	6%	7%	8%	9%	10%	11%	12%	13%	14%	15%	16%	17%	18%	19%	20%
1	1.0000	1.0000	1.0000	1.0000	1.0000	1.0000	1.0000	1.0000	1.0000	1.0000	1.0000	1.0000	1.0000	1.0000	1.0000	1.0000	1.0000	1.0000	1.0000	1.0000
2	2.0100	2.0200	2.0300	2.0400	2.0500	2.0600	2.0700	2.0800	2.0900	2.1000	2.1100	2.1200	2.1300	2.1400	2.1500	2.1600	2.1700	2.1800	2.1900	2.2000
3	3.0301	3.0604	3.0909	3.1216	3.1525	3.1836	3.2149	3.2464	3.2781	3.3100	3.3421	3.3744	3.4069	3.4396	3.4725	3.5056	3.5389	3.5724	3.6061	3.6400
4	4.0604	4.1216	4.1836	4.2465	4.3101	4.3746	4.4399	4.5061	4.5731	4.6410	4.7097	4.7793	4.8498	4.9211	4.9934	5.0665	5.1405	5.2154	5.2913	5.3680
5	5.1010	5.2040	5.3091	5.4163	5.5256	5.6371	5.7507	5.8666	5.9847	6.1051	6.2278	6.3528	6.4803	6.6101	6.7424	6.8771	7.0144	7.1542	7.2966	7.4416
6	6.1520	6.3081	6.4684	6.6330	6.8019	6.9753	7.1533	7.3359	7.5233	7.7156	7.9129	8.1152	8.3227	8.5355	8.7537	8.9775	9.2068	9.4420	9.6830	9.9299
7	7.2135	7.4343	7.6625	7.8983	8.1420	8.3938	8.6540	8.9228	9.2004	9.4872	9.7833	10.0890	10.4047	10.7305	11.0668	11.4139	11.7720	12.1415	12.5227	12.9159
8	8.2857	8.5830	8.8923	9.2142	9.5491	9.8975	10.2598	10.6366	11.0285	11.4359	11.8594	12.2997	12.7573	13.2328	13.7268	14.2401	14.7733	15.3270	15.9020	16.4991
9	9.3685	9.7546	10.1591	10.5828	11.0266	11.4913	11.9780	12.4876	13.0210	13.5795	14.1640	14.7757	15.4157	16.0853	16.7858	17.5185	18.2847	19.0859	19.9234	20.7989
10	10.4622	10.9497	11.4639	12.0061	12.5779	13.1808	13.8164	14.4866	15.1929	15.9374	16.7220	17.5487	18.4197	19.3373	20.3037	21.3215	22.3931	23.5213	24.7089	25.9587
11	11.5668	12.1687	12.8078	13.4864	14.2068	14.9716	15.7836	16.6455	17.5603	18.5312	19.5614	20.6546	21.8143	23.0445	24.3493	25.7329	27.1999	28.7551	30.4035	32.1504
12	12.6825	13.4121	14.1920	15.0258	15.9171	16.8699	17.8885	18.9771	20.1407	21.3843	22.7132	24.1331	25.6502	27.2707	29.0017	30.8502	32.8239	34.9311	37.1802	39.5805
13	13.8093	14.6803	15.6178	16.6268	17.7130	18.8821	20.1406	21.4953	22.9534	24.5227	26.2116	28.0291	29.9847	32.0887	34.3519	36.7862	39.4040	42.2187	45.2445	48.4966
14	14.9474	15.9739	17.0863	18.2919	19.5986	21.0151	22.5505	24.2149	26.0192	27.9750	30.0949	32.3926	34.8827	37.5811	40.5047	43.6720	47.1027	50.8180	54.8409	59.1959
15	16.0969	17.2934	18.5989	20.0236	21.5786	23.2760	25.1290	27.1521	29.3609	31.7725	34.4054	37.2797	40.4175	43.8424	47.5804	51.6595	56.1101	60.9653	66.2607	72.0351
16	17.2579	18.6393	20.1569	21.8245	23.6575	25.6725	27.8881	30.3243	33.0034	35.9497	39.1899	42.7533	46.6717	50.9804	55.7175	60.9250	66.6488	72.9390	79.8502	87.4421
17	18.4304	20.0121	21.7616	23.6975	25.8404	28.2129	30.8402	33.7502	36.9737	40.5447	44.5008	48.8837	53.7391	59.1176	65.0751	71.6730	78.9791	87.0680	96.0217	105.9306
18	19.6147	21.4123	23.4144	25.6454	28.1324	30.9057	33.9990	37.4502	41.3013	45.5992	50.3959	55.7497	61.7251	68.3941	75.8364	84.1407	93.4056	103.7403	115.2659	128.1167
19	20.8109	22.8406	25.1169	27.6712	30.5390	33.7600	37.3790	41.4463	46.0185	51.1591	56.9395	63.4397	70.7494	78.9692	88.2118	98.6032	110.2846	123.4135	138.1664	154.7400
20	22.0190	24.2974	26.8704	29.7781	33.0660	36.7856	40.9955	45.7620	51.1601	57.2750	64.2028	72.0524	80.9468	91.0249	102.4436	115.3797	130.0329	146.6280	165.4180	186.6880
21	23.2392	25.7833	28.6765	31.9692	35.7193	39.9927	44.8652	50.4229	56.7645	64.0025	72.2651	81.6987	92.4699	104.7684	118.8101	134.8405	153.1385	174.0210	197.8474	225.0256
22	24.4716	27.2990	30.5368	34.2480	38.5052	43.3923	49.0057	55.4568	62.8733	71.4027	81.2143	92.5026	105.4910	120.4360	137.6316	157.4150	180.1721	206.3448	236.4384	271.0307
23	25.7163	28.8450	32.4529	36.6179	41.4305	46.9958	53.4361	60.8933	69.5319	79.5430	91.1479	104.6029	120.2048	138.2970	159.2764	183.6014	211.8013	244.4868	282.3618	326.2368
24	26.9735	30.4219	34.4265	39.0826	44.5020	50.8156	58.1767	66.7648	76.7898	88.4973	102.1741	118.1552	136.8315	158.6586	184.1678	213.9776	248.8075	289.4945	337.0105	392.4842
25	28.2432	32.0303	36.4593	41.6459	47.7271	54.8645	63.2490	73.1059	84.7009	98.3471	114.4133	133.3339	155.6196	181.8708	212.7930	249.2140	292.1048	342.6035	402.0424	471.9811
26	29.5256	33.6709	38.5530	44.3117	51.1135	59.1564	68.6765	79.9544	93.3240	109.1818	127.9988	150.3339	176.8501	208.3327	245.7120	290.0883	342.7626	405.2721	479.4305	567.3773
27	30.8209	35.3443	40.7096	47.0842	54.6691	63.7058	74.4838	87.3508	102.7231	121.0999	143.0786	169.3740	200.8406	238.4993	283.5688	337.5024	402.0323	479.2211	571.5223	681.8527
28	32.1291	37.0512	42.9309	49.9676	58.4026	68.5281	80.6977	95.3388	112.9682	134.2099	159.8173	190.6989	227.9499	272.8892	327.1041	392.5027	471.3778	566.4808	681.1116	819.2233
29	33.4504	38.7922	45.2188	52.9663	62.3227	73.6398	87.3465	103.9659	124.1354	148.6309	178.3972	214.5827	258.5834	312.0937	377.1697	456.3032	552.5120	669.4474	811.5228	984.0679
30	34.7849	40.5681	47.5754	56.0849	66.4389	79.0582	94.4608	113.2832	136.3075	164.4940	199.0209	241.3327	293.1992	356.7868	434.7451	530.3117	647.4390	790.9479	966.7121	1181.882
40	48.8864	60.4020	75.4013	95.0255	120.7998	154.7620	199.6351	259.0565	337.8824	442.5925	581.8260	767.0914	1013.704	1342.025	1779.090	2360.757	3134.522	4163.212	5529.829	7343.856
50	64.4632	84.5794	112.7969	152.6671	209.3480	290.3359	406.5289	573.7701	815.0834	1163.908	1668.771	2400.018	3459.507	4994.522	7217.714	10435.65	15089.50	21813.09	31515.33	45497.17

Illustrations Using Appendix A.4: Present Value of Series of Equal Amounts (an Annuity of $1 per Period)

To use this table, locate the present value factor for the time period and the interest rate.

1. You are entering into a contract that will provide you with an income of $1000 at the end of the year for the next 10 years. If the annual interest rate is 7 percent, what is the present value of that stream of payments?

   The present value factor is 7.024; hence, the solution is $1000 × 7.024, or $7024.

2. You expect to have $250,000 available in a retirement plan when you retire. If the amount invested yields 8 percent and you hope to live an additional 20 years, how much can you withdraw each year so that the fund will just be liquidated after 20 years?

   The present value factor for 20 years at 8 percent is 9.818. Hence, the solution is $250,000 ÷ 9.818, or $25,463.

3. You have received an inheritance of $60,000 that you invested so that it earns 9 percent. If you withdraw $8000 annually to supplement your income, in how many years will the fund run out?

   Solving for n, $60,000 ÷ $8000 = 7.5. Scan down the 9 percent column until you find a present value factor close to 7.5, which is 7.487. The row indicates 13 years; thus, the fund will be depleted in approximately 13 years with $8000 annual withdrawals.

4. A seller offers to finance the sale of a building to you as an investment. The mortgage loan of $280,000 will be for 20 years and requires an annual mortgage payment of $24,000. Should you finance the purchase through the seller or borrow the funds from a financial institution at a current rate of 10 percent?

   $280,000 ÷ $24,000 = 11.667. Scan down the periods (n) column to 20 years and then read across to locate the figure closest to 11.667, which is 11.470. The column indicates 6 percent; thus, seller financing offers a lower interest rate.

5. You have the opportunity to purchase an office building for $750,000 with an expected life of 20 years. Looking over the financial details, you see that the before-tax net rental income is $90,000. If you want a return of at least 15 percent, how much should you pay for the building?

   The present value factor for 20 years at 15 percent is 6.259, and $90,000 × 6.259 = $563,310. Thus, the price is too high for you to earn a return of 15 percent.

An alternative approach is to use a calculator to determine the present value, *PV*, of a stream of payments. The equation is

$$PV = \frac{[1.0 - 1.0/(1.0 + i)^n] \times A}{i}$$ (A.4)

where

PV = *Present Value* of the investment
i = *Interest* rate per period
n = *Number* of periods the *PV* is invested
A = *Amount* of the annuity

Appendix A.4 Present Value of a Series of Equal Amounts (an Annuity of $1 Received at the End of Each Period)
(Used to Compute the Discounted Present Value of a Stream of Income Payments)

n	1%	2%	3%	4%	5%	6%	7%	8%	9%	10%	11%	12%	13%	14%	15%	16%	17%	18%	19%	20%
1	0.9901	0.9804	0.9709	0.9615	0.9524	0.9434	0.9346	0.9259	0.9174	0.9091	0.9009	0.8929	0.8850	0.8772	0.8696	0.8621	0.8547	0.8475	0.8403	0.8333
2	1.9704	1.9416	1.9135	1.8861	1.8594	1.8334	1.8080	1.7833	1.7591	1.7355	1.7125	1.6901	1.6681	1.6467	1.6257	1.6052	1.5852	1.5656	1.5465	1.5278
3	2.9410	2.8839	2.8286	2.7751	2.7232	2.6730	2.6243	2.5771	2.5313	2.4869	2.4437	2.4018	2.3612	2.3216	2.2832	2.2459	2.2096	2.1743	2.1399	2.1065
4	3.9020	3.8077	3.7171	3.6299	3.5460	3.4651	3.3872	3.3121	3.2397	3.1699	3.1024	3.0373	2.9745	2.9137	2.8550	2.7982	2.7432	2.6901	2.6386	2.5887
5	4.8534	4.7135	4.5797	4.4518	4.3295	4.2124	4.1002	3.9927	3.8897	3.7908	3.6959	3.6048	3.5172	3.4331	3.3522	3.2743	3.1993	3.1272	3.0576	2.9906
6	5.7955	5.6014	5.4172	5.2421	5.0757	4.9173	4.7665	4.6229	4.4859	4.3553	4.2305	4.1114	3.9975	3.8887	3.7845	3.6847	3.5892	3.4976	3.4098	3.3255
7	6.7282	6.4720	6.2303	6.0021	5.7864	5.5824	5.3893	5.2064	5.0330	4.8684	4.7122	4.5638	4.4226	4.2883	4.1604	4.0386	3.9224	3.8115	3.7057	3.6046
8	7.6517	7.3255	7.0197	6.7327	6.4632	6.2098	5.9713	5.7466	5.5348	5.3349	5.1461	4.9676	4.7988	4.6389	4.4873	4.3436	4.2072	4.0776	3.9544	3.8372
9	8.5660	8.1622	7.7861	7.4353	7.1078	6.8017	6.5152	6.2469	5.9952	5.7590	5.5370	5.3282	5.1317	4.9464	4.7716	4.6065	4.4506	4.3030	4.1633	4.0310
10	9.4713	8.9826	8.5302	8.1109	7.7217	7.3601	7.0236	6.7101	6.4177	6.1446	5.8892	5.6502	5.4262	5.2161	5.0188	4.8332	4.6586	4.4941	4.3389	4.1925
11	10.3676	9.7868	9.2526	8.7605	8.3064	7.8869	7.4987	7.1390	6.8052	6.4951	6.2065	5.9377	5.6869	5.4527	5.2337	5.0286	4.8364	4.6560	4.4865	4.3271
12	11.2551	10.5753	9.9540	9.3851	8.8633	8.3838	7.9427	7.5361	7.1607	6.8137	6.4924	6.1944	5.9176	5.6603	5.4206	5.1971	4.9884	4.7932	4.6105	4.4392
13	12.1337	11.3484	10.6350	9.9856	9.3936	8.8527	8.3577	7.9038	7.4869	7.1034	6.7499	6.4235	6.1218	5.8424	5.5831	5.3423	5.1183	4.9095	4.7147	4.5327
14	13.0037	12.1062	11.2961	10.5631	9.8986	9.2950	8.7455	8.2442	7.7862	7.3667	6.9819	6.6282	6.3025	6.0021	5.7245	5.4675	5.2293	5.0081	4.8023	4.6106
15	13.8651	12.8493	11.9379	11.1184	10.3797	9.7122	9.1079	8.5595	8.0607	7.6061	7.1909	6.8109	6.4624	6.1422	5.8474	5.5755	5.3242	5.0916	4.8759	4.6755
16	14.7179	13.5777	12.5611	11.6523	10.8378	10.1059	9.4466	8.8514	8.3126	7.8237	7.3792	6.9740	6.6039	6.2651	5.9542	5.6685	5.4053	5.1624	4.9377	4.7296
17	15.5623	14.2919	13.1661	12.1657	11.2741	10.4773	9.7632	9.1216	8.5436	8.0216	7.5488	7.1196	6.7291	6.3729	6.0472	5.7487	5.4746	5.2223	4.9897	4.7746
18	16.3983	14.9920	13.7535	12.6593	11.6896	10.8276	10.0591	9.3719	8.7556	8.2014	7.7016	7.2497	6.8399	6.4674	6.1280	5.8178	5.5339	5.2732	5.0333	4.8122
19	17.2260	15.6785	14.3238	13.1339	12.0853	11.1581	10.3356	9.6036	8.9501	8.3649	7.8393	7.3658	6.9380	6.5504	6.1982	5.8775	5.5845	5.3162	5.0700	4.8435
20	18.0456	16.3514	14.8775	13.5903	12.4622	11.4699	10.5940	9.8181	9.1285	8.5136	7.9633	7.4694	7.0248	6.6231	6.2593	5.9288	5.6278	5.3527	5.1009	4.8696
21	18.8570	17.0112	15.4150	14.0292	12.8212	11.7641	10.8355	10.0168	9.2922	8.6487	8.0751	7.5620	7.1016	6.6870	6.3125	5.9731	5.6648	5.3837	5.1268	4.8913
22	19.6604	17.6580	15.9369	14.4511	13.1630	12.0416	11.0612	10.2007	9.4424	8.7715	8.1757	7.6446	7.1695	6.7429	6.3587	6.0113	5.6964	5.4099	5.1486	4.9094
23	20.4558	18.2922	16.4436	14.8568	13.4886	12.3034	11.2722	10.3711	9.5802	8.8832	8.2664	7.7184	7.2297	6.7921	6.3988	6.0442	5.7234	5.4321	5.1668	4.9245
24	21.2434	18.9139	16.9355	15.2470	13.7986	12.5504	11.4693	10.5288	9.7066	8.9847	8.3481	7.7843	7.2829	6.8351	6.4338	6.0726	5.7465	5.4509	5.1822	4.9371
25	22.0232	19.5235	17.4131	15.6221	14.0939	12.7834	11.6536	10.6748	9.8226	9.0770	8.4217	7.8431	7.3300	6.8729	6.4641	6.0971	5.7662	5.4669	5.1951	4.9476
26	22.7952	20.1210	17.8768	15.9828	14.3752	13.0032	11.8258	10.8100	9.9290	9.1609	8.4881	7.8957	7.3717	6.9061	6.4906	6.1182	5.7831	5.4804	5.2060	4.9563
27	23.5596	20.7069	18.3270	16.3296	14.6430	13.2105	11.9867	10.9352	10.0266	9.2372	8.5478	7.9426	7.4086	6.9352	6.5135	6.1364	5.7975	5.4919	5.2151	4.9636
28	24.3164	21.2813	18.7641	16.6631	14.8981	13.4062	12.1371	11.0511	10.1161	9.3066	8.6016	7.9844	7.4412	6.9607	6.5335	6.1520	5.8099	5.5016	5.2228	4.9697
29	25.0658	21.8444	19.1885	16.9837	15.1411	13.5907	12.2777	11.1584	10.1983	9.3696	8.6501	8.0218	7.4701	6.9830	6.5509	6.1656	5.8204	5.5098	5.2292	4.9747
30	25.8077	22.3965	19.6004	17.2920	15.3725	13.7648	12.4090	11.2578	10.2737	9.4269	8.6938	8.0552	7.4957	7.0027	6.5660	6.1772	5.8294	5.5168	5.2347	4.9789
40	32.8347	27.3555	23.1148	19.7928	17.1591	15.0463	13.3317	11.9246	10.7574	9.7791	8.9511	8.2438	7.6344	7.1050	6.6418	6.2335	5.8713	5.5482	5.2582	4.9966
50	39.1961	31.4236	25.7298	21.4822	18.2559	15.7619	13.8007	12.2335	10.9617	9.9148	9.0417	8.3045	7.6752	7.1327	6.6605	6.2463	5.8801	5.5541	5.2623	4.9995

Estimating Social Security Benefits

The Social Security Administration (SSA) provides basic benefits for your retirement, for a period of disability, or for your survivors. To qualify, you must have earned the number of credits required for each benefit program. Once you qualify, the level of benefits received is based on your income in years past that was subject to the Federal Insurance Contributions Act (FICA) taxes, commonly known as Social Security taxes. Benefits increase each year based on a cost of living adjustment (COLA) announced by the SSA each October for the following year. Over the past ten years, COLA adjustments have averaged 2.6 percent. The discussion and Appendix B.1 provide the authors' estimates of Social Security benefits for 2010 for various income levels using calculators found at http://www.ssa.gov/planners/calculators.htm. The amounts are for a 30-year-old worker but would not differ significantly for workers ten years older or younger.

Social Security Retirement Benefits

To qualify for Social Security retirement benefits, any worker born after 1928 must have earned 40 credits of coverage. As noted in the text, it is possible to receive a maximum of four credits per year. In 2009, a worker would earn one credit for each $1,090 of income subject to Social Security taxes (this figure is adjusted upward each year for inflation). Dependent children, spouses caring for dependent children, and retired spouses at age 62 (including former spouses if the marriage lasted at least ten years) may also collect benefits based on the eligibility of the retired worker.

You can use Appendix B.1 to estimate a person's Social Security retirement benefits in today's dollars, assuming the retiree worked steadily, received average pay raises, and retired at the full-benefit retirement age. If more than one person would receive a benefit under the retiree's account (retiree and spouse, for example), the amount of the second person's benefit would be one-half of the retiree's benefit, giving a couple a total benefit 50 percent higher than the individual figure listed in Appendix B.1.

Social Security Disability Benefits

Social Security will pay disability benefits to an insured worker, dependent children up to age 18 (or 19 if the child is still in high school), a spouse caring for a dependent child who is younger than age 16 or disabled, and a spouse (even if divorced, but not remarried, provided that the marriage lasted ten years) age 62 or older. The benefit amount depends on two factors. The first factor is the eligibility of the disabled worker. To qualify for disability benefits, workers need at least 40 credits of coverage under Social Security, with at least 20 of the credits attained in the previous ten years (depending on year of birth). A worker younger than age 31 must have attained at least six credits or one more than one-half of the total credits possible after age 21, whichever is greater. (For example, a 26-year-old worker would have five years, or 20 credits, possible and would need ten credits of coverage.) The second factor affecting benefit levels is the predisability income of the covered individual that was subject to the FICA tax.

You can use Appendix B.1 to estimate an individual's Social Security disability benefits, assuming the disabled person worked steadily and received average pay raises. To obtain figures more specific than those given in Appendix B.1, contact the Social Security Administration to obtain your Social Security Statement as described in Chapter 17 or log on to http://www.ssa.gov/mystatement/ or http://www.ssa.gov/planners/calculators.htm.

Social Security Survivors Benefits

Social Security will pay benefits to surviving children younger than age 18 (or 19 if the child is still in high school), to a surviving spouse (even if divorced from the deceased, but not remarried) caring for surviving children who are younger than age 16, and to a surviving spouse (even if divorced, if the marriage lasted at least ten years) age 60 or older. Two factors are important in such cases. The first factor is the eligibility of the covered worker. The deceased worker who has accrued at least 40 credits of coverage is considered to be "fully insured." Workers who have earned at least as many credits of coverage as years since turning age 21 will be fully insured as well. Other individuals may be considered "currently insured" if they have earned six credits of coverage out of the previous 13 possible calendar credits. The survivors of currently insured workers receive limited types of benefits compared with those available to fully insured workers. The second factor is the covered worker's level of earnings, as indicated in Appendix B.1.

You can use Appendix B.1 to estimate monthly survivors benefits from Social Security in today's dollars for eligible surviving family members. The table assumes that the deceased worker worked steadily and received average pay raises.

Appendix B.1 **Estimates* of Social Security Benefits for the Three Major Social Security Programs**

	Present Annual Earnings					
	$30,000	**$40,000**	**$50,000**	**$60,000**	**$75,000**	**$100,000**
Monthly Retirement Benefits at Age 67 in Today's Dollars						
Per month	$ 1,276	$ 1,543	$ 1,816	$ 1,943	$ 2,195	$ 2,516
Per year	$15,312	$18,156	$21,792	$23,316	$26,340	$ 30,192
As a percentage of income	51%	46%	44%	39%	35%	30%
Monthly Retirement Benefits at Age 67 in Future Dollars						
Per month	$ 4,772	$ 5,743	$ 6,743	$ 7,623	$ 8,327	$ 9,501
Per year	$57,264	$68,916	$80,916	$91,476	$99,924	$ 114,012
Monthly Disability Benefits If You Became Disabled in 2010						
Individual benefit per month	$ 1,150	$ 1,387	$ 1,623	$ 1,858	$ 2,058	$ 2,334
Individual benefit per year	$13,800	$16,644	$19,476	$22,296	$24,696	$ 28,008
As a percentage of income	46%	42%	39%	37%	33%	28%
Maximum family benefit per month	$ 1,955	$ 2,358	$ 2,759	$ 3,159	$ 3,499	$ 3,968
Maximum family benefit per year	$23,460	$28,296	$33,108	$37,908	$41,988	$ 47,616
Monthly Survivor's Benefits If You Died in 2010						
Individual benefit per month†	$ 889	$ 1,074	$ 1,259	$ 1,443	$ 1,573	$ 1,790
Individual benefit per year	$10,668	$12,888	$15,108	$17,316	$18,876	$ 21,480
As a percentage of income	36%	32%	30%	29%	25%	21%
Maximum family benefit per month	$ 1,974	$ 2,676	$ 3,005	$ 3,368	$ 3,671	$ 4,179
Maximum family benefit per year	$23,688	$32,112	$36,060	$40,416	$44,052	$ 50,148

*Authors' estimates in 2010 for a 30-year-old worker using Social Security Administration website calculators.
†A surviving spouse age 65 or older would receive a retirement benefit approximately one-third higher than these figures.

Glossary

10-K report A firm's financial statements and activity details for any publicly traded company appear in this mandatory report sent to the SEC annually.

12b-1 fees/distribution fees Annual fees that some "no-load" fund companies deduct from a fund's assets to compensate salespeople and pay other expenses.

401(k) plan Defined-contribution plan designed for employees of private corporations.

403(b) plan Defined-contribution plan designed for eligible employees of not-for-profit institutions, such as colleges, hospitals, and religious organizations.

529 plan Provides a tax-free way to save for college in a state-run investment plan whereby the deposits into the fund are not deductible but the earnings at withdrawal are tax-free if used for qualified educational expenses.

above-the-line deductions Adjustments subtracted from gross income whether taxpayer itemizes deductions or not.

acceleration clause Part of a credit contract stating that after a specific number of payments are unpaid (often just one), the loan is considered in default and all remaining installments are due and payable upon demand of the creditor.

account reconciliation Comparing your records with your bank's records, checking the accuracy of both and identifying and correcting any errors.

active investor An investor who wishes to manage her own account by carefully studying the economy, market trends, and investment alternatives; regularly monitoring these factors; and buying and selling three to four times a year to rebalance her or his portfolio.

activities of daily living (ADLs) Insurance companies use the inability to perform a certain number of such activities as a criterion for deciding when the insured becomes eligible for long-term care benefits.

actual cash value (of personal property) Represents the purchase price of the property less depreciation.

add-on interest method Interest is calculated by applying an interest rate to the amount borrowed times the number of years to arrive at the total interest to be charged.

adjustable-rate mortgage (ARM)/variable-rate mortgage Mortgage in which the borrower's interest rate fluctuates according to some index of interest rates based on the rising or falling cost of credit in the economy—thus transferring interest rate risk to the borrower.

adjusted capitalized cost (adjusted cap cost) Subtracting the capitalized cost reductions from the gross capitalized cost.

adjusted gross income (AGI) Gross income less any exclusions and adjustments.

adjustments to income Allowable subtractions from gross income.

adoption tax credit A nonrefundable tax credit of up to $12,150 available for the qualifying costs of an adoption.

advance medical directive Statement of medical preferences, including designation of surrogate decision maker if patients become unable to make medical decisions for themselves in case of coma, dementia, or brain death.

adverse selection A situation involving certain types of perils such as earthquakes and floods where only those people with high probabilities of loss will want to buy the coverage, thereby violating the law of large numbers.

after-tax dollars Money on which employee has already paid taxes.

after-tax money Funds put into regular investment accounts; subject to income taxes.

after-tax profit Money left over after a firm has paid expenses, bondholder interest, and taxes.

after-tax yield The percentage yield on a taxable investment after subtracting the effect of federal income taxes that will need to be paid on the investment.

aggressive growth funds Funds that invest in speculative stocks with volatile price swings, seeking the greatest long-term capital appreciation possible. Also known as maximum capital gains funds and capital appreciation funds.

aggressive investment philosophy (risk seeker) Investors with this philosophy primarily seek capital gains, often with a short time horizon.

all-risk (open-perils) policies Cover losses caused by all perils other than those that the policy specifically excludes.

alpha statistic Quantifies the difference between an investment's expected return and its actual recent performance (outperforming or underperforming) given its risk; positive values indicate better-than-market performance.

alternative dispute resolution programs Industry- or government-sponsored programs that provide an avenue to resolve disputes outside the formal court system.

alternative minimum tax (AMT) A special higher tax rate of 26 or 28 percent that must be paid rather than the regular tax called for in the standard marginal tax brackets for certain high-income taxpayers that is triggered for people with excessive deductions.

American Opportunity Tax Credit A partially refundable tax credit of up to $2500 a year that to help defray college expenses for the first four years of postsecondary education.

amortization Loan repayment method in which part of the payment goes to pay interest and part goes to repay principal. Extra payments toward principal shorten the life of the loan and decrease total amount of interest paid.

amortization schedule List that shows all the monthly payments, the portions that will go toward interest and principal, and the debt remaining after each payment is made throughout the life of the loan.

annual fees Charges levied against cardholders for the privilege of having an open account but that are not included in the advertised APR.

annual fund operating expenses Normal operating costs of the business that are deducted from fund assets before shareholders receive earnings.

annual percentage rate (APR) Expresses the cost of credit on a yearly basis as a percentage rate.

annual percentage yield (APY) Return on total interest received on $100 deposit for 365-day period, given institution's simple annual interest rate and compounding frequency.

annual report Legally required yearly report about financial performance, activities, and prospects sent to major stockholders and made available to the general public.

annuitant Person covered by an annuity who is to receive the benefits.

annuity Contract made with an insurance company that provides for a series of payments to be received at stated intervals (usually monthly) for a fixed or variable time period.

any-occupation policy Provides full benefits only if you cannot perform any occupation.

appraisal fee Fee charged for a professionally prepared estimate of the fair market value of the property by an objective party.

approximate compound yield (ACY) A measure of the annualized compound growth of any long-term investment stated as a percentage.

aptitudes The natural abilities and talents that individuals possess.

"as is" Way for seller to get around legal requirements for warranties; buyer takes all risk of nonperformance or other problems despite any salesperson's verbal assurances.

ask price Declared lowest price that anyone is willing to accept to sell a security.

asset Property owned by a taxpayer for personal use or as an investment that has monetary value.

asset allocation Form of diversification in which investor decides on proportions of an investment portfolio that will be devoted to various categories of assets.

asset allocation funds Investments in a mix of assets (usually stocks, bonds, and cash equivalents and sometimes international assets, gold, and real estate); they buy and sell regularly to reduce risk while trying to outperform the market.

asset management account (AMA, central asset accounts, or all-in-one account) Multiple-purpose, coordinated package that gathers most monetary asset management vehicles into a unified account and reports activity on a single monthly statement to the client.

assets Everything you own that has monetary value.

asset-to-debt ratio Compares total assets with total liabilities.

assumable mortgage Buyer pays the seller a down payment generally equal to the seller's equity in the home and takes responsibility for the mortgage loan payments for the remaining term of the seller's existing mortgage loan.

ATM transaction fee Payments levied each time an automated teller machine (ATM) is used.

automatic enrollment plan Plan in which the employer withholds up to 6 percent of an employee's salary and places it into a defined-contribution retirement plan.

automatic funds transfer agreement Agreement whereby the amount necessary to cover a bad check is transferred from your savings account to your checking account.

automatic premium loan Provision allows any premium not paid by the end of the grace period to be paid automatically with a policy loan if sufficient cash value or dividends have accumulated.

automatic reinvestment Investor's option to choose to automatically reinvest any interest, dividends, and capital gains payments to purchase additional fund shares.

automobile bodily injury liability Occurs when a driver or car owner is held legally responsible for bodily injury losses that other people, including pedestrians, suffer.

automobile insurance Combines the liability and property insurance coverages that most car owners and drivers need into a single-package policy.

automobile medical payments insurance Insurance that covers bodily injury losses suffered by the driver of the insured vehicle and any passengers, regardless of who is at fault.

automobile property damage liability Occurs when a driver or car owner is held legally responsible for damage to others' property.

average-balance account Checking account for which service fees are assessed if the account's average daily balance drops below a certain level during specified time.

average daily balance Sum of the outstanding balances owed each day during the billing period divided by the number of days in the period.

average share cost Actual cost basis of the investment used for income tax purposes, calculated by dividing the total amount invested by the total shares purchased.

average share price Calculated by dividing the share price total by the number of investment periods.

average tax rate Proportion of total income paid in income taxes.

back-end ratio Compares the total of all monthly PITI expenditures plus auto loans and other debts with gross monthly income.

balanced funds Funds that keep a set mix of stocks and bonds, often 60 percent stocks and 40 percent bonds, in order to earn a well-balanced return of income and long-term capital gains.

balance sheet (or net worth statement) Snapshot of assets, liabilities, and net worth on a particular date.

balance transfer Full or partial payment on the balance of one credit card using a cash advance from another.

balloon automobile loan A loan that has a low monthly payment similar in amount to that required if the vehicle had been leased and with a large final payment similar in amount to the residual value under a lease.

bank credit card account Open-ended credit account with a financial institution that allows the holder to make purchases almost anywhere.

bankruptcy Constitutionally guaranteed right that permits people (and businesses) to ask a court to find them officially unable to meet their debts.

basic (homeowner's insurance) form (HO-1) Named-perils policy that covers 11 property-damage–causing perils and provides three areas of liability-related protection: personal liability, property damage liability, and medical payments.

basic liquidity ratio Number of months you could meet expenses using only monetary assets if all income ceases.

basic retirement benefit/primary insurance amount Amount of Social Security benefits a worker would receive at his or her full-benefit retirement age, which is 67 for those born after 1960.

bear market Market in which securities prices have declined in value by 20 percent or more from previous highs, often over the course of several weeks or months.

below-average costs Average costs of an investment if more shares are purchased when the price is down and fewer shares when the price is high.

beneficiary A person or organization designated to receive a benefit from a life insurance policy or estate or investment/savings account.

beneficiary designation form A form signed when opening a retirement account that contractually determines who will inherit the funds in that retirement account in case you die before the funds are distributed.

beneficiary designation Allowance of fund holder to name one or more beneficiaries so that the proceeds bypass probate proceedings if the original shareholder dies.

benefit amount Long-term care plans are generally written to provide a specific dollar benefit per day of care.

benefit period Length of time that the individual for whom a policy is written would likely need the care.

best buy Product or service that, in the buyer's opinion, represents acceptable quality at a fair or low price for that quality level.

beta value/beta coefficient A measure of stock volatility; that is, how much the stock price varies relative to the rest of the market.

bid price Declared highest price anyone wants to pay for a security.

billing/closing/statement date The last day for which any transactions are reported on the credit statement.

biweekly mortgage A form of growing-equity mortgage (GEM) that calls for payments of half of the normal payment to be made every two weeks; the borrower thus makes 26 payments a year and reduces the principal amount by one full payment each year; this reduces the mortgage term to about 20 years on a 30-year mortgage.

blue-chip stock A public corporation that has been around for a long time, has a well-regarded reputation, dominates its industry, and is known for being a solid, relatively safe investment.

board of directors A group of individuals at a corporation that sets policy and names the principal officers of the company.

bond A debt instrument issued by an organization that promises repayment at a specific time and the right to receive regular interest payments during the life of the bond; from investor's standpoint, a loan that the investor makes to a government or a corporation.

bond funds Fixed-income funds that aim to earn current income higher than a money market fund without incurring undue risk by investing in a portfolio of bonds and other low-risk investments that pay high dividends and offer capital appreciation.

bond rating An impartial outsider's opinion of the quality—or creditworthiness—of the issuing organization.

bonds Interest-bearing negotiable certificates of long-term debt issued by a corporation, a municipality (such as a city or state), or the federal government.

book-entry form Bond certificates aren't issued; rather, account is set up in name of the issuing organization or the brokerage firm that sold the bond, and interest is paid into this account when due.

book value per share Reflects the book value of a company divided by the number of shares of common stock outstanding.

book value/shareholder's equity Net worth of a company, determined by subtracting total liabilities from assets.

breakeven price The point at which the cost of a options contract is negated by a profit (or the cost is reduced by hedging a loss).

broker/dealer A brokerage firm representing a buyer that communicates with another brokerage firm that has the desired securities, thus in effect "making a market" for one or more securities.

broker's commission Largest selling cost in selling a home; these commissions often amount to 6 percent of the selling price of the home.

budget Paper or electronic document used to record both planned and actual income and expenditures over a period of time.

budget estimates Projected dollar amounts to receive or spend in a budgeting period.

budget exceptions When budget estimates differ from actual expenditures.

budget variance Difference between amount budgeted and actual amount spent or received.

bull market Market in which securities prices have risen 20 percent or more over time.

bunching deductions A technique to save on income taxes by prepaying tax deductible expenses in a year in advance so as to increase one's itemizations higher than the standard deduction threshold and taking the standard deduction in the following year.

business cycle/economic cycle Business cycles can be depicted as a wavelike pattern of rising and falling economic activity; the phases of the business cycle include expansion, peak, contraction (which may turn into recession), and trough.

business-cycle risk The risk that economic growth or the lack thereof will impact the profits of a particular business.

business failure risk (also called financial risk) The possibility that a business will fail, perhaps go bankrupt, and result in a massive or total loss of one's invested funds.

buy and hold/buy to hold Investment strategy in which investors buy a widely diversified mix of stocks and/or mutual funds, reinvest the dividends by buying more stocks and mutual funds, and hold on to those investments almost indefinitely.

buyer's order Written offer that names a specific vehicle and all charges; only sign such offers after the salesperson and sales manager have signed *first*.

buying long Buying a security (especially on margin) with the hope that the stock price will rise.

call option Stipulation in an indenture that allows issuer to repurchase the bond at par value or by paying a premium, often one year's worth of interest. Bonds are thus callable.

capital gain Net income received from sale of an asset above its purchase price.

capital gains distributions Distributions representing the net gains (capital gains minus capital losses) that a fund realizes when it sells securities that were held in the fund's portfolio.

capital improvements Costs incurred in making value-enhancing changes (beyond maintenance and repair) in real property.

capital loss The net loss of income that results when the sale of an asset brings less income than the costs of purchasing and selling an asset.

card registration service Firm that will notify all companies with which you have debit and credit cards if your cards are lost or stolen.

career The lifework chosen by a person to use personal talent, education, and training.

career fairs University-, community- and employer-sponsored events for job seekers to meet with many employers quickly to screen potential employers.

career goal Identifying what you want to do for a living, whether a specific job or field of employment.

career plan A plan that identifies employment that interests you; fits your abilities, skills, work style, and lifestyle; and provides strategic guidance to help you reach your career goal.

career planning Finding employment that will use your interests and abilities and that will support you financially.

cash Cash equivalents such as Treasury securities.

cash account A brokerage account that requires an initial deposit (perhaps as little as $100) and specifies that full settlement is due to the brokerage firm within three business days after a buy or sell order has been given.

cash advance A cash advance is the use of a credit card to obtain cash rather than to make a purchase.

cash advance (or convenience) checks A check-equivalent way to take a cash advance on a credit card.

cash-balance plan Defined-benefit plan funded solely by an employer that gives each participant an interest-earning account credited with a percentage of pay on a monthly basis.

cash basis Only transactions involving actual cash received or cash spent are recorded.

cash dividends Distributions made in cash to holders of common and preferred stock typically paid 4 times a year.

cash flow Amount of rental income you have left after paying all operating expenses.

cash-flow calendar Budget estimates for monthly income and expenses.

cash-flow statement (or income and expense statement) Summary of all income and expense transactions over a specific time period.

cash surrender value Represents the cash value of a policy minus any surrender charges.

cash-value life insurance Pays benefits at death and includes a savings/investment element that can provide a reduced level of benefits to the policyholder prior to the death of the insured person.

catch-up provision Permits workers age 50 or older to contribute an additional $5500 to most employer-sponsored plans ($1000 limit on IRA accounts).

certificate of deposit (CD) An interest-earning savings instrument purchased for a fixed period of time.

certificate of insurance Paper or booklet that outlines group health insurance benefits.

certified check Personal check on which your financial institution imprints the word *certified*, signifying that the account has sufficient funds to cover its payment.

Chapter 7 of the Bankruptcy Act (straight bankruptcy) Provides for the liquidation of assets with proceeds applied to paying off excusable debts to the degree possible.

Chapter 13 of the Bankruptcy Act (wage earner or regular income plan) Designed for individuals with regular incomes who might be able to pay off some or all of their debts given certain court protections.

chargeback The amount of the transaction is charged back to the business where the transaction originated in the case of a dispute or challenge by the cardholder.

checking accounts At depository institutions, allow depositors to write checks against their deposited funds, which transfer deposited funds to other people and organizations.

child and dependent care credit A nonrefundable tax credit that may be claimed by workers who pay employment-related expenses for care of a child or other dependent if that care gives them the freedom to work, seek work, or attend school full time.

child tax credit A refundable tax credit of $1000 or more that may be taken by low and moderate income families for each qualifying child younger than age 17 claimed as a dependent.

chronological format Résumé that provides your information in reverse order, with most recent first.

city indexes Comparing wages and cost of living for various employment locations.

claims adjuster Person designated by the insurance company to assess whether the loss is covered and to determine the dollar amount that the company will pay.

cliff vesting A time schedule under which an employee is fully vested in an employer-sponsored retirement plan within three years of employment.

closed-end lease/walkaway lease Agreement in which the lessee pays no charge if the end-of-lease market value of the vehicle is lower than the originally projected residual value.

closed-end mutual funds Funds that issue a limited and fixed number of shares at inception and do not buy them back; after purchase, fund shares trade at market prices.

closing costs Include fees and charges other than the down payment and may vary from 2 to 10 percent of the mortgage loan amount.

COBRA rights The Consolidated Omnibus Budget Reconciliation Act of 1985 that allows a former employee to remain a member of a group health plan for as long as 18 months if the employee worked for an employer with more than 20 workers.

codicil Legal instrument with which one can make minor changes to a will.

coinsurance Method by which the insured and the insurer share proportionately in the payment for a loss.

coinsurance clause Requires insured to pay a proportion of any loss suffered.

collectibles Cultural artifacts that have value because of their beauty, age, scarcity, or popularity, such as antiques, stamps, rare coins, art, baseball cards, and so on.

college savings plan One of the two types of qualified tuition programs that is set up for a designated beneficiary.

collision insurance Reimburses insureds for losses to their vehicles resulting from a collision with another car or object or from a rollover.

commissions Fees or percentages of the selling price paid to salespeople, agents, and companies for their services in buying or selling an investment.

common stock Most basic form of ownership of a corporation.

comparison shopping Process of comparing products or services to find the best buy.

compounding When interest on an investment itself earns interest.

compound interest When interest on an investment itself earns interest.

comprehensive automobile insurance Protects against property damage losses to an insured vehicle caused by perils other than collision and rollover.

comprehensive health insurance Insurance that provides protection against financial losses resulting from hospital, surgical, and medical expenditures with policy limits as high as $1 million or more.

condominium Form of ownership with the owners holding legal title to their own housing unit among many with common grounds and facilities owned by the developer or homeowner's association.

conservative investment philosophy (risk aversion) Investors with this philosophy accept very little risk and are generally rewarded with relatively low rates of return for seeking the twin goals of a moderate amount of current income and preservation of capital.

consumer-driven health care An approach to health care protection where the consumer elects a health care plan with a high deductible and high overall policy limits.

consumer finance company/small loan company Firm that specializes in making relatively small secured or unsecured loans that require monthly installment payments.

consumer price index (CPI) A broad measure of changes in the prices of all goods and services purchased for consumption by urban households.

consumer statement Your version of a credit issue that shows up on your credit report when the credit bureau refuses to drop a disputed claim.

contents replacement-cost protection Option sometimes available in homeowner's insurance policies (including the renter's form) that pays the full replacement cost of any personal property.

contingency clauses Specify that certain conditions must be satisfied before a contract is binding.

contingent (or secondary) beneficiary The beneficiary in case the first-named beneficiary has died; also called the secondary beneficiary.

contingent deferred sales charge A sales commission that is imposed only when shares are sold; often charges are on a sliding scale, with the fee dropping 1 percentage point per year that the investor stays in the fund.

contributory plan The most common type of employee-sponsored defined-contribution retirement plan; accepts employee as well as employer contributions.

conventional mortgage A fixed-rate, fixed-term, fixed-payment mortgage loan.

convertible preferred stock Can be exchanged at the option of the stockholder for a specified number of shares of common stock.

convertible term insurance Offers policyholders option of exchanging a term policy for a cash-value policy without evidence of insurability.

cooperative (co-op) Form of ownership in which owner holds a share of the corporation that owns and manages a group of housing units as well as common grounds and facilities.

coordination-of-benefits clause Prevents an individual from collecting insurance benefits that exceed the loss suffered by noting the order in which plans will pay if the insured individual is covered by multiple plans.

copayment A variation of a deductible, requires you to pay a specific dollar amount each time you use your benefits for a specific covered expense item.

corporate bonds Interest-bearing certificates of long-term debt issued by a corporation.

corporate earnings The profits a company makes during a specific time period indicate to many analysts whether to buy or sell a stock.

corporation A state-chartered legal entity that can conduct business operations in its own name.

countercyclical (or defensive) stock A stock that exhibits price changes contrary to movements in the business cycle.

coupon rate/coupon/coupon yield/stated interest rate Interest rate printed on the certificate when the bond is issued.

cover letter A letter of introduction sent to a prospective employer to get an interview.

Coverage C—uninsured and underinsured motorist insurance Coverage that an insured can purchase as part of automobile insurance that covers the insured in an accident with an uninsured or underinsured driver at fault.

Coverdell education savings account (or education savings account) An IRS approved way to pay the future education costs for a child younger than age 18 whereby the earnings accumulate tax free and withdrawals for qualified expenses are tax free.

covered option Option for a security that the writer owns and thus the writer can settle any call options contract with relatively little risk.

covering a position When an investor using a margin account buys back securities sold short or sells securities bought long.

credit A term used to describe an arrangement in which goods, services, or money is received in exchange for a promise to repay at a future date.

credit agreement Contract that stipulates repayment terms for credit cards.

credit application Form or interview that provides information about your ability and willingness to repay debts.

credit bureau Firm that collects and keeps records of many borrowers' credit histories.

credit card blocking Hotels or other service providers use a credit card number to secure reservations and charge the anticipated cost of services.

credit cards Cards that allow repeated use of credit as long as the consumer makes regular monthly payments.

credit counseling agency (CCA) Agency that can arrange payment schedules with unsecured creditors for overly indebted consumers and can provide individuals with credit counseling.

credit history Continuing record of a person's credit usage and repayment of debts.

credit limit Maximum outstanding debt that a lender will allow on an open-ended credit account.

credit receipt Written evidence of any items returned that notes the specific amount and date of the transaction.

credit repair company (credit clinic) Firm that offers to help improve or fix a person's credit history for a (usually hefty) fee.

credit report Information compiled by a credit bureau from merchants, utility companies, banks, court records, and creditors about your payment history.

credit reporting service Allows you to access your credit report as often as daily and obtain your credit score for an annual fee.

credit score (risk score) Statistical measure used to rate applicants based on various factors deemed relevant to creditworthiness and the likelihood of repayment.

credit statement The monthly bill on a credit card account showing the charges and payments made, minimum payment required, and due date among other information; also called a *periodic statement*.

credit union (CU) Member-owned, not-for-profit federally insured financial institutions that provide checking, savings, and loan services to members.

crude annual rate of return A rough measure of the yield on amounts invested that assumes that equal portions of the gain are earned each year.

cumulative preferred stock Preferred stock for which dividends must be paid, including any skipped dividends, before dividends go to common stockholders.

current income Money received while you own an investment; usually received regularly as interest, rent, or dividends.

currently insured status Requires workers to earn six credits in the most recent three years; provides for some survivors or disability benefits but no retirement benefits.

current rate Rate of return the insurance company has recently paid to policyholders.

current yield Equals the bond's fixed annual interest payment divided by its bond price.

cyclical stock the stock of a company whose profits are greatly influenced by changes in the economic business cycle.

day trading Occurs when an investor buys and sells stocks quickly throughout a day with the hope that prices will move enough to cover transaction costs and earn some profits.

dealer holdback/dealer rebate Dealer incentive in which the manufacturer allows dealers to hold back a percentage of invoice price, thereby providing the dealer with additional profit on the vehicle.

death benefit Amount that will be paid to beneficiary when the insured dies.

debt Any obligation to repay an amount borrowed.

debt collection agency Firm that specializes in collecting debts that the original lender could not collect.

debt-consolidation loan A loan taken out to pay off several smaller debts.

debt limit Overall maximum you believe you should owe based on your ability to meet repayment obligations.

debt management plan (DMP) Arrangement whereby consumer provides one monthly payment (usually somewhat smaller than the total of previous credit payments) that is distributed to all creditors.

debt payments-to-disposable income method Percentage of disposable personal income available for regular debt repayments aside from set obligations.

debt payments-to-disposable income ratio Divides monthly disposable personal income into monthly debt repayments.

debts Lending investments that typically offer both a fixed maturity and a fixed income.

debt service-to-income ratio Compares dollars spent on gross annual debt.

debt-to-equity ratio Ratio of your consumer debt to your assets.

declining-balance method Interest calculation method in which interest is assessed during each billing period (usually each month) based on the outstanding balance of the installment loan that billing period.

deductible clause Requires that the policyholder pays an initial portion of any loss.

deductibles Clauses in health care plans that require you to pay an initial portion of health expenses annually before receiving reimbursement.

deed Written document used to convey real estate ownership.

deeded timesharing The buyer obtains a legal title or deed to limited time periods of use of real estate and becomes a secured creditor.

default rate Percentage of bonds that do not repay principal at maturity and sometimes cease interest payments in the interim.

default risk/credit risk Uncertainty associated with not receiving the promised periodic interest payments and the principal amount when it becomes due at maturity.

deferred annuity Annuity plan in which annuitants pay premiums during their working lives, then take income payments at some future date, such as retirement.

deficiency amount The difference between the amount owed on a mortgage loan and what the lender collects at a short sale of the property.

deficiency balance Occurs when money raised by sale of repossessed collateral doesn't cover the amount owed on the debt plus any repossession expenses.

deficit (or net loss) when expenses exceed income such as reported on a cash flow statement.

defined-benefit retirement plan Employer-sponsored retirement plan that pays lifetime monthly annuity payments to retirees based on a predetermined formula.

defined-contribution retirement plan IRS-approved retirement plan sponsored by employers that allows employees to make pretax contributions that lower their tax liability.

dental expense insurance Insurance that provides reimbursement for dental care expenses.

depository institutions Organizations licensed to take deposits and make loans.

depreciation Decline in value of an asset over time due to normal wear and tear and obsolescence.

derivative/derivative security A financial instrument that people trade in order to more easily manage the underlying asset upon which these instruments are based, which can be used to reduce risk or take on additional risk.

direct ownership Results when investor holds actual legal title to property.

direct sellers Companies that market insurance policies through salaried employees, mail-order promotions, newspapers, the Internet, and even vending machines.

disability benefits Substantially reduced benefits paid to employees who become disabled prior to retirement.

disability income insurance Insurance that covers a portion of the income lost when you cannot work because of illness or injury.

discharged debts Debts (or portions thereof) that are excused as a result of a bankruptcy.

discount brokers Charge commissions to execute trades that are often 30 to 80 percent less than the fees charged by full-service brokers, but also offer fewer services.

discounted cash-flow method Effective way to estimate the value or asking price of a real estate investment based on after-tax cash flow and the return on the invested dollars discounted over time to reflect a discounted yield.

discount method of calculating interest Interest is calculated based on discount rate multiplied by the amount borrowed and by number of years to repay. Interest is then subtracted from the amount of the loan and the difference is given to the borrower. In this method, interest is paid up front before any part of the payment is applied toward the principal.

discount yield Difference between the original purchase price of a T-bill and what the Treasury pays you at maturity—the gain, or "par," is interest.

discretionary income The money left over once the necessities of living are covered, such as paying for housing, food, and other necessities; the money that is "controllable" and often makes up the bulk of money available to pay for one's variable expenses.

disposable income Amount of income remaining after taxes and withholding for such purposes as insurance and union dues.

diversification Process of reducing risk by spreading investment money among several investment opportunities.

dividend A portion of a company's earnings that the firm pays out to its shareholders.

dividend payout ratio Dividends per share divided by earnings per share (EPS); helps judge likelihood of future dividends.

dividends per share Translates the total cash dividends paid out by a company to common stockholders into a per-share figure.

dividend yield Cash dividend to an investor expressed as a percentage of the current market price of a security.

dollar-cost averaging/cost averaging Systematic program of investing equal sums of money at regular intervals regardless of the price of the investment.

Dow Jones Industrial Average (DJIA) The most widely reported of all stock market indexes that tracks prices of only 30 actively traded blue-chip stocks, including well-known companies such as American Express and AT&T.

down payment Portion of the purchase price that is not borrowed.

due-on-sale clause Requires that the mortgage loan be fully paid off if the home is sold. It can impose a burden on the seller because it prohibits a buyer from assuming the mortgage loan.

dunning letters Notices that make insistent demands for repayment.

durable power of attorney for finances Document that appoints someone, called an attorney-in-fact, to handle your legal or business matters and sign your name to documents if illness prevents you from doing so yourself.

earned income credit (EIC) A refundable tax credit that may be claimed by workers with a qualifying child and in certain cases by childless workers.

earnest money Funds given to seller as a deposit to hold the property until a purchase contract can be negotiated.

earnings per share (EPS) A firm's profit divided by the number of outstanding shares.

earnings yield Inverse of the P/E ratio; helps investors more clearly see investment expectations.

earthquake insurance Can be purchased only from a private insurance company either as a separate policy or as an endorsement to an existing homeowner's or renter's insurance policy.

economic growth A condition of increasing production (business spending) and consumption (consumer spending) in the economy and hence increasing national income.

effective marginal tax rate The total marginal rate reflects all taxes on a person's income, including federal, state, and local income taxes as well as Social Security and Medicare taxes.

Electronic funds transfers (EFTs) Funds shifted electronically (rather than by check or cash) among various accounts or to and from other people and businesses.

employee benefit Compensation for employment that does not take the form of wages, salaries, commissions, or other cash payments.

Employee Retirement Income Security Act (ERISA) Regulates employer-sponsored plans by calling for proper plan reporting and disclosure to participants in defined-contribution, defined-benefit, and cash-balance plans.

employee stock option A contractual option to purchase a stock without putting any money down that is sometimes given to employees who might benefit from a hoped for increase in the employer's stock price.

employee stock-ownership plan (ESOP) Benefit plan in which employers make tax-deductible gifts of company stock into trusts, which are then allocated into employee accounts.

employer-sponsored retirement plan An IRS-approved retirement plan offered by an employer (also called **qualified** plans).

employment agency Firm that locates employment for certain types of employees.

envelope system Placing exact amounts into envelopes for each budgetary purpose.

equities Stocks and/or stock mutual funds.

equity Dollar value of the home in excess of the amount owed on it.

escrow account Special reserve account at a financial institution in which funds are held until they are paid to a third party—in this case, for home insurance and for property taxes.

estate Your worldly possessions and financial assets less any debts you owe.

estate planning The definite arrangements you make during your lifetime that are consistent with your wishes for the administration and distribution of your estate when you die.

estimated taxes People who are self-employed or receive substantial income from an employer that is not required to practice payroll withholding (such as lawyers and owners of rental property) are required by the IRS to estimate their tax liability and pay them in advance in quarterly installments.

estimate of the required rate of return on an investment A calculation that multiplies the beta value of an investment by the estimated market risk and adds the risk-free T-bill rate that suggests to investors the return required to put their money at risk.

excess mileage charge Fees assessed at the end of a lease if the vehicle was driven more miles than originally specified in the lease contract.

exchange fees Small amount charged to move money among funds within a mutual fund family.

exchange privilege Allowance for mutual fund shareholders to easily swap shares on a dollar-for-dollar basis for shares in another mutual fund within a mutual fund family. Also called switching, conversion, or transfer privilege.

exchange-traded fund (ETF) Basket of passively managed securities structured like an index fund; owns all or a representative set of securities that duplicate the performance of a market segment or index.

exclusion amount The value of assets that may be transferred to heirs without incurring an estate tax—currently $3.5 million.

exclusions Income not subject to federal taxation.

executor/personal representative Person responsible for carrying out the provisions of a will and managing the assets until the estate is passed on to heirs.

exemption (or personal exemption) Legally permitted amount deducted from AGI based on number of people that taxpayer's income supports.

expense ratio Expense per dollar of assets under management.

expenses Total expenditures made in a specified time such as reported on a cash-flow statement.

expiration date An exact date, typically three, six, or nine months in the future from the date of purchase of an options contract after which the investor may not exercise the option to buy or sell shares of stock specified in the contract.

extended warranty/service contract/maintenance agreement/buyer protection plan Agreement between the seller and buyer of product to repair or replace covered product components for some specified time period; purchased separately from product itself.

face amount Dollar value of protection as listed in the policy and used to calculate the premium.

Fair Credit Billing Act (FCBA) Helps people who wish to dispute billing errors on revolving credit accounts.

Fair Credit Reporting Act (FCRA) Requires that credit reports contain accurate, relevant, and recent information and that only bona fide users be permitted to review a file for approved purposes.

Fair Debt Collection Practices Act (FDCPA) Prohibits third-party debt collection agencies from using abusive, deceptive, or unfair practices to collect past-due debts.

fair market value Amount a willing buyer would pay to a willing seller for a charitable item.

federal deposit insurance Insures deposits, both principal amounts and accrued interest, up to $100,000 per account for most accounts.

federal estate tax Assessed against a deceased person's estate before property (real estate, stocks and bonds, business interests, and so on) is transferred to heirs or assigned according to terms of a will or state intestacy laws.

federal funds rate The rate that banks charge one another for overnight loans; set by the Federal Reserve Board.

Federal Housing Administration (FHA) An arm of the U.S. Department of Housing and Urban Development (HUD) that insures loans that meet its standards to encourage home ownership.

Federal Insurance Contributions Act (FICA) Act that authorizes Social Security and Medicare tax withdrawals from employee paychecks; amounts withheld go into Social Security trust fund accounts, which pay benefits to current retirees.

filing status Description of a taxpayer's marital status on last day of tax year.

final expenses One-time expenses occurring just prior to or after a death.

finance charge Total dollar amount paid to use credit.

financial goals Specific objectives addressed by planning and managing finances.

financial literacy Knowledge of facts, concepts, principles, and technological tools that are fundamental to being smart about money.

financial planner An investment professional who evaluates the personal finances of an individual or family and recommends strategies to set and achieve long-term financial goals.

financial planning Managing income and wealth continuously through life to meet financial goals.

financial ratios Calculations designed to simplify evaluation of financial strength and progress.

financial records Documents that evidence financial transactions.

financial responsibility Means that you are accountable for your future financial well-being and that you strive to make wise personal financial decisions.

financial risk Possibility that an investment will fail to pay a return to the investor.

financial services industry Companies that provide monetary asset management and other services.

financial statements Snapshots that describe an individual or family's current financial condition.

financial strategies Preestablished action plans implemented in specific situations.

first-time home buyer credit An $8000 refundable tax credit for those who purchased a home between April 2008 and July 2009. (This credit may be extended by Congress.)

fixed expenses Expenses that recur at fixed intervals.

fixed income Specific rate of return that borrower agrees to pay the investor for use of the principal (initial investment).

fixed maturity Specific date on which borrower agrees to repay the principal to the investor.

fixed yield Interest income payment remains the same regardless of bond's price.

flexible benefit plan An employer-sponsored plan that gives the employee a choice of selecting either cash or one or more qualifying nontaxable benefits; also known as a cafeteria plan.

flexible spending account (FSA) An employer-sponsored account that allows employee-paid expenses for medical or dependent care to be paid with an employee's pretax dollars rather than after-tax income.

flexible spending account (FSA) (or expense reimbursement account) An IRS approved plan for employers that allows an employee to fund qualified medical expenses on a pretax basis through salary reduction to pay for out-of-pocket unreimbursed expenses for health and dependent care that are not covered by insurance.

flexible spending arrangements Employer arrangements that allow employees to place a portion of their salary into an account that is used to pay some of their health care expenditures, including employee-paid health plan premiums.

floater policies Provide all-risk protection for accident and theft losses to movable property regardless of where the loss occurs.

floor broker Brokerage firm's contact person at an exchange.

foreclosure Process in which the lender sues the borrower to prove default and asks the court to order the sale of the property to pay the debt.

front-end load A sales charge paid when an individual buys an investment, reducing the amount available to purchase fund shares.

front-end ratio Compares the total annual PITI expenditures for housing with the loan applicant's gross annual income to assess the borrower's ability to pay the mortgage.

FSBO For sale by owner; commonly pronounced "fizbo"; home sold directly by the homeowner to save on sales commission paid to a real estate broker.

full warranty Warranty that meets three stringent promises: product must be fixed at no cost to buyer within reasonable time, owner will not have to undertake an unreasonable task to return product for repair, and defective product will be replaced with a new one or the buyer's money will be returned if product cannot be fixed.

full-benefit retirement age Age at which a retiree is entitled to full Social Security benefits; 67 for those born in 1960 or later.

fully insured Social Security status Requires 40 credits and provides workers and their families with benefits under the retirement, survivors, and disability programs; once status is earned, it cannot be taken away even if the eligible worker never works again.

functional format Résumé that emphasizes career-related experiences.

fundamental analysis School of thought in market analysis that assumes each stock has an intrinsic (or true) value based on its expected stream of future earnings.

fund investment advisers Money managers, securities analysts, and traders of a mutual fund that have access to the best research; they select, buy, sell, and monitor the performance of the securities purchased; thus, they oversee the portfolio.

fund screener/fund-screening tool Permits investors to screen all of the mutual funds in the market to gauge performance.

futures contract Type of exchange-traded standardized forward contract that specifies the size of the contract, quality of product to be delivered, and delivery date.

future value The valuation of an asset projected to the end of a particular time period in the future.

garnishment Court-sanctioned procedure by which a portion of debtors' wages are set aside by their employers to pay debts.

general (full-service) brokerage firms Offer a full range of services to customers, including investment advice and research.

generic products Goods that carry store brand names or a general commodity name rather than an advertsised brand, such as Del Monte.

gold bullion A refined and stamped weight of precious metal.

gold bullion coins Various world mints issue these coins, which contain 1 troy ounce (31.15 grams) of pure gold.

good-faith estimate Lender's list of all the costs associated with the loan, including the annual percentage rate (APR), application and processing fees, closing costs, and any other charges that must be paid when the deal is legally consummated.

government securities money market funds Funds that appeal to investor concerns about safety by investing solely in U.S. Treasury bills and other short-term securities backed by the U.S. government.

grace period Period (in days) for which deposits or withdrawals can be made without any penalty.

graduated-payment mortgage Mortgage in which borrower pays smaller-than-normal payments in the early years but payments gradually increase to larger-than-normal payments in later years.

graduated vesting Schedule under which employees must be at least 20 percent vested after two years of service and gain an additional 20 percent of vesting for each subsequent year until, at the end of year six, the account is fully vested.

grantor Creator of a trust—the person who makes a grant of assets to establish a trust. Also called the *settler, donor,* or *trustor.*

gross capitalized cost (gross cap cost) Includes vehicle price plus cost of any extra features such as insurance or maintenance agreements.

gross domestic product (GDP) The nation's broadest measure of economic health; it reports how much economic activity (all goods and services) has occurred within the U.S. borders during a given period.

gross income All income in the form of money, goods, services, and/or property.

group health plan Sold collectively to an entire group of people rather than to individuals, such as the group health care policies offered by employers.

growth and income funds Funds that invest in companies that have a high likelihood of both dividend income and price appreciation; less risk-oriented than aggressive growth funds or growth funds.

growth funds Funds that seek long-term capital appreciation by investing in common stocks of companies with higher-than-average revenue and earnings growth, often the larger and well-established firms.

growth stock The stock of a company that offers the promise of much higher profits tomorrow and has a consistent record of relatively rapid growth in earnings in all economic conditions.

guaranteed insurability (guaranteed purchase option) Permits the cash-value policyholder to buy additional stated amounts of cash-value life insurance at stated times in the future without evidence of insurability.

guaranteed insurance contracts (GIC) An investment offered by an insurance company that guarantees the owner a fixed or floating interest rate for a predetermined period of time and the return of principal.

guaranteed minimum rate of return Minimum rate that, by contract, the insurance company is legally obligated to pay.

guaranteed portability Provision that allows an individual to convert group coverage to individual coverage within 180 days before COBRA ends.

guaranteed renewable policies Policies that must be continued in force as long as the policyholder pays the required premium.

guaranteed renewable term insurance Protects you against the possibility of becoming uninsurable.

guardian Person responsible for caring for and raising any child under the age of 18 and for managing the child's estate.

hazard Any condition that increases the probability that a peril will occur.

health care plan Generic name for any program that pays or provides reimbursement for direct health care expenditures.

health care proxy/durable power of attorney for health care Legal document that appoints another person to make health care decisions if the writer of the proxy is rendered incapable of making his or her wishes known.

health maintenance organizations (HMOs) Health insurance plans that provide a broad range of health care services for a set monthly fee on a prepaid basis.

health reimbursement account (HRA) Funds that employers set aside to reimburse employees for qualified health expenses.

health savings accounts (HSAs) Special savings account intended for people who have a high-deductible health care plan (with annual deductibles of at least $1000 for individuals and $2000 for families).

hedge funds Freewheeling risky investment pools for the extremely wealthy that are global companies beyond the regulations of the U.S. Securities and Exchange Commission (SEC) that use unconventional investment strategies.

heir Person who inherits or is entitled by law or by the terms of a will to inherit some asset.

high-balling Sales tactic in which dealer offers a trade-in allowance that is much higher than the vehicle is worth.

high-deductible health care plan Can either be traditional health insurance or an HMO that follows the consumer-driven health care philosophy by charging relatively high deductibles.

high-risk investments Alternative investments that have the potential for significant fluctuations in return over short time periods, perhaps only days or weeks, such as collectibles, precious metals and stones, and options and futures contracts.

high-risk/speculative investments Present potential for significant fluctuations in return, sometimes over short time periods.

home inspection Conducted to ensure that the home is physically sound and that all operating systems are in proper order.

homeowner's general liability protection Applies when you are legally liable for another person's losses, other than those that arise out of use of vehicles or your professional duties.

homeowner's insurance Combines liability and property insurance coverages that homeowners and renters typically need into single-package policies.

I bonds Nonmarketable savings bonds backed by the U.S. government that pay an earnings rate that combines two rates: a fixed interest rate set when the investor buys the bond and a semiannual variable interest rate tied to inflation that protects the investor's purchasing power.

immediate annuity Annuity, often funded by a lump sum from the death benefit of a life insurance policy or lump sum from a defined-contribution plan, that begins payments one month after purchase.

income Total income received such as reported on a cash-flow statement.

income stock A stock that may not grow too quickly, but year after year it pays a cash dividend higher than that offered by most companies.

incontestability clause Places a time limit on the right of the insurance company to deny a claim.

indenture Written, legal agreement between bondholders and debtor that describes terms of the debt by setting forth the maturity date, interest rate, and other details.

indexed A procedure used by the Social Security Administration to adjust the earnings during one's working years to reflect increases in average wages for all workers over time; used in the process of calculating SSA benefits.

index fund Mutual fund that seeks to achieve the same return as a particular market index by buying and holding all or a representative selection of securities in it.

indexing Yearly adjustments to tax brackets that reduce inflation's effects on tax brackets.

index of leading economic indicators (LEI) A composite index reported monthly by the Conference Board that suggests the future direction of the U.S. economy.

individual account Has one owner who is solely responsible for the account and its activity.

individual retirement account (IRA) Investment accounts that reduce current year income and that are allowed to accumulate tax free.

inflation A steady and sustained rise in general price levels across economic sectors; measured by the changing cost over time of a "market basket" of goods and services that a typical household might purchase.

inflation risk (also called purchasing power risk) The danger that money saved or invested will not grow as fast as inflation and therefore not be worth as much in the future as it is today.

inheritance tax A tax imposed by eight states (i.e., Connecticut, Indiana, Iowa, Kentucky, Maryland, Nebraska, New Jersey, and Pennsylvania) that is assessed on the decedent's beneficiaries who receive inherited property.

initial public offerings (IPOs) New issues of stock issued by a public corporation.

insolvent A situation where a person's liabilities exceed their assets resulting in a negative net worth.

installment-certain annuity Provides monthly payments for the rest of the life of the annuitant with a guarantee that if the person dies before receiving a specific number of payments, the beneficiary will receive a certain number of payments for a particular time period.

installment credit (closed-end credit) Credit arrangement in which the borrower must repay the amount owed plus interest in a specific number of equal payments.

insurance Mechanism for transferring and reducing pure risk through which a large number of individuals share in the financial losses suffered by members of the group as a whole.

insurance agent Representative of an insurance company authorized to sell, modify, service, and terminate insurance contracts.

insurance claim Formal request to the insurance company for reimbursement for a covered loss.

insurance dividends Surplus earnings of insurance company when the difference between the total premium charged exceeds the cost to the company of providing insurance.

insurance policy Contract between the person buying insurance (the insured) and the insurance company (the insurer).

insured Individual whose life is insured.

interest Charge for borrowing money; investors in bonds earn interest.

interest-adjusted net payment index (IANPI) If a policy will remain in force until death, this method allows you to effectively measure the cost of cash-value insurance. The lower the IANPI, the lower the cost of the policy.

interest-earning checking account Any account on which you can write checks that pays interest.

interest inventories Scaled surveys that assess career interests and activities.

interest-only mortgage Mortgage in which the borrower pays only the interest on the mortgage in monthly payments for a fixed term, then either refinances the principal, pays off the principal, or starts paying the higher monthly payment with the principal payments added in.

interest rate risk Risk that interest rates will rise and bond prices will fall, thereby lowering the prices on older bond issues.

intermediate-term goals Financial targets that can be achieved within one to five years.

intestate When a person dies without a legal will.

introductory rate A temporarily low initial interest rate to entice borrowers to apply for a credit card.

investing Putting saved money to work so that it makes you even more money.

investment (capital) assets Tangible and intangible items acquired for their monetary benefits.

investment assets-to-total assets ratio Compares investment asset value with total assets.

investment banking firms Financial organizations that serve as intermediaries between public companies issuing new stocks and bonds and the investing public.

investment-grade bonds Offer investors a reasonable certainty of regularly receiving periodic income (interest) and retrieving the amount originally invested (principal).

investment philosophy Investor's general tolerance for risk in investments, whether it is conservative, moderate, or aggressive, given the investor's financial goals.

investment plan An explanation of your investment philosophy and your logic on investing to reach specific goals.

investment risk The possibility that the yield on an investment will deviate from its expected return.

investments Assets purchased with the goal of providing additional income from the asset itself.

invoice price/seller's cost Reflects the price the dealer has been billed from the manufacturer.

irrevocable living trust Arrangement in which the grantor permanently gives up ownership and the right to control of the property, to change the beneficiaries, and to change the trustees.

IRS tax table Used to figure income tax returns for incomes up to $100,000.

itemized deductions Tax-deductible expenses.

item limits Specify the maximum reimbursement for a particular health care expense.

job interview Formal meeting between employer and potential employee to discuss job qualifications and suitability.

joint and survivor benefit/survivor's benefit Annuity whose payments continue to a surviving spouse after the participant's death; often equals at least 50 percent of participant's benefit.

joint-and-survivor annuity Provides monthly payments for as long as one of the two people—usually a husband and wife—is alive.

joint tenancy with right of survivorship Type of account ownership whereby each person owns the whole of the asset and can dispose of it without the approval of the other(s).

Keogh Tax-deferred retirement account designed for self-employed and small-business owners.

kiddie tax A tax on a portion of the unearned income of those 24 and younger typically earned on money placed in a savings or investment account by a parent in an effort to avoid capital-gains taxes.

land contract/contract for deed Brings greater risk for the buyer because all terms in the contract (including payment of the debt) must be satisfied before transfer of title will occur.

large-cap stocks Those public corporations that are capitalized by issuing $3 billion to $4 billion (or more) of stocks; most are considered blue-chip companies.

large-loss principal A basic rule of risk management that encourages us to insure the risks that we cannot afford and retain the risks that we can reasonably afford.

law of large numbers As the number of members in a group increases, predictions about the group's behavior become increasingly accurate.

layering term insurance policies Purchasing level-premium term policies so that coverage grows when you need it most and then can be decreased as your needs change.

LEAP (Long-term Equity AnticiPation Security) An option with a much longer term than traditional stock or index options.

lease In this context, a contract specifying both tenant and landlord legal responsibilities.

leasing Renting a product while ownership title remains with lease grantor.

lemon laws State laws that provide guidelines for arbitrators to use to order a dealer's buyback of a "lemon" as defined under the law—commonly if a car that has been in the shop four or more times to fix the same problem.

lesser-known growth stocks Growth stocks that are not as popular with investors as more well known growth stocks; examples include regional businesses with strong earnings or companies that may be the third or fourth leading firm in an industry.

letter of last instructions Nonlegal instrument that may contain preferences regarding funeral and burial, material to be included in the obituary, and other information useful to the survivors.

level-premium term insurance Term policy with long term under which premiums remain constant. Also called guaranteed level-premium term insurance.

leverage Using borrowed funds to invest with the goal of earning a rate of return in excess of the after-tax costs of borrowing.

liabilities What you owe.

liability insurance Protection from financial losses suffered when you are held liable for others' losses.

lien A legal right to seize and dispose of (usually sell) property to obtain payment of a claim. Once loan is paid, lien is removed.

life insurance An insurance contract that promises to pay a dollar benefit to a beneficiary upon the death of the insured person.

lifestyle trade-offs Weighing the demands of particular jobs with your social and cultural preferences.

lifetime/aggregate limit Places an overall maximum on the total amount of reimbursement available under a policy.

lifetime learning credit A nonrefundable tax credit that may be claimed every year for tuition and related expenses paid for all years of postsecondary education undertaken to acquire or improve job skills.

limited liability The responsibility for business losses to stockholders is limited to the amount invested in the shares of stock owned. Stockholders vote to elect the company's.

limited managed account Services sometimes provided by a vender to employees in the employer-sponsored retirement plan that automatically rebalance (buy and sell) the retirement assets of employees according to their preferred asset allocations.

limited-pay whole life insurance Whole life insurance that allows premium payments to cease before the insured reaches the age of 100.

limited warranty Any warranty that offers less than the three conditions for full warranty.

limit order Instructs the stockbroker to buy or sell a stock at a specific price.

liquidity Speed and ease with which an asset can be converted to cash.

listing agreement Agreement that brokers require homeowners to sign that permits the broker to list the property exclusively or with a multiple-listing service.

living trust A trust that takes effect while the grantor is still alive.

load funds Mutual funds that always charge a "load" or sales charge upon purchase; the load is the commission used to compensate brokers.

loan Consumer credit that is repaid in equal amounts over a set period of time.

loan commitment/loan preapproval Lender's promise to grant a loan.

loan preapproval Oral commitment from a bank or credit union agreeing to furnish credit for a purchase; lets buyers know how much they can borrow and at what interest rate.

loan-to-value ratio Measures the amount of leverage in a real estate investment project by dividing the total amount of debt by the market price of the investment.

long-term care insurance Provides reimbursement for costs associated with intermediate-term and custodial care in a nursing facility or at home.

long-term disability income insurance plan Replaces a portion of one's income for an extended period of time of five years or more.

long-term gain/or loss A profit or loss on the sale of an asset that has been held for more than a year.

long-term goals Financial targets to achieve more than five years in the future.

long-term liability Debt that comes due in more than one year.

loss control Designing specific mechanisms to reduce loss frequency and loss severity.

low-balling A sales tactic where the seller quote and artificially low price to obtain a verbal agreement from a buyer and then attempts to raise the negotiated price when it comes time to finalize the written contract.

low-load funds Funds carrying sales charges of perhaps 1 to 3 percent; sold by brokers, via mail, and sometimes through mutual fund retailers located in shopping centers.

managed care plans Any health care plan that controls the conditions under which health care can be obtained.

managed funds Funds that employ professional managers who constantly evaluate and choose securities to buy or sell, using a specific investment approach.

management Those who run a corporation's day-to-day operations, such as the president and the chief financial officer.

manufacturer's suggested retail price (MSRP)/sticker price Suggested initial asking price.

margin account Account at a brokerage firm that requires a substantial deposit of cash or securities and permits the purchase of other securities using credit granted by the brokerage firm.

marginal cost The additional (marginal) cost of one more incremental unit of some item.

marginal tax bracket (MTB)/marginal tax rate One of six income-range segments at which income is taxed at increasing rates. Also known as **marginal tax rate**.

marginal tax rate The tax rates that apply to income in each tax bracket range. Also known as **marginal tax bracket**.

marginal utility The extra satisfaction derived from gaining one more incremental unit of a product or service.

margin buying Using a margin account to buy securities; allows the investor to apply leverage that magnifies returns—or losses.

margin call If a stock price declines to the point that the investor's equity is less than the required percentage, a representative of the brokerage firm makes a phone call and tells the investor to either put up more money or securities or face having the position bought on margin (liquidated).

margin rate Set by the Fed, percentage of the value (or equity) in an investment that is not borrowed—recently 25 to 40 percent.

marital deduction Allows an estate to pass on an unlimited amount of assets to a surviving spouse free of estate taxes.

marketability risk The risk that when you have to sell a certain asset quickly, it may not sell at or near the market price.

market efficiency The speed at which new information is reflected in investment prices suggesting that security prices are reflective of their true value at all times because publicly available information has driven market prices to the correct level.

market interest rates Current long- and short-term interest rates paid on various types of corporate and government debts that carry similar levels of risk.

market making a broker/dealer who both buys and sells securities by maintaining an inventory of specific securities to sell to other brokerage firms and stands ready to buy reasonable quantities of the same securities at market prices.

market order Instructs the stockbroker to execute an order at the prevailing market price—that is, the current selling price of the stock.

market price the current price of a share of stock that a buyer is willing to pay a willing seller.

market risk/systematic risk/undiversifiable risk Risk that the value of an investment may drop due to influences and events that affect all similar investments.

market timers Long-term investors who pull out of stocks or bonds in anticipation of a market decline or hold back from investing until the market "settles down"—that is, when they expect prices to climb.

market timing Investing, perhaps speculatively, in an effort to "time" the markets by buying or selling on the anticipated direction of the overall market, hope to capture most of the upside of rising stock prices while avoiding most of the downside.

market volatility the likelihood of large price swings in securities due to a company's success (or lack of it) and various market conditions.

market–volatility risk All investments are subject to occasional sharp changes in price as a result of events affecting a particular company or the overall market for similar investments.

matching contribution Employer benefit that offers a full or partial matching contribution to a participating employee's account in proportion to each dollar of contributions made by the participant.

maturity date Date upon which the principal is returned to the bondholder.

maximum taxable yearly earnings (MTYE) The maximum amount To which the FICA tax is applied.

Medicaid A government health care program for low-income people funded jointly by the federal and state governments.

medicare The federal government's health care program for the elderly.

microcap stocks Stocks of public corporations with less than $100 million in capitalization, and perhaps as little as $10 million.

midcap stocks Stocks of public corporations that are quite substantial in terms of capitalization—perhaps $750 million to $3 billion in size—but not among the very largest firms. *Small-cap stocks*—stocks of public corporations that have a capitalization of less than $750 million.

minimum-balance account Checking account that requires customers to keep a certain minimum amount for a specified time period to avoid fees.

minimum payment Payment that must be made to a credit account each month to cover interest and a portion of the amount owed.

minimum payment amount Lowest allowable monthly payment required by the lender.

moderate investment philosophy (risk indifference) Investors with this philosophy accept some risk as they seek capital gains through slow and steady growth in investment value along with current income.

modern portfolio theory (MPT) Goal is to identify the investor's acceptable level of risk tolerance and then find an optimal portfolio of assets that will have the highest expected returns for that level of risk.

monetary asset (cash) management How you handle your monetary assets.

monetary assets Cash and low-risk, near-cash items that can quickly be converted into cash.

money market account Interest-earning accounts that pay relatively high interest rates and offer limited check-writing privileges.

money market deposit account (MMDA) Government-insured money market account with minimum-balance requirements and tiered interest rates.

money market mutual fund (MMMF) Money market account in a mutual fund rather than at a depository institution.

Monte Carlo analysis Technique that performs a large number of trial runs of a particular portfolio mix of investments, called simulations, to find an optimal allocation for a particular investor's goals and risk tolerance.

Monte Carlo simulations Mathematical calculations that can be used to find an optimal portfolio of mutual funds and stocks that will have the highest expected returns for a certain level of risk.

mortgage broker Individual or company that acts as an intermediary between borrowers and lenders.

mortgage insurance Insures the difference between the amount of down payment required by an 80 percent LTV ratio and the actual, lower down payment.

mortgage interest tax credit A nonrefundable income tax credit of up to $2000 for persons who borrow money to buy a home under certain state and local government programs.

mortgage interest tax credit A nonrefundable tax credit of up to $2000 for mortgage interest paid may be claimed under special state and local government programs that provide a "mortgage credit certificate" for people who purchase a principal residence or borrow funds for certain home improvements.

mortgage life insurance A life insurance policy specifically focused on paying the remaining balance on a mortgage loan.

mortgage loan Loan to purchase real estate in which the property itself serves as collateral.

municipal bonds (munis) Long-term debt issued by state and local governments and their agencies to finance public improvement projects; usually tax-free interest to buyer.

municipal government bonds (munis) Long-term debts (bonds) issued by local governments (cities, states, and various districts and political subdivisions) and their agencies.

mutual fund Investment company that pools funds by selling shares to investors and makes diversified investments to achieve financial goals of income or growth, or both.

mutual fund ask (or offer) price Price at which an investor can purchase a mutual fund's shares; current NAV per share plus sales charges.

mutual fund bid price Shareholders receive this amount per share when they redeem their shares, which is the same dollar amount as the NAV.

mutual fund dividend Income paid to investors out of profits earned by the mutual fund from its investments.

mutual fund family Investment management company that offers a number of different funds to the investing public, each with its own investment objectives or philosophies of investing.

mutual funds Investment companies that raise money by selling shares to the public and then invest that money in a diversified investment portfolio.

naked option Speculative option that the writer does not own, thus exposing the writer to unlimited risk (if selling a call) or substantial risk (if selling a put).

named-perils policies Cover only losses caused by perils that the policy specifically mentions.

NASDAQ National Association of Securities Dealers Automated Quotations system, which provides instantaneous information on securities offered by more than 3200 domestic and foreign companies.

National Flood Insurance Program A federal government program that makes flood insurance available in counties where flooding is common.

need Item thought to be necessary.

needs-based approach A superior method of calculating the amount of insurance needed that considers all of the factors that might potentially affect the level of need.

negative amortization Occurs when monthly payments are actually smaller than necessary to pay interest on the loan, which will result in a rising principal loan balance.

negative option plans You are automatically signed up for a purchase or subscription plan and your membership renews automatically unless you notify them that you want it to end.

negotiating/haggling Process of discussing actual terms of agreement with a seller, usually on higher-priced items.

net asset value (NAV) Per-share value of a mutual fund.

net surplus Amount remaining after all budget classification deficits are subtracted from those with surpluses.

net worth What's left when you subtract liabilities from assets.

new-vehicle buying service No-fee organization that arranges discount purchases for new-car buyers who are referred to nearby participating automobile dealers that have agreed to charge specific discount prices.

no-load funds Funds that allow investors to purchase shares directly at the net asset value (NAV) without the addition of sales charges.

nominal income Also called money income; income that has not been adjusted for inflation and decreasing purchasing power.

noncontributory plan An employer-sponsored defined-contribution retirement plan in which only the employer makes contributions.

nondeeded timesharing A timeshare property sold without a deed that gives the buyer a legal right-to-use purchase of a limited, preplanned timesharing period of use of a property; in effect a long-term lease that expires in 20 to 25 years.

nonforfeiture values Amounts stipulated in a life insurance policy that protect the cash value, if any, in the event that the policyholder chooses not to pay or fails to pay required premiums.

nonprobate property Does not go through probate; includes assets transferred to survivors by contract (such as beneficiaries listed on retirement accounts and bank accounts held with another person).

nonrefundable tax credit A tax credit that can reduce one's tax liability only to zero, however, if the credit is more than the tax liability, the excess is not refunded.

nonsalary benefits Forms of remuneration provided by employers to employees that result in the employee not having to pay out-of-pocket money for certain expenses; also known as employee benefits.

odd lot An amount of a security that is less than the normal unit of trading for that particular security; for stocks, any transaction less than 100 shares is usually considered to be an odd lot.

online brokers Such brokers, also called Internet or electronic brokers, have reduced the cost of executing a trade to perhaps $20 or even $10 because their primary business is online trading.

open-ended (revolving) credit Arrangement in which credit is extended in advance of any transaction so that borrowers do not need to reapply each time they need to use credit.

open-end mutual funds Investment that issues redeemable shares that investors purchase directly from the fund (or through a broker for the fund).

opportunity cost Most valuable alternative that must be sacrificed to satisfy a want or need.

option Contract to buy or sell a financial asset at a specified point in the future at a specified price.

option ARMs Adjustable-rate loans with low initial rates that give the borrower the option of paying the standard payment, an interest-only payment, and even worse, a less than interest payment resulting in negative amortization.

option holder Person who buys and then owns an option contract.

option premium Price of an option contract.

option writer Agrees to sell an option contract that promises either to buy or to sell a specified asset for a fixed striking price.

ordinary income dividend distributions Distributions that occur when the fund pays out dividend income and interest (monthly, quarterly, or annually) it has received from securities held in the fund.

organized exchanges Actual physical location for a market, at which some securities prices are set by open outcry.

overindebted When one's excessive personal debts make repayment difficult and cause financial distress.

over-the-counter (OTC) marketplace Electronic marketplace for securities transactions.

owner/policyholder Retains all rights and privileges granted by the policy, including the right to amend the policy and the right to designate who receives the proceeds.

paid-up Point at which the owner of a whole life policy can stop paying premiums.

participating policies Life insurance policies that pay dividends.

par value/face value Some multiple of $1000 that is printed on a bond when issued and repaid at maturity.

passive investor An investor who does not actively engage in trading securities or monitoring his or her investments; seeks to match the market return via mutual funds or other managed investments in the longer term.

payable-on-death designation Status granted to individuals who are not joint tenants and who might need to access accounts without going through probate—the deceased signs the designation before death and the designee simply presents a death certificate to access the accounts.

payroll withholding The IRS requirement that an employer withhold a certain amount from an employee's income as a prepayment of that individual's tax liability for the year, and it is sent to the government where it is credited to the taxpayer's account.

pay yourself first Treating savings as the first expenditure after—or even before—getting paid rather than simply the money left over at the end of the month.

penny stock A speculative stock that sells for less than $1 per share typically issued by new companies with erratic sales, few profits, and only some hope of success; sometimes sold over the telephone by high-pressure salespeople to unsophisticated investors.

pension Sum of money paid regularly as a retirement benefit.

peril Any event that can cause a financial loss.

periodic rate The APR for a charge account divided by the number of billing cycles per year (usually 12).

periodic statements Consumer-protecting recaps that show all electronic transfers to and from accounts, fees charged, and opening and closing balances.

personal finance The study of personal and family resources considered important in achieving financial success; it involves how people spend, save, protect, and invest their financial resources.

personal injury protection (PIP) Medical payments coverage for the driver and any passengers for bodily injury losses as well as possibly lost wages and rehabilitation expenses common in no-fault accident states.

personal line of credit Form of open-ended credit in which the lender allows the borrower access to a prearranged revolving line of credit.

PITI Elements of a monthly real estate payment consisting of principal, interest, real estate taxes, and homeowner's insurance.

plan See qualified tuition plan.

planned buying Thinking through all the details of a purchase from the initial desire to buy to your satisfaction after the purchase.

point/interest point Fee equal to 1 percent of the total mortgage loan amount.

policy limits Specify the maximum dollar amounts that will be paid under the policy.

portability Upon termination of employment, employees with portable benefits can keep their savings in tax-sheltered accounts, transferring retirement funds from employer's account directly to another account without penalty.

portfolio Collection of investments assembled to meet your investment goals.

portfolio diversification Practice of selecting a collection of different asset classes of investments (such as stocks, bonds, mutual funds, real estate, and cash) that are chosen not only for their potential returns but also for their dissimilar risk–return characteristics.

portfolio tracking Automatically updates the value of your portfolio after you enter the symbols of the stocks you own and the number of shares held.

potential rate of return A calculation of the approximate compound yield of an investment that sums up projected income and price appreciation, and the resulting figure may then be compared with returns on other investments.

predatory lending Dishonest or deceptive practices by lenders taking advantage of a borrower's lack of understanding of credit matters.

preemptive right Right of common stockholders to purchase additional shares before a firm offers new shares to the public.

preexisting conditions Medical conditions or symptoms that the plan participant knew about or had been diagnosed within a certain time period before the plan effective date.

preferred employer Identifying employers that would suit you best.

preferred provider organization (PPO) Group of health care providers (doctors, hospitals, and other health care providers) who contract with a health insurance company to provide services at a discount.

preferred stock Type of fixed-income ownership security in a corporation that pays fixed dividends.

premium Comparatively small, predictable fee with which individuals or companies can replace an uncertain—and possibly large—financial loss.

premium conversion plans With premium conversion, the employee's share of the premiums is paid with pretax dollars; those amounts are not included when the employer reports the employee's income to the IRS.

premium-only plan (POP) An IRS approved plan offered by some employers that allows employees to withhold a portion of their pretax salary to pay their premium contributions for employer-provided health benefits.

premium quote service Offers computer-generated comparisons among 20 to 80 different companies.

prepaid educational service plan Type of qualified tuition program that allows purchase of a child's future college education at today's prices, locking in tuition prices. Also known as **prepaid tuition plan**.

prepayment penalty Special charge assessed to the borrower for paying off a loan early.

present value The current value of an asset (or stream of assets) that will be received in the future; also known as discounted value.

preservation of capital A concept suggesting that an investor does not want to lose any of the money invested thus they are risk averse.

preshopping research Gathering information before actually beginning to interact with sellers.

pretax dollars Money income that has not been taxed by the government.

pretax income The amount of income withheld from a worker's salary before taxes are calculated.

pretax money Investing with pretax money to a tax-sheltered retirement account comes out of your earnings before income taxes are calculated, thus gaining an immediate elimination of part of your income tax liability for the current year.

price/earnings (P/E) ratio (or multiple) The current market price of a stock divided by earnings per share (EPS) over the past four quarters; used as the primary means of valuing a stock.

price/sales ratio (P/S ratio) Tells the number of dollars it takes to buy a dollar's worth of a company's annual revenues; calculated by dividing company's total market capitalization by its sales for the past four quarters.

price-to-book ratio (P/B ratio) Current stock price divided by the per-share net value of a firm's plant, equipment, and other assets (book value).

price-to-rent ratio Measures the current income in a real estate market; multiply the monthly rent by 12 and then divide the property price by this figure. The higher the number, the less likely you are to make money.

principal Face amount of a bond, or price originally paid for a bond.

principle of indemnity Insurance will pay *no more* than the actual financial loss suffered.

privately-held corporation One that issues stock purchased by a relatively small number of people and is not traded on a public stock exchange.

private mortgage insurance (PMI) Mortgage insurance obtained from a private company.

probate Court-supervised process that allows creditors to present claims against an estate and ensures the transfer of a decedent's assets to the rightful beneficiaries according to a properly executed and valid will or, when no will exists, to the people, agencies, or organizations required by state law.

probate property All assets other than nonprobate property.

professional abilities Job-related activities that you can perform physically, mentally, artistically, mechanically, and financially.

professional interests Long-standing topics and activities that engage your attention.

professional liability insurance/malpractice insurance Protects individuals and organizations that provide professional services when they are held liable for their clients' losses.

professional networking Making and using contacts with individuals, groups, and other firms to exchange career information.

profile prospectus/fund profile Publication that describes the mutual fund, its investment objectives, and how it tries to achieve its objectives in lay terms rather than the legal language used in a regular prospectus.

profit Money left over after a firm pays all expenses and interest to bondholders.

profit-sharing plan Employer-sponsored plan that allocates some of the employer profits to employees in the form of end-of-year cash or common stock contributions to employees' 401(k) accounts.

progressive income tax Tax rate increases as taxable income increases.

projected P/E ratio Because investors need to look to the future rather than the past, this measure divides price by projected earnings over the coming four quarters. Also known as forward price/earnings ratio.

promissory note (note) Contract that stipulates repayment terms for a loan.

property insurance Protection from financial losses resulting from the damage to or destruction of your property or possessions.

prospectus Highly legalistic information presented by a firm to the SEC and to the public with any new issue of stock.

public corporation One that issues stock purchased by the general public and traded on stock markets such as the New York Stock Exchange.

purchase contract/sales contract Formal legal document that outlines the actual agreement that results from the real estate negotiations.

purchase offer/offer to purchase Written offer to purchase real estate.

purchasing power Measure of the goods and services that one's income will buy.

pure risk A situation that exists when there is no potential for gain.

put option Gives option holder the right to sell the optioned asset to the option writer at the striking price at any time before the option expires.

qualified retirement accounts IRS-approved retirement savings programs.

qualified tuition (Section 529) program Provides tax-sheltering when saving for a child's education.

qualified tuition program IRS approved plans whereby individuals may save and invest after-tax money for college and the withdrawals are free if made for qualified education expenses.

random/unsystematic risk Risk associated with owning only one investment of a particular type (such as stock in one company) that, by chance, may do very poorly in the future due to uncontrollable or random factors that do not affect the rest of the market.

rate of return/yield Total return on an investment expressed as a percentage of its price.

real estate Property consisting of land, all structures permanently attached to that land, and accompanying rights and privileges, such as crops and mineral rights.

real estate (or housing) bubble Rapid and unsustainable increases in home prices followed by sharp declines in values.

real estate broker Person licensed by a state to provide advice and assistance, for a fee, to buyer or sellers of real estate.

real estate investment trust (REIT) Special kind of closed-end mutual fund that invests in a portfolio of assets, such as properties, like office buildings and shopping centers, or mortgages.

real estate transfer taxes Community-assessed taxes paid by the seller and also sometimes by the buyer based on the purchase price of the home or the equity the seller has in the home.

real income Income measured in constant prices relative to some base time period. It reflects the actual buying power of the money you have as measured in constant dollars.

real rate of return Return on an investment after subtracting the effects of inflation and income taxes.

rebate A partial refund of a purchase price offered as an inducement to buy.

recession A recurring period of decline in total output, income, employment, and trade, usually lasting from six months to a year and marked by widespread contractions in many sectors of the economy.

record date Date that an issuer establishes to determine who is eligible to receive a dividend or distribution.

record keeping Recording sources and amounts of dollars earned and spent.

redeems When an investor sells shares.

redemption charge/exit fee Similar to a deferred load but often much lower; used to reduce excessive trading of fund shares.

redress Process of righting a wrong.

refundable tax credit A tax credit that can reduce one's income tax liability to below zero and the excess is refunded to taxpayer.

registered bond Bondholder's name is recorded so that checks or electronic funds transfers for payment of interest and principal can be safely forwarded when due.

reinvestment risk (or duration risk) The risk that the return on a future investment will not be the same as the return earned by the original investment in part because of falling interest rates.

release Insurance document affirming that the dollar amount of the loss settlement is accepted as full and complete reimbursement.

rent Cost charged for using an apartment or other housing space.

rental yield A computation of how much income the investor might pocket from rent each year (before mortgage payments) as a percentage of the purchase price; divide the annual rent by 2 and then divide by the purchase price.

renter's contents broad form (HO-4) Named-perils policy that protects the insured from losses to the contents of a rented dwelling rather than the dwelling itself.

repairs Usually tax-deductible expenses necessary to maintain property value.

replacement-cost requirement Stipulates that a home *must* be insured for 80 percent of its replacement value (some companies require 100 percent) in order for any loss to be fully covered.

repossession/foreclosure Legal proceeding by which the lender seizes an asset.

residual claim Common stockholders have a right to share in the income and assets of a corporation after higher-priority claims are satisfied.

residual clause Feature of own-occupation policies that allows for some reduced level of disability income benefits when a partial—rather than full—disability strikes.

residual value Projected value of leased asset at end of lease time period.

résumé Summary record of your education, training, experience, and other qualifications.

retail credit cards Allow customers to make purchases on credit at any of the outlets of a particular retailer.

retained earnings Money left over after firm has paid expenses, bondholder interest, taxes, preferred stockholder dividends, and common stockholder dividends.

retirement The time in life when the major sources of income change from earned income (such as salary or wages) to employer-based retirement benefits, private savings and investments, income from Social Security, and perhaps parttime employment.

retirement plan contribution credit/saver's tax credit Program to encourage low-income individuals to save for retirement, this tax credit ranges from 10 to 50 percent of every dollar they contribute to an IRA or employer-sponsored retirement plan up to $2000.

retirement savings contribution credit A nonrefundable tax credit (also known as a **saver credit**) of up to $1000 available for some low and moderate income taxpayers.

retirement savings goal/retirement nest egg Total amount of accumulated savings and investments needed to support desired retirement lifestyle.

reverse mortgage/home-equity conversion loan Allows a homeowner older than age 61 to continue living in the home and to borrow against the equity in a home that is fully paid for and to receive the proceeds in a series of monthly payments, often over a period of 5 to 15 years or for life.

revocable living trust Grantor maintains the right to change the trust's terms or cancel it at any time, for any reason, during his or her lifetime.

revolving savings fund Variable budgeting tool that places funds in savings to cover emergency or higher-than-usual expenses.

risk Uncertainty about the outcome of a situation or event.

risk management Process of identifying and evaluating purely risky situations to determine and implement appropriate management.

risk premium Amount that risk-averse investors require for taking on a riskier investment rather than a risk-free investment like U.S. government securities. The riskier the investment, the greater the premium demanded.

risk reduction Includes mechanisms, such as insurance, that reduce the overall uncertainty about the magnitude of loss.

risk retention Consciously accepting that some risks simply arise in the course of one's life and consciously retaining that risk.

risk tolerance An investor's ability and willingness to weather changes in security prices, that is, to weather market risk.

Roth IRA An individual retirement account of investments made with after-tax money; the interest on such accounts is allowed to grow tax free, and withdrawals are also tax free.

round lots Standard units of trading of 100 shares of stock and $1000 or $5000 par value for bonds.

rule of 72 A formula for figuring the number of years it takes to double the principal using compound interest; simply divide the interest rate that the money will earn *into* the number 72.

rule of 78s method/sum of the digits method for calculating prepayment penalties A common method of calculating the prepayment penalty on a loan which uses the add-on method for calculating the interest.

sales finance company Seller-related lender whose primary business is financing sales for its parent company.

savings Income not spent on current consumption.

savings account Account that provides an accessible source of emergency cash and a temporary holding place for extra funds that will earn some interest.

S-CHIP program A government program similar to Medicaid that covers children whose parents are middle income and lower and do not have access to a private health care plan.

secured bond Pledges specific assets as collateral in indenture or has the principal and interest guaranteed by another corporation or government agency.

secured loan Loan that is backed by collateral or a cosigner.

securities Assets suitable for investment, including stocks, bonds, and mutual funds.

securities exchange/stock market Market where agents of buyers and sellers can find each other easily by providing an orderly, open plan to trade securities.

securities market index Measures the average value of a number of securities chosen as a sample to reflect the behavior of a more general market.

securities markets Places where stocks and bonds are traded (or in the case of electronic trading, the way in which securities are traded).

security freeze With a freeze you tell the credit bureaus not to release your financial records to anyone without your consent.

security's street name Securities certificates kept in the brokerage firm's name instead of the name of the individual investor.

self-directed In defined-contribution plans, employees control the assets in their account—how often to make contributions to the account, how much to contribute, how much risk to take, and how to invest.

seller financing/owner financing When seller self-finances a buyer's loan by accepting a promissory note from buyer, who makes monthly mortgage payments.

selling short Investors selling securities they do not own (borrowing them from a broker) and later buying the same number of shares of the security at a lower price (returning them to the broker).

serial bonds Bonds that are retired serially; that is, each bond is numbered consecutively and matures according to a prenumbered schedule at stated intervals.

Series EE savings bonds Nonmarketable, interest-bearing bonds issued by the federal government that are issued at a sharp [MLC5] discount from face value and pay no annual interest, an they may be redeemed at full value upon maturity.

settlement options Choices from which the policyholder can choose in how the death benefit payment will be structured.

shareholder fees Fees charged directly to investors for specific transactions, such as purchases, redemptions, or exchanges.

short sale A circumstance in housing when a home is being foreclosed and a lender agrees to accept less than the full mortgage amount and often forgive whatever debt is left unpaid.

short-term (current) liability Obligation paid off within one year.

short-term disability income insurance plan Replaces a portion of one's income for a short period of time; perhaps up to two years.

short-term gain/loss A profit or loss on the sale of an asset that has been held for one year or less.

short-term health insurance Health care plans that can be paid for monthly for a term of 6-months or a year and may be renewable.

simplified employee pension–individual retirement account (SEP-IRA) A retirement savings account for sole proprietor's self-employment income and owners of small businesses looking to save only in profitable years.

single-family dwelling Housing unit that is detached from other units.

sinking fund Bond feature through which money is set aside with a trustee each year for repayment of the principal portion of the debt at maturity.

skilled nursing care Intended for people who need intensive care, that is, 24-hour-a-day supervision and treatment by a registered nurse under the direction of a doctor.

skills format Résumé that emphasizes your aptitudes and qualities.

small-cap stocks Stocks of a company that has a capitalization of $300 million to $2 billion.

small-claims court State courts in which civil matters are often resolved without attorney assistance.

socially conscious funds Funds that invest in companies that meet some predefined standard of moral and ethical behavior.

Social Security credits Accumulated quarterly credits to qualify for Social Security benefits obtained by paying FICA taxes.

Social Security Disability Income Insurance Under this government program, eligible workers can collect some income for up to one year if their disabilities are total, meaning that they cannot work at any job.

Social Security rider Provides an extra dollar amount of protection if a person fails to qualify for Social Security disability benefits (70 percent of all applicants are rejected).

Social Security Statement A document that the Social Security Administration periodically sends to all workers, which includes earnings history, Social Security taxes paid, and an estimated benefit amount.

Social Security survivor's benefits Government program benefits paid to a surviving spouse and children.

special (homeowner's insurance) form (HO-3) Provides open-perils protection (except for the commonly excluded perils of war, earthquake, and flood) for four types of property losses.

specialist Person on floor of an exchange who handles trades of a particular stock in an effort to maintain a fair and orderly market.

speculative-grade bonds Long-term, high-risk, high-interest-rate corporate (or municipal) IOUs issued by companies (or municipalities) with poor or no credit ratings. Also called junk bonds or high-yield bonds.

speculative risk Involves the potential for either gain or loss; equity investments might do either.

speculative stock A company that has a potential for substantial earnings at some time in the future although those earnings may never be realized.

speculator An investor who buys in the hope that someone else will pay more for an asset in the not-too-distant future.

spousal consent requirement Federal law that protects surviving rights of spouse or ex-spouse to retirement or pension benefits unless the person signs a waiver of those rights.

spousal IRA Account set up for spouse who does not work for wages; offers tax-deferred growth and tax deductibility.

spread Represents difference between bid price at which a broker/dealer will buy shares and higher ask price at which the broker/dealer will sell shares.

springing power of attorney "Springs" into effect when a specified event occurs, usually mental incapacitation or disability.

standard deduction Fixed amount that all taxpayers may subtract from their adjusted gross income if they do not itemize their deductions.

standard deviation A measure of a security's or mutual fund's volatility; also known as beta.

standardized expense table SEC-required information that describes and illustrates mutual fund charges in an identical manner so that investors can accurately compare the effects of all of a fund's fees and other expenses relative to other funds.

standard of living Material well-being and peace of mind that individuals or groups earnestly desire and seek to attain, to maintain if attained, to preserve if threatened, and to regain if lost.

start-up capital Funds initially invested in a business enterprise.

stated commission The sales charge as a percentage of the amount invested.

stockbroker/account executive Professional who is licensed to buy and sell securities on behalf of the brokerage firm's clients.

stock dividend A non-cash dividend declared by a public corporation in the form of shares of common stock given to current shareholders.

stockholder/shareholder Each person who owns a share of a company's stock holds a proportionate interest in firm ownership (a very small slice) and, therefore, in the assets and income of the corporation.

stock option Security that gives the holder the right to buy or sell a specific number of shares (normally 100) of a certain stock at a specified (striking) price before a specified expiration date.

stocks Shares of ownership in the assets and earnings of a business corporation.

stock-screening tools Enable you to quickly sift through vast databases of hundreds of companies to find those that best suit your investment objectives.

stock split When the shares of a stock owned by existing shareholders are divided into a larger number of shares.

stop order Instructs a stockbroker to sell your shares of stock at the market price if a stock declines to or goes below a specified price.

stop-payment order Notifying your bank not to honor a check when it's presented for payment.

straight annuity Provides lifetime payments for the life of the annuitant only.

striking price A specific price before a specified date in an options contract when the holder has the right, but not the obligation, to buy or sell a specific number of shares of a certain stock at a specified price.

subleasing An arrangement in which the original tenant leases the property to another tenant.

subordinate budget Detailed listing of planned expenses within a single budgeting classification.

subprime lending This market focuses on lending to people who normally would not qualify for credit due to low credit scores. The interest rates are commensurately higher.

subrogation rights Allow an insurer to take action against a negligent third party (and that party's insurance company) to obtain reimbursement for payments made to an insured.

surplus (or net gain or net income) When total income exceeds total expenses such as reported on a cash-flow statement.

sweat equity property Property that needs repairs but that has good underlying value; an investor buys the property at a favorable price and fixes it up to rent or sell at a profit.

take-home pay/disposable income Pay received after employer withholdings for taxes, insurance, and union dues.

tangible (use) assets Personal property used to maintain your everyday lifestyle.

target-date retirement funds/life-cycle funds Asset allocation funds that offer investors premixed portfolios of stocks, bonds, and cash that investors of a certain age and risk tolerance might prefer.

taxable income Income upon which income taxes are levied.

tax avoidance Reducing tax liability through legal techniques.

tax balance due Money you must pay to the IRS if withholding and quarterly payments are insufficient to cover tax liability.

tax credit Dollar-for-dollar decrease in tax liability; also known as credit.

tax deferred The individual does not have to pay current income taxes on the earnings (interest, dividends, and capital gains) reinvested in a retirement account.

tax-deferred compounding Tax-free growth of tax-deferred investments.

taxes Compulsory government-imposed charges levied on citizens and their property.

tax evasion Deliberately and willfully hiding income from the IRS, falsely claiming deductions, or otherwise cheating the government out of taxes owed; it is illegal.

tax-exempt income Income that is totally and permanently free of taxes.

tax-exempt money market funds Funds that limit their investments to tax-exempt municipal securities with maturities of 90 days or less.

tax free Withdrawals from retirement accounts that IRS regulations deem are never taxed, such as money taken out of Roth IRA accounts.

tax-free exchange Arises when a real estate investor trades equity in one property for equity in a similar property and no other forms of property or money change hands.

tax losses Paper losses that may not represent actual losses created when deductions generated from an investment exceed income from the investment.

tax planning Seeking legal ways to reduce, eliminate, or defer income taxes.

tax rate schedules Equations to figure taxes for returns with incomes above $100,000.

tax refund Amount the IRS sends back to taxpayer if withholding and estimated payments exceed tax liability.

tax-sheltered income Income exempt from income taxes in the current year but that will be subject to taxation in a later tax year.

tax-sheltered investments Investments that yield returns that are tax advantaged.

tax-sheltered retirement accounts Retirement account for which all earnings from the invested funds are not subject to income taxes.

tax-sheltered retirement plan Employer-sponsored, defined-contribution retirement plans including 401(k) plans and similar 403(b) and 457 plans.

T-bill One form of Treasury securities is the short-term Treasury bill, or T-bill, which is a government IOU of one year of less.

teaser rate Low interest rate that lenders sometimes use to lure buyers; these rates will be low for the first year or so and then will rise to more realistic rates.

technical analysis Method of evaluating securities that uses statistics generated by market activity, such as past prices and volume, over time to determine when to buy or sell a stock.

tech stocks Stock in the technology sector that offer technology-based products and services, biotechnology, Internet services, network services, wireless communications, and more.

term life insurance "Pure protection" against early death; pays benefits only if the insured dies within the time period (term) that the policy covers.

testamentary trust Becomes effective upon death of the grantor according to the terms of the grantor's will or a revocable living trust. Such trusts can provide money or asset management after the grantor's death for the heirs' benefit.

tiered interest Common type of NOW account that pays lower interest on smaller deposits and higher interest on larger balances.

time deposits Savings accounts that financial institutions expect to remain on deposit for an extended period.

time risk The more time your money is invested, the more it is at risk, thus the sooner your invested money is supposed to be returned to you—the **time horizon** of an investment—the less the likelihood that something could go wrong.

timesharing The joint ownership or lease of vacation property through which the principals occupy the property individually for set periods of time.

time value of money (TVM) A method by which one can compare cash flows across time, either as what a future cash flow is worth today (present value) or what an investment made today will be worth in the future (future value).

title Legal right of ownership interest to real property.

title insurance Protects the lender's interest if the title search is later found faulty.

total income Compensation from all sources.

total return Income an investment generates from current income and capital gains.

trade-off Giving up one thing for another.

traditional (regular) IRA Account that offers tax-deferred growth; the initial contribution may be tax deductible for the year that the IRA was funded.

trailing commission Compensation paid to salespeople for months or years in the future.

trailing P/E ratio Calculated using recently reported earnings, usually from the previous four quarters.

transaction fee Charge levied against cardholders per use of the card and are not included in the APR advertised.

transportation reimbursement plan An IRS approved plan offered by some employers that allows employees the opportunity to withhold a portion of their pretax salary to pay for work-related transportation expenses because it reduces the individual's income tax liability.

travel and entertainment (T&E) cards Bank credit cards that allow holders to make purchases at numerous businesses but that require the holder to repay the entire balance charged within 30 days.

treasury bills Known as T-bills, U.S. government securities with maturities of one year or less.

treasury Inflation-Protected Securities (TIPS) Marketable Treasury bonds whose value increases with inflation. These inflation-indexed $1000 bonds are the only investment that guarantees that the investor's return will outpace inflation.

treasury note/treasury bond Fixed-principal, fixed-interest-rate government security issued for an intermediate term or long term. Notes mature in ten years or less; bonds mature in more than ten years.

treasury securities Known as Treasuries, securities issued by the U.S. government, including bills, notes, and bonds.

trust Legal arrangement between you as the creator of the trust and the trustee, the person designated to faithfully and wisely manage any assets in the trust to your benefit and to the benefit of your heirs.

trustee Person charged with carrying out the trust for the benefit of the grantor(s) and heirs.

Truth in Lending Act (TIL) Requires lenders to disclose to credit applicants both the interest rate expressed as an annual percentage rate (APR) and the finance charge.

U.S. government savings bonds Nonmarketable, interest-bearing bonds issued by the U.S. Treasury.

umbrella (excess) liability insurance Catastrophic liability policy that covers liability losses in excess of those covered by any underlying homeowner's, automobile, or professional liability policy.

unearned income Investment returns in the form of rents, dividends, capital gains, interest, or royalties.

uniform settlement statement Lists all of the costs and fees to be paid at the closing.

unit investment trust (UIT) Closed-end investment company that makes a one-time public offering of only a specific, fixed number of units; once the UIT closes, it becomes an unmanaged fund that is somewhat illiquid.

universal life insurance Provides the pure protection of term insurance and the cash-value buildup of whole life insurance, along with face amount variability, rate of cash-value accumulation, premiums, and rate of return.

unmanaged fund Fund with very low management fees since managers do not evaluate or select individual securities; ETFs and index funds are examples.

unsecured bond/debenture Does not name collateral as security for debt; backed only by the good faith and reputation of the issuing agency.

unsecured loan/signature loan Loan granted based solely on borrower's good creditworthiness.

use-it-or-lose-it rule An IRS regulation requiring that unspent dollars in a flexible spending account at the end of a calendar year be forfeited, unless the employer allows a 2½ month grace period for spending the funds.

value funds Funds specializing in stocks that are fundamentally sound whose prices appear to be low (low P/E ratios) based on the logic that such stocks are currently out of favor and undervalued by the market.

value investing Seeing to invest, in stocks for example, when they are underpriced and sell them when they rise.

value investor One who believes that the market isn't always efficient and that it is possible to find companies trading for less than they are worth, thus they try to buy stocks when they are quoted below their fair value and sell them when they rise above that level.

value stock A stock that tends to trade at a low price relative to its company fundamentals (dividends, earnings, sales, and so on) and thus is considered undervalued by a value investor.

values The principles, standards, or qualities that you consider desirable.

variable annuity Annuity whose value rises and falls like mutual funds and pays a limited death benefit via an insurance contract. Not as efficient as a mutual fund; costs are high for little return.

variable expenses Expenses over which you have substantial control.

variable interest rate cards Have rates that change monthly or annually according to general changes in the economy as a whole.

variable-rate (adjustable-rate) loans Loans for which the interest rate varies with the monthly payment going up or down, allowing the loan to be paid off by the original end date.

variable-universal life insurance Form of universal life insurance that gives the policyholder some choice in the investments made with the cash value accumulated by the policy. Also called flexible-premium variable life insurance.

variable value Because interest rates change, bonds may trade at a premium (more than face value) or at a discount (less than par) so that the yield equals the current yield for bonds with similar maturities and risk levels.

vesting Ensures that a retirement plan participant has the right to take full possession of all employer contributions and earnings if employee is dismissed, resigns, or retires.

volatility A mutual fund's (or any security's) tendency to rise or fall in price over time.

voting rights Proportionate authority to express an opinion or choice in matters affecting the company.

waiting period Long-term care policies can pay benefits from the first day of nursing home care or they can include a waiting period. Premiums drop with longer waiting periods.

waiver of premium Sets certain conditions under which an insurance policy would be kept in full force by the company without the payment of premiums.

want Item not necessary but desired.

warranty Sellers' assurances that goods are as promised and that certain steps will be taken to rectify problems if they arise.

well-known growth stocks Stocks of companies that are leaders in their fields, that dominate their markets, and that have several consecutive years of above-industry-average earnings.

whole life insurance Form of cash-value life insurance that provides lifetime life insurance protection and expects the insured to pay premiums for life. Also called straight life insurance.

will Written document in which a person tells how his or her remaining assets should be given away after death; without a will, the property will be distributed according to state probate law.

withdrawal A removal of assets from an account.

withdrawal options/systematic withdrawal plans Arrangements with a mutual fund company for shareholders who want to receive income on a regular basis from their mutual fund investments.

work-style personality Your own ways of working with and responding to job requirements, surroundings, and associates.

yield to maturity (YTM) Total annual effective rate of return earned by a bondholder on a bond if the security is held to maturity—takes into consideration both the price at which the bond sold and the coupon interest rate to arrive at effective rate of return.

zero-coupon bonds (zeros or deep discount bonds) Municipal, corporate, and Treasury bonds that are issued at a sharp discount from face value and pay no annual interest but are redeemed at full face value upon maturity.

zero-sum game Situation in which the wealth of all investors remains the same; the trading simply redistributes the wealth among those traders. Each profit must be offset by an equivalent loss; therefore, the average rate of return for all investors in futures is zero.

Index

Note: **Boldface** type indicates key terms defined in text.